The 50 States

The 50 States

Third Edition
Volume 1

Edited by
Rodney Carlisle
Rutgers University

Second Edition Edited by
Charles F. Bahmueller
Center for Civic Education
Calabasas, California

Contributors

Carl L. Bankston III
Tulane University

Rose Secrest
Chattanooga, Tennessee

Sarah Hilbert
Pasadena, California

R. Baird Shuman
University of Illinois

Kevin M. Mitchell
Glendale, California

Rowena Wildin
Altadena, California

Lauren M. Mitchell
Glendale, California

Michael Witkoski
University of South Carolina

Salem Press

A Division of EBSCO Information Services, Inc.
Ipswich, Massachusetts

GREY HOUSE PUBLISHING

Editor, third edition: **Rodney Carlisle**
Editor, second edition: **Charles F. Bahmueller**

ISBN 978-1-61925-208-0

Library of Congress Cataloging-in-Publication Data

The 50 states / edited by Charles F. Bahmueller ; managing editor, R.
  Kent Rasmussen ; contributors, Carl L. Bankston, III ... [et al.]. --
  3rd ed.

    2 v. : ill., maps ; cm.

  First published in 2000.
  Additional comparative ranking tables available online allow users to sort and rank states and regions of the U.S. by hundreds of different criteria.
  Includes bibliographical references and index.
  ISBN: 978-1-61925-208-0 (set)

  1. U.S. states--Miscellanea. 2. United States--Miscellanea. I. Bahmueller, Charles F. II. Rasmussen, R. Kent.
III. Bankston, Carl L. (Carl Leon), 1952- IV. Title: Fifty states

E180 .A15 2013
973/.02

First Printing

CONTENTS

Contents

Contents

Contents

Publisher's Note

Salem Press's popular *The 50 States* was first published in 2000. Like its predecessors, this 3rd edition is designed to serve the needs of students, researchers and the general public seeking basic and up-to-date information on individual American states. Unlike its predecessors, this 3rd edition is two volumes, making handling easier and research more focused.

Content in this 3rd edition is completely revised. State chapters include several new features, including current survey results, new color photographs, and new statistical tables.

State Stories—Past to Present

State Profile Notes: Each state chapter opens with a profile listing basic data on population, geography, history, and other facts, complete with the state flag and seal. A brief history of the state emphasizes the events and forces that have worked to make the state what it is today, and includes a map of the state's physical features. Additional historical facts are summarized in an up-to-the-minute Time Line, which is followed by a detailed Notes for Further Study. This section is visually punctuated by a number of photographs, both black and white and color.

Coastline and Shoreline Notes: When describing the state's physical features, "coastline" mileage reflects the broad contours of marine seacoasts. "Shoreline" mileage encompasses seacoasts, offshore islands, and all inland shores touching tidal waters, including rivers and creeks that are at least one hundred feet wide.

Survey Says: This feature shows how the state ranked in more than 30 interesting and important areas – best for families, job growth, and transportation, for example— from sources like *Money Magazine, Huffington Post, U.S. News and World Report,* and *America's Health Rankings.*

County Data Notes: Every state chapter also contains a list of its counties, with population and area. These lists include each county's rank in both area and population within its state. Every county list is complemented by a county map. Following county data is city data—a list of all the state's cities and towns of at least ten thousand residents—or six thousand residents for states lacking

sufficient towns with ten thousand residents—and a city/ town map.

Statistical Tables

Following each state narrative are 46 valuable statistical tables—six more than the last edition – and organized under 11 main categories:

- Demographics
- Vital Statistics
- Economy
- Land and Water
- Health and Medical Care
- Housing
- Education
- Transportation and Travel
- Crime and Law Enforcement
- Government and Finance
- Politics

The data in these tables come from both the latest federal government statistics—U.S. 2010 Census, CDC Wonder Online, U.S. Departments of Commerce, Agriculture, Transportation and Justice—and from private sources, like the National Association of Realtors and the U.S. Travel Association. These tables have a new look, designed with consistency, understandability, and accessibility in mind.

The tables offer comprehensive population data, including projections of each state's population growth through the year 2030. Other tables summarize such vital statistics as infant mortality rates and marriage, divorce, and death rates. Economic data includes statistics on housing, gross state products, personal income, and agricultural data. This edition also offers statistics on state government revenue and expenditures. Political data includes lists of all state governors and the political make-up of state and federal legislators through mid-2013, and voter participation in presidential elections. Other tables offer data on transportation, health, education, crime, and law enforcement.

Most tables include not only state and U.S. numbers, but how the state compares to the national data.

New Tables: New topics in this edition include Population by Hispanic Origin and Race, Death Rates by Selected Causes, Educational Attainment, State Expenditures by Function, State Government Cash and Debt, and **Composition of the House of Representatives.**

State by State Comparisons and Rankings

This section includes 51 state by state ranking tables—15 more than the last edition. You'll see at a glance that Wyoming uses the most energy per capita and Texas has the highest percentage of residents without health insurance.

A new feature of this ranking section is regional rankings. Each of the 51 ranking topics are not only ranked by state, but also by region of the country. For example, you'll see that in the Northeast, Maine has the highest percentage of adult smokers and that, of the Midwest states, Indiana has the smallest percentage of residents with a bachelor's degree or higher.

This 3rd edition of *The 50 States* ends with three valuable elements: **General Bibliography** covers publications on the states collectively; **Guide to Web Resources** is annotated with useful strategies and descriptions; and **General Index.**

A brand new feature of the online format of *The 50 States* is that the ranking tables are interactive, so the user can customize rankings by state and topic right online. Salem Press will provide you with your instant link, free with purchase of the print. Call 800-221-1592.

Abbreviations Used in Maps

NB National Battlefield
NBP National Battlefield Park
NBS National Battlefield Site
NHP National Historical Park
NHS National Historic Site
NL National Lakeshore
NM National Monument
NMem National Memorial
NMP National Military Park
NP National Park

NPres National Preserve
NR National River
NRA National Recreation Area
NRes National Reserve
NS National Seashore
NST National Scenic Trail
NVM National Volcanic Monument
Pkwy National Parkway
WSR Wild and Scenic River

The 50 States

United States of America

Alabama

Location: Southeast

Area and rank: 50,750 square miles (131,443 square kilometers); 52,423 square miles (135,776 square kilometers) including water; twenty-eighth largest state in area

Coastline: 53 miles (85 kilometers) on the Gulf of Mexico

Shoreline: 607 miles (977 kilometers)

Population and rank: 4,822,023 (2012 est.); twenty-third largest state in population

Capital city: Montgomery (205,764 people in 2010 census)

Largest city: Birmingham (212,237 people in 2010 census)

Became territory: March 3, 1817

Entered Union and rank: December 14, 1819; twenty-second state

Present constitution adopted: 1901

Counties: 67

State name: "Alabama" is thought to have come from a Choctaw word meaning "thicket

State capitol building at Montgomery. (Wikimedia Commons)

clearers" or "vegetation gatherers"

State nickname: Yellowhammer

State Motto: *Audemus jura nostra defendere* (We dare defend our rights)

State flag: White field with crimson cross of Saint Andrew

Highest point: Cheaha Mountain—2,405 feet (733 meters)

Lowest point: Gulf of Mexico— sea level

Highest recorded temperature: 112 degrees Fahrenheit (44 degrees Celsius)— Centerville, 1925

Lowest recorded temperature: –27 degrees Fahrenheit (–33 degrees Celsius)—New Market, 1966

State song: "Alabama" ("Sweet Home Alabama" is unofficial)

State tree: Southern pine (longleaf)

State flower: Camellia

State bird: Yellowhammer

State fish: Tarpon (saltwater); Largemouth bass (freshwater)

Alabama History

Alabama is in the southeastern part of the United States, between Mississippi to the west and Georgia and Florida to the east. Most of Alabama's southern border adjoins Florida, but a small portion of the state extends down to the Gulf of Mexico. The northern part of Alabama, just below Tennessee, is known as the Appalachian region. It is made up of high plateaus, ridges, valleys, and the high Talladega Mountains. The Piedmont Plateau, another rocky region, extends from the Talladega Mountains to the Georgia border. Until well into the twentieth century, many of the people in the high lands of Alabama lived the isolated lives of mountain and hill dwellers. The Interior Low Plateau region is the part of northern Alabama drained by the Tennessee River. Below the northern uplands, the Gulf Coastal Plains extend south to the Gulf of Mexico. The Gulf Coastal Plains include the Black Belt, a dark-soiled prairie.

The Tennessee River area and the Black Belt have rich soil. Together with Alabama's hot, humid climate, this has made these territories ideal for agriculture. As a result, agriculture tended to dominate the state's economic activities until the second half of the twentieth century. Worldwide demand for cotton in the nineteenth century led the state to specialize in cotton production. Since cotton was a crop that required a great deal of unskilled labor, this created a reliance on slavery that profoundly affected the state's history.

Early History. Before the arrival of the Europeans, Alabama was dominated by Native Americans known as the Mound Builders, after their ceremonial earth mounds. The best-known archeological site of the Mound Builders in Alabama is at Moundville on the Black Warrior River in central Alabama. Moundville was a large and complex society, second in size and organization only to the Cahokia site of Mound Builder culture in Illinois. Both a populous town and a political and religious center, the Moundville community itself probably housed about one thousand people at its height and was surrounded by around ten thousand people living in the Black Warrior River Valley. This settlement lasted from about 1000 C.E. to about 1450.

In the eighteenth century, the Creek were one of the largest and predominant Native American groups in Alabama. The Creek, who lived in villages of log houses, sided with the British against the Americans in both the Revolutionary War and the War of 1812. At war with the Americans, they were defeated by General Andrew Jackson, and by 1828 they agreed to give up all of their lands and move to Indian Territory in modern Oklahoma. The Cherokee, who were spread throughout the Southeast, were also well represented in Alabama. In 1838, most of the Cherokee were also forced to relocate to Indian Territory. Similarly, most of the Choctaw and the Chickasaw were removed from Alabama and the adjacent states.

Exploration and Settlement. Spanish explorers reached Alabama around 1540. The Spanish attempted to establish a settlement at Mobile Bay but soon deserted it, leaving cattle, hogs, and horses behind, all of which became part of local Native American ways of life. The French claimed much of Alabama as part of their vast Louisiana territory, and they built forts and trading posts. After France and Great Britain fought the French and Indian Wars (1754-1763), Alabama fell under the control of the British. The coastal area, including Mobile Bay, became part of West Florida. North of West Florida, all of Alabama was reserved by the British for the Native Americans.

During the American Revolution, Spain captured Mobile from the British, shutting the British out of Alabama. After the Revolution, West Florida became Spanish land, and interior Alabama was turned over to the new United States. After several years of border disputes, the United States and Spain finally agreed in 1795 that latitude thirty-one degrees north would be the boundary between U.S. land and West Florida; this would continue to be the boundary between Alabama and the Florida Panhandle. In 1798, the U.S. Congress formed the Mississippi Territory, made up of modern Mississippi and Alabama. The portion of the territory along the Mississippi River became the state of Mississippi in 1817, and in 1819 Alabama was admitted to the Union as the twenty-second state.

Slavery and Civil War. Alabama's rich soil led to an influx of settlers. Worldwide demand for cotton made this crop enormously profitable for a few wealthy landowners. Black slaves worked the cotton plantations, and between 1830 and 1860 the state's slave population grew by 270 percent, while the white population grew by only 170 percent. Although the big plantation owners made up only about 6 to 7 percent of Alabama's population, they were enormously influential and dominated the state's society. The majority of white Alabamians, especially in the hills and mountains, were small subsistence farmers.

Slavery became a contentious issue in the United States in the first half of the nineteenth century. As new territories entered the United States, many northern leaders opposed the spread of slavery. The southern political leadership, dominated by the plantation owners, saw slavery as essential to the southern agricultural way of life and feared falling under the control of the populous north.

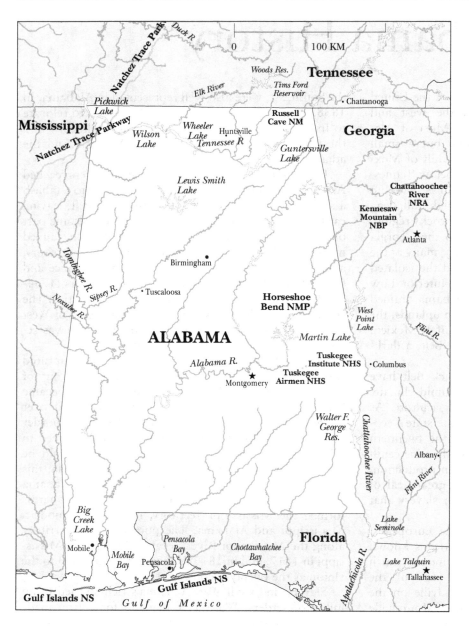

Alabamian blacks were able to take positions of political leadership because of the former slaves' lack of education and experience. By 1874, white southern Democrats managed to take control of the state government. Throughout the nineteenth century, the white state government established legal segregation and restriction of the rights of African Americans.

The Civil Rights Era. During the 1950's and 1960's, African Americans in Alabama and other southern states began organizing to oppose segregation and racial discrimination. In 1955, Rosa Parks, a black citizen of Montgomery, Alabama, was arrested when she refused to give up her seat on a bus to a white passenger. In response, the African American residents of Montgomery, under the leadership of the clergyman Dr. Martin Luther King, Jr., organized a boycott of the city's public transportation system. The successful boycott made King a national civil rights leader, and he went on to advocate desegregation campaigns and marches throughout the South.

Alabama Governor George Wallace, first elected in 1962, came to national prominence as a result of his opposition to integration. Wallace had experienced defeat in a first run for governor in 1959, when he refused the support of the Ku Klux Klan and ran a campaign of racial moderation. After that defeat, he became a staunch segregationist and attempted to block the integration of Alabama's schools

In 1861, Alabama joined other southern states in seceding from the United States and forming the Confederate States of America. The bitter Civil War ensued. By 1865 Alabama and the other southern states were defeated and occupied by northern troops.

With the end of the Civil War, Alabama's slaves received freedom. However, there were few economic opportunities for them and most had to take jobs working as low-income agricultural laborers for white landowners. The American Missionary Association and the Federal Freedmen's Bureau helped to establish schools that formed a basis for future African American education. Although African Americans received the right to vote during Reconstruction, the period from after the Civil War to 1877, when Union troops withdrew from the South, relatively few

and universities. On the basis of the national recognition brought by his segregationist policies, Wallace ran for president of the United States in 1968 as the candidate of the American Independent Party.

Although racial inequality continued to be a problem in Alabama, segregation became illegal, and black Alabamians achieved substantial social and political influence. From 1969 to 1970, the percentage of African American students attending integrated schools increased from 15 percent to 80 percent. In 1982, when George Wallace was elected to his third term as governor, he actively appealed to black voters and renounced his earlier racial positions.

Alabama's Industrialization. Alabama saw substantial industrialization over the course of the twentieth century.

In 1907, United States Steel Corporation established a steel industry in Birmingham. Iron and steel became leading products of Alabama, concentrated mainly in the Birmingham area.

The port city of Mobile became a center of ship-building during World War I. Shipbuilding and ship repair continued to be important on the Alabama Gulf Coast, but the area around Mobile also began to produce paper and chemical products. The city of Huntsville became a focal point of U.S. government missile manufacturing and the aerospace industry after World War II. Cutbacks in federal government spending caused Huntsville to diversify its economy after the 1970's, and other high technology industries located there.

Despite the rapid industrialization, agriculture continued to be a major economic activity. However, most modern agricultural activities in Alabama are heavily mechanized and use relatively little labor. Cotton remains important, but many of the old cotton fields now produce peanuts, soybeans, corn, and other crops.

As Alabama has industrialized, its population has shifted from rural areas to urban areas. In 1990, 60 percent of the people in the state lived in places with more than 2,500 inhabitants. Birmingham was the largest concentration, with a population of 266,000. African Americans, who lived almost entirely in rural areas during the early twentieth century, were heavily concentrated in larger cities in the southern and central parts of the state by 1990.

Alabama in the Twenty-first Century. Just before and after the turn of the twenty-first century, Alabama faced a series of issues that gave an uneven texture to its public life. In 1999, the state's politics were roiled when a dispute between the Democratic leadership of the state senate and the lieutenant governor closed the senate down for twelve of the thirty days devoted annually to its meetings. The state's conservative leaning was evident when in 2002 Judge Roy Moore of the Alabama Supreme Court denounced homosexuality as an "inherent evil" and an "abhorrent, immoral, detestable, crime against nature." Two years later, Moore failed in his attempt to place the Ten Commandments in the court's lobby and was removed from the bench for defying the court's rulings against him. The U.S. Supreme Court refused to hear his appeal. Within national politics, the state found itself among the "red states" that supported George W. Bush's election to the presidency both in 2000 and in 2004.

The state's prominent place as a battleground of the Civil Rights movement once again figured prominently in its public life. The turn of the twenty-first century saw the perpetrators of the 1963 Birmingham church bombing that took the lives of four African American girls finally charged with murder and placed on trial; those found guilty were jailed for life. A library named for renowned civil rights activist Rosa Parks was dedicated in 2000.

The somewhat whimsical Boll Weevil Monument in Enterprise recalls the important part cotton has played in Alabama's history. (Alabama Bureau of Tourism & Travel/ Dan Brothers)

Parks herself received national accolades for moral courage when she died in 2005.

Two hurricanes wreaked havoc on the state's Gulf coast. In September, 2004, the Gulf coast was badly damaged by Hurricane Ivan. In August of the following year, it was devastated by Hurricane Katrina but received scant attention nationally, since attention was focused on the catastrophe that the hurricane had visited upon New Orleans and its vicinity.

Deepwater Horizon. On April 20, 2010, an explosion aboard the offshore drilling rig Deepwater Horizon destroyed the rig, and the subsequent oil spill affected Alabama, Mississippi, Louisiana, and Florida. Despite several attempts, the well was not capped successfully until mid September, 2010. By July 2011,

Dauphin Street in Mobile, Alabama's second-largest city. (Alabama Bureau of Tourism & Travel/Karim Shamsi Basha)

about 491 miles of coastline in the four states had been contaminated by oil. In 2013, tar balls were still being recovered from Alabama beaches. A major step in the response of Alabama to the oil spill was the formation of the Coastal Alabama Leadership Council. The Leadership Council, a non-profit coalition of regional leaders, was an outgrowth of the Coastal Recovery Commission of Alabama created by executive order of then Governor Bob Riley, who served 2003-2011. In 2013, Alabama Attorney General Luther Strange took an active role in working with Alabamans with claims for damages against British Petroleum, the operator of Deepwater Horizon.

Energy and Environment. Coal mining in Alabama has long represented a threat to the natural environment, particularly to the water supply of the state. The Black Warrior River system is a major source of drinking water for Birmingham, Tuscaloosa, and other Alabama communities. In 2008, a mining company, Shepherd Bend proposed a 1,773-acre surface coal mine in Walker County, a short distance upstream from one of the largest intakes for Birmingham's water system. The Birmingham Water Works Board and environmentalists expressed grave concerns, but the Alabama Department of Environmental Management (ADEM) issued a permit in July 2008. The permit allowed the company to discharge waste water into Mulberry Fork, a tributary of the Black Warrior River. Like other surface mining effluents, the waste water would contain iron, sulfates, and other contaminants.

In October 2009, the Alabama Environmental Management Commission agreed to a hearing on whether water quality would be negatively impacted by the mine, but eventually the commission sided with ADEM on the pollution-abatement plan. The Southern Environmental Law Center continued its campaign to stop expansion of surface coal mining into regions that would impact water supply.

Carl L. Bankston III
Updated by the Editor

Alabama Time Line

700-1300	Mound Builders of the Mississippian culture build ceremonial mounds in the eastern part of North America, including Moundville in Alabama's Hale County.
1519	Spaniard Alonzo Alvárez de Piñeda sails into Mobile Bay.
July 2, 1540	Spanish explorer Hernando de Soto reaches Mobile, Alabama, while exploring southeastern North America.
1682	French explorer René-Robert Cavalier, sieur de La Salle, travels down the Mississippi to its mouth and claims all lands along the river in the name of France.
1712	French settlement and fort are established at Mobile, on the Gulf of Mexico.
1763	Great Britain takes control of Alabama and other parts of the Mississippi region after winning the French and Indian War. a

Operated by the government of Alabama, the Huntsville U.S. Space and Rocket Center received construction financing approval through a citizens initiative in 1968. (Alabama Bureau of Tourism & Travel)

Mar. 4, 1780	Spanish capture Mobile during the American Revolution.
1799	American surveyor marks the thirty-first latitude as the boundary between Spanish West Florida and the United States.
1802	State of Georgia gives up its claims on most of the lands of modern Alabama.
1805-1806	Choctaw, Chickasaw, and Cherokee lands are opened up to settlement by non-Native Americans.
Apr. 15, 1813	Spanish surrender Mobile to American forces; United States annexes part of Spanish West Florida, including the Alabama coast.
July, 1813	Creek Indian Wars begin between the United States and the Creeks.
Dec. 14, 1819	Alabama becomes the twenty-second state of the Union.
1826	Alabama's capital is moved from St. Stephens to Tuscaloosa.
Sept. 27, 1830	Choctaws cede the rest of their lands to Alabama and are removed to Oklahoma.
1846	Alabama's general assembly votes to move the capital to Montgomery.
1856	Large-scale coal mining begins when the Alabama Coal Mining Company establishes underground mines.
Jan. 11, 1861	Alabama convention votes to secede from the Union.
May 26, 1865	Last Confederate army unit surrenders, ending the Civil War.
1868	Alabama ratifies a new constitution, recognizing the right of blacks to vote; is then readmitted to the United States.
1871	Birmingham is founded.
1874	Conservative Democrats regain control of the Alabama state government.
Feb. 10, 1881	Booker T. Washington founds Tuskegee Institute (later Tuskegee University), a renowned African American center of higher education.
1901	New state constitution is ratified that effectively disenfranchises black Alabamians and greatly reduces the number of poor white voters.
1907	U.S. Steel Corporation establishes a steel industry in Birmingham.
1948	Democratic president Harry S. Truman's support for civil rights prompts conservative southern Democrats to form Dixiecrat Party, which nominates Strom Thurmond for president.
1955-1956	Montgomery bus boycott follows refusal of seamstress Rosa Parks to give up her bus seat to a white passenger.
1963	George C. Wallace begins the first of his four terms as governor.
1965	Civil rights march from Montgomery to Selma calls national attention to the need for a national voting rights bill.
1982	George Wallace is elected with black support to his third term as governor.
1987	Guy Hunt becomes the first Republican governor since Reconstruction.
1991	Alabama's state universities are ordered by a federal district judge to hire more minority faculty members.
2000-2003	Perpetrators of the 1963 church bombings are criminally charged and those found guilty are jailed.
2000	Library named for civil rights hero Rosa Parks is dedicated.
2003	Judge Roy Moore is removed from the state supreme court over his insistence that the Ten Commandments be posted on state property.
Sept. 16, 2004	Hurricane Ivan causes disastrous damage on state's Gulf of Mexico coast.
Aug. 29, 2005	Hurricane Katrina devastates Alabama's Gulf coast.
2008-2009	The Birmingham Water Works Board and environmentalists expresses grave concerns, but the Alabama Department of Environmental Management (ADEM) issues a permit in July 2008 allowing coal mining in The Black Warrior River, the major water source for Birmingham and other cities/communities nearby. In October 2009, a hearing on whether water quality would be negatively impacted by the mine, but eventually the commission sided with ADEM on the pollution-abatement plan. The Southern Environmental Law Center continued its campaign to stop expansion of surface coal mining into regions that would impact water supply.
April 10, 2011	An explosion aboard the British Petroleum (BP) offshore drilling rig Deepwater Horizon destroys the rig, and the subsequent oil spill affects Alabama, Mississippi, Louisiana, and Florida. By July 2011, about 491 miles of coastline in the four states are been contaminated by oil.
2013	Tar balls are still being recovered from Alabama beaches from the Deepwater Horizons explosion and oil spill.

Notes for Further Study

Published Sources. *Alabama: The History of a Deep South State* (1994) by William Warren Rogers, Robert David Ward, Willia Rogers, and Leah R. Atkins is an excellent history of Alabama. It is divided into three sections. The first ends with Alabama's Civil War defeat in 1865, the second covers the state from the end of the war to the 1920's, and the third covers Alabama to 1993. Allen Cronenberg's *Forth to the Mighty Conflict: Alabama and World War II* (1995) is an intriguing examination of the impact of World War II on the state and of the role played by Alabamians in this modern struggle. Some of the most interesting parts of the book concern the Tuskegee Army Air Field, where African American pilots learned to fly, and the prisoner-of-war camps for German soldiers in Alabama.

Readers will find an in-depth look at the beginnings of the Civil Rights movement in *Alabama in Daybreak of Freedom: The Montgomery Bus Boycott* (1997), a documentary history assembled by editor Stewart Burns. Historian Glenn T. Eskew provides a look at another center of the Civil Rights movement in

But for Birmingham: The Local and National Movements in the Civil Rights Struggle (1997), which describes the movement in Birmingham from the end of World War II onward. Winner of the 2002 Pulitzer Prize for General Nonfiction, Diane McWhorter's *Carry Me Home: Birmingham, Alabama—The Climactic Battle of the Civil Rights Revolution* (2001) details a pivotal year—1963—in the Civil Rights movement.

Marshall Frady's *Wallace* (1996) is a political biography of the controversial Alabama governor and U.S. presidential candidate George Wallace. Frady provides a detailed portrait of this complex individual, and he argues that Wallace's 1968 campaign for president helped to build a conservative working-class voting block that later contributed to the election of President Ronald Reagan. *Alabama Governors: A Political History of the State* (2001), edited by Samuel L. Webb and Margaret E. Armbrester, brings together biographical essays written by thirty-four noted historians and political scientists. Wayne Flint's *Alabama in the Twentieth Century* (2004) is an engaging, academic discussion of the state's achievements and failures. Young adults will appreciate the work of three books in particular: *Alabama Native Americans* (2004) by Carole Marsh, *Alabama* (2005) by Vanessa Brown, and *Alabama: The Heart of Dixie* (2002) by Michael A. Martin.

Web Resources. The Alabama Department of Archives and History has a wide range of Internet links available (www.archives.state.al.us). Use the About Alabama link to access information on nearly any aspect of Alabama history or modern life in Alabama. Those interested in learning about their family connections to Alabama's Civil War history will want to look at the Alabama Civil War Roots Homepage (www.rootsweb.ancestry.com/~alcwroot). The purpose of this page is to help people find their Alabama Civil War ancestors on both the Union and Confederate sides. Outdoor enthusiasts planning a trip to Alabama might want to consult Outdoor Alabama (www.outdooralabama.com/) for information on hunting, fishing, state parks, and wildlife watching. The Alabama Bureau of Tourism also has an informative site for visitors (http://alabama.travel/).

Horseshoe Bend National Military Park located in Daviston, Alabama, is managed by the National Park Service. It is the site of the last battle of the Creek War on March 27, 1814—the largest loss of life for Native Americans in a single battle in the history of United States. (Alabama Bureau of Tourism & Travel)

Counties

County	2012 Population	Pop. Rank	Land Area (sq. miles)	Area Rank	County	2012 Population	Pop. Rank	Land Area (sq. miles)	Area Rank
Autauga	55,514	24	594.44	55	Colbert	54,446	25	592.62	56
Baldwin	190,790	7	1,589.78	1	Conecuh	12,981	61	850.16	18
Barbour	27,201	39	884.88	16	Coosa	10,966	63	650.93	36
Bibb	22,597	46	622.58	45	Covington	37,955	33	1,030.46	8
Blount	57,826	22	644.78	38	Crenshaw	14,083	57	608.84	49
Bullock	10,474	65	622.80	44	Cullman	80,440	19	734.84	27
Butler	20,307	49	776.83	24	Dale	50,444	28	561.15	63
Calhoun	117,296	10	605.87	51	Dallas	42,864	30	978.69	10
Chambers	34,064	34	596.53	54	DeKalb	71,080	20	777.09	23
Cherokee	26,021	41	553.70	66	Elmore	80,629	18	618.48	46
Chilton	43,819	29	692.85	31	Escambia	37,994	32	945.08	12
Choctaw	13,633	58	913.50	13	Etowah	104,392	11	534.99	67
Clarke	25,161	42	1,238.46	3	Fayette	16,983	53	627.66	43
Clay	13,435	59	603.96	53	Franklin	31,761	37	633.82	41
Cleburne	14,832	55	560.10	64	Geneva	26,931	40	574.41	60
Coffee	51,252	27	678.97	33	Greene	8,876	67	647.11	37

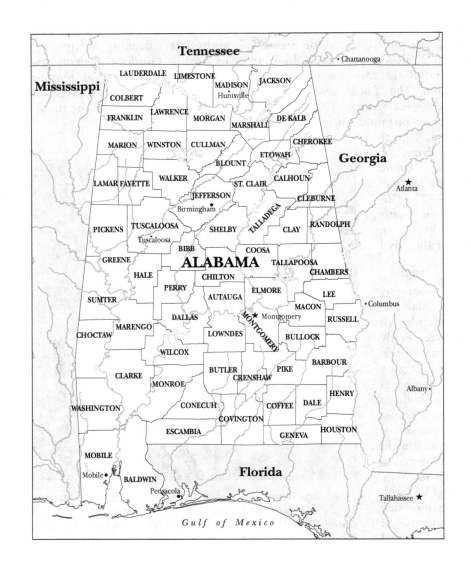

County	2012 Population	Pop. Rank	Land Area (sq. miles)	Area Rank
Hale	15,388	54	643.94	39
Henry	17,287	51	561.75	62
Houston	103,402	12	579.82	58
Jackson	53,019	26	1,077.87	7
Jefferson	660,009	1	1,111.28	5
Lamar	14,259	56	604.85	52
Lauderdale	92,542	14	667.70	35
Lawrence	33,838	35	690.68	32
Lee	147,257	8	607.54	50
Limestone	87,654	15	559.94	65
Lowndes	10,857	64	715.91	30
Macon	20,535	47	608.89	48
Madison	343,080	3	801.59	19
Marengo	20,401	48	976.88	11
Marion	30,327	38	742.29	25
Marshall	94,776	13	565.84	61
Mobile	413,936	2	1,229.44	4
Monroe	22,602	45	1,025.67	9
Montgomery	230,149	4	784.25	22
Morgan	120,395	9	579.34	59
Perry	10,181	66	719.66	28
Pickens	19,405	50	881.41	17
Pike	33,182	36	672.09	34
Randolph	22,675	44	580.55	57
Russell	57,820	23	641.14	40
Shelby	200,941	5	784.93	21
St. Clair	85,237	16	631.90	42
Sumter	13,427	60	903.89	14
Talladega	81,762	17	736.78	26
Tallapoosa	41,168	31	716.52	29
Tuscaloosa	198,596	6	1,321.75	2
Walker	66,221	21	791.19	20
Washington	17,109	52	1,080.21	6
Wilcox	11,431	62	888.50	15
Winston	24,108	43	612.98	47

Source: U.S. Census Bureau, 2012 Population Estimates

Cities
With 10,000 or more residents

Legal Name	2010 Population	Pop. Rank	Land Area (sq. miles)	Area Rank
Alabaster city	30,352	16	25.04	33
Albertville city	21,160	28	26.56	29
Alexander City city	14,875	40	40.84	15
Anniston city	23,106	22	45.64	14
Athens city	21,897	24	39.54	17
Atmore city	10,194	61	21.85	41
Auburn city	53,380	9	58.07	9
Bessemer city	27,456	17	39.85	16
Birmingham city	212,237	1	146.07	3
Calera city	11,620	58	24.09	36
Center Point city	16,921	34	6.12	63
Chelsea city	10,183	62	21.34	42
Cullman city	14,775	41	19.38	47
Daphne city	21,570	25	16.24	51
Decatur city	55,683	8	53.67	11
Dothan city	65,496	7	89.40	5
Enterprise city	26,562	18	31.24	23
Eufaula city	13,137	51	59.39	8
Fairfield city	11,117	59	3.47	64
Fairhope city	15,326	38	12.06	58
Florence city	39,319	11	26.00	30
Foley city	14,618	44	25.76	31
Forestdale CDP	10,162	63	6.86	62
Fort Payne city	14,012	47	55.49	10
Gadsden city	36,856	12	37.16	19
Gardendale city	13,893	48	22.55	40
Hartselle city	14,255	46	16.26	50
Helena city	16,793	35	20.34	43

Legal Name	2010 Population	Pop. Rank	Land Area (sq. miles)	Area Rank
Homewood city	25,167	20	8.36	61
Hoover city	81,619	6	47.16	13
Hueytown city	16,105	36	19.45	45
Huntsville city	180,105	4	209.05	1
Irondale city	12,349	55	17.31	48
Jacksonville city	12,548	54	9.84	60
Jasper city	14,352	45	28.46	26
Leeds city	11,773	56	22.86	39
Madison city	42,938	10	29.59	25
Millbrook city	14,640	43	12.81	55
Mobile city	195,111	3	139.11	4
Montgomery city	205,764	2	159.57	2
Moody city	11,726	57	24.40	35
Mountain Brook city	20,413	30	12.79	56
Muscle Shoals city	13,146	50	15.53	52
Northport city	23,330	21	16.75	49
Opelika city	26,477	19	59.59	7
Oxford city	21,348	27	30.67	24
Ozark city	14,907	39	34.09	20

Legal Name	2010 Population	Pop. Rank	Land Area (sq. miles)	Area Rank
Pelham city	21,352	26	39.02	18
Pell City city	12,695	53	24.75	34
Phenix City city	32,822	15	27.75	27
Pleasant Grove city	10,110	64	9.89	59
Prattville city	33,960	14	32.85	22
Prichard city	22,659	23	25.29	32
Saks CDP	10,744	60	12.15	57
Saraland city	13,405	49	23.18	38
Scottsboro city	14,770	42	50.65	12
Selma city	20,756	29	13.81	53
Sylacauga city	12,749	52	19.49	44
Talladega city	15,676	37	23.98	37
Tillmans Corner CDP	17,398	33	12.97	54
Troy city	18,033	32	27.63	28
Trussville city	19,933	31	33.03	21
Tuscaloosa city	90,468	5	60.23	6
Vestavia Hills city	34,033	13	19.41	46

Note: CDP–Census Designated Place
Source: U.S. Census Bureau, 2010 Census

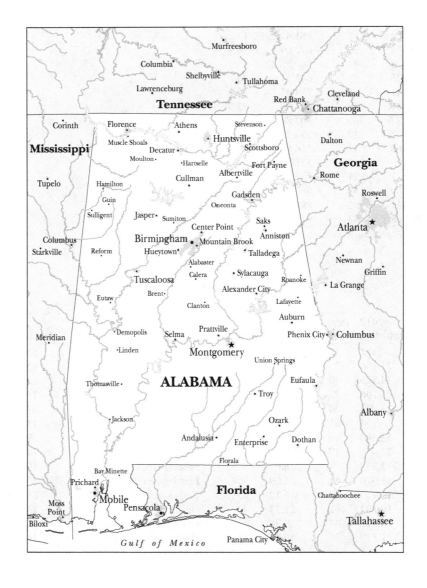

Survey Says...

This section presents current rankings from dozens of public and private sources. It shows how this state ranks in a number of critical categories, including education, job growth, cost of living, teen drivers, energy efficiency, and business environment. Sources include *Forbes, Reuters, U.S. News and World Report, CNN Money, Gallup,* and *Huffington Post.*

- Alabama ranked #39 in a government study measuring real gross domestic product (GDP)—the output of goods and services produced by labor and property located in the United States. The ranking is based on the percentage change compared with 2011 GDP.
  U.S. Department of Commerce, Bureau of Economic Analysis, June 2013; www.bea.gov

- Alabama ranked #26 in a government study measuring real gross domestic product (GDP)—the output of goods and services produced by labor and property located in the United States. The ranking is based on the dollar value of its GDP.
  U.S. Department of Commerce, Bureau of Economic Analysis, June 2013; www.bea.gov

- Alabama ranked #30 in the 17th edition of "Quality Counts; State of the States," Education Week's "report card" surveying key education indicators, policy efforts, and educational outcomes.
  Education Week, January 4, 2013 (online) and January 10, 2013 (print); www.edweek.org

- SERI (Science and Engineering Readiness Index) weighs the performance of the states' K-12 schools in preparing students in physics and calculus, the high school subjects considered most important for future scientists and engineers. Alabama ranked #47.
  Newsletter of the Forum on Education of the American Physical Society, Summer 2011 issue; www.huffingtonpost.com, July 11, 2011; updated October 1, 2012

- Business website 24/7 Wall St. identified the states with the highest and lowest percentages of residents 25 or older with a college degree or higher. Of "America's Worst Educated States," Alabama ranked #6 (#1 = worst).
  247wallst.com, posted October 15, 2012; consulted July 18, 2013

- MoneyRates.com ranked Alabama #39 on its list of the best to worst states for making a living. Criteria: average income; inflation; employment prospects; and workers' Workplace Environment assessments according to the Gallup-Healthways Well-Being Index.
  www.money-rates.com, posted April 1, 2013

- *Forbes* analyzed business costs, labor supply, regulatory environment, current economic climate, growth prospects, and quality of life, to compile its "Best States for Business" rankings. Alabama ranked #40.
  www.forbes.com. posted December 12, 2012

- The 2012 Gallup-Healthways Well-Being Index, surveyed American's opinions on economic confidence, workplace perceptions, community climate, personal choices, and health predictors to assess the "future livability" of each state. Alabama ranked #44.
  "Utah Poised to Be the Best State to Live In," Gallup Wellbeing, www.gallup.com, August 7, 2012

- On CNBC's list of "America's Top States for Business 2013," Alabama ranked #33. Criteria: measures of competitiveness developed with input from the National Association of Manufacturers, the Council on Competitiveness, and other business groups weighed with the states' own marketing criteria.
  www.cnbc.com, consulted July 19, 2013

- Alabama ranked #25 on MoneyRates list of "Best-and Worst-States to Retire 2012." Criteria: life expectancy, crime rate, climate, economic conditions, taxes, job opportunities, and cost of living.
  www.money-rates.com, October 22, 2012

- Alabama ranked #8 on the 2013 Bankrate "Best Places to Retire" list ranking the states and District of Columbia on various criteria relating to health, safety, and cost.
  www.bankrate.com, May 6, 2013

- Alabama ranked #47 on the Social Science Research Council's "American Human Development Report: The Measure of America," assessing the 50 states plus the District of Columbia on health, education, and living-standard criteria.
  The Measure of America 2013-2014, posted June 19, 2013; www.measureofamerica.org

- Alabama ranked #44 on the Foundation for Child Development's (FCD) Child Well-being Index (CWI). The FCD used the KIDS COUNT report and the National Survey of Children's Health, the only state-level source for several key indicators of child well-being.
  Foundation for Child Development, January 18, 2012; fcd-us.org

- Alabama ranked #44 overall according to the 2013 KIDS COUNT Data Book, a project of the Annie E. Casey Foundation. Criteria: children's economic well-being, education, health, and family and community indicators.
  KIDS COUNT Data Center's Data Book, released June 20, 2013; http://datacenter.kidscount.org

- Alabama ranked #40 in the children's economic well-being category by the 2013 KIDS COUNT Data Book, a project of the Annie E. Casey Foundation.
  KIDS COUNT Data Center's Data Book, released June 20, 2013; http://datacenter.kidscount.org

- Alabama ranked #44 in the children's educational opportunities and attainments category by the 2013 KIDS COUNT Data Book, a project of the Annie E. Casey Foundation.
  KIDS COUNT Data Center's Data Book, released June 20, 2013; http://datacenter.kidscount.org

- Alabama ranked #35 in the children's health category by the 2013 KIDS COUNT Data Book, a project of the Annie E. Casey Foundation.
  KIDS COUNT Data Center's Data Book, released June 20, 2013; http://datacenter.kidscount.org

- Alabama ranked #44 in the family and community circumstances that factor into children's well-being category by the 2013 KIDS COUNT Data Book, a project of the Annie E. Casey Foundation.
  KIDS COUNT Data Center's Data Book, released June 20, 2013; http://datacenter.kidscount.org

- Alabama ranked #45 in the 2012 Gallup-Healthways Well-Being Index. Criteria: emotional health; physical health; healthy behavior; work environment; basic access to food, shelter, health care; and a safe and satisfying place to live.
  2012 State of Well-Being, Gallup-Healthways Well-Being Index, released February 28, 2013; www.well-beingindex.com

- *U.S. News and World Report's* "Best States for Teen Drivers" rankings are based on driving and road safety laws, federal reports on driver's licenses, car accident fatality, and road-quality statistics. Alabama ranked #32.
  U.S. News and World Report, March 18, 2010; www.usnews.com

- The Yahoo! Sports service Rivals.com ranks the states according to the strength of their high school football programs. Alabama ranked #7.
  "Ranking the States: Where Is the Best Football Played?," November 18, 2011; highschool.rivals.com

- iVillage ranked the states by hospitable living conditions for women. Criteria: economic success, access to affordable childcare, health care, reproductive rights, female representation in government, and educational attainment. Alabama ranked #45.
  iVillage, "50 Best to Worst States for Women," March 14, 2012; www.ivillage.com

- The League of American Bicyclists's "Bicycle Friendly States" ranked Alabama #49. Criteria: legislation and enforcement, policies and programs, infrastructure and funding, education and advocacy, and evaluation and planning.
  "Washington Tops the Bicycle-Friendly State Ranking," May 1, 2013; bicycling.com

- The federal Corporation for National and Community Service ranked the states and the District of Columbia by volunteer rates. Alabama ranked #41 for community service.
  "Volunteering and Civic Life in America 2012," www.volunteeringinamerica.gov, accessed July 24, 2013

- The Hospital Safety Score ranked states and the District of Columbia on their hospitals' performance scores. Alabama ranked #18. Criteria: avoiding preventable harm and medical errors, as demonstrated by 26 hospital safety metrics.
  Spring 2013 Hospital Safety Score, May 8, 2013; www.hospitalsafetyscore.org

- GMAC Insurance ranked the states and the District of Columbia by the performance of their drivers on the GMAC Insurance National Drivers Test, comprised of DMV test questions. Alabama ranked #30.
  "2011 GMAC Insurance National Drivers Test," www.gmacinsurance.com, accessed July 23, 2013

- Alabama ranked #17 in a "State Integrity Investigation" analysis of laws and practices intended to deter corruption and promote accountability and openness in campaign finance, ethics laws, lobbying regulations and management of state pension funds.
  "What's Your State's Grade?," www.publicintegrity.org, accessed July 23, 2013

- Alabama ranked #17 among the states and the District of Columbia in total rail miles, as tracked by the Association of American Railroads.
  "U.S. Freight Railroad Industry Snapshot: Railroads and States: Total Rail Miles by State: 2011"; www.aar.org, accessed July 23, 2013

- According to statistics compiled by the Beer Institute, Alabama ranked #22 among the states and the District of Columbia in per capita beer consumption of persons 21 years or older.
  "Shipments of Malt Beverages and Per Capita Consumption by State 2012;" www.beerinstitute.org

- According to Concordia University's "Public Education Costs per Pupil by State Rankings," based on statistics gathered by the U.S. Census Bureau, which includes the District of Columbia, Alabama ranked #39.
  Concordia University Online; education.cu-portland.edu, accessed July 24, 2013

- Alabama ranked #27 among the states and the District of Columbia in population density based on U.S. Census Bureau data for resident population and total land area. "List of U.S. States by Population Density."
  www.wikipedia.org, accessed July 24, 2013

- In "America's Health Rankings, 2012 Edition," by the United Health Foundation, Alabama ranked #45. Criteria included: rate of high school graduation; violent crime rate; incidence of infectious disease; childhood immunizations; prevalence of diabetes; per capita public-health funding; percentage of uninsured population; rate of children in poverty; and availability of primary-care physicians.
  United Health Foundation; www.americashealthrankings.org, accessed July 24, 2013

- The TechNet 2012 "State Broadband Index" ranked Alabama #38 on the following criteria: broadband adoption; network quality; and economic structure. Improved broadband use is hoped to promote economic development, build strong communities, improve delivery of government services and upgrade educational systems.
  TechNet; www.technet.org, accessed July 24, 2013

- Alabama was ranked #40 among the states and District of Columbia on the American Council for an Energy-Efficient Economy's "State Energy Efficiency Scorecard" for 2012.
  American Council for an Energy-Efficient Economy; aceee.org/sector/state-policy/scorecard, accessed July 24, 2013

Statistical Tables

DEMOGRAPHICS
Resident State and National Population, 1950-2012
Projected State and National Population, 2000-2030
Population by Age, 2012
Population by Race, 2012
Population by Hispanic Origin and Race, 2012

VITAL STATISTICS
Death Rates by Leading Causes, 2010
Death Rates by Selected Causes, 2010
Abortion Rates, 2009
Infant Mortality Rates, 1995-2009
Marriage and Divorce Rates, 2000-2011

ECONOMY
Nominal Gross Domestic Product by Industry, 2012
Real Gross Domestic Product, 2000-2012
Personal Income Per Capita, 1930-2012
Non-Farm Employment by Sector, 2012
Foreign Exports, 2000-2012
Energy Consumption, 2011

LAND AND WATER
Surface Area and Federally-Owned Land, 2007
Land Cover/Use of Non-Federal Rural Land, 2007
Farms and Crop Acreage, 2012

HEALTH AND MEDICAL CARE
Medical Professionals, 2012
Health Insurance Coverage, 2011
HIV, STD, and Tuberculosis Cases and Rates, 2011
Cigarette Smoking, 2011

HOUSING
Home Ownership Rates, 1995-2012
Home Sales, 2000-2010
Value of Owner-Occupied Homes, 2011

EDUCATION
School Enrollment, 2011
Educational Attainment, 2011
Public College Finances, FY 2012

TRANSPORTATION AND TRAVEL
Motor Vehicle Registrations and Drivers Licenses, 2011
Domestic Travel Expenditures, 2009
Retail Gasoline Prices, 2013
Public Road Length, 2011

CRIME AND LAW ENFORCEMENT
Full-Time Law Enforcement Officers, 2011
Prison Population, 2000-2012
Crime Rate, 2011

GOVERNMENT AND FINANCE
Local Governments by Type, 2012
State Government Revenue, 2011
State Government Expenditures, 2011
State Government General Expenditures by Function, 2011
State Government Finances, Cash and Debt, 2011

POLITICS
Composition of the Senate, 1995-2013
Composition of the House of Representatives, 1995-2013
Composition of State Legislature, 2004-2013
Voter Participation in Presidential Elections, 1980-2012
Governors Since Statehood

DEMOGRAPHICS

Resident State and National Population, 1950–2012

Year	State Population	U.S. Population	State Share
1950	3,062,000	151,326,000	2.02%
1960	3,267,000	179,323,000	1.82%
1970	3,444,354	203,302,031	1.69%
1980	3,893,888	226,545,805	1.72%
1990	4,040,587	248,709,873	1.62%
2000	4,447,207	281,424,600	1.58%
2010	4,779,736	308,745,538	1.55%
2012	4,822,023	313,914,040	1.54%

Note: 1950/1960 population figures are rounded to the nearest thousand.
Source: U.S. Census Bureau, Decennial Census 1950–2010; U.S. Census Bureau, 2012 Population Estimates

Projected State and National Population, 2000–2030

Year	State Population	U.S. Population	State Share
2000	4,447,100	281,421,906	1.58%
2005	4,527,166	295,507,134	1.53%
2010	4,596,330	308,935,581	1.49%
2015	4,663,111	322,365,787	1.45%
2020	4,728,915	335,804,546	1.41%
2025	4,800,092	349,439,199	1.37%
2030	4,874,243	363,584,435	1.34%
State population growth, 2000–2030			427,143
State percentage growth, 2000–2030			9.6%

Source: U.S. Census Bureau, Population Division, Interim State Population Projections, 2005

Population by Age, 2012

Age Group	State Population	Percent of Total Population	
		State	U.S.
Under 5 years	305,267	6.3%	6.4%
5 to 14 years	627,468	13.0%	13.1%
15 to 24 years	676,612	14.0%	14.0%
25 to 34 years	617,757	12.8%	13.5%
35 to 44 years	606,667	12.6%	12.9%
45 to 54 years	673,464	14.0%	14.1%
55 to 64 years	615,408	12.8%	12.3%
65 to 74 years	402,571	8.3%	7.6%
75 to 84 years	216,705	4.5%	4.2%
85 years and older	80,104	1.7%	1.9%
Under 18 years	1,124,406	23.3%	23.5%
65 years and older	699,380	14.5%	13.7%
Median age (years)	–	38.2	37.4

Source: U.S. Census Bureau, Annual Estimates of the Resident Population for Selected Age Groups by Sex for the United States, States, Counties, and Puerto Rico Commonwealth and Municipios: April 1, 2010 to July 1, 2012

Population by Race, 2012

Race	State Population	Percent of Total Population	
		State	U.S.
All residents	4,822,023	100.00%	100.00%
White	3,373,844	69.97%	77.89%
African American	1,279,805	26.54%	13.13%
Native American	33,579	0.70%	1.23%
Asian	59,602	1.24%	5.14%
Native Hawaiian	5,270	0.11%	0.23%
Two or more races	69,923	1.45%	2.39%

Source: U.S. Census Bureau, Population Division, Annual Estimates of the Resident Population by Sex, Race and Hispanic Origin for the United States, States, and Counties: April 1, 2010 to July 1, 2012

Population by Hispanic Origin and Race, 2012

Hispanic Origin/Race	State Population	Percent of Total Population	
		State	U.S.
All residents	4,822,023	100.00%	100.00%
All Hispanic residents	196,032	4.07%	16.89%
Hispanic			
White	163,666	3.39%	14.91%
African American	13,980	0.29%	0.79%
Native American	7,125	0.15%	0.49%
Asian	1,619	0.03%	0.17%
Native Hawaiian	3,090	0.06%	0.06%
Two or more races	6,552	0.14%	0.48%
Not Hispanic			
White	3,210,178	66.57%	62.98%
African American	1,265,825	26.25%	12.34%
Native American	26,454	0.55%	0.74%
Asian	57,983	1.20%	4.98%
Native Hawaiian	2,180	0.05%	0.17%
Two or more races	63,371	1.31%	1.91%

Source: U.S. Census Bureau, Population Division, Annual Estimates of the Resident Population by Sex, Race and Hispanic Origin for the United States, States, and Counties: April 1, 2010 to July 1, 2012

VITAL STATISTICS

Death Rates by Leading Causes, 2010

Cause	State	U.S.
Malignant neoplasms	207.4	186.2
Ischaemic heart diseases	116.1	122.9
Other forms of heart disease	121.8	53.4
Chronic lower respiratory diseases	58.8	44.7
Cerebrovascular diseases	55.3	41.9
Organic, incl. symptomatic, mental disorders	48.4	35.7
Other degenerative diseases of the nervous sys.	34.4	28.4
Other external causes of accidental injury	29.6	26.5
Diabetes mellitus	26.9	22.4
Hypertensive diseases	21.4	20.4
All causes	1,004.3	799.5

Note: Figures are age-adjusted death rates per 100,000 population
Source: CDC/NCHS, Underlying Cause of Death 1999–2010 on CDC WONDER Online Database

Death Rates by Selected Causes, 2010

Cause	State	U.S.
Assault	8.2	5.2
Diseases of the liver	15.4	13.9
Human immunodeficiency virus (HIV) disease	3.2	2.7
Influenza and pneumonia	20.0	16.2
Intentional self-harm	14.2	12.4
Malnutrition	1.2	0.9
Obesity and other hyperalimentation	1.3	1.8
Renal failure	22.9	14.4
Transport accidents	20.4	12.1
Viral hepatitis	2.1	2.4

Note: Figures are age-adjusted death rates per 100,000 population; A dash indicates that data was not available or was suppressed
Source: CDC/NCHS, Underlying Cause of Death 1999–2010 on CDC WONDER Online Database

Abortion Rates, 2009

Category	2009
By state of residence	
Total abortions	9,749
Abortion rate[1]	10.3%
Abortion ratio[2]	156
By state of occurrence	
Total abortions	10,882
Abortion rate[1]	11.5%
Abortion ratio[2]	174
Abortions obtained by out-of-state residents	18.2%
U.S. abortion rate[1]	15.1%
U.S. abortion ratio[2]	227

Note: (1) Number of abortions per 1,000 women aged 15–44 years; (2) Number of abortions per 1,000 live births; A dash indicates that data was not available
Source: CDC/NCHS, Morbidity and Mortality Weekly Report, November 23, 2012 (Abortion Surveillance, United States, 2009)

Infant Mortality Rates, 1995–2009

Category	1995	2000	2005	2009
All state residents	9.78	9.51	9.53	8.28
All U.S. residents	7.57	6.89	6.86	6.39
All state white residents	7.22	6.68	7.39	6.41
All U.S. white residents	6.30	5.71	5.73	5.33
All state black residents	14.90	15.45	14.61	12.65
All U.S. black residents	14.58	13.48	13.26	12.12

Note: Figures represent deaths per 1,000 live births of resident infants under one year old, exclusive of fetal deaths; A dash indicates that data was not available or was suppressed.
Source: Centers of Disease Control and Prevention, Division of Vital Statistics, Linked Birth/Infant Death Records on CDC Wonder Online

Marriage and Divorce Rates, 2000–2011

Year	Marriage Rate		Divorce Rate	
	State	U.S.	State	U.S.
2000	10.1	8.2	5.5	4.0
2002	9.9	8.0	5.4	3.9
2004	9.4	7.8	4.9	3.7
2006	9.2	7.5	4.9	3.7
2008	8.6	7.1	4.3	3.5
2010	8.2	6.8	4.4	3.6
2011	8.4	6.8	4.3	3.6

Note: Rates are based on provisional counts of marriages/divorces by state of occurrence and are per 1,000 total population residing in area
Source: CDC/NCHS, National Vital Statistics System

ECONOMY

Nominal Gross Domestic Product by Industry, 2012
In millions of current dollars

Industry	State GDP
Accommodation and food services	5,118
Administrative and waste management services	4,619
Agriculture, forestry, fishing, and hunting	1,863
Arts, entertainment, and recreation	635
Construction	7,784
Educational services	1,073
Finance and insurance	11,280
Health care and social assistance	13,390
Information	4,047
Management of companies and enterprises	1,770
Manufacturing	30,001
Mining	2,072
Other services, except government	5,587
Professional, scientific, and technical services	11,461
Real estate and rental and leasing	17,899
Retail trade	13,263
Transportation and warehousing	5,308
Utilities	6,092
Wholesale trade	9,994

Source: U.S. Department of Commerce, Bureau of Economic Analysis, Survey of Current Business

Real Gross Domestic Product, 2000–2012
In millions of chained 2005 dollars

Year	State GDP	U.S. GDP	State Share
2000	132,699	11,225,406	1.18%
2005	150,968	12,539,116	1.20%
2010	153,839	12,897,088	1.19%
2012	157,272	13,430,576	1.17%

Source: U.S. Department of Commerce, Bureau of Economic Analysis, Survey of Current Business

Personal Income Per Capita, 1930–2012

Year	State	U.S.
1930	$263	$618
1940	$279	$593
1950	$904	$1,503
1960	$1,539	$2,268
1970	$2,962	$4,084
1980	$7,825	$10,091
1990	$15,618	$19,354
2000	$24,067	$30,319
2010	$33,710	$39,791
2012	$35,625	$42,693

Source: U.S. Department of Commerce, Bureau of Economic Analysis, Regional Economic Accounts

Non-Farm Employment by Sector, 2012
In thousands

Sector	Employment
Construction	79.1
Education and health services	218.5
Financial activities	92.5
Government	376.5
Information	22.5
Leisure and hospitality	173.7
Mining and logging	12.6
Manufacturing	243.0
Other services	80.5
Professional and business services	218.4
Trade, transportation, and utilities	365.3
All sectors	1,882.6

Source: U.S. Bureau of Labor Statistics, State and Area Employment

Foreign Exports, 2000–2012
In millions of dollars

Year	State Exports	U.S. Exports	State Share
2000	7,317	712,054	1.03%
2002	8,256	649,940	1.27%
2004	9,062	768,554	1.18%
2006	13,898	973,994	1.43%
2008	15,879	1,222,545	1.30%
2010	15,495	1,208,080	1.28%
2012	19,572	1,478,268	1.32%

Note: U.S. figures exclude data from Puerto Rico, U.S. Virgin Islands, and unallocated exports
Source: U.S. Department of Commerce, International Trade Admin., Office of Trade and Industry Information, Manufacturing and Services

Energy Consumption, 2011
In trillions of BTUs, except as noted

Total energy consumption
Total state energy consumption	1,931.3
Total U.S. energy consumption	97,387.3
State share of U.S. total	1.98%

Per capita consumption (in millions of BTUs)
Total state per capita consumption	402.0
Total U.S. per capita consumption	312.6

End-use sectors
Residential	376.9
Commercial	257.2
Industrial	810.0
Transportation	487.2

Sources of energy
Petroleum	549.5
Natural gas	614.8
Coal	651.0
Renewable energy	260.6
Nuclear electric power	411.8

Source: U.S. Energy Information Administration, State Energy Data 2011: Consumption

LAND AND WATER

Surface Area and Federally-Owned Land, 2007
In thousands of acres

Category	State	U.S.	State Share
Total surface area	33,423.8	1,937,664.2	1.72%
Total land area	32,133.7	1,886,846.9	1.70%
Non-federal land	31,135.8	1,484,910.0	2.10%
Developed	2,942.9	111,251.2	2.65%
Rural	28,192.9	1,373,658.8	2.05%
Federal land	997.9	401,936.9	0.25%
Water area	1,290.1	50,817.3	2.54%

Source: U.S. Department of Agriculture, Natural Resources Conservation Service, 2007 National Resources Inventory

Land Cover/Use of Non-Federal Rural Land, 2007
In thousands of acres

Category	State	U.S.	State Share
Total rural land	28,192.9	1,373,658.8	2.05%
Cropland	2,221.9	357,023.5	0.62%
CRP[1] land	456.6	32,850.2	1.39%
Pastureland	3,464.2	118,615.7	2.92%
Rangeland	73.3	409,119.4	0.02%
Forest land	21,529.4	406,410.4	5.30%
Other rural land	447.5	49,639.6	0.90%

Note: (1) Conservation Reserve Program was created to assist private landowners in converting highly erodible cropland to vegetative cover.
Source: U.S. Department of Agriculture, Natural Resources Conservation Service, 2007 National Resources Inventory

Farms and Crop Acreage, 2012

Category	State	U.S.	State Share
Farms (in thousands)	46.5	2,170.0	2.14%
Acres (in millions)	8.9	914.0	0.97%
Acres per farm	190.3	421.2	–

Source: U.S. Department of Agriculture, National Agricultural Statistical Service, Quick Stats, 2012 Survey Data

HEALTH AND MEDICAL CARE

Medical Professionals, 2012

Profession	State Number	U.S. Number	State Share	State Rate[1]	U.S. Rate[1]
Physicians[2]	10,601	894,637	1.18%	220.7	287.1
Dentists	2,089	193,587	1.08%	43.5	62.1
Podiatrists	140	17,469	0.80%	2.9	5.6
Optometrists	669	45,638	1.47%	13.9	14.6
Chiropractors	681	77,494	0.88%	14.2	24.9

Note: (1) Rates are per 100,000 population; (2) Includes total, active Doctors of Osteopathic Medicine and Doctors of Medicine in 2011.
Source: U.S. Department of Health and Human Services, Bureau of Health Professions, Area Health Resource File, 2012-2013

Health Insurance Coverage, 2011

Category	State	U.S.
Total persons covered	4,143,000	260,214,000
Total persons not covered	622,000	48,613,000
Percent not covered	13.1%	15.7%
Children under age 18 covered	1,090,000	67,143,000
Children under age 18 not covered	86,000	6,965,000
Percent of children not covered	7.3%	9.4%

Source: U.S. Census Bureau, Current Population Survey, 2012 Annual Social and Economic Supplement

HIV, STD, and Tuberculosis Cases and Rates, 2011

Disease	State Cases	State Rate[1]	U.S. Rate[1]
Chlamydia	29,626	619.8	457.6
Gonorrhea	9,132	191.1	104.2
HIV diagnosis	837	20.9	15.8
HIV, stage 3 (AIDS)	391	9.8	10.3
Syphilis, early latent	268	5.6	4.3
Syphilis, primary/secondary	228	4.8	4.5
Tuberculosis	161	3.4	3.4

Note: (1) Rates are per 100,000 population
Source: Centers for Disease Control and Prevention

Cigarette Smoking, 2011

Category	State	U.S.
Adults who are current smokers	24.3%	21.2%
Adults who smoke everyday	18.6%	15.4%
Adults who smoke some days	5.8%	5.7%
Adults who are former smokers	25.1%	25.1%
Adults who never smoked	50.6%	52.9%

Source: Centers for Disease Control and Prevention, Behaviorial Risk Factor Surveillance System, Tobacco Use, 2011

HOUSING

Home Ownership Rates, 1995–2012

Area	1995	2000	2005	2010	2012
State	70.1%	73.2%	76.6%	73.2%	71.9%
U.S.	64.7%	67.4%	68.9%	66.9%	65.4%

Source: U.S. Census Bureau, Housing Vacancies and Homeownership, Annual Statistics

Home Sales, 2000–2010
In thousands of units

Year	State Sales	U.S. Sales	State Share
2000	67.0	5,174	1.29%
2002	82.2	5,632	1.46%
2004	112.0	6,778	1.65%
2006	125.8	6,478	1.94%
2008	86.0	4,913	1.75%
2010	71.6	4,908	1.46%

Note: Units include single-family homes, condos and co-ops
Source: National Association of Realtors, Real Estate Outlook, Market Trends & Insights

Value of Owner-Occupied Homes, 2011

Value	Total Units in State	Percent of Total, State	Percent of Total, U.S.
Less than $50,000	206,692	16.0%	8.8%
$50,000 to $99,000	310,299	24.1%	16.0%
$100,000 to $149,000	250,739	19.4%	16.5%
$150,000 to $199,000	206,216	16.0%	15.4%
$200,000 to $299,000	177,195	13.7%	18.2%
$300,000 to $499,000	95,094	7.4%	15.2%
$500,000 to $999,000	32,740	2.5%	7.9%
$1,000,000 or more	10,242	0.8%	2.0%
Median value	–	$122,700	$173,600

Source: U.S. Census Bureau, 2011 American Community Survey 1-Year Estimates

EDUCATION

School Enrollment, 2011

Educational Level	Students Enrolled in State	Percent of Total, State	Percent of Total, U.S.
All levels	1,241,786	100.0%	100.0%
Nursery school, preschool	65,528	5.3%	6.0%
Kindergarten	66,517	5.4%	5.1%
Elementary (grades 1–8)	513,567	41.4%	39.5%
Secondary (grades 9–12)	259,573	20.9%	20.7%
College or graduate school	336,601	27.1%	28.7%

Note: Figures cover the population 3 years and over enrolled in school
Source: U.S. Census Bureau, 2011 American Community Survey 1-Year Estimates

Educational Attainment, 2011

Highest Level of Education	State	U.S.
High school diploma	82.7%	85.9%
Bachelor's degree	22.3%	28.5%
Graduate/Professional degree	8.4%	10.6%

Note: Figures cover the population 25 years and over
Source: U.S. Census Bureau, 2011 American Community Survey 1-Year Estimates

Public College Finances, FY 2012

Category	State	U.S.
Full-time equivalent enrollment (FTE)[1]	205,317	11,548,974
Educational appropriations per FTE[2]	$5,855	$5,906
Net tuition revenue per FTE[3]	$8,553	$5,189
Total educational revenue per FTE[4]	$13,785	$11,043

(1) Full-time equivalent enrollment equates student credit hours to full time, academic year students, but excludes medical students; (2) Educational appropriations measure state and local support available for public higher education operating expenses including ARRA funds and excludes appropriations for independent institutions, financial aid for students attending independent institutions, research, hospitals, and medical education; (3) Net tuition revenue is calculated by taking the gross amount of tuition and fees, less state and institutional financial aid, tuition waivers or discounts, and medical student tuition and fees. Net tuition revenue used for capital debt service is included in the net tuition revenue figures; (4) Total educational revenue is the sum of educational appropriations and net tuition excluding net tuition revenue used for capital debt service.
Source: State Higher Education Executive Officers, State Higher Education Finance FY 2012

TRANSPORTATION AND TRAVEL

Motor Vehicle Registrations and Drivers Licenses, 2011

Vehicle Type	State	U.S.	State Share
Automobiles[1]	2,307,668	125,656,528	1.84%
Buses	12,373	666,064	1.86%
Trucks	2,364,601	118,455,587	2.00%
Motorcycles	127,301	8,437,502	1.51%
Drivers licenses	3,798,552	211,874,649	1.79%

Note: Motor vehicle registrations include private, commercial, and publicly-owned vehicles; (1) Includes taxicabs
Source: U.S. Department of Transportation, Federal Highway Administration

Domestic Travel Expenditures, 2009
In millions of dollars

Category	State	U.S.	State Share
Travel expenditures	$7,123	$610,200	1.17%

Note: Figures represent U.S. spending on domestic overnight trips and day trips of 50 miles or more, one way, away from home. Excludes spending by foreign visitors.
Source: U.S. Travel Association, Impact of Travel on State Economies, 2009

Retail Gasoline Prices, 2013

Gasoline Grade	State Average	U.S. Average
Regular	$3.40	$3.65
Mid	$3.60	$3.81
Premium	$3.78	$3.98
Diesel	$3.78	$3.88
Excise tax[1]	39.3 cents	49.4 cents

Note: Gasoline prices as of 7/26/2013; (1) Includes state and federal excise taxes and other state taxes as of July 1, 2013
Source: American Automobile Association, Daily Fuel Guage Report; American Petroleum Institute, State Motor Fuel Taxes, 2013

Public Road Length, 2011

Type	State Mileage	U.S. Mileage	State Share
Interstate highways	906	46,960	1.93%
Other highways	129	15,719	0.82%
Principal arterial	3,179	156,262	2.03%
Minor arterial	6,118	242,942	2.52%
Major collector	15,473	534,592	2.89%
Minor collector	6,699	266,357	2.52%
Local	69,165	2,814,925	2.46%
Urban	25,252	1,095,373	2.31%
Rural	76,416	2,982,383	2.56%
Total	101,668	4,077,756	2.49%

Note: Combined urban and rural road mileage equals the total of the other road types
Source: U.S. Department of Transportation, Federal Highway Administration, Public Road Length, 2011

CRIME AND LAW ENFORCEMENT

Full-Time Law Enforcement Officers, 2011

Gender	State Number	State Rate[1]	U.S. Rate[1]
Male officers	10,019	224.5	210.3
Female officers	756	16.9	28.1
Total officers	10,775	241.4	238.3

Note: (1) Rates are per 100,000 population
Source: Federal Bureau of Investigation, Uniform Crime Reports, Crime in the United States 2011

Prison Population, 2000–2012

Year	State Population	U.S. Population	State Share
2000	26,332	1,391,261	1.89%
2005	27,888	1,527,929	1.83%
2010	31,764	1,613,803	1.97%
2011	32,270	1,598,783	2.02%
2012	32,431	1,571,013	2.06%

Note: Figures include prisoners under the jurisdiction of state or federal correctional authorities.
Source: U.S. Department of Justice, Bureau of Justice Statistics, Prisoners in 2006, 2011, 2012 (Advance Counts)

Crime Rate, 2011
Incidents per 100,000 residents

Category	State	U.S.
Violent crimes	420.1	386.3
Murder	6.3	4.7
Forcible rape	28.5	26.8
Robbery	102.2	113.7
Aggravated assault	283.0	241.1
Property crimes	3,606.1	2,908.7
Burglary	1,064.3	702.2
Larceny/theft	2,319.7	1,976.9
Motor vehicle theft	222.0	229.6
All crimes	4,026.2	3,295.0

Source: Federal Bureau of Investigation, Uniform Crime Reports, Crime in the United States 2011

GOVERNMENT AND FINANCE

Local Governments by Type, 2012

Government Type	State	U.S.	State Share
All local governments	1,208	89,004	1.36%
County	67	3,031	2.21%
Municipality	461	19,522	2.36%
Town/Township	0	16,364	0.00%
Special District	548	37,203	1.47%
Ind. School District	132	12,884	1.02%

Source: U.S. Census Bureau, 2012 Census of Governments: Organization Component Preliminary Estimates

State Government Revenue, 2011
In thousands of dollars, except for per capita figures

Total revenue	**$26,305,162**
Total revenue per capita, State	$5,476
Total revenue per capita, U.S.	$7,271
General revenue	$23,276,781
Intergovernmental revenue	$8,881,520
Taxes	$8,635,527
General sales	$2,174,639
Selective sales	$2,400,488
License taxes	$496,117
Individual income taxes	$2,795,906
Corporate income taxes	$301,178
Other taxes	$467,199
Current charges	$4,452,308
Miscellaneous general revenue	$1,307,426
Utility revenue	$0
Liquor store revenue	$266,951
Insurance trust revenue[1]	$2,761,430

Note: (1) Within insurance trust revenue, net earnings of state retirement systems is a calculated statistic, and thus can be positive or negative. Net earnings is the sum of earnings on investments plus gains on investments minus losses on investments.
Source: U.S. Census Bureau, 2011 Annual Survey of State Government Finances

State Government Expenditures, 2011
In thousands of dollars, except for per capita figures

Total expenditure	$28,061,237
Total expenditure per capita, State	$5,842
Total expenditure per capita, U.S.	$6,427
Intergovernmental expenditure	$6,800,787
Direct expenditure	$21,260,450
Current operation	$14,898,156
Capital outlay	$1,920,251
Insurance benefits and repayments	$3,526,164
Assistance and subsidies	$565,447
Interest on debt	$350,432
Utility expenditure	$0
Liquor store expenditure	$244,605
Insurance trust expenditure	$3,526,164

Source: U.S. Census Bureau, 2011 Annual Survey of State Government Finances

State Government General Expenditures by Function, 2011
In thousands of dollars

Education	$10,938,129
Public welfare	$5,961,891
Hospitals	$1,948,230
Health	$609,367
Highways	$1,616,245
Police protection	$183,957
Correction	$563,058
Natural resources	$270,950
Parks and recreation	$36,497
Governmental administration	$579,928
Interest on general debt	$350,432
Other and unallocable	$1,231,784

Source: U.S. Census Bureau, 2011 Annual Survey of State Government Finances

State Government Finances, Cash and Debt, 2011
In thousands of dollars, except for per capita figures

Debt at end of fiscal year	
State, total	$9,067,280
State, per capita	$1,888
U.S., per capita	$3,635
Cash and security holdings	
State, total	$34,335,207
State, per capita	$7,148
U.S., per capita	$11,759

Source: U.S. Census Bureau, 2011 Annual Survey of State Government Finances

POLITICS

Composition of the Senate, 1995–2013

Congress (Year)	State/U.S	Dem	Rep	Total
104th (1995)	State delegates	1	1	2
	Total U.S.	48	52	100
105th (1997)	State delegates	0	2	2
	Total U.S.	45	55	100
106th (1999)	State delegates	0	2	2
	Total U.S.	45	55	100
107th (2001)	State delegates	0	2	2
	Total U.S.	50	50	100
108th (2003)	State delegates	0	2	2
	Total U.S.	48	51	100
109th (2005)	State delegates	0	2	2
	Total U.S.	44	55	100
110th (2007)	State delegates	0	2	2
	Total U.S.	49	49	100
111th (2009)	State delegates	0	2	2
	Total U.S.	57	41	100
112th (2011)	State delegates	0	2	2
	Total U.S.	51	47	100
113th (2013)	State delegates	0	2	2
	Total U.S.	54	45	100

Note: Figures are for the starts of first sessions; Totals include Democratic (Dem) and Republican (Rep) members as well as vacancies and seats held by independent party members
Source: U.S. Congress, Congressional Directory

Composition of the House of Representatives, 1995–2013

Congress (Year)	State/U.S	Dem	Rep	Total
104th (1995)	State delegates	4	3	7
	Total U.S.	204	230	435
105th (1997)	State delegates	2	5	7
	Total U.S.	207	226	435
106th (1999)	State delegates	2	5	7
	Total U.S.	211	223	435
107th (2001)	State delegates	2	5	7
	Total U.S.	212	221	435
108th (2003)	State delegates	2	5	7
	Total U.S.	205	229	435
109th (2005)	State delegates	2	5	7
	Total U.S.	202	231	435
110th (2007)	State delegates	2	5	7
	Total U.S.	233	198	435
111th (2009)	State delegates	3	4	7
	Total U.S.	256	178	435
112th (2011)	State delegates	1	6	7
	Total U.S.	193	242	435
113th (2013)	State delegates	1	6	7
	Total U.S.	201	234	435

Note: Figures are for the starts of first sessions; Totals include Democratic (Dem) and Republican (Rep) members as well as vacancies and seats held by independent party members
Source: U.S. Congress, Congressional Directory

Composition of State Legislature, 2004–2013

Year	Democrats	Republicans	Total
State Senate			
2004	25	10	35
2005	25	10	35
2006	25	10	35
2007	23	12	35
2008	23	12	35
2009	19	13	35
2010	21	14	35
2011	12	22	35
2012	12	22	35
2013	11	22	35
State House			
2004	63	42	105
2005	62	40	105
2006	63	42	105
2007	62	43	105
2008	62	43	105
2009	62	43	105
2010	60	45	105
2011	39	65	105
2012	40	65	105
2013	37	65	105

Note: Totals may include minor party members and vacancies
Source: The Council of State Governments, State Legislatures

Voter Participation in Presidential Elections, 1980–2012

Year	Voting-eligible State Population	State Voter Turnout Rate	U.S. Voter Turnout Rate
1980	2,726,249	49.2	54.2
1984	2,831,099	50.9	55.2
1988	2,901,744	47.5	52.8
1992	3,030,549	55.7	58.1
1996	3,144,249	48.8	51.7
2000	3,241,682	51.6	54.2
2004	3,292,608	57.2	60.1
2008	3,454,510	60.8	61.6
2012	3,522,336	58.9	58.2

Note: All figures are based on the voting-eligible population which excludes person ineligible to vote such as non-citizens, felons (depending on state law), and mentally-incapacitated persons. U.S. figures include the overseas eligible population (including military personnel).
Source: McDonald, Michael P., United States Election Project, Presidential Voter Turnout Rates, 1980–2012

Governors Since Statehood

William W. Bibb (O) . . . . (d) 1819-1820
Thomas Bibb (O) 1820-1821
Israel Pickens (O) 1821-1825
John Murphy (D) 1825-1829
Gabriel Moore (D) . . . . (r) 1829-1831
Samuel B. Moore (D) 1831
John Gayle (D) 1831-1835
Clement C. Clay (D) . . . . (r) 1835-1837
Hugh McVay (D) 1837
Arthur P. Bagby (D) 1837-1841
Benjamin Fitzpatrick (D) 1841-1845

Joshua L. Martin (O) 1845-1847
Reuben Chapman (D) 1847-1849
Henry W. Collier (D) 1849-1853
John A. Winston (D) 1853-1857
Andrew B. Moore (D) 1857-1861
John G. Shorter (D) 1861-1863
Thomas H. Watts (D). . . . . (i) 1863-1865
Lewis E. Parsons 1865
Robert M. Patton 1865-1868
William H. Smith (R) 1868-1870
Robert B. Lindsay (D) 1870-1872
David P. Lewis (R). 1872-1874
George S. Houston (D). 1874-1878
Rufus W. Cobb (D) 1878-1882
Edward A. O'Neal (D) 1882-1886
Thomas Seay (D) 1886-1890
Thomas G. Jones (D) 1890-1894
William C. Oates (D) 1894-1896
Joseph F. Johnston (D) 1896-1900
William D. Jelks (D) 1900
William J. Samford (D) . . . . (d) 1900-1901
William D. Jelks (D) 1901-1907
Braxton B. Comer (D) 1907-1911
Emmet O'Neal (D). 1911-1915
Charles Henderson (D). 1915-1919
Thomas E. Kilby (D) 1919-1923
William W. Brandon (D) 1923-1927
(David) Bibb Graves (D) 1927-1931
Benjamin M. Miller (D) 1931-1935
(David) Bibb Graves (D) 1935-1939
Frank M. Dixon (D) 1939-1943
Chauncey M. Sparks (D) 1943-1947
James E. Folsom (D) 1947-1951
(Seth) Gordon Persons (D) 1951-1955
James E. Folsom (D) 1955-1959
John M. Patterson (D) 1959-1963
George C. Wallace Jr. (D) 1963-1967
Lurleen B. Wallace (D). . . . . (d) 1967-1968
Albert P. Brewer (D) 1968-1971
George C. Wallace Jr. (D) 1971-1979
Forrest ("Fob") H. James (D) 1979-1983
George C. Wallace Jr. (D) 1983-1987
Guy Hunt (R) 1987-1993
James E. Folsom (D) 1993-1995
Forrest ("Fob") H. James (D). 1995-1999
Don Siegelman (D). 1999-2003
Robert R. Riley (R) 2003-2011
Robert Bentley (R) 2011-2015

Note: (D) Democrat; (R) Republican; (O) Other party; (r) resigned; (d) died in office; (i) removed from office

Alaska

Location: Northwest of Canada

Area and rank: 570,374 square miles (1,477,267 square kilometers); 656,424 square miles (1,700,138 square kilometers) including water; largest state in area

Coastline: 6,640 miles (10,686 kilometers) on the Pacific and Arctic Oceans

Shoreline: 33,904 miles (54,563 kilometers)

Population and rank: 731,449 (2012 estimate); forty-seventh state in population

Capital city: Juneau (31,275 people in 2010 census)

Largest city: Anchorage (291,826 people in 2010 census)

Became territory: 1912

Entered Union and rank: January 3, 1959; forty-ninth state

Alaska Governor's Mansion in Juneau, Alaska. (Wikimedia Commons)

Present constitution adopted: April 24, 1956

Boroughs: 16

State name: "Alaska" comes from an Aleut word meaning "great land" or "that which the sea breaks against"

State nicknames: The Last Frontier; Land of the Midnight Sun

Motto: North to the Future

State flag: Blue field with eight Gold stars forming Ursa Major and the North Star

Highest point: Mount McKinley—20,320 feet (6,194 meters)

Lowest point: Pacific Ocean—sea level

Highest recorded temperature: 100 degrees Fahrenheit (38 degrees Celsius)— Fort Yukon, 1915

Lowest recorded temperature: –80 degrees Fahrenheit (–62 degrees Celsius)—Prospect Creek, 1971

State song: "Alaska's Flag"

State tree: Sitka spruce

State flower: Forget-me-not

State bird: Willow ptarmigan

State fish: King salmon

National parks: Denali, Gates of the Arctic, Glacier Bay, Katmai, Kenai Fjords, Kobuk Valley, Lake Clark, Wrangell-St. Elias

Alaska History

Alaska must be described in terms of absolutes and superlatives. When it was admitted to the Union in 1959, it became the first state outside the forty-eight contiguous states. It is the northernmost state, and remarkably, it is also the westernmost and easternmost state, extending from 130 degrees west latitude, across the 180 degree meridian, to 172 degrees east latitude. Its longitude runs from Barrow in the Arctic at 72 degrees north to the southernmost point in the Aleutian Islands, where its longitude is 52 degrees north, giving it greater longitude than the entire forty-eight contiguous states and almost as much latitude. Alaska lies geographically in four time zones, although, for practical purposes, two official time zones have been established.

Alaska is the only state that borders the Arctic Ocean and extends into the Arctic Circle. It lies closest to Asia of any of the states, its western extreme on Little Diomede Island being just two miles from the Russian island of Big Diomede. On the east and north, its border with Canada is the longest of any state. The shortest air routes between the United States and Asia are directly over Alaska, which has the largest oil and natural gas reserves in the United States. With a land mass of 570,374 square miles, it is the largest state, more than twice the size of Texas. Alaska has the largest glaciers and the most volcanoes of any U.S. state. With 1.1 persons per square mile, it has the lowest population density in the United States. Alaska's Mount McKinley, at 20,320 feet, is the highest point in the North American continent.

Early History. Alaska's earliest inhabitants were the Tlingit-Haidas and members of the Athabascan Tribes. The Aleuts and Eskimos, or Inuits, crossed the Bering Strait from Russia more than four thousand years ago and settled along the coast, surviving largely by fishing and hunting. These migrants were likely Asians who came to the region when what is now Alaska was linked to mainland Asia by a land bridge. By 1750, some seventy thousand native Inuits lived in Alaska (that number has not significantly changed). Aleuts were driven from the Aleutian Islands by the Russians in the eighteenth and nineteenth centuries and by the American military forces during World War II.

The earliest incursions by westerners occurred in 1741, when Vitus Bering, a Dane supported in his ventures by Russia, sailed to Alaska and established the first settlement on Kodiak Island in 1784. The fur business, important and lucrative in early Alaska, thrived with the establishment in 1799 of the Russian-American Company. It controlled the fur trade from its headquarters in Archangel, present-day Sitka.

Russia owned Alaska until 1867, when President Andrew Johnson's secretary of state, William H. Seward, negotiated its purchase by the United States for $7.2 million. Although the U.S. Senate approved this purchase

The discovery of gold in 1898 drew prospectors from all over the world to Alaska and Canada's Klondike in one of the last great gold rushes. (Alaska Division of Tourism)

the country. Many U.S. citizens had gone there to work during the last half of the nineteenth century, but communication and transportation were limited. With the advent of radios and telephones, these problems began to fade, although it was many years before telephone communication with the "lower 48," as the United States mainland was called, was perfected. Almost simultaneously with better telephone communication came the development of air transportation, which had evolved rapidly during World War I and was, by the 1920's, becoming a major factor in transportation worldwide.

Alaska's enormous spaces made it an ideal venue for private aircraft. During the late 1920's and the 1930's, many Alaskans owned private planes, shrinking perceptibly the time they needed to cover the state's huge expanses. Commercial aircraft began to serve Alaska's major cities, and Anchorage became a refueling stop for planes flying from the United States and Canada to Asia.

These factors eliminated some of the earlier objections to statehood. Also, because the Japanese attacked and eventually occupied some of the Aleutian Islands during World War II, Americans became increasingly aware of Alaska's defensive importance.

Alaska's Economy. From its earliest days, Alaska had a stable economy. While mainland America struggled economically during the Great Depression of the 1930's, Alaska was undergoing an economic rebirth brought on largely by gold mining. Alaska had thriving copper mines as well. As revenues increased, the territorial government built much-needed roads, whose construction employed thousands of workers, many of whom came to Alaska and remained there as permanent residents.

World War II had a profound effect on the Alaskan economy. With Japan's invasion of the Aleutian Islands in 1942, the United States deployed about 200,000 military personnel to Alaska, where major military installations were built at Adak, Anchorage, Fairbanks, Kodiak, and Sitka. The Alcan highway was completed, creating a road link among Alaska's major cities.

Throughout the 1950's, military construction in Alaska continued at a brisk pace. This activity brought both construction workers and military personnel to the area in large numbers. Many, impressed by Alaska's grandeur and economic opportunities, remained there when the work that originally brought them to Alaska was completed.

In 1957, huge oil deposits were discovered in Alaska's Kenai Peninsula, and shortly thereafter other vast fields

enthusiastically, buying this little-known area, which most people considered a frozen wasteland, was unpopular and known as "Seward's Folly." This "folly" paid off handsomely when a major gold strike was made near Juneau in 1880, unleashing a gold rush to the region and stimulating the exploration of Alaska for its mineral wealth.

In 1896, gold was discovered in Canada's Klondike, and, in 1898, at Fairbanks, causing another gold rush. Fish canneries built in the southeastern part of the area during the 1880's and 1890's imported workers from the United States. American traders moving to Alaska in search of riches established a route along the Yukon, the fourth longest river in the northern hemisphere.

Steps Toward Statehood. As Alaska became more viable economically, Congress viewed it with increased interest. In 1884, Alaska was made a judicial district, with Sitka as its capital. In 1906, it was permitted one elected delegate in the United States House of Representatives. The region was granted territorial status in 1912, and Juneau was declared its capital. Its political powers, however, were limited. Statehood was first proposed in Congress in 1916 but was rejected. In 1946, however, Alaskans, in a state referendum, approved statehood. Ten years later, a state constitution was adopted. On January 3, 1959, Alaska was admitted to the Union as the forty-ninth state.

When statehood was first proposed for Alaska in 1916, the state was extremely isolated from the rest of were found at Prudhoe Bay. Despite the harsh climate and great distances involved, the eight hundred-mile long trans-Alaska oil pipeline was completed in 1977. Alaska became so oil rich that it was able to finance a giant expansion and still give each of its citizens more than one thousand dollars a year as a cash bonus for several years. It had no need for a state income tax.

The oil boom waned during the 1980's and by the mid-1980's was virtually over. The state by this time had attracted many new residents who viewed Alaska as the land of opportunity. Its population increased by 36.9 percent between 1980 and 1990, reaching just over 550,000 in 1990. The 1997 population registered a more than 10 percent increase, having grown to almost 610,000.

Following the oil boom, Alaska struggled to attract tourist dollars. It also began establishing trade with such Asian countries as South Korea, Taiwan, and Japan, although the slowing of the Asian economy in 1998 and 1999 temporarily stalled some of these efforts. Alaska's abundance of many resources that Asia does not have makes trade enviable. Natural gas development also became vigorously pursued within the state, which also did a great deal to increase the amount of metal mining done within its boundaries. Alaska has deposits of every known mineral except bauxite.

The Threat of Oil Spills. Environmentalists were concerned about the building of the Trans-Alaska Pipeline because portions of it were laid in areas with geological faults. However, the pipelines have been fashioned to resist the earthquakes that are common in fault areas. A severe earthquake in 1964, followed by a tsunami, a huge tidal wave, devastated much of coastal Alaska, doing considerable damage in Anchorage, Kodiak, Seward, and Valdez. At this time, there was no pipeline that might rupture. The potential for destruction of the pipeline is slight, but still a cause for concern.

In 1989, a huge supertanker, the *Exxon Valdez*, foundered in Prince William Sound and spilled more than 240,000 barrels of oil into the surrounding water. The result was catastrophic: Commercial fishing was so negatively impacted that many who fished for a living were forced out of business. The wholesale destruction of wildlife would take the area years from which to recover completely. If any good came out of the *Exxon Valdez* disaster, it is that the shipping of oil on supertankers became more strenuously regulated. Many new tankers have double hulls so that if the hull is punctured, the oil will not leak into the surrounding ocean.

The conflict between those who wish to exploit Alaska's natural resources and those who oppose these policies on environmentalist grounds played a considerable role in

Completion of the Trans-Alaska Pipeline in 1977 raised Alaska to an unprecedented level of prosperity. (©Luca Galuzzi/ Wikimedia Commons)

the state's public life during the early twenty-first century. These debates were heightened by a 150,000-gallon oil spill from the Trans-Alaska Pipeline in 2001.

The question of oil drilling in the state's Arctic National Wildlife Refuge (ANWR) was as much a national as a state issue, roiling national politics year after year following the era of the Carter administration. Drilling became an intense issue in the new century as oil prices rose and national security became a greater public concern. In 2002, for example, after considerable debate and a negative National Research Council report, Congress rejected ANWR oil drilling. The next year, despite a national security appeal from President George W. Bush, the Senate narrowly rejected drilling. In 2005, however, the Senate accepted it, and the provision was dropped from the House version of the energy bill. Drilling in ANWR continued to be unapproved at mid-decade.

National Security and Politics. Another issue that affected public life in Alaska was the state's security from attack by the missiles of the Democratic People's Republic of Korea (DPRK). Following 1998, the North Koreans maintained a moratorium on missile testing after receiving stern warnings from the United States and its allies. However, in the summer of 2006, the issue again arose when the DPRK tested a number of short-range and long-range missiles. Although the long-range test was a failure, Alaska was put on notice that it was a possible future target. The DPRK claim, backed by Western intelligence, that it had nuclear weapons made Alaska's security a serious public issue.

To counter these security concerns, the Bush administration increased funding for a missile defense system, some of which would be deployed in Alaska. Critics wondered, however, how effective the system really was, especially after test failures, including one in 2004. Nevertheless, in late 2004, six ground-based missiles were placed in silos at Fort Greely.

Politically, Alaska remained split between Republican and Democrat office holders, with Republicans in Congress and a Democrat in the statehouse in Juneau. If

The Anchorage Fur Rendezvous is Alaska's largest and oldest winter festival. The event includes the Rondy World Championship Sled Dog Races, where dog teams and their mushers compete for the fastest elapsed time out of three 25-mile loop races taking place over three days.

anything, however, the state leaned to the political right, voting for the Republican presidential candidate, Bush, in 2000 and 2004. On social issues, the state also leaned to the right, rejecting same-sex marriage and the partial legalization of marijuana. In August, 2006, former U.S. senator and current governor Frank Murkowski, who had very low approval ratings from the public, lost his bid for reelection in the Republican primary election in what was a landslide victory for former Wasilla mayor Sarah Palin, who took 50 percent of the vote. Murkowski got only 19 percent—identical to his approval rating.

The Alaska 2010 election for the U.S. Senate was one of the most unusual in recent history. Primary elections on August 24, 2010 selected the major party candidates. Scott McAdams, the Mayor of Sitka, was elected the Democratic Party nominee for U.S. Senate, while Joe Miller, an attorney and former federal magistrate, became the Republican nominee, defeating incumbent Senator Lisa Murkowski. Miller was endorsed by the Tea Party movement and former Alaska Governor Sarah Palin. However, Senator Murkowski decided to run in the general election as a write-in candidate, and she got more than 100,000 votes.

Miller challenged her election on the basis that many of the write-ins were misspelled or had other errors. On December 10, the Alaska Superior Court ruled that Murkowski was the victor, a ruling upheld later by the Alaska Supreme Court and by a federal court. On December 30, 2010, Alaska state election officials certified Lisa Murkowski's election, making her the first U.S. Senate candidate to be elected by a write-in vote since 1954. The next day, Miller conceded the election.

Exxon Valdez Punitive Damages. In the early years of the 21st century, the continuing issue of damages from the 1989 *Exxon Valdez* oil spill continued to work through the courts. Exxon appealed the original ruling that set direct damages at $287 million and punitive damages at $5 billion, and on December 6, 2002, the judge announced that he had reduced the punitive damages to $4 billion. When Exxon appealed again, the judge reset punitive damages at $4.5 billion, plus interest. After another appeal before the 9th Circuit Court of Appeals on January 27, 2006, punitive damages were cut to $2.5 billion in December 2006. Exxon appealed this amount in 2007, but the 9th Circuit Court of Appeals denied ExxonMobil's request for a third hearing and let stand the $2.5 billion.

The case went to the U.S. Supreme Court on February 27, 2008. In a June 25, 2008, decision, the court vacated the $2.5 billion award and remanded the case back to a lower court, finding the damages were excessive. Exxon argued that punitive damages greater than $25 million were not justified on the grounds that the spill resulted from an accident. Furthermore, the company spent an estimated $2 billion cleaning up the spill and about another $1 billion to settle related civil and criminal charges. Even so, by December 2009, Exxon paid another $507.5 million in direct and indirect damages that included lawsuit costs and interest to thousands of plaintiffs, bringing the total paid out to about $3.5 billion.

R. Baird Shuman
Updated by the Editor

Alaska Time Line

c. 10,000 B.C.E.	Human habitation of the area toward the end of the last Ice Age is documented.
c. 650 C.E.	Aleuts and Eskimos separate; Eskimos divide into Yupic and Inupiaq.
c. 1000 C.E.	Eskimos migrate from Alaska to Greenland.
1741	Vitus Bering lands off Kayak Island.
1774–1792	Spanish explore Alaska's west coast.
1778	British captain James Cook surveys Alaska coast.
1784	Russian Grigori Sheilikhov establishes Russian settlement near present-day Kodiak.
1791	British captain George Vancouver charts southeastern Alaska.
1799	Czar Paul I charters Russian-American Company.
1802	Tlingit Indians attack Russian-American Company, killing 408.
1823	Father Ivan Veniaminov works among the Aleuts.
1824–1825	Boundaries of Russian settlement in Alaska are fixed.
Mar. 30, 1867	United States purchases Alaska from Russia for $7.2 million.
1876	First Protestant mission in Alaska is established at Wrangell.
1878	First salmon cannery is built at Klawock.
1880	Gold is discovered at Juneau.
1884	Alaska becomes a judicial district with the capital at Sitka; native land rights are preserved and laws of Oregon are enforced.

1891	Sheldon Jackson introduces reindeer into Alaska to compensate for near-extinction of whales and walrus.
1898	Klondike gold rush begins, continuing for twenty years.
1900	United States Congress reforms Alaska's civil government, making Juneau the capital.
1906	Alaska is permitted to elect one delegate to the United States House of Representatives.
1911	Alaska signs international agreement to restrict seal hunting off Pribilof and other islands.
Aug. 24, 1912	Alaska is granted territorial status.
1913	Women receive voting rights.
1916	Alaskan statehood is first proposed in Congress.
1917	University of Alaska is founded.
1923	Alaska Railroad is completed, connecting Anchorage and Seward with Fairbanks.
1923	Alaska Agricultural College and School of Mines opens.
1924	Lieutenant Carl Ben Eielson flies first airmail.
1931	Federal Building is completed in Juneau.
1935	Matanuska agricultural colony is established under New Deal.
1942	Japanese bomb Dutch Harbor.
June 7, 1942	Japan invades and occupies Kiska and Attu in the Aleutian Islands.
Nov. 20, 1942	Alcan Highway, running from Great Falls, Montana, to Fairbanks, is completed.
1943	United States recaptures Aleutians from the Japanese.
1945	Racial discrimination in public accommodations is ruled illegal.
1946	Alaskans approve statehood in statewide referendum.
1952	First pulp and paper mill is built outside Ketchikan.
1955	Eklutna Power Project opens near Palmer.
1955	Military fuel pipeline opens between Haines and Fairbanks.
1956	Alaskans adopt state constitution.
1957	Oil is discovered on Kenai Peninsula.
Jan. 3, 1959	Alaska is granted statehood.
1963	Alaska's first oil refinery opens.
Mar. 27, 1964	Most severe earthquake in North America's history strikes; tsunamis devastate Anchorage, Kodiak, Seward, and Valdez.
Aug. 14-15, 1967	Record floods damage Fairbanks.
1971	Alaska Native Land Claims Settlement bill is enacted.
1977	Trans-Alaska oil pipeline is completed.
1981	Alaska National Interest Lands Conservation bill is enacted.
1988	Forest fires destroy over two million acres.
1988	Border between Alaska and eastern Soviet Union opens.
Mar. 24, 1989	Exxon Valdez spills 240,000 barrels of oil into Prince William Sound.
1996	Exxon Corporation pays Alaska $900 million for clean-up following Exxon Valdez oil spill.
1997	Congress passes bill to phase out largest factory trawlers for bottom fishing on the Bering Sea.
1997	Alaska ranks among the top three states in per-pupil expenditures for public education.
1998	Federal budget gives Alaska pollock processors $100 million.
1999	Alaska and Canada sign pact to protect endangered salmon species.
2003	Wildfires burn 3.6 million acres across the state.
2003	U.S. Senate rejects ANWR oil drilling.
2005	U.S. Senate approves ANWR drilling, but the House omits it from energy bill.
July 4, 2006	Alaska's security is threatened by the resumption of missile testing by North Korea.
Aug. 22, 2006	Governor Frank Murkowski loses reelection bid in Republican primary, gaining just 19 percent of the vote. His opponent, Sarah Palin, would go on to win the general election to become Alaska's first female governor.
July 2009	Governor Sarah Palin resigns and passes power to Sean Parnell. Parnell would win re-election in 2010.
December 2009	Exxon pays another $507.5 million in direct and indirect damages; this includes lawsuit costs and interest, to thousands of plaintiffs, bringing the total paid out to about $3.5 billion.
2010	Lisa Murkowski is the first U.S. Senate candidate to be elected by a write-in vote since 1954.

Notes for Further Study

Published Sources. Robert Hedin and Gary Holthaus's *The Great Land: Reflections on Alaska* (1994) offers comprehensive overviews of the state. George W. Rogers, in *Change in Alaska: People, Petroleum, Politics* (1970), considers what the oil discoveries at Kenai Peninsula and Prudhoe mean to the state and is especially useful when read in conjunction with Robert

B. Weeden's *Messages from Earth: Nature and Human Prospect in Alaska* (1992) and Craig A. Doherty and Katherine M. Doherty's *The Alaska Pipeline* (1998). Bryan Cooper's *Alaska: The Last Frontier* (1973) also focuses on the effect that the petroleum discoveries of the late 1960's and early 1970's had upon the ecology and economy of Alaska. Jeff Wheelwright's

Degrees of Disaster: Prince William Sound—How Nature Reels and Rebounds (1994) considers the aftermath of the *Exxon Valdez* oil spill. Taking a step further back into the state's history, Lydia T. Black uses text, detailed maps, and color illustrations to examine

the merging of Russian and Alaskan history in *Russians in Alaska, 1732-1867* (2004).

Owen K. Mason, William J. Neal, and Orrin H. Pilkey consider threats to the Alaskan coastline in *Living with the Coast of Alaska* (1997). David S. Case considers how native Alaskans adapt to American laws in *Alaska Natives and American Laws* (1997), while Michael Jenning, in *Alaska Native Political Leadership and Higher Education: One University, Two Universes* (2004), focuses on the ways in which imperial notions of education altered indigenous peoples' relationship to and understanding of their land. Theodore Lane considers the special climatic conditions of Alaska and how to cope with them in *Developing America's Northern Frontier* (1987).

The state's harsh elements provide the backbone for two "true story" adventure books: *The Last Frontier: Incredible Tales of Survival, Exploration, and Adventure from "Alaska Magazine"* (2004), which tells stories of

Rising to an altitude of 20,320 feet, Alaska's Mount McKinley is the tallest mountain in North America. (PhotoDisc)

Alaska's largest city, Anchorage has four times as many residents as the state's next two largest cities, Fairbanks and Juneau, combined. (PhotoDisc)

events as disparate as earthquakes, tidal waves, bear attacks, and influenza epidemics in its lively focus on Alaska's wilderness; and *Tales from the Edge: True Adventures in Alaska* (2005), edited by Larry Kaniut, which thrills readers with stories of humans struggling against the oftentimes inhospitable environment. In *Looking for Alaska* (2001), Peter Jenkins examines the lives and cultures he encounters during his eighteen-month sojourn across the state. Carole Marsh's *Alaska Timeline: A Chronology of Alaska History, Mystery, Trivia, Legend, Lore, and More* (1992) is aimed at the juvenile market and is a worthwhile study. Kathleen Thompson's *Alaska* (1988) is also written with juveniles in mind.

Web Resources. Alaska's government Web site (www.alaska.gov) is a well-organized portal for a wealth of information about the state. The home page is divided into three main categories, and readers will likely find the most interesting information under the headings Residents, Business, and Visitors. The state's tourist Web site (www.travelalaska.com) is directed at the traveler and includes interactive maps and photo galleries, as well as the requisite tourist amenity information for numerous cities and towns. Those planning outdoor activities in the state should consult the Alaska Travel Adventures Web site (www.alaskaadventures.com). Alaska national parklands are described on the National Parklands Web site (www.nps.gov/akso), while an insider's guide to traveling in the state can be found on the Alaska Travel Tips Web site (www.alaskaparks.com).

For scientific information about Alaska's Arctic regions, the Arctic Research Consortium's Web site (www.arcus.org) is helpful. The University of Alaska Anchorage Justice Center (justice.uaa.alaska.edu/) operates a Web page index to numerous resources about the state's native peoples, including information on specific tribes, self-governance, environment, and organizations and associations. The Klondike Gold Rush was a preeminent event in the state's history and several Web sites are dedicated to it, including the Klondike Gold Rush National Park (http://www.nps.gov/klse/index.htm), Explore North's index listing (www.explorenorth.com/library/ya/bl22y.htm) to a wide variety of Klondike resources, and the Klondike Gold Rush site (library.thinkquest.org/5181/).

Counties

Borough/Census Area	2012 Population	Pop. Rank	Land Area (sq. miles)	Area Rank
Aleutians East (b)	3,161	21	6,981.94	17
Aleutians West (ca)	5,547	18	4,390.28	20
Anchorage	298,610	1	1,704.68	27
Bethel (ca)	17,746	6	40,540.73	3
Bristol Bay (b)	991	27	503.84	28
Denali (b)	1,875	25	12,751.41	13
Dillingham (ca)	5,034	19	18,568.78	10
Fairbanks North Star (b)	100,272	2	7,338.21	16
Haines (b)	2,552	22	2,318.60	26
Hoonah-Angoon (ca)	2,129	24	7,524.91	15
Juneau City and (b)	32,556	5	2,701.93	24
Kenai Peninsula (b)	56,900	4	16,075.33	12
Ketchikan Gateway (b)	13,779	8	4,858.41	19
Kodiak Island (b)	14,239	7	6,549.58	18
Lake and Peninsula (b)	1,654	26	23,652.01	8
Matanuska-Susitna (b)	93,925	3	24,607.90	7

Borough/Census Area	2012 Population	Pop. Rank	Land Area (sq. miles)	Area Rank
Nome (ca)	9,915	9	22,961.76	9
North Slope (b)	9,643	11	88,803.50	2
Northwest Arctic (b)	7,810	13	35,572.58	4
Petersburg (ca)	3,844	20	3,281.98	22
Prince of Wales-Hyder (ca)	5,751	17	3,922.87	21
Sitka City and (b)	9,046	12	2,870.34	23
Skagway	959	28	452.32	29
Southeast Fairbanks (ca)	7,144	15	24,768.81	6
Valdez-Cordova (ca)	9,717	10	34,239.88	5
Wade Hampton (ca)	7,809	14	17,081.43	11
Wrangell City and (b)	2,403	23	2,541.48	25
Yakutat City and (b)	668	29	7,649.46	14
Yukon-Koyukuk (ca)	5,770	16	145,560.51	1

Note: (b) borough; (ca) census area
Source: U.S. Census Bureau, 2012 Population Estimates

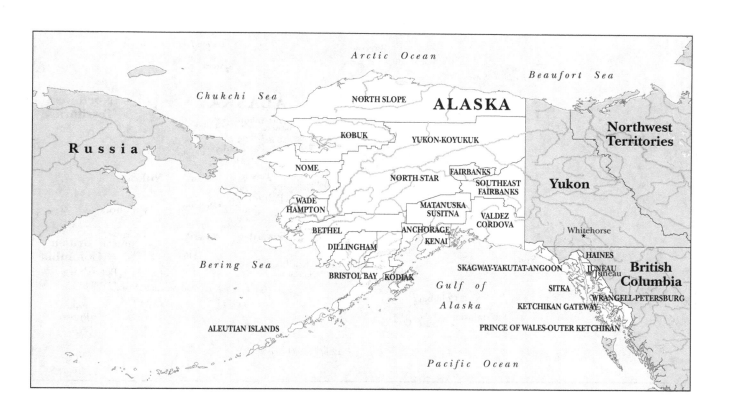

Cities

With 5,000 or more residents

Legal Name	2010 Population	Pop. Rank	Land Area (sq. miles)	Area Rank
Anchorage municipality	291,826	1	1,704.68	3
Badger CDP	19,482	4	65.63	9
Bethel city	6,080	17	43.18	10
Chena Ridge CDP	5,791	19	36.47	11
College CDP	12,964	6	18.78	16
Fairbanks city	31,535	2	31.69	12
Gateway CDP	5,552	21	21.55	15
Homer city	5,003	22	13.83	17
Juneau city and borough	31,275	3	2,701.93	2
Kalifornsky CDP	7,850	11	68.87	8
Kenai city	7,100	14	28.59	14
Ketchikan city	8,050	10	4.35	21

Legal Name	2010 Population	Pop. Rank	Land Area (sq. miles)	Area Rank
Knik-Fairview CDP	14,923	5	83.10	5
Kodiak city	6,130	16	3.49	22
Lakes CDP	8,364	8	12.57	18
Meadow Lakes CDP	7,570	13	75.22	7
Palmer city	5,937	18	5.15	20
Sitka city and borough	8,881	7	2,870.34	1
Steele Creek CDP	6,662	15	92.84	4
Sterling CDP	5,617	20	77.76	6
Tanaina CDP	8,197	9	30.38	13
Wasilla city	7,831	12	12.38	19

Note: CDP–Census Designated Place
Source: U.S. Census Bureau, 2010 Census

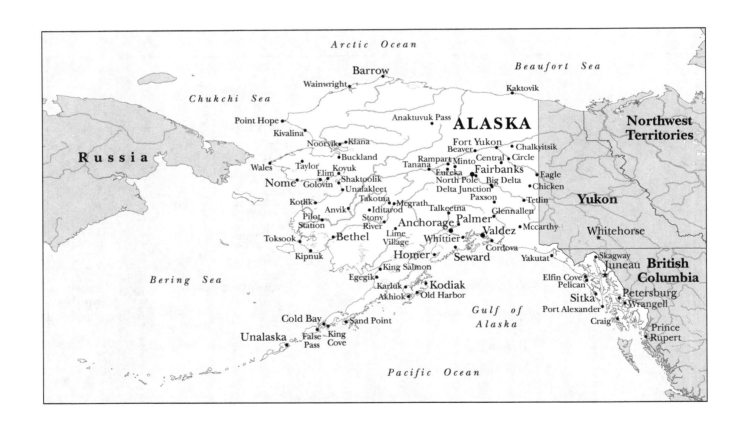

Survey Says...

This section presents current rankings from dozens of public and private sources. It shows how this state ranks in a number of critical categories, including education, job growth, cost of living, teen drivers, energy efficiency, and business environment. Sources include *Forbes, Reuters, U.S. News and World Report, CNN Money, Gallup,* and *Huffington Post.*

- CNN Money compiled a list of "Ten Most Entrepreneurial States" based on the Kauffman Index of Entrepreneurial Activity. Alaska ranked #4 among the 50 states in 2012 for number of startups per 100,000 adult residents.
  CNN Money, June 20, 2013; money.cnn.com

- Alaska ranked #41 in a government study measuring real gross domestic product (GDP)—the output of goods and services produced by labor and property located in the United States. The ranking is based on the percentage change compared with 2011 GDP.
  U.S. Department of Commerce, Bureau of Economic Analysis, June 2013; www.bea.gov

- Alaska ranked #46 in a government study measuring real gross domestic product (GDP)—the output of goods and services produced by labor and property located in the United States. The ranking is based on the dollar value of its GDP.
  U.S. Department of Commerce, Bureau of Economic Analysis, June 2013; www.bea.gov

- Alaska ranked #47 in the 17th edition of "Quality Counts; State of the States," Education Week's "report card" surveying key education indicators, policy efforts, and educational outcomes.
  Education Week, January 4, 2013 (online) and January 10, 2013 (print); www.edweek.org

- SERI (Science and Engineering Readiness Index) weighs the performance of the states' K-12 schools in preparing students in physics and calculus, the high school subjects considered most important for future scientists and engineers. Alaska ranked #39.
  Newsletter of the Forum on Education of the American Physical Society, Summer 2011 issue; www.huffingtonpost.com, July 11, 2011; updated October 1, 2012

- ND Parks, the "site for North Dakota Parks," named Alaska as one of the "Top Five States to Visit for RV Camping Trips."
  www.ndparks.com, consulted 18 July 2013

- MoneyRates.com ranked Alaska #42 on its list of the best to worst states for making a living. Criteria: average income; inflation; employment prospects; and workers' Workplace Environment assessments according to the Gallup-Healthways Well-Being Index.
  www.money-rates.com, posted April 1, 2013

- *Forbes* analyzed business costs, labor supply, regulatory environment, current economic climate, growth prospects, and quality of life, to compile its "Best States for Business" rankings. Alaska ranked #37.
  www.forbes.com. posted December 12, 2012

- The 2012 Gallup-Healthways Well-Being Index, surveyed American's opinions on economic confidence, workplace perceptions, community climate, personal choices, and health predictors to assess the "future livability" of each state. Alaska ranked #14.
  "Utah Poised to Be the Best State to Live In," Gallup Wellbeing, www.gallup.com, August 7, 2012

- On CNBC's list of "America's Top States for Business 2013," Alaska ranked #44. Criteria: measures of competitiveness developed with input from the National Association of Manufacturers, the Council on Competitiveness, and other business groups weighed with the states' own marketing criteria.
  www.cnbc.com, consulted July 19, 2013

- Alaska ranked #48 on MoneyRates list of "Best-and Worst-States to Retire 2012." Criteria: life expectancy, crime rate, climate, economic conditions, taxes, job opportunities, and cost of living.
  www.money-rates.com, October 22, 2012

- Alaska ranked #50 on the 2013 Bankrate "Best Places to Retire" list ranking the states and District of Columbia on various criteria relating to health, safety, and cost.
  www.bankrate.com, May 6, 2013

- Reuters ranked Alaska #9 on its list of the "Ten Most Expensive States in America." Rankings are based on the U.S. Commerce Department's prototype cost-of-living index comparing price levels across the states for a standardized mix of goods and services.
  www.huffingtonpost.com, posted June 12, 2013

- Alaska ranked #21 on the Social Science Research Council's "American Human Development Report: The Measure of America," assessing the 50 states plus the District of Columbia on health, education, and living-standard criteria.
  The Measure of America 2013-2014, posted June 19, 2013; www.measureofamerica.org

- Alaska ranked #42 on the Foundation for Child Development's (FCD) Child Well-being Index (CWI). The FCD used the KIDS COUNT report and the National Survey of Children's Health, the only state-level source for several key indicators of child well-being.
  Foundation for Child Development, January 18, 2012; fcd-us.org

- Alaska ranked #33 overall according to the 2013 KIDS COUNT Data Book, a project of the Annie E. Casey Foundation. Criteria: children's economic well-being, education, health, and family and community indicators.
  KIDS COUNT Data Center's Data Book, released June 20, 2013; http://datacenter.kidscount.org

- Alaska ranked #24 in the children's economic well-being category by the 2013 KIDS COUNT Data Book, a project of the Annie E. Casey Foundation.
  KIDS COUNT Data Center's Data Book, released June 20, 2013; http://datacenter.kidscount.org

- Alaska ranked #43 in the children's educational opportunities and attainments category by the 2013 KIDS COUNT Data Book, a project of the Annie E. Casey Foundation.
  KIDS COUNT Data Center's Data Book, released June 20, 2013; http://datacenter.kidscount.org

- Alaska ranked #46 in the children's health category by the 2013 KIDS COUNT Data Book, a project of the Annie E. Casey Foundation.
  KIDS COUNT Data Center's Data Book, released June 20, 2013; http://datacenter.kidscount.org

- Alaska ranked #19 in the family and community circumstances that factor into children's well-being category by the 2013 KIDS COUNT Data Book, a project of the Annie E. Casey Foundation.
  KIDS COUNT Data Center's Data Book, released June 20, 2013; http://datacenter.kidscount.org

- Alaska ranked #31 in the 2012 Gallup-Healthways Well-Being Index. Criteria: emotional health; physical health; healthy behavior; work environment; basic access to food, shelter, health care; and a safe and satisfying place to live.
  2012 State of Well-Being, Gallup-Healthways Well-Being Index, released February 28, 2013; www.well-beingindex.com

- *U.S. News and World Report's* "Best States for Teen Drivers" rankings are based on driving and road safety laws, federal reports on driver's licenses, car accident fatality, and road-quality statistics. Alaska ranked #16.
  U.S. News and World Report, March 18, 2010; www.usnews.com

- The Yahoo! Sports service Rivals.com ranks the states according to the strength of their high school football programs. Alaska ranked #43.
  "Ranking the States: Where Is the Best Football Played?," November 18, 2011; highschool.rivals.com

- iVillage ranked the states by hospitable living conditions for women. Criteria: economic success, access to affordable childcare, health care, reproductive rights, female representation in government, and educational attainment. Alaska ranked #15.
  iVillage, "50 Best to Worst States for Women," March 14, 2012; www.ivillage.com

- The League of American Bicyclists's "Bicycle Friendly States" ranked Alaska #45. Criteria: legislation and enforcement, policies and programs, infrastructure and funding, education and advocacy, and evaluation and planning.
  "Washington Tops the Bicycle-Friendly State Ranking," May 1, 2013; bicycling.com

- The federal Corporation for National and Community Service ranked the states and the District of Columbia by volunteer rates. Alaska ranked #11 for community service.
  "Volunteering and Civic Life in America 2012," www.volunteeringinamerica.gov, accessed July 24, 2013

- The Hospital Safety Score ranked states and the District of Columbia on their hospitals' performance scores. Alaska ranked #36. Criteria: avoiding preventable harm and medical errors, as demonstrated by 26 hospital safety metrics.
  Spring 2013 Hospital Safety Score, May 8, 2013; www.hospitalsafetyscore.org

- GMAC Insurance ranked the states and the District of Columbia by the performance of their drivers on the GMAC Insurance National Drivers Test, comprised of DMV test questions. Alaska ranked #40.
  "2011 GMAC Insurance National Drivers Test," www.gmacinsurance.com, accessed July 23, 2013

- Alaska ranked #32 in a "State Integrity Investigation" analysis of laws and practices intended to deter corruption and promote accountability and openness in campaign finance, ethics laws, lobbying regulations and management of state pension funds.
  "What's Your State's Grade?," www.publicintegrity.org, accessed July 23, 2013

- Alaska ranked #45 among the states and the District of Columbia in total rail miles, as tracked by the Association of American Railroads.
  "U.S. Freight Railroad Industry Snapshot: Railroads and States: Total Rail Miles by State: 2011"; www.aar.org, accessed July 23, 2013

- According to statistics compiled by the Beer Institute, Alaska ranked #27 among the states and the District of Columbia in per capita beer consumption of persons 21 years or older.
  "Shipments of Malt Beverages and Per Capita Consumption by State 2012;" www.beerinstitute.org

- According to Concordia University's "Public Education Costs per Pupil by State Rankings," based on statistics gathered by the U.S. Census Bureau, which includes the District of Columbia, Alaska ranked #4.
  Concordia University Online; education.cu-portland.edu, accessed July 24, 2013

- Alaska ranked #50 among the states and the District of Columbia in population density based on U.S. Census Bureau data for resident population and total land area. "List of U.S. States by Population Density."
  www.wikipedia.org, accessed July 24, 2013

- In "America's Health Rankings, 2012 Edition," by the United Health Foundation, Alaska ranked #28. Criteria included: rate of high school graduation; violent crime rate; incidence of infectious disease; childhood immunizations; prevalence of diabetes; per capita public-health funding; percentage of uninsured population; rate of children in poverty; and availability of primary-care physicians.
  United Health Foundation; www.americashealthrankings.org, accessed July 24, 2013

- The TechNet 2012 "State Broadband Index" ranked Alaska #49 on the following criteria: broadband adoption; network quality; and economic structure. Improved broadband use is hoped to promote economic development, build strong communities, improve delivery of government services and upgrade educational systems.
  TechNet; www.technet.org, accessed July 24, 2013

- Alaska was ranked #46 among the states and District of Columbia on the American Council for an Energy-Efficient Economy's "State Energy Efficiency Scorecard" for 2012.
  American Council for an Energy-Efficient Economy; aceee.org/sector/state-policy/scorecard, accessed July 24, 2013

Statistical Tables

DEMOGRAPHICS
Resident State and National Population, 1950-2012
Projected State and National Population, 2000-2030
Population by Age, 2012
Population by Race, 2012
Population by Hispanic Origin and Race, 2012

VITAL STATISTICS
Death Rates by Leading Causes, 2010
Death Rates by Selected Causes, 2010
Abortion Rates, 2009
Infant Mortality Rates, 1995-2009
Marriage and Divorce Rates, 2000-2011

ECONOMY
Nominal Gross Domestic Product by Industry, 2012
Real Gross Domestic Product, 2000-2012
Personal Income Per Capita, 1930-2012
Non-Farm Employment by Sector, 2012
Foreign Exports, 2000-2012
Energy Consumption, 2011

LAND AND WATER
Surface Area and Federally-Owned Land, 2007
Land Cover/Use of Non-Federal Rural Land, 2007
Farms and Crop Acreage, 2012

HEALTH AND MEDICAL CARE
Medical Professionals, 2012
Health Insurance Coverage, 2011
HIV, STD, and Tuberculosis Cases and Rates, 2011
Cigarette Smoking, 2011

HOUSING
Home Ownership Rates, 1995-2012
Home Sales, 2000-2010
Value of Owner-Occupied Homes, 2011

EDUCATION
School Enrollment, 2011
Educational Attainment, 2011
Public College Finances, FY 2012

TRANSPORTATION AND TRAVEL
Motor Vehicle Registrations and Drivers Licenses, 2011
Domestic Travel Expenditures, 2009
Retail Gasoline Prices, 2013
Public Road Length, 2011

CRIME AND LAW ENFORCEMENT
Full-Time Law Enforcement Officers, 2011
Prison Population, 2000-2012
Crime Rate, 2011

GOVERNMENT AND FINANCE
Local Governments by Type, 2012
State Government Revenue, 2011
State Government Expenditures, 2011
State Government General Expenditures by Function, 2011
State Government Finances, Cash and Debt, 2011

POLITICS
Composition of the Senate, 1995-2013
Composition of the House of Representatives, 1995-2013
Composition of State Legislature, 2004-2013
Voter Participation in Presidential Elections, 1980-2012
Governors Since Statehood

DEMOGRAPHICS

Resident State and National Population, 1950–2012

Year	State Population	U.S. Population	State Share
1950	129,000	151,326,000	0.09%
1960	226,000	179,323,000	0.13%
1970	302,583	203,302,031	0.15%
1980	401,851	226,545,805	0.18%
1990	550,043	248,709,873	0.22%
2000	626,933	281,424,600	0.22%
2010	710,231	308,745,538	0.23%
2012	731,449	313,914,040	0.23%

Note: 1950/1960 population figures are rounded to the nearest thousand.
Source: U.S. Census Bureau, Decennial Census 1950–2010; U.S. Census Bureau, 2012 Population Estimates

Projected State and National Population, 2000–2030

Year	State Population	U.S. Population	State Share
2000	626,932	281,421,906	0.22%
2005	661,110	295,507,134	0.22%
2010	694,109	308,935,581	0.22%
2015	732,544	322,365,787	0.23%
2020	774,421	335,804,546	0.23%
2025	820,881	349,439,199	0.23%
2030	867,674	363,584,435	0.24%
State population growth, 2000–2030			240,742
State percentage growth, 2000–2030			38.4%

Source: U.S. Census Bureau, Population Division, Interim State Population Projections, 2005

Population by Age, 2012

Age Group	State Population	Percent of Total Population	
		State	U.S.
Under 5 years	54,791	7.5%	6.4%
5 to 14 years	101,874	13.9%	13.1%
15 to 24 years	110,102	15.1%	14.0%
25 to 34 years	111,110	15.2%	13.5%
35 to 44 years	91,993	12.6%	12.9%
45 to 54 years	106,266	14.5%	14.1%
55 to 64 years	92,816	12.7%	12.3%
65 to 74 years	41,000	5.6%	7.6%
75 to 84 years	16,124	2.2%	4.2%
85 years and older	5,373	0.7%	1.9%
Under 18 years	187,100	25.6%	23.5%
65 years and older	62,497	8.5%	13.7%
Median age (years)	–	33.7	37.4

Source: U.S. Census Bureau, Annual Estimates of the Resident Population for Selected Age Groups by Sex for the United States, States, Counties, and Puerto Rico Commonwealth and Municipios: April 1, 2010 to July 1, 2012

Population by Race, 2012

Race	State Population	Percent of Total Population	
		State	U.S.
All residents	731,449	100.00%	100.00%
White	493,430	67.46%	77.89%
African American	27,373	3.74%	13.13%
Native American	108,249	14.80%	1.23%
Asian	41,986	5.74%	5.14%
Native Hawaiian	8,558	1.17%	0.23%
Two or more races	51,853	7.09%	2.39%

Source: U.S. Census Bureau, Population Division, Annual Estimates of the Resident Population by Sex, Race and Hispanic Origin for the United States, States, and Counties: April 1, 2010 to July 1, 2012

Population by Hispanic Origin and Race, 2012

Hispanic Origin/Race	State Population	Percent of Total Population	
		State	U.S.
All residents	731,449	100.00%	100.00%
All Hispanic residents	44,869	6.13%	16.89%
Hispanic			
White	32,222	4.41%	14.91%
African American	2,482	0.34%	0.79%
Native American	3,793	0.52%	0.49%
Asian	1,239	0.17%	0.17%
Native Hawaiian	429	0.06%	0.06%
Two or more races	4,704	0.64%	0.48%
Not Hispanic			
White	461,208	63.05%	62.98%
African American	24,891	3.40%	12.34%
Native American	104,456	14.28%	0.74%
Asian	40,747	5.57%	4.98%
Native Hawaiian	8,129	1.11%	0.17%
Two or more races	47,149	6.45%	1.91%

Source: U.S. Census Bureau, Population Division, Annual Estimates of the Resident Population by Sex, Race and Hispanic Origin for the United States, States, and Counties: April 1, 2010 to July 1, 2012

VITAL STATISTICS

Death Rates by Leading Causes, 2010

Cause	State	U.S.
Malignant neoplasms	187.9	186.2
Ischaemic heart diseases	89.7	122.9
Other forms of heart disease	58.3	53.4
Chronic lower respiratory diseases	44.0	44.7
Cerebrovascular diseases	44.0	41.9
Organic, incl. symptomatic, mental disorders	51.8	35.7
Other degenerative diseases of the nervous sys.	28.8	28.4
Other external causes of accidental injury	43.0	26.5
Diabetes mellitus	20.7	22.4
Hypertensive diseases	17.6	20.4
All causes	822.0	799.5

Note: Figures are age-adjusted death rates per 100,000 population
Source: CDC/NCHS, Underlying Cause of Death 1999–2010 on CDC WONDER Online Database

Death Rates by Selected Causes, 2010

Cause	State	U.S.
Assault	5.7	5.2
Diseases of the liver	15.0	13.9
Human immunodeficiency virus (HIV) disease	–	2.7
Influenza and pneumonia	17.0	16.2
Intentional self-harm	23.3	12.4
Malnutrition	–	0.9
Obesity and other hyperalimentation	0.0	1.8
Renal failure	11.7	14.4
Transport accidents	16.5	12.1
Viral hepatitis	3.6	2.4

Note: Figures are age-adjusted death rates per 100,000 population; A dash indicates that data was not available or was suppressed
Source: CDC/NCHS, Underlying Cause of Death 1999–2010 on CDC WONDER Online Database

Abortion Rates, 2009

Category	2009
By state of residence	
Total abortions	2,079
Abortion rate[1]	14.4%
Abortion ratio[2]	184
By state of occurrence	
Total abortions	1,938
Abortion rate[1]	13.4%
Abortion ratio[2]	171
Abortions obtained by out-of-state residents	1.4%
U.S. abortion rate[1]	15.1%
U.S. abortion ratio[2]	227

Note: (1) Number of abortions per 1,000 women aged 15–44 years; (2) Number of abortions per 1,000 live births; A dash indicates that data was not available
Source: CDC/NCHS, Morbidity and Mortality Weekly Report, November 23, 2012 (Abortion Surveillance, United States, 2009)

Infant Mortality Rates, 1995–2009

Category	1995	2000	2005	2009
All state residents	7.52	6.92	5.93	6.89
All U.S. residents	7.57	6.89	6.86	6.39
All state white residents	5.70	5.81	4.59	4.76
All U.S. white residents	6.30	5.71	5.73	5.33
All state black residents	–	–	–	–
All U.S. black residents	14.58	13.48	13.26	12.12

Note: Figures represent deaths per 1,000 live births of resident infants under one year old, exclusive of fetal deaths; A dash indicates that data was not available or was suppressed.
Source: Centers of Disease Control and Prevention, Division of Vital Statistics, Linked Birth/Infant Death Records on CDC Wonder Online

Marriage and Divorce Rates, 2000–2011

Year	Marriage Rate		Divorce Rate	
	State	U.S.	State	U.S.
2000	8.9	8.2	3.9	4.0
2002	8.3	8.0	4.6	3.9
2004	8.5	7.8	4.3	3.7
2006	8.2	7.5	4.2	3.7
2008	8.4	7.1	4.4	3.5
2010	8.0	6.8	4.7	3.6
2011	7.8	6.8	4.8	3.6

Note: Rates are based on provisional counts of marriages/divorces by state of occurrence and are per 1,000 total population residing in area
Source: CDC/NCHS, National Vital Statistics System

ECONOMY

Nominal Gross Domestic Product by Industry, 2012
In millions of current dollars

Industry	State GDP
Accommodation and food services	1,311
Administrative and waste management services	994
Agriculture, forestry, fishing, and hunting	469
Arts, entertainment, and recreation	302
Construction	2,143
Educational services	139
Finance and insurance	1,658
Health care and social assistance	3,180
Information	1,161
Management of companies and enterprises	186
Manufacturing	1,671
Mining	11,053
Other services, except government	847
Professional, scientific, and technical services	2,331
Real estate and rental and leasing	4,339
Retail trade	2,083
Transportation and warehousing	6,250
Utilities	798
Wholesale trade	1,109

Source: U.S. Department of Commerce, Bureau of Economic Analysis, Survey of Current Business

Real Gross Domestic Product, 2000–2012
In millions of chained 2005 dollars

Year	State GDP	U.S. GDP	State Share
2000	34,192	11,225,406	0.30%
2005	37,774	12,539,116	0.30%
2010	43,472	12,897,088	0.34%
2012	44,732	13,430,576	0.33%

Source: U.S. Department of Commerce, Bureau of Economic Analysis, Survey of Current Business

Personal Income Per Capita, 1930–2012

Year	State	U.S.
1930	–	$618
1940	–	$593
1950	$2,401	$1,503
1960	$3,062	$2,268
1970	$5,248	$4,084
1980	$14,975	$10,091
1990	$22,594	$19,354
2000	$30,508	$30,319
2010	$43,749	$39,791
2012	$46,778	$42,693

Source: U.S. Department of Commerce, Bureau of Economic Analysis, Regional Economic Accounts

Non-Farm Employment by Sector, 2012
In thousands

Sector	Employment
Construction	16.6
Education and health services	46.4
Financial activities	13.3
Government	84.0
Information	6.2
Leisure and hospitality	33.0
Mining and logging	17.0
Manufacturing	13.5
Other services	11.6
Professional and business services	28.6
Trade, transportation, and utilities	63.8
All sectors	334.1

Source: U.S. Bureau of Labor Statistics, State and Area Employment

Foreign Exports, 2000–2012
In millions of dollars

Year	State Exports	U.S. Exports	State Share
2000	2,464	712,054	0.35%
2002	2,504	649,940	0.39%
2004	3,157	768,554	0.41%
2006	4,046	973,994	0.42%
2008	3,541	1,222,545	0.29%
2010	4,154	1,208,080	0.34%
2012	4,543	1,478,268	0.31%

Note: U.S. figures exclude data from Puerto Rico, U.S. Virgin Islands, and unallocated exports
Source: U.S. Department of Commerce, International Trade Admin., Office of Trade and Industry Information, Manufacturing and Services

Energy Consumption, 2011

In trillions of BTUs, except as noted

Total energy consumption	
Total state energy consumption	637.9
Total U.S. energy consumption	97,387.3
State share of U.S. total	0.66%
Per capita consumption (in millions of BTUs)	
Total state per capita consumption	881.2
Total U.S. per capita consumption	312.6
End-use sectors	
Residential	53.7
Commercial	68.2
Industrial	315.4
Transportation	200.7
Sources of energy	
Petroleum	267.1
Natural gas	337.0
Coal	15.5
Renewable energy	18.4
Nuclear electric power	0.0

Source: U.S. Energy Information Administration, State Energy Data 2011: Consumption

LAND AND WATER

Surface Area and Federally-Owned Land, 2007

In thousands of acres

Category	State	U.S.	State Share
Total surface area	387,977.0	1,937,664.2	20.02%
Total land area	353,359.5	1,886,846.9	18.73%
Non-federal land	133,357.0	1,484,910.0	8.98%
Developed	365.8	111,251.2	0.33%
Rural	132,991.2	1,373,658.8	9.68%
Federal land	220,002.5	401,936.9	54.74%
Water area	34,617.5	50,817.3	68.12%

Source: U.S. Department of Agriculture, Natural Resources Conservation Service, 2007 National Resources Inventory

Land Cover/Use of Non-Federal Rural Land, 2007

In thousands of acres

Category	State	U.S.	State Share
Total rural land	352,950.3	1,373,658.8	25.69%
Cropland[2]	109.5	357,023.5	0.03%
CRP[1] land[2]	0.0	32,850.2	0.00%
Pastureland[2]	0.0	118,615.7	0.00%
Rangeland	201,528.5	409,119.4	49.26%
Forest land	101,918.5	406,410.4	25.08%
Other rural land	49,393.8	49,639.6	99.50%

Note: (1) Conservation Reserve Program was created to assist private landowners in converting highly erodible cropland to vegetative cover; (2) CRP and pastureland are combined with cropland
Source: U.S. Department of Agriculture, Natural Resources Conservation Service, 2007 National Resources Inventory

Farms and Crop Acreage, 2012

Category	State	U.S.	State Share
Farms (in thousands)	0.7	2,170.0	0.03%
Acres (in millions)	0.9	914.0	0.10%
Acres per farm	1,294.1	421.2	–

Source: U.S. Department of Agriculture, National Agricultural Statistical Service, Quick Stats, 2012 Survey Data

HEALTH AND MEDICAL CARE

Medical Professionals, 2012

Profession	State Number	U.S. Number	State Share	State Rate[1]	U.S. Rate[1]
Physicians[2]	1,653	894,637	0.18%	228.4	287.1
Dentists	615	193,587	0.32%	85.0	62.1
Podiatrists	20	17,469	0.11%	2.8	5.6
Optometrists	132	45,638	0.29%	18.2	14.6
Chiropractors	258	77,494	0.33%	35.6	24.9

Note: (1) Rates are per 100,000 population; (2) Includes total, active Doctors of Osteopathic Medicine and Doctors of Medicine in 2011.
Source: U.S. Department of Health and Human Services, Bureau of Health Professions, Area Health Resource File, 2012-2013

Health Insurance Coverage, 2011

Category	State	U.S.
Total persons covered	584,000	260,214,000
Total persons not covered	129,000	48,613,000
Percent not covered	18.1%	15.7%
Children under age 18 covered	170,000	67,143,000
Children under age 18 not covered	21,000	6,965,000
Percent of children not covered	11.0%	9.4%

Source: U.S. Census Bureau, Current Population Survey, 2012 Annual Social and Economic Supplement

HIV, STD, and Tuberculosis Cases and Rates, 2011

Disease	State Cases	State Rate[1]	U.S. Rate[1]
Chlamydia	5,739	808.0	457.6
Gonorrhea	984	138.5	104.2
HIV diagnosis	27	4.6	15.8
HIV, stage 3 (AIDS)	29	5.0	10.3
Syphilis, early latent	3	0.4	4.3
Syphilis, primary/secondary	5	0.7	4.5
Tuberculosis	67	9.3	3.4

Note: (1) Rates are per 100,000 population
Source: Centers for Disease Control and Prevention

Cigarette Smoking, 2011

Category	State	U.S.
Adults who are current smokers	22.9%	21.2%
Adults who smoke everyday	15.9%	15.4%
Adults who smoke some days	7.0%	5.7%
Adults who are former smokers	27.9%	25.1%
Adults who never smoked	49.1%	52.9%

Source: Centers for Disease Control and Prevention, Behaviorial Risk Factor Surveillance System, Tobacco Use, 2011

HOUSING

Home Ownership Rates, 1995–2012

Area	1995	2000	2005	2010	2012
State	60.9%	66.4%	66.0%	65.7%	63.7%
U.S.	64.7%	67.4%	68.9%	66.9%	65.4%

Source: U.S. Census Bureau, Housing Vacancies and Homeownership, Annual Statistics

Home Sales, 2000–2010
In thousands of units

Year	State Sales	U.S. Sales	State Share
2000	14.3	5,174	0.28%
2002	17.2	5,632	0.31%
2004	23.0	6,778	0.34%
2006	30.7	6,478	0.47%
2008	23.2	4,913	0.47%
2010	22.4	4,908	0.46%

Note: Units include single-family homes, condos and co-ops
Source: National Association of Realtors, Real Estate Outlook, Market Trends & Insights

Value of Owner-Occupied Homes, 2011

Value	Total Units in State	Percent of Total, State	Percent of Total, U.S.
Less than $50,000	9,372	5.8%	8.8%
$50,000 to $99,000	11,297	7.0%	16.0%
$100,000 to $149,000	12,930	8.0%	16.5%
$150,000 to $199,000	26,180	16.1%	15.4%
$200,000 to $299,000	51,355	31.6%	18.2%
$300,000 to $499,000	40,241	24.8%	15.2%
$500,000 to $999,000	9,971	6.1%	7.9%
$1,000,000 or more	966	0.6%	2.0%
Median value	–	$238,300	$173,600

Source: U.S. Census Bureau, 2011 American Community Survey 1-Year Estimates

EDUCATION

School Enrollment, 2011

Educational Level	Students Enrolled in State	Percent of Total, State	Percent of Total, U.S.
All levels	196,240	100.0%	100.0%
Nursery school, preschool	9,140	4.7%	6.0%
Kindergarten	10,259	5.2%	5.1%
Elementary (grades 1–8)	83,021	42.3%	39.5%
Secondary (grades 9–12)	42,751	21.8%	20.7%
College or graduate school	51,069	26.0%	28.7%

Note: Figures cover the population 3 years and over enrolled in school
Source: U.S. Census Bureau, 2011 American Community Survey 1-Year Estimates

Educational Attainment, 2011

Highest Level of Education	State	U.S.
High school diploma	91.8%	85.9%
Bachelor's degree	26.4%	28.5%
Graduate/Professional degree	9.5%	10.6%

Note: Figures cover the population 25 years and over
Source: U.S. Census Bureau, 2011 American Community Survey 1-Year Estimates

Public College Finances, FY 2012

Category	State	U.S.
Full-time equivalent enrollment (FTE)[1]	21,819	11,548,974
Educational appropriations per FTE[2]	$11,909	$5,906
Net tuition revenue per FTE[3]	$4,545	$5,189
Total educational revenue per FTE[4]	$16,454	$11,043

(1) Full-time equivalent enrollment equates student credit hours to full time, academic year students, but excludes medical students; (2) Educational appropriations measure state and local support available for public higher education operating expenses including ARRA funds and excludes appropriations for independent institutions, financial aid for students attending independent institutions, research, hospitals, and medical education; (3) Net tuition revenue is calculated by taking the gross amount of tuition and fees, less state and institutional financial aid, tuition waivers or discounts, and medical student tuition and fees. Net tuition revenue used for capital debt service is included in the net tuition revenue figures; (4) Total educational revenue is the sum of educational appropriations and net tuition excluding net tuition revenue used for capital debt service.
Source: State Higher Education Executive Officers, State Higher Education Finance FY 2012

TRANSPORTATION AND TRAVEL

Motor Vehicle Registrations and Drivers Licenses, 2011

Vehicle Type	State	U.S.	State Share
Automobiles[1]	215,688	125,656,528	0.17%
Buses	2,346	666,064	0.35%
Trucks	508,900	118,455,587	0.43%
Motorcycles	31,020	8,437,502	0.37%
Drivers licenses	521,280	211,874,649	0.25%

Note: Motor vehicle registrations include private, commercial, and publicly-owned vehicles; (1) Includes taxicabs
Source: U.S. Department of Transportation, Federal Highway Administration

Domestic Travel Expenditures, 2009
In millions of dollars

Category	State	U.S.	State Share
Travel expenditures	$1,721	$610,200	0.28%

Note: Figures represent U.S. spending on domestic overnight trips and day trips of 50 miles or more, one way, away from home. Excludes spending by foreign visitors.
Source: U.S. Travel Association, Impact of Travel on State Economies, 2009

Retail Gasoline Prices, 2013

Gasoline Grade	State Average	U.S. Average
Regular	$4.07	$3.65
Mid	$4.12	$3.81
Premium	$4.24	$3.98
Diesel	$4.30	$3.88
Excise tax[1]	30.9 cents	49.4 cents

Note: Gasoline prices as of 7/26/2013; (1) Includes state and federal excise taxes and other state taxes as of July 1, 2013
Source: American Automobile Association, Daily Fuel Guage Report; American Petroleum Institute, State Motor Fuel Taxes, 2013

Public Road Length, 2011

Type	State Mileage	U.S. Mileage	State Share
Interstate highways	1,084	46,960	2.31%
Other highways	0	15,719	0.00%
Principal arterial	940	156,262	0.60%
Minor arterial	636	242,942	0.26%
Major collector	1,629	534,592	0.30%
Minor collector	1,652	266,357	0.62%
Local	10,734	2,814,925	0.38%
Urban	2,688	1,095,373	0.25%
Rural	13,987	2,982,383	0.47%
Total	16,675	4,077,756	0.41%

Note: Combined urban and rural road mileage equals the total of the other road types
Source: U.S. Department of Transportation, Federal Highway Administration, Public Road Length, 2011

CRIME AND LAW ENFORCEMENT

Full-Time Law Enforcement Officers, 2011

Gender	State Number	State Rate[1]	U.S. Rate[1]
Male officers	1,179	163.3	210.3
Female officers	106	14.7	28.1
Total officers	1,285	177.9	238.3

Note: (1) Rates are per 100,000 population
Source: Federal Bureau of Investigation, Uniform Crime Reports, Crime in the United States 2011

Prison Population, 2000–2012

Year	State Population	U.S. Population	State Share
2000	4,173	1,391,261	0.30%
2005	4,812	1,527,929	0.31%
2010	5,391	1,613,803	0.33%
2011	5,412	1,598,783	0.34%
2012	5,533	1,571,013	0.35%

Note: Figures include prisoners under the jurisdiction of state or federal correctional authorities.
Source: U.S. Department of Justice, Bureau of Justice Statistics, Prisoners in 2006, 2011, 2012 (Advance Counts)

Crime Rate, 2011
Incidents per 100,000 residents

Category	State	U.S.
Violent crimes	606.5	386.3
Murder	4.0	4.7
Forcible rape	58.1	26.8
Robbery	79.7	113.7
Aggravated assault	464.6	241.1
Property crimes	2,632.8	2,908.7
Burglary	391.0	702.2
Larceny/theft	2,056.0	1,976.9
Motor vehicle theft	185.8	229.6
All crimes	3,239.3	3,295.0

Source: Federal Bureau of Investigation, Uniform Crime Reports, Crime in the United States 2011

GOVERNMENT AND FINANCE

Local Governments by Type, 2012

Government Type	State	U.S.	State Share
All local governments	177	89,004	0.20%
County	14	3,031	0.46%
Municipality	148	19,522	0.76%
Town/Township	0	16,364	0.00%
Special District	15	37,203	0.04%
Ind. School District	0	12,884	0.00%

Source: U.S. Census Bureau, 2012 Census of Governments: Organization Component Preliminary Estimates

State Government Revenue, 2011
In thousands of dollars, except for per capita figures

Total revenue	$14,920,900
Total revenue per capita, State	$20,613
Total revenue per capita, U.S.	$7,271
General revenue	$12,665,675
Intergovernmental revenue	$3,040,677
Taxes	$5,537,679
General sales	$0
Selective sales	$256,014
License taxes	$137,889
Individual income taxes	$0
Corporate income taxes	$720,733
Other taxes	$4,423,043
Current charges	$586,262
Miscellaneous general revenue	$3,501,057
Utility revenue	$17,613
Liquor store revenue	$0
Insurance trust revenue[1]	$2,237,612

Note: (1) Within insurance trust revenue, net earnings of state retirement systems is a calculated statistic, and thus can be positive or negative. Net earnings is the sum of earnings on investments plus gains on investments minus losses on investments.
Source: U.S. Census Bureau, 2011 Annual Survey of State Government Finances

State Government Expenditures, 2011

In thousands of dollars, except for per capita figures

Total expenditure	$11,320,127
Total expenditure per capita, State	$15,639
Total expenditure per capita, U.S.	$6,427
Intergovernmental expenditure	$1,723,023
Direct expenditure	$9,597,104
Current operation	$6,661,701
Capital outlay	$1,218,201
Insurance benefits and repayments	$1,244,060
Assistance and subsidies	$183,766
Interest on debt	$289,376
Utility expenditure	$119,933
Liquor store expenditure	$0
Insurance trust expenditure	$1,244,060

Source: U.S. Census Bureau, 2011 Annual Survey of State Government Finances

State Government General Expenditures by Function, 2011

In thousands of dollars

Education	$2,475,486
Public welfare	$1,917,737
Hospitals	$66,227
Health	$362,760
Highways	$1,412,087
Police protection	$118,154
Correction	$283,764
Natural resources	$391,462
Parks and recreation	$21,012
Governmental administration	$585,703
Interest on general debt	$283,836
Other and unallocable	$2,037,906

Source: U.S. Census Bureau, 2011 Annual Survey of State Government Finances

State Government Finances, Cash and Debt, 2011

In thousands of dollars, except for per capita figures

Debt at end of fiscal year	
State, total	$6,417,682
State, per capita	$8,866
U.S., per capita	$3,635
Cash and security holdings	
State, total	$69,279,035
State, per capita	$95,708
U.S., per capita	$11,759

Source: U.S. Census Bureau, 2011 Annual Survey of State Government Finances

POLITICS

Composition of the Senate, 1995–2013

Congress (Year)	State/U.S	Dem	Rep	Total
104th (1995)	State delegates	0	2	2
	Total U.S.	48	52	100
105th (1997)	State delegates	0	2	2
	Total U.S.	45	55	100
106th (1999)	State delegates	0	2	2
	Total U.S.	45	55	100
107th (2001)	State delegates	0	2	2
	Total U.S.	50	50	100
108th (2003)	State delegates	0	2	2
	Total U.S.	48	51	100
109th (2005)	State delegates	0	2	2
	Total U.S.	44	55	100
110th (2007)	State delegates	0	2	2
	Total U.S.	49	49	100
111th (2009)	State delegates	1	1	2
	Total U.S.	57	41	100
112th (2011)	State delegates	1	1	2
	Total U.S.	51	47	100
113th (2013)	State delegates	1	1	2
	Total U.S.	54	45	100

Note: Figures are for the starts of first sessions; Totals include Democratic (Dem) and Republican (Rep) members as well as vacancies and seats held by independent party members
Source: U.S. Congress, Congressional Directory

Composition of the House of Representatives, 1995–2013

Congress (Year)	State/U.S	Dem	Rep	Total
104th (1995)	State delegates	0	1	1
	Total U.S.	204	230	435
105th (1997)	State delegates	0	1	1
	Total U.S.	207	226	435
106th (1999)	State delegates	0	1	1
	Total U.S.	211	223	435
107th (2001)	State delegates	0	1	1
	Total U.S.	212	221	435
108th (2003)	State delegates	0	1	1
	Total U.S.	205	229	435
109th (2005)	State delegates	0	1	1
	Total U.S.	202	231	435
110th (2007)	State delegates	0	1	1
	Total U.S.	233	198	435
111th (2009)	State delegates	0	1	1
	Total U.S.	256	178	435
112th (2011)	State delegates	0	1	1
	Total U.S.	193	242	435
113th (2013)	State delegates	0	1	1
	Total U.S.	201	234	435

Note: Figures are for the starts of first sessions; Totals include Democratic (Dem) and Republican (Rep) members as well as vacancies and seats held by independent party members
Source: U.S. Congress, Congressional Directory

Composition of State Legislature, 2004–2013

Year	Democrats	Republicans	Total
State Senate			
2004	8	12	20
2005	8	12	20
2006	8	12	20
2007	9	11	20
2008	9	11	20
2009	10	10	20
2010	10	10	20
2011	10	10	20
2012	10	10	20
2013	7	13	20
State House			
2004	13	27	40
2005	14	26	40
2006	14	26	40
2007	17	23	40
2008	17	23	40
2009	18	22	40
2010	18	22	40
2011	16	24	40
2012	16	24	40
2013	14	26	40

Note: Totals may include minor party members and vacancies
Source: The Council of State Governments, State Legislatures

Voter Participation in Presidential Elections, 1980–2012

Year	Voting-eligible State Population	State Voter Turnout Rate	U.S. Voter Turnout Rate
1980	270,122	58.7	54.2
1984	343,030	60.5	55.2
1988	355,023	56.4	52.8
1992	389,898	66.3	58.1
1996	404,180	59.8	51.7
2000	419,111	68.1	54.2
2004	452,124	69.1	60.1
2008	479,429	68.0	61.6
2012	509,785	58.9	58.2

Note: All figures are based on the voting-eligible population which excludes person ineligible to vote such as non-citizens, felons (depending on state law), and mentally-incapacitated persons. U.S. figures include the overseas eligible population (including military personnel).
Source: McDonald, Michael P., United States Election Project, Presidential Voter Turnout Rates, 1980–2012

Governors Since Statehood

William A. Egan (D)	1959-1966
Walter J. Hickel (R)	(r) 1966-1969
Keith H. Miller (R)	1969-1970
William A. Egan (D)	1970-1974
Jay S. Hammond (R)	1974-1982
William Sheffield (D)	1982-1986
Steve Cowper (D)	1986-1990
Walter J. Hickel (O)	1990-1994
Tony Knowles (D)	1994-2002
Frank Murkowski (R)	2002-2006
Sarah Palin (R)	(r) 2006-2009
Sean Parnell (R)	2009-2014

Note: (D) Democrat; (R) Republican; (O) Other party; (r) resigned; (d) died in office; (i) removed from office

Arizona

Location: Southwest

Area and rank: 114,000 square miles (295,249 square kilometers); 114,006 square miles (295,276 square kilometers) including water; sixth largest state in area

Coastline: none (c. 40 miles from Gulf of California)

Population and rank: 6,553,255 (2012 estimate); fifteenth largest state in population

Capital and largest city: Phoenix (1,445,632 people in 2010 census)

Became territory: February 24, 1863

Entered Union and rank: February 14, 1912; forty-eighth state

Present constitution adopted: 1911

Counties: 15

A 2009 view of downtown skyscrapers of Arizona's capital and largest city, Phoenix. Camelback Mountain is visible in the center background. (Wikimedia Commons)

State name: "Arizona" derives from the American Indian "Arizonac," which means "little spring" or "young spring"

State nickname: Grand Canyon State

Motto: *Ditat Deus* (God enriches)

State flag: Blue field on bottom half; thirteen red and yellow rays and a copper star on top half

Highest point: Humphreys Peak—12,633 feet (3,851 meters)

Lowest point: Colorado River—70 feet (21 meters)

Highest recorded temperature: 127 degrees Fahrenheit (53 degrees Celsius)— Parker, 1905

Lowest recorded temperature: –40 degrees Fahrenheit (–40 degrees Celsius)— Hawley Lake, 1971

State song: "Arizona March Song"
State tree: Palo Verde

State flower: Saguaro cactus blossom

State bird: Cactus wren

State fish: Apache trout

National parks: Grand Canyon, Petrified Forest, Saguaro

Arizona History

Arizona's arid climate and southwest location combined to play influential roles in its history. Lack of rain has placed water at the center of Arizona's concerns, because without water, economic development is impossible. During the 1850's, the federal government even imported camels for a route through Arizona. The state was later than others in developing, with a population of barely forty thousand in 1880. On the other hand, the completion of a number of significant dams before and after World War II provided copious water and electric power, and the state's warm winters attract millions of new arrivals.

Early History. American Indians are believed to have inhabited Arizona for thousands of years, probably as early as 25,000 B.C.E. First to have settled were the Anasazi, ancestors of today's Pueblo, Hohokam, and Mogollon peoples. Not long before the entrance of Europeans to the region, the Navajos and Apaches arrived.

In the sixteenth century, Spanish and Native Americans came in contact with each other. A succession of Spanish expeditions arrived, headed by priests such as Franciscan friar Marcos de Niza, who came in 1539 searching for the fabled Seven Cities of Cibola. Other adventurers arrived, such as Francisco Vásquez de Coronado, who explored the region from 1540 to 1542. More explorers entered the region later in the century searching for precious metals.

In the next century a number of priests came in search of American Indian souls to save and began erecting missions. Perhaps the most illustrious was Father Eusebio Francisco Kino, a Jesuit mathematics professor of German origin, who went to Mexico in 1680. Kino thoroughly explored the region, covering twenty thousand miles and finding an overland route to California. Kino also founded several missions, including San Xavier del Bac Mission, located near Tucson, established

Apache leaders Geronimo (center left with arms on knees) and Nana (to Geromino's right) negotiating with General George Crook (second from right with white hat) around 1886, during one of several attempts to end the region's Apache wars. (Library of Congress)

The Hoover Dam in 2011. The dam was completed in the mid-1930's. (©Antoine Taveneaux/Wikimedia Commons)

and was active more than thirty years later when he led gold-hunting parties. In these yearsmodern Arizona was part of Mexico,which gained independence from Spain after its War of Independence, begun in 1810.

From Spanish to American Rule. Arizona passed from Mexican to American hands as a consequence of the Mexican-American War (1846–1848). The terms of the Treaty of Guadalupe Hidalgo called for Mexico to cede all lands north of the Gila River, which runs through southern Arizona. Thus Arizona became part of New Mexico, which became a territory after its annexation to the United States.

The Gila River border proved problematic, however, when plans for a transcontinental railroad were being drawn up, since the best route ran south of the river. Accordingly, an American diplomat, James Gadsden, American Minister to Mexico, negotiated transfer of the required land. In 1853, by the terms of the Gadsden Purchase, Mexico agreed to sell a strip of territory along its northern border between Texas and California for $10 million.

Arizona was still part of New Mexico when the Civil War broke out. In 1861, when southern President Jefferson Davis declared New Mexico part of the Confederacy, Kit Carson was asked to raise a force to defend the territory against invasion. When the Confederacy sent troops to the region in 1862, the only Civil War battle on Arizona soil occurred, resulting in Union victory. Thereafter, claims of the Confederacy to the region rang hollow. To ensure its status, however, Congress made Arizona a separate territory in 1863. Prescott was the new territory's first capital, though the site changed from one place to another until Phoenix became the permanent capital in 1889.

Native American Relations. During the Civil War, the area was nearly emptied of European settlers. Yet after the war, when miners and ranchers returned, American Indian attacks became a serious matter. In 1864, Kit Carson led a successful campaign against the Navahos. The defeated Navahos were then required to trek, many of them on foot, to Bosque Redondo, New Mexico, some three hundred miles away. The event became known as the Long Walk. They remained there until 1868, when they made the Long Walk Home. The Apaches, however, remained hostile and active in Arizona. With such leaders as Cochise, Mangas Coloradas, and Geronimo, the Apaches were a formidable threat, attacking not only ranches but also towns and even forts. Not until 1886 did the last raiding party led

in 1692. It is the only surviving Mexican Baroque church in the United States.

In the eighteenth century Spanish activity continued. In 1776, when the American colonies declared independence from Britain, Spanish cleric Father Francisco Silvestre Vélez de Escalante undertook important explorations of the Colorado River region. The previous year, Tucson had been founded when a fortress, Old Pueblo, was constructed there. In succeeding years, Spanish troops were busy dealing with hostile American Indians. During the 1780's they conquered the Yumas, and in 1790 negotiations with the Apaches resulted in a peace lasting until 1822. Peace with the Navahos after their military defeat in 1806 lasted thirteen years.

American involvement in the region began during the 1820's, when traders and trappers entered the territory. From 1828, trapper, scout, and soldier Kit Carson used Taos, New Mexico, as a base for expeditions, which in some cases traveled through Arizona. Another famous trapper and scout, Pauline Weaver, arrived in 1830

by Geronimo surrender to federal forces.

Despite problems with Native Americans, much economic progress was made. Mining made great strides during the 1870's, and after 1886 grazing prospered despite frequent range wars between cattle and sheep ranchers. During the 1880's copper was discovered near Bisbee, in the southeast. Eventually copper became an important state resource. Settlement of the territory was assisted by several congressional acts, such as the Homestead Act (1862), which gave land to settlers but required them to develop it to make good their claims. A tremendous boost to the state's development occurred when the first transcontinental railroad appeared in 1877. Six years later, track for a second railroad was laid in northern Arizona. Population, which was a dismal 9,658 in 1870, jumped to more than 40,000 ten years later and reached 88,000 in 1890. At the close of the century, it was 123,000, and in 1910, just prior to statehood, it passed 200,000.

From Territory to Statehood. With the American Indian menace behind them, Arizonans of the 1890's agitated for statehood. Not until 1910, however, could Congress be persuaded to pass enabling legislation. Accordingly, a constitution was adopted. Like those

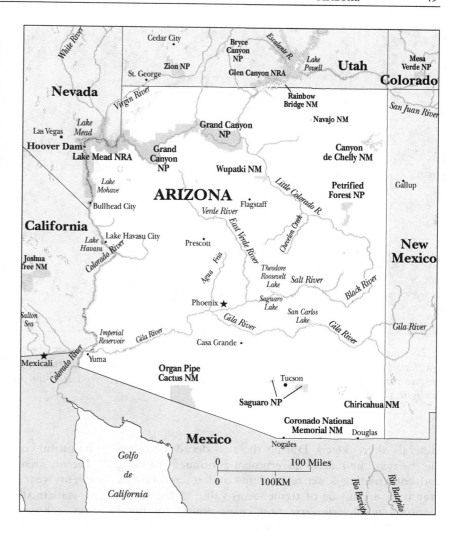

of other western states, it provided for the initiative and referendum and allowed recall of public officials. This provision included recall of judges by voters, but President William Howard Taft strongly objected and refused to agree to Arizona statehood unless it was removed. He believed that judicial independence, essential for constitutional government, would be fatally compromised by such a provision. The offending provision was therefore deleted. Upon attaining statehood, however, voters restored the provision.

The constitution provides for a governor elected for no more than two four-year terms. Four other executive branch officials are elected—a secretary of state, attorney general, treasurer, and superintendent of public instruction. These officials form a line of succession if a governor dies, resigns, or is removed from office; they, too, are limited to two four-year terms. Members of the bicameral legislature can be elected to a maximum of four two-year terms. The state's supreme court justices are appointed by the governor to six-year terms, at the end of which voters decide whether to retain them. The recall provision was

most notably used in 1988 to remove a sitting governor.

Social and Economic Progress. By the time Arizona achieved statehood, it had begun the process of advancing from an extraction to a manufacturing economy. With the emergence of labor unions in mines, labor strife became familiar. Among militant labor organizers were the Marxist International Workers of the World (IWW). A notorious event in the state's labor history involving the IWW was the "Bisbee deportation" of July 12, 1917, during World War I. In this incident, some two thousand persons, most of them copper miners called out on strike by the IWW, were arrested by armed civilians, headed by the sheriff. Those who refused to abandon the strike, nearly 1,200 men, were loaded onto cattle cars and taken across the New Mexico border. There, they were unloaded in the desert, where they spent two unsheltered days before U.S. troops arrived. Hundreds of civil suits were filed afterward and settled out of court.

Along with neighboring states, the American entrance into World War I gave a significant, though temporary, boost to Arizona's economy, when the price of

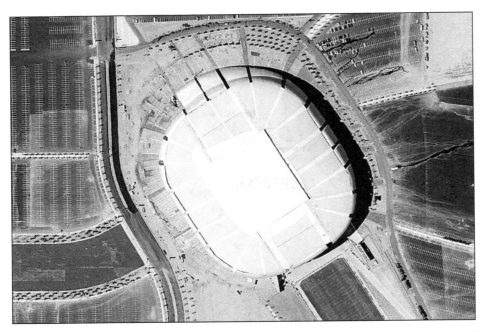

In 2006, after playing before sweltering crowds in Arizona's desert heat, the National Football League's Cardinals began playing in a new air-conditioned stadium with a unique innovation: a real-grass field that rolls out of the covered stadium into the sunlight. (NASA)

minerals skyrocketed. During the two decades following the war, the federal government continued planning and constructing a series of dams and reservoirs that eventually would be of tremendous value to the state's economy by allowing irrigation, cheap power, and flood control. The Roosevelt Dam had been constructed prior to statehood. After the war, further projects included the Coolidge Dam on the Upper Gila River in south central Arizona, other dams on the Verde and Salt Rivers, and the great Hoover Dam, one of the century's great engineering projects, on the Arizona-Nevada border. In 1922, the Colorado River Compact devised a scheme for water sharing among seven states, including Arizona. As further irrigation became possible, agriculture prospered. The 1930's Depression years, however, were as difficult for Arizona as for the rest of the nation.

World War II and Postwar Developments. The state's economy rebounded through federal spending during World War II, when numerous air bases were opened due to the state's ideal flying weather. After the war the boom continued. Between 1940 and 1960, population nearly tripled, reaching 1.3 million. Adequate water supplies allowed manufacturing to expand, especially after 1963, when the U.S. Supreme Court awarded the state rights to 2.8 million acre feet of water a year from the Colorado River. By then, Arizona's extraction economy had been transformed by industrialization.

By the 1990's the state had undergone a second transformation. Manufacturing accounted for only 12 percent of its income, though high-tech industries were making their mark. Agriculture was just 2 percent and mining a scant 1 percent of state income. The lion's share was now taken up by services, including a thriving tourist industry. Society had also been transformed by a postwar flight from the eastern and Midwestern "rust belt" to the warmer climate and economic opportunities of the Southwest. From a raw frontier territory at the start of the century, Arizona had become a prosperous modern, postindustrial society, with a rich and colorful past and a confident future.

Twenty-first Century Prosperity. As the new millennium approached, Arizona could find much satisfaction in its growing prosperity. People flocked to the state, where a bountiful economy beckoned, especially in the Phoenix-Tucson area. In 1999, the U.S. poverty rate reached a twenty-year low; Arizona was one of seven states with a statistically significant drop in poverty. Following the 2000 census, which reflected the state's population increase, Arizona gained two new members in the U.S. House of Representatives.

Politically, the state remained somewhat right of center, voting for the Republican presidential candidate, George W. Bush, in both 2000 and 2004. Both of its U.S. senators and four of its five members of the House were Republican, and the two seats created in 2002 went to Republicans. The state governor elected in 2002, Janet Napolitano, however, was a Democrat.

Wildfires. Many of the Western states struggled with historic droughts during the 1990's and into the early twenty-first century, and Arizona was no exception. One serious consequence of the droughts was the recurrence of wildfires, some of which consumed hundreds of thousands of acres. The wildfires in 1999 were so prevalent and destructive that they were said to be "the worst wildfire season in a generation." Other fires, not all of them of natural origin, followed annually. The devastating Rodeo-Chediski fire of 2002, in east-central Arizona, burned more than 400,000 acres.

Illegal Immigration. By the late 1990's, a simmering controversy plagued the state regarding illegal immigrants flowing north from the Mexican border. In 2000,

Arizonans sought to shore up social cohesion by passing an initiative, Proposition 203, abolishing bilingual education and replacing it with English immersion education for immigrant students. Four years later, in 2004, the state's voters, fearful of noncitizen influence at the polls, passed an initiative requiring proof of U.S. citizenship for voting.

Tragic circumstances surrounded other aspects of illegal immigration. In 2001, fourteen illegal immigrants who had been abandoned by smugglers in the Arizona desert were found dead some thirty miles north of the Mexican border. Others, more fortunate, were found alive but dehydrated and exhausted. Several years later, on August 15, 2005, Governor Napolitano declared a state of emergency in four counties bordering Mexico because of problems caused by a heavy influx of illegal immigrants.

During the same year, about thirteen hundred citizen volunteers—declaring themselves part of the Minuteman Project after the Revolutionary-era defenders of the American colonies—spent a month patrolling border areas for illegal immigrants and informing Border Patrol agents of immigrant activity they witnessed.

Despite its problems, Arizona entered the third millennium in a dynamically prosperous position, with the continued arrival of Americans from other parts to the country eager to take advantage of the state's warm climate and its growing economic opportunities.

Shooting. On January 8, 2011, U.S. Member of Congress Gabrielle Giffords and eighteen others were shot during a public meeting held in a lot in Casas Adobes, Arizona, in the Tucson metropolitan area. Six people died, including Arizona District Court Chief Judge John Roll; Gabe Zimmerman, a member of Giffords' staff; and a nine-year-old girl, Christina-Taylor Green. The assailant, Jared Lee Loughner, shot Giffords in the head before shooting the other victims. Loughner was immediately arrested and charged with federal crimes, including attempted assassination of a member of Congress and the assassination of a federal judge. In January 2012, a federal judge found Loughner was incompetent to stand trial due to a diagnosis of paranoid schizophrenia. However, on August 7, 2012 Loughner was judged competent; he then pleaded guilty, and in November 2012, he was sentenced to seven consecutive life terms plus 140 years in prison without parole.

The shooting was immediately followed by claims that hostile political rhetoric had inspired Loughner, with some focus on the fact that Sarah Palin had used gun imagery in her speeches; some of Palin's campaign literature had shown certain congressional districts as "targeted," including that of Giffords. For several weeks, this claim was widely circulated; however, many saw the claim as an effort to libel Giffords' political opponents. One longer-term consequence was a renewed effort at gun-control; a number of figures on both the conservative and liberal extremes argued for reduced angry rhetoric in political discourse. Representative Giffords made a recovery, and spoke before Congress on January 22, 2012, announcing she was resigning her seat to concentrate on physical therapy.

State Immigration Law. Arizona passed a controversial immigration enforcement act, SB1070, signed into law by Governor Jan Brewer on April 23, 2010. Under federal law, adult aliens in the United States must carry documentation if they are in the United States more than 30 days. The state law requires police to determine the immigration status of someone arrested or detained when there is "reasonable suspicion" that the person arrested is not in the United States legally. Following Arizona's enactment of SB 1070, five other states—Alabama, Georgia, Indiana, South Carolina and Utah passed similar laws.

In June 2012, the U.S. Supreme Court ruled on the case *Arizona v. United States*. The Court upheld the provision requiring immigration status checks during law enforcement stops, but struck down three other provisions as violations of the Supremacy Clause of the United States Constitution.

Charles F. Bahmueller
Updated by the Editor

Arizona Time Line

500 C.E.–1450   Hohokam tribes flourish; build more than two hundred miles of canals for water for irrigation and domestic use.
c. 1000   Cochise tribe settles near present-day Bisbee.
1526   Don José de Basconales crosses part of Arizona.
1536   Explorer Alvar Núñez Cabeza de Vaca crosses part of southwest Arizona.
1539   Franciscan friar Marcos de Niza explores in Arizona, searching for rich Seven Cities of Cibola.
1540   Francisco Vásquez de Coronado explores Arizona region.
1581–1583   Spanish expeditions through Arizona find precious metals.
1620   Franciscan missionaries appeal to Hopi tribe.

1680	Father Eusebio Francisco Kino begins missionary work.
1700	Father Kino founds San Xavier del Bac Mission.
1752	First white settlement is founded by Spanish at Tubac.
1776	Tucson is founded as Spanish fort.
1776	Father Francisco Silvestre Vélez de Escalante explores Colorado River region.
1782	Spanish military forces conquer Yuma tribe.
1804–1806	Navaho Indians are defeated by Spanish military; peace endures for thirteen years.
1821	Arizona becomes province of Mexico; Santa Fe Trail opens.
1824	American traders begin exploring Apache territory.
1827	Mexican Republic expels Franciscans, ending missionary era.
1830	American trapper and scout Pauline Weaver begins Arizona travels.
Dec. 17, 1846	Mormon battalion occupies Tucson; raises U.S. flag on road from Santa Fe to the Pacific.
1848	Mexico cedes all land north of Gila River to United States in Treaty of Guadalupe Hidalgo.
Sept. 9, 1850	Territory of New Mexico, which includes Arizona, is established.
1853	Gadsden Purchase makes southern Arizona U.S. land.
1860	First newspaper, the Weekly Arizonan, begins publication.
1860	Apache chief Cochise leads raids on settlers.
1861	Southern president Jefferson Davis declares Arizona a Confederate territory.
1862	Sole Civil War battle in Arizona fought at Picacho Peak, near Tucson; results in Union victory.
Feb. 24, 1863	Union president Abraham Lincoln creates Arizona Territory; Prescott is made capital.
1864	Navahos are forced to walk three hundred miles from Arizona to Fort Sumner, New Mexico, after military defeat in an event remembered as The Long Walk.
1866	First public schools open, in Prescott and Tucson.
1867	Treaty establishing Navaho Reservation is signed.
Apr. 30, 1871	Grant Camp Massacre occurs, in which 108 Apaches are killed by whites.
1875	First copper is mined at Clifton.
1879	Tombstone is founded after gold is discovered.
1880	First railroad crosses state.
Oct. 26, 1881	Gunfight at the O.K. Corral, among Wyatt Earp, Doc Holliday, and others, takes place in Tombstone.
1883	Santa Fe Railroad crosses northern region of Arizona.
1907	Arizona is nation's leading copper producer.
1911	Roosevelt Dam is dedicated.
Feb. 14, 1912	Arizona becomes forty-eighth state.
1919	Grand Canyon National Park is established.
1928	Coolidge Dam is dedicated.
1936	Boulder (now Hoover) Dam, on Arizona-Nevada border, is completed.
1942	Almost eighteen thousand Japanese Americans are interned in Poston.
1948	Arizona's Native Americans win right to vote.
1962	U.S. Supreme Court gives Arizona Colorado River water rights.
1963	Judge Lorna Lockwood becomes first female state supreme court chief justice.
1969	Navajo Community College, the first college on an Indian reservation, opens in Tsaile.
1974	Construction begins on Central Arizona Project, designed to assure Arizona sufficient water.
1991	Central Arizona Project is completed.
1997	Arizona's population is estimated at 4,554,966.
May 23–24, 2001	Fourteen illegal immigrants, abandoned by smugglers, are found dead in the Arizona desert.
Oct. 16, 2003	Colorado River Water Pact is signed guaranteeing stable access to water from the Colorado River to Arizona and to seven other Colorado River Basin states.
Nov. 4, 2003	Mexico's president Vicente Fox visits the state in search of agreement on the regularization of the status of illegal Mexican immigrants; he meets with Arizona governor and governors of three other border states.
Aug. 15, 2005	Governor declares a state of emergency in border counties because of a heavy influx of illegal immigrants.

Aug. 12, 2006	State-of-the-art, retractable roof, air-conditioned Cardinals Stadium, which cost $455 million to build, opens in Glendale, Arizona.
April 23, 2010	Arizona passes a controversial immigration enforcement act giving police the right to determine the immigration status of individuals under "reasonable suspicion."
Jan. 8, 2011	U.S. Representative Gabrielle Giffords and eighteen others are shot during a public meeting held in a lot in Casas Adobes, Arizona, in the Tucson metropolitan area. Six people die, including Arizona District Court Chief Judge John Roll. The assailant, Jared Lee Loughner, is immediately arrested.
June 2012	U.S. Supreme Court ruled on the case *Arizona v. United States* with mixed results, upholding status checks during typical law enforcement stops, but striking down three other provisions in the Arizona law.

Notes for Further Study

Published Sources. Among books useful for an understanding of government in Arizona are David R. Berman's *Arizona Politics and Government: The Quest for Autonomy, Democracy, and Development* (1998), Gerald E. Hansen and Douglas

A. Brown's *Arizona: Its Constitution and Government* (1993), and *The Arizona Constitution Study Guide* (8th ed., 2005). There is also an annually updated yearbook series, *Arizona Yearbook: A Guide to Government in the Grand Canyon State.*On Arizona's geography, see Malcolm L. Comeaux's *Arizona: A Geography* (1982); for place names, there is Will Croft Barnes's *Arizona Place Names* (1988); and for a historical atlas, one should consult Henry Pickering Walker's *Historical Atlas of Arizona* (1987).

For natural history, an excellent source is *The Smithsonian Guide to Natural America: The Southwest—New Mexico and Arizona* (1995). For an overview of Arizona history, see Robert Wozinicki's *History of Arizona* (1987); Donald Gawronski's *An Introduction to Arizona and Government* (1988); and Thomas G. Aylesworth, et al. *The West: Arizona, Nevada, Utah* (1995). Eminent folk historian Marshall Trimble has also written *Arizona: A Cavalcade of History* (Rev. ed., 2003), a solid overview of the state's past. Travelers should also consult Trimble's *Roadside History of Arizona* (2d ed., 2004) and Anne O'Brien's *Traveling Indian Arizona* (2006), which introduces readers to the modern-day culture, traditions, cuisine, and arts of the state's twenty-one tribal communities. Studies on Native Americans include W. E. Coffer's *Sipapu: The Story of the Indians of Arizona and New Mexico* (1986). Regarding individual tribes, Ruth Underhill studies *The Papago and Pima Indians of Arizona* (1990), and Franck C. Lockwood examines *The Apache Indians* (1987). Ancient Indian culture is explored in James J. Reid and Stephanie Whittlesey's *The Archeology of Ancient Arizona* (1997). Few

Americans know that the Civil War was fought as far west as the territory that was to become Arizona. In *The Civil War in Arizona: The Story of the California Volunteers, 1861–1865* (2006), Andrew E. Masich chronicles the struggles of the California Column, a group of volunteer soldiers who served in the U.S. Army from 1861 to 1866 and played a key role in creating and shaping Arizona Territory. Young audiences will appreciate the survey of the state found in *Arizona* (2005) by Vanessa Brown.

Web Resources. The official state of Arizona Web site (http://az.gov) is a good starting place for information on the state, especially by using the Find by Category heading on the home page. Arizona Travel (www.arizonaguide.com/) is a comprehensive site with a wealth of information for those planning a trip to the state. The governor's site (governor.state.az.us/) and the State of Arizona Legislative Information System (www.azleg.state.az.us/) offer resources on the political workings in the state. Pages on individual counties are good resources for statistical information on state demographics (quickfacts.census.gov/qfd/states/04000.html). Useful links to Arizona history sites include the Prescott site (prescott.org/history.htm) and the Arizona Heritage Traveler (arizonaheritagetraveler.org); click on Attractions A-Z in the top navigation bar. For a taste of the state's varied ethnic history, see the Promise of Gold Mountain: Tucson's Chinese Heritage (parentseyes.arizona.edu/promise/).

The Arizona state historical society maintains information on library archives on Arizona history (www.arizonahistoricalsociety.org/). Access Genealogy (www.accessgenealogy.com/native/arizona/) maintains a very useful page on the history of many of the state's tribal communities, as does AzCentral (www.azcentral.com/news/native-americans). Information on individual tribes may also be researched; consult pages on the Hopi (www.crystalinks.com/hopi1.html).

Counties

County	2012 Population	Pop. Rank	Land Area (sq. miles)	Area Rank
Apache	73,195	10	11,197.52	3
Cochise	132,088	8	6,165.69	8
Coconino	136,011	7	18,618.88	1
Gila	53,144	11	4,757.93	11
Graham	37,416	13	4,622.60	12
Greenlee	8,802	15	1,843.13	14
La Paz	20,281	14	4,499.63	13
Maricopa	3,942,169	1	9,200.14	5

County	2012 Population	Pop. Rank	Land Area (sq. miles)	Area Rank
Mohave	203,334	5	13,311.08	2
Navajo	107,094	9	9,950.42	4
Pima	992,394	2	9,187.04	6
Pinal	387,365	3	5,365.61	10
Santa Cruz	47,303	12	1,236.92	15
Yavapai	212,637	4	8,123.50	7
Yuma	200,022	6	5,513.99	9

Source: U.S. Census Bureau, 2012 Population Estimates

Cities
With 10,000 or more residents

Legal Name	2010 Population	Pop. Rank	Land Area (sq. miles)	Area Rank
Anthem CDP	21,700	40	7.98	60
Apache Junction city	35,840	28	34.99	37
Arizona City CDP	10,475	63	6.11	63
Avondale city	76,238	13	45.60	26
Buckeye town	50,876	18	375.26	2
Bullhead City city	39,540	25	59.38	21
Camp Verde town	10,873	60	43.14	28
Casa Grande city	48,571	20	109.67	13
Casas Adobes CDP	66,795	14	26.75	44
Catalina Foothills CDP	50,796	19	42.01	29
Chandler city	236,123	4	64.41	16

Legal Name	2010 Population	Pop. Rank	Land Area (sq. miles)	Area Rank
Chino Valley town	10,817	61	63.37	18
Coolidge city	11,825	57	56.49	22
Cottonwood city	11,265	59	16.41	53
Douglas city	17,378	44	9.98	59
Drexel Heights CDP	27,749	32	20.20	49
El Mirage city	31,797	30	10.03	58
Eloy city	16,631	46	111.51	11
Flagstaff city	65,870	15	63.87	17
Florence town	25,536	35	52.45	24
Flowing Wells CDP	16,419	47	4.02	66
Fort Mohave CDP	14,364	51	16.70	52

Legal Name	2010 Population	Pop. Rank	Land Area (sq. miles)	Area Rank
Fortuna Foothills CDP	26,265	34	40.17	32
Fountain Hills town	22,489	39	20.33	48
Gilbert town	208,453	7	67.96	15
Glendale city	226,721	5	59.98	20
Gold Canyon CDP	10,159	65	22.39	46
Goodyear city	65,275	16	191.48	4
Green Valley CDP	21,391	41	32.24	40
Kingman city	28,068	31	34.82	38
Lake Havasu City city	52,527	17	44.43	27
Marana town	34,961	29	121.47	9
Maricopa city	43,482	22	47.47	25
Mesa city	439,041	3	136.45	8
New Kingman-Butler CDP	12,134	56	4.97	65
New River CDP	14,952	49	55.75	23
Nogales city	20,837	42	20.82	47
Oro Valley town	41,011	23	35.53	36
Paradise Valley town	12,820	54	15.43	54
Payson town	15,301	48	19.47	50
Peoria city	154,065	9	174.40	6
Phoenix city	1,445,632	1	516.70	1
Prescott city	39,843	24	41.34	30
Prescott Valley town	38,822	26	38.65	34
Queen Creek town	26,361	33	28.04	43
Rio Rico CDP	18,962	43	62.26	19
Sahuarita town	25,259	37	31.04	42
San Luis city	25,505	36	32.03	41
San Tan Valley CDP	81,321	12	35.78	35
Scottsdale city	217,385	6	183.92	5
Sedona city	10,031	66	19.14	51
Show Low city	10,660	62	40.94	31
Sierra Vista city	43,888	21	152.27	7
Sierra Vista Southeast CDP	14,797	50	110.90	12
Somerton city	14,287	52	7.29	61
Sun City CDP	37,499	27	14.36	55
Sun City West CDP	24,535	38	10.93	57
Sun Lakes CDP	13,975	53	5.32	64
Surprise city	117,517	10	105.75	14
Tanque Verde CDP	16,901	45	32.98	39
Tempe city	161,719	8	39.93	33
Tucson city	520,116	2	226.71	3
Tucson Estates CDP	12,192	55	13.00	56
Vail CDP	10,208	64	22.66	45
Verde Village CDP	11,605	58	6.98	62
Yuma city	93,064	11	120.28	10

Note: CDP–Census Designated Place
Source: U.S. Census Bureau, 2010 Census

Survey Says...

This section presents current rankings from dozens of public and private sources. It shows how this state ranks in a number of critical categories, including education, job growth, cost of living, teen drivers, energy efficiency, and business environment. Sources include *Forbes, Reuters, U.S. News and World Report, CNN Money, Gallup,* and *Huffington Post.*

- Arizona ranked #13 in a government study measuring real gross domestic product (GDP)—the output of goods and services produced by labor and property located in the United States. The ranking is based on the percentage change compared with 2011 GDP.
  U.S. Department of Commerce, Bureau of Economic Analysis, June 2013; www.bea.gov

- Arizona ranked #20 in a government study measuring real gross domestic product (GDP)—the output of goods and services produced by labor and property located in the United States. The ranking is based on the dollar value of its GDP.
  U.S. Department of Commerce, Bureau of Economic Analysis, June 2013; www.bea.gov

- Arizona ranked #43 in the 17th edition of "Quality Counts; State of the States," Education Week's "report card" surveying key education indicators, policy efforts, and educational outcomes.
  Education Week, January 4, 2013 (online) and January 10, 2013 (print); www.edweek.org

- SERI (Science and Engineering Readiness Index) weighs the performance of the states' K-12 schools in preparing students in physics and calculus, the high school subjects considered most important for future scientists and engineers. Arizona ranked #45.
  Newsletter of the Forum on Education of the American Physical Society, Summer 2011 issue; www.huffingtonpost.com, July 11, 2011; updated October 1, 2012

- MoneyRates.com ranked Arizona #11 on its list of the best to worst states for making a living. Criteria: average income; inflation; employment prospects; and workers' Workplace Environment assessments according to the Gallup-Healthways Well-Being Index.
  www.money-rates.com, posted April 1, 2013

- *Forbes* analyzed business costs, labor supply, regulatory environment, current economic climate, growth prospects, and quality of life, to compile its "Best States for Business" rankings. Arizona ranked #25.
  www.forbes.com. posted December 12, 2012

- The 2012 Gallup-Healthways Well-Being Index, surveyed American's opinions on economic confidence, workplace perceptions, community climate, personal choices, and health predictors to assess the "future livability" of each state. Arizona ranked #23.
  "Utah Poised to Be the Best State to Live In," Gallup Wellbeing, www.gallup.com, August 7, 2012

- On CNBC's list of "America's Top States for Business 2013," Arizona ranked #20. Criteria: measures of competitiveness developed with input from the National Association of Manufacturers, the Council on Competitiveness, and other business groups weighed with the states' own marketing criteria.
  www.cnbc.com, consulted July 19, 2013

- Kiplinger identified "Ten States with the Biggest Rate of Job Growth in 2013" using data from the U.S. Bureau of Labor Statistics, IHS Global Insights, Moody's Analytics, and state economic data. Arizona ranked #10.
  www.kiplinger.com, March 2013

- Arizona ranked #4 on MoneyRates list of "Best-and Worst-States to Retire 2012." Criteria: life expectancy, crime rate, climate, economic conditions, taxes, job opportunities, and cost of living.
  www.money-rates.com, October 22, 2012

- Arizona ranked #33 on the 2013 Bankrate "Best Places to Retire" list ranking the states and District of Columbia on various criteria relating to health, safety, and cost.
  www.bankrate.com, May 6, 2013

- Arizona ranked #27 on the Social Science Research Council's "American Human Development Report: The Measure of America," assessing the 50 states plus the District of Columbia on health, education, and living-standard criteria.
  The Measure of America 2013-2014, posted June 19, 2013; www.measureofamerica.org

- Arizona ranked #45 on the Foundation for Child Development's (FCD) Child Well-being Index (CWI). The FCD used the KIDS COUNT report and the National Survey of Children's Health, the only state-level source for several key indicators of child well-being.
  Foundation for Child Development, January 18, 2012; fcd-us.org

- Arizona ranked #47 overall according to the 2013 KIDS COUNT Data Book, a project of the Annie E. Casey Foundation. Criteria: children's economic well-being, education, health, and family and community indicators.
  KIDS COUNT Data Center's Data Book, released June 20, 2013; http://datacenter.kidscount.org

- Arizona ranked #47 in the children's economic well-being category by the 2013 KIDS COUNT Data Book, a project of the Annie E. Casey Foundation.
  KIDS COUNT Data Center's Data Book, released June 20, 2013; http://datacenter.kidscount.org

- Arizona ranked #46 in the children's educational opportunities and attainments category by the 2013 KIDS COUNT Data Book, a project of the Annie E. Casey Foundation.
  KIDS COUNT Data Center's Data Book, released June 20, 2013; http://datacenter.kidscount.org

- Arizona ranked #45 in the children's health category by the 2013 KIDS COUNT Data Book, a project of the Annie E. Casey Foundation.
  KIDS COUNT Data Center's Data Book, released June 20, 2013; http://datacenter.kidscount.org

- Arizona ranked #46 in the family and community circumstances that factor into children's well-being category by the 2013 KIDS COUNT Data Book, a project of the Annie E. Casey Foundation.
  KIDS COUNT Data Center's Data Book, released June 20, 2013; http://datacenter.kidscount.org

- Arizona ranked #23 in the 2012 Gallup-Healthways Well-Being Index. Criteria: emotional health; physical health; healthy behavior; work environment; basic access to food, shelter, health care; and a safe and satisfying place to live.
  2012 State of Well-Being, Gallup-Healthways Well-Being Index, released February 28, 2013; www.well-beingindex.com

- *U.S. News and World Report's* "Best States for Teen Drivers" rankings are based on driving and road safety laws, federal reports on driver's licenses, car accident fatality, and road-quality statistics. Arizona ranked #27.
  U.S. News and World Report, March 18, 2010; www.usnews.com

- The Yahoo! Sports service Rivals.com ranks the states according to the strength of their high school football programs. Arizona ranked #15.
  "Ranking the States: Where Is the Best Football Played?," November 18, 2011; highschool.rivals.com

- iVillage ranked the states by hospitable living conditions for women. Criteria: economic success, access to affordable childcare, health care, reproductive rights, female representation in government, and educational attainment. Arizona ranked #22.
  iVillage, "50 Best to Worst States for Women," March 14, 2012; www.ivillage.com

- The League of American Bicyclists's "Bicycle Friendly States" ranked Arizona #10. Criteria: legislation and enforcement, policies and programs, infrastructure and funding, education and advocacy, and evaluation and planning.
  "Washington Tops the Bicycle-Friendly State Ranking," May 1, 2013; bicycling.com

- The federal Corporation for National and Community Service ranked the states and the District of Columbia by volunteer rates. Arizona ranked #38 for community service.
  "Volunteering and Civic Life in America 2012," www.volunteeringinamerica.gov, accessed July 24, 2013

- The Hospital Safety Score ranked states and the District of Columbia on their hospitals' performance scores. Arizona ranked #20. Criteria: avoiding preventable harm and medical errors, as demonstrated by 26 hospital safety metrics.
  Spring 2013 Hospital Safety Score, May 8, 2013; www.hospitalsafetyscore.org

- GMAC Insurance ranked the states and the District of Columbia by the performance of their drivers on the GMAC Insurance National Drivers Test, comprised of DMV test questions. Arizona ranked #28.
  "2011 GMAC Insurance National Drivers Test," www.gmacinsurance.com, accessed July 23, 2013

- Arizona ranked #30 in a "State Integrity Investigation" analysis of laws and practices intended to deter corruption and promote accountability and openness in campaign finance, ethics laws, lobbying regulations and management of state pension funds.
  "What's Your State's Grade?," www.publicintegrity.org, accessed July 23, 2013

- Arizona ranked #36 among the states and the District of Columbia in total rail miles, as tracked by the Association of American Railroads.
  "U.S. Freight Railroad Industry Snapshot: Railroads and States: Total Rail Miles by State: 2011"; www.aar.org, accessed July 23, 2013

- According to statistics compiled by the Beer Institute, Arizona ranked #25 among the states and the District of Columbia in per capita beer consumption of persons 21 years or older.
  "Shipments of Malt Beverages and Per Capita Consumption by State 2012;" www.beerinstitute.org

- According to Concordia University's "Public Education Costs per Pupil by State Rankings," based on statistics gathered by the U.S. Census Bureau, which includes the District of Columbia, Arizona ranked #49.
  Concordia University Online; education.cu-portland.edu, accessed July 24, 2013

- Arizona ranked #33 among the states and the District of Columbia in population density based on U.S. Census Bureau data for resident population and total land area. "List of U.S. States by Population Density."
  www.wikipedia.org, accessed July 24, 2013

- In "America's Health Rankings, 2012 Edition," by the United Health Foundation, Arizona ranked #25. Criteria included: rate of high school graduation; violent crime rate; incidence of infectious disease; childhood immunizations; prevalence of diabetes; per capita public-health funding; percentage of uninsured population; rate of children in poverty; and availability of primary-care physicians.
  United Health Foundation; www.americashealthrankings.org, accessed July 24, 2013

- The TechNet 2012 "State Broadband Index" ranked Arizona #23 on the following criteria: broadband adoption; network quality; and economic structure. Improved broadband use is hoped to promote economic development, build strong communities, improve delivery of government services and upgrade educational systems.
  TechNet; www.technet.org, accessed July 24, 2013

- Arizona was ranked #12 among the states and District of Columbia on the American Council for an Energy-Efficient Economy's "State Energy Efficiency Scorecard" for 2012.
  American Council for an Energy-Efficient Economy; aceee.org/sector/state-policy/scorecard, accessed July 24, 2013

Statistical Tables

DEMOGRAPHICS
Resident State and National Population, 1950-2012
Projected State and National Population, 2000-2030
Population by Age, 2012
Population by Race, 2012
Population by Hispanic Origin and Race, 2012

VITAL STATISTICS
Death Rates by Leading Causes, 2010
Death Rates by Selected Causes, 2010
Abortion Rates, 2009
Infant Mortality Rates, 1995-2009
Marriage and Divorce Rates, 2000-2011

ECONOMY
Nominal Gross Domestic Product by Industry, 2012
Real Gross Domestic Product, 2000-2012
Personal Income Per Capita, 1930-2012
Non-Farm Employment by Sector, 2012
Foreign Exports, 2000-2012
Energy Consumption, 2011

LAND AND WATER
Surface Area and Federally-Owned Land, 2007
Land Cover/Use of Non-Federal Rural Land, 2007
Farms and Crop Acreage, 2012

HEALTH AND MEDICAL CARE
Medical Professionals, 2012
Health Insurance Coverage, 2011
HIV, STD, and Tuberculosis Cases and Rates, 2011
Cigarette Smoking, 2011

HOUSING
Home Ownership Rates, 1995-2012
Home Sales, 2000-2010
Value of Owner-Occupied Homes, 2011

EDUCATION
School Enrollment, 2011
Educational Attainment, 2011
Public College Finances, FY 2012

TRANSPORTATION AND TRAVEL
Motor Vehicle Registrations and Drivers Licenses, 2011
Domestic Travel Expenditures, 2009
Retail Gasoline Prices, 2013
Public Road Length, 2011

CRIME AND LAW ENFORCEMENT
Full-Time Law Enforcement Officers, 2011
Prison Population, 2000-2012
Crime Rate, 2011

GOVERNMENT AND FINANCE
Local Governments by Type, 2012
State Government Revenue, 2011
State Government Expenditures, 2011
State Government General Expenditures by Function, 2011
State Government Finances, Cash and Debt, 2011

POLITICS
Composition of the Senate, 1995-2013
Composition of the House of Representatives, 1995-2013
Composition of State Legislature, 2004-2013
Voter Participation in Presidential Elections, 1980-2012
Governors Since Statehood

DEMOGRAPHICS

Resident State and National Population, 1950–2012

Year	State Population	U.S. Population	State Share
1950	750,000	151,326,000	0.50%
1960	1,302,000	179,323,000	0.73%
1970	1,775,399	203,302,031	0.87%
1980	2,718,215	226,545,805	1.20%
1990	3,665,228	248,709,873	1.47%
2000	5,130,247	281,424,600	1.82%
2010	6,392,017	308,745,538	2.07%
2012	6,553,255	313,914,040	2.09%

Note: 1950/1960 population figures are rounded to the nearest thousand.
Source: U.S. Census Bureau, Decennial Census 1950–2010; U.S. Census Bureau, 2012 Population Estimates

Projected State and National Population, 2000–2030

Year	State Population	U.S. Population	State Share
2000	5,130,632	281,421,906	1.82%
2005	5,868,004	295,507,134	1.99%
2010	6,637,381	308,935,581	2.15%
2015	7,495,238	322,365,787	2.33%
2020	8,456,448	335,804,546	2.52%
2025	9,531,537	349,439,199	2.73%
2030	10,712,397	363,584,435	2.95%
State population growth, 2000–2030			5,581,765
State percentage growth, 2000–2030			108.8%

Source: U.S. Census Bureau, Population Division, Interim State Population Projections, 2005

Population by Age, 2012

Age Group	State Population	Percent of Total Population	
		State	U.S.
Under 5 years	439,633	6.7%	6.4%
5 to 14 years	911,968	13.9%	13.1%
15 to 24 years	922,244	14.1%	14.0%
25 to 34 years	877,831	13.4%	13.5%
35 to 44 years	826,174	12.6%	12.9%
45 to 54 years	839,039	12.8%	14.1%
55 to 64 years	764,833	11.7%	12.3%
65 to 74 years	558,589	8.5%	7.6%
75 to 84 years	298,519	4.6%	4.2%
85 years and older	114,425	1.7%	1.9%
Under 18 years	1,620,894	24.7%	23.5%
65 years and older	971,533	14.8%	13.7%
Median age (years)	–	36.5	37.4

Source: U.S. Census Bureau, Annual Estimates of the Resident Population for Selected Age Groups by Sex for the United States, States, Counties, and Puerto Rico Commonwealth and Municipios: April 1, 2010 to July 1, 2012

Population by Race, 2012

Race	State Population	Percent of Total Population	
		State	U.S.
All residents	6,553,255	100.00%	100.00%
White	5,522,144	84.27%	77.89%
African American	297,985	4.55%	13.13%
Native American	345,622	5.27%	1.23%
Asian	204,840	3.13%	5.14%
Native Hawaiian	16,922	0.26%	0.23%
Two or more races	165,742	2.53%	2.39%

Source: U.S. Census Bureau, Population Division, Annual Estimates of the Resident Population by Sex, Race and Hispanic Origin for the United States, States, and Counties: April 1, 2010 to July 1, 2012

Population by Hispanic Origin and Race, 2012

Hispanic Origin/Race	State Population	Percent of Total Population	
		State	U.S.
All residents	6,553,255	100.00%	100.00%
All Hispanic residents	1,976,106	30.15%	16.89%
Hispanic			
White	1,783,106	27.21%	14.91%
African American	42,339	0.65%	0.79%
Native American	81,061	1.24%	0.49%
Asian	17,011	0.26%	0.17%
Native Hawaiian	5,240	0.08%	0.06%
Two or more races	47,349	0.72%	0.48%
Not Hispanic			
White	3,739,038	57.06%	62.98%
African American	255,646	3.90%	12.34%
Native American	264,561	4.04%	0.74%
Asian	187,829	2.87%	4.98%
Native Hawaiian	11,682	0.18%	0.17%
Two or more races	118,393	1.81%	1.91%

Source: U.S. Census Bureau, Population Division, Annual Estimates of the Resident Population by Sex, Race and Hispanic Origin for the United States, States, and Counties: April 1, 2010 to July 1, 2012

VITAL STATISTICS

Death Rates by Leading Causes, 2010

Cause	State	U.S.
Malignant neoplasms	166.4	186.2
Ischaemic heart diseases	114.6	122.9
Other forms of heart disease	29.3	53.4
Chronic lower respiratory diseases	45.6	44.7
Cerebrovascular diseases	34.3	41.9
Organic, incl. symptomatic, mental disorders	27.4	35.7
Other degenerative diseases of the nervous sys.	39.3	28.4
Other external causes of accidental injury	34.4	26.5
Diabetes mellitus	21.9	22.4
Hypertensive diseases	19.5	20.4
All causes	742.9	799.5

Note: Figures are age-adjusted death rates per 100,000 population
Source: CDC/NCHS, Underlying Cause of Death 1999–2010 on CDC WONDER Online Database

Death Rates by Selected Causes, 2010

Cause	State	U.S.
Assault	6.5	5.2
Diseases of the liver	16.7	13.9
Human immunodeficiency virus (HIV) disease	1.7	2.7
Influenza and pneumonia	12.3	16.2
Intentional self-harm	17.5	12.4
Malnutrition	0.6	0.9
Obesity and other hyperalimentation	2.3	1.8
Renal failure	7.0	14.4
Transport accidents	13.4	12.1
Viral hepatitis	3.7	2.4

Note: Figures are age-adjusted death rates per 100,000 population; A dash indicates that data was not available or was suppressed
Source: CDC/NCHS, Underlying Cause of Death 1999–2010 on CDC WONDER Online Database

Abortion Rates, 2009

Category	2009
By state of residence	
Total abortions	10,298
Abortion rate[1]	7.9%
Abortion ratio[2]	111
By state of occurrence	
Total abortions	10,271
Abortion rate[1]	7.9%
Abortion ratio[2]	111
Abortions obtained by out-of-state residents	2.4%
U.S. abortion rate[1]	15.1%
U.S. abortion ratio[2]	227

Note: (1) Number of abortions per 1,000 women aged 15–44 years; (2) Number of abortions per 1,000 live births; A dash indicates that data was not available
Source: CDC/NCHS, Morbidity and Mortality Weekly Report, November 23, 2012 (Abortion Surveillance, United States, 2009)

Infant Mortality Rates, 1995–2009

Category	1995	2000	2005	2009
All state residents	7.62	6.75	6.85	5.97
All U.S. residents	7.57	6.89	6.86	6.39
All state white residents	7.40	6.37	6.60	5.36
All U.S. white residents	6.30	5.71	5.73	5.33
All state black residents	13.40	15.07	10.15	13.32
All U.S. black residents	14.58	13.48	13.26	12.12

Note: Figures represent deaths per 1,000 live births of resident infants under one year old, exclusive of fetal deaths; A dash indicates that data was not available or was suppressed.
Source: Centers of Disease Control and Prevention, Division of Vital Statistics, Linked Birth/Infant Death Records on CDC Wonder Online

Marriage and Divorce Rates, 2000–2011

Year	Marriage Rate		Divorce Rate	
	State	U.S.	State	U.S.
2000	7.5	8.2	4.6	4.0
2002	6.7	8.0	4.8	3.9
2004	6.7	7.8	4.3	3.7
2006	6.5	7.5	4.0	3.7
2008	6.0	7.1	3.8	3.5
2010	5.9	6.8	3.5	3.6
2011	5.7	6.8	3.9	3.6

Note: Rates are based on provisional counts of marriages/divorces by state of occurrence and are per 1,000 total population residing in area
Source: CDC/NCHS, National Vital Statistics System

ECONOMY

Nominal Gross Domestic Product by Industry, 2012

In millions of current dollars

Industry	State GDP
Accommodation and food services	9,539
Administrative and waste management services	10,877
Agriculture, forestry, fishing, and hunting	2,115
Arts, entertainment, and recreation	2,669
Construction	12,857
Educational services	3,210
Finance and insurance	23,951
Health care and social assistance	22,136
Information	7,148
Management of companies and enterprises	2,889
Manufacturing	21,934
Mining	5,085
Other services, except government	5,928
Professional, scientific, and technical services	16,064
Real estate and rental and leasing	37,375
Retail trade	19,911
Transportation and warehousing	8,053
Utilities	6,320
Wholesale trade	14,647

Source: U.S. Department of Commerce, Bureau of Economic Analysis, Survey of Current Business

Real Gross Domestic Product, 2000–2012

In millions of chained 2005 dollars

Year	State GDP	U.S. GDP	State Share
2000	178,845	11,225,406	1.59%
2005	222,569	12,539,116	1.77%
2010	221,016	12,897,088	1.71%
2012	230,641	13,430,576	1.72%

Source: U.S. Department of Commerce, Bureau of Economic Analysis, Survey of Current Business

Personal Income Per Capita, 1930–2012

Year	State	U.S.
1930	$514	$618
1940	$502	$593
1950	$1,360	$1,503
1960	$2,063	$2,268
1970	$3,829	$4,084
1980	$9,484	$10,091
1990	$16,806	$19,354
2000	$26,293	$30,319
2010	$33,773	$39,791
2012	$35,979	$42,693

Source: U.S. Department of Commerce, Bureau of Economic Analysis, Regional Economic Accounts

Non-Farm Employment by Sector, 2012

In thousands

Sector	Employment
Construction	115.7
Education and health services	366.2
Financial activities	176.5
Government	410.7
Information	38.2
Leisure and hospitality	266.7
Mining and logging	12.7
Manufacturing	155.2
Other services	85.6
Professional and business services	354.4
Trade, transportation, and utilities	478.5
All sectors	2,460.3

Source: U.S. Bureau of Labor Statistics, State and Area Employment

Foreign Exports, 2000–2012

In millions of dollars

Year	State Exports	U.S. Exports	State Share
2000	14,333	712,054	2.01%
2002	11,860	649,940	1.82%
2004	13,481	768,554	1.75%
2006	18,299	973,994	1.88%
2008	19,784	1,222,545	1.62%
2010	15,720	1,208,080	1.30%
2012	18,405	1,478,268	1.25%

Note: U.S. figures exclude data from Puerto Rico, U.S. Virgin Islands, and unallocated exports
Source: U.S. Department of Commerce, International Trade Admin., Office of Trade and Industry Information, Manufacturing and Services

Energy Consumption, 2011

In trillions of BTUs, except as noted

Total energy consumption

Total state energy consumption	1,431.5
Total U.S. energy consumption	97,387.3
State share of U.S. total	1.47%

Per capita consumption (in millions of BTUs)

Total state per capita consumption	221.3
Total U.S. per capita consumption	312.6

End-use sectors

Residential	394.7
Commercial	345.5
Industrial	221.2
Transportation	470.1

Sources of energy

Petroleum	500.9
Natural gas	293.7
Coal	459.9
Renewable energy	136.6
Nuclear electric power	327.3

Source: U.S. Energy Information Administration, State Energy Data 2011: Consumption

LAND AND WATER

Surface Area and Federally-Owned Land, 2007

In thousands of acres

Category	State	U.S.	State Share
Total surface area	72,964.4	1,937,664.2	3.77%
Total land area	72,774.7	1,886,846.9	3.86%
Non-federal land	42,348.5	1,484,910.0	2.85%
Developed	2,006.2	111,251.2	1.80%
Rural	40,342.3	1,373,658.8	2.94%
Federal land	30,426.2	401,936.9	7.57%
Water area	189.7	50,817.3	0.37%

Source: U.S. Department of Agriculture, Natural Resources Conservation Service, 2007 National Resources Inventory

Land Cover/Use of Non-Federal Rural Land, 2007

In thousands of acres

Category	State	U.S.	State Share
Total rural land	40,342.3	1,373,658.8	2.94%
Cropland	753.4	357,023.5	0.21%
CRP[1] land	0.0	32,850.2	0.00%
Pastureland	90.8	118,615.7	0.08%
Rangeland	32,497.2	409,119.4	7.94%
Forest land	4,094.8	406,410.4	1.01%
Other rural land	2,906.1	49,639.6	5.85%

Note: (1) Conservation Reserve Program was created to assist private landowners in converting highly erodible cropland to vegetative cover.
Source: U.S. Department of Agriculture, Natural Resources Conservation Service, 2007 National Resources Inventory

Farms and Crop Acreage, 2012

Category	State	U.S.	State Share
Farms (in thousands)	15.5	2,170.0	0.71%
Acres (in millions)	26.1	914.0	2.86%
Acres per farm	1,683.9	421.2	–

Source: U.S. Department of Agriculture, National Agricultural Statistical Service, Quick Stats, 2012 Survey Data

HEALTH AND MEDICAL CARE

Medical Professionals, 2012

Profession	State Number	U.S. Number	State Share	State Rate[1]	U.S. Rate[1]
Physicians[2]	15,855	894,637	1.77%	245.2	287.1
Dentists	3,674	193,587	1.90%	56.8	62.1
Podiatrists	329	17,469	1.88%	5.1	5.6
Optometrists	846	45,638	1.85%	13.1	14.6
Chiropractors	1,807	77,494	2.33%	27.9	24.9

Note: (1) Rates are per 100,000 population; (2) Includes total, active Doctors of Osteopathic Medicine and Doctors of Medicine in 2011.
Source: U.S. Department of Health and Human Services, Bureau of Health Professions, Area Health Resource File, 2012-2013

Health Insurance Coverage, 2011

Category	State	U.S.
Total persons covered	5,424,000	260,214,000
Total persons not covered	1,137,000	48,613,000
Percent not covered	17.3%	15.7%
Children under age 18 covered	1,410,000	67,143,000
Children under age 18 not covered	219,000	6,965,000
Percent of children not covered	13.4%	9.4%

Source: U.S. Census Bureau, Current Population Survey, 2012 Annual Social and Economic Supplement

HIV, STD, and Tuberculosis Cases and Rates, 2011

Disease	State Cases	State Rate[1]	U.S. Rate[1]
Chlamydia	29,251	457.6	457.6
Gonorrhea	4,564	71.4	104.2
HIV diagnosis	708	13.3	15.8
HIV, stage 3 (AIDS)	430	8.1	10.3
Syphilis, early latent	187	2.9	4.3
Syphilis, primary/secondary	274	4.3	4.5
Tuberculosis	255	3.9	3.4

Note: (1) Rates are per 100,000 population
Source: Centers for Disease Control and Prevention

Cigarette Smoking, 2011

Category	State	U.S.
Adults who are current smokers	19.3%	21.2%
Adults who smoke everyday	13.1%	15.4%
Adults who smoke some days	6.2%	5.7%
Adults who are former smokers	24.9%	25.1%
Adults who never smoked	55.9%	52.9%

Source: Centers for Disease Control and Prevention, Behaviorial Risk Factor Surveillance System, Tobacco Use, 2011

HOUSING

Home Ownership Rates, 1995–2012

Area	1995	2000	2005	2010	2012
State	62.9%	68.0%	71.1%	66.6%	65.3%
U.S.	64.7%	67.4%	68.9%	66.9%	65.4%

Source: U.S. Census Bureau, Housing Vacancies and Homeownership, Annual Statistics

Home Sales, 2000–2010
In thousands of units

Year	State Sales	U.S. Sales	State Share
2000	104.8	5,174	2.03%
2002	128.2	5,632	2.28%
2004	186.8	6,778	2.76%
2006	142.9	6,478	2.21%
2008	116.1	4,913	2.36%
2010	147.5	4,908	3.01%

Note: Units include single-family homes, condos and co-ops
Source: National Association of Realtors, Real Estate Outlook, Market Trends & Insights

Value of Owner-Occupied Homes, 2011

Value	Total Units in State	Percent of Total, State	Percent of Total, U.S.
Less than $50,000	153,268	10.2%	8.8%
$50,000 to $99,000	276,105	18.4%	16.0%
$100,000 to $149,000	297,177	19.8%	16.5%
$150,000 to $199,000	249,026	16.6%	15.4%
$200,000 to $299,000	257,432	17.1%	18.2%
$300,000 to $499,000	179,153	11.9%	15.2%
$500,000 to $999,000	69,300	4.6%	7.9%
$1,000,000 or more	20,067	1.3%	2.0%
Median value	–	$153,800	$173,600

Source: U.S. Census Bureau, 2011 American Community Survey 1-Year Estimates

EDUCATION

School Enrollment, 2011

Educational Level	Students Enrolled in State	Percent of Total, State	Percent of Total, U.S.
All levels	1,751,916	100.0%	100.0%
Nursery school, preschool	81,638	4.7%	6.0%
Kindergarten	83,383	4.8%	5.1%
Elementary (grades 1–8)	728,593	41.6%	39.5%
Secondary (grades 9–12)	363,517	20.7%	20.7%
College or graduate school	494,785	28.2%	28.7%

Note: Figures cover the population 3 years and over enrolled in school
Source: U.S. Census Bureau, 2011 American Community Survey 1-Year Estimates

Educational Attainment, 2011

Highest Level of Education	State	U.S.
High school diploma	85.7%	85.9%
Bachelor's degree	26.6%	28.5%
Graduate/Professional degree	9.5%	10.6%

Note: Figures cover the population 25 years and over
Source: U.S. Census Bureau, 2011 American Community Survey 1-Year Estimates

Public College Finances, FY 2012

Category	State	U.S.
Full-time equivalent enrollment (FTE)[1]	275,238	11,548,974
Educational appropriations per FTE[2]	$4,567	$5,906
Net tuition revenue per FTE[3]	$5,086	$5,189
Total educational revenue per FTE[4]	$9,375	$11,043

(1) Full-time equivalent enrollment equates student credit hours to full time, academic year students, but excludes medical students; (2) Educational appropriations measure state and local support available for public higher education operating expenses including ARRA funds and excludes appropriations for independent institutions, financial aid for students attending independent institutions, research, hospitals, and medical education; (3) Net tuition revenue is calculated by taking the gross amount of tuition and fees, less state and institutional financial aid, tuition waivers or discounts, and medical student tuition and fees. Net tuition revenue used for capital debt service is included in the net tuition revenue figures; (4) Total educational revenue is the sum of educational appropriations and net tuition excluding net tuition revenue used for capital debt service.
Source: State Higher Education Executive Officers, State Higher Education Finance FY 2012

TRANSPORTATION AND TRAVEL

Motor Vehicle Registrations and Drivers Licenses, 2011

Vehicle Type	State	U.S.	State Share
Automobiles[1]	2,363,015	125,656,528	1.88%
Buses	11,759	666,064	1.77%
Trucks	2,555,552	118,455,587	2.16%
Motorcycles	178,928	8,437,502	2.12%
Drivers licenses	4,592,398	211,874,649	2.17%

Note: Motor vehicle registrations include private, commercial, and publicly-owned vehicles; (1) Includes taxicabs
Source: U.S. Department of Transportation, Federal Highway Administration

Domestic Travel Expenditures, 2009
In millions of dollars

Category	State	U.S.	State Share
Travel expenditures	$11,448	$610,200	1.88%

Note: Figures represent U.S. spending on domestic overnight trips and day trips of 50 miles or more, one way, away from home. Excludes spending by foreign visitors.
Source: U.S. Travel Association, Impact of Travel on State Economies, 2009

Retail Gasoline Prices, 2013

Gasoline Grade	State Average	U.S. Average
Regular	$3.58	$3.65
Mid	$3.70	$3.81
Premium	$3.83	$3.98
Diesel	$3.79	$3.88
Excise tax[1]	37.4 cents	49.4 cents

Note: Gasoline prices as of 7/26/2013; (1) Includes state and federal excise taxes and other state taxes as of July 1, 2013
Source: American Automobile Association, Daily Fuel Guage Report; American Petroleum Institute, State Motor Fuel Taxes, 2013

Public Road Length, 2011

Type	State Mileage	U.S. Mileage	State Share
Interstate highways	1,168	46,960	2.49%
Other highways	203	15,719	1.29%
Principal arterial	2,702	156,262	1.73%
Minor arterial	3,116	242,942	1.28%
Major collector	6,064	534,592	1.13%
Minor collector	2,034	266,357	0.76%
Local	49,804	2,814,925	1.77%
Urban	23,498	1,095,373	2.15%
Rural	41,594	2,982,383	1.39%
Total	65,092	4,077,756	1.60%

Note: Combined urban and rural road mileage equals the total of the other road types
Source: U.S. Department of Transportation, Federal Highway Administration, Public Road Length, 2011

CRIME AND LAW ENFORCEMENT

Full-Time Law Enforcement Officers, 2011

Gender	State Number	State Rate[1]	U.S. Rate[1]
Male officers	10,810	176.5	210.3
Female officers	1,259	20.6	28.1
Total officers	12,069	197.1	238.3

Note: (1) Rates are per 100,000 population
Source: Federal Bureau of Investigation, Uniform Crime Reports, Crime in the United States 2011

Prison Population, 2000–2012

Year	State Population	U.S. Population	State Share
2000	26,510	1,391,261	1.91%
2005	33,565	1,527,929	2.20%
2010	40,209	1,613,803	2.49%
2011	40,020	1,598,783	2.50%
2012	40,013	1,571,013	2.55%

Note: Figures include prisoners under the jurisdiction of state or federal correctional authorities.
Source: U.S. Department of Justice, Bureau of Justice Statistics, Prisoners in 2006, 2011, 2012 (Advance Counts)

Crime Rate, 2011

Incidents per 100,000 residents

Category	State	U.S.
Violent crimes	405.9	386.3
Murder	6.2	4.7
Forcible rape	34.9	26.8
Robbery	109.9	113.7
Aggravated assault	254.8	241.1
Property crimes	3,554.5	2,908.7
Burglary	847.3	702.2
Larceny/theft	2,401.3	1,976.9
Motor vehicle theft	305.9	229.6
All crimes	3,960.4	3,295.0

Source: Federal Bureau of Investigation, Uniform Crime Reports, Crime in the United States 2011

GOVERNMENT AND FINANCE

Local Governments by Type, 2012

Government Type	State	U.S.	State Share
All local governments	659	89,004	0.74%
County	15	3,031	0.49%
Municipality	91	19,522	0.47%
Town/Township	0	16,364	0.00%
Special District	309	37,203	0.83%
Ind. School District	244	12,884	1.89%

Source: U.S. Census Bureau, 2012 Census of Governments: Organization Component Preliminary Estimates

State Government Revenue, 2011

In thousands of dollars, except for per capita figures

Total revenue	**$36,611,494**
Total revenue per capita, State	$5,661
Total revenue per capita, U.S.	$7,271
General revenue	$27,048,737
Intergovernmental revenue	$12,360,358
Taxes	$10,848,179
General sales	$4,462,557
Selective sales	$1,743,812
License taxes	$418,938
Individual income taxes	$2,863,658
Corporate income taxes	$560,236
Other taxes	$798,978
Current charges	$2,277,144
Miscellaneous general revenue	$1,563,056
Utility revenue	$29,511
Liquor store revenue	$0
Insurance trust revenue[1]	$9,533,246

Note: (1) Within insurance trust revenue, net earnings of state retirement systems is a calculated statistic, and thus can be positive or negative. Net earnings is the sum of earnings on investments plus gains on investments minus losses on investments.
Source: U.S. Census Bureau, 2011 Annual Survey of State Government Finances

State Government Expenditures, 2011

In thousands of dollars, except for per capita figures

Total expenditure	$32,875,412
Total expenditure per capita, State	$5,083
Total expenditure per capita, U.S.	$6,427
Intergovernmental expenditure	$8,668,387
Direct expenditure	$24,207,025
Current operation	$16,547,532
Capital outlay	$1,648,490
Insurance benefits and repayments	$4,720,412
Assistance and subsidies	$627,999
Interest on debt	$662,592
Utility expenditure	$31,905
Liquor store expenditure	$0
Insurance trust expenditure	$4,720,412

Source: U.S. Census Bureau, 2011 Annual Survey of State Government Finances

State Government General Expenditures by Function, 2011

In thousands of dollars

Education	$9,121,942
Public welfare	$9,511,299
Hospitals	$52,314
Health	$1,822,334
Highways	$2,038,165
Police protection	$240,169
Correction	$906,213
Natural resources	$256,522
Parks and recreation	$97,087
Governmental administration	$655,362
Interest on general debt	$660,422
Other and unallocable	$2,761,266

Source: U.S. Census Bureau, 2011 Annual Survey of State Government Finances

State Government Finances, Cash and Debt, 2011

In thousands of dollars, except for per capita figures

Debt at end of fiscal year	
State, total	$14,163,076
State, per capita	$2,190
U.S., per capita	$3,635
Cash and security holdings	
State, total	$47,487,739
State, per capita	$7,343
U.S., per capita	$11,759

Source: U.S. Census Bureau, 2011 Annual Survey of State Government Finances

POLITICS

Composition of the Senate, 1995–2013

Congress (Year)	State/U.S	Dem	Rep	Total
104th (1995)	State delegates	0	2	2
	Total U.S.	48	52	100
105th (1997)	State delegates	0	2	2
	Total U.S.	45	55	100
106th (1999)	State delegates	0	2	2
	Total U.S.	45	55	100
107th (2001)	State delegates	0	2	2
	Total U.S.	50	50	100
108th (2003)	State delegates	0	2	2
	Total U.S.	48	51	100
109th (2005)	State delegates	0	2	2
	Total U.S.	44	55	100
110th (2007)	State delegates	0	2	2
	Total U.S.	49	49	100
111th (2009)	State delegates	0	2	2
	Total U.S.	57	41	100
112th (2011)	State delegates	0	2	2
	Total U.S.	51	47	100
113th (2013)	State delegates	0	2	2
	Total U.S.	54	45	100

Note: Figures are for the starts of first sessions; Totals include Democratic (Dem) and Republican (Rep) members as well as vacancies and seats held by independent party members
Source: U.S. Congress, Congressional Directory

Composition of the House of Representatives, 1995–2013

Congress (Year)	State/U.S	Dem	Rep	Total
104th (1995)	State delegates	1	5	6
	Total U.S.	204	230	435
105th (1997)	State delegates	1	5	6
	Total U.S.	207	226	435
106th (1999)	State delegates	1	5	6
	Total U.S.	211	223	435
107th (2001)	State delegates	1	5	6
	Total U.S.	212	221	435
108th (2003)	State delegates	2	6	8
	Total U.S.	205	229	435
109th (2005)	State delegates	2	6	8
	Total U.S.	202	231	435
110th (2007)	State delegates	4	4	8
	Total U.S.	233	198	435
111th (2009)	State delegates	5	3	8
	Total U.S.	256	178	435
112th (2011)	State delegates	3	5	8
	Total U.S.	193	242	435
113th (2013)	State delegates	5	4	9
	Total U.S.	201	234	435

Note: Figures are for the starts of first sessions; Totals include Democratic (Dem) and Republican (Rep) members as well as vacancies and seats held by independent party members
Source: U.S. Congress, Congressional Directory

Composition of State Legislature, 2004–2013

Year	Democrats	Republicans	Total
State Senate			
2004	13	17	30
2005	12	18	30
2006	12	18	30
2007	13	17	30
2008	13	17	30
2009	12	18	30
2010	12	18	30
2011	9	21	30
2012	9	21	30
2013	13	17	30
State House			
2004	21	39	60
2005	22	38	60
2006	21	39	60
2007	27	33	60
2008	27	33	60
2009	24	36	60
2010	25	35	60
2011	20	40	60
2012	20	40	60
2013	24	36	60

Note: Totals may include minor party members and vacancies
Source: The Council of State Governments, State Legislatures

Voter Participation in Presidential Elections, 1980–2012

Year	Voting-eligible State Population	State Voter Turnout Rate	U.S. Voter Turnout Rate
1980	1,890,167	46.2	54.2
1984	2,151,391	47.7	55.2
1988	2,454,254	47.7	52.8
1992	2,671,933	55.7	58.1
1996	3,079,908	45.6	51.7
2000	3,357,701	45.6	54.2
2004	3,717,055	54.1	60.1
2008	4,046,075	56.7	61.6
2012	4,360,076	52.9	58.2

*Note: All figures are based on the voting-eligible population which
excludes person ineligible to vote such as non-citizens, felons (depending
on state law), and mentally-incapacitated persons. U.S. figures include
the overseas eligible population (including military personnel).*
*Source: McDonald, Michael P., United States Election Project,
Presidential Voter Turnout Rates, 1980–2012*

Governors Since Statehood

George W. P. Hunt (D)	1912-1917
Thomas E. Campbell (R)	(i) 1917
George W. P. Hunt (D)	1917-1919
Thomas E. Campbell (R)	1919-1923
George W. P. Hunt (D)	1923-1929
John C. Phillips (R)	1929-1931
George W. P. Hunt (D)	1931-1933
Benjamin B. Moeur (D)	1933-1937
Rawghlie C. Stanford (D)	1937-1939
Robert T. Jones (D)	1939-1941
Sidney P. Osborn (D)	(d) 1941-1948
Daniel E. Garvey (D)	1948-1951
(John) Howard Pyle (R)	1951-1955
Ernest W. McFarland (D)	1955-1959
Paul J. Fannin (R)	1959-1965
Samuel P. Goddard Jr. (D)	1965-1967
John R. (Jack) Williams (R)	1967-1975
Raul H. Castro (D)	(r) 1975-1977
Wesley Bolin (D)	(d) 1977-1978
Bruce Babbitt (D)	1978-1987
Evan Mecham (R)	1987-1988
Rose Mofford (R)	1988-1991
Fife Symington (R)	(r) 1991-1997
Jane Dee Hull (R)	1997-2003
Janet Napolitano (D)	2003-2009
Jan Brewer (R)	2009-2015 (term limits)

*Note: (D) Democrat; (R) Republican; (O) Other party; (r) resigned;
(d) died in office; (i) removed from office*

Arkansas

Location: South

Area and rank: 52,075 square miles (134,875 square kilometers); 53,182 square miles (137,741 square kilometers) including water; twenty-seventh largest state in area

Coastline: none

Population and rank: 2,949,131 (2012 estimate); thirty-second largest state in population

Capital and Largest city: Little Rock (193,524 people in 2010 census)

Became territory: March 2, 1819

Entered Union and rank: June 15, 1836; twenty-fifth state

Present constitution adopted: 1874

Counties: 75

State capitol building in Little Rock on the Fourth of July, 2013. (Wikimedia Commons)

State name: "Arkansas" comes from a Quapaw Indian word

State nickname: The Natural State

Motto: *Regnat populus* (The people rule)

State flag: Red field with four stars and white diamond with name "Arkansas"

Highest point: Magazine Mountain—2,753 feet (839 meters)

Lowest point: Ouachita River—55 feet (17 meters)

Highest recorded temperature: 120 degrees Fahrenheit (49 degrees Celsius)—Ozark, 1936

Lowest recorded temperature: –29 degrees Fahrenheit (–34 degrees Celsius)—Pond, 1905

State songs: "Arkansas"; "Oh, Arkansas"

State tree: Pine
State flower: Apple blossom

State bird: Mockingbird

National parks: Hot Springs

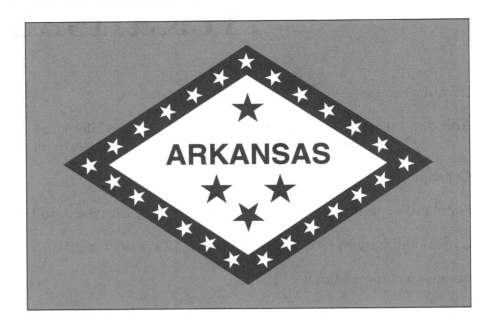

Arkansas History

The history of Arkansas was greatly influenced by the natural division of the area into northwestern highlands and southeastern lowlands. Running through these two regions as it flows in a southeasterly direction to meet the Mississippi River, the Arkansas River has also been of major importance in the area's history. As long as ten thousand years ago, hunters and gatherers wandered the land surrounding the Arkansas River, attracted by the abundant wildlife. About one thousand years ago, bluff dwellers and mound builders grew crops in the area's fertile soil. By the time Europeans arrived in the New World, the primary groups of Native Americans inhabiting the area were the Osage, in Missouri and northwestern Arkansas; the Caddo, in Louisiana and southwestern Arkansas; and the Quapaw, along the Arkansas River. All three groups were forced into Oklahoma by the middle of the nineteenth century.

Exploration and Settlement. The first Europeans to reach the area were led northwest from Florida by Spanish explorer Hernando de Soto in 1541. A French expedition led by Jacques Marquette and Louis Jolliet reached the area in 1673 by traveling south from Michigan. In 1682, a similar expedition was led by René-Robert Cavelier, sieur de La Salle. La Salle claimed the entire valley of the Mississippi River, including all of Arkansas, for France. This enormous area was named Louisiana in honor of King Louis XIV of France.

Despite La Salle's claim to the area, European settlement of the area began modestly. In 1686, French explorer Henri de Tonti established Arkansas Post, the first permanent European settlement in the area, near the point where the Arkansas River meets the Mississippi River. Starting with a population of six residents, Arkansas Post grew to become the largest city in Arkansas until the nineteenth century. In 1722, French explorer Bernard de la Harpe led an expedition along the Arkansas River and named a natural rock formation Little Rock. Nearly a century later, a city of the same name was founded there.

Road to Statehood. Settlement of the area continued slowly throughout the eighteenth century. In 1762, France ceded Louisiana to Spain. In order to encourage settlers, Spain offered free land and freedom from taxes to all who chose to live there. In 1783, British forces attacked Arkansas Post but were defeated by the Spanish and Quapaw. By 1799 Arkansas had nearly four hundred European settlers.

In 1800, Louisiana was returned to France. Three years later, the United States purchased this vast area, doubling the size of the young nation, for a payment of more than twenty-seven million dollars. At first a part of the huge Louisiana Territory, in 1812 Arkansas became part of the newly created Missouri Territory, then became a separate territory in 1819. In 1824, the western section of the area became part of the Indian Territory (Oklahoma), giving Arkansas its modern boundaries. By 1836 Arkansas had the sixty thousand residents necessary for statehood, primarily settlers from eastern states, and it was admitted as the twenty-fifth state.

The Civil War. Along with those who arrived from the eastern United States, the 1840's and 1850's brought large numbers of Irish and German immigrants to the area. The mountains and plateaus of the northwest supported small farms, while the lowlands of the southeast developed large cotton plantations dependent on slaves. By 1860 the population of Arkansas reached 435,000. About one-quarter of the inhabitants were slaves.

Arkansas seceded from the Union on May 6, 1861, nearly a month after the Civil War broke out. The delay in joining the Confederacy may have been due to strong Union sympathies in the northwest part of the state. About six thousand residents of the state fought for the Union, while about fifty-eight thousand fought for the Confederacy. Several important Civil War battles were fought in northern Arkansas, near the border with Missouri. The Battle of Pea Ridge (March 7-8, 1862) led to heavy losses on both sides, as Union forces drove back an attack by the Confederates, ending the threat of a Confederate invasion of Missouri. In September of 1863, Union forces took control of Little Rock.

From the end of the war until the middle of the 1870's, a period known as Reconstruction, Arkansas and the other former Confederate states were occupied by federal troops and ruled by state governments dominated by the Republican Party. Arkansas was readmitted to the Union under Republican control in 1868. The Republican government, which attempted to win civil rights for freed slaves, was seen as an artificial structure imposed by the northern states. It was opposed, often violently, by many white Arkansans, leading to increased repression of African Americans after Reconstruction. After federal troops were withdrawn, the Democratic Party returned to power in 1874, completely dominating state politics for nearly a century.

After the War. Economic recovery after the devastation of the Civil War was difficult for Arkansans. The plantation system of the southeastern region of the state, which relied on slavery, was replaced with sharecropping. Under this system, tenants lived on and farmed a landowner's property, paying rent in the form of crops, usually cotton. The social and economic gap between the farmer and the landlord was often a large one.

An economic depression in the southern states during the late nineteenth century led to widespread poverty. The situation became even worse in 1885, when the state government defaulted on huge debts, including fourteen million dollars of interest payments. Race relations were also a severe problem, with the state government completely controlled by the Democratic Party, which excluded African Americans.

The Twentieth Century. Along with the rest of the country, Arkansas experienced a large increase in the number of European immigrants at the end of the nineteenth century. Although the pace of economic growth remained slow, the state began to develop new resources during the early years of the twentieth century. Rice, which would later become a major crop, was first planted in 1904. With the rise of the automobile and the increasing industrialization of the United States, the discovery of oil and natural gas deposits in 1921 was an important boost to the economy. The many rivers in Arkansas became an important resource, and modern dams were built beginning during the 1920's.

Arkansas, along with the rest of the United States, suffered a severe economic setback with the Great Depression of the 1930's. Adding to the problem, years of drought forced many farmers to abandon their lands. The Southern Farm Tenants Union, created by Arkansas sharecroppers at this time, had an important influence on national farm policies. It was not until the United States entered World War II in 1941 that the economy began to recover. The enormous defense industry created by the war effort, as well as the technological and economic growth that followed the war, led to major changes in Arkansas society.

The number of Arkansans living in rural areas decreased, and many small family farms were replaced by large agricultural enterprises. Little Rock and other major cities experienced a rapid increase in population. Women entered the workplace in greater numbers. The most important social change during the middle of the twentieth century was the struggle to win civil rights for African Americans.

The attention of the world was focused on race relations in Arkansas in September of 1957. Three years earlier, the Supreme Court had declared public school segregation unconstitutional. To comply with the Court's decision, the school board of Little Rock created a plan to desegregate the city's schools. When nine African American students attempted to attend the city's Central High School, Governor Orval E. Faubus ordered the state militia to prevent them from entering. In response, President Dwight David Eisenhower sent federal troops to enforce the desegregation process.

Economic Growth. Economic development continued steadily throughout the second half of the twentieth century. During the 1960's, rice, soybeans, and poultry replaced cotton as the most important agricultural products. The McClellan-Kerr Arkansas River Navigation System, an ambitious project of building dams and locks, was completed after twenty-five years of work, in January of 1971. The project, the largest ever undertaken by the United States Army Corps of Engineers, made Little Rock an important river port and contributed greatly to the state's economy.

By the end of the twentieth century, important sources of income included fish farming, hydroelectric and nuclear power production, food processing,

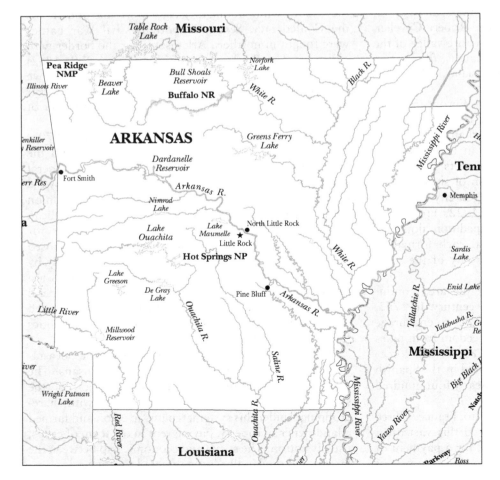

retail merchandising, computer software development, and financial services. The manufacturing sector of the economy produced clothing, furniture, machinery, electrical equipment, metal products, and electronic devices. With improvements in transportation, tourism became a particularly important source of revenue, with thousands of visitors traveling to attractions such as Hot Springs National Park and the Ozark Mountains each year. Despite this growth, Arkansas continued to have one of the lowest per-capita incomes in the United States.

Former Governor Clinton. At the close of the last decade of the twentieth century, Arkansas's close ties to President Bill Clinton, its former attorney general and governor, continued to affect the state. In May of 2000, the Arkansas Supreme Court Committee of Professional Conduct recommended barring Clinton from practicing law in the state on account of his denying under oath the nature of his liaison with White House intern Monica Lewinsky. In September, in Washington, D.C., Independent Counsel Robert Ray announced in his final report that there was insufficient evidence to prosecute President Clinton and First Lady Hillary Rodham Clinton for criminal wrongdoing in the scandal involving the Whitewater real estate partnership in northern Arkansas. This report concluded the investigation of the Clintons, which began in 1994 and eventually cost taxpayers $65 million.

At the end of the year, the outgoing president again figured in Arkansas news when he pardoned a vice president of Arkansas-based giant Tyson Foods, Archibald Schaffer III. Schaffer was convicted of a felony in making illegal gifts in 1993 to Secretary of Agriculture Mike Espy and subsequently lying about them to investigators. In January, 2001, former president Clinton reached an agreement with the independent counsel that suspended his license to practice law in Arkansas for five years, imposed a twenty-five thousand-dollar fine, and required Clinton to agree not to seek repayment of legal fees. The agreement shielded him from being tried for perjury and obstruction of justice.

Politics and Elections. Notwithstanding Arkansas's strong previous support of the Democratic Party, in the 2000 election, the state sent its six electoral votes to presidential candidate George W. Bush, who defeated Democrat Al Gore by 51-46 percent. Independent Ralph Nader, with just 1.5 percent of the vote, did not figure in the outcome. One Republican congressional incumbent was unseated by a Democratic challenger, giving the Democrats a 3-1 edge in the state's congressional delegation. Two years later, Arkansas reelected its colorful and sometimes controversial governor Mike Huckabee, who won by a 53-47 percent margin. In 2004, Bush again claimed the state's electoral votes, defeating John Kerry 56 to 44 percent. U.S. senator Blanche Lincoln, a Democrat, was also reelected.

Huckabee, frequently mentioned as a possible presidential candidate in 2008, became governor in 1996 when the sitting governor resigned after a felony conviction in the Whitewater scandal. He subsequently showed a marked interest in health care matters and created a health insurance program for the needy shortly after assuming office. Huckabee also made an example of himself in shedding more than one hundred pounds after being

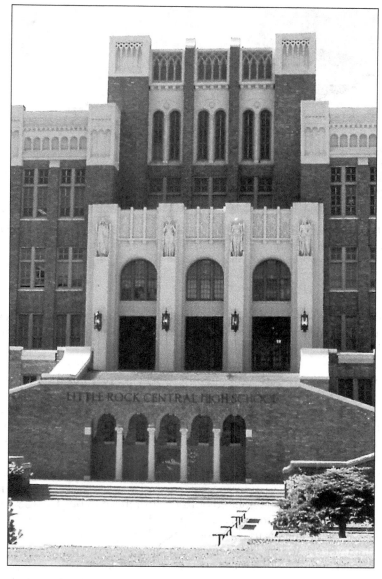

Little Rock's Central High School was the scene of a major civil rights confrontation. The school is now designated a National Historic Site. (National Archives and Records Administration.)

Duck hunting in Arkansas. The state is famed for small game hunting, and duck hunting along the Mississippi Flyway in the Arkansas Delta is particularly popular. (Arkansas Parks & Tourism)

diagnosed a diabetic. He successfully advocated using all funds from the state's tobacco settlement revenues for health care.

After about 70,000 refugees from Hurricane Katrina entered the state in the fall of 2006, Huckabee organized a program to shelter them throughout the state and expedited prescription drug and other health care needs. Huckabee's critics, however, contend that the governor, a devoutly religious graduate of Baptist educational institutions, failed to abide by separation of church and state practices, especially in his dealings with Reclaim America for Christ conferences.

He has also been criticized both for his refusal to open his financial affairs to public scrutiny and for his purchase of a jet plane and his use of it for personal travel. His most controversial action as governor was his pardoning of a convicted rapist. Upon release, the pardoned man, Wayne DuMond, raped and murdered a woman in Missouri.

Mike Huckabee announced his run for the White House on January 28, 2007, and at the August 11 Iowa Straw Poll, Huckabee took second place with 2,587 votes, about 18 percent. Huckabee spent less than $58 per vote received in the Straw Poll, the lowest among the top three candidates. In November 2007, Huckabee drew endorsements from a large number of religious leaders, including a director and vice president of the Christian Coalition of America, founded in 1988 by a previous presidential candidate, Pat Robertson.

On January 3, 2008, Huckabee won the Iowa Republican caucuses, receiving 34 percent of the electorate and 17 delegates, ahead of Mitt Romney who finished second, earning 12 delegates. After gaining good support in other primaries, including Kansas, Huckabee withdrew from the race in March 2008, when polls indicated he would lose in Texas. Despite rumors he was to be included on the ticket as John McCain's running mate, Huckabee went on to a career in television, as a commentator on Fox news, and later, replacing Paul Harvey, who passed away in 2009, with a show called "The Huckabee Report."

Environmental Issues. In the early 21st century, environmental advocacy groups in Arkansas have focused on maintaining water quality in the states rivers and streams, supplementing underfunded state agencies with publicity, published reports, volunteer testing and studies, and protests. An additional concern has been pesticide run-off from rice growing operations.

Floods. Like several other states in the center of the nation, Arkansas was struck by the 2011 Mississippi River floods beginning in early May. In Arkansas, fourteen people were killed and Interstate 40, connecting Memphis and Little Rock, was flooded west of Memphis along the White River. Between the towns of Hazen and Brinkley, the interstate was closed in both directions. The Arkansas Farm Bureau announced that more than 1 million acres of cropland were under water, calculated to have caused at least $500 million in damage, including both already-planted crops, as well as future losses. The flood came at the optimum planting season for rice, cotton and corn. The $500 million loss calculation did not include costs to repair roads and other infrastructure, farm equipment, farmland itself, or the loss of stored grain. Particularly hard hit was the rice crop. Some 300,000 acres of rice farmland was endangered, resulting in an estimated loss of $300 million in rice production.

Rose Secrest
Updated by the Editor

Arkansas Time Line

June 18, 1541	Hernando de Soto crosses the Mississippi River and leads the first Europeans to the area.
July, 1673	Jacques Marquette and Louis Jolliet lead the first French expedition to the area.
Mar. 13, 1682	René-Robert Cavelier, sieur de La Salle, explores the area and claims the entire Mississippi valley for France, naming it Louisiana.
1686	Henri de Tonti establishes the first permanent European settlement at Arkansas Post.
1722	Bernard de la Harpe explores the Arkansas River and names Little Rock.
1762	Louisiana is ceded to Spain.
1783	British forces attack Arkansas Post.
1800	Louisiana is returned to France.
1803	United States purchases Louisiana.
1811-1812	Series of large earthquakes centered in New Madrid, Missouri, damage the area.
1812	Arkansas becomes part of the Missouri Territory.
1817	First post office is established.
Mar. 2, 1819	Arkansas Territory is created.
Nov. 20, 1819	First Arkansas newspaper, the *Arkansas Gazette*, is established.
1820	Border between Missouri and Arkansas is established as the line dividing future slave states and free states.
Oct. 25, 1821	Capital is moved from Arkansas Post to Little Rock.
1824	Western part of Arkansas becomes part of the Indian Territory.
1830	Congress marks boundary between Arkansas and Indian Territory.
June 15, 1836	Arkansas becomes the twenty-fifth state.
1858	First railroad is established.
1859	All free blacks are ordered out of the state by the end of the year.
1860	Population reaches 435,450, including 111,115 slaves.

Arkansas's first capitol building, the Old State House, covers an entire block of the city and has been preserved and set aside as a museum since the early 1940's. (Arkansas Department of Parks & Tourism)

May 6, 1861	Arkansas secedes from the Union.
Sept. 10, 1863	Union forces occupy Little Rock.
1864	State government dominated by the Republican Party is established.
1864	Unionists abolish slavery in Arkansas and adopt a new state constitution.
Aug. 1866	Laws passed prohibiting blacks from jury duty, militia service, and attendance at white schools.
Mar. 2, 1867	Reconstruction Act is passed in Congress, voiding the government of Arkansas and nine other southern states.
Mar. 13, 1868	New constitution is adopted, freeing blacks and disenfranchising ex-Confederate soldiers.
June 22, 1868	Arkansas is readmitted to the Union.
Nov., 1868	Martial law is declared in much of the state, as battles with the Ku Klux Klan become more frequent.
1872	University of Arkansas is established.
Oct. 13, 1874	New constitution restores franchise to all whites and gives full civil rights to blacks.
1885	State government defaults on millions of dollars of debt.
1891	Jim Crow laws go into effect, segregating trains and waiting stations.
1898	Whites-only primary elections are established.
1900	Population reaches 1.3 million.
1904	First rice crop is planted.
1906	Diamonds are discovered near Murfreesboro, leading to the only diamond-mining site in the United States.
1908	Ozark National Forest is established.
1921	Hot Springs National Park is established.
1921	Oil and natural gas are discovered.
1921	Commercial radio broadcasts begin.
1928	Law is passed prohibiting teaching of evolution theory in public schools, which would not be over-turned until 1968, by the U.S. Supreme Court.
1930's	Drought and economic depression lead to widespread poverty.
1930's	Southern Farm Tenants Union is created.
1931	Hattie W. Caraway is first woman elected to U.S. Senate.
1940's	World War II defense industry leads to economic recovery.
1953	Commercial television broadcasts begin.
1957	Federal troops enter Little Rock after the state militia is called out to prevent school integration.
1960's	Rice, soybeans, and poultry replace cotton as the leading agricultural products.
1966	Winthrop Rockefeller is elected the first Republican governor since 1874.
1971	McClellan-Kerr Arkansas River Navigation System is completed.
1983	Arkansas requires teachers to pass basic skills tests, becoming the first state to do so.
1990	Population reaches 2.35 million.
Nov. 3, 1992	Bill Clinton becomes the first Arkansan elected president of the United States.
1993	M. Jocelyn Elders, former director of the state Department of Health, becomes the first African American Surgeon General of the United States.
1996	Severe tornadoes kill at least twelve people and do more than $300 million worth of property damage.
1998	Eleven-year-old and thirteen-year-old boys kill four fellow students and a teacher, wounding ten others, in a schoolyard shooting in Jonesboro, leading to a national debate on the issue of school violence.
May 2000	Committee of the Arkansas State Bar Association recommends disbarring President Bill Clinton for lying under oath.
Sept. 19, 2000	Independent Counsel Robert Ray closes books on Whitewater real estate partnership of northern Arkansas.
Jan. 2001	Bill Clinton agrees to five-year suspension of his Arkansas law license on account of false statements made under oath.
Nov. 5, 2002	Mike Huckabee is reelected governor.
Nov. 2, 2004	George W. Bush wins Arkansas presidential election by 54 to 46 percent; Democratic U.S. senator Blanche Lincoln is reelected 56 to 44 percent.
2007	Arkansas's 44th governor, Mike Huckabee, announces his bid for the 2008 Presidential election. He would eventually fail to carry the Republican ticket against John McCain.
2011	The Mississippi River begins flooding in May, causing damage across several states. The Arkansas Farm Bureau announces at least $500 million in damages.

Notes for Further Study

Published Sources. For an overall view of Arkansas's physical geography, the *Arkansas Atlas and Gazetteer* (1997) from the DeLorme Mapping Company is an excellent resource. The state government can be understood by reading *The Arkansas Constitution: A Reference Guide* (1993) by Kay Collett Goss. The botany of the state is discussed in *Keys to the Flora of Arkansas* (1994) by Edwin B. Smith.

Among the many outstanding books devoted to the state's past are *Cultural Encounters in the Early South: Indians and Europeans in Arkansas* (1995) by Jeannie M. Whayne; *Colonial Arkansas, 1686-1804: A Social and Cultural History* (1991) by Morris S. Arnold; *Territorial Ambition: Land and Society in Arkansas, 1800-1840* (1993) by Charles S. Bolton; *Rebellion and Realignment: Arkansas's Road to Secession* (1987) by James M. Woods; *Rugged and Sublime: The Civil War in Arkansas* (1994), edited by Mark K. Christ; *War and Wartime Changes: The Transformation of Arkansas, 1940–1945* (1986) by Calvin C. Smith; and *Warriors Don't Cry: A Searing Memoir of the Battle to Integrate Little Rock's Central High* (1994) by Melba Pattillo Beals. Younger audiences will appreciate the scholarly but still accessible account of the state's history published by the University of Arkansas Press, *Arkansas History for Young People* (3d ed., 2003) by T. Harri Baker and Jane Browning. Carole Marsh's *Arkansas Native Americans* (2004) is also designed for younger readers.

During the 1930's, the Federal Writers' Project, sponsored by the Works Progress Administration (WPA), worked to interview as many former slaves as possible. Employed authors interviewed more than two thousand former slaves, over one third of them in Arkansas. Editor George E. Lankford brings together all 176 of the testimonies describing slavery in Arkansas in *Bearing Witness: Memories of Arkansas Slavery—Narratives from the 1930's WPA Collections* (2003). Immense changes occurred within the state as it changed from a primarily rural society in the early 1900's to an expanded manufacturing economy in subsequent decades. Ben F. Johnson details this evolution in *Arkansas in Modern America: 1930–1999* (2000). For travelers planning a visit to the state, Patti DeLano's *Arkansas: Off the Beaten Path* (2006) is a solid resource.

Web Resources. A number of excellent Web sites devoted to Arkansas have been developed by government agencies, universities, and private organizations and individuals. A good place to start is the official state government site (www.state.ar.us/), which provides links to agencies dealing with government, tourism, and business, as well as links to local communities and information about state laws. More specific sites include Arkansas—The Natural State (www.arkansas.com) from the Arkansas Department of Parks and Tourism; the Arkansas Department of Economic Development (www.1-800-arkansas.com) for information on business; and Arkansas Quickfacts (quickfacts.census.gov/qfd/states/05000.html) from the United States Census Bureau, providing numerous demographic statistics for every major town and city in the state.

Barge loaded with agricultural produce on the Arkansas River, a major tributary of the Mississippi. (A. C. Haralson/Arkansas)

Counties

County	2012 Population	Pop. Rank	Land Area (sq. miles)	Area Rank	County	2012 Population	Pop. Rank	Land Area (sq. miles)	Area Rank
Arkansas	18,892	38	988.77	3	Cross	17,683	43	616.38	49
Ashley	21,524	34	925.35	6	Dallas	7,987	71	667.39	32
Baxter	41,048	18	554.28	69	Desha	12,545	57	768.15	19
Benton	232,268	2	847.36	12	Drew	18,743	39	828.36	14
Boone	37,327	20	590.23	61	Faulkner	118,704	5	647.88	38
Bradley	11,397	60	649.23	36	Franklin	18,045	40	608.86	52
Calhoun	5,307	75	628.58	45	Fulton	12,318	58	618.19	47
Carroll	27,610	24	630.09	44	Garland	96,903	8	677.78	31
Chicot	11,433	59	644.30	39	Grant	17,986	41	631.81	43
Clark	22,936	30	866.07	10	Greene	43,163	17	577.70	66
Clay	15,684	50	639.46	40	Hempstead	22,373	31	727.52	25
Cleburne	25,808	26	553.69	70	Hot Spring	33,394	22	615.20	50
Cleveland	8,627	67	597.78	58	Howard	13,735	53	588.55	62
Columbia	24,473	28	766.05	20	Independence	37,025	21	763.95	21
Conway	21,287	35	552.25	71	Izard	13,474	54	580.58	65
Craighead	99,735	7	707.21	29	Jackson	17,600	44	633.94	42
Crawford	61,946	13	593.09	60	Jefferson	74,723	10	870.75	9
Crittenden	50,021	14	609.76	51	Johnson	25,901	25	659.80	34

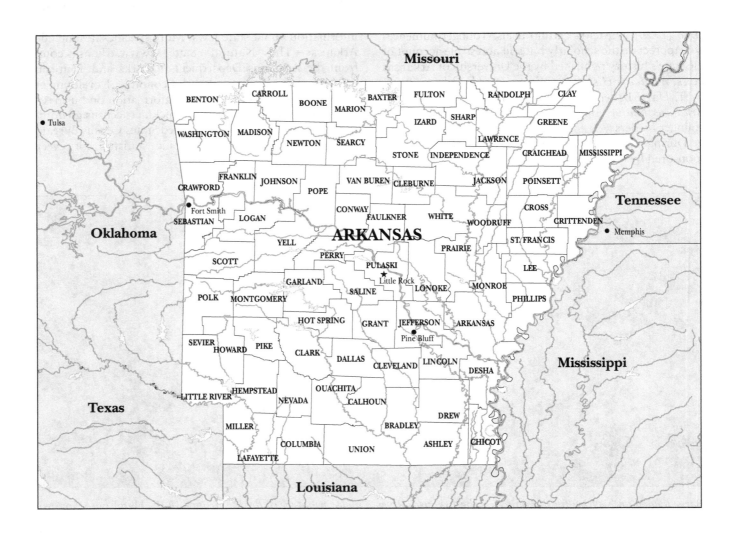

County	2012 Population	Pop. Rank	Land Area (sq. miles)	Area Rank
Lafayette	7,447	73	528.27	75
Lawrence	17,012	48	587.61	63
Lee	10,216	64	602.62	56
Lincoln	14,101	52	561.52	68
Little River	12,919	55	532.25	73
Logan	21,983	32	708.12	28
Lonoke	69,839	11	770.73	18
Madison	15,645	51	834.26	13
Marion	16,568	49	597.01	59
Miller	43,634	16	625.58	46
Mississippi	45,562	15	900.57	7
Monroe	7,828	72	607.12	53
Montgomery	9,340	65	779.88	17
Nevada	8,925	66	617.84	48
Newton	8,086	69	820.90	15
Ouachita	25,396	27	732.78	24
Perry	10,339	63	551.40	72
Phillips	20,784	36	695.66	30
Pike	11,247	61	600.62	57
Poinsett	24,307	29	758.39	23
Polk	20,471	37	857.68	11
Pope	62,765	12	812.55	16
Prairie	8,458	68	647.96	37
Pulaski	388,953	1	759.76	22
Randolph	17,930	42	652.19	35
Saline	111,845	6	723.60	26
Scott	11,010	62	892.32	8
Searcy	8,007	70	666.09	33
Sebastian	127,304	4	531.91	74
Sevier	17,177	45	565.13	67
Sharp	17,054	46	604.44	55
St. Francis	27,858	23	634.77	41
Stone	12,663	56	606.40	54
Union	40,867	19	1,039.21	1
Van Buren	17,030	47	708.14	27
Washington	211,411	3	941.97	4
White	78,493	9	1,035.08	2
Woodruff	7,100	74	586.79	64
Yell	21,932	33	929.98	5

Source: U.S. Census Bureau, 2012 Population Estimates

Cities
With 10,000 or more residents

Legal Name	2010 Population	Pop. Rank	Land Area (sq. miles)	Area Rank	Legal Name	2010 Population	Pop. Rank	Land Area (sq. miles)	Area Rank
Arkadelphia city	10,714	36	7.26	39	El Dorado city	18,884	23	16.27	28
Batesville city	10,248	38	10.98	36	Fayetteville city	73,580	3	53.85	4
Bella Vista town	26,461	17	44.26	9	Forrest City city	15,371	27	16.29	27
Benton city	30,681	12	22.24	19	Fort Smith city	86,209	2	61.97	3
Bentonville city	35,301	10	31.29	14	Harrison city	12,943	29	11.08	34
Blytheville city	15,620	26	20.79	21	Helena-West Helena city	12,282	33	13.33	30
Bryant city	16,688	25	20.80	20	Hope city	10,095	39	10.08	37
Cabot city	23,776	20	20.12	24	Hot Springs city	35,193	11	35.02	13
Camden city	12,183	34	16.45	26	Hot Springs Village CDP	12,807	30	53.52	5
Conway city	58,908	7	45.34	7	Jacksonville city	28,364	15	28.10	18

Legal Name	2010 Population	Pop. Rank	Land Area (sq. miles)	Area Rank
Jonesboro city	67,263	5	79.87	2
Little Rock city	193,524	1	119.20	1
Magnolia city	11,577	35	13.24	31
Malvern city	10,318	37	8.66	38
Marion city	12,345	32	20.42	23
Maumelle city	17,163	24	12.05	32
Mountain Home city	12,448	31	11.73	33
North Little Rock city	62,304	6	51.50	6
Paragould city	26,113	19	31.20	15
Pine Bluff city	49,083	9	44.58	8
Rogers city	55,964	8	37.94	12
Russellville city	27,920	16	28.28	17
Searcy city	22,858	21	18.34	25
Sherwood city	29,523	14	20.61	22
Siloam Springs city	15,039	28	11.07	35
Springdale city	69,797	4	41.80	10
Texarkana city	29,919	13	41.65	11
Van Buren city	22,791	22	15.45	29
West Memphis city	26,245	18	28.44	16

Note: CDP–Census Designated Place
Source: U.S. Census Bureau, 2010 Census

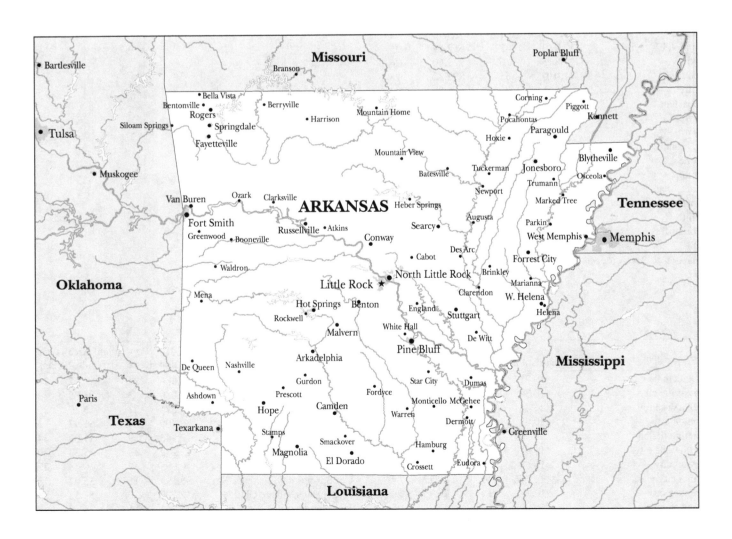

Survey Says...

This section presents current rankings from dozens of public and private sources. It shows how this state ranks in a number of critical categories, including education, job growth, cost of living, teen drivers, energy efficiency, and business environment. Sources include *Forbes, Reuters, U.S. News and World Report, CNN Money, Gallup,* and *Huffington Post.*

- Arkansas ranked #38 in a government study measuring real gross domestic product (GDP)—the output of goods and services produced by labor and property located in the United States. The ranking is based on the percentage change compared with 2011 GDP.
  U.S. Department of Commerce, Bureau of Economic Analysis, June 2013; www.bea.gov

- Arkansas ranked #34 in a government study measuring real gross domestic product (GDP)—the output of goods and services produced by labor and property located in the United States. The ranking is based on the dollar value of its GDP.
  U.S. Department of Commerce, Bureau of Economic Analysis, June 2013; www.bea.gov

- Arkansas ranked #5 in the 17th edition of "Quality Counts; State of the States," Education Week's "report card" surveying key education indicators, policy efforts, and educational outcomes.
  Education Week, January 4, 2013 (online) and January 10, 2013 (print); www.edweek.org

- SERI (Science and Engineering Readiness Index) weighs the performance of the states' K-12 schools in preparing students in physics and calculus, the high school subjects considered most important for future scientists and engineers. Arkansas ranked #41.
  Newsletter of the Forum on Education of the American Physical Society, Summer 2011 issue; www.huffingtonpost.com, July 11, 2011; updated October 1, 2012

- Business website 24/7 Wall St. identified the states with the highest and lowest percentages of residents 25 or older with a college degree or higher. Of "America's Worst Educated States," Arkansas ranked #3 (#1 = worst).
  247wallst.com, posted October 15, 2012; consulted July 18, 2013

- MoneyRates.com ranked Arkansas #31 on its list of the best to worst states for making a living. Criteria: average income; inflation; employment prospects; and workers' Workplace Environment assessments according to the Gallup-Healthways Well-Being Index.
  www.money-rates.com, posted April 1, 2013

- *Forbes* analyzed business costs, labor supply, regulatory environment, current economic climate, growth prospects, and quality of life, to compile its "Best States for Business" rankings. Arkansas ranked #35.
  www.forbes.com. posted December 12, 2012

- The 2012 Gallup-Healthways Well-Being Index, surveyed American's opinions on economic confidence, workplace perceptions, community climate, personal choices, and health predictors to assess the "future livability" of each state. Arkansas ranked #45.
  "Utah Poised to Be the Best State to Live In," Gallup Wellbeing, www.gallup.com, August 7, 2012

- On CNBC's list of "America's Top States for Business 2013," Arkansas ranked #24. Criteria: measures of competitiveness developed with input from the National Association of Manufacturers, the Council on Competitiveness, and other business groups weighed with the states' own marketing criteria.
  www.cnbc.com, consulted July 19, 2013

- Arkansas ranked #5 on the "worst" end of the Christian Science Monitor's list of "States with the Best (and Worst) Job Growth," as indicated by year-over-year growth rates from May 2012 to May 2013.
  www.csmonitor.com, July 5, 2013

- Arkansas ranked #24 on MoneyRates list of "Best-and Worst-States to Retire 2012." Criteria: life expectancy, crime rate, climate, economic conditions, taxes, job opportunities, and cost of living.
  www.money-rates.com, October 22, 2012

- Arkansas ranked #28 on the 2013 Bankrate "Best Places to Retire" list ranking the states and District of Columbia on various criteria relating to health, safety, and cost.
  www.bankrate.com, May 6, 2013

- Arkansas ranked #50 on the Social Science Research Council's "American Human Development Report: The Measure of America," assessing the 50 states plus the District of Columbia on health, education, and living-standard criteria.
  The Measure of America 2013-2014, posted June 19, 2013; www.measureofamerica.org

- Arkansas ranked #47 on the Foundation for Child Development's (FCD) Child Well-being Index (CWI). The FCD used the KIDS COUNT report and the National Survey of Children's Health, the only state-level source for several key indicators of child well-being.
  Foundation for Child Development, January 18, 2012; fcd-us.org

- Arkansas ranked #40 overall according to the 2013 KIDS COUNT Data Book, a project of the Annie E. Casey Foundation. Criteria: children's economic well-being, education, health, and family and community indicators.
  KIDS COUNT Data Center's Data Book, released June 20, 2013; http://datacenter.kidscount.org

- Arkansas ranked #39 in the children's economic well-being category by the 2013 KIDS COUNT Data Book, a project of the Annie E. Casey Foundation.
  KIDS COUNT Data Center's Data Book, released June 20, 2013; http://datacenter.kidscount.org

- Arkansas ranked #36 in the children's educational opportunities and attainments category by the 2013 KIDS COUNT Data Book, a project of the Annie E. Casey Foundation.
  KIDS COUNT Data Center's Data Book, released June 20, 2013; http://datacenter.kidscount.org

- Arkansas ranked #30 in the children's health category by the 2013 KIDS COUNT Data Book, a project of the Annie E. Casey Foundation.
  KIDS COUNT Data Center's Data Book, released June 20, 2013; http://datacenter.kidscount.org

- Arkansas ranked #45 in the family and community circumstances that factor into children's well-being category by the 2013 KIDS COUNT Data Book, a project of the Annie E. Casey Foundation.
  KIDS COUNT Data Center's Data Book, released June 20, 2013; http://datacenter.kidscount.org

- Arkansas ranked #46 in the 2012 Gallup-Healthways Well-Being Index. Criteria: emotional health; physical health; healthy behavior; work environment; basic access to food, shelter, health care; and a safe and satisfying place to live.
  2012 State of Well-Being, Gallup-Healthways Well-Being Index, released February 28, 2013; www.well-beingindex.com

- *U.S. News and World Report's* "Best States for Teen Drivers" rankings are based on driving and road safety laws, federal reports on driver's licenses, car accident fatality, and road-quality statistics. Arkansas ranked #11.
  U.S. News and World Report, March 18, 2010; www.usnews.com

- The Yahoo! Sports service Rivals.com ranks the states according to the strength of their high school football programs. Arkansas ranked #24.
  "Ranking the States: Where Is the Best Football Played?," November 18, 2011; highschool.rivals.com

- iVillage ranked the states by hospitable living conditions for women. Criteria: economic success, access to affordable childcare, health care, reproductive rights, female representation in government, and educational attainment. Arkansas ranked #48.
  iVillage, "50 Best to Worst States for Women," March 14, 2012; www.ivillage.com

- The League of American Bicyclists's "Bicycle Friendly States" ranked Arkansas #37. Criteria: legislation and enforcement, policies and programs, infrastructure and funding, education and advocacy, and evaluation and planning.
  "Washington Tops the Bicycle-Friendly State Ranking," May 1, 2013; bicycling.com

- The federal Corporation for National and Community Service ranked the states and the District of Columbia by volunteer rates. Arkansas ranked #44 for community service.
  "Volunteering and Civic Life in America 2012," www.volunteeringinamerica.gov, accessed July 24, 2013

- The Hospital Safety Score ranked states and the District of Columbia on their hospitals' performance scores. Arkansas ranked #38. Criteria: avoiding preventable harm and medical errors, as demonstrated by 26 hospital safety metrics.
  Spring 2013 Hospital Safety Score, May 8, 2013; www.hospitalsafetyscore.org

- GMAC Insurance ranked the states and the District of Columbia by the performance of their drivers on the GMAC Insurance National Drivers Test, comprised of DMV test questions. Arkansas ranked #27.
  "2011 GMAC Insurance National Drivers Test," www.gmacinsurance.com, accessed July 23, 2013

- Arkansas ranked #28 in a "State Integrity Investigation" analysis of laws and practices intended to deter corruption and promote accountability and openness in campaign finance, ethics laws, lobbying regulations and management of state pension funds.
  "What's Your State's Grade?," www.publicintegrity.org, accessed July 23, 2013

- Arkansas ranked #25 among the states and the District of Columbia in total rail miles, as tracked by the Association of American Railroads.
  "U.S. Freight Railroad Industry Snapshot: Railroads and States: Total Rail Miles by State: 2011"; www.aar.org, accessed July 23, 2013

- According to statistics compiled by the Beer Institute, Arkansas ranked #37 among the states and the District of Columbia in per capita beer consumption of persons 21 years or older.
  "Shipments of Malt Beverages and Per Capita Consumption by State 2012;" www.beerinstitute.org

- According to Concordia University's "Public Education Costs per Pupil by State Rankings," based on statistics gathered by the U.S. Census Bureau, which includes the District of Columbia, Arkansas ranked #36.
  Concordia University Online; education.cu-portland.edu, accessed July 24, 2013

- Arkansas ranked #34 among the states and the District of Columbia in population density based on U.S. Census Bureau data for resident population and total land area. "List of U.S. States by Population Density."
  www.wikipedia.org, accessed July 24, 2013

- In "America's Health Rankings, 2012 Edition," by the United Health Foundation, Arkansas ranked #48. Criteria included: rate of high school graduation; violent crime rate; incidence of infectious disease; childhood immunizations; prevalence of diabetes; per capita public-health funding; percentage of uninsured population; rate of children in poverty; and availability of primary-care physicians.
  United Health Foundation; www.americashealthrankings.org, accessed July 24, 2013

- The TechNet 2012 "State Broadband Index" ranked Arkansas #50 on the following criteria: broadband adoption; network quality; and economic structure. Improved broadband use is hoped to promote economic development, build strong communities, improve delivery of government services and upgrade educational systems.
  TechNet; www.technet.org, accessed July 24, 2013

- Arkansas was ranked #37 among the states and District of Columbia on the American Council for an Energy-Efficient Economy's "State Energy Efficiency Scorecard" for 2012.
  American Council for an Energy-Efficient Economy; aceee.org/sector/state-policy/scorecard, accessed July 24, 2013

Statistical Tables

DEMOGRAPHICS
Resident State and National Population, 1950-2012
Projected State and National Population, 2000-2030
Population by Age, 2012
Population by Race, 2012
Population by Hispanic Origin and Race, 2012

VITAL STATISTICS
Death Rates by Leading Causes, 2010
Death Rates by Selected Causes, 2010
Abortion Rates, 2009
Infant Mortality Rates, 1995-2009
Marriage and Divorce Rates, 2000-2011

ECONOMY
Nominal Gross Domestic Product by Industry, 2012
Real Gross Domestic Product, 2000-2012
Personal Income Per Capita, 1930-2012
Non-Farm Employment by Sector, 2012
Foreign Exports, 2000-2012
Energy Consumption, 2011

LAND AND WATER
Surface Area and Federally-Owned Land, 2007
Land Cover/Use of Non-Federal Rural Land, 2007
Farms and Crop Acreage, 2012

HEALTH AND MEDICAL CARE
Medical Professionals, 2012
Health Insurance Coverage, 2011
HIV, STD, and Tuberculosis Cases and Rates, 2011
Cigarette Smoking, 2011

HOUSING
Home Ownership Rates, 1995-2012
Home Sales, 2000-2010
Value of Owner-Occupied Homes, 2011

EDUCATION
School Enrollment, 2011
Educational Attainment, 2011
Public College Finances, FY 2012

TRANSPORTATION AND TRAVEL
Motor Vehicle Registrations and Drivers Licenses, 2011
Domestic Travel Expenditures, 2009
Retail Gasoline Prices, 2013
Public Road Length, 2011

CRIME AND LAW ENFORCEMENT
Full-Time Law Enforcement Officers, 2011
Prison Population, 2000-2012
Crime Rate, 2011

GOVERNMENT AND FINANCE
Local Governments by Type, 2012
State Government Revenue, 2011
State Government Expenditures, 2011
State Government General Expenditures by Function, 2011
State Government Finances, Cash and Debt, 2011

POLITICS
Composition of the Senate, 1995-2013
Composition of the House of Representatives, 1995-2013
Composition of State Legislature, 2004-2013
Voter Participation in Presidential Elections, 1980-2012
Governors Since Statehood

DEMOGRAPHICS

Resident State and National Population, 1950–2012

Year	State Population	U.S. Population	State Share
1950	1,910,000	151,326,000	1.26%
1960	1,786,000	179,323,000	1.00%
1970	1,923,322	203,302,031	0.95%
1980	2,286,435	226,545,805	1.01%
1990	2,350,725	248,709,873	0.95%
2000	2,673,293	281,424,600	0.95%
2010	2,915,918	308,745,538	0.94%
2012	2,949,131	313,914,040	0.94%

Note: 1950/1960 population figures are rounded to the nearest thousand.
Source: U.S. Census Bureau, Decennial Census 1950–2010; U.S. Census Bureau, 2012 Population Estimates

Projected State and National Population, 2000–2030

Year	State Population	U.S. Population	State Share
2000	2,673,400	281,421,906	0.95%
2005	2,777,007	295,507,134	0.94%
2010	2,875,039	308,935,581	0.93%
2015	2,968,913	322,365,787	0.92%
2020	3,060,219	335,804,546	0.91%
2025	3,151,005	349,439,199	0.90%
2030	3,240,208	363,584,435	0.89%
State population growth, 2000–2030			566,808
State percentage growth, 2000–2030			21.2%

Source: U.S. Census Bureau, Population Division, Interim State Population Projections, 2005

Population by Age, 2012

Age Group	State Population	Percent of Total Population	
		State	U.S.
Under 5 years	194,019	6.6%	6.4%
5 to 14 years	399,465	13.5%	13.1%
15 to 24 years	404,089	13.7%	14.0%
25 to 34 years	384,233	13.0%	13.5%
35 to 44 years	363,648	12.3%	12.9%
45 to 54 years	396,935	13.5%	14.1%
55 to 64 years	364,152	12.3%	12.3%
65 to 74 years	252,770	8.6%	7.6%
75 to 84 years	135,900	4.6%	4.2%
85 years and older	53,920	1.8%	1.9%
Under 18 years	710,881	24.1%	23.5%
65 years and older	442,590	15.0%	13.7%
Median age (years)	–	37.6	37.4

Source: U.S. Census Bureau, Annual Estimates of the Resident Population for Selected Age Groups by Sex for the United States, States, Counties, and Puerto Rico Commonwealth and Municipios: April 1, 2010 to July 1, 2012

Population by Race, 2012

Race	State Population	Percent of Total Population	
		State	U.S.
All residents	2,949,131	100.00%	100.00%
White	2,359,569	80.01%	77.89%
African American	459,739	15.59%	13.13%
Native American	27,647	0.94%	1.23%
Asian	41,338	1.40%	5.14%
Native Hawaiian	7,495	0.25%	0.23%
Two or more races	53,343	1.81%	2.39%

Source: U.S. Census Bureau, Population Division, Annual Estimates of the Resident Population by Sex, Race and Hispanic Origin for the United States, States, and Counties: April 1, 2010 to July 1, 2012

Population by Hispanic Origin and Race, 2012

Hispanic Origin/Race	State Population	Percent of Total Population	
		State	U.S.
All residents	2,949,131	100.00%	100.00%
All Hispanic residents	199,693	6.77%	16.89%
Hispanic			
White	178,837	6.06%	14.91%
African American	6,560	0.22%	0.79%
Native American	6,373	0.22%	0.49%
Asian	1,495	0.05%	0.17%
Native Hawaiian	1,076	0.04%	0.06%
Two or more races	5,352	0.18%	0.48%
Not Hispanic			
White	2,180,732	73.94%	62.98%
African American	453,179	15.37%	12.34%
Native American	21,274	0.72%	0.74%
Asian	39,843	1.35%	4.98%
Native Hawaiian	6,419	0.22%	0.17%
Two or more races	47,991	1.63%	1.91%

Source: U.S. Census Bureau, Population Division, Annual Estimates of the Resident Population by Sex, Race and Hispanic Origin for the United States, States, and Counties: April 1, 2010 to July 1, 2012

VITAL STATISTICS

Death Rates by Leading Causes, 2010

Cause	State	U.S.
Malignant neoplasms	210.3	186.2
Ischaemic heart diseases	155.9	122.9
Other forms of heart disease	65.1	53.4
Chronic lower respiratory diseases	57.2	44.7
Cerebrovascular diseases	57.5	41.9
Organic, incl. symptomatic, mental disorders	37.0	35.7
Other degenerative diseases of the nervous sys.	32.5	28.4
Other external causes of accidental injury	27.2	26.5
Diabetes mellitus	28.0	22.4
Hypertensive diseases	19.0	20.4
All causes	954.8	799.5

Note: Figures are age-adjusted death rates per 100,000 population
Source: CDC/NCHS, Underlying Cause of Death 1999–2010 on CDC WONDER Online Database

Death Rates by Selected Causes, 2010

Cause	State	U.S.
Assault	6.4	5.2
Diseases of the liver	15.3	13.9
Human immunodeficiency virus (HIV) disease	2.2	2.7
Influenza and pneumonia	21.4	16.2
Intentional self-harm	15.5	12.4
Malnutrition	1.9	0.9
Obesity and other hyperalimentation	2.0	1.8
Renal failure	22.2	14.4
Transport accidents	22.4	12.1
Viral hepatitis	2.0	2.4

Note: Figures are age-adjusted death rates per 100,000 population; A dash indicates that data was not available or was suppressed
Source: CDC/NCHS, Underlying Cause of Death 1999–2010 on CDC WONDER Online Database

Abortion Rates, 2009

Category	2009
By state of residence	
Total abortions	4,820
Abortion rate[1]	8.5%
Abortion ratio[2]	121
By state of occurrence	
Total abortions	4,580
Abortion rate[1]	8.1%
Abortion ratio[2]	115
Abortions obtained by out-of-state residents	13.5%
U.S. abortion rate[1]	15.1%
U.S. abortion ratio[2]	227

Note: (1) Number of abortions per 1,000 women aged 15–44 years; (2) Number of abortions per 1,000 live births; A dash indicates that data was not available
Source: CDC/NCHS, Morbidity and Mortality Weekly Report, November 23, 2012 (Abortion Surveillance, United States, 2009)

Infant Mortality Rates, 1995–2009

Category	1995	2000	2005	2009
All state residents	8.64	8.23	7.83	7.56
All U.S. residents	7.57	6.89	6.86	6.39
All state white residents	7.23	7.19	6.36	6.47
All U.S. white residents	6.30	5.71	5.73	5.33
All state black residents	13.55	12.55	14.05	11.66
All U.S. black residents	14.58	13.48	13.26	12.12

Note: Figures represent deaths per 1,000 live births of resident infants under one year old, exclusive of fetal deaths; A dash indicates that data was not available or was suppressed.
Source: Centers of Disease Control and Prevention, Division of Vital Statistics, Linked Birth/Infant Death Records on CDC Wonder Online

Marriage and Divorce Rates, 2000–2011

Year	Marriage Rate		Divorce Rate	
	State	U.S.	State	U.S.
2000	15.4	8.2	6.4	4.0
2002	14.3	8.0	6.2	3.9
2004	13.4	7.8	6.1	3.7
2006	12.4	7.5	5.8	3.7
2008	10.6	7.1	5.5	3.5
2010	10.8	6.8	5.7	3.6
2011	10.4	6.8	5.3	3.6

Note: Rates are based on provisional counts of marriages/divorces by state of occurrence and are per 1,000 total population residing in area
Source: CDC/NCHS, National Vital Statistics System

ECONOMY

Nominal Gross Domestic Product by Industry, 2012
In millions of current dollars

Industry	State GDP
Accommodation and food services	2,953
Administrative and waste management services	2,458
Agriculture, forestry, fishing, and hunting	2,794
Arts, entertainment, and recreation	432
Construction	4,355
Educational services	573
Finance and insurance	5,183
Health care and social assistance	8,788
Information	2,575
Management of companies and enterprises	3,912
Manufacturing	15,604
Mining	2,134
Other services, except government	2,698
Professional, scientific, and technical services	4,044
Real estate and rental and leasing	11,535
Retail trade	8,095
Transportation and warehousing	5,016
Utilities	3,241
Wholesale trade	7,753

Source: U.S. Department of Commerce, Bureau of Economic Analysis, Survey of Current Business

Real Gross Domestic Product, 2000–2012
In millions of chained 2005 dollars

Year	State GDP	U.S. GDP	State Share
2000	77,539	11,225,406	0.69%
2005	88,501	12,539,116	0.71%
2010	92,075	12,897,088	0.71%
2012	93,892	13,430,576	0.70%

Source: U.S. Department of Commerce, Bureau of Economic Analysis, Survey of Current Business

Personal Income Per Capita, 1930–2012

Year	State	U.S.
1930	$224	$618
1940	$255	$593
1950	$840	$1,503
1960	$1,397	$2,268
1970	$2,840	$4,084
1980	$7,521	$10,091
1990	$14,402	$19,354
2000	$22,574	$30,319
2010	$32,373	$39,791
2012	$34,723	$42,693

Source: U.S. Department of Commerce, Bureau of Economic Analysis, Regional Economic Accounts

Non-Farm Employment by Sector, 2012
In thousands

Sector	Employment
Construction	47.4
Education and health services	171.8
Financial activities	49.1
Government	215.9
Information	14.5
Leisure and hospitality	102.8
Mining and logging	10.7
Manufacturing	155.9
Other services	43.5
Professional and business services	123.0
Trade, transportation, and utilities	242.8
All sectors	1,177.4

Source: U.S. Bureau of Labor Statistics, State and Area Employment

Foreign Exports, 2000–2012
In millions of dollars

Year	State Exports	U.S. Exports	State Share
2000	2,599	712,054	0.37%
2002	2,807	649,940	0.43%
2004	3,481	768,554	0.45%
2006	4,264	973,994	0.44%
2008	5,775	1,222,545	0.47%
2010	5,219	1,208,080	0.43%
2012	7,619	1,478,268	0.52%

Note: U.S. figures exclude data from Puerto Rico, U.S. Virgin Islands, and unallocated exports
Source: U.S. Department of Commerce, International Trade Admin., Office of Trade and Industry Information, Manufacturing and Services

Energy Consumption, 2011

In trillions of BTUs, except as noted

Total energy consumption	
Total state energy consumption	1,117.1
Total U.S. energy consumption	97,387.3
State share of U.S. total	1.15%
Per capita consumption (in millions of BTUs)	
Total state per capita consumption	380.1
Total U.S. per capita consumption	312.6
End-use sectors	
Residential	246.3
Commercial	174.7
Industrial	405.0
Transportation	291.2
Sources of energy	
Petroleum	335.7
Natural gas	288.6
Coal	306.1
Renewable energy	123.7
Nuclear electric power	148.5

Source: U.S. Energy Information Administration, State Energy Data 2011: Consumption

LAND AND WATER

Surface Area and Federally-Owned Land, 2007

In thousands of acres

Category	State	U.S.	State Share
Total surface area	34,036.9	1,937,664.2	1.76%
Total land area	33,134.8	1,886,846.9	1.76%
Non-federal land	30,030.6	1,484,910.0	2.02%
Developed	1,809.3	111,251.2	1.63%
Rural	28,221.3	1,373,658.8	2.05%
Federal land	3,104.2	401,936.9	0.77%
Water area	902.1	50,817.3	1.78%

Source: U.S. Department of Agriculture, Natural Resources Conservation Service, 2007 National Resources Inventory

Land Cover/Use of Non-Federal Rural Land, 2007

In thousands of acres

Category	State	U.S.	State Share
Total rural land	28,221.3	1,373,658.8	2.05%
Cropland	7,379.5	357,023.5	2.07%
CRP[1] land	156.3	32,850.2	0.48%
Pastureland	5,167.5	118,615.7	4.36%
Rangeland	37.6	409,119.4	0.01%
Forest land	15,095.9	406,410.4	3.71%
Other rural land	384.5	49,639.6	0.77%

Note: (1) Conservation Reserve Program was created to assist private landowners in converting highly erodible cropland to vegetative cover.
Source: U.S. Department of Agriculture, Natural Resources Conservation Service, 2007 National Resources Inventory

Farms and Crop Acreage, 2012

Category	State	U.S.	State Share
Farms (in thousands)	47.8	2,170.0	2.20%
Acres (in millions)	13.5	914.0	1.48%
Acres per farm	282.4	421.2	–

Source: U.S. Department of Agriculture, National Agricultural Statistical Service, Quick Stats, 2012 Survey Data

HEALTH AND MEDICAL CARE

Medical Professionals, 2012

Profession	State Number	U.S. Number	State Share	State Rate[1]	U.S. Rate[1]
Physicians[2]	6,070	894,637	0.68%	206.6	287.1
Dentists	1,228	193,587	0.63%	41.8	62.1
Podiatrists	72	17,469	0.41%	2.5	5.6
Optometrists	404	45,638	0.89%	13.7	14.6
Chiropractors	495	77,494	0.64%	16.8	24.9

Note: (1) Rates are per 100,000 population; (2) Includes total, active Doctors of Osteopathic Medicine and Doctors of Medicine in 2011.
Source: U.S. Department of Health and Human Services, Bureau of Health Professions, Area Health Resource File, 2012-2013

Health Insurance Coverage, 2011

Category	State	U.S.
Total persons covered	2,401,000	260,214,000
Total persons not covered	508,000	48,613,000
Percent not covered	17.5%	15.7%
Children under age 18 covered	636,000	67,143,000
Children under age 18 not covered	56,000	6,965,000
Percent of children not covered	8.1%	9.4%

Source: U.S. Census Bureau, Current Population Survey, 2012 Annual Social and Economic Supplement

HIV, STD, and Tuberculosis Cases and Rates, 2011

Disease	State Cases	State Rate[1]	U.S. Rate[1]
Chlamydia	16,052	550.5	457.6
Gonorrhea	4,687	160.7	104.2
HIV diagnosis	243	10.0	15.8
HIV, stage 3 (AIDS)	138	5.7	10.3
Syphilis, early latent	167	5.7	4.3
Syphilis, primary/secondary	182	6.2	4.5
Tuberculosis	85	2.9	3.4

Note: (1) Rates are per 100,000 population
Source: Centers for Disease Control and Prevention

Cigarette Smoking, 2011

Category	State	U.S.
Adults who are current smokers	27.0%	21.2%
Adults who smoke everyday	20.1%	15.4%
Adults who smoke some days	6.8%	5.7%
Adults who are former smokers	25.1%	25.1%
Adults who never smoked	48.0%	52.9%

Source: Centers for Disease Control and Prevention, Behavioral Risk Factor Surveillance System, Tobacco Use, 2011

HOUSING

Home Ownership Rates, 1995–2012

Area	1995	2000	2005	2010	2012
State	67.2%	68.9%	69.2%	67.9%	66.0%
U.S.	64.7%	67.4%	68.9%	66.9%	65.4%

Source: U.S. Census Bureau, Housing Vacancies and Homeownership, Annual Statistics

Home Sales, 2000–2010
In thousands of units

Year	State Sales	U.S. Sales	State Share
2000	45.0	5,174	0.87%
2002	52.2	5,632	0.93%
2004	60.9	6,778	0.90%
2006	82.6	6,478	1.28%
2008	64.2	4,913	1.31%
2010	59.9	4,908	1.22%

Note: Units include single-family homes, condos and co-ops
Source: National Association of Realtors, Real Estate Outlook, Market Trends & Insights

Value of Owner-Occupied Homes, 2011

Value	Total Units in State	Percent of Total, State	Percent of Total, U.S.
Less than $50,000	136,420	18.2%	8.8%
$50,000 to $99,000	218,636	29.1%	16.0%
$100,000 to $149,000	146,731	19.5%	16.5%
$150,000 to $199,000	109,048	14.5%	15.4%
$200,000 to $299,000	83,340	11.1%	18.2%
$300,000 to $499,000	40,898	5.4%	15.2%
$500,000 to $999,000	12,890	1.7%	7.9%
$1,000,000 or more	3,021	0.4%	2.0%
Median value	–	$106,300	$173,600

Source: U.S. Census Bureau, 2011 American Community Survey 1-Year Estimates

EDUCATION

School Enrollment, 2011

Educational Level	Students Enrolled in State	Percent of Total, State	Percent of Total, U.S.
All levels	752,121	100.0%	100.0%
Nursery school, preschool	51,732	6.9%	6.0%
Kindergarten	36,735	4.9%	5.1%
Elementary (grades 1–8)	316,819	42.1%	39.5%
Secondary (grades 9–12)	154,329	20.5%	20.7%
College or graduate school	192,506	25.6%	28.7%

Note: Figures cover the population 3 years and over enrolled in school
Source: U.S. Census Bureau, 2011 American Community Survey 1-Year Estimates

Educational Attainment, 2011

Highest Level of Education	State	U.S.
High school diploma	83.8%	85.9%
Bachelor's degree	20.3%	28.5%
Graduate/Professional degree	7.2%	10.6%

Note: Figures cover the population 25 years and over
Source: U.S. Census Bureau, 2011 American Community Survey 1-Year Estimates

Public College Finances, FY 2012

Category	State	U.S.
Full-time equivalent enrollment (FTE)[1]	125,981	11,548,974
Educational appropriations per FTE[2]	$6,873	$5,906
Net tuition revenue per FTE[3]	$3,595	$5,189
Total educational revenue per FTE[4]	$9,600	$11,043

(1) Full-time equivalent enrollment equates student credit hours to full time, academic year students, but excludes medical students; (2) Educational appropriations measure state and local support available for public higher education operating expenses including ARRA funds and excludes appropriations for independent institutions, financial aid for students attending independent institutions, research, hospitals, and medical education; (3) Net tuition revenue is calculated by taking the gross amount of tuition and fees, less state and institutional financial aid, tuition waivers or discounts, and medical student tuition and fees. Net tuition revenue used for capital debt service is included in the net tuition revenue figures; (4) Total educational revenue is the sum of educational appropriations and net tuition excluding net tuition revenue used for capital debt service.
Source: State Higher Education Executive Officers, State Higher Education Finance FY 2012

TRANSPORTATION AND TRAVEL

Motor Vehicle Registrations and Drivers Licenses, 2011

Vehicle Type	State	U.S.	State Share
Automobiles[1]	1,021,817	125,656,528	0.81%
Buses	3,350	666,064	0.50%
Trucks	1,346,842	118,455,587	1.14%
Motorcycles	76,301	8,437,502	0.90%
Drivers licenses	1,956,091	211,874,649	0.92%

Note: Motor vehicle registrations include private, commercial, and publicly-owned vehicles; (1) Includes taxicabs
Source: U.S. Department of Transportation, Federal Highway Administration

Domestic Travel Expenditures, 2009
In millions of dollars

Category	State	U.S.	State Share
Travel expenditures	$5,237	$610,200	0.86%

Note: Figures represent U.S. spending on domestic overnight trips and day trips of 50 miles or more, one way, away from home. Excludes spending by foreign visitors.
Source: U.S. Travel Association, Impact of Travel on State Economies, 2009

Retail Gasoline Prices, 2013

Gasoline Grade	State Average	U.S. Average
Regular	$3.46	$3.65
Mid	$3.61	$3.81
Premium	$3.78	$3.98
Diesel	$3.78	$3.88
Excise tax[1]	40.2 cents	49.4 cents

Note: Gasoline prices as of 7/26/2013; (1) Includes state and federal excise taxes and other state taxes as of July 1, 2013
Source: American Automobile Association, Daily Fuel Guage Report; American Petroleum Institute, State Motor Fuel Taxes, 2013

Public Road Length, 2011

Type	State Mileage	U.S. Mileage	State Share
Interstate highways	655	46,960	1.39%
Other highways	221	15,719	1.41%
Principal arterial	2,755	156,262	1.76%
Minor arterial	4,320	242,942	1.78%
Major collector	13,930	534,592	2.61%
Minor collector	7,032	266,357	2.64%
Local	71,168	2,814,925	2.53%
Urban	13,013	1,095,373	1.19%
Rural	87,069	2,982,383	2.92%
Total	100,082	4,077,756	2.45%

Note: Combined urban and rural road mileage equals the total of the other road types
Source: U.S. Department of Transportation, Federal Highway Administration, Public Road Length, 2011

CRIME AND LAW ENFORCEMENT

Full-Time Law Enforcement Officers, 2011

Gender	State Number	State Rate[1]	U.S. Rate[1]
Male officers	5,265	179.9	210.3
Female officers	498	17.0	28.1
Total officers	5,763	197.0	238.3

Note: (1) Rates are per 100,000 population
Source: Federal Bureau of Investigation, Uniform Crime Reports, Crime in the United States 2011

Prison Population, 2000–2012

Year	State Population	U.S. Population	State Share
2000	11,915	1,391,261	0.86%
2005	13,541	1,527,929	0.89%
2010	16,204	1,613,803	1.00%
2011	16,108	1,598,783	1.01%
2012	14,654	1,571,013	0.93%

Note: Figures include prisoners under the jurisdiction of state or federal correctional authorities.
Source: U.S. Department of Justice, Bureau of Justice Statistics, Prisoners in 2006, 2011, 2012 (Advance Counts)

Crime Rate, 2011

Incidents per 100,000 residents

Category	State	U.S.
Violent crimes	480.9	386.3
Murder	5.5	4.7
Forcible rape	41.3	26.8
Robbery	82.6	113.7
Aggravated assault	351.5	241.1
Property crimes	3,754.1	2,908.7
Burglary	1,173.3	702.2
Larceny/theft	2,383.0	1,976.9
Motor vehicle theft	197.8	229.6
All crimes	4,235.0	3,295.0

Source: Federal Bureau of Investigation, Uniform Crime Reports, Crime in the United States 2011

GOVERNMENT AND FINANCE

Local Governments by Type, 2012

Government Type	State	U.S.	State Share
All local governments	1,543	89,004	1.73%
County	75	3,031	2.47%
Municipality	502	19,522	2.57%
Town/Township	0	16,364	0.00%
Special District	727	37,203	1.95%
Ind. School District	239	12,884	1.86%

Source: U.S. Census Bureau, 2012 Census of Governments: Organization Component Preliminary Estimates

State Government Revenue, 2011

In thousands of dollars, except for per capita figures

Total revenue	**$22,807,859**
Total revenue per capita, State	$7,762
Total revenue per capita, U.S.	$7,271
General revenue	$17,453,870
Intergovernmental revenue	$6,313,263
Taxes	$7,975,526
General sales	$2,736,946
Selective sales	$1,140,036
License taxes	$361,548
Individual income taxes	$2,270,383
Corporate income taxes	$376,874
Other taxes	$1,089,739
Current charges	$2,319,881
Miscellaneous general revenue	$845,200
Utility revenue	$0
Liquor store revenue	$0
Insurance trust revenue[1]	$5,353,989

Note: (1) Within insurance trust revenue, net earnings of state retirement systems is a calculated statistic, and thus can be positive or negative. Net earnings is the sum of earnings on investments plus gains on investments minus losses on investments.
Source: U.S. Census Bureau, 2011 Annual Survey of State Government Finances

State Government Expenditures, 2011

In thousands of dollars, except for per capita figures

Total expenditure	$18,861,507
Total expenditure per capita, State	$6,419
Total expenditure per capita, U.S.	$6,427
Intergovernmental expenditure	$5,151,981
Direct expenditure	$13,709,526
Current operation	$10,101,909
Capital outlay	$898,800
Insurance benefits and repayments	$2,001,596
Assistance and subsidies	$555,837
Interest on debt	$151,384
Utility expenditure	$0
Liquor store expenditure	$0
Insurance trust expenditure	$2,001,596

Source: U.S. Census Bureau, 2011 Annual Survey of State Government Finances

State Government General Expenditures by Function, 2011

In thousands of dollars

Education	$7,508,042
Public welfare	$4,493,896
Hospitals	$856,818
Health	$278,329
Highways	$1,081,300
Police protection	$97,386
Correction	$411,436
Natural resources	$339,085
Parks and recreation	$59,730
Governmental administration	$576,327
Interest on general debt	$151,384
Other and unallocable	$1,006,178

Source: U.S. Census Bureau, 2011 Annual Survey of State Government Finances

State Government Finances, Cash and Debt, 2011

In thousands of dollars, except for per capita figures

Debt at end of fiscal year	
State, total	$3,748,749
State, per capita	$1,276
U.S., per capita	$3,635
Cash and security holdings	
State, total	$26,065,733
State, per capita	$8,870
U.S., per capita	$11,759

Source: U.S. Census Bureau, 2011 Annual Survey of State Government Finances

POLITICS

Composition of the Senate, 1995–2013

Congress (Year)	State/U.S	Dem	Rep	Total
104th (1995)	State delegates	2	0	2
	Total U.S.	48	52	100
105th (1997)	State delegates	1	1	2
	Total U.S.	45	55	100
106th (1999)	State delegates	1	1	2
	Total U.S.	45	55	100
107th (2001)	State delegates	1	1	2
	Total U.S.	50	50	100
108th (2003)	State delegates	2	0	2
	Total U.S.	48	51	100
109th (2005)	State delegates	2	0	2
	Total U.S.	44	55	100
110th (2007)	State delegates	2	0	2
	Total U.S.	49	49	100
111th (2009)	State delegates	2	0	2
	Total U.S.	57	41	100
112th (2011)	State delegates	1	1	2
	Total U.S.	51	47	100
113th (2013)	State delegates	1	1	2
	Total U.S.	54	45	100

Note: Figures are for the starts of first sessions; Totals include Democratic (Dem) and Republican (Rep) members as well as vacancies and seats held by independent party members
Source: U.S. Congress, Congressional Directory

Composition of the House of Representatives, 1995–2013

Congress (Year)	State/U.S	Dem	Rep	Total
104th (1995)	State delegates	2	2	4
	Total U.S.	204	230	435
105th (1997)	State delegates	2	2	4
	Total U.S.	207	226	435
106th (1999)	State delegates	2	2	4
	Total U.S.	211	223	435
107th (2001)	State delegates	3	1	4
	Total U.S.	212	221	435
108th (2003)	State delegates	3	1	4
	Total U.S.	205	229	435
109th (2005)	State delegates	3	1	4
	Total U.S.	202	231	435
110th (2007)	State delegates	3	1	4
	Total U.S.	233	198	435
111th (2009)	State delegates	3	1	4
	Total U.S.	256	178	435
112th (2011)	State delegates	3	1	4
	Total U.S.	193	242	435
113th (2013)	State delegates	0	4	4
	Total U.S.	201	234	435

Note: Figures are for the starts of first sessions; Totals include Democratic (Dem) and Republican (Rep) members as well as vacancies and seats held by independent party members
Source: U.S. Congress, Congressional Directory

Composition of State Legislature, 2004–2013

Year	Democrats	Republicans	Total
State Senate			
2004	27	8	35
2005	27	8	35
2006	27	8	35
2007	27	8	35
2008	27	8	35
2009	27	8	35
2010	27	8	35
2011	20	15	35
2012	20	15	35
2013	14	21	35
State House			
2004	70	30	100
2005	72	28	100
2006	72	28	100
2007	75	25	100
2008	75	25	100
2009	71	28	100
2010	71	28	100
2011	54	44	100
2012	54	46	100
2013	49	51	100

Note: Totals may include minor party members and vacancies
Source: The Council of State Governments, State Legislatures

Voter Participation in Presidential Elections, 1980–2012

Year	Voting-eligible State Population	State Voter Turnout Rate	U.S. Voter Turnout Rate
1980	1,610,104	52.0	54.2
1984	1,668,136	53.0	55.2
1988	1,689,491	49.0	52.8
1992	1,751,083	54.3	58.1
1996	1,844,689	47.9	51.7
2000	1,925,961	47.9	54.2
2004	1,969,208	53.6	60.1
2008	2,071,563	52.5	61.6
2012	2,116,668	50.5	58.2

Note: All figures are based on the voting-eligible population which excludes person ineligible to vote such as non-citizens, felons (depending on state law), and mentally-incapacitated persons. U.S. figures include the overseas eligible population (including military personnel).
Source: McDonald, Michael P., United States Election Project, Presidential Voter Turnout Rates, 1980–2012

Governors Since Statehood

James S. Conway (D) 1836-1840
Archibald Yell (D). . . . . (r) 1840-1844
Samuel Adams (D) 1844
Thomas S. Drew (D) 1844-1849
Richard C. Byrd (D) 1849
John S. Roane (D) 1849-1852
Elias N. Conway (D) 1852-1860
Henry M. Rector (D) . . . . (r) 1860-1862
Thomas Fletcher (D) 1862
Harris Flanagin (D) . . . . (i) 1862-1864
Isaac Murphy (O) 1864-1868

Powell Clayton (R) . . . . (r) 1868-1871
Ozra A. Hadley (R) 1871-1873
Elisha Baxter (R) 1873-1874
Augustus H. Garland (D) 1874-1877
William R. Miller (D). 1877-1881
Thomas J. Churchill (D). 1881-1883
James H. Berry (D). 1883-1885
Simon P. Hughes (D) 1885-1889
James P. Eagle (D) 1889-1893
William M. Fishback (D) 1893-1895
James P. Clarke (D) 1895-1897
Daniel W. Jones (D). 1897-1901
Jefferson Davis (D) 1901-1907
John S. Little (D) 1907-1909
George W. Donaghey (D). 1909-1913
James T. Robinson (D) . . . . (r) 1913
William K. Oldham (D). 1913
J. Marion Futrell (D) 1913
George W. Hays (D). 1913-1917
Charles H. Brough (D) 1917-1921
Thomas C. McRae (D) 1921-1925
Thomas J. Terral (D) 1925-1927
John E. Martineau (D). . . . . (r) 1927-1928
Harvey Parnell (D) 1928-1933
J. Marion Futrell (D) 1933-1937
Carl E. Bailey (D). 1937-1941
Homer M. Adkins (D) 1941-1945
Benjamin T. Laney (D) 1945-1949
Sidney S. McMath (D) 1949-1953
Francis A. Cherry (D). 1953-1955
Orval E. Faubus (D) 1955-1967
Winthrop Rockefeller (R). 1967-1971
Dale L. Bumpers (D) . . . . (r) 1971-1975
Robert C. Riley (D) 1975
David H. Pryor (D). 1975-1979
William J. Clinton (D) 1979-1992
Jim Guy Tucker (D) . . . . (r) 1992-1996
Mike Huckabee (R) 1996-2007
Mike Beebe (D). . . . . 2007-2015 (term limits)

Note: (D) Democrat; (R) Republican; (O) Other party; (r) resigned;
(d) died in office; (i) removed from office

California

Location: Pacific coast

Area and rank: 155,973 square miles (403,970 square kilometers); 163,707 square miles (424,000 square kilometers) including water; third largest state in area

Coastline: 840 miles (1,394 kilometers) on the Pacific Ocean

Shoreline: 3,427 miles (5,512 kilometers)

Population and rank: 38,041,430 (2012 estimate); largest state in population

Capital city: Sacramento (466,488 people in 2010 census)

Largest city: Los Angeles (3,792,621 people in 2010 census)

Sacramento's state capitol building after its major renovation was completed in 1982. (Wikimedia Commons)

Entered Union and rank:
September 9, 1850;
thirty-first state

Present constitution adopted:
1879

Counties: 58

State name: "California" is
believed to have derived from
a name in a Spanish romance
written around 1500

State nickname: Golden State

Motto: *Eureka*! (Greek for "I have
found it!")

State flag: Star above grizzly bear on white background above red stripe

Highest point: Mount Whitney—14,494 feet (4,418 meters); highest point in continental
United States

Lowest point: Death Valley—282 feet (87 meters) below sea level; lowest point in United States

Highest recorded temperature: 134 degrees Fahrenheit (57 degrees Celsius)— Death Valley, 1913

Lowest recorded temperature: −45
degrees Fahrenheit (−43 degrees
Celsius)—Boca, 1937

State song: "I Love You, California"
("California, Here I Come" is
unofficial)

State tree: California redwoods

State flower: Golden poppy

State bird: California valley quail

State fish: Golden trout

State animal: California grizzly bear

National parks: Channel Islands,
Death Valley, Joshua Tree, Kings
Canyon, Lassen Volcanic, Redwood,
Sequoia, Yosemite

California History

To an extent much greater than in other states, California is a naturally defined region with a distinct history of its own. Its differences begin with its natural geography. Bounded by the Pacific Ocean on the west and the Sierra Madre range along the east, California had limited contacts with the outside world until the mid-nineteenth century. Until then, little was known about its abundant natural resources beyond the fact it had an equable climate and fertile land.

An estimated 300,000 Native Americans inhabited the region before Europeans arrived. Though they were among the most numerous and prosperous native societies in North America, most of them lived outside the main currents of Native American history. Compared to many cultures outside California, their culture was simple. Metallurgy, pottery, intensive cultivation, horses and draft animals were all unknown to them. With economies based mostly on fishing, hunting, and gathering, they nevertheless achieved comparatively high levels of prosperity and lived largely peaceful lives.

Early Exploration. European contact with California began in 1542, when the Spanish navigator Juan Rodríguez Cabrillo found San Diego Bay. English navigator Francis Drake followed thirty-seven years later, when he reached Northern California. Little came out of these early explorations. Busy colonizing Mexico, Spain paid little attention to the California region over the next two centuries. Permanent European interest in the region finally began during the late eighteenth century, when Spain authorized members of the Franciscan order to build a chain of mission stations up the California coast. Father Junipero Serra founded California's first mission at San Diego in 1769; twenty other mission stations followed over the next fifty-four years.

During those years California was nominally a Spanish colony, but the government exercised only light control, and the burden of imposing European culture on California's peoples was left to the Franciscans. The missionaries began systematic agricultural development and gathered American Indian communities around their mission stations. Meanwhile, Russian traders established posts north of the mission chain without interference. After a half century of formal Spanish colonization, the non-native residents of California numbered only about 3,300—a fraction of the number of Native Americans.

Mexican Rule. By this time, Spain was losing its hold on its New World empire and Mexico was in open revolt. When Mexico won its independence from Spain in 1821, California's Spanish governor peacefully recognized Mexican rule, and California became a Mexican province. Mexico then followed Spain's example by taking little active interest in the region until the early 1830's, when it began secularizing California's mission stations and distributing titles to large blocs of land among favored families. In 1837, the Mexican government granted California's administration a large measure of autonomy, continuing California's tradition of comparative isolation.

Secularization was a disaster to the American Indian communities attached to the former mission stations. The departure of the Franciscans left the indigenous peoples at the mercy of private landlords, who had little interest in their welfare. Most Native Americans left the missions for their original homes, where harsh economic conditions and European diseases reduced their numbers greatly. By the turn of the twentieth century their numbers fell to their lowest level ever—about 15,000 people, about one-twentieth their precolonial number.

By the early 1840's, Americans hungry for land and new opportunities were moving west and settling in California. Conflicts soon arose between these new, non-Spanish-speaking residents and the established Spanish and Mexican settlers, known as *Californios.* Soon, the U.S. government was taking an interest in the region, which it feared might be occupied by Great Britain or Russia. In 1845, it instructed its consul in Monterey to promote local interest in annexation to the United States. The following year, disgruntled American settlers in northern California found an excuse for rebelling against the Mexican regime and proclaimed an independent republic in Sonoma—a short-lived rebellion known as the "Bear Flag Revolt," after the flag the rebels used.

For reasons largely unrelated to California, the United States declared war against Mexico in 1846. Placed under military rule by Mexico, California played a small role in the Mexican-American War. The Mexican government surrendered California to the United States when John C. Frémont arrived with an occupation force in 1847. In the peace accord that followed, Mexico formally ceded California, along with most of what became the American Southwest, to the United States. California's territorial status was short-lived. Two years later, before its territorial government was fully organized, California entered the Union as a state. Its rapid transition to statehood owed much to an unexpected and spectacular event that fundamentally changed the region's future: the discovery of gold near Sacramento.

The Gold Rush and Statehood. Scarcely a week before the treaty ending the Mexican-American War was signed, news of the discovery of gold in northern California became public, and the seeds of one of the world's great gold rushes began. The effect the gold rush had on

California would be difficult to overstate. Within a matter of only a few years, California was transformed from a sleepy backwater to perhaps the fastest-growing economy in the world. Hundreds of thousands of people poured into the state from the East and other parts of the world. Within ten years California's non-Indian population rose from less than 10,000 to several hundred thousands. Meanwhile, San Francisco grew from little more than a village to a booming metropolitan center offering virtually every service and amenity available in big eastern cities and controlling the commerce of the West Coast.

The multitudes who rushed to California dreamt of striking it rich from mineral wealth; however, the real fortunes made there grew mostly out of the many enterprises that arose to support the gold industry. Great profits were made in agriculture, retail trade, transportation, and countless other industries and services. For the first time, agriculture was undertaken on a large scale. As the gold rush made food production a critical priority, the agricultural potential of California's great Central Valley was finally recognized. Eventually, California's agricultural production would not only lead the

nation, but reach a level exceeded by only a handful of nations in the world.

The gold rush peaked during the early 1850's. By 1861, when the Civil War began, it was essentially over. Nevertheless, California's economy continued to expand. The war interrupted commerce with the eastern United States but actually helped the local economy. Once again isolated from the East, California had to diversify its production to make up for what it could not import. Pro-Unionists outnumbered Confederate sympathizers within California, but the state played no direct role in the war.

Communications. When California attained statehood in 1850, it was separated from the rest of the states by the Central Plains, Rocky Mountains, and arid Southwest. With people and goods arriving at increasing rates, cheaper and more rapid transportation became a paramount need. With overland slow and expensive, much goods and people reaching the state came by ship—by way of Central America. In 1860, the Pony Express was begun to speed mail service between California and the East. It lasted little more than a year—but only because it was displaced by transcontinental telegraph service. Completion of the first transcontinental railroad in 1869 linked California's capital, Sacramento, with St. Joseph, Missouri. These new links with the East were major steps in ending California's isolation.

With the building of the railway and the end of the Civil War, California settled down to a period of steady growth and development. Settlers continued to pour in from the East, doubling the state's population every decade—a rate of growth that continued through most of the twentieth century. As the proportion of European Americans rose, their tolerance for other immigrants diminished and racially discriminatory laws were passed. Particular targets of white intolerance were the thousands of Chinese workers who had come to California to help build the railroads. Most of these people stayed working at low-paying jobs shunned by whites, who pressed the state government to legislate against Asians.

Agricultural production grew and diversified until California led the nation in production during the late 1940's. Meanwhile, other industries arose to contribute to the state's growing economy. In 1895, oil was discovered in Southern California, just as the invention of motor-driven automobiles was creating new demand for petroleum products. Through the first four decades of the twentieth century, California led all states in oil production.

Completed in 1937, the Golden Gate Bridge spans the mile-wide gap separating San Francisco Bay from the Pacific Ocean. (PhotoDisc)

Most of California's early development occurred in the northern part of the state. During the twentieth century, the balance shifted to the south, where such new industries as petrochemicals, aeronautics, and entertainment attracted new immigrants from the East. By 1920 most of the state's population resided in southern counties. However, its bicameral legislative system left the balance of political power in the north. With most of the water resources also in the north, supplying water to the largely arid south be came a critical issue in state politics. Correction of the political imbalance finally came during the early 1960's, after a U.S. Supreme Court decision forced reapportionment of the state legislature. By this time, California ranked as the most populous state in the nation.

Over the next four decades, a central issue in state politics was the changing composition of the population. Opposition to immigrants of all kinds is an issue with roots going back to the late nineteenth century. During

Aerial view of Hollywood's Capitol Records building, which was designed to resemble a record turntable. (PhotoDisc)

the Great Depression of the 1930's, for example, the state tried, unsuccessfully, to keep out swarms of poor farmers fleeing the drought-stricken Midwest. After World War II, Californians became alarmed by the rising influx of Mexicans seeking higher-paying jobs—particularly in agriculture. Immigration from Asia, Mexico, and Central America grew through the rest of the twentieth century, making California the most multicultural state in the Union.

Twenty-first Century Developments. As California moved toward the new millennium, it faced new challenges arising from its burgeoning population and the consequent pressure on its resources. During the late 1990's, the energy supply became a critical issue. The year 2000 saw a sharp rise in energy prices that was soon followed by unprecedented power blackouts due to a shortage of electricity. In January, 2001, Governor Grey Davis declared a state of emergency, and North Califor-

nia's largest power utility, Pacific Gas and Electric, filed for bankruptcy. Over the next several years, the power shortage was alleviated, but dissatisfaction over the governor's handling of the crisis led to calls for an unprecedented recall election.

In October, 2003, after more than 1.3 million signatures on recall petitions were validated, a special recall election was held. Voters were asked to decide on two issues: first, whether Governor Davis should be recalled; second, who should replace him if a majority of voters endorsed his recall. Requirements for candidacy were so low that 135 people qualified for listing on the ballot. Davis, a Democrat, was voted out of office by a decisive margin and became only the second U.S. governor in history to be recalled (the first was North Dakota's governor in 1921). Actor Arnold Schwarzenegger was elected to replace him.

Candidates in the special election did not run on party affiliations, but Schwarzenegger was known to be a registered Republican. Schwarzenegger was first elected on October 7, 2003, in the special recall election to replace Governor Gray Davis. Schwarzenegger was sworn in November 17, 2003, and served out the remainder of Davis's term. Schwarzenegger was re-elected in California's 2006 gubernatorial election to serve a full term as governor, defeating Democrat Phil Angelides, California State Treasurer. In 2011, Schwarzenegger completed his second term as governor. He announced that he had separated from Maria Shriver, his wife for 25 years, who is a member of the influential Kennedy clan and a niece of John F. Kennedy.

Same-sex marriage. In the November 2008 elections, Californians passed Proposition 8. "Prop Eight" was drafted by those opposed to same-sex marriage. The proposition was intended to override a ruling by the California Supreme Court in May, 2008, which had ruled unconstitutional an earlier proposition, also designed to prohibit same-sex marriage, passed in 2000.

Proposition 8 was intended to get around the 2008 ruling by adding an amendment to the California Constitution that would state "only marriage between a man and a woman is valid or recognized in California." At first, the California Supreme Court ruled that the amendment was constitutional, in *Strauss v. Horton*, in 2009, because it "carved out a limited [or 'narrow'] exception to the state equal protection clause." After being ruled constitutional in state court, a case brought by two same-sex married couples involving Prop Eight went to federal court and the proposition was ruled unconstitutional in 2010, and finally confirmed after appeals on June 26, 2013.

R. Kent Rasmussen
Updated by the Editor

California Time Line

1521	Spain conquers Mexico.
Sept. 28, 1542	Juan Rodríguez Cabrillo is the first European to sight California's coast.
1579	Sir Francis Drake lands in Northern California.
1602	Sebastían Vizcaíno sails along California coast.
1700's	Estimated American Indian population is nearly 300,000 people.
1769–1823	Franciscans build twenty-one mission stations between San Diego and Sonoma.
1773	Spanish colonization begins.
1812	Russians establish trading posts in Northern California.
1820	Estimated *non*-Native American population is 3,270.
1821	Newly independent, Mexico makes California a province.
1833–1840	Mexico secularizes California missions and distributes lands among favored families.
1837	Mexico grants California government considerable autonomy.
1841	American settlers begin migrating to California from Missouri.
June 14, 1846	Americans raise "Bear Flag" republic revolt in Sonoma.
May, 1846	United States declares war on Mexico, which places California under military rule.
1847	California becomes U.S. territory when Mexico surrenders it to John C. Frémont's force.
1848	Signing of Treaty of Guadalupe Hidalgo ends Mexican-American War.
Jan. 24, 1848	Discovery of gold near Sacramento launches gold rush, promoting rapid, long-term development.
1849	Convention votes against forming a territorial government, instead drafts bilingual state constitution, which voters ratify.
Sept. 9, 1850	California is admitted to the Union.
1854	Sacramento becomes permanent state capital.
1860-1861	Pony Express improves mail service with the East.
Oct. 1861	Transcontinental telegraph reaches California.
1868	University of California is founded in Berkeley.
1869	Completion of transcontinental railroad ends California's isolation.
1872	State laws are codified for the first time.
May 7, 1879	Voters ratify new constitution.
1890	Yosemite becomes state's first national park.
1895	Oil is discovered in Southern California.
1900	Native American population drops to about 15,500 people.
Oct. 1906	Earthquake and fire level San Francisco.
1908	Film industry begins in Los Angeles.
1914	Opening of Panama Canal improves communications with the East Coast, lowering shipping and transportation costs.
1920	Southern California overtakes the north in population, but legislature refuses to reapportion.
Feb. 3, 1923	Mount Lassen erupts.
1930's	Great Depression sends many farmers from the Great Plains to California, which tries to keep them out.
1931	Master plan for distributing water throughout the state is created.
Nov. 1934	Voters endorse calling of new constitutional convention, but legislature never acts to organize it.
1937	Golden Gate Bridge opens in San Francisco Bay.
Nov. 1938	Culbert Olson is first Democrat elected governor.
1940	First freeway in United States opens in Pasadena.
Feb. 1942	Federal government orders internment of state's Japanese American population after World War II begins.
1942–1945	World War II spurs industrial and economic growth.
1945	State Water Resources Board is created to distribute state's limited water supplies.
1947	State's agriculture ranks first among U.S. states.
1953	Governor Earl Warren becomes chief justice of the United States.
1959	California is first state to adopt master highway plan.

1960	State prepares master plan for higher education.
1964	California surpasses New York as most populous state.
Nov., 1964	Ronald Reagan is elected governor.
Aug., 1965	Nation's first modern racially motivated rioting erupts in Los Angeles's Watts district.
Nov., 1966	First elections after reapportionment are held.
Feb. 9, 1971	Massive earthquake devastates Los Angeles area.
June 6, 1978	Voters approve referendum Prop 13, mandating statewide reduction in property tax of 57 percent.
Nov., 1980	Ronald Reagan is elected president of the United States.
Oct. 17, 1989	Earthquake devastates San Francisco Bay Area.
Oct. 20, 1991	Most destructive urban wildfire in U.S. history burns parts of Berkeley and Oakland.
Apr. 29, 1992	Acquittal of policemen charged with beating Rodney King touches off rioting in Los Angeles.
Jan. 17, 1994	Massive earthquake devastates Southern California.
Nov., 1998	Grey Davis is first Democrat elected governor since 1978.
2000	Significant rise in energy prices signals beginning of energy crisis that worsens as power blackouts occur.
Jan. 17, 2000	Governor Davis responds to energy crisis by declaring a state of emergency.
Nov., 2002	Despite energy crisis, Davis is reelected governor by a wide margin.
Feb. 5, 2003	Movement to recall Davis is launched.
Oct. 7, 2003	In special recall election, Davis is voted out of office, and actor Arnold Schwarzenegger is elected from among 135 candidates to complete his term.
Nov. 13, 2003	Davis ends the state of emergency four days before leaving office.
Nov. 8, 2005	In another special selection, voters reject all four ballot initiatives proposed by Schwarzenegger to reform the state government.
Nov., 2006	Schwarzenegger defeats Democrat Phil Angelides in his first bid for reelection.
Jan., 2007	San Francisco congresswoman Nancy Pelosi becomes the Speaker of the House of Representatives.
2008-2013	Californians battle in elections and courts over same-sex marriage and Prop Eight. Eventually, a case regarding a same sex couple reaches the Supreme Court in 2013, which confirms the unconstitutionality of banning same-sex marriages.

Notes for Further Study

Published Sources. As the largest state in the nation, California offers the most abundant resources for further study. Thousands of published books cover every imaginable aspect of the state's history, peoples, politics, economy, and natural resources. Especially abundant are travel guides. These not only provide practical guides to the state as a whole, its major cities, and regions, but also are filled with statistics, historical facts, and other useful information. Vast amounts of diverse information can also be obtained from government agencies at all levels. A good starting point for general information on the state is *California Almanac* (7th ed., 1996), edited by James S. Fay. Warren A. Beck and Ynez D. Haase's *Historical Atlas of California* (1975) remains a standard source on historical geography. For an updated version of a classic history text emphasizing forces that have made California unique, see Carey McWilliams and Lewis H. Lapham's *California: The Great Exception* (1999). Another overview can be found in *California: An Interpretive History* (8th ed., 2003) by James J. Rawls and Walton Bean. California historian Kevin Starr brings together a discussion of the state's history and the myths surrounding it in *California: A History* (2005).

Agriculture forms a substantial portion of California's economy, and Richard A. Walker examines the modern agroindustrial system of production in the state in *The Conquest of Bread: One Hundred Fifty Years of Agribusiness in California*. Editors Charles F. Hohm and James A. Glynn focus the chapters in *California's Social Problems* (2d ed., 2002) on the important challenges facing the state's communities, including those involving health, institutional change, population growth, and environmental decline. C. L. Keyworth's *California Indians* (1999) is a comprehensive guide to the history, cultures, and modern condition of the state's diverse Native American peoples. An authoritative analysis of how government works in the state can be found both in Mona Field and Charles P. Sohner's *California Government and Politics Today* (8th ed., 1999) and in *California Politics and Government: A Practical Approach* (8th ed., 2006) by Larry N. Gerston and Terry Christensen.

Web Resources. The range of Web sites offering useful information on California is too broad even to summarize. However, many of the sites are so well connected by links and are so easy to find with Web search engines that the addresses of only a few will suffice to direct users to most of the rest. An excellent starting point is the official California Tourist Bureau site (http://www.visitcalifornia.com/), providing links to maps and travel information. The State of California's Web site (www.ca.gov/) is a thorough site, providing residents and visitors with information on the state's history and culture, travel and transportation, environmental and natural resources, and health and safety, among many other topics. Among specialized sites, readers will find interest in California State Library (www.library.ca.gov/), which hosts a page detailing all the state's insignia, such as the state flower, state gemstone, and state seal; California Coastal Geography (ceres.ca.gov/ceres/calweb/coastal/geography.html); Gold Rush! (www.museumca.org/goldrush/), detailing the influx of settlers and miners following the 1848 discovery of gold; and A History of Mexican Americans in California (www.cr.nps.gov/history/online-books/5views/5views5.htm.).

Another good starting point on the Web is the Law Library of Congress (www.loc.gov/law/guide/us-ca.html), which provides links to the office of the governor, state agencies, and the California Legislative Assembly, among many others. The California State Association of Counties Web site (www.csac.counties.org/) offers profiles of every county, as well as links to individual Web sites for most of them. The county sites, in turn, provide additional information on local matters and government agencies. The Official California Legislative Information site (www.leginfo.ca.gov) provides full information on current legislative activity as well as pending legislation.

The Hollywood Sign is situated on Mount Lee in the Hollywood Hills area of the Santa Monica Mountains in Los Angeles, California. First erected as an advertisement in 1923, this cultural icon is 45 feet tall (14 m) and 350 feet long (110 m). (Wikimedia Commons)

Counties

County	2012 Population	Pop. Rank	Land Area (sq. miles)	Area Rank
Alameda	1,554,720	7	739.02	49
Alpine	1,129	58	738.33	50
Amador	37,035	46	594.58	54
Butte	221,539	27	1,636.46	28
Calaveras	44,742	44	1,020.01	40
Colusa	21,411	50	1,150.73	39
Contra Costa	1,079,597	9	715.94	51
Del Norte	28,290	48	1,006.37	42

County	2012 Population	Pop. Rank	Land Area (sq. miles)	Area Rank
El Dorado	180,561	29	1,707.88	27
Fresno	947,895	10	5,957.99	6
Glenn	27,992	49	1,313.95	36
Humboldt	134,827	35	3,567.99	14
Imperial	176,948	31	4,176.60	10
Inyo	18,495	52	10,180.88	2
Kern	856,158	11	8,131.92	3
Kings	151,364	33	1,389.42	34

County	2012 Population	Pop. Rank	Land Area (sq. miles)	Area Rank
Lake	63,983	40	1,256.46	38
Lassen	33,658	47	4,541.18	8
Los Angeles	9,962,789	1	4,057.88	11
Madera	152,218	32	2,137.07	24
Marin	256,069	26	520.31	55
Mariposa	17,905	53	1,448.82	31
Mendocino	87,428	38	3,506.34	15
Merced	262,305	25	1,934.97	25
Modoc	9,327	56	3,917.77	12
Mono	14,348	54	3,048.98	19
Monterey	426,762	20	3,280.60	17
Napa	139,045	34	748.36	48
Nevada	98,292	36	957.77	44
Orange	3,090,132	3	790.57	47
Placer	361,682	22	1,407.01	32
Plumas	19,399	51	2,553.04	22
Riverside	2,268,783	4	7,206.48	4
Sacramento	1,450,121	8	964.64	43
San Benito	56,884	42	1,388.71	35
San Bernardino	2,081,313	5	20,056.94	1
San Diego	3,177,063	2	4,206.63	9
San Francisco	825,863	13	46.87	58
San Joaquin	702,612	15	1,391.32	33
San Luis Obispo	274,804	23	3,298.57	16
San Mateo	739,311	14	448.41	56
Santa Barbara	431,249	19	2,735.09	21
Santa Clara	1,837,504	6	1,290.10	37
Santa Cruz	266,776	24	445.17	57
Shasta	178,586	30	3,775.40	13
Sierra	3,086	57	953.21	45
Siskiyou	44,154	45	6,277.89	5
Solano	420,757	21	821.76	46
Sonoma	491,829	17	1,575.85	29
Stanislaus	521,726	16	1,494.83	30
Sutter	95,022	37	602.41	53
Tehama	63,406	41	2,949.71	20
Trinity	13,526	55	3,179.25	18
Tulare	451,977	18	4,824.21	7
Tuolumne	54,008	43	2,220.88	23
Ventura	835,981	12	1,843.13	26
Yolo	204,118	28	1,014.69	41
Yuba	72,926	39	631.84	52

Source: U.S. Census Bureau, 2012 Population Estimates

Cities

With 10,000 or more residents

Legal Name	2010 Population	Pop. Rank	Land Area (sq. miles)	Area Rank
Adelanto city	31,765	249	56.01	22
Agoura Hills city	20,330	337	7.79	284
Alameda city	73,812	110	10.61	228
Alamo CDP	14,570	401	9.67	242
Albany city	18,539	352	1.79	465
Alhambra city	83,089	92	7.63	289
Aliso Viejo city	47,823	185	7.47	292

Legal Name	2010 Population	Pop. Rank	Land Area (sq. miles)	Area Rank
Alpine CDP	14,236	409	26.78	83
Altadena CDP	42,777	198	8.71	262
Alum Rock CDP	15,536	383	1.20	477
American Canyon city	19,454	346	4.84	367
Anaheim city	336,265	10	49.84	30
Antelope CDP	45,770	192	6.84	312
Antioch city	102,372	65	28.35	75

Legal Name	2010 Population	Pop. Rank	Land Area (sq. miles)	Area Rank
Apple Valley town	69,135	117	73.19	13
Arcadia city	56,364	156	10.93	223
Arcata city	17,231	366	9.10	252
Arden-Arcade CDP	92,186	78	17.83	143
Arroyo Grande city	17,252	365	5.84	341
Artesia city	16,522	372	1.62	469
Arvin city	19,304	347	4.82	369
Ashland CDP	21,925	320	1.84	462
Atascadero city	28,310	267	25.64	87
Atwater city	28,168	269	6.09	334
Auburn city	13,330	423	7.14	304

Legal Name	2010 Population	Pop. Rank	Land Area (sq. miles)	Area Rank
Avenal city	15,505	384	19.42	126
Avocado Heights CDP	15,411	385	2.71	433
Azusa city	46,361	190	9.66	243
Bakersfield city	347,483	9	142.16	5
Baldwin Park city	75,390	107	6.63	317
Banning city	29,603	258	23.10	100
Barstow city	22,639	316	41.38	41
Bay Point CDP	21,349	326	6.55	320
Beaumont city	36,877	220	30.91	65
Bell city	35,477	227	2.50	442
Bell Gardens city	42,072	204	2.46	443

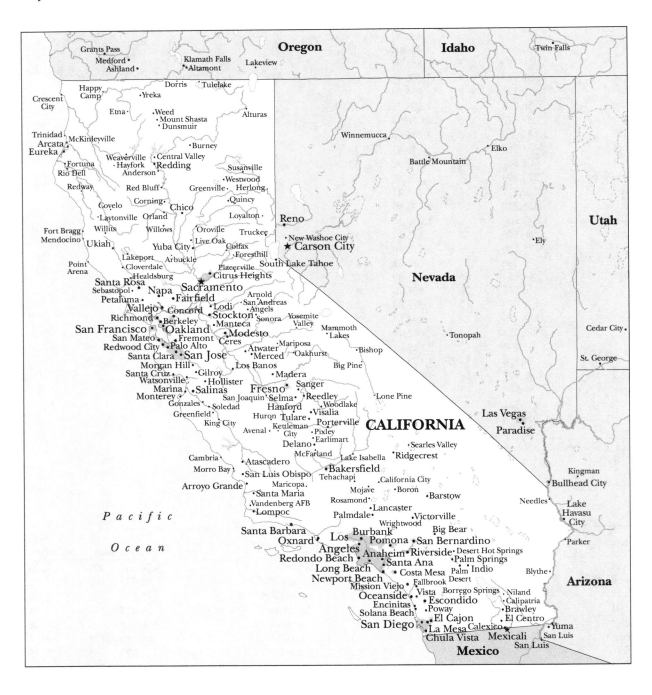

Legal Name	2010 Population	Pop. Rank	Land Area (sq. miles)	Area Rank
Bellflower city	76,616	104	6.12	332
Belmont city	25,835	282	4.62	376
Benicia city	26,997	277	12.93	196
Berkeley city	112,580	53	10.47	230
Beverly Hills city	34,109	237	5.71	345
Big Bear City CDP	12,304	442	31.95	63
Bloomington CDP	23,851	299	5.99	337
Blythe city	20,817	329	26.19	85
Bonita CDP	12,538	438	5.00	364
Bostonia CDP	15,379	386	1.93	456
Brawley city	24,953	289	7.68	285
Brea city	39,282	213	12.08	209
Brentwood city	51,481	172	14.79	174
Buena Park city	80,530	95	10.52	229
Burbank city	103,340	64	17.34	150
Burlingame city	28,806	265	4.41	383
Calabasas city	23,058	309	12.90	197
Calexico city	38,572	215	8.39	272
California City city	14,120	410	203.52	3
Camarillo city	65,201	125	19.53	122
Cameron Park CDP	18,228	356	11.11	219
Camp Pendleton South CDP	10,616	474	3.91	395
Campbell city	39,349	212	5.80	344
Canyon Lake city	10,561	477	3.93	394
Carlsbad city	105,328	60	37.72	49
Carmichael CDP	61,762	139	13.53	189
Carpinteria city	13,040	427	2.59	438
Carson city	91,714	79	18.72	134
Casa de Oro-Mount Helix CDP	18,762	350	6.85	311
Castaic CDP	19,015	348	7.26	300
Castro Valley CDP	61,388	141	16.63	156
Cathedral City city	51,200	174	21.50	112
Ceres city	45,417	193	8.01	276
Cerritos city	49,041	178	8.73	261
Cherryland CDP	14,728	397	1.20	477
Chico city	86,187	85	32.92	61
Chino city	77,983	99	29.64	71
Chino Hills city	74,799	108	44.68	37
Chowchilla city	18,720	351	7.66	287
Chula Vista city	243,916	14	49.63	31
Citrus CDP	10,866	464	0.89	485
Citrus Heights city	83,301	91	14.23	180
Claremont city	34,926	231	13.35	191
Clayton city	10,897	463	3.84	397
Clearlake city	15,250	387	10.13	232
Clovis city	95,631	73	23.28	98
Coachella city	40,704	209	28.95	73
Coalinga city	13,380	421	6.12	332
Colton city	52,154	169	15.32	166
Commerce city	12,823	432	6.54	321
Compton city	96,455	72	10.01	234
Concord city	122,067	47	30.55	67
Corcoran city	24,813	292	7.47	292
Corona city	152,374	33	38.83	47
Coronado city	18,912	349	7.93	279
Costa Mesa city	109,960	55	15.65	164
Coto de Caza CDP	14,866	395	7.95	278

Legal Name	2010 Population	Pop. Rank	Land Area (sq. miles)	Area Rank
Covina city	47,796	188	7.03	306
Crestline CDP	10,770	467	13.84	185
Cudahy city	23,805	300	1.18	480
Culver City city	38,883	214	5.11	361
Cupertino city	58,302	149	11.26	216
Cypress city	47,802	187	6.58	318
Daly City city	101,123	66	7.66	287
Dana Point city	33,351	240	6.50	323
Danville town	42,039	205	18.03	140
Davis city	65,622	124	9.89	237
Del Aire CDP	10,001	487	1.01	483
Delano city	53,041	168	14.30	179
Delhi CDP	10,755	468	3.51	407
Desert Hot Springs city	25,938	281	23.62	96
Diamond Bar city	55,544	157	14.88	171
Diamond Springs CDP	11,037	458	16.64	155
Dinuba city	21,453	324	6.47	325
Discovery Bay CDP	13,352	422	6.22	328
Dixon city	18,351	355	7.00	307
Downey city	111,772	54	12.41	205
Duarte city	21,321	327	6.69	313
Dublin city	46,036	191	14.91	170
East Hemet CDP	17,418	364	5.21	358
East Los Angeles CDP	126,496	44	7.45	295
East Palo Alto city	28,155	270	2.51	441
East Rancho Dominguez CDP	15,135	389	0.82	486
East San Gabriel CDP	14,874	394	1.56	470
Eastvale CDP	53,668	165	11.41	213
El Cajon city	99,478	69	14.43	177
El Centro city	42,598	200	11.08	220
El Cerrito city	23,549	303	3.69	404
El Dorado Hills CDP	42,108	203	48.45	32
El Monte city	113,475	52	9.56	245
El Paso de Robles (Paso Robles) city	29,793	257	19.12	131
El Segundo city	16,654	371	5.46	351
El Sobrante CDP	12,723	433	7.21	302
El Sobrante CDP	12,669	436	2.77	428
Elk Grove city	153,015	31	42.19	39
Emeryville city	10,080	485	1.25	476
Encinitas city	59,518	145	18.81	132
Escondido city	143,911	38	36.81	52
Eureka city	27,191	275	9.38	249
Exeter city	10,334	479	2.46	443
Fair Oaks CDP	30,912	251	10.79	226
Fairfield city	105,321	61	37.39	50
Fairview CDP	10,003	486	2.76	429
Fallbrook CDP	30,534	253	17.53	149
Farmersville city	10,588	476	2.26	449
Fillmore city	15,002	393	3.36	413
Florence-Graham CDP	63,387	133	3.58	405
Florin CDP	47,513	189	8.70	263
Folsom city	72,203	112	21.95	108
Fontana city	196,069	20	42.43	38
Foothill Farms CDP	33,121	242	4.20	386
Fortuna city	11,926	445	4.85	366
Foster City city	30,567	252	3.76	400

Legal Name	2010 Population	Pop. Rank	Land Area (sq. miles)	Area Rank
Fountain Valley city	55,313	159	9.02	255
Fremont city	214,089	15	77.46	12
French Valley CDP	23,067	308	10.87	225
Fresno city	494,665	5	111.96	6
Fullerton city	135,161	42	22.35	104
Galt city	23,647	301	5.93	339
Garden Acres CDP	10,648	471	2.59	438
Garden Grove city	170,883	25	17.94	141
Gardena city	58,829	147	5.83	342
Gilroy city	48,821	180	16.15	160
Glen Avon CDP	20,199	341	8.10	275
Glendale city	191,719	22	30.45	68
Glendora city	50,073	177	19.39	128
Goleta city	29,888	256	7.90	281
Grand Terrace city	12,040	444	3.50	408
Granite Bay CDP	20,402	336	21.53	111
Grass Valley city	12,860	431	4.74	372
Greenfield city	16,330	373	2.14	452
Grover Beach city	13,156	424	2.31	447
Hacienda Heights CDP	54,038	162	11.18	217
Half Moon Bay city	11,324	454	6.42	326
Hanford city	53,967	163	16.59	157
Hawaiian Gardens city	14,254	408	0.95	484
Hawthorne city	84,293	89	6.08	335
Hayward city	144,186	37	45.32	36
Healdsburg city	11,254	456	4.46	380
Hemet city	78,657	98	27.85	78
Hercules city	24,060	297	6.21	329
Hermosa Beach city	19,506	345	1.43	475
Hesperia city	90,173	80	73.10	15
Highland city	53,104	167	18.76	133
Hillsborough town	10,825	465	6.19	331
Hollister city	34,928	230	7.29	297
Home Gardens CDP	11,570	449	1.56	470
Huntington Beach city	189,992	23	26.75	84
Huntington Park city	58,114	150	3.01	423
Imperial city	14,758	396	5.86	340
Imperial Beach city	26,324	279	4.16	387
Indio city	76,036	105	29.18	72
Inglewood city	109,673	56	9.07	254
Irvine city	212,375	16	66.11	16
Isla Vista CDP	23,096	307	1.85	459
Kerman city	13,544	419	3.23	417
King City city	12,874	429	3.84	397
Kingsburg city	11,382	453	2.83	427
La Cañada Flintridge city	20,246	340	8.63	266
La Crescenta-Montrose CDP	19,653	344	3.43	411
La Habra city	60,239	143	7.37	296
La Mesa city	57,065	154	9.08	253
La Mirada city	48,527	182	7.84	282
La Palma city	15,568	381	1.81	464
La Presa CDP	34,169	236	5.50	349
La Puente city	39,816	210	3.48	409
La Quinta city	37,467	218	35.12	57
La Riviera CDP	10,802	466	1.85	459
La Verne city	31,063	250	8.43	270
Ladera Ranch CDP	22,980	310	4.90	365

Legal Name	2010 Population	Pop. Rank	Land Area (sq. miles)	Area Rank
Lafayette city	23,893	298	15.22	168
Laguna Beach city	22,723	313	8.85	259
Laguna Hills city	30,344	254	6.67	315
Laguna Niguel city	62,979	135	14.83	173
Laguna Woods city	16,192	375	3.12	420
Lake Arrowhead CDP	12,424	439	17.73	146
Lake Elsinore city	51,821	171	36.21	55
Lake Forest city	77,264	101	17.82	144
Lake Los Angeles CDP	12,328	441	9.74	240
Lakeland Village CDP	11,541	451	8.68	265
Lakeside CDP	20,648	332	6.90	309
Lakewood city	80,048	96	9.41	248
Lamont CDP	15,120	390	4.59	377
Lancaster city	156,633	30	94.28	9
Larkspur city	11,926	445	3.03	422
Lathrop city	18,023	358	21.93	109
Lawndale city	32,769	244	1.97	455
Lemon Grove city	25,320	287	3.88	396
Lemon Hill CDP	13,729	416	1.63	468
Lemoore city	24,531	293	8.52	268
Lennox CDP	22,753	312	1.09	482
Lincoln city	42,819	197	20.11	118
Linda CDP	17,773	360	8.55	267
Lindsay city	11,768	447	2.61	437
Live Oak CDP	17,158	368	3.24	416
Livermore city	80,968	94	25.17	88
Livingston city	13,058	426	3.72	403
Lodi city	62,134	138	13.61	186
Loma Linda city	23,261	305	7.52	291
Lomita city	20,256	339	1.91	457
Lompoc city	42,434	202	11.60	211
Long Beach city	462,257	7	50.29	28
Los Alamitos city	11,449	452	4.05	391
Los Altos city	28,976	263	6.49	324
Los Angeles city	3,792,621	1	468.67	1
Los Banos city	35,972	224	9.99	235
Los Gatos town	29,413	259	11.08	220
Los Osos CDP	14,276	407	12.76	200
Lynwood city	69,772	115	4.84	367
Madera city	61,416	140	15.79	163
Magalia CDP	11,310	455	14.01	182
Malibu city	12,645	437	19.78	119
Manhattan Beach city	35,135	229	3.94	393
Manteca city	67,096	121	17.73	146
Marina city	19,718	343	8.88	257
Martinez city	35,824	225	12.13	207
Marysville city	12,072	443	3.46	410
Maywood city	27,395	274	1.18	480
McFarland city	12,707	434	2.67	435
McKinleyville CDP	15,177	388	20.80	115
Mead Valley CDP	18,510	353	19.17	130
Mendota city	11,014	460	3.28	414
Menifee city	77,519	100	46.47	34
Menlo Park city	32,026	247	9.79	239
Merced city	78,958	97	23.32	97
Mill Valley city	13,903	413	4.76	371
Millbrae city	21,532	323	3.25	415
Milpitas city	66,790	122	13.59	188

Legal Name	2010 Population	Pop. Rank	Land Area (sq. miles)	Area Rank
Mira Loma CDP	21,930	319	8.00	277
Mission Viejo city	93,305	76	17.74	145
Modesto city	201,165	18	36.87	51
Monrovia city	36,590	222	13.60	187
Montclair city	36,664	221	5.52	347
Montebello city	62,500	137	8.33	273
Monterey city	27,810	272	8.47	269
Monterey Park city	60,269	142	7.67	286
Moorpark city	34,421	233	12.58	204
Moraga town	16,016	378	9.43	246
Moreno Valley city	193,365	21	51.27	27
Morgan Hill city	37,882	217	12.88	198
Morro Bay city	10,234	481	5.30	355
Mountain View city	74,066	109	12.00	210
Murrieta city	103,466	63	33.58	59
Muscoy CDP	10,644	473	3.14	419
Napa city	76,915	102	17.84	142
National City city	58,582	148	7.28	298
Newark city	42,573	201	13.87	184
Newman city	10,224	482	2.10	453
Newport Beach city	85,186	87	23.80	94
Nipomo CDP	16,714	370	14.85	172
Norco city	27,063	276	13.96	183
North Auburn CDP	13,022	428	7.80	283
North Fair Oaks CDP	14,687	398	1.20	477
North Highlands CDP	42,694	199	8.83	260
North Tustin CDP	24,917	290	6.67	315
Norwalk city	105,549	59	9.71	241
Novato city	51,904	170	27.44	79
Oak Park CDP	13,811	414	5.29	357
Oakdale city	20,675	331	6.04	336
Oakland city	390,724	8	55.79	23
Oakley city	35,432	228	15.85	162
Oceanside city	167,086	27	41.23	43
Oildale CDP	32,684	245	6.53	322
Olivehurst CDP	13,656	418	7.47	292
Ontario city	163,924	29	49.94	29
Orange city	136,416	41	24.80	89
Orangevale CDP	33,960	238	11.52	212
Orcutt CDP	28,905	264	11.12	218
Orinda city	17,643	361	12.68	202
Oroville city	15,546	382	12.99	194
Oxnard city	197,899	19	26.89	81
Pacific Grove city	15,041	392	2.86	425
Pacifica city	37,234	219	12.66	203
Palm Desert city	48,445	183	26.81	82
Palm Springs city	44,552	195	94.12	10
Palmdale city	152,750	32	105.96	7
Palo Alto city	64,403	128	23.88	93
Palos Verdes Estates city	13,438	420	4.77	370
Paradise town	26,218	280	18.31	138
Paramount city	54,098	161	4.73	373
Parkway CDP	14,670	399	2.42	445
Parlier city	14,494	402	2.19	450
Pasadena city	137,122	40	22.97	101
Patterson city	20,413	335	5.95	338
Pedley CDP	12,672	435	5.08	362
Perris city	68,386	120	31.39	64

Legal Name	2010 Population	Pop. Rank	Land Area (sq. miles)	Area Rank
Petaluma city	57,941	151	14.38	178
Phelan CDP	14,304	405	60.10	18
Pico Rivera city	62,942	136	8.30	274
Piedmont city	10,667	470	1.68	467
Pinole city	18,390	354	5.32	353
Pittsburg city	63,264	134	17.22	151
Placentia city	50,533	176	6.57	319
Placerville city	10,389	478	5.81	343
Pleasant Hill city	33,152	241	7.07	305
Pleasanton city	70,285	114	24.11	92
Pomona city	149,058	35	22.95	102
Port Hueneme city	21,723	321	4.45	381
Porterville city	54,165	160	17.61	148
Poway city	47,811	186	39.08	46
Prunedale CDP	17,560	362	46.05	35
Quartz Hill CDP	10,912	462	3.76	400
Ramona CDP	20,292	338	38.41	48
Rancho Cordova city	64,776	127	33.51	60
Rancho Cucamonga city	165,269	28	39.85	45
Rancho Mirage city	17,218	367	24.45	90
Rancho Palos Verdes city	41,643	206	13.46	190
Rancho San Diego CDP	21,208	328	8.70	263
Rancho Santa Margarita city	47,853	184	12.96	195
Red Bluff city	14,076	411	7.56	290
Redding city	89,861	81	59.65	19
Redlands city	68,747	118	36.13	56
Redondo Beach city	66,748	123	6.20	330
Redwood City city	76,815	103	19.42	126
Reedley city	24,194	295	5.08	362
Rialto city	99,171	70	22.35	104
Richmond city	103,701	62	30.07	70
Ridgecrest city	27,616	273	20.77	116
Rio Linda CDP	15,106	391	9.90	236
Ripon city	14,297	406	5.30	355
Riverbank city	22,678	315	4.09	390
Riverside city	303,871	12	81.14	11
Rocklin city	56,974	155	19.54	121
Rohnert Park city	40,971	208	7.00	307
Rosamond CDP	18,150	357	52.12	26
Rosedale CDP	14,058	412	33.96	58
Rosemead city	53,764	164	5.16	359
Rosemont CDP	22,681	314	4.35	385
Roseville city	118,788	48	36.22	54
Rossmoor CDP	10,244	480	1.54	472
Rowland Heights CDP	48,993	179	13.08	193
Rubidoux CDP	34,280	235	9.66	243
Sacramento city	466,488	6	97.92	8
Salida CDP	13,722	417	5.32	353
Salinas city	150,441	34	23.18	99
San Anselmo town	12,336	440	2.68	434
San Bernardino city	209,924	17	59.20	20
San Bruno city	41,114	207	5.48	350
San Buenaventura (Ventura) city	106,433	57	21.65	110
San Carlos city	28,406	266	5.54	346
San Clemente city	63,522	132	18.71	135
San Diego city	1,307,402	2	325.19	2

Legal Name	2010 Population	Pop. Rank	Land Area (sq. miles)	Area Rank
San Diego Country Estates CDP	10,109	484	16.85	154
San Dimas city	33,371	239	15.04	169
San Fernando city	23,645	302	2.37	446
San Francisco city	805,235	4	46.87	33
San Gabriel city	39,718	211	4.14	388
San Jacinto city	44,199	196	25.72	86
San Jose city	945,942	3	176.53	4
San Juan Capistrano city	34,593	232	14.12	181
San Leandro city	84,950	88	13.34	192
San Lorenzo CDP	23,452	304	2.76	429
San Luis Obispo city	45,119	194	12.78	199
San Marcos city	83,781	90	24.37	91
San Marino city	13,147	425	3.77	399
San Mateo city	97,207	71	12.13	207
San Pablo city	29,139	262	2.63	436
San Rafael city	57,713	152	16.47	158
San Ramon city	72,148	113	18.06	139
Sanger city	24,270	294	5.52	347
Santa Ana city	324,528	11	27.27	80
Santa Barbara city	88,410	84	19.47	124
Santa Clara city	116,468	49	18.41	137
Santa Clarita city	176,320	24	52.72	25
Santa Cruz city	59,946	144	12.74	201
Santa Fe Springs city	16,223	374	8.87	258
Santa Maria city	99,553	68	22.76	103
Santa Monica city	89,736	82	8.41	271
Santa Paula city	29,321	260	4.59	377
Santa Rosa city	167,815	26	41.29	42
Santee city	53,413	166	16.24	159
Saratoga city	29,926	255	12.38	206
Scotts Valley city	11,580	448	4.59	377
Seal Beach city	24,168	296	11.29	215
Seaside city	33,025	243	9.24	250
Selma city	23,219	306	5.14	360
Shafter city	16,988	369	27.94	76
Shasta Lake city	10,164	483	10.92	224
Sierra Madre city	10,917	461	2.95	424
Signal Hill city	11,016	459	2.19	450
Simi Valley city	124,237	46	41.48	40
Solana Beach city	12,867	430	3.52	406
Soledad city	25,738	283	4.41	383
Sonoma city	10,648	471	2.74	431
South El Monte city	20,116	342	2.84	426
South Gate city	94,396	74	7.24	301
South Lake Tahoe city	21,403	325	10.16	231
South Pasadena city	25,619	284	3.41	412
South San Francisco city	63,632	131	9.14	251
South San Jose Hills CDP	20,551	334	1.51	473
South Whittier CDP	57,156	153	5.34	352
Spring Valley CDP	28,205	268	7.17	303
Stanford CDP	13,809	415	2.73	432
Stanton city	38,186	216	3.15	418
Stevenson Ranch CDP	17,557	363	6.36	327
Stockton city	291,707	13	61.67	17
Suisun City city	28,111	271	4.11	389
Sun Village CDP	11,565	450	10.69	227
Sunnyvale city	140,081	39	21.99	107
Susanville city	17,947	359	7.93	279
Tamalpais-Homestead Valley CDP	10,735	469	4.64	375
Tehachapi city	14,414	403	9.87	238
Temecula city	100,097	67	30.15	69
Temescal Valley CDP	22,535	318	19.30	129
Temple City city	35,558	226	4.01	392
Thousand Oaks city	126,683	43	55.03	24
Torrance city	145,438	36	20.48	117
Tracy city	82,922	93	22.00	106
Truckee town	16,180	376	32.32	62
Tulare city	59,278	146	20.93	114
Turlock city	68,549	119	16.93	153
Tustin city	75,540	106	11.08	220
Twentynine Palms city	25,048	288	59.14	21
Ukiah city	16,075	377	4.67	374
Union City city	69,516	116	19.47	124
Upland city	73,732	111	15.62	165
Vacaville city	92,428	77	28.37	74
Valinda CDP	22,822	311	2.01	454
Valle Vista CDP	14,578	400	6.87	310
Vallejo city	115,942	50	30.67	66
Victorville city	115,903	51	73.18	14
View Park-Windsor Hills CDP	11,075	457	1.84	462
Vincent CDP	15,922	380	1.47	474
Vineyard CDP	24,836	291	17.21	152
Visalia city	124,442	45	36.25	53
Vista city	93,834	75	18.68	136
Walnut city	29,172	261	8.99	256
Walnut Creek city	64,173	130	19.76	120
Walnut Park CDP	15,966	379	0.75	487
Wasco city	25,545	285	9.43	246
Watsonville city	51,199	175	6.69	313
West Carson CDP	21,699	322	2.27	448
West Covina city	106,098	58	16.04	161
West Hollywood city	34,399	234	1.89	458
West Puente Valley CDP	22,636	317	1.76	466
West Sacramento city	48,744	181	21.43	113
West Whittier-Los Nietos CDP	25,540	286	2.52	440
Westminster city	89,701	83	10.05	233
Westmont CDP	31,853	248	1.85	459
Whittier city	85,331	86	14.65	175
Wildomar city	32,176	246	23.69	95
Willowbrook CDP	35,983	223	3.76	400
Windsor town	26,801	278	7.27	299
Winter Gardens CDP	20,631	333	4.43	382
Winton CDP	10,613	475	3.04	421
Woodcrest CDP	14,347	404	11.41	213
Woodland city	55,468	158	15.30	167
Yorba Linda city	64,234	129	19.48	123
Yuba City city	64,925	126	14.58	176
Yucaipa city	51,367	173	27.89	77
Yucca Valley town	20,700	330	40.02	44

Note: CDP–Census Designated Place
Source: U.S. Census Bureau, 2010 Census

Survey Says...

This section presents current rankings from dozens of public and private sources. It shows how this state ranks in a number of critical categories, including education, job growth, cost of living, teen drivers, energy efficiency, and business environment. Sources include *Forbes, Reuters, U.S. News and World Report, CNN Money, Gallup,* and *Huffington Post.*

- CNN Money compiled a list of "Ten Most Entrepreneurial States" based on the Kauffman Index of Entrepreneurial Activity. California ranked #6 among the 50 states in 2012 for number of startups per 100,000 adult residents.
  CNN Money, June 20, 2013; money.cnn.com

- California ranked #6 in a government study measuring real gross domestic product (GDP)—the output of goods and services produced by labor and property located in the United States. The ranking is based on the percentage change compared with 2011 GDP.
  U.S. Department of Commerce, Bureau of Economic Analysis, June 2013; www.bea.gov

- California ranked #1 in a government study measuring real gross domestic product (GDP)—the output of goods and services produced by labor and property located in the United States. The ranking is based on the dollar value of its GDP.
  U.S. Department of Commerce, Bureau of Economic Analysis, June 2013; www.bea.gov

- California ranked #36 in the 17th edition of "Quality Counts; State of the States," Education Week's "report card" surveying key education indicators, policy efforts, and educational outcomes.
  Education Week, January 4, 2013 (online) and January 10, 2013 (print); www.edweek.org

- SERI (Science and Engineering Readiness Index) weighs the performance of the states' K-12 schools in preparing students in physics and calculus, the high school subjects considered most important for future scientists and engineers. California ranked #34.
  Newsletter of the Forum on Education of the American Physical Society, Summer 2011 issue; www.huffingtonpost.com, July 11, 2011; updated October 1, 2012

- ND Parks, the "site for North Dakota Parks," named California as one of the "Top Five States to Visit for RV Camping Trips."
  www.ndparks.com, consulted 18 July 2013

- MoneyRates.com ranked California #29 on its list of the best to worst states for making a living. Criteria: average income; inflation; employment prospects; and workers' Workplace Environment assessments according to the Gallup-Healthways Well-Being Index.
  www.money-rates.com, posted April 1, 2013

- *Forbes* analyzed business costs, labor supply, regulatory environment, current economic climate, growth prospects, and quality of life, to compile its "Best States for Business" rankings. California ranked #41.
  www.forbes.com. posted December 12, 2012

- The 2012 Gallup-Healthways Well-Being Index, surveyed American's opinions on economic confidence, workplace perceptions, community climate, personal choices, and health predictors to assess the "future livability" of each state. California ranked #18.
  "Utah Poised to Be the Best State to Live In," Gallup Wellbeing, www.gallup.com, August 7, 2012

- On CNBC's list of "America's Top States for Business 2013," California ranked #47. Criteria: measures of competitiveness developed with input from the National Association of Manufacturers, the Council on Competitiveness, and other business groups weighed with the states' own marketing criteria.
  www.cnbc.com, consulted July 19, 2013

- California ranked #1 on the "best" end of the Christian Science Monitor's list of "States with the Best (and Worst) Job Growth," as indicated by year-over-year growth rates from May 2012 to May 2013.
  www.csmonitor.com, July 5, 2013

- California ranked #10 on MoneyRates list of "Best-and Worst-States to Retire 2012." Criteria: life expectancy, crime rate, climate, economic conditions, taxes, job opportunities, and cost of living.
  www.money-rates.com, October 22, 2012

- California ranked #48 on the 2013 Bankrate "Best Places to Retire" list ranking the states and District of Columbia on various criteria relating to health, safety, and cost.
  www.bankrate.com, May 6, 2013

- Reuters ranked California #6 on its list of the "Ten Most Expensive States in America." Rankings are based on the U.S. Commerce Department's prototype cost-of-living index comparing price levels across the states for a standardized mix of goods and services.
  www.huffingtonpost.com, posted June 12, 2013

- California ranked #12 on the Social Science Research Council's "American Human Development Report: The Measure of America," assessing the 50 states plus the District of Columbia on health, education, and living-standard criteria.
  The Measure of America 2013-2014, posted June 19, 2013; www.measureofamerica.org

- California ranked #30 on the Foundation for Child Development's (FCD) Child Well-being Index (CWI). The FCD used the KIDS COUNT report and the National Survey of Children's Health, the only state-level source for several key indicators of child well-being.
  Foundation for Child Development, January 18, 2012; fcd-us.org

- California ranked #41 overall according to the 2013 KIDS COUNT Data Book, a project of the Annie E. Casey Foundation. Criteria: children's economic well-being, education, health, and family and community indicators.
  KIDS COUNT Data Center's Data Book, released June 20, 2013; http://datacenter.kidscount.org

- California ranked #46 in the children's economic well-being category by the 2013 KIDS COUNT Data Book, a project of the Annie E. Casey Foundation.
KIDS COUNT Data Center's Data Book, released June 20, 2013; http://datacenter.kidscount.org

- California ranked #39 in the children's educational opportunities and attainments category by the 2013 KIDS COUNT Data Book, a project of the Annie E. Casey Foundation.
KIDS COUNT Data Center's Data Book, released June 20, 2013; http://datacenter.kidscount.org

- California ranked #29 in the children's health category by the 2013 KIDS COUNT Data Book, a project of the Annie E. Casey Foundation.
KIDS COUNT Data Center's Data Book, released June 20, 2013; http://datacenter.kidscount.org

- California ranked #42 in the family and community circumstances that factor into children's well-being category by the 2013 KIDS COUNT Data Book, a project of the Annie E. Casey Foundation.
KIDS COUNT Data Center's Data Book, released June 20, 2013; http://datacenter.kidscount.org

- California ranked #18 in the 2012 Gallup-Healthways Well-Being Index. Criteria: emotional health; physical health; healthy behavior; work environment; basic access to food, shelter, health care; and a safe and satisfying place to live.
2012 State of Well-Being, Gallup-Healthways Well-Being Index, released February 28, 2013; www.well-beingindex.com

- *U.S. News and World Report's* "Best States for Teen Drivers" rankings are based on driving and road safety laws, federal reports on driver's licenses, car accident fatality, and road-quality statistics. California ranked #2.
U.S. News and World Report, March 18, 2010; www.usnews.com

- The Yahoo! Sports service Rivals.com ranks the states according to the strength of their high school football programs. California ranked #5.
"Ranking the States: Where Is the Best Football Played?," November 18, 2011; highschool.rivals.com

- iVillage ranked the states by hospitable living conditions for women. Criteria: economic success, access to affordable childcare, health care, reproductive rights, female representation in government, and educational attainment. California ranked #5.
iVillage, "50 Best to Worst States for Women," March 14, 2012; www.ivillage.com

- The League of American Bicyclists's "Bicycle Friendly States" ranked California #19. Criteria: legislation and enforcement, policies and programs, infrastructure and funding, education and advocacy, and evaluation and planning.
"Washington Tops the Bicycle-Friendly State Ranking," May 1, 2013; bicycling.com

- The federal Corporation for National and Community Service ranked the states and the District of Columbia by volunteer rates. California ranked #37 for community service.
"Volunteering and Civic Life in America 2012," www.volunteeringinamerica.gov, accessed July 24, 2013

- The Hospital Safety Score ranked states and the District of Columbia on their hospitals' performance scores. California ranked #11. Criteria: avoiding preventable harm and medical errors, as demonstrated by 26 hospital safety metrics.
Spring 2013 Hospital Safety Score, May 8, 2013; www.hospitalsafetyscore.org

- GMAC Insurance ranked the states and the District of Columbia by the performance of their drivers on the GMAC Insurance National Drivers Test, comprised of DMV test questions. California ranked #34.
"2011 GMAC Insurance National Drivers Test," www.gmacinsurance.com, accessed July 23, 2013

- California ranked #4 in a "State Integrity Investigation" analysis of laws and practices intended to deter corruption and promote accountability and openness in campaign finance, ethics laws, lobbying regulations and management of state pension funds.
"What's Your State's Grade?," www.publicintegrity.org, accessed July 23, 2013

- California ranked #4 among the states and the District of Columbia in total rail miles, as tracked by the Association of American Railroads.
"U.S. Freight Railroad Industry Snapshot: Railroads and States: Total Rail Miles by State: 2011"; www.aar.org, accessed July 23, 2013

- According to statistics compiled by the Beer Institute, California ranked #44 among the states and the District of Columbia in per capita beer consumption of persons 21 years or older.
"Shipments of Malt Beverages and Per Capita Consumption by State 2012;" www.beerinstitute.org

- According to Concordia University's "Public Education Costs per Pupil by State Rankings," based on statistics gathered by the U.S. Census Bureau, which includes the District of Columbia, California ranked #35.
Concordia University Online; education.cu-portland.edu, accessed July 24, 2013

- California ranked #10 among the states and the District of Columbia in population density based on U.S. Census Bureau data for resident population and total land area. "List of U.S. States by Population Density."
www.wikipedia.org, accessed July 24, 2013

- In "America's Health Rankings, 2012 Edition," by the United Health Foundation, California ranked #22. Criteria included: rate of high school graduation; violent crime rate; incidence of infectious disease; childhood immunizations; prevalence of diabetes; per capita public-health funding; percentage of uninsured population; rate of children in poverty; and availability of primary-care physicians.
United Health Foundation; www.americashealthrankings.org, accessed July 24, 2013

- The TechNet 2012 "State Broadband Index" ranked California #5 on the following criteria: broadband adoption; network quality; and economic structure. Improved broadband use is hoped to promote economic development, build strong communities, improve delivery of government services and upgrade educational systems.
TechNet; www.technet.org, accessed July 24, 2013

- California was ranked #2 among the states and District of Columbia on the American Council for an Energy-Efficient Economy's "State Energy Efficiency Scorecard" for 2012.
American Council for an Energy-Efficient Economy; aceee.org/sector/state-policy/scorecard, accessed July 24, 2013

Statistical Tables

DEMOGRAPHICS
Resident State and National Population, 1950-2012
Projected State and National Population, 2000-2030
Population by Age, 2012
Population by Race, 2012
Population by Hispanic Origin and Race, 2012

VITAL STATISTICS
Death Rates by Leading Causes, 2010
Death Rates by Selected Causes, 2010
Abortion Rates, 2009
Infant Mortality Rates, 1995-2009
Marriage and Divorce Rates, 2000-2011

ECONOMY
Nominal Gross Domestic Product by Industry, 2012
Real Gross Domestic Product, 2000-2012
Personal Income Per Capita, 1930-2012
Non-Farm Employment by Sector, 2012
Foreign Exports, 2000-2012
Energy Consumption, 2011

LAND AND WATER
Surface Area and Federally-Owned Land, 2007
Land Cover/Use of Non-Federal Rural Land, 2007
Farms and Crop Acreage, 2012

HEALTH AND MEDICAL CARE
Medical Professionals, 2012
Health Insurance Coverage, 2011
HIV, STD, and Tuberculosis Cases and Rates, 2011
Cigarette Smoking, 2011

HOUSING
Home Ownership Rates, 1995-2012
Home Sales, 2000-2010
Value of Owner-Occupied Homes, 2011

EDUCATION
School Enrollment, 2011
Educational Attainment, 2011
Public College Finances, FY 2012

TRANSPORTATION AND TRAVEL
Motor Vehicle Registrations and Drivers Licenses, 2011
Domestic Travel Expenditures, 2009
Retail Gasoline Prices, 2013
Public Road Length, 2011

CRIME AND LAW ENFORCEMENT
Full-Time Law Enforcement Officers, 2011
Prison Population, 2000-2012
Crime Rate, 2011

GOVERNMENT AND FINANCE
Local Governments by Type, 2012
State Government Revenue, 2011
State Government Expenditures, 2011
State Government General Expenditures by Function, 2011
State Government Finances, Cash and Debt, 2011

POLITICS
Composition of the Senate, 1995-2013
Composition of the House of Representatives, 1995-2013
Composition of State Legislature, 2004-2013
Voter Participation in Presidential Elections, 1980-2012
Governors Since Statehood

DEMOGRAPHICS

Resident State and National Population, 1950–2012

Year	State Population	U.S. Population	State Share
1950	10,586,000	151,326,000	7.00%
1960	15,717,000	179,323,000	8.76%
1970	19,971,069	203,302,031	9.82%
1980	23,667,902	226,545,805	10.45%
1990	29,760,021	248,709,873	11.97%
2000	33,871,653	281,424,600	12.04%
2010	37,253,956	308,745,538	12.07%
2012	38,041,430	313,914,040	12.12%

Note: 1950/1960 population figures are rounded to the nearest thousand.
Source: U.S. Census Bureau, Decennial Census 1950–2010; U.S. Census Bureau, 2012 Population Estimates

Projected State and National Population, 2000–2030

Year	State Population	U.S. Population	State Share
2000	33,871,648	281,421,906	12.04%
2005	36,038,859	295,507,134	12.20%
2010	38,067,134	308,935,581	12.32%
2015	40,123,232	322,365,787	12.45%
2020	42,206,743	335,804,546	12.57%
2025	44,305,177	349,439,199	12.68%
2030	46,444,861	363,584,435	12.77%
State population growth, 2000–2030			12,573,213
State percentage growth, 2000–2030			37.1%

Source: U.S. Census Bureau, Population Division, Interim State Population Projections, 2005

Population by Age, 2012

Age Group	State Population	Percent of Total Population	
		State	U.S.
Under 5 years	2,541,497	6.7%	6.4%
5 to 14 years	5,086,457	13.4%	13.1%
15 to 24 years	5,633,508	14.8%	14.0%
25 to 34 years	5,482,640	14.4%	13.5%
35 to 44 years	5,161,434	13.6%	12.9%
45 to 54 years	5,231,936	13.8%	14.1%
55 to 64 years	4,303,873	11.3%	12.3%
65 to 74 years	2,539,119	6.7%	7.6%
75 to 84 years	1,406,685	3.7%	4.2%
85 years and older	654,281	1.7%	1.9%
Under 18 years	9,240,219	24.3%	23.5%
65 years and older	4,600,085	12.1%	13.7%
Median age (years)	–	35.5	37.4

Source: U.S. Census Bureau, Annual Estimates of the Resident Population for Selected Age Groups by Sex for the United States, States, Counties, and Puerto Rico Commonwealth and Municipios: April 1, 2010 to July 1, 2012

Population by Race, 2012

Race	State Population	Percent of Total Population	
		State	U.S.
All residents	38,041,430	100.00%	100.00%
White	28,033,826	73.69%	77.89%
African American	2,515,716	6.61%	13.13%
Native American	639,740	1.68%	1.23%
Asian	5,294,255	13.92%	5.14%
Native Hawaiian	187,855	0.49%	0.23%
Two or more races	1,370,038	3.60%	2.39%

Source: U.S. Census Bureau, Population Division, Annual Estimates of the Resident Population by Sex, Race and Hispanic Origin for the United States, States, and Counties: April 1, 2010 to July 1, 2012

Population by Hispanic Origin and Race, 2012

Hispanic Origin/Race	State Population	Percent of Total Population	
		State	U.S.
All residents	38,041,430	100.00%	100.00%
All Hispanic residents	14,537,666	38.22%	16.89%
Hispanic			
White	13,062,484	34.34%	14.91%
African American	313,676	0.82%	0.79%
Native American	474,518	1.25%	0.49%
Asian	230,682	0.61%	0.17%
Native Hawaiian	50,922	0.13%	0.06%
Two or more races	405,384	1.07%	0.48%
Not Hispanic			
White	14,971,342	39.36%	62.98%
African American	2,202,040	5.79%	12.34%
Native American	165,222	0.43%	0.74%
Asian	5,063,573	13.31%	4.98%
Native Hawaiian	136,933	0.36%	0.17%
Two or more races	964,654	2.54%	1.91%

Source: U.S. Census Bureau, Population Division, Annual Estimates of the Resident Population by Sex, Race and Hispanic Origin for the United States, States, and Counties: April 1, 2010 to July 1, 2012

VITAL STATISTICS

Death Rates by Leading Causes, 2010

Cause	State	U.S.
Malignant neoplasms	168.7	186.2
Ischaemic heart diseases	118.8	122.9
Other forms of heart disease	39.5	53.4
Chronic lower respiratory diseases	39.2	44.7
Cerebrovascular diseases	40.9	41.9
Organic, incl. symptomatic, mental disorders	20.4	35.7
Other degenerative diseases of the nervous sys.	33.7	28.4
Other external causes of accidental injury	20.0	26.5
Diabetes mellitus	21.1	22.4
Hypertensive diseases	24.4	20.4
All causes	693.5	799.5

Note: Figures are age-adjusted death rates per 100,000 population
Source: CDC/NCHS, Underlying Cause of Death 1999–2010 on CDC WONDER Online Database

Death Rates by Selected Causes, 2010

Cause	State	U.S.
Assault	4.9	5.2
Diseases of the liver	14.8	13.9
Human immunodeficiency virus (HIV) disease	2.0	2.7
Influenza and pneumonia	17.6	16.2
Intentional self-harm	10.8	12.4
Malnutrition	0.6	0.9
Obesity and other hyperalimentation	1.4	1.8
Renal failure	7.3	14.4
Transport accidents	8.6	12.1
Viral hepatitis	3.8	2.4

Note: Figures are age-adjusted death rates per 100,000 population; A dash indicates that data was not available or was suppressed
Source: CDC/NCHS, Underlying Cause of Death 1999–2010 on CDC WONDER Online Database

Abortion Rates, 2009

Category	2009
By state of residence	
Total abortions	–
Abortion rate[1]	–%
Abortion ratio[2]	–
By state of occurrence	
Total abortions	–
Abortion rate[1]	–%
Abortion ratio[2]	–
Abortions obtained by out-of-state residents	–%
U.S. abortion rate[1]	15.1%
U.S. abortion ratio[2]	227

Note: (1) Number of abortions per 1,000 women aged 15–44 years; (2) Number of abortions per 1,000 live births; A dash indicates that data was not available
Source: CDC/NCHS, Morbidity and Mortality Weekly Report, November 23, 2012 (Abortion Surveillance, United States, 2009)

Infant Mortality Rates, 1995–2009

Category	1995	2000	2005	2009
All state residents	6.30	5.42	5.32	4.91
All U.S. residents	7.57	6.89	6.86	6.39
All state white residents	5.78	5.02	4.99	4.58
All U.S. white residents	6.30	5.71	5.73	5.33
All state black residents	13.29	11.61	11.84	10.11
All U.S. black residents	14.58	13.48	13.26	12.12

Note: Figures represent deaths per 1,000 live births of resident infants under one year old, exclusive of fetal deaths; A dash indicates that data was not available or was suppressed.
Source: Centers of Disease Control and Prevention, Division of Vital Statistics, Linked Birth/Infant Death Records on CDC Wonder Online

Marriage and Divorce Rates, 2000–2011

Year	Marriage Rate		Divorce Rate	
	State	U.S.	State	U.S.
2000	6.5	8.2	0.0	4.0
2002	6.1	8.0	0.0	3.9
2004	6.4	7.8	0.0	3.7
2006	6.2	7.5	0.0	3.7
2008	5.8	7.1	0.0	3.5
2010	5.8	6.8	0.0	3.6
2011	1.0	6.8	0.0	3.6

Note: Rates are based on provisional counts of marriages/divorces by state of occurrence and are per 1,000 total population residing in area
Source: CDC/NCHS, National Vital Statistics System

ECONOMY

Nominal Gross Domestic Product by Industry, 2012
In millions of current dollars

Industry	State GDP
Accommodation and food services	57,327
Administrative and waste management services	62,410
Agriculture, forestry, fishing, and hunting	30,177
Arts, entertainment, and recreation	26,951
Construction	62,210
Educational services	21,866
Finance and insurance	114,577
Health care and social assistance	130,265
Information	144,099
Management of companies and enterprises	29,178
Manufacturing	213,257
Mining	19,552
Other services, except government	49,011
Professional, scientific, and technical services	188,733
Real estate and rental and leasing	309,148
Retail trade	124,973
Transportation and warehousing	49,883
Utilities	33,652
Wholesale trade	112,606

Source: U.S. Department of Commerce, Bureau of Economic Analysis, Survey of Current Business

Real Gross Domestic Product, 2000–2012
In millions of chained 2005 dollars

Year	State GDP	U.S. GDP	State Share
2000	1,472,323	11,225,406	13.12%
2005	1,688,949	12,539,116	13.47%
2010	1,672,473	12,897,088	12.97%
2012	1,751,002	13,430,576	13.04%

Source: U.S. Department of Commerce, Bureau of Economic Analysis, Survey of Current Business

Personal Income Per Capita, 1930–2012

Year	State	U.S.
1930	$887	$618
1940	$845	$593
1950	$1,871	$1,503
1960	$2,822	$2,268
1970	$4,801	$4,084
1980	$11,928	$10,091
1990	$21,380	$19,354
2000	$33,404	$30,319
2010	$41,893	$39,791
2012	$44,980	$42,693

Source: U.S. Department of Commerce, Bureau of Economic Analysis, Regional Economic Accounts

Non-Farm Employment by Sector, 2012
In thousands

Sector	Employment
Construction	587.5
Education and health services	1,879.2
Financial activities	774.6
Government	2,375.1
Information	430.4
Leisure and hospitality	1,599.1
Mining and logging	30.1
Manufacturing	1,252.8
Other services	505.7
Professional and business services	2,235.1
Trade, transportation, and utilities	2,725.1
All sectors	14,394.5

Source: U.S. Bureau of Labor Statistics, State and Area Employment

Foreign Exports, 2000–2012
In millions of dollars

Year	State Exports	U.S. Exports	State Share
2000	119,640	712,054	16.80%
2002	92,177	649,940	14.18%
2004	110,143	768,554	14.33%
2006	127,770	973,994	13.12%
2008	144,805	1,222,545	11.84%
2010	143,208	1,208,080	11.85%
2012	161,879	1,478,268	10.95%

Note: U.S. figures exclude data from Puerto Rico, U.S. Virgin Islands, and unallocated exports
Source: U.S. Department of Commerce, International Trade Admin., Office of Trade and Industry Information, Manufacturing and Services

Energy Consumption, 2011

In trillions of BTUs, except as noted

Total energy consumption	
Total state energy consumption	7,858.4
Total U.S. energy consumption	97,387.3
State share of U.S. total	8.07%
Per capita consumption (in millions of BTUs)	
Total state per capita consumption	208.5
Total U.S. per capita consumption	312.6
End-use sectors	
Residential	1,516.1
Commercial	1,556.1
Industrial	1,785.7
Transportation	3,000.5
Sources of energy	
Petroleum	3,405.8
Natural gas	2,196.6
Coal	55.3
Renewable energy	928.5
Nuclear electric power	383.6

Source: U.S. Energy Information Administration, State Energy Data 2011: Consumption

LAND AND WATER

Surface Area and Federally-Owned Land, 2007

In thousands of acres

Category	State	U.S.	State Share
Total surface area	101,510.2	1,937,664.2	5.24%
Total land area	99,635.3	1,886,846.9	5.28%
Non-federal land	52,996.3	1,484,910.0	3.57%
Developed	6,173.8	111,251.2	5.55%
Rural	46,822.5	1,373,658.8	3.41%
Federal land	46,639.0	401,936.9	11.60%
Water area	1,874.9	50,817.3	3.69%

Source: U.S. Department of Agriculture, Natural Resources Conservation Service, 2007 National Resources Inventory

Land Cover/Use of Non-Federal Rural Land, 2007

In thousands of acres

Category	State	U.S.	State Share
Total rural land	46,822.5	1,373,658.8	3.41%
Cropland	9,489.4	357,023.5	2.66%
CRP[1] land	174.3	32,850.2	0.53%
Pastureland	1,119.5	118,615.7	0.94%
Rangeland	17,531.9	409,119.4	4.29%
Forest land	14,389.9	406,410.4	3.54%
Other rural land	4,117.5	49,639.6	8.29%

Note: (1) Conservation Reserve Program was created to assist private landowners in converting highly erodible cropland to vegetative cover.
Source: U.S. Department of Agriculture, Natural Resources Conservation Service, 2007 National Resources Inventory

Farms and Crop Acreage, 2012

Category	State	U.S.	State Share
Farms (in thousands)	80.5	2,170.0	3.71%
Acres (in millions)	25.4	914.0	2.78%
Acres per farm	315.5	421.2	–

Source: U.S. Department of Agriculture, National Agricultural Statistical Service, Quick Stats, 2012 Survey Data

HEALTH AND MEDICAL CARE

Medical Professionals, 2012

Profession	State Number	U.S. Number	State Share	State Rate[1]	U.S. Rate[1]
Physicians[2]	103,744	894,637	11.60%	275.3	287.1
Dentists	28,699	193,587	14.82%	76.2	62.1
Podiatrists	1,817	17,469	10.40%	4.8	5.6
Optometrists	5,986	45,638	13.12%	15.9	14.6
Chiropractors	10,396	77,494	13.42%	27.6	24.9

Note: (1) Rates are per 100,000 population; (2) Includes total, active Doctors of Osteopathic Medicine and Doctors of Medicine in 2011.
Source: U.S. Department of Health and Human Services, Bureau of Health Professions, Area Health Resource File, 2012-2013

Health Insurance Coverage, 2011

Category	State	U.S.
Total persons covered	30,209,000	260,214,000
Total persons not covered	7,425,000	48,613,000
Percent not covered	19.7%	15.7%
Children under age 18 covered	8,320,000	67,143,000
Children under age 18 not covered	1,008,000	6,965,000
Percent of children not covered	10.8%	9.4%

Source: U.S. Census Bureau, Current Population Survey, 2012 Annual Social and Economic Supplement

HIV, STD, and Tuberculosis Cases and Rates, 2011

Disease	State Cases	State Rate[1]	U.S. Rate[1]
Chlamydia	166,773	447.7	457.6
Gonorrhea	27,516	73.9	104.2
HIV diagnosis	5,965	19.2	15.8
HIV, stage 3 (AIDS)	3,622	11.6	10.3
Syphilis, early latent	2,030	5.4	4.3
Syphilis, primary/secondary	2,443	6.6	4.5
Tuberculosis	2,320	6.2	3.4

Note: (1) Rates are per 100,000 population
Source: Centers for Disease Control and Prevention

Cigarette Smoking, 2011

Category	State	U.S.
Adults who are current smokers	13.7%	21.2%
Adults who smoke everyday	8.6%	15.4%
Adults who smoke some days	5.0%	5.7%
Adults who are former smokers	23.9%	25.1%
Adults who never smoked	62.5%	52.9%

Source: Centers for Disease Control and Prevention, Behaviorial Risk Factor Surveillance System, Tobacco Use, 2011

HOUSING

Home Ownership Rates, 1995–2012

Area	1995	2000	2005	2010	2012
State	55.4%	57.1%	59.7%	56.1%	54.5%
U.S.	64.7%	67.4%	68.9%	66.9%	65.4%

Source: U.S. Census Bureau, Housing Vacancies and Homeownership, Annual Statistics

Home Sales, 2000–2010
In thousands of units

Year	State Sales	U.S. Sales	State Share
2000	573.5	5,174	11.08%
2002	565.1	5,632	10.03%
2004	610.1	6,778	9.00%
2006	459.9	6,478	7.10%
2008	439.9	4,913	8.95%
2010	468.4	4,908	9.54%

Note: Units include single-family homes, condos and co-ops
Source: National Association of Realtors, Real Estate Outlook, Market Trends & Insights

Value of Owner-Occupied Homes, 2011

Value	Total Units in State	Percent of Total, State	Percent of Total, U.S.
Less than $50,000	263,488	3.9%	8.8%
$50,000 to $99,000	328,995	4.8%	16.0%
$100,000 to $149,000	469,223	6.9%	16.5%
$150,000 to $199,000	589,284	8.6%	15.4%
$200,000 to $299,000	1,165,024	17.0%	18.2%
$300,000 to $499,000	1,860,313	27.2%	15.2%
$500,000 to $999,000	1,680,288	24.6%	7.9%
$1,000,000 or more	486,754	7.1%	2.0%
Median value	–	$355,600	$173,600

Source: U.S. Census Bureau, 2011 American Community Survey 1-Year Estimates

EDUCATION

School Enrollment, 2011

Educational Level	Students Enrolled in State	Percent of Total, State	Percent of Total, U.S.
All levels	10,584,220	100.0%	100.0%
Nursery school, preschool	588,092	5.6%	6.0%
Kindergarten	512,746	4.8%	5.1%
Elementary (grades 1–8)	4,064,276	38.4%	39.5%
Secondary (grades 9–12)	2,258,239	21.3%	20.7%
College or graduate school	3,160,867	29.9%	28.7%

Note: Figures cover the population 3 years and over enrolled in school
Source: U.S. Census Bureau, 2011 American Community Survey 1-Year Estimates

Educational Attainment, 2011

Highest Level of Education	State	U.S.
High school diploma	81.1%	85.9%
Bachelor's degree	30.3%	28.5%
Graduate/Professional degree	11.1%	10.6%

Note: Figures cover the population 25 years and over
Source: U.S. Census Bureau, 2011 American Community Survey 1-Year Estimates

Public College Finances, FY 2012

Category	State	U.S.
Full-time equivalent enrollment (FTE)[1]	1,495,868	11,548,974
Educational appropriations per FTE[2]	$6,577	$5,906
Net tuition revenue per FTE[3]	$2,265	$5,189
Total educational revenue per FTE[4]	$8,842	$11,043

(1) Full-time equivalent enrollment equates student credit hours to full time, academic year students, but excludes medical students; (2) Educational appropriations measure state and local support available for public higher education operating expenses including ARRA funds and excludes appropriations for independent institutions, financial aid for students attending independent institutions, research, hospitals, and medical education; (3) Net tuition revenue is calculated by taking the gross amount of tuition and fees, less state and institutional financial aid, tuition waivers or discounts, and medical student tuition and fees. Net tuition revenue used for capital debt service is included in the net tuition revenue figures; (4) Total educational revenue is the sum of educational appropriations and net tuition excluding net tuition revenue used for capital debt service.
Source: State Higher Education Executive Officers, State Higher Education Finance FY 2012

TRANSPORTATION AND TRAVEL

Motor Vehicle Registrations and Drivers Licenses, 2011

Vehicle Type	State	U.S.	State Share
Automobiles[1]	14,549,841	125,656,528	11.58%
Buses	36,876	666,064	5.54%
Trucks	13,771,330	118,455,587	11.63%
Motorcycles	818,650	8,437,502	9.70%
Drivers licenses	23,856,600	211,874,649	11.26%

Note: Motor vehicle registrations include private, commercial, and publicly-owned vehicles; (1) Includes taxicabs
Source: U.S. Department of Transportation, Federal Highway Administration

Domestic Travel Expenditures, 2009
In millions of dollars

Category	State	U.S.	State Share
Travel expenditures	$75,514	$610,200	12.38%

Note: Figures represent U.S. spending on domestic overnight trips and day trips of 50 miles or more, one way, away from home. Excludes spending by foreign visitors.
Source: U.S. Travel Association, Impact of Travel on State Economies, 2009

Retail Gasoline Prices, 2013

Gasoline Grade	State Average	U.S. Average
Regular	$4.02	$3.65
Mid	$4.12	$3.81
Premium	$4.22	$3.98
Diesel	$4.14	$3.88
Excise tax[1]	71.9 cents	49.4 cents

Note: Gasoline prices as of 7/26/2013; (1) Includes state and federal excise taxes and other state taxes as of July 1, 2013
Source: American Automobile Association, Daily Fuel Guage Report; American Petroleum Institute, State Motor Fuel Taxes, 2013

Public Road Length, 2011

Type	State Mileage	U.S. Mileage	State Share
Interstate highways	2,453	46,960	5.22%
Other highways	1,539	15,719	9.79%
Principal arterial	10,078	156,262	6.45%
Minor arterial	17,431	242,942	7.17%
Major collector	24,169	534,592	4.52%
Minor collector	8,131	266,357	3.05%
Local	108,403	2,814,925	3.85%
Urban	90,324	1,095,373	8.25%
Rural	81,877	2,982,383	2.75%
Total	172,202	4,077,756	4.22%

Note: Combined urban and rural road mileage equals the total of the other road types
Source: U.S. Department of Transportation, Federal Highway Administration, Public Road Length, 2011

CRIME AND LAW ENFORCEMENT

Full-Time Law Enforcement Officers, 2011

Gender	State Number	State Rate[1]	U.S. Rate[1]
Male officers	67,432	208.5	210.3
Female officers	10,152	31.4	28.1
Total officers	77,584	239.9	238.3

Note: (1) Rates are per 100,000 population
Source: Federal Bureau of Investigation, Uniform Crime Reports, Crime in the United States 2011

Prison Population, 2000–2012

Year	State Population	U.S. Population	State Share
2000	163,001	1,391,261	11.72%
2005	170,676	1,527,929	11.17%
2010	165,062	1,613,803	10.23%
2011	149,569	1,598,783	9.36%
2012	134,534	1,571,013	8.56%

Note: Figures include prisoners under the jurisdiction of state or federal correctional authorities.
Source: U.S. Department of Justice, Bureau of Justice Statistics, Prisoners in 2006, 2011, 2012 (Advance Counts)

Crime Rate, 2011

Incidents per 100,000 residents

Category	State	U.S.
Violent crimes	411.1	386.3
Murder	4.8	4.7
Forcible rape	20.3	26.8
Robbery	144.0	113.7
Aggravated assault	242.0	241.1
Property crimes	2,583.8	2,908.7
Burglary	610.4	702.2
Larceny/theft	1,583.8	1,976.9
Motor vehicle theft	389.6	229.6
All crimes	2,994.9	3,295.0

Source: Federal Bureau of Investigation, Uniform Crime Reports, Crime in the United States 2011

GOVERNMENT AND FINANCE

Local Governments by Type, 2012

Government Type	State	U.S.	State Share
All local governments	4,350	89,004	4.89%
County	57	3,031	1.88%
Municipality	482	19,522	2.47%
Town/Township	0	16,364	0.00%
Special District	2,786	37,203	7.49%
Ind. School District	1,025	12,884	7.96%

Source: U.S. Census Bureau, 2012 Census of Governments: Organization Component Preliminary Estimates

State Government Revenue, 2011

In thousands of dollars, except for per capita figures

Total revenue	**$334,233,317**
Total revenue per capita, State	$8,869
Total revenue per capita, U.S.	$7,271
General revenue	$211,358,143
Intergovernmental revenue	$68,430,680
Taxes	$116,695,284
General sales	$30,996,372
Selective sales	$14,151,285
License taxes	$8,186,412
Individual income taxes	$50,508,441
Corporate income taxes	$9,613,594
Other taxes	$3,239,180
Current charges	$16,701,739
Miscellaneous general revenue	$9,530,440
Utility revenue	$2,496,154
Liquor store revenue	$0
Insurance trust revenue[1]	$120,379,020

Note: (1) Within insurance trust revenue, net earnings of state retirement systems is a calculated statistic, and thus can be positive or negative. Net earnings is the sum of earnings on investments plus gains on investments minus losses on investments.
Source: U.S. Census Bureau, 2011 Annual Survey of State Government Finances

State Government Expenditures, 2011

In thousands of dollars, except for per capita figures

Total expenditure	$280,212,581
Total expenditure per capita, State	$7,436
Total expenditure per capita, U.S.	$6,427
Intergovernmental expenditure	$91,501,553
Direct expenditure	$188,711,028
Current operation	$117,525,130
Capital outlay	$7,881,389
Insurance benefits and repayments	$52,116,136
Assistance and subsidies	$3,537,207
Interest on debt	$7,651,166
Utility expenditure	$3,104,288
Liquor store expenditure	$0
Insurance trust expenditure	$52,116,136

Source: U.S. Census Bureau, 2011 Annual Survey of State Government Finances

State Government General Expenditures by Function, 2011

In thousands of dollars

Education	$74,992,505
Public welfare	$77,464,948
Hospitals	$11,297,876
Health	$7,352,206
Highways	$10,623,812
Police protection	$1,646,807
Correction	$6,589,627
Natural resources	$3,843,151
Parks and recreation	$538,898
Governmental administration	$8,496,967
Interest on general debt	$7,302,166
Other and unallocable	$14,843,194

Source: U.S. Census Bureau, 2011 Annual Survey of State Government Finances

State Government Finances, Cash and Debt, 2011

In thousands of dollars, except for per capita figures

Debt at end of fiscal year	
State, total	$149,670,954
State, per capita	$3,972
U.S., per capita	$3,635
Cash and security holdings	
State, total	$535,101,067
State, per capita	$14,200
U.S., per capita	$11,759

Source: U.S. Census Bureau, 2011 Annual Survey of State Government Finances

POLITICS

Composition of the Senate, 1995–2013

Congress (Year)	State/U.S	Dem	Rep	Total
104th (1995)	State delegates	2	0	2
	Total U.S.	48	52	100
105th (1997)	State delegates	2	0	2
	Total U.S.	45	55	100
106th (1999)	State delegates	2	0	2
	Total U.S.	45	55	100
107th (2001)	State delegates	2	0	2
	Total U.S.	50	50	100
108th (2003)	State delegates	2	0	2
	Total U.S.	48	51	100
109th (2005)	State delegates	2	0	2
	Total U.S.	44	55	100
110th (2007)	State delegates	2	0	2
	Total U.S.	49	49	100
111th (2009)	State delegates	2	0	2
	Total U.S.	57	41	100
112th (2011)	State delegates	2	0	2
	Total U.S.	51	47	100
113th (2013)	State delegates	2	0	2
	Total U.S.	54	45	100

Note: Figures are for the starts of first sessions; Totals include Democratic (Dem) and Republican (Rep) members as well as vacancies and seats held by independent party members
Source: U.S. Congress, Congressional Directory

Composition of the House of Representatives, 1995–2013

Congress (Year)	State/U.S	Dem	Rep	Total
104th (1995)	State delegates	27	25	52
	Total U.S.	204	230	435
105th (1997)	State delegates	29	23	52
	Total U.S.	207	226	435
106th (1999)	State delegates	28	24	52
	Total U.S.	211	223	435
107th (2001)	State delegates	32	20	52
	Total U.S.	212	221	435
108th (2003)	State delegates	33	20	53
	Total U.S.	205	229	435
109th (2005)	State delegates	33	20	53
	Total U.S.	202	231	435
110th (2007)	State delegates	34	19	53
	Total U.S.	233	198	435
111th (2009)	State delegates	34	19	53
	Total U.S.	256	178	435
112th (2011)	State delegates	34	19	53
	Total U.S.	193	242	435
113th (2013)	State delegates	38	15	53
	Total U.S.	201	234	435

Note: Figures are for the starts of first sessions; Totals include Democratic (Dem) and Republican (Rep) members as well as vacancies and seats held by independent party members
Source: U.S. Congress, Congressional Directory

Composition of State Legislature, 2004–2013

Year	Democrats	Republicans	Total
State Senate			
2004	25	15	40
2005	25	15	40
2006	25	15	40
2007	25	15	40
2008	25	15	40
2009	25	14	40
2010	25	14	40
2011	25	15	40
2012	25	15	40
2013	26	11	40
State House			
2004	48	32	80
2005	48	32	80
2006	48	32	80
2007	48	32	80
2008	47	32	80
2009	51	29	80
2010	49	29	80
2011	52	27	80
2012	52	28	80
2013	55	25	80

Note: Totals may include minor party members and vacancies
Source: The Council of State Governments, State Legislatures

Voter Participation in Presidential Elections, 1980–2012

Year	Voting-eligible State Population	State Voter Turnout Rate	U.S. Voter Turnout Rate
1980	15,610,966	55.0	54.2
1984	16,618,345	57.2	55.2
1988	17,738,700	55.7	52.8
1992	18,460,157	60.3	58.1
1996	18,644,593	53.7	51.7
2000	19,685,258	55.7	54.2
2004	21,132,533	58.8	60.1
2008	22,261,504	60.9	61.6
2012	23,620,070	55.2	58.2

Note: All figures are based on the voting-eligible population which excludes person ineligible to vote such as non-citizens, felons (depending on state law), and mentally-incapacitated persons. U.S. figures include the overseas eligible population (including military personnel).
Source: McDonald, Michael P., United States Election Project, Presidential Voter Turnout Rates, 1980–2012

Governors Since Statehood

Peter H. Burnett (D) . . . . (r) 1849-1851
John McDougal (D) 1851-1852
John Bigler (D). 1852-1856
John Neely Johnson (O) 1856-1858
John B. Weller (D) 1858-1860
Milton S. Latham (D) . . . . (r) 1860-1860
John G. Downey (D) 1860-1862
Leland Stanford (R) 1862-1863
Frederick F. Low (O) 1863-1867
Henry H. Haight (D). 1867-1871
Newton Booth (R) . . . . (r) 1871-1875
Romualdo Pacheco (R). 1875-1875
William Irwin (D). 1875-1880
George C. Perkins (R) 1880-1883
George Stoneman (D). 1883-1887
Washington Bartlett (D) . . . . (d) 1887-1887
Robert W. Waterman (R) 1887-1891
Henry H. Markham (R) 1891-1895
James H. Budd (D). 1895-1899
Henry T. Gage (R) 1899-1903
George C. Pardee (R) 1903-1907
James N. Gillette (R) 1907-1911
Hiram W. Johnson (R). . . . . (r) 1911-1917
William D. Stephens (R) 1917-1923
Friend W. Richardson (R) 1923-1927
Clement C. Young (R) 1927-1931
James Rolph Jr. (R). (d) 1931-1934
Frank F. Merriam (R). 1934-1939
Culbert L. Olson (D) 1939-1943
Earl Warren (R). . . . . (r) 1943-1953
Goodwin J. Knight (R) 1953-1959
Edmund G. ("Pat") Brown (D). 1959-1967
Ronald W. Reagan (R) 1967-1975
Edmund G. ("Jerry") Brown Jr. (D) 1975-1983
George Deukmejian (R) 1983-1991
Pete Wilson (R) 1991-1999
Gray Davis (D) . . . . (i) 1999-2003
Arnold Schwarzenegger (R). 2003-2011
Jerry Brown (D) 2011-2015

Note: (D) Democrat; (R) Republican; (O) Other party; (r) resigned; (d) died in office; (i) removed from office

Colorado

Location: Rocky Mountains

Area and rank: 103,730 square miles (268,660 square kilometers); 104,100 square miles (269,619 square kilometers) including water; eighth largest state in area

Coastline: none

Population and rank: 5,187,582 (2012 estimate); twenty-second largest state in population

Capital and largest city: Denver (600,158 people in 2010 census)

Became territory: February 28, 1861

State capitol building in Denver. (Denver Metro Convention & Visitors Bureau)

Entered Union and rank:
August 1, 1876; thirty-
eighth state

Present constitution adopted:
1876

Counties: 63

State name: "Colorado" is
derived from the Spanish
for "ruddy" or "red"

State nickname: Centennial
State

Motto: *Nil sine numine*
(Nothing without
providence)

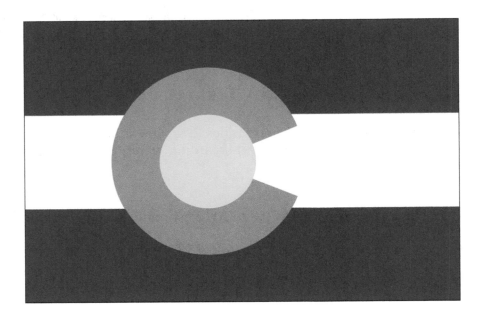

State flag: Blue and white stripes with red
letter C and yellow disk in center

Highest point: Mount Elbert—14,433 feet
(4,399 meters)

Lowest point: Arkansas River—3,350 feet
(1,021 meters)

Highest recorded temperature: 118 degrees
Fahrenheit (48 degrees Celsius)—
Bennett, 1888

Lowest recorded temperature: –61 degrees
Fahrenheit (–52 degrees Celsius)—
Maybell, 1985

State song: "Where the Columbines Grow"

State tree: Colorado blue spruce

State flower: Rocky Mountain columbine
State bird: Lark bunting **State fish:**
Greenback cutthroat trout

State animal: Rocky Mountain bighorn
sheep

National parks: Black Canyon of the
Gunnison, Mesa Verde, Rocky
Mountain

Colorado History

The history of Colorado is marked by its geographical features, divided as it is by the Rocky Mountains, with rugged territory lying to the west and agriculturally productive plains to the east. Mining in the central and western parts of the state was influential in its early history; while agriculture, and its thirst for water in the parched eastern plains, was influential in later decades. Colorado's mountainous terrain has attracted generations of tourists, who flock to winter and summer recreational attractions.

Early History. The earliest inhabitants of the area were nomadic hunters, around 10,000 B.C.E. About the first century C.E., the southwestern area of the state was populated by a people known as the Basket Makers. By 800, the Cliff Dwellers had established their civilization in the state's mesa country. From 1000 the civilization of the Cliff Dwellers flourished, but around 1300, for unknown reasons, it died out.

Though their origins are unknown, many other Native American peoples populated today's Colorado when whites arrived. A number of Apache bands raided Colorado territory, but only one such band, the Jicarilla, lived permanently in Colorado and its environs, mainly in the southeastern portion. Bannock and Shoshone tribes roamed over the northwest corner of the state. The Cheyenne, Arapaho, and Comanche tribes hunted and made war in eastern areas, as did the Kiowa and the Kiowa Apaches, who always accompanied them. The Navahos occasionally entered the state from New Mexico, but the Ute occupied the state's entire central and western portions. Most of the Pueblos inhabited the state's southwest, in Colorado's famous cliff ruins, sometimes intermarrying with the Utes.

Spanish Exploration. In the sixteenth century the Spanish became the area's first European explorers. Searching for rich cities of gold, Francisco Vásquez de

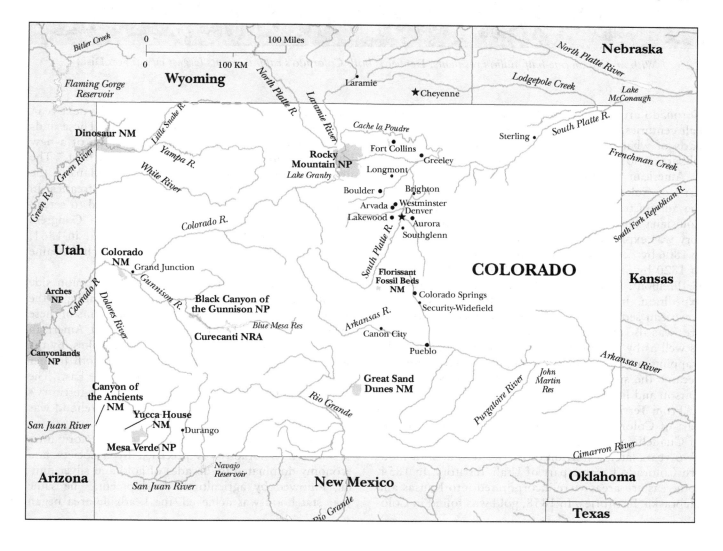

With more than one-half million residents, Denver is both Colorado's capital and its largest city. (PhotoDisc)

Coronado arrived in 1541. During the next two-and-a-half centuries, a number of Spanish explorers traversed parts of what became Colorado, among them Juan de Ulibarri, who claimed the territory for the Spanish crown.

American Exploration and Settlement. In 1803, parts of Colorado were sold to the United States when the administration of Thomas Jefferson concluded the Louisiana Purchase with France. Thereafter, the territory was explored by a series of American expeditions: in 1806 by Zebulon Pike, for whom Pikes Peak is named; in 1820 by Stephen Long; from 1842 to 1853 by John C. Frémont; and in 1853 by the Gunnison-Beckwith expedition. In 1833, Bent's Fort, the first permanent American settlement in Colorado, was completed. The area was also inhabited by various nomadic Indian tribes, as well as by American "mountain men," who lived by trapping and fur trading. Among them were those who became the subjects of American folklore, such as Kit Carson and Jim Bridger.

From Territory to Statehood. In 1848, Mexico ceded part of Colorado to the United States with the Treaty of Guadelupe Hidalgo, which ended the Mexican War. Two years later, a portion of the western area of modern Colorado became part of Utah Territory. In 1854, some eastern areas were incorporated into Kansas and Nebraska Territories. In 1858, gold was found in Colo-

rado, first at Cherry Creek, near Denver. The next year, a rich vein was discovered in Central City. These finds brought thousands of adventurers in search of a new life, who adopted the slogan "Pikes Peak or Bust." The miners ignored the claims of American Indians to the land that had been deeded to them in past treaties. In place of Indian lands, newcomers attempted to set up a new, so-called Jefferson Territory, which Congress did not approve. After Kansas became a state in 1861, Colorado Territory was organized, with much the same boundaries as the subsequent state.

Colorado entered the Civil War on the Union side in 1861 and was the scene of significant fighting in the western phases of the war. Other notable events of these early years were wars between whites and American Indians, and a number of gold and silver strikes. By the late 1860's new mining methods brought both further prosperity and more immigration from the East. The increased population was a key factor in the territory's seeking statehood. After several failures, statehood was finally attained in 1876.

Economic and Social Development. The formation of modern Colorado was preceded by a society and economy dominated by decades of gold and silver mining followed by agricultural development. The same year statehood was achieved, the Leadville area began to surrender its millions of dollars of gold and silver ore. More than a decade later, Cripple Creek was the scene of another notable gold strike. This discovery was especially welcome, because the free coinage of silver sent silver mining into a tailspin that the Cripple Creek find helped to offset.

The last of the battles with American Indian tribes came in 1879, when the Utes rebelled. In the last uprising by Native Americans in the American West, the Utes massacred Nathan Meeker, an Indian agent, and his workers in what would become the town of Meeker, in the White River Valley in northwestern Colorado. This massacre resulted in the Utes' forcible removal to eastern Utah. Some Native Americans, however, appear to have maintained their presence, though in modest numbers. For example, in 1845, the Jicarilla Apaches were said to number 800. According to the census of 1910, there were 694, and in 1937, the Report of the U.S. Indian Office said there were 714.

If Indian wars were at an end, other conflicts were not long in arriving. When a depression struck in 1893, serious labor problems erupted after the federal government canceled its agreement to purchase substantial amounts of silver. Silver miners were thrown out of work; strikes by miners, now employees of mining companies, not independent adventurers, occurred in silver mines in 1893-1894 and 1903-1904 and in coal mines in 1913-1914. These strikes were settled with military force, a graphic reminder that the days of the romantic West were over.

The Twentieth Century. The opening of the twentieth century saw the beginning of the natural conservation movement that attracted tourists. In 1906, Congress created Mesa Verde National Park to preserve the remains of ancient Indian culture, and nine years later Rocky Mountain National Park was established. During these years, the economy depended on agriculture, as Colorado became the most irrigated state in the Union. Canning and other industries grew along with agriculture. In 1899, Colorado's first sugar beet factory began operations at Grand Junction; seven years later the U.S. Mint opened in Denver.

The advent of another industry, however, augured well for the future, when oil production and refining

Last occupied during the thirteenth century, the Cliff Palace ruins in Mesa Verde National Park contain some of the oldest and best-preserved pre-Columbian dwellings in North America. (National Park Service)

became prominent sources of income. With the plentiful availability of oil throughout the nation came the advent of the automobile. America's love affair with the automobile, coupled with the unsurpassed beauty of western Colorado, gave rise to the state's considerable tourist industry, which developed rapidly after World War I. Colorado, moreover, has its own oil sources.

Small amounts of oil had been discovered in the nineteenth century, when in 1862 the first oil well was drilled near Canon City. But in the next century more, and larger, fields were found. By the 1920's, the importance of oil surpassed all other minerals, though not until after World War II and the development of the Rangley oil field in 1946 in northwest Colorado did oil production approach its zenith. Oil production rose from 1.7 million barrels in 1940 to 23 million barrels in 1950.

Like the rest of the nation, Colorado suffered considerably during the Great Depression of the 1930's. World War II lifted the state from its doldrums, as its oil and minerals were in great demand. Military and other federal installations opened in several areas, especially around Denver, the state's capital.

Postwar Developments. Colorado's population, which had grown to 800,000 in 1910, grew swiftly after World War II. With population increase and demand for expansion of agriculture came the need for water. Irrigation had begun in the nineteenth century. Large irrigation projects existed from the 1860's, but after the war a series of irrigation projects was carried out. In 1947, the Alva B. Adams Tunnel, which carries water eastward through the Rocky Mountains, was completed. Two years later Cherry Creek Dam, near Denver, was finished. In 1959, the Colorado-Big Thompson Project, a series of dams, reservoirs, and tunnels, was completed, of which the Adams Tunnel is a part. More water-conservation projects were carried out between the 1950's and the 1980's, such as the Colorado River Storage Project, begun in 1956, and the Frying Pan-Arkansas project, begun during the early 1960's and completed in 1985.

Other significant postwar changes in the state's economy changed the complexion of its society. Manufacturing replaced agriculture in importance by the mid-1950's. Federal agencies sank important new roots in the state, opening the laboratory of the National Bureau of Standards in Boulder in 1954, the United States Air Force Academy in 1958, and the North American Air Defense Command in 1966, sunk some twelve hundred feet deep in Cheyenne Mountain.

By the 1990's Colorado had emerged as both a significant area of urban development below the eastern slopes of the Rocky Mountains and one of the nation's most popular recreation areas. The upscale mountain community of Vail, for example, serves as an icon of winter sports, and the state's national parks and other scenic wonders draw millions of vacationers each year. At the same time, the nation's academic life benefited from its universities, and several of its political figures reached national stature. If in its early decades, Colorado, seemingly connected more to the West, felt marginal to powerful eastern states, a century after its admittance to the Union the state became fully integrated into the nation's life. Signs of this integration include its thriving urban life, especially in its capital and environs; its significant defense installations; and its sports teams, such as those in professional baseball, basketball, and football.

At the end of the twentieth century, Colorado's prosperity continued. Population increase gained the state a further representative in Congress after the census in 2000. Greater Denver experienced more than 30 percent growth over the previous decade; more than one third of the state was now Hispanic. In 2000, the state's reputation as a tourist destination was enhanced when President Bill Clinton created a new national monument, Canyon of the Ancients, in Colorado's southwest. Natural forces, however, did not always cooperate with the state's upbeat economic life. Wildfires bedeviled the state throughout the first half of the new decade; those of 2000 were called the "worst in a generation."

Headline Cases. Tragedy also touched the state. On April 20, 1999, the nation was shocked when two disturbed high school students, Eric Harris and Dylan Klebold, opened fire on classmates and faculty at Columbine High School in Littleton. The students, who timed the attack to coincide with Adolf Hitler's birthday, killed twelve students and one teacher in the span of sixteen minutes, an act caught on the school's video cameras. Much soul-searching ensued, but the affair was not concluded before two more Columbine students were slain at a restaurant near the school on Valentine's Day, 2000, and another Columbine student took his life in May. The school library, where most of the shooting took place, was demolished and another opened later in its place in June, 2001.

The state also made national headlines for several months when, in July, 2003, a hotel employee in Eagle, a small town near Vail, accused a famous basketball player of rape. A complex set of legal actions began, including an indictment of Kobe Bryant of the Los Angeles Lakers on a sexual assault charge. The case reached a climax just before a trial was to start, when the accuser decided not to testify, and Bryant issued a quasi-apologetic statement. A civil lawsuit by the accuser eventuated in an out-of-court settlement of unspecified terms.

Finally, the state's best-known institution of higher learning, the University of Colorado at Boulder, became the focus of national attention in January, 2005, when the public became aware of controversial statements made by professor Ward Churchill about the victims of the September 11, 2001, terrorist attacks on the World Trade Center in New York. Churchill said that they were no more than "little Eichmanns," a reference to a Nazi bureaucrat who was a principal organizer of the Holocaust of the Jews during World War II. A university investigation accused the professor, who refused to retract his remarks, of plagiarism and other academic misdeeds but stopped short of recommending that he be fired. His removal, however, which had been called for by Colorado's governor, remained a possibility.

Political Developments. Politically, Colorado moved from being a more Republican state to a centrist position during the early twenty-first century. In 2003, its congressional representation included two Republican U.S. senators and five Republican members of the House of Representatives. By 2006, however, it had one senator of each party and four Republicans and three Democrats in the House. Governor William F. "Bill" Owens, a Republican, was re-elected in 2002.

Marijuana. In the November 2012 elections, Colorado voters passed Amendment 64 to the state constitution, which legalized the possession of one ounce of marijuana for adults over the age of 21 and allowed individuals to grow up to six plants for personal use. However, Colorado did not immediately pass legislation on how to regulate marijuana stores. Furthermore, some areas, such as Douglas County, prohibit sales by local ordinance. The state amendment also prohibits smoking marijuana in public places such as on the street or in parks. The federal government continued to take the position that any possession of marijuana is illegal, so a federal-state clash over the issue was anticipated.

Oil Shale. In 2010 the federal Government Accounting Office (GAO) released a report that drew considerable attention in Colorado. The report stated that the Green River Formation, which represents a 1000-foot layer of sedimentary rocks, contained the world's largest deposits of oil shale. The richest section, the Piceance Basin, lies in northwest Colorado and in neighboring regions in Utah and Wyoming. The Green River Formation is estimated to contain some 3 trillion barrels of oil, representing an amount equal to twice the oil discovered everywhere else in the world. The Rand Institute estimated that, using methods known today, somewhere between 30 and 60 percent of the oil could be recovered, enough to guarantee that the United States would become a major oil supplier, rather than a net importer. Much of the Green River Formation lies under federal lands. However, with current technologies, the cost of the recovered oil would far exceed the current world prices for petroleum. Despite the fact that no immediate development was to be expected, the GAO report spurred controversy among environmental advocates, who feared the exploitation of the resource would result in damage to the ecosystem.

Charles F. Bahmueller
Updated by the Editor

Colorado Time Line

c. 1000 C.E.	Indian cliff dwellers live in southwestern part of state.
1500's	Spanish explorers searching for legendary golden cities travel through parts of the state.
1541	Spaniard Francisco Vásquez de Coronado probably crosses southeastern corner of the state.
1700	French explorers reach the Rocky Mountains.
1706	Juan de Uribarri, leader of a Spanish expedition to capture runaway Indian slaves, claims the area for Philip V of Spain.
c. 1776	Two Franciscan monks explore much of western and southwestern areas seeking a route to the California missions.
1779	Juan Bautista de Anza explores territory for Spain.
1803	Portions of Colorado become part of the United States through the Louisiana Purchase.
1806	Zebulon Pike explores Pikes Peak. 1820 Stephen Long explores western boundary of Colorado.
1835	Bent's Old Fort is founded; first permanent American settlement of future state.
1842–1853	Sponsored by the federal government, John C. Frémont explores Colorado on five occasions.
1845	Portion of future state is acquired in connection with annexation of Texas.
1848	Entirety of Colorado is acquired in the Treaty of Guadalupe Hidalgo, which ended the Mexican War.
1854	Parts of Colorado are incorporated in the Kansas and Nebraska Territories.
1858	Gold is discovered at Cherry Creek, near Denver.
1858–1859	Agricultural irrigation begins.
1859	Rich gold vein is discovered in Central City; Colorado Gold Rush attracts thousands of fortune hunters.
1859	Production of gold begins; reaches peak in 1900.

1860's	Wars with American Indians take place.
Feb. 28, 1861	Colorado Territory is organized; Cheyenne tribes give up most of their lands.
1861–1865	Entering on Union side, Colorado Territory is scene of Civil War fighting.
1867	Denver becomes permanent capital.
1867	Treaty of Medicine Lodge is signed; Cheyenne and Arapaho move to Indian Territory (Oklahoma).
1870	Denver Pacific Railroad is completed to Denver.
1876	Convention meeting in Denver adopts state constitution (March), which is ratified by voters (July).
1876	Gold mining in Leadville area is especially productive.
Aug. 1, 1876	Colorado enters the Union as the thirty-eighth state.
1877	University of Colorado at Boulder is founded.
1878	Adoption of Bland-Allison Act stimulates production of silver, causing silver boom.
1879	Ute tribes, originally given most of western Colorado, are relocated after massacre of Indian agent Nathan Meeker and his colleagues.
1890's	Following rapid growth, state experiences economic depression and severe labor strife.
1891	Gold production begins at Cripple Creek mine.
Nov. 2, 1893	Women receive voting rights.
1906	U.S. Mint opens in Denver.
1906	Congress establishes Mesa Verde National Park.
Apr. 20, 1914	National Guardsmen burn a tent colony of striking Colorado Fuel and Iron Corporation miners, killing twenty; ten-day uprising follows, resulting in dispatch of federal troops.
1915	Rocky Mountain National Park is established.
1924	Ku Klux Klan members are elected to major state offices; Klan-endorsed politicians become

Nineteenth-century painter Frederic Remington's fanciful depiction of Coronado's march through Colorado in 1541. (Library of Congress)

	governor and senator.
1927	Moffat Tunnel through the Rocky Mountains is completed.
1942	Relocation center for West Coast Japanese Americans is established near Granada.
1954	Air Force Academy is authorized by Congress, with temporary quarters at Lowry Air Force Base; permanent quarters at Colorado Springs opens four years later.
1957	North American Air Defense Command (NORAD) is established in Colorado Springs.
1959	Series of dams for irrigation, known as the Colorado-Big Thompson Project, is completed.
1961	National Center for Atmospheric Research is created at Boulder.
Apr. 25, 1967	Colorado is first to pass liberal abortion laws.
1990's	Economic boom turns state's electorate toward political right.
1998	Marked Republican plurality of 120,000 voters replaces previous slight Democratic Party advantage.
Apr. 20, 1999	Two disturbed students at Columbine High School in Littleton murder twelve students and one teacher and injure twenty-four in a planned shooting attack.
June, 2002	Hayman wildfire near Denver is the largest wildfire recorded in state's history.
July 18, 2003	Basketball star Kobe Bryant is accused of raping a hotel employee in Eagle; charges are later dropped after he issues apology.
Jan. 2005	University of Colorado professor Ward Churchill becomes center of national controversy after he calls World Trade Center 9/11 victims "little Eichmanns."
2010	The federal Government Accounting Office releases a report that the the Green River Formation, a 1,000-foot layer of sedimentary rock, is estimated to contain some 3 trillion barrels of oil in shale form, though only an estimated 30–60 percent of it is recoverable.
Nov. 2012	Colorado voters pass Amendment 64, which legalizes possession of up to one ounce of marijuana.

Notes for Further Study

Published Sources. A standard history of Colorado is *Colorado: A History of the Centennial State* (4th ed., 2005) by Carl Abbott et al. and *Colorado History* (9th ed., 2006) by Carl Ubbelohde, Duane A. Smith, and Maxine Benson. Informal volumes of colorful incidents and facets of the state's past constitute Abott Fay's *I Never Knew That About Colorado: A Quaint Volume of Forgotten Lore* (1997) and Muriel Marshall's *Where Rivers Meet: Lore from the Colorado Frontier* (1996). Maxine Benson's *1001 Colorado Place Names* (1995) discusses place names chosen for their historical, geographical, or geological significance. A good guide to the state is *Colorado* (4th ed., 1998) by Jon Klusmire and Paul Chesley. For the state's politicsand government, readers should consult Roger A. Walton's *Colorado: A Practical Guide to Its Government and Politics* (6th rev. ed., 1991) or *Cornerstones and Communities: A Historical Overview of Colorado's County Seats and Court Houses* (2001), edited by William Virden and Barbara Teel. A useful guide to the state's geography is *Colorado: A Geography* (1983) by Mel Griffiths and Lynell Rubright. Sally Crum's *People of the Red Earth: Native Americans of Colorado* (1998) uses archaeological evidence in discussing Colorado's original inhabitants.

Web Resources. Those visiting the state or wishing to know more about it might begin with the State of Colorado home page (www.state.co.us). The site includes pages on points of interest; road, ski, weather, and air pollution conditions; doing business in Colorado; and information on the state's elected officials, among other topics. Colorado.com (www.colorado.com/) is another good site for travelers. For those traveling to the state's national parks, the National Park service has informative Web sites (www.nps.gov/romo/ and www.nps.gov/meve/). The U.S. Census Bureau Quickfacts (quickfacts.census.gov/qfd/states/08000.html) allows one to select any county or city in the state and view a range of related demographic statistics.

Counties

County	2012 Population	Pop. Rank	Land Area (sq. miles)	Area Rank	County	2012 Population	Pop. Rank	Land Area (sq. miles)	Area Rank
Adams	459,598	5	1,167.65	39	Eagle	51,874	15	1,684.53	27
Alamosa	16,148	29	722.64	53	El Paso	644,964	1	2,126.80	19
Arapahoe	595,546	3	798.10	48	Elbert	23,383	23	1,850.85	21
Archuleta	12,070	36	1,350.18	33	Fremont	46,788	16	1,533.07	31
Baca	3,751	55	2,554.97	11	Garfield	56,953	13	2,947.56	8
Bent	5,773	47	1,512.86	32	Gilpin	5,491	48	149.90	63
Boulder	305,318	7	726.29	52	Grand	14,195	33	1,846.33	22
Broomfield	58,298	12	33.03	64	Gunnison	15,475	31	3,239.10	5
Chaffee	18,150	27	1,013.40	43	Hinsdale	810	62	1,117.25	41
Cheyenne	1,874	59	1,778.28	24	Huerfano	6,596	45	1,591.00	30
Clear Creek	9,026	39	395.23	59	Jackson	1,348	61	1,613.72	29
Conejos	8,275	40	1,287.39	34	Jefferson	545,358	4	764.21	50
Costilla	3,594	56	1,226.95	38	Kiowa	1,444	60	1,767.77	25
Crowley	5,365	50	787.42	49	Kit Carson	8,094	41	2,160.82	18
Custer	4,249	54	738.63	51	La Plata	52,401	14	1,692.08	26
Delta	30,432	18	1,142.05	40	Lake	7,338	43	376.91	61
Denver	634,265	2	153.00	62	Larimer	310,487	6	2,596.00	9
Dolores	1,994	58	1,067.05	42	Las Animas	14,945	32	4,772.67	1
Douglas	298,215	8	840.25	47	Lincoln	5,453	49	2,577.63	10

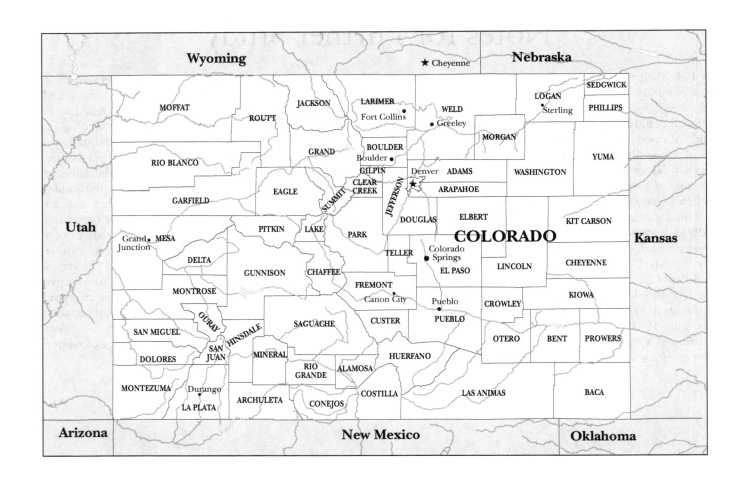

County	2012 Population	Pop. Rank	Land Area (sq. miles)	Area Rank
Logan	22,631	25	1,838.55	23
Mesa	147,848	11	3,328.97	4
Mineral	709	63	875.67	46
Moffat	13,200	34	4,743.29	2
Montezuma	25,431	21	2,029.53	20
Montrose	40,725	17	2,240.69	16
Morgan	28,472	19	1,280.43	36
Otero	18,698	26	1,261.96	37
Ouray	4,530	52	541.59	58
Park	16,029	30	2,193.85	17
Phillips	4,367	53	687.93	54
Pitkin	17,263	28	970.70	44
Prowers	12,389	35	1,638.39	28
Pueblo	160,852	10	2,386.10	13
Rio Blanco	6,857	44	3,220.93	6
Rio Grande	11,943	37	911.96	45
Routt	23,334	24	2,362.03	15
Saguache	6,304	46	3,168.52	7
San Juan	690	64	387.49	60
San Miguel	7,580	42	1,286.61	35
Sedgwick	2,383	57	548.04	57
Summit	28,044	20	608.36	55
Teller	23,389	22	557.06	56
Washington	4,766	51	2,518.03	12
Weld	263,691	9	3,987.24	3
Yuma	10,119	38	2,364.40	14

Source: U.S. Census Bureau, 2012 Population Estimates

Cities
With 10,000 or more residents

Legal Name	2010 Population	Pop. Rank	Land Area (sq. miles)	Area Rank
Arvada city	106,433	8	35.14	11
Aurora city	325,078	3	154.73	2
Berkley CDP	11,207	54	3.71	56
Black Forest CDP	13,116	48	100.65	4
Boulder city	97,385	11	24.66	21
Brighton city	33,352	23	19.98	26
Broomfield city	55,889	17	33.03	16
Castle Pines North city	10,360	57	9.01	43
Castle Rock town	48,231	18	33.79	14
Cañon City city	16,400	42	12.50	31
Centennial city	100,377	10	28.72	18
Cherry Creek CDP	11,120	55	1.68	60
Cimarron Hills CDP	16,161	43	6.06	52
Clifton CDP	19,889	33	6.00	53
Colorado Springs city	416,427	2	194.54	1
Columbine CDP	24,280	32	6.65	50
Commerce City city	45,913	19	34.29	13
Dakota Ridge CDP	32,005	26	9.28	42
Denver city	600,158	1	153.00	3
Durango city	16,887	41	9.92	36
Edwards CDP	10,266	58	26.64	19
Englewood city	30,255	27	6.56	51
Erie town	18,135	40	17.18	28
Evans city	18,537	37	10.20	34
Federal Heights city	11,467	52	1.78	59
Firestone town	10,147	60	10.37	32
Fort Carson CDP	13,813	47	8.71	44
Fort Collins city	143,986	4	54.28	6
Fort Morgan city	11,315	53	3.93	55
Fountain city	25,846	30	23.98	24
Fruita city	12,646	49	7.12	49
Golden city	18,867	35	9.92	36
Grand Junction city	58,566	16	38.22	10
Greeley city	92,889	13	46.55	8
Greenwood Village city	13,925	46	8.27	45
Highlands Ranch CDP	96,713	12	24.26	23
Ken Caryl CDP	32,438	25	9.72	38
Lafayette city	24,453	31	9.46	40
Lakewood city	142,980	5	42.88	9
Littleton city	41,737	21	12.98	30
Lone Tree city	10,218	59	9.57	39
Longmont city	86,270	14	26.19	20
Louisville city	18,376	38	7.89	46
Loveland city	66,859	15	33.59	15
Montrose city	19,132	34	17.80	27
Northglenn city	35,789	22	7.41	48

Legal Name	2010 Population	Pop. Rank	Land Area (sq. miles)	Area Rank
Parker town	45,297	20	20.48	25
Pueblo city	106,595	7	53.64	7
Pueblo West CDP	29,637	29	70.43	5
Security-Widefield CDP	32,882	24	13.64	29
Sherrelwood CDP	18,287	39	2.43	58
Steamboat Springs city	12,088	51	10.14	35
Sterling city	14,777	45	7.61	47
Superior town	12,483	50	3.96	54
The Pinery CDP	10,517	56	10.36	33
Thornton city	118,772	6	34.84	12
Welby CDP	14,846	44	3.69	57
Westminster city	106,114	9	31.55	17
Wheat Ridge city	30,166	28	9.30	41
Windsor town	18,644	36	24.44	22

Note: CDP–Census Designated Place
Source: U.S. Census Bureau, 2010 Census

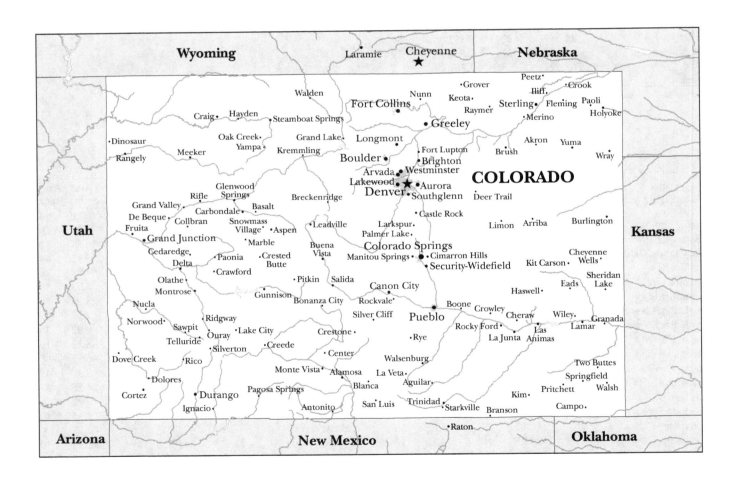

Survey Says...

This section presents current rankings from dozens of public and private sources. It shows how this state ranks in a number of critical categories, including education, job growth, cost of living, teen drivers, energy efficiency, and business environment. Sources include *Forbes*, *Reuters*, *U.S. News and World Report*, *CNN Money*, *Gallup*, and *Huffington Post*.

- Colorado ranked #22 in a government study measuring real gross domestic product (GDP)—the output of goods and services produced by labor and property located in the United States. The ranking is based on the percentage change compared with 2011 GDP.
  U.S. Department of Commerce, Bureau of Economic Analysis, June 2013; www.bea.gov

- Colorado ranked #19 in a government study measuring real gross domestic product (GDP)—the output of goods and services produced by labor and property located in the United States. The ranking is based on the dollar value of its GDP.
  U.S. Department of Commerce, Bureau of Economic Analysis, June 2013; www.bea.gov

- Colorado ranked #32 in the 17th edition of "Quality Counts; State of the States," Education Week's "report card" surveying key education indicators, policy efforts, and educational outcomes.
  Education Week, January 4, 2013 (online) and January 10, 2013 (print); www.edweek.org

- SERI (Science and Engineering Readiness Index) weighs the performance of the states' K-12 schools in preparing students in physics and calculus, the high school subjects considered most important for future scientists and engineers. Colorado ranked #15.
  Newsletter of the Forum on Education of the American Physical Society, Summer 2011 issue; www.huffingtonpost.com, July 11, 2011; updated October 1, 2012

- Business website 24/7 Wall St. identified the states with the highest and lowest percentages of residents 25 or older with a college degree or higher. Of "America's Best Educated States," Colorado ranked #3 (#1 = best).
  247wallst.com, posted October 15, 2012; consulted July 18, 2013

- MoneyRates.com ranked Colorado #3 on its list of the best to worst states for making a living. Criteria: average income; inflation; employment prospects; and workers' Workplace Environment assessments according to the Gallup-Healthways Well-Being Index.
  www.money-rates.com, posted April 1, 2013

- *Forbes* analyzed business costs, labor supply, regulatory environment, current economic climate, growth prospects, and quality of life, to compile its "Best States for Business" rankings. Colorado ranked #5.
  www.forbes.com. posted December 12, 2012

- The 2012 Gallup-Healthways Well-Being Index, surveyed American's opinions on economic confidence, workplace perceptions, community climate, personal choices, and health predictors to assess the "future livability" of each state. Colorado ranked #3.
  "Utah Poised to Be the Best State to Live In," Gallup Wellbeing, www.gallup.com, August 7, 2012

- On CNBC's list of "America's Top States for Business 2013," Colorado ranked #7. Criteria: measures of competitiveness developed with input from the National Association of Manufacturers, the Council on Competitiveness, and other business groups weighed with the states' own marketing criteria.
  www.cnbc.com, consulted July 19, 2013

- Kiplinger identified "Ten States with the Biggest Rate of Job Growth in 2013" using data from the U.S. Bureau of Labor Statistics, IHS Global Insights, Moody's Analytics, and state economic data. Colorado ranked #5.
  www.kiplinger.com, March 2013

- Colorado ranked #6 on MoneyRates list of "Best-and Worst-States to Retire 2012." Criteria: life expectancy, crime rate, climate, economic conditions, taxes, job opportunities, and cost of living.
  www.money-rates.com, October 22, 2012

- Colorado ranked #38 on the 2013 Bankrate "Best Places to Retire" list ranking the states and District of Columbia on various criteria relating to health, safety, and cost.
  www.bankrate.com, May 6, 2013

- Colorado ranked #9 on the Social Science Research Council's "American Human Development Report: The Measure of America," assessing the 50 states plus the District of Columbia on health, education, and living-standard criteria.
  The Measure of America 2013-2014, posted June 19, 2013; www.measureofamerica.org

- Colorado ranked #26 on the Foundation for Child Development's (FCD) Child Well-being Index (CWI). The FCD used the KIDS COUNT report and the National Survey of Children's Health, the only state-level source for several key indicators of child well-being.
  Foundation for Child Development, January 18, 2012; fcd-us.org

- Colorado ranked #21 overall according to the 2013 KIDS COUNT Data Book, a project of the Annie E. Casey Foundation. Criteria: children's economic well-being, education, health, and family and community indicators.
  KIDS COUNT Data Center's Data Book, released June 20, 2013; http://datacenter.kidscount.org

- Colorado ranked #19 in the children's economic well-being category by the 2013 KIDS COUNT Data Book, a project of the Annie E. Casey Foundation.
  KIDS COUNT Data Center's Data Book, released June 20, 2013; http://datacenter.kidscount.org

- Colorado ranked #9 in the children's educational opportunities and attainments category by the 2013 KIDS COUNT Data Book, a project of the Annie E. Casey Foundation.
  KIDS COUNT Data Center's Data Book, released June 20, 2013; http://datacenter.kidscount.org

- Colorado ranked #42 in the children's health category by the 2013 KIDS COUNT Data Book, a project of the Annie E. Casey Foundation.
  KIDS COUNT Data Center's Data Book, released June 20, 2013; http://datacenter.kidscount.org

- Colorado ranked #21 in the family and community circumstances that factor into children's well-being category by the 2013 KIDS COUNT Data Book, a project of the Annie E. Casey Foundation.
  KIDS COUNT Data Center's Data Book, released June 20, 2013; http://datacenter.kidscount.org

- Colorado ranked #2 in the 2012 Gallup-Healthways Well-Being Index. Criteria: emotional health; physical health; healthy behavior; work environment; basic access to food, shelter, health care; and a safe and satisfying place to live.
  2012 State of Well-Being, Gallup-Healthways Well-Being Index, released February 28, 2013; www.well-beingindex.com

- *U.S. News and World Report's* "Best States for Teen Drivers" rankings are based on driving and road safety laws, federal reports on driver's licenses, car accident fatality, and road-quality statistics. Colorado ranked #3.
  U.S. News and World Report, March 18, 2010; www.usnews.com

- The Yahoo! Sports service Rivals.com ranks the states according to the strength of their high school football programs. Colorado ranked #30.
  "Ranking the States: Where Is the Best Football Played?," November 18, 2011; highschool.rivals.com

- iVillage ranked the states by hospitable living conditions for women. Criteria: economic success, access to affordable childcare, health care, reproductive rights, female representation in government, and educational attainment. Colorado ranked #12.
  iVillage, "50 Best to Worst States for Women," March 14, 2012; www.ivillage.com

- The League of American Bicyclists's "Bicycle Friendly States" ranked Colorado #2. Criteria: legislation and enforcement, policies and programs, infrastructure and funding, education and advocacy, and evaluation and planning.
  "Washington Tops the Bicycle-Friendly State Ranking," May 1, 2013; bicycling.com

- The federal Corporation for National and Community Service ranked the states and the District of Columbia by volunteer rates. Colorado ranked #13 for community service.
  "Volunteering and Civic Life in America 2012," www.volunteeringinamerica.gov, accessed July 24, 2013

- The Hospital Safety Score ranked states and the District of Columbia on their hospitals' performance scores. Colorado ranked #8. Criteria: avoiding preventable harm and medical errors, as demonstrated by 26 hospital safety metrics.
  Spring 2013 Hospital Safety Score, May 8, 2013; www.hospitalsafetyscore.org

- GMAC Insurance ranked the states and the District of Columbia by the performance of their drivers on the GMAC Insurance National Drivers Test, comprised of DMV test questions. Colorado ranked #3.
  "2011 GMAC Insurance National Drivers Test," www.gmacinsurance.com, accessed July 23, 2013

- Colorado ranked #33 in a "State Integrity Investigation" analysis of laws and practices intended to deter corruption and promote accountability and openness in campaign finance, ethics laws, lobbying regulations and management of state pension funds.
  "What's Your State's Grade?," www.publicintegrity.org, accessed July 23, 2013

- Colorado ranked #26 among the states and the District of Columbia in total rail miles, as tracked by the Association of American Railroads.
  "U.S. Freight Railroad Industry Snapshot: Railroads and States: Total Rail Miles by State: 2011"; www.aar.org, accessed July 23, 2013

- According to statistics compiled by the Beer Institute, Colorado ranked #24 among the states and the District of Columbia in per capita beer consumption of persons 21 years or older.
  "Shipments of Malt Beverages and Per Capita Consumption by State 2012;" www.beerinstitute.org

- According to Concordia University's "Public Education Costs per Pupil by State Rankings," based on statistics gathered by the U.S. Census Bureau, which includes the District of Columbia, Colorado ranked #41.
  Concordia University Online; education.cu-portland.edu, accessed July 24, 2013

- Colorado ranked #37 among the states and the District of Columbia in population density based on U.S. Census Bureau data for resident population and total land area. "List of U.S. States by Population Density."
  www.wikipedia.org, accessed July 24, 2013

- In "America's Health Rankings, 2012 Edition," by the United Health Foundation, Colorado ranked #11. Criteria included: rate of high school graduation; violent crime rate; incidence of infectious disease; childhood immunizations; prevalence of diabetes; per capita public-health funding; percentage of uninsured population; rate of children in poverty; and availability of primary-care physicians.
  United Health Foundation; www.americashealthrankings.org, accessed July 24, 2013

- The TechNet 2012 "State Broadband Index" ranked Colorado #22 on the following criteria: broadband adoption; network quality; and economic structure. Improved broadband use is hoped to promote economic development, build strong communities, improve delivery of government services and upgrade educational systems.
  TechNet; www.technet.org, accessed July 24, 2013

- Colorado was ranked #14 among the states and District of Columbia on the American Council for an Energy-Efficient Economy's "State Energy Efficiency Scorecard" for 2012.
  American Council for an Energy-Efficient Economy; aceee.org/sector/state-policy/scorecard, accessed July 24, 2013

Statistical Tables

DEMOGRAPHICS
Resident State and National Population, 1950-2012
Projected State and National Population, 2000-2030
Population by Age, 2012
Population by Race, 2012
Population by Hispanic Origin and Race, 2012

VITAL STATISTICS
Death Rates by Leading Causes, 2010
Death Rates by Selected Causes, 2010
Abortion Rates, 2009
Infant Mortality Rates, 1995-2009
Marriage and Divorce Rates, 2000-2011

ECONOMY
Nominal Gross Domestic Product by Industry, 2012
Real Gross Domestic Product, 2000-2012
Personal Income Per Capita, 1930-2012
Non-Farm Employment by Sector, 2012
Foreign Exports, 2000-2012
Energy Consumption, 2011

LAND AND WATER
Surface Area and Federally-Owned Land, 2007
Land Cover/Use of Non-Federal Rural Land, 2007
Farms and Crop Acreage, 2012

HEALTH AND MEDICAL CARE
Medical Professionals, 2012
Health Insurance Coverage, 2011
HIV, STD, and Tuberculosis Cases and Rates, 2011
Cigarette Smoking, 2011

HOUSING
Home Ownership Rates, 1995-2012
Home Sales, 2000-2010
Value of Owner-Occupied Homes, 2011

EDUCATION
School Enrollment, 2011
Educational Attainment, 2011
Public College Finances, FY 2012

TRANSPORTATION AND TRAVEL
Motor Vehicle Registrations and Drivers Licenses, 2011
Domestic Travel Expenditures, 2009
Retail Gasoline Prices, 2013
Public Road Length, 2011

CRIME AND LAW ENFORCEMENT
Full-Time Law Enforcement Officers, 2011
Prison Population, 2000-2012
Crime Rate, 2011

GOVERNMENT AND FINANCE
Local Governments by Type, 2012
State Government Revenue, 2011
State Government Expenditures, 2011
State Government General Expenditures by Function, 2011
State Government Finances, Cash and Debt, 2011

POLITICS
Composition of the Senate, 1995-2013
Composition of the House of Representatives, 1995-2013
Composition of State Legislature, 2004-2013
Voter Participation in Presidential Elections, 1980-2012
Governors Since Statehood

DEMOGRAPHICS

Resident State and National Population, 1950–2012

Year	State Population	U.S. Population	State Share
1950	1,325,000	151,326,000	0.88%
1960	1,754,000	179,323,000	0.98%
1970	2,209,596	203,302,031	1.09%
1980	2,889,964	226,545,805	1.28%
1990	3,294,394	248,709,873	1.32%
2000	4,302,086	281,424,600	1.53%
2010	5,029,196	308,745,538	1.63%
2012	5,187,582	313,914,040	1.65%

Note: 1950/1960 population figures are rounded to the nearest thousand.
Source: U.S. Census Bureau, Decennial Census 1950–2010; U.S. Census Bureau, 2012 Population Estimates

Projected State and National Population, 2000–2030

Year	State Population	U.S. Population	State Share
2000	4,301,261	281,421,906	1.53%
2005	4,617,962	295,507,134	1.56%
2010	4,831,554	308,935,581	1.56%
2015	5,049,493	322,365,787	1.57%
2020	5,278,867	335,804,546	1.57%
2025	5,522,803	349,439,199	1.58%
2030	5,792,357	363,584,435	1.59%
State population growth, 2000–2030			1,491,096
State percentage growth, 2000–2030			34.7%

Source: U.S. Census Bureau, Population Division, Interim State Population Projections, 2005

Population by Age, 2012

Age Group	State Population	Percent of Total Population State	Percent of Total Population U.S.
Under 5 years	337,568	6.5%	6.4%
5 to 14 years	695,760	13.4%	13.1%
15 to 24 years	704,700	13.6%	14.0%
25 to 34 years	761,670	14.7%	13.5%
35 to 44 years	707,346	13.6%	12.9%
45 to 54 years	725,419	14.0%	14.1%
55 to 64 years	641,878	12.4%	12.3%
65 to 74 years	358,320	6.9%	7.6%
75 to 84 years	178,411	3.4%	4.2%
85 years and older	76,510	1.5%	1.9%
Under 18 years	1,231,358	23.7%	23.5%
65 years and older	613,241	11.8%	13.7%
Median age (years)	–	36.3	37.4

Source: U.S. Census Bureau, Annual Estimates of the Resident Population for Selected Age Groups by Sex for the United States, States, Counties, and Puerto Rico Commonwealth and Municipios: April 1, 2010 to July 1, 2012

Population by Race, 2012

Race	State Population	Percent of Total Population State	Percent of Total Population U.S.
All residents	5,187,582	100.00%	100.00%
White	4,572,022	88.13%	77.89%
African American	225,390	4.34%	13.13%
Native American	81,688	1.57%	1.23%
Asian	155,031	2.99%	5.14%
Native Hawaiian	9,231	0.18%	0.23%
Two or more races	144,220	2.78%	2.39%

Source: U.S. Census Bureau, Population Division, Annual Estimates of the Resident Population by Sex, Race and Hispanic Origin for the United States, States, and Counties: April 1, 2010 to July 1, 2012

Population by Hispanic Origin and Race, 2012

Hispanic Origin/Race	State Population	Percent of Total Population State	Percent of Total Population U.S.
All residents	5,187,582	100.00%	100.00%
All Hispanic residents	1,088,744	20.99%	16.89%
Hispanic			
White	963,935	18.58%	14.91%
African American	26,264	0.51%	0.79%
Native American	48,684	0.94%	0.49%
Asian	8,478	0.16%	0.17%
Native Hawaiian	2,890	0.06%	0.06%
Two or more races	38,493	0.74%	0.48%
Not Hispanic			
White	3,608,087	69.55%	62.98%
African American	199,126	3.84%	12.34%
Native American	33,004	0.64%	0.74%
Asian	146,553	2.83%	4.98%
Native Hawaiian	6,341	0.12%	0.17%
Two or more races	105,727	2.04%	1.91%

Source: U.S. Census Bureau, Population Division, Annual Estimates of the Resident Population by Sex, Race and Hispanic Origin for the United States, States, and Counties: April 1, 2010 to July 1, 2012

VITAL STATISTICS

Death Rates by Leading Causes, 2010

Cause	State	U.S.
Malignant neoplasms	160.2	186.2
Ischaemic heart diseases	84.7	122.9
Other forms of heart disease	43.5	53.4
Chronic lower respiratory diseases	52.4	44.7
Cerebrovascular diseases	38.7	41.9
Organic, incl. symptomatic, mental disorders	38.5	35.7
Other degenerative diseases of the nervous sys.	34.5	28.4
Other external causes of accidental injury	34.1	26.5
Diabetes mellitus	16.4	22.4
Hypertensive diseases	13.6	20.4
All causes	729.1	799.5

Note: Figures are age-adjusted death rates per 100,000 population
Source: CDC/NCHS, Underlying Cause of Death 1999–2010 on CDC WONDER Online Database

Death Rates by Selected Causes, 2010

Cause	State	U.S.
Assault	3.3	5.2
Diseases of the liver	15.8	13.9
Human immunodeficiency virus (HIV) disease	1.3	2.7
Influenza and pneumonia	13.3	16.2
Intentional self-harm	17.2	12.4
Malnutrition	0.9	0.9
Obesity and other hyperalimentation	1.7	1.8
Renal failure	8.8	14.4
Transport accidents	10.7	12.1
Viral hepatitis	2.0	2.4

Note: Figures are age-adjusted death rates per 100,000 population; A dash indicates that data was not available or was suppressed
Source: CDC/NCHS, Underlying Cause of Death 1999–2010 on CDC WONDER Online Database

Abortion Rates, 2009

Category	2009
By state of residence	
Total abortions	10,735
Abortion rate[1]	10.4%
Abortion ratio[2]	156
By state of occurrence	
Total abortions	11,598
Abortion rate[1]	11.3%
Abortion ratio[2]	169
Abortions obtained by out-of-state residents	8.0%
U.S. abortion rate[1]	15.1%
U.S. abortion ratio[2]	227

Note: (1) Number of abortions per 1,000 women aged 15–44 years; (2) Number of abortions per 1,000 live births; A dash indicates that data was not available
Source: CDC/NCHS, Morbidity and Mortality Weekly Report, November 23, 2012 (Abortion Surveillance, United States, 2009)

Infant Mortality Rates, 1995–2009

Category	1995	2000	2005	2009
All state residents	6.41	6.14	6.44	6.24
All U.S. residents	7.57	6.89	6.86	6.39
All state white residents	5.94	5.61	6.11	5.85
All U.S. white residents	6.30	5.71	5.73	5.33
All state black residents	14.89	16.50	14.73	13.41
All U.S. black residents	14.58	13.48	13.26	12.12

Note: Figures represent deaths per 1,000 live births of resident infants under one year old, exclusive of fetal deaths; A dash indicates that data was not available or was suppressed.
Source: Centers of Disease Control and Prevention, Division of Vital Statistics, Linked Birth/Infant Death Records on CDC Wonder Online

Marriage and Divorce Rates, 2000–2011

Year	Marriage Rate State	Marriage Rate U.S.	Divorce Rate State	Divorce Rate U.S.
2000	8.3	8.2	4.7	4.0
2002	8.0	8.0	4.7	3.9
2004	7.4	7.8	4.4	3.7
2006	7.2	7.5	4.5	3.7
2008	7.4	7.1	4.3	3.5
2010	6.9	6.8	4.3	3.6
2011	7.0	6.8	4.4	3.6

Note: Rates are based on provisional counts of marriages/divorces by state of occurrence and are per 1,000 total population residing in area
Source: CDC/NCHS, National Vital Statistics System

ECONOMY

Nominal Gross Domestic Product by Industry, 2012
In millions of current dollars

Industry	State GDP
Accommodation and food services	9,659
Administrative and waste management services	8,787
Agriculture, forestry, fishing, and hunting	2,287
Arts, entertainment, and recreation	3,515
Construction	10,015
Educational services	2,230
Finance and insurance	16,974
Health care and social assistance	16,964
Information	22,484
Management of companies and enterprises	5,909
Manufacturing	19,992
Mining	10,201
Other services, except government	6,840
Professional, scientific, and technical services	26,678
Real estate and rental and leasing	34,621
Retail trade	15,977
Transportation and warehousing	7,328
Utilities	4,233
Wholesale trade	14,432

Source: U.S. Department of Commerce, Bureau of Economic Analysis, Survey of Current Business

Real Gross Domestic Product, 2000–2012
In millions of chained 2005 dollars

Year	State GDP	U.S. GDP	State Share
2000	195,300	11,225,406	1.74%
2005	217,329	12,539,116	1.73%
2010	230,976	12,897,088	1.79%
2012	239,884	13,430,576	1.79%

Source: U.S. Department of Commerce, Bureau of Economic Analysis, Survey of Current Business

Personal Income Per Capita, 1930–2012

Year	State	U.S.
1930	$571	$618
1940	$542	$593
1950	$1,512	$1,503
1960	$2,331	$2,268
1970	$4,040	$4,084
1980	$10,714	$10,091
1990	$19,377	$19,354
2000	$33,986	$30,319
2010	$42,107	$39,791
2012	$45,135	$42,693

Source: U.S. Department of Commerce, Bureau of Economic Analysis, Regional Economic Accounts

Non-Farm Employment by Sector, 2012
In thousands

Sector	Employment
Construction	115.1
Education and health services	282.3
Financial activities	146.1
Government	394.6
Information	69.7
Leisure and hospitality	280.3
Mining and logging	30.3
Manufacturing	132.1
Other services	95.5
Professional and business services	355.1
Trade, transportation, and utilities	409.0
All sectors	2,310.0

Source: U.S. Bureau of Labor Statistics, State and Area Employment

Foreign Exports, 2000–2012
In millions of dollars

Year	State Exports	U.S. Exports	State Share
2000	6,592	712,054	0.93%
2002	5,525	649,940	0.85%
2004	6,659	768,554	0.87%
2006	7,954	973,994	0.82%
2008	7,712	1,222,545	0.63%
2010	6,726	1,208,080	0.56%
2012	8,167	1,478,268	0.55%

Note: U.S. figures exclude data from Puerto Rico, U.S. Virgin Islands, and unallocated exports
Source: U.S. Department of Commerce, International Trade Admin., Office of Trade and Industry Information, Manufacturing and Services

Energy Consumption, 2011

In trillions of BTUs, except as noted

Total energy consumption	
Total state energy consumption	1,480.8
Total U.S. energy consumption	97,387.3
State share of U.S. total	1.52%
Per capita consumption (in millions of BTUs)	
Total state per capita consumption	289.4
Total U.S. per capita consumption	312.6
End-use sectors	
Residential	353.0
Commercial	287.2
Industrial	423.6
Transportation	416.9
Sources of energy	
Petroleum	472.9
Natural gas	476.5
Coal	368.9
Renewable energy	102.9
Nuclear electric power	0.0

Source: U.S. Energy Information Administration, State Energy Data 2011: Consumption

LAND AND WATER

Surface Area and Federally-Owned Land, 2007

In thousands of acres

Category	State	U.S.	State Share
Total surface area	66,624.5	1,937,664.2	3.44%
Total land area	66,292.4	1,886,846.9	3.51%
Non-federal land	42,495.5	1,484,910.0	2.86%
Developed	1,934.3	111,251.2	1.74%
Rural	40,561.2	1,373,658.8	2.95%
Federal land	23,796.9	401,936.9	5.92%
Water area	332.1	50,817.3	0.65%

Source: U.S. Department of Agriculture, Natural Resources Conservation Service, 2007 National Resources Inventory

Land Cover/Use of Non-Federal Rural Land, 2007

In thousands of acres

Category	State	U.S.	State Share
Total rural land	40,561.2	1,373,658.8	2.95%
Cropland	7,609.4	357,023.5	2.13%
CRP[1] land	2,446.9	32,850.2	7.45%
Pastureland	1,032.9	118,615.7	0.87%
Rangeland	25,275.8	409,119.4	6.18%
Forest land	3,243.8	406,410.4	0.80%
Other rural land	952.4	49,639.6	1.92%

Note: (1) Conservation Reserve Program was created to assist private landowners in converting highly erodible cropland to vegetative cover.
Source: U.S. Department of Agriculture, Natural Resources Conservation Service, 2007 National Resources Inventory

Farms and Crop Acreage, 2012

Category	State	U.S.	State Share
Farms (in thousands)	36.3	2,170.0	1.67%
Acres (in millions)	31.3	914.0	3.42%
Acres per farm	862.3	421.2	–

Source: U.S. Department of Agriculture, National Agricultural Statistical Service, Quick Stats, 2012 Survey Data

HEALTH AND MEDICAL CARE

Medical Professionals, 2012

Profession	State Number	U.S. Number	State Share	State Rate[1]	U.S. Rate[1]
Physicians[2]	14,253	894,637	1.59%	278.6	287.1
Dentists	3,739	193,587	1.93%	73.1	62.1
Podiatrists	183	17,469	1.05%	3.6	5.6
Optometrists	885	45,638	1.94%	17.3	14.6
Chiropractors	1,838	77,494	2.37%	35.9	24.9

Note: (1) Rates are per 100,000 population; (2) Includes total, active Doctors of Osteopathic Medicine and Doctors of Medicine in 2011.
Source: U.S. Department of Health and Human Services, Bureau of Health Professions, Area Health Resource File, 2012-2013

Health Insurance Coverage, 2011

Category	State	U.S.
Total persons covered	4,239,000	260,214,000
Total persons not covered	789,000	48,613,000
Percent not covered	15.7%	15.7%
Children under age 18 covered	1,122,000	67,143,000
Children under age 18 not covered	131,000	6,965,000
Percent of children not covered	10.5%	9.4%

Source: U.S. Census Bureau, Current Population Survey, 2012 Annual Social and Economic Supplement

HIV, STD, and Tuberculosis Cases and Rates, 2011

Disease	State Cases	State Rate[1]	U.S. Rate[1]
Chlamydia	21,811	433.7	457.6
Gonorrhea	2,363	47.0	104.2
HIV diagnosis	404	9.6	15.8
HIV, stage 3 (AIDS)	256	6.1	10.3
Syphilis, early latent	154	3.1	4.3
Syphilis, primary/secondary	133	2.6	4.5
Tuberculosis	70	1.4	3.4

Note: (1) Rates are per 100,000 population
Source: Centers for Disease Control and Prevention

Cigarette Smoking, 2011

Category	State	U.S.
Adults who are current smokers	18.3%	21.2%
Adults who smoke everyday	12.3%	15.4%
Adults who smoke some days	6.0%	5.7%
Adults who are former smokers	27.2%	25.1%
Adults who never smoked	54.6%	52.9%

Source: Centers for Disease Control and Prevention, Behaviorial Risk Factor Surveillance System, Tobacco Use, 2011

HOUSING

Home Ownership Rates, 1995–2012

Area	1995	2000	2005	2010	2012
State	64.6%	68.3%	71.0%	68.5%	65.3%
U.S.	64.7%	67.4%	68.9%	66.9%	65.4%

Source: U.S. Census Bureau, Housing Vacancies and Homeownership, Annual Statistics

Home Sales, 2000–2010

In thousands of units

Year	State Sales	U.S. Sales	State Share
2000	111.5	5,174	2.16%
2002	109.4	5,632	1.94%
2004	126.0	6,778	1.86%
2006	123.7	6,478	1.91%
2008	106.8	4,913	2.17%
2010	90.5	4,908	1.84%

Note: Units include single-family homes, condos and co-ops
Source: National Association of Realtors, Real Estate Outlook, Market Trends & Insights

Value of Owner-Occupied Homes, 2011

Value	Total Units in State	Percent of Total, State	Percent of Total, U.S.
Less than $50,000	60,085	4.7%	8.8%
$50,000 to $99,000	69,195	5.4%	16.0%
$100,000 to $149,000	145,451	11.4%	16.5%
$150,000 to $199,000	225,217	17.7%	15.4%
$200,000 to $299,000	355,644	28.0%	18.2%
$300,000 to $499,000	273,909	21.5%	15.2%
$500,000 to $999,000	115,316	9.1%	7.9%
$1,000,000 or more	26,987	2.1%	2.0%
Median value	–	$233,700	$173,600

Source: U.S. Census Bureau, 2011 American Community Survey 1-Year Estimates

EDUCATION

School Enrollment, 2011

Educational Level	Students Enrolled in State	Percent of Total, State	Percent of Total, U.S.
All levels	1,377,803	100.0%	100.0%
Nursery school, preschool	89,850	6.5%	6.0%
Kindergarten	67,775	4.9%	5.1%
Elementary (grades 1–8)	545,345	39.6%	39.5%
Secondary (grades 9–12)	272,164	19.8%	20.7%
College or graduate school	402,669	29.2%	28.7%

Note: Figures cover the population 3 years and over enrolled in school
Source: U.S. Census Bureau, 2011 American Community Survey 1-Year Estimates

Educational Attainment, 2011

Highest Level of Education	State	U.S.
High school diploma	90.2%	85.9%
Bachelor's degree	36.7%	28.5%
Graduate/Professional degree	13.4%	10.6%

Note: Figures cover the population 25 years and over
Source: U.S. Census Bureau, 2011 American Community Survey 1-Year Estimates

Public College Finances, FY 2012

Category	State	U.S.
Full-time equivalent enrollment (FTE)[1]	192,541	11,548,974
Educational appropriations per FTE[2]	$2,551	$5,906
Net tuition revenue per FTE[3]	$6,171	$5,189
Total educational revenue per FTE[4]	$8,722	$11,043

(1) Full-time equivalent enrollment equates student credit hours to full time, academic year students, but excludes medical students; (2) Educational appropriations measure state and local support available for public higher education operating expenses including ARRA funds and excludes appropriations for independent institutions, financial aid for students attending independent institutions, research, hospitals, and medical education; (3) Net tuition revenue is calculated by taking the gross amount of tuition and fees, less state and institutional financial aid, tuition waivers or discounts, and medical student tuition and fees. Net tuition revenue used for capital debt service is included in the net tuition revenue figures; (4) Total educational revenue is the sum of educational appropriations and net tuition excluding net tuition revenue used for capital debt service.
Source: State Higher Education Executive Officers, State Higher Education Finance FY 2012

TRANSPORTATION AND TRAVEL

Motor Vehicle Registrations and Drivers Licenses, 2011

Vehicle Type	State	U.S.	State Share
Automobiles[1]	1,798,922	125,656,528	1.43%
Buses	10,005	666,064	1.50%
Trucks	2,350,093	118,455,587	1.98%
Motorcycles	173,231	8,437,502	2.05%
Drivers licenses	3,669,816	211,874,649	1.73%

Note: Motor vehicle registrations include private, commercial, and publicly-owned vehicles; (1) Includes taxicabs
Source: U.S. Department of Transportation, Federal Highway Administration

Domestic Travel Expenditures, 2009

In millions of dollars

Category	State	U.S.	State Share
Travel expenditures	$12,028	$610,200	1.97%

Note: Figures represent U.S. spending on domestic overnight trips and day trips of 50 miles or more, one way, away from home. Excludes spending by foreign visitors.
Source: U.S. Travel Association, Impact of Travel on State Economies, 2009

Retail Gasoline Prices, 2013

Gasoline Grade	State Average	U.S. Average
Regular	$3.56	$3.65
Mid	$3.67	$3.81
Premium	$3.79	$3.98
Diesel	$3.80	$3.88
Excise tax[1]	40.4 cents	49.4 cents

Note: Gasoline prices as of 7/26/2013; (1) Includes state and federal excise taxes and other state taxes as of July 1, 2013
Source: American Automobile Association, Daily Fuel Guage Report; American Petroleum Institute, State Motor Fuel Taxes, 2013

Public Road Length, 2011

Type	State Mileage	U.S. Mileage	State Share
Interstate highways	953	46,960	2.03%
Other highways	353	15,719	2.25%
Principal arterial	3,494	156,262	2.24%
Minor arterial	5,386	242,942	2.22%
Major collector	7,296	534,592	1.36%
Minor collector	8,963	266,357	3.37%
Local	61,970	2,814,925	2.20%
Urban	19,531	1,095,373	1.78%
Rural	68,883	2,982,383	2.31%
Total	88,415	4,077,756	2.17%

Note: Combined urban and rural road mileage equals the total of the other road types
Source: U.S. Department of Transportation, Federal Highway Administration, Public Road Length, 2011

CRIME AND LAW ENFORCEMENT

Full-Time Law Enforcement Officers, 2011

Gender	State Number	State Rate[1]	U.S. Rate[1]
Male officers	9,864	194.9	210.3
Female officers	1,391	27.5	28.1
Total officers	11,255	222.4	238.3

Note: (1) Rates are per 100,000 population
Source: Federal Bureau of Investigation, Uniform Crime Reports, Crime in the United States 2011

Prison Population, 2000–2012

Year	State Population	U.S. Population	State Share
2000	16,833	1,391,261	1.21%
2005	21,456	1,527,929	1.40%
2010	22,815	1,613,803	1.41%
2011	21,978	1,598,783	1.37%
2012	20,462	1,571,013	1.30%

Note: Figures include prisoners under the jurisdiction of state or federal correctional authorities.
Source: U.S. Department of Justice, Bureau of Justice Statistics, Prisoners in 2006, 2011, 2012 (Advance Counts)

Crime Rate, 2011
Incidents per 100,000 residents

Category	State	U.S.
Violent crimes	320.2	386.3
Murder	2.9	4.7
Forcible rape	44.5	26.8
Robbery	64.6	113.7
Aggravated assault	208.1	241.1
Property crimes	2,606.3	2,908.7
Burglary	503.6	702.2
Larceny/theft	1,886.8	1,976.9
Motor vehicle theft	215.9	229.6
All crimes	2,926.5	3,295.0

Source: Federal Bureau of Investigation, Uniform Crime Reports, Crime in the United States 2011

GOVERNMENT AND FINANCE

Local Governments by Type, 2012

Government Type	State	U.S.	State Share
All local governments	2,818	89,004	3.17%
County	62	3,031	2.05%
Municipality	271	19,522	1.39%
Town/Township	0	16,364	0.00%
Special District	2,305	37,203	6.20%
Ind. School District	180	12,884	1.40%

Source: U.S. Census Bureau, 2012 Census of Governments: Organization Component Preliminary Estimates

State Government Revenue, 2011
In thousands of dollars, except for per capita figures

Total revenue	$30,248,080
Total revenue per capita, State	$5,912
Total revenue per capita, U.S.	$7,271
General revenue	$21,864,224
Intergovernmental revenue	$7,007,888
Taxes	$9,467,684
General sales	$2,173,882
Selective sales	$1,623,488
License taxes	$599,455
Individual income taxes	$4,540,586
Corporate income taxes	$383,513
Other taxes	$146,760
Current charges	$3,333,064
Miscellaneous general revenue	$2,055,588
Utility revenue	$0
Liquor store revenue	$0
Insurance trust revenue[1]	$8,383,856

Note: (1) Within insurance trust revenue, net earnings of state retirement systems is a calculated statistic, and thus can be positive or negative. Net earnings is the sum of earnings on investments plus gains on investments minus losses on investments.
Source: U.S. Census Bureau, 2011 Annual Survey of State Government Finances

State Government Expenditures, 2011

In thousands of dollars, except for per capita figures

Total expenditure	$29,169,425
Total expenditure per capita, State	$5,701
Total expenditure per capita, U.S.	$6,427
Intergovernmental expenditure	$7,090,961
Direct expenditure	$22,078,464
Current operation	$13,061,655
Capital outlay	$1,698,430
Insurance benefits and repayments	$6,108,159
Assistance and subsidies	$313,645
Interest on debt	$896,575
Utility expenditure	$30,937
Liquor store expenditure	$0
Insurance trust expenditure	$6,108,159

Source: U.S. Census Bureau, 2011 Annual Survey of State Government Finances

State Government General Expenditures by Function, 2011

In thousands of dollars

Education	$9,250,143
Public welfare	$5,663,074
Hospitals	$660,019
Health	$1,232,255
Highways	$1,436,154
Police protection	$137,732
Correction	$1,023,871
Natural resources	$336,507
Parks and recreation	$127,871
Governmental administration	$926,146
Interest on general debt	$872,349
Other and unallocable	$1,364,208

Source: U.S. Census Bureau, 2011 Annual Survey of State Government Finances

State Government Finances, Cash and Debt, 2011

In thousands of dollars, except for per capita figures

Debt at end of fiscal year	
State, total	$16,335,260
State, per capita	$3,193
U.S., per capita	$3,635
Cash and security holdings	
State, total	$62,786,242
State, per capita	$12,272
U.S., per capita	$11,759

Source: U.S. Census Bureau, 2011 Annual Survey of State Government Finances

POLITICS

Composition of the Senate, 1995–2013

Congress (Year)	State/U.S	Dem	Rep	Total
104th (1995)	State delegates	0	2	2
	Total U.S.	48	52	100
105th (1997)	State delegates	0	2	2
	Total U.S.	45	55	100
106th (1999)	State delegates	0	2	2
	Total U.S.	45	55	100
107th (2001)	State delegates	0	2	2
	Total U.S.	50	50	100
108th (2003)	State delegates	0	2	2
	Total U.S.	48	51	100
109th (2005)	State delegates	1	1	2
	Total U.S.	44	55	100
110th (2007)	State delegates	1	1	2
	Total U.S.	49	49	100
111th (2009)	State delegates	2	0	2
	Total U.S.	57	41	100
112th (2011)	State delegates	2	0	2
	Total U.S.	51	47	100
113th (2013)	State delegates	2	0	2
	Total U.S.	54	45	100

Note: Figures are for the starts of first sessions; Totals include Democratic (Dem) and Republican (Rep) members as well as vacancies and seats held by independent party members
Source: U.S. Congress, Congressional Directory

Composition of the House of Representatives, 1995–2013

Congress (Year)	State/U.S	Dem	Rep	Total
104th (1995)	State delegates	2	4	6
	Total U.S.	204	230	435
105th (1997)	State delegates	2	4	6
	Total U.S.	207	226	435
106th (1999)	State delegates	2	4	6
	Total U.S.	211	223	435
107th (2001)	State delegates	2	4	6
	Total U.S.	212	221	435
108th (2003)	State delegates	2	5	7
	Total U.S.	205	229	435
109th (2005)	State delegates	3	4	7
	Total U.S.	202	231	435
110th (2007)	State delegates	4	3	7
	Total U.S.	233	198	435
111th (2009)	State delegates	5	2	7
	Total U.S.	256	178	435
112th (2011)	State delegates	3	4	7
	Total U.S.	193	242	435
113th (2013)	State delegates	3	4	7
	Total U.S.	201	234	435

Note: Figures are for the starts of first sessions; Totals include Democratic (Dem) and Republican (Rep) members as well as vacancies and seats held by independent party members
Source: U.S. Congress, Congressional Directory

Composition of State Legislature, 2004–2013

Year	Democrats	Republicans	Total
State Senate			
2004	17	18	35
2005	18	17	35
2006	18	17	35
2007	20	15	35
2008	20	15	35
2009	21	14	35
2010	21	14	35
2011	20	15	35
2012	20	15	35
2013	20	15	35
State House			
2004	28	37	65
2005	35	30	65
2006	35	30	65
2007	39	26	65
2008	40	25	65
2009	38	27	65
2010	38	27	65
2011	32	33	65
2012	32	33	65
2013	37	28	65

Note: Totals may include minor party members and vacancies
Source: The Council of State Governments, State Legislatures

Voter Participation in Presidential Elections, 1980–2012

Year	Voting-eligible State Population	State Voter Turnout Rate	U.S. Voter Turnout Rate
1980	2,071,959	57.2	54.2
1984	2,267,668	57.1	55.2
1988	2,327,768	59.0	52.8
1992	2,494,998	62.9	58.1
1996	2,770,252	54.5	51.7
2000	3,026,316	57.5	54.2
2004	3,192,647	66.7	60.1
2008	3,382,959	71.0	61.6
2012	3,654,045	70.3	58.2

Note: All figures are based on the voting-eligible population which excludes person ineligible to vote such as non-citizens, felons (depending on state law), and mentally-incapacitated persons. U.S. figures include the overseas eligible population (including military personnel).
Source: McDonald, Michael P., United States Election Project, Presidential Voter Turnout Rates, 1980–2012

Governors Since Statehood

John L. Routt (R) 1876-1879
Frederick W. Pitkin (R) 1879-1883
James B. Grant (D). 1883-1885
Benjamin H. Eaton (R) 1885-1887
Alva Adams (D) 1887-1889
Job A. Cooper (R) 1889-1891
John L. Routt (R) 1891-1893
Davis H. Waite (D). 1893-1895
Albert W. McIntire (R). 1895-1897
Alva Adams (D) 1897-1899
Charles S. Thomas (O) 1899-1901

James B. Orman (O). 1901-1903
James H. Peabody (R) 1903-1905
Alva Adams (D) . . . . (r) 1905
James H. Peabody (R) 1905
Jesse F. McDonald (R) 1905-1907
Henry A. Buchtel (R) 1907-1909
John F. Shafroth (D). 1909-1913
Elias M. Ammons (D) 1913-1915
George A. Carlson (R) 1915-1917
Julius C. Gunter (D) 1917-1919
Oliver H. Shoup (R) 1919-1923
William E. Sweet (D) 1923-1925
Clarence J. Morley (R). 1925-1927
William H. Adams (D). 1927-1933
Edwin C. Johnson (D) . . . . (r) 1933-1937
Ray H. Talbot (D) 1937
Teller Ammons (D) 1937-1939
Ralph L. Carr (R) 1939-1943
John C. Vivian (R) 1943-1947
William L. Knous (D) . . . . (r) 1947-1950
Walter W. Johnson (D). 1950-1951
Daniel I. J. Thornton (R) 1951-1955
Edwin C. Johnson (D) 1955-1957
Stephen L. R. McNichols (D). 1957-1963
John A. Love (R) . . . . (r) 1963-1973
John D. Vanderhoof (R) 1973-1975
Richard D. Lamm (D) 1975-1987
Roy Romer (D). 1987-1999
Bill Owens (R) 1999-2007
Bill Ritter (D). 2007-2011
John Hickenlooper (D) 2011-2015

Note: (D) Democrat; (R) Republican; (O) Other party; (r) resigned; (d) died in office; (i) removed from office

Connecticut

Location: New England

Area and rank: 4,845 square miles (12,550 square kilometers); 5,544 square miles (14,359 square kilometers) including water; forty-eighth largest state in area

Shoreline: 618 miles (995 kilometers) on Long Island Sound

Population and rank: 3,590,347 (2012 estimate); twenty-ninth largest state in population

Capital city: Hartford (124,775 people in 2010 census)

Largest city: Bridgeport (144,229 people in 2010 census)

Entered Union and rank: January 9, 1788; fifth state

Present constitution adopted: December 30, 1965

A mixture of Gothic and Renaissance architectural styles, the state capitol building in Hartford was completed in 1878. Almost a century later, it was designated a National Historic Landmark. (Wikimedia Commons)

Counties: 8

State name: "Connecticut" is derived from the Indian word "Quinnehtukqut," meaning "beside the long tidal river"

State nickname: Nutmeg State

Motto: *Qui transtulit sustinet* (He who transplanted still sustains)

State flag: Azure field with state coat of arms above banner with state motto

Highest point: Mount Frissell—2,380 feet (725 meters)

Lowest point: Long Island Sound—sea level

Highest recorded temperature: 105 degrees Fahrenheit (41 degrees Celsius)—Waterbury, 1926

Lowest recorded temperature: –32 degrees Fahrenheit (–36 degrees Celsius)—Falls Village, 1943

State song: "Yankee Doodle"

State tree: White Oak

State flower: Mountain Laurel

State bird: American robin

State fish: (none)

State animal: Sperm whale

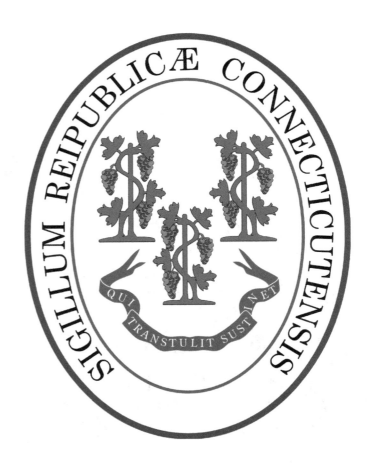

Connecticut History

Connecticut is the third smallest state in area in the Union, after Rhode Island and Delaware. It is also the fourth most densely populated state. Positioned at the southernmost part of New England, Connecticut is bordered by New York on the west, Rhode Island on the east, Massachusetts on the north, and Long Island Sound—an arm of the Atlantic Ocean—on the south. Like most New England states, Connecticut is shaped by its abundance of water. It has more than 1,000 lakes and 8,400 miles of rivers and streams. The three major rivers flowing through the state, the Connecticut, the Housatonic, and the Thames, provide ports, fishing, and power for industry.

The Connecticut River Valley has very fertile land; potatoes, corn, onions, lettuce, tobacco, and other crops are grown there. Forests cover 60 percent of the state, making Connecticut one of the most wooded states in the Union. Maple trees are used to supply sugar and syrup. Until the nineteenth century, salmon fishing was a highly profitable industry. After a dam was built on the Connecticut River, preventing salmon from reaching their spawning grounds, the salmon supply was depleted.

Early History. Connecticut was inhabited by American Indian tribes for thousands of years before the first Europeans came to North America. By the seventeenth century, approximately twenty thousand Algonquian Indians lived in the region. The dominant tribe was the Pequot, a warrior group who conquered most of the Connecticut River Valley during the sixteenth century. Other tribes included the Narragansetts, Quinnipiacs, Mohegans, and Saukiogs, who hunted moose, deer, and bear and grew corn, beans, and squash.

Dutch explorer Adriaen Block sailed the Connecticut River in 1614, meeting friendly Podunk Indians. In 1633, Dutch settlers built the House of Good Hope trading post near modern Hartford, where they traded with the Native Americans. In the same year, English settlers founded Windsor. Violence erupted between the settlers and the Pequots in 1637 over land disputes. The Native Americans were defeated during the Pequot War, with losses of six hundred people. Many remaining Native Americans left the state, and by 1990, Indians made up only 0.2 percent of the population.

Colonization. In 1638, 250 Puritans from the Massachusetts Bay Colony established the New Haven Colony. The government was based on the Fundamental Agreement, which stated that the Bible was the supreme law. The colony was not inclusive; only Puritans were allowed to vote or hold office.

The residents of Wethersfield, Windsor, and Hartford joined to form the Colony of Connecticut in 1639.

This colony's government was based on the teachings of Reverend Thomas Hooker, which were known as the Fundamental Orders. A Puritan preacher, Hooker believed that the right to vote should belong to all, regardless of their religion. The Fundamental Orders, which served as Connecticut's constitution for many years, were the first document in the New World to give the government its power from the "free consent of the people."

In 1643, Connecticut, New Haven, Massachussetts, and Plymouth colonies banded together, forming the Confederation of New England. The colonies stayed independent of each other but made a pact to act together in times of war. In 1662, the Connecticut colony received a royal charter, allowing it self-rule. The charter was revoked, however, twenty-three years later by King James. Edmund Andros, acting for the duke of York, tried to claim the area west of the Connecticut River for the New York colony. The residents of Connecticut refused to turn over their charter, supposedly hiding it in an oak tree, and they were able to resume self-rule in 1689. Connecticut became a state, the fifth in the Union, in 1788.

The American Revolution. Connecticut played a major role in the American Revolution. It sent thirty thousand soldiers into action—more, in relation to its population, than any other colony. These men included more than three hundred black soldiers. General George Washington called Connecticut the "Provisions State" because it sent so many supplies and munitions to the soldiers. The colony's navy captured more than forty British ships.

Connecticut produced both villains and heroes. One of its residents, Benedict Arnold, became a spy for the British, led English troops in an attack at Fort Griswold, and burned down the city of New London. Connecticut's Nathan Hale was a spy for the Union and became famous for the last words he uttered before the British hanged him.

Slavery in Connecticut. During the mid-eighteenth century, about three to five thousand black people lived in the colony, most of them slaves. A law was passed in 1774 prohibiting residents from bringing in new slaves, and the 1784 Connecticut Emancipation Law allowed children born to slaves to be freed at the age of twenty-five. After the Revolution, all slaves who fought were freed.

A well-publicized Connecticut court case in 1839 brought the issue of slavery to national attention. Africans carried in the Spanish slave ship *Amistad* mutinied and tried to force the crew to to turn the ship back to Africa. The crew instead secretly headed for Long Island, and the rebels, led by Joseph Cinqué, stood trial in Hartford for murder and piracy. In 1840, the U.S. Supreme Court ruled that the Africans were born free and taken as

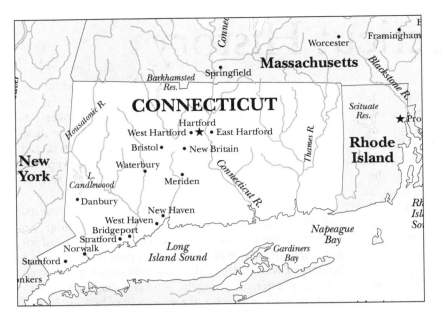

slaves against their will, so they were returned home. Slavery was banished in Connecticut in 1848. Later, the antislavery state sent more than fifty-seven thousand men to fight in the Civil War on the Union side.

Industry. In its early days, Connecticut's economy depended on agriculture and fishing. Its economy grew during the early ninteenth century with the construction of cotton, wool, and paper mills. Samuel Colt invented the six-shooter, the first repeating pistol, and its factories boomed. A machine to remove seeds from cotton, the cotton gin, invented in 1793 by Eli Whitney, added to the growth of industry.

Connecticut was hit hard by the Great Depression of the 1930's, with 22 percent of the state's workers unemployed. However, its economy bounced back during World War II. Connecticut produced more war supplies per person than any other state. During the late 1940's, more than half of its adult population worked in factories. Most of the industry was centered in ten towns, especially New Haven, Bridgeport, and Danbury, and half of Connecticut residents lived in these factory towns.

After the 1950's, textile production and other factory work subsided, and service jobs grew. Most middle-class families left the cities, and poverty increased in urban areas. Urban renewal programs initiated during the 1950's–1970's could not counter the riots that took place in poor areas in 1967.

Economy. By the end of the twentieth century, Hartford was the insurance capital of the world, a position it had held since the late eighteenth century. Groton was the submarine capital of the world during the early part of the century, but massive layoffs in the defense industry during the 1990's forced the closure of many shipyards and factories. Connecticut's population fell by several thousand during this period.

The state's economy was revitalized by the Mashantucket Pequot Indian Foxwoods Casino, which opened in 1993 as the largest casino in the Western Hemisphere. Paying the state one-quarter of its earnings, the casino pumps about $1 billion per year into Connecticut's economy. Nevertheless, the state imposed its first income tax in 1993, to the dismay of many.

Politics. Connecticut traditionally has been a Republican state. In 1974, however, Ella T. Grasso, a Democrat and the first Connecticut governor of Italian descent, became the first woman governor of a state elected in her own right. In 1981, Thirman Milner of Hartford became the first African American mayor of a New England city.

In 2000 Connecticut was honored when one of its U.S. senators, Joe Lieberman, was chosen running mate of Vice President Al Gore in his bid for the presidency. The state voted for the Democratic ticket, which lost in a narrow defeat. Lieberman, however, was reelected senator.

Social Issues and Headline Cases. Crime rates fell during the 1990's, and efforts were made to clean up Connecticut's deteriorating inner cities. The state government instituted a drug-policy reform in which drug addicts received methadone (a heroin substitute) treatments and thereby possibly avoided long-term imprisonment. Connecticut was the first state to place drug courts in every jurisdiction. About 75 percent of the defendants stay in the program, compared to about 25 percent in regular drug-treatment programs.

In July, 2000, West Nile virus was found in a dead bird, and authorities announced that the disease had circulated undetected in the state in 1999. In addition, the new national census did not benefit the state; it lost a representative in Congress as a result of declining population. In 2001, the state took a leading role in the national debate over the death penalty when Governor John Rowland signed a measure into law that mandated a study of the state's death penalty system. The study was to determine if racial or economic factors are used in decisions for execution. In 2002, Connecticut was the site of a sensational murder trial involving Michael Skakel, a nephew of Ethel and Robert Kennedy. The case involved the 1975 murder of a young woman. The defendant was convicted and sentenced to twenty years to life.

Two important public controversies erupted in the first years of the new century. One of them concerned pedophilia in the Roman Catholic Church. In 2002, Cardinal Edward Egan was accused of mishandling child molestation cases. Written evidence from previous years indicated both that he allowed priests accused of such crimes to continue working and that he failed to inform the authorities, contrary to legal requirements. In 2003, the matter was concluded when a suit involving forty people molested by sixteen priests was settled for $21 million. Finally, Governor Rowland became implicated in a bribery scandal when he was found to have accepted cash and gifts from state contractors. His resignation was effective on July 1, 2004.

2006 Democratic Primary. On August 8, 2006, Ned Lamont, scion of a wealthy Connecticut family, defeated Senator Lieberman in the Democratic primary election to gain the party's formal endorsement in the election for the senator's seat in November. The outcome caused a sensation both in the state and in the nation, since Lieberman had been Al Gore's running mate in 2000 and a strong fixture in the Democratic Party in Connecticut for many years. However, Lieberman's strong support for the Iraq War—which, for many Connecticut Democrats, tied him too closely to President George W. Bush—hurt his support. Many Democratic voters had soured on the war, and Lamont took full advantage of these sentiments. On August 9, however, Lieberman announced that he would run in the November election as an "independent Democrat." He won the ensuing contest.

Recent Politics. Several political developments from 2008 to 2012 showed Democrats gaining solid strength in statewide elections. In 2008, Christopher Shays, the lone conservative member of Congress from the region, was defeated by a Democratic businessman from Greenwich, Jim Himes. Shays was criticized for his backing the national financial bailout bill. His support for the war in Iraq and President Bush were seen as contributing to his defeat. Himes, 42, a former investment banker for Goldman Sachs, ended up representing the Connecticut district, one of the wealthiest in the nation. Meanwhile, the other Democrats in the state's delegation to Congress won re-election.

In the 2010 elections, Republican Tom Foley was defeated in the race for governor by Dan Malloy, candidate of both the Democratic Party and the local Working Families Party. In 2012, incumbent Senator Joe Lieberman, an independent who caucused with the Democratic Party, decided to retire. Republican Linda McMahon ran against Democratic member of Congress, Chris Murphy, with Murphy winning the seat.

Superstorm Sandy. In 2012, in response to Hurricane Sandy, which reached the shore as a severe tropical storm, Connecticut Governor Dan Malloy signed a Declaration of Emergency on October 29, also ordering road closures for all state highways. As the storm came ashore, local officials issued numerous mandatory and partial evacuations in cities across Connecticut.

Lauren M. Mitchell
Updated by the Editor

Replica of the Amistad *slave ship at Mystic Harbor.* (PhotoDisc)

Connecticut Time Line

1600's	Connecticut area is inhabited by Native American Algonquians dominated by Pequots.
1614	Dutch explorer Adriaen Block sails up Connecticut River and claims region for Holland.
1633	English settle Windsor.
June 6, 1633	Dutch buy land from Pequot Indians and build trading post at modern Hartford.
1636	Thomas Hooker and followers settle at Hartford.
1637	Pequot War ends with defeat of Indians.
1638	New Haven is founded.
Jan. 14, 1639	Fundamental Orders of Connecticut, the first written constitution, is adopted.
1639	Hartford, Wethersfield, and Windsor unite, forming Connecticut Colony.
1647	Connecticut is first New England colony to hang a woman convicted of witchcraft.
1662	Connecticut Colony is officially chartered.
Jan. 5, 1665	New Haven becomes part of Connecticut Colony.
1701	Yale University is founded in New Haven.
1740	First tinware in New World is made in central Connecticut by Edward and William Pattison.
1779	New Haven is attacked, and Fairfield and Norwalk are burned during Revolutionary War.
1781	Benedict Arnold, a Connecticut traitor leading British troops, burns New London.
1784	First American law school is founded in New Litchfield.
1784	Connecticut Emancipation Law rules children born to slaves become free at age twenty-five.
Jan. 9, 1788	Connecticut becomes fifth state in Union.
1794	Eli Whitney of Connecticut invents cotton gin.
1798	Whitney establishes mass production at gun-making plant in Whitneyville.
1810	First silk mill in the Union is built in Mansfield.
1818	New state constitution is ratified.
1833	Hartford and New Haven Railroad opens.
1835	Samuel Colt of Connecticut invents six-shooter pistol.
1841	Africans sold into slavery win freedom in Hartford trials after mutiny of *Amistad*.
1861–1865	Connecticut sends more than 57,000 men to fight in the Civil War for the Union.
1882	Knights of Columbus brotherhood is founded in New Haven.
1888	Great Blizzard of 1888 leaves hundreds dead.
1910	U.S. Coast Guard Academy moves to New London.
1917	U.S. naval submarine base opens at Groton.
1917-1918	During World War I, Connecticut is supply center; sends more than 60,000 men to fight.
1930's	Great Depression hits the industrial state hard; 150,000 are unemployed.
1941-1945	During World War II, Connecticut is supply center.
1943	Connecticut is first state to establish a civil rights commission.
Jan. 1954	First atomic-powered submarine, *Nautilus*, is launched at Groton.
1965	New state constitution is ratified.
1969	Race riots occur in black and Puerto Rican parts of Hartford.
1973	Waste agency opens, to combat widespread pollution.
1974	Connecticut's Ella Grasso is first woman to be elected a state governor without succeeding her husband.
1979	State bans construction of new nuclear plants.
1981	Thirman Milner of Hartford becomes first black mayor of a New England city.
1984	Ellen Ash Peters is first woman named to Connecticut supreme court.
1991	City of Bridgeport files for bankruptcy.
1991	First Connecticut state income tax is established.
1996	*Sheff v. O'Neill* case, claiming racial segregation in schools, reaches state supreme court.
July 5, 2000	Potentially deadly West Nile virus reported found in Fairfield County, as well as in adjoining states; the disease is also found to have circulated undetected in 1999.
Nov. 21, 2001	Elderly Connecticut resident Ottilie Lundgren dies mysteriously of inhalation anthrax.
Oct. 2003	Lawsuit settling child molestation in the Roman Catholic Church involving forty Connecticut victims is settled for $21 million.

June 20, 2004	Governor John G. Rowland announces his resignation as governor, effective July 1.
Aug. 8, 2006	Ned Lamont defeats Senator Joe Lieberman in Democratic Party primary election for U.S. Senate.
2008–2012	Connecticut voters almost unanimously elect Democrats over Republicans in several key races, including congressional and senatorial seats.
October 2012	Superstorm Sandy ravages most of the East Coast states, including Connecticut. Mandatory and partial evacuations occur throughout the state.

Notes for Further Study

Published Sources. Among the many books on Connecticut state history, a good place to start is *Connecticut* (1989) by William Hubbell and Roger Eddy. *Connecticut: An Explorer's Guide* (1999) by Barnett D. Laschever and Andi Marie Fusco and *Connecticut: Driving Through History* (1998) by Suzanne Staubach are excellent travel books that give tourist information and history lessons. Two accessible books for young adults on the state's history are *Connecticut* (2004) by Emily Lauren and Dina McClellan and *Primary Source History of the Colony of Connecticut* (2005) by Ann Malaspina. Richard Radune explores a particular aspect the colonial history of Connecticut in *Pequot Plantation: The Story of an Early Colonial Settlement* (2005).

Useful books on Native Americans in Connecticut include *Algonquians of the East Coast* (1996), published by Time-Life Books. It reveals the history, customs, and mythology of this important Connecticut tribe, with many photographs. Alfred A. Cave's *The Pequot War* (1997) explains the Puritan belief that Native Americans were "agents of Satan" and were to be destroyed. *The Puritan Family: Religion and Domestic Relations in Seventeenth Century New England* (1990), by Edmund Sears Morgan, discusses the Puritan ideal of social virtue and the communities established by Puritans in New England.

Howard Jones's *Mutiny on the "Amistad": The Saga of a Slave Revolt and Its Impact on American Abolition, Law, and Diplomacy* (1988) is a full-scale treatment of the infamous case in which African slaves won their freedom. Another excellent study is *Black Mutiny: The Revolt on the Schooner "Amistad"* (1953) by William A. Owens and Michael E. Dyson, which provides one of the most detailed accounts of the *Amistad* mutiny. *Colt: The Making of an American Legend* (1996) by William Hosley, Constance McLaughlin Green's *Eli Whitney and the Birth of American Technology* (1998), and *Eli Whitney, Great Inventor: Discovery Biography* (1991) by Jean Lee Latham and Louis F. Cary are good biographies of these important Connecticut industrial leaders.

Web Resources. The best starting place on the Internet is the official state of Connecticut site (www.state.ct.us), which covers government information, news, history, and tourist attractions. Other good tourist sites are Visit Connecticut (www.visitconnecticut.com), and Connecticut.com (www.connecticut.com), which provides a state photograph gallery and other features.

For state and county data from the U.S. Census Bureau, see Connecticut QuickFacts (quickfacts.census.gov/qfd/states/09000.html). Two good resources for state news, which are updated daily, are Connecticut Central (www.ctcentral.com), with news from the *New Haven Register* and *The Middletown Press*, and *The Hartford Courant* (www.courant.com), which also provides the history of the newspaper. For specific history, the Pequot Web site (www.pequotwar.com/) has much data on the Pequot War in Connecticut. More information on Native Americans can be found at Nipmuc Indian Association of Connecticut (www.nativetech.org/Nipmuc/), with news of Nipmucs and links to other American Indian Web sites. The Fundamental Orders of 1639 site (www.constitution.org/bcp/fo_1639.htm) gives the history of the constitution and reprints it. The *Amistad* mutiny is discussed at the Amistad Case (www.archives.gov/education/lessons/amistad/), which provides legal documents. The Connecticut Society of the Sons of the American Revolution (www.connecticutsar.org/) provides links to biographies of state patriots, a list of articles detailing the state's involvement in the war, and a timeline of events.

Counties

County	2012 Population	Pop. Rank	Land Area (sq. miles)	Area Rank
Fairfield	933,835	1	624.89	4
Hartford	897,259	2	735.10	2
Litchfield	187,530	5	920.56	1
Middlesex	165,602	6	369.30	8
New Haven	862,813	3	604.51	5
New London	274,170	4	664.88	3
Tolland	151,539	7	410.21	7
Windham	117,599	8	512.91	6

Source: U.S. Census Bureau, 2012 Population Estimates

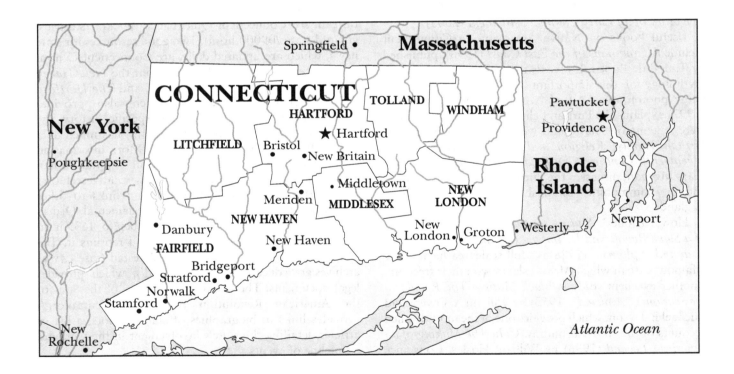

Cities

With 10,000 or more residents

Legal Name	2010 Population	Pop. Rank	Land Area (sq. miles)	Area Rank
Ansonia city	19,249	62	6.02	98
Avon town	18,098	68	23.15	60
Berlin town	19,866	56	26.32	52
Bethel town	18,584	64	16.89	80
Bloomfield town	20,486	54	26.09	54
Branford town	28,026	39	21.83	67
Bridgeport city	144,229	1	15.97	83

Legal Name	2010 Population	Pop. Rank	Land Area (sq. miles)	Area Rank
Bristol city	60,477	13	26.41	51
Brookfield town	16,452	75	19.77	73
Canton town	10,292	102	24.59	57
Cheshire town	29,261	34	33.07	33
Clinton town	13,260	87	16.21	82
Colchester town	16,068	76	48.98	5
Coventry town	12,435	93	37.57	23

Legal Name	2010 Population	Pop. Rank	Land Area (sq. miles)	Area Rank
Cromwell town	14,005	84	12.45	90
Danbury city	80,893	7	41.89	13
Darien town	20,732	53	12.66	89
Derby city	12,902	90	5.06	101
East Hampton town	12,959	88	35.65	26
East Hartford town	51,252	20	18.00	75
East Haven town	29,257	35	12.30	92
East Lyme town	19,159	63	34.00	30
East Windsor town	11,162	100	26.25	53
Ellington town	15,602	78	34.06	29
Enfield town	44,654	23	33.27	32
Fairfield town	59,404	14	29.90	40
Farmington town	25,340	46	28.02	47
Glastonbury town	34,427	30	51.27	4
Granby town	11,282	98	40.68	15
Greenwich town	61,171	10	47.62	7
Greenwich CDP	12,942	89	4.11	103
Griswold town	11,951	96	34.71	27
Groton town	40,115	26	31.03	38
Groton city	10,389	101	3.08	104
Guilford town	22,375	52	47.12	8
Hamden town	60,960	11	32.65	36
Hartford city	124,775	3	17.38	78
Killingly town	17,370	72	48.31	6
Ledyard town	15,051	82	38.22	21
Madison town	18,269	66	36.15	24
Manchester town	58,241	15	27.40	48
Manchester CDP	30,577	32	6.46	97
Mansfield town	26,543	43	44.60	9
Meriden city	60,868	12	23.79	58
Middletown city	47,648	21	41.02	14
Milford town	52,759	17	22.18	63
Milford city (balance)	51,271	19	21.90	64
Monroe town	19,479	61	26.07	55
Montville town	19,571	59	41.95	12
Naugatuck borough and town	31,862	31	16.31	81
New Britain city	73,206	8	13.39	87
New Canaan town	19,738	57	22.19	62
New Fairfield town	13,881	86	20.44	69
New Haven city	129,779	2	18.68	74
New London city	27,620	40	5.62	99
New Milford town	28,142	38	61.57	1
Newington town	30,562	33	13.14	88
Newtown town	27,560	41	57.66	3
North Branford town	14,407	83	24.76	56
North Haven town	24,093	49	20.84	68
Norwalk city	85,603	6	22.86	61
Norwich city	40,493	25	28.06	45
Old Saybrook town	10,242	103	15.04	84
Orange town	13,956	85	17.18	79
Oxford town	12,683	91	32.74	35
Plainfield town	15,405	79	42.36	10
Plainville town	17,716	71	9.71	94
Plymouth town	12,243	94	21.89	65
Ridgefield town	24,638	48	34.52	28
Rocky Hill town	19,709	58	13.45	86
Seymour town	16,540	74	14.52	85

Legal Name	2010 Population	Pop. Rank	Land Area (sq. miles)	Area Rank
Shelton city	39,559	27	30.63	39
Simsbury town	23,511	50	33.92	31
Somers town	11,444	97	28.37	44
South Windsor town	25,709	45	28.06	45
Southbury town	19,904	55	38.99	19
Southington town	43,069	24	35.91	25
Stafford town	12,087	95	58.04	2
Stamford city	122,643	4	37.64	22
Stonington town	18,545	65	38.66	20
Storrs CDP	15,344	80	5.59	100
Stratford town	51,384	18	17.48	77
Suffield town	15,735	77	42.26	11
Tolland town	15,052	81	39.63	17
Torrington city	36,383	28	39.75	16
Trumbull town	36,018	29	23.32	59
Vernon town	29,179	36	17.70	76
Wallingford town	45,135	22	39.04	18
Wallingford Center CDP	18,209	67	7.26	96
Waterbury city	110,366	5	28.52	43
Waterford town	19,517	60	32.77	34
Watertown town	22,514	51	29.01	42
West Hartford town	63,268	9	21.84	66
West Haven city	55,564	16	10.75	93
Weston town	10,179	104	19.80	72
Westport town	26,391	44	19.96	71
Wethersfield town	26,668	42	12.31	91
Willimantic CDP	17,737	70	4.40	102
Wilton town	18,062	69	26.80	50
Winchester town	11,242	99	32.51	37
Windham town	25,268	47	26.97	49
Windsor town	29,044	37	29.50	41
Windsor Locks town	12,498	92	9.02	95
Wolcott town	16,680	73	20.43	70

Note: CDP–Census Designated Place
Source: U.S. Census Bureau, 2010 Census

Survey Says...

This section presents current rankings from dozens of public and private sources. It shows how this state ranks in a number of critical categories, including education, job growth, cost of living, teen drivers, energy efficiency, and business environment. Sources include *Forbes, Reuters, U.S. News and World Report, CNN Money, Gallup,* and *Huffington Post.*

- Connecticut ranked #50 in a government study measuring real gross domestic product (GDP)—the output of goods and services produced by labor and property located in the United States. The ranking is based on the percentage change compared with 2011 GDP.
  U.S. Department of Commerce, Bureau of Economic Analysis, June 2013; www.bea.gov

- Connecticut ranked #24 in a government study measuring real gross domestic product (GDP)—the output of goods and services produced by labor and property located in the United States. The ranking is based on the dollar value of its GDP.
  U.S. Department of Commerce, Bureau of Economic Analysis, June 2013; www.bea.gov

- Connecticut ranked #16 in the 17th edition of "Quality Counts; State of the States," Education Week's "report card" surveying key education indicators, policy efforts, and educational outcomes.
  Education Week, January 4, 2013 (online) and January 10, 2013 (print); www.edweek.org

- SERI (Science and Engineering Readiness Index) weighs the performance of the states' K-12 schools in preparing students in physics and calculus, the high school subjects considered most important for future scientists and engineers. Connecticut ranked #8.
  Newsletter of the Forum on Education of the American Physical Society, Summer 2011 issue; www.huffingtonpost.com, July 11, 2011; updated October 1, 2012

- Business website 24/7 Wall St. identified the states with the highest and lowest percentages of residents 25 or older with a college degree or higher. Of "America's Best Educated States," Connecticut ranked #4 (#1 = best).
  247wallst.com, posted October 15, 2012; consulted July 18, 2013

- MoneyRates.com ranked Connecticut #37 on its list of the best to worst states for making a living. Criteria: average income; inflation; employment prospects; and workers' Workplace Environment assessments according to the Gallup-Healthways Well-Being Index.
  www.money-rates.com, posted April 1, 2013

- *Forbes* analyzed business costs, labor supply, regulatory environment, current economic climate, growth prospects, and quality of life, to compile its "Best States for Business" rankings. Connecticut ranked #39.
  www.forbes.com. posted December 12, 2012

- In "The States People Are Fleeing in 2013," *Forbes* reported the results of United Van Lines's thirty-sixth annual survey of its "customer migration patterns." In percentage of outbound moves, Connecticut ranked #7 (1 = most).
  www.forbes.com, posted February 7, 2013

- The 2012 Gallup-Healthways Well-Being Index, surveyed American's opinions on economic confidence, workplace perceptions, community climate, personal choices, and health predictors to assess the "future livability" of each state. Connecticut ranked #22.
  "Utah Poised to Be the Best State to Live In," Gallup Wellbeing, www.gallup.com, August 7, 2012

- On CNBC's list of "America's Top States for Business 2013," Connecticut ranked #45. Criteria: measures of competitiveness developed with input from the National Association of Manufacturers, the Council on Competitiveness, and other business groups weighed with the states' own marketing criteria.
  www.cnbc.com, consulted July 19, 2013

- Connecticut ranked #37 on MoneyRates list of "Best-and Worst-States to Retire 2012." Criteria: life expectancy, crime rate, climate, economic conditions, taxes, job opportunities, and cost of living.
  www.money-rates.com, October 22, 2012

- Connecticut ranked #41 on the 2013 Bankrate "Best Places to Retire" list ranking the states and District of Columbia on various criteria relating to health, safety, and cost.
  www.bankrate.com, May 6, 2013

- Reuters ranked Connecticut #7 on its list of the "Ten Most Expensive States in America." Rankings are based on the U.S. Commerce Department's prototype cost-of-living index comparing price levels across the states for a standardized mix of goods and services.
  www.huffingtonpost.com, posted June 12, 2013

- Connecticut ranked #1 on the Social Science Research Council's "American Human Development Report: The Measure of America," assessing the 50 states plus the District of Columbia on health, education, and living-standard criteria.
  The Measure of America 2013-2014, posted June 19, 2013; www.measureofamerica.org

- Connecticut ranked #5 on the Foundation for Child Development's (FCD) Child Well-being Index (CWI). The FCD used the KIDS COUNT report and the National Survey of Children's Health, the only state-level source for several key indicators of child well-being.
  Foundation for Child Development, January 18, 2012; fcd-us.org

- Connecticut ranked #9 overall according to the 2013 KIDS COUNT Data Book, a project of the Annie E. Casey Foundation. Criteria: children's economic well-being, education, health, and family and community indicators.
  KIDS COUNT Data Center's Data Book, released June 20, 2013; http://datacenter.kidscount.org

- Connecticut ranked #16 in the children's economic well-being category by the 2013 KIDS COUNT Data Book, a project of the Annie E. Casey Foundation.
  KIDS COUNT Data Center's Data Book, released June 20, 2013; http://datacenter.kidscount.org

- Connecticut ranked #6 in the children's educational opportunities and attainments category by the 2013 KIDS COUNT Data Book, a project of the Annie E. Casey Foundation.
  KIDS COUNT Data Center's Data Book, released June 20, 2013; http://datacenter.kidscount.org

- Connecticut ranked #2 in the children's health category by the 2013 KIDS COUNT Data Book, a project of the Annie E. Casey Foundation.
  KIDS COUNT Data Center's Data Book, released June 20, 2013; http://datacenter.kidscount.org

- Connecticut ranked #11 in the family and community circumstances that factor into children's well-being category by the 2013 KIDS COUNT Data Book, a project of the Annie E. Casey Foundation.
  KIDS COUNT Data Center's Data Book, released June 20, 2013; http://datacenter.kidscount.org

- Connecticut ranked #16 in the 2012 Gallup-Healthways Well-Being Index. Criteria: emotional health; physical health; healthy behavior; work environment; basic access to food, shelter, health care; and a safe and satisfying place to live.
  2012 State of Well-Being, Gallup-Healthways Well-Being Index, released February 28, 2013; www.well-beingindex.com

- *U.S. News and World Report's* "Best States for Teen Drivers" rankings are based on driving and road safety laws, federal reports on driver's licenses, car accident fatality, and road-quality statistics. Connecticut ranked #22.
  U.S. News and World Report, March 18, 2010; www.usnews.com

- The Yahoo! Sports service Rivals.com ranks the states according to the strength of their high school football programs. Connecticut ranked #41.
  "Ranking the States: Where Is the Best Football Played?," November 18, 2011; highschool.rivals.com

- iVillage ranked the states by hospitable living conditions for women. Criteria: economic success, access to affordable childcare, health care, reproductive rights, female representation in government, and educational attainment. Connecticut ranked #1.
  iVillage, "50 Best to Worst States for Women," March 14, 2012; www.ivillage.com

- The League of American Bicyclists's "Bicycle Friendly States" ranked Connecticut #18. Criteria: legislation and enforcement, policies and programs, infrastructure and funding, education and advocacy, and evaluation and planning.
  "Washington Tops the Bicycle-Friendly State Ranking," May 1, 2013; bicycling.com

- The federal Corporation for National and Community Service ranked the states and the District of Columbia by volunteer rates. Connecticut ranked #22 for community service.
  "Volunteering and Civic Life in America 2012," www.volunteeringinamerica.gov, accessed July 24, 2013

- The Hospital Safety Score ranked states and the District of Columbia on their hospitals' performance scores. Connecticut ranked #37. Criteria: avoiding preventable harm and medical errors, as demonstrated by 26 hospital safety metrics.
  Spring 2013 Hospital Safety Score, May 8, 2013; www.hospitalsafetyscore.org

- GMAC Insurance ranked the states and the District of Columbia by the performance of their drivers on the GMAC Insurance National Drivers Test, comprised of DMV test questions. Connecticut ranked #35.
  "2011 GMAC Insurance National Drivers Test," www.gmacinsurance.com, accessed July 23, 2013

- Connecticut ranked #2 in a "State Integrity Investigation" analysis of laws and practices intended to deter corruption and promote accountability and openness in campaign finance, ethics laws, lobbying regulations and management of state pension funds.
  "What's Your State's Grade?," www.publicintegrity.org, accessed July 23, 2013

- Connecticut ranked #46 among the states and the District of Columbia in total rail miles, as tracked by the Association of American Railroads.
  "U.S. Freight Railroad Industry Snapshot: Railroads and States: Total Rail Miles by State: 2011"; www.aar.org, accessed July 23, 2013

- According to statistics compiled by the Beer Institute, Connecticut ranked #50 among the states and the District of Columbia in per capita beer consumption of persons 21 years or older.
  "Shipments of Malt Beverages and Per Capita Consumption by State 2012;" www.beerinstitute.org

- According to Concordia University's "Public Education Costs per Pupil by State Rankings," based on statistics gathered by the U.S. Census Bureau, which includes the District of Columbia, Connecticut ranked #7.
  Concordia University Online; education.cu-portland.edu, accessed July 24, 2013

- Connecticut ranked #4 among the states and the District of Columbia in population density based on U.S. Census Bureau data for resident population and total land area. "List of U.S. States by Population Density."
  www.wikipedia.org, accessed July 24, 2013

- In "America's Health Rankings, 2012 Edition," by the United Health Foundation, Connecticut ranked #6. Criteria included: rate of high school graduation; violent crime rate; incidence of infectious disease; childhood immunizations; prevalence of diabetes; per capita public-health funding; percentage of uninsured population; rate of children in poverty; and availability of primary-care physicians.
  United Health Foundation; www.americashealthrankings.org, accessed July 24, 2013

- The TechNet 2012 "State Broadband Index" ranked Connecticut #17 on the following criteria: broadband adoption; network quality; and economic structure. Improved broadband use is hoped to promote economic development, build strong communities, improve delivery of government services and upgrade educational systems.
  TechNet; www.technet.org, accessed July 24, 2013

- Connecticut was ranked #6 among the states and District of Columbia on the American Council for an Energy-Efficient Economy's "State Energy Efficiency Scorecard" for 2012.
  American Council for an Energy-Efficient Economy; aceee.org/sector/state-policy/scorecard, accessed July 24, 2013

Statistical Tables

DEMOGRAPHICS
Resident State and National Population, 1950-2012
Projected State and National Population, 2000-2030
Population by Age, 2012
Population by Race, 2012
Population by Hispanic Origin and Race, 2012

VITAL STATISTICS
Death Rates by Leading Causes, 2010
Death Rates by Selected Causes, 2010
Abortion Rates, 2009
Infant Mortality Rates, 1995-2009
Marriage and Divorce Rates, 2000-2011

ECONOMY
Nominal Gross Domestic Product by Industry, 2012
Real Gross Domestic Product, 2000-2012
Personal Income Per Capita, 1930-2012
Non-Farm Employment by Sector, 2012
Foreign Exports, 2000-2012
Energy Consumption, 2011

LAND AND WATER
Surface Area and Federally-Owned Land, 2007
Land Cover/Use of Non-Federal Rural Land, 2007
Farms and Crop Acreage, 2012

HEALTH AND MEDICAL CARE
Medical Professionals, 2012
Health Insurance Coverage, 2011
HIV, STD, and Tuberculosis Cases and Rates, 2011
Cigarette Smoking, 2011

HOUSING
Home Ownership Rates, 1995-2012
Home Sales, 2000-2010
Value of Owner-Occupied Homes, 2011

EDUCATION
School Enrollment, 2011
Educational Attainment, 2011
Public College Finances, FY 2012

TRANSPORTATION AND TRAVEL
Motor Vehicle Registrations and Drivers Licenses, 2011
Domestic Travel Expenditures, 2009
Retail Gasoline Prices, 2013
Public Road Length, 2011

CRIME AND LAW ENFORCEMENT
Full-Time Law Enforcement Officers, 2011
Prison Population, 2000-2012
Crime Rate, 2011

GOVERNMENT AND FINANCE
Local Governments by Type, 2012
State Government Revenue, 2011
State Government Expenditures, 2011
State Government General Expenditures by Function, 2011
State Government Finances, Cash and Debt, 2011

POLITICS
Composition of the Senate, 1995-2013
Composition of the House of Representatives, 1995-2013
Composition of State Legislature, 2004-2013
Voter Participation in Presidential Elections, 1980-2012
Governors Since Statehood

DEMOGRAPHICS

Resident State and National Population, 1950–2012

Year	State Population	U.S. Population	State Share
1950	2,007,000	151,326,000	1.33%
1960	2,535,000	179,323,000	1.41%
1970	3,032,217	203,302,031	1.49%
1980	3,107,576	226,545,805	1.37%
1990	3,287,116	248,709,873	1.32%
2000	3,405,650	281,424,600	1.21%
2010	3,574,097	308,745,538	1.16%
2012	3,590,347	313,914,040	1.14%

Note: 1950/1960 population figures are rounded to the nearest thousand.
Source: U.S. Census Bureau, Decennial Census 1950–2010; U.S. Census Bureau, 2012 Population Estimates

Projected State and National Population, 2000–2030

Year	State Population	U.S. Population	State Share
2000	3,405,565	281,421,906	1.21%
2005	3,503,185	295,507,134	1.19%
2010	3,577,490	308,935,581	1.16%
2015	3,635,414	322,365,787	1.13%
2020	3,675,650	335,804,546	1.09%
2025	3,691,016	349,439,199	1.06%
2030	3,688,630	363,584,435	1.01%
State population growth, 2000–2030			283,065
State percentage growth, 2000–2030			8.3%

Source: U.S. Census Bureau, Population Division, Interim State Population Projections, 2005

Population by Age, 2012

Age Group	State Population	Percent of Total Population State	Percent of Total Population U.S.
Under 5 years	193,456	5.4%	6.4%
5 to 14 years	452,548	12.6%	13.1%
15 to 24 years	484,622	13.5%	14.0%
25 to 34 years	434,550	12.1%	13.5%
35 to 44 years	458,449	12.8%	12.9%
45 to 54 years	566,537	15.8%	14.1%
55 to 64 years	467,473	13.0%	12.3%
65 to 74 years	281,617	7.8%	7.6%
75 to 84 years	162,927	4.5%	4.2%
85 years and older	88,168	2.5%	1.9%
Under 18 years	793,558	22.1%	23.5%
65 years and older	532,712	14.8%	13.7%
Median age (years)	–	40.5	37.4

Source: U.S. Census Bureau, Annual Estimates of the Resident Population for Selected Age Groups by Sex for the United States, States, Counties, and Puerto Rico Commonwealth and Municipios: April 1, 2010 to July 1, 2012

Population by Race, 2012

Race	State Population	Percent of Total Population State	Percent of Total Population U.S.
All residents	3,590,347	100.00%	100.00%
White	2,942,335	81.95%	77.89%
African American	401,496	11.18%	13.13%
Native American	17,688	0.49%	1.23%
Asian	150,529	4.19%	5.14%
Native Hawaiian	3,641	0.10%	0.23%
Two or more races	74,658	2.08%	2.39%

Source: U.S. Census Bureau, Population Division, Annual Estimates of the Resident Population by Sex, Race and Hispanic Origin for the United States, States, and Counties: April 1, 2010 to July 1, 2012

Population by Hispanic Origin and Race, 2012

Hispanic Origin/Race	State Population	Percent of Total Population State	Percent of Total Population U.S.
All residents	3,590,347	100.00%	100.00%
All Hispanic residents	510,645	14.22%	16.89%
Hispanic			
White	419,465	11.68%	14.91%
African American	55,923	1.56%	0.79%
Native American	10,344	0.29%	0.49%
Asian	3,889	0.11%	0.17%
Native Hawaiian	2,366	0.07%	0.06%
Two or more races	18,658	0.52%	0.48%
Not Hispanic			
White	2,522,870	70.27%	62.98%
African American	345,573	9.63%	12.34%
Native American	7,344	0.20%	0.74%
Asian	146,640	4.08%	4.98%
Native Hawaiian	1,275	0.04%	0.17%
Two or more races	56,000	1.56%	1.91%

Source: U.S. Census Bureau, Population Division, Annual Estimates of the Resident Population by Sex, Race and Hispanic Origin for the United States, States, and Counties: April 1, 2010 to July 1, 2012

VITAL STATISTICS

Death Rates by Leading Causes, 2010

Cause	State	U.S.
Malignant neoplasms	175.3	186.2
Ischaemic heart diseases	96.5	122.9
Other forms of heart disease	60.4	53.4
Chronic lower respiratory diseases	31.1	44.7
Cerebrovascular diseases	31.5	41.9
Organic, incl. symptomatic, mental disorders	35.0	35.7
Other degenerative diseases of the nervous sys.	19.3	28.4
Other external causes of accidental injury	24.5	26.5
Diabetes mellitus	16.4	22.4
Hypertensive diseases	14.0	20.4
All causes	697.9	799.5

Note: Figures are age-adjusted death rates per 100,000 population
Source: CDC/NCHS, Underlying Cause of Death 1999–2010 on CDC WONDER Online Database

Death Rates by Selected Causes, 2010

Cause	State	U.S.
Assault	4.1	5.2
Diseases of the liver	11.7	13.9
Human immunodeficiency virus (HIV) disease	2.2	2.7
Influenza and pneumonia	13.1	16.2
Intentional self-harm	9.6	12.4
Malnutrition	0.7	0.9
Obesity and other hyperalimentation	1.5	1.8
Renal failure	12.6	14.4
Transport accidents	9.5	12.1
Viral hepatitis	1.4	2.4

Note: Figures are age-adjusted death rates per 100,000 population; A dash indicates that data was not available or was suppressed
Source: CDC/NCHS, Underlying Cause of Death 1999–2010 on CDC WONDER Online Database

Abortion Rates, 2009

Category	2009
By state of residence	
Total abortions	13,651
Abortion rate[1]	19.8%
Abortion ratio[2]	351
By state of occurrence	
Total abortions	13,732
Abortion rate[1]	20.0%
Abortion ratio[2]	353
Abortions obtained by out-of-state residents	3.4%
U.S. abortion rate[1]	15.1%
U.S. abortion ratio[2]	227

Note: (1) Number of abortions per 1,000 women aged 15–44 years; (2) Number of abortions per 1,000 live births; A dash indicates that data was not available
Source: CDC/NCHS, Morbidity and Mortality Weekly Report, November 23, 2012 (Abortion Surveillance, United States, 2009)

Infant Mortality Rates, 1995–2009

Category	1995	2000	2005	2009
All state residents	7.13	6.51	5.85	5.55
All U.S. residents	7.57	6.89	6.86	6.39
All state white residents	6.35	5.61	4.53	4.66
All U.S. white residents	6.30	5.71	5.73	5.33
All state black residents	12.23	13.84	15.15	11.54
All U.S. black residents	14.58	13.48	13.26	12.12

Note: Figures represent deaths per 1,000 live births of resident infants under one year old, exclusive of fetal deaths; A dash indicates that data was not available or was suppressed.
Source: Centers of Disease Control and Prevention, Division of Vital Statistics, Linked Birth/Infant Death Records on CDC Wonder Online

Marriage and Divorce Rates, 2000–2011

Year	Marriage Rate		Divorce Rate	
	State	U.S.	State	U.S.
2000	5.7	8.2	3.3	4.0
2002	5.7	8.0	3.3	3.9
2004	5.8	7.8	3.1	3.7
2006	5.5	7.5	3.1	3.7
2008	5.4	7.1	3.4	3.5
2010	5.6	6.8	2.9	3.6
2011	5.5	6.8	3.1	3.6

Note: Rates are based on provisional counts of marriages/divorces by state of occurrence and are per 1,000 total population residing in area
Source: CDC/NCHS, National Vital Statistics System

ECONOMY

Nominal Gross Domestic Product by Industry, 2012
In millions of current dollars

Industry	State GDP
Accommodation and food services	5,131
Administrative and waste management services	6,465
Agriculture, forestry, fishing, and hunting	314
Arts, entertainment, and recreation	1,680
Construction	6,163
Educational services	4,683
Finance and insurance	36,851
Health care and social assistance	18,837
Information	9,614
Management of companies and enterprises	6,571
Manufacturing	24,079
Mining	73
Other services, except government	5,048
Professional, scientific, and technical services	16,547
Real estate and rental and leasing	33,527
Retail trade	12,141
Transportation and warehousing	3,859
Utilities	3,939
Wholesale trade	12,771

Source: U.S. Department of Commerce, Bureau of Economic Analysis, Survey of Current Business

Real Gross Domestic Product, 2000–2012
In millions of chained 2005 dollars

Year	State GDP	U.S. GDP	State Share
2000	184,776	11,225,406	1.65%
2005	196,307	12,539,116	1.57%
2010	197,613	12,897,088	1.53%
2012	197,202	13,430,576	1.47%

Source: U.S. Department of Commerce, Bureau of Economic Analysis, Survey of Current Business

Personal Income Per Capita, 1930–2012

Year	State	U.S.
1930	$923	$618
1940	$920	$593
1950	$1,884	$1,503
1960	$2,799	$2,268
1970	$5,071	$4,084
1980	$12,321	$10,091
1990	$26,198	$19,354
2000	$41,920	$30,319
2010	$55,427	$39,791
2012	$58,908	$42,693

Source: U.S. Department of Commerce, Bureau of Economic Analysis, Regional Economic Accounts

Non-Farm Employment by Sector, 2012
In thousands

Sector	Employment
Construction	51.1
Education and health services	317.7
Financial activities	132.3
Government	238.7
Information	31.1
Leisure and hospitality	142.6
Mining and logging	0.6
Manufacturing	165.0
Other services	61.5
Professional and business services	203.1
Trade, transportation, and utilities	295.3
All sectors	1,639.0

Source: U.S. Bureau of Labor Statistics, State and Area Employment

Foreign Exports, 2000–2012
In millions of dollars

Year	State Exports	U.S. Exports	State Share
2000	8,046	712,054	1.13%
2002	8,310	649,940	1.28%
2004	8,573	768,554	1.12%
2006	12,248	973,994	1.26%
2008	15,384	1,222,545	1.26%
2010	16,028	1,208,080	1.33%
2012	15,961	1,478,268	1.08%

Note: U.S. figures exclude data from Puerto Rico, U.S. Virgin Islands, and unallocated exports
Source: U.S. Department of Commerce, International Trade Admin., Office of Trade and Industry Information, Manufacturing and Services

Energy Consumption, 2011

In trillions of BTUs, except as noted

Total energy consumption	
Total state energy consumption	741.6
Total U.S. energy consumption	97,387.3
State share of U.S. total	0.76%
Per capita consumption (in millions of BTUs)	
Total state per capita consumption	206.8
Total U.S. per capita consumption	312.6
End-use sectors	
Residential	239.4
Commercial	184.4
Industrial	80.4
Transportation	237.4
Sources of energy	
Petroleum	315.6
Natural gas	235.7
Coal	6.1
Renewable energy	43.8
Nuclear electric power	166.7

Source: U.S. Energy Information Administration, State Energy Data 2011: Consumption

LAND AND WATER

Surface Area and Federally-Owned Land, 2007

In thousands of acres

Category	State	U.S.	State Share
Total surface area	3,194.7	1,937,664.2	0.16%
Total land area	3,066.1	1,886,846.9	0.16%
Non-federal land	3,051.6	1,484,910.0	0.21%
Developed	1,051.6	111,251.2	0.95%
Rural	2,000.0	1,373,658.8	0.15%
Federal land	14.5	401,936.9	0.00%
Water area	128.6	50,817.3	0.25%

Source: U.S. Department of Agriculture, Natural Resources Conservation Service, 2007 National Resources Inventory

Land Cover/Use of Non-Federal Rural Land, 2007

In thousands of acres

Category	State	U.S.	State Share
Total rural land	2,000.0	1,373,658.8	0.15%
Cropland	172.0	357,023.5	0.05%
CRP[1] land	0.0	32,850.2	0.00%
Pastureland	105.2	118,615.7	0.09%
Rangeland	0.0	409,119.4	0.00%
Forest land	1,620.4	406,410.4	0.40%
Other rural land	102.4	49,639.6	0.21%

Note: (1) Conservation Reserve Program was created to assist private landowners in converting highly erodible cropland to vegetative cover.
Source: U.S. Department of Agriculture, Natural Resources Conservation Service, 2007 National Resources Inventory

Farms and Crop Acreage, 2012

Category	State	U.S.	State Share
Farms (in thousands)	4.9	2,170.0	0.23%
Acres (in millions)	0.4	914.0	0.04%
Acres per farm	81.6	421.2	–

Source: U.S. Department of Agriculture, National Agricultural Statistical Service, Quick Stats, 2012 Survey Data

HEALTH AND MEDICAL CARE

Medical Professionals, 2012

Profession	State Number	U.S. Number	State Share	State Rate[1]	U.S. Rate[1]
Physicians[2]	13,897	894,637	1.55%	387.5	287.1
Dentists	2,710	193,587	1.40%	75.6	62.1
Podiatrists	255	17,469	1.46%	7.1	5.6
Optometrists	502	45,638	1.10%	14.0	14.6
Chiropractors	855	77,494	1.10%	23.8	24.9

Note: (1) Rates are per 100,000 population; (2) Includes total, active Doctors of Osteopathic Medicine and Doctors of Medicine in 2011.
Source: U.S. Department of Health and Human Services, Bureau of Health Professions, Area Health Resource File, 2012-2013

Health Insurance Coverage, 2011

Category	State	U.S.
Total persons covered	3,215,000	260,214,000
Total persons not covered	302,000	48,613,000
Percent not covered	8.6%	15.7%
Children under age 18 covered	766,000	67,143,000
Children under age 18 not covered	43,000	6,965,000
Percent of children not covered	5.3%	9.4%

Source: U.S. Census Bureau, Current Population Survey, 2012 Annual Social and Economic Supplement

HIV, STD, and Tuberculosis Cases and Rates, 2011

Disease	State Cases	State Rate[1]	U.S. Rate[1]
Chlamydia	13,649	381.9	457.6
Gonorrhea	2,449	68.5	104.2
HIV diagnosis	430	14.2	15.8
HIV, stage 3 (AIDS)	327	10.8	10.3
Syphilis, early latent	57	1.6	4.3
Syphilis, primary/secondary	65	1.8	4.5
Tuberculosis	83	2.3	3.4

Note: (1) Rates are per 100,000 population
Source: Centers for Disease Control and Prevention

Cigarette Smoking, 2011

Category	State	U.S.
Adults who are current smokers	17.1%	21.2%
Adults who smoke everyday	11.8%	15.4%
Adults who smoke some days	5.3%	5.7%
Adults who are former smokers	27.8%	25.1%
Adults who never smoked	55.1%	52.9%

Source: Centers for Disease Control and Prevention, Behaviorial Risk Factor Surveillance System, Tobacco Use, 2011

HOUSING

Home Ownership Rates, 1995–2012

Area	1995	2000	2005	2010	2012
State	68.2%	70.0%	70.5%	70.8%	68.8%
U.S.	64.7%	67.4%	68.9%	66.9%	65.4%

Source: U.S. Census Bureau, Housing Vacancies and Homeownership, Annual Statistics

Home Sales, 2000–2010
In thousands of units

Year	State Sales	U.S. Sales	State Share
2000	61.5	5,174	1.19%
2002	63.8	5,632	1.13%
2004	75.1	6,778	1.11%
2006	70.8	6,478	1.09%
2008	47.4	4,913	0.96%
2010	46.2	4,908	0.94%

Note: Units include single-family homes, condos and co-ops
Source: National Association of Realtors, Real Estate Outlook, Market Trends & Insights

Value of Owner-Occupied Homes, 2011

Value	Total Units in State	Percent of Total, State	Percent of Total, U.S.
Less than $50,000	17,669	1.9%	8.8%
$50,000 to $99,000	24,913	2.7%	16.0%
$100,000 to $149,000	65,406	7.2%	16.5%
$150,000 to $199,000	137,241	15.1%	15.4%
$200,000 to $299,000	262,157	28.8%	18.2%
$300,000 to $499,000	250,385	27.5%	15.2%
$500,000 to $999,000	113,294	12.4%	7.9%
$1,000,000 or more	39,994	4.4%	2.0%
Median value	–	$278,700	$173,600

Source: U.S. Census Bureau, 2011 American Community Survey 1-Year Estimates

EDUCATION

School Enrollment, 2011

Educational Level	Students Enrolled in State	Percent of Total, State	Percent of Total, U.S.
All levels	943,212	100.0%	100.0%
Nursery school, preschool	59,983	6.4%	6.0%
Kindergarten	43,015	4.6%	5.1%
Elementary (grades 1–8)	369,804	39.2%	39.5%
Secondary (grades 9–12)	209,490	22.2%	20.7%
College or graduate school	260,920	27.7%	28.7%

Note: Figures cover the population 3 years and over enrolled in school
Source: U.S. Census Bureau, 2011 American Community Survey 1-Year Estimates

Educational Attainment, 2011

Highest Level of Education	State	U.S.
High school diploma	89.1%	85.9%
Bachelor's degree	36.2%	28.5%
Graduate/Professional degree	15.7%	10.6%

Note: Figures cover the population 25 years and over
Source: U.S. Census Bureau, 2011 American Community Survey 1-Year Estimates

Public College Finances, FY 2012

Category	State	U.S.
Full-time equivalent enrollment (FTE)[1]	85,683	11,548,974
Educational appropriations per FTE[2]	$7,354	$5,906
Net tuition revenue per FTE[3]	$6,662	$5,189
Total educational revenue per FTE[4]	$14,016	$11,043

(1) Full-time equivalent enrollment equates student credit hours to full time, academic year students, but excludes medical students; (2) Educational appropriations measure state and local support available for public higher education operating expenses including ARRA funds and excludes appropriations for independent institutions, financial aid for students attending independent institutions, research, hospitals, and medical education; (3) Net tuition revenue is calculated by taking the gross amount of tuition and fees, less state and institutional financial aid, tuition waivers or discounts, and medical student tuition and fees. Net tuition revenue used for capital debt service is included in the net tuition revenue figures; (4) Total educational revenue is the sum of educational appropriations and net tuition excluding net tuition revenue used for capital debt service.
Source: State Higher Education Executive Officers, State Higher Education Finance FY 2012

TRANSPORTATION AND TRAVEL

Motor Vehicle Registrations and Drivers Licenses, 2011

Vehicle Type	State	U.S.	State Share
Automobiles[1]	1,719,536	125,656,528	1.37%
Buses	7,496	666,064	1.13%
Trucks	1,003,799	118,455,587	0.85%
Motorcycles	97,963	8,437,502	1.16%
Drivers licenses	2,986,267	211,874,649	1.41%

Note: Motor vehicle registrations include private, commercial, and publicly-owned vehicles; (1) Includes taxicabs
Source: U.S. Department of Transportation, Federal Highway Administration

Domestic Travel Expenditures, 2009
In millions of dollars

Category	State	U.S.	State Share
Travel expenditures	$8,611	$610,200	1.41%

Note: Figures represent U.S. spending on domestic overnight trips and day trips of 50 miles or more, one way, away from home. Excludes spending by foreign visitors.
Source: U.S. Travel Association, Impact of Travel on State Economies, 2009

Retail Gasoline Prices, 2013

Gasoline Grade	State Average	U.S. Average
Regular	$4.03	$3.65
Mid	$4.19	$3.81
Premium	$4.33	$3.98
Diesel	$4.23	$3.88
Excise tax[1]	67.7 cents	49.4 cents

Note: Gasoline prices as of 7/26/2013; (1) Includes state and federal excise taxes and other state taxes as of July 1, 2013
Source: American Automobile Association, Daily Fuel Guage Report; American Petroleum Institute, State Motor Fuel Taxes, 2013

Public Road Length, 2011

Type	State Mileage	U.S. Mileage	State Share
Interstate highways	346	46,960	0.74%
Other highways	279	15,719	1.77%
Principal arterial	808	156,262	0.52%
Minor arterial	1,918	242,942	0.79%
Major collector	2,772	534,592	0.52%
Minor collector	435	266,357	0.16%
Local	14,889	2,814,925	0.53%
Urban	15,193	1,095,373	1.39%
Rural	6,252	2,982,383	0.21%
Total	21,445	4,077,756	0.53%

Note: Combined urban and rural road mileage equals the total of the other road types
Source: U.S. Department of Transportation, Federal Highway Administration, Public Road Length, 2011

CRIME AND LAW ENFORCEMENT

Full-Time Law Enforcement Officers, 2011

Gender	State Number	State Rate[1]	U.S. Rate[1]
Male officers	7,570	211.4	210.3
Female officers	785	21.9	28.1
Total officers	8,355	233.3	238.3

Note: (1) Rates are per 100,000 population
Source: Federal Bureau of Investigation, Uniform Crime Reports, Crime in the United States 2011

Prison Population, 2000–2012

Year	State Population	U.S. Population	State Share
2000	18,355	1,391,261	1.32%
2005	19,442	1,527,929	1.27%
2010	19,321	1,613,803	1.20%
2011	18,324	1,598,783	1.15%
2012	17,530	1,571,013	1.12%

Note: Figures include prisoners under the jurisdiction of state or federal correctional authorities.
Source: U.S. Department of Justice, Bureau of Justice Statistics, Prisoners in 2006, 2011, 2012 (Advance Counts)

Crime Rate, 2011
Incidents per 100,000 residents

Category	State	U.S.
Violent crimes	272.8	386.3
Murder	3.6	4.7
Forcible rape	19.2	26.8
Robbery	102.7	113.7
Aggravated assault	147.3	241.1
Property crimes	2,167.4	2,908.7
Burglary	437.9	702.2
Larceny/theft	1,542.1	1,976.9
Motor vehicle theft	187.4	229.6
All crimes	2,440.2	3,295.0

Source: Federal Bureau of Investigation, Uniform Crime Reports, Crime in the United States 2011

GOVERNMENT AND FINANCE

Local Governments by Type, 2012

Government Type	State	U.S.	State Share
All local governments	644	89,004	0.72%
County	0	3,031	0.00%
Municipality	30	19,522	0.15%
Town/Township	149	16,364	0.91%
Special District	448	37,203	1.20%
Ind. School District	17	12,884	0.13%

Source: U.S. Census Bureau, 2012 Census of Governments: Organization Component Preliminary Estimates

State Government Revenue, 2011
In thousands of dollars, except for per capita figures

Total revenue	**$28,927,902**
Total revenue per capita, State	$8,065
Total revenue per capita, U.S.	$7,271
General revenue	$23,508,277
Intergovernmental revenue	$6,561,366
Taxes	$13,432,252
General sales	$3,252,123
Selective sales	$2,270,657
License taxes	$446,755
Individual income taxes	$6,469,246
Corporate income taxes	$672,816
Other taxes	$320,655
Current charges	$2,096,873
Miscellaneous general revenue	$1,417,786
Utility revenue	$31,060
Liquor store revenue	$0
Insurance trust revenue[1]	$5,388,565

Note: (1) Within insurance trust revenue, net earnings of state retirement systems is a calculated statistic, and thus can be positive or negative. Net earnings is the sum of earnings on investments plus gains on investments minus losses on investments.
Source: U.S. Census Bureau, 2011 Annual Survey of State Government Finances

State Government Expenditures, 2011

In thousands of dollars, except for per capita figures

Total expenditure	$28,094,106
Total expenditure per capita, State	$7,833
Total expenditure per capita, U.S.	$6,427
Intergovernmental expenditure	$4,485,808
Direct expenditure	$23,608,298
Current operation	$14,822,195
Capital outlay	$1,522,409
Insurance benefits and repayments	$5,228,718
Assistance and subsidies	$551,181
Interest on debt	$1,483,795
Utility expenditure	$616,309
Liquor store expenditure	$0
Insurance trust expenditure	$5,228,718

Source: U.S. Census Bureau, 2011 Annual Survey of State Government Finances

State Government General Expenditures by Function, 2011

In thousands of dollars

Education	$6,747,698
Public welfare	$6,362,163
Hospitals	$1,475,928
Health	$932,699
Highways	$1,013,420
Police protection	$201,969
Correction	$698,030
Natural resources	$143,541
Parks and recreation	$35,864
Governmental administration	$1,177,686
Interest on general debt	$1,483,795
Other and unallocable	$1,976,286

Source: U.S. Census Bureau, 2011 Annual Survey of State Government Finances

State Government Finances, Cash and Debt, 2011

In thousands of dollars, except for per capita figures

Debt at end of fiscal year	
State, total	$30,523,708
State, per capita	$8,510
U.S., per capita	$3,635
Cash and security holdings	
State, total	$42,652,669
State, per capita	$11,892
U.S., per capita	$11,759

Source: U.S. Census Bureau, 2011 Annual Survey of State Government Finances

POLITICS

Composition of the Senate, 1995–2013

Congress (Year)	State/U.S	Dem	Rep	Total
104th (1995)	State delegates	2	0	2
	Total U.S.	48	52	100
105th (1997)	State delegates	2	0	2
	Total U.S.	45	55	100
106th (1999)	State delegates	2	0	2
	Total U.S.	45	55	100
107th (2001)	State delegates	2	0	2
	Total U.S.	50	50	100
108th (2003)	State delegates	2	0	2
	Total U.S.	48	51	100
109th (2005)	State delegates	2	0	2
	Total U.S.	44	55	100
110th (2007)	State delegates	2	0	2
	Total U.S.	49	49	100
111th (2009)	State delegates	2	0	2
	Total U.S.	57	41	100
112th (2011)	State delegates	2	0	2
	Total U.S.	51	47	100
113th (2013)	State delegates	2	0	2
	Total U.S.	54	45	100

Note: Figures are for the starts of first sessions; Totals include Democratic (Dem) and Republican (Rep) members as well as vacancies and seats held by independent party members
Source: U.S. Congress, Congressional Directory

Composition of the House of Representatives, 1995–2013

Congress (Year)	State/U.S	Dem	Rep	Total
104th (1995)	State delegates	3	3	6
	Total U.S.	204	230	435
105th (1997)	State delegates	4	2	6
	Total U.S.	207	226	435
106th (1999)	State delegates	4	2	6
	Total U.S.	211	223	435
107th (2001)	State delegates	3	3	6
	Total U.S.	212	221	435
108th (2003)	State delegates	2	3	5
	Total U.S.	205	229	435
109th (2005)	State delegates	2	3	5
	Total U.S.	202	231	435
110th (2007)	State delegates	4	1	5
	Total U.S.	233	198	435
111th (2009)	State delegates	5	0	5
	Total U.S.	256	178	435
112th (2011)	State delegates	5	0	5
	Total U.S.	193	242	435
113th (2013)	State delegates	5	0	5
	Total U.S.	201	234	435

Note: Figures are for the starts of first sessions; Totals include Democratic (Dem) and Republican (Rep) members as well as vacancies and seats held by independent party members
Source: U.S. Congress, Congressional Directory

Composition of State Legislature, 2004–2013

Year	Democrats	Republicans	Total
State Senate			
2004	21	15	36
2005	24	12	36
2006	24	12	36
2007	24	12	36
2008	24	12	36
2009	24	12	36
2010	24	12	36
2011	22	14	36
2012	22	14	36
2013	22	14	36
State House			
2004	95	56	151
2005	99	52	151
2006	99	52	151
2007	107	44	151
2008	107	44	151
2009	114	36	151
2010	114	37	151
2011	98	52	151
2012	99	52	151
2013	99	52	151

Note: Totals may include minor party members and vacancies
Source: The Council of State Governments, State Legislatures

Voter Participation in Presidential Elections, 1980–2012

Year	Voting-eligible State Population	State Voter Turnout Rate	U.S. Voter Turnout Rate
1980	2,201,356	63.9	54.2
1984	2,300,533	63.8	55.2
1988	2,379,699	60.7	52.8
1992	2,356,937	68.6	58.1
1996	2,337,160	59.6	51.7
2000	2,357,687	61.9	54.2
2004	2,429,634	65.0	60.1
2008	2,471,082	66.6	61.6
2012	2,558,470	60.9	58.2

Note: All figures are based on the voting-eligible population which excludes person ineligible to vote such as non-citizens, felons (depending on state law), and mentally-incapacitated persons. U.S. figures include the overseas eligible population (including military personnel).
Source: McDonald, Michael P., United States Election Project, Presidential Voter Turnout Rates, 1980–2012

Governors Since Statehood

Jonathan Trumbull	1776-1784
Matthew Griswold	1784-1786
Samuel Huntington (O)	(d) 1786-1796
Oliver Wolcott (O)	(d) 1796-1797
Jonathan Trumbull Jr. (O)	(d) 1797-1809
John Treadwell (O)	1809-1811
Robert Griswold (O)	(d) 1811-1812
John Cotton Smith (O)	1812-1817
Oliver Wolcott II (O)	1817-1827
Gideon Tomlinson (O)	1827-1831
John S. Peters (O)	1831-1833
Henry W. Edwards (D)	1833-1834
Samuel A. Foot (O)	1834-1835
Henry W. Edwards (D)	1835-1838
William W. Ellsworth (O)	1838-1842
Chauncey F. Cleveland (D)	1842-1844
Roger S. Baldwin (O)	1844-1846
Isaac Toucey (D)	1846-1847
Clark Bissell (O)	1847-1849
Joseph Trumbull (O)	1849-1850
Thomas H. Seymour (D)	(r) 1850-1853
Charles H. Pond (D)	1853-1854
Henry Dutton (O)	1854-1855
William T. Minor (O)	1855-1857
Alexander H. Holley (R)	1857-1858
William A. Buckingham (R)	1858-1866
Joseph R. Hawley (R)	1866-1867
James E. English (D)	1867-1869
Marshall Jewell (R)	1869-1870
James E. English (D)	1870-1871
Marshall Jewell (R)	1871-1873
Charles R. Ingersoll (R)	1873-1877
Richard D. Hubbard (D)	1877-1879
Charles B. Andrews (R)	1879-1881
Hobart B. Bigelow (R)	1881-1883
Thomas M. Waller (D)	1883-1885
Henry B. Harrison (R)	1885-1887
Phineas C. Lounsbury (R)	1887-1889
Morgan G. Bulkeley (R)	1889-1893
Luzon B. Morris (D)	1893-1895
Owen Vincent Coffin (R)	1895-1897
Lorrin A. Cooke (R)	1897-1899
George S. Lounsbury (R)	1899-1901
George P. McLean (R)	1901-1903
Abiram Chamberlain (R)	1903-1905
Harry Roberts (R)	1905-1907
Rollin S. Woodruff (R)	1907-1909
George L. Lilley (R)	(d) 1909
Frank B. Weeks (R)	1909-1911
Simeon E. Baldwin (D)	1911-1915
Marcus H. Holcomb (R)	1915-1921
Everett J. Lake (R)	1921-1923
Charles A. Templeton (R)	1923-1925
Hiram Bingham (R)	(r) 1925
John H. Trumbull (R)	1925-1931
Wilbur L. Cross (D)	1931-1939
Raymond E. Baldwin (R)	1939-1941
Robert A. Hurley (D)	1941-1943
Raymond E. Baldwin (R)	(r) 1943-1946
Wilbert Snow (D)	1946-1947
James L. McConaughty (R)	(d) 1947-1948
James C. Shannon (R)	1948-1949
Charles B. Bowles (D)	1949-1951
John D. Lodge (R)	1951-1955
Abraham Ribicoff (D)	(r) 1955-1961
John N. Dempsey (D)	1961-1971
Thomas J. Meskill (R)	1971-1975
Ella T. Grasso (D)	1975-1980
William A. O'Neill (D)	1981-1991
Lowell P. Weicker Jr. (O)	1991-1995
John G. Rowland (R)	1995-2004
M. Jodi Rell (R)	2004-2011
Dan Malloy (D)	2011-2015

Note: (D) Democrat; (R) Republican; (O) Other party; (r) resigned; (d) died in office; (i) removed from office

Delaware

Location: Atlantic coast

Area and rank: 1,982 square miles (5,153 square kilometers); 2,489 square miles (6,447 square kilometers) including water; forty-ninth largest state in area

Coastline: 28 miles (45 kilometers) on the Atlantic Ocean

Shoreline: 381 miles (613 kilometers)

Population and rank: 917,092 (2012 estimate); forty-fifth largest state in population

Capital city: Dover (36,047 people in 2012 census)

Largest city: Wilmington (70,851 people in 2010 census)

Entered Union and rank: December 7, 1787; first state
Present constitution adopted: 1897

Counties: 3

Governor Ross mansion in Dover. (Courtesy, Delaware Tourism Office)

State name: "Delaware" was named after the Delaware River and Bay, which was named for Sir Thomas West, Baron De La Warr

State nickname: Diamond State; First State; Small Wonder

Motto: Liberty and independence

State flag: Blue field with yellow diamond with state coat of arms and date of entrance to Union

DECEMBER 7, 1787

Highest point: Ebright Road—442 feet (135 meters)

Lowest point: Atlantic Ocean—sea level

Highest recorded temperature: 110 degrees Fahrenheit (43 degrees Celsius)—Millsboro, 1930

Lowest recorded temperature: –17 degrees Fahrenheit (–27 degrees Celsius)—Millsboro, 1893

State song: "Our Delaware"

State tree: American holly

State flower: Peach blossom

State bird: Blue Hen chicken

State fish: Weakfish

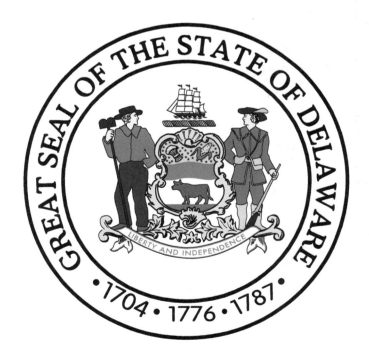

Delaware History

Of the fifty states, only Rhode Island is smaller in land mass than Delaware, which stretches one hundred miles from north to south and varies in width from ten to thirty-five miles. Bounded on the north by Pennsylvania, on the south and west by Maryland, and on the east by the Atlantic Ocean and the Delaware River, whose east bank is in New Jersey, this small state, with a land mass of 1,982 square miles, has just three counties, New Castle in the north, Kent in the middle, and Sussex in the south. The state's mean elevation is about sixty feet.

Early History. As early as 1609, English explorer Henry Hudson sailed on what became known as the Delaware River and the Delaware Bay. By 1631, the Dutch had established the first European settlement in the area around present-day Lewes, in the southeastern part of the state. Long before European settlement began in the region, prehistoric Indians occupied the area. Archaeological excavations at Island Field, twenty miles south of Dover, Delaware's capital, unearthed Indian graves that were close to one thousand years old. The Native Americans in this area are thought to have been the Owascos, a tribe related to the Iroquois, who inhabited the Finger Lakes region in New York.

Later American Indian inhabitants in northern Delaware included the Lenni-Lenape, also called the Delaware. Near the ocean and on the Delaware Bay lived the Nanticoke and Assateague tribes. These Indians massacred the first Dutch settlers in the area near Lewes. When more permanent settlement occurred with the arrival of the Swedes, these tribes disappeared from the area.

Permanent Settlements in Delaware. By 1638 a permanent Swedish settlement was established at Fort Christina, which is close to Wilmington on the Delaware River in the state's north. Peter Minuit, who had been colonial governor of New Amsterdam (present-day New York), helped create this settlement for the New Sweden Company, partly sponsored by the Dutch. They soon withdrew their support, leaving a hearty band of Swedes

The architecture of the center of the University of Delaware campus, in Newark, recalls that of the University of Virginia, whose main buildings were designed by Thomas Jefferson. (Wikimedia Commons)

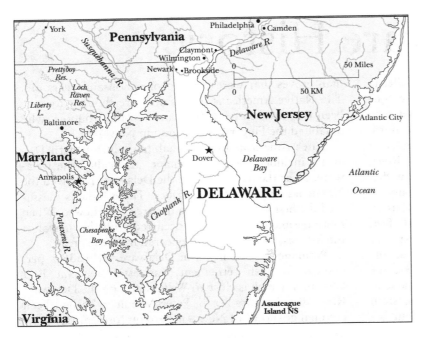

In 1777, British forces making their way from the Chesapeake Bay to Philadelphia invaded Delaware. George Washington's army had dug in close to Wilmington, but the British troops cut into Pennsylvania south of Wilmington and finally met Washington's men at Brandywine. After the Battle of Brandywine, the British took Wilmington and controlled it until they gained complete control of the Delaware River in June, 1778.

After the Revolutionary War, Delaware, in 1787, became the first of the newly formed states to ratify the United States Constitution, thereby earning one of its nicknames, the First State. Because of its size, Delaware feared it would be viewed as politically inferior to larger states. During the Constitutional Convention in 1787, Delaware called for equal representation for all states. Finally, the Delaware delegation accepted a compromise whereby every state would have two senators but would have representation in the House of Representatives based on each state's population.

The War of 1812. Delaware, which was a Federalist state, opposed the War of 1812. Once the United States entered that war, however, Delaware gave its reluctant support. Residents of the state feared an invasion when the British took Washington and, after burning the executive mansion, attacked Baltimore. Delaware was spared by the British, whose only assault on it was an abortive bombardment of Lewes in 1813.

The du Pont Company. In 1802, E. I. du Pont built a munitions factory on the Brandywine River. This marked the beginning of the highly influential enterprise E. I. du Pont de Nemours and Company, which grew into one of the most important chemical companies in the world. The presence of this company in Delaware eventually attracted other corporations to the region.

In time changing its name to the du Pont Company, having long since expanded from its original munitions manufacturing, it boasts a large nylon plant in Seaford, in the southwestern part of Delaware, and two major pigment factories in other parts of the state. Its home offices and laboratories are located in both Wilmington and Newark, Delaware. A large refinery in Delaware City drew many petrochemical companies to the state.

The Civil War. In 1790, Delaware had about nine thousand slaves, although the state was divided on the slavery issue and many abolitionists were active in helping African slaves escape from the South through Delaware. The state's first constitution, in 1776, made the further importation of slaves illegal. Because the state's tobacco industry was dependent upon slave labor, abolition bills introduced during the 1790's and again in

to manage as well as they could on their own. Their governor, Johan Printz, was an able leader who almost singlehandedly sustained the beleaguered community.

This settlement, which eventually extended from below Wilmington to Philadelphia, had about one thousand inhabitants. It was eventually overcome in 1655 by Dutch forces sent from New Amsterdam. In 1664, however, the British, rankling at the inroads the Dutch were making on English trade, assaulted New Amsterdam and captured it, then, after a considerable battle, took the Dutch fort at New Castle. The whole of New York and Delaware became part of the province of New York. Delaware remained so until 1682, when the duke of York gave Delaware to William Penn, who owned Pennsylvania.

At first, Penn, whose colony needed more direct access to the ocean, tried to merge his two holdings, but the people in southern Delaware feared that their colony might in time be overwhelmed by Pennsylvania, many times its size. In 1704, Penn finally permitted the people of Delaware to form their own assembly and, although the area had the same governor as Pennsylvania, to make their own laws.

The Revolt Against England. Although sentiment about gaining independence from England was spreading, Delaware had many loyalists among its inhabitants. George Read, one of Delaware's three delegates to the Continental Congress in 1774, voted against the colonies' declaring independence from England. Had another delegate, Caesar Rodney, not ridden on horseback all night from Dover, Delaware, to Philadelphia to cast the deciding vote, Delaware might not have joined the twelve other colonies in supporting the Declaration of Independence.

1847 were narrowly defeated. Nevertheless, by 1860, the slave population in the state had declined to about two thousand.

Although Delaware was staunchly opposed to secession, Abraham Lincoln won no electoral votes from the state in 1860 or in 1864. Delaware was more northern in its outlook and orientation than states in the Deep South. Some men from Delaware joined the Confederate forces, but most Delawareans fought on the Union side.

Despite its Union leanings, Delaware was occupied during the war by Union troops sent by President Lincoln to disarm some of the militia whose loyalty was suspect and to guard the polling places during elections. At war's end, many of the people in Delaware were so incensed by the federal government's punitive measures that the state became solidly Democrat, as did much of the Deep South.

Economy. Strategically situated on the Delaware River, Wilmington became a center of industrial activity in the state. In the city and its environs are textile mills, a steel foundry, automobile assembly operations, paper mills, and tanneries. Many large national corporations established their headquarters in Delaware, primarily in Wilmington, because of state's favorable business climate.

Because of its location near the point where the Delaware River flows into the Atlantic Ocean, Wilmington has proved an ideal location for shipbuilders, who built iron-hulled ships during the nineteenth century. During World War II, the largest employer in the state was a shipbuilding company based in Wilmington that produced ships for the U.S. Navy and Merchant Marine.

The Dover Air Force Base helped Delaware's economy substantially. The national headquarters of the International Reading Association in Newark, whose outreach is enormous, serves ninety thousand members in ninety-nine countries and employs more than eighty people in its headquarters. In 1998, nearly one-third of the people who worked in Delaware worked in the service sector, whereas slightly more than 20 percent were engaged in construction and about 15 percent in some aspect of manufacturing. The unemployment rate in that year was about 4 percent. The 1997 per-capita income was $29,022, up from $10,339 in 1980. The state had 2,667 federal employees in 1997 with average annual salaries of $40,159.

Despite its size, Delaware has a thriving agricultural industry that produces soybeans, lima beans, corn, potatoes, mushrooms, and various grains. It also produces considerable livestock, mainly chickens, hogs, and cattle. Its timber industry produced fifteen million board feet in 1998. Although it is not rich in minerals, Delaware produces magnesium, as well as sand, gravel, and gemstones.

Delaware's Population. A few of Delaware's Native American population, especially descendants of the Nanticoke and Moor tribes, remain in Kent and Sussex counties, although most of the native population was driven out or killed in combat with the Europeans who settled the state. In 1770, more than 20 percent of Delaware's population was African American; in 1998, 16.9 percent was black and less than 3 percent Hispanic.

During the mid-nineteenth century, many Germans and Irish came to Delaware. By the end of the century, southern and eastern Europeans began to arrive in large numbers, seeking work in the state's thriving industries. The first decades of the twentieth century saw the arrival of many Ukrainians and Greeks. As industry grew, many people arrived from other states to take advantage of Delaware's economic opportunities. In 1998, about 3 percent of the state's population was foreign born.

Delaware, lying in the highly urbanized corridor that runs from Boston to Richmond, Virginia, experienced rapid population growth in the last third of the twentieth century. Its population density of 340.8 people per square mile is among the greatest in the United States, and its population of nearly a million from 2012 should exceed the million mark sometime in the first decade of the twenty-first century.

Politics. As Delaware approached the twenty-first century, it was clear that change in its political landscape was imminent. This small state had just four major offices—governor, one member of the House of Representatives, and two U.S. senators. These offices had been held by a few individuals for a considerable period. The incumbent member of the House, Michael Castle, had been a popular governor before term limits directed him to Washington, D.C. William Roth had been senator since 1970—a duration of thirty years by the end of his term— and was nearly eighty years old. The popular governor, Thomas R. Carper, was also barred from reelection by term limits. The other U.S. senator, Democrat Joe Biden, was a well-regarded and stable fixture in the state; he was not up for reelection in 2000.

Although Castle aspired to the U.S. Senate, he was unwilling to challenge fellow Republican Roth in election primaries. However, Democrat Carper had no such inhibitions. When the election took place, Carper ousted Roth, mostly, it was said, because of Roth's advanced age. Veteran state politician Ruth Ann Minner was elected governor. Castle fended off his Democrat opponent without difficulty and remained the state's congress member in 2000 and in succeeding elections. In 2002, Biden easily overwhelmed his Republican opposition, winning by 58 to 41 percent of the vote. In 2004, Minner was reelected by a 51–46 percent margin.

For decades, Delaware was considered "a bellwether state," that is, reflecting and predicting national political trends. Delaware had voted for the winner in every presidential election from 1953 to 1996. However, in 2000 and 2004, the state supported Al Gore and John Kerry, while George W. Bush took the national presidential elections. Through the first years of the 21st century, Delaware has been regarded as part of the solid bloc of states that vote Democratic in the Northeast.

When Delaware Senator Joe Biden was nominated to run with Barack Obama in 2008, it was clear that the Democratic national ticket would take the state. With only three counties, the two northern urban counties, New Castle (basically suburban to Philadelphia), and Kent, which contains the state capital, Dover, racked up solid Democratic majorities. The third and most southerly county, Sussex, is more rural and tends to vote more conservatively, supporting Hillary Clinton in the 2008 Democratic Primaries over Barack Obama, and voting for Mitt Romney in the 2012 general election. In the 2008 election, Democrats gained control of both houses of the state legislature, as well as the governorship under former State Treasurer Jack Markell, the first time since the 1970's that Democrats had won both houses as well as elected the governor.

Court Cases. Delaware found itself at the center of national attention in the autumn of 2004. In a bitter dispute, top Walt Disney Company management, in particular Chief Executive Michael Eisner, fought a courtroom battle in Delaware with Disney shareholders, led by Walt Disney's nephew Roy E. Disney, over business decisions costing the company hundreds of millions of dollars. At issue was a severance payment to former Eisner friend and Disney president Michael Ovitz. In the end, after dramatic and emotional testimony, Disney management prevailed. Critics said that pertinent Delaware law affecting the central issue of the trial, the "business judgment rule," reflected a race to the bottom of bad law. In June, 2006, the Delaware Supreme Court affirmed the decision. In 2003, in a quite different case, the Delaware-based DuPont Company, the chemical giant, agreed to a $348 million settlement of a site over its perfluorooctanoic chemical, which was found in a West Virginia water supply.

Hurricanes. Situated partially on the Atlantic Ocean in the direct path of storms moving up the Atlantic Coast from the south, Delaware has long been prey to hurricanes. Even though many are downgraded to lesser storms when they reach Delaware's shores, some still pack a sufficient punch to cause damage. Thus, when the remnants of Hurricane Gordon in September, 2000, and Tropical Storm Allison in June, 2001, passed through the state, they dumped considerable rain, though they did little damage. However, in July, 2003, torrential rains from the remains of Tropical Storm Bill flooded hundreds of homes, trapped motorists, and damaged infrastructure. A few months later, in September, Hurricane Isabel did enough damage, including prolonged power outages, that President George W. Bush declared the state a disaster area. Storms in later years did similar damage and in some cases caused tornadoes.

R. Baird Shuman
Updated by the Editor

Kent County farm country. (Courtesy, Delaware Tourism Office)

Delaware Time Line

1609	Henry Hudson explores the Delaware River and Delaware Bay for the Dutch East Indies.
1610	Samuel Argall of Virginia blown off course into a bay that he names for his governor, Lord De La Warr.
1631	Dutch found a settlement near present-day Lewes.
1632	Native Americans destroy the Dutch settlement.
1638	Swedish settlement is established at Fort Christina.
1655	Dutch conquer the Swedish settlement and add it to the New Netherland settlement.
1664	New Netherland is taken by the British and renamed New York.
1682	Duke of York gives Delaware to William Penn.
1704	Delaware's General Assembly meets apart from Pennsylvania's legislature and makes its own laws.
1739	Wilmington receives its royal charter.
1743	University of Delaware opens in Newark.
1776	Delaware breaks from England, writes constitution for Delaware State.
1777	British capture Wilmington; Delaware General Assembly moves to Dover from New Castle.
Dec. 7, 1787	Delaware becomes the first state to ratify the United States Constitution.
1792	Delaware adopts second state constitution.
1802	E. I. du Pont opens powder mill on the Brandywine.
1813	British bombard Lewes in War of 1812.
1829	Chesapeake and Delaware Canal opens.
1829	Free public schools are mandated.
1831	Third state constitution is adopted.
1838	Philadelphia, Wilmington, and Baltimore Railroad is completed.
1861	Delaware refuses to join secession movement.
1897	New state constitution is adopted.
1912	Wilmington Society of the Fine Arts opens its museum, which grows into the Delaware Art Museum.
1917	Passage of state income and inheritance taxes.
1924	Completion of first highway running the length of Delaware.
1951	Delaware Memorial Bridge opens, linking Delaware and New Jersey.
1956	International Reading Association is established in Newark.
1966	Reorganized state government is established in New Castle County.
1968	Legislative reapportionment is completed.
1969	Henry Francis du Pont dies, leaving Winterthur, his 125-room residence, and most of its contents as a public museum in Wilmington.
1976	Rockwood Museum opens in New Castle; Willington Square with its six restored colonial homes relocated in a Wilmington park.
1981	Financial Center Development Act is enacted.
1987	Senator Joseph Biden withdraws presidential bid after being charged with plagiarism.
1988	Legislature passes law restricting hostile takeovers of businesses incorporated in-state.
1990	Laws passed enabling banks to sell and underwrite insurance.
1997	Seventeen hazardous waste sites placed on National Priority List.
Nov. 7, 2000	Al Gore wins Delaware's presidential electoral votes; Governor Thomas R. Carper defeats Senator William Roth for U.S. Senate seat. Ruth Ann Minner is elected governor.
Sept. 2003	Hurricane Isabel causes severe power outages and millions of dollars in damage.
Dec. 13, 2003	Former senator Roth, responsible for the tax-free Individual Retirement Accounts (IRAs) that bear his name, dies in Washington, D.C.
Nov. 2, 2004	John Kerry defeats George W. Bush in presidential balloting, despite his national loss; Bush is re-elected president.
Jan. 20, 2009	Democrat Jack Markell becomes governor.
July 1, 2013	Delaware's same-sex marraige law goes into effect.

Notes for Further Study

Published Sources. One of the best comprehensive histories of Delaware is John A. Munroe's *History of Delaware* (5th ed., 2006). It relates how the state came into being and is especially effective in outlining clearly the chaotic situation that resulted in Delaware once being a part of New York. Historical maps, archival illustrations, and first-person accounts help tell the story of the state's history in National Geographic's *Delaware 1638–1776* (2006). Slavery existed but never really flourished in Delaware; Alice Dunbar-Nelson's essay "Delaware: A Jewel of Inconsistencies," written in the 1920's and reproduced in *These "Colored" United States: African American Essays from the 1920's* (1996), edited by Tom Lutz and Susanne Ashton, offers an interesting retrospective view of the situation by an African American who was affected by the ambivalent situation regarding people of color in the state. William H. Williams's *Slavery and Freedom in Delaware, 1639–1865* (1996) examines how slavery existed in a state that had few slave owners and many active abolitionists. William W. Boyer examines politics and public policy in *Governing Delaware: Policy Problems of the First State* (2000). For young adults, Roberta Wiener and James R. Arnold provide a concise history of the state with *Delaware* (2004), while Aaron Raymond discusses the colonial era for this audience in *Primary Source History of the Colony of Delaware* (2006).

Jay F. Custer's *Delaware Prehistoric Archaeology: An Ecological Approach* (1984) reaches useful conclusions about the earliest history of the Delaware area based on archeological findings. His *Prehistoric Culture in the Delmarva Peninsula: An Archeological Study* (1989) also delves into some of the state's ancient history as revealed in artifacts and ancient burial grounds. David McCutchen offers cogent insights into early Indian cultures in *The Red Record: The Wallam Plum—the Oldest Native North American History* (1993). A reliable study of later Native Americans in Delaware is found in C. A. Weslager's *The Delaware Indians: A History* (1972) and in John Bierhorst's *Myth of the Lenape: Guide and Texts* (1995). The latter presents the folk traditions of these Delaware Indians. In *New Sweden in America* (1995), edited by Carol E. Hoffecker and others, one will find six informative essays that touch on the early Swedish settlement of Delaware in the seventeenth century.

Web Resources. A reasonable starting point for finding out more about Delaware and for locating other Web sites and their addresses is the state's Web site (www.delaware.gov/). This Web site offers material about many aspects of state government, tourism, history, commerce, economy, and population. A Web site run by the state's department of tourism (www.visitdelaware.com/) also provides comprehensive information about many of the state's attractions and facilities.

Research resources can be found on the University of Delaware Library's Web site (www.lib.udel.edu/). A good source of information about business and commerce is found on the Delaware State Chamber of Commerce Web site (www.dscc.com/). For those interested in visiting any of the state's history museums, detailed information about their collections and visitor information can be found using the links on Census Finder Historical Museums of Delaware (www.censusfinder.com/delaware-historical-museums.htm). For those interested in researching state history or one's ancestry in the state, the Historical Society of Delaware (www.hsd.org/) is a good destination.

Counties

County	2012 Population	Pop. Rank	Land Area (sq. miles)	Area Rank
Kent	167,626	3	586.18	2
New Castle	546,076	1	426.29	3
Sussex	203,390	2	936.08	1

Source: U.S. Census Bureau, 2012 Population Estimates

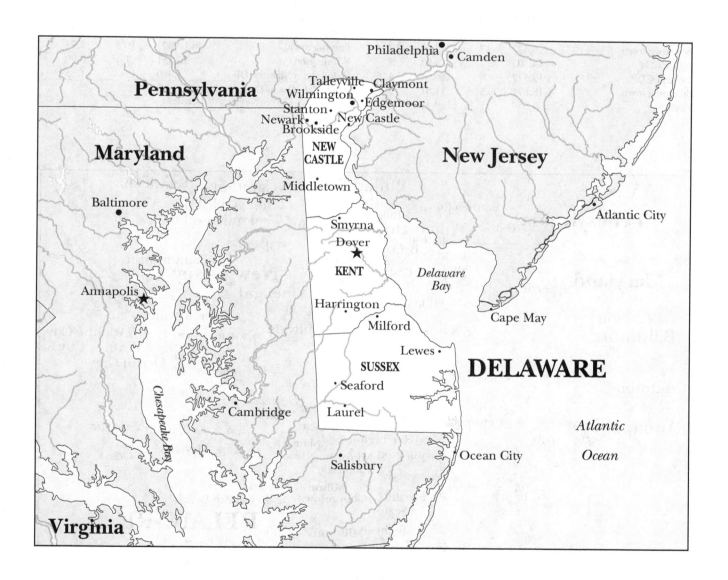

Cities

With 5,000 or more residents

Legal Name	2010 Population	Pop. Rank	Land Area (sq. miles)	Area Rank
Bear CDP	19,371	4	5.71	10
Brookside CDP	14,353	6	3.95	13
Claymont CDP	8,253	12	2.15	17
Dover city	36,047	2	23.15	1
Edgemoor CDP	5,677	19	1.87	18
Elsmere town	6,131	18	1.01	20
Georgetown town	6,422	17	5.04	12
Glasgow CDP	14,303	7	9.93	5
Hockessin CDP	13,527	8	10.04	4
Middletown town	18,871	5	11.61	2
Milford city	9,559	11	9.45	6

Legal Name	2010 Population	Pop. Rank	Land Area (sq. miles)	Area Rank
New Castle city	5,285	20	3.40	14
Newark city	31,454	3	9.19	7
North Star CDP	7,980	13	6.80	8
Pike Creek CDP	7,898	14	2.76	15
Pike Creek Valley CDP	11,217	9	2.58	16
Seaford city	6,928	16	5.21	11
Smyrna town	10,023	10	5.93	9
Wilmington city	70,851	1	10.90	3
Wilmington Manor CDP	7,889	15	1.55	19

Note: CDP–Census Designated Place
Source: U.S. Census Bureau, 2010 Census

Survey Says...

This section presents current rankings from dozens of public and private sources. It shows how this state ranks in a number of critical categories, including education, job growth, cost of living, teen drivers, energy efficiency, and business environment. Sources include *Forbes, Reuters, U.S. News and World Report, CNN Money, Gallup,* and *Huffington Post.*

- Delaware ranked #49 in a government study measuring real gross domestic product (GDP)—the output of goods and services produced by labor and property located in the United States. The ranking is based on the percentage change compared with 2011 GDP.
  U.S. Department of Commerce, Bureau of Economic Analysis, June 2013; www.bea.gov

- Delaware ranked #42 in a government study measuring real gross domestic product (GDP)—the output of goods and services produced by labor and property located in the United States. The ranking is based on the dollar value of its GDP.
  U.S. Department of Commerce, Bureau of Economic Analysis, June 2013; www.bea.gov

- Delaware ranked #19 in the 17th edition of "Quality Counts; State of the States," Education Week's "report card" surveying key education indicators, policy efforts, and educational outcomes.
  Education Week, January 4, 2013 (online) and January 10, 2013 (print); www.edweek.org

- SERI (Science and Engineering Readiness Index) weighs the performance of the states' K-12 schools in preparing students in physics and calculus, the high school subjects considered most important for future scientists and engineers. Delaware ranked #25.
  Newsletter of the Forum on Education of the American Physical Society, Summer 2011 issue; www.huffingtonpost.com, July 11, 2011; updated October 1, 2012

- MoneyRates.com ranked Delaware #27 on its list of the best to worst states for making a living. Criteria: average income; inflation; employment prospects; and workers' Workplace Environment assessments according to the Gallup-Healthways Well-Being Index.
  www.money-rates.com, posted April 1, 2013

- *Forbes* analyzed business costs, labor supply, regulatory environment, current economic climate, growth prospects, and quality of life, to compile its "Best States for Business" rankings. Delaware ranked #21.
  www.forbes.com. posted December 12, 2012

- The 2012 Gallup-Healthways Well-Being Index, surveyed American's opinions on economic confidence, workplace perceptions, community climate, personal choices, and health predictors to assess the "future livability" of each state. Delaware ranked #41.
  "Utah Poised to Be the Best State to Live In," Gallup Wellbeing, www.gallup.com, August 7, 2012

- On CNBC's list of "America's Top States for Business 2013," Delaware ranked #31. Criteria: measures of competitiveness developed with input from the National Association of Manufacturers, the Council on Competitiveness, and other business groups weighed with the states' own marketing criteria.
  www.cnbc.com, consulted July 19, 2013

- Delaware ranked #4 on the "worst" end of the Christian Science Monitor's list of "States with the Best (and Worst) Job Growth," as indicated by year-over-year growth rates from May 2012 to May 2013.
  www.csmonitor.com, July 5, 2013

- Delaware ranked #19 on MoneyRates list of "Best-and Worst-States to Retire 2012." Criteria: life expectancy, crime rate, climate, economic conditions, taxes, job opportunities, and cost of living.
  www.money-rates.com, October 22, 2012

- Delaware ranked #42 on the 2013 Bankrate "Best Places to Retire" list ranking the states and District of Columbia on various criteria relating to health, safety, and cost.
  www.bankrate.com, May 6, 2013

- Delaware ranked #17 on the Social Science Research Council's "American Human Development Report: The Measure of America," assessing the 50 states plus the District of Columbia on health, education, and living-standard criteria.
  The Measure of America 2013-2014, posted June 19, 2013; www.measureofamerica.org

- Delaware ranked #21 on the Foundation for Child Development's (FCD) Child Well-being Index (CWI). The FCD used the KIDS COUNT report and the National Survey of Children's Health, the only state-level source for several key indicators of child well-being.
  Foundation for Child Development, January 18, 2012; fcd-us.org

- Delaware ranked #22 overall according to the 2013 KIDS COUNT Data Book, a project of the Annie E. Casey Foundation. Criteria: children's economic well-being, education, health, and family and community indicators.
  KIDS COUNT Data Center's Data Book, released June 20, 2013; http://datacenter.kidscount.org

- Delaware ranked #21 in the children's economic well-being category by the 2013 KIDS COUNT Data Book, a project of the Annie E. Casey Foundation.
  KIDS COUNT Data Center's Data Book, released June 20, 2013; http://datacenter.kidscount.org

- Delaware ranked #23 in the children's educational opportunities and attainments category by the 2013 KIDS COUNT Data Book, a project of the Annie E. Casey Foundation.
  KIDS COUNT Data Center's Data Book, released June 20, 2013; http://datacenter.kidscount.org

- Delaware ranked #19 in the children's health category by the 2013 KIDS COUNT Data Book, a project of the Annie E. Casey Foundation.
  KIDS COUNT Data Center's Data Book, released June 20, 2013; http://datacenter.kidscount.org

- Delaware ranked #28 in the family and community circumstances that factor into children's well-being category by the 2013 KIDS COUNT Data Book, a project of the Annie E. Casey Foundation.
  KIDS COUNT Data Center's Data Book, released June 20, 2013; http://datacenter.kidscount.org

- Delaware ranked #26 in the 2012 Gallup-Healthways Well-Being Index. Criteria: emotional health; physical health; healthy behavior; work environment; basic access to food, shelter, health care; and a safe and satisfying place to live.
  2012 State of Well-Being, Gallup-Healthways Well-Being Index, released February 28, 2013; www.well-beingindex.com

- *U.S. News and World Report's* "Best States for Teen Drivers" rankings are based on driving and road safety laws, federal reports on driver's licenses, car accident fatality, and road-quality statistics. Delaware ranked #17.
  U.S. News and World Report, March 18, 2010; www.usnews.com

- The Yahoo! Sports service Rivals.com ranks the states according to the strength of their high school football programs. Delaware ranked #40.
  "Ranking the States: Where Is the Best Football Played?," November 18, 2011; highschool.rivals.com

- iVillage ranked the states by hospitable living conditions for women. Criteria: economic success, access to affordable childcare, health care, reproductive rights, female representation in government, and educational attainment. Delaware ranked #17.
  iVillage, "50 Best to Worst States for Women," March 14, 2012; www.ivillage.com

- The League of American Bicyclists's "Bicycle Friendly States" ranked Delaware #5. Criteria: legislation and enforcement, policies and programs, infrastructure and funding, education and advocacy, and evaluation and planning.
  "Washington Tops the Bicycle-Friendly State Ranking," May 1, 2013; bicycling.com

- The federal Corporation for National and Community Service ranked the states and the District of Columbia by volunteer rates. Delaware ranked #29 for community service.
  "Volunteering and Civic Life in America 2012," www.volunteeringinamerica.gov, accessed July 24, 2013

- The Hospital Safety Score ranked states and the District of Columbia on their hospitals' performance scores. Delaware ranked #14. Criteria: avoiding preventable harm and medical errors, as demonstrated by 26 hospital safety metrics.
  Spring 2013 Hospital Safety Score, May 8, 2013; www.hospitalsafetyscore.org

- GMAC Insurance ranked the states and the District of Columbia by the performance of their drivers on the GMAC Insurance National Drivers Test, comprised of DMV test questions. Delaware ranked #31.
  "2011 GMAC Insurance National Drivers Test," www.gmacinsurance.com, accessed July 23, 2013

- Delaware ranked #22 in a "State Integrity Investigation" analysis of laws and practices intended to deter corruption and promote accountability and openness in campaign finance, ethics laws, lobbying regulations and management of state pension funds.
  "What's Your State's Grade?," www.publicintegrity.org, accessed July 23, 2013

- Delaware ranked #48 among the states and the District of Columbia in total rail miles, as tracked by the Association of American Railroads.
  "U.S. Freight Railroad Industry Snapshot: Railroads and States: Total Rail Miles by State: 2011"; www.aar.org, accessed July 23, 2013

- According to statistics compiled by the Beer Institute, Delaware ranked #14 among the states and the District of Columbia in per capita beer consumption of persons 21 years or older.
  "Shipments of Malt Beverages and Per Capita Consumption by State 2012;" www.beerinstitute.org

- According to Concordia University's "Public Education Costs per Pupil by State Rankings," based on statistics gathered by the U.S. Census Bureau, which includes the District of Columbia, Delaware ranked #12.
  Concordia University Online; education.cu-portland.edu, accessed July 24, 2013

- Delaware ranked #6 among the states and the District of Columbia in population density based on U.S. Census Bureau data for resident population and total land area. "List of U.S. States by Population Density."
  www.wikipedia.org, accessed July 24, 2013

- In "America's Health Rankings, 2012 Edition," by the United Health Foundation, Delaware ranked #31. Criteria included: rate of high school graduation; violent crime rate; incidence of infectious disease; childhood immunizations; prevalence of diabetes; per capita public-health funding; percentage of uninsured population; rate of children in poverty; and availability of primary-care physicians.
  United Health Foundation; www.americashealthrankings.org, accessed July 24, 2013

- The TechNet 2012 "State Broadband Index" ranked Delaware #3 on the following criteria: broadband adoption; network quality; and economic structure. Improved broadband use is hoped to promote economic development, build strong communities, improve delivery of government services and upgrade educational systems.
  TechNet; www.technet.org, accessed July 24, 2013

- Delaware was ranked #27 among the states and District of Columbia on the American Council for an Energy-Efficient Economy's "State Energy Efficiency Scorecard" for 2012.
  American Council for an Energy-Efficient Economy; aceee.org/sector/state-policy/scorecard, accessed July 24, 2013

Statistical Tables

DEMOGRAPHICS
Resident State and National Population, 1950-2012
Projected State and National Population, 2000-2030
Population by Age, 2012
Population by Race, 2012
Population by Hispanic Origin and Race, 2012

VITAL STATISTICS
Death Rates by Leading Causes, 2010
Death Rates by Selected Causes, 2010
Abortion Rates, 2009
Infant Mortality Rates, 1995-2009
Marriage and Divorce Rates, 2000-2011

ECONOMY
Nominal Gross Domestic Product by Industry, 2012
Real Gross Domestic Product, 2000-2012
Personal Income Per Capita, 1930-2012
Non-Farm Employment by Sector, 2012
Foreign Exports, 2000-2012
Energy Consumption, 2011

LAND AND WATER
Surface Area and Federally-Owned Land, 2007
Land Cover/Use of Non-Federal Rural Land, 2007
Farms and Crop Acreage, 2012

HEALTH AND MEDICAL CARE
Medical Professionals, 2012
Health Insurance Coverage, 2011
HIV, STD, and Tuberculosis Cases and Rates, 2011
Cigarette Smoking, 2011

HOUSING
Home Ownership Rates, 1995-2012
Home Sales, 2000-2010
Value of Owner-Occupied Homes, 2011

EDUCATION
School Enrollment, 2011
Educational Attainment, 2011
Public College Finances, FY 2012

TRANSPORTATION AND TRAVEL
Motor Vehicle Registrations and Drivers Licenses, 2011
Domestic Travel Expenditures, 2009
Retail Gasoline Prices, 2013
Public Road Length, 2011

CRIME AND LAW ENFORCEMENT
Full-Time Law Enforcement Officers, 2011
Prison Population, 2000-2012
Crime Rate, 2011

GOVERNMENT AND FINANCE
Local Governments by Type, 2012
State Government Revenue, 2011
State Government Expenditures, 2011
State Government General Expenditures by Function, 2011
State Government Finances, Cash and Debt, 2011

POLITICS
Composition of the Senate, 1995-2013
Composition of the House of Representatives, 1995-2013
Composition of State Legislature, 2004-2013
Voter Participation in Presidential Elections, 1980-2012
Governors Since Statehood

DEMOGRAPHICS

Resident State and National Population, 1950–2012

Year	State Population	U.S. Population	State Share
1950	318,000	151,326,000	0.21%
1960	446,000	179,323,000	0.25%
1970	548,104	203,302,031	0.27%
1980	594,338	226,545,805	0.26%
1990	666,168	248,709,873	0.27%
2000	783,559	281,424,600	0.28%
2010	897,934	308,745,538	0.29%
2012	917,092	313,914,040	0.29%

Note: 1950/1960 population figures are rounded to the nearest thousand.
Source: U.S. Census Bureau, Decennial Census 1950–2010; U.S. Census Bureau, 2012 Population Estimates

Projected State and National Population, 2000–2030

Year	State Population	U.S. Population	State Share
2000	783,600	281,421,906	0.28%
2005	836,687	295,507,134	0.28%
2010	884,342	308,935,581	0.29%
2015	927,400	322,365,787	0.29%
2020	963,209	335,804,546	0.29%
2025	990,694	349,439,199	0.28%
2030	1,012,658	363,584,435	0.28%
State population growth, 2000–2030			229,058
State percentage growth, 2000–2030			29.2%

Source: U.S. Census Bureau, Population Division, Interim State Population Projections, 2005

Population by Age, 2012

Age Group	State Population	Percent of Total Population	
		State	U.S.
Under 5 years	56,279	6.1%	6.4%
5 to 14 years	114,131	12.4%	13.1%
15 to 24 years	128,301	14.0%	14.0%
25 to 34 years	116,298	12.7%	13.5%
35 to 44 years	111,481	12.2%	12.9%
45 to 54 years	132,413	14.4%	14.1%
55 to 64 years	117,715	12.8%	12.3%
65 to 74 years	81,042	8.8%	7.6%
75 to 84 years	42,612	4.6%	4.2%
85 years and older	16,820	1.8%	1.9%
Under 18 years	205,050	22.4%	23.5%
65 years and older	140,474	15.3%	13.7%
Median age (years)	–	39.2	37.4

Source: U.S. Census Bureau, Annual Estimates of the Resident Population for Selected Age Groups by Sex for the United States, States, Counties, and Puerto Rico Commonwealth and Municipios: April 1, 2010 to July 1, 2012

Population by Race, 2012

Race	State Population	Percent of Total Population	
		State	U.S.
All residents	917,092	100.00%	100.00%
White	654,352	71.35%	77.89%
African American	202,090	22.04%	13.13%
Native American	6,161	0.67%	1.23%
Asian	32,141	3.50%	5.14%
Native Hawaiian	766	0.08%	0.23%
Two or more races	21,582	2.35%	2.39%

Source: U.S. Census Bureau, Population Division, Annual Estimates of the Resident Population by Sex, Race and Hispanic Origin for the United States, States, and Counties: April 1, 2010 to July 1, 2012

Population by Hispanic Origin and Race, 2012

Hispanic Origin/Race	State Population	Percent of Total Population	
		State	U.S.
All residents	917,092	100.00%	100.00%
All Hispanic residents	78,813	8.59%	16.89%
Hispanic			
White	62,338	6.80%	14.91%
African American	9,399	1.02%	0.79%
Native American	3,222	0.35%	0.49%
Asian	534	0.06%	0.17%
Native Hawaiian	479	0.05%	0.06%
Two or more races	2,841	0.31%	0.48%
Not Hispanic			
White	592,014	64.55%	62.98%
African American	192,691	21.01%	12.34%
Native American	2,939	0.32%	0.74%
Asian	31,607	3.45%	4.98%
Native Hawaiian	287	0.03%	0.17%
Two or more races	18,741	2.04%	1.91%

Source: U.S. Census Bureau, Population Division, Annual Estimates of the Resident Population by Sex, Race and Hispanic Origin for the United States, States, and Counties: April 1, 2010 to July 1, 2012

VITAL STATISTICS

Death Rates by Leading Causes, 2010

Cause	State	U.S.
Malignant neoplasms	199.5	186.2
Ischaemic heart diseases	121.8	122.9
Other forms of heart disease	52.5	53.4
Chronic lower respiratory diseases	46.3	44.7
Cerebrovascular diseases	43.5	41.9
Organic, incl. symptomatic, mental disorders	48.2	35.7
Other degenerative diseases of the nervous sys.	24.4	28.4
Other external causes of accidental injury	26.2	26.5
Diabetes mellitus	20.8	22.4
Hypertensive diseases	16.7	20.4
All causes	822.8	799.5

Note: Figures are age-adjusted death rates per 100,000 population
Source: CDC/NCHS, Underlying Cause of Death 1999–2010 on CDC WONDER Online Database

Death Rates by Selected Causes, 2010

Cause	State	U.S.
Assault	6.9	5.2
Diseases of the liver	14.3	13.9
Human immunodeficiency virus (HIV) disease	5.0	2.7
Influenza and pneumonia	14.9	16.2
Intentional self-harm	11.7	12.4
Malnutrition	–	0.9
Obesity and other hyperalimentation	2.6	1.8
Renal failure	14.8	14.4
Transport accidents	12.9	12.1
Viral hepatitis	3.2	2.4

Note: Figures are age-adjusted death rates per 100,000 population; A dash indicates that data was not available or was suppressed
Source: CDC/NCHS, Underlying Cause of Death 1999–2010 on CDC WONDER Online Database

Abortion Rates, 2009

Category	2009
By state of residence	
Total abortions	–
Abortion rate[1]	–%
Abortion ratio[2]	–
By state of occurrence	
Total abortions	–
Abortion rate[1]	–%
Abortion ratio[2]	–
Abortions obtained by out-of-state residents	–%
U.S. abortion rate[1]	15.1%
U.S. abortion ratio[2]	227

Note: (1) Number of abortions per 1,000 women aged 15–44 years; (2) Number of abortions per 1,000 live births; A dash indicates that data was not available
Source: CDC/NCHS, Morbidity and Mortality Weekly Report, November 23, 2012 (Abortion Surveillance, United States, 2009)

Infant Mortality Rates, 1995–2009

Category	1995	2000	2005	2009
All state residents	7.40	9.59	9.02	7.96
All U.S. residents	7.57	6.89	6.86	6.39
All state white residents	6.37	8.12	5.98	4.50
All U.S. white residents	6.30	5.71	5.73	5.33
All state black residents	11.43	13.29	17.86	16.69
All U.S. black residents	14.58	13.48	13.26	12.12

Note: Figures represent deaths per 1,000 live births of resident infants under one year old, exclusive of fetal deaths; A dash indicates that data was not available or was suppressed.
Source: Centers of Disease Control and Prevention, Division of Vital Statistics, Linked Birth/Infant Death Records on CDC Wonder Online

Marriage and Divorce Rates, 2000–2011

Year	Marriage Rate		Divorce Rate	
	State	U.S.	State	U.S.
2000	6.5	8.2	3.9	4.0
2002	6.4	8.0	3.5	3.9
2004	6.1	7.8	3.7	3.7
2006	5.9	7.5	3.8	3.7
2008	5.5	7.1	3.5	3.5
2010	5.2	6.8	3.5	3.6
2011	5.2	6.8	3.6	3.6

Note: Rates are based on provisional counts of marriages/divorces by state of occurrence and are per 1,000 total population residing in area
Source: CDC/NCHS, National Vital Statistics System

ECONOMY

Nominal Gross Domestic Product by Industry, 2012
In millions of current dollars

Industry	State GDP
Accommodation and food services	1,239
Administrative and waste management services	1,172
Agriculture, forestry, fishing, and hunting	0
Arts, entertainment, and recreation	460
Construction	1,569
Educational services	383
Finance and insurance	24,608
Health care and social assistance	4,090
Information	1,160
Management of companies and enterprises	1,363
Manufacturing	4,393
Mining	0
Other services, except government	987
Professional, scientific, and technical services	4,617
Real estate and rental and leasing	6,979
Retail trade	2,584
Transportation and warehousing	878
Utilities	983
Wholesale trade	2,173

Source: U.S. Department of Commerce, Bureau of Economic Analysis, Survey of Current Business

Real Gross Domestic Product, 2000–2012
In millions of chained 2005 dollars

Year	State GDP	U.S. GDP	State Share
2000	46,453	11,225,406	0.41%
2005	54,422	12,539,116	0.43%
2010	55,496	12,897,088	0.43%
2012	56,110	13,430,576	0.42%

Source: U.S. Department of Commerce, Bureau of Economic Analysis, Survey of Current Business

Personal Income Per Capita, 1930–2012

Year	State	U.S.
1930	$855	$618
1940	$1,028	$593
1950	$2,066	$1,503
1960	$2,817	$2,268
1970	$4,594	$4,084
1980	$10,756	$10,091
1990	$21,209	$19,354
2000	$31,009	$30,319
2010	$39,425	$39,791
2012	$41,940	$42,693

Source: U.S. Department of Commerce, Bureau of Economic Analysis, Regional Economic Accounts

Non-Farm Employment by Sector, 2012
In thousands

Sector	Employment
Construction	18.4
Education and health services	68.1
Financial activities	42.3
Government	63.5
Information	5.5
Leisure and hospitality	43.4
Mining and logging (combined with construction)	0.0
Manufacturing	25.8
Other services	19.6
Professional and business services	56.3
Trade, transportation, and utilities	75.6
All sectors	418.5

Source: U.S. Bureau of Labor Statistics, State and Area Employment

Foreign Exports, 2000–2012
In millions of dollars

Year	State Exports	U.S. Exports	State Share
2000	2,197	712,054	0.31%
2002	2,017	649,940	0.31%
2004	2,055	768,554	0.27%
2006	3,896	973,994	0.40%
2008	4,898	1,222,545	0.40%
2010	4,945	1,208,080	0.41%
2012	5,113	1,478,268	0.35%

Note: U.S. figures exclude data from Puerto Rico, U.S. Virgin Islands, and unallocated exports
Source: U.S. Department of Commerce, International Trade Admin., Office of Trade and Industry Information, Manufacturing and Services

Energy Consumption, 2011

In trillions of BTUs, except as noted

Total energy consumption	
Total state energy consumption	271.6
Total U.S. energy consumption	97,387.3
State share of U.S. total	0.28%
Per capita consumption (in millions of BTUs)	
Total state per capita consumption	299.1
Total U.S. per capita consumption	312.6
End-use sectors	
Residential	67.8
Commercial	58.9
Industrial	82.7
Transportation	62.2
Sources of energy	
Petroleum	101.5
Natural gas	81.7
Coal	17.9
Renewable energy	7.1
Nuclear electric power	0.0

Source: U.S. Energy Information Administration, State Energy Data 2011: Consumption

LAND AND WATER

Surface Area and Federally-Owned Land, 2007

In thousands of acres

Category	State	U.S.	State Share
Total surface area	1,533.5	1,937,664.2	0.08%
Total land area	1,243.3	1,886,846.9	0.07%
Non-federal land	1,212.3	1,484,910.0	0.08%
Developed	280.1	111,251.2	0.25%
Rural	932.2	1,373,658.8	0.07%
Federal land	31.0	401,936.9	0.01%
Water area	290.2	50,817.3	0.57%

Source: U.S. Department of Agriculture, Natural Resources Conservation Service, 2007 National Resources Inventory

Land Cover/Use of Non-Federal Rural Land, 2007

In thousands of acres

Category	State	U.S.	State Share
Total rural land	932.2	1,373,658.8	0.07%
Cropland	420.5	357,023.5	0.12%
CRP[1] land	0.0	32,850.2	0.00%
Pastureland	37.4	118,615.7	0.03%
Rangeland	0.0	409,119.4	0.00%
Forest land	339.4	406,410.4	0.08%
Other rural land	134.9	49,639.6	0.27%

Note: (1) Conservation Reserve Program was created to assist private landowners in converting highly erodible cropland to vegetative cover.
Source: U.S. Department of Agriculture, Natural Resources Conservation Service, 2007 National Resources Inventory

Farms and Crop Acreage, 2012

Category	State	U.S.	State Share
Farms (in thousands)	2.5	2,170.0	0.12%
Acres (in millions)	0.5	914.0	0.05%
Acres per farm	196.0	421.2	–

Source: U.S. Department of Agriculture, National Agricultural Statistical Service, Quick Stats, 2012 Survey Data

HEALTH AND MEDICAL CARE

Medical Professionals, 2012

Profession	State Number	U.S. Number	State Share	State Rate[1]	U.S. Rate[1]
Physicians[2]	2,483	894,637	0.28%	273.4	287.1
Dentists	408	193,587	0.21%	44.9	62.1
Podiatrists	60	17,469	0.34%	6.6	5.6
Optometrists	113	45,638	0.25%	12.4	14.6
Chiropractors	188	77,494	0.24%	20.7	24.9

Note: (1) Rates are per 100,000 population; (2) Includes total, active Doctors of Osteopathic Medicine and Doctors of Medicine in 2011.
Source: U.S. Department of Health and Human Services, Bureau of Health Professions, Area Health Resource File, 2012-2013

Health Insurance Coverage, 2011

Category	State	U.S.
Total persons covered	812,000	260,214,000
Total persons not covered	91,000	48,613,000
Percent not covered	10.1%	15.7%
Children under age 18 covered	192,000	67,143,000
Children under age 18 not covered	13,000	6,965,000
Percent of children not covered	6.3%	9.4%

Source: U.S. Census Bureau, Current Population Survey, 2012 Annual Social and Economic Supplement

HIV, STD, and Tuberculosis Cases and Rates, 2011

Disease	State Cases	State Rate[1]	U.S. Rate[1]
Chlamydia	4,508	502.0	457.6
Gonorrhea	827	92.1	104.2
HIV diagnosis	127	16.7	15.8
HIV, stage 3 (AIDS)	105	13.8	10.3
Syphilis, early latent	49	5.5	4.3
Syphilis, primary/secondary	27	3.0	4.5
Tuberculosis	21	2.3	3.4

Note: (1) Rates are per 100,000 population
Source: Centers for Disease Control and Prevention

Cigarette Smoking, 2011

Category	State	U.S.
Adults who are current smokers	21.8%	21.2%
Adults who smoke everyday	16.3%	15.4%
Adults who smoke some days	5.5%	5.7%
Adults who are former smokers	28.3%	25.1%
Adults who never smoked	50.0%	52.9%

Source: Centers for Disease Control and Prevention, Behavioral Risk Factor Surveillance System, Tobacco Use, 2011

HOUSING

Home Ownership Rates, 1995–2012

Area	1995	2000	2005	2010	2012
State	71.7%	72.0%	75.8%	74.7%	73.4%
U.S.	64.7%	67.4%	68.9%	66.9%	65.4%

Source: U.S. Census Bureau, Housing Vacancies and Homeownership, Annual Statistics

Home Sales, 2000–2010
In thousands of units

Year	State Sales	U.S. Sales	State Share
2000	12.9	5,174	0.25%
2002	14.5	5,632	0.26%
2004	18.9	6,778	0.28%
2006	17.8	6,478	0.27%
2008	11.5	4,913	0.23%
2010	10.9	4,908	0.22%

Note: Units include single-family homes, condos and co-ops
Source: National Association of Realtors, Real Estate Outlook, Market Trends & Insights

Value of Owner-Occupied Homes, 2011

Value	Total Units in State	Percent of Total, State	Percent of Total, U.S.
Less than $50,000	14,069	5.9%	8.8%
$50,000 to $99,000	9,650	4.0%	16.0%
$100,000 to $149,000	22,503	9.4%	16.5%
$150,000 to $199,000	40,577	17.0%	15.4%
$200,000 to $299,000	77,563	32.5%	18.2%
$300,000 to $499,000	58,982	24.7%	15.2%
$500,000 to $999,000	12,033	5.0%	7.9%
$1,000,000 or more	3,183	1.3%	2.0%
Median value	–	$236,900	$173,600

Source: U.S. Census Bureau, 2011 American Community Survey 1-Year Estimates

EDUCATION

School Enrollment, 2011

Educational Level	Students Enrolled in State	Percent of Total, State	Percent of Total, U.S.
All levels	237,520	100.0%	100.0%
Nursery school, preschool	14,665	6.2%	6.0%
Kindergarten	13,437	5.7%	5.1%
Elementary (grades 1–8)	90,971	38.3%	39.5%
Secondary (grades 9–12)	47,238	19.9%	20.7%
College or graduate school	71,209	30.0%	28.7%

Note: Figures cover the population 3 years and over enrolled in school
Source: U.S. Census Bureau, 2011 American Community Survey 1-Year Estimates

Educational Attainment, 2011

Highest Level of Education	State	U.S.
High school diploma	87.0%	85.9%
Bachelor's degree	28.8%	28.5%
Graduate/Professional degree	11.7%	10.6%

Note: Figures cover the population 25 years and over
Source: U.S. Census Bureau, 2011 American Community Survey 1-Year Estimates

Public College Finances, FY 2012

Category	State	U.S.
Full-time equivalent enrollment (FTE)[1]	34,672	11,548,974
Educational appropriations per FTE[2]	$4,663	$5,906
Net tuition revenue per FTE[3]	$12,330	$5,189
Total educational revenue per FTE[4]	$16,913	$11,043

(1) Full-time equivalent enrollment equates student credit hours to full time, academic year students, but excludes medical students; (2) Educational appropriations measure state and local support available for public higher education operating expenses including ARRA funds and excludes appropriations for independent institutions, financial aid for students attending independent institutions, research, hospitals, and medical education; (3) Net tuition revenue is calculated by taking the gross amount of tuition and fees, less state and institutional financial aid, tuition waivers or discounts, and medical student tuition and fees. Net tuition revenue used for capital debt service is included in the net tuition revenue figures; (4) Total educational revenue is the sum of educational appropriations and net tuition excluding net tuition revenue used for capital debt service.
Source: State Higher Education Executive Officers, State Higher Education Finance FY 2012

TRANSPORTATION AND TRAVEL

Motor Vehicle Registrations and Drivers Licenses, 2011

Vehicle Type	State	U.S.	State Share
Automobiles[1]	490,696	125,656,528	0.39%
Buses	3,128	666,064	0.47%
Trucks	405,093	118,455,587	0.34%
Motorcycles	30,498	8,437,502	0.36%
Drivers licenses	716,109	211,874,649	0.34%

Note: Motor vehicle registrations include private, commercial, and publicly-owned vehicles; (1) Includes taxicabs
Source: U.S. Department of Transportation, Federal Highway Administration

Domestic Travel Expenditures, 2009
In millions of dollars

Category	State	U.S.	State Share
Travel expenditures	$1,334	$610,200	0.22%

Note: Figures represent U.S. spending on domestic overnight trips and day trips of 50 miles or more, one way, away from home. Excludes spending by foreign visitors.
Source: U.S. Travel Association, Impact of Travel on State Economies, 2009

Retail Gasoline Prices, 2013

Gasoline Grade	State Average	U.S. Average
Regular	$3.68	$3.65
Mid	$3.88	$3.81
Premium	$4.06	$3.98
Diesel	$3.81	$3.88
Excise tax[1]	41.4 cents	49.4 cents

Note: Gasoline prices as of 7/26/2013; (1) Includes state and federal excise taxes and other state taxes as of July 1, 2013
Source: American Automobile Association, Daily Fuel Guage Report; American Petroleum Institute, State Motor Fuel Taxes, 2013

Public Road Length, 2011

Type	State Mileage	U.S. Mileage	State Share
Interstate highways	41	46,960	0.09%
Other highways	30	15,719	0.19%
Principal arterial	338	156,262	0.22%
Minor arterial	308	242,942	0.13%
Major collector	820	534,592	0.15%
Minor collector	224	266,357	0.08%
Local	4,598	2,814,925	0.16%
Urban	2,997	1,095,373	0.27%
Rural	3,361	2,982,383	0.11%
Total	6,358	4,077,756	0.16%

Note: Combined urban and rural road mileage equals the total of the other road types
Source: U.S. Department of Transportation, Federal Highway Administration, Public Road Length, 2011

CRIME AND LAW ENFORCEMENT

Full-Time Law Enforcement Officers, 2011

Gender	State Number	State Rate[1]	U.S. Rate[1]
Male officers	1,954	215.5	210.3
Female officers	320	35.3	28.1
Total officers	2,274	250.8	238.3

Note: (1) Rates are per 100,000 population
Source: Federal Bureau of Investigation, Uniform Crime Reports, Crime in the United States 2011

Prison Population, 2000–2012

Year	State Population	U.S. Population	State Share
2000	6,921	1,391,261	0.50%
2005	6,966	1,527,929	0.46%
2010	6,615	1,613,803	0.41%
2011	6,739	1,598,783	0.42%
2012	6,914	1,571,013	0.44%

Note: Figures include prisoners under the jurisdiction of state or federal correctional authorities.
Source: U.S. Department of Justice, Bureau of Justice Statistics, Prisoners in 2006, 2011, 2012 (Advance Counts)

Crime Rate, 2011
Incidents per 100,000 residents

Category	State	U.S.
Violent crimes	559.5	386.3
Murder	4.5	4.7
Forcible rape	31.9	26.8
Robbery	169.5	113.7
Aggravated assault	353.5	241.1
Property crimes	3,410.6	2,908.7
Burglary	830.2	702.2
Larceny/theft	2,411.8	1,976.9
Motor vehicle theft	168.7	229.6
All crimes	3,970.1	3,295.0

Source: Federal Bureau of Investigation, Uniform Crime Reports, Crime in the United States 2011

GOVERNMENT AND FINANCE

Local Governments by Type, 2012

Government Type	State	U.S.	State Share
All local governments	338	89,004	0.38%
County	3	3,031	0.10%
Municipality	57	19,522	0.29%
Town/Township	0	16,364	0.00%
Special District	259	37,203	0.70%
Ind. School District	19	12,884	0.15%

Source: U.S. Census Bureau, 2012 Census of Governments: Organization Component Preliminary Estimates

State Government Revenue, 2011
In thousands of dollars, except for per capita figures

Total revenue	$9,105,971
Total revenue per capita, State	$10,027
Total revenue per capita, U.S.	$7,271
General revenue	$7,309,677
Intergovernmental revenue	$1,890,925
Taxes	$3,017,837
General sales	$0
Selective sales	$493,195
License taxes	$1,172,354
Individual income taxes	$962,321
Corporate income taxes	$322,537
Other taxes	$67,430
Current charges	$1,134,111
Miscellaneous general revenue	$1,266,804
Utility revenue	$16,142
Liquor store revenue	$0
Insurance trust revenue[1]	$1,780,152

Note: (1) Within insurance trust revenue, net earnings of state retirement systems is a calculated statistic, and thus can be positive or negative. Net earnings is the sum of earnings on investments plus gains on investments minus losses on investments.
Source: U.S. Census Bureau, 2011 Annual Survey of State Government Finances

State Government Expenditures, 2011

In thousands of dollars, except for per capita figures

Total expenditure	$7,936,467
Total expenditure per capita, State	$8,739
Total expenditure per capita, U.S.	$6,427
Intergovernmental expenditure	$1,293,106
Direct expenditure	$6,643,361
Current operation	$4,731,765
Capital outlay	$666,590
Insurance benefits and repayments	$752,501
Assistance and subsidies	$225,552
Interest on debt	$266,953
Utility expenditure	$126,249
Liquor store expenditure	$0
Insurance trust expenditure	$752,501

Source: U.S. Census Bureau, 2011 Annual Survey of State Government Finances

State Government General Expenditures by Function, 2011

In thousands of dollars

Education	$2,543,765
Public welfare	$1,762,406
Hospitals	$51,908
Health	$395,092
Highways	$460,695
Police protection	$114,070
Correction	$266,666
Natural resources	$99,770
Parks and recreation	$37,934
Governmental administration	$439,594
Interest on general debt	$266,953
Other and unallocable	$618,864

Source: U.S. Census Bureau, 2011 Annual Survey of State Government Finances

State Government Finances, Cash and Debt, 2011

In thousands of dollars, except for per capita figures

Debt at end of fiscal year	
State, total	$5,807,957
State, per capita	$6,395
U.S., per capita	$3,635
Cash and security holdings	
State, total	$14,799,103
State, per capita	$16,296
U.S., per capita	$11,759

Source: U.S. Census Bureau, 2011 Annual Survey of State Government Finances

POLITICS

Composition of the Senate, 1995–2013

Congress (Year)	State/U.S	Dem	Rep	Total
104th (1995)	State delegates	1	1	2
	Total U.S.	48	52	100
105th (1997)	State delegates	1	1	2
	Total U.S.	45	55	100
106th (1999)	State delegates	1	1	2
	Total U.S.	45	55	100
107th (2001)	State delegates	2	0	2
	Total U.S.	50	50	100
108th (2003)	State delegates	2	0	2
	Total U.S.	48	51	100
109th (2005)	State delegates	2	0	2
	Total U.S.	44	55	100
110th (2007)	State delegates	2	0	2
	Total U.S.	49	49	100
111th (2009)	State delegates	2	0	2
	Total U.S.	57	41	100
112th (2011)	State delegates	2	0	2
	Total U.S.	51	47	100
113th (2013)	State delegates	2	0	2
	Total U.S.	54	45	100

Note: Figures are for the starts of first sessions; Totals include Democratic (Dem) and Republican (Rep) members as well as vacancies and seats held by independent party members
Source: U.S. Congress, Congressional Directory

Composition of the House of Representatives, 1995–2013

Congress (Year)	State/U.S	Dem	Rep	Total
104th (1995)	State delegates	0	1	1
	Total U.S.	204	230	435
105th (1997)	State delegates	0	1	1
	Total U.S.	207	226	435
106th (1999)	State delegates	0	1	1
	Total U.S.	211	223	435
107th (2001)	State delegates	0	1	1
	Total U.S.	212	221	435
108th (2003)	State delegates	0	1	1
	Total U.S.	205	229	435
109th (2005)	State delegates	0	1	1
	Total U.S.	202	231	435
110th (2007)	State delegates	0	1	1
	Total U.S.	233	198	435
111th (2009)	State delegates	0	1	1
	Total U.S.	256	178	435
112th (2011)	State delegates	1	0	1
	Total U.S.	193	242	435
113th (2013)	State delegates	1	0	1
	Total U.S.	201	234	435

Note: Figures are for the starts of first sessions; Totals include Democratic (Dem) and Republican (Rep) members as well as vacancies and seats held by independent party members
Source: U.S. Congress, Congressional Directory

Composition of State Legislature, 2004–2013

Year	Democrats	Republicans	Total
State Senate			
2004	13	8	21
2005	13	8	21
2006	13	8	21
2007	13	8	21
2008	13	8	21
2009	16	5	21
2010	15	6	21
2011	14	7	21
2012	14	7	21
2013	13	8	21
State House			
2004	12	29	41
2005	15	25	41
2006	15	25	41
2007	18	23	41
2008	19	22	41
2009	24	17	41
2010	24	17	41
2011	26	15	41
2012	26	15	41
2013	27	14	41

Note: Totals may include minor party members and vacancies
Source: The Council of State Governments, State Legislatures

Voter Participation in Presidential Elections, 1980–2012

Year	Voting-eligible State Population	State Voter Turnout Rate	U.S. Voter Turnout Rate
1980	421,344	56.0	54.2
1984	442,354	57.5	55.2
1988	472,441	52.9	52.8
1992	499,266	58.0	58.1
1996	528,630	51.2	51.7
2000	554,863	59.0	54.2
2004	584,817	64.2	60.1
2008	628,200	65.6	61.6
2012	660,580	62.7	58.2

Note: All figures are based on the voting-eligible population which excludes person ineligible to vote such as non-citizens, felons (depending on state law), and mentally-incapacitated persons. U.S. figures include the overseas eligible population (including military personnel).
Source: McDonald, Michael P., United States Election Project, Presidential Voter Turnout Rates, 1980–2012

Governors Since Statehood

John McKinly	1777
Thomas McKean	1777
George Read	1777-1778
Caesar Rodney	1778-1781
John Dickinson	(r) 1781-1782
John Cook	1782-1783
Nicholas Van Dyke	1783-1786
Thomas Collins	(d) 1786-1789
Jehu Davis	1789
Joshua Clayton (O)	1789-1796
Gunning Bedford (O)	(d) 1796-1797
Daniel Rogers (O)	1797-1799
Richard Bassett (O)	(r) 1799-1801
James Sykes (O)	1801-1802
David Hall (O)	1802-1805
Nathaniel Mitchell (O)	1805-1808
George Truitt (O)	1808-1811
Joseph Haslet (O)	1811-1814
Daniel Rodney (O)	1814-1817
John Clark (O)	1817-1820
Jacob Stout (O)	1820-1821
John Collins (O)	(d) 1821-1822
Caleb Rodney (O)	1822-1823
Joseph Haslet (O)	(d) 1823
Charles Thomas (O)	1823-1824
Samuel Paynter (O)	1824-1827
Charles Polk (O)	1827-1830
David Hazzard (D)	1830-1833
Caleb P. Bennett (D)	(d) 1833-1836
Charles Polk (O)	1836-1837
Cornelius P. Comegys (O)	1837-1841
William B. Cooper (O)	1841-1845
Thomas Stockton (O)	(d) 1845-1846
Joseph Maull (O)	(d) 1846
William Temple (O)	1846-1847
William Tharp (D)	1847-1851
William H. H. Ross (D)	1851-1855
Peter F. Causey (O)	1855-1859
William Burton (D)	1859-1863
William Cannon (O)	(d) 1863-1865
Gove Saulsbury (D)	1865-1871
James Ponder (D)	1871-1875
John P. Cochran (D)	1875-1879
John W. Hall (D)	1879-1883
Charles C. Stockley (D)	1883-1887
Benjamin T. Biggs (D)	1887-1891
Robert J. Reynolds (D)	1891-1895
Joshua H. Marvel (R)	(d) 1895
William T. Watson (D)	1895-1897
Ebe W. Tunnell (D)	1897-1901
John Hunn (R)	1901-1905
Preston Lea (R)	1905-1909
Simeon S. Pennewell (R)	1909-1913
Charles R. Miller (R)	1913-1917
John G. Townsend Jr. (R)	1917-1921
William D. Denney (R)	1921-1925
Robert P. Robinson (R)	1925-1929
Clayton Douglass Buck (R)	1929-1937
Richard C. McMullen (D)	1937-1941
Walter W. Bacon (R)	1941-1949
Elbert N. Carvel (D)	1949-1953
James Caleb Boggs (R)	(r) 1953-1960
David P. Buckson (R)	1960-1961
Elbert N. Carvel (D)	1961-1965
Charles L. Terry Jr. (D)	1965-1969
Russell W. Peterson (R)	1969-1973
Sherman W. Tribbitt (D)	1973-1977
Pierre Samuel du Pont IV (R)	1977-1985
Michael N. Castle (R)	1985-1993
Thomas R. Carper (D)	(r) 1993-2001
Ruth Ann Minner (D)	2001-2009
Jack Markell (D)	2009-2017 (term limits)

Note: Governors were called state presidents before 1792; (D) Democrat; (R) Republican; (O) Other party; (r) resigned; (d) died in office; (i) removed from office

Florida

Location: Southeast coast

Area and rank: 53,997 square miles (139,852 square kilometers); 65,758 square miles (170,313 square kilometers) including water; twenty-sixth largest state in area

Coastline: 1,350 miles (2,173 kilometers) on the Atlantic Ocean and Gulf of Mexico

Shoreline: 8,426 miles (13,560 kilometers)

Population and rank: 19,317,568 (2012); fourth largest state in population

Capital city: Tallahassee (181,376 people in 2010 census)

State capitol building in Tallahassee. (Wikimedia Commons)

Largest city: Jacksonville (consolidated city, coextensive with Duval County; 821,784 people in 2010 census)

Became territory: March 30, 1822

Entered Union and rank: March 3, 1845; twenty-seventh state

Present constitution adopted: 1968

Counties: 67

State name: "Florida" comes from the Spanish for "feast of flowers," which relates to Easter celebrations

State nickname: Sunshine State

Motto: In God we trust

State flag: White field with red cross of Saint Andrew and state seal in center

Highest point: Geological survey section 30, T6 north, R20 west—345 feet (105 meters)

Lowest point: Atlantic Ocean—sea level

Highest recorded temperature: 109 degrees Fahrenheit (43 degrees Celsius)—Monticello, 1931

Lowest recorded temperature: –2 degrees Fahrenheit (–19 degrees Celsius)—Tallahassee, 1899

State songs: "Swannee River"; "Florida, My Florida"

State flower: Orange blossom

State bird: Mockingbird

National parks: Biscayne, Dry Tortugas, Everglades

Florida History

Although Florida has a long and varied history, many of the most important developments in the state, especially in terms of economic, political, and demographic changes, took place after the 1950's. Because of its geographic location, which promotes the influence of West Indian and Caribbean cultures, and its pleasant, tropical climate, which has attracted large numbers of residents from both the Northern and Southern Hemispheres, Florida developed a unique and distinctive character.

Early History. Native Americans arrived in Florida sometime around 10,000 B.C.E. and slowly made their way south, not reaching the southern tip of the peninsula until about 1400 B.C.E. Archaeological evidence from northeastern Florida and southeastern Georgia indicates that inhabitants of these areas invented pottery in the period around 2000 B.C.E. This would place their development of pottery approximately eight hundred years before other North American cultures.

Because of the abundance of game and marine life, early Native Americans in the Florida area were primarily hunters and fishers, rather than farmers. Great respect was paid to the dead, who were interred in large burial mounds. By 1500 C.E., a sun worship cult, also centered around large earthen mounds, spread through the region. The tribes discovered agriculture and grew corn, beans, and squash, among other crops.

Along the northern Gulf coast lived the Panzacola, Chatot, and Apalachicola; farther west were the Apalachee. The lower part of the peninsula, from Tampa Bay extending south, was inhabited by the warrior Calusa, for whom warfare seemed to be part of religious practice. In the north, the dominant group was the Timucua, who were the first Native Americans to encounter Europeans. By far the most famous of Florida tribes, however, were the Seminoles, who entered the state in 1750. The word *seminole* means "runaway" in the Creek language, and the people themselves were Creek Indians who came from Alabama and Georgia. At first scattered in small groups, the Seminoles united against those who wanted to remove them from Florida, first the Spanish and English and later the Americans.

Exploration and Settlement. The first European contact with Florida began in 1513, when Juan Ponce

Hernando de Soto landing at Tampa Bay in 1539. (Library of Congress)

de León landed on the coast, claimed the land for Spain, and bestowed its current name, either because it was Easter (*Pascua Florida*, in Spanish) or because of the many flowering plants he discovered (*florida* also means "flowery" in Spanish). After Ponce de León's death during a battle with Native Americans in 1521, several other Spanish explorers, including Hernando de Soto, sought to establish a permanent presence in Florida. It was not until 1565, however, that a Spanish colony was founded at St. Augustine, becoming the first permanent European settlement in what is now the United States.

As they did elsewhere with their New World colonies, the Spanish implemented both imperial rule and the Catholic religion. Settlements and missions were established throughout Florida, but these were destroyed during the early eighteenth century in raids by Native Americans and British settlers from South Carolina. In 1763, as part of the treaties which ended the French and Indian War, Spain ceded Florida to the British in exchange for Cuba. The British divided the colony into East and West Florida.

Immigration increased the English population of Florida, and during the American Revolution the residents remained loyal to that crown. However, in 1778, Spain, which had become an American ally, seized West Florida. In 1783, at the end of the Revolution, Spain regained all of Florida. While many English settlers left for British possessions in the West Indies, others remained behind, stubbornly defiant to the Spanish and fearful of possible takeover by French forces.

Steps to Statehood. During the War of 1812 the British used Pensacola as a naval base, prompting its capture by American forces under General Andrew Jackson. In 1819, Spain ceded Florida to the United States, and Jackson returned in 1822 as military governor of the new territory. The northwestern portion of the region, along the panhandle, became the site of numerous cotton plantations worked by slaves. Tallahassee was named the capital in 1823. In 1845, Florida was admitted to the Union.

Even before Florida officially became part of the United States, efforts had been under way to remove Native Americans from the territory. This ongoing conflict was concentrated on the Seminoles, who had formed a formidable presence against the threat from the Americans. From 1835 to 1842 the United States waged the Seminole War against the tribe. The war was begun when Osceola, a young Seminole chief, publicly rejected a harsh treaty with the United States by plunging

his dagger through the document. Outnumbered by the Americans, Osceola led the Seminoles into the Everglades and conducted guerrilla warfare. He was captured while under a flag of truce and imprisoned in Fort Moultrie at Charleston, South Carolina; he died there in 1838. Without his leadership, the tide turned against the Seminoles, and after their final defeat they were removed to lands in the western United States. Only a handful remained behind, hidden in the swamps and wilderness of Florida. The number of Seminoles increased in the state during the twentieth century, however.

Civil War and Reconstruction. In 1861, Florida joined other southern states in seceding from the Union. During the Civil War, Union naval forces quickly captured strong points along the coast, including Fernandina, Pensacola, and St. Augustine. However, when Union troops attempted an invasion of the interior, they were defeated at the battle of Olustee in 1864. A second Union attempt to capture Tallahassee failed in March, 1865; the Florida capital and Austin, Texas, were the only two Confederate capitals never captured during the war.

After being readmitted to the Union in 1868, Florida entered Reconstruction and began a period of trans-

Highway connecting the islands of the Florida Keys at the sourthern tip of the state's mainland. (PhotoDisc)

Space Shuttle launch at Cape Canaveral in Brevard County, Florida. (National Aeronautics and Space Administration)

economy, which was severely affected by the Great Depression of 1929. President Franklin Roosevelt's New Deal brought relief and massive defense spending before and during World War II, helping bring the state into the modern age.

A Mixed Economy. Cape Canaveral on the east coast of Florida was one of the oldest sites to be named by Europeans on the North American continent. During the 1950's and 1960's it became the site of the nation's newest explorers, as the National Aeronautics and Space Administration (NASA) chose it for the site of the American space program. In 1958, it saw the launch of the first U.S. satellite, in 1961 and 1962 the first American manned space flight and orbital mission, and in 1969 the first lunar mission.

Modern Florida developed a mixed economy that depends upon traditional areas such as manufacturing and agriculture and also relies heavily on tourism. Companies that produce computer equipment and accessories have taken the lead in manufacturing. Citrus fruits, first introduced to Florida during the 1570's, are a strong staple, with Florida producing more than three-quarters of the total U.S. harvest of grapefruit and oranges. In addition, the state's pine forests are valuable sources of materials for pulp and paper, as well as turpentine and other products. The almost year-round growing season has made Florida a leader in truck-farm agriculture; Florida ships tomatoes, vegetables, and other produce throughout the nation.

A Multicultural State. The Cuban Revolution of 1959, which brought Fidel Castro and the Communist Party to power, saw a massive emigration from that island, largely among the professional, upper, and middle classes. Conservative in politics and religion, Cubans brought with them a tradition of respect for learning and for the free enterprise system. Although their initial plans had been for an early return to their home, these immigrants established themselves in southern Florida, especially in the Miami area, where they developed a strong economy and thriving culture. By the late 1970's, southern Florida had become a multicultural, bilingual area.

These developments were not without difficulty. In 1986, Bob Martinez became the first Hispanic to be elected governor of Florida. Significantly, he won election as a Republican. However, many conservatives, disturbed at the increasing power of Hispanic voters, pushed hard to win approval in 1988 of an amendment to the state constitution that made English the official language of

formation of the state's economic base. Citrus fruits replaced cotton as the major cash crop, and phosphate mining for fertilizer became a dominant industry. Tourism, almost unknown before the Civil War, began to become a key economic factor during the 1880's, especially with the development of railroads. Henry B. Plant completed the Kissimmee-Tampa cross-state railroad in 1884, and Henry M. Flagler inaugurated the Jacksonville-Miami Line in 1896. The two systems linked Florida and its produce to the rich markets of the Northeast and encouraged the growth of the tourism and retirement industries. Starting during the early twentieth century, the state's population began to double approximately every twenty years.

The Florida real estate boom of the 1920's saw a dramatic increase in settlers, but by the middle of the decade the boom had ended. In addition, massive hurricanes in 1926 and 1928 further damaged the state's state government. Adding to the situation were sometimes tense relations between the white, Hispanic, and African American populations; during the early 1980's these tensions caused riots to flare in the Miami area.

Tourism and Nature. Tourism, long a staple of the modern Florida economy, received a major boost in 1971 with the opening of Walt Disney World near Orlando. Disney's Epcot Center followed in 1982. Soon, Disney World became the single most popular tourist destination in the United States. Other attractions, including Sea World, Universal Studios theme park, and Busch Gardens, increased Florida's appeal as a tourist destination. Added to these are the state's natural attractions, such as the Everglades, the Florida Keys, and the unique John Pennekamp Coral Reef State Park near Key Largo, which is entirely underwater and features living coral formations. In 1990, a record-breaking 41 million visitors from around the world visited Florida.

Although much of Florida's appeal rested upon its environment, much of that environment had been devastated by natural forces or harmed by human intervention. In 1992, the state was struck by Hurricane An-drew, at that time the costliest natural disaster in U.S. history. The storm raged through southern Florida, ruining entire communities and causing more than $20 billion in damages.

As the state entered the twenty-first century, it began to address a potentially fatal threat to its environment. Decades of systematic draining of wetlands, including the vast expanse of the Everglades, to accommodate expanding human population and development seriously endangered the environment and wildlife. Finally realizing the seriousness of the situation, the U.S. Army Corps of Engineers and other organizations abandoned long-standing projects such as the Cross Florida Barge Canal and began efforts to reverse years of neglect and active damage. These efforts became critical for a state more dependent than most on its natural environment for its prosperity and continued growth.

Headlines and Controversy. Florida gained national attention at the end of the twentieth century as the center of a series of controversies. One regarded the fate of a six-year-old Cuban boy, Elián González. In late November, 1999, the boy's mother drowned while

President Harry S. Truman as he walks to the beach at Key West, Florida, on March 20, 1951. (National Archives and Records Administration)

Hurricane Andrew approaching the Bahamas and South Florida on August 23, 1992. At the time of its occurrence, Andrew, a Category 5 strorm, was the costliest hurricane in United States. (U.S. Department of Commerce)

escaping from Cuba. Rescued by American fishermen, the boy was taken in by relatives in Miami, where his plight captured the nation's imagination. Miami's large Cuban émigré community was adamant that he stay in the United States, while many felt that he should be returned to his father in Cuba. In the end, he was forcibly seized by federal agents and sent back to Cuba to be with his father.

A second controversy occurred in November, 2000, when the state nearly deadlocked in the presidential election between George W. Bush and Al Gore. Questions surrounding what recounting of votes should be done and who had authority to order such recounts were at the center of the intense weeks-long political controversy. After a flurry of legal maneuvers, including decisions by the Florida Supreme Court, the issue landed at the U.S. Supreme Court. On December 12, 2000, the Court ruled in favor of the Bush campaign, ordering a halt to a vote recount. The following day, Gore conceded. His supporters remained embittered. It was later determined, however, that the recount method most favored by the Gore campaign was the one that would have most increased Bush's lead.

A third cause célèbre centered upon a forty-two year-old woman, Terri Schiavo, who, by 2005, had been comatose for fifteen years. Doctors pronounced her in a persistent vegetative state and said she would never regain consciousness. A long conflict had taken place between her parents and her husband over whether, in these circumstances, life support should be withdrawn and she be allowed to die. Americans followed the debate, with some arguing that Schiavo was a human being and that

it was not right, as her husband wished, to allow her to die. In the end, after attempts in Congress and the Florida State legislature, as well as extensive legal maneuvering, failed, a judge's order on March 18, 2005, that her feeding tube be withdrawn was carried out. On March 31, Schiavo died.

Hurricane Alley. A series of hurricanes battered the state in the twenty-first century, following Hurricane Gordon, a storm in 2000 that was relatively weak but nonetheless killed one person and displaced twenty thousand. However, in August, 2004, Hurricane Charley, the second most costly hurricane in Florida's history, made landfall, causing some $20 billion in damage. One million people were without electricity, and the infrastructure of southwestern Florida was devastated. Charley was followed on September 13 by Hurricane Francis, on September 16 by Hurricane Ivan, and on September 25 by Hurricane Jeanne. Each was a considerable, damaging storm. Altogether, Florida's four hurricanes in August and September of 2004 did $42 billion in damage and destroyed twenty-five thousand homes, with another forty thousand sustaining major damage.

In 2005, Hurricane Katrina swept across the state, en route to catastrophic destruction on the Gulf Coast, especially in Louisiana. In Florida, Katrina killed fourteen people and left one million people in the dark, but its winds were relatively modest. The storm developed its most destructive force after leaving the state and traveling across the Gulf of Mexico.

Despite its hurricane destruction, Florida remained prosperous. Its population gains were enough to gain it another member of Congress to its delegation following the 2000 census. Retirees continued to flock to the state, which has no state income tax.

Deepwater Horizon. On April 20, 2010 the Deepwater Horizon oil rig, located about 41 miles off the coast of Louisiana, exploded. The resultant oil spill caused severe damage to the economy and natural environment of Louisiana and nearby states, including the beaches and shoreline of the Gulf Coast of Florida. The accident is estimated to have released more than 4.9 million barrels of crude oil into Gulf waters. The oil spill affected about 68,000 square miles of ocean, and oil washed ashore along some 125 miles of the Gulf states by June 2010. A year later, the impacted shoreline was estimated to exceed 1000 miles.

The Florida Attorney General's Office filed a lawsuit against British Petroleum and Halliburton in the Northern

District of Florida on April 20, 2013. The suit sought to recover damages for the State of Florida's economic losses. That lawsuit was merged into a multidistrict litigation case in New Orleans; however, the trial regarding the State's economic losses would take place within Florida.

Zimmerman Case. An incident in Florida became a matter of intense national media interest in 2012–2013. A young African American man, Trayvon Martin, was shot and killed in Sanford, Florida by a civic watch patrolman, George Zimmerman, on February 26, 2012. After Zimmerman voluntarily surrendered to police, the State of Florida charged that Zimmerman profiled and confronted Martin and shot him to death while Martin was committing no crimes. Zimmerman said he shot Martin in self-defense. National media coverage of the crime focused on the issue of racial profiling and on the fact that there was no evidence that Zimmerman had been assaulted or in any danger. After sixteen hours of deliberations the six-member jury found Zimmerman not guilty on all counts on July 13, 2013.

Michael Witkoski
Updated by the Editor

Florida Time Line

Apr. 3, 1513	Juan Ponce de León discovers territory he calls Florida and claims for Spain.
May, 1539	Hernando de Soto lands near what is now Tampa Bay and begins exploration.
1564	French Huguenots establish settlement on St. Johns River.
1565	Spanish mariner Pedro Menéndez de Avilés founds St. Augustine, the oldest city in the Union, and kills French Huguenot colonists, establishing Spanish power.
1570's	Citrus trees are introduced into Florida.
1698	Spanish establish settlement at Pensacola.
1750	Seminoles migrate to Florida from Georgia.
1763	Spain trades Florida to Britain.
1783	Britain cedes Florida back to Spain.
1814	General Andrew Jackson seizes Pensacola in War of 1812.
1819	Spain cedes East Florida to United States.
Mar. 30, 1822	Territory of Florida is established.
1835–1842	Seminole War rages as settlers try to push Native Americans from area.
Mar. 3, 1845	Florida enters the Union as the twenty-seventh state.
1853	University of Florida is founded at Gainesville.
Jan. 10, 1861	Florida is the third state to secede from the Union.
July 4, 1868	Florida is readmitted to the Union.
1884	Phosphate deposits are found on Peace River.
1884	Henry B. Plant completes cross-state railroad.
1886	Henry M. Flagler opens Jacksonville-Miami railroad.
1906	Draining operations begin in the Everglades.
1947	Everglades National Park is created.
1954	Sunshine Skyway across Tampa Bay opens.
1958	NASA begins administration of Cape Canaveral aerospace center.
1963	Cape Canaveral is renamed Cape Kennedy.
1968	New state constitution is adopted.
1969	All public schools, including colleges and universities, come under a unified system.
1971	Construction on Cross Florida Barge Canal halted for environmental reasons.
1971	Walt Disney World opens.
1973	Cape Kennedy is renamed Cape Canaveral.
1982	Epcot Center opens at Walt Disney World.
1985	Xavier Suarez becomes first Cuban American elected mayor of Miami.
1986	Republican Bob Martinez becomes first Hispanic elected governor.
1988	English is made the official language of state government through a constitutional amendment.
1990	41 million people visit Florida, a state record.
Aug. 24, 1992	Hurricane Andrew devastates southern Florida.
June 28, 2000	Six-year-old Elián González is returned to his father in Cuba.

Nov. 7–Dec. 13, 2000	Florida is center of national political controversy when presidential voting is nearly equal between the major party candidates. In the U.S. Supreme Court decision *Bush v. Gore*, Florida's 25 electoral votes were given to George W. Bush, and he became the president.
Aug.–Sept 2004	Series of hurricanes hits the state, causing the deaths of eighty-six people and more than $42 billion in damage.
Mar. 31, 2005	The national controversy over continuance of life support for Terri Schiavo ends with her death.
Aug. 25, 2005	Hurricane Katrina cuts a swath through the state, killing fourteen persons.
April 20, 2010	Deepwater Horizon, an offshore British Petroleum oil rig about 41 miles off the coast of Louisiana, explodes, releasing a total of more than 4.9 million barrels of crude oil into the Gulf.
2012–2013	A young African American, Trayvon Martin, is shot to death by civic watch patrolman George Zimmerman. The case gains national media attention as details emerge that Martin, 17, was unarmed and in fact being pursued by Zimmerman against police orders. In July 2013 Zimmerman was acquitted on all possible counts, ranging from 1st degree murder to manslaughter.

Notes for Further Study

Published Sources. Charlton Tebeau's *A History of Florida* (3d rev. ed., 1999) provides a good start to understanding the growth and development of the state, especially from statehood to Civil War and Reconstruction. *Florida: A Short History* (1993) by Michael Gannon is another excellent introductory survey of the state and its development. David Nolan's *Fifty Feet in Paradise: The Booming of Florida* (1984) discusses Florida's checkered history in the modern era, as the state went through several periods of growth and recession. *Land of Sunshine, State of Dreams: A Social History of Modern Florida* (2005) by Gary R. Mormino examines the state's explosive growth following 1950 as a result of immigration and the combined pull of tourism, retirement communities, and new technology sectors. Michael Grunwald, in *The Swamp: The Everglades, Florida, and the Politics of Paradise* (2006), examines the region's population growth from another angle: the environmental destruction of the Everglades and efforts to restore them.

Tourism is a critical sector in Florida, and two books explore the early efforts of railroad tycoon Henry Flagler to establish the state as a vacationer's destination: *Last Train to Paradise: Henry Flagler and the Spectacular Rise and Fall of the Railroad That Crossed an Ocean* (2002) by Les Standiford and *The Architecture of Leisure: The Florida Resort Hotels of Henry Flagler and Henry Plant* (2002) by Susan R. Braden. David R. Colburn and Lance de Haven-Smith's work, *Government in the Sunshine State: Florida Since Statehood* (1999), examines several aspects of state politics.

Hernando de Soto and the Indians of Florida (1993) by Jerald T. Milanich and Charles Hudson looks at the beginning of an often troubled relationship between Native Americans and later-arriving European settlers.

David Colburn's *The African American Heritage of Florida* (1995) is an important and interesting survey of African American contributions to the state during its history.

Web Resources. Practically every aspect of Florida history, culture, politics, economics, and leisure can be accessed through a Web site, and most of the general sites provide easy reference to specific areas. Perhaps the best portal site is My Florida (www.myflorida.com/). Using the navigation on the left-hand side, site visitors will need to choose the category that pertains to them— Visitor, Floridian, Business, or Government—wherein one can find numerous links to specific information on that category.

For official information about the state, including statistics and links to agencies and departments, choose the Government category on My Florida (www. myflorida.com/taxonomy/government/). My Florida also has a comprehensive section for students (www. flheritage.com/kids/), which explains the state's history, culture, and Native American history, among other topics.

For those who are interested in Florida history, a variety of sites offer valuable information and links to other pages. Florida Smart (www.floridasmart.com/commculture/history.htm) offers countless links to historical information and associations and to facts about the state. For those who wish information about Florida's Native Americans, the Seminole Tribe of Florida has its own site (www.seminoletribe.com). One of the many legacies of Henry Flagler, the railroad tycoon and resort developer, is the Flagler Museum in Palm Beach (www. flagler.org/). Its Web site offers a thorough biography of Flagler and a description of the collections one will find when visiting the museum.

Counties

County	2012 Population	Pop. Rank	Land Area (sq. miles)	Area Rank
Alachua	251,417	23	875.02	22
Baker	27,086	51	585.23	46
Bay	171,903	28	758.46	29
Bradford	27,049	52	293.96	65
Brevard	547,307	10	1,015.66	15
Broward	1,815,137	2	1,209.79	7
Calhoun	14,723	61	567.33	50
Charlotte	162,449	29	680.28	36
Citrus	139,360	33	581.70	48
Clay	194,345	25	604.36	43

County	2012 Population	Pop. Rank	Land Area (sq. miles)	Area Rank
Collier	332,427	17	1,998.32	1
Columbia	67,966	40	797.57	25
DeSoto	34,712	48	637.06	41
Dixie	16,126	58	705.05	33
Duval	879,602	7	762.19	28
Escambia	302,715	19	656.46	38
Flagler	98,359	35	485.46	60
Franklin	11,686	65	534.72	56
Gadsden	46,528	43	516.33	57
Gilchrist	16,815	57	349.68	63

County	2012 Population	Pop. Rank	Land Area (sq. miles)	Area Rank
Glades	13,107	64	806.01	24
Gulf	15,718	59	564.01	51
Hamilton	14,708	62	513.79	58
Hardee	27,514	50	637.78	40
Hendry	37,447	47	1,152.75	8
Hernando	173,422	27	472.54	62
Highlands	98,128	36	1,016.61	14
Hillsborough	1,277,746	4	1,020.21	13
Holmes	19,804	55	478.78	61
Indian River	140,567	32	502.87	59
Jackson	48,968	42	917.76	20
Jefferson	14,256	63	598.10	45
Lafayette	8,804	66	543.41	55
Lake	303,186	18	938.38	18
Lee	645,293	8	784.51	26
Leon	283,769	22	666.85	37
Levy	40,025	45	1,118.21	9
Liberty	8,276	67	835.56	23
Madison	18,907	56	695.95	34
Manatee	333,895	16	742.93	31
Marion	335,125	15	1,584.55	5
Martin	148,817	31	543.46	54
Miami-Dade	2,591,035	1	1,897.72	3
Monroe	74,809	37	983.28	17
Nassau	74,629	38	648.64	39
Okaloosa	190,083	26	930.25	19
Okeechobee	39,467	46	768.91	27
Orange	1,202,234	5	903.43	21
Osceola	287,416	20	1,327.45	6
Palm Beach	1,356,545	3	1,969.76	2
Pasco	470,391	12	746.89	30
Pinellas	921,319	6	273.80	66
Polk	616,158	9	1,797.84	4
Putnam	73,263	39	727.62	32
Santa Rosa	158,512	30	1,011.60	16
Sarasota	386,147	14	555.87	52
Seminole	430,838	13	309.22	64
St. Johns	202,188	24	600.66	44
St. Lucie	283,866	21	571.93	49
Sumter	101,620	34	546.93	53
Suwannee	43,656	44	688.55	35
Taylor	22,744	54	1,043.31	11
Union	15,212	60	243.56	67
Volusia	496,950	11	1,101.03	10
Wakulla	30,818	49	606.42	42
Walton	57,582	41	1,037.62	12
Washington	24,892	53	582.80	47

Source: U.S. Census Bureau, 2012 Population Estimates

Cities

With 10,000 or more residents

Legal Name	2010 Population	Pop. Rank	Land Area (sq. miles)	Area Rank
Alafaya CDP	78,113	32	37.96	29
Altamonte Springs city	41,496	80	9.01	166
Apollo Beach CDP	14,055	230	19.84	78
Apopka city	41,542	78	31.24	42
Atlantic Beach city	12,655	257	3.49	270
Auburndale city	13,507	244	13.49	123
Aventura city	35,762	92	2.65	289
Azalea Park CDP	12,556	259	3.18	280

Legal Name	2010 Population	Pop. Rank	Land Area (sq. miles)	Area Rank
Bartow city	17,298	195	45.87	22
Bayonet Point CDP	23,467	144	5.74	216
Bayshore Gardens CDP	16,323	206	3.50	268
Bellair-Meadowbrook Terrace CDP	13,343	248	4.20	248
Belle Glade city	17,467	194	5.62	218
Bellview CDP	23,355	146	11.64	139
Bloomingdale CDP	22,711	152	8.13	178

Legal Name	2010 Population	Pop. Rank	Land Area (sq. miles)	Area Rank
Boca Raton city	84,392	30	29.33	47
Bonita Springs city	43,914	75	38.60	28
Boynton Beach city	68,217	39	16.17	96
Bradenton city	49,546	68	14.18	115
Brandon CDP	103,483	18	33.10	38
Brent CDP	21,804	163	10.38	149
Brownsville CDP	15,313	216	2.27	300
Buenaventura Lakes CDP	26,079	132	5.58	220
Callaway city	14,405	223	9.01	166
Cape Coral city	154,305	11	105.67	4
Carrollwood CDP	33,365	106	9.21	162
Casselberry city	26,241	130	6.99	198
Cheval CDP	10,702	297	5.96	211
Citrus Park CDP	24,252	138	10.16	155
Clearwater city	107,685	16	25.56	58
Clermont city	28,742	123	13.63	121
Cocoa city	17,140	198	13.32	124
Cocoa Beach city	11,231	288	4.66	235
Coconut Creek city	52,909	63	11.85	138
Conway CDP	13,467	247	3.42	273
Cooper City city	28,547	124	8.04	184
Coral Gables city	46,780	72	12.92	125
Coral Springs city	121,096	15	23.79	64
Coral Terrace CDP	24,376	137	3.38	275
Country Club CDP	47,105	71	4.14	250
Country Walk CDP	15,997	208	2.58	292
Crestview city	20,978	169	16.02	99
Cutler Bay town	40,286	84	9.83	158
Cypress Lake CDP	11,846	273	3.86	258
Dania Beach city	29,639	119	8.09	180
Davie town	91,992	24	34.89	33
Daytona Beach city	61,005	43	58.41	16
DeBary city	19,320	184	18.97	81
DeLand city	27,031	128	17.60	90
Deerfield Beach city	75,018	37	15.09	109
Delray Beach city	60,522	44	15.81	101
Deltona city	85,182	27	37.53	30
Destin city	12,305	263	7.69	188
Doctor Phillips CDP	10,981	291	3.39	274
Doral city	45,704	73	13.88	118
Dunedin city	35,321	96	10.36	151
East Lake CDP	30,962	116	28.91	49
East Lake-Orient Park CDP	22,753	151	16.32	94
East Milton CDP	11,074	289	28.81	50
Edgewater city	20,750	171	22.22	70
Egypt Lake-Leto CDP	35,282	97	5.91	213
Elfers CDP	13,986	232	3.54	266
Englewood CDP	14,863	221	9.79	159
Ensley CDP	20,602	173	12.17	132
Estero CDP	22,612	155	20.02	77
Eustis city	18,558	188	10.50	148
Fairview Shores CDP	10,239	305	3.03	282
Fernandina Beach city	11,487	284	11.13	146
Ferry Pass CDP	28,921	122	13.94	116
Fish Hawk CDP	14,087	229	16.21	95
Fleming Island CDP	27,126	127	15.83	100
Florida City city	11,245	287	5.95	212
Florida Ridge CDP	18,164	192	10.77	147

Legal Name	2010 Population	Pop. Rank	Land Area (sq. miles)	Area Rank
Forest City CDP	13,854	237	4.26	245
Fort Lauderdale city	165,521	8	34.77	34
Fort Myers city	62,298	42	39.96	27
Fort Pierce city	41,590	77	20.57	76
Fort Walton Beach city	19,507	182	7.48	190
Fountainebleau CDP	59,764	48	4.26	245
Four Corners CDP	26,116	131	46.36	20
Fruit Cove CDP	29,362	120	16.06	98
Fruitville CDP	13,224	251	6.80	202
Gainesville city	124,354	13	61.30	14
Gibsonton CDP	14,234	226	12.79	126
Gladeview CDP	11,535	280	2.56	293
Glenvar Heights CDP	16,898	199	4.12	251
Golden Gate CDP	23,961	142	3.90	256
Golden Glades CDP	33,145	109	4.88	231
Goldenrod CDP	12,039	268	2.52	294
Gonzalez CDP	13,273	250	15.11	108
Goulds CDP	10,103	307	2.91	284
Greenacres city	37,573	88	5.79	215
Gulf Gate Estates CDP	10,911	292	2.71	288
Gulfport city	12,029	269	2.76	286
Haines City city	20,535	174	18.39	83
Hallandale Beach city	37,113	89	4.22	247
Hialeah city	224,669	6	21.45	74
Hialeah Gardens city	21,744	165	3.25	278
Highland City CDP	10,834	294	8.01	186
Hobe Sound CDP	11,521	282	5.27	225
Holiday CDP	22,403	157	5.37	223
Holly Hill city	11,659	276	3.93	255
Hollywood city	140,768	12	27.37	53
Homestead city	60,512	45	15.14	107
Homosassa Springs CDP	13,791	240	25.14	60
Horizon West CDP	14,000	231	32.94	39
Hudson CDP	12,158	266	6.32	209
Hunters Creek CDP	14,321	225	3.83	259
Immokalee CDP	24,154	139	22.70	68
Iona CDP	15,369	215	6.60	207
Ives Estates CDP	19,525	181	2.50	295
Jacksonville city	821,784	1	747.00	1
Jacksonville Beach city	21,362	166	7.33	194
Jasmine Estates CDP	18,989	186	3.55	265
Jensen Beach CDP	11,707	275	6.76	203
Jupiter town	55,156	58	21.47	73
Jupiter Farms CDP	11,994	272	14.98	111
Kendale Lakes CDP	56,148	55	8.10	179
Kendall CDP	75,371	35	16.08	97
Kendall West CDP	36,154	91	2.75	287
Key Biscayne village	12,344	261	1.23	307
Key Largo CDP	10,433	302	12.05	134
Key West city	24,649	135	5.59	219
Keystone CDP	24,039	140	35.13	32
Kissimmee city	59,682	49	21.19	75
Lady Lake town	13,926	236	8.07	183
Lake Butler CDP	15,400	214	12.22	130
Lake City city	12,046	267	12.02	135
Lake Magdalene CDP	28,509	125	10.23	153
Lake Mary city	13,822	238	9.16	163
Lake Wales city	14,225	227	18.69	82

Legal Name	2010 Population	Pop. Rank	Land Area (sq. miles)	Area Rank
Lake Worth city	34,910	99	5.87	214
Lakeland city	97,422	23	65.27	12
Lakeland Highlands CDP	11,056	290	4.85	232
Lakeside CDP	30,943	117	13.52	122
Lakewood Park CDP	11,323	285	6.65	204
Land O' Lakes CDP	31,996	112	19.04	80
Lantana town	10,423	303	2.29	299
Largo city	77,648	33	17.62	89
Lauderdale Lakes city	32,593	110	3.68	262
Lauderhill city	66,887	40	8.53	174
Lealman CDP	19,879	179	4.01	252
Leesburg city	20,117	176	30.80	44
Lehigh Acres CDP	86,784	26	92.56	8
Leisure City CDP	22,655	154	3.33	276
Lighthouse Point city	10,344	304	2.31	298
Lockhart CDP	13,060	252	4.42	243
Longwood city	13,657	241	5.45	222
Lutz CDP	19,344	183	24.65	61
Lynn Haven city	18,493	189	10.37	150
Maitland city	15,751	211	5.27	225
Mango CDP	11,313	286	4.66	235
Marco Island city	16,413	204	12.14	133
Margate city	53,284	61	8.85	169
Meadow Woods CDP	25,558	133	11.39	144
Melbourne city	76,068	34	33.86	36
Merritt Island CDP	34,743	100	17.51	91
Miami city	399,457	2	35.87	31
Miami Beach city	87,779	25	7.63	189
Miami Gardens city	107,167	17	18.23	85
Miami Lakes town	29,361	121	5.63	217
Miami Shores village	10,493	300	2.50	295
Miami Springs city	13,809	239	2.88	285
Middleburg CDP	13,008	254	19.56	79
Midway CDP	16,115	207	12.01	136
Miramar city	122,041	14	29.52	45
Mount Dora city	12,370	260	8.02	185
Myrtle Grove CDP	15,870	210	6.64	206
Naples city	19,537	180	12.31	128
Navarre CDP	31,378	114	23.00	66
New Port Richey city	14,911	220	4.53	241
New Port Richey East CDP	10,036	309	3.70	261
New Smyrna Beach city	22,464	156	34.64	35
Niceville city	12,749	256	11.42	143
North Fort Myers CDP	39,407	85	49.48	19
North Lauderdale city	41,023	83	4.59	239
North Miami city	58,786	50	8.41	176
North Miami Beach city	41,523	79	4.83	233
North Palm Beach village	12,015	271	3.59	263
North Port city	57,357	52	99.58	7
Northdale CDP	22,079	159	8.08	182
Oak Ridge CDP	22,685	153	3.57	264
Oakland Park city	41,363	81	7.46	191
Oakleaf Plantation CDP	20,315	175	16.57	93
Ocala city	56,315	54	44.83	24
Ocoee city	35,579	94	14.71	112
Ojus CDP	18,036	193	2.65	289
Oldsmar city	13,591	242	8.70	170
Olympia Heights CDP	13,488	246	2.65	289

Legal Name	2010 Population	Pop. Rank	Land Area (sq. miles)	Area Rank
Opa-locka city	15,219	218	4.30	244
Orange City city	10,599	298	7.08	196
Orlando city	238,300	5	102.40	5
Ormond Beach city	38,137	87	31.93	40
Oviedo city	33,342	107	15.21	106
Pace CDP	20,039	177	24.23	62
Palatka city	10,558	299	8.55	173
Palm Bay city	103,190	19	65.70	11
Palm Beach Gardens city	48,452	70	55.09	18
Palm City CDP	23,120	148	13.91	117
Palm Coast city	75,180	36	89.87	9
Palm Harbor CDP	57,439	51	17.38	92
Palm River-Clair Mel CDP	21,024	168	11.55	141
Palm Springs village	18,928	187	3.30	277
Palm Valley CDP	20,019	178	12.21	131
Palmetto city	12,606	258	5.37	223
Palmetto Bay village	23,410	145	8.29	177
Palmetto Estates CDP	13,535	243	2.16	303
Panama City city	36,484	90	29.28	48
Panama City Beach city	12,018	270	18.39	83
Parkland city	23,962	141	12.33	127
Pembroke Pines city	154,750	10	33.12	37
Pensacola city	51,923	64	22.54	69
Pine Castle CDP	10,805	295	2.49	297
Pine Hills CDP	60,076	47	12.25	129
Pinecrest village	18,223	191	7.44	192
Pinellas Park city	49,079	69	15.51	103
Pinewood CDP	16,520	203	1.76	305
Plant City city	34,721	101	27.18	54
Plantation city	84,955	28	21.74	72
Poinciana CDP	53,193	62	71.88	10
Pompano Beach city	99,845	21	24.00	63
Port Charlotte CDP	54,392	59	28.43	52
Port Orange city	56,048	56	26.66	56
Port St. John CDP	12,267	264	3.87	257
Port St. Lucie city	164,603	9	113.95	2
Port Salerno CDP	10,091	308	3.53	267
Princeton CDP	22,038	160	7.38	193
Punta Gorda city	16,641	202	15.01	110
Richmond West CDP	31,973	113	4.17	249
Riverview CDP	71,050	38	46.19	21
Riviera Beach city	32,488	111	8.53	174
Rockledge city	24,926	134	11.94	137
Royal Palm Beach village	34,140	104	11.20	145
Ruskin CDP	17,208	197	18.01	87
Safety Harbor city	16,884	200	4.90	229
St. Augustine city	12,975	255	9.43	161
St. Cloud city	35,183	98	17.76	88
St. Petersburg city	244,769	4	61.74	13
San Carlos Park CDP	16,824	201	4.72	234
Sanford city	53,570	60	22.96	67
Sarasota city	51,917	65	14.66	114
Sarasota Springs CDP	14,395	224	3.50	268
Satellite Beach city	10,109	306	2.92	283
Sebastian city	21,929	162	13.66	120
Sebring city	10,491	301	9.98	156
Seminole city	17,233	196	5.10	227
Shady Hills CDP	11,523	281	28.57	51

Legal Name	2010 Population	Pop. Rank	Land Area (sq. miles)	Area Rank
South Bradenton CDP	22,178	158	4.47	242
South Daytona city	12,252	265	3.71	260
South Miami city	11,657	277	2.27	300
South Miami Heights CDP	35,696	93	4.89	230
South Venice CDP	13,949	235	6.02	210
Southchase CDP	15,921	209	6.84	201
Spring Hill CDP	98,621	22	59.81	15
Stuart city	15,593	213	6.65	204
Sun City Center CDP	19,258	185	15.74	102
Sunny Isles Beach city	20,832	170	1.02	308
Sunrise city	84,439	29	18.10	86
Sunset CDP	16,389	205	3.48	271
Sweetwater city	13,499	245	0.79	309
Tallahassee city	181,376	7	100.25	6
Tamarac city	60,427	46	11.62	140
Tamiami CDP	55,271	57	7.07	197
Tampa city	335,709	3	113.41	3
Tarpon Springs city	23,484	143	9.11	164
Tavares city	13,951	234	9.50	160
Temple Terrace city	24,541	136	6.85	200
The Acreage CDP	38,704	86	40.84	26
The Crossings CDP	22,758	150	3.46	272
The Hammocks CDP	51,003	67	7.88	187
The Villages CDP	51,442	66	30.81	43
Thonotosassa CDP	13,014	253	26.50	57
Three Lakes CDP	15,047	219	3.20	279
Titusville city	43,761	76	29.37	46
Town 'n' Country CDP	78,442	31	22.11	71
Trinity CDP	10,907	293	4.62	238
University CDP	31,084	115	9.08	165
University CDP	41,163	82	6.42	208
University Park CDP	26,995	129	3.97	253
Upper Grand Lagoon CDP	13,963	233	8.09	180
Valrico CDP	35,545	95	13.81	119
Venice city	20,748	172	15.27	105
Vero Beach city	15,220	217	11.44	142
Vero Beach South CDP	23,092	149	10.25	152
Viera East CDP	10,757	296	5.07	228
Villas CDP	11,569	279	4.65	237
Warrington CDP	14,531	222	6.93	199
Wekiwa Springs CDP	21,998	161	8.59	172
Wellington village	56,508	53	44.89	23
Wesley Chapel CDP	44,092	74	43.90	25
West Lealman CDP	15,651	212	3.13	281
West Little River CDP	34,699	102	4.56	240
West Melbourne city	18,355	190	10.20	154
West Palm Beach city	99,919	20	55.29	17
West Park city	14,156	228	2.19	302
West Pensacola CDP	21,339	167	7.18	195
Westchase CDP	21,747	164	9.87	157
Westchester CDP	29,862	118	3.94	254
Weston city	65,333	41	25.16	59
Westwood Lakes CDP	11,838	274	1.64	306
Wilton Manors city	11,632	278	1.96	304
Winter Garden city	34,568	103	15.41	104
Winter Haven city	33,874	105	31.30	41
Winter Park city	27,852	126	8.68	171
Winter Springs city	33,282	108	14.67	113

Legal Name	2010 Population	Pop. Rank	Land Area (sq. miles)	Area Rank
World Golf Village CDP	12,310	262	26.86	55
Wright CDP	23,127	147	5.52	221
Yulee CDP	11,491	283	23.16	65
Zephyrhills city	13,288	249	8.88	168

Note: CDP–Census Designated Place
Source: U.S. Census Bureau, 2010 Census

Survey Says...

This section presents current rankings from dozens of public and private sources. It shows how this state ranks in a number of critical categories, including education, job growth, cost of living, teen drivers, energy efficiency, and business environment. Sources include *Forbes, Reuters, U.S. News and World Report, CNN Money, Gallup,* and *Huffington Post.*

- Florida ranked #14 in a government study measuring real gross domestic product (GDP)—the output of goods and services produced by labor and property located in the United States. The ranking is based on the percentage change compared with 2011 GDP.
  U.S. Department of Commerce, Bureau of Economic Analysis, June 2013; www.bea.gov

- Florida ranked #4 in a government study measuring real gross domestic product (GDP)—the output of goods and services produced by labor and property located in the United States. The ranking is based on the dollar value of its GDP.
  U.S. Department of Commerce, Bureau of Economic Analysis, June 2013; www.bea.gov

- Florida ranked #6 in the 17th edition of "Quality Counts; State of the States," Education Week's "report card" surveying key education indicators, policy efforts, and educational outcomes.
  Education Week, January 4, 2013 (online) and January 10, 2013 (print); www.edweek.org

- SERI (Science and Engineering Readiness Index) weighs the performance of the states' K-12 schools in preparing students in physics and calculus, the high school subjects considered most important for future scientists and engineers. Florida ranked #11.
  Newsletter of the Forum on Education of the American Physical Society, Summer 2011 issue; www.huffingtonpost.com, July 11, 2011; updated October 1, 2012

- ND Parks, the "site for North Dakota Parks," named Florida as one of the "Top Five States to Visit for RV Camping Trips."
  www.ndparks.com, consulted 18 July 2013

- MoneyRates.com ranked Florida #28 on its list of the best to worst states for making a living. Criteria: average income; inflation; employment prospects; and workers' Workplace Environment assessments according to the Gallup-Healthways Well-Being Index.
  www.money-rates.com, posted April 1, 2013

- *Forbes* analyzed business costs, labor supply, regulatory environment, current economic climate, growth prospects, and quality of life, to compile its "Best States for Business" rankings. Florida ranked #27.
  www.forbes.com. posted December 12, 2012

- The 2012 Gallup-Healthways Well-Being Index, surveyed American's opinions on economic confidence, workplace perceptions, community climate, personal choices, and health predictors to assess the "future livability" of each state. Florida ranked #45.
  "Utah Poised to Be the Best State to Live In," Gallup Wellbeing, www.gallup.com, August 7, 2012

- On CNBC's list of "America's Top States for Business 2013," Florida ranked #30. Criteria: measures of competitiveness developed with input from the National Association of Manufacturers, the Council on Competitiveness, and other business groups weighed with the states' own marketing criteria.
  www.cnbc.com, consulted July 19, 2013

- Florida ranked #3 on the "best" end of the Christian Science Monitor's list of "States with the Best (and Worst) Job Growth," as indicated by year-over-year growth rates from May 2012 to May 2013.
  www.csmonitor.com, July 5, 2013

- Kiplinger identified "Ten States with the Biggest Rate of Job Growth in 2013" using data from the U.S. Bureau of Labor Statistics, IHS Global Insights, Moody's Analytics, and state economic data. Florida ranked #7.
  www.kiplinger.com, March 2013

- Florida ranked #7 on MoneyRates list of "Best-and Worst-States to Retire 2012." Criteria: life expectancy, crime rate, climate, economic conditions, taxes, job opportunities, and cost of living.
  www.money-rates.com, October 22, 2012

- Florida ranked #19 on the 2013 Bankrate "Best Places to Retire" list ranking the states and District of Columbia on various criteria relating to health, safety, and cost.
  www.bankrate.com, May 6, 2013

- Florida ranked #30 on the Social Science Research Council's "American Human Development Report: The Measure of America," assessing the 50 states plus the District of Columbia on health, education, and living-standard criteria.
  The Measure of America 2013-2014, posted June 19, 2013; www.measureofamerica.org

- Florida ranked #34 on the Foundation for Child Development's (FCD) Child Well-being Index (CWI). The FCD used the KIDS COUNT report and the National Survey of Children's Health, the only state-level source for several key indicators of child well-being.
  Foundation for Child Development, January 18, 2012; fcd-us.org

- Florida ranked #38 overall according to the 2013 KIDS COUNT Data Book, a project of the Annie E. Casey Foundation. Criteria: children's economic well-being, education, health, and family and community indicators.
  KIDS COUNT Data Center's Data Book, released June 20, 2013; http://datacenter.kidscount.org

- Florida ranked #45 in the children's economic well-being category by the 2013 KIDS COUNT Data Book, a project of the Annie E. Casey Foundation.
  KIDS COUNT Data Center's Data Book, released June 20, 2013; http://datacenter.kidscount.org

- Florida ranked #35 in the children's educational opportunities and attainments category by the 2013 KIDS COUNT Data Book, a project of the Annie E. Casey Foundation.
  KIDS COUNT Data Center's Data Book, released June 20, 2013; http://datacenter.kidscount.org

- Florida ranked #37 in the children's health category by the 2013 KIDS COUNT Data Book, a project of the Annie E. Casey Foundation.
  KIDS COUNT Data Center's Data Book, released June 20, 2013; http://datacenter.kidscount.org

- Florida ranked #35 in the family and community circumstances that factor into children's well-being category by the 2013 KIDS COUNT Data Book, a project of the Annie E. Casey Foundation.
  KIDS COUNT Data Center's Data Book, released June 20, 2013; http://datacenter.kidscount.org

- Florida ranked #34 in the 2012 Gallup-Healthways Well-Being Index. Criteria: emotional health; physical health; healthy behavior; work environment; basic access to food, shelter, health care; and a safe and satisfying place to live.
  2012 State of Well-Being, Gallup-Healthways Well-Being Index, released February 28, 2013; www.well-beingindex.com

- *U.S. News and World Report's* "Best States for Teen Drivers" rankings are based on driving and road safety laws, federal reports on driver's licenses, car accident fatality, and road-quality statistics. Florida ranked #21.
  U.S. News and World Report, March 18, 2010; www.usnews.com

- The Yahoo! Sports service Rivals.com ranks the states according to the strength of their high school football programs. Florida ranked #3.
  "Ranking the States: Where Is the Best Football Played?," November 18, 2011; highschool.rivals.com

- iVillage ranked the states by hospitable living conditions for women. Criteria: economic success, access to affordable childcare, health care, reproductive rights, female representation in government, and educational attainment. Florida ranked #31.
  iVillage, "50 Best to Worst States for Women," March 14, 2012; www.ivillage.com

- The League of American Bicyclists's "Bicycle Friendly States" ranked Florida #31. Criteria: legislation and enforcement, policies and programs, infrastructure and funding, education and advocacy, and evaluation and planning.
  "Washington Tops the Bicycle-Friendly State Ranking," May 1, 2013; bicycling.com

- The federal Corporation for National and Community Service ranked the states and the District of Columbia by volunteer rates. Florida ranked #45 for community service.
  "Volunteering and Civic Life in America 2012," www.volunteeringinamerica.gov, accessed July 24, 2013

- The Hospital Safety Score ranked states and the District of Columbia on their hospitals' performance scores. Florida ranked #10. Criteria: avoiding preventable harm and medical errors, as demonstrated by 26 hospital safety metrics.
  Spring 2013 Hospital Safety Score, May 8, 2013; www.hospitalsafetyscore.org

- GMAC Insurance ranked the states and the District of Columbia by the performance of their drivers on the GMAC Insurance National Drivers Test, comprised of DMV test questions. Florida ranked #37.
  "2011 GMAC Insurance National Drivers Test," www.gmacinsurance.com, accessed July 23, 2013

- Florida ranked #18 in a "State Integrity Investigation" analysis of laws and practices intended to deter corruption and promote accountability and openness in campaign finance, ethics laws, lobbying regulations and management of state pension funds.
  "What's Your State's Grade?," www.publicintegrity.org, accessed July 23, 2013

- Florida ranked #24 among the states and the District of Columbia in total rail miles, as tracked by the Association of American Railroads.
  "U.S. Freight Railroad Industry Snapshot: Railroads and States: Total Rail Miles by State: 2011"; www.aar.org, accessed July 23, 2013

- According to statistics compiled by the Beer Institute, Florida ranked #34 among the states and the District of Columbia in per capita beer consumption of persons 21 years or older.
  "Shipments of Malt Beverages and Per Capita Consumption by State 2012;" www.beerinstitute.org

- According to Concordia University's "Public Education Costs per Pupil by State Rankings," based on statistics gathered by the U.S. Census Bureau, which includes the District of Columbia, Florida ranked #43.
  Concordia University Online; education.cu-portland.edu, accessed July 24, 2013

- Florida ranked #8 among the states and the District of Columbia in population density based on U.S. Census Bureau data for resident population and total land area. "List of U.S. States by Population Density."
  www.wikipedia.org, accessed July 24, 2013

- In "America's Health Rankings, 2012 Edition," by the United Health Foundation, Florida ranked #34. Criteria included: rate of high school graduation; violent crime rate; incidence of infectious disease; childhood immunizations; prevalence of diabetes; per capita public-health funding; percentage of uninsured population; rate of children in poverty; and availability of primary-care physicians.
  United Health Foundation; www.americashealthrankings.org, accessed July 24, 2013

- The TechNet 2012 "State Broadband Index" ranked Florida #20 on the following criteria: broadband adoption; network quality; and economic structure. Improved broadband use is hoped to promote economic development, build strong communities, improve delivery of government services and upgrade educational systems.
  TechNet; www.technet.org, accessed July 24, 2013

- Florida was ranked #29 among the states and District of Columbia on the American Council for an Energy-Efficient Economy's "State Energy Efficiency Scorecard" for 2012.
  American Council for an Energy-Efficient Economy; aceee.org/sector/state-policy/scorecard, accessed July 24, 2013

Statistical Tables

DEMOGRAPHICS
Resident State and National Population, 1950-2012
Projected State and National Population, 2000-2030
Population by Age, 2012
Population by Race, 2012
Population by Hispanic Origin and Race, 2012

VITAL STATISTICS
Death Rates by Leading Causes, 2010
Death Rates by Selected Causes, 2010
Abortion Rates, 2009
Infant Mortality Rates, 1995-2009
Marriage and Divorce Rates, 2000-2011

ECONOMY
Nominal Gross Domestic Product by Industry, 2012
Real Gross Domestic Product, 2000-2012
Personal Income Per Capita, 1930-2012
Non-Farm Employment by Sector, 2012
Foreign Exports, 2000-2012
Energy Consumption, 2011

LAND AND WATER
Surface Area and Federally-Owned Land, 2007
Land Cover/Use of Non-Federal Rural Land, 2007
Farms and Crop Acreage, 2012

HEALTH AND MEDICAL CARE
Medical Professionals, 2012
Health Insurance Coverage, 2011
HIV, STD, and Tuberculosis Cases and Rates, 2011
Cigarette Smoking, 2011

HOUSING
Home Ownership Rates, 1995-2012
Home Sales, 2000-2010
Value of Owner-Occupied Homes, 2011

EDUCATION
School Enrollment, 2011
Educational Attainment, 2011
Public College Finances, FY 2012

TRANSPORTATION AND TRAVEL
Motor Vehicle Registrations and Drivers Licenses, 2011
Domestic Travel Expenditures, 2009
Retail Gasoline Prices, 2013
Public Road Length, 2011

CRIME AND LAW ENFORCEMENT
Full-Time Law Enforcement Officers, 2011
Prison Population, 2000-2012
Crime Rate, 2011

GOVERNMENT AND FINANCE
Local Governments by Type, 2012
State Government Revenue, 2011
State Government Expenditures, 2011
State Government General Expenditures by Function, 2011
State Government Finances, Cash and Debt, 2011

POLITICS
Composition of the Senate, 1995-2013
Composition of the House of Representatives, 1995-2013
Composition of State Legislature, 2004-2013
Voter Participation in Presidential Elections, 1980-2012
Governors Since Statehood

DEMOGRAPHICS

Resident State and National Population, 1950–2012

Year	State Population	U.S. Population	State Share
1950	2,771,000	151,326,000	1.83%
1960	4,952,000	179,323,000	2.76%
1970	6,791,418	203,302,031	3.34%
1980	9,746,324	226,545,805	4.30%
1990	12,937,926	248,709,873	5.20%
2000	15,982,571	281,424,600	5.68%
2010	18,801,310	308,745,538	6.09%
2012	19,317,568	313,914,040	6.15%

Note: 1950/1960 population figures are rounded to the nearest thousand.
Source: U.S. Census Bureau, Decennial Census 1950–2010; U.S. Census Bureau, 2012 Population Estimates

Projected State and National Population, 2000–2030

Year	State Population	U.S. Population	State Share
2000	15,982,378	281,421,906	5.68%
2005	17,509,827	295,507,134	5.93%
2010	19,251,691	308,935,581	6.23%
2015	21,204,132	322,365,787	6.58%
2020	23,406,525	335,804,546	6.97%
2025	25,912,458	349,439,199	7.42%
2030	28,685,769	363,584,435	7.89%
State population growth, 2000–2030			12,703,391
State percentage growth, 2000–2030			79.5%

Source: U.S. Census Bureau, Population Division, Interim State Population Projections, 2005

Population by Age, 2012

Age Group	State Population	Percent of Total Population	
		State	U.S.
Under 5 years	1,071,463	5.5%	6.4%
5 to 14 years	2,229,160	11.5%	13.1%
15 to 24 years	2,492,842	12.9%	14.0%
25 to 34 years	2,401,234	12.4%	13.5%
35 to 44 years	2,403,067	12.4%	12.9%
45 to 54 years	2,746,309	14.2%	14.1%
55 to 64 years	2,463,778	12.8%	12.3%
65 to 74 years	1,894,785	9.8%	7.6%
75 to 84 years	1,132,177	5.9%	4.2%
85 years and older	482,753	2.5%	1.9%
Under 18 years	4,002,480	20.7%	23.5%
65 years and older	3,509,715	18.2%	13.7%
Median age (years)	–	41.3	37.4

Source: U.S. Census Bureau, Annual Estimates of the Resident Population for Selected Age Groups by Sex for the United States, States, Counties, and Puerto Rico Commonwealth and Municipios: April 1, 2010 to July 1, 2012

Population by Race, 2012

Race	State Population	Percent of Total Population	
		State	U.S.
All residents	19,317,568	100.00%	100.00%
White	15,120,082	78.27%	77.89%
African American	3,206,350	16.60%	13.13%
Native American	95,218	0.49%	1.23%
Asian	511,960	2.65%	5.14%
Native Hawaiian	20,454	0.11%	0.23%
Two or more races	363,504	1.88%	2.39%

Source: U.S. Census Bureau, Population Division, Annual Estimates of the Resident Population by Sex, Race and Hispanic Origin for the United States, States, and Counties: April 1, 2010 to July 1, 2012

Population by Hispanic Origin and Race, 2012

Hispanic Origin/Race	State Population	Percent of Total Population	
		State	U.S.
All residents	19,317,568	100.00%	100.00%
All Hispanic residents	4,484,199	23.21%	16.89%
Hispanic			
White	4,111,686	21.28%	14.91%
African American	222,778	1.15%	0.79%
Native American	44,840	0.23%	0.49%
Asian	19,099	0.10%	0.17%
Native Hawaiian	8,458	0.04%	0.06%
Two or more races	77,338	0.40%	0.48%
Not Hispanic			
White	11,008,396	56.99%	62.98%
African American	2,983,572	15.44%	12.34%
Native American	50,378	0.26%	0.74%
Asian	492,861	2.55%	4.98%
Native Hawaiian	11,996	0.06%	0.17%
Two or more races	286,166	1.48%	1.91%

Source: U.S. Census Bureau, Population Division, Annual Estimates of the Resident Population by Sex, Race and Hispanic Origin for the United States, States, and Counties: April 1, 2010 to July 1, 2012

VITAL STATISTICS

Death Rates by Leading Causes, 2010

Cause	State	U.S.
Malignant neoplasms	179.4	186.2
Ischaemic heart diseases	120.6	122.9
Other forms of heart disease	39.1	53.4
Chronic lower respiratory diseases	42.9	44.7
Cerebrovascular diseases	35.3	41.9
Organic, incl. symptomatic, mental disorders	33.0	35.7
Other degenerative diseases of the nervous sys.	24.5	28.4
Other external causes of accidental injury	29.5	26.5
Diabetes mellitus	21.8	22.4
Hypertensive diseases	19.8	20.4
All causes	752.5	799.5

Note: Figures are age-adjusted death rates per 100,000 population
Source: CDC/NCHS, Underlying Cause of Death 1999–2010 on CDC WONDER Online Database

Death Rates by Selected Causes, 2010

Cause	State	U.S.
Assault	6.0	5.2
Diseases of the liver	15.4	13.9
Human immunodeficiency virus (HIV) disease	5.6	2.7
Influenza and pneumonia	9.5	16.2
Intentional self-harm	14.2	12.4
Malnutrition	0.5	0.9
Obesity and other hyperalimentation	1.8	1.8
Renal failure	12.1	14.4
Transport accidents	14.0	12.1
Viral hepatitis	2.8	2.4

Note: Figures are age-adjusted death rates per 100,000 population; A dash indicates that data was not available or was suppressed
Source: CDC/NCHS, Underlying Cause of Death 1999–2010 on CDC WONDER Online Database

Abortion Rates, 2009

Category	2009
By state of residence	
Total abortions	–
Abortion rate[1]	–%
Abortion ratio[2]	–
By state of occurrence	
Total abortions	81,918
Abortion rate[1]	23.5%
Abortion ratio[2]	370
Abortions obtained by out-of-state residents	–%
U.S. abortion rate[1]	15.1%
U.S. abortion ratio[2]	227

Note: (1) Number of abortions per 1,000 women aged 15–44 years; (2) Number of abortions per 1,000 live births; A dash indicates that data was not available
Source: CDC/NCHS, Morbidity and Mortality Weekly Report, November 23, 2012 (Abortion Surveillance, United States, 2009)

Infant Mortality Rates, 1995–2009

Category	1995	2000	2005	2009
All state residents	7.54	6.91	7.24	6.90
All U.S. residents	7.57	6.89	6.86	6.39
All state white residents	6.01	5.29	5.64	5.17
All U.S. white residents	6.30	5.71	5.73	5.33
All state black residents	12.74	12.31	12.14	12.07
All U.S. black residents	14.58	13.48	13.26	12.12

Note: Figures represent deaths per 1,000 live births of resident infants under one year old, exclusive of fetal deaths; A dash indicates that data was not available or was suppressed.
Source: Centers of Disease Control and Prevention, Division of Vital Statistics, Linked Birth/Infant Death Records on CDC Wonder Online

Marriage and Divorce Rates, 2000–2011

Year	Marriage Rate		Divorce Rate	
	State	U.S.	State	U.S.
2000	8.9	8.2	5.1	4.0
2002	9.4	8.0	5.1	3.9
2004	9.0	7.8	4.7	3.7
2006	8.6	7.5	4.7	3.7
2008	8.0	7.1	4.3	3.5
2010	7.3	6.8	4.4	3.6
2011	7.4	6.8	4.5	3.6

Note: Rates are based on provisional counts of marriages/divorces by state of occurrence and are per 1,000 total population residing in area
Source: CDC/NCHS, National Vital Statistics System

ECONOMY

Nominal Gross Domestic Product by Industry, 2012
In millions of current dollars

Industry	State GDP
Accommodation and food services	35,588
Administrative and waste management services	29,121
Agriculture, forestry, fishing, and hunting	6,076
Arts, entertainment, and recreation	14,845
Construction	30,646
Educational services	7,819
Finance and insurance	54,333
Health care and social assistance	67,456
Information	30,986
Management of companies and enterprises	12,112
Manufacturing	37,023
Mining	1,665
Other services, except government	21,571
Professional, scientific, and technical services	55,693
Real estate and rental and leasing	123,451
Retail trade	60,190
Transportation and warehousing	24,100
Utilities	17,708
Wholesale trade	51,074

Source: U.S. Department of Commerce, Bureau of Economic Analysis, Survey of Current Business

Real Gross Domestic Product, 2000–2012
In millions of chained 2005 dollars

Year	State GDP	U.S. GDP	State Share
2000	549,269	11,225,406	4.89%
2005	681,225	12,539,116	5.43%
2010	650,291	12,897,088	5.04%
2012	672,287	13,430,576	5.01%

Source: U.S. Department of Commerce, Bureau of Economic Analysis, Survey of Current Business

Personal Income Per Capita, 1930–2012

Year	State	U.S.
1930	$466	$618
1940	$522	$593
1950	$1,299	$1,503
1960	$2,016	$2,268
1970	$3,998	$4,084
1980	$9,921	$10,091
1990	$19,437	$19,354
2000	$29,079	$30,319
2010	$38,345	$39,791
2012	$40,344	$42,693

Source: U.S. Department of Commerce, Bureau of Economic Analysis, Regional Economic Accounts

Non-Farm Employment by Sector, 2012
In thousands

Sector	Employment
Construction	341.5
Education and health services	1,109.9
Financial activities	497.5
Government	1,078.6
Information	133.4
Leisure and hospitality	997.7
Mining and logging	5.6
Manufacturing	316.8
Other services	314.4
Professional and business services	1,067.5
Trade, transportation, and utilities	1,537.1
All sectors	7,400.1

Source: U.S. Bureau of Labor Statistics, State and Area Employment

Foreign Exports, 2000–2012
In millions of dollars

Year	State Exports	U.S. Exports	State Share
2000	26,542	712,054	3.73%
2002	24,461	649,940	3.76%
2004	29,042	768,554	3.78%
2006	38,557	973,994	3.96%
2008	54,238	1,222,545	4.44%
2010	55,399	1,208,080	4.59%
2012	66,201	1,478,268	4.48%

Note: U.S. figures exclude data from Puerto Rico, U.S. Virgin Islands, and unallocated exports
Source: U.S. Department of Commerce, International Trade Admin., Office of Trade and Industry Information, Manufacturing and Services

Energy Consumption, 2011

In trillions of BTUs, except as noted

Total energy consumption	
Total state energy consumption	4,217.1
Total U.S. energy consumption	97,387.3
State share of U.S. total	4.33%
Per capita consumption (in millions of BTUs)	
Total state per capita consumption	221.0
Total U.S. per capita consumption	312.6
End-use sectors	
Residential	1,230.5
Commercial	971.6
Industrial	477.0
Transportation	1,538.0
Sources of energy	
Petroleum	1,611.9
Natural gas	1,236.6
Coal	552.7
Renewable energy	335.1
Nuclear electric power	230.4

Source: U.S. Energy Information Administration, State Energy Data 2011: Consumption

LAND AND WATER

Surface Area and Federally-Owned Land, 2007

In thousands of acres

Category	State	U.S.	State Share
Total surface area	37,533.7	1,937,664.2	1.94%
Total land area	34,400.1	1,886,846.9	1.82%
Non-federal land	30,615.9	1,484,910.0	2.06%
Developed	5,515.2	111,251.2	4.96%
Rural	25,100.7	1,373,658.8	1.83%
Federal land	3,784.2	401,936.9	0.94%
Water area	3,133.6	50,817.3	6.17%

Source: U.S. Department of Agriculture, Natural Resources Conservation Service, 2007 National Resources Inventory

Land Cover/Use of Non-Federal Rural Land, 2007

In thousands of acres

Category	State	U.S.	State Share
Total rural land	25,100.7	1,373,658.8	1.83%
Cropland	2,880.4	357,023.5	0.81%
CRP[1] land	82.8	32,850.2	0.25%
Pastureland	3,633.1	118,615.7	3.06%
Rangeland	2,636.0	409,119.4	0.64%
Forest land	13,169.7	406,410.4	3.24%
Other rural land	2,698.7	49,639.6	5.44%

Note: (1) Conservation Reserve Program was created to assist private landowners in converting highly erodible cropland to vegetative cover.
Source: U.S. Department of Agriculture, Natural Resources Conservation Service, 2007 National Resources Inventory

Farms and Crop Acreage, 2012

Category	State	U.S.	State Share
Farms (in thousands)	47.5	2,170.0	2.19%
Acres (in millions)	9.3	914.0	1.01%
Acres per farm	194.7	421.2	–

Source: U.S. Department of Agriculture, National Agricultural Statistical Service, Quick Stats, 2012 Survey Data

HEALTH AND MEDICAL CARE

Medical Professionals, 2012

Profession	State Number	U.S. Number	State Share	State Rate[1]	U.S. Rate[1]
Physicians[2]	50,225	894,637	5.61%	263.2	287.1
Dentists	9,965	193,587	5.15%	52.2	62.1
Podiatrists	1,348	17,469	7.72%	7.1	5.6
Optometrists	2,467	45,638	5.41%	12.9	14.6
Chiropractors	4,747	77,494	6.13%	24.9	24.9

Note: (1) Rates are per 100,000 population; (2) Includes total, active Doctors of Osteopathic Medicine and Doctors of Medicine in 2011.
Source: U.S. Department of Health and Human Services, Bureau of Health Professions, Area Health Resource File, 2012-2013

Health Insurance Coverage, 2011

Category	State	U.S.
Total persons covered	15,247,000	260,214,000
Total persons not covered	3,765,000	48,613,000
Percent not covered	19.8%	15.7%
Children under age 18 covered	3,455,000	67,143,000
Children under age 18 not covered	517,000	6,965,000
Percent of children not covered	13.0%	9.4%

Source: U.S. Census Bureau, Current Population Survey, 2012 Annual Social and Economic Supplement

HIV, STD, and Tuberculosis Cases and Rates, 2011

Disease	State Cases	State Rate[1]	U.S. Rate[1]
Chlamydia	76,033	404.4	457.6
Gonorrhea	19,689	104.7	104.2
HIV diagnosis	5,394	33.2	15.8
HIV, stage 3 (AIDS)	3,440	21.2	10.3
Syphilis, early latent	1,212	6.4	4.3
Syphilis, primary/secondary	1,257	6.7	4.5
Tuberculosis	754	4.0	3.4

Note: (1) Rates are per 100,000 population
Source: Centers for Disease Control and Prevention

Cigarette Smoking, 2011

Category	State	U.S.
Adults who are current smokers	19.3%	21.2%
Adults who smoke everyday	13.5%	15.4%
Adults who smoke some days	5.8%	5.7%
Adults who are former smokers	28.0%	25.1%
Adults who never smoked	52.8%	52.9%

Source: Centers for Disease Control and Prevention, Behaviorial Risk Factor Surveillance System, Tobacco Use, 2011

HOUSING

Home Ownership Rates, 1995–2012

Area	1995	2000	2005	2010	2012
State	66.6%	68.4%	72.4%	69.3%	67.0%
U.S.	64.7%	67.4%	68.9%	66.9%	65.4%

Source: U.S. Census Bureau, Housing Vacancies and Homeownership, Annual Statistics

Home Sales, 2000–2010
In thousands of units

Year	State Sales	U.S. Sales	State Share
2000	393.6	5,174	7.61%
2002	429.3	5,632	7.62%
2004	526.5	6,778	7.77%
2006	395.3	6,478	6.10%
2008	262.5	4,913	5.34%
2010	396.5	4,908	8.08%

Note: Units include single-family homes, condos and co-ops
Source: National Association of Realtors, Real Estate Outlook, Market Trends & Insights

Value of Owner-Occupied Homes, 2011

Value	Total Units in State	Percent of Total, State	Percent of Total, U.S.
Less than $50,000	464,550	9.8%	8.8%
$50,000 to $99,000	994,868	21.0%	16.0%
$100,000 to $149,000	891,772	18.8%	16.5%
$150,000 to $199,000	767,443	16.2%	15.4%
$200,000 to $299,000	798,789	16.8%	18.2%
$300,000 to $499,000	522,708	11.0%	15.2%
$500,000 to $999,000	224,259	4.7%	7.9%
$1,000,000 or more	76,780	1.6%	2.0%
Median value	–	$151,000	$173,600

Source: U.S. Census Bureau, 2011 American Community Survey 1-Year Estimates

EDUCATION

School Enrollment, 2011

Educational Level	Students Enrolled in State	Percent of Total, State	Percent of Total, U.S.
All levels	4,682,575	100.0%	100.0%
Nursery school, preschool	298,557	6.4%	6.0%
Kindergarten	219,985	4.7%	5.1%
Elementary (grades 1–8)	1,796,841	38.4%	39.5%
Secondary (grades 9–12)	948,343	20.3%	20.7%
College or graduate school	1,418,849	30.3%	28.7%

Note: Figures cover the population 3 years and over enrolled in school
Source: U.S. Census Bureau, 2011 American Community Survey 1-Year Estimates

Educational Attainment, 2011

Highest Level of Education	State	U.S.
High school diploma	85.9%	85.9%
Bachelor's degree	25.8%	28.5%
Graduate/Professional degree	9.3%	10.6%

Note: Figures cover the population 25 years and over
Source: U.S. Census Bureau, 2011 American Community Survey 1-Year Estimates

Public College Finances, FY 2012

Category	State	U.S.
Full-time equivalent enrollment (FTE)[1]	638,018	11,548,974
Educational appropriations per FTE[2]	$5,130	$5,906
Net tuition revenue per FTE[3]	$3,084	$5,189
Total educational revenue per FTE[4]	$8,213	$11,043

(1) Full-time equivalent enrollment equates student credit hours to full time, academic year students, but excludes medical students; (2) Educational appropriations measure state and local support available for public higher education operating expenses including ARRA funds and excludes appropriations for independent institutions, financial aid for students attending independent institutions, research, hospitals, and medical education; (3) Net tuition revenue is calculated by taking the gross amount of tuition and fees, less state and institutional financial aid, tuition waivers or discounts, and medical student tuition and fees. Net tuition revenue used for capital debt service is included in the net tuition revenue figures; (4) Total educational revenue is the sum of educational appropriations and net tuition excluding net tuition revenue used for capital debt service.
Source: State Higher Education Executive Officers, State Higher Education Finance FY 2012

TRANSPORTATION AND TRAVEL

Motor Vehicle Registrations and Drivers Licenses, 2011

Vehicle Type	State	U.S.	State Share
Automobiles[1]	7,981,816	125,656,528	6.35%
Buses	34,942	666,064	5.25%
Trucks	6,878,085	118,455,587	5.81%
Motorcycles	574,346	8,437,502	6.81%
Drivers licenses	13,882,423	211,874,649	6.55%

Note: Motor vehicle registrations include private, commercial, and publicly-owned vehicles; (1) Includes taxicabs
Source: U.S. Department of Transportation, Federal Highway Administration

Domestic Travel Expenditures, 2009
In millions of dollars

Category	State	U.S.	State Share
Travel expenditures	$48,394	$610,200	7.93%

Note: Figures represent U.S. spending on domestic overnight trips and day trips of 50 miles or more, one way, away from home. Excludes spending by foreign visitors.
Source: U.S. Travel Association, Impact of Travel on State Economies, 2009

Retail Gasoline Prices, 2013

Gasoline Grade	State Average	U.S. Average
Regular	$3.62	$3.65
Mid	$3.83	$3.81
Premium	$4.00	$3.98
Diesel	$3.91	$3.88
Excise tax[1]	53.8 cents	49.4 cents

Note: Gasoline prices as of 7/26/2013; (1) Includes state and federal excise taxes and other state taxes as of July 1, 2013
Source: American Automobile Association, Daily Fuel Guage Report; American Petroleum Institute, State Motor Fuel Taxes, 2013

Public Road Length, 2011

Type	State Mileage	U.S. Mileage	State Share
Interstate highways	1,495	46,960	3.18%
Other highways	747	15,719	4.75%
Principal arterial	6,289	156,262	4.02%
Minor arterial	6,520	242,942	2.68%
Major collector	11,227	534,592	2.10%
Minor collector	3,296	266,357	1.24%
Local	92,185	2,814,925	3.27%
Urban	81,471	1,095,373	7.44%
Rural	40,288	2,982,383	1.35%
Total	121,759	4,077,756	2.99%

Note: Combined urban and rural road mileage equals the total of the other road types
Source: U.S. Department of Transportation, Federal Highway Administration, Public Road Length, 2011

CRIME AND LAW ENFORCEMENT

Full-Time Law Enforcement Officers, 2011

Gender	State Number	State Rate[1]	U.S. Rate[1]
Male officers	38,145	210.6	210.3
Female officers	6,468	35.7	28.1
Total officers	44,613	246.4	238.3

Note: (1) Rates are per 100,000 population
Source: Federal Bureau of Investigation, Uniform Crime Reports, Crime in the United States 2011

Prison Population, 2000–2012

Year	State Population	U.S. Population	State Share
2000	71,319	1,391,261	5.13%
2005	89,768	1,527,929	5.88%
2010	104,306	1,613,803	6.46%
2011	103,055	1,598,783	6.45%
2012	101,930	1,571,013	6.49%

Note: Figures include prisoners under the jurisdiction of state or federal correctional authorities.
Source: U.S. Department of Justice, Bureau of Justice Statistics, Prisoners in 2006, 2011, 2012 (Advance Counts)

Crime Rate, 2011
Incidents per 100,000 residents

Category	State	U.S.
Violent crimes	515.3	386.3
Murder	5.2	4.7
Forcible rape	27.7	26.8
Robbery	134.4	113.7
Aggravated assault	348.0	241.1
Property crimes	3,522.0	2,908.7
Burglary	892.9	702.2
Larceny/theft	2,421.1	1,976.9
Motor vehicle theft	207.9	229.6
All crimes	4,037.3	3,295.0

Source: Federal Bureau of Investigation, Uniform Crime Reports, Crime in the United States 2011

GOVERNMENT AND FINANCE

Local Governments by Type, 2012

Government Type	State	U.S.	State Share
All local governments	1,554	89,004	1.75%
County	66	3,031	2.18%
Municipality	410	19,522	2.10%
Town/Township	0	16,364	0.00%
Special District	983	37,203	2.64%
Ind. School District	95	12,884	0.74%

Source: U.S. Census Bureau, 2012 Census of Governments: Organization Component Preliminary Estimates

State Government Revenue, 2011
In thousands of dollars, except for per capita figures

Total revenue	**$106,165,531**
Total revenue per capita, State	$5,564
Total revenue per capita, U.S.	$7,271
General revenue	$75,290,282
Intergovernmental revenue	$27,804,346
Taxes	$32,557,946
General sales	$19,353,000
Selective sales	$7,803,056
License taxes	$2,132,280
Individual income taxes	$0
Corporate income taxes	$1,869,870
Other taxes	$1,399,740
Current charges	$9,034,401
Miscellaneous general revenue	$5,893,589
Utility revenue	$20,342
Liquor store revenue	$0
Insurance trust revenue[1]	$30,854,907

Note: (1) Within insurance trust revenue, net earnings of state retirement systems is a calculated statistic, and thus can be positive or negative. Net earnings is the sum of earnings on investments plus gains on investments minus losses on investments.
Source: U.S. Census Bureau, 2011 Annual Survey of State Government Finances

State Government Expenditures, 2011

In thousands of dollars, except for per capita figures

Total expenditure	$84,633,065
Total expenditure per capita, State	$4,435
Total expenditure per capita, U.S.	$6,427
Intergovernmental expenditure	$19,725,217
Direct expenditure	$64,907,848
Current operation	$43,852,094
Capital outlay	$5,059,074
Insurance benefits and repayments	$12,509,675
Assistance and subsidies	$2,055,395
Interest on debt	$1,431,610
Utility expenditure	$138,504
Liquor store expenditure	$0
Insurance trust expenditure	$12,509,675

Source: U.S. Census Bureau, 2011 Annual Survey of State Government Finances

State Government General Expenditures by Function, 2011

In thousands of dollars

Education	$24,882,722
Public welfare	$22,302,600
Hospitals	$948,858
Health	$3,749,538
Highways	$5,449,166
Police protection	$439,294
Correction	$2,465,017
Natural resources	$1,133,964
Parks and recreation	$116,607
Governmental administration	$2,757,756
Interest on general debt	$1,431,610
Other and unallocable	$6,307,754

Source: U.S. Census Bureau, 2011 Annual Survey of State Government Finances

State Government Finances, Cash and Debt, 2011

In thousands of dollars, except for per capita figures

Debt at end of fiscal year	
State, total	$43,471,755
State, per capita	$2,278
U.S., per capita	$3,635
Cash and security holdings	
State, total	$191,713,677
State, per capita	$10,047
U.S., per capita	$11,759

Source: U.S. Census Bureau, 2011 Annual Survey of State Government Finances

POLITICS

Composition of the Senate, 1995–2013

Congress (Year)	State/U.S	Dem	Rep	Total
104th (1995)	State delegates	1	1	2
	Total U.S.	48	52	100
105th (1997)	State delegates	1	1	2
	Total U.S.	45	55	100
106th (1999)	State delegates	1	1	2
	Total U.S.	45	55	100
107th (2001)	State delegates	2	0	2
	Total U.S.	50	50	100
108th (2003)	State delegates	2	0	2
	Total U.S.	48	51	100
109th (2005)	State delegates	1	1	2
	Total U.S.	44	55	100
110th (2007)	State delegates	1	1	2
	Total U.S.	49	49	100
111th (2009)	State delegates	1	1	2
	Total U.S.	57	41	100
112th (2011)	State delegates	1	1	2
	Total U.S.	51	47	100
113th (2013)	State delegates	1	1	2
	Total U.S.	54	45	100

Note: Figures are for the starts of first sessions; Totals include Democratic (Dem) and Republican (Rep) members as well as vacancies and seats held by independent party members
Source: U.S. Congress, Congressional Directory

Composition of the House of Representatives, 1995–2013

Congress (Year)	State/U.S	Dem	Rep	Total
104th (1995)	State delegates	8	15	23
	Total U.S.	204	230	435
105th (1997)	State delegates	8	15	23
	Total U.S.	207	226	435
106th (1999)	State delegates	8	15	23
	Total U.S.	211	223	435
107th (2001)	State delegates	8	15	23
	Total U.S.	212	221	435
108th (2003)	State delegates	7	18	25
	Total U.S.	205	229	435
109th (2005)	State delegates	7	18	25
	Total U.S.	202	231	435
110th (2007)	State delegates	9	16	25
	Total U.S.	233	198	435
111th (2009)	State delegates	10	15	25
	Total U.S.	256	178	435
112th (2011)	State delegates	6	19	27
	Total U.S.	193	242	435
113th (2013)	State delegates	10	17	27
	Total U.S.	201	234	435

Note: Figures are for the starts of first sessions; Totals include Democratic (Dem) and Republican (Rep) members as well as vacancies and seats held by independent party members
Source: U.S. Congress, Congressional Directory

Composition of State Legislature, 2004–2013

Year	Democrats	Republicans	Total
State Senate			
2004	14	26	40
2005	14	26	40
2006	14	26	40
2007	14	26	40
2008	14	26	40
2009	14	26	40
2010	14	26	40
2011	12	28	40
2012	12	28	40
2013	14	26	40
State House			
2004	39	81	120
2005	36	84	120
2006	36	84	120
2007	41	79	120
2008	42	78	120
2009	44	76	120
2010	44	76	120
2011	38	81	120
2012	39	81	120
2013	44	76	120

Note: Totals may include minor party members and vacancies
Source: The Council of State Governments, State Legislatures

Voter Participation in Presidential Elections, 1980–2012

Year	Voting-eligible State Population	State Voter Turnout Rate	U.S. Voter Turnout Rate
1980	7,088,658	52.0	54.2
1984	7,976,805	52.4	55.2
1988	8,777,510	49.0	52.8
1992	9,506,230	55.9	58.1
1996	10,219,294	51.9	51.7
2000	10,667,193	55.9	54.2
2004	11,811,921	64.4	60.1
2008	12,687,407	66.1	61.6
2012	13,348,802	63.5	58.2

Note: All figures are based on the voting-eligible population which excludes person ineligible to vote such as non-citizens, felons (depending on state law), and mentally-incapacitated persons. U.S. figures include the overseas eligible population (including military personnel).
Source: McDonald, Michael P., United States Election Project, Presidential Voter Turnout Rates, 1980–2012

Governors Since Statehood

William D. Moseley (D) 1845-1849
Thomas Brown (O) 1849-1853
James E. Broome (D) 1853-1857
Madison S. Perry (D) 1857-1861
John Milton (D) . . . . (d) 1861-1865
Abram K. Allison (D) . . . . (i) 1865
William Marvin 1865
David S. Walker 1865-1868
Harrison Reed (R) 1868-1873
Ossian B. Hart (R) . . . . (d) 1873-1874
Marcellus L. Stearns (R) 1874-1877

George F. Drew (D) 1877-1881
William D. Bloxham (D) 1881-1885
Edward A. Perry (D) 1885-1889
Francis P. Fleming (D) 1889-1893
Henry L. Mitchell (D) 1893-1897
William D. Bloxham (D) 1897-1901
William S. Jennings (D) 1901-1905
Napoleon B. Broward (D) 1905-1909
Albert W. Gilchrist (D) 1909-1913
Park Trammell (D) 1913-1917
Sidney J. Catts (O) 1917-1921
Gary A. Hardee (D) 1921-1925
John W. Martin (D) 1925-1929
Doyle E. Carlton (D) 1929-1933
David Sholtz (D) 1933-1937
Frederick P. Cone (D) 1937-1941
Spessard L. Holland (D) 1941-1945
Millard F. Caldwell Jr. (D) 1945-1949
Fuller Warren (D) 1949-1953
Daniel T. McCarty (D) . . . . (d) 1953
Charles E. Johns (D) 1953-1955
Thomas Leroy Collins (D) 1955-1961
Cecil Farris Bryant (D) 1961-1965
William Hayden Burns (D) 1965-1967
Claude R. Kirk Jr. (R) 1967-1971
Reubin O. Askew (D) 1971-1979
Robert Graham (D) 1979-1987
Bob Martinez (R) 1987-1991
Lawton Chiles (D) 1991-1999
Jeb Bush (R) 1999-2007
Charlie Crist (R) 2007-2011
Rick Scott (R) 2011-2015

Note: (D) Democrat; (R) Republican; (O) Other party; (r) resigned; (d) died in office; (i) removed from office

Georgia

Location: Southeast coast

Area and rank: 57,919 square miles (150,010 square kilometers); 59,441 square miles (153,952 square kilometers) including water; twenty-second largest state in area

Coastline: 100 miles (161 kilometers) on the Atlantic Ocean

Shoreline: 2,344 miles (3,772 kilometers)

Population and rank: 9,919,945 (2012 estimate); eighth largest state in population

Capital and largest city: Atlanta (420,003 people in 2010 census)

Entered Union and rank: January 2, 1788; fourth state

Present constitution adopted: 1983

Counties: 159

State name: Georgia takes its name from King George II of England

State nickname: Peach State; Empire State of the South

State capitol building in Atlanta. The statue in the foreground is of former governor Richard B. Russell. (Wikimedia Commons)

Motto: Wisdom, justice, and moderation

State flag: One-third is blue field with state coat of arms; two-thirds are the Confederate flag— red field with blue and white cross of Saint Andrew and thirteen white stars

Highest point: Brasstown Bald—4,784 feet (1,458 meters)

Lowest point: Atlantic Ocean—sea level

Highest recorded temperature: 113 degrees Fahrenheit (45 degrees Celsius)—Greenville, 1978

Lowest recorded temperature: –17 degrees Fahrenheit (–27 degrees Celsius)—CCC Camp F-16, 1940

State song: "Georgia on My Mind"

State tree: Live oak

State flower: Cherokee rose

State bird: Brown thrasher

Georgia History

The last of the original thirteen English colonies to be founded, and the largest state east of the Mississippi River, Georgia has twice led its region in being the forerunner of the "New South," first following the Civil War and then during the second half of the twentieth century. A state of immense geographical variation, changing in elevation from nearly a mile to sea level, it transformed itself from a primarily agricultural state to one that embraced modern manufacturing and technology. Its capital, Atlanta, is one of the largest and fastest-growing cities in the South and a metropolis of truly international distinction.

Early History. In approximately 12,000 B.C.E. the first inhabitants lived along the rivers and coasts of what would become Georgia with a diet of fish and shellfish. They were followed first by nomadic hunters and then by more settled residents who developed agriculture. When Europeans arrived during the mid-sixteenth century, the Native American Cherokee and Creek tribes were dominant in the eastern and coastal areas. Along the coast the Yamacraw, a group of the Creek, were well established. The Chickasaw and Choctaw inhabited the western portion of the territory.

A Native American chief named Guale was the first to make lasting contact with the Europeans, meeting the Spanish soldier Pedro Menéndez de Avilés in 1566. As a result, for a time the entire coastal region was called Guale. The British, French, and Spanish competed to make the Native American tribes their allies, with hopes of using them to defend their own colonies and eliminate those of their competitors. After the Yamasee War (1715-1728) nearly destroyed the British colony of Carolina, the British were determined to settle a buffer colony between themselves and the Spanish in Florida. That colony would become Georgia.

Exploration and Settlement. Spain, with strongholds established throughout the Caribbean and in Florida, sent the first European explorers into the area of Georgia. In 1540, Hernando de Soto passed through Georgia on his lengthy and difficult expedition in search of the fabled Seven Cities of Gold, which were rumored to possess wealth in excess of anything yet found in the New World. French Huguenots under Jean Ribaut landed along the coast in 1562, the same year Ribaut sought to colonize the Port Royal region to the north, in what is now South Carolina. Both attempts were failures. In order to strengthen its position and defend its Florida possessions, Spain established a string of missions and forts running along the coast from northern Florida to the sea islands.

The English responded by thrusting south, forcing the Spanish back to St. Augustine. To create a barrier between the Spanish and the rapidly growing colonies to the north, King George II granted a charter for a colony in 1732. General James Edward Oglethorpe, who wished to open the colony for debtors to give them a fresh start on life, was placed in command of the venture. In 1733, with just over one hundred colonists, Oglethorpe arrived at the bluffs of the Savannah River and struck a deal with Yamacraw chief Tomochichi for land along the river. Oglethorpe laid out the city of Savannah with a grid like pattern of squares, which would remain.

The Spanish threat was effectively ended in 1742 with Oglethorpe's victory at the battle of Bloody Marsh on Saint Simons Island. Georgia grew rapidly with an economy based on rice, indigo, and cotton. Slave imports were banned in the colony in 1735, but crops were grown best under the plantation system, and in 1749 the slave trade was legalized. The territory up the Savannah River was explored and settled; in 1753 the city of Augusta was founded. In 1754, Georgia became a royal colony.

Revolution and the New Nation. As the colonies moved toward independence, Georgia convened a Provincial Congress in 1775, and its Council of Safety sent delegates to the Continental Congress in Philadelphia. The year following the declaration of American independence, Georgia ratified its first state constitution. In 1778, as the British pursued a southern strategy to pacify the rebellion, their troops seized Savannah. American and French troops were repulsed in a bloody attempt to retake the city, which the British continued to hold until the end of the Revolution.

Georgia became the fourth state to ratify the Constitution, and it joined the Union in 1788, with Augusta, on the Savannah River, as its capital. Its western lands were rapidly developed, and this growth led to the Yazoo Fraud, during which members of the state legislature sold 50 million acres to phantom land companies (most of which were owned by the legislators themselves), which resold them to the public. In the end, the federal government had to pay more than $4 million to settle claims from the incident.

The western movement also prompted the removal of the Cherokee and Creek Indians from Georgia. The Creek began selling their lands in 1827 and moved to Arkansas. Although the Cherokee had tried to fashion a compromise with the European settlers, the discovery of gold on their territory doomed those efforts. Georgia ordered the removal of the Native Americans in 1832, and six years later the tribe began its Trail of Tears to Indian Territory, now the state of Oklahoma.

One of the most important developments in American history occurred near Savannah in 1793, when Eli

Whitney invented the cotton gin. This device automatically separated cotton seed from cotton fiber, a time-consuming task which before had been done only by hand. The cotton gin made possible the booming growth of cotton farming in the South, including Georgia, where the rich soil in the central part of the state made the crop highly profitable.

Civil War and Reconstruction. In 1861, Georgia joined with seven other southern states and seceded from the Union. Laterthat year, in thetemporary capital of Montgomery, Alabama, Alexander H. Stephens of Georgia was elected vice president of the Confederacy. While Georgia soldiers were fighting along the front lines in Tennessee and Virginia, Union forces bombarded and captured Fort Pulaski at the mouth of the Savannah River and clamped a tight blockade on the Georgia coastline. In 1863, after capturing Chattanooga, Tennessee, a Union army advancing into Georgia was surprised and overcome at the Battle of Chickamauga. The following year, the Federals returned under General William Tecumseh Sherman to strike at the strategic railroad center of Atlanta. After months of siege, Atlanta fell and was burned. Sherman then embarked on his March to the Sea, leaving a swath of destruction through Georgia sixty miles wide and capturing Savannah in December.

Following the war, Georgia, like the rest of the defeated South, entered a period of Reconstruction. It attempted to rejoin the Union in 1868 but was refused reentry in 1869 because it refused to ratify the Fifteenth Amendment,

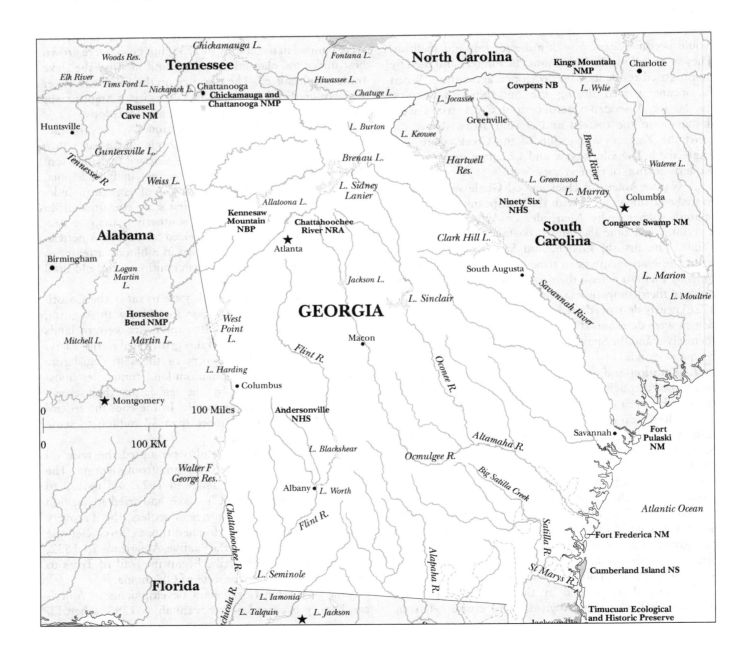

This monumental relief carved on Stone Mountain, near Atlanta, honors (left to right), Confederate leaders Jefferson Davis, Robert E. Lee, and Thomas "Stonewall" Jackson. (PhotoDisc)

which prohibits denying voting rights because of race. When Georgia complied with this amendment it was readmitted to the Union, in 1870.

During Reconstruction, Georgia began to rebuild its economy, repairing and expanding its railroad system, which had been largely destroyed during the Civil War, and diversifying its agricultural base to include corn, fruit—especially peaches—tobacco, and livestock. However, cotton, which had been a major crop before the Civil War, remained an essential part of the state's economy, and when a boll weevil infestation struck during the 1920's, it was a severe blow to Georgia's farmers and the entire state.

The state was making strides in other areas. In 1879, Henry Grady had become one of the owners of the Atlanta *Constitution*, the state's largest newspaper. As an unofficial spokesperson for Georgia, Grady prophesied the "New South," which would embrace progress, introduce industry and manufacturing, and move away from the wounds of the Civil War. Atlanta took as its symbol the phoenix, since the city had literally risen anew from the ashes of destruction. It became the headquarters of large regional companies, an economic powerhouse in the Southeast, and a literal symbol of Grady's New South. Among the local success stories was the rise of Coca-Cola, invented by pharmacist John

Styth Pemberton in 1886 and, after a few years, the most popular soft drink in the nation.

The Modern Age. During the 1940's and 1950's, manufacturing in Georgia passed agriculture, forestry, and fishing as the major source of income. Textile mills, in particular, became a major force in the state's economy. Georgia became one of the world's largest sources of kaolin and fuller's earth, the first used in producing paper and dishware, the second used for cat litter. High-quality granite was also mined in the upper portion of the state. Meanwhile, the growth of banking and financial institutions continued to the point that Atlanta became known as the "Wall Street of the South," while businesses involved with modern technology also contributed to the growth of the state.

Georgia's passage through the civil rights era was aided by a tradition of moderation among its political leadership. From 1877 on, the state had only Democratic governors. Although Democrat Lester Maddox was elected governor in 1966 with an openly segregationist agenda, broad-minded Atlanta mayor Ivan Allen and progressive governors such as Ellis Arnall, Carl Sanders, and Jimmy Carter were more representative and helped bring the state through a potentially difficult period. Carter in 1976 was elected president of the United States. In 1972, Maynard Jackson was elected mayor of

Atlanta, the first African American chosen to lead a large southern city. Also that year, Andrew Young became the first African American elected to Congress from Georgia since the end of Reconstruction. This period of Georgia's history is regarded as marking the birth of the second "New South," which combined economic development with racial progress.

Georgia's economy is strong, with its deep-water port of Savannah one of the most active on the East Coast. Atlanta's Hartsville International Airport is one of the largest and best equipped in the world. Natural resources contribute to the state's revenues.

The New South. As the new millennium approached, Georgia remained at the head of the economy and society of the New South. With Atlanta at its economic heart, Georgia was modern, forward looking, and prosperous. The city's gleaming international airport was one of the busiest in the United States. Emblematic of the state's growing economic status was the announcement in 2000 that Atlanta-based United Parcel Service (UPS) received permission for six flights a week to be initiated to China. Population growth in greater Atlanta pointed in the same upward trajectory, with a 39 percent increase over the previous decade. The state had outgrown most other states and earned an additional two seats in the U.S. House of Representatives in Washington, D.C.

Political Change and Legal Controversy. Also symbolic of the dynamics of the New South's politics was the aftermath of the election of Zell Miller, a Democrat, to the U.S. Senate over Republican senator Mack Mattingly. Miller had been appointed to the seat upon the death of Senator Paul Coverdell. Miller, however, turned against Democrats and critics of the administration of George W. Bush to back the president's reelectionin2004. He delivered a fiery keynote speech at the Republican National Convention in New York, all the while remaining a Democrat.

On July 24, 2000, the University of Georgia at Athens lost a closely watched affirmative action suit before the U.S. Eleventh Circuit Court of Appeals. Three women sued the university when minority candidates gained admission to the university, notwithstanding the plaintiffs' high scores on the Scholastic Aptitude Test. The awarding of bonus points for race by the university was found unconstitutional. The Court demanded that admissions officials "fully and fairly" analyze applicants "as individuals and not merely as members of groups."

In the 2002 midterm elections, Republican Saxby Chambliss, by 53 to 46 percent, took the seat of U.S. senator Max Cleland, a decorated Vietnam War veteran and a member of the Senate's liberal wing. Once again, the politics of the New South rejected the domination of

One of the great plantation houses of nineteenth-century Savannah. (Georgia Department of Industry, Trade & Tourism)

the "Solid South" of yore, when the real race for public office took place in the Democratic Party primaries and not in the general election, where the outcome was typically a foregone conclusion. Further evidence of these changes lay in the fact that a black Republican candidate for Congress beat a white Democrat in a heavily Democratic redrawn congressional district.

In both the 2008 and 2012 presidential elections, Georgia supported the Republican candidate. In 2008, Senator John McCain won the state by a clear majority of over 52 percent of the popular vote; in 2012, former Massachusetts Governor Mitt Romney took more than 53 percent of the vote, a margin of more than 7.8 percent. Democratic support was concentrated largely in 33 of the state's 159 counties.

Peanuts. Fluctuations in the price and supply of peanuts through the first years of the 21st century remained a central fact of the Georgia economy. After a peanut shortage in 2011, growers across Georgia planted a record crop of peanuts, leading to a fall in prices from an expected $700 a ton to some $355 per ton at the low point. With over 3 million tons of peanuts raised across the nation, Georgia farmers were hard hit by the bumper crop and glut on the market. The huge crop in Georgia was partly due to a favorable growing season, yielding an average of 4,550 pounds per acre. Over half the nation's peanut crop came from the state of Georgia in 2012, with about 1.67 million tons harvested in the state.

Michael Witkoski
Updated by the Editor

Georgia Time Line

1540	Spanish explorer Hernando de Soto marches through part of Georgia in his quest for gold.
1566	Spanish mariner Pedro Menéndez de Avilés builds a fort on Saint Catherine's Island.
June 9, 1732	George II grants charter giving imprisoned English debtors the right to settle in Georgia.
Feb. 12, 1733	General James Oglethorpe founds Savannah.
1735	Georgia bans importation of slaves.
1736	Methodist preachers John and Charles Wesley arrive at Savannah.
1742	Oglethorpe's troops defeat Spaniards at battle of Bloody Marsh on Saint Simons Island.
1749	Slave trade is legalized.
1754	Georgia becomes a royal colony.
1775	Provincial Congress meets in Savannah.
Feb. 5, 1777	First state constitution is ratified in Savannah.
1778	British troops capture Savannah during the Revolution.
July 12, 1782	British abandon Savannah.
1785	University of Georgia is founded at Athens.
1786	Augusta is named state capital.
Jan. 2, 1788	Georgia enters the Union as the fourth state.
June 20, 1793	Eli Whitney invents the cotton gin near Savannah.
1795	Louisville is named state capital.
1804	Milledgeville is named state capital.
1827	Creek Indians begin selling their lands east of Flint River to Georgia.
1828-1838	Conflicts with Cherokee over land claims lead to their removal from Georgia.
1836	Georgia Female College, now Wesleyan College, the first college chartered to grant degrees to women, opens in Macon.
1837	City of Terminus, later Atlanta, is founded.
Jan. 19, 1861	Georgia secedes from Union.
Feb. 18, 1861	Georgian Alexander H. Stephens becomes vice president of the Confederacy.
Sept. 20, 1863	Union army is defeated at Battle of Chickamauga.
1864	Union general William Tecumseh Sherman captures and burns Atlanta; Union army marches to the sea and captures Savannah.
1868	Federal troops leave state.
1868	Atlanta is named state capital.
July 15, 1870	Georgia is readmitted to Union.
1875	First commercial peach orchard in Georgia is established.

The Atlanta home in which civil rights leader Martin Luther King, Jr. was born is now a National Historic Site. (Georgia Department of Industry, Trade & Tourism)

1886	Pharmacist John Styth Pemberton of Atlanta invents Coca-Cola.
1888	Georgia Institute of Technology opens in Atlanta.
1912	Girl Scouts of America are formed by Juliette Gordon Low of Savannah.
1921	Boll weevil infestation damages Georgia's cotton crop.
1960	Future governor Lester Maddox organizes Georgians Unwilling to Surrender (GUTS), which boycotts businesses that change their segregation policies.
1966	Race riots take place in Atlanta.
1972	Maynard Jackson becomes the first African American elected mayor of Atlanta.
1972	Andrew Young is elected the first African American congressman from Georgia since Reconstruction.
1976	Former governor Jimmy Carter is elected president of the United States.
1980	World's largest airport terminal opens in Atlanta.
1983	New state constitution is adopted.
1987	Gwinnet County in Atlanta is the fastest-growing county in the United States for the second year.
1991	Georgia carries out the most executions in the country.
1992	Governor Zell Miller announces legislation to remove the Confederate battle symbol from the state flag.
2000	Georgia gains two seats in the U.S. House of Representatives after the 2000 census shows substantial population growth in the state compared with other states.
July 24, 2000	Three women candidates for admission at the University of Georgia at Athens who were denied admission in favor of less-qualified minority candidates win their case in U.S. federal court.
Nov. 5, 2002	Republican Saxby Chambliss, a conservative, defeats Democratic senator MaxCleland, a veteran of the Vietnam War and one-term senator.
Dec. 10, 2004	Former president and former Georgia governor Jimmy Carter receives the Nobel Peace Prize in Oslo, Norway.
2012	After a peanut shortage in 2011, growers across Georgia plant a record crop of peanuts, leading to a fall in prices from an expected $700 a ton to some $355 per ton at the low point.

Notes for Further Study

Published Sources. A good starting place for information on the state is *A History of Georgia* (2d ed., 1991), edited by Kenneth Coleman. This is a solid traditional history of the state, well researched and documented, which explores a wide range of topics. Robin S. Doak takes an accessible approach to the history of the state with *Georgia* (2005), a book for young adults. Another book for the younger audience is *Primary Source History of the Colony of Georgia* (2005) by Liz Sonneborn. Two good sources on Georgia residents are James C. Cobb's *Georgia Odyssey* (1997) and Lane Mills's *The People of Georgia: An Illustrated History* (2d ed., 1992), a popular history on individuals and groups, from the earliest times to the modern era, who shaped developments in the Peach State. *Civil War Savannah* (1997) by Derek Smith explores one of the South's most important cities during the Civil War. *The Archaeology and History of the Native Georgia Tribes* (2002) by Max E. White uses evidence from select archaeological sites, maps, photographs, and vivid fictional vignettes to highlight the history of the state's indigenous communities. During the Great Depression, unemployed writers and researchers were recruited by the Federal Writers' Project of the Works Progress Administration (WPA) to interview former slaves and collect the memories of their enslaved years. *On Jordan's Stormy Banks: Personal Accounts of Slavery in Georgia* (2000) is one result of this project, a collection of dramatic reminiscences brought together by Andrew White. Rebecca S. Montgomery's *Politics of Education in the New South: Women and Reform in Georgia, 1890-1930* (2006) is a fascinating study of the way in which post-Civil War women activists advocated a fair and just system of education as a way of providing economic opportunity for women and the rural and urban poor.

Web Resources. The state of Georgia has a Web site that provides a wealth of information and directs visitors to other locations (http:georgiagov/). A valuable source of information for tourists, businesspeople, and residents can be found at the site hosted by the Georgia Department of Industry, Trade and Tourism (www .georgia.org). Roadside America Attractions also has a good site for visitors to the state (www.roadsideamerica. com/map/ga.html). For information specifically about Georgia's rich historical heritage, the Georgia History site (http://georgiainfo.galileo.usg.edu/) is an excellent starting place. It is well supplemented and amplified by a visit to the site of the Georgia Department of Archives and History (www.georgiaarchives.org/who_are_we/ default.htm). For those interested in Georgia's natural resources, an excellent site is Links to Georgia Geoscience Sites (facstaff.gpc.edu/~pgore/georgia.htm).

Skyline of Atlanta, Georgia's capital and largest city. (Georgia Department of Industry, Trade & Tourism)

Counties

County	2012 Population	Pop. Rank	Land Area (sq. miles)	Area Rank
Appling	18,368	94	507.08	22
Atkinson	8,284	141	339.38	83
Bacon	11,198	121	258.58	115
Baker	3,366	154	341.94	80
Baldwin	46,367	43	257.84	116
Banks	18,316	95	232.09	127
Barrow	70,169	32	160.31	153
Bartow	100,661	25	459.54	35
Ben Hill	17,538	99	250.12	118
Berrien	19,041	91	451.90	38
Bibb	156,462	13	249.76	119
Bleckley	12,913	117	215.87	133
Brantley	18,587	93	442.36	41
Brooks	15,403	107	493.05	27

County	2012 Population	Pop. Rank	Land Area (sq. miles)	Area Rank
Bryan	32,214	54	435.97	45
Bulloch	72,694	31	672.81	8
Burke	23,125	79	826.97	2
Butts	23,524	76	184.39	144
Calhoun	6,504	148	280.37	108
Camden	51,402	41	613.03	11
Candler	11,117	122	243.04	122
Carroll	111,580	21	499.08	24
Catoosa	65,046	36	162.16	152
Charlton	13,295	115	773.58	5
Chatham	276,434	5	426.44	49
Chattahoochee	13,037	116	248.74	121
Chattooga	25,725	71	313.34	94
Cherokee	221,315	7	421.67	51

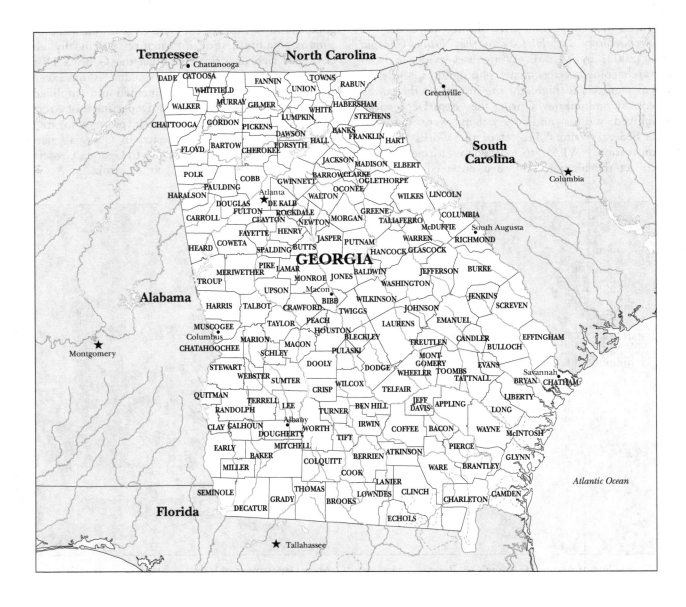

County	2012 Population	Pop. Rank	Land Area (sq. miles)	Area Rank	County	2012 Population	Pop. Rank	Land Area (sq. miles)	Area Rank
Clarke	120,266	19	119.20	159	Laurens	48,041	42	807.30	3
Clay	3,116	156	195.38	140	Lee	28,746	59	355.78	73
Clayton	265,888	6	141.57	157	Liberty	65,471	35	489.80	28
Clinch	6,718	146	800.22	4	Lincoln	7,737	143	210.38	135
Cobb	707,442	3	339.55	82	Long	16,048	106	400.29	56
Coffee	43,170	47	575.10	13	Lowndes	114,552	20	496.07	25
Colquitt	46,137	44	544.15	16	Lumpkin	30,611	56	282.93	104
Columbia	131,627	17	290.09	101	Macon	14,263	111	400.64	55
Cook	16,923	100	227.16	129	Madison	27,922	63	282.31	106
Coweta	130,929	18	440.89	42	Marion	8,711	137	366.00	69
Crawford	12,600	118	324.89	88	McDuffie	21,663	84	257.46	117
Crisp	23,606	75	272.58	110	McIntosh	13,839	113	424.30	50
Dade	16,490	101	173.98	149	Meriwether	21,273	87	501.22	23
Dawson	22,422	81	210.83	134	Miller	5,969	150	282.42	105
DeKalb	707,089	4	267.58	112	Mitchell	23,144	78	512.08	20
Decatur	27,509	66	597.14	12	Monroe	26,637	68	395.66	57
Dodge	21,329	86	495.89	26	Montgomery	8,913	136	239.52	124
Dooly	14,318	110	391.94	60	Morgan	17,881	97	347.35	76
Dougherty	94,501	27	328.69	86	Murray	39,392	50	344.47	79
Douglas	133,971	16	200.07	137	Muscogee	198,413	10	216.39	131
Early	10,594	124	512.59	19	Newton	101,505	24	272.16	111
Echols	3,988	153	414.89	53	Oconee	33,619	52	184.29	145
Effingham	53,293	40	477.70	31	Oglethorpe	14,618	109	439.01	43
Elbert	19,684	90	351.06	75	Paulding	144,800	15	312.22	95
Emanuel	22,898	80	680.60	6	Peach	27,622	64	150.27	155
Evans	10,689	123	182.85	147	Pickens	29,268	58	232.06	128
Fannin	23,492	77	386.72	63	Pierce	18,844	92	316.49	93
Fayette	107,524	22	194.34	142	Pike	17,810	98	216.09	132
Floyd	96,177	26	509.91	21	Polk	41,188	48	310.33	96
Forsyth	187,928	11	224.02	130	Pulaski	11,720	119	249.03	120
Franklin	21,894	82	261.50	113	Putnam	21,198	88	344.64	78
Fulton	977,773	1	526.63	17	Quitman	2,404	158	151.24	154
Gilmer	28,190	62	426.54	48	Rabun	16,297	104	369.99	67
Glascock	3,142	155	143.74	156	Randolph	7,327	144	428.24	47
Glynn	81,022	30	419.75	52	Richmond	202,587	9	324.33	89
Gordon	55,766	39	355.81	72	Rockdale	85,820	28	129.79	158
Grady	25,440	73	454.53	37	Schley	4,990	152	166.91	150
Greene	16,092	105	387.44	62	Screven	14,202	112	645.10	9
Gwinnett	842,046	2	430.38	46	Seminole	8,947	135	235.23	125
Habersham	43,520	46	276.74	109	Spalding	63,865	37	196.47	139
Hall	185,416	12	392.78	59	Stephens	25,891	70	179.13	148
Hancock	8,996	134	471.84	32	Stewart	6,042	149	458.73	36
Haralson	28,400	61	282.17	107	Sumter	31,554	55	482.70	29
Harris	32,550	53	463.87	34	Talbot	6,517	147	391.39	61
Hart	25,518	72	232.39	126	Taliaferro	1,680	159	194.61	141
Heard	11,633	120	296.03	98	Tattnall	25,384	74	479.40	30
Henry	209,053	8	322.13	91	Taylor	8,420	139	376.69	65
Houston	146,136	14	375.54	66	Telfair	16,349	103	437.30	44
Irwin	9,600	129	354.34	74	Terrell	9,045	133	335.44	84
Jackson	60,571	38	339.66	81	Thomas	44,724	45	544.60	15
Jasper	13,630	114	368.16	68	Tift	41,064	49	258.91	114
Jeff Davis	15,156	108	330.74	85	Toombs	27,315	67	364.00	70
Jefferson	16,432	102	526.48	18	Towns	10,495	125	166.56	151
Jenkins	9,213	131	347.28	77	Treutlen	6,769	145	199.44	138
Johnson	9,897	128	303.01	97	Troup	68,468	33	413.99	54
Jones	28,577	60	393.93	58	Turner	8,410	140	285.39	102
Lamar	18,057	96	183.50	146	Twiggs	8,447	138	358.40	71
Lanier	10,400	126	185.26	143	Union	21,451	85	321.93	92

County	2012 Population	Pop. Rank	Land Area (sq. miles)	Area Rank
Upson	26,630	69	323.44	90
Walker	68,094	34	446.38	40
Walton	84,575	29	325.68	87
Ware	35,821	51	892.46	1
Warren	5,578	151	284.30	103
Washington	20,879	89	678.45	7
Wayne	30,305	57	641.78	10
Webster	2,793	157	209.12	136
Wheeler	7,888	142	295.48	99
White	27,556	65	240.69	123
Whitfield	103,359	23	290.46	100
Wilcox	9,068	132	377.70	64
Wilkes	10,076	127	469.49	33
Wilkinson	9,577	130	447.31	39
Worth	21,741	83	570.70	14

Source: U.S. Census Bureau, 2012 Population Estimates

Cities

With 10,000 or more residents

Legal Name	2010 Population	Pop. Rank	Land Area (sq. miles)	Area Rank
Acworth city	20,425	44	8.24	78
Albany city	77,434	9	55.13	8
Alpharetta city	57,551	12	26.91	21
Americus city	17,041	56	11.24	66
Athens-Clarke County unified government	115,452	5	116.36	5
Atlanta city	420,003	1	133.15	4
Augusta-Richmond County consolidated government	195,844	2	302.47	1
Bainbridge city	12,697	82	18.80	34
Belvedere Park CDP	15,152	67	4.92	90
Brunswick city	15,383	64	17.07	38
Buford city	12,225	83	17.01	39
Calhoun city	15,650	62	14.93	49
Candler-McAfee CDP	23,025	41	7.01	85
Canton city	22,958	42	18.59	35
Carrollton city	24,388	38	22.29	28
Cartersville city	19,731	45	29.15	20
College Park city	13,942	75	10.07	73
Columbus city	189,885	3	216.39	3
Conyers city	15,195	66	11.66	65
Cordele city	11,147	91	10.14	72
Covington city	13,118	79	15.46	45
Cusseta-Chattahoochee County unified govt	11,267	89	248.74	2
Dallas city	11,544	88	7.06	84
Dalton city	33,128	25	20.54	30
Decatur city	19,335	47	4.27	93
Douglas city	11,589	86	13.39	56
Douglasville city	30,961	29	22.46	27
Druid Hills CDP	14,568	71	4.18	94
Dublin city	16,201	59	15.49	44
Duluth city	26,600	36	9.99	74
Dunwoody city	46,267	16	12.94	59
East Point city	33,712	23	14.67	50

Legal Name	2010 Population	Pop. Rank	Land Area (sq. miles)	Area Rank
Evans CDP	29,011	32	25.27	23
Fairburn city	12,950	80	16.85	40
Fayetteville city	15,945	61	10.89	68
Forest Park city	18,468	51	9.28	77
Gainesville city	33,804	22	31.93	16
Georgetown CDP	11,823	84	8.23	79
Griffin city	23,643	40	13.92	53
Grovetown city	11,216	90	4.82	91
Hinesville city	33,437	24	20.37	32
Jesup city	10,214	95	16.41	41
Johns Creek city	76,728	10	30.73	18
Kennesaw city	29,783	30	9.44	76
Kingsland city	15,946	60	42.72	9
LaGrange city	29,588	31	39.51	11
Lawrenceville city	28,546	33	13.39	56
Lilburn city	11,596	85	6.32	86
Lithia Springs CDP	15,491	63	13.60	54
Loganville city	10,458	94	7.34	82
Mableton CDP	37,115	18	20.57	29
Macon city	91,351	7	55.72	7
Marietta city	56,579	13	23.08	25
Martinez CDP	35,795	20	14.51	51
McDonough city	22,084	43	12.71	60
Milledgeville city	17,715	54	20.41	31
Milton city	32,661	28	38.52	12
Monroe city	13,234	78	15.12	47
Moultrie city	14,268	72	16.34	42
Mountain Park CDP	11,554	87	5.67	87
Newnan city	33,039	26	18.32	36
North Atlanta CDP	40,456	17	7.64	81
North Decatur CDP	16,698	57	4.98	89
North Druid Hills CDP	18,947	49	5.04	88
Peachtree City city	34,364	21	24.54	24
Perry city	13,839	77	26.18	22

Legal Name	2010 Population	Pop. Rank	Land Area (sq. miles)	Area Rank
Pooler city	19,140	48	29.39	19
Powder Springs city	13,940	76	7.17	83
Redan CDP	33,015	27	9.61	75
Riverdale city	15,134	69	4.53	92
Rome city	36,303	19	30.91	17
Roswell city	88,346	8	40.72	10
St. Marys city	17,121	55	22.51	26
St. Simons CDP	12,743	81	15.94	43
Sandy Springs city	93,853	6	37.64	13
Savannah city	136,286	4	103.15	6
Scottdale CDP	10,631	92	3.50	95
Smyrna city	51,271	15	15.35	46
Snellville city	18,242	53	10.45	71
Statesboro city	28,422	34	13.50	55
Stockbridge city	25,636	37	13.31	58
Sugar Hill city	18,522	50	10.60	70

Legal Name	2010 Population	Pop. Rank	Land Area (sq. miles)	Area Rank
Suwanee city	15,355	65	10.88	69
Thomasville city	18,413	52	14.95	48
Tifton city	16,350	58	12.49	61
Tucker CDP	27,581	35	11.98	63
Union City city	19,456	46	19.11	33
Valdosta city	54,518	14	35.83	14
Vidalia city	10,473	93	17.27	37
Villa Rica city	13,956	74	14.24	52
Warner Robins city	66,588	11	35.07	15
Waycross city	14,649	70	11.71	64
Wilmington Island CDP	15,138	68	8.20	80
Winder city	14,099	73	12.41	62
Woodstock city	23,896	39	11.16	67

Note: CDP–Census Designated Place
Source: U.S. Census Bureau, 2010 Census

Survey Says...

This section presents current rankings from dozens of public and private sources. It shows how this state ranks in a number of critical categories, including education, job growth, cost of living, teen drivers, energy efficiency, and business environment. Sources include *Forbes, Reuters, U.S. News and World Report, CNN Money, Gallup,* and *Huffington Post.*

- Georgia ranked #24 in a government study measuring real gross domestic product (GDP)—the output of goods and services produced by labor and property located in the United States. The ranking is based on the percentage change compared with 2011 GDP.
  U.S. Department of Commerce, Bureau of Economic Analysis, June 2013; www.bea.gov

- Georgia ranked #11 in a government study measuring real gross domestic product (GDP)—the output of goods and services produced by labor and property located in the United States. The ranking is based on the dollar value of its GDP.
  U.S. Department of Commerce, Bureau of Economic Analysis, June 2013; www.bea.gov

- Georgia ranked #7 in the 17th edition of "Quality Counts; State of the States," Education Week's "report card" surveying key education indicators, policy efforts, and educational outcomes.
  Education Week, January 4, 2013 (online) and January 10, 2013 (print); www.edweek.org

- SERI (Science and Engineering Readiness Index) weighs the performance of the states' K-12 schools in preparing students in physics and calculus, the high school subjects considered most important for future scientists and engineers. Georgia ranked #19.
  Newsletter of the Forum on Education of the American Physical Society, Summer 2011 issue; www.huffingtonpost.com, July 11, 2011; updated October 1, 2012

- MoneyRates.com ranked Georgia #23 on its list of the best to worst states for making a living. Criteria: average income; inflation; employment prospects; and workers' Workplace Environment assessments according to the Gallup-Healthways Well-Being Index.
  www.money-rates.com, posted April 1, 2013

- *Forbes* analyzed business costs, labor supply, regulatory environment, current economic climate, growth prospects, and quality of life, to compile its "Best States for Business" rankings. Georgia ranked #8.
  www.forbes.com. posted December 12, 2012

- The 2012 Gallup-Healthways Well-Being Index, surveyed American's opinions on economic confidence, workplace perceptions, community climate, personal choices, and health predictors to assess the "future livability" of each state. Georgia ranked #20.
  "Utah Poised to Be the Best State to Live In," Gallup Wellbeing, www.gallup.com, August 7, 2012

- On CNBC's list of "America's Top States for Business 2013," Georgia ranked #8. Criteria: measures of competitiveness developed with input from the National Association of Manufacturers, the Council on Competitiveness, and other business groups weighed with the states' own marketing criteria.
  www.cnbc.com, consulted July 19, 2013

- Georgia ranked #21 on MoneyRates list of "Best-and Worst-States to Retire 2012." Criteria: life expectancy, crime rate, climate, economic conditions, taxes, job opportunities, and cost of living.
  www.money-rates.com, October 22, 2012

- Georgia ranked #18 on the 2013 Bankrate "Best Places to Retire" list ranking the states and District of Columbia on various criteria relating to health, safety, and cost.
  www.bankrate.com, May 6, 2013

- Georgia ranked #36 on the Social Science Research Council's "American Human Development Report: The Measure of America," assessing the 50 states plus the District of Columbia on health, education, and living-standard criteria.
  The Measure of America 2013-2014, posted June 19, 2013; www.measureofamerica.org

- Georgia ranked #35 on the Foundation for Child Development's (FCD) Child Well-being Index (CWI). The FCD used the KIDS COUNT report and the National Survey of Children's Health, the only state-level source for several key indicators of child well-being.
  Foundation for Child Development, January 18, 2012; fcd-us.org

- Georgia ranked #43 overall according to the 2013 KIDS COUNT Data Book, a project of the Annie E. Casey Foundation. Criteria: children's economic well-being, education, health, and family and community indicators.
  KIDS COUNT Data Center's Data Book, released June 20, 2013; http://datacenter.kidscount.org

- Georgia ranked #43 in the children's economic well-being category by the 2013 KIDS COUNT Data Book, a project of the Annie E. Casey Foundation.
  KIDS COUNT Data Center's Data Book, released June 20, 2013; http://datacenter.kidscount.org

- Georgia ranked #38 in the children's educational opportunities and attainments category by the 2013 KIDS COUNT Data Book, a project of the Annie E. Casey Foundation.
  KIDS COUNT Data Center's Data Book, released June 20, 2013; http://datacenter.kidscount.org

- Georgia ranked #40 in the children's health category by the 2013 KIDS COUNT Data Book, a project of the Annie E. Casey Foundation.
  KIDS COUNT Data Center's Data Book, released June 20, 2013; http://datacenter.kidscount.org

- Georgia ranked #40 in the family and community circumstances that factor into children's well-being category by the 2013 KIDS COUNT Data Book, a project of the Annie E. Casey Foundation.
  KIDS COUNT Data Center's Data Book, released June 20, 2013; http://datacenter.kidscount.org

- Georgia ranked #33 in the 2012 Gallup-Healthways Well-Being Index. Criteria: emotional health; physical health; healthy behavior; work environment; basic access to food, shelter, health care; and a safe and satisfying place to live.
  2012 State of Well-Being, Gallup-Healthways Well-Being Index, released February 28, 2013; www.well-beingindex.com

- *U.S. News and World Report's* "Best States for Teen Drivers" rankings are based on driving and road safety laws, federal reports on driver's licenses, car accident fatality, and road-quality statistics. Georgia ranked #19.
  U.S. News and World Report, March 18, 2010; www.usnews.com

- The Yahoo! Sports service Rivals.com ranks the states according to the strength of their high school football programs. Georgia ranked #1.
  "Ranking the States: Where Is the Best Football Played?," November 18, 2011; highschool.rivals.com

- iVillage ranked the states by hospitable living conditions for women. Criteria: economic success, access to affordable childcare, health care, reproductive rights, female representation in government, and educational attainment. Georgia ranked #25.
  iVillage, "50 Best to Worst States for Women," March 14, 2012; www.ivillage.com

- The League of American Bicyclists's "Bicycle Friendly States" ranked Georgia #24. Criteria: legislation and enforcement, policies and programs, infrastructure and funding, education and advocacy, and evaluation and planning.
  "Washington Tops the Bicycle-Friendly State Ranking," May 1, 2013; bicycling.com

- The federal Corporation for National and Community Service ranked the states and the District of Columbia by volunteer rates. Georgia ranked #34 for community service.
  "Volunteering and Civic Life in America 2012," www.volunteeringinamerica.gov, accessed July 24, 2013

- The Hospital Safety Score ranked states and the District of Columbia on their hospitals' performance scores. Georgia ranked #33. Criteria: avoiding preventable harm and medical errors, as demonstrated by 26 hospital safety metrics.
  Spring 2013 Hospital Safety Score, May 8, 2013; www.hospitalsafetyscore.org

- GMAC Insurance ranked the states and the District of Columbia by the performance of their drivers on the GMAC Insurance National Drivers Test, comprised of DMV test questions. Georgia ranked #43.
  "2011 GMAC Insurance National Drivers Test," www.gmacinsurance.com, accessed July 23, 2013

- Georgia ranked #50 in a "State Integrity Investigation" analysis of laws and practices intended to deter corruption and promote accountability and openness in campaign finance, ethics laws, lobbying regulations and management of state pension funds.
  "What's Your State's Grade?," www.publicintegrity.org, accessed July 23, 2013

- Georgia ranked #7 among the states and the District of Columbia in total rail miles, as tracked by the Association of American Railroads.
  "U.S. Freight Railroad Industry Snapshot: Railroads and States: Total Rail Miles by State: 2011"; www.aar.org, accessed July 23, 2013

- According to statistics compiled by the Beer Institute, Georgia ranked #43 among the states and the District of Columbia in per capita beer consumption of persons 21 years or older.
  "Shipments of Malt Beverages and Per Capita Consumption by State 2012;" www.beerinstitute.org

- According to Concordia University's "Public Education Costs per Pupil by State Rankings," based on statistics gathered by the U.S. Census Bureau, which includes the District of Columbia, Georgia ranked #33.
  Concordia University Online; education.cu-portland.edu, accessed July 24, 2013

- Georgia ranked #18 among the states and the District of Columbia in population density based on U.S. Census Bureau data for resident population and total land area. "List of U.S. States by Population Density."
  www.wikipedia.org, accessed July 24, 2013

- In "America's Health Rankings, 2012 Edition," by the United Health Foundation, Georgia ranked #36. Criteria included: rate of high school graduation; violent crime rate; incidence of infectious disease; childhood immunizations; prevalence of diabetes; per capita public-health funding; percentage of uninsured population; rate of children in poverty; and availability of primary-care physicians.
  United Health Foundation; www.americashealthrankings.org, accessed July 24, 2013

- The TechNet 2012 "State Broadband Index" ranked Georgia #16 on the following criteria: broadband adoption; network quality; and economic structure. Improved broadband use is hoped to promote economic development, build strong communities, improve delivery of government services and upgrade educational systems.
  TechNet; www.technet.org, accessed July 24, 2013

- Georgia was ranked #33 among the states and District of Columbia on the American Council for an Energy-Efficient Economy's "State Energy Efficiency Scorecard" for 2012.
  American Council for an Energy-Efficient Economy; aceee.org/sector/state-policy/scorecard, accessed July 24, 2013

Statistical Tables

DEMOGRAPHICS
Resident State and National Population, 1950-2012
Projected State and National Population, 2000-2030
Population by Age, 2012
Population by Race, 2012
Population by Hispanic Origin and Race, 2012

VITAL STATISTICS
Death Rates by Leading Causes, 2010
Death Rates by Selected Causes, 2010
Abortion Rates, 2009
Infant Mortality Rates, 1995-2009
Marriage and Divorce Rates, 2000-2011

ECONOMY
Nominal Gross Domestic Product by Industry, 2012
Real Gross Domestic Product, 2000-2012
Personal Income Per Capita, 1930-2012
Non-Farm Employment by Sector, 2012
Foreign Exports, 2000-2012
Energy Consumption, 2011

LAND AND WATER
Surface Area and Federally-Owned Land, 2007
Land Cover/Use of Non-Federal Rural Land, 2007
Farms and Crop Acreage, 2012

HEALTH AND MEDICAL CARE
Medical Professionals, 2012
Health Insurance Coverage, 2011
HIV, STD, and Tuberculosis Cases and Rates, 2011
Cigarette Smoking, 2011

HOUSING
Home Ownership Rates, 1995-2012
Home Sales, 2000-2010
Value of Owner-Occupied Homes, 2011

EDUCATION
School Enrollment, 2011
Educational Attainment, 2011
Public College Finances, FY 2012

TRANSPORTATION AND TRAVEL
Motor Vehicle Registrations and Drivers Licenses, 2011
Domestic Travel Expenditures, 2009
Retail Gasoline Prices, 2013
Public Road Length, 2011

CRIME AND LAW ENFORCEMENT
Full-Time Law Enforcement Officers, 2011
Prison Population, 2000-2012
Crime Rate, 2011

GOVERNMENT AND FINANCE
Local Governments by Type, 2012
State Government Revenue, 2011
State Government Expenditures, 2011
State Government General Expenditures by Function, 2011
State Government Finances, Cash and Debt, 2011

POLITICS
Composition of the Senate, 1995-2013
Composition of the House of Representatives, 1995-2013
Composition of State Legislature, 2004-2013
Voter Participation in Presidential Elections, 1980-2012
Governors Since Statehood

DEMOGRAPHICS

Resident State and National Population, 1950–2012

Year	State Population	U.S. Population	State Share
1950	3,445,000	151,326,000	2.28%
1960	3,943,000	179,323,000	2.20%
1970	4,587,930	203,302,031	2.26%
1980	5,463,105	226,545,805	2.41%
1990	6,478,216	248,709,873	2.60%
2000	8,186,653	281,424,600	2.91%
2010	9,687,653	308,745,538	3.14%
2012	9,919,945	313,914,040	3.16%

Note: 1950/1960 population figures are rounded to the nearest thousand.
Source: U.S. Census Bureau, Decennial Census 1950–2010; U.S. Census Bureau, 2012 Population Estimates

Projected State and National Population, 2000–2030

Year	State Population	U.S. Population	State Share
2000	8,186,453	281,421,906	2.91%
2005	8,925,796	295,507,134	3.02%
2010	9,589,080	308,935,581	3.10%
2015	10,230,578	322,365,787	3.17%
2020	10,843,753	335,804,546	3.23%
2025	11,438,622	349,439,199	3.27%
2030	12,017,838	363,584,435	3.31%
State population growth, 2000–2030			3,831,385
State percentage growth, 2000–2030			46.8%

Source: U.S. Census Bureau, Population Division, Interim State Population Projections, 2005

Population by Age, 2012

Age Group	State Population	Percent of Total Population	
		State	U.S.
Under 5 years	675,032	6.8%	6.4%
5 to 14 years	1,403,553	14.1%	13.1%
15 to 24 years	1,427,822	14.4%	14.0%
25 to 34 years	1,366,607	13.8%	13.5%
35 to 44 years	1,378,173	13.9%	12.9%
45 to 54 years	1,394,548	14.1%	14.1%
55 to 64 years	1,134,511	11.4%	12.3%
65 to 74 years	686,935	6.9%	7.6%
75 to 84 years	329,281	3.3%	4.2%
85 years and older	123,483	1.2%	1.9%
Under 18 years	2,490,125	25.1%	23.5%
65 years and older	1,139,699	11.5%	13.7%
Median age (years)	–	35.7	37.4

Source: U.S. Census Bureau, Annual Estimates of the Resident Population for Selected Age Groups by Sex for the United States, States, Counties, and Puerto Rico Commonwealth and Municipios: April 1, 2010 to July 1, 2012

Population by Race, 2012

Race	State Population	Percent of Total Population	
		State	U.S.
All residents	9,919,945	100.00%	100.00%
White	6,231,978	62.82%	77.89%
African American	3,091,904	31.17%	13.13%
Native American	50,539	0.51%	1.23%
Asian	351,734	3.55%	5.14%
Native Hawaiian	11,061	0.11%	0.23%
Two or more races	182,729	1.84%	2.39%

Source: U.S. Census Bureau, Population Division, Annual Estimates of the Resident Population by Sex, Race and Hispanic Origin for the United States, States, and Counties: April 1, 2010 to July 1, 2012

Population by Hispanic Origin and Race, 2012

Hispanic Origin/Race	State Population	Percent of Total Population	
		State	U.S.
All residents	9,919,945	100.00%	100.00%
All Hispanic residents	909,902	9.17%	16.89%
Hispanic			
White	762,036	7.68%	14.91%
African American	79,800	0.80%	0.79%
Native American	27,996	0.28%	0.49%
Asian	7,526	0.08%	0.17%
Native Hawaiian	5,196	0.05%	0.06%
Two or more races	27,348	0.28%	0.48%
Not Hispanic			
White	5,469,942	55.14%	62.98%
African American	3,012,104	30.36%	12.34%
Native American	22,543	0.23%	0.74%
Asian	344,208	3.47%	4.98%
Native Hawaiian	5,865	0.06%	0.17%
Two or more races	155,381	1.57%	1.91%

Source: U.S. Census Bureau, Population Division, Annual Estimates of the Resident Population by Sex, Race and Hispanic Origin for the United States, States, and Counties: April 1, 2010 to July 1, 2012

VITAL STATISTICS

Death Rates by Leading Causes, 2010

Cause	State	U.S.
Malignant neoplasms	188.9	186.2
Ischaemic heart diseases	97.0	122.9
Other forms of heart disease	86.0	53.4
Chronic lower respiratory diseases	49.3	44.7
Cerebrovascular diseases	49.7	41.9
Organic, incl. symptomatic, mental disorders	48.2	35.7
Other degenerative diseases of the nervous sys.	31.5	28.4
Other external causes of accidental injury	26.7	26.5
Diabetes mellitus	24.9	22.4
Hypertensive diseases	32.2	20.4
All causes	905.8	799.5

Note: Figures are age-adjusted death rates per 100,000 population
Source: CDC/NCHS, Underlying Cause of Death 1999–2010 on CDC WONDER Online Database

Death Rates by Selected Causes, 2010

Cause	State	U.S.
Assault	6.5	5.2
Diseases of the liver	13.3	13.9
Human immunodeficiency virus (HIV) disease	5.2	2.7
Influenza and pneumonia	19.6	16.2
Intentional self-harm	12.0	12.4
Malnutrition	1.4	0.9
Obesity and other hyperalimentation	2.4	1.8
Renal failure	20.4	14.4
Transport accidents	14.8	12.1
Viral hepatitis	1.6	2.4

Note: Figures are age-adjusted death rates per 100,000 population; A dash indicates that data was not available or was suppressed
Source: CDC/NCHS, Underlying Cause of Death 1999–2010 on CDC WONDER Online Database

Abortion Rates, 2009

Category	2009
By state of residence	
Total abortions	30,264
Abortion rate[1]	14.5%
Abortion ratio[2]	214
By state of occurrence	
Total abortions	32,925
Abortion rate[1]	15.8%
Abortion ratio[2]	233
Abortions obtained by out-of-state residents	9.4%
U.S. abortion rate[1]	15.1%
U.S. abortion ratio[2]	227

Note: (1) Number of abortions per 1,000 women aged 15–44 years; (2) Number of abortions per 1,000 live births; A dash indicates that data was not available
Source: CDC/NCHS, Morbidity and Mortality Weekly Report, November 23, 2012 (Abortion Surveillance, United States, 2009)

Infant Mortality Rates, 1995–2009

Category	1995	2000	2005	2009
All state residents	9.55	8.45	8.07	7.33
All U.S. residents	7.57	6.89	6.86	6.39
All state white residents	6.59	5.99	5.84	5.28
All U.S. white residents	6.30	5.71	5.73	5.33
All state black residents	15.26	13.54	12.56	11.11
All U.S. black residents	14.58	13.48	13.26	12.12

Note: Figures represent deaths per 1,000 live births of resident infants under one year old, exclusive of fetal deaths; A dash indicates that data was not available or was suppressed.
Source: Centers of Disease Control and Prevention, Division of Vital Statistics, Linked Birth/Infant Death Records on CDC Wonder Online

Marriage and Divorce Rates, 2000–2011

Year	Marriage Rate		Divorce Rate	
	State	U.S.	State	U.S.
2000	6.8	8.2	3.3	4.0
2002	6.5	8.0	2.5	3.9
2004	7.9	7.8	0.0	3.7
2006	7.3	7.5	0.0	3.7
2008	6.0	7.1	0.0	3.5
2010	7.3	6.8	0.0	3.6
2011	6.6	6.8	0.0	3.6

Note: Rates are based on provisional counts of marriages/divorces by state of occurrence and are per 1,000 total population residing in area
Source: CDC/NCHS, National Vital Statistics System

ECONOMY

Nominal Gross Domestic Product by Industry, 2012
In millions of current dollars

Industry	State GDP
Accommodation and food services	13,225
Administrative and waste management services	15,003
Agriculture, forestry, fishing, and hunting	3,703
Arts, entertainment, and recreation	2,968
Construction	15,109
Educational services	4,755
Finance and insurance	29,458
Health care and social assistance	28,588
Information	27,666
Management of companies and enterprises	7,762
Manufacturing	48,599
Mining	406
Other services, except government	9,758
Professional, scientific, and technical services	31,652
Real estate and rental and leasing	48,270
Retail trade	26,887
Transportation and warehousing	17,808
Utilities	9,757
Wholesale trade	32,514

Source: U.S. Department of Commerce, Bureau of Economic Analysis, Survey of Current Business

Real Gross Domestic Product, 2000–2012
In millions of chained 2005 dollars

Year	State GDP	U.S. GDP	State Share
2000	329,292	11,225,406	2.93%
2005	363,177	12,539,116	2.90%
2010	358,843	12,897,088	2.78%
2012	374,000	13,430,576	2.78%

Source: U.S. Department of Commerce, Bureau of Economic Analysis, Survey of Current Business

Personal Income Per Capita, 1930–2012

Year	State	U.S.
1930	$302	$618
1940	$333	$593
1950	$1,058	$1,503
1960	$1,685	$2,268
1970	$3,379	$4,084
1980	$8,408	$10,091
1990	$17,563	$19,354
2000	$28,541	$30,319
2010	$34,531	$39,791
2012	$36,869	$42,693

Source: U.S. Department of Commerce, Bureau of Economic Analysis, Regional Economic Accounts

Non-Farm Employment by Sector, 2012
In thousands

Sector	Employment
Construction	141.0
Education and health services	495.8
Financial activities	227.2
Government	681.8
Information	100.5
Leisure and hospitality	394.8
Mining and logging	8.6
Manufacturing	354.6
Other services	153.1
Professional and business services	562.4
Trade, transportation, and utilities	833.2
All sectors	3,952.8

Source: U.S. Bureau of Labor Statistics, State and Area Employment

Foreign Exports, 2000–2012
In millions of dollars

Year	State Exports	U.S. Exports	State Share
2000	14,925	712,054	2.10%
2002	14,424	649,940	2.22%
2004	19,720	768,554	2.57%
2006	20,113	973,994	2.07%
2008	27,513	1,222,545	2.25%
2010	28,898	1,208,080	2.39%
2012	36,067	1,478,268	2.44%

Note: U.S. figures exclude data from Puerto Rico, U.S. Virgin Islands, and unallocated exports
Source: U.S. Department of Commerce, International Trade Admin., Office of Trade and Industry Information, Manufacturing and Services

Energy Consumption, 2011

In trillions of BTUs, except as noted

Total energy consumption	
Total state energy consumption	3,002.1
Total U.S. energy consumption	97,387.3
State share of U.S. total	3.08%
Per capita consumption (in millions of BTUs)	
Total state per capita consumption	305.9
Total U.S. per capita consumption	312.6
End-use sectors	
Residential	745.9
Commercial	564.4
Industrial	747.7
Transportation	944.0
Sources of energy	
Petroleum	996.6
Natural gas	531.6
Coal	634.8
Renewable energy	236.7
Nuclear electric power	338.1

Source: U.S. Energy Information Administration, State Energy Data 2011: Consumption

LAND AND WATER

Surface Area and Federally-Owned Land, 2007

In thousands of acres

Category	State	U.S.	State Share
Total surface area	37,740.5	1,937,664.2	1.95%
Total land area	36,681.2	1,886,846.9	1.94%
Non-federal land	34,557.2	1,484,910.0	2.33%
Developed	4,639.9	111,251.2	4.17%
Rural	29,917.3	1,373,658.8	2.18%
Federal land	2,124.0	401,936.9	0.53%
Water area	1,059.3	50,817.3	2.08%

Source: U.S. Department of Agriculture, Natural Resources Conservation Service, 2007 National Resources Inventory

Land Cover/Use of Non-Federal Rural Land, 2007

In thousands of acres

Category	State	U.S.	State Share
Total rural land	29,917.3	1,373,658.8	2.18%
Cropland	3,995.0	357,023.5	1.12%
CRP[1] land	300.3	32,850.2	0.91%
Pastureland	2,809.7	118,615.7	2.37%
Rangeland	0.0	409,119.4	0.00%
Forest land	21,963.9	406,410.4	5.40%
Other rural land	848.4	49,639.6	1.71%

Note: (1) Conservation Reserve Program was created to assist private landowners in converting highly erodible cropland to vegetative cover.
Source: U.S. Department of Agriculture, Natural Resources Conservation Service, 2007 National Resources Inventory

Farms and Crop Acreage, 2012

Category	State	U.S.	State Share
Farms (in thousands)	47.0	2,170.0	2.17%
Acres (in millions)	10.4	914.0	1.14%
Acres per farm	221.3	421.2	–

Source: U.S. Department of Agriculture, National Agricultural Statistical Service, Quick Stats, 2012 Survey Data

HEALTH AND MEDICAL CARE

Medical Professionals, 2012

Profession	State Number	U.S. Number	State Share	State Rate[1]	U.S. Rate[1]
Physicians[2]	21,904	894,637	2.45%	223.2	287.1
Dentists	4,625	193,587	2.39%	47.1	62.1
Podiatrists	371	17,469	2.12%	3.8	5.6
Optometrists	1,064	45,638	2.33%	10.8	14.6
Chiropractors	2,371	77,494	3.06%	24.2	24.9

Note: (1) Rates are per 100,000 population; (2) Includes total, active Doctors of Osteopathic Medicine and Doctors of Medicine in 2011.
Source: U.S. Department of Health and Human Services, Bureau of Health Professions, Area Health Resource File, 2012-2013

Health Insurance Coverage, 2011

Category	State	U.S.
Total persons covered	7,821,000	260,214,000
Total persons not covered	1,862,000	48,613,000
Percent not covered	19.2%	15.7%
Children under age 18 covered	2,262,000	67,143,000
Children under age 18 not covered	277,000	6,965,000
Percent of children not covered	10.9%	9.4%

Source: U.S. Census Bureau, Current Population Survey, 2012 Annual Social and Economic Supplement

HIV, STD, and Tuberculosis Cases and Rates, 2011

Disease	State Cases	State Rate[1]	U.S. Rate[1]
Chlamydia	54,403	561.6	457.6
Gonorrhea	16,428	169.6	104.2
HIV diagnosis	2,520	31.4	15.8
HIV, stage 3 (AIDS)	2,234	27.9	10.3
Syphilis, early latent	436	4.5	4.3
Syphilis, primary/secondary	678	7.0	4.5
Tuberculosis	347	3.5	3.4

Note: (1) Rates are per 100,000 population
Source: Centers for Disease Control and Prevention

Cigarette Smoking, 2011

Category	State	U.S.
Adults who are current smokers	21.2%	21.2%
Adults who smoke everyday	14.3%	15.4%
Adults who smoke some days	6.9%	5.7%
Adults who are former smokers	22.1%	25.1%
Adults who never smoked	56.7%	52.9%

Source: Centers for Disease Control and Prevention, Behaviorial Risk Factor Surveillance System, Tobacco Use, 2011

HOUSING

Home Ownership Rates, 1995–2012

Area	1995	2000	2005	2010	2012
State	66.6%	69.8%	67.9%	67.1%	64.3%
U.S.	64.7%	67.4%	68.9%	66.9%	65.4%

Source: U.S. Census Bureau, Housing Vacancies and Homeownership, Annual Statistics

Home Sales, 2000–2010
In thousands of units

Year	State Sales	U.S. Sales	State Share
2000	143.6	5,174	2.78%
2002	173.9	5,632	3.09%
2004	215.8	6,778	3.18%
2006	248.8	6,478	3.84%
2008	174.9	4,913	3.56%
2010	162.7	4,908	3.31%

Note: Units include single-family homes, condos and co-ops
Source: National Association of Realtors, Real Estate Outlook, Market Trends & Insights

Value of Owner-Occupied Homes, 2011

Value	Total Units in State	Percent of Total, State	Percent of Total, U.S.
Less than $50,000	239,693	10.6%	8.8%
$50,000 to $99,000	446,572	19.8%	16.0%
$100,000 to $149,000	466,905	20.7%	16.5%
$150,000 to $199,000	388,056	17.2%	15.4%
$200,000 to $299,000	375,166	16.6%	18.2%
$300,000 to $499,000	236,614	10.5%	15.2%
$500,000 to $999,000	84,674	3.8%	7.9%
$1,000,000 or more	19,023	0.8%	2.0%
Median value	–	$147,100	$173,600

Source: U.S. Census Bureau, 2011 American Community Survey 1-Year Estimates

EDUCATION

School Enrollment, 2011

Educational Level	Students Enrolled in State	Percent of Total, State	Percent of Total, U.S.
All levels	2,782,980	100.0%	100.0%
Nursery school, preschool	177,581	6.4%	6.0%
Kindergarten	153,712	5.5%	5.1%
Elementary (grades 1–8)	1,125,570	40.4%	39.5%
Secondary (grades 9–12)	559,081	20.1%	20.7%
College or graduate school	767,036	27.6%	28.7%

Note: Figures cover the population 3 years and over enrolled in school
Source: U.S. Census Bureau, 2011 American Community Survey 1-Year Estimates

Educational Attainment, 2011

Highest Level of Education	State	U.S.
High school diploma	84.3%	85.9%
Bachelor's degree	27.6%	28.5%
Graduate/Professional degree	9.8%	10.6%

Note: Figures cover the population 25 years and over
Source: U.S. Census Bureau, 2011 American Community Survey 1-Year Estimates

Public College Finances, FY 2012

Category	State	U.S.
Full-time equivalent enrollment (FTE)[1]	379,004	11,548,974
Educational appropriations per FTE[2]	$6,644	$5,906
Net tuition revenue per FTE[3]	$3,872	$5,189
Total educational revenue per FTE[4]	$10,501	$11,043

(1) Full-time equivalent enrollment equates student credit hours to full time, academic year students, but excludes medical students; (2) Educational appropriations measure state and local support available for public higher education operating expenses including ARRA funds and excludes appropriations for independent institutions, financial aid for students attending independent institutions, research, hospitals, and medical education; (3) Net tuition revenue is calculated by taking the gross amount of tuition and fees, less state and institutional financial aid, tuition waivers or discounts, and medical student tuition and fees. Net tuition revenue used for capital debt service is included in the net tuition revenue figures; (4) Total educational revenue is the sum of educational appropriations and net tuition excluding net tuition revenue used for capital debt service.
Source: State Higher Education Executive Officers, State Higher Education Finance FY 2012

TRANSPORTATION AND TRAVEL

Motor Vehicle Registrations and Drivers Licenses, 2011

Vehicle Type	State	U.S.	State Share
Automobiles[1]	3,430,165	125,656,528	2.73%
Buses	27,227	666,064	4.09%
Trucks	3,876,723	118,455,587	3.27%
Motorcycles	199,620	8,437,502	2.37%
Drivers licenses	6,505,690	211,874,649	3.07%

Note: Motor vehicle registrations include private, commercial, and publicly-owned vehicles; (1) Includes taxicabs
Source: U.S. Department of Transportation, Federal Highway Administration

Domestic Travel Expenditures, 2009
In millions of dollars

Category	State	U.S.	State Share
Travel expenditures	$17,570	$610,200	2.88%

Note: Figures represent U.S. spending on domestic overnight trips and day trips of 50 miles or more, one way, away from home. Excludes spending by foreign visitors.
Source: U.S. Travel Association, Impact of Travel on State Economies, 2009

Retail Gasoline Prices, 2013

Gasoline Grade	State Average	U.S. Average
Regular	$3.52	$3.65
Mid	$3.70	$3.81
Premium	$3.88	$3.98
Diesel	$3.86	$3.88
Excise tax[1]	46.9 cents	49.4 cents

Note: Gasoline prices as of 7/26/2013; (1) Includes state and federal excise taxes and other state taxes as of July 1, 2013
Source: American Automobile Association, Daily Fuel Guage Report; American Petroleum Institute, State Motor Fuel Taxes, 2013

Public Road Length, 2011

Type	State Mileage	U.S. Mileage	State Share
Interstate highways	1,248	46,960	2.66%
Other highways	147	15,719	0.94%
Principal arterial	4,598	156,262	2.94%
Minor arterial	9,538	242,942	3.93%
Major collector	15,584	534,592	2.92%
Minor collector	7,489	266,357	2.81%
Local	84,943	2,814,925	3.02%
Urban	39,998	1,095,373	3.65%
Rural	83,548	2,982,383	2.80%
Total	123,546	4,077,756	3.03%

Note: Combined urban and rural road mileage equals the total of the other road types
Source: U.S. Department of Transportation, Federal Highway Administration, Public Road Length, 2011

CRIME AND LAW ENFORCEMENT

Full-Time Law Enforcement Officers, 2011

Gender	State Number	State Rate[1]	U.S. Rate[1]
Male officers	21,368	234.5	210.3
Female officers	3,964	43.5	28.1
Total officers	25,332	278.1	238.3

Note: (1) Rates are per 100,000 population
Source: Federal Bureau of Investigation, Uniform Crime Reports, Crime in the United States 2011

Prison Population, 2000–2012

Year	State Population	U.S. Population	State Share
2000	44,232	1,391,261	3.18%
2005	48,749	1,527,929	3.19%
2010	56,432	1,613,803	3.50%
2011	55,944	1,598,783	3.50%
2012	55,457	1,571,013	3.53%

Note: Figures include prisoners under the jurisdiction of state or federal correctional authorities.
Source: U.S. Department of Justice, Bureau of Justice Statistics, Prisoners in 2006, 2011, 2012 (Advance Counts)

Crime Rate, 2011

Incidents per 100,000 residents

Category	State	U.S.
Violent crimes	373.2	386.3
Murder	5.6	4.7
Forcible rape	20.9	26.8
Robbery	123.8	113.7
Aggravated assault	222.9	241.1
Property crimes	3,626.5	2,908.7
Burglary	974.6	702.2
Larceny/theft	2,351.7	1,976.9
Motor vehicle theft	300.3	229.6
All crimes	3,999.7	3,295.0

Source: Federal Bureau of Investigation, Uniform Crime Reports, Crime in the United States 2011

GOVERNMENT AND FINANCE

Local Governments by Type, 2012

Government Type	State	U.S.	State Share
All local governments	1,365	89,004	1.53%
County	153	3,031	5.05%
Municipality	535	19,522	2.74%
Town/Township	0	16,364	0.00%
Special District	497	37,203	1.34%
Ind. School District	180	12,884	1.40%

Source: U.S. Census Bureau, 2012 Census of Governments: Organization Component Preliminary Estimates

State Government Revenue, 2011

In thousands of dollars, except for per capita figures

Total revenue	$52,294,783
Total revenue per capita, State	$5,329
Total revenue per capita, U.S.	$7,271
General revenue	$37,167,825
Intergovernmental revenue	$15,266,487
Taxes	$16,003,250
General sales	$5,080,777
Selective sales	$2,027,885
License taxes	$477,056
Individual income taxes	$7,658,782
Corporate income taxes	$670,410
Other taxes	$88,340
Current charges	$3,922,860
Miscellaneous general revenue	$1,975,228
Utility revenue	$9,824
Liquor store revenue	$0
Insurance trust revenue[1]	$15,117,134

Note: (1) Within insurance trust revenue, net earnings of state retirement systems is a calculated statistic, and thus can be positive or negative. Net earnings is the sum of earnings on investments plus gains on investments minus losses on investments.
Source: U.S. Census Bureau, 2011 Annual Survey of State Government Finances

State Government Expenditures, 2011

In thousands of dollars, except for per capita figures

Total expenditure	$44,750,297
Total expenditure per capita, State	$4,561
Total expenditure per capita, U.S.	$6,427
Intergovernmental expenditure	$10,600,099
Direct expenditure	$34,150,198
Current operation	$22,210,411
Capital outlay	$2,639,401
Insurance benefits and repayments	$7,296,018
Assistance and subsidies	$1,316,050
Interest on debt	$688,318
Utility expenditure	$43,813
Liquor store expenditure	$0
Insurance trust expenditure	$7,296,018

Source: U.S. Census Bureau, 2011 Annual Survey of State Government Finances

State Government General Expenditures by Function, 2011

In thousands of dollars

Education	$17,429,181
Public welfare	$10,366,884
Hospitals	$838,523
Health	$1,159,244
Highways	$1,640,847
Police protection	$298,050
Correction	$1,462,044
Natural resources	$559,431
Parks and recreation	$195,353
Governmental administration	$810,105
Interest on general debt	$688,318
Other and unallocable	$1,962,486

Source: U.S. Census Bureau, 2011 Annual Survey of State Government Finances

State Government Finances, Cash and Debt, 2011

In thousands of dollars, except for per capita figures

Debt at end of fiscal year	
State, total	$13,402,568
State, per capita	$1,366
U.S., per capita	$3,635
Cash and security holdings	
State, total	$77,103,782
State, per capita	$7,858
U.S., per capita	$11,759

Source: U.S. Census Bureau, 2011 Annual Survey of State Government Finances

POLITICS

Composition of the Senate, 1995–2013

Congress (Year)	State/U.S	Dem	Rep	Total
104th (1995)	State delegates	1	1	2
	Total U.S.	48	52	100
105th (1997)	State delegates	1	1	2
	Total U.S.	45	55	100
106th (1999)	State delegates	2	0	2
	Total U.S.	45	55	100
107th (2001)	State delegates	2	0	2
	Total U.S.	50	50	100
108th (2003)	State delegates	1	1	2
	Total U.S.	48	51	100
109th (2005)	State delegates	0	2	2
	Total U.S.	44	55	100
110th (2007)	State delegates	0	2	2
	Total U.S.	49	49	100
111th (2009)	State delegates	0	2	2
	Total U.S.	57	41	100
112th (2011)	State delegates	0	2	2
	Total U.S.	51	47	100
113th (2013)	State delegates	0	2	2
	Total U.S.	54	45	100

Note: Figures are for the starts of first sessions; Totals include Democratic (Dem) and Republican (Rep) members as well as vacancies and seats held by independent party members
Source: U.S. Congress, Congressional Directory

Composition of the House of Representatives, 1995–2013

Congress (Year)	State/U.S	Dem	Rep	Total
104th (1995)	State delegates	4	7	11
	Total U.S.	204	230	435
105th (1997)	State delegates	3	8	11
	Total U.S.	207	226	435
106th (1999)	State delegates	3	8	11
	Total U.S.	211	223	435
107th (2001)	State delegates	3	8	11
	Total U.S.	212	221	435
108th (2003)	State delegates	5	8	13
	Total U.S.	205	229	435
109th (2005)	State delegates	6	7	13
	Total U.S.	202	231	435
110th (2007)	State delegates	6	7	13
	Total U.S.	233	198	435
111th (2009)	State delegates	6	7	13
	Total U.S.	256	178	435
112th (2011)	State delegates	5	8	13
	Total U.S.	193	242	435
113th (2013)	State delegates	5	9	14
	Total U.S.	201	234	435

Note: Figures are for the starts of first sessions; Totals include Democratic (Dem) and Republican (Rep) members as well as vacancies and seats held by independent party members
Source: U.S. Congress, Congressional Directory

Composition of State Legislature, 2004–2013

Year	Democrats	Republicans	Total
State Senate			
2004	26	30	56
2005	22	34	56
2006	22	34	56
2007	22	34	56
2008	22	34	56
2009	22	34	56
2010	22	34	56
2011	20	36	56
2012	20	36	56
2013	18	38	56
State House			
2004	107	72	180
2005	80	99	180
2006	80	99	180
2007	74	106	180
2008	72	107	180
2009	73	107	180
2010	74	105	180
2011	63	116	180
2012	63	115	180
2013	60	119	180

Note: Totals may include minor party members and vacancies
Source: The Council of State Governments, State Legislatures

Voter Participation in Presidential Elections, 1980–2012

Year	Voting-eligible State Population	State Voter Turnout Rate	U.S. Voter Turnout Rate
1980	3,791,652	42.1	54.2
1984	4,119,852	43.1	55.2
1988	4,459,739	40.6	52.8
1992	4,766,958	48.5	58.1
1996	5,181,708	44.4	51.7
2000	5,639,668	45.8	54.2
2004	5,878,186	56.2	60.1
2008	6,281,872	62.5	61.6
2012	6,682,600	58.4	58.2

Note: All figures are based on the voting-eligible population which excludes person ineligible to vote such as non-citizens, felons (depending on state law), and mentally-incapacitated persons. U.S. figures include the overseas eligible population (including military personnel).
Source: McDonald, Michael P., United States Election Project, Presidential Voter Turnout Rates, 1980–2012

Governors Since Statehood

John A. Treutlen	1777-1778
John Houstoun	1778-1779
George Walton	1779-1780
Richard Howley	1780-1781
Nathan Brownson	1781-1782
John Martin	1782-1783
Lyman Hall	1783-1784
John Houstoun	1784-1785
Samuel Elbert	1785-1786
Edward Telfair	1786-1787
George Mathews	1787-1788
George Handley	1788-1789
George Walton (O)	1789
Edward Telfair (O)	1789-1793
George Mathews (O)	1793-1796
Jared Irwin (O)	1796-1798
James Jackson (O)	(r) 1798-1801
David Emanuel (O)	1801
Josiah Tattnall (O)	(r) 1801-1802
John Milledge (O)	(r) 1802-1806
Jared Irwin (O)	1806-1809
David B. Mitchell (O)	1809-1813
William Rabun (O)	(d) 1813-1819
Matthew Talbot (O)	1819
John Clark (O)	1819-1823
George M. Troup (O)	1823-1827
John Forsyth (O)	1827-1829
George R. Gilmer (D)	1829-1831
Wilson Lumpkin (D)	1831-1835
William Schley (D)	1835-1837
George R. Gilmer (O)	1837-1839
Charles J. McDonald (D)	1839-1843
George W. Crawford (O)	1843-1847
George W. B. Towns (D)	1847-1851
Howell Cobb (D)	1851-1853
Herschel V. Johnson (D)	1853-1857
Joseph E. Brown (D)	(i) 1857-1865
James Johnson (D)	1865
Charles J. Jenkins (D)	(i) 1865-1868
Thomas H. Ruger	(i) 1868
Rufus B. Bullock (R)	(r) 1868-1871
Benjamin Conley (R)	1871-1872
James M. Smith (R)	1872-1877
Alfred M. Colquitt (D)	1877-1882
Alexander H. Stephens (D)	(d) 1882-1883
James S. Boynton (D)	1883
Henry D. McDaniel (D)	1883-1886
John B. Gordon (D)	1886-1890
William J. Northern (D)	1890-1894
William Y. Atkinson (D)	1894-1898
Allen D. Candler (D)	1898-1902
Joseph M. Terrell (D)	1902-1907
Michael Hoke Smith (D)	1907-1909
Joseph M. Brown (D)	1909-1911
Michael Hoke Smith (D)	(r) 1911
John M. Slaton (D)	1911-1912
Joseph M. Brown (D)	1912-1913
John M. Slaton (D)	1913-1915
Nathaniel E. Harris (D)	1915-1917
Hugh M. Dorsey (D)	1917-1921
Thomas W. Hardwick (D)	1921-1923
Clifford M. Walker (D)	1923-1927
Lamartine G. Hardman (D)	1927-1931
Richard B. Russell Jr. (D)	1931-1933
Eugene Talmadge (D)	1933-1937
Eurith D. Rivers (D)	1937-1941
Eugene Talmadge (D)	1941-1943
Ellis G. Arnall (D)	1943-1947
Herman Talmadge (D)	(i) 1947
Ellis G. Arnall (D)	(r) 1947
Melvin E. Thompson (D)	1947-1948
Herman Talmadge (D)	1948-1955
Samuel Marvin Griffin (D)	1955-1959
Samuel Ernest Vandiver Jr. (D)	1959-1963

Carl E. Sanders (D) 1963-1967
Lester G. Maddox (D) 1967-1971
Jimmy (James E.) Carter (D) 1971-1975
George D. Busbee (D) 1975-1983
Joe Frank Harris (D)........................... 1983-1991
Zell Miller (D) 1991-1999
Roy Barnes (D)................................ 1999-2003
George E. "Sonny" Perdue III (R) 2003-2011
Nathan Deal (R)............................... 2011-2015

Note: (D) Democrat; (R) Republican; (O) Other party; (r) resigned;
(d) died in office; (i) removed from office

Hawaii

Location: South Pacific Ocean

Area and rank: 6,423 square miles (16,637 square kilometers); 10,932 square miles (28,314 square kilometers) including water; forty-seventh largest state in area

Coastline: 750 miles (1,207 kilometers) on the Pacific Ocean

Shoreline: 1,052 miles (1,693 kilometers)

Population and rank: 1,392,313 (2012 estimate); fortieth largest state in population

Capital and largest city: Honolulu (390,738 people in 2010 census)

Became territory: 1900

Entered Union and rank: August 21, 1959; fiftieth state

Present constitution adopted: 1950

Honolulu, Hawaii's capital city, is home to a third of the state's residents, as well as a large, changing tourist population.
(Wikimedia Commons)

Counties: 4 and Kalawao, a nonfunctioning county

State name: Hawaii appears to have taken its name from either Hawaii Loa, the islands' traditional discoverer, or the traditional home of the Polynesians, known as Hawaii or Hawaiki.

State nickname: Aloha State

Motto: *Ua mau ke ea o ka aina i ka pono* (The life of the land is perpetuated in righteousness)

State flag: Eight stripes of red, white, and blue, with the Union Jack in the upper left corner

Highest point: Puu Wekiu—13,796 feet (4,205 meters)

Lowest point: Pacific Ocean—sea level

Highest recorded temperature: 100 degrees Fahrenheit (38 degrees Celsius)—Pahala, 1931

Lowest recorded temperature: 14 degrees Fahrenheit (–10 degrees Celsius)—Haleukala, 1961

State song: "Hawai'i Pono'i"

State tree: Kukui (Candlenut)

State flower: Pua Aloalo (Hibiscus)

State bird: Nene (Hawaiian goose)

National parks: Haleakala; Hawaii

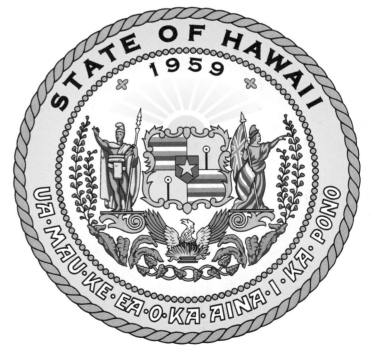

Hawaii History

Hawaii is unique in many ways. It is the only one of the fifty United States that lies outside the northern hemisphere and is, with Alaska, one of two states that is not part of the contiguous forty-eight states that, until 1959, constituted the United States of America. It is the only state that is composed of a group of islands, running from the big island of Hawaii to the islet of Kure at Hawaii's northwest extreme. Ka Lae, or South Cape, on the big island, is the southernmost point in the United States.

Hawaii is also the most multiethnic state in the Union. Some 40 percent of Hawaiian marriages are interracial. In this state of idyllic islands with inviting beaches, one can ascend the big island's Mauna Loa volcano in winter and, at an altitude of almost fourteen thousand feet, go skiiing. Although 80 percent of the state's population lives in bustling, crowded cities, mainly Honolulu, Hawaiians are probably the most relaxed of all Americans.

Early History. As early as the middle of the eighth century, people sailed from the South Seas to Hawaii, presumably intent on colonizing some of its islands. Most of these people were Southeast Asians who had made their arduous way to Tahiti and the Marquesa Islands. In time, sailing in large double-hulled canoes, they continued to Hawaii, carrying with them roots and seeds to plant, as well as animals, mostly pigs and chickens, to raise.

These seamen knew enough about sailing and about the currents of the Pacific Ocean, presumably, to make trips from Tahiti to Hawaii and safely back to Tahiti. Seemingly they did this regularly between 1100 and 1400. An influx of foreigners resumed, however, in the eighteenth century, this time from Europe as well as Asia. The native Hawaiian population, which exceeded 225,000 toward the end of that century, plummeted to about 50,000 one hundred years later, as many natives fell victim to diseases that visitors brought to the islands.

Although Spanish seamen sailed from Manila in the Philippines to the west coast of Mexico in the seventeenth century, they seem to have passed north of the Hawaiian archipelago and were unaware of this chain of volcanic islands. Captain James Cook, in January, 1778, was probably the first European to find the Hawaiian islands, calling them the Sandwich Islands after the earl of Sandwich, from whom he had financial support for his explorations. In February, 1779,

Captain Cook was killed by natives on the big island of Hawaii in an argument over some thefts from his ship. In time, trade with white merchants began to flourish, Hawaii's chief export being sandalwood. As foreign merchants came to Hawaii to trade, the social structure of the islands began to change.

The Kingdom of Hawaii. In 1810, Kamehameha I, a warrior chief, founded the Kingdom of Hawaii after gaining the loyal support of Kauai's chieftain. Although a native Hawaiian gained political control, the islands had already been altered appreciably by the influx of people from the West who came there to do business. Upon the king's death in 1819, Kamehameha II, who

Waimoku Waterfall in Haleakala National Park. Containing some of the world's most spectacular tropical scenery, the Hawaiian islands are frequently used as film locations. (©Paul Keeler/Wikimedia Commons)

welcomed traders from the West, was given the reins of power. Under his jurisdiction, the kapu system, based on the ancient laws and taboos that had long prevailed in the islands, began to give way to Western customs.

The following year, the first Christian missionaries arrived from New England. These Congregationalists were soon followed by Methodists from the United States, Roman Catholics from France, Anglicans from Britain, and Lutherans from Germany. Mormon missionaries arrived considerably later and had such great success in winning Hawaiians to Mormonism that they ultimately established a branch of Brigham Young University and a Mormon temple and information center on Oahu's northeast coast.

The pusillanimous Hawaiians, who were traditionally polytheistic, were easy to convert to Christianity, although they still preserved the myths of many of their deities, such as Pele and Maui. The arrival of the missionaries marked a wave of immigration to the islands and also heralded an era of interracial interchanges and interracial marriage, thereby minimizing many of the ethnic divisions that characterize some societies.

The next wave of immigration came during the 1850's, when large numbers of Chinese immigrants arrived, drawn to Hawaii by its climate, its strategic location, and its commercial possibilities. The Chinese, many of whom initially worked on the sugar and pineapple plantations, soon gravitated to urban centers, mostly to Honolulu, to establish businesses. Soon they had the highest family income of all the ethnic groups in the islands.

During the nineteenth century, significant numbers of immigrants arrived, first from Japan around 1860, then from Scandinavia, Spain, Madeira, the Azores, Puerto Rico, and Germany. The overwhelming influx was from Asia. About half of Hawaii's population is of Asian ancestry. Intermarriage reduced the number of full-blooded Hawaiians from about 225,000 at the end of the eighteenth century to less than 10,000 at the end of the twentieth century.

Land Ownership. The king originally owned most of the state's land, held as crown lands. These properties, broken up in 1848, eventually reverted to the territorial government, which now owns about 40 percent of Hawaii's land. The federal government owns another 10 percent, and private land barons own all but about 3 percent of the remaining land. As a result, many people who own houses or other buildings in Hawaii built them on leased land. Long-term leases offer homeowners some protection, but when the leases come up for renewal, substantial increases are usually imposed.

The Bishop Estate is the largest private landowner in Hawaii, holding about 9 percent of all the land in the state. It uses the large income that these lands produce to fund the Kamehameha School, initially established to educate children of Hawaiian blood and thought to be the most affluent secondary school in the world.

The Annexation of Hawaii. By the middle of the nineteenth century, during the reign of Kamehameha III, the kingdom was increasingly influenced by American missionaries. Kamehameha III in 1843 ceded the islands to Britain, but within a few months, the United States had strongly protested this action, and, shortly thereafter, both Britain and France acknowledged Hawaii's independence. The kingdom was reformed under the Organic Acts of 1845-1847.

The reigns of Kamehameha IV and Kamehameha V witnessed the growth of huge sugar plantations owned mostly by Americans. U.S. financial interests in Hawaii grew before the reign of Queen Liliuokalani, who ascended to the throne in 1891. She showed signs of becoming a more absolute ruler than her predecessors, so in 1893 she was deposed, and a republic, whose president was American Sanford B. Dole, was soon created. Dole and his legislature requested that the United States annex Hawaii, which, after some hesitation, it did in 1898. It officially became a United States territory in 1900.

Moving Toward Statehood. With the advent of military aircraft during World War I, Hawaii began to be viewed by military leaders as a first line of defense for the continental United States. With the bombing of Pearl Harbor on December 7, 1941, Americans soon realized how vulnerable Hawaii was to attack and how vital it was both as a line of defense and as a staging area for a Pacific war.

During the early days of the war, Nisei (second-generation) Japanese in Hawaii were viewed with a combination of distrust and contempt. They were barred from service in the U.S. armed forces, although they were not incarcerated in camps, as their counterparts on the mainland West Coast had been. Eventually they were admitted to the armed forces and, as members of the 100th Infantry Battalion and the 442d Regimental Combat Team, performed heroically in some of the most desperate battles of the conflict, proving their loyalty.

Shortly after the war, mainland labor unions called plantation strikes in Hawaii that paralyzed shipping. The five business cartels that controlled a great deal of the islands' economy were forced to make substantial concessions to plantation workers. Many Japanese Americans rose to political power and did a great deal to reform state government. As the territory attracted large numbers of new inhabitants and gained considerable affluence, agitation for statehood grew. In 1959, statehood was conferred.

The Growth of Tourism. Hawaii's economy during the nineteenth century and the first half of the twentieth came largely from the sale of sandalwood, sugar, and pineapples, although the federal and territorial governments increasingly provided jobs that bolstered the economy. In

1970, seventy thousand of the islands' population of less than one million were employed in state and federal jobs. By 1997 the federal government employed only 20,221 people in Hawaii at an average salary of $39,984.

Although the federal government spends a billion dollars a year in Hawaii, its expenditures are far exceeded by the revenues generated for the state through tourism, which in 1996 amounted to more than fourteen billion dollars. The Hawaiian Chamber of Commerce is among the most efficient and accommodating in the United States. The five islands that are most often visited, Oahu, Maui, Hawaii, Molokai, and Kauai, have excellent tourist facilities and offer breathtaking beaches and waves that attract surfers from around the world. Of the inhabited islands, only Lanai, owned by the Dole Corporation, discourages tourism.

Honolulu is Hawaii's most-visited city. Waikiki Beach, close to the main section of Honolulu, is lined with elegant hotels. Its beaches are filled with tourists and surfers throughout the year. Such natural attractions as the Haleakala Volcano on Maui, the Mauna Loa and Mauna Kea volcanoes on Hawaii, Diamond Head on Oahu, and the Waimea Canyon on Kauai are popular among tourists.

Political Developments and Controversies. At the end of last decade of the twentieth century, Hawaii continued to lean to the political left in its congressional representation and in its legislature, with one significant exception. In 2000, with the election of Linda Lingle, the state elected its first Republican governor. In doing so, the state also elected its first woman governor and its first Jewish governor. However, the state continued it practice of electing a Democrat to the U.S. House of Representatives. In 2002, Representative Patsy Takemoto Mink, a twelve-term Democratic congresswoman, died prior to the general election but was elected nonetheless by a margin of 56-40 percent.

During the same period, the state was involved in two political controversies that drew national attention. During 1999, the state's Office of Hawaiian Affairs decided that it would allow only Hawaiians of indigenous descent to vote for Trustees of the Office. This policy was challenged in the courts as unconstitutionally discriminatory. Early in 2000, the U.S. Supreme Court, in *Rice v. Cayetano*, denied the legitimacy of allowing only native Hawaiians to vote for trustees of the Office of Hawaiian Affairs as unconstitutional racial discrimination.

A second controversy regarded a law proposed by Hawaiian senator Daniel Akaka known as the Native Hawaiian Governmental Reorganization Act of 2005. The proposed law would allow Hawaiians of indigenous descent to group themselves as a sovereign, autonomous nation, just as American Indian tribes are constituted. Opponents dissented from this proposal, which nonetheless passed the U.S. House of Representatives. In June, 2006, however, the bill was effectively killed before being voted upon in the Senate because a procedural vote denied the bill the sixty votes required to cut off debate (called "cloture" in the Senate). The matter was not necessarily settled, however, because the bill could be reintroduced at a later time.

Tragedy and Natural Disaster. Another noteworthy event was the tragic accident that took place in the waters off Hawaii early in 2001. On February 9, during a training exercise, the submarine USS *Greeneville* collided with a Japanese fishing and high school training ship, the *Ehime Maru*. The Japanese vessel sank, drowning nine

A statue of Hawaii's King Kamehameha I stands in front of Hawaii's judiciary building in Honolulu. (Hawaii Visitors & Convention Bureau/ Robert Coello)

Japan's surprise attack on the U.S. Naval Base at Pearl Harbor on December 7, 1941, brought the United States into World War II. (National Archives)

persons, including four high school students. Relations between the United States and Japan were strained for some time afterward.

In spring, 2006, nature played a role in the islands' history, as rains of biblical proportions descended upon the islands, especially Oahu and Kauai. The rains, which began on February 19, lasted for forty days and nights, killing seven persons on Kauai and leaving untold damage.

Hawaiian Sovereignty Issue. Over the period 2000-2013, the "Akaka bill" or Native Hawaiian Government Reorganization Act passed several times in the House of Representatives, but was defeated in the U.S. Senate. Named for Senator Daniel Akaka, who introduced the bill several times, it remained the most controversial aspect of Hawaiian politics through the early years of the 21st century.

Despite support from Senator Daniel Inouye and President Barack Obama, the bill's opponents were able to defeat the controversial measure. Supporters claim that the bill would guarantee protection and rights to native Hawaiians, similar to those extended to native American Indian tribes in Alaska and the lower 48 states. Opponents claim that the bill is flawed, and would be racially discriminatory against people of non-native ancestry who are citizens of the State of Hawaii. Native Hawaiians are found on both sides of the issue. Some believe it does not go far enough, opting for complete sovereignty and independence for Hawaii, based on the grounds that the original U.S. seizure of power and overthrow of the Hawaiian monarchy was illegal. Others argue that the bill is unworkable or agree that it is discriminatory. Local groups in Hawaii, including Asian Americans and others, also find it discriminatory, as do many U.S. Senators and members of Congress.

The bill itself and supporters point to the 1993 "Apology" resolution signed by President Clinton, apologizing for the overthrow of the royal government. The 2005 version of the Akaka bill quoted the 1993 apology: "the Apology Resolution acknowledges that the overthrow of the Kingdom of Hawaii occurred with the active participation of agents and citizens of the United States and further acknowledges that the Native Hawaiian people never directly relinquished to the United States their claims to their inherent sovereignty as a people over their national lands."

R. Baird Shuman
Updated by the Editor

Hawaii Time Line

750–800	First Polynesians begin to colonize the islands.
Jan. 18, 1778	James Cook discovers the Hawaiian archipelago and calls it the Sandwich Islands.
1810	Kamehameha I conquers the islands and establishes the Kingdom of Hawaii.
1819	Kamehameha I dies; Kamehameha II abolishes the kapu system.
1820	First Christian missionaries arrive from the United States.
1835	Ladd and Company establishes first sugar plantation on Kauai.
1840	Kamehameha III drafts first Hawaiian constitution.
1843	Kamehameha III cedes islands to Great Britain.
1845	Britain and France recognize Hawaii's independence.
1846	Redistribution of Hawaiian land begins, most going to the state.
1851	First Chinese laborers arrive to work on sugar plantations.
1868	First Japanese laborers arrive to work on Hawaiian plantations.
Jan. 17, 1893	Queen Liliuokalani deposed; republic is established by American business leaders.
July 4, 1894	New constitution introduced, establishing Republic of Hawaii; Sanford B. Dole is president.
Aug. 12, 1898	United States annexes Hawaii.
1900	Hawaii given territorial status by Organic Act; Sanford Dole named first territorial governor.
1901	First successful pineapple cannery is established.
1903	Territorial legislature asks Congress for statehood.
1907	University of Hawaii is established.
1916	Hawaii Volcanoes National Park and Haleakala National Park are established.
1927	First nonstop flight is made from American mainland.
1929	Regular air service is established among Hawaii's islands.
1935	Pan American Airlines launches first commercial flight across the Pacific with the China Clipper.
Dec. 7, 1941	Japanese attack Pearl Harbor.
1943	100th Infantry Battalion and 442d Regimental Combat Team admit Nisei Japanese.
1946	Plantation strikes launched by International Longshoremen's and Warehousemen's Union (ILWU).
1947	First statehood bill fails in U.S. Congress.
1949	Hawaiian waterfront is paralyzed for 178 days by ILWU strike.
1950	Constitutional Convention drafts constitution for state of Hawaii.
1955	Democrats take control of both legislative houses for the first time in Hawaii's history.
Aug. 21, 1959	Hawaii becomes fiftieth state.
May 23, 1960	Thirty-five-foot tidal wave kills fifty-seven, causes $50 million in damage.
1967	Mauna Kea Observatory opens.
1968	President Lyndon B. Johnson confers with South Vietnam's President Nguyen Van Thieu in Honolulu.
1972	First full Hawaiian medical school is approved.
1973	First Hawaiian school of law is established.
1985	Marijuana crop is estimated at $4 billion, ten times the worth of the sugar crop.
1986	Kilauea volcano erupts, destroying everything in its path.
1994	United States Navy negates 1941 agreement that gave it Kahoolawe Island as a gunnery site.
Feb. 23, 2000	U.S. Supreme Court's *Rice v. Cayetano* ruling denies the legitimacy of allowing only Native Hawaiians to vote for trustees of the Office of Hawaiian Affairs.
Nov. 7, 2000	Linda Lingle elected Hawaii's first Republican, first female, and first Jewish governor.
Feb. 9, 2001	Submarine USS *Greeneville* collides with a Japanese training ship off Hawaii, drowning nine persons, including four high school students.
Nov. 5, 2002	Hawaii re-elects a recently deceased congresswoman, Patsy Takemoto Mink, a twelve-term member of Congress.
Aug. 19, 2004	Hiram Fong, one of Hawaii's first senators and the state's first Chinese American senator, dies at the age of ninety-six.
June 6, 2006	Vote of the U.S. Senate fails to allow a vote on the Native Hawaiian Governmental Act of 2005.
Oct. 15, 2006	Earthquake with magnitude of 6.6 hits island of Hawaii.
Jan. 20, 2009	Barack Obama, who was born in Hawaii, becomes president of the United States
Dec. 6, 2010	Democrat Neil Abercrombie becomes governor.

Notes for Further Study

Published Sources. One of the best brief accounts of Hawaii's ethnic situation is found in William Petersen's *Ethnicity Counts* (1997), which devotes ten pages to the multi-ethnicity of the islands. The book is excellent for its comparisons and contrasts with other places. Wayne S. Wooden's *Return to Paradise: Continuity and Change in Hawaii* (1995) also touches on the islands' ethnicity, as does Mary Ann Lynch's *Hawaii: The Land, the People, the Cities* (1991), which is richly illustrated. Eleanor C. Nordyke's second edition of *The Peopling of Hawai'i* (1989) offers specifics about the origins of the Hawaiian people and about the state's ethnicity. Nancy J. Morris and Love Dean compiled *Hawai'i* (1992), a fine source about the prehistory and languages of the islands. Bonnie Friedman, Paul Wood, and others offer eyewitness views of the islands in *Hawaii* (1998) and provide useful maps of the areas about which the many contributors write.

Two books cover interesting historical aspects of the islands' local communities: *The Colony: The Harrowing True Story of the Exiles of Molokai* by John Tayman (2006) explores the history and survival of nine thousand exiled leprosy sufferers on the island of Molokai between 1866 and 1969. In another fascinating historical account, Noenoe K. Silva, while doing preliminary research into her book, discovered numerous primary documents that detailed native Hawaiians' organization of a substantial petition drive to protest the late nineteenth century plans to allow the United States to annex Hawaii. Her work, *Aloha Betrayed: Native Hawaiian Resistance to American Colonialism* (2004), fills a gap in Hawaiian history and gives voice to a group that was once considered acquiescent to white imperialism.

For young readers interested in knowing more about Hawaii, the second revised edition of Joyce Johnson's *Hawaii* (2001), part of the Hello USA! series, is a short, attractive book filled with entertaining facts about daily life, history, and environmental issues. Also of interest is Penelope J. Neri's *Hawaii* (2003), which covers the state's topography, climate, history, government, and culture for a young-adult audience. For a reader-friendly guide to the state, John H. Chambers's *Hawaii* (2006), part of the On the Road Histories series, begins with the volcanic origins of the islands, covers the exploration of Captain Cook, and continues up through the modern era and the process of statehood.

Web Resources. The most comprehensive Web site on Hawaii is that run by the state government (www.hawaii.gov). The Visitors' Department Web site (www.gohawaii.com) offers extensive, up-to-date information about every aspect of tourism in the state. The Web site of Honolulu's newspaper, *The Star-Bulletin* (www.starbulletin.com), is excellent for covering developments in the state generally and in Honolulu specifically. It includes classified advertisements that can be useful. The individual islands most visited by tourists have their own Web sites: Maui (www.visitmaui.com), Molokai (visitmolokai.com/), Hawaii (www.bigisland.com/ and www.hawaiibigisland.com), Kauai (www.kauaivisitorsbureau.org), and Oahu (www.oahuvacations.com). Those interested in Hawaii's volcanoes or in volcanology should consult the sites for Hawaii Volcanoes National Park (www.nps.gov.havo and www.hawaii.volcanoes.national-park.com/) or the Hawaii Center for Volcanology Web site (www.soest.hawaii.edu/GG/hcv.html). Users interested in the cultural aspects of the islands will find valuable information on the Web site of the Honolulu Academy of Arts (www.honoluluacademy.org) or the Hawaii Art Web site (www.hawaiiart.com). Those wishing to learn more about business in Hawaii should consult Hawaii Business (www.hawaiibusiness.com). For information on the islands' history or genealogy research, consult Hawaiian Roots (www.hawaiian-roots.com/). The Hawaiian Historical Society also has a good Internet site (www.hawaiianhistory.org/).

Mount Kilauea, on the island of Hawaii, has the largest crater of any active volcano in the world. (Hawaii Visitors & Convention Bureau/Warren Bolster)

Counties

County	2012 Population	Pop. Rank	Land Area (sq. miles)	Area Rank
Hawaii	189,191	2	4,028.42	1
Honolulu	976,372	1	600.74	4
Kalawao	90	5	11.99	5
Kauai	68,434	4	619.96	3
Maui	158,226	3	1,161.52	2

Source: U.S. Census Bureau, 2012 Population Estimates

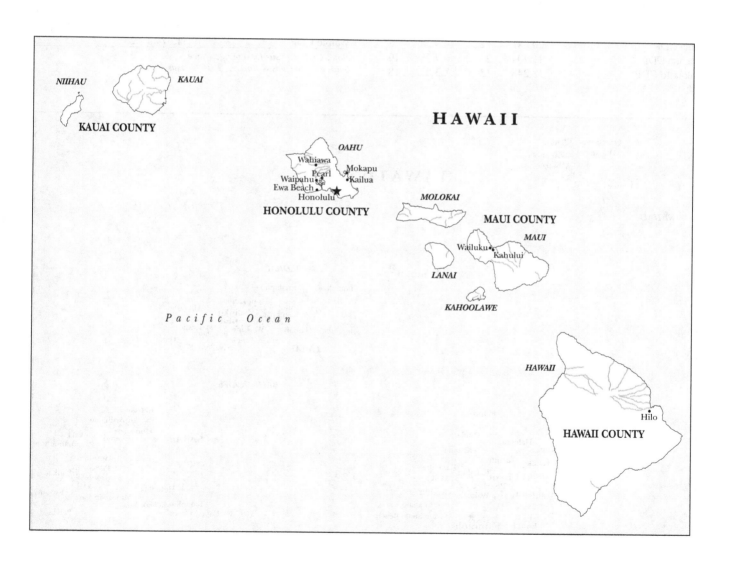

Cities

With 10,000 or more residents

Legal Name	2010 Population	Pop. Rank	Land Area (sq. miles)	Area Rank
East Honolulu CDP	49,914	2	23.01	4
Ewa Beach CDP	14,955	18	1.21	28
Ewa Gentry CDP	22,690	10	2.18	24
Halawa CDP	14,014	20	2.37	23
Hawaiian Paradise Park CDP	11,404	27	15.21	5
Hilo CDP	43,263	4	53.39	2
Kahului CDP	26,337	9	14.45	6
Kailua CDP	11,975	24	35.63	3
Kailua CDP	38,635	5	7.76	11
Kaneohe CDP	34,597	7	6.53	12
Kapaa CDP	10,699	28	10.01	7
Kapolei CDP	15,186	17	4.14	15
Kihei CDP	20,881	12	9.28	8
Lahaina CDP	11,704	25	7.78	10
Makakilo CDP	18,248	13	3.82	18

Legal Name	2010 Population	Pop. Rank	Land Area (sq. miles)	Area Rank
Mililani Mauka CDP	21,039	11	3.98	17
Mililani Town CDP	27,629	8	4.01	16
Nanakuli CDP	12,666	23	2.99	20
Pearl City CDP	47,698	3	9.11	9
Royal Kunia CDP	14,525	19	3.02	19
Schofield Barracks CDP	16,370	15	2.77	22
Urban Honolulu CDP	337,256	1	60.52	1
Wahiawa CDP	17,821	14	2.07	25
Waianae CDP	13,177	22	5.36	13
Wailuku CDP	15,313	16	5.32	14
Waimalu CDP	13,730	21	1.83	26
Waipahu CDP	38,216	6	2.80	21
Waipio CDP	11,674	26	1.25	27

Note: CDP–Census Designated Place
Source: U.S. Census Bureau, 2010 Census

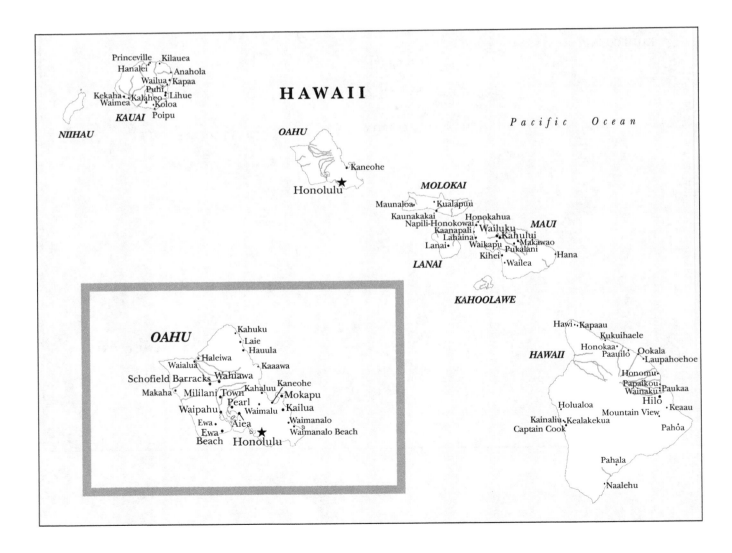

Survey Says...

This section presents current rankings from dozens of public and private sources. It shows how this state ranks in a number of critical categories, including education, job growth, cost of living, teen drivers, energy efficiency, and business environment. Sources include *Forbes, Reuters, U.S. News and World Report, CNN Money, Gallup,* and *Huffington Post.*

- CNN Money compiled a list of "Ten Most Entrepreneurial States" based on the Kauffman Index of Entrepreneurial Activity. Hawaii ranked #8 among the 50 states in 2012 for number of startups per 100,000 adult residents.
  CNN Money, June 20, 2013; money.cnn.com

- Hawaii ranked #28 in a government study measuring real gross domestic product (GDP)—the output of goods and services produced by labor and property located in the United States. The ranking is based on the percentage change compared with 2011 GDP.
  U.S. Department of Commerce, Bureau of Economic Analysis, June 2013; www.bea.gov

- Hawaii ranked #39 in a government study measuring real gross domestic product (GDP)—the output of goods and services produced by labor and property located in the United States. The ranking is based on the dollar value of its GDP.
  U.S. Department of Commerce, Bureau of Economic Analysis, June 2013; www.bea.gov

- Hawaii ranked #29 in the 17th edition of "Quality Counts; State of the States," Education Week's "report card" surveying key education indicators, policy efforts, and educational outcomes.
  Education Week, January 4, 2013 (online) and January 10, 2013 (print); www.edweek.org

- SERI (Science and Engineering Readiness Index) weighs the performance of the states' K-12 schools in preparing students in physics and calculus, the high school subjects considered most important for future scientists and engineers. Hawaii ranked #37.
  Newsletter of the Forum on Education of the American Physical Society, Summer 2011 issue; www.huffingtonpost.com, July 11, 2011; updated October 1, 2012

- MoneyRates.com ranked Hawaii #50 on its list of the best to worst states for making a living. Criteria: average income; inflation; employment prospects; and workers' Workplace Environment assessments according to the Gallup-Healthways Well-Being Index.
  www.money-rates.com, posted April 1, 2013

- *Forbes* analyzed business costs, labor supply, regulatory environment, current economic climate, growth prospects, and quality of life, to compile its "Best States for Business" rankings. Hawaii ranked #48.
  www.forbes.com. posted December 12, 2012

- The 2012 Gallup-Healthways Well-Being Index, surveyed American's opinions on economic confidence, workplace perceptions, community climate, personal choices, and health predictors to assess the "future livability" of each state. Hawaii ranked #8.
  "Utah Poised to Be the Best State to Live In," Gallup Wellbeing, www.gallup.com, August 7, 2012

- On CNBC's list of "America's Top States for Business 2013," Hawaii ranked #50. Criteria: measures of competitiveness developed with input from the National Association of Manufacturers, the Council on Competitiveness, and other business groups weighed with the states' own marketing criteria.
  www.cnbc.com, consulted July 19, 2013

- Kiplinger identified "Ten States with the Biggest Rate of Job Growth in 2013" using data from the U.S. Bureau of Labor Statistics, IHS Global Insights, Moody's Analytics, and state economic data. Hawaii ranked #3.
  www.kiplinger.com, March 2013

- Hawaii ranked #1 on MoneyRates list of "Best-and Worst-States to Retire 2012." Criteria: life expectancy, crime rate, climate, economic conditions, taxes, job opportunities, and cost of living.
  www.money-rates.com, October 22, 2012

- Hawaii ranked #35 on the 2013 Bankrate "Best Places to Retire" list ranking the states and District of Columbia on various criteria relating to health, safety, and cost.
  www.bankrate.com, May 6, 2013

- Reuters ranked Hawaii #1 on its list of the "Ten Most Expensive States in America." Rankings are based on the U.S. Commerce Department's prototype cost-of-living index comparing price levels across the states for a standardized mix of goods and services.
  www.huffingtonpost.com, posted June 12, 2013

- Hawaii ranked #10 on the Social Science Research Council's "American Human Development Report: The Measure of America," assessing the 50 states plus the District of Columbia on health, education, and living-standard criteria.
  The Measure of America 2013-2014, posted June 19, 2013; www.measureofamerica.org

- Hawaii ranked #19 on the Foundation for Child Development's (FCD) Child Well-being Index (CWI). The FCD used the KIDS COUNT report and the National Survey of Children's Health, the only state-level source for several key indicators of child well-being.
  Foundation for Child Development, January 18, 2012; fcd-us.org

- Hawaii ranked #25 overall according to the 2013 KIDS COUNT Data Book, a project of the Annie E. Casey Foundation. Criteria: children's economic well-being, education, health, and family and community indicators.
  KIDS COUNT Data Center's Data Book, released June 20, 2013; http://datacenter.kidscount.org

- Hawaii ranked #34 in the children's economic well-being category by the 2013 KIDS COUNT Data Book, a project of the Annie E. Casey Foundation.
  KIDS COUNT Data Center's Data Book, released June 20, 2013; http://datacenter.kidscount.org

- Hawaii ranked #33 in the children's educational opportunities and attainments category by the 2013 KIDS COUNT Data Book, a project of the Annie E. Casey Foundation.
  KIDS COUNT Data Center's Data Book, released June 20, 2013; http://datacenter.kidscount.org

- Hawaii ranked #18 in the children's health category by the 2013 KIDS COUNT Data Book, a project of the Annie E. Casey Foundation.
  KIDS COUNT Data Center's Data Book, released June 20, 2013; http://datacenter.kidscount.org

- Hawaii ranked #16 in the family and community circumstances that factor into children's well-being category by the 2013 KIDS COUNT Data Book, a project of the Annie E. Casey Foundation.
  KIDS COUNT Data Center's Data Book, released June 20, 2013; http://datacenter.kidscount.org

- Hawaii ranked #1 in the 2012 Gallup-Healthways Well-Being Index. Criteria: emotional health; physical health; healthy behavior; work environment; basic access to food, shelter, health care; and a safe and satisfying place to live.
  2012 State of Well-Being, Gallup-Healthways Well-Being Index, released February 28, 2013; www.well-beingindex.com

- *U.S. News and World Report's* "Best States for Teen Drivers" rankings are based on driving and road safety laws, federal reports on driver's licenses, car accident fatality, and road-quality statistics. Hawaii ranked #26.
  U.S. News and World Report, March 18, 2010; www.usnews.com

- The Yahoo! Sports service Rivals.com ranks the states according to the strength of their high school football programs. Hawaii ranked #39.
  "Ranking the States: Where Is the Best Football Played?," November 18, 2011; highschool.rivals.com

- iVillage ranked the states by hospitable living conditions for women. Criteria: economic success, access to affordable childcare, health care, reproductive rights, female representation in government, and educational attainment. Hawaii ranked #2.
  iVillage, "50 Best to Worst States for Women," March 14, 2012; www.ivillage.com

- The League of American Bicyclists's "Bicycle Friendly States" ranked Hawaii #35. Criteria: legislation and enforcement, policies and programs, infrastructure and funding, education and advocacy, and evaluation and planning.
  "Washington Tops the Bicycle-Friendly State Ranking," May 1, 2013; bicycling.com

- The federal Corporation for National and Community Service ranked the states and the District of Columbia by volunteer rates. Hawaii ranked #49 for community service.
  "Volunteering and Civic Life in America 2012," www.volunteeringinamerica.gov, accessed July 24, 2013

- The Hospital Safety Score ranked states and the District of Columbia on their hospitals' performance scores. Hawaii ranked #15. Criteria: avoiding preventable harm and medical errors, as demonstrated by 26 hospital safety metrics.
  Spring 2013 Hospital Safety Score, May 8, 2013; www.hospitalsafetyscore.org

- GMAC Insurance ranked the states and the District of Columbia by the performance of their drivers on the GMAC Insurance National Drivers Test, comprised of DMV test questions. Hawaii ranked #50.
  "2011 GMAC Insurance National Drivers Test," www.gmacinsurance.com, accessed July 23, 2013

- Hawaii ranked #13 in a "State Integrity Investigation" analysis of laws and practices intended to deter corruption and promote accountability and openness in campaign finance, ethics laws, lobbying regulations and management of state pension funds.
  "What's Your State's Grade?," www.publicintegrity.org, accessed July 23, 2013

- Hawaii ranked #51 among the states and the District of Columbia in total rail miles, as tracked by the Association of American Railroads.
  "U.S. Freight Railroad Industry Snapshot: Railroads and States: Total Rail Miles by State: 2011"; www.aar.org, accessed July 23, 2013

- According to statistics compiled by the Beer Institute, Hawaii ranked #19 among the states and the District of Columbia in per capita beer consumption of persons 21 years or older.
  "Shipments of Malt Beverages and Per Capita Consumption by State 2012;" www.beerinstitute.org

- According to Concordia University's "Public Education Costs per Pupil by State Rankings," based on statistics gathered by the U.S. Census Bureau, which includes the District of Columbia, Hawaii ranked #15.
  Concordia University Online; education.cu-portland.edu, accessed July 24, 2013

- Hawaii ranked #13 among the states and the District of Columbia in population density based on U.S. Census Bureau data for resident population and total land area. "List of U.S. States by Population Density."
  www.wikipedia.org, accessed July 24, 2013

- In "America's Health Rankings, 2012 Edition," by the United Health Foundation, Hawaii ranked #2. Criteria included: rate of high school graduation; violent crime rate; incidence of infectious disease; childhood immunizations; prevalence of diabetes; per capita public-health funding; percentage of uninsured population; rate of children in poverty; and availability of primary-care physicians.
  United Health Foundation; www.americashealthrankings.org, accessed July 24, 2013

- The TechNet 2012 "State Broadband Index" ranked Hawaii #48 on the following criteria: broadband adoption; network quality; and economic structure. Improved broadband use is hoped to promote economic development, build strong communities, improve delivery of government services and upgrade educational systems.
  TechNet; www.technet.org, accessed July 24, 2013

- Hawaii was ranked #18 among the states and District of Columbia on the American Council for an Energy-Efficient Economy's "State Energy Efficiency Scorecard" for 2012.
  American Council for an Energy-Efficient Economy; aceee.org/sector/state-policy/scorecard, accessed July 24, 2013

Statistical Tables

DEMOGRAPHICS
Resident State and National Population, 1950-2012
Projected State and National Population, 2000-2030
Population by Age, 2012
Population by Race, 2012
Population by Hispanic Origin and Race, 2012

VITAL STATISTICS
Death Rates by Leading Causes, 2010
Death Rates by Selected Causes, 2010
Abortion Rates, 2009
Infant Mortality Rates, 1995-2009
Marriage and Divorce Rates, 2000-2011

ECONOMY
Nominal Gross Domestic Product by Industry, 2012
Real Gross Domestic Product, 2000-2012
Personal Income Per Capita, 1930-2012
Non-Farm Employment by Sector, 2012
Foreign Exports, 2000-2012
Energy Consumption, 2011

LAND AND WATER
Surface Area and Federally-Owned Land, 2007
Land Cover/Use of Non-Federal Rural Land, 2007
Farms and Crop Acreage, 2012

HEALTH AND MEDICAL CARE
Medical Professionals, 2012
Health Insurance Coverage, 2011
HIV, STD, and Tuberculosis Cases and Rates, 2011
Cigarette Smoking, 2011

HOUSING
Home Ownership Rates, 1995-2012
Home Sales, 2000-2010
Value of Owner-Occupied Homes, 2011

EDUCATION
School Enrollment, 2011
Educational Attainment, 2011
Public College Finances, FY 2012

TRANSPORTATION AND TRAVEL
Motor Vehicle Registrations and Drivers Licenses, 2011
Domestic Travel Expenditures, 2009
Retail Gasoline Prices, 2013
Public Road Length, 2011

CRIME AND LAW ENFORCEMENT
Full-Time Law Enforcement Officers, 2011
Prison Population, 2000-2012
Crime Rate, 2011

GOVERNMENT AND FINANCE
Local Governments by Type, 2012
State Government Revenue, 2011
State Government Expenditures, 2011
State Government General Expenditures by Function, 2011
State Government Finances, Cash and Debt, 2011

POLITICS
Composition of the Senate, 1995-2013
Composition of the House of Representatives, 1995-2013
Composition of State Legislature, 2004-2013
Voter Participation in Presidential Elections, 1980-2012
Governors Since Statehood

DEMOGRAPHICS

Resident State and National Population, 1950–2012

Year	State Population	U.S. Population	State Share
1950	500,000	151,326,000	0.33%
1960	633,000	179,323,000	0.35%
1970	769,913	203,302,031	0.38%
1980	964,691	226,545,805	0.43%
1990	1,108,229	248,709,873	0.45%
2000	1,211,497	281,424,600	0.43%
2010	1,360,301	308,745,538	0.44%
2012	1,392,313	313,914,040	0.44%

Note: 1950/1960 population figures are rounded to the nearest thousand.
Source: U.S. Census Bureau, Decennial Census 1950–2010; U.S. Census Bureau, 2012 Population Estimates

Projected State and National Population, 2000–2030

Year	State Population	U.S. Population	State Share
2000	1,211,537	281,421,906	0.43%
2005	1,276,552	295,507,134	0.43%
2010	1,340,674	308,935,581	0.43%
2015	1,385,952	322,365,787	0.43%
2020	1,412,373	335,804,546	0.42%
2025	1,438,720	349,439,199	0.41%
2030	1,466,046	363,584,435	0.40%
State population growth, 2000–2030			254,509
State percentage growth, 2000–2030			21.0%

Source: U.S. Census Bureau, Population Division, Interim State Population Projections, 2005

Population by Age, 2012

Age Group	State Population	Percent of Total Population	
		State	U.S.
Under 5 years	89,149	6.4%	6.4%
5 to 14 years	165,092	11.9%	13.1%
15 to 24 years	185,640	13.3%	14.0%
25 to 34 years	199,305	14.3%	13.5%
35 to 44 years	174,744	12.6%	12.9%
45 to 54 years	186,382	13.4%	14.1%
55 to 64 years	181,200	13.0%	12.3%
65 to 74 years	112,147	8.1%	7.6%
75 to 84 years	64,031	4.6%	4.2%
85 years and older	34,623	2.5%	1.9%
Under 18 years	303,011	21.8%	23.5%
65 years and older	210,801	15.1%	13.7%
Median age (years)	–	38.3	37.4

Source: U.S. Census Bureau, Annual Estimates of the Resident Population for Selected Age Groups by Sex for the United States, States, Counties, and Puerto Rico Commonwealth and Municipios: April 1, 2010 to July 1, 2012

Population by Race, 2012

Race	State Population	Percent of Total Population	
		State	U.S.
All residents	1,392,313	100.00%	100.00%
White	363,544	26.11%	77.89%
African American	29,905	2.15%	13.13%
Native American	5,507	0.40%	1.23%
Asian	532,599	38.25%	5.14%
Native Hawaiian	140,112	10.06%	0.23%
Two or more races	320,646	23.03%	2.39%

Source: U.S. Census Bureau, Population Division, Annual Estimates of the Resident Population by Sex, Race and Hispanic Origin for the United States, States, and Counties: April 1, 2010 to July 1, 2012

Population by Hispanic Origin and Race, 2012

Hispanic Origin/Race	State Population	Percent of Total Population	
		State	U.S.
All residents	1,392,313	100.00%	100.00%
All Hispanic residents	131,744	9.46%	16.89%
Hispanic			
White	45,426	3.26%	14.91%
African American	3,061	0.22%	0.79%
Native American	2,328	0.17%	0.49%
Asian	15,940	1.14%	0.17%
Native Hawaiian	9,288	0.67%	0.06%
Two or more races	55,701	4.00%	0.48%
Not Hispanic			
White	318,118	22.85%	62.98%
African American	26,844	1.93%	12.34%
Native American	3,179	0.23%	0.74%
Asian	516,659	37.11%	4.98%
Native Hawaiian	130,824	9.40%	0.17%
Two or more races	264,945	19.03%	1.91%

Source: U.S. Census Bureau, Population Division, Annual Estimates of the Resident Population by Sex, Race and Hispanic Origin for the United States, States, and Counties: April 1, 2010 to July 1, 2012

VITAL STATISTICS

Death Rates by Leading Causes, 2010

Cause	State	U.S.
Malignant neoplasms	151.6	186.2
Ischaemic heart diseases	76.3	122.9
Other forms of heart disease	60.7	53.4
Chronic lower respiratory diseases	19.2	44.7
Cerebrovascular diseases	38.6	41.9
Organic, incl. symptomatic, mental disorders	36.8	35.7
Other degenerative diseases of the nervous sys.	12.4	28.4
Other external causes of accidental injury	20.5	26.5
Diabetes mellitus	17.9	22.4
Hypertensive diseases	9.8	20.4
All causes	629.9	799.5

Note: Figures are age-adjusted death rates per 100,000 population
Source: CDC/NCHS, Underlying Cause of Death 1999–2010 on CDC WONDER Online Database

Death Rates by Selected Causes, 2010

Cause	State	U.S.
Assault	1.7	5.2
Diseases of the liver	10.4	13.9
Human immunodeficiency virus (HIV) disease	0.0	2.7
Influenza and pneumonia	18.2	16.2
Intentional self-harm	15.1	12.4
Malnutrition	–	0.9
Obesity and other hyperalimentation	0.0	1.8
Renal failure	12.1	14.4
Transport accidents	9.3	12.1
Viral hepatitis	2.8	2.4

Note: Figures are age-adjusted death rates per 100,000 population; A dash indicates that data was not available or was suppressed
Source: CDC/NCHS, Underlying Cause of Death 1999–2010 on CDC WONDER Online Database

Abortion Rates, 2009

Category	2009
By state of residence	
Total abortions	3,342
Abortion rate[1]	13.4%
Abortion ratio[2]	177
By state of occurrence	
Total abortions	3,342
Abortion rate[1]	13.4%
Abortion ratio[2]	177
Abortions obtained by out-of-state residents	0.4%
U.S. abortion rate[1]	15.1%
U.S. abortion ratio[2]	227

Note: (1) Number of abortions per 1,000 women aged 15–44 years; (2) Number of abortions per 1,000 live births; A dash indicates that data was not available
Source: CDC/NCHS, Morbidity and Mortality Weekly Report, November 23, 2012 (Abortion Surveillance, United States, 2009)

Infant Mortality Rates, 1995–2009

Category	1995	2000	2005	2009
All state residents	5.65	8.09	6.58	5.93
All U.S. residents	7.57	6.89	6.86	6.39
All state white residents	4.83	7.71	4.11	4.23
All U.S. white residents	6.30	5.71	5.73	5.33
All state black residents	–	–	–	–
All U.S. black residents	14.58	13.48	13.26	12.12

Note: Figures represent deaths per 1,000 live births of resident infants under one year old, exclusive of fetal deaths; A dash indicates that data was not available or was suppressed.
Source: Centers of Disease Control and Prevention, Division of Vital Statistics, Linked Birth/Infant Death Records on CDC Wonder Online

Marriage and Divorce Rates, 2000–2011

Year	Marriage Rate		Divorce Rate	
	State	U.S.	State	U.S.
2000	20.6	8.2	3.9	4.0
2002	20.8	8.0	3.7	3.9
2004	22.6	7.8	0.0	3.7
2006	21.9	7.5	0.0	3.7
2008	19.1	7.1	0.0	3.5
2010	17.6	6.8	0.0	3.6
2011	17.6	6.8	0.0	3.6

Note: Rates are based on provisional counts of marriages/divorces by state of occurrence and are per 1,000 total population residing in area
Source: CDC/NCHS, National Vital Statistics System

ECONOMY

Nominal Gross Domestic Product by Industry, 2012
In millions of current dollars

Industry	State GDP
Accommodation and food services	5,876
Administrative and waste management services	2,232
Agriculture, forestry, fishing, and hunting	406
Arts, entertainment, and recreation	666
Construction	3,925
Educational services	803
Finance and insurance	2,784
Health care and social assistance	4,506
Information	1,598
Management of companies and enterprises	813
Manufacturing	1,274
Mining	17
Other services, except government	1,766
Professional, scientific, and technical services	3,282
Real estate and rental and leasing	12,797
Retail trade	4,789
Transportation and warehousing	2,936
Utilities	2,248
Wholesale trade	2,105

Source: U.S. Department of Commerce, Bureau of Economic Analysis, Survey of Current Business

Real Gross Domestic Product, 2000–2012
In millions of chained 2005 dollars

Year	State GDP	U.S. GDP	State Share
2000	48,819	11,225,406	0.43%
2005	56,901	12,539,116	0.45%
2010	59,673	12,897,088	0.46%
2012	61,877	13,430,576	0.46%

Source: U.S. Department of Commerce, Bureau of Economic Analysis, Survey of Current Business

Personal Income Per Capita, 1930–2012

Year	State	U.S.
1930	–	$618
1940	–	$593
1950	$1,430	$1,503
1960	$2,326	$2,268
1970	$5,077	$4,084
1980	$11,394	$10,091
1990	$21,818	$19,354
2000	$29,024	$30,319
2010	$40,952	$39,791
2012	$44,024	$42,693

Source: U.S. Department of Commerce, Bureau of Economic Analysis, Regional Economic Accounts

Non-Farm Employment by Sector, 2012
In thousands

Sector	Employment
Construction	29.5
Education and health services	76.7
Financial activities	27.0
Government	126.3
Information	8.3
Leisure and hospitality	107.0
Mining and logging (combined with construction)	0.0
Manufacturing	13.3
Other services	26.4
Professional and business services	76.4
Trade, transportation, and utilities	114.6
All sectors	605.3

Source: U.S. Bureau of Labor Statistics, State and Area Employment

Foreign Exports, 2000–2012
In millions of dollars

Year	State Exports	U.S. Exports	State Share
2000	386	712,054	0.05%
2002	514	649,940	0.08%
2004	411	768,554	0.05%
2006	692	973,994	0.07%
2008	959	1,222,545	0.08%
2010	684	1,208,080	0.06%
2012	731	1,478,268	0.05%

Note: U.S. figures exclude data from Puerto Rico, U.S. Virgin Islands, and unallocated exports
Source: U.S. Department of Commerce, International Trade Admin., Office of Trade and Industry Information, Manufacturing and Services

Energy Consumption, 2011
In trillions of BTUs, except as noted

Total energy consumption	
Total state energy consumption	286.0
Total U.S. energy consumption	97,387.3
State share of U.S. total	0.29%
Per capita consumption (in millions of BTUs)	
Total state per capita consumption	207.5
Total U.S. per capita consumption	312.6
End-use sectors	
Residential	35.1
Commercial	40.7
Industrial	64.3
Transportation	146.0
Sources of energy	
Petroleum	246.2
Natural gas	0.2
Coal	16.1
Renewable energy	23.5
Nuclear electric power	0.0

Source: U.S. Energy Information Administration, State Energy Data 2011: Consumption

LAND AND WATER

Surface Area and Federally-Owned Land, 2007
In thousands of acres

Category	State	U.S.	State Share
Total surface area	4,158.4	1,937,664.2	0.21%
Total land area	4,105.9	1,886,846.9	0.22%
Non-federal land	3,744.7	1,484,910.0	0.25%
Developed	217.6	111,251.2	0.20%
Rural	3,527.1	1,373,658.8	0.26%
Federal land	361.2	401,936.9	0.09%
Water area	52.5	50,817.3	0.10%

Source: U.S. Department of Agriculture, Natural Resources Conservation Service, 2007 National Resources Inventory

Land Cover/Use of Non-Federal Rural Land, 2007
In thousands of acres

Category	State	U.S.	State Share
Total rural land	3,527.1	1,373,658.8	0.26%
Cropland	126.9	357,023.5	0.04%
CRP[1] land	0.0	32,850.2	0.00%
Pastureland	60.3	118,615.7	0.05%
Rangeland	1,082.4	409,119.4	0.26%
Forest land	1,627.4	406,410.4	0.40%
Other rural land	630.1	49,639.6	1.27%

Note: (1) Conservation Reserve Program was created to assist private landowners in converting highly erodible cropland to vegetative cover.
Source: U.S. Department of Agriculture, Natural Resources Conservation Service, 2007 National Resources Inventory

Farms and Crop Acreage, 2012

Category	State	U.S.	State Share
Farms (in thousands)	7.5	2,170.0	0.35%
Acres (in millions)	1.1	914.0	0.12%
Acres per farm	148.0	421.2	–

Source: U.S. Department of Agriculture, National Agricultural Statistical Service, Quick Stats, 2012 Survey Data

HEALTH AND MEDICAL CARE

Medical Professionals, 2012

Profession	State Number	U.S. Number	State Share	State Rate[1]	U.S. Rate[1]
Physicians[2]	4,061	894,637	0.45%	294.7	287.1
Dentists	1,131	193,587	0.58%	82.1	62.1
Podiatrists	38	17,469	0.22%	2.8	5.6
Optometrists	261	45,638	0.57%	18.9	14.6
Chiropractors	272	77,494	0.35%	19.7	24.9

Note: (1) Rates are per 100,000 population; (2) Includes total, active Doctors of Osteopathic Medicine and Doctors of Medicine in 2011.
Source: U.S. Department of Health and Human Services, Bureau of Health Professions, Area Health Resource File, 2012-2013

Health Insurance Coverage, 2011

Category	State	U.S.
Total persons covered	1,235,000	260,214,000
Total persons not covered	105,000	48,613,000
Percent not covered	7.8%	15.7%
Children under age 18 covered	297,000	67,143,000
Children under age 18 not covered	13,000	6,965,000
Percent of children not covered	4.2%	9.4%

Source: U.S. Census Bureau, Current Population Survey, 2012 Annual Social and Economic Supplement

HIV, STD, and Tuberculosis Cases and Rates, 2011

Disease	State Cases	State Rate[1]	U.S. Rate[1]
Chlamydia	6,001	441.2	457.6
Gonorrhea	685	50.4	104.2
HIV diagnosis	78	6.8	15.8
HIV, stage 3 (AIDS)	44	3.8	10.3
Syphilis, early latent	5	0.4	4.3
Syphilis, primary/secondary	14	1.0	4.5
Tuberculosis	123	8.9	3.4

Note: (1) Rates are per 100,000 population
Source: Centers for Disease Control and Prevention

Cigarette Smoking, 2011

Category	State	U.S.
Adults who are current smokers	16.8%	21.2%
Adults who smoke everyday	12.2%	15.4%
Adults who smoke some days	4.7%	5.7%
Adults who are former smokers	25.9%	25.1%
Adults who never smoked	57.3%	52.9%

Source: Centers for Disease Control and Prevention, Behaviorial Risk Factor Surveillance System, Tobacco Use, 2011

HOUSING

Home Ownership Rates, 1995–2012

Area	1995	2000	2005	2010	2012
State	50.2%	55.2%	59.8%	56.1%	57.2%
U.S.	64.7%	67.4%	68.9%	66.9%	65.4%

Source: U.S. Census Bureau, Housing Vacancies and Homeownership, Annual Statistics

Home Sales, 2000–2010
In thousands of units

Year	State Sales	U.S. Sales	State Share
2000	22.1	5,174	0.43%
2002	28.1	5,632	0.50%
2004	35.5	6,778	0.52%
2006	31.5	6,478	0.49%
2008	20.0	4,913	0.41%
2010	20.9	4,908	0.43%

Note: Units include single-family homes, condos and co-ops
Source: National Association of Realtors, Real Estate Outlook, Market Trends & Insights

Value of Owner-Occupied Homes, 2011

Value	Total Units in State	Percent of Total, State	Percent of Total, U.S.
Less than $50,000	2,818	1.1%	8.8%
$50,000 to $99,000	5,140	2.0%	16.0%
$100,000 to $149,000	6,632	2.6%	16.5%
$150,000 to $199,000	8,734	3.4%	15.4%
$200,000 to $299,000	29,500	11.6%	18.2%
$300,000 to $499,000	79,071	31.0%	15.2%
$500,000 to $999,000	102,778	40.4%	7.9%
$1,000,000 or more	20,027	7.9%	2.0%
Median value	–	$487,400	$173,600

Source: U.S. Census Bureau, 2011 American Community Survey 1-Year Estimates

EDUCATION

School Enrollment, 2011

Educational Level	Students Enrolled in State	Percent of Total, State	Percent of Total, U.S.
All levels	336,724	100.0%	100.0%
Nursery school, preschool	19,353	5.7%	6.0%
Kindergarten	16,286	4.8%	5.1%
Elementary (grades 1–8)	130,416	38.7%	39.5%
Secondary (grades 9–12)	69,938	20.8%	20.7%
College or graduate school	100,731	29.9%	28.7%

Note: Figures cover the population 3 years and over enrolled in school
Source: U.S. Census Bureau, 2011 American Community Survey 1-Year Estimates

Educational Attainment, 2011

Highest Level of Education	State	U.S.
High school diploma	90.6%	85.9%
Bachelor's degree	29.1%	28.5%
Graduate/Professional degree	9.9%	10.6%

Note: Figures cover the population 25 years and over
Source: U.S. Census Bureau, 2011 American Community Survey 1-Year Estimates

Public College Finances, FY 2012

Category	State	U.S.
Full-time equivalent enrollment (FTE)[1]	40,612	11,548,974
Educational appropriations per FTE[2]	$6,898	$5,906
Net tuition revenue per FTE[3]	$3,548	$5,189
Total educational revenue per FTE[4]	$10,446	$11,043

(1) Full-time equivalent enrollment equates student credit hours to full time, academic year students, but excludes medical students; (2) Educational appropriations measure state and local support available for public higher education operating expenses including ARRA funds and excludes appropriations for independent institutions, financial aid for students attending independent institutions, research, hospitals, and medical education; (3) Net tuition revenue is calculated by taking the gross amount of tuition and fees, less state and institutional financial aid, tuition waivers or discounts, and medical student tuition and fees. Net tuition revenue used for capital debt service is included in the net tuition revenue figures; (4) Total educational revenue is the sum of educational appropriations and net tuition excluding net tuition revenue used for capital debt service.
Source: State Higher Education Executive Officers, State Higher Education Finance FY 2012

TRANSPORTATION AND TRAVEL

Motor Vehicle Registrations and Drivers Licenses, 2011

Vehicle Type	State	U.S.	State Share
Automobiles[1]	534,815	125,656,528	0.43%
Buses	2,330	666,064	0.35%
Trucks	580,398	118,455,587	0.49%
Motorcycles	30,498	8,437,502	0.36%
Drivers licenses	911,660	211,874,649	0.43%

Note: Motor vehicle registrations include private, commercial, and publicly-owned vehicles; (1) Includes taxicabs
Source: U.S. Department of Transportation, Federal Highway Administration

Domestic Travel Expenditures, 2009
In millions of dollars

Category	State	U.S.	State Share
Travel expenditures	$8,631	$610,200	1.41%

Note: Figures represent U.S. spending on domestic overnight trips and day trips of 50 miles or more, one way, away from home. Excludes spending by foreign visitors.
Source: U.S. Travel Association, Impact of Travel on State Economies, 2009

Retail Gasoline Prices, 2013

Gasoline Grade	State Average	U.S. Average
Regular	$4.36	$3.65
Mid	$4.45	$3.81
Premium	$4.54	$3.98
Diesel	$4.91	$3.88
Excise tax[1]	69.0 cents	49.4 cents

Note: Gasoline prices as of 7/26/2013; (1) Includes state and federal excise taxes and other state taxes as of July 1, 2013
Source: American Automobile Association, Daily Fuel Guage Report; American Petroleum Institute, State Motor Fuel Taxes, 2013

Public Road Length, 2011

Type	State Mileage	U.S. Mileage	State Share
Interstate highways	55	46,960	0.12%
Other highways	34	15,719	0.22%
Principal arterial	340	156,262	0.22%
Minor arterial	416	242,942	0.17%
Major collector	706	534,592	0.13%
Minor collector	122	266,357	0.05%
Local	2,732	2,814,925	0.10%
Urban	2,355	1,095,373	0.21%
Rural	2,050	2,982,383	0.07%
Total	4,405	4,077,756	0.11%

Note: Combined urban and rural road mileage equals the total of the other road types
Source: U.S. Department of Transportation, Federal Highway Administration, Public Road Length, 2011

CRIME AND LAW ENFORCEMENT

Full-Time Law Enforcement Officers, 2011

Gender	State Number	State Rate[1]	U.S. Rate[1]
Male officers	2,666	193.9	210.3
Female officers	294	21.4	28.1
Total officers	2,960	215.3	238.3

Note: (1) Rates are per 100,000 population
Source: Federal Bureau of Investigation, Uniform Crime Reports, Crime in the United States 2011

Prison Population, 2000–2012

Year	State Population	U.S. Population	State Share
2000	5,053	1,391,261	0.36%
2005	6,146	1,527,929	0.40%
2010	5,912	1,613,803	0.37%
2011	6,037	1,598,783	0.38%
2012	5,831	1,571,013	0.37%

Note: Figures include prisoners under the jurisdiction of state or federal correctional authorities.
Source: U.S. Department of Justice, Bureau of Justice Statistics, Prisoners in 2006, 2011, 2012 (Advance Counts)

Crime Rate, 2011

Incidents per 100,000 residents

Category	State	U.S.
Violent crimes	287.2	386.3
Murder	1.2	4.7
Forcible rape	31.6	26.8
Robbery	75.8	113.7
Aggravated assault	178.6	241.1
Property crimes	3,337.8	2,908.7
Burglary	728.0	702.2
Larceny/theft	2,305.6	1,976.9
Motor vehicle theft	304.3	229.6
All crimes	3,625.0	3,295.0

Source: Federal Bureau of Investigation, Uniform Crime Reports, Crime in the United States 2011

GOVERNMENT AND FINANCE

Local Governments by Type, 2012

Government Type	State	U.S.	State Share
All local governments	21	89,004	0.02%
County	3	3,031	0.10%
Municipality	1	19,522	0.01%
Town/Township	0	16,364	0.00%
Special District	17	37,203	0.05%
Ind. School District	0	12,884	0.00%

Source: U.S. Census Bureau, 2012 Census of Governments: Organization Component Preliminary Estimates

State Government Revenue, 2011

In thousands of dollars, except for per capita figures

Total revenue	$12,931,811
Total revenue per capita, State	$9,384
Total revenue per capita, U.S.	$7,271
General revenue	$10,203,676
Intergovernmental revenue	$2,918,445
Taxes	$4,857,729
General sales	$2,495,807
Selective sales	$839,755
License taxes	$151,525
Individual income taxes	$1,247,291
Corporate income taxes	$67,859
Other taxes	$55,492
Current charges	$1,599,757
Miscellaneous general revenue	$827,745
Utility revenue	$0
Liquor store revenue	$0
Insurance trust revenue[1]	$2,728,135

Note: (1) Within insurance trust revenue, net earnings of state retirement systems is a calculated statistic, and thus can be positive or negative. Net earnings is the sum of earnings on investments plus gains on investments minus losses on investments.
Source: U.S. Census Bureau, 2011 Annual Survey of State Government Finances

State Government Expenditures, 2011

In thousands of dollars, except for per capita figures

Total expenditure	$11,475,771
Total expenditure per capita, State	$8,327
Total expenditure per capita, U.S.	$6,427
Intergovernmental expenditure	$207,988
Direct expenditure	$11,267,783
Current operation	$8,411,885
Capital outlay	$862,111
Insurance benefits and repayments	$1,507,373
Assistance and subsidies	$125,206
Interest on debt	$361,208
Utility expenditure	$5,151
Liquor store expenditure	$0
Insurance trust expenditure	$1,507,373

Source: U.S. Census Bureau, 2011 Annual Survey of State Government Finances

State Government General Expenditures by Function, 2011

In thousands of dollars

Education	$3,345,134
Public welfare	$2,086,752
Hospitals	$666,713
Health	$620,003
Highways	$357,387
Police protection	$31,656
Correction	$191,030
Natural resources	$97,119
Parks and recreation	$110,006
Governmental administration	$417,053
Interest on general debt	$361,208
Other and unallocable	$1,679,186

Source: U.S. Census Bureau, 2011 Annual Survey of State Government Finances

State Government Finances, Cash and Debt, 2011

In thousands of dollars, except for per capita figures

Debt at end of fiscal year	
State, total	$7,912,833
State, per capita	$5,742
U.S., per capita	$3,635
Cash and security holdings	
State, total	$15,603,693
State, per capita	$11,322
U.S., per capita	$11,759

Source: U.S. Census Bureau, 2011 Annual Survey of State Government Finances

POLITICS

Composition of the Senate, 1995–2013

Congress (Year)	State/U.S	Dem	Rep	Total
104th (1995)	State delegates	2	0	2
	Total U.S.	48	52	100
105th (1997)	State delegates	2	0	2
	Total U.S.	45	55	100
106th (1999)	State delegates	2	0	2
	Total U.S.	45	55	100
107th (2001)	State delegates	2	0	2
	Total U.S.	50	50	100
108th (2003)	State delegates	2	0	2
	Total U.S.	48	51	100
109th (2005)	State delegates	2	0	2
	Total U.S.	44	55	100
110th (2007)	State delegates	2	0	2
	Total U.S.	49	49	100
111th (2009)	State delegates	2	0	2
	Total U.S.	57	41	100
112th (2011)	State delegates	2	0	2
	Total U.S.	51	47	100
113th (2013)	State delegates	2	0	2
	Total U.S.	54	45	100

Note: Figures are for the starts of first sessions; Totals include Democratic (Dem) and Republican (Rep) members as well as vacancies and seats held by independent party members
Source: U.S. Congress, Congressional Directory

Composition of the House of Representatives, 1995–2013

Congress (Year)	State/U.S	Dem	Rep	Total
104th (1995)	State delegates	2	0	2
	Total U.S.	204	230	435
105th (1997)	State delegates	2	0	2
	Total U.S.	207	226	435
106th (1999)	State delegates	2	0	2
	Total U.S.	211	223	435
107th (2001)	State delegates	2	0	2
	Total U.S.	212	221	435
108th (2003)	State delegates	2	0	2
	Total U.S.	205	229	435
109th (2005)	State delegates	2	0	2
	Total U.S.	202	231	435
110th (2007)	State delegates	2	0	2
	Total U.S.	233	198	435
111th (2009)	State delegates	1	1	2
	Total U.S.	256	178	435
112th (2011)	State delegates	2	0	2
	Total U.S.	193	242	435
113th (2013)	State delegates	2	0	2
	Total U.S.	201	234	435

Note: Figures are for the starts of first sessions; Totals include Democratic (Dem) and Republican (Rep) members as well as vacancies and seats held by independent party members
Source: U.S. Congress, Congressional Directory

Composition of State Legislature, 2004–2013

Year	Democrats	Republicans	Total
State Senate			
2004	20	5	25
2005	20	5	25
2006	20	5	25
2007	20	5	25
2008	21	4	25
2009	23	2	25
2010	23	2	25
2011	24	1	25
2012	24	1	25
2013	24	1	25
State House			
2004	36	15	51
2005	41	10	51
2006	41	10	51
2007	43	8	51
2008	44	7	51
2009	45	6	51
2010	45	6	51
2011	43	8	51
2012	42	8	51
2013	44	7	51

Note: Totals may include minor party members and vacancies
Source: The Council of State Governments, State Legislatures

Voter Participation in Presidential Elections, 1980–2012

Year	Voting-eligible State Population	State Voter Turnout Rate	U.S. Voter Turnout Rate
1980	646,583	46.9	54.2
1984	694,187	48.4	55.2
1988	739,890	47.9	52.8
1992	795,148	46.9	58.1
1996	820,055	43.9	51.7
2000	832,642	44.2	54.2
2004	889,540	48.2	60.1
2008	930,067	48.8	61.6
2012	982,943	44.2	58.2

Note: All figures are based on the voting-eligible population which excludes person ineligible to vote such as non-citizens, felons (depending on state law), and mentally-incapacitated persons. U.S. figures include the overseas eligible population (including military personnel).
Source: McDonald, Michael P., United States Election Project, Presidential Voter Turnout Rates, 1980–2012

Governors Since Statehood

William F. Quinn (R) 1959-1962
John A. Burns (D) 1962-1974
George R. Ariyoshi (D) 1974-1986
John Waihee (D). 1986-1998
Benjamin J. Cayetano (D) 1998-2002
Linda Lingle (R). 2002-2010
Neil Abercrombie (D) 2010-2014

Note: (D) Democrat; (R) Republican; (O) Other party; (r) resigned;
(d) died in office; (i) removed from office

Idaho

Location: Northwest

Area and rank: 82,751 square miles (214,325 square kilometers); 83,574 square miles (216,457 square kilometers) including water; eleventh largest state in area

Coastline: none

Population and rank: 1,595,728 (2012 estimate); thirty ninth largest state in population

Capital and largest city: Boise (205,671 people in 2010 census)

Became territory: March 4, 1863

Entered Union and rank: July 3, 1890; forty-third state

Present constitution adopted: 1890

Counties: 44, as well as a small part of Yellowstone National Park

Boise skyline, showing the capitol building. (Idaho Department of Commerce)

State name: "Idaho" is an invented name whose meaning is unknown

State nicknames: Gem State; Spud State; Panhandle State

Motto: *Esto perpetua* (It is forever)

State flag: Blue field with state seal and red band with words "State of Idaho"

Highest point: Borah Peak—12,662 feet (3,859 meters)

Lowest point: Snake River—5,000 feet (1,524 meters)

Highest recorded temperature: 118 degrees Fahrenheit (48 degrees Celsius)—Orotino, 1934

Lowest recorded temperature: –60 degrees Fahrenheit (–51 degrees Celsius)—Island Park Dam, 1943

State song: "Here We Have Idaho"

State tree: White pine

State flower: Syringa

State bird: Mountain bluebird

State fish: Cutthroat trout

National parks: Yellowstone

Idaho History

Idaho's history is marked by its frontier origins. The state was settled later than neighboring Washington and Oregon, as pioneers passed through during the 1840's without stopping to settle until valuable gold strikes brought miners in significant numbers. The rough character of Idaho's early days was reflected in the violence of its first decades as a state, which came to a close only around the time of the U.S. entrance into World War I. This background is sometimes still apparent in extremist political groups, some of which are racist or anarchist.

Early History. Idaho was first inhabited by various American Indian tribes, such as the Nez Perce, Coeur d'Alene, Pend d'Oreille, Kutenai, Paiute Shoshone, and Bannock. The origins of the indigenous inhabitants extend back around fourteen thousand years. Other ancient cultures flourished from eight thousand years ago until about the seventeenth century. By the eighteenth century, Shoshone bands (fragments of tribes) had obtained horses from European contacts, but these contacts decimated the native population by spreading smallpox.

No whites are known to have explored Idaho before Meriwether Lewis and William Clark led their famous expedition through Lemhi Pass in Idaho in 1805. Traveling through the Bitterroot Mountains, the explorers built canoes with the assistance of the Shoshone and Nez Perce and floated down the Clearwater and Snake Rivers to the Columbia. Four years later, Canadian explorer David Thompson built Kullyspell House, known as the first non-native house in the Pacific Northwest, near Pend Oreille Lake. Decades later, during the 1830's, Forts Hall and Boise, site of the future state's capital, were founded.

Pre-settlement Decades. Missionaries, a constant feature of the early days of the Pacific Northwest, soon made their appearance in Idaho, bringing Christianity and—in their eyes—civilization to the native tribes. Henry Spalding arrived in 1836 and established the state's first school. He also created its first irrigation system and planted its first potatoes, both of which were to play significant roles in Idaho's later economic development. The 1840's saw the arrival of the wagon trains headed west on the Oregon Trail.

The steady stream of humanity became a flood in 1849, as twenty thousand forty-niners came through on their way to California's goldfields. Continuing heavy traffic led to the establishment of the U.S. military post Cantonment Loring near Fort Hall. There were still no settlers, however, even after French Canadians discovered gold on the Pend Oreille River in 1852, the year before a large piece of Oregon Territory broke off to form Washington Territory, of which Idaho was a part. The first permanent community had not even been founded when Oregon was admitted to the Union at the end of the decade. Mormon missionaries had established the Salmon River Mission (Fort Lemhi) in mid-decade, but it was not a success and was abandoned in 1858.

From Territory to Statehood. Only in 1860, when much of the rest of the nation was gearing up for a

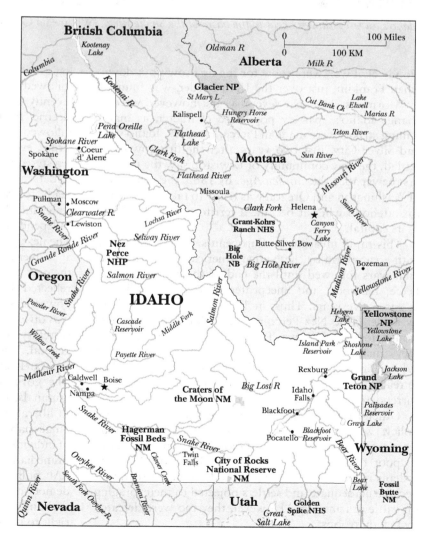

Idaho's lowest altitudes occur in the basin of the Snake River. (Wikimedia Commons)

Economic Development and Statehood. In the meantime, other events were unfolding that foretold the new territory's social and economic future. The first wave of modern technology made its appearance in 1866, as the first telegraph service reached the territory. A harbinger of modern social conflict arrived the next year, when the Owyhee Miners' League, Idaho's first labor union, made its appearance. Early in the following decade the first U.S. assay office and Idaho's first prison were built. Soon after, railroad service came to Franklin, and the way was open for even greater emigration from the restless east. By the next century these immigrants included English, Chinese, Czech, Dutch, French, French Canadian, German, Mexican, and Scandinavian settlers.

From the 1880's on, technological developments and their economic consequences followed with stunning speed for a region that was so recently an untamed wilderness. During the early 1880's electric light was introduced, and telephone service followed in 1883. The following year, an enormous silver strike, eventually recognized as the nation's largest, was registered in the Coeur d'Alene mining district, and more settlers arrived. By the close of the decade, Idaho was ready to trade its position as territory for the status of state. In 1889, a constitutional convention convened on Independence Day to institute a new frame of government. The next year Idaho was admitted to the Union.

Government and Social Conflict. Government under the new state constitution, as in neighboring Washington, reflected the frontier distrust of power in the form of a powerful state governor. Accordingly, executive control was divided into a number of elective offices in which the secretary of state, state controller, state treasurer, attorney general, and superintendent of public instruction are separately elected rather than appointed by the governor. The governor is also denied the power of pardoning criminals. The state constitution underlines a commitment to liberal democracy. It opens with a declaration of the "inalienable rights of man" and a detailed enumeration of individual rights, the central idea of classical liberalism. Immediately following is the forthright statement that "All political power is inherent in the people," the key democratic idea of popular sovereignty. In keeping with a strong tradition of frontier democracy, voters have the right to the initiative, referendum, and recall.

bloody civil war, were roots for the first town put down, when Franklin, just over the Utah border, was founded by Mormons. The next several years, however, were to change Idaho's sparsely populated character, as major mining strikes were made in Pierce, Florence, Idaho City, and Silver City. Just two years after the first town was settled, the new community of Lewiston saw the region's first newspaper, the *Golden Age.* By 1863, the region east of Washington and Oregon was ready to take a giant step to statehood when it became a territory, with Lewiston as its capital.

This rapid invasion by European settlers was viewed with great alarm by the Native Americans. American Indian wars followed until the end of the 1870's, as Nez Perce, Bannock, and Sheepeater Indian wars followed in successive years. Thus, in 1877, after years of abuse by settlers, the Nez Perce resisted efforts to send them from Oregon to Lapwai Reservation in Idaho. In June, they crushed U.S. Army troops and settler volunteers at White Bird Canyon, in north-central Idaho. Forced to retreat after federal reinforcements arrived, the Nez Perce surrendered in Montana in October.

Other American Indians, in accordance with federal policy, were also settled on reservations provided by treaties. Conditions on reservations were in some cases so poor that rebellions took place. Thus, the Bannock Indians rebelled in 1878, when food on their reservation became inadequate and settlers objected to their foraging on cattle grazing land. However, they too were defeated by federal troops.

While a framework for orderly government was in place, Idaho's rough-and-ready frontier origins could hardly disappear overnight. This became evident during the 1890's as serious violence broke out between union miners and mine owners. In 1892, the Coeur d'Alene mining area was the scene of dynamiting and shootings. More violence broke out when a new strike occurred in 1899. The strike was broken when the governor, Frank Steunenberg, called out federal troops.

Much bitterness remained, however. In 1905, former governor Steunenberg was murdered by a bomb. The perpetrator, a member of the Western Federation of Miners, an organization of the militant Marxist International Workers of the World (IWW), confessed but implicated three union officials. When a sensational trial was held in 1907, renowned defense attorney Clarence Darrow gained acquittals of two officials, and charges against the third were dropped. The prosecutor, William E. Borah, nevertheless won national fame and was elected six times to the U.S. Senate, where he became a stalwart foreign policy isolationist.

Two World Wars and Depression. Before World War I, the state's economy benefited from irrigation projects. A dam on the Snake River completed in 1906, for example, opened more than 100,000 acres of land for agriculture.

The war created an agricultural boom when wartime food shortages brought demand for farm products. The end of the war, however, brought an economic downturn, whose effects were felt into the 1920's. Matters were worse in the Great Depression of the 1930's, when many banks collapsed. Federal spending helped to a degree through a highway construction program and employment in the Civilian Conservation Corps (CCC).

World War II brought renewed prosperity, as in the rest of the nation, with massive federal spending for war needs. People of Japanese descent who were relocated from western portions of Oregon and Washington went to work in agriculture, where conscription had made labor scarce. Wartime industry made a lasting change in the economy, since in the postwar period manufacturing begun by defense needs continued, resulting in increased urbanization. By 1960, half of the population lived in cities or towns.

Postwar Economy and Society. As in neighboring states, postwar economic growth was also stimulated by development of cheap hydroelectric power. A series of dams was built during the 1950's, and projects continued during the 1960's. In 1976, one of the dams collapsed, and several rural communities were inundated, causing loss of life and considerable damage. During the

Frederic Remington's depiction of Chief Joseph surrendering the Nez Perce to U.S. cavalry troops in northern Montana in 1877, after leading five thousand troops on a five-month chase. (Library of Congress)

Harvesting potatoes in Idaho's Boise Valley in 1920. Today, the Idaho potato industry harvests approximately 13 billion pounds annually and produces roughly one-third of all the potatoes grown in the United States. (Wikimedia Commons)

1970's, the state's prosperity brought a rapid increase in population, which rose nearly one-third between 1970 and 1980.

By the 1990's, Idaho's economy was balanced between agriculture, mining, and nonagricultural industries. Various high-tech industries moved to the Boise area; food processing and wood products remained important. A tourist industry that, led by development of winter sports in Sun Valley, had grown up beginning during the 1950's was also important. Politically, the state was divided between conservationists and their opponents, and outsiders frequently noted the activity of unsavory fringe political groups, such as anarchists and neo-Nazis. Observers noted that the wise and efficient use of the state's natural resources would principally determine its future prosperity.

At the end of the twentieth century, Idaho's politics remained predominantly Republican. The state voted for Texas governor George W. Bush and Richard Cheney, a former congressman from neighboring Wyoming, in the presidential election on November 7, by a 68–28 percent margin, and again in 2004 by a similar margin (68-30 percent). Indicative of the political leanings of the state was the wide margin by which Idaho's new congressman in Washington, D.C., C. L. (Butch) Otter, defeated his opponent by a 65–32 percent margin in 2000.

Wildfires and Wildlife. Idaho, as common in other Western states, was the victim of annual wildfires, exacerbated by lingering drought. The state had experienced wildfires in the past, but they seemed to intensify around the turn of the new century. Fires during the 2000 season were said to be the worst on record, destroying some 6.7 million acres in the seven most stricken states, including

Idaho. The federal government became involved in helping to organize a plan among the states to limit the damage that the fires were causing. Acting in a nonpartisan spirit, the seven states unanimously endorsed the plan proposed by the U.S. Secretary of the Interior and the Secretary of Agriculture. The plan avoided discussion of contentious issues such as harvesting timber but instead emphasized fire prevention and local decision making. The federal government paid the states $800 million to replenish emergency funds that were depleted during the fire season.

Aside from the fire problem, the state was involved in other environmental controversies involving natural resources. One of these involved a plan to reintroduce grizzly bears in the Selway-Bitterroot Wilderness area in Idaho and Montana. The return of the bears did not take place because a federal judge in Boise, Idaho's state capital, ruled that introducing the animals would cause irreplaceable harm to the Idaho economy and put its mining and timber industries out of business.

Aryan Nations Lawsuit. Also during 2000, the victims of a 1998 neo-Nazi assault outside the compound of the so-called Aryan Nations founded by Richard Butler won a $6.3 million settlement in their lawsuit over the incident, effectively putting Butler and his group out of business. As a result, Butler agreed to give up the name Aryan Nations. The following year, the victims bought Butler's compound, where the group had been headquartered, and converted it into a human rights center.

Politics. Former lieutenant governor and U.S. Representative Butch Otter (R) won the governorship of Idaho in 2006 against Democratic Party nominee Jerry Brady with 52.67 percent of the vote. He was re-elected in 2010, defeating his Democratic opponent Keith G. Allred. In the 2008 and 2012 presidential elections, the Republican candidates, John McCain and Mitt Romney won the state with over 60 percent of the popular vote.

Wolf Introduction Program. Despite opposition from the Idaho state government, wolves were introduced into Idaho as part of a federal project in 1995. The state wolf population peaked in 2009 at 856. As a consequence of the rapid increase and continued opposition from Idaho ranchers, hunters, and the general population to the wolf introduction program, the state introduced a management plan to limit the wolf population in 2008. Through the next years, Idaho continued to attempt to limit the population of grey wolves in the state. The federally monitored state report indicated a population of 683 wolves in the state at the end of 2012, down some 11 percent from the previous year. State wildlife managers had hoped to decrease the pack further, despite the fact that hunters and trappers had killed some 418 wolves in 2012.

The state further reported that there were additional smaller packs of wolves, averaging about five per pack. The limitation program of granting hunting and trapping licenses as part of the control program began to show some success, despite outcries from environmentalists and endangered species advocates. The state carefully monitors the locations of packs, and tracks a number that are interstate, ranging into bordering Washington and Montana.

Charles F. Bahmueller
Updated by the Editor

Idaho Time Line

6000 B.C.E.–1700's	American Indian cultures flourish.
1810	Fort Henry, first American fur post west of Rocky Mountains, is established near St. Anthony.
1811	Party based at Astoria on the Pacific Coast explores portions of the future Oregon Trail in Idaho.
1819	Canadian Donald Mackenzie holds rendezvous with American Indians on the Boise River; attempts to establish post.
1820	Mackenzie negotiates peace treaty with the Shoshone on Little Lost River.
1821	Hudson's Bay Company and North West Company merge.
1822	Founding of Rocky Mountain Fur Company.
1830	Captain B. L. E. Bonneville leads wagon train across South Pass to Green River.
1834	Forts Laramie, Boise, and Hall are established.
1843	First Oregon Trail wagons cross Idaho.
Aug. 14, 1848	Oregon Territory is created, which includes Idaho.
1852	French Canadians discover gold on the Pend Oreille River.
1853	Idaho becomes part of Washington Territory.
1863	Major mining strikes take place near Pierce, Florence, Idaho City, and Silver City.
Mar. 4, 1863	Idaho Territory is established.
1864	Territorial legislature approves moving capital to Boise.
1867	Owyhee Miners' League, state's first labor union, is organized.
1874	First railroad service in Idaho begins at Franklin.
1877–1879	Nez Perce, Bannock, and Sheepeater Indians war with settlers.
1884	Silver is discovered in the Coeur d'Alene mining district.
Nov. 5, 1889	State constitution is ratified.
1889	Territorial legislature establishes University of Idaho.
July 3, 1890	Idaho becomes the forty-third state.
1904	Completion of Milner Dam brings irrigation to the south side of the Snake River.
1910	Forest fires consume one-sixth of north Idaho's forests.
1912	State Board of Education is established.
1914	Moses Alexander is elected the first Jewish governor in the United States.
1924	Craters of the Moon National Monument is established.
1926	First commercial airmail service in the United States begins in Boise.
1934	Idaho is nation's leading silver producer.
1936	Sun Valley winter sports resort is established by Union Pacific Railroad; world's first ski chair lift opens there.
1942	Almost ten thousand Japanese Americans are placed in an internment camp near Eden.
1949	National Reactor Testing Station (NRTS) is established.
1951	NRTS becomes site of the world's first use of nuclear fission to produce electricity.
1958	Idaho leads the nation in mining of silver, lead, and cobalt.
1966	Voters uphold 3 percent state sales tax.
1975	Port of Lewiston opens Idaho to oceangoing shipping.
June 5, 1976	Teton Dam collapses, killing eleven and forcing thousands to flee.

1978	Voters approve tax limitation placing severe restrictions on use of the property tax.
1985	Idaho produces one-fourth of U.S. potatoes.
1986	Voters adopt constitutional amendment prohibiting the payment of union dues as a necessity for employment.
1992	First woman appointed to Idaho Supreme Court.
June–Sept., 2000	Idaho experiences extensive, destructive wildfires that also severely affect many other western States.
Nov. 7, 2000	Idaho votes for George W. Bush and Richard Cheney for president and vice president, respectively. The state's other representatives in Washington remain Republican.
2006	Former Lieutenant Governor and U.S. Representative Butch Otter (R) wins the governorship of Idaho against Democratic Party nominee Jerry Brady with 52.67 percent of the vote. He is re-elected in 2010.
2012	After grey wolves are introduced to the state in 1995, hunters and trappers try to decrease the burgeoning population against the wishes of environmentalists.

Notes for Further Study

Published Sources. For an introduction to the state, see Rick Ardinger and M. L. Peterson's *Celebrating Idaho: The Centennial in Words and Pictures* (1991). Books on Idaho's history include Leonard J. Arrington's *History of Idaho* (2 vols., 1994) and Dorothy Dutton's *A Rendezvous with Idaho History* (1994). One facet of ethnic history is described in *History of the Jews in Utah and Idaho, 1853–1950* (1973) by Juanita Brooks.

Good books on Idaho geography include Lalia Phipps Boone's *Idaho Place Names: A Geographical Dictionary* (1988) and Delorme Mapping's *Idaho Atlas and Gazetteer* (5th ed., 2002). American Indian history is surveyed in *Indians of Idaho* (1978) by Deward Walker. For information on the great Nez Perce leader Chief Joseph, readers should consult Clifford E. Trafzer's *Chief Joseph's Allies: The Palouse Indians and the Nez Perce* (1992) or *Chief Joseph: Guardian of the People* (2005) by Candy Moulton. The Bannock Indians are studied both in Brigham D. Mardsen's *The Bannock of Idaho* (1996) and, along with the Shoshone, in John W. Heaton's *The Shoshone-Bannocks: Culture and Commerce at Fort Hall, 1870–1940* (2005). Laura Woodworth-Ney uses a number of historical documents to examine the development of one of Idaho's reservations in *Mapping Identity: The Creation of the Coeur d'Alene Indian Reservation, 1805–1902* (2004). The life and work of an important Idaho photographer is detailed in Joanna Cohan Scherer's *A Danish Photographer of Idaho Indians: Benedicte Wrensted* (2005).

The state's government is discussed in *Governing Idaho: Politics, People, and Power* (2005) by James Weatherby and Randy Strapilus. Idaho's constitution is examined in Dennis C. Colson's *Idaho's Constitution: The Tie That Binds* (rev. ed., 2003). Jennifer Eastman Attebery's *Building Idaho: An Architectural History* (1991) treats the state's architecture. Those interested in archaeology of the state should see Mark Plew's *Introduction to the Archaeology*

of Southern Idaho (1986). For those interested in general travel in Idaho, Cort Conley's *Idaho for the Curious: A Guide* (2003) and *Idaho Off the Beaten Path* (5th ed., 2004) by Julie Fanselow are excellent guides.

Web Resources. For information on politics and government in Idaho, a good place to start is the state of Idaho home page (www.accessidaho.org/), which contains information on and links to state agencies and major offices, as well as commerce, education, the environment, and many related topics. A federal government agency particularly significant in Idaho is the Bureau of Land Management (BLM), whose work is outlined on its home page (www.id.blm.gov/). The Idaho section of the American Local History Network (www.usgennet.org/usa/id/state1/alhn/index.htm) has a variety of information and links, including local, ethnic, and cultural history; schools and education; genealogy; geography; government (including the Idaho Constitution); military records; museums; and other topics. Other information on the state is found on the Libraries Linking Idaho home page (www.lili.org/lili/). The state historical society home page (www.idahohistory.net/) is useful for learning about the early days of Idaho. State geography information especially suitable to young people can be accessed at Kidport (kidport.com/RefLib/UsaGeography/Facts/Idaho.htm). Travelers may wish to consult Virtual Tourist: Travel in Idaho (www.virtualtourist.com/travel/North_America/United_States_of_America/Idaho/TravelGuide-Idaho.html).

For information on Native Americans, readers should view the home pages maintained by various tribes—for example, the Nez Perce home page (www.nezperce.org/). The sites for Bannock, Cayuse, and other Idaho Native Americans (www.rootsweb.com/~idreserv/fhhist.html), along with that for Coeur d'Alene tribal history (www.rootsweb.com/~idreserv/cdhist.html), are also informative.

Counties

County	2012 Population	Pop. Rank	Land Area (sq. miles)	Area Rank
Ada	409,061	1	1,052.58	31
Adams	3,915	40	1,363.06	22
Bannock	83,800	5	1,111.99	27
Bear Lake	5,907	36	974.78	32
Benewah	9,117	30	776.62	34
Bingham	45,474	7	2,093.98	12
Blaine	21,146	17	2,643.59	7
Boise	6,835	34	1,899.24	14
Bonner	40,476	8	1,734.57	19
Bonneville	106,684	4	1,866.08	15
Boundary	10,808	26	1,268.56	23
Butte	2,740	42	2,231.67	11
Camas	1,077	43	1,074.49	30
Canyon	193,888	2	587.37	39
Caribou	6,787	35	1,764.15	18
Cassia	23,249	14	2,565.08	9
Clark	869	44	1,764.19	17
Clearwater	8,590	31	2,457.27	10
Custer	4,331	38	4,920.94	3
Elmore	26,223	13	3,074.74	6
Franklin	12,786	23	663.64	37
Fremont	12,957	22	1,863.53	16
Gem	16,673	19	560.90	40

County	2012 Population	Pop. Rank	Land Area (sq. miles)	Area Rank
Gooding	15,291	21	728.97	36
Idaho	16,308	20	8,477.35	1
Jefferson	26,684	12	1,093.50	28
Jerome	22,499	16	597.18	38
Kootenai	142,357	3	1,244.12	24
Latah	38,184	10	1,076.00	29
Lemhi	7,758	33	4,563.39	4
Lewis	3,889	41	478.80	41
Lincoln	5,277	37	1,201.41	25
Madison	37,456	11	469.21	42
Minidoka	20,037	18	757.59	35
Nez Perce	39,531	9	848.09	33
Oneida	4,215	39	1,200.06	26
Owyhee	11,439	25	7,665.51	2
Payette	22,639	15	406.87	44
Power	7,778	32	1,404.24	21
Shoshone	12,702	24	2,629.66	8
Teton	10,052	28	449.46	43
Twin Falls	78,595	6	1,921.21	13
Valley	9,545	29	3,664.52	5
Washington	10,099	27	1,452.98	20

Source: U.S. Census Bureau, 2012 Population Estimates

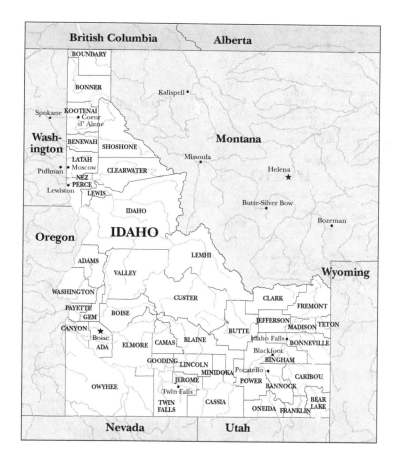

Cities

With 10,000 or more residents

Legal Name	2010 Population	Pop. Rank	Land Area (sq. miles)	Area Rank
Ammon city	13,816	17	7.26	15
Blackfoot city	11,899	19	5.83	19
Boise City city	205,671	1	79.36	1
Burley city	10,345	22	6.12	17
Caldwell city	46,237	6	22.06	7
Chubbuck city	13,922	16	4.19	21
Coeur d'Alene city	44,137	7	15.57	11
Eagle city	19,908	13	28.92	4
Garden City city	10,972	20	4.04	22
Hayden city	13,294	18	9.60	14
Idaho Falls city	56,813	4	22.35	6
Jerome city	10,890	21	5.52	20

Legal Name	2010 Population	Pop. Rank	Land Area (sq. miles)	Area Rank
Kuna city	15,210	14	18.08	9
Lewiston city	31,894	9	17.23	10
Meridian city	75,092	3	26.79	5
Moscow city	23,800	12	6.85	16
Mountain Home city	14,206	15	6.07	18
Nampa city	81,557	2	31.19	3
Pocatello city	54,255	5	32.22	2
Post Falls city	27,574	10	14.07	12
Rexburg city	25,484	11	9.76	13
Twin Falls city	44,125	8	18.10	8

Note: CDP–Census Designated Place
Source: U.S. Census Bureau, 2010 Census

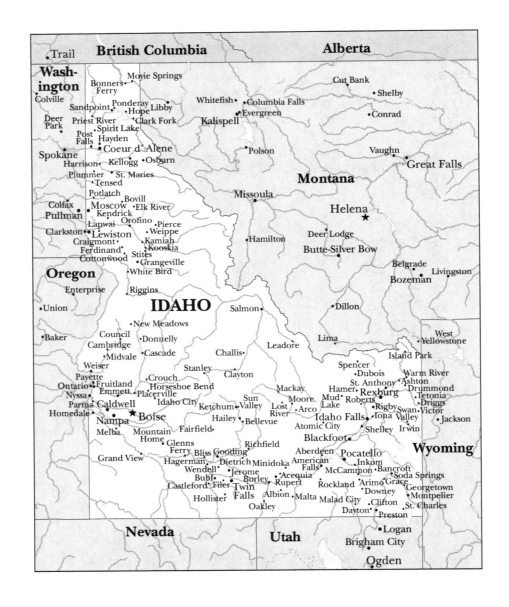

Survey Says...

This section presents current rankings from dozens of public and private sources. It shows how this state ranks in a number of critical categories, including education, job growth, cost of living, teen drivers, energy efficiency, and business environment. Sources include *Forbes, Reuters, U.S. News and World Report, CNN Money, Gallup,* and *Huffington Post.*

- CNN Money compiled a list of "Ten Most Entrepreneurial States" based on the Kauffman Index of Entrepreneurial Activity. Idaho ranked #7 among the 50 states in 2012 for number of startups per 100,000 adult residents.
  CNN Money, June 20, 2013; money.cnn.com

- Idaho ranked #45 in a government study measuring real gross domestic product (GDP)—the output of goods and services produced by labor and property located in the United States. The ranking is based on the percentage change compared with 2011 GDP.
  U.S. Department of Commerce, Bureau of Economic Analysis, June 2013; www.bea.gov

- Idaho ranked #43 in a government study measuring real gross domestic product (GDP)—the output of goods and services produced by labor and property located in the United States. The ranking is based on the dollar value of its GDP.
  U.S. Department of Commerce, Bureau of Economic Analysis, June 2013; www.bea.gov

- Idaho ranked #49 in the 17th edition of "Quality Counts; State of the States," Education Week's "report card" surveying key education indicators, policy efforts, and educational outcomes.
  Education Week, January 4, 2013 (online) and January 10, 2013 (print); www.edweek.org

- SERI (Science and Engineering Readiness Index) weighs the performance of the states' K-12 schools in preparing students in physics and calculus, the high school subjects considered most important for future scientists and engineers. Idaho ranked #30.
  Newsletter of the Forum on Education of the American Physical Society, Summer 2011 issue; www.huffingtonpost.com, July 11, 2011; updated October 1, 2012

- MoneyRates.com ranked Idaho #20 on its list of the best to worst states for making a living. Criteria: average income; inflation; employment prospects; and workers' Workplace Environment assessments according to the Gallup-Healthways Well-Being Index.
  www.money-rates.com, posted April 1, 2013

- *Forbes* analyzed business costs, labor supply, regulatory environment, current economic climate, growth prospects, and quality of life, to compile its "Best States for Business" rankings. Idaho ranked #19.
  www.forbes.com. posted December 12, 2012

- The 2012 Gallup-Healthways Well-Being Index, surveyed American's opinions on economic confidence, workplace perceptions, community climate, personal choices, and health predictors to assess the "future livability" of each state. Idaho ranked #15.
  "Utah Poised to Be the Best State to Live In," Gallup Wellbeing, www.gallup.com, August 7, 2012

- On CNBC's list of "America's Top States for Business 2013," Idaho ranked #10. Criteria: measures of competitiveness developed with input from the National Association of Manufacturers, the Council on Competitiveness, and other business groups weighed with the states' own marketing criteria.
  www.cnbc.com, consulted July 19, 2013

- Kiplinger identified "Ten States with the Biggest Rate of Job Growth in 2013" using data from the U.S. Bureau of Labor Statistics, IHS Global Insights, Moody's Analytics, and state economic data. Idaho ranked #6.
  www.kiplinger.com, March 2013

- Idaho ranked #2 on MoneyRates list of "Best-and Worst-States to Retire 2012." Criteria: life expectancy, crime rate, climate, economic conditions, taxes, job opportunities, and cost of living.
  www.money-rates.com, October 22, 2012

- Idaho ranked #24 on the 2013 Bankrate "Best Places to Retire" list ranking the states and District of Columbia on various criteria relating to health, safety, and cost.
  www.bankrate.com, May 6, 2013

- Idaho ranked #42 on the Social Science Research Council's "American Human Development Report: The Measure of America," assessing the 50 states plus the District of Columbia on health, education, and living-standard criteria.
  The Measure of America 2013-2014, posted June 19, 2013; www.measureofamerica.org

- Idaho ranked #24 on the Foundation for Child Development's (FCD) Child Well-being Index (CWI). The FCD used the KIDS COUNT report and the National Survey of Children's Health, the only state-level source for several key indicators of child well-being.
  Foundation for Child Development, January 18, 2012; fcd-us.org

- Idaho ranked #20 overall according to the 2013 KIDS COUNT Data Book, a project of the Annie E. Casey Foundation. Criteria: children's economic well-being, education, health, and family and community indicators.
  KIDS COUNT Data Center's Data Book, released June 20, 2013; http://datacenter.kidscount.org

- Idaho ranked #23 in the children's economic well-being category by the 2013 KIDS COUNT Data Book, a project of the Annie E. Casey Foundation.
  KIDS COUNT Data Center's Data Book, released June 20, 2013; http://datacenter.kidscount.org

- Idaho ranked #29 in the children's educational opportunities and attainments category by the 2013 KIDS COUNT Data Book, a project of the Annie E. Casey Foundation.
  KIDS COUNT Data Center's Data Book, released June 20, 2013; http://datacenter.kidscount.org

- Idaho ranked #28 in the children's health category by the 2013 KIDS COUNT Data Book, a project of the Annie E. Casey Foundation.

  KIDS COUNT Data Center's Data Book, released June 20, 2013; http://datacenter.kidscount.org

- Idaho ranked #10 in the family and community circumstances that factor into children's well-being category by the 2013 KIDS COUNT Data Book, a project of the Annie E. Casey Foundation.

  KIDS COUNT Data Center's Data Book, released June 20, 2013; http://datacenter.kidscount.org

- Idaho ranked #22 in the 2012 Gallup-Healthways Well-Being Index. Criteria: emotional health; physical health; healthy behavior; work environment; basic access to food, shelter, health care; and a safe and satisfying place to live.

  2012 State of Well-Being, Gallup-Healthways Well-Being Index, released February 28, 2013; www.well-beingindex.com

- *U.S. News and World Report's* "Best States for Teen Drivers" rankings are based on driving and road safety laws, federal reports on driver's licenses, car accident fatality, and road-quality statistics. Idaho ranked #45.

  U.S. News and World Report, March 18, 2010; www.usnews.com

- The Yahoo! Sports service Rivals.com ranks the states according to the strength of their high school football programs. Idaho ranked #34.

  "Ranking the States: Where Is the Best Football Played?," November 18, 2011; highschool.rivals.com

- iVillage ranked the states by hospitable living conditions for women. Criteria: economic success, access to affordable childcare, health care, reproductive rights, female representation in government, and educational attainment. Idaho ranked #41.

  iVillage, "50 Best to Worst States for Women," March 14, 2012; www.ivillage.com

- The League of American Bicyclists's "Bicycle Friendly States" ranked Idaho #26. Criteria: legislation and enforcement, policies and programs, infrastructure and funding, education and advocacy, and evaluation and planning.

  "Washington Tops the Bicycle-Friendly State Ranking," May 1, 2013; bicycling.com

- The federal Corporation for National and Community Service ranked the states and the District of Columbia by volunteer rates. Idaho ranked #2 for community service.

  "Volunteering and Civic Life in America 2012," www.volunteeringinamerica.gov, accessed July 24, 2013

- The Hospital Safety Score ranked states and the District of Columbia on their hospitals' performance scores. Idaho ranked #45. Criteria: avoiding preventable harm and medical errors, as demonstrated by 26 hospital safety metrics.

  Spring 2013 Hospital Safety Score, May 8, 2013; www.hospitalsafetyscore.org

- GMAC Insurance ranked the states and the District of Columbia by the performance of their drivers on the GMAC Insurance National Drivers Test, comprised of DMV test questions. Idaho ranked #11.

  "2011 GMAC Insurance National Drivers Test," www.gmacinsurance.com, accessed July 23, 2013

- Idaho ranked #41 in a "State Integrity Investigation" analysis of laws and practices intended to deter corruption and promote accountability and openness in campaign finance, ethics laws, lobbying regulations and management of state pension funds.

  "What's Your State's Grade?," www.publicintegrity.org, accessed July 23, 2013

- Idaho ranked #37 among the states and the District of Columbia in total rail miles, as tracked by the Association of American Railroads.

  "U.S. Freight Railroad Industry Snapshot: Railroads and States: Total Rail Miles by State: 2011"; www.aar.org, accessed July 23, 2013

- According to statistics compiled by the Beer Institute, Idaho ranked #33 among the states and the District of Columbia in per capita beer consumption of persons 21 years or older.

  "Shipments of Malt Beverages and Per Capita Consumption by State 2012;" www.beerinstitute.org

- According to Concordia University's "Public Education Costs per Pupil by State Rankings," based on statistics gathered by the U.S. Census Bureau, which includes the District of Columbia, Idaho ranked #50.

  Concordia University Online; education.cu-portland.edu, accessed July 24, 2013

- Idaho ranked #44 among the states and the District of Columbia in population density based on U.S. Census Bureau data for resident population and total land area. "List of U.S. States by Population Density."

  www.wikipedia.org, accessed July 24, 2013

- In "America's Health Rankings, 2012 Edition," by the United Health Foundation, Idaho ranked #17. Criteria included: rate of high school graduation; violent crime rate; incidence of infectious disease; childhood immunizations; prevalence of diabetes; per capita public-health funding; percentage of uninsured population; rate of children in poverty; and availability of primary-care physicians.

  United Health Foundation; www.americashealthrankings.org, accessed July 24, 2013

- The TechNet 2012 "State Broadband Index" ranked Idaho #41 on the following criteria: broadband adoption; network quality; and economic structure. Improved broadband use is hoped to promote economic development, build strong communities, improve delivery of government services and upgrade educational systems.

  TechNet; www.technet.org, accessed July 24, 2013

- Idaho was ranked #22 among the states and District of Columbia on the American Council for an Energy-Efficient Economy's "State Energy Efficiency Scorecard" for 2012.

  American Council for an Energy-Efficient Economy; aceee.org/sector/state-policy/scorecard, accessed July 24, 2013

Statistical Tables

DEMOGRAPHICS
Resident State and National Population, 1950-2012
Projected State and National Population, 2000-2030
Population by Age, 2012
Population by Race, 2012
Population by Hispanic Origin and Race, 2012

VITAL STATISTICS
Death Rates by Leading Causes, 2010
Death Rates by Selected Causes, 2010
Abortion Rates, 2009
Infant Mortality Rates, 1995-2009
Marriage and Divorce Rates, 2000-2011

ECONOMY
Nominal Gross Domestic Product by Industry, 2012
Real Gross Domestic Product, 2000-2012
Personal Income Per Capita, 1930-2012
Non-Farm Employment by Sector, 2012
Foreign Exports, 2000-2012
Energy Consumption, 2011

LAND AND WATER
Surface Area and Federally-Owned Land, 2007
Land Cover/Use of Non-Federal Rural Land, 2007
Farms and Crop Acreage, 2012

HEALTH AND MEDICAL CARE
Medical Professionals, 2012
Health Insurance Coverage, 2011
HIV, STD, and Tuberculosis Cases and Rates, 2011
Cigarette Smoking, 2011

HOUSING
Home Ownership Rates, 1995-2012
Home Sales, 2000-2010
Value of Owner-Occupied Homes, 2011

EDUCATION
School Enrollment, 2011
Educational Attainment, 2011
Public College Finances, FY 2012

TRANSPORTATION AND TRAVEL
Motor Vehicle Registrations and Drivers Licenses, 2011
Domestic Travel Expenditures, 2009
Retail Gasoline Prices, 2013
Public Road Length, 2011

CRIME AND LAW ENFORCEMENT
Full-Time Law Enforcement Officers, 2011
Prison Population, 2000-2012
Crime Rate, 2011

GOVERNMENT AND FINANCE
Local Governments by Type, 2012
State Government Revenue, 2011
State Government Expenditures, 2011
State Government General Expenditures by Function, 2011
State Government Finances, Cash and Debt, 2011

POLITICS
Composition of the Senate, 1995-2013
Composition of the House of Representatives, 1995-2013
Composition of State Legislature, 2004-2013
Voter Participation in Presidential Elections, 1980-2012
Governors Since Statehood

DEMOGRAPHICS

Resident State and National Population, 1950–2012

Year	State Population	U.S. Population	State Share
1950	589,000	151,326,000	0.39%
1960	667,000	179,323,000	0.37%
1970	713,015	203,302,031	0.35%
1980	943,935	226,545,805	0.42%
1990	1,006,749	248,709,873	0.40%
2000	1,293,957	281,424,600	0.46%
2010	1,567,582	308,745,538	0.51%
2012	1,595,728	313,914,040	0.51%

Note: 1950/1960 population figures are rounded to the nearest thousand.
Source: U.S. Census Bureau, Decennial Census 1950–2010; U.S. Census Bureau, 2012 Population Estimates

Projected State and National Population, 2000–2030

Year	State Population	U.S. Population	State Share
2000	1,293,953	281,421,906	0.46%
2005	1,407,060	295,507,134	0.48%
2010	1,517,291	308,935,581	0.49%
2015	1,630,045	322,365,787	0.51%
2020	1,741,333	335,804,546	0.52%
2025	1,852,627	349,439,199	0.53%
2030	1,969,624	363,584,435	0.54%
State population growth, 2000–2030			675,671
State percentage growth, 2000–2030			52.2%

Source: U.S. Census Bureau, Population Division, Interim State Population Projections, 2005

Population by Age, 2012

Age Group	State Population	Percent of Total Population	
		State	U.S.
Under 5 years	115,972	7.3%	6.4%
5 to 14 years	241,430	15.1%	13.1%
15 to 24 years	226,098	14.2%	14.0%
25 to 34 years	210,527	13.2%	13.5%
35 to 44 years	193,924	12.2%	12.9%
45 to 54 years	203,034	12.7%	14.1%
55 to 64 years	192,165	12.0%	12.3%
65 to 74 years	123,343	7.7%	7.6%
75 to 84 years	62,625	3.9%	4.2%
85 years and older	26,610	1.7%	1.9%
Under 18 years	426,653	26.7%	23.5%
65 years and older	212,578	13.3%	13.7%
Median age (years)	–	35.2	37.4

Source: U.S. Census Bureau, Annual Estimates of the Resident Population for Selected Age Groups by Sex for the United States, States, Counties, and Puerto Rico Commonwealth and Municipios: April 1, 2010 to July 1, 2012

Population by Race, 2012

Race	State Population	Percent of Total Population	
		State	U.S.
All residents	1,595,728	100.00%	100.00%
White	1,497,404	93.84%	77.89%
African American	12,037	0.75%	13.13%
Native American	26,684	1.67%	1.23%
Asian	21,899	1.37%	5.14%
Native Hawaiian	2,916	0.18%	0.23%
Two or more races	34,788	2.18%	2.39%

Source: U.S. Census Bureau, Population Division, Annual Estimates of the Resident Population by Sex, Race and Hispanic Origin for the United States, States, and Counties: April 1, 2010 to July 1, 2012

Population by Hispanic Origin and Race, 2012

Hispanic Origin/Race	State Population	Percent of Total Population	
		State	U.S.
All residents	1,595,728	100.00%	100.00%
All Hispanic residents	185,160	11.60%	16.89%
Hispanic			
White	165,754	10.39%	14.91%
African American	2,180	0.14%	0.79%
Native American	8,679	0.54%	0.49%
Asian	1,409	0.09%	0.17%
Native Hawaiian	590	0.04%	0.06%
Two or more races	6,548	0.41%	0.48%
Not Hispanic			
White	1,331,650	83.45%	62.98%
African American	9,857	0.62%	12.34%
Native American	18,005	1.13%	0.74%
Asian	20,490	1.28%	4.98%
Native Hawaiian	2,326	0.15%	0.17%
Two or more races	28,240	1.77%	1.91%

Source: U.S. Census Bureau, Population Division, Annual Estimates of the Resident Population by Sex, Race and Hispanic Origin for the United States, States, and Counties: April 1, 2010 to July 1, 2012

VITAL STATISTICS

Death Rates by Leading Causes, 2010

Cause	State	U.S.
Malignant neoplasms	171.5	186.2
Ischaemic heart diseases	102.5	122.9
Other forms of heart disease	54.3	53.4
Chronic lower respiratory diseases	49.7	44.7
Cerebrovascular diseases	44.4	41.9
Organic, incl. symptomatic, mental disorders	41.2	35.7
Other degenerative diseases of the nervous sys.	30.0	28.4
Other external causes of accidental injury	27.5	26.5
Diabetes mellitus	24.1	22.4
Hypertensive diseases	16.5	20.4
All causes	781.0	799.5

Note: Figures are age-adjusted death rates per 100,000 population
Source: CDC/NCHS, Underlying Cause of Death 1999–2010 on CDC WONDER Online Database

Death Rates by Selected Causes, 2010

Cause	State	U.S.
Assault	1.4	5.2
Diseases of the liver	13.5	13.9
Human immunodeficiency virus (HIV) disease	–	2.7
Influenza and pneumonia	14.4	16.2
Intentional self-harm	19.3	12.4
Malnutrition	0.0	0.9
Obesity and other hyperalimentation	2.3	1.8
Renal failure	10.7	14.4
Transport accidents	15.4	12.1
Viral hepatitis	2.8	2.4

Note: Figures are age-adjusted death rates per 100,000 population; A dash indicates that data was not available or was suppressed
Source: CDC/NCHS, Underlying Cause of Death 1999–2010 on CDC WONDER Online Database

Abortion Rates, 2009

Category	2009
By state of residence	
Total abortions	2,381
Abortion rate[1]	7.8%
Abortion ratio[2]	100
By state of occurrence	
Total abortions	1,650
Abortion rate[1]	5.4%
Abortion ratio[2]	70
Abortions obtained by out-of-state residents	4.1%
U.S. abortion rate[1]	15.1%
U.S. abortion ratio[2]	227

Note: (1) Number of abortions per 1,000 women aged 15–44 years; (2) Number of abortions per 1,000 live births; A dash indicates that data was not available
Source: CDC/NCHS, Morbidity and Mortality Weekly Report, November 23, 2012 (Abortion Surveillance, United States, 2009)

Infant Mortality Rates, 1995–2009

Category	1995	2000	2005	2009
All state residents	6.15	7.56	5.98	5.48
All U.S. residents	7.57	6.89	6.86	6.39
All state white residents	6.01	7.41	5.97	5.38
All U.S. white residents	6.30	5.71	5.73	5.33
All state black residents	–	–	–	–
All U.S. black residents	14.58	13.48	13.26	12.12

Note: Figures represent deaths per 1,000 live births of resident infants under one year old, exclusive of fetal deaths; A dash indicates that data was not available or was suppressed.
Source: Centers of Disease Control and Prevention, Division of Vital Statistics, Linked Birth/Infant Death Records on CDC Wonder Online

Marriage and Divorce Rates, 2000–2011

Year	Marriage Rate		Divorce Rate	
	State	U.S.	State	U.S.
2000	10.8	8.2	5.5	4.0
2002	11.0	8.0	5.3	3.9
2004	10.8	7.8	5.0	3.7
2006	10.1	7.5	5.0	3.7
2008	9.5	7.1	4.8	3.5
2010	8.8	6.8	5.2	3.6
2011	8.6	6.8	4.9	3.6

Note: Rates are based on provisional counts of marriages/divorces by state of occurrence and are per 1,000 total population residing in area
Source: CDC/NCHS, National Vital Statistics System

ECONOMY

Nominal Gross Domestic Product by Industry, 2012
In millions of current dollars

Industry	State GDP
Accommodation and food services	1,636
Administrative and waste management services	1,719
Agriculture, forestry, fishing, and hunting	3,158
Arts, entertainment, and recreation	433
Construction	2,556
Educational services	424
Finance and insurance	2,968
Health care and social assistance	4,557
Information	1,242
Management of companies and enterprises	722
Manufacturing	7,556
Mining	492
Other services, except government	1,363
Professional, scientific, and technical services	3,927
Real estate and rental and leasing	6,819
Retail trade	4,527
Transportation and warehousing	1,752
Utilities	1,185
Wholesale trade	3,198

Source: U.S. Department of Commerce, Bureau of Economic Analysis, Survey of Current Business

Real Gross Domestic Product, 2000–2012
In millions of chained 2005 dollars

Year	State GDP	U.S. GDP	State Share
2000	39,402	11,225,406	0.35%
2005	48,683	12,539,116	0.39%
2010	50,734	12,897,088	0.39%
2012	50,976	13,430,576	0.38%

Source: U.S. Department of Commerce, Bureau of Economic Analysis, Survey of Current Business

Personal Income Per Capita, 1930–2012

Year	State	U.S.
1930	$486	$618
1940	$456	$593
1950	$1,321	$1,503
1960	$1,882	$2,268
1970	$3,539	$4,084
1980	$8,637	$10,091
1990	$15,603	$19,354
2000	$24,685	$30,319
2010	$31,556	$39,791
2012	$33,749	$42,693

Source: U.S. Department of Commerce, Bureau of Economic Analysis, Regional Economic Accounts

Non-Farm Employment by Sector, 2012
In thousands

Sector	Employment
Construction	31.3
Education and health services	88.7
Financial activities	30.3
Government	116.7
Information	9.3
Leisure and hospitality	61.1
Mining and logging	4.0
Manufacturing	56.8
Other services	21.5
Professional and business services	76.2
Trade, transportation, and utilities	126.1
All sectors	622.0

Source: U.S. Bureau of Labor Statistics, State and Area Employment

Foreign Exports, 2000–2012
In millions of dollars

Year	State Exports	U.S. Exports	State Share
2000	3,558	712,054	0.50%
2002	1,962	649,940	0.30%
2004	2,916	768,554	0.38%
2006	3,726	973,994	0.38%
2008	5,005	1,222,545	0.41%
2010	5,156	1,208,080	0.43%
2012	6,119	1,478,268	0.41%

Note: U.S. figures exclude data from Puerto Rico, U.S. Virgin Islands, and unallocated exports
Source: U.S. Department of Commerce, International Trade Admin., Office of Trade and Industry Information, Manufacturing and Services

Energy Consumption, 2011
In trillions of BTUs, except as noted

Total energy consumption	
Total state energy consumption	525.6
Total U.S. energy consumption	97,387.3
State share of U.S. total	0.54%
Per capita consumption (in millions of BTUs)	
Total state per capita consumption	331.9
Total U.S. per capita consumption	312.6
End-use sectors	
Residential	124.9
Commercial	85.3
Industrial	183.8
Transportation	131.7
Sources of energy	
Petroleum	161.3
Natural gas	83.9
Coal	7.8
Renewable energy	179.7
Nuclear electric power	0.0

Source: U.S. Energy Information Administration, State Energy Data 2011: Consumption

LAND AND WATER

Surface Area and Federally-Owned Land, 2007
In thousands of acres

Category	State	U.S.	State Share
Total surface area	53,487.5	1,937,664.2	2.76%
Total land area	52,929.9	1,886,846.9	2.81%
Non-federal land	19,366.6	1,484,910.0	1.30%
Developed	907.3	111,251.2	0.82%
Rural	18,459.3	1,373,658.8	1.34%
Federal land	33,563.3	401,936.9	8.35%
Water area	557.6	50,817.3	1.10%

Source: U.S. Department of Agriculture, Natural Resources Conservation Service, 2007 National Resources Inventory

Land Cover/Use of Non-Federal Rural Land, 2007
In thousands of acres

Category	State	U.S.	State Share
Total rural land	18,459.3	1,373,658.8	1.34%
Cropland	5,246.1	357,023.5	1.47%
CRP[1] land	797.2	32,850.2	2.43%
Pastureland	1,307.6	118,615.7	1.10%
Rangeland	6,514.3	409,119.4	1.59%
Forest land	4,015.9	406,410.4	0.99%
Other rural land	578.2	49,639.6	1.16%

Note: (1) Conservation Reserve Program was created to assist private landowners in converting highly erodible cropland to vegetative cover.
Source: U.S. Department of Agriculture, Natural Resources Conservation Service, 2007 National Resources Inventory

Farms and Crop Acreage, 2012

Category	State	U.S.	State Share
Farms (in thousands)	24.5	2,170.0	1.13%
Acres (in millions)	11.4	914.0	1.25%
Acres per farm	465.3	421.2	–

Source: U.S. Department of Agriculture, National Agricultural Statistical Service, Quick Stats, 2012 Survey Data

HEALTH AND MEDICAL CARE

Medical Professionals, 2012

Profession	State Number	U.S. Number	State Share	State Rate[1]	U.S. Rate[1]
Physicians[2]	2,830	894,637	0.32%	178.7	287.1
Dentists	998	193,587	0.52%	63.0	62.1
Podiatrists	59	17,469	0.34%	3.7	5.6
Optometrists	264	45,638	0.58%	16.7	14.6
Chiropractors	516	77,494	0.67%	32.6	24.9

Note: (1) Rates are per 100,000 population; (2) Includes total, active Doctors of Osteopathic Medicine and Doctors of Medicine in 2011.
Source: U.S. Department of Health and Human Services, Bureau of Health Professions, Area Health Resource File, 2012-2013

Health Insurance Coverage, 2011

Category	State	U.S.
Total persons covered	1,308,000	260,214,000
Total persons not covered	266,000	48,613,000
Percent not covered	16.9%	15.7%
Children under age 18 covered	379,000	67,143,000
Children under age 18 not covered	48,000	6,965,000
Percent of children not covered	11.2%	9.4%

Source: U.S. Census Bureau, Current Population Survey, 2012 Annual Social and Economic Supplement

HIV, STD, and Tuberculosis Cases and Rates, 2011

Disease	State Cases	State Rate[1]	U.S. Rate[1]
Chlamydia	4,699	299.8	457.6
Gonorrhea	162	10.3	104.2
HIV diagnosis	38	3.0	15.8
HIV, stage 3 (AIDS)	23	1.8	10.3
Syphilis, early latent	11	0.7	4.3
Syphilis, primary/secondary	13	0.8	4.5
Tuberculosis	12	0.8	3.4

Note: (1) Rates are per 100,000 population
Source: Centers for Disease Control and Prevention

Cigarette Smoking, 2011

Category	State	U.S.
Adults who are current smokers	17.2%	21.2%
Adults who smoke everyday	12.4%	15.4%
Adults who smoke some days	4.8%	5.7%
Adults who are former smokers	24.4%	25.1%
Adults who never smoked	58.5%	52.9%

Source: Centers for Disease Control and Prevention, Behaviorial Risk Factor Surveillance System, Tobacco Use, 2011

HOUSING

Home Ownership Rates, 1995–2012

Area	1995	2000	2005	2010	2012
State	72.0%	70.5%	74.2%	72.4%	73.0%
U.S.	64.7%	67.4%	68.9%	66.9%	65.4%

Source: U.S. Census Bureau, Housing Vacancies and Homeownership, Annual Statistics

Home Sales, 2000–2010
In thousands of units

Year	State Sales	U.S. Sales	State Share
2000	24.1	5,174	0.47%
2002	25.7	5,632	0.46%
2004	32.0	6,778	0.47%
2006	0.0	6,478	0.00%
2008	26.5	4,913	0.54%
2010	38.8	4,908	0.79%

Note: Units include single-family homes, condos and co-ops
Source: National Association of Realtors, Real Estate Outlook, Market Trends & Insights

Value of Owner-Occupied Homes, 2011

Value	Total Units in State	Percent of Total, State	Percent of Total, U.S.
Less than $50,000	30,564	7.7%	8.8%
$50,000 to $99,000	59,260	14.9%	16.0%
$100,000 to $149,000	91,271	22.9%	16.5%
$150,000 to $199,000	86,189	21.6%	15.4%
$200,000 to $299,000	77,400	19.4%	18.2%
$300,000 to $499,000	38,132	9.6%	15.2%
$500,000 to $999,000	12,331	3.1%	7.9%
$1,000,000 or more	3,669	0.9%	2.0%
Median value	–	$158,800	$173,600

Source: U.S. Census Bureau, 2011 American Community Survey 1-Year Estimates

EDUCATION

School Enrollment, 2011

Educational Level	Students Enrolled in State	Percent of Total, State	Percent of Total, U.S.
All levels	452,340	100.0%	100.0%
Nursery school, preschool	23,824	5.3%	6.0%
Kindergarten	23,546	5.2%	5.1%
Elementary (grades 1–8)	189,345	41.9%	39.5%
Secondary (grades 9–12)	94,891	21.0%	20.7%
College or graduate school	120,734	26.7%	28.7%

Note: Figures cover the population 3 years and over enrolled in school
Source: U.S. Census Bureau, 2011 American Community Survey 1-Year Estimates

Educational Attainment, 2011

Highest Level of Education	State	U.S.
High school diploma	88.6%	85.9%
Bachelor's degree	25.2%	28.5%
Graduate/Professional degree	7.8%	10.6%

Note: Figures cover the population 25 years and over
Source: U.S. Census Bureau, 2011 American Community Survey 1-Year Estimates

Public College Finances, FY 2012

Category	State	U.S.
Full-time equivalent enrollment (FTE)[1]	58,980	11,548,974
Educational appropriations per FTE[2]	$5,661	$5,906
Net tuition revenue per FTE[3]	$3,329	$5,189
Total educational revenue per FTE[4]	$8,990	$11,043

(1) Full-time equivalent enrollment equates student credit hours to full time, academic year students, but excludes medical students; (2) Educational appropriations measure state and local support available for public higher education operating expenses including ARRA funds and excludes appropriations for independent institutions, financial aid for students attending independent institutions, research, hospitals, and medical education; (3) Net tuition revenue is calculated by taking the gross amount of tuition and fees, less state and institutional financial aid, tuition waivers or discounts, and medical student tuition and fees. Net tuition revenue used for capital debt service is included in the net tuition revenue figures; (4) Total educational revenue is the sum of educational appropriations and net tuition excluding net tuition revenue used for capital debt service.
Source: State Higher Education Executive Officers, State Higher Education Finance FY 2012

TRANSPORTATION AND TRAVEL

Motor Vehicle Registrations and Drivers Licenses, 2011

Vehicle Type	State	U.S.	State Share
Automobiles[1]	610,646	125,656,528	0.49%
Buses	4,553	666,064	0.68%
Trucks	947,382	118,455,587	0.80%
Motorcycles	62,623	8,437,502	0.74%
Drivers licenses	1,083,992	211,874,649	0.51%

Note: Motor vehicle registrations include private, commercial, and publicly-owned vehicles; (1) Includes taxicabs
Source: U.S. Department of Transportation, Federal Highway Administration

Domestic Travel Expenditures, 2009
In millions of dollars

Category	State	U.S.	State Share
Travel expenditures	$2,889	$610,200	0.47%

Note: Figures represent U.S. spending on domestic overnight trips and day trips of 50 miles or more, one way, away from home. Excludes spending by foreign visitors.
Source: U.S. Travel Association, Impact of Travel on State Economies, 2009

Retail Gasoline Prices, 2013

Gasoline Grade	State Average	U.S. Average
Regular	$3.78	$3.65
Mid	$3.88	$3.81
Premium	$4.00	$3.98
Diesel	$3.98	$3.88
Excise tax[1]	43.4 cents	49.4 cents

Note: Gasoline prices as of 7/26/2013; (1) Includes state and federal excise taxes and other state taxes as of July 1, 2013
Source: American Automobile Association, Daily Fuel Guage Report; American Petroleum Institute, State Motor Fuel Taxes, 2013

Public Road Length, 2011

Type	State Mileage	U.S. Mileage	State Share
Interstate highways	612	46,960	1.30%
Other highways	0	15,719	0.00%
Principal arterial	2,198	156,262	1.41%
Minor arterial	2,045	242,942	0.84%
Major collector	6,491	534,592	1.21%
Minor collector	4,015	266,357	1.51%
Local	33,194	2,814,925	1.18%
Urban	5,553	1,095,373	0.51%
Rural	43,000	2,982,383	1.44%
Total	48,553	4,077,756	1.19%

Note: Combined urban and rural road mileage equals the total of the other road types
Source: U.S. Department of Transportation, Federal Highway Administration, Public Road Length, 2011

CRIME AND LAW ENFORCEMENT

Full-Time Law Enforcement Officers, 2011

Gender	State Number	State Rate[1]	U.S. Rate[1]
Male officers	2,588	163.8	210.3
Female officers	171	10.8	28.1
Total officers	2,759	174.6	238.3

Note: (1) Rates are per 100,000 population
Source: Federal Bureau of Investigation, Uniform Crime Reports, Crime in the United States 2011

Prison Population, 2000–2012

Year	State Population	U.S. Population	State Share
2000	5,535	1,391,261	0.40%
2005	6,818	1,527,929	0.45%
2010	7,431	1,613,803	0.46%
2011	7,739	1,598,783	0.48%
2012	7,985	1,571,013	0.51%

Note: Figures include prisoners under the jurisdiction of state or federal correctional authorities.
Source: U.S. Department of Justice, Bureau of Justice Statistics, Prisoners in 2006, 2011, 2012 (Advance Counts)

Crime Rate, 2011

Incidents per 100,000 residents

Category	State	U.S.
Violent crimes	200.9	386.3
Murder	2.3	4.7
Forcible rape	27.4	26.8
Robbery	11.6	113.7
Aggravated assault	159.6	241.1
Property crimes	2,068.6	2,908.7
Burglary	436.6	702.2
Larceny/theft	1,547.9	1,976.9
Motor vehicle theft	84.1	229.6
All crimes	2,269.5	3,295.0

Source: Federal Bureau of Investigation, Uniform Crime Reports, Crime in the United States 2011

GOVERNMENT AND FINANCE

Local Governments by Type, 2012

Government Type	State	U.S.	State Share
All local governments	1,161	89,004	1.30%
County	44	3,031	1.45%
Municipality	200	19,522	1.02%
Town/Township	0	16,364	0.00%
Special District	799	37,203	2.15%
Ind. School District	118	12,884	0.92%

Source: U.S. Census Bureau, 2012 Census of Governments: Organization Component Preliminary Estimates

State Government Revenue, 2011

In thousands of dollars, except for per capita figures

Total revenue	**$10,776,454**
Total revenue per capita, State	$6,804
Total revenue per capita, U.S.	$7,271
General revenue	$7,344,101
Intergovernmental revenue	$2,804,663
Taxes	$3,261,722
General sales	$1,187,070
Selective sales	$425,655
License taxes	$297,648
Individual income taxes	$1,169,247
Corporate income taxes	$170,214
Other taxes	$11,888
Current charges	$801,841
Miscellaneous general revenue	$475,875
Utility revenue	$0
Liquor store revenue	$121,520
Insurance trust revenue[1]	$3,310,833

Note: (1) Within insurance trust revenue, net earnings of state retirement systems is a calculated statistic, and thus can be positive or negative. Net earnings is the sum of earnings on investments plus gains on investments minus losses on investments.
Source: U.S. Census Bureau, 2011 Annual Survey of State Government Finances

State Government Expenditures, 2011

In thousands of dollars, except for per capita figures

Total expenditure	$8,733,485
Total expenditure per capita, State	$5,514
Total expenditure per capita, U.S.	$6,427
Intergovernmental expenditure	$2,036,312
Direct expenditure	$6,697,173
Current operation	$4,430,640
Capital outlay	$691,443
Insurance benefits and repayments	$1,235,285
Assistance and subsidies	$163,543
Interest on debt	$176,262
Utility expenditure	$0
Liquor store expenditure	$93,451
Insurance trust expenditure	$1,235,285

Source: U.S. Census Bureau, 2011 Annual Survey of State Government Finances

State Government General Expenditures by Function, 2011

In thousands of dollars

Education	$2,700,603
Public welfare	$2,174,866
Hospitals	$44,305
Health	$159,152
Highways	$836,014
Police protection	$52,386
Correction	$219,042
Natural resources	$194,745
Parks and recreation	$35,329
Governmental administration	$272,690
Interest on general debt	$176,262
Other and unallocable	$539,355

Source: U.S. Census Bureau, 2011 Annual Survey of State Government Finances

State Government Finances, Cash and Debt, 2011

In thousands of dollars, except for per capita figures

Debt at end of fiscal year	
State, total	$3,928,080
State, per capita	$2,480
U.S., per capita	$3,635
Cash and security holdings	
State, total	$18,352,520
State, per capita	$11,588
U.S., per capita	$11,759

Source: U.S. Census Bureau, 2011 Annual Survey of State Government Finances

POLITICS

Composition of the Senate, 1995–2013

Congress (Year)	State/U.S	Dem	Rep	Total
104th (1995)	State delegates	0	2	2
	Total U.S.	48	52	100
105th (1997)	State delegates	0	2	2
	Total U.S.	45	55	100
106th (1999)	State delegates	0	2	2
	Total U.S.	45	55	100
107th (2001)	State delegates	0	2	2
	Total U.S.	50	50	100
108th (2003)	State delegates	0	2	2
	Total U.S.	48	51	100
109th (2005)	State delegates	0	2	2
	Total U.S.	44	55	100
110th (2007)	State delegates	0	2	2
	Total U.S.	49	49	100
111th (2009)	State delegates	0	2	2
	Total U.S.	57	41	100
112th (2011)	State delegates	0	2	2
	Total U.S.	51	47	100
113th (2013)	State delegates	0	2	2
	Total U.S.	54	45	100

Note: Figures are for the starts of first sessions; Totals include Democratic (Dem) and Republican (Rep) members as well as vacancies and seats held by independent party members
Source: U.S. Congress, Congressional Directory

Composition of the House of Representatives, 1995–2013

Congress (Year)	State/U.S	Dem	Rep	Total
104th (1995)	State delegates	0	2	2
	Total U.S.	204	230	435
105th (1997)	State delegates	0	2	2
	Total U.S.	207	226	435
106th (1999)	State delegates	0	2	2
	Total U.S.	211	223	435
107th (2001)	State delegates	0	2	2
	Total U.S.	212	221	435
108th (2003)	State delegates	0	2	2
	Total U.S.	205	229	435
109th (2005)	State delegates	0	2	2
	Total U.S.	202	231	435
110th (2007)	State delegates	0	2	2
	Total U.S.	233	198	435
111th (2009)	State delegates	1	1	2
	Total U.S.	256	178	435
112th (2011)	State delegates	0	2	2
	Total U.S.	193	242	435
113th (2013)	State delegates	0	2	2
	Total U.S.	201	234	435

Note: Figures are for the starts of first sessions; Totals include Democratic (Dem) and Republican (Rep) members as well as vacancies and seats held by independent party members
Source: U.S. Congress, Congressional Directory

Composition of State Legislature, 2004–2013

Year	Democrats	Republicans	Total
State Senate			
2004	7	28	35
2005	7	28	35
2006	7	28	35
2007	7	28	35
2008	7	28	35
2009	7	28	35
2010	7	28	35
2011	7	28	35
2012	7	28	35
2013	7	28	35
State House			
2004	16	54	70
2005	13	57	70
2006	13	57	70
2007	19	51	70
2008	19	51	70
2009	18	52	70
2010	18	52	70
2011	13	57	70
2012	13	57	70
2013	13	57	70

Note: Totals may include minor party members and vacancies
Source: The Council of State Governments, State Legislatures

Voter Participation in Presidential Elections, 1980–2012

Year	Voting-eligible State Population	State Voter Turnout Rate	U.S. Voter Turnout Rate
1980	633,624	69.0	54.2
1984	662,771	62.0	55.2
1988	667,345	61.3	52.8
1992	734,855	65.6	58.1
1996	825,329	59.3	51.7
2000	877,406	57.2	54.2
2004	946,160	63.2	60.1
2008	1,029,416	63.6	61.6
2012	1,094,490	59.6	58.2

Note: All figures are based on the voting-eligible population which excludes person ineligible to vote such as non-citizens, felons (depending on state law), and mentally-incapacitated persons. U.S. figures include the overseas eligible population (including military personnel).
Source: McDonald, Michael P., United States Election Project, Presidential Voter Turnout Rates, 1980–2012

Governors Since Statehood

George L. Shoup (R)	(r) 1890
Norman B. Willey (R)	1890-1893
William J. McConnell (R)	1893-1897
Frank Steunenberg (D)	1897-1901
Frank W. Hunt (D)	1901-1903
John T. Morrison (R)	1903-1905
Frank R. Gooding (R)	1905-1909
James H. Brady (R)	1909-1911
James W. Hawley (D)	1911-1913
John M. Haines (R)	1913-1915
Moses Alexander (D)	1915-1919
David W. Davis (R)	1919-1923
Charles C. Moore (R)	1923-1927
H. Clarence Baldridge (R)	1927-1931
Charles Ben Ross (D)	1931-1937
Barzilla W. Clark (D)	1937-1939
Clarence A. Bottolfsen (R)	1939-1941
Chase A. Clark (D)	1941-1943
Clarence A. Bottolfsen (R)	1943-1945
Charles C. Gossett (D)	(r) 1945
Arnold Williams (D)	1945-1947
Charles A. Robins (R)	1947-1951
Leonard B. Jordan (R)	1951-1955
Robert E. Smylie (R)	1955-1967
Donald W. Samuelson (R)	1967-1971
Cecil D. Andrus (D)	(r) 1971-1977
John V. Evans (D)	1977-1987
Cecil D. Andrus (D)	1987-1995
Phillip E. Batt (R)	1995-1999
Dirk Kempthorne (R)	(r) 1999-2006
Jim Risch (R)	2006-2007
C. L. "Butch" Otter (R)	2007-2015

Note: (D) Democrat; (R) Republican; (O) Other party; (r) resigned; (d) died in office; (i) removed from office

Illinois

Location: Midwest

Area and rank: 55,593 square miles (143,987 square kilometers); 57,918 square miles (150,008 square kilometers) including water; twenty-fourth largest state in area

Coastline: none

Population and rank: 12,875,255 (2012 estimate); fifth largest state in population

Capital city: Springfield (116,250 people in 2010 census)

Illinois's chief city, Chicago is the third largest city in the United States. (Wikimedia Commons)

Largest city: Chicago (2,695,598 people in 2010 census)

Became territory: February 3, 1809

Entered Union and rank: December 3, 1818; twenty-first state

Present constitution adopted: 1970

Counties: 102

State name: "Illinois" is an Algonquin word for "tribe of superior men"

State nickname: Prairie State

Motto: State sovereignty, national union

State flag: White field with state seal and name "Illinois" in blue

Highest point: Charles Mound—1,235 feet (376 meters)

Lowest point: Mississippi River—279 feet (85 meters)

Highest recorded temperature: 117 degrees Fahrenheit (47 degrees Celsius)—East St. Louis, 1954

Lowest recorded temperature: –35 degrees Fahrenheit (–37 degrees Celsius)—Mount Carroll, 1930

State song: "Illinois"

State tree: White oak

State flower: Purple violet

State bird: Cardinal

State fish: Bluegill

State animal: White-tailed deer

ILLINOIS

Illinois History

Situated between the major waterways of the Mississippi River and Lake Michigan, and possessing unusually rich soil for agricultural purposes, Illinois has been an important area of human activity since the earliest days of habitation. The historical development of the region has been sharply divided among the urban northeast area, dominated by Chicago; the central area, a mixture of urban and rural cultures; and the rural southern area, which resembles its southern neighbors, Missouri and Kentucky, more than it does the rest of the state.

Early History. The earliest humans to inhabit the area were hunters and gatherers who roamed the southern part of the region ten thousand years ago. Over the next several thousand years, cultures developed that built permanent villages and depended primarily on the growing of corn. By the year 1300, the Mississippian culture, a highly developed society based on the raising of corn, squash, and beans, dominated central North America. This society, the largest Native American culture north of Mexico, built large, fortified cities and extensive earth-mound monuments. The largest of these monuments were found at Cahokia, the culture's religious center, located in southwestern Illinois.

By the time Europeans arrived in the New World, a large number of Native American peoples, belonging to the Algonquin language group, inhabited the region. Among these were the Kickapoo, Sauk, and Fox in the north; the Potawatomi, Ottawa, and Ojibwa near Lake Michigan; the Illinois, a confederation of five peoples, in the central prairies; and the Cahokia and Tamaroa in the south. These societies relied on agriculture and buffalo hunting for survival. By the end of the first third of the nineteenth century, all these peoples had sold, ceded, or been forced off their native lands and had settled in other areas.

Exploration and Settlement. The first Europeans to visit the Illinois area were led by the French explorers Louis Jolliet and Jacques Marquette in 1673 as they traveled south from Wisconsin along the Mississippi River as far as Arkansas. This expedition also explored the Illinois River on its return journey north. In 1680, the French explorers René-Robert Cavelier, sieur de La Salle, and

Henri de Tonti founded Fort Crevecoeur near the modern city of Peoria, followed two years later by Fort Saint Louis near the modern city of Ottawa. After a century of French settlement, the area became British territory at the end of the French and Indian War.

British policy was unfavorable to the economic development of the area, and settlements often lacked any form of government. Combined with violent encounters with Native Americans living in the area, these factors tended to discourage settlers. By 1773, the num-

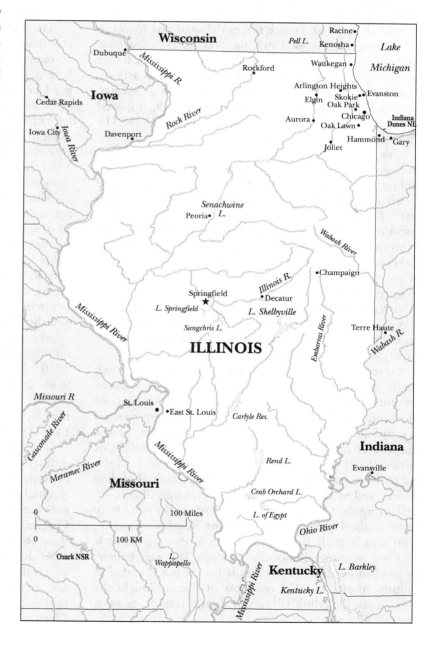

ber of Europeans in Illinois had declined to about one thousand. The population also included a few hundred slaves.

During the American Revolution, American forces under George Rogers Clark captured British settlements at Kaskaskia and Cahokia in May of 1778, winning the region for the newly created United States. American control of the area was confirmed by the Treaty of Paris, which ended the war in 1783. At first a part of the state of Virginia, the region became part of the new Northwest Territory in 1787; part of the new Indiana Territory in 1800; a separate territory, including parts of modern Wisconsin and Minnesota, in 1809; and a state, with its modern borders, in 1818.

Conflict with Native Americans. Battles between European settlers and Native Americans began long before statehood. In 1730, French forces defeated Fox forces in east central Illinois. In 1803, the Kaskaskia ceded their lands to the United States. In 1812, Potawatomi forces killed fifty-two Americans and destroyed Fort Dearborn, a military establishment on the site of modern Chicago. The Kickapoo left their native lands in 1819, followed by the Ojibwa, Ottawa, and Potawatomi in 1829. The Illinois sold their land in 1832.

One of the most violent encounters between settlers and American Indians was the Black Hawk War of 1832. Although some leaders of the Sauk and Fox had ceded their lands to the United States in 1804, others refused to leave. Black Hawk, a leader of these people, was driven into Iowa in 1831 but crossed back over the Mississippi River into Illinois the next year with about one thousand followers. Although at first Black Hawk was able to defeat the Illinois militia, lack of supplies forced him to retreat northward into Wisconsin, where most of his followers were killed. The destruction of Black Hawk's people, including women, children, and the elderly, was an important factor in the decision of nearly all Native Americans to leave the area by 1837.

Slavery and the Civil War. At the time of statehood, slaves in Illinois were given the status of indentured servants, due to the fear that permitting slavery would block admission to the Union. In 1824, voters rejected a proposal to hold a constitutional convention for the purpose of making slavery legal. Increasing numbers of settlers from free states during the 1830's and 1840's led to a new state constitution in 1848, which abolished slavery and made it illegal to bring slaves into Illinois.

During the Civil War, most residents of the state were loyal to the Union and to President Abraham Lincoln, who was himself from Illinois. An attempt was made to unite southern Illinois, which was less sympathetic to the Union cause, to the Confederacy, but it ended in failure. About 250,000 residents of Illinois fought for the Union, including Ulysses S. Grant, one of its most capable generals.

The Rise of Chicago. During the early nineteenth century, about two-thirds of the population of Illinois lived in the southern part of the state. Although Jean Baptist Point du Sable, known as the father of Chicago, founded a trading post at the site in 1779, it remained a small settlement for nearly half a century. The opening of the Erie Canal in 1825, linking the Hudson River to Lake Erie, made transportation from eastern states to northern Illinois much easier. In 1837, Chicago had a population of 4,200 and was incorporated as a city.

The opening of the Illinois and Michigan canal in 1848 linked Lake Michigan and the Illinois River, providing Chicago with a waterway to the Mississippi River. By 1852 two railroad lines linked Chicago to eastern states. By 1856 it was the nation's most important railroad center.

The second half of the nineteenth century saw rapid economic growth in Chicago, with the city becoming dominant in iron and steel production, lumber distribution, slaughtering and meat packing, and marketing of produce. The Great Chicago Fire, lasting for two days in October, 1871, killed more than two hundred people, left ninety thousand homeless, and destroyed $200 million worth of property. Despite this disaster, Chicago continued to experience rapid growth. From 1850 to 1880 the population of the city grew from about thirty thousand to more than half a million.

The Twentieth Century. Although Illinois harbored a number of German and Irish immigrants during the 1840's, it was not until the turn of the century that large numbers of immigrants from other nations, including Poland, Hungary, Italy, Norway, Sweden, Austria, and Russia, arrived in the state. Chicago was the center of immigration, with more than three-fourths of its population in 1900 consisting of those born in other countries and their children.

The same period also saw a large increase in the number of African Americans in Illinois. From 1870 to 1910, the population of African Americans increased from 29,000 to more than 100,000. Prior to World War II, large numbers of European Jews immigrated to Illinois. In later years, increasing numbers of Asians and Latin Americans immigrated to the state.

The late nineteenth century and the early twentieth century brought Illinois a reputation for violence, particularly in Chicago, where the Haymarket Riot of 1886 resulted in numerous deaths in a confrontation between police and labor activists. Railroad worker strikes in Chicago in 1894 also led to violence. Elsewhere in the state, strikes by mine workers led to violence in 1898 and 1922. Race riots broke out in Springfield in 1908, in East St. Louis in 1917, and in Chicago in 1919. The 1920's saw an increase in violence against African Americans by the Ku Klux Klan. During the 1920's and 1930's, Chicago was a center of organized crime. Perhaps the most infamous event in the history of crime in Chicago occurred in 1929, when crime leader Al Capone had seven rivals killed in the Saint Valentine's Day Massacre.

Throughout the twentieth century, the Democratic and Republican parties struggled for control of Illinois. This fact, combined with the state's large number of electoral votes, made Illinois a key target of presidential election campaigns. In general, the city of Chicago has been strongly Democratic, the suburbs and farmlands of the north and central regions strongly Republican, and the southern region mixed.

After the economic recession of the 1970's, the electronic and computer technology industries in Illinois became an important part of the state's economy during the 1980's. Illinois also became a leader in nuclear-power production during the 1990's, when it had thirteen operating nuclear power plants, more than any other state. These plants supplied more than half of the state's electricity.

Politics. Illinois underwent several political changes at the end of the twentieth century. In the 2000 presidential elections, the state voted for Vice President Al Gore. The state also replaced congressional Democrats with two Republicans, one by a margin of 51 to 49 percent, the other by 53-47 percent. The U.S. Senate remained the same. Following the 2000 census, Illinois lost one seat in the U.S. House of Representatives.

Another notable political event in 2000 was President Bill Clinton's pardoning of former Representative Dan Rostenkowski, the once-powerful chairman of the House Ways and Means Committee. In 1996, Rostenkowski had been convicted of embezzlement and sent to prison for fifteen months. In 2000, Governor George Ryan declared a moratorium on the application of the death penalty after he learned that following 1987 the state had removed more prison inmates than it had executed from death row as a result of wrongful conviction. A national study had shown that more than two-thirds of all death sentences were overturned on appeal because of procedural or other flaws.

By 2002, the political climate turned decidedly frosty for Governor Ryan, whose campaign committee and two of his former top aides were indicted with a variety of crimes, including racketeering. The indictment forced the governor to abandon a reelection bid. Instead, Democrat Rod Blagojevich resigned his seat in Congress, ran for governor, and won.

Two years later, in 2004, a newly vacated seat in the

Contemporary magazine illustration of the Haymarket Riot. (Library of Congress)

U.S. Senate was won by Democrat Barack Obama, a lecturer at the University of Chicago Law School. Obama, whose father was an immigrant from Kenya, handily beat Republican candidate Alan Keyes. At the same time, the state remained in the Democrats' column in presidential elections, as John Kerry, aided by a large margin in Cook County where Chicago is located, defeated President George W. Bush, 55-44 percent.

Rahm Emanuel, Obama's chief of staff and a former member of Congress, won the 2011 Chicago mayoral election after a contentious campaign, becoming the city's first Jewish mayor. Early in his political career,

Emanuel served as director of the finance committee for Bill Clinton's 1992 presidential campaign. The following year he became a member of the Clinton administration, serving as assistant to the president for policy and strategy. From 1999 to 2002, Emanuel worked at the investment bank Wassertein Perella and Co. and served on the board of Freddie Mac.

Emanuel received 55 percent of the vote in the nonpartisan election and took over for Richard M. Daley, who had been mayor for 22 years.

Rose Secrest
Updated by the Editor

The Great Chicago Fire of October 9, 1871, depicted in a lithograph from the same year. (Library of Congress)

Illinois Time Line

1673	Louis Jolliet and Jacques Marquette lead the first European expedition to the area.
1680	René-Robert Cavelier, sieur de La Salle, and Henri de Tonti found Fort Crevecoeur.
1682	La Salle and Tonti found Fort Saint Louis.
1730	Fox forces are defeated in a battle with French settlers.
1763	End of the French and Indian War brings the area under British control.
1778	George Rogers Clark leads American forces to victory over British forces in Kaskaskia and Cahokia.
1779	Jean Baptist Point du Sable founds a trading post at Chicago.
1783	End of the American Revolution brings the area under American control.
1787	Illinois becomes part of the Northwest Territory.
1803	Kaskaskia cede their land to the United States.
1803	Fort Dearborn is established at Chicago. 1809 Illinois Territory is established.
1811–1812	Earthquakes centered near New Madrid, Missouri, cause extensive damage in southern Illinois. 1812 Potawatomi forces destroy Fort Dearborn.
1814	First newspaper, the *Illinois Herald*, is established.
1816	Fort Dearborn is rebuilt.
1816	First bank in Illinois is established.
1818	Population is nearly thirty-five thousand.
Dec. 3, 1818	Illinois becomes the twenty-first state.
1819	Kickapoo leave their native lands.
1820	Capital is moved from Kaskaskia to Vandalia.
1824	Voters defeat a plan for a constitutional convention which would legalize slavery in the state.
1825	Opening of the Erie Canal brings more settlers to Chicago.
1827	Rock Spring Seminary, the first college, is established.
1829	Ojibwa, Ottawa, and Potawatomi cede their lands to the United States.
1832	Black Hawk War leads to the defeat of the Sauk and Fox.
1837	Chicago is incorporated as a city.
1839	Capital is moved to Springfield.
1848	New state constitution abolishes slavery.
1850	Population reaches 850,000; Chicago is home to 30,000.
1852	Railroads connect Chicago with eastern cities.
1867	University of Illinois is established.
1871	Great Chicago Fire devastates the city.
1880	Population of Chicago reaches 500,000.
1883	Ten-story Home Insurance Building, the world's first skyscraper, is built in Chicago.
1886	Haymarket Riot, a confrontation between police and labor activists, breaks out in Chicago.
1894	Strike by railroad workers leads to violence in Chicago.
1898	Strike by mine workers leads to violence in Pana and Virden.
1900	Population reaches nearly five million.
1908	Race riot breaks out in Springfield.
1917	Race riot breaks out in East St. Louis.
1919	Race riot breaks out in Chicago.
1922	Strike by mine workers leads to violence in Williamson County.
1929	Seven Chicago crime leaders are murdered in the Saint Valentine's Day Massacre.
1942	First controlled nuclear chain reaction is achieved at the University of Chicago.
1950	Population reaches nearly nine million.
1957	First nuclear power plant in the United States is established.
1968	Violence breaks out between police and protesters during the Democratic National Convention.
1990	Population reaches 11.5 million.
1992	Carol Moseley-Braun of Chicago becomes the first African American woman elected to the United States Senate.
1993	Worst floods in the state's history do $1.5billion worth of damage in western and southern Illinois.

Lake Michigan in northeast Illinois offers miles of sandy beaches. (PhotoDisc)

1994	Members of the Republican Party hold all statewide offices and control both chambers of the state assembly.
1997	Population reaches nearly 12 million, with 85 percent living in urban areas, including 65 percent in the Chicago metropolitan area.
Jan. 31, 2000	Governor George Ryan declares a moratorium on the death penalty.
Nov. 7, 2000	Illinois votes its twenty-two electoral votes for Vice President Al Gore.
Dec. 2000	President Bill Clinton pardons former Illinois congressman Dan Rostenkowski, who had served prison time for embezzling funds.
2002	Indictment of Governor Ryan's campaign committee and two of his former top aides leads to his withdrawal from a reelection bid.
Nov. 2, 2004	Democrat Barack Obama defeats Alan Keyes for the vacant U.S. Senate seat.
2011	Rahm Israel Emanuel wins election as the 55th Mayor of Chicago in 2011, defeating Richard M. Daley who had held the position for 22 years.
March 2012	Former governor of Illinois Rod Blagojevich begins a 14-year prison sentence for corruption.

Notes for Further Study

Published Sources. Two good places for the beginning student to start are Andrew Santella's *Illinois* (1998)—a simple but clear account of the state's history, geography, ecology, people, economy, cities, and attractions—and his *All Around Illinois: Regions and Resources* (2002). An extremely detailed discussion of the state's physical structure can be found in A. Doyne Horsley's *Illinois: A Geography* (1986), which includes extensive maps. The land and its inhabitants are described in *The Natural Resources of Illinois* (1987), compiled by R. Dan Neely and Carla G. Heister. Two of the best books dealing with the early history of the state are *Frontier Illinois* (1998) by James E. Davis and *French Roots in the Illinois Country: The Mississippi Frontier in Colonial Times* (1998) by Carl J. Ekberg. Two worthwhile books detail specific aspects of the slavery period in Illinois: *Democracy and Slavery in Frontier Illinois: The Bottomland Republic* (2000) by James Simeone and *Escape Betwixt Two Suns: A True Tale of the Underground Railroad in Illinois* (2000) by Carol Pirtle. For more detailed information on the state's history, the University of Illinois publishes numerous volumes dealing with all aspects of the state's past.

Of the many books dealing with Chicago, one of the best for the general reader is *Chicago Sketches: Urban Tales, Stories, and Legends from Chicago History* (1995) by June Skinner Sawyers, a collection of seventy-two colorful essays. A more serious book about the city is David Farber's *Chicago '68* (1988), a dramatic account of the riots that occurred during the Democratic National Convention in 1968. John C. Hudson's *Chicago: A Geography of the City and its Region* (2006) is a thorough book that brings forth a topical and chronological focus to the city's history. In *Chicago Dreaming: Midwesterners and the City, 1871–1919* (2005), Timothy B. Spears examines the influx of rural midwesterners into Chicago during a period of fifty years and how it shaped the young city's identity.

Web Resources. An excellent place to start one's research on the state of Illinois is its official government site (www.state.il.us). It provides information on governmental agencies, tourism, cities and counties, and state facts. For local information, Illinois Counties (www.outfitters.com/illinois/index2 .html) provides brief data on all the state's counties, while Living in Ilinois (illinoisgis.ito.state.il.us/communities/) offers users in-depth information about counties when one uses the drop-down menu, or about cities when one types in a city name. Tourist attractions in the state are discussed in the Illinois @ Travel Notes site (www.travelnotes.org/NorthAmerica/illinois.htm). The physical structure of the region is described in the Illinois States Geologic Survey Web site (lsgs.illinois.edu/).

One of the many Web sites devoted to Illinois history, with discussions of Chicago, Abraham Lincoln, Native Americans, early settlers, and the history of transportation, is the Illinois History Resource Page (www.historyillinois.org/files/Links/hist.html). An excellent time line can be found at Illinois Historic Preservation Agency (www.state.il.us/hpa/lib/ILChronology.htm). Illinois Digital Archives (www.idaillinois.org/) is a unique online history project which covers Illinois in its first century of statehood, 1818-1918. The Encyclopedia of Chicago (www.encyclopedia.chicagohistory.org/) offers comprehensive information on the city, while the Chicago's History from the Kids' View (http://library.thinkquest .org/CR0215480/) is an entertaining site for young learners.

At the time of its completion in 1973, the Willis Tower (formerly Sears Tower) was the tallest building in the world. (©Daniel Schwen/Wikimedia Commons)

Counties

County	2012 Population	Pop. Rank	Land Area (sq. miles)	Area Rank	County	2012 Population	Pop. Rank	Land Area (sq. miles)	Area Rank
Adams	67,197	22	855.20	12	Macon	110,122	19	580.69	38
Alexander	7,748	90	235.51	97	Macoupin	47,231	32	862.91	11
Bond	17,644	64	380.28	76	Madison	267,883	9	715.58	22
Boone	53,940	26	280.72	93	Marion	38,894	36	572.36	40
Brown	6,914	93	305.61	91	Marshall	12,327	85	386.79	74
Bureau	34,323	45	869.03	8	Mason	14,327	78	539.24	48
Calhoun	5,014	100	253.82	94	Massac	15,234	73	237.22	96
Carroll	15,011	74	444.81	60	McDonough	32,537	48	589.41	36
Cass	13,338	82	375.82	79	McHenry	308,145	6	603.17	34
Champaign	203,276	10	996.27	5	McLean	172,281	13	1,183.38	1
Christian	34,638	43	709.38	24	Menard	12,722	84	314.44	90
Clark	16,209	71	501.42	53	Mercer	16,219	70	561.20	45
Clay	13,766	80	468.32	59	Monroe	33,357	46	385.01	75
Clinton	38,061	39	474.08	58	Montgomery	29,620	50	703.69	25
Coles	53,655	27	508.29	52	Morgan	35,272	41	568.79	42
Cook	5,231,351	1	945.33	6	Moultrie	14,933	75	335.94	86
Crawford	19,600	59	443.63	62	Ogle	52,848	28	758.57	17
Cumberland	10,968	87	346.02	84	Peoria	187,254	12	619.21	32
De Witt	16,434	68	397.51	73	Perry	22,058	56	441.76	63
DeKalb	104,704	20	631.31	30	Piatt	16,504	67	439.20	64
Douglas	19,853	58	416.66	70	Pike	16,308	69	831.38	14
DuPage	927,987	2	327.50	87	Pope	4,272	101	368.77	82
Edgar	18,191	61	623.37	31	Pulaski	5,998	95	199.18	100
Edwards	6,684	94	222.42	99	Putnam	5,886	97	160.16	102
Effingham	34,353	44	478.78	57	Randolph	32,956	47	575.50	39
Fayette	22,014	57	716.48	20	Richland	16,176	72	359.99	83
Ford	14,008	79	485.62	56	Rock Island	147,457	14	427.64	67
Franklin	39,407	34	408.89	72	Saline	24,946	52	379.82	77
Fulton	36,651	40	865.59	10	Sangamon	199,271	11	868.30	9
Gallatin	5,430	98	323.07	88	Schuyler	7,457	91	437.27	65
Greene	13,576	81	543.02	46	Scott	5,290	99	250.91	95
Grundy	50,281	30	418.04	69	Shelby	22,196	55	758.52	18
Hamilton	8,370	89	434.67	66	St. Clair	268,858	8	657.76	28
Hancock	18,891	60	793.73	16	Stark	5,946	96	288.08	92
Hardin	4,258	102	177.53	101	Stephenson	46,959	33	564.52	43
Henderson	7,043	92	378.87	78	Tazewell	135,949	15	648.97	29
Henry	50,155	31	822.99	15	Union	17,647	63	413.46	71
Iroquois	29,240	51	1,117.32	3	Vermilion	80,727	21	898.37	7
Jackson	60,071	24	584.08	37	Wabash	11,727	86	223.25	98
Jasper	9,614	88	494.51	55	Warren	17,731	62	542.41	47
Jefferson	38,720	37	571.17	41	Washington	14,598	76	562.57	44
Jersey	22,742	53	369.27	81	Wayne	16,574	66	713.81	23
Jo Daviess	22,549	54	601.09	35	White	14,568	77	494.77	54
Johnson	12,760	83	343.91	85	Whiteside	57,846	25	684.25	26
Kane	522,487	5	520.06	50	Will	682,518	4	836.91	13
Kankakee	113,040	17	676.56	27	Williamson	66,674	23	420.15	68
Kendall	118,105	16	320.34	89	Winnebago	292,069	7	513.36	51
Knox	52,247	29	716.39	21	Woodford	38,971	35	527.80	49
LaSalle	112,973	18	1,135.12	2					
Lake	702,120	3	443.67	61					
Lawrence	16,604	65	372.18	80					
Lee	35,037	42	724.90	19					
Livingston	38,647	38	1,044.29	4					
Logan	30,013	49	618.06	33					

Source: U.S. Census Bureau, 2012 Population Estimates

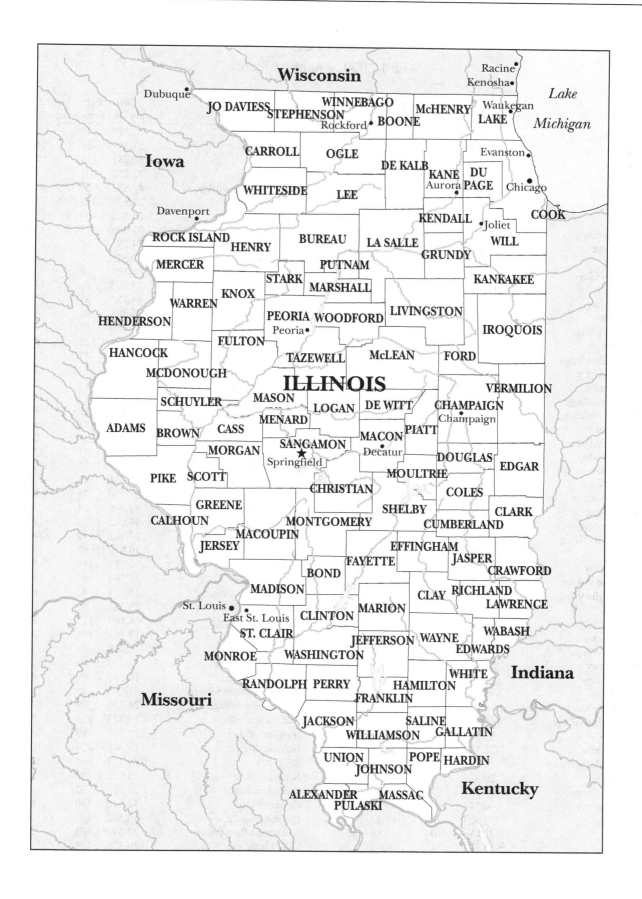

Cities

With 10,000 or more residents

Legal Name	2010 Population	Pop. Rank	Land Area (sq. miles)	Area Rank	Legal Name	2010 Population	Pop. Rank	Land Area (sq. miles)	Area Rank
Addison village	36,942	52	9.77	93	Deerfield village	18,225	141	5.58	160
Algonquin village	30,046	66	12.23	67	Des Plaines city	58,364	20	14.28	55
Alsip village	19,277	128	6.39	147	Dixon city	15,733	158	7.43	130
Alton city	27,865	76	15.47	43	Dolton village	23,153	107	4.56	181
Antioch village	14,430	170	8.21	115	Downers Grove village	47,833	30	14.31	54
Arlington Heights village	75,101	14	16.61	34	East Moline city	21,302	118	14.76	47
Aurora city	197,899	2	44.94	6	East Peoria city	23,402	105	19.96	21
Barrington village	10,327	217	4.62	179	East St. Louis city	27,006	81	13.99	58
Bartlett village	41,208	39	15.63	41	Edwardsville city	24,293	97	19.56	22
Batavia city	26,045	83	9.64	96	Effingham city	12,328	197	9.86	90
Beach Park village	13,638	178	7.10	135	Elgin city	108,188	8	37.16	9
Belleville city	44,478	32	22.74	15	Elk Grove Village village	33,127	56	11.34	75
Bellwood village	19,071	129	2.40	211	Elmhurst city	44,121	33	10.25	84
Belvidere city	25,585	86	12.08	69	Elmwood Park village	24,883	91	1.91	219
Bensenville village	18,352	137	5.57	161	Evanston city	74,486	15	7.78	125
Berwyn city	56,657	24	3.91	190	Evergreen Park village	19,852	122	3.16	198
Bloomingdale village	22,018	112	6.78	142	Fairview Heights city	17,078	147	11.42	73
Bloomington city	76,610	12	27.22	11	Forest Park village	14,167	172	2.40	211
Blue Island city	23,706	103	4.07	188	Fox Lake village	10,579	214	8.12	119
Bolingbrook village	73,366	17	24.05	12	Frankfort village	17,782	143	14.98	45
Bourbonnais village	18,631	134	9.31	105	Franklin Park village	18,333	138	4.77	175
Bradley village	15,895	157	7.24	132	Freeport city	25,638	85	11.78	71
Bridgeview village	16,446	153	4.15	187	Gages Lake CDP	10,198	220	2.99	201
Brookfield village	18,978	131	3.06	199	Galesburg city	32,195	61	17.75	29
Buffalo Grove village	41,496	37	9.50	98	Geneva city	21,495	117	9.75	94
Burbank city	28,925	71	4.17	186	Glen Carbon village	12,934	188	10.04	88
Burr Ridge village	10,559	215	7.00	137	Glen Ellyn village	27,450	78	6.61	145
Cahokia village	15,241	163	9.40	102	Glendale Heights village	34,208	53	5.37	166
Calumet City city	37,042	51	7.19	133	Glenview village	44,692	31	13.95	59
Campton Hills village	11,131	205	16.91	32	Godfrey village	17,982	142	34.64	10
Canton city	14,704	166	7.90	121	Granite City city	29,849	67	19.29	23
Carbondale city	25,902	84	17.09	31	Grayslake village	20,957	119	9.87	89
Carol Stream village	39,711	43	9.09	107	Gurnee village	31,295	62	13.50	62
Carpentersville village	37,691	48	7.90	121	Hanover Park village	37,973	47	6.33	148
Cary village	18,271	140	6.27	150	Harvey city	25,282	89	6.30	149
Centralia city	13,032	185	8.19	116	Hazel Crest village	14,100	173	3.39	196
Champaign city	81,055	11	22.43	16	Herrin city	12,501	196	9.23	106
Channahon village	12,560	193	14.99	44	Hickory Hills city	14,049	174	2.83	203
Charleston city	21,838	116	8.92	110	Highland Park city	29,763	69	12.20	68
Chatham village	11,500	202	5.72	157	Hinsdale village	16,816	149	4.60	180
Chicago city	2,695,598	1	227.63	1	Hoffman Estates village	51,895	28	20.80	19
Chicago Heights city	30,276	65	10.07	86	Homer Glen village	24,220	99	22.17	17
Chicago Ridge village	14,305	171	2.25	215	Homewood village	19,323	126	5.21	168
Cicero town	83,891	10	5.86	155	Huntley village	24,291	98	14.07	57
Collinsville city	25,579	87	14.68	49	Jacksonville city	19,446	124	10.47	79
Country Club Hills city	16,541	152	4.82	174	Joliet city	147,433	4	62.11	2
Crest Hill city	20,837	120	9.03	108	Justice village	12,926	189	2.84	202
Crestwood village	10,950	207	3.05	200	Kankakee city	27,537	77	14.14	56
Crystal Lake city	40,743	40	18.35	26	Kewanee city	12,916	190	6.71	144
Danville city	33,027	57	17.89	28	La Grange village	15,550	160	2.52	209
Darien city	22,086	110	6.18	152	La Grange Park village	13,579	181	2.23	216
DeKalb city	43,862	34	14.65	50	Lake Forest city	19,375	125	17.18	30
Decatur city	76,122	13	42.22	7	Lake Zurich village	19,631	123	6.77	143

Legal Name	2010 Population	Pop. Rank	Land Area (sq. miles)	Area Rank
Lake in the Hills village	28,965	70	10.38	80
Lansing village	28,331	72	6.79	141
Lemont village	16,000	156	7.97	120
Libertyville village	20,315	121	8.81	112
Lincoln city	14,504	168	6.40	146
Lincolnwood village	12,590	192	2.69	208
Lindenhurst village	14,462	169	4.44	182
Lisle village	22,390	109	6.84	140
Lockport city	24,839	92	11.40	74
Lombard village	43,165	36	10.25	84
Loves Park city	23,996	102	16.03	36
Lyons village	10,729	212	2.18	217
Machesney Park village	23,499	104	12.68	66
Macomb city	19,288	127	10.69	78
Marion city	17,193	146	15.99	38
Markham city	12,508	195	5.31	167
Matteson village	19,009	130	9.32	104
Mattoon city	18,555	135	10.34	82
Maywood village	24,090	101	2.72	207
McHenry city	26,992	82	14.74	48
Melrose Park village	25,411	88	4.24	184
Midlothian village	14,819	165	2.82	204
Minooka village	10,924	208	9.45	99
Mokena village	18,740	133	8.89	111
Moline city	43,483	35	16.43	35
Montgomery village	18,438	136	9.34	103
Morris city	13,636	179	9.44	100
Morton village	16,267	154	12.95	65
Morton Grove village	23,270	106	5.09	169
Mount Prospect village	54,167	25	10.34	82
Mount Vernon city	15,277	162	13.07	64
Mundelein village	31,064	63	9.57	97
Naperville city	141,853	5	38.77	8
New Lenox village	24,394	96	15.66	40
Niles village	29,803	68	5.85	156
Normal town	52,497	27	18.35	26
Norridge village	14,572	167	1.81	220
North Aurora village	16,760	150	7.18	134
North Chicago city	32,574	60	7.90	121
Northbrook village	33,170	55	13.19	63
Northlake city	12,323	198	3.17	197
O'Fallon city	28,281	73	14.35	53
Oak Forest city	27,962	75	5.95	154
Oak Lawn village	56,690	23	8.59	114
Oak Park village	51,878	29	4.70	178
Orland Park village	56,767	21	21.88	18
Oswego village	30,355	64	15.53	42
Ottawa city	18,768	132	12.00	70
Palatine village	68,557	18	13.62	60
Palos Heights city	12,515	194	3.78	193
Palos Hills city	17,484	145	4.25	183
Park Forest village	21,975	114	4.96	173
Park Ridge city	37,480	50	7.09	136
Pekin city	34,094	54	14.56	52
Peoria city	115,007	7	48.01	5
Peru city	10,295	218	8.96	109
Plainfield village	39,581	45	23.22	14
Plano city	10,856	209	7.46	129
Pontiac city	11,931	200	7.73	127

Legal Name	2010 Population	Pop. Rank	Land Area (sq. miles)	Area Rank
Prospect Heights city	16,256	155	4.24	184
Quincy city	40,633	41	15.91	39
Rantoul village	12,941	187	8.15	118
Richton Park village	13,646	177	3.98	189
River Forest village	11,172	204	2.48	210
River Grove village	10,227	219	2.39	213
Riverdale village	13,549	182	3.57	195
Rock Island city	39,018	46	16.85	33
Rockford city	152,871	3	61.08	3
Rolling Meadows city	24,099	100	5.63	159
Romeoville village	39,680	44	18.44	25
Roscoe village	10,785	211	10.36	81
Roselle village	22,763	108	5.41	164
Round Lake village	18,289	139	5.47	162
Round Lake Beach village	28,175	74	5.06	170
St. Charles city	32,974	58	14.61	51
Sauk Village village	10,506	216	3.84	191
Schaumburg village	74,227	16	19.22	24
Schiller Park village	11,793	201	2.77	206
Shiloh village	12,651	191	10.86	77
Shorewood village	15,615	159	7.77	126
Skokie village	64,784	19	10.06	87
South Elgin village	21,985	113	6.99	138
South Holland village	22,030	111	7.27	131
Springfield city	116,250	6	59.48	4
Sterling city	15,370	161	5.71	158
Streamwood village	39,858	42	7.82	124
Streator city	13,710	176	6.07	153
Summit village	11,054	206	2.12	218
Swansea village	13,430	183	6.26	151
Sycamore city	17,519	144	9.73	95
Taylorville city	11,246	203	9.86	90
Tinley Park village	56,703	22	16.02	37
Urbana city	41,250	38	11.65	72
Vernon Hills village	25,113	90	7.71	128
Villa Park village	21,904	115	4.71	177
Warrenville city	13,140	184	5.46	163
Washington city	15,134	164	8.17	117
Wauconda village	13,603	180	5.05	171
Waukegan city	89,078	9	23.67	13
West Chicago city	27,086	80	14.80	46
Westchester village	16,718	151	3.69	194
Western Springs village	12,975	186	2.79	205
Westmont village	24,685	94	5.03	172
Wheaton city	52,894	26	11.25	76
Wheeling village	37,648	49	8.70	113
Wilmette village	27,087	79	5.40	165
Winnetka village	12,187	199	3.81	192
Wood Dale city	13,770	175	4.72	176
Wood River city	10,657	213	6.98	139
Woodridge village	32,971	59	9.42	101
Woodstock city	24,770	93	13.55	61
Worth village	10,789	210	2.37	214
Yorkville city	16,921	148	19.97	20
Zion city	24,413	95	9.81	92

Note: CDP–Census Designated Place
Source: U.S. Census Bureau, 2010 Census

Survey Says...

This section presents current rankings from dozens of public and private sources. It shows how this state ranks in a number of critical categories, including education, job growth, cost of living, teen drivers, energy efficiency, and business environment. Sources include *Forbes, Reuters, U.S. News and World Report, CNN Money, Gallup,* and *Huffington Post.*

- Illinois ranked #26 in a government study measuring real gross domestic product (GDP)—the output of goods and services produced by labor and property located in the United States. The ranking is based on the percentage change compared with 2011 GDP.
  U.S. Department of Commerce, Bureau of Economic Analysis, June 2013; www.bea.gov

- Illinois ranked #5 in a government study measuring real gross domestic product (GDP)—the output of goods and services produced by labor and property located in the United States. The ranking is based on the dollar value of its GDP.
  U.S. Department of Commerce, Bureau of Economic Analysis, June 2013; www.bea.gov

- Illinois ranked #28 in the 17th edition of "Quality Counts; State of the States," Education Week's "report card" surveying key education indicators, policy efforts, and educational outcomes.
  Education Week, January 4, 2013 (online) and January 10, 2013 (print); www.edweek.org

- SERI (Science and Engineering Readiness Index) weighs the performance of the states' K-12 schools in preparing students in physics and calculus, the high school subjects considered most important for future scientists and engineers. Illinois ranked #12.
  Newsletter of the Forum on Education of the American Physical Society, Summer 2011 issue; www.huffingtonpost.com, July 11, 2011; updated October 1, 2012

- MoneyRates.com ranked Illinois #22 on its list of the best to worst states for making a living. Criteria: average income; inflation; employment prospects; and workers' Workplace Environment assessments according to the Gallup-Healthways Well-Being Index.
  www.money-rates.com, posted April 1, 2013

- *Forbes* analyzed business costs, labor supply, regulatory environment, current economic climate, growth prospects, and quality of life, to compile its "Best States for Business" rankings. Illinois ranked #38.
  www.forbes.com. posted December 12, 2012

- In "The States People Are Fleeing in 2013," *Forbes* reported the results of United Van Lines's thirty-sixth annual survey of its "customer migration patterns." In percentage of outbound moves, Illinois ranked #2 (1 = most).
  www.forbes.com, posted February 7, 2013

- The 2012 Gallup-Healthways Well-Being Index, surveyed American's opinions on economic confidence, workplace perceptions, community climate, personal choices, and health predictors to assess the "future livability" of each state. Illinois ranked #28.
  "Utah Poised to Be the Best State to Live In," Gallup Wellbeing, www.gallup.com, August 7, 2012

- On CNBC's list of "America's Top States for Business 2013," Illinois ranked #37. Criteria: measures of competitiveness developed with input from the National Association of Manufacturers, the Council on Competitiveness, and other business groups weighed with the states' own marketing criteria.
  www.cnbc.com, consulted July 19, 2013

- Illinois ranked #3 on the "worst" end of the Christian Science Monitor's list of "States with the Best (and Worst) Job Growth," as indicated by year-over-year growth rates from May 2012 to May 2013.
  www.csmonitor.com, July 5, 2013

- Illinois ranked #47 on MoneyRates list of "Best-and Worst-States to Retire 2012." Criteria: life expectancy, crime rate, climate, economic conditions, taxes, job opportunities, and cost of living.
  www.money-rates.com, October 22, 2012

- Illinois ranked #20 on the 2013 Bankrate "Best Places to Retire" list ranking the states and District of Columbia on various criteria relating to health, safety, and cost.
  www.bankrate.com, May 6, 2013

- Illinois ranked #16 on the Social Science Research Council's "American Human Development Report: The Measure of America," assessing the 50 states plus the District of Columbia on health, education, and living-standard criteria.
  The Measure of America 2013-2014, posted June 19, 2013; www.measureofamerica.org

- Illinois ranked #16 on the Foundation for Child Development's (FCD) Child Well-being Index (CWI). The FCD used the KIDS COUNT report and the National Survey of Children's Health, the only state-level source for several key indicators of child well-being.
  Foundation for Child Development, January 18, 2012; fcd-us.org

- Illinois ranked #23 overall according to the 2013 KIDS COUNT Data Book, a project of the Annie E. Casey Foundation. Criteria: children's economic well-being, education, health, and family and community indicators.
  KIDS COUNT Data Center's Data Book, released June 20, 2013; http://datacenter.kidscount.org

- Illinois ranked #29 in the children's economic well-being category by the 2013 KIDS COUNT Data Book, a project of the Annie E. Casey Foundation.
  KIDS COUNT Data Center's Data Book, released June 20, 2013; http://datacenter.kidscount.org

- Illinois ranked #14 in the children's educational opportunities and attainments category by the 2013 KIDS COUNT Data Book, a project of the Annie E. Casey Foundation.
  KIDS COUNT Data Center's Data Book, released June 20, 2013; http://datacenter.kidscount.org

- Illinois ranked #12 in the children's health category by the 2013 KIDS COUNT Data Book, a project of the Annie E. Casey Foundation.
  KIDS COUNT Data Center's Data Book, released June 20, 2013; http://datacenter.kidscount.org

- Illinois ranked #29 in the family and community circumstances that factor into children's well-being category by the 2013 KIDS COUNT Data Book, a project of the Annie E. Casey Foundation.
  KIDS COUNT Data Center's Data Book, released June 20, 2013; http://datacenter.kidscount.org

- Illinois ranked #28 in the 2012 Gallup-Healthways Well-Being Index. Criteria: emotional health; physical health; healthy behavior; work environment; basic access to food, shelter, health care; and a safe and satisfying place to live.
  2012 State of Well-Being, Gallup-Healthways Well-Being Index, released February 28, 2013; www.well-beingindex.com

- *U.S. News and World Report's* "Best States for Teen Drivers" rankings are based on driving and road safety laws, federal reports on driver's licenses, car accident fatality, and road-quality statistics. Illinois ranked #5.
  U.S. News and World Report, March 18, 2010; www.usnews.com

- The Yahoo! Sports service Rivals.com ranks the states according to the strength of their high school football programs. Illinois ranked #18.
  "Ranking the States: Where Is the Best Football Played?," November 18, 2011; highschool.rivals.com

- iVillage ranked the states by hospitable living conditions for women. Criteria: economic success, access to affordable childcare, health care, reproductive rights, female representation in government, and educational attainment. Illinois ranked #14.
  iVillage, "50 Best to Worst States for Women," March 14, 2012; www.ivillage.com

- The League of American Bicyclists's "Bicycle Friendly States" ranked Illinois #9. Criteria: legislation and enforcement, policies and programs, infrastructure and funding, education and advocacy, and evaluation and planning.
  "Washington Tops the Bicycle-Friendly State Ranking," May 1, 2013; bicycling.com

- The federal Corporation for National and Community Service ranked the states and the District of Columbia by volunteer rates. Illinois ranked #25 for community service.
  "Volunteering and Civic Life in America 2012," www.volunteeringinamerica.gov, accessed July 24, 2013

- The Hospital Safety Score ranked states and the District of Columbia on their hospitals' performance scores. Illinois ranked #5. Criteria: avoiding preventable harm and medical errors, as demonstrated by 26 hospital safety metrics.
  Spring 2013 Hospital Safety Score, May 8, 2013; www.hospitalsafetyscore.org

- GMAC Insurance ranked the states and the District of Columbia by the performance of their drivers on the GMAC Insurance National Drivers Test, comprised of DMV test questions. Illinois ranked #41.
  "2011 GMAC Insurance National Drivers Test," www.gmacinsurance.com, accessed July 23, 2013

- Illinois ranked #11 in a "State Integrity Investigation" analysis of laws and practices intended to deter corruption and promote accountability and openness in campaign finance, ethics laws, lobbying regulations and management of state pension funds.
  "What's Your State's Grade?," www.publicintegrity.org, accessed July 23, 2013

- Illinois ranked #2 among the states and the District of Columbia in total rail miles, as tracked by the Association of American Railroads.
  "U.S. Freight Railroad Industry Snapshot: Railroads and States: Total Rail Miles by State: 2011"; www.aar.org, accessed July 23, 2013

- According to statistics compiled by the Beer Institute, Illinois ranked #26 among the states and the District of Columbia in per capita beer consumption of persons 21 years or older.
  "Shipments of Malt Beverages and Per Capita Consumption by State 2012;" www.beerinstitute.org

- According to Concordia University's "Public Education Costs per Pupil by State Rankings," based on statistics gathered by the U.S. Census Bureau, which includes the District of Columbia, Illinois ranked #16.
  Concordia University Online; education.cu-portland.edu, accessed July 24, 2013

- Illinois ranked #12 among the states and the District of Columbia in population density based on U.S. Census Bureau data for resident population and total land area. "List of U.S. States by Population Density."
  www.wikipedia.org, accessed July 24, 2013

- In "America's Health Rankings, 2012 Edition," by the United Health Foundation, Illinois ranked #30. Criteria included: rate of high school graduation; violent crime rate; incidence of infectious disease; childhood immunizations; prevalence of diabetes; per capita public-health funding; percentage of uninsured population; rate of children in poverty; and availability of primary-care physicians.
  United Health Foundation; www.americashealthrankings.org, accessed July 24, 2013

- The TechNet 2012 "State Broadband Index" ranked Illinois #24 on the following criteria: broadband adoption; network quality; and economic structure. Improved broadband use is hoped to promote economic development, build strong communities, improve delivery of government services and upgrade educational systems.
  TechNet; www.technet.org, accessed July 24, 2013

- Illinois was ranked #14 among the states and District of Columbia on the American Council for an Energy-Efficient Economy's "State Energy Efficiency Scorecard" for 2012.
  American Council for an Energy-Efficient Economy; aceee.org/sector/state-policy/scorecard, accessed July 24, 2013

Statistical Tables

DEMOGRAPHICS

Resident State and National Population, 1950–2012

Year	State Population	U.S. Population	State Share
1950	8,712,000	151,326,000	5.76%
1960	10,081,000	179,323,000	5.62%
1970	11,110,285	203,302,031	5.46%
1980	11,426,518	226,545,805	5.04%
1990	11,430,602	248,709,873	4.60%
2000	12,419,927	281,424,600	4.41%
2010	12,830,632	308,745,538	4.16%
2012	12,875,255	313,914,040	4.10%

Note: 1950/1960 population figures are rounded to the nearest thousand.
Source: U.S. Census Bureau, Decennial Census 1950–2010; U.S. Census Bureau, 2012 Population Estimates

Projected State and National Population, 2000–2030

Year	State Population	U.S. Population	State Share
2000	12,419,293	281,421,906	4.41%
2005	12,699,336	295,507,134	4.30%
2010	12,916,894	308,935,581	4.18%
2015	13,097,218	322,365,787	4.06%
2020	13,236,720	335,804,546	3.94%
2025	13,340,507	349,439,199	3.82%
2030	13,432,892	363,584,435	3.69%
State population growth, 2000–2030			1,013,599
State percentage growth, 2000–2030			8.2%

Source: U.S. Census Bureau, Population Division, Interim State Population Projections, 2005

Population by Age, 2012

Age Group	State Population	Percent of Total Population State	U.S.
Under 5 years	816,278	6.3%	6.4%
5 to 14 years	1,713,823	13.3%	13.1%
15 to 24 years	1,788,611	13.9%	14.0%
25 to 34 years	1,786,326	13.9%	13.5%
35 to 44 years	1,693,816	13.2%	12.9%
45 to 54 years	1,824,083	14.2%	14.1%
55 to 64 years	1,557,881	12.1%	12.3%
65 to 74 years	923,499	7.2%	7.6%
75 to 84 years	523,100	4.1%	4.2%
85 years and older	247,838	1.9%	1.9%
Under 18 years	3,064,065	23.8%	23.5%
65 years and older	1,694,437	13.2%	13.7%
Median age (years)	–	37.0	37.4

Source: U.S. Census Bureau, Annual Estimates of the Resident Population for Selected Age Groups by Sex for the United States, States, Counties, and Puerto Rico Commonwealth and Municipios: April 1, 2010 to July 1, 2012

Population by Race, 2012

Race	State Population	Percent of Total Population State	U.S.
All residents	12,875,255	100.00%	100.00%
White	10,028,832	77.89%	77.89%
African American	1,900,578	14.76%	13.13%
Native American	75,948	0.59%	1.23%
Asian	638,108	4.96%	5.14%
Native Hawaiian	7,877	0.06%	0.23%
Two or more races	223,912	1.74%	2.39%

Source: U.S. Census Bureau, Population Division, Annual Estimates of the Resident Population by Sex, Race and Hispanic Origin for the United States, States, and Counties: April 1, 2010 to July 1, 2012

Population by Hispanic Origin and Race, 2012

Hispanic Origin/Race	State Population	Percent of Total Population State	U.S.
All residents	12,875,255	100.00%	100.00%
All Hispanic residents	2,101,208	16.32%	16.89%
Hispanic			
White	1,914,273	14.87%	14.91%
African American	66,700	0.52%	0.79%
Native American	56,460	0.44%	0.49%
Asian	15,597	0.12%	0.17%
Native Hawaiian	4,484	0.03%	0.06%
Two or more races	43,694	0.34%	0.48%
Not Hispanic			
White	8,114,559	63.02%	62.98%
African American	1,833,878	14.24%	12.34%
Native American	19,488	0.15%	0.74%
Asian	622,511	4.83%	4.98%
Native Hawaiian	3,393	0.03%	0.17%
Two or more races	180,218	1.40%	1.91%

Source: U.S. Census Bureau, Population Division, Annual Estimates of the Resident Population by Sex, Race and Hispanic Origin for the United States, States, and Counties: April 1, 2010 to July 1, 2012

VITAL STATISTICS

Death Rates by Leading Causes, 2010

Cause	State	U.S.
Malignant neoplasms	192.3	186.2
Ischaemic heart diseases	120.3	122.9
Other forms of heart disease	56.3	53.4
Chronic lower respiratory diseases	41.6	44.7
Cerebrovascular diseases	42.0	41.9
Organic, incl. symptomatic, mental disorders	34.4	35.7
Other degenerative diseases of the nervous sys.	23.6	28.4
Other external causes of accidental injury	22.3	26.5
Diabetes mellitus	19.9	22.4
Hypertensive diseases	21.0	20.4
All causes	788.4	799.5

Note: Figures are age-adjusted death rates per 100,000 population
Source: CDC/NCHS, Underlying Cause of Death 1999–2010 on CDC WONDER Online Database

Death Rates by Selected Causes, 2010

Cause	State	U.S.
Assault	6.0	5.2
Diseases of the liver	12.0	13.9
Human immunodeficiency virus (HIV) disease	2.4	2.7
Influenza and pneumonia	17.3	16.2
Intentional self-harm	9.2	12.4
Malnutrition	0.9	0.9
Obesity and other hyperalimentation	1.6	1.8
Renal failure	18.5	14.4
Transport accidents	8.6	12.1
Viral hepatitis	1.1	2.4

Note: Figures are age-adjusted death rates per 100,000 population; A dash indicates that data was not available or was suppressed
Source: CDC/NCHS, Underlying Cause of Death 1999–2010 on CDC WONDER Online Database

Abortion Rates, 2009

Category	2009
By state of residence	
Total abortions	42,226
Abortion rate[1]	16.0%
Abortion ratio[2]	247
By state of occurrence	
Total abortions	46,077
Abortion rate[1]	17.4%
Abortion ratio[2]	269
Abortions obtained by out-of-state residents	8.1%
U.S. abortion rate[1]	15.1%
U.S. abortion ratio[2]	227

Note: (1) Number of abortions per 1,000 women aged 15–44 years; (2) Number of abortions per 1,000 live births; A dash indicates that data was not available
Source: CDC/NCHS, Morbidity and Mortality Weekly Report, November 23, 2012 (Abortion Surveillance, United States, 2009)

Infant Mortality Rates, 1995–2009

Category	1995	2000	2005	2009
All state residents	9.36	8.48	7.38	6.92
All U.S. residents	7.57	6.89	6.86	6.39
All state white residents	7.12	6.62	5.77	5.50
All U.S. white residents	6.30	5.71	5.73	5.33
All state black residents	18.32	16.52	15.14	13.78
All U.S. black residents	14.58	13.48	13.26	12.12

Note: Figures represent deaths per 1,000 live births of resident infants under one year old, exclusive of fetal deaths; A dash indicates that data was not available or was suppressed.
Source: Centers of Disease Control and Prevention, Division of Vital Statistics, Linked Birth/Infant Death Records on CDC Wonder Online

Marriage and Divorce Rates, 2000–2011

Year	Marriage Rate		Divorce Rate	
	State	U.S.	State	U.S.
2000	6.9	8.2	3.2	4.0
2002	6.6	8.0	2.9	3.9
2004	6.2	7.8	2.6	3.7
2006	6.2	7.5	2.5	3.7
2008	5.9	7.1	2.5	3.5
2010	5.7	6.8	2.6	3.6
2011	5.6	6.8	2.6	3.6

Note: Rates are based on provisional counts of marriages/divorces by state of occurrence and are per 1,000 total population residing in area
Source: CDC/NCHS, National Vital Statistics System

ECONOMY

Nominal Gross Domestic Product by Industry, 2012
In millions of current dollars

Industry	State GDP
Accommodation and food services	19,536
Administrative and waste management services	22,347
Agriculture, forestry, fishing, and hunting	5,781
Arts, entertainment, and recreation	5,971
Construction	21,335
Educational services	9,737
Finance and insurance	67,198
Health care and social assistance	48,805
Information	23,216
Management of companies and enterprises	16,627
Manufacturing	92,383
Mining	1,946
Other services, except government	17,616
Professional, scientific, and technical services	59,852
Real estate and rental and leasing	85,612
Retail trade	40,369
Transportation and warehousing	25,451
Utilities	13,117
Wholesale trade	48,535

Source: U.S. Department of Commerce, Bureau of Economic Analysis, Survey of Current Business

Real Gross Domestic Product, 2000–2012
In millions of chained 2005 dollars

Year	State GDP	U.S. GDP	State Share
2000	537,369	11,225,406	4.79%
2005	568,114	12,539,116	4.53%
2010	571,228	12,897,088	4.43%
2012	594,201	13,430,576	4.42%

Source: U.S. Department of Commerce, Bureau of Economic Analysis, Survey of Current Business

Personal Income Per Capita, 1930–2012

Year	State	U.S.
1930	$806	$618
1940	$751	$593
1950	$1,827	$1,503
1960	$2,670	$2,268
1970	$4,568	$4,084
1980	$10,980	$10,091
1990	$20,835	$19,354
2000	$32,645	$30,319
2010	$42,025	$39,791
2012	$44,815	$42,693

Source: U.S. Department of Commerce, Bureau of Economic Analysis, Regional Economic Accounts

Non-Farm Employment by Sector, 2012
In thousands

Sector	Employment
Construction	187.9
Education and health services	864.0
Financial activities	366.1
Government	831.9
Information	100.1
Leisure and hospitality	534.8
Mining and logging	10.2
Manufacturing	582.9
Other services	249.3
Professional and business services	861.5
Trade, transportation, and utilities	1,155.7
All sectors	5,744.4

Source: U.S. Bureau of Labor Statistics, State and Area Employment

Foreign Exports, 2000–2012
In millions of dollars

Year	State Exports	U.S. Exports	State Share
2000	31,437	712,054	4.42%
2002	25,674	649,940	3.95%
2004	30,313	768,554	3.94%
2006	42,134	973,994	4.33%
2008	53,677	1,222,545	4.39%
2010	50,060	1,208,080	4.14%
2012	68,127	1,478,268	4.61%

Note: U.S. figures exclude data from Puerto Rico, U.S. Virgin Islands, and unallocated exports
Source: U.S. Department of Commerce, International Trade Admin., Office of Trade and Industry Information, Manufacturing and Services

Energy Consumption, 2011

In trillions of BTUs, except as noted

Total energy consumption	
Total state energy consumption	3,977.8
Total U.S. energy consumption	97,387.3
State share of U.S. total	4.08%
Per capita consumption (in millions of BTUs)	
Total state per capita consumption	309.3
Total U.S. per capita consumption	312.6
End-use sectors	
Residential	980.1
Commercial	789.1
Industrial	1,229.5
Transportation	979.1
Sources of energy	
Petroleum	1,201.3
Natural gas	986.4
Coal	1,052.2
Renewable energy	212.1
Nuclear electric power	1,002.7

Source: U.S. Energy Information Administration, State Energy Data 2011: Consumption

LAND AND WATER

Surface Area and Federally-Owned Land, 2007

In thousands of acres

Category	State	U.S.	State Share
Total surface area	36,058.7	1,937,664.2	1.86%
Total land area	35,326.2	1,886,846.9	1.87%
Non-federal land	34,835.1	1,484,910.0	2.35%
Developed	3,383.3	111,251.2	3.04%
Rural	31,451.8	1,373,658.8	2.29%
Federal land	491.1	401,936.9	0.12%
Water area	732.5	50,817.3	1.44%

Source: U.S. Department of Agriculture, Natural Resources Conservation Service, 2007 National Resources Inventory

Land Cover/Use of Non-Federal Rural Land, 2007

In thousands of acres

Category	State	U.S.	State Share
Total rural land	31,451.8	1,373,658.8	2.29%
Cropland	23,910.5	357,023.5	6.70%
CRP[1] land	664.6	32,850.2	2.02%
Pastureland	2,249.5	118,615.7	1.90%
Rangeland	0.0	409,119.4	0.00%
Forest land	3,934.8	406,410.4	0.97%
Other rural land	692.4	49,639.6	1.39%

Note: (1) Conservation Reserve Program was created to assist private landowners in converting highly erodible cropland to vegetative cover.
Source: U.S. Department of Agriculture, Natural Resources Conservation Service, 2007 National Resources Inventory

Farms and Crop Acreage, 2012

Category	State	U.S.	State Share
Farms (in thousands)	74.3	2,170.0	3.42%
Acres (in millions)	26.6	914.0	2.91%
Acres per farm	358.0	421.2	–

Source: U.S. Department of Agriculture, National Agricultural Statistical Service, Quick Stats, 2012 Survey Data

HEALTH AND MEDICAL CARE

Medical Professionals, 2012

Profession	State Number	U.S. Number	State Share	State Rate[1]	U.S. Rate[1]
Physicians[2]	39,183	894,637	4.38%	304.7	287.1
Dentists	8,605	193,587	4.45%	66.9	62.1
Podiatrists	1,017	17,469	5.82%	7.9	5.6
Optometrists	2,091	45,638	4.58%	16.3	14.6
Chiropractors	4,032	77,494	5.20%	31.4	24.9

Note: (1) Rates are per 100,000 population; (2) Includes total, active Doctors of Osteopathic Medicine and Doctors of Medicine in 2011.
Source: U.S. Department of Health and Human Services, Bureau of Health Professions, Area Health Resource File, 2012-2013

Health Insurance Coverage, 2011

Category	State	U.S.
Total persons covered	10,837,000	260,214,000
Total persons not covered	1,874,000	48,613,000
Percent not covered	14.7%	15.7%
Children under age 18 covered	2,914,000	67,143,000
Children under age 18 not covered	191,000	6,965,000
Percent of children not covered	6.2%	9.4%

Source: U.S. Census Bureau, Current Population Survey, 2012 Annual Social and Economic Supplement

HIV, STD, and Tuberculosis Cases and Rates, 2011

Disease	State Cases	State Rate[1]	U.S. Rate[1]
Chlamydia	64,939	506.1	457.6
Gonorrhea	17,037	132.8	104.2
HIV diagnosis	2,137	20.0	15.8
HIV, stage 3 (AIDS)	1,304	12.2	10.3
Syphilis, early latent	581	4.5	4.3
Syphilis, primary/secondary	881	6.9	4.5
Tuberculosis	359	2.8	3.4

Note: (1) Rates are per 100,000 population
Source: Centers for Disease Control and Prevention

Cigarette Smoking, 2011

Category	State	U.S.
Adults who are current smokers	20.9%	21.2%
Adults who smoke everyday	14.3%	15.4%
Adults who smoke some days	6.6%	5.7%
Adults who are former smokers	24.4%	25.1%
Adults who never smoked	54.7%	52.9%

Source: Centers for Disease Control and Prevention, Behaviorial Risk Factor Surveillance System, Tobacco Use, 2011

HOUSING

Home Ownership Rates, 1995–2012

Area	1995	2000	2005	2010	2012
State	66.4%	67.9%	70.9%	68.8%	66.8%
U.S.	64.7%	67.4%	68.9%	66.9%	65.4%

Source: U.S. Census Bureau, Housing Vacancies and Homeownership, Annual Statistics

Home Sales, 2000–2010
In thousands of units

Year	State Sales	U.S. Sales	State Share
2000	246.8	5,174	4.77%
2002	269.0	5,632	4.78%
2004	307.5	6,778	4.54%
2006	289.0	6,478	4.46%
2008	183.1	4,913	3.73%
2010	176.7	4,908	3.60%

Note: Units include single-family homes, condos and co-ops
Source: National Association of Realtors, Real Estate Outlook, Market Trends & Insights

Value of Owner-Occupied Homes, 2011

Value	Total Units in State	Percent of Total, State	Percent of Total, U.S.
Less than $50,000	224,056	7.0%	8.8%
$50,000 to $99,000	493,848	15.5%	16.0%
$100,000 to $149,000	523,741	16.4%	16.5%
$150,000 to $199,000	549,647	17.2%	15.4%
$200,000 to $299,000	681,656	21.4%	18.2%
$300,000 to $499,000	494,325	15.5%	15.2%
$500,000 to $999,000	180,295	5.7%	7.9%
$1,000,000 or more	42,714	1.3%	2.0%
Median value	–	$178,500	$173,600

Source: U.S. Census Bureau, 2011 American Community Survey 1-Year Estimates

EDUCATION

School Enrollment, 2011

Educational Level	Students Enrolled in State	Percent of Total, State	Percent of Total, U.S.
All levels	3,516,919	100.0%	100.0%
Nursery school, preschool	240,046	6.8%	6.0%
Kindergarten	170,538	4.8%	5.1%
Elementary (grades 1–8)	1,377,626	39.2%	39.5%
Secondary (grades 9–12)	742,710	21.1%	20.7%
College or graduate school	985,999	28.0%	28.7%

Note: Figures cover the population 3 years and over enrolled in school
Source: U.S. Census Bureau, 2011 American Community Survey 1-Year Estimates

Educational Attainment, 2011

Highest Level of Education	State	U.S.
High school diploma	87.2%	85.9%
Bachelor's degree	31.0%	28.5%
Graduate/Professional degree	11.7%	10.6%

Note: Figures cover the population 25 years and over
Source: U.S. Census Bureau, 2011 American Community Survey 1-Year Estimates

Public College Finances, FY 2012

Category	State	U.S.
Full-time equivalent enrollment (FTE)[1]	422,261	11,548,974
Educational appropriations per FTE[2]	$8,554	$5,906
Net tuition revenue per FTE[3]	$4,473	$5,189
Total educational revenue per FTE[4]	$12,855	$11,043

(1) Full-time equivalent enrollment equates student credit hours to full time, academic year students, but excludes medical students; (2) Educational appropriations measure state and local support available for public higher education operating expenses including ARRA funds and excludes appropriations for independent institutions, financial aid for students attending independent institutions, research, hospitals, and medical education; (3) Net tuition revenue is calculated by taking the gross amount of tuition and fees, less state and institutional financial aid, tuition waivers or discounts, and medical student tuition and fees. Net tuition revenue used for capital debt service is included in the net tuition revenue figures; (4) Total educational revenue is the sum of educational appropriations and net tuition excluding net tuition revenue used for capital debt service.
Source: State Higher Education Executive Officers, State Higher Education Finance FY 2012

TRANSPORTATION AND TRAVEL

Motor Vehicle Registrations and Drivers Licenses, 2011

Vehicle Type	State	U.S.	State Share
Automobiles[1]	5,563,757	125,656,528	4.43%
Buses	33,428	666,064	5.02%
Trucks	4,497,731	118,455,587	3.80%
Motorcycles	350,292	8,437,502	4.15%
Drivers licenses	8,373,969	211,874,649	3.95%

Note: Motor vehicle registrations include private, commercial, and publicly-owned vehicles; (1) Includes taxicabs
Source: U.S. Department of Transportation, Federal Highway Administration

Domestic Travel Expenditures, 2009
In millions of dollars

Category	State	U.S.	State Share
Travel expenditures	$25,134	$610,200	4.12%

Note: Figures represent U.S. spending on domestic overnight trips and day trips of 50 miles or more, one way, away from home. Excludes spending by foreign visitors.
Source: U.S. Travel Association, Impact of Travel on State Economies, 2009

Retail Gasoline Prices, 2013

Gasoline Grade	State Average	U.S. Average
Regular	$3.89	$3.65
Mid	$4.09	$3.81
Premium	$4.34	$3.98
Diesel	$3.97	$3.88
Excise tax[1]	57.5 cents	49.4 cents

Note: Gasoline prices as of 7/26/2013; (1) Includes state and federal excise taxes and other state taxes as of July 1, 2013
Source: American Automobile Association, Daily Fuel Guage Report; American Petroleum Institute, State Motor Fuel Taxes, 2013

Public Road Length, 2011

Type	State Mileage	U.S. Mileage	State Share
Interstate highways	2,182	46,960	4.65%
Other highways	99	15,719	0.63%
Principal arterial	5,494	156,262	3.52%
Minor arterial	9,183	242,942	3.78%
Major collector	18,566	534,592	3.47%
Minor collector	3,361	266,357	1.26%
Local	100,614	2,814,925	3.57%
Urban	41,273	1,095,373	3.77%
Rural	98,226	2,982,383	3.29%
Total	139,498	4,077,756	3.42%

Note: Combined urban and rural road mileage equals the total of the other road types
Source: U.S. Department of Transportation, Federal Highway Administration, Public Road Length, 2011

CRIME AND LAW ENFORCEMENT

Full-Time Law Enforcement Officers, 2011

Gender	State Number	State Rate[1]	U.S. Rate[1]
Male officers	27,917	234.6	210.3
Female officers	5,163	43.4	28.1
Total officers	33,080	278.0	238.3

Note: (1) Rates are per 100,000 population
Source: Federal Bureau of Investigation, Uniform Crime Reports, Crime in the United States 2011

Prison Population, 2000–2012

Year	State Population	U.S. Population	State Share
2000	45,281	1,391,261	3.25%
2005	44,919	1,527,929	2.94%
2010	48,418	1,613,803	3.00%
2011	48,427	1,598,783	3.03%
2012	0	1,571,013	0.00%

Note: Figures include prisoners under the jurisdiction of state or federal correctional authorities.
Source: U.S. Department of Justice, Bureau of Justice Statistics, Prisoners in 2006, 2011, 2012 (Advance Counts)

Crime Rate, 2011

Incidents per 100,000 residents

Category	State	U.S.
Violent crimes	429.3	386.3
Murder	5.6	4.7
Forcible rape	28.8	26.8
Robbery	157.4	113.7
Aggravated assault	237.5	241.1
Property crimes	2,688.8	2,908.7
Burglary	604.1	702.2
Larceny/theft	1,861.1	1,976.9
Motor vehicle theft	223.5	229.6
All crimes	3,118.1	3,295.0

Source: Federal Bureau of Investigation, Uniform Crime Reports, Crime in the United States 2011

GOVERNMENT AND FINANCE

Local Governments by Type, 2012

Government Type	State	U.S.	State Share
All local governments	6,968	89,004	7.83%
County	102	3,031	3.37%
Municipality	1,298	19,522	6.65%
Town/Township	1,431	16,364	8.74%
Special District	3,232	37,203	8.69%
Ind. School District	905	12,884	7.02%

Source: U.S. Census Bureau, 2012 Census of Governments: Organization Component Preliminary Estimates

State Government Revenue, 2011

In thousands of dollars, except for per capita figures

Total revenue	**$79,512,457**
Total revenue per capita, State	$6,183
Total revenue per capita, U.S.	$7,271
General revenue	$58,202,342
Intergovernmental revenue	$19,586,991
Taxes	$29,433,475
General sales	$7,420,829
Selective sales	$6,192,798
License taxes	$2,525,341
Individual income taxes	$11,225,000
Corporate income taxes	$1,851,000
Other taxes	$218,507
Current charges	$4,731,611
Miscellaneous general revenue	$4,450,265
Utility revenue	$0
Liquor store revenue	$0
Insurance trust revenue[1]	$21,310,115

Note: (1) Within insurance trust revenue, net earnings of state retirement systems is a calculated statistic, and thus can be positive or negative. Net earnings is the sum of earnings on investments plus gains on investments minus losses on investments.
Source: U.S. Census Bureau, 2011 Annual Survey of State Government Finances

State Government Expenditures, 2011
In thousands of dollars, except for per capita figures

Total expenditure	$74,655,351
Total expenditure per capita, State	$5,805
Total expenditure per capita, U.S.	$6,427
Intergovernmental expenditure	$15,711,058
Direct expenditure	$58,944,293
Current operation	$35,433,844
Capital outlay	$3,867,268
Insurance benefits and repayments	$15,150,850
Assistance and subsidies	$1,235,360
Interest on debt	$3,256,971
Utility expenditure	$0
Liquor store expenditure	$0
Insurance trust expenditure	$15,150,850

Source: U.S. Census Bureau, 2011 Annual Survey of State Government Finances

State Government General Expenditures by Function, 2011
In thousands of dollars

Education	$17,130,559
Public welfare	$19,508,223
Hospitals	$1,183,689
Health	$2,233,917
Highways	$5,110,368
Police protection	$440,245
Correction	$1,514,033
Natural resources	$253,236
Parks and recreation	$179,401
Governmental administration	$1,313,020
Interest on general debt	$3,256,971
Other and unallocable	$7,380,839

Source: U.S. Census Bureau, 2011 Annual Survey of State Government Finances

State Government Finances, Cash and Debt, 2011
In thousands of dollars, except for per capita figures

Debt at end of fiscal year	
State, total	$64,801,423
State, per capita	$5,039
U.S., per capita	$3,635
Cash and security holdings	
State, total	$123,283,282
State, per capita	$9,587
U.S., per capita	$11,759

Source: U.S. Census Bureau, 2011 Annual Survey of State Government Finances

POLITICS

Composition of the Senate, 1995–2013

Congress (Year)	State/U.S	Dem	Rep	Total
104th (1995)	State delegates	2	0	2
	Total U.S.	48	52	100
105th (1997)	State delegates	2	0	2
	Total U.S.	45	55	100
106th (1999)	State delegates	1	1	2
	Total U.S.	45	55	100
107th (2001)	State delegates	1	1	2
	Total U.S.	50	50	100
108th (2003)	State delegates	1	1	2
	Total U.S.	48	51	100
109th (2005)	State delegates	2	0	2
	Total U.S.	44	55	100
110th (2007)	State delegates	2	0	2
	Total U.S.	49	49	100
111th (2009)	State delegates	2	0	2
	Total U.S.	57	41	100
112th (2011)	State delegates	1	1	2
	Total U.S.	51	47	100
113th (2013)	State delegates	1	1	2
	Total U.S.	54	45	100

Note: Figures are for the starts of first sessions; Totals include Democratic (Dem) and Republican (Rep) members as well as vacancies and seats held by independent party members
Source: U.S. Congress, Congressional Directory

Composition of the House of Representatives, 1995–2013

Congress (Year)	State/U.S	Dem	Rep	Total
104th (1995)	State delegates	10	10	20
	Total U.S.	204	230	435
105th (1997)	State delegates	10	10	20
	Total U.S.	207	226	435
106th (1999)	State delegates	10	10	20
	Total U.S.	211	223	435
107th (2001)	State delegates	10	10	20
	Total U.S.	212	221	435
108th (2003)	State delegates	9	10	19
	Total U.S.	205	229	435
109th (2005)	State delegates	10	9	19
	Total U.S.	202	231	435
110th (2007)	State delegates	10	9	19
	Total U.S.	233	198	435
111th (2009)	State delegates	12	7	19
	Total U.S.	256	178	435
112th (2011)	State delegates	8	11	19
	Total U.S.	193	242	435
113th (2013)	State delegates	12	6	18
	Total U.S.	201	234	435

Note: Figures are for the starts of first sessions; Totals include Democratic (Dem) and Republican (Rep) members as well as vacancies and seats held by independent party members
Source: U.S. Congress, Congressional Directory

Composition of State Legislature, 2004–2013

Year	Democrats	Republicans	Total
State Senate			
2004	26	32	59
2005	31	27	59
2006	31	27	59
2007	37	22	59
2008	37	22	59
2009	37	22	59
2010	37	22	59
2011	34	24	59
2012	35	24	59
2013	40	19	59
State House			
2004	66	52	118
2005	65	53	118
2006	65	53	118
2007	66	52	118
2008	67	51	118
2009	70	48	118
2010	70	48	118
2011	64	54	118
2012	64	54	118
2013	71	47	118

Note: Totals may include minor party members and vacancies
Source: The Council of State Governments, State Legislatures

Voter Participation in Presidential Elections, 1980–2012

Year	Voting-eligible State Population	State Voter Turnout Rate	U.S. Voter Turnout Rate
1980	7,868,300	60.4	54.2
1984	7,922,605	60.8	55.2
1988	7,950,848	57.3	52.8
1992	8,113,900	62.2	58.1
1996	8,215,662	52.5	51.7
2000	8,432,600	56.2	54.2
2004	8,576,696	61.5	60.1
2008	8,681,138	63.6	61.6
2012	8,903,001	58.9	58.2

Note: All figures are based on the voting-eligible population which excludes person ineligible to vote such as non-citizens, felons (depending on state law), and mentally-incapacitated persons. U.S. figures include the overseas eligible population (including military personnel).
Source: McDonald, Michael P., United States Election Project, Presidential Voter Turnout Rates, 1980–2012

Governors Since Statehood

Shadrach Bond (O)	1818-1822
Edward Coles (O)	1822-1826
Ninian Edwards (O)	1826-1830
John Reynolds (O)	(r) 1830-1834
William L. D. Ewing (O)	1834
Joseph Duncan (O)	1834-1838
Thomas Carlin (D)	1838-1842
Thomas Ford (D)	1842-1846
Augustus C. French (D)	1846-1853
Joel A. Matteson (D)	1853-1857
William H. Bissell (R)	(d) 1857-1860
John Wood (R)	1860-1861
Richard Yates (R)	1861-1865
Richard J. Oglesby (R)	1865-1869
John M. Palmer (R)	1869-1873
Richard J. Oglesby (R)	(r) 1873
John L. Beveridge (R)	1873-1877
Shelby L. Cullom (R)	(r) 1877-1883
John M. Hamilton (R)	1883-1885
Richard J. Oglesby (R)	1885-1889
Joseph W. Fifer (R)	1889-1893
John P. Altgeld (D)	1893-1897
John R. Tanner (R)	1897-1901
Richard Yates Jr. (R)	1901-1905
Charles S. Deneen (R)	1905-1913
Edward F. Dunne (D)	1913-1917
Frank O. Lowden (R)	1917-1921
Lennington Small (R)	1921-1929
Louis L. Emmerson (R)	1929-1933
Henry Horner (D)	(d) 1933-1940
John H. Stelle (D)	1940-1941
Dwight H. Green (R)	1941-1949
Adlai E. Stevenson II (D)	1949-1953
William G. Stratton (R)	1953-1961
Otto Kerner Jr. (D)	(r) 1961-1968
Samuel H. Shapiro (D)	1968-1969
Richard B. Ogilvie (R)	1969-1973
Daniel Walker (D)	1973-1977
James R. Thompson (R)	1977-1991
Jim Edgar (R)	1991-1999
George H. Ryan (R)	1999-2003
Rod R. Blagojevich (D)	(i) 2003-2009
Pat Quinn (D)	2009-2015

Note: (D) Democrat; (R) Republican; (O) Other party; (r) resigned; (d) died in office; (i) removed from office

Indiana

Location: Midwest

Area and rank: 35,870 square miles (92,904 square kilometers); 36,420 square miles (94,328 square kilometers) including water; thirty-eighth largest state in area

Coastline: none

Population and rank: 6,537,334 (2012); sixteenth largest state in population

Capital and largest city: Indianapolis (829,445 people in 2010 census)

Became territory: May 7, 1800

Entered Union and rank: December 11, 1816; nineteenth state

Present constitution adopted: 1851

Counties: 92

State name: "Indiana" means "land of Indians"

State nickname: Hoosier State

Motto: The Crossroads of America

State capitol building in Indianapolis. (Jim West)

State flag: Blue field with gold torch surrounded by an outer circle of thirteen stars and an inner half circle of five stars

Highest point: Franklin Township—1,257 feet (383 meters)

Lowest point: Ohio River— 320 feet (98 meters)

Highest recorded temperature: 116 degrees Fahrenheit (47 degrees Celsius)— Collegeville, 1936

Lowest recorded temperature: –35 degrees Fahrenheit (–37 degrees Celsius)— Greensburg, 1951

State song: "On the Banks of the Wabash"

State tree: Tulip tree

State flower: Peony

State bird: Cardinal

Indiana History

Indiana's central position between earlier settled regions to the east and south and more recently settled regions to the north and west has made it an important area of commerce and transportation since the early years of the United States. Urban areas of the state, particularly in the northwest corner, which is located near the giant city of Chicago, have developed a multiethnic culture in sharp contrast to the white, western European, Protestant culture which dominates the rest of the state.

Early History. Several thousand years ago, early hunting, gathering, and crop-growing societies inhabited areas near the Ohio River. The oldest artifacts from this period have been discovered at Angel Mounds, a large archaeological site near Evansville. By the time Europeans arrived in the New World, the northern and central regions of the area were inhabited by the Miami Confederation, a group of Native Americans belonging to the Algonquin language group. The Miami, who depended largely on the growing of corn and the hunting of buffalo for survival, were organized into a confederation in order to protect their lands from the Iroquois, a large group of various Native American peoples living to the east. During the nineteenth century, the Miami ceded most of their land to the United States. Most of the Miami moved to Oklahoma, but some remained in Indiana.

French and British Settlement. During the seventeenth century, the Iroquois, who were generally hostile to the French, agreed to treaties which allowed the French to trade with the Miami. In 1679, the French explorer René-Robert Cavelier, sieur de La Salle, led an expedition into the northern part of the region by traveling south from Michigan down the Saint Joseph River. At about the same time, traders from the British colonies along the Atlantic coast began to settle in the region along the Wabash River and the Ohio River.

In order to protect their access to the Wabash River, which led to the vital waterway of the Mississippi River, the French built a series of forts in the area. The first was Fort Miami, built in 1704, followed by Fort Ouiatanon, built in 1719, and Fort Vincennes, built in 1732. The effort to win the region for France ended in failure in 1763, when the Treaty of Paris, which ended the French and Indian War, brought the area under British control. Although the British officially banned any further European settlement of the area, this prohibition was largely ignored. The area became part of the British province of Quebec in 1774.

American Settlement. During the American Revolution, American forces led by George Rogers Clark brought the region under the control of the newly created United States in 1779 in a surprise attack on British forces in Vincennes. The Peace of Paris, which ended the war in 1783, officially made the area part of the new nation. The first American settlement in the region was established in 1784 in Clarkville, across the Ohio River from Louisville, Kentucky. The area was part of the Northwest Territory from 1787 to 1800, when the Indiana Territory, which

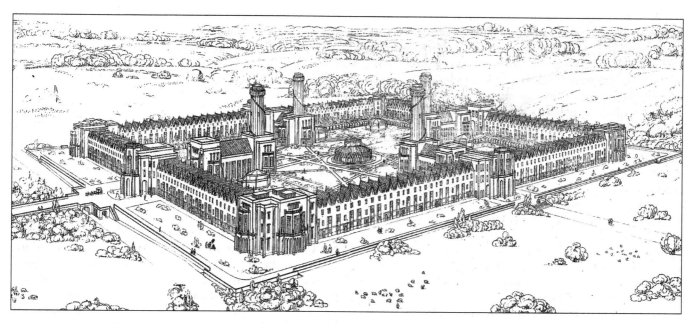

New Harmony community founded by the Wabash River in 1815. (Library of Congress)

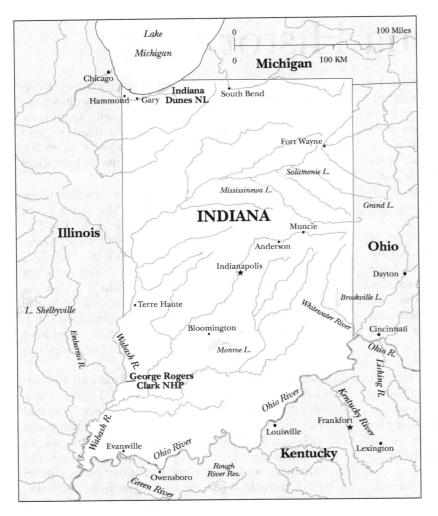

As a result, Indiana became culturally more southern than other states in the area and was inhabited primarily by Protestants of English, Scottish, Irish, and German ancestry. This rapid increase in the rate of European settlement led to an increase in the number of violent encounters with Native Americans.

The second phase of Native American resistance ended on November 7, 1811, at the Battle of Tippecanoe, near the modern city of Lafayette. During the battle, American forces led by William Henry Harrison defeated Shawnee forces led by Tenskwatawa. Although the two sides suffered equal losses, the battle was generally considered a decisive American victory, and it helped Harrison, a war hero, become president in 1840. Between 1820 and 1840 most Native Americans left the state.

Indianapolis. Settlement in Indiana in the first half of the nineteenth century was centered in the southern part of the state. The economy was based primarily on agriculture and transportation of goods along the Ohio River and the Wabash River. Indianapolis, a planned city designed to resemble Washington, D.C., was founded in 1821 in the center of the state and became the state capital in 1825. With the rise of railroads during the middle of the nineteenth century and the increase in motor-vehicle traffic in the twentieth century, Indianapolis became one of the largest cities in the world not located on a major waterway. It also went on to be served by more major highways than any other city in the United States.

Education and Industry. The first college in Indiana was founded in Vincennes in 1801. The first major institute of higher education, Indiana University, was founded in Bloomington in 1820. This university went on to become one of the most respected in the United States, with a particularly well-regarded university press. Indiana later became the home of other outstanding universities, with the founding of the University of Notre Dame, near South Bend, in 1842, and Purdue University, in West Lafayette, in 1869.

The Civil War, in which many Indianans fought for the Union, brought a rapid increase in the growth of industry in the state, particularly in the northern region. Natural resources that contributed to this growth included limestone, found in the southern part of the state, and coal, found in the southwest area. The south ern half of the state was also the site of the world's larg-

included Michigan, Illinois, Wisconsin, and part of Minnesota, was created. The Michigan Territory was created in 1805, giving the region its modern northern border. In 1809, the Illinois Territory was created, giving the area its modern western border. Indiana became a state in 1816, with its first capital at Corydon.

Wars with Native Americans. Violent conflict with the Native Americans inhabiting the region began as soon as European settlers entered the area. The first phase of American Indian resistance ended in 1794 with the Battle of Fallen Timbers, near the border between Ohio and Indiana. About one thousand Americans led by Anthony Wayne defeated about two thousand Native Americans of the Northwest Indian Confederation, including members of the Miami, Potawatomi, Shawnee, Delaware, Ottawa, Ojibwa, and Iroquois, led by Shawnee chief Bluejacket. As a result of the battle, in 1795 Miami chief Little Turtle ceded much of his people's land to the United States in the Treaty of Fort Greenville.

The opening of this land to non-Indians led to a large increase in the number of settlers from southern states.

est natural gas field in 1880's, but this resource was depleted by 1898.

Steel production became one of the state's most important industries, particularly with the founding of Gary, located near Chicago, in 1906. At about the same time, automobile manufacturing began in South Bend and Indianapolis. Certain cities specialized in the manufacturing of particular products. Elkhart became known for producing musical instruments in 1875, while Fort Wayne produces a large part of the world's diamond tools. Overall, Indiana is one of the top ten manufacturing states in the nation. Manufacturing accounts for about 40 percent of the state's income. Environmental destruction to the state's unique sand dunes along Lake Michigan, an indirect result of industrial growth, was slowed by the creation of Indiana Dunes National Lakeshore in 1972.

The Twentieth Century. Although much of Indiana retains its character as an enclave of white, Anglo-Saxon, Protestant culture, the growth of the state's cities and the powerful influence of Chicago on the northwest region brought a mixture of ethnic groups to the area. World War I brought a steady flow of African Americans to the industrial centers of the state. By the late twentieth century, African Americans made up about 20 percent of the population of Indianapolis and about 70 percent of the population of Gary. Indianans of Polish ancestry constitute an important ethnic group in South Bend. Other ethnic groups in the state, particularly in northern cities, include Indianans whose ancestors arrived from Hungary, Belgium, and Italy. These groups give northern Indiana a higher percentage of Roman Catholics than the rest of the state, which is about two-thirds Protestant.

Politically, Indiana is generally conservative. The state spends less per capita on education, welfare, and health care than most other states. The amount of federal aid which the state receives per capita is one of the lowest in the nation. Change is slow to come to the state's political system, which still uses the state constitution of 1851. Although this constitution requires changes to be made in legislative districts based on population changes, this rule was disregarded from 1923 to 1963, giving the rural areas more political power than their dwindling

Notre Dame University in South Bend, Indiana, is famous for its legendary football team and is also one of the nation's top-ranked universities. (Derek Jensen)

population should have allowed. It was not until 1970 that voters approved a proposal to have the state legislature meet annually rather than every two years.

Despite this conservatism, the Republican Party held only a slight advantage in the state after the Civil War. Indiana counties are about one-third Republican, one-third Democratic, and one-third variable. Almost as many liberals and Democrats have been elected from the state as conservatives and Republicans. Indiana state politics are sometimes surprisingly innovative, as when Indianapolis merged with Marion County in 1969 to form a unique type of city/ county government.

Church and State. Indiana ended the twentieth century with a political controversy. On March 14, 2000, Governor Frank O'Bannon, a Democrat, signed a bill allowing schools and other government entities to display the Ten Commandments on state property, challenging the constitutional prohibition of an "establishment" of religion. The law made Indiana the first state to allow such an action. Two weeks later, however, after suit was filed by the Indiana American Civil Liberties Union, a federal judge barred placing a Ten Commandments monument on the State House lawn. The judge argued that the monument lacked a secular purpose and implied endorsement of religious belief, contradicting the U.S. Constitution. The following year a similar decision was made by the U.S. Supreme Court. The city of Elkhart placed a stone pillar on its lawn displaying the Ten Commandments. A lower court ruled that the display violated the U.S. Constitution's separation of church and state provision found in the First Amendment. While the city maintained that the pillar stated no religious preference, Justice John Paul Stevens, speaking for the Court, disagreed.

Republican Gains. Politically, Indiana leaned Republican in national politics, though not necessarily in state politics. In the 2000 presidential election, George W. Bush and his running mate Richard Cheney collected the state's twelve electoral votes by a 57-41 percent margin. Both of Indiana's newly elected members of Congress were Republicans. One exception to the Republican preponderance was Governor O'Bannon, a Democrat, who was reelected by the comfortable margin of 56 to 42 percent.

Following the 2000 census, Indiana lost a member of Congress to states with larger population increases. Also in 2000, Indiana's highly respected senior senator, Richard Lugar, was elected by landslide proportions (67 to 32 percent). The luster of Senator Lugar's public image was burnished by his nomination for a Nobel Peace Prize for his efforts to reduce Russia's dangerously exposed stockpile of nuclear weapons and materials. In the 2002 and 2004 elections, Republican strength asserted itself.

In 2002, a vacated seat in Congress was won by the Republican candidate, though not by a large margin (50-46 percent). In 2004, President Bush took the state by 55-45 percent; a Republican won over a Democrat in a newly created district; and the governorship went to a Republican, Mitch Daniels, by 53-45 percent over Democratic incumbent Joe Kernan, who had been the successor to Governor O'Bannon, who had died in office. The state legislature, previously Democratically controlled, became tied in party affiliation.

Weak Economy. During the early twenty-first century, Indiana's economy turned in a less than stellar performance, as the national economy declined especially after the September 11, 2001, terrorist attacks. A study found that welfare caseloads in 2001 rose in thirty-three states across the nation before and after the attacks; the largest increases came in Indiana and two other states. The economic recovery regarding unemployment in later years was weak in Indiana, partly because gross national product was lifted by increases in productivity, and new hiring was accordingly less prevalent.

Politics. The elections of 2008, 2010, and 2012 continued to show that Indiana was fairly evenly split between Democrats and Republicans, and that it remained a swing state. In 2008, Barack Obama won the popular vote for president by the slim margin of just over 1 percent. Prior to the election, news organizations had regarded the state as too close to call. The 2008 election was the first since 1964 in which a Democrat won the state's vote for president.

In 2010, Democratic Senator Evan Bayh decided not to seek reelection. Democrats nominated Member of Congress Brad Ellsworth for the Senate. The Republicans nominated lobbyist Dan Coats who won the election with over 54 percent of the vote. In the 2012 election, incumbent Republican Senator Richard Lugar was defeated in the primary elections by Tea Party Republican Richard Mourdock. In the general election, Mourdock was defeated by Democratic Congressman Joe Donnelly. However, that same year, in the 2012 Presidential Election, the Democrats did not campaign seriously in Indiana, and Mitt Romney, the Republican candidate, won in the state by a comfortable 10 percent margin.

In 2013, an investigation and trial revealed that in the 2008 primary elections in the state, which had put both Hillary Clinton and Barack Obama on the ballot as presidential candidates, serious election fraud had occurred. Close examination revealed that local Democratic Party officials in South Bend had forged hundreds of signatures to get both candidates on the primary election ballot. Page after page of the nominating petitions were in the same handwriting; two officials were convicted of fraud and forgery. However, since the charges had not been contested during the election, none of the results were affected.

Rose Secrest
Updated by the Editor

Indiana Time Line

Dec. 5, 1679	René-Robert Cavelier, sieur de La Salle, leads a French expedition down the Saint Joseph River from Michigan into Indiana.
1686	Trading post is established at the future site of Fort Wayne.
1704	Fort Miami is founded.
1719	Fort Ouiatanon is founded.
1732	Fort Vincennes is founded.
1763	Defeat of the French in the French and Indian War brings the region under British control.
1774	Indiana becomes part of the British province of Quebec.
Feb. 25, 1779	American forces led by George Rogers Clark defeat British forces at Vincennes.
1783	Defeat of the British in the American Revolution brings the region under American control.
1784	First American settlement in Indiana is founded at Clarkville.
1787	Indiana becomes part of the Northwest Territory.
1794	Battle of Fallen Timbers results in the defeat of a confederation of Native Americans.
1795	Miami people cede much of their land to the United States.
May 7, 1800	Indiana Territory is created.
1801	First college is founded at Vincennes.
1805	Michigan Territory is created from the northern part of the Indiana Territory.
1809	Illinois Territory is created from the western part of the Indiana Territory.
Nov. 7, 1811	Battle of Tippecanoe results in the defeat of the Shawnee.
1815	New Harmony, a utopian community, is founded on the Wabash River.
Dec. 11, 1816	Indiana becomes the nineteenth state.
1818	Bloomington is founded.
1820	Trading post is founded at the future site of South Bend.
1820	Indiana University is founded.
1821	Indianapolis is founded.
1825	Indianapolis becomes the state capital.
1832	Elkhart is founded.
1835	First railroad in the state, a horse-drawn single car, arrives in Shelbyville.
1840	William Henry Harrison, hero of the Battle of Tippecanoe, is elected president of the United States.
1842	University of Notre Dame is founded.
1851	State constitution is adopted.
1869	Purdue University is founded.
1880's	Indiana's "Gas Belt" contains the world's largest producing natural gas field.
1888	Indianapolis resident Benjamin Harrison, grandson of William Henry Harrison, is elected president.
1893	American Railway Union, the first industrial union in the United States, is founded in Terre Haute.
1894	Strike by the American Railway Union leads to violence and intervention by federal troops.
1898	Indiana's natural gas supplies are depleted.
1906	Gary is founded.
May 30, 1911	First Indianapolis 500 automobile race is held.
1912	Indiana native Thomas R. Marshall is elected vice president.
1923–1963	State legislature disregards the state constitution requirement that legislative districts be changed to reflect changes in population.
1969	Indianapolis merges with Marion County to form a single government.
1970	Port of Indiana, an artificial harbor, is opened on Lake Michigan, linking the state to worldwide water traffic.
1972	University of Notre Dame begins accepting female students.
1972	Indiana Dunes National Lakeshore is created.
1975	Indiana and Michigan Electric Company begins generating nuclear power.
1988	Indiana native Dan Quayle is elected vice president.
Oct. 7, 1991	Rose-Hulman Institute of Terre Haute, an all-male school for 117 years, admits women.
Mar. 14, 2000	Governor Frank O'Bannon signs bill allowing schools and other government entities to display the Ten Commandments on state property.

Mar. 28, 2000	Federal court finds that placing a monument with the Ten Commandments on the lawn of the Indiana State House violates the Bill of Rights guarantee of a separation of church and state.
Nov. 7, 2000	Governor Frank O'Bannon reelected by a 56-42 percent margin.
May 29, 2001	U.S. Supreme Court lets stand a ruling that City of Elkhart's Ten Commandments display is unconstitutional.
Nov. 2, 2004	President George Bush wins the state by 55–45 percent and Mitch Daniels wins the governorship by a 53-45 percent margin.
2010	Republican Dan Coats narrowly wins the Senatorial election with 54 percent of the vote.
2012	Tea Party Republican Richard Murdock defeats Republican Senator Richard Lugar in the primary, but loses to Democrat Joe Donnelly in the general election.
2013	Investigations begin over the 2008 presidential primary elections in the state.

Notes for Further Study

Published Sources. For those unfamiliar with basic facts about the history of Indiana, an excellent starting point is Howard Henry Peckham's *Indiana: A Bicentennial History* (1978), a clear, concise, colorful account of the state's past. For more advanced students, the Indiana Historical Bureau and the Indiana Historical Society, based in Indianapolis, have published several volumes in a series, which includes *Indiana to 1816: The Colonial Period* (1971) by John D. Barnhart and Dorothy L. Riker; *Indiana, 1816–1850: The Pioneer Era* (1998) by Donald F. Carmony; *Indiana in the Civil War Era, 1850–1880* (1965) by Emma Lou Thornburgh; *Indiana in Transition: The Emergence of an Industrial Commonwealth, 1880–1920* (1968) by Clifton J. Phillips; and *Indiana Through Transition and Change: A History of the Hoosier State and Its People, 1920–1945* (1968) by James H. Madison.

A detailed and scholarly account of the early years of the state can be found in *Frontier Indiana* by Andrew R. L. Cayton (1996), one of many outstanding historical works published by Indiana University Press, located in Bloomington. *Destination Indiana: Travels Through Hoosier History* (2000) written by Ray E. Boomhower (photography by Darryl Jones) brings together carefully researched text with beautiful photographs of public historic sites throughout Indiana. Two books that focus more on niche history are *At Home in the Hoosier Hills: Agriculture, Politics, and Religion in Southern Indiana, 1810–1870* (2005) by Richard F. Nation and *Centennial Farms of Indiana* (2003), edited by M. Teresa Baer et al., which traces the history of Hoosier farmers, including Native Americans to modern-day agribusiness. *An Amish Patchwork: Indiana's Old Orders in the Modern World* (2005) by Thomas J. Meyers and Steven M.

Nolt provides an overview of the beliefs and values of the Amish, their migration history, and the differences between the state's two major Amish ethnic groups (Pennsylvania Dutch and Swiss). The often overlooked story of African Americans in the state is found in a series of articles collected in *Indiana's African-American Heritage: Essays from Black History News and Notes* (1993), edited by Wilma L. Gibbs.

Web Resources. Several excellent Web sites, supplied by government agencies, private organizations, and individuals, are dedicated to the history of Indiana. A good place to start is the official Web site of the state government of Indiana (www.in.gov/). It offers basic information on the state, a list of famous Indianans and the accomplishments for which they are noted, a discussion of the structure of the state government, and links to historical Web sites, among many other features. Visit Indiana (www.visitindiana.net/) provides several links and articles for the visitor to the state.

A unique, detailed, and interactive time line is found at the Indiana Historical Society (www.indianahistory.org). This site is particularly helpful for information on the prehistory of the state, pre-Columbian Native American archaeology, French settlement, and early statehood. Two historical organizations in the state maintain Web sites which are frequently updated. The Indiana Historical Bureau (www.in.gov/history/) includes numerous historical documents and links to historical periodicals, while the Center for Indiana History (centerforhistory.org/learn-history/indiana-history) includes links to publications and a collection of essays on subjects ranging from biographies of noted Indianans to a history of the state's constitution.

Counties

County	2012 Population	Pop. Rank	Land Area (sq. miles)	Area Rank	County	2012 Population	Pop. Rank	Land Area (sq. miles)	Area Rank
Adams	34,365	45	339.03	71	Clay	26,837	59	357.54	70
Allen	360,412	3	657.31	1	Clinton	33,022	50	405.07	40
Bartholomew	79,129	19	406.91	37	Crawford	10,665	86	305.64	80
Benton	8,804	89	406.42	39	Daviess	32,064	54	429.49	26
Blackford	12,502	85	165.08	89	DeKalb	42,321	35	362.82	68
Boone	58,944	27	422.91	28	Dearborn	49,831	28	305.03	81
Brown	15,083	81	311.98	76	Decatur	26,042	60	372.57	63
Carroll	20,095	73	372.22	64	Delaware	117,364	14	392.12	51
Cass	38,581	38	412.15	32	Dubois	42,071	36	427.27	27
Clark	111,951	15	372.86	62	Elkhart	199,619	6	463.17	16

County	2012 Population	Pop. Rank	Land Area (sq. miles)	Area Rank
Fayette	24,029	64	215.01	87
Floyd	75,283	21	147.93	91
Fountain	17,119	76	395.66	48
Franklin	22,969	67	384.43	55
Fulton	20,737	72	368.39	65
Gibson	33,458	47	487.49	13
Grant	69,330	24	414.07	30
Greene	32,940	51	542.49	4
Hamilton	289,495	4	394.27	50
Hancock	70,933	22	306.02	79
Harrison	39,134	37	484.52	14
Hendricks	150,434	10	406.91	37
Henry	49,345	29	391.88	52
Howard	82,849	18	293.06	82
Huntington	36,987	43	382.65	57
Jackson	43,083	34	509.31	8
Jasper	33,456	48	559.62	3
Jay	21,366	69	383.91	56
Jefferson	32,554	52	360.63	69
Jennings	28,161	56	376.58	60
Johnson	143,191	11	320.43	75
Knox	38,122	40	516.03	6
Kosciusko	77,609	20	531.38	5
LaGrange	37,521	42	379.62	59
LaPorte	111,246	16	598.30	2
Lake	493,618	2	498.96	12
Lawrence	46,078	32	449.17	20
Madison	130,348	13	451.92	19
Marion	918,977	1	396.30	47
Marshall	47,024	31	443.63	24
Martin	10,260	88	335.74	72
Miami	36,486	44	373.84	61
Monroe	141,019	12	394.51	49
Montgomery	38,254	39	504.61	10
Morgan	69,356	23	403.97	41
Newton	14,044	82	401.76	43
Noble	47,582	30	410.84	34
Ohio	6,079	92	86.14	92
Orange	19,690	74	398.39	45
Owen	21,380	68	385.29	53
Parke	17,069	78	444.66	23
Perry	19,462	75	381.73	58
Pike	12,766	84	334.24	74
Porter	165,682	9	418.15	29
Posey	25,599	62	409.57	35
Pulaski	13,124	83	433.65	25
Putnam	37,750	41	480.53	15
Randolph	25,815	61	452.38	18
Ripley	28,583	55	446.43	22
Rush	17,095	77	408.12	36
Scott	23,791	65	190.40	88
Shelby	44,471	33	411.15	33
Spencer	20,837	71	396.74	46
St. Joseph	266,344	5	457.85	17
Starke	23,213	66	309.13	77
Steuben	34,124	46	308.94	78
Sullivan	21,188	70	447.14	21
Switzerland	10,424	87	220.63	86

County	2012 Population	Pop. Rank	Land Area (sq. miles)	Area Rank
Tippecanoe	177,513	8	499.81	11
Tipton	15,695	80	260.54	83
Union	7,362	91	161.22	90
Vanderburgh	180,858	7	233.48	85
Vermillion	16,040	79	256.88	84
Vigo	108,428	17	403.31	42
Wabash	32,361	53	412.43	31
Warren	8,342	90	364.68	67
Warrick	60,463	26	384.82	54
Washington	27,921	57	513.73	7
Wayne	68,346	25	401.74	44
Wells	27,652	58	368.09	66
White	24,426	63	505.12	9
Whitley	33,342	49	335.57	73

Source: U.S. Census Bureau, 2012 Population Estimates

Cities

With 10,000 or more residents

Legal Name	2010 Population	Pop. Rank	Land Area (sq. miles)	Area Rank
Anderson city	56,129	13	41.37	7
Auburn city	12,731	65	7.10	68
Avon town	12,446	67	14.24	37
Bedford city	13,413	63	12.16	42
Beech Grove city	14,192	59	4.39	77
Bloomington city	80,405	6	23.16	22
Brownsburg town	21,285	43	11.08	48
Carmel city	79,191	8	47.46	4
Cedar Lake town	11,560	72	8.22	60
Chesterton town	13,068	64	9.33	52
Clarksville town	21,724	42	9.97	50
Columbus city	44,061	21	27.50	14
Connersville city	13,481	62	7.74	61

Legal Name	2010 Population	Pop. Rank	Land Area (sq. miles)	Area Rank
Crawfordsville city	15,915	54	9.15	54
Crown Point city	27,317	37	17.71	29
Dyer town	16,390	53	6.10	71
East Chicago city	29,698	32	14.09	38
Elkhart city	50,949	15	23.45	21
Evansville city	117,429	3	44.15	5
Fishers town	76,794	9	33.59	10
Fort Wayne city	253,691	2	110.62	2
Frankfort city	16,422	52	6.31	70
Franklin city	23,712	39	13.01	40
Gary city	80,294	7	49.87	3
Goshen city	31,719	27	16.23	31
Granger CDP	30,465	29	25.57	19

Legal Name	2010 Population	Pop. Rank	Land Area (sq. miles)	Area Rank
Greencastle city	10,326	77	5.24	72
Greenfield city	20,602	44	12.55	41
Greensburg city	11,492	74	9.27	53
Greenwood city	49,791	16	21.23	25
Griffith town	16,893	51	7.73	62
Hammond city	80,830	5	22.78	23
Highland town	23,727	38	6.94	69
Hobart city	29,059	35	26.33	17
Huntington city	17,391	50	8.71	57
Indianapolis city (balance)	820,445	1	361.43	1
Jasper city	15,038	56	13.10	39
Jeffersonville city	44,953	20	34.06	9
Kokomo city	45,468	19	18.50	28
La Porte city	22,053	41	11.66	43
Lafayette city	67,140	11	27.74	13
Lake Station city	12,572	66	8.30	59
Lawrence city	46,001	18	20.13	26
Lebanon city	15,792	55	15.55	33
Logansport city	18,396	47	8.75	56
Madison city	11,967	69	8.57	58
Marion city	29,948	31	15.71	32
Martinsville city	11,828	70	4.49	76
Merrillville town	35,246	25	33.22	11
Michigan City city	31,479	28	19.59	27
Mishawaka city	48,252	17	17.00	30
Muncie city	70,085	10	27.20	15
Munster town	23,603	40	7.57	64
New Albany city	36,372	24	14.94	35
New Castle city	18,114	48	7.29	67
New Haven city	14,794	58	9.87	51
Noblesville city	51,969	14	31.37	12
Peru city	11,417	75	5.10	73
Plainfield town	27,631	36	22.27	24
Plymouth city	10,033	78	7.53	65
Portage city	36,828	22	25.63	18
Purdue University CDP	12,183	68	1.30	78
Richmond city	36,812	23	23.91	20
St. John town	14,850	57	11.39	47
Schererville town	29,243	34	14.71	36
Seymour city	17,503	49	11.42	46
Shelbyville city	19,191	45	11.56	45
South Bend city	101,168	4	41.46	6
Speedway town	11,812	71	4.76	74
Terre Haute city	60,785	12	34.54	8
Valparaiso city	31,730	26	15.53	34
Vincennes city	18,423	46	7.41	66
Wabash city	10,666	76	8.89	55
Warsaw city	13,559	61	11.58	44
Washington city	11,509	73	4.73	75
West Lafayette city	29,596	33	7.62	63
Westfield town	30,068	30	26.84	16
Zionsville town	14,160	60	10.26	49

Note: CDP–Census Designated Place
Source: U.S. Census Bureau, 2010 Census

Survey Says...

This section presents current rankings from dozens of public and private sources. It shows how this state ranks in a number of critical categories, including education, job growth, cost of living, teen drivers, energy efficiency, and business environment. Sources include *Forbes, Reuters, U.S. News and World Report, CNN Money, Gallup,* and *Huffington Post.*

- Indiana ranked #8 in a government study measuring real gross domestic product (GDP)—the output of goods and services produced by labor and property located in the United States. The ranking is based on the percentage change compared with 2011 GDP.
  U.S. Department of Commerce, Bureau of Economic Analysis, June 2013; www.bea.gov

- Indiana ranked #16 in a government study measuring real gross domestic product (GDP)—the output of goods and services produced by labor and property located in the United States. The ranking is based on the dollar value of its GDP.
  U.S. Department of Commerce, Bureau of Economic Analysis, June 2013; www.bea.gov

- Indiana ranked #20 in the 17th edition of "Quality Counts; State of the States," Education Week's "report card" surveying key education indicators, policy efforts, and educational outcomes.
  Education Week, January 4, 2013 (online) and January 10, 2013 (print); www.edweek.org

- SERI (Science and Engineering Readiness Index) weighs the performance of the states' K-12 schools in preparing students in physics and calculus, the high school subjects considered most important for future scientists and engineers. Indiana ranked #9.
  Newsletter of the Forum on Education of the American Physical Society, Summer 2011 issue; www.huffingtonpost.com, July 11, 2011; updated October 1, 2012

- Business website 24/7 Wall St. identified the states with the highest and lowest percentages of residents 25 or older with a college degree or higher. Of "America's Worst Educated States," Indiana ranked #8 (#1 = worst).
  247wallst.com, posted October 15, 2012; consulted July 18, 2013

- MoneyRates.com ranked Indiana #15 on its list of the best to worst states for making a living. Criteria: average income; inflation; employment prospects; and workers' Workplace Environment assessments according to the Gallup-Healthways Well-Being Index.
  www.money-rates.com, posted April 1, 2013

- *Forbes* analyzed business costs, labor supply, regulatory environment, current economic climate, growth prospects, and quality of life, to compile its "Best States for Business" rankings. Indiana ranked #18.
  www.forbes.com. posted December 12, 2012

- The 2012 Gallup-Healthways Well-Being Index, surveyed American's opinions on economic confidence, workplace perceptions, community climate, personal choices, and health predictors to assess the "future livability" of each state. Indiana ranked #31.
  "Utah Poised to Be the Best State to Live In," Gallup Wellbeing, www.gallup.com, August 7, 2012

- On CNBC's list of "America's Top States for Business 2013," Indiana ranked #18. Criteria: measures of competitiveness developed with input from the National Association of Manufacturers, the Council on Competitiveness, and other business groups weighed with the states' own marketing criteria.
  www.cnbc.com, consulted July 19, 2013

- Indiana ranked #5 on the "worst" end of the Christian Science Monitor's list of "States with the Best (and Worst) Job Growth," as indicated by year-over-year growth rates from May 2012 to May 2013.
  www.csmonitor.com, July 5, 2013

- Indiana ranked #25 on MoneyRates list of "Best-and Worst-States to Retire 2012." Criteria: life expectancy, crime rate, climate, economic conditions, taxes, job opportunities, and cost of living.
  www.money-rates.com, October 22, 2012

- Indiana ranked #26 on the 2013 Bankrate "Best Places to Retire" list ranking the states and District of Columbia on various criteria relating to health, safety, and cost.
  www.bankrate.com, May 6, 2013

- Indiana ranked #39 on the Social Science Research Council's "American Human Development Report: The Measure of America," assessing the 50 states plus the District of Columbia on health, education, and living-standard criteria.
  The Measure of America 2013-2014, posted June 19, 2013; www.measureofamerica.org

- Indiana ranked #28 on the Foundation for Child Development's (FCD) Child Well-being Index (CWI). The FCD used the KIDS COUNT report and the National Survey of Children's Health, the only state-level source for several key indicators of child well-being.
  Foundation for Child Development, January 18, 2012; fcd-us.org

- Indiana ranked #30 overall according to the 2013 KIDS COUNT Data Book, a project of the Annie E. Casey Foundation. Criteria: children's economic well-being, education, health, and family and community indicators.
  KIDS COUNT Data Center's Data Book, released June 20, 2013; http://datacenter.kidscount.org

- Indiana ranked #26 in the children's economic well-being category by the 2013 KIDS COUNT Data Book, a project of the Annie E. Casey Foundation.
  KIDS COUNT Data Center's Data Book, released June 20, 2013; http://datacenter.kidscount.org

- Indiana ranked #34 in the children's educational opportunities and attainments category by the 2013 KIDS COUNT Data Book, a project of the Annie E. Casey Foundation.
  KIDS COUNT Data Center's Data Book, released June 20, 2013; http://datacenter.kidscount.org

- Indiana ranked #21 in the children's health category by the 2013 KIDS COUNT Data Book, a project of the Annie E. Casey Foundation.
  KIDS COUNT Data Center's Data Book, released June 20, 2013; http://datacenter.kidscount.org

- Indiana ranked #30 in the family and community circumstances that factor into children's well-being category by the 2013 KIDS COUNT Data Book, a project of the Annie E. Casey Foundation.
  KIDS COUNT Data Center's Data Book, released June 20, 2013; http://datacenter.kidscount.org

- Indiana ranked #42 in the 2012 Gallup-Healthways Well-Being Index. Criteria: emotional health; physical health; healthy behavior; work environment; basic access to food, shelter, health care; and a safe and satisfying place to live.
  2012 State of Well-Being, Gallup-Healthways Well-Being Index, released February 28, 2013; www.well-beingindex.com

- *U.S. News and World Report's* "Best States for Teen Drivers" rankings are based on driving and road safety laws, federal reports on driver's licenses, car accident fatality, and road-quality statistics. Indiana ranked #38.
  U.S. News and World Report, March 18, 2010; www.usnews.com

- The Yahoo! Sports service Rivals.com ranks the states according to the strength of their high school football programs. Indiana ranked #8.
  "Ranking the States: Where Is the Best Football Played?," November 18, 2011; highschool.rivals.com

- iVillage ranked the states by hospitable living conditions for women. Criteria: economic success, access to affordable childcare, health care, reproductive rights, female representation in government, and educational attainment. Indiana ranked #43.
  iVillage, "50 Best to Worst States for Women," March 14, 2012; www.ivillage.com

- The League of American Bicyclists's "Bicycle Friendly States" ranked Indiana #42. Criteria: legislation and enforcement, policies and programs, infrastructure and funding, education and advocacy, and evaluation and planning.
  "Washington Tops the Bicycle-Friendly State Ranking," May 1, 2013; bicycling.com

- The federal Corporation for National and Community Service ranked the states and the District of Columbia by volunteer rates. Indiana ranked #24 for community service.
  "Volunteering and Civic Life in America 2012," www.volunteeringinamerica.gov, accessed July 24, 2013

- The Hospital Safety Score ranked states and the District of Columbia on their hospitals' performance scores. Indiana ranked #25. Criteria: avoiding preventable harm and medical errors, as demonstrated by 26 hospital safety metrics.
  Spring 2013 Hospital Safety Score, May 8, 2013; www.hospitalsafetyscore.org

- GMAC Insurance ranked the states and the District of Columbia by the performance of their drivers on the GMAC Insurance National Drivers Test, comprised of DMV test questions. Indiana ranked #7.
  "2011 GMAC Insurance National Drivers Test," www.gmacinsurance.com, accessed July 23, 2013

- Indiana ranked #23 in a "State Integrity Investigation" analysis of laws and practices intended to deter corruption and promote accountability and openness in campaign finance, ethics laws, lobbying regulations and management of state pension funds.
  "What's Your State's Grade?," www.publicintegrity.org, accessed July 23, 2013

- Indiana ranked #9 among the states and the District of Columbia in total rail miles, as tracked by the Association of American Railroads.
  "U.S. Freight Railroad Industry Snapshot: Railroads and States: Total Rail Miles by State: 2011"; www.aar.org, accessed July 23, 2013

- According to statistics compiled by the Beer Institute, Indiana ranked #42 among the states and the District of Columbia in per capita beer consumption of persons 21 years or older.
  "Shipments of Malt Beverages and Per Capita Consumption by State 2012;" www.beerinstitute.org

- According to Concordia University's "Public Education Costs per Pupil by State Rankings," based on statistics gathered by the U.S. Census Bureau, which includes the District of Columbia, Indiana ranked #31.
  Concordia University Online; education.cu-portland.edu, accessed July 24, 2013

- Indiana ranked #16 among the states and the District of Columbia in population density based on U.S. Census Bureau data for resident population and total land area. "List of U.S. States by Population Density."
  www.wikipedia.org, accessed July 24, 2013

- In "America's Health Rankings, 2012 Edition," by the United Health Foundation, Indiana ranked #41. Criteria included: rate of high school graduation; violent crime rate; incidence of infectious disease; childhood immunizations; prevalence of diabetes; per capita public-health funding; percentage of uninsured population; rate of children in poverty; and availability of primary-care physicians.
  United Health Foundation; www.americashealthrankings.org, accessed July 24, 2013

- The TechNet 2012 "State Broadband Index" ranked Indiana #28 on the following criteria: broadband adoption; network quality; and economic structure. Improved broadband use is hoped to promote economic development, build strong communities, improve delivery of government services and upgrade educational systems.
  TechNet; www.technet.org, accessed July 24, 2013

- Indiana was ranked #33 among the states and District of Columbia on the American Council for an Energy-Efficient Economy's "State Energy Efficiency Scorecard" for 2012.
  American Council for an Energy-Efficient Economy; aceee.org/sector/state-policy/scorecard, accessed July 24, 2013

Statistical Tables

DEMOGRAPHICS
Resident State and National Population, 1950-2012
Projected State and National Population, 2000-2030
Population by Age, 2012
Population by Race, 2012
Population by Hispanic Origin and Race, 2012

VITAL STATISTICS
Death Rates by Leading Causes, 2010
Death Rates by Selected Causes, 2010
Abortion Rates, 2009
Infant Mortality Rates, 1995-2009
Marriage and Divorce Rates, 2000-2011

ECONOMY
Nominal Gross Domestic Product by Industry, 2012
Real Gross Domestic Product, 2000-2012
Personal Income Per Capita, 1930-2012
Non-Farm Employment by Sector, 2012
Foreign Exports, 2000-2012
Energy Consumption, 2011

LAND AND WATER
Surface Area and Federally-Owned Land, 2007
Land Cover/Use of Non-Federal Rural Land, 2007
Farms and Crop Acreage, 2012

HEALTH AND MEDICAL CARE
Medical Professionals, 2012
Health Insurance Coverage, 2011
HIV, STD, and Tuberculosis Cases and Rates, 2011
Cigarette Smoking, 2011

HOUSING
Home Ownership Rates, 1995-2012
Home Sales, 2000-2010
Value of Owner-Occupied Homes, 2011

EDUCATION
School Enrollment, 2011
Educational Attainment, 2011
Public College Finances, FY 2012

TRANSPORTATION AND TRAVEL
Motor Vehicle Registrations and Drivers Licenses, 2011
Domestic Travel Expenditures, 2009
Retail Gasoline Prices, 2013
Public Road Length, 2011

CRIME AND LAW ENFORCEMENT
Full-Time Law Enforcement Officers, 2011
Prison Population, 2000-2012
Crime Rate, 2011

GOVERNMENT AND FINANCE
Local Governments by Type, 2012
State Government Revenue, 2011
State Government Expenditures, 2011
State Government General Expenditures by Function, 2011
State Government Finances, Cash and Debt, 2011

POLITICS
Composition of the Senate, 1995-2013
Composition of the House of Representatives, 1995-2013
Composition of State Legislature, 2004-2013
Voter Participation in Presidential Elections, 1980-2012
Governors Since Statehood

DEMOGRAPHICS

Resident State and National Population, 1950–2012

Year	State Population	U.S. Population	State Share
1950	3,934,000	151,326,000	2.60%
1960	4,662,000	179,323,000	2.60%
1970	5,195,392	203,302,031	2.56%
1980	5,490,224	226,545,805	2.42%
1990	5,544,159	248,709,873	2.23%
2000	6,080,827	281,424,600	2.16%
2010	6,483,802	308,745,538	2.10%
2012	6,537,334	313,914,040	2.08%

Note: 1950/1960 population figures are rounded to the nearest thousand.
Source: U.S. Census Bureau, Decennial Census 1950–2010; U.S. Census Bureau, 2012 Population Estimates

Projected State and National Population, 2000–2030

Year	State Population	U.S. Population	State Share
2000	6,080,485	281,421,906	2.16%
2005	6,249,617	295,507,134	2.11%
2010	6,392,139	308,935,581	2.07%
2015	6,517,631	322,365,787	2.02%
2020	6,627,008	335,804,546	1.97%
2025	6,721,322	349,439,199	1.92%
2030	6,810,108	363,584,435	1.87%
State population growth, 2000–2030			729,623
State percentage growth, 2000–2030			12.0%

Source: U.S. Census Bureau, Population Division, Interim State Population Projections, 2005

Population by Age, 2012

Age Group	State Population	Percent of Total Population	
		State	U.S.
Under 5 years	425,503	6.5%	6.4%
5 to 14 years	894,823	13.7%	13.1%
15 to 24 years	933,631	14.3%	14.0%
25 to 34 years	836,003	12.8%	13.5%
35 to 44 years	825,294	12.6%	12.9%
45 to 54 years	920,303	14.1%	14.1%
55 to 64 years	812,629	12.4%	12.3%
65 to 74 years	493,554	7.5%	7.6%
75 to 84 years	273,667	4.2%	4.2%
85 years and older	121,927	1.9%	1.9%
Under 18 years	1,591,477	24.3%	23.5%
65 years and older	889,148	13.6%	13.7%
Median age (years)	–	37.2	37.4

Source: U.S. Census Bureau, Annual Estimates of the Resident Population for Selected Age Groups by Sex for the United States, States, Counties, and Puerto Rico Commonwealth and Municipios: April 1, 2010 to July 1, 2012

Population by Race, 2012

Race	State Population	Percent of Total Population	
		State	U.S.
All residents	6,537,334	100.00%	100.00%
White	5,659,668	86.57%	77.89%
African American	616,199	9.43%	13.13%
Native American	25,494	0.39%	1.23%
Asian	116,029	1.77%	5.14%
Native Hawaiian	3,769	0.06%	0.23%
Two or more races	116,175	1.78%	2.39%

Source: U.S. Census Bureau, Population Division, Annual Estimates of the Resident Population by Sex, Race and Hispanic Origin for the United States, States, and Counties: April 1, 2010 to July 1, 2012

Population by Hispanic Origin and Race, 2012

Hispanic Origin/Race	State Population	Percent of Total Population	
		State	U.S.
All residents	6,537,334	100.00%	100.00%
All Hispanic residents	412,609	6.31%	16.89%
Hispanic			
White	364,157	5.57%	14.91%
African American	19,993	0.31%	0.79%
Native American	10,860	0.17%	0.49%
Asian	2,833	0.04%	0.17%
Native Hawaiian	1,681	0.03%	0.06%
Two or more races	13,085	0.20%	0.48%
Not Hispanic			
White	5,295,511	81.00%	62.98%
African American	596,206	9.12%	12.34%
Native American	14,634	0.22%	0.74%
Asian	113,196	1.73%	4.98%
Native Hawaiian	2,088	0.03%	0.17%
Two or more races	103,090	1.58%	1.91%

Source: U.S. Census Bureau, Population Division, Annual Estimates of the Resident Population by Sex, Race and Hispanic Origin for the United States, States, and Counties: April 1, 2010 to July 1, 2012

VITAL STATISTICS

Death Rates by Leading Causes, 2010

Cause	State	U.S.
Malignant neoplasms	203.6	186.2
Ischaemic heart diseases	125.4	122.9
Other forms of heart disease	65.6	53.4
Chronic lower respiratory diseases	58.7	44.7
Cerebrovascular diseases	47.6	41.9
Organic, incl. symptomatic, mental disorders	36.1	35.7
Other degenerative diseases of the nervous sys.	30.8	28.4
Other external causes of accidental injury	26.5	26.5
Diabetes mellitus	24.5	22.4
Hypertensive diseases	15.5	20.4
All causes	877.5	799.5

Note: Figures are age-adjusted death rates per 100,000 population
Source: CDC/NCHS, Underlying Cause of Death 1999–2010 on CDC WONDER Online Database

Death Rates by Selected Causes, 2010

Cause	State	U.S.
Assault	4.9	5.2
Diseases of the liver	13.6	13.9
Human immunodeficiency virus (HIV) disease	1.4	2.7
Influenza and pneumonia	18.2	16.2
Intentional self-harm	13.5	12.4
Malnutrition	1.1	0.9
Obesity and other hyperalimentation	2.0	1.8
Renal failure	20.8	14.4
Transport accidents	12.3	12.1
Viral hepatitis	1.5	2.4

Note: Figures are age-adjusted death rates per 100,000 population; A dash indicates that data was not available or was suppressed
Source: CDC/NCHS, Underlying Cause of Death 1999–2010 on CDC WONDER Online Database

Abortion Rates, 2009

Category	2009
By state of residence	
Total abortions	11,687
Abortion rate[1]	9.1%
Abortion ratio[2]	135
By state of occurrence	
Total abortions	10,557
Abortion rate[1]	8.2%
Abortion ratio[2]	122
Abortions obtained by out-of-state residents	4.5%
U.S. abortion rate[1]	15.1%
U.S. abortion ratio[2]	227

Note: (1) Number of abortions per 1,000 women aged 15–44 years; (2) Number of abortions per 1,000 live births; A dash indicates that data was not available
Source: CDC/NCHS, Morbidity and Mortality Weekly Report, November 23, 2012 (Abortion Surveillance, United States, 2009)

Infant Mortality Rates, 1995–2009

Category	1995	2000	2005	2009
All state residents	8.39	7.79	8.04	7.82
All U.S. residents	7.57	6.89	6.86	6.39
All state white residents	7.44	6.92	7.24	6.80
All U.S. white residents	6.30	5.71	5.73	5.33
All state black residents	16.37	14.91	14.98	15.04
All U.S. black residents	14.58	13.48	13.26	12.12

Note: Figures represent deaths per 1,000 live births of resident infants under one year old, exclusive of fetal deaths; A dash indicates that data was not available or was suppressed.
Source: Centers of Disease Control and Prevention, Division of Vital Statistics, Linked Birth/Infant Death Records on CDC Wonder Online

Marriage and Divorce Rates, 2000–2011

Year	Marriage Rate		Divorce Rate	
	State	U.S.	State	U.S.
2000	7.9	8.2	0.0	4.0
2002	7.9	8.0	0.0	3.9
2004	7.8	7.8	0.0	3.7
2006	7.0	7.5	0.0	3.7
2008	8.0	7.1	0.0	3.5
2010	6.3	6.8	0.0	3.6
2011	6.8	6.8	0.0	3.6

Note: Rates are based on provisional counts of marriages/divorces by state of occurrence and are per 1,000 total population residing in area
Source: CDC/NCHS, National Vital Statistics System

ECONOMY

Nominal Gross Domestic Product by Industry, 2012
In millions of current dollars

Industry	State GDP
Accommodation and food services	7,464
Administrative and waste management services	7,987
Agriculture, forestry, fishing, and hunting	3,965
Arts, entertainment, and recreation	3,242
Construction	11,324
Educational services	2,892
Finance and insurance	18,418
Health care and social assistance	23,401
Information	6,180
Management of companies and enterprises	3,417
Manufacturing	84,150
Mining	927
Other services, except government	7,072
Professional, scientific, and technical services	12,158
Real estate and rental and leasing	27,670
Retail trade	17,519
Transportation and warehousing	10,344
Utilities	6,725
Wholesale trade	15,012

Source: U.S. Department of Commerce, Bureau of Economic Analysis, Survey of Current Business

Real Gross Domestic Product, 2000–2012
In millions of chained 2005 dollars

Year	State GDP	U.S. GDP	State Share
2000	222,254	11,225,406	1.98%
2005	239,321	12,539,116	1.91%
2010	241,927	12,897,088	1.88%
2012	255,380	13,430,576	1.90%

Source: U.S. Department of Commerce, Bureau of Economic Analysis, Survey of Current Business

Personal Income Per Capita, 1930–2012

Year	State	U.S.
1930	$511	$618
1940	$549	$593
1950	$1,515	$1,503
1960	$2,201	$2,268
1970	$3,791	$4,084
1980	$9,353	$10,091
1990	$17,454	$19,354
2000	$27,459	$30,319
2010	$34,028	$39,791
2012	$36,902	$42,693

Source: U.S. Department of Commerce, Bureau of Economic Analysis, Regional Economic Accounts

Non-Farm Employment by Sector, 2012
In thousands

Sector	Employment
Construction	124.4
Education and health services	438.0
Financial activities	130.3
Government	428.5
Information	35.5
Leisure and hospitality	286.2
Mining and logging	7.0
Manufacturing	482.0
Other services	110.2
Professional and business services	298.4
Trade, transportation, and utilities	561.6
All sectors	2,902.1

Source: U.S. Bureau of Labor Statistics, State and Area Employment

Foreign Exports, 2000–2012
In millions of dollars

Year	State Exports	U.S. Exports	State Share
2000	15,385	712,054	2.16%
2002	14,955	649,940	2.30%
2004	19,212	768,554	2.50%
2006	22,666	973,994	2.33%
2008	26,502	1,222,545	2.17%
2010	28,764	1,208,080	2.38%
2012	34,431	1,478,268	2.33%

Note: U.S. figures exclude data from Puerto Rico, U.S. Virgin Islands, and unallocated exports
Source: U.S. Department of Commerce, International Trade Admin., Office of Trade and Industry Information, Manufacturing and Services

Energy Consumption, 2011

In trillions of BTUs, except as noted

Total energy consumption	
Total state energy consumption	2,869.2
Total U.S. energy consumption	97,387.3
State share of U.S. total	2.95%
Per capita consumption (in millions of BTUs)	
Total state per capita consumption	440.3
Total U.S. per capita consumption	312.6
End-use sectors	
Residential	556.7
Commercial	376.9
Industrial	1,314.0
Transportation	621.7
Sources of energy	
Petroleum	763.6
Natural gas	635.2
Coal	1,333.4
Renewable energy	148.2
Nuclear electric power	0.0

Source: U.S. Energy Information Administration, State Energy Data 2011: Consumption

LAND AND WATER

Surface Area and Federally-Owned Land, 2007

In thousands of acres

Category	State	U.S.	State Share
Total surface area	23,158.4	1,937,664.2	1.20%
Total land area	22,785.3	1,886,846.9	1.21%
Non-federal land	22,312.9	1,484,910.0	1.50%
Developed	2,446.0	111,251.2	2.20%
Rural	19,866.9	1,373,658.8	1.45%
Federal land	472.4	401,936.9	0.12%
Water area	373.1	50,817.3	0.73%

Source: U.S. Department of Agriculture, Natural Resources Conservation Service, 2007 National Resources Inventory

Land Cover/Use of Non-Federal Rural Land, 2007

In thousands of acres

Category	State	U.S.	State Share
Total rural land	19,866.9	1,373,658.8	1.45%
Cropland	13,219.9	357,023.5	3.70%
CRP[1] land	213.1	32,850.2	0.65%
Pastureland	1,926.1	118,615.7	1.62%
Rangeland	0.0	409,119.4	0.00%
Forest land	3,829.2	406,410.4	0.94%
Other rural land	678.6	49,639.6	1.37%

Note: (1) Conservation Reserve Program was created to assist private landowners in converting highly erodible cropland to vegetative cover.
Source: U.S. Department of Agriculture, Natural Resources Conservation Service, 2007 National Resources Inventory

Farms and Crop Acreage, 2012

Category	State	U.S.	State Share
Farms (in thousands)	60.0	2,170.0	2.76%
Acres (in millions)	14.7	914.0	1.61%
Acres per farm	245.0	421.2	–

Source: U.S. Department of Agriculture, National Agricultural Statistical Service, Quick Stats, 2012 Survey Data

HEALTH AND MEDICAL CARE

Medical Professionals, 2012

Profession	State Number	U.S. Number	State Share	State Rate[1]	U.S. Rate[1]
Physicians[2]	14,830	894,637	1.66%	227.6	287.1
Dentists	3,245	193,587	1.68%	49.8	62.1
Podiatrists	291	17,469	1.67%	4.5	5.6
Optometrists	1,210	45,638	2.65%	18.6	14.6
Chiropractors	1,073	77,494	1.38%	16.5	24.9

Note: (1) Rates are per 100,000 population; (2) Includes total, active Doctors of Osteopathic Medicine and Doctors of Medicine in 2011.
Source: U.S. Department of Health and Human Services, Bureau of Health Professions, Area Health Resource File, 2012-2013

Health Insurance Coverage, 2011

Category	State	U.S.
Total persons covered	5,589,000	260,214,000
Total persons not covered	764,000	48,613,000
Percent not covered	12.0%	15.7%
Children under age 18 covered	1,489,000	67,143,000
Children under age 18 not covered	88,000	6,965,000
Percent of children not covered	5.6%	9.4%

Source: U.S. Census Bureau, Current Population Survey, 2012 Annual Social and Economic Supplement

HIV, STD, and Tuberculosis Cases and Rates, 2011

Disease	State Cases	State Rate[1]	U.S. Rate[1]
Chlamydia	27,801	428.8	457.6
Gonorrhea	6,569	101.3	104.2
HIV diagnosis	512	9.5	15.8
HIV, stage 3 (AIDS)	353	6.6	10.3
Syphilis, early latent	95	1.5	4.3
Syphilis, primary/secondary	173	2.7	4.5
Tuberculosis	100	1.5	3.4

Note: (1) Rates are per 100,000 population
Source: Centers for Disease Control and Prevention

Cigarette Smoking, 2011

Category	State	U.S.
Adults who are current smokers	25.6%	21.2%
Adults who smoke everyday	19.4%	15.4%
Adults who smoke some days	6.2%	5.7%
Adults who are former smokers	24.7%	25.1%
Adults who never smoked	49.7%	52.9%

Source: Centers for Disease Control and Prevention, Behaviorial Risk Factor Surveillance System, Tobacco Use, 2011

HOUSING

Home Ownership Rates, 1995–2012

Area	1995	2000	2005	2010	2012
State	71.0%	74.9%	75.0%	71.2%	72.1%
U.S.	64.7%	67.4%	68.9%	66.9%	65.4%

Source: U.S. Census Bureau, Housing Vacancies and Homeownership, Annual Statistics

Home Sales, 2000–2010
In thousands of units

Year	State Sales	U.S. Sales	State Share
2000	111.0	5,174	2.15%
2002	125.2	5,632	2.22%
2004	130.5	6,778	1.93%
2006	147.4	6,478	2.28%
2008	118.6	4,913	2.41%
2010	97.7	4,908	1.99%

Note: Units include single-family homes, condos and co-ops
Source: National Association of Realtors, Real Estate Outlook, Market Trends & Insights

Value of Owner-Occupied Homes, 2011

Value	Total Units in State	Percent of Total, State	Percent of Total, U.S.
Less than $50,000	175,877	10.2%	8.8%
$50,000 to $99,000	468,182	27.2%	16.0%
$100,000 to $149,000	432,559	25.1%	16.5%
$150,000 to $199,000	291,874	17.0%	15.4%
$200,000 to $299,000	212,994	12.4%	18.2%
$300,000 to $499,000	104,416	6.1%	15.2%
$500,000 to $999,000	27,304	1.6%	7.9%
$1,000,000 or more	6,856	0.4%	2.0%
Median value	–	$122,400	$173,600

Source: U.S. Census Bureau, 2011 American Community Survey 1-Year Estimates

EDUCATION

School Enrollment, 2011

Educational Level	Students Enrolled in State	Percent of Total, State	Percent of Total, U.S.
All levels	1,761,848	100.0%	100.0%
Nursery school, preschool	107,054	6.1%	6.0%
Kindergarten	88,256	5.0%	5.1%
Elementary (grades 1–8)	717,155	40.7%	39.5%
Secondary (grades 9–12)	362,046	20.5%	20.7%
College or graduate school	487,337	27.7%	28.7%

Note: Figures cover the population 3 years and over enrolled in school
Source: U.S. Census Bureau, 2011 American Community Survey 1-Year Estimates

Educational Attainment, 2011

Highest Level of Education	State	U.S.
High school diploma	87.3%	85.9%
Bachelor's degree	23.0%	28.5%
Graduate/Professional degree	8.2%	10.6%

Note: Figures cover the population 25 years and over
Source: U.S. Census Bureau, 2011 American Community Survey 1-Year Estimates

Public College Finances, FY 2012

Category	State	U.S.
Full-time equivalent enrollment (FTE)[1]	261,765	11,548,974
Educational appropriations per FTE[2]	$4,258	$5,906
Net tuition revenue per FTE[3]	$6,138	$5,189
Total educational revenue per FTE[4]	$10,396	$11,043

(1) Full-time equivalent enrollment equates student credit hours to full time, academic year students, but excludes medical students; (2) Educational appropriations measure state and local support available for public higher education operating expenses including ARRA funds and excludes appropriations for independent institutions, financial aid for students attending independent institutions, research, hospitals, and medical education; (3) Net tuition revenue is calculated by taking the gross amount of tuition and fees, less state and institutional financial aid, tuition waivers or discounts, and medical student tuition and fees. Net tuition revenue used for capital debt service is included in the net tuition revenue figures; (4) Total educational revenue is the sum of educational appropriations and net tuition excluding net tuition revenue used for capital debt service.
Source: State Higher Education Executive Officers, State Higher Education Finance FY 2012

TRANSPORTATION AND TRAVEL

Motor Vehicle Registrations and Drivers Licenses, 2011

Vehicle Type	State	U.S.	State Share
Automobiles[1]	2,882,224	125,656,528	2.29%
Buses	21,518	666,064	3.23%
Trucks	3,024,623	118,455,587	2.55%
Motorcycles	204,407	8,437,502	2.42%
Drivers licenses	6,569,665	211,874,649	3.10%

Note: Motor vehicle registrations include private, commercial, and publicly-owned vehicles; (1) Includes taxicabs
Source: U.S. Department of Transportation, Federal Highway Administration

Domestic Travel Expenditures, 2009
In millions of dollars

Category	State	U.S.	State Share
Travel expenditures	$8,362	$610,200	1.37%

Note: Figures represent U.S. spending on domestic overnight trips and day trips of 50 miles or more, one way, away from home. Excludes spending by foreign visitors.
Source: U.S. Travel Association, Impact of Travel on State Economies, 2009

Retail Gasoline Prices, 2013

Gasoline Grade	State Average	U.S. Average
Regular	$3.63	$3.65
Mid	$3.74	$3.81
Premium	$3.87	$3.98
Diesel	$3.90	$3.88
Excise tax[1]	57.3 cents	49.4 cents

Note: Gasoline prices as of 7/26/2013; (1) Includes state and federal excise taxes and other state taxes as of July 1, 2013
Source: American Automobile Association, Daily Fuel Guage Report; American Petroleum Institute, State Motor Fuel Taxes, 2013

Public Road Length, 2011

Type	State Mileage	U.S. Mileage	State Share
Interstate highways	1,171	46,960	2.49%
Other highways	170	15,719	1.08%
Principal arterial	3,450	156,262	2.21%
Minor arterial	5,074	242,942	2.09%
Major collector	13,430	534,592	2.51%
Minor collector	9,017	266,357	3.39%
Local	64,754	2,814,925	2.30%
Urban	26,895	1,095,373	2.46%
Rural	70,171	2,982,383	2.35%
Total	97,066	4,077,756	2.38%

Note: Combined urban and rural road mileage equals the total of the other road types
Source: U.S. Department of Transportation, Federal Highway Administration, Public Road Length, 2011

CRIME AND LAW ENFORCEMENT

Full-Time Law Enforcement Officers, 2011

Gender	State Number	State Rate[1]	U.S. Rate[1]
Male officers	9,878	161.4	210.3
Female officers	761	12.4	28.1
Total officers	10,639	173.9	238.3

Note: (1) Rates are per 100,000 population
Source: Federal Bureau of Investigation, Uniform Crime Reports, Crime in the United States 2011

Prison Population, 2000–2012

Year	State Population	U.S. Population	State Share
2000	20,125	1,391,261	1.45%
2005	24,455	1,527,929	1.60%
2010	28,028	1,613,803	1.74%
2011	28,906	1,598,783	1.81%
2012	28,831	1,571,013	1.84%

Note: Figures include prisoners under the jurisdiction of state or federal correctional authorities.
Source: U.S. Department of Justice, Bureau of Justice Statistics, Prisoners in 2006, 2011, 2012 (Advance Counts)

Crime Rate, 2011
Incidents per 100,000 residents

Category	State	U.S.
Violent crimes	331.8	386.3
Murder	4.8	4.7
Forcible rape	27.0	26.8
Robbery	107.1	113.7
Aggravated assault	193.0	241.1
Property crimes	3,161.8	2,908.7
Burglary	775.7	702.2
Larceny/theft	2,158.8	1,976.9
Motor vehicle theft	227.3	229.6
All crimes	3,493.6	3,295.0

Source: Federal Bureau of Investigation, Uniform Crime Reports, Crime in the United States 2011

GOVERNMENT AND FINANCE

Local Governments by Type, 2012

Government Type	State	U.S.	State Share
All local governments	2,694	89,004	3.03%
County	91	3,031	3.00%
Municipality	569	19,522	2.91%
Town/Township	1,006	16,364	6.15%
Special District	737	37,203	1.98%
Ind. School District	291	12,884	2.26%

Source: U.S. Census Bureau, 2012 Census of Governments: Organization Component Preliminary Estimates

State Government Revenue, 2011
In thousands of dollars, except for per capita figures

Total revenue	**$38,894,976**
Total revenue per capita, State	$5,969
Total revenue per capita, U.S.	$7,271
General revenue	$31,449,911
Intergovernmental revenue	$10,858,319
Taxes	$14,909,416
General sales	$6,269,721
Selective sales	$2,562,091
License taxes	$625,782
Individual income taxes	$4,583,977
Corporate income taxes	$717,207
Other taxes	$150,638
Current charges	$3,709,260
Miscellaneous general revenue	$1,972,916
Utility revenue	$0
Liquor store revenue	$0
Insurance trust revenue[1]	$7,445,065

Note: (1) Within insurance trust revenue, net earnings of state retirement systems is a calculated statistic, and thus can be positive or negative. Net earnings is the sum of earnings on investments plus gains on investments minus losses on investments.
Source: U.S. Census Bureau, 2011 Annual Survey of State Government Finances

State Government Expenditures, 2011

In thousands of dollars, except for per capita figures

Total expenditure	$35,261,522
Total expenditure per capita, State	$5,411
Total expenditure per capita, U.S.	$6,427
Intergovernmental expenditure	$9,265,386
Direct expenditure	$25,996,136
Current operation	$17,396,095
Capital outlay	$2,268,396
Insurance benefits and repayments	$4,359,127
Assistance and subsidies	$973,086
Interest on debt	$999,432
Utility expenditure	$0
Liquor store expenditure	$0
Insurance trust expenditure	$4,359,127

Source: U.S. Census Bureau, 2011 Annual Survey of State Government Finances

State Government General Expenditures by Function, 2011

In thousands of dollars

Education	$14,055,154
Public welfare	$8,396,983
Hospitals	$177,353
Health	$565,707
Highways	$2,680,023
Police protection	$226,750
Correction	$661,358
Natural resources	$303,525
Parks and recreation	$73,011
Governmental administration	$551,909
Interest on general debt	$999,432
Other and unallocable	$2,211,190

Source: U.S. Census Bureau, 2011 Annual Survey of State Government Finances

State Government Finances, Cash and Debt, 2011

In thousands of dollars, except for per capita figures

Debt at end of fiscal year	
State, total	$22,144,251
State, per capita	$3,398
U.S., per capita	$3,635
Cash and security holdings	
State, total	$56,822,466
State, per capita	$8,720
U.S., per capita	$11,759

Source: U.S. Census Bureau, 2011 Annual Survey of State Government Finances

POLITICS

Composition of the Senate, 1995–2013

Congress (Year)	State/U.S	Dem	Rep	Total
104th (1995)	State delegates	0	2	2
	Total U.S.	48	52	100
105th (1997)	State delegates	0	2	2
	Total U.S.	45	55	100
106th (1999)	State delegates	1	1	2
	Total U.S.	45	55	100
107th (2001)	State delegates	1	1	2
	Total U.S.	50	50	100
108th (2003)	State delegates	1	1	2
	Total U.S.	48	51	100
109th (2005)	State delegates	1	1	2
	Total U.S.	44	55	100
110th (2007)	State delegates	1	1	2
	Total U.S.	49	49	100
111th (2009)	State delegates	1	1	2
	Total U.S.	57	41	100
112th (2011)	State delegates	0	2	2
	Total U.S.	51	47	100
113th (2013)	State delegates	1	1	2
	Total U.S.	54	45	100

Note: Figures are for the starts of first sessions; Totals include Democratic (Dem) and Republican (Rep) members as well as vacancies and seats held by independent party members
Source: U.S. Congress, Congressional Directory

Composition of the House of Representatives, 1995–2013

Congress (Year)	State/U.S	Dem	Rep	Total
104th (1995)	State delegates	4	6	10
	Total U.S.	204	230	435
105th (1997)	State delegates	4	6	10
	Total U.S.	207	226	435
106th (1999)	State delegates	4	6	10
	Total U.S.	211	223	435
107th (2001)	State delegates	4	6	10
	Total U.S.	212	221	435
108th (2003)	State delegates	3	6	9
	Total U.S.	205	229	435
109th (2005)	State delegates	2	7	9
	Total U.S.	202	231	435
110th (2007)	State delegates	5	4	9
	Total U.S.	233	198	435
111th (2009)	State delegates	5	4	9
	Total U.S.	256	178	435
112th (2011)	State delegates	3	6	9
	Total U.S.	193	242	435
113th (2013)	State delegates	2	7	9
	Total U.S.	201	234	435

Note: Figures are for the starts of first sessions; Totals include Democratic (Dem) and Republican (Rep) members as well as vacancies and seats held by independent party members
Source: U.S. Congress, Congressional Directory

Composition of State Legislature, 2004–2013

Year	Democrats	Republicans	Total
State Senate			
2004	18	32	50
2005	17	33	50
2006	17	33	50
2007	17	33	50
2008	17	33	50
2009	17	33	50
2010	17	33	50
2011	13	37	50
2012	13	37	50
2013	13	37	50
State House			
2004	51	49	100
2005	48	52	100
2006	48	52	100
2007	51	49	100
2008	51	49	100
2009	52	48	100
2010	52	48	100
2011	40	60	100
2012	40	60	100
2013	31	69	100

Note: Totals may include minor party members and vacancies
Source: The Council of State Governments, State Legislatures

Voter Participation in Presidential Elections, 1980–2012

Year	Voting-eligible State Population	State Voter Turnout Rate	U.S. Voter Turnout Rate
1980	3,846,321	58.3	54.2
1984	3,916,362	57.0	55.2
1988	3,996,319	54.3	52.8
1992	4,162,678	55.4	58.1
1996	4,302,745	49.6	51.7
2000	4,424,909	49.3	54.2
2004	4,504,260	54.8	60.1
2008	4,653,019	59.1	61.6
2012	4,759,100	55.1	58.2

Note: All figures are based on the voting-eligible population which excludes person ineligible to vote such as non-citizens, felons (depending on state law), and mentally-incapacitated persons. U.S. figures include the overseas eligible population (including military personnel).
Source: McDonald, Michael P., United States Election Project, Presidential Voter Turnout Rates, 1980–2012

Governors Since Statehood

Jonathan Jennings (O) . . . . (r) 1816-1822
Ratliff Boon (O) 1822
William Hendricks (O) . . . . (r) 1822-1825
James B. Ray (O) 1825-1831
Noah Noble (O) 1831-1837
David Wallace (O) 1837-1840
Samuel Rigger (O) 1840-1843
James Whitcomb (D) . . . . (r) 1843-1848
Paris C. Dunning (D) 1848-1849
Joseph A. Wright (D) 1849-1857
Ashbel P. Willard (D) . . . . (d) 1857-1860

Abram A. Hammond (D) 1860-1861
Henry S. Lane (R) . . . . (r) 1861
Oliver H. P. T. Morton (R) . . . . (r) 1861-1865
Conrad Baker (R) 1865-1873
Thomas A. Hendricks (D) 1873-1877
James D. Williams (D) . . . . (d) 1877-1880
Isaac P. Gray (D) 1880-1881
Albert G. Porter (R) 1881-1885
Isaac P. Gray (D) 1885-1889
Alvin P. Hovey (R) . . . . (d) 1889-1891
Ira J. Chase (R) 1891-1893
Claude Matthews (D) 1893-1897
James A. Mount (R) 1897-1901
Winfield T. Durbin (R) 1901-1905
James Franklin Hanly (R) 1905-1909
Thomas R. Marshall (D) 1909-1913
Samuel M. Ralston (D) 1913-1917
James P. Goodrich (R) 1917-1921
Warren T. McCray (R) . . . . (i) 1921-1924
Emmett F. Branch (R) 1924-1925
Edward F. Jackson (R) 1925-1929
Harry G. Leslie (R) 1929-1933
Paul V. McNutt (D) 1933-1937
Maurice Clifford Townsend (D) 1937-1941
Henry F. Schricker (D) 1941-1945
Ralph F. Gates (R) 1945-1949
Henry F. Schricker (D) 1949-1953
George N. Craig (R) 1953-1957
Harold W. Handley (R) 1957-1961
Matthew E. Welsh (D) 1961-1965
Roger D. Branigan (D) 1965-1969
Edgar D. Whitcomb (R) 1969-1973
Otis R. Bowen (R) 1973-1981
Robert D. Orr (R) 1981-1989
Evan Bayh (D) 1989-1997
Frank O'Bannon (D) . . . . (d) 1997-2003
Joe Kernan (D) 2003-2005
Mitch Daniels (R) 2005-2013
Mike Pence (R) 2013-2017

Note: (D) Democrat; (R) Republican; (O) Other party; (r) resigned; (d) died in office; (i) removed from office

Iowa

Location: Midwest

Area and rank: 55,875 square miles (144,716 square kilometers); 56,276 square miles (145,755 square kilometers) including water; twenty-third largest state in area

Coastline: none

Population and rank: 3,074,186 (2012 estimate); thirtieth largest state in population

Capital and largest city: Des Moines (203,433 people in 2000 census)

Became territory: June 12, 1838

Entered Union and rank: December 28, 1846; twenty-ninth state

Present constitution adopted: 1857

Iowa's state capitol building in Des Moines has the largest dome of any state capitol. (Wikimedia Commons)

Counties: 99

State name: "Iowa" probably
derives from an Indian
word meaning either
"this is the place" or
"the beautiful land"

State nickname: Hawkeye
State

Motto: Our liberties we prize
and our rights we will
maintain

State flag: Red, white, and
blue stripes with a detail
from the state seal and
the name "Iowa"

Highest point: Geographical survey section 29, T100N, R41W—1,670 feet
(509 meters)

Lowest point: Mississippi River—480 feet (146 meters)

Highest recorded temperature:
118 degrees Fahrenheit (48
degrees Celsius)—Keokuk,
1934

Lowest recorded temperature:
–47 degrees Fahrenheit (–44
degrees Celsius)—Washta,
1912

State songs: "Song of Iowa";
"Iowa State Fight Song";
"The Bells of Iowa State"

State flower: Wild prairie rose

State bird: Eastern goldfinch

Iowa History

Defined by the Mississippi River on the east and the Missouri River on the west, Iowa is a rolling stretch of lush, green prairie with rich, black soil and ample rainfall for growing crops. The fertility of the earth and the lack of trees make for excellent farmland, and as a result, Iowa has been and remains a state focused on agriculture.

Early History. The Paleo-Indians, nomadic hunters and gatherers, lived in the Iowa region more than ten thousand years ago. They were followed by other nomadic tribes and the mound builders. The Ioway, who controlled most of Iowa in the seventeenth century, left their name to the state and to one of its rivers but gave up all claim to land in the state in 1838, settling in Kansas and Nebraska. About seventeen different tribes are believed to have lived in what became Iowa.

In 1673, Father Jacques Marquette and mapmaker-explorer Louis Jolliet entered the Mississippi River from the Wisconsin River and gazed on Iowa, the "land across the river." They went ashore on June 25, finding members of the Illini tribe, who probably actually lived on the east side of the Mississippi. In 1682, France claimed all the lands along the Mississippi River, and in 1803, in the Louisiana Purchase, the United States bought the land from France. The following year, Meriwether Lewis and William Clark traveled up the Missouri River searching for a waterway that would take them to the Pacific Ocean.

In 1812, Iowa became part of the Territory of Missouri. Eight years later, Missouri became a state, and in 1834, the Territory of Michigan was expanded to include Iowa. In 1838, the Territory of Iowa was created.

The Native Americans. The U.S. government pushed the Sauk and the Mesquaki (Fox) tribes out of western Illinois and into Iowa, where the Sioux already lived. In 1832, Chief Black Hawk, a respected Sauk leader, sought to reclaim his tribe's land on the Illinois side of the Mississippi River. For three months, in what is known as the Black Hawk War, the Illinois militia pursued Black Hawk, chasing him to the mouth of the Bad Axe River in Wisconsin, where he gave up. In a treaty signed on September 21, 1832, the Mesquaki and Sauk were required to relinquish a strip of land along the Mississippi River and vacate the land by June 1, 1833. Large numbers of white settlers began to move into Iowa, pushing the tribes farther west or into Missouri. In 1842, the Sauk and Mesquaki signed a treaty agreeing to leave Iowa by May, 1845. By 1851 the Sioux had also been forced to give up all land in Iowa. In 1856, a few Mesquaki negotiated with the governor of Iowa to buy back a portion of their former land in modern-day Tama County, eventually buying back about 3,200 acres.

White Settlement and Statehood. In 1838, 23,000 people settled on land in the newly established Territory of Iowa, buying the land for $1.25 an acre. The first settlers were primarily of northern European ancestry.

Usher's Ferry Historic Village, a re-creation of a turn-of-the-twentieth-century Iowa farming town in Cedar Rapids. (Paul Rehn)

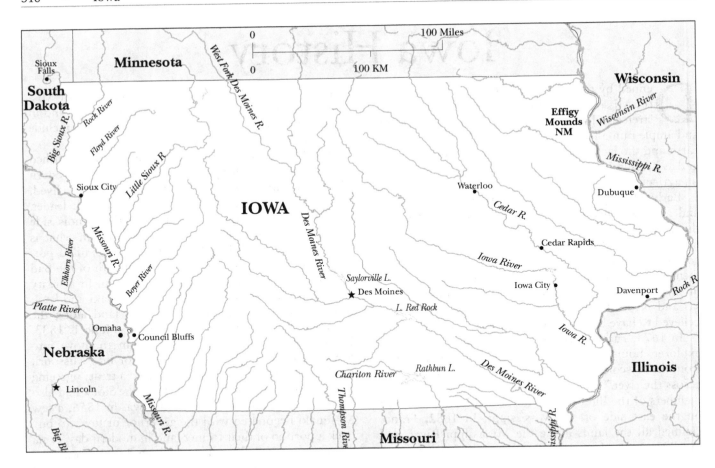

Many were families who had lived in eastern states such as New York, Pennsylvania, or Ohio, and many were originally from Germany. The 1840 census showed Iowa to have a population of 43,000, exclusive of American Indians. By 1846 the population of Iowa had reached 96,088. Iowa became the twenty-ninth state of the Union in 1846.

Industry, Education, and Religion. During the early 1850's, railroad companies sprung up in Iowa. The Chicago, Iowa, and Nebraska line became the first railroad to cross the state, in 1867. Soon tracks crisscrossed Iowa, providing year-round transportation to markets and giving birth to new industries such as an oat-processing plant that would come to be known as Quaker Oats.

Early settlers soon established township elementary schools, but high schools were not common until after 1900. State officials created the University of Iowa in 1855 to provide traditional and professional education, Iowa State College of Science and Technology (later Iowa State University) in 1858 for agricultural and technical training, and Iowa State Teachers' College (later University of Northern Iowa) in 1876 for teacher training. Many religious groups, including Congregationalists, Roman Catholics, and Methodists, which had come to the state beginning during the 1830's, founded private colleges.

Although major religious denominations usually set up churches across the state, smaller religious groups tended to settle in specific areas. The Quakers settled in West Branch and Springdale, the Reorganized Church of the Latter-day Saints (a Mormon offshoot) in Lamoni, and the Mennonites in Johnson and Washington Counties. From 1855 to 1865, a group of German Pietists established the seven cities of Amana in Iowa County. The residents of the Amana colonies practiced communal living for about eighty years. The Amana name lives on in refrigerators, air-conditioners, and microwaves, although the colonies sold the business in 1937.

The Civil War. The biggest change the Civil War brought in Iowa was to create a one-party state. At the beginning of Iowa's statehood, the state was largely Democratic, although it contained some Whigs. However, many Iowans opposed slavery, and Iowa would later become an important station in the Underground Railroad. The identification of the Democratic Party with a proslavery stance, among other issues, caused many Iowans to turn to the new Republican Party. By the mid-1850's, the state was solidly Republican and would stay that way through the first half of the twentieth century.

After the outbreak of the war, Iowans quickly responded to President Abraham Lincoln's call for troops.

During the course of the war, the state sent 70,000 soldiers, of whom 13,001 died and 8,500 were seriously wounded. Iowans fought at Wilson's Creek to keep Missouri in the Union, accompanied Ulysses S. Grant to Vicksburg, and participated in Sherman's March to the Sea.

Immigration. The population of Iowa grew from 674,913 in 1860 to 1,194,020 in 1870. The state encouraged immigration from northern Europe and attracted many Germans, Swedes, Norwegians, Danes, and Hollanders, as well as people from the British Isles. Many of these immigrant groups created rural neighborhoods with distinct ethnic identities and churches. The coal mines in central and southern Iowa, which promised immediate employment and required few skills, drew people from Italy and Wales and large numbers of former slaves, who formed camps near the mines.

Farming and Economic Growth. By the 1870's, Iowa had become blanketed by small towns and family farms, connected by railroads. Farmers were raising cattle and hogs and increasingly corn instead of wheat. Scientific research led to the introduction during the early twentieth century of soybeans, which eventually became second only to corn in terms of acreage and value. During World War I, farmers prospered, but after the war ended and farm subsidies were eliminated, farmers began to experience difficulties in paying off the money they had borrowed during boom times. A group of farmers formed the Farm Holiday Association, which attempted to withhold farm products from the market in order to force prices up, but the association's efforts had little impact.

Native Iowan Henry A. Wallace became secretary of agriculture under President Franklin D. Roosevelt in 1933. He believed that farmers would prosper if production was restricted and farmers were compensated for withholding land from production, and he incorporated these ideas into the Agricultural Adjustment Act of 1933, part of the New Deal. In 1926, Wallace and a

Iowa's location along the Mississippi River has enhanced the value of its farm produce by providing easy access to relatively inexpensive bulk cargo carriage on the river. (PhotoDisc)

partner founded what became Pioneer Seed Company, the first commercial company to produce hybrid seed corn, which led to increased yields and a more uniform plant that made mechanization of the harvest much easier. By 1944 nearly all corn planted in Iowa came from hybrid seed.

Farmers prospered when World War II and the Korean War boosted corn prices and again during the 1970's, when land prices rose and many farmers borrowed money to expand their operations. During the 1980's, however, land prices crashed, and many farmers lost their farms, initiating a trend away from family farms and toward farming corporations. In 1985, the Iowa legislature introduced legislation designed to help troubled farmers deal with creditors and keep their farms. During the 1990's, the family farm was challenged on another front as large-scale hog-producing corporations moved into the state, driving down hog prices and forcing small hog producers out of business.

Although agriculture dominates Iowa's economy, the state has also supported business and manufacturing operations, some of which are farm-related. Major concerns include farm-implement producer John Deere, the washing machine and appliance company Maytag, Winnebago motor-homes, the Sheaffer pen company, and Iowa Beef Processors. In 1991, Iowa legalized riverboat gambling, creating a somewhat controversial source of revenue.

Middle America. Iowa is largely rural, an assemblage of small towns and family farms. In 1994, the state's population reached 2.8 million, and the population of its largest city, Des Moines, was 193,422. During the 1970's, 1980's, and to a lesser extent during the 1990's, the state became the focus of national attention early in each presidential election year during the Iowa caucuses. These early tests of presidential strength provided boosts to some candidates, including Jimmy Carter in 1976 and George H. W. Bush in 1980. Although the state is not a microcosm of the nation, its reputation as Middle America—a stable place where family values dominate—lends weight to its preferences. As more and more farm corporations are formed and the number of family farms decreases, the nature of Iowa, its character and makeup, which reflect this rural dominance, may undergo a transformation.

2000 Elections. The state of Iowa perennially gained national attention in the run-up to presidential elections through the institution of "Iowa caucuses," informal gatherings of Democratic and Republican state political party members, who cast votes on their choices for president. Because the caucuses are held early in election years, they have become a kind of barometer of political strength, attracting national candidates in profusion.

Thus, the results of the 2000 caucuses on January 24 were of some significance. Vice President Al Gore won the caucus over former senator Bill Bradley by a large margin, 63 to 35 percent, harming the former New Jersey senator's campaign and boosting his own. Similarly, Texas governor George W. Bush came in first in the Republican caucuses, gaining 41 percent of the vote to industrialist Steve Forbes's 30 percent, former diplomat Alan Keyes's 14 percent, and Senator John McCain's 5 percent.

In the general election later that year, the state went by a small margin to Vice President Gore, while all congressional incumbents, as well as state assembly incumbents, were victorious. The 4,144 margin was small enough for Governor Bush to threaten to demand a recount if Gore persisted in his calls for recounts in the wafer-thin Republican margin in Florida. Wildcard candidate Ralph Nader took 2 percent. The state's congressional delegation remained at four Republicans and one Democrat.

Controversies. In October and November, 2001, when anthrax attacks followed the September 11, 2001, terror attacks on New York City and the Pentagon, the national spotlight played on Iowa intermittently. The reason was that Iowa State University at Ames had first isolated a strain of anthrax that Tom Ridge, director of the Office of Homeland Security, said was the type used in all recent anthrax attacks. On November 9, however, the university reported that it had destroyed its anthrax samples after the first reported death from anthrax was identified as the Ames strain. The university did so because of security concerns but not before asking the Federal Bureau of Investigation (FBI) and the Centers for Disease Control (CDC) for their approval.

Another issue that affected Iowa, a premier farming state, concerned genetically modified crops (GM). In 2003, GM farming rules were reported to have been broken. Farmers were obligated to plant at least 20 percent of their crops in conventional seed, but a study showed that farmers in a number of midwestern states did not do so. Planting of crops, however, was a difficult matter to police in the absence of voluntary farmer compliance.

Politics. John Kerry, destined to become the Democratic Party's presidential candidate, won the Iowa caucuses in January, 2004. When Election Day arrived on November 2, another election cliff-hanger soon became evident. When Kerry conceded the election to President Bush, Iowa had not been called for either candidate. By morning, however, it was clear that the president had won by a small margin—33,500 votes—though not nearly as small as the margin that he had lost the state in 2000.

In the general election in 2008, Barack Obama won the state vote with 53.9 percent of the vote, compared to 44.4 percent for Senator John McCain. The state was considered safely in the Democratic column, despite the fact that in 2004, President George W. Bush narrowly won the Iowa vote. Analysts regarded Obama's victory in the state as due to the troubled economy and the unpopularity of the Republican administration by 2008.

As in past elections, the Iowa caucuses in 2012 to choose the major party candidates made national news as the first event of the long drawn-out national political process. The 2012 Republican caucuses in January, resulted in the closest caucus race in the state's history. Former Senator Rick Santorum of Pennsylvania received 29,839 votes against former Massachusetts Governor Mitt Romney, with 29,805. The 34 votes separating the two represented a record; the third candidate, member of Congress Ron Paul of Texas, got 26,306 votes. Newt Gingrich, Texas Governor Rick Perry, and member of Congress Michele Bachman received smaller numbers. The Republican caucus turnout was a record for the party in the state, with over 121,000 votes cast (although this was less than the 239,000 Democrats who turned out for the 2008 caucuses.)

The caucuses are non-binding, despite the national attention focused on them. As a consequence, Ron Paul had a majority of the Iowa Republican delegates at the state convention, despite the fact that he had placed third in the state caucus popular vote. The 2012 caucuses in the state set a record for the dollar amount expended, much from out-of state political action committees, that ran "attack ads" on opponents. Despite the closeness of the race, the high amounts of out-of-state money spent, and the non-binding nature of the caucuses, the votes still influenced candidate decisions. Michele Bachmann, who placed sixth among the candidates, dropped out of the race; Governor Rick Perry, who finished fifth, "reassessed" his campaign, but stayed in for primaries in New Hampshire and South Carolina before withdrawing.

Rowena Wildin
Updated by the Editor

Downtown Des Moines viewed through the Center Street footbridge. Des Moines is Iowa's capital and largest city. (Wikimedia Commons)

Iowa Time Line

1673	French explorers Jacques Marquette and Louis Jolliet are the first Europeans to reach Iowa.
1788	French trader Julien Dubuque begins mining lead near modern-day Dubuque, with the permission of the Mesquaki Indians.
Dec. 30, 1803	United States purchases the Louisiana Territory, which includes Iowa, from France.
1804	Explorers Meriwether Lewis and William Clark cross Iowa on their journey to the Pacific Ocean.
1832	Sauk chief Black Hawk signs a treaty in which the Sauk and Mesquaki agree to vacate a strip of land near the Mississippi River by June, 1833.
June 12, 1838	Territory of Iowa is created.
1838	Land offices begin to sell Iowa land for $1.25 per acre.
Oct. 11, 1842	Sauk and Fox agree to leave Iowa within three years.
1846	Mormons begin crossing Iowa on their trek to Utah from Navuvoo, Illinois.
Dec. 28, 1846	Iowa becomes the twenty-ninth state of the Union.
1851	The Sioux, the last Native Americans with land in the state, agree to leave Iowa.
1855	University of Iowa is founded.
1855–1865	German immigrants form the Amana colonies, a communal society that lasts for eighty years.
1857	Group of Mesquaki purchase land in Tama County, part of their former homeland.
1857	Group of Sioux kill thirty-four settlers along the shores of Spirit Lake and capture four women, two of whom are later ransomed.
1857	State capital moves from Iowa City to Des Moines.
1858	Iowa State University is founded.
1858	"Cardiff Giant," a prehistoric man, is found to be a hoax.
1861–1865	Iowa sends seventy thousand soldiers to the Civil War; thirteen thousand die.
1867	First railroad, the Chicago, Iowa, and Nebraska line, reaches the state's western edge.
1868	Iowa supreme court rules that segregated schools are unconstitutional in Iowa; African Americans are given voting rights.
1876	University of Northern Iowa is founded.
1880	Five major and spur railroad lines, more than five thousand miles of track, cover Iowa.
1896	Free rural mail delivery begins.
1900–1918	Buxton, a town in Monroe county inhabited predominantly by African American coal miners, flourishes until its coal mines are depleted.
1906-1920	Bicycle shop owner Fred Duesenberg and attorney Edward R. Mason build cars, designed by Duesenberg, in Iowa.
1910	Iowa State Experiment Station tests soybeans as a potential crop.
1912	Walter Sheaffer, a jeweler in Fort Madison, develops an easily inked fountain pen.
1926	Henry A. Wallace creates Pioneer Seed Corn, devoted to producing hybrid seed corn.
Mar. 4, 1929	Herbert Hoover, from Iowa, becomes president of the United States.
1935	Rural Electrification Administration brings electricity to Iowa farms.
1950's	Forrest City furniture dealer John Hanon creates the Winnebago motor-home.
1965	Des Moines students are suspended for wearing black armbands protesting the Vietnam War; four years later, the U.S. Supreme Court supports their right to protest.
1985	Musician Willie Nelson holds Farm Aid benefit concert for farmers suffering from falling land values.
1991	Iowa legalizes riverboat gambling.
1998	More than two hundred methamphetamine labs or dumpsites are found in Iowa, a record for the state.
Jan. 24, 2000	Presidential candidates Al Gore (Democrat) and George W. Bush (Republican) win Iowa caucuses.
Nov. 7, 2000	Gore wins Iowa's seven electoral votes by slightly more than four thousand votes.
Oct.–Nov. 2001	Iowa State University at Ames destroys its strain of anthrax samples after the same strain is said to be responsible for anthrax attacks in Washington, D.C., New York, New Jersey, and Connecticut.
2003	Study of Midwestern states, including Iowa, shows that farmers fail to follow the rule providing that they plant at least 20 percent of their crops in conventional seed.
Nov. 2, 2004	President George W. Bush wins Iowa's electoral votes by a slim margin, 33,500 votes.
2008	Senator Barack Obama wins 53.9 percent of the state's popular vote for the presidency.
Jan. 3, 2012	In a recount of the Iowa caucus, Rick Santorum beats Mitt Romney by just a few votes.

Notes for Further Study

Published Sources. *Iowa: The Middle Land* (1996) by Dorothy Schwieder presents a thorough history of Iowa from its earliest days to the mid-1990's. Allan Carpenter's *Between the Two Rivers: Iowa Year by Year, 1846-1996* (1997) examines the first 150 years of Iowa's statehood. Two older but still useful books on Iowa history are Joseph F. Wall's *Iowa, a Bicentennial History* (1978) and Leland L. Sage's *A History of Iowa* (1974). For young adults, David C. King and Rick Petreycik's *Iowa* (2006) offers an accessible account of the state's history. *Iowa History Reader* (1996), edited by Marvin Bergman, offers readings in Iowa history selected by the State Historical Society of Iowa. *Iowa's Ethnic Roots* (1993), edited by Ron E. Roberts, examines the ethnic history of Iowa. In *Iowa Letters: Dutch Immigrants on the American Frontier* (2005), compiled by Johan Stellingwerff and edited by Robert P. Swierenga, more than two hundred immigrant letters relating to the midwestern frontier and brought together from archives and private holdings provide insight into key issues in the minds of immigrants themselves and of their relatives in Holland. *Hook and Eye: A History of the Iowa Central Railway* (2005) by Don L. Hofsommer details the history of the Iowa Central Railway, a north-south route across the state which linked Minneapolis and St. Paul with St. Louis and provided transportation for the state's agricultural and industrial trade. Using primary sources that include memoirs, diaries, and census data, Patricia Riney-Kehrberg examines what life was like for rural children in Iowa and the greater Midwest between the end of the Civil War and the Progressive Era in *Childhood on the Farm: Work, Play, and Coming of Age in the Midwest* (2005). Charles O. Musser's *Soldier Boy: The Civil War Letters of Charles O. Musser, 29th Iowa* (1995), edited by Barry Popchock, presents a look at the Civil War through the eyes of a soldier with the 29th Iowa Infantry Regiment. Although Iowa is not necessarily a sought-after tourist destination, Mike Whye argues in his *The Great Iowa Touring Book* (2004) that if travelers leave the major routes and take to the back roads, numerous intriguing attractions can be found in the state's rural and urban landscapes.

Web Resources. A good place to start searching for information about Iowa on the Internet is through the state of Iowa's site (www.iowa.gov/state/main/index.html). It provides current Iowa news and weather; information on tourism, travel, and special events; and links to many other sites. Another excellent source of information is the many links furnished by the Iowa secretary of state (www.sos.state.ia.us). The Iowa general assembly's site (www.legis.iowa.gov/) contains information about the assembly and legislation.

An essay found on the University of Iowa's Web site (www.uiowa.edu/~osa/learn/historic/hisper.htm) presents an interesting and informative look at various aspects of Iowa history, while the Iowa History Project (iagenweb. org/history/) brings together a number of pamphlets, newspaper articles, and journals related to the state's history. Another good source is the Iowa Tourism Bureau's site (www.traveliowa.com), which offers a brief history of Iowa, interesting facts, and travel-related information, including events and attractions. The online version of *Iowan* magazine (www.iowan.com) provides articles about the state and allows a search of back issues.

Corn is an agricultural product with which Iowa has almost become synonymous. (PhotoDisc)

Counties

County	2012 Population	Pop. Rank	Land Area (sq. miles)	Area Rank
Adair	7,481	89	569.27	53
Adams	3,911	99	423.44	92
Allamakee	14,237	56	639.08	18
Appanoose	12,700	60	497.29	73
Audubon	5,910	97	442.96	78
Benton	25,827	24	716.26	11
Black Hawk	131,820	5	565.77	57
Boone	26,195	23	571.57	44
Bremer	24,479	26	435.48	82
Buchanan	20,942	30	571.02	45
Buena Vista	20,592	34	574.91	39
Butler	14,986	53	580.13	30
Calhoun	9,909	77	569.97	48
Carroll	20,631	33	569.44	51
Cass	13,723	58	564.27	58
Cedar	18,416	38	579.44	31
Cerro Gordo	43,788	13	568.31	55
Cherokee	11,946	65	576.91	35
Chickasaw	12,276	63	504.38	69
Clarke	9,370	80	431.17	88
Clay	16,599	46	567.24	56
Clayton	17,835	39	778.54	5
Clinton	48,717	11	694.91	15
Crawford	17,309	42	714.19	13

County	2012 Population	Pop. Rank	Land Area (sq. miles)	Area Rank
Dallas	71,967	10	588.45	24
Davis	8,689	85	502.19	70
Decatur	8,253	86	531.88	65
Delaware	17,574	40	577.76	33
Des Moines	40,340	16	416.12	93
Dickinson	16,972	44	380.61	99
Dubuque	95,097	7	608.30	21
Emmet	10,120	76	395.88	98
Fayette	20,793	31	730.81	7
Floyd	16,056	48	500.63	72
Franklin	10,554	73	581.97	28
Fremont	7,147	92	511.15	68
Greene	9,153	82	569.57	50
Grundy	12,448	62	501.86	71
Guthrie	10,777	69	590.62	23
Hamilton	15,344	52	576.75	36
Hancock	11,134	68	571.00	46
Hardin	17,302	43	569.31	52
Harrison	14,548	55	696.85	14
Henry	20,236	35	434.33	84
Howard	9,563	79	473.25	75
Humboldt	9,729	78	434.35	83
Ida	7,108	93	431.51	87
Iowa	16,189	47	586.46	26

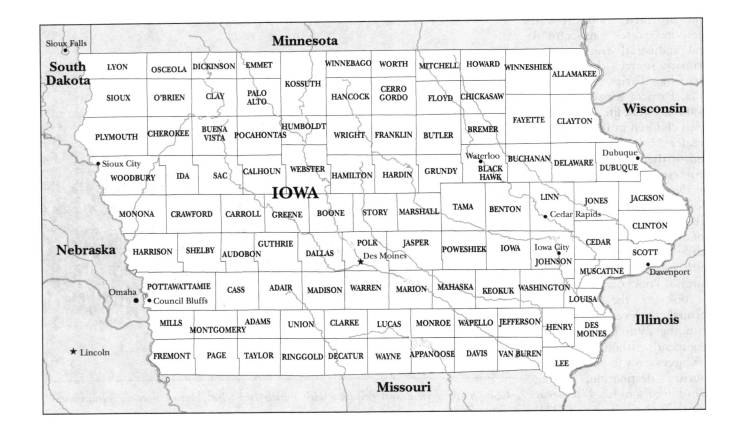

County	2012 Population	Pop. Rank	Land Area (sq. miles)	Area Rank
Jackson	19,712	36	636.04	19
Jasper	36,602	18	730.42	8
Jefferson	16,867	45	435.51	81
Johnson	136,317	4	614.04	20
Jones	20,639	32	575.62	37
Keokuk	10,374	74	579.18	32
Kossuth	15,346	51	972.72	1
Lee	35,617	19	517.52	67
Linn	215,295	2	716.88	10
Louisa	11,278	67	401.77	94
Lucas	8,760	84	430.59	89
Lyon	11,757	66	587.65	25
Madison	15,654	50	561.01	60
Mahaska	22,443	27	570.86	47
Marion	33,419	22	554.53	61
Marshall	40,857	15	572.50	43
Mills	14,837	54	437.44	80
Mitchell	10,725	70	469.13	76
Monona	9,124	83	694.07	16
Monroe	8,063	87	433.72	85
Montgomery	10,566	72	424.10	90
Muscatine	42,879	14	437.47	79
O'Brien	14,172	57	573.04	41
Osceola	6,193	96	398.68	97
Page	15,713	49	534.94	63
Palo Alto	9,275	81	563.84	59
Plymouth	24,907	25	862.89	4
Pocahontas	7,150	91	577.24	34
Polk	443,710	1	573.79	40
Pottawattamie	92,913	8	950.28	2
Poweshiek	18,736	37	584.93	27
Ringgold	5,096	98	535.50	62
Sac	10,153	75	575.01	38
Scott	168,799	3	458.09	77
Shelby	12,069	64	590.78	22
Sioux	34,268	21	768.33	6
Story	91,140	9	572.82	42
Tama	17,536	41	721.01	9
Taylor	6,208	95	531.90	64
Union	12,594	61	423.65	91
Van Buren	7,449	90	484.79	74
Wapello	35,366	20	431.83	86
Warren	46,891	12	569.83	49
Washington	21,914	28	568.84	54
Wayne	6,344	94	525.44	66
Webster	37,273	17	715.62	12
Winnebago	10,600	71	400.49	95
Winneshiek	21,061	29	689.87	17
Woodbury	102,323	6	872.83	3
Worth	7,519	88	400.12	96
Wright	12,991	59	580.42	29

Source: U.S. Census Bureau, 2012 Population Estimates

Cities
With 10,000 or more residents

Legal Name	2010 Population	Pop. Rank	Land Area (sq. miles)	Area Rank
Altoona city	14,541	28	9.35	30
Ames city	58,965	8	24.21	14
Ankeny city	45,582	11	29.33	10
Bettendorf city	33,217	15	21.22	16
Boone city	12,661	31	9.02	32
Burlington city	25,663	19	14.48	23
Carroll city	10,103	38	5.69	37
Cedar Falls city	39,260	13	28.75	11
Cedar Rapids city	126,326	2	70.80	2
Clinton city	26,885	18	35.15	8
Clive city	15,447	25	7.59	35
Coralville city	18,907	23	12.01	25
Council Bluffs city	62,230	7	40.97	6
Davenport city	99,685	3	62.95	3
Des Moines city	203,433	1	80.87	1
Dubuque city	57,637	9	29.97	9
Fort Dodge city	25,206	20	16.05	20
Fort Madison city	11,051	34	9.49	29
Indianola city	14,782	27	11.25	26
Iowa City city	67,862	6	25.01	13

Legal Name	2010 Population	Pop. Rank	Land Area (sq. miles)	Area Rank
Johnston city	17,278	24	17.16	19
Keokuk city	10,780	35	9.13	31
Marion city	34,768	14	16.05	20
Marshalltown city	27,552	17	19.28	17
Mason City city	28,079	16	27.81	12
Muscatine city	22,886	22	17.30	18
Newton city	15,254	26	11.19	27
North Liberty city	13,374	30	7.83	34
Oskaloosa city	11,463	32	7.43	36
Ottumwa city	25,023	21	15.86	22
Pella city	10,352	37	8.73	33
Sioux City city	82,684	4	57.35	5
Spencer city	11,233	33	11.01	28
Storm Lake city	10,600	36	4.08	38
Urbandale city	39,463	12	21.92	15
Waterloo city	68,406	5	61.39	4
Waukee city	13,790	29	12.97	24
West Des Moines city	56,609	10	38.59	7

Note: CDP–Census Designated Place
Source: U.S. Census Bureau, 2010 Census

Survey Says...

This section presents current rankings from dozens of public and private sources. It shows how this state ranks in a number of critical categories, including education, job growth, cost of living, teen drivers, energy efficiency, and business environment. Sources include *Forbes, Reuters, U.S. News and World Report, CNN Money, Gallup,* and *Huffington Post.*

- Iowa ranked #16 in a government study measuring real gross domestic product (GDP)—the output of goods and services produced by labor and property located in the United States. The ranking is based on the percentage change compared with 2011 GDP.

  U.S. Department of Commerce, Bureau of Economic Analysis, June 2013; www.bea.gov

- Iowa ranked #30 in a government study measuring real gross domestic product (GDP)—the output of goods and services produced by labor and property located in the United States. The ranking is based on the dollar value of its GDP.

  U.S. Department of Commerce, Bureau of Economic Analysis, June 2013; www.bea.gov

- Iowa ranked #34 in the 17th edition of "Quality Counts; State of the States," Education Week's "report card" surveying key education indicators, policy efforts, and educational outcomes.

  Education Week, January 4, 2013 (online) and January 10, 2013 (print); www.edweek.org

- SERI (Science and Engineering Readiness Index) weighs the performance of the states' K-12 schools in preparing students in physics and calculus, the high school subjects considered most important for future scientists and engineers. Iowa ranked #38.

  Newsletter of the Forum on Education of the American Physical Society, Summer 2011 issue; www.huffingtonpost.com, July 11, 2011; updated October 1, 2012

- MoneyRates.com ranked Iowa #12 on its list of the best to worst states for making a living. Criteria: average income; inflation; employment prospects; and workers' Workplace Environment assessments according to the Gallup-Healthways Well-Being Index.

  www.money-rates.com, posted April 1, 2013

- *Forbes* analyzed business costs, labor supply, regulatory environment, current economic climate, growth prospects, and quality of life, to compile its "Best States for Business" rankings. Iowa ranked #10.

  www.forbes.com. posted December 12, 2012

- The 2012 Gallup-Healthways Well-Being Index, surveyed American's opinions on economic confidence, workplace perceptions, community climate, personal choices, and health predictors to assess the "future livability" of each state. Iowa ranked #7.

  "Utah Poised to Be the Best State to Live In," Gallup Wellbeing, www.gallup.com, August 7, 2012

- On CNBC's list of "America's Top States for Business 2013," Iowa ranked #11. Criteria: measures of competitiveness developed with input from the National Association of Manufacturers, the Council on Competitiveness, and other business groups weighed with the states' own marketing criteria.

  www.cnbc.com, consulted July 19, 2013

- Iowa ranked #14 on MoneyRates list of "Best-and Worst-States to Retire 2012." Criteria: life expectancy, crime rate, climate, economic conditions, taxes, job opportunities, and cost of living.

  www.money-rates.com, October 22, 2012

- Iowa ranked #22 on the 2013 Bankrate "Best Places to Retire" list ranking the states and District of Columbia on various criteria relating to health, safety, and cost.

  www.bankrate.com, May 6, 2013

- Iowa ranked #22 on the Social Science Research Council's "American Human Development Report: The Measure of America," assessing the 50 states plus the District of Columbia on health, education, and living-standard criteria.

  The Measure of America 2013-2014, posted June 19, 2013; www.measureofamerica.org

- Iowa ranked #7 on the Foundation for Child Development's (FCD) Child Well-being Index (CWI). The FCD used the KIDS COUNT report and the National Survey of Children's Health, the only state-level source for several key indicators of child well-being.

  Foundation for Child Development, January 18, 2012; fcd-us.org

- Iowa ranked #7 overall according to the 2013 KIDS COUNT Data Book, a project of the Annie E. Casey Foundation. Criteria: children's economic well-being, education, health, and family and community indicators.

  KIDS COUNT Data Center's Data Book, released June 20, 2013; http://datacenter.kidscount.org

- Iowa ranked #5 in the children's economic well-being category by the 2013 KIDS COUNT Data Book, a project of the Annie E. Casey Foundation.

  KIDS COUNT Data Center's Data Book, released June 20, 2013; http://datacenter.kidscount.org

- Iowa ranked #15 in the children's educational opportunities and attainments category by the 2013 KIDS COUNT Data Book, a project of the Annie E. Casey Foundation.

  KIDS COUNT Data Center's Data Book, released June 20, 2013; http://datacenter.kidscount.org

- Iowa ranked #7 in the children's health category by the 2013 KIDS COUNT Data Book, a project of the Annie E. Casey Foundation.

  KIDS COUNT Data Center's Data Book, released June 20, 2013; http://datacenter.kidscount.org

- Iowa ranked #8 in the family and community circumstances that factor into children's well-being category by the 2013 KIDS COUNT Data Book, a project of the Annie E. Casey Foundation.

  KIDS COUNT Data Center's Data Book, released June 20, 2013; http://datacenter.kidscount.org

- Iowa ranked #9 in the 2012 Gallup-Healthways Well-Being Index. Criteria: emotional health; physical health; healthy behavior; work environment; basic access to food, shelter, health care; and a safe and satisfying place to live.
  2012 State of Well-Being, Gallup-Healthways Well-Being Index, released February 28, 2013; www.well-beingindex.com

- *U.S. News and World Report's* "Best States for Teen Drivers" rankings are based on driving and road safety laws, federal reports on driver's licenses, car accident fatality, and road-quality statistics. Iowa ranked #49.
  U.S. News and World Report, March 18, 2010; www.usnews.com

- The Yahoo! Sports service Rivals.com ranks the states according to the strength of their high school football programs. Iowa ranked #36.
  "Ranking the States: Where Is the Best Football Played?," November 18, 2011; highschool.rivals.com

- iVillage ranked the states by hospitable living conditions for women. Criteria: economic success, access to affordable childcare, health care, reproductive rights, female representation in government, and educational attainment. Iowa ranked #28.
  iVillage, "50 Best to Worst States for Women," March 14, 2012; www.ivillage.com

- The League of American Bicyclists's "Bicycle Friendly States" ranked Iowa #21. Criteria: legislation and enforcement, policies and programs, infrastructure and funding, education and advocacy, and evaluation and planning.
  "Washington Tops the Bicycle-Friendly State Ranking," May 1, 2013; bicycling.com

- The federal Corporation for National and Community Service ranked the states and the District of Columbia by volunteer rates. Iowa ranked #3 for community service.
  "Volunteering and Civic Life in America 2012," www.volunteeringinamerica.gov, accessed July 24, 2013

- The Hospital Safety Score ranked states and the District of Columbia on their hospitals' performance scores. Iowa ranked #27. Criteria: avoiding preventable harm and medical errors, as demonstrated by 26 hospital safety metrics.
  Spring 2013 Hospital Safety Score, May 8, 2013; www.hospitalsafetyscore.org

- GMAC Insurance ranked the states and the District of Columbia by the performance of their drivers on the GMAC Insurance National Drivers Test, comprised of DMV test questions. Iowa ranked #2.
  "2011 GMAC Insurance National Drivers Test," www.gmacinsurance.com, accessed July 23, 2013

- Iowa ranked #7 in a "State Integrity Investigation" analysis of laws and practices intended to deter corruption and promote accountability and openness in campaign finance, ethics laws, lobbying regulations and management of state pension funds.
  "What's Your State's Grade?," www.publicintegrity.org, accessed July 23, 2013

- Iowa ranked #11 among the states and the District of Columbia in total rail miles, as tracked by the Association of American Railroads.
  "U.S. Freight Railroad Industry Snapshot: Railroads and States: Total Rail Miles by State: 2011"; www.aar.org, accessed July 23, 2013

- According to statistics compiled by the Beer Institute, Iowa ranked #13 among the states and the District of Columbia in per capita beer consumption of persons 21 years or older.
  "Shipments of Malt Beverages and Per Capita Consumption by State 2012;" www.beerinstitute.org

- According to Concordia University's "Public Education Costs per Pupil by State Rankings," based on statistics gathered by the U.S. Census Bureau, which includes the District of Columbia, Iowa ranked #28.
  Concordia University Online; education.cu-portland.edu, accessed July 24, 2013

- Iowa ranked #36 among the states and the District of Columbia in population density based on U.S. Census Bureau data for resident population and total land area. "List of U.S. States by Population Density."
  www.wikipedia.org, accessed July 24, 2013

- In "America's Health Rankings, 2012 Edition," by the United Health Foundation, Iowa ranked #20. Criteria included: rate of high school graduation; violent crime rate; incidence of infectious disease; childhood immunizations; prevalence of diabetes; per capita public-health funding; percentage of uninsured population; rate of children in poverty; and availability of primary-care physicians.
  United Health Foundation; www.americashealthrankings.org, accessed July 24, 2013

- The TechNet 2012 "State Broadband Index" ranked Iowa #34 on the following criteria: broadband adoption; network quality; and economic structure. Improved broadband use is hoped to promote economic development, build strong communities, improve delivery of government services and upgrade educational systems.
  TechNet; www.technet.org, accessed July 24, 2013

- Iowa was ranked #11 among the states and District of Columbia on the American Council for an Energy-Efficient Economy's "State Energy Efficiency Scorecard" for 2012.
  American Council for an Energy-Efficient Economy; aceee.org/sector/state-policy/scorecard, accessed July 24, 2013

Statistical Tables

DEMOGRAPHICS
Resident State and National Population, 1950-2012
Projected State and National Population, 2000-2030
Population by Age, 2012
Population by Race, 2012
Population by Hispanic Origin and Race, 2012

VITAL STATISTICS
Death Rates by Leading Causes, 2010
Death Rates by Selected Causes, 2010
Abortion Rates, 2009
Infant Mortality Rates, 1995-2009
Marriage and Divorce Rates, 2000-2011

ECONOMY
Nominal Gross Domestic Product by Industry, 2012
Real Gross Domestic Product, 2000-2012
Personal Income Per Capita, 1930-2012
Non-Farm Employment by Sector, 2012
Foreign Exports, 2000-2012
Energy Consumption, 2011

LAND AND WATER
Surface Area and Federally-Owned Land, 2007
Land Cover/Use of Non-Federal Rural Land, 2007
Farms and Crop Acreage, 2012

HEALTH AND MEDICAL CARE
Medical Professionals, 2012
Health Insurance Coverage, 2011
HIV, STD, and Tuberculosis Cases and Rates, 2011
Cigarette Smoking, 2011

HOUSING
Home Ownership Rates, 1995-2012
Home Sales, 2000-2010
Value of Owner-Occupied Homes, 2011

EDUCATION
School Enrollment, 2011
Educational Attainment, 2011
Public College Finances, FY 2012

TRANSPORTATION AND TRAVEL
Motor Vehicle Registrations and Drivers Licenses, 2011
Domestic Travel Expenditures, 2009
Retail Gasoline Prices, 2013
Public Road Length, 2011

CRIME AND LAW ENFORCEMENT
Full-Time Law Enforcement Officers, 2011
Prison Population, 2000-2012
Crime Rate, 2011

GOVERNMENT AND FINANCE
Local Governments by Type, 2012
State Government Revenue, 2011
State Government Expenditures, 2011
State Government General Expenditures by Function, 2011
State Government Finances, Cash and Debt, 2011

POLITICS
Composition of the Senate, 1995-2013
Composition of the House of Representatives, 1995-2013
Composition of State Legislature, 2004-2013
Voter Participation in Presidential Elections, 1980-2012
Governors Since Statehood

DEMOGRAPHICS

Resident State and National Population, 1950–2012

Year	State Population	U.S. Population	State Share
1950	2,621,000	151,326,000	1.73%
1960	2,758,000	179,323,000	1.54%
1970	2,825,368	203,302,031	1.39%
1980	2,913,808	226,545,805	1.29%
1990	2,776,755	248,709,873	1.12%
2000	2,926,538	281,424,600	1.04%
2010	3,046,355	308,745,538	0.99%
2012	3,074,186	313,914,040	0.98%

Note: 1950/1960 population figures are rounded to the nearest thousand.
Source: U.S. Census Bureau, Decennial Census 1950–2010; U.S. Census Bureau, 2012 Population Estimates

Projected State and National Population, 2000–2030

Year	State Population	U.S. Population	State Share
2000	2,926,324	281,421,906	1.04%
2005	2,973,700	295,507,134	1.01%
2010	3,009,907	308,935,581	0.97%
2015	3,026,380	322,365,787	0.94%
2020	3,020,496	335,804,546	0.90%
2025	2,993,222	349,439,199	0.86%
2030	2,955,172	363,584,435	0.81%
State population growth, 2000–2030			28,848
State percentage growth, 2000–2030			1.0%

Source: U.S. Census Bureau, Population Division, Interim State Population Projections, 2005

Population by Age, 2012

Age Group	State Population	Percent of Total Population	
		State	U.S.
Under 5 years	196,366	6.4%	6.4%
5 to 14 years	405,010	13.2%	13.1%
15 to 24 years	435,867	14.2%	14.0%
25 to 34 years	390,200	12.7%	13.5%
35 to 44 years	359,269	11.7%	12.9%
45 to 54 years	423,537	13.8%	14.1%
55 to 64 years	393,632	12.8%	12.3%
65 to 74 years	240,544	7.8%	7.6%
75 to 84 years	152,389	5.0%	4.2%
85 years and older	77,372	2.5%	1.9%
Under 18 years	722,953	23.5%	23.5%
65 years and older	470,305	15.3%	13.7%
Median age (years)	–	38.1	37.4

Source: U.S. Census Bureau, Annual Estimates of the Resident Population for Selected Age Groups by Sex for the United States, States, Counties, and Puerto Rico Commonwealth and Municipios: April 1, 2010 to July 1, 2012

Population by Race, 2012

Race	State Population	Percent of Total Population	
		State	U.S.
All residents	3,074,186	100.00%	100.00%
White	2,851,533	92.76%	77.89%
African American	97,080	3.16%	13.13%
Native American	14,179	0.46%	1.23%
Asian	60,004	1.95%	5.14%
Native Hawaiian	2,634	0.09%	0.23%
Two or more races	48,756	1.59%	2.39%

Source: U.S. Census Bureau, Population Division, Annual Estimates of the Resident Population by Sex, Race and Hispanic Origin for the United States, States, and Counties: April 1, 2010 to July 1, 2012

Population by Hispanic Origin and Race, 2012

Hispanic Origin/Race	State Population	Percent of Total Population	
		State	U.S.
All residents	3,074,186	100.00%	100.00%
All Hispanic residents	162,894	5.30%	16.89%
Hispanic			
White	145,939	4.75%	14.91%
African American	4,313	0.14%	0.79%
Native American	5,398	0.18%	0.49%
Asian	1,135	0.04%	0.17%
Native Hawaiian	590	0.02%	0.06%
Two or more races	5,519	0.18%	0.48%
Not Hispanic			
White	2,705,594	88.01%	62.98%
African American	92,767	3.02%	12.34%
Native American	8,781	0.29%	0.74%
Asian	58,869	1.91%	4.98%
Native Hawaiian	2,044	0.07%	0.17%
Two or more races	43,237	1.41%	1.91%

Source: U.S. Census Bureau, Population Division, Annual Estimates of the Resident Population by Sex, Race and Hispanic Origin for the United States, States, and Counties: April 1, 2010 to July 1, 2012

VITAL STATISTICS

Death Rates by Leading Causes, 2010

Cause	State	U.S.
Malignant neoplasms	184.8	186.2
Ischaemic heart diseases	136.9	122.9
Other forms of heart disease	35.8	53.4
Chronic lower respiratory diseases	47.2	44.7
Cerebrovascular diseases	40.7	41.9
Organic, incl. symptomatic, mental disorders	28.8	35.7
Other degenerative diseases of the nervous sys.	37.5	28.4
Other external causes of accidental injury	24.8	26.5
Diabetes mellitus	20.7	22.4
Hypertensive diseases	16.2	20.4
All causes	772.1	799.5

Note: Figures are age-adjusted death rates per 100,000 population
Source: CDC/NCHS, Underlying Cause of Death 1999–2010 on CDC WONDER Online Database

Death Rates by Selected Causes, 2010

Cause	State	U.S.
Assault	1.8	5.2
Diseases of the liver	11.3	13.9
Human immunodeficiency virus (HIV) disease	0.0	2.7
Influenza and pneumonia	14.7	16.2
Intentional self-harm	12.3	12.4
Malnutrition	0.5	0.9
Obesity and other hyperalimentation	1.5	1.8
Renal failure	7.2	14.4
Transport accidents	13.4	12.1
Viral hepatitis	1.4	2.4

Note: Figures are age-adjusted death rates per 100,000 population; A dash indicates that data was not available or was suppressed
Source: CDC/NCHS, Underlying Cause of Death 1999–2010 on CDC WONDER Online Database

Abortion Rates, 2009

Category	2009
By state of residence	
Total abortions	5,132
Abortion rate[1]	8.9%
Abortion ratio[2]	129
By state of occurrence	
Total abortions	5,821
Abortion rate[1]	10.1%
Abortion ratio[2]	147
Abortions obtained by out-of-state residents	16.3%
U.S. abortion rate[1]	15.1%
U.S. abortion ratio[2]	227

Note: (1) Number of abortions per 1,000 women aged 15–44 years; (2) Number of abortions per 1,000 live births; A dash indicates that data was not available
Source: CDC/NCHS, Morbidity and Mortality Weekly Report, November 23, 2012 (Abortion Surveillance, United States, 2009)

Infant Mortality Rates, 1995–2009

Category	1995	2000	2005	2009
All state residents	8.26	6.43	5.44	4.61
All U.S. residents	7.57	6.89	6.86	6.39
All state white residents	7.99	6.13	5.14	4.38
All U.S. white residents	6.30	5.71	5.73	5.33
All state black residents	–	–	–	11.15
All U.S. black residents	14.58	13.48	13.26	12.12

Note: Figures represent deaths per 1,000 live births of resident infants under one year old, exclusive of fetal deaths; A dash indicates that data was not available or was suppressed.
Source: Centers of Disease Control and Prevention, Division of Vital Statistics, Linked Birth/Infant Death Records on CDC Wonder Online

Marriage and Divorce Rates, 2000–2011

Year	Marriage Rate		Divorce Rate	
	State	U.S.	State	U.S.
2000	6.9	8.2	3.3	4.0
2002	7.0	8.0	3.1	3.9
2004	6.9	7.8	2.8	3.7
2006	6.7	7.5	2.7	3.7
2008	6.5	7.1	2.6	3.5
2010	6.9	6.8	2.4	3.6
2011	6.7	6.8	2.4	3.6

Note: Rates are based on provisional counts of marriages/divorces by state of occurrence and are per 1,000 total population residing in area
Source: CDC/NCHS, National Vital Statistics System

ECONOMY

Nominal Gross Domestic Product by Industry, 2012
In millions of current dollars

Industry	State GDP
Accommodation and food services	3,422
Administrative and waste management services	3,047
Agriculture, forestry, fishing, and hunting	10,162
Arts, entertainment, and recreation	1,212
Construction	5,650
Educational services	1,349
Finance and insurance	19,285
Health care and social assistance	10,326
Information	4,056
Management of companies and enterprises	1,626
Manufacturing	25,406
Mining	125
Other services, except government	3,471
Professional, scientific, and technical services	5,069
Real estate and rental and leasing	15,066
Retail trade	9,029
Transportation and warehousing	5,400
Utilities	2,783
Wholesale trade	8,882

Source: U.S. Department of Commerce, Bureau of Economic Analysis, Survey of Current Business

Real Gross Domestic Product, 2000–2012
In millions of chained 2005 dollars

Year	State GDP	U.S. GDP	State Share
2000	105,338	11,225,406	0.94%
2005	119,998	12,539,116	0.96%
2010	124,011	12,897,088	0.96%
2012	129,799	13,430,576	0.97%

Source: U.S. Department of Commerce, Bureau of Economic Analysis, Survey of Current Business

Personal Income Per Capita, 1930–2012

Year	State	U.S.
1930	$499	$618
1940	$492	$593
1950	$1,530	$1,503
1960	$2,058	$2,268
1970	$3,878	$4,084
1980	$9,573	$10,091
1990	$17,350	$19,354
2000	$27,285	$30,319
2010	$37,882	$39,791
2012	$42,126	$42,693

Source: U.S. Department of Commerce, Bureau of Economic Analysis, Regional Economic Accounts

Non-Farm Employment by Sector, 2012
In thousands

Sector	Employment
Construction	64.4
Education and health services	220.5
Financial activities	101.6
Government	254.2
Information	27.1
Leisure and hospitality	134.0
Mining and logging	2.2
Manufacturing	210.5
Other services	57.7
Professional and business services	129.5
Trade, transportation, and utilities	306.8
All sectors	1,508.4

Source: U.S. Bureau of Labor Statistics, State and Area Employment

Foreign Exports, 2000–2012
In millions of dollars

Year	State Exports	U.S. Exports	State Share
2000	4,465	712,054	0.63%
2002	4,754	649,940	0.73%
2004	6,414	768,554	0.83%
2006	8,428	973,994	0.87%
2008	12,124	1,222,545	0.99%
2010	10,879	1,208,080	0.90%
2012	14,635	1,478,268	0.99%

Note: U.S. figures exclude data from Puerto Rico, U.S. Virgin Islands, and unallocated exports
Source: U.S. Department of Commerce, International Trade Admin., Office of Trade and Industry Information, Manufacturing and Services

Energy Consumption, 2011

In trillions of BTUs, except as noted

Total energy consumption	
Total state energy consumption	1,512.6
Total U.S. energy consumption	97,387.3
State share of U.S. total	1.55%
Per capita consumption (in millions of BTUs)	
Total state per capita consumption	493.7
Total U.S. per capita consumption	312.6
End-use sectors	
Residential	245.9
Commercial	207.9
Industrial	745.9
Transportation	312.9
Sources of energy	
Petroleum	422.6
Natural gas	277.6
Coal	463.1
Renewable energy	351.9
Nuclear electric power	54.6

Source: U.S. Energy Information Administration, State Energy Data 2011: Consumption

LAND AND WATER

Surface Area and Federally-Owned Land, 2007

In thousands of acres

Category	State	U.S.	State Share
Total surface area	36,016.5	1,937,664.2	1.86%
Total land area	35,530.6	1,886,846.9	1.88%
Non-federal land	35,358.2	1,484,910.0	2.38%
Developed	1,892.3	111,251.2	1.70%
Rural	33,465.9	1,373,658.8	2.44%
Federal land	172.4	401,936.9	0.04%
Water area	485.9	50,817.3	0.96%

Source: U.S. Department of Agriculture, Natural Resources Conservation Service, 2007 National Resources Inventory

Land Cover/Use of Non-Federal Rural Land, 2007

In thousands of acres

Category	State	U.S.	State Share
Total rural land	33,465.9	1,373,658.8	2.44%
Cropland	25,446.2	357,023.5	7.13%
CRP[1] land	1,427.5	32,850.2	4.35%
Pastureland	3,304.8	118,615.7	2.79%
Rangeland	0.0	409,119.4	0.00%
Forest land	2,354.7	406,410.4	0.58%
Other rural land	932.7	49,639.6	1.88%

Note: (1) Conservation Reserve Program was created to assist private landowners in converting highly erodible cropland to vegetative cover.
Source: U.S. Department of Agriculture, Natural Resources Conservation Service, 2007 National Resources Inventory

Farms and Crop Acreage, 2012

Category	State	U.S.	State Share
Farms (in thousands)	92.2	2,170.0	4.25%
Acres (in millions)	30.7	914.0	3.36%
Acres per farm	333.0	421.2	–

Source: U.S. Department of Agriculture, National Agricultural Statistical Service, Quick Stats, 2012 Survey Data

HEALTH AND MEDICAL CARE

Medical Professionals, 2012

Profession	State Number	U.S. Number	State Share	State Rate[1]	U.S. Rate[1]
Physicians[2]	6,859	894,637	0.77%	223.9	287.1
Dentists	1,827	193,587	0.94%	59.6	62.1
Podiatrists	178	17,469	1.02%	5.8	5.6
Optometrists	545	45,638	1.19%	17.8	14.6
Chiropractors	1,547	77,494	2.00%	50.5	24.9

Note: (1) Rates are per 100,000 population; (2) Includes total, active Doctors of Osteopathic Medicine and Doctors of Medicine in 2011.
Source: U.S. Department of Health and Human Services, Bureau of Health Professions, Area Health Resource File, 2012-2013

Health Insurance Coverage, 2011

Category	State	U.S.
Total persons covered	2,730,000	260,214,000
Total persons not covered	303,000	48,613,000
Percent not covered	10.0%	15.7%
Children under age 18 covered	686,000	67,143,000
Children under age 18 not covered	36,000	6,965,000
Percent of children not covered	5.0%	9.4%

Source: U.S. Census Bureau, Current Population Survey, 2012 Annual Social and Economic Supplement

HIV, STD, and Tuberculosis Cases and Rates, 2011

Disease	State Cases	State Rate[1]	U.S. Rate[1]
Chlamydia	10,705	351.4	457.6
Gonorrhea	1,920	63.0	104.2
HIV diagnosis	128	5.0	15.8
HIV, stage 3 (AIDS)	93	3.6	10.3
Syphilis, early latent	11	0.4	4.3
Syphilis, primary/secondary	20	0.7	4.5
Tuberculosis	40	1.3	3.4

Note: (1) Rates are per 100,000 population
Source: Centers for Disease Control and Prevention

Cigarette Smoking, 2011

Category	State	U.S.
Adults who are current smokers	20.4%	21.2%
Adults who smoke everyday	15.5%	15.4%
Adults who smoke some days	4.8%	5.7%
Adults who are former smokers	25.0%	25.1%
Adults who never smoked	54.6%	52.9%

Source: Centers for Disease Control and Prevention, Behaviorial Risk Factor Surveillance System, Tobacco Use, 2011

HOUSING

Home Ownership Rates, 1995–2012

Area	1995	2000	2005	2010	2012
State	71.4%	75.2%	73.9%	71.1%	70.2%
U.S.	64.7%	67.4%	68.9%	66.9%	65.4%

Source: U.S. Census Bureau, Housing Vacancies and Homeownership, Annual Statistics

Home Sales, 2000–2010
In thousands of units

Year	State Sales	U.S. Sales	State Share
2000	53.3	5,174	1.03%
2002	58.4	5,632	1.04%
2004	71.1	6,778	1.05%
2006	74.6	6,478	1.15%
2008	55.7	4,913	1.13%
2010	55.7	4,908	1.13%

Note: Units include single-family homes, condos and co-ops
Source: National Association of Realtors, Real Estate Outlook, Market Trends & Insights

Value of Owner-Occupied Homes, 2011

Value	Total Units in State	Percent of Total, State	Percent of Total, U.S.
Less than $50,000	101,321	11.5%	8.8%
$50,000 to $99,000	225,583	25.6%	16.0%
$100,000 to $149,000	212,034	24.1%	16.5%
$150,000 to $199,000	145,653	16.5%	15.4%
$200,000 to $299,000	126,054	14.3%	18.2%
$300,000 to $499,000	52,369	5.9%	15.2%
$500,000 to $999,000	13,343	1.5%	7.9%
$1,000,000 or more	4,011	0.5%	2.0%
Median value	–	$123,400	$173,600

Source: U.S. Census Bureau, 2011 American Community Survey 1-Year Estimates

EDUCATION

School Enrollment, 2011

Educational Level	Students Enrolled in State	Percent of Total, State	Percent of Total, U.S.
All levels	809,863	100.0%	100.0%
Nursery school, preschool	55,477	6.9%	6.0%
Kindergarten	41,290	5.1%	5.1%
Elementary (grades 1–8)	314,946	38.9%	39.5%
Secondary (grades 9–12)	165,367	20.4%	20.7%
College or graduate school	232,783	28.7%	28.7%

Note: Figures cover the population 3 years and over enrolled in school
Source: U.S. Census Bureau, 2011 American Community Survey 1-Year Estimates

Educational Attainment, 2011

Highest Level of Education	State	U.S.
High school diploma	90.6%	85.9%
Bachelor's degree	25.8%	28.5%
Graduate/Professional degree	8.1%	10.6%

Note: Figures cover the population 25 years and over
Source: U.S. Census Bureau, 2011 American Community Survey 1-Year Estimates

Public College Finances, FY 2012

Category	State	U.S.
Full-time equivalent enrollment (FTE)[1]	132,423	11,548,974
Educational appropriations per FTE[2]	$4,390	$5,906
Net tuition revenue per FTE[3]	$7,060	$5,189
Total educational revenue per FTE[4]	$11,449	$11,043

(1) Full-time equivalent enrollment equates student credit hours to full time, academic year students, but excludes medical students; (2) Educational appropriations measure state and local support available for public higher education operating expenses including ARRA funds and excludes appropriations for independent institutions, financial aid for students attending independent institutions, research, hospitals, and medical education; (3) Net tuition revenue is calculated by taking the gross amount of tuition and fees, less state and institutional financial aid, tuition waivers or discounts, and medical student tuition and fees. Net tuition revenue used for capital debt service is included in the net tuition revenue figures; (4) Total educational revenue is the sum of educational appropriations and net tuition excluding net tuition revenue used for capital debt service.
Source: State Higher Education Executive Officers, State Higher Education Finance FY 2012

TRANSPORTATION AND TRAVEL

Motor Vehicle Registrations and Drivers Licenses, 2011

Vehicle Type	State	U.S.	State Share
Automobiles[1]	1,645,916	125,656,528	1.31%
Buses	8,951	666,064	1.34%
Trucks	1,667,446	118,455,587	1.41%
Motorcycles	174,263	8,437,502	2.07%
Drivers licenses	2,191,715	211,874,649	1.03%

Note: Motor vehicle registrations include private, commercial, and publicly-owned vehicles; (1) Includes taxicabs
Source: U.S. Department of Transportation, Federal Highway Administration

Domestic Travel Expenditures, 2009
In millions of dollars

Category	State	U.S.	State Share
Travel expenditures	$6,056	$610,200	0.99%

Note: Figures represent U.S. spending on domestic overnight trips and day trips of 50 miles or more, one way, away from home. Excludes spending by foreign visitors.
Source: U.S. Travel Association, Impact of Travel on State Economies, 2009

Retail Gasoline Prices, 2013

Gasoline Grade	State Average	U.S. Average
Regular	$3.62	$3.65
Mid	$3.53	$3.81
Premium	$3.85	$3.98
Diesel	$3.79	$3.88
Excise tax[1]	40.4 cents	49.4 cents

Note: Gasoline prices as of 7/26/2013; (1) Includes state and federal excise taxes and other state taxes as of July 1, 2013
Source: American Automobile Association, Daily Fuel Guage Report; American Petroleum Institute, State Motor Fuel Taxes, 2013

Public Road Length, 2011

Type	State Mileage	U.S. Mileage	State Share
Interstate highways	782	46,960	1.67%
Other highways	0	15,719	0.00%
Principal arterial	4,282	156,262	2.74%
Minor arterial	5,463	242,942	2.25%
Major collector	15,457	534,592	2.89%
Minor collector	16,162	266,357	6.07%
Local	72,241	2,814,925	2.57%
Urban	11,401	1,095,373	1.04%
Rural	102,986	2,982,383	3.45%
Total	114,387	4,077,756	2.81%

Note: Combined urban and rural road mileage equals the total of the other road types
Source: U.S. Department of Transportation, Federal Highway Administration, Public Road Length, 2011

CRIME AND LAW ENFORCEMENT

Full-Time Law Enforcement Officers, 2011

Gender	State Number	State Rate[1]	U.S. Rate[1]
Male officers	4,676	156.4	210.3
Female officers	400	13.4	28.1
Total officers	5,076	169.7	238.3

Note: (1) Rates are per 100,000 population
Source: Federal Bureau of Investigation, Uniform Crime Reports, Crime in the United States 2011

Prison Population, 2000–2012

Year	State Population	U.S. Population	State Share
2000	7,955	1,391,261	0.57%
2005	8,737	1,527,929	0.57%
2010	9,455	1,613,803	0.59%
2011	9,116	1,598,783	0.57%
2012	8,733	1,571,013	0.56%

Note: Figures include prisoners under the jurisdiction of state or federal correctional authorities.
Source: U.S. Department of Justice, Bureau of Justice Statistics, Prisoners in 2006, 2011, 2012 (Advance Counts)

Crime Rate, 2011

Incidents per 100,000 residents

Category	State	U.S.
Violent crimes	255.6	386.3
Murder	1.5	4.7
Forcible rape	27.2	26.8
Robbery	26.9	113.7
Aggravated assault	199.9	241.1
Property crimes	2,330.3	2,908.7
Burglary	568.2	702.2
Larceny/theft	1,633.6	1,976.9
Motor vehicle theft	128.5	229.6
All crimes	2,585.9	3,295.0

Source: Federal Bureau of Investigation, Uniform Crime Reports, Crime in the United States 2011

GOVERNMENT AND FINANCE

Local Governments by Type, 2012

Government Type	State	U.S.	State Share
All local governments	1,939	89,004	2.18%
County	99	3,031	3.27%
Municipality	947	19,522	4.85%
Town/Township	0	16,364	0.00%
Special District	527	37,203	1.42%
Ind. School District	366	12,884	2.84%

Source: U.S. Census Bureau, 2012 Census of Governments: Organization Component Preliminary Estimates

State Government Revenue, 2011

In thousands of dollars, except for per capita figures

Total revenue	$24,088,747
Total revenue per capita, State	$7,862
Total revenue per capita, U.S.	$7,271
General revenue	$18,097,362
Intergovernmental revenue	$7,043,992
Taxes	$7,236,476
General sales	$2,232,028
Selective sales	$1,094,387
License taxes	$731,560
Individual income taxes	$2,851,449
Corporate income taxes	$250,272
Other taxes	$76,780
Current charges	$2,629,644
Miscellaneous general revenue	$1,187,250
Utility revenue	$0
Liquor store revenue	$213,972
Insurance trust revenue[1]	$5,777,413

Note: (1) Within insurance trust revenue, net earnings of state retirement systems is a calculated statistic, and thus can be positive or negative. Net earnings is the sum of earnings on investments plus gains on investments minus losses on investments.
Source: U.S. Census Bureau, 2011 Annual Survey of State Government Finances

State Government Expenditures, 2011
In thousands of dollars, except for per capita figures

Total expenditure	$19,937,080
Total expenditure per capita, State	$6,507
Total expenditure per capita, U.S.	$6,427
Intergovernmental expenditure	$5,151,627
Direct expenditure	$14,785,453
Current operation	$9,984,903
Capital outlay	$1,449,045
Insurance benefits and repayments	$2,571,457
Assistance and subsidies	$536,240
Interest on debt	$243,808
Utility expenditure	$0
Liquor store expenditure	$146,710
Insurance trust expenditure	$2,571,457

Source: U.S. Census Bureau, 2011 Annual Survey of State Government Finances

State Government General Expenditures by Function, 2011
In thousands of dollars

Education	$6,269,650
Public welfare	$4,900,757
Hospitals	$1,090,080
Health	$252,373
Highways	$1,590,730
Police protection	$96,692
Correction	$332,291
Natural resources	$314,102
Parks and recreation	$24,953
Governmental administration	$551,375
Interest on general debt	$243,808
Other and unallocable	$1,552,102

Source: U.S. Census Bureau, 2011 Annual Survey of State Government Finances

State Government Finances, Cash and Debt, 2011
In thousands of dollars, except for per capita figures

Debt at end of fiscal year	
State, total	$7,573,811
State, per capita	$2,472
U.S., per capita	$3,635
Cash and security holdings	
State, total	$35,356,891
State, per capita	$11,539
U.S., per capita	$11,759

Source: U.S. Census Bureau, 2011 Annual Survey of State Government Finances

POLITICS

Composition of the Senate, 1995–2013

Congress (Year)	State/U.S	Dem	Rep	Total
104th (1995)	State delegates	1	1	2
	Total U.S.	48	52	100
105th (1997)	State delegates	1	1	2
	Total U.S.	45	55	100
106th (1999)	State delegates	1	1	2
	Total U.S.	45	55	100
107th (2001)	State delegates	1	1	2
	Total U.S.	50	50	100
108th (2003)	State delegates	1	1	2
	Total U.S.	48	51	100
109th (2005)	State delegates	1	1	2
	Total U.S.	44	55	100
110th (2007)	State delegates	1	1	2
	Total U.S.	49	49	100
111th (2009)	State delegates	1	1	2
	Total U.S.	57	41	100
112th (2011)	State delegates	1	1	2
	Total U.S.	51	47	100
113th (2013)	State delegates	1	1	2
	Total U.S.	54	45	100

Note: Figures are for the starts of first sessions; Totals include Democratic (Dem) and Republican (Rep) members as well as vacancies and seats held by independent party members
Source: U.S. Congress, Congressional Directory

Composition of the House of Representatives, 1995–2013

Congress (Year)	State/U.S	Dem	Rep	Total
104th (1995)	State delegates	0	5	5
	Total U.S.	204	230	435
105th (1997)	State delegates	1	4	5
	Total U.S.	207	226	435
106th (1999)	State delegates	1	4	5
	Total U.S.	211	223	435
107th (2001)	State delegates	1	4	5
	Total U.S.	212	221	435
108th (2003)	State delegates	1	4	5
	Total U.S.	205	229	435
109th (2005)	State delegates	1	4	5
	Total U.S.	202	231	435
110th (2007)	State delegates	3	2	5
	Total U.S.	233	198	435
111th (2009)	State delegates	3	2	5
	Total U.S.	256	178	435
112th (2011)	State delegates	3	2	5
	Total U.S.	193	242	435
113th (2013)	State delegates	2	2	4
	Total U.S.	201	234	435

Note: Figures are for the starts of first sessions; Totals include Democratic (Dem) and Republican (Rep) members as well as vacancies and seats held by independent party members
Source: U.S. Congress, Congressional Directory

Composition of State Legislature, 2004–2013

Year	Democrats	Republicans	Total
State Senate			
2004	21	29	50
2005	25	25	50
2006	25	25	50
2007	30	20	50
2008	30	20	50
2009	32	18	50
2010	32	18	50
2011	26	24	50
2012	26	24	50
2013	26	24	50
State House			
2004	47	53	100
2005	49	51	100
2006	49	51	100
2007	54	46	100
2008	53	47	100
2009	56	44	100
2010	56	44	100
2011	40	60	100
2012	40	60	100
2013	47	53	100

Note: Totals may include minor party members and vacancies
Source: The Council of State Governments, State Legislatures

Voter Participation in Presidential Elections, 1980–2012

Year	Voting-eligible State Population	State Voter Turnout Rate	U.S. Voter Turnout Rate
1980	2,070,935	63.6	54.2
1984	2,057,482	64.1	55.2
1988	2,021,793	60.6	52.8
1992	2,057,690	65.8	58.1
1996	2,098,332	58.8	51.7
2000	2,082,950	63.2	54.2
2004	2,156,389	69.9	60.1
2008	2,216,094	69.4	61.6
2012	2,263,375	69.9	58.2

Note: All figures are based on the voting-eligible population which excludes person ineligible to vote such as non-citizens, felons (depending on state law), and mentally-incapacitated persons. U.S. figures include the overseas eligible population (including military personnel).
Source: McDonald, Michael P., United States Election Project, Presidential Voter Turnout Rates, 1980–2012

Governors Since Statehood

Ansel Briggs (D)	1846-1850
Stephen P. Hempstead (D)	1850-1854
James W. Grimes (R)	1854-1858
Ralph P. Lowe (R)	1858-1860
Samuel J. Kirkwood (R)	1860-1864
William H. Stone (O)	1864-1868
Samuel Merrill (R)	1868-1872
Cyrus C. Carpenter (R)	1872-1876
Samuel J. Kirkwood (R)	(r) 1876-1877
Joshua G. Newbold (R)	1877-1878
John H. Gear (R)	1878-1882
Buren R. Sherman (R)	1882-1886
William Larrabee (R)	1886-1890
Horace Boies (D)	1890-1894
Frank D. Jackson (R)	1894-1896
Francis M. Drake (R)	1896-1898
Leslie M. Shaw (R)	1898-1902
Albert B. Cummins (R)	(r) 1902-1908
Warren Garst (R)	1908-1909
Beryl F. Carroll (R)	1909-1913
George W. Clarke (R)	1913-1917
William L. Harding (R)	1917-1921
Nathan E. Kendall (R)	1921-1925
John Hammill (R)	1925-1931
Daniel W. Turner (R)	1931-1933
Clyde L. Herring (D)	1933-1937
Nelson C. Kraschel (D)	1937-1939
George A. Wilson (R)	1939-1943
Bourke B. Hickenlooper (R)	1943-1945
Robert D. Blue (R)	1945-1949
William S. Beardsley (R)	(d) 1949-1954
Leo Elthon (R)	1954-1955
Leo A. Hoegh (R)	1955-1957
Herschel C. Loveless (D)	1957-1961
Norman A. Erbe (R)	1961-1963
Harold E. Hughes (D)	(r) 1963-1969
Robert D. Fulton (D)	1969
Robert D. Ray (R)	1969-1983
Terry E. Branstad (R)	1983-1999
Thomas Vilsack (D)	1999-2007
Chet Culver (D)	2007-2011
Terry Branstad (R)	2011-2015

Note: (D) Democrat; (R) Republican; (O) Other party; (r) resigned; (d) died in office; (i) removed from office

Kansas

Location: Midwest

Area and rank: 81,823 square miles (211,922 square kilometers); 82,282 square miles (213,110 square kilometers) including water; thirteenth largest state in area

Coastline: none

Population and rank: 2,885,905 (2012 estimate); thirty-third largest state in population

Capital city: Topeka (127,473 people in 2010 census)

Largest city: Wichita (382,368 people in 2010 census)

State capitol building in Topeka. (©James Blank/Weststock)

Became territory: May 30, 1854

Entered Union and rank: January 29, 1861; thirty-fourth state

Present constitution adopted: 1859

Counties: 105

State name: "Kansas" derives from a Sioux name for "people of the south wind"

State nickname: Sunflower State; Jayhawk State

Motto: *Ad astra per aspera* (To the stars through difficulties)

State flag: Blue field with state seal, state flower, and name "Kansas"

Highest point: Mount Sunflower—4,039 feet (1,231 meters)

Lowest point: Verdigris River—679 feet (207 meters)

Highest recorded temperature: 121 degrees Fahrenheit (49 degrees Celsius)—near Alton, 1936

Lowest recorded temperature: –40 degrees Fahrenheit (–40 degrees Celsius)—Lebanon, 1905

State song: "Home on the Range"

State tree: Cottonwood

State flower: Sunflower

State bird: Western meadowlark

State animal: Buffalo

Kansas History

Within Kansas, slightly northwest of Lebanon, is the geographical center of the forty-eight contiguous states. The Spanish explorer Francisco Vásquez de Coronado first ventured into the area in 1541 seeking gold. Native Americans had occupied the region since prehistoric times, possibly as early as 14,000 B.C.E. The Pawnee, Osage, Wichita, and Kansa Indians lived there during the early Spanish exploration. They were mostly hunters and farmers living along the Kansas River.

Later members of various semi-nomadic tribes, mainly the Kiowa, Cheyenne, Arapaho, and Comanche, also dwelled in the area. After 1830, however, the federal government forcibly moved many Native Americans from eastern tribes into the territory it had acquired through the Louisiana Purchase of 1803. Among the tribes whose members were relocated were the Cherokee, Miami, Potawatomi, Ottawa, Creek, Chickasaw, Choctaw, Delaware, and Shawnee. In all, about thirty tribes were assigned to Kansas for relocation.

French and American Settlement. The French moved into the area after the Spanish had been defeated by the Pawnee Indians in Nebraska. During the early eighteenth century, the French, attracted by the fur trade, built a trading post and military outpost, Fort Cavagnial, near present-day Leavenworth.

With the Louisiana Purchase, American exploration began. Meriwether Lewis and William Clark set out to explore the newly acquired area, which included all but a small part of southwestern Kansas bought in 1850 from Texas.

These explorers were followed in 1806 by Zebulon Pike, who made an east-west journey across the territory. As the eastern United States began to be developed, the federal government was under pressure to claim Native American lands for development. Relocating American Indians to the West provided the government with a convenient solution to a difficult problem. The Native Americans who were relocated are usually referred to as the emigrant tribes.

Between 1827 and 1853, Kansas was inhabited mostly by Native Americans. Some thirty-four thousand Indians from over thirty tribes and only fifteen hundred white inhabitants, mostly missionaries and the person-

The building of the transcontinental railroad accelerated the development of Kansas, while also hastening the destruction of the region's once-great buffalo herds. (Library of Congress)

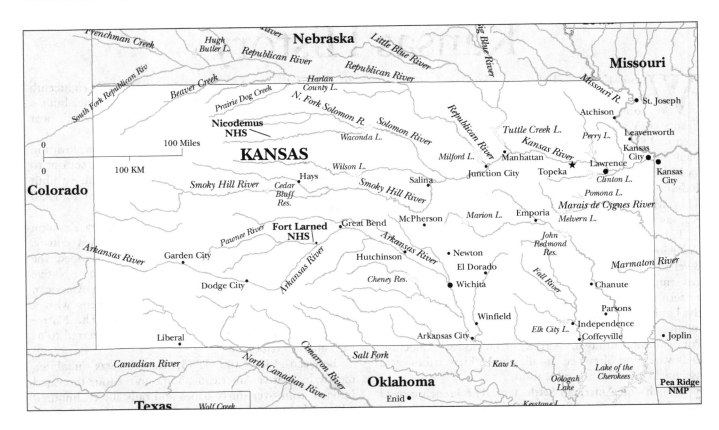

nel that maintained the government forts constructed at Leavenworth, Fort Scott, and Fort Riley, lived there.

The Kansas-Nebraska Act and Statehood. So great was the incursion of European settlers to the area after 1854 that the Native Americans who lived there, both original dwellers and the emigrant tribes, were removed from the state and settled elsewhere. In 1854, Kansas was created as a territory in the western part of what had previously been called the Missouri Territory. The early borders of the rectangular-shaped territory were much as they are today. Kansas is bounded by Missouri on the east and Colorado on the west. To the north, the boundary is Nebraska, and the southern border is Oklahoma. The only natural boundary is in the northeast, where the Missouri River constitutes part of the state line.

Soon after Kansas gained territorial status, the Kansas-Nebraska Act of 1854, which replaced the Missouri Compromise, opened the territory to settlement. Under the terms of this act, citizens of a territory decided whether it would be slave or free, whereas under the Missouri Compromise, an artificial balance between slave and free states was imposed.

Opinions were strongly divided about which choice Kansas should make. Its neighboring state, Missouri, had slaves. Nebraska opted to be free, but proslavery sentiment was strong in Kansas. When the issue came to a vote, hundreds of land-hungry people who had come to Kansas stuffed the ballot boxes.

Kansas was plunged into controversy between the pro-and antislavery forces. Abolitionists were recruited to come to Kansas from New England and make it a free state. Abolitionist John Brown led the Pottawatomie Massacre in May of 1856. In 1863, an angry proslavery mob, led by William Clarke Quantrill, attacked Lawrence, Kansas, killing around 150 of its citizens.

With the pro-and antislavery forces fighting against each other, both sides drew up constitutions, neither of them acceptable to the United States Congress. Finally, in 1859, the antislavery Wyandotte Constitution was approved. This cleared the way for Kansas to achieve statehood on January 29, 1861, just as many southern states were seceding from the Union. Kansas was the thirty-fourth state admitted to the Union.

The Homestead Act of 1862. Following passage of the Homestead Act of 1862, Kansas grew rapidly. Under the terms of this act, upon the payment of a ten-dollar filing fee, heads of family or anyone over twenty-one years old could receive 160 acres of government land, which they would own if they lived on it for five years and improved the property. This opportunity was a magnet that drew thousands of easterners to Kansas.

The railroads that served the area received large land grants, chunks of which they sold to the early settlers. The Union Pacific Railroad began operating in Kansas in 1857, the Atchison and Topeka Railroad was chartered in 1859, and the Missouri, Kansas, and Texas line soon followed. Eventually twelve railroads operated on more than six thousand miles of track in Kansas.

The Kansas Economy. Because of the nature of its founding, Kansas was originally a rural state concentrating heavily on agriculture. During the Civil War, it sided with the North, and many of its citizens joined the Union army. Shortly after the war, cow towns began to develop in Kansas. These were towns that had railway connections, notably Abilene, Dodge City, Ellsworth, and Wichita.

Texas at this time had no railroad service, so until the mid-1880's, when rail service became available, Texan cattle ranchers drove their herds across Oklahoma to the railroad towns of Kansas, from which they were shipped to other destinations.

Eastern Kansas was settled early, but soon other settlers moved into the central and western regions, as far as Great Bend near the Colorado border. A diverse population developed as Europeans from Russia, Germany, Bohemia, France, England, and Italy came to the state, which also had a sizable African American population, being one of the free states that attracted freed slaves following the Civil War in what was called the "exodus movement."

Kansas, with a growing season of about 150 days in its northern reaches and more than 200 days in the southeast, is hospitable to agriculture. The rainfall ranges from sixteen inches annually in the west to more than forty inches in the east, although droughts are a frequent problem. During the early to mid-1930's, the dust bowls of Kansas and Oklahoma put many farmers out of business.

The state constructed more than twenty large reservoirs to control flooding, provide drinking water, and afford irrigation to farmers. Also, early Russian immigrants into Kansas brought with them a drought-resistant strain of wheat, Turkey Red, which is grown extensively in the state.

Although Kansas was originally rural, it increasingly moved toward manufacturing, commerce, and service occupations, causing a population shift to urban areas. Of its more than six hundred incorporated cities, fifty have populations exceeding five thousand. Nevertheless, more than two-thirds of the total 1990 population of about 2.5 million lived in urban areas.

Besides its agricultural and cattle industries, Kansas has a thriving aircraft industry centered in Wichita, where both private planes and commercial aircraft are produced by such companies as Boeing and Cessna. One of the nation's leading mental hospitals, the Menninger Neuropsychiatric Clinic, is located in Topeka. Kansas also has impressive oil reserves, as well as natural gas, coal, lead, salt, and zinc.

Kansas Conservatism. Kansas has traditionally been a conservative state, largely a Republican stronghold, although it has strong Populist leanings as well and has elected Populists as governors and representatives. It gave a moderate, Nancy Landon Kassebaum, three terms in the United States Senate.

In 1880, the state adopted prohibition and essentially remained a dry state. In 1899, Kansan Carry Nation single-handedly undertook the enforcement of Kansas's prohibition law by destroying saloons with her renowned axe.

The Twentieth-Century Economy. The economy of Kansas had a significant resurgence during World War I,

Arapaho and Comanche council in 1867 at Medicine Lodge Creek, where tribal leaders signed a treaty with the U.S. government designed to end their wars on the southern plains. (Library of Congress)

when the price of wheat escalated, bringing considerable money into the state's economy. The economy grew until the 1930's, when a drought that continued for several years devastated wheat farming.

The financial woes of the 1930's did not end until World War II again stimulated the economy and brought considerable industry into the state. The road building in the state during and after World War II resulted in one of the best road systems in the country. Kansas is served by 125 public and 250 private airports that provide excellent commercial air transport and encourage private ownership of airplanes.

Religion, Education, and Science. In 2000, controversy resulted from decisions of the Kansas State Board of Education. During 1999, the board had voted 6-4 to make teaching the theory of evolution optional for local school districts. Schools could also teach the biblical account of Creation or others in addition to or instead of evolution. In 2000, the board also rewrote state science standards to make the age of the earth ten thousand years, and it removed the big bang theory of the origin of the universe from its teaching standards. In the state's primary elections in 2000, some Democrats were said to have changed party affiliation in order to vote in the Republican primary for pro-evolution candidates. In the state's Republican primary, voters rejected three incumbent candidates for the state school board who rejected evolution. The outcome of the controversy was that the teaching of evolution was restored to the state curriculum in 2001, when the Kansas State Board of Education voted 7-3 to adopt new state science standards.

The new state education standards made provision for religious dissent from evolution among students and cautioned educators that students were free to accept or reject the concepts presented. Teachers were not to ridicule dissenting students and were to suggest that students bring the subject up with parents or others. In 2004, however, conservatives won the board back, and controversial standards calling evolution into question were again in place. However, in August, 2006, voters elected one new science-oriented member to the school board that appeared to be split between the two camps.

Law and Public Policy Controversies. In other controversial issues in social policy, in mid-2002, a Kansas law barring alien Asian immigrants from inheriting real property was repealed. Florida and New Mexico were the only states left with such laws. The following year, the U.S. Supreme Court vacated a Kansas Court of Appeals decision that upheld a sentence of seventeen years for a developmentally disabled eighteen-year-old male, who was convicted of having consensual oral sex with a similarly disabled fourteen-year-old male. The court ordered Kansas to reconsider the case in the light of the court's decision in *Lawrence v. Texas* (2003), a case that struck down Texas antisodomy law. Late in 2005, the Kansas Supreme Court struck down the law under which the defendant was convicted.

Electoral Politics. In the 2000 general election, Kansas voted its six electoral votes for George W. Bush by a 58-37 percent margin; independent candidate Ralph Nader received thirty-five thousand votes, not nearly enough to make a difference in the outcome. All of the state's incumbent congressional delegation were re-elected, but not all seats were easy wins. Democratic congressman Dennis Moore had a close call when his opponent, a state legislator, won 48 percent of the vote to Moore's 50 percent.

In the 2002 general election, Kansas voters elected a new governor. Democrat Kathleen Sebelius, the state insurance commissioner, won over Tim Shallenburger, a staunch conservative, by a margin of 53 to 45 percent.

In the 2004 election, U.S. senator Sam Brownback easily beat the challenger for his seat by a 62-27 percent margin. This was a wider margin in the popular vote than that of President Bush, who nevertheless handily took the state's six electoral votes by a 62-27 percent margin. Also in this election, former Olympic runner Jim Ryun won his fifth term in Congress by a 56-41 percent margin.

The 2010 gubernatorial election saw the victory by a wide margin of Sam Brownback (R), who had entered his name as a candidate for president in the 2008 primary election season. Due to his popularity as a member of the U.S. Senate, Brownback defeated his Democratic opponent, Tom Holland, by a wide margin, with more than 63 percent of the popular vote.

Environment. In the early years of the 21st century, Kansas faced a series of environmental issues, some of which were also common in nearby states. These included confined animal feeding facilities; pollution issues on three rivers: the Arkansas, Kansas, and Missouri rivers; prairie grass conservation; and issues associated with wind power. As in neighboring Missouri, environmentalists were concerned about the water waste emitted from facilities which housed tens of thousands of turkeys, pigs, or chickens. New regulations passed in the late 1990's were deemed generally inadequate to protect the Ogallala aquifer from waste produced by such operations and reportedly did little to protect neighbors from dust and noxious odors. The regulations imposed more reporting of data, which helped environmentalists monitor the impacts of the facilities. Environmental activists were concerned about the effect of dredging on rivers in the state and the leaching of pesticides and excess nutrients from fertilizer and from sewage plants, especially nitrogen and phosphorus, into the state's waterways.

R. Baird Shuman
Updated by the Editor

Kansas Time Line

1541	Francisco Vásquez de Coronado explores central Kansas.
1723	Fort Orleans is built by French explorer Etienne de Bourgmont.
1744	French establish trading post at Fort Cavagnial, near Leavenworth.
1803	Area that becomes Kansas becomes part of the United States through the Louisiana Purchase.
1804	Meriwether Lewis and William Clark explore Kansas on their way to the Pacific Coast.
1806	Captain Zebulon Pike crosses Kansas from east to west.
June 4, 1812	Territory of Missouri is established, which includes Kansas.
Aug. 10, 1819	Stephen H. Long makes first steamboat expedition in Kansas.
1821	William Becknell establishes Santa Fe Trail.
1824	Founding of Presbyterian mission on Neosho River.
1827	Fort Leavenworth becomes the first permanent white settlement in Kansas.
1827	Daniel Boone establishes American Indian school in Jefferson County.
1830	United States government relocates Native Americans from the eastern states to Kansas.
1830	Shawnee Methodist Mission for Indians is established near Turner.
June 20, 1834	Kansas is declared Indian Country by Congress.
1839	Shawnee Methodist Mission moved to location near Shawnee.
1842	First of several expeditions by John C. Frémont passes through Kansas.
1842	Fort Scott is established.
1843	Great migration to Oregon begins.
1853	Fort Riley is established.

Silhouette figures of cattle drivers erected near Caldwell, at Kansas's Oklahoma border, recall the days when great herds of cattle moved between Abilene, in east central Kansas, and Texas on the Chisholm Trail. (Kansas Department of Commerce & Housing, Travel and Tourism)

May 30, 1854	Kansas-Nebraska Act passed, giving Kansas territorial status.
July 2, 1855	First territorial legislature meeting at Pawnee and later at the Shawnee Mission legalizes slavery in Kansas.
1855	Free State antislavery party is established as conflict grows over slavery.
May 21, 1856	Lawrence Massacre results in 150 deaths when proslavery groups attack.
May 23–24, 1856	John Brown leads free-state massacre along Pottawatomie Creek.
1858	Congress rejects proslavery Lecompton Constitution.
1859	Atchison and Topeka Railroad chartered.
Oct. 4, 1859	Antislavery Wyandotte Constitution is adopted.
1860	First oil well drilled in Kansas near Paola.
Apr., 1860	Pony Express crosses Kansas.
Jan. 29, 1861	Kansas admitted to Union as thirty-fourth state.
1863	William Quantrill's Confederate troops attack Lawrence.
1864	University of Kansas opens at Lawrence.
1864	Confederate general Sterling Price leads his troops to Kansas.
1867	First Texas cattle run to Kansas.
1874	Mennonites from Russia introduce drought-resistant Turkey Red wheat to Kansas.
1878	Last Native American skirmish launched by Cheyenne Indians.
1880	Kansas imposes prohibition.
1899	Carry Nation begins her antisaloon raids.
1903	State capitol is completed.
1918	Economy bolstered by wheat sales during World War I.
1935	Dust storms devastate Kansas farmland.
1936	Alfred M. Landon is Republican candidate for president, losing with only 8 electoral votes.
1945	Growth of Kansas aircraft industry following World War II.
1948	Kanopolis Dam is completed on Smoky Hill River.
1949	Fall River Dam is completed.
1951	Cedar Bluff Dam on Smoky Hill River is completed.
1951	Kansas is devastated by floods.
1952	Kansan Dwight D. Eisenhower becomes thirty-fourth president of the United States.
1954	Eisenhower Museum opens in Abilene.
1954	U.S. Supreme Court rules against school board of Topeka in segregation case *Brown v. Board of Education of Topeka*.
1956	Kansas Turnpike is completed.
1965	Agricultural Hall of Fame and National Center opens near Kansas City.
1965	Fort Scott named a national historic monument.
1972	Terms of governor and other state officials increased from two to four years.
1976	Mid-American All-Indian Center opens in Wichita.
1988	Drought and wind erosion destroy more than 865,000 acres in Kansas.
1991	Largest remaining plot of Kansas prairie is plowed under.
Nov. 1991	Joan Finney is first woman elected governor of Kansas.
1999	Kansas State Board of Education votes 6–4 to make teaching the theory of evolution optional for local school districts.
2000	State Board of Education votes to replace the age of the earth in state education standards from three to four billion years to ten thousand years, a move that repudiates the theory of evolution. It also votes to remove the big bang as the prevailing theory of the origin of the universe.
2001	Newly seated members of the State Board of Education introduce new state science education standards that restore the theory of evolution to the curriculum.
2003	U.S. Supreme Court vacates conviction under Kansas law forbidding sex between consensual same-sex partners.
2010	Running on the Republican ticket, two years after running for president, the enormously popular Senator Sam Brownback wins the gubernatorial election with 63 percent of the vote.
Aug. 21, 2013	Kansas files a lawsuit against the federal government seeking approval to require proof of citizenship when registering to vote.

Notes for Further Study

Published Sources. *Natural Kansas* (1985), edited by Joseph T. Collins, provides interesting essays about biological, geological, geographical, and physical aspects of Kansas. Robert Richmond's *Kansas: A Land of Contrasts* (3d. ed., 1989) also presents varied information about the state, emphasizing that it is not entirely flat, soaring to an elevation of 4,039 feet at Mount Sunflower and having a mean elevation of 2,000 feet. *Kansas Archaeology* (2006) provides insight into the state's Native American past.

A thorough overview of the state's history can be found in *Kansas: The History of the Sunflower State, 1854-2000* (2002) by H. Craig Miner. *Bleeding Kansas: Contested Liberty in the Civil War Era* (2004) by Nicole Etcheson details the state's role in the struggle over slavery. Robert S. Bader's *Prohibition in Kansas: A History* (1986) offers interesting information about this phase of the state's history and the state's role in the passage of the Eighteenth Amendment to the U.S. Constitution. Thomas Goodrich relates details of the Lawrence Massacre of 1863 in *Bloody Dawn: The Story of the Lawrence Massacre* (1991). Pamela Riney-Kehrbert's *Rooted in Dust: Surviving Drought and Depression in Southwestern Kansas* (1994) offers the best coverage of how widespread droughts in the early 1930's led to a rapid deterioration of the Kansas economy, followed by the Great Depression. James R. Shortridge's *Cities on the Plains: The Evolution of Urban Kansas* (2004) offers a comparative history of the development of cities and the roles of railroads, the mining industry, and the cattle trade, among other factors.

Numerous books on Kansas are directed primarily to juvenile readers. Allen Carpenter's *Kansas* (1979) remains a useful resource despite being an older title. Zachary Kent's later *Kansas* (1990) is an excellent brief account of the state. Both of these books can be supplemented by Dennis Fradin's *Kansas: In Words and Pictures* (1980), Patricia D. Netzley's *Kansas* (2002), and Patricia K. Kummer's *Kansas* (Rev. ed., 2002).

Web Resources. The state of Kansas maintains a Web site (www.kansas.gov/) that provides useful information about the state and its government. The state's department of tourism has a Web site (www.travelks.com/) that includes information about tourist attractions, lodging, restaurants, and public transportation. The Web site of the University of Kansas (www.ku.edu/) offers information about the various branches of the university and their attractions. Various libraries around the state have Web sites through which their catalogs can be accessed. Chief among these are the libraries of Kansas City (www.kcpl.lib.mo.us), the Mid-American Library Alliance (www.kcmlin.org), Manhattan (www.manhattan.lib.ks.us), Hutchinson (hutchpl.org/), Southeast Kansas (www.sekls.lib.ks.us), and Topeka (www.tscpl.org).

News developments that affect Kansas can be found on the *Wichita Eagle* site (www.kansas.com/mld/kansas/). For a wide range of historical information, visit Kansas History Online (www.kansashistoryonline.org/ksh/), the Kansas State Historical Society (www.kshs.org/research/topics/index.htm), and the History Gateway of Kansas (www.ku.edu/history/).

On May 4, 2007, an EF5 tornado touched down in Kiowa County where it destroyed 95 percent of the city of Greensburg, Kansas. Thirteen people were killed and sixty were injured. (Wikimedia Commons)

Counties

County	2012 Population	Pop. Rank	Land Area (sq. miles)	Area Rank	County	2012 Population	Pop. Rank	Land Area (sq. miles)	Area Rank
Allen	13,319	36	500.30	97	Franklin	25,906	23	571.76	90
Anderson	7,917	50	579.65	86	Geary	38,013	12	384.62	104
Atchison	16,813	31	431.17	102	Gove	2,729	90	1,071.66	12
Barber	4,861	70	1,134.07	6	Graham	2,578	94	898.52	25
Barton	27,557	22	895.40	29	Grant	7,923	49	574.80	89
Bourbon	14,897	34	635.47	79	Gray	6,030	61	868.87	39
Brown	9,881	41	570.87	92	Greeley	1,298	105	778.45	49
Butler	65,827	8	1,429.86	1	Greenwood	6,454	57	1,143.30	5
Chase	2,757	89	773.06	50	Hamilton	2,639	93	996.51	17
Chautauqua	3,571	78	638.88	78	Harper	5,911	62	801.27	45
Cherokee	21,226	28	587.57	85	Harvey	34,852	15	539.75	95
Cheyenne	2,678	92	1,019.89	15	Haskell	4,256	74	577.52	87
Clark	2,181	99	974.63	19	Hodgeman	1,963	101	859.99	41
Clay	8,531	46	645.30	73	Jackson	13,449	35	656.22	72
Cloud	9,397	44	715.34	67	Jefferson	18,945	30	532.57	96
Coffey	8,502	47	626.95	80	Jewell	3,046	84	909.78	22
Comanche	1,913	102	788.30	48	Johnson	559,913	1	473.37	99
Cowley	36,288	14	1,125.75	7	Kearny	3,968	75	870.54	38
Crawford	39,361	11	589.76	84	Kingman	7,863	52	863.36	40
Decatur	2,871	87	893.52	31	Kiowa	2,496	97	722.64	56
Dickinson	19,762	29	847.07	43	Labette	21,284	27	645.29	74
Doniphan	7,864	51	393.41	103	Lane	1,704	103	717.46	63
Douglas	112,864	5	455.87	101	Leavenworth	77,739	6	462.83	100
Edwards	2,979	86	621.89	81	Lincoln	3,174	81	719.40	59
Elk	2,720	91	644.26	75	Linn	9,441	43	594.06	83
Ellis	29,053	21	899.91	24	Logan	2,784	88	1,072.99	11
Ellsworth	6,494	56	715.85	66	Lyon	33,748	18	847.47	42
Finney	37,200	13	1,301.97	2	Marion	12,347	37	944.29	20
Ford	34,752	16	1,098.27	8	Marshall	10,022	39	900.18	23

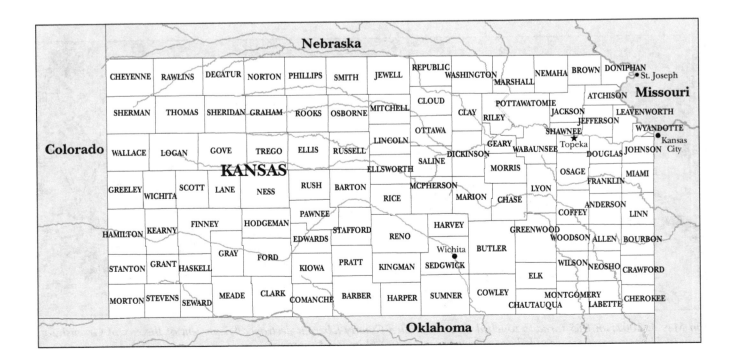

County	2012 Population	Pop. Rank	Land Area (sq. miles)	Area Rank
McPherson	29,356	20	898.27	26
Meade	4,396	72	978.09	18
Miami	32,612	19	575.66	88
Mitchell	6,355	58	701.79	69
Montgomery	34,459	17	643.53	76
Morris	5,854	63	695.28	70
Morton	3,169	82	729.73	53
Nemaha	10,132	38	717.43	64
Neosho	16,406	32	571.47	91
Ness	3,068	83	1,074.75	9
Norton	5,612	66	878.13	37
Osage	16,142	33	705.52	68
Osborne	3,806	76	892.50	32
Ottawa	6,072	60	720.73	57
Pawnee	6,928	55	754.26	51
Phillips	5,519	67	885.88	36
Pottawatomie	22,302	26	841.02	44
Pratt	9,728	42	735.04	52
Rawlins	2,560	95	1,069.42	13
Reno	64,438	9	1,255.35	3
Republic	4,858	71	717.37	65
Rice	9,985	40	726.24	55
Riley	75,508	7	609.77	82
Rooks	5,223	68	890.53	33
Rush	3,220	80	717.76	61
Russell	6,946	54	886.26	35
Saline	55,988	10	720.22	58
Scott	4,937	69	717.54	62
Sedgwick	503,889	2	997.51	16
Seward	23,547	25	639.50	77
Shawnee	178,991	3	544.02	94
Sheridan	2,538	96	895.96	27
Sherman	6,113	59	1,056.07	14
Smith	3,765	77	895.46	28
Stafford	4,358	73	792.05	47
Stanton	2,175	100	680.35	71
Stevens	5,756	65	727.29	54
Sumner	23,674	24	1,181.94	4
Thomas	7,941	48	1,074.69	10
Trego	2,986	85	889.48	34
Wabaunsee	7,039	53	794.30	46
Wallace	1,517	104	913.65	21
Washington	5,758	64	894.76	30
Wichita	2,256	98	718.57	60
Wilson	9,105	45	570.42	93
Woodson	3,278	79	497.82	98
Wyandotte	159,129	4	151.60	105

Source: U.S. Census Bureau, 2012 Population Estimates

Cities

With 10,000 or more residents

Legal Name	2010 Population	Pop. Rank	Land Area (sq. miles)	Area Rank
Andover city	11,791	31	9.99	25
Arkansas City city	12,415	29	9.36	27
Atchison city	11,021	33	7.82	32
Coffeyville city	10,295	37	7.43	33
Derby city	22,158	18	9.55	26
Dodge City city	27,340	14	14.44	14
El Dorado city	13,021	27	8.86	29
Emporia city	24,916	16	11.83	19
Garden City city	26,658	15	8.82	30
Gardner city	19,123	24	10.12	24
Great Bend city	15,995	25	10.60	23
Hays city	20,510	21	7.95	31
Haysville city	10,826	35	4.61	36
Hutchinson city	42,080	11	22.69	11
Junction City city	23,353	17	12.15	18
Kansas City city	145,786	3	124.81	2
Lansing city	11,265	32	12.38	17
Lawrence city	87,643	6	33.56	8
Leavenworth city	35,251	12	24.04	10
Leawood city	31,867	13	15.06	13

Legal Name	2010 Population	Pop. Rank	Land Area (sq. miles)	Area Rank
Lenexa city	48,190	9	34.10	7
Liberal city	20,525	20	11.61	20
Manhattan city	52,281	8	18.76	12
McPherson city	13,155	26	7.18	34
Merriam city	11,003	34	4.32	37
Newton city	19,132	23	12.60	16
Olathe city	125,872	5	59.66	5
Ottawa city	12,649	28	9.33	28
Overland Park city	173,372	2	74.84	3
Parsons city	10,500	36	10.61	22
Pittsburg city	20,233	22	12.80	15
Prairie Village city	21,447	19	6.20	35
Salina city	47,707	10	25.11	9
Shawnee city	62,209	7	41.85	6
Topeka city	127,473	4	60.17	4
Wichita city	382,368	1	159.29	1
Winfield city	12,301	30	11.56	21

Note: CDP–Census Designated Place
Source: U.S. Census Bureau, 2010 Census

Survey Says...

This section presents current rankings from dozens of public and private sources. It shows how this state ranks in a number of critical categories, including education, job growth, cost of living, teen drivers, energy efficiency, and business environment. Sources include *Forbes, Reuters, U.S. News and World Report, CNN Money, Gallup,* and *Huffington Post.*

- Kansas ranked #35 in a government study measuring real gross domestic product (GDP)—the output of goods and services produced by labor and property located in the United States. The ranking is based on the percentage change compared with 2011 GDP.
  U.S. Department of Commerce, Bureau of Economic Analysis, June 2013; www.bea.gov

- Kansas ranked #31 in a government study measuring real gross domestic product (GDP)—the output of goods and services produced by labor and property located in the United States. The ranking is based on the dollar value of its GDP.
  U.S. Department of Commerce, Bureau of Economic Analysis, June 2013; www.bea.gov

- Kansas ranked #37 in the 17th edition of "Quality Counts; State of the States," Education Week's "report card" surveying key education indicators, policy efforts, and educational outcomes.
  Education Week, January 4, 2013 (online) and January 10, 2013 (print); www.edweek.org

- SERI (Science and Engineering Readiness Index) weighs the performance of the states' K-12 schools in preparing students in physics and calculus, the high school subjects considered most important for future scientists and engineers. Kansas ranked #16.
  Newsletter of the Forum on Education of the American Physical Society, Summer 2011 issue; www.huffingtonpost.com, July 11, 2011; updated October 1, 2012

- MoneyRates.com ranked Kansas #9 on its list of the best to worst states for making a living. Criteria: average income; inflation; employment prospects; and workers' Workplace Environment assessments according to the Gallup-Healthways Well-Being Index.
  www.money-rates.com, posted April 1, 2013

- *Forbes* analyzed business costs, labor supply, regulatory environment, current economic climate, growth prospects, and quality of life, to compile its "Best States for Business" rankings. Kansas ranked #13.
  www.forbes.com. posted December 12, 2012

- The 2012 Gallup-Healthways Well-Being Index, surveyed American's opinions on economic confidence, workplace perceptions, community climate, personal choices, and health predictors to assess the "future livability" of each state. Kansas ranked #13.
  "Utah Poised to Be the Best State to Live In," Gallup Wellbeing, www.gallup.com, August 7, 2012

- On CNBC's list of "America's Top States for Business 2013," Kansas ranked #14. Criteria: measures of competitiveness developed with input from the National Association of Manufacturers, the Council on Competitiveness, and other business groups weighed with the states' own marketing criteria.
  www.cnbc.com, consulted July 19, 2013

- Kansas ranked #28 on MoneyRates list of "Best-and Worst-States to Retire 2012." Criteria: life expectancy, crime rate, climate, economic conditions, taxes, job opportunities, and cost of living.
  www.money-rates.com, October 22, 2012

- Kansas ranked #13 on the 2013 Bankrate "Best Places to Retire" list ranking the states and District of Columbia on various criteria relating to health, safety, and cost.
  www.bankrate.com, May 6, 2013

- Kansas ranked #24 on the Social Science Research Council's "American Human Development Report: The Measure of America," assessing the 50 states plus the District of Columbia on health, education, and living-standard criteria.
  The Measure of America 2013-2014, posted June 19, 2013; www.measureofamerica.org

- Kansas ranked #20 on the Foundation for Child Development's (FCD) Child Well-being Index (CWI). The FCD used the KIDS COUNT report and the National Survey of Children's Health, the only state-level source for several key indicators of child well-being.
  Foundation for Child Development, January 18, 2012; fcd-us.org

- Kansas ranked #16 overall according to the 2013 KIDS COUNT Data Book, a project of the Annie E. Casey Foundation. Criteria: children's economic well-being, education, health, and family and community indicators.
  KIDS COUNT Data Center's Data Book, released June 20, 2013; http://datacenter.kidscount.org

- Kansas ranked #8 in the children's economic well-being category by the 2013 KIDS COUNT Data Book, a project of the Annie E. Casey Foundation.
  KIDS COUNT Data Center's Data Book, released June 20, 2013; http://datacenter.kidscount.org

- Kansas ranked #11 in the children's educational opportunities and attainments category by the 2013 KIDS COUNT Data Book, a project of the Annie E. Casey Foundation.
  KIDS COUNT Data Center's Data Book, released June 20, 2013; http://datacenter.kidscount.org

- Kansas ranked #26 in the children's health category by the 2013 KIDS COUNT Data Book, a project of the Annie E. Casey Foundation.
  KIDS COUNT Data Center's Data Book, released June 20, 2013; http://datacenter.kidscount.org

- Kansas ranked #23 in the family and community circumstances that factor into children's well-being category by the 2013 KIDS COUNT Data Book, a project of the Annie E. Casey Foundation.
  KIDS COUNT Data Center's Data Book, released June 20, 2013; http://datacenter.kidscount.org

- Kansas ranked #17 in the 2012 Gallup-Healthways Well-Being Index. Criteria: emotional health; physical health; healthy behavior; work environment; basic access to food, shelter, health care; and a safe and satisfying place to live.
  2012 State of Well-Being, Gallup-Healthways Well-Being Index, released February 28, 2013; www.well-beingindex.com

- *U.S. News and World Report's* "Best States for Teen Drivers" rankings are based on driving and road safety laws, federal reports on driver's licenses, car accident fatality, and road-quality statistics. Kansas ranked #46.
  U.S. News and World Report, March 18, 2010; www.usnews.com

- The Yahoo! Sports service Rivals.com ranks the states according to the strength of their high school football programs. Kansas ranked #28.
  "Ranking the States: Where Is the Best Football Played?," November 18, 2011; highschool.rivals.com

- iVillage ranked the states by hospitable living conditions for women. Criteria: economic success, access to affordable childcare, health care, reproductive rights, female representation in government, and educational attainment. Kansas ranked #29.
  iVillage, "50 Best to Worst States for Women," March 14, 2012; www.ivillage.com

- The League of American Bicyclists's "Bicycle Friendly States" ranked Kansas #40. Criteria: legislation and enforcement, policies and programs, infrastructure and funding, education and advocacy, and evaluation and planning.
  "Washington Tops the Bicycle-Friendly State Ranking," May 1, 2013; bicycling.com

- The federal Corporation for National and Community Service ranked the states and the District of Columbia by volunteer rates. Kansas ranked #7 for community service.
  "Volunteering and Civic Life in America 2012," www.volunteeringinamerica.gov, accessed July 24, 2013

- The Hospital Safety Score ranked states and the District of Columbia on their hospitals' performance scores. Kansas ranked #47. Criteria: avoiding preventable harm and medical errors, as demonstrated by 26 hospital safety metrics.
  Spring 2013 Hospital Safety Score, May 8, 2013; www.hospitalsafetyscore.org

- GMAC Insurance ranked the states and the District of Columbia by the performance of their drivers on the GMAC Insurance National Drivers Test, comprised of DMV test questions. Kansas ranked #1.
  "2011 GMAC Insurance National Drivers Test," www.gmacinsurance.com, accessed July 23, 2013

- Kansas ranked #10 in a "State Integrity Investigation" analysis of laws and practices intended to deter corruption and promote accountability and openness in campaign finance, ethics laws, lobbying regulations and management of state pension funds.
  "What's Your State's Grade?," www.publicintegrity.org, accessed July 23, 2013

- Kansas ranked #6 among the states and the District of Columbia in total rail miles, as tracked by the Association of American Railroads.
  "U.S. Freight Railroad Industry Snapshot: Railroads and States: Total Rail Miles by State: 2011"; www.aar.org, accessed July 23, 2013

- According to statistics compiled by the Beer Institute, Kansas ranked #31 among the states and the District of Columbia in per capita beer consumption of persons 21 years or older.
  "Shipments of Malt Beverages and Per Capita Consumption by State 2012;" www.beerinstitute.org

- According to Concordia University's "Public Education Costs per Pupil by State Rankings," based on statistics gathered by the U.S. Census Bureau, which includes the District of Columbia, Kansas ranked #27.
  Concordia University Online; education.cu-portland.edu, accessed July 24, 2013

- Kansas ranked #40 among the states and the District of Columbia in population density based on U.S. Census Bureau data for resident population and total land area. "List of U.S. States by Population Density."
  www.wikipedia.org, accessed July 24, 2013

- In "America's Health Rankings, 2012 Edition," by the United Health Foundation, Kansas ranked #24. Criteria included: rate of high school graduation; violent crime rate; incidence of infectious disease; childhood immunizations; prevalence of diabetes; per capita public-health funding; percentage of uninsured population; rate of children in poverty; and availability of primary-care physicians.
  United Health Foundation; www.americashealthrankings.org, accessed July 24, 2013

- The TechNet 2012 "State Broadband Index" ranked Kansas #25 on the following criteria: broadband adoption; network quality; and economic structure. Improved broadband use is hoped to promote economic development, build strong communities, improve delivery of government services and upgrade educational systems.
  TechNet; www.technet.org, accessed July 24, 2013

- Kansas was ranked #45 among the states and District of Columbia on the American Council for an Energy-Efficient Economy's "State Energy Efficiency Scorecard" for 2012.
  American Council for an Energy-Efficient Economy; aceee.org/sector/state-policy/scorecard, accessed July 24, 2013

Statistical Tables

DEMOGRAPHICS
Resident State and National Population, 1950-2012
Projected State and National Population, 2000-2030
Population by Age, 2012
Population by Race, 2012
Population by Hispanic Origin and Race, 2012

VITAL STATISTICS
Death Rates by Leading Causes, 2010
Death Rates by Selected Causes, 2010
Abortion Rates, 2009
Infant Mortality Rates, 1995-2009
Marriage and Divorce Rates, 2000-2011

ECONOMY
Nominal Gross Domestic Product by Industry, 2012
Real Gross Domestic Product, 2000-2012
Personal Income Per Capita, 1930-2012
Non-Farm Employment by Sector, 2012
Foreign Exports, 2000-2012
Energy Consumption, 2011

LAND AND WATER
Surface Area and Federally-Owned Land, 2007
Land Cover/Use of Non-Federal Rural Land, 2007
Farms and Crop Acreage, 2012

HEALTH AND MEDICAL CARE
Medical Professionals, 2012
Health Insurance Coverage, 2011
HIV, STD, and Tuberculosis Cases and Rates, 2011
Cigarette Smoking, 2011

HOUSING
Home Ownership Rates, 1995-2012
Home Sales, 2000-2010
Value of Owner-Occupied Homes, 2011

EDUCATION
School Enrollment, 2011
Educational Attainment, 2011
Public College Finances, FY 2012

TRANSPORTATION AND TRAVEL
Motor Vehicle Registrations and Drivers Licenses, 2011
Domestic Travel Expenditures, 2009
Retail Gasoline Prices, 2013
Public Road Length, 2011

CRIME AND LAW ENFORCEMENT
Full-Time Law Enforcement Officers, 2011
Prison Population, 2000-2012
Crime Rate, 2011

GOVERNMENT AND FINANCE
Local Governments by Type, 2012
State Government Revenue, 2011
State Government Expenditures, 2011
State Government General Expenditures by Function, 2011
State Government Finances, Cash and Debt, 2011

POLITICS
Composition of the Senate, 1995-2013
Composition of the House of Representatives, 1995-2013
Composition of State Legislature, 2004-2013
Voter Participation in Presidential Elections, 1980-2012
Governors Since Statehood

DEMOGRAPHICS

Resident State and National Population, 1950–2012

Year	State Population	U.S. Population	State Share
1950	1,905,000	151,326,000	1.26%
1960	2,179,000	179,323,000	1.22%
1970	2,249,071	203,302,031	1.11%
1980	2,363,679	226,545,805	1.04%
1990	2,477,574	248,709,873	1.00%
2000	2,688,925	281,424,600	0.96%
2010	2,853,118	308,745,538	0.92%
2012	2,885,905	313,914,040	0.92%

Note: 1950/1960 population figures are rounded to the nearest thousand.
Source: U.S. Census Bureau, Decennial Census 1950–2010; U.S. Census Bureau, 2012 Population Estimates

Projected State and National Population, 2000–2030

Year	State Population	U.S. Population	State Share
2000	2,688,418	281,421,906	0.96%
2005	2,751,509	295,507,134	0.93%
2010	2,805,470	308,935,581	0.91%
2015	2,852,690	322,365,787	0.88%
2020	2,890,566	335,804,546	0.86%
2025	2,919,002	349,439,199	0.84%
2030	2,940,084	363,584,435	0.81%
State population growth, 2000–2030			251,666
State percentage growth, 2000–2030			9.4%

Source: U.S. Census Bureau, Population Division, Interim State Population Projections, 2005

Population by Age, 2012

Age Group	State Population	Percent of Total Population	
		State	U.S.
Under 5 years	203,267	7.0%	6.4%
5 to 14 years	403,341	14.0%	13.1%
15 to 24 years	414,638	14.4%	14.0%
25 to 34 years	387,451	13.4%	13.5%
35 to 44 years	343,038	11.9%	12.9%
45 to 54 years	388,791	13.5%	14.1%
55 to 64 years	351,110	12.2%	12.3%
65 to 74 years	206,830	7.2%	7.6%
75 to 84 years	125,271	4.3%	4.2%
85 years and older	62,168	2.2%	1.9%
Under 18 years	724,304	25.1%	23.5%
65 years and older	394,269	13.7%	13.7%
Median age (years)	–	36.0	37.4

Source: U.S. Census Bureau, Annual Estimates of the Resident Population for Selected Age Groups by Sex for the United States, States, Counties, and Puerto Rico Commonwealth and Municipios: April 1, 2010 to July 1, 2012

Population by Race, 2012

Race	State Population	Percent of Total Population	
		State	U.S.
All residents	2,885,905	100.00%	100.00%
White	2,517,663	87.24%	77.89%
African American	178,820	6.20%	13.13%
Native American	33,909	1.17%	1.23%
Asian	74,598	2.58%	5.14%
Native Hawaiian	2,953	0.10%	0.23%
Two or more races	77,962	2.70%	2.39%

Source: U.S. Census Bureau, Population Division, Annual Estimates of the Resident Population by Sex, Race and Hispanic Origin for the United States, States, and Counties: April 1, 2010 to July 1, 2012

Population by Hispanic Origin and Race, 2012

Hispanic Origin/Race	State Population	Percent of Total Population	
		State	U.S.
All residents	2,885,905	100.00%	100.00%
All Hispanic residents	317,061	10.99%	16.89%
Hispanic			
White	282,227	9.78%	14.91%
African American	10,592	0.37%	0.79%
Native American	10,376	0.36%	0.49%
Asian	2,031	0.07%	0.17%
Native Hawaiian	868	0.03%	0.06%
Two or more races	10,967	0.38%	0.48%
Not Hispanic			
White	2,235,436	77.46%	62.98%
African American	168,228	5.83%	12.34%
Native American	23,533	0.82%	0.74%
Asian	72,567	2.51%	4.98%
Native Hawaiian	2,085	0.07%	0.17%
Two or more races	66,995	2.32%	1.91%

Source: U.S. Census Bureau, Population Division, Annual Estimates of the Resident Population by Sex, Race and Hispanic Origin for the United States, States, and Counties: April 1, 2010 to July 1, 2012

VITAL STATISTICS

Death Rates by Leading Causes, 2010

Cause	State	U.S.
Malignant neoplasms	184.9	186.2
Ischaemic heart diseases	104.8	122.9
Other forms of heart disease	62.9	53.4
Chronic lower respiratory diseases	52.9	44.7
Cerebrovascular diseases	44.4	41.9
Organic, incl. symptomatic, mental disorders	39.8	35.7
Other degenerative diseases of the nervous sys.	27.0	28.4
Other external causes of accidental injury	27.3	26.5
Diabetes mellitus	22.2	22.4
Hypertensive diseases	9.2	20.4
All causes	816.1	799.5

Note: Figures are age-adjusted death rates per 100,000 population
Source: CDC/NCHS, Underlying Cause of Death 1999–2010 on CDC WONDER Online Database

Death Rates by Selected Causes, 2010

Cause	State	U.S.
Assault	3.6	5.2
Diseases of the liver	13.1	13.9
Human immunodeficiency virus (HIV) disease	1.0	2.7
Influenza and pneumonia	17.7	16.2
Intentional self-harm	14.3	12.4
Malnutrition	1.3	0.9
Obesity and other hyperalimentation	1.8	1.8
Renal failure	17.7	14.4
Transport accidents	17.6	12.1
Viral hepatitis	2.3	2.4

Note: Figures are age-adjusted death rates per 100,000 population; A dash indicates that data was not available or was suppressed
Source: CDC/NCHS, Underlying Cause of Death 1999–2010 on CDC WONDER Online Database

Abortion Rates, 2009

Category	2009
By state of residence	
Total abortions	4,987
Abortion rate[1]	9.0%
Abortion ratio[2]	120
By state of occurrence	
Total abortions	9,410
Abortion rate[1]	17.0%
Abortion ratio[2]	227
Abortions obtained by out-of-state residents	49.9%
U.S. abortion rate[1]	15.1%
U.S. abortion ratio[2]	227

Note: (1) Number of abortions per 1,000 women aged 15–44 years; (2) Number of abortions per 1,000 live births; A dash indicates that data was not available
Source: CDC/NCHS, Morbidity and Mortality Weekly Report, November 23, 2012 (Abortion Surveillance, United States, 2009)

Infant Mortality Rates, 1995–2009

Category	1995	2000	2005	2009
All state residents	6.88	6.55	7.37	7.10
All U.S. residents	7.57	6.89	6.86	6.39
All state white residents	6.16	6.35	6.78	6.35
All U.S. white residents	6.30	5.71	5.73	5.33
All state black residents	15.57	10.10	15.35	15.60
All U.S. black residents	14.58	13.48	13.26	12.12

Note: Figures represent deaths per 1,000 live births of resident infants under one year old, exclusive of fetal deaths; A dash indicates that data was not available or was suppressed.
Source: Centers of Disease Control and Prevention, Division of Vital Statistics, Linked Birth/Infant Death Records on CDC Wonder Online

Marriage and Divorce Rates, 2000–2011

Year	Marriage Rate		Divorce Rate	
	State	U.S.	State	U.S.
2000	8.3	8.2	3.6	4.0
2002	7.3	8.0	3.6	3.9
2004	7.0	7.8	3.3	3.7
2006	6.8	7.5	3.1	3.7
2008	6.7	7.1	3.5	3.5
2010	6.4	6.8	3.7	3.6
2011	6.3	6.8	3.9	3.6

Note: Rates are based on provisional counts of marriages/divorces by state of occurrence and are per 1,000 total population residing in area
Source: CDC/NCHS, National Vital Statistics System

ECONOMY

Nominal Gross Domestic Product by Industry, 2012
In millions of current dollars

Industry	State GDP
Accommodation and food services	3,700
Administrative and waste management services	4,406
Agriculture, forestry, fishing, and hunting	5,428
Arts, entertainment, and recreation	675
Construction	4,558
Educational services	853
Finance and insurance	9,542
Health care and social assistance	10,423
Information	6,201
Management of companies and enterprises	1,641
Manufacturing	20,503
Mining	1,659
Other services, except government	3,386
Professional, scientific, and technical services	7,182
Real estate and rental and leasing	12,288
Retail trade	9,206
Transportation and warehousing	5,309
Utilities	2,917
Wholesale trade	8,469

Source: U.S. Department of Commerce, Bureau of Economic Analysis, Survey of Current Business

Real Gross Domestic Product, 2000–2012
In millions of chained 2005 dollars

Year	State GDP	U.S. GDP	State Share
2000	97,940	11,225,406	0.87%
2005	104,869	12,539,116	0.84%
2010	113,324	12,897,088	0.88%
2012	118,523	13,430,576	0.88%

Source: U.S. Department of Commerce, Bureau of Economic Analysis, Survey of Current Business

Personal Income Per Capita, 1930–2012

Year	State	U.S.
1930	$460	$618
1940	$421	$593
1950	$1,461	$1,503
1960	$2,141	$2,268
1970	$3,824	$4,084
1980	$9,939	$10,091
1990	$18,034	$19,354
2000	$28,468	$30,319
2010	$38,545	$39,791
2012	$41,835	$42,693

Source: U.S. Department of Commerce, Bureau of Economic Analysis, Regional Economic Accounts

Non-Farm Employment by Sector, 2012
In thousands

Sector	Employment
Construction	55.1
Education and health services	186.1
Financial activities	74.6
Government	259.0
Information	28.3
Leisure and hospitality	119.7
Mining and logging	9.9
Manufacturing	163.1
Other services	51.6
Professional and business services	153.2
Trade, transportation, and utilities	257.2
All sectors	1,357.8

Source: U.S. Bureau of Labor Statistics, State and Area Employment

Foreign Exports, 2000–2012
In millions of dollars

Year	State Exports	U.S. Exports	State Share
2000	5,145	712,054	0.72%
2002	4,988	649,940	0.77%
2004	4,939	768,554	0.64%
2006	8,636	973,994	0.89%
2008	12,513	1,222,545	1.02%
2010	9,899	1,208,080	0.82%
2012	11,696	1,478,268	0.79%

Note: U.S. figures exclude data from Puerto Rico, U.S. Virgin Islands, and unallocated exports
Source: U.S. Department of Commerce, International Trade Admin., Office of Trade and Industry Information, Manufacturing and Services

Energy Consumption, 2011

In trillions of BTUs, except as noted

Total energy consumption	
Total state energy consumption	1,162.5
Total U.S. energy consumption	97,387.3
State share of U.S. total	1.19%
Per capita consumption (in millions of BTUs)	
Total state per capita consumption	405.0
Total U.S. per capita consumption	312.6
End-use sectors	
Residential	244.9
Commercial	216.4
Industrial	421.0
Transportation	280.2
Sources of energy	
Petroleum	398.1
Natural gas	284.6
Coal	346.5
Renewable energy	77.6
Nuclear electric power	76.6

Source: U.S. Energy Information Administration, State Energy Data 2011: Consumption

LAND AND WATER

Surface Area and Federally-Owned Land, 2007

In thousands of acres

Category	State	U.S.	State Share
Total surface area	52,660.8	1,937,664.2	2.72%
Total land area	52,106.4	1,886,846.9	2.76%
Non-federal land	51,602.4	1,484,910.0	3.48%
Developed	2,095.7	111,251.2	1.88%
Rural	49,506.7	1,373,658.8	3.60%
Federal land	504.0	401,936.9	0.13%
Water area	554.4	50,817.3	1.09%

Source: U.S. Department of Agriculture, Natural Resources Conservation Service, 2007 National Resources Inventory

Land Cover/Use of Non-Federal Rural Land, 2007

In thousands of acres

Category	State	U.S.	State Share
Total rural land	49,506.7	1,373,658.8	3.60%
Cropland	25,635.6	357,023.5	7.18%
CRP[1] land	3,164.9	32,850.2	9.63%
Pastureland	2,497.6	118,615.7	2.11%
Rangeland	15,787.5	409,119.4	3.86%
Forest land	1,685.5	406,410.4	0.41%
Other rural land	735.6	49,639.6	1.48%

Note: (1) Conservation Reserve Program was created to assist private landowners in converting highly erodible cropland to vegetative cover.
Source: U.S. Department of Agriculture, Natural Resources Conservation Service, 2007 National Resources Inventory

Farms and Crop Acreage, 2012

Category	State	U.S.	State Share
Farms (in thousands)	65.5	2,170.0	3.02%
Acres (in millions)	46.0	914.0	5.03%
Acres per farm	702.3	421.2	–

Source: U.S. Department of Agriculture, National Agricultural Statistical Service, Quick Stats, 2012 Survey Data

HEALTH AND MEDICAL CARE

Medical Professionals, 2012

Profession	State Number	U.S. Number	State Share	State Rate[1]	U.S. Rate[1]
Physicians[2]	7,108	894,637	0.79%	247.6	287.1
Dentists	1,486	193,587	0.77%	51.8	62.1
Podiatrists	86	17,469	0.49%	3.0	5.6
Optometrists	597	45,638	1.31%	20.8	14.6
Chiropractors	1,067	77,494	1.38%	37.2	24.9

Note: (1) Rates are per 100,000 population; (2) Includes total, active Doctors of Osteopathic Medicine and Doctors of Medicine in 2011.
Source: U.S. Department of Health and Human Services, Bureau of Health Professions, Area Health Resource File, 2012-2013

Health Insurance Coverage, 2011

Category	State	U.S.
Total persons covered	2,434,000	260,214,000
Total persons not covered	380,000	48,613,000
Percent not covered	13.5%	15.7%
Children under age 18 covered	652,000	67,143,000
Children under age 18 not covered	68,000	6,965,000
Percent of children not covered	9.4%	9.4%

Source: U.S. Census Bureau, Current Population Survey, 2012 Annual Social and Economic Supplement

HIV, STD, and Tuberculosis Cases and Rates, 2011

Disease	State Cases	State Rate[1]	U.S. Rate[1]
Chlamydia	10,598	371.5	457.6
Gonorrhea	2,209	77.4	104.2
HIV diagnosis	146	6.2	15.8
HIV, stage 3 (AIDS)	105	4.5	10.3
Syphilis, early latent	34	1.2	4.3
Syphilis, primary/secondary	24	0.8	4.5
Tuberculosis	36	1.3	3.4

Note: (1) Rates are per 100,000 population
Source: Centers for Disease Control and Prevention

Cigarette Smoking, 2011

Category	State	U.S.
Adults who are current smokers	22.0%	21.2%
Adults who smoke everyday	16.9%	15.4%
Adults who smoke some days	5.1%	5.7%
Adults who are former smokers	22.4%	25.1%
Adults who never smoked	55.6%	52.9%

Source: Centers for Disease Control and Prevention, Behaviorial Risk Factor Surveillance System, Tobacco Use, 2011

HOUSING

Home Ownership Rates, 1995–2012

Area	1995	2000	2005	2010	2012
State	67.5%	69.3%	69.5%	67.4%	63.2%
U.S.	64.7%	67.4%	68.9%	66.9%	65.4%

Source: U.S. Census Bureau, Housing Vacancies and Homeownership, Annual Statistics

Home Sales, 2000–2010
In thousands of units

Year	State Sales	U.S. Sales	State Share
2000	52.6	5,174	1.02%
2002	60.0	5,632	1.07%
2004	73.4	6,778	1.08%
2006	76.1	6,478	1.17%
2008	60.4	4,913	1.23%
2010	51.8	4,908	1.06%

Note: Units include single-family homes, condos and co-ops
Source: National Association of Realtors, Real Estate Outlook, Market Trends & Insights

Value of Owner-Occupied Homes, 2011

Value	Total Units in State	Percent of Total, State	Percent of Total, U.S.
Less than $50,000	104,151	13.9%	8.8%
$50,000 to $99,000	178,990	24.0%	16.0%
$100,000 to $149,000	153,637	20.6%	16.5%
$150,000 to $199,000	127,429	17.1%	15.4%
$200,000 to $299,000	110,083	14.7%	18.2%
$300,000 to $499,000	51,362	6.9%	15.2%
$500,000 to $999,000	18,384	2.5%	7.9%
$1,000,000 or more	3,043	0.4%	2.0%
Median value	–	$128,300	$173,600

Source: U.S. Census Bureau, 2011 American Community Survey 1-Year Estimates

EDUCATION

School Enrollment, 2011

Educational Level	Students Enrolled in State	Percent of Total, State	Percent of Total, U.S.
All levels	801,598	100.0%	100.0%
Nursery school, preschool	51,416	6.4%	6.0%
Kindergarten	40,669	5.1%	5.1%
Elementary (grades 1–8)	320,055	39.9%	39.5%
Secondary (grades 9–12)	158,457	19.8%	20.7%
College or graduate school	231,001	28.8%	28.7%

Note: Figures cover the population 3 years and over enrolled in school
Source: U.S. Census Bureau, 2011 American Community Survey 1-Year Estimates

Educational Attainment, 2011

Highest Level of Education	State	U.S.
High school diploma	90.0%	85.9%
Bachelor's degree	30.1%	28.5%
Graduate/Professional degree	10.4%	10.6%

Note: Figures cover the population 25 years and over
Source: U.S. Census Bureau, 2011 American Community Survey 1-Year Estimates

Public College Finances, FY 2012

Category	State	U.S.
Full-time equivalent enrollment (FTE)[1]	142,967	11,548,974
Educational appropriations per FTE[2]	$4,647	$5,906
Net tuition revenue per FTE[3]	$4,665	$5,189
Total educational revenue per FTE[4]	$9,313	$11,043

(1) Full-time equivalent enrollment equates student credit hours to full time, academic year students, but excludes medical students; (2) Educational appropriations measure state and local support available for public higher education operating expenses including ARRA funds and excludes appropriations for independent institutions, financial aid for students attending independent institutions, research, hospitals, and medical education; (3) Net tuition revenue is calculated by taking the gross amount of tuition and fees, less state and institutional financial aid, tuition waivers or discounts, and medical student tuition and fees. Net tuition revenue used for capital debt service is included in the net tuition revenue figures; (4) Total educational revenue is the sum of educational appropriations and net tuition excluding net tuition revenue used for capital debt service.
Source: State Higher Education Executive Officers, State Higher Education Finance FY 2012

TRANSPORTATION AND TRAVEL

Motor Vehicle Registrations and Drivers Licenses, 2011

Vehicle Type	State	U.S.	State Share
Automobiles[1]	1,141,601	125,656,528	0.91%
Buses	5,083	666,064	0.76%
Trucks	1,217,921	118,455,587	1.03%
Motorcycles	81,361	8,437,502	0.96%
Drivers licenses	2,025,581	211,874,649	0.96%

Note: Motor vehicle registrations include private, commercial, and publicly-owned vehicles; (1) Includes taxicabs
Source: U.S. Department of Transportation, Federal Highway Administration

Domestic Travel Expenditures, 2009
In millions of dollars

Category	State	U.S.	State Share
Travel expenditures	$5,094	$610,200	0.83%

Note: Figures represent U.S. spending on domestic overnight trips and day trips of 50 miles or more, one way, away from home. Excludes spending by foreign visitors.
Source: U.S. Travel Association, Impact of Travel on State Economies, 2009

Retail Gasoline Prices, 2013

Gasoline Grade	State Average	U.S. Average
Regular	$3.60	$3.65
Mid	$3.70	$3.81
Premium	$3.87	$3.98
Diesel	$3.84	$3.88
Excise tax[1]	43.4 cents	49.4 cents

Note: Gasoline prices as of 7/26/2013; (1) Includes state and federal excise taxes and other state taxes as of July 1, 2013
Source: American Automobile Association, Daily Fuel Guage Report; American Petroleum Institute, State Motor Fuel Taxes, 2013

Public Road Length, 2011

Type	State Mileage	U.S. Mileage	State Share
Interstate highways	874	46,960	1.86%
Other highways	187	15,719	1.19%
Principal arterial	3,876	156,262	2.48%
Minor arterial	5,644	242,942	2.32%
Major collector	24,362	534,592	4.56%
Minor collector	9,230	266,357	3.47%
Local	96,341	2,814,925	3.42%
Urban	12,980	1,095,373	1.18%
Rural	127,532	2,982,383	4.28%
Total	140,513	4,077,756	3.45%

Note: Combined urban and rural road mileage equals the total of the other road types
Source: U.S. Department of Transportation, Federal Highway Administration, Public Road Length, 2011

CRIME AND LAW ENFORCEMENT

Full-Time Law Enforcement Officers, 2011

Gender	State Number	State Rate[1]	U.S. Rate[1]
Male officers	6,004	236.2	210.3
Female officers	590	23.2	28.1
Total officers	6,594	259.5	238.3

Note: (1) Rates are per 100,000 population
Source: Federal Bureau of Investigation, Uniform Crime Reports, Crime in the United States 2011

Prison Population, 2000–2012

Year	State Population	U.S. Population	State Share
2000	8,344	1,391,261	0.60%
2005	9,068	1,527,929	0.59%
2010	9,051	1,613,803	0.56%
2011	9,327	1,598,783	0.58%
2012	9,682	1,571,013	0.62%

Note: Figures include prisoners under the jurisdiction of state or federal correctional authorities.
Source: U.S. Department of Justice, Bureau of Justice Statistics, Prisoners in 2006, 2011, 2012 (Advance Counts)

Crime Rate, 2011

Incidents per 100,000 residents

Category	State	U.S.
Violent crimes	353.9	386.3
Murder	3.8	4.7
Forcible rape	37.8	26.8
Robbery	50.8	113.7
Aggravated assault	261.5	241.1
Property crimes	3,080.1	2,908.7
Burglary	654.4	702.2
Larceny/theft	2,193.2	1,976.9
Motor vehicle theft	232.5	229.6
All crimes	3,434.0	3,295.0

Source: Federal Bureau of Investigation, Uniform Crime Reports, Crime in the United States 2011

GOVERNMENT AND FINANCE

Local Governments by Type, 2012

Government Type	State	U.S.	State Share
All local governments	3,806	89,004	4.28%
County	103	3,031	3.40%
Municipality	626	19,522	3.21%
Town/Township	1,268	16,364	7.75%
Special District	1,503	37,203	4.04%
Ind. School District	306	12,884	2.38%

Source: U.S. Census Bureau, 2012 Census of Governments: Organization Component Preliminary Estimates

State Government Revenue, 2011

In thousands of dollars, except for per capita figures

Total revenue	$18,613,184
Total revenue per capita, State	$6,485
Total revenue per capita, U.S.	$7,271
General revenue	$15,019,196
Intergovernmental revenue	$4,940,903
Taxes	$6,828,477
General sales	$2,487,499
Selective sales	$845,468
License taxes	$333,916
Individual income taxes	$2,720,819
Corporate income taxes	$246,518
Other taxes	$194,257
Current charges	$2,369,426
Miscellaneous general revenue	$880,390
Utility revenue	$0
Liquor store revenue	$0
Insurance trust revenue[1]	$3,593,988

Note: (1) Within insurance trust revenue, net earnings of state retirement systems is a calculated statistic, and thus can be positive or negative. Net earnings is the sum of earnings on investments plus gains on investments minus losses on investments.
Source: U.S. Census Bureau, 2011 Annual Survey of State Government Finances

State Government Expenditures, 2011

In thousands of dollars, except for per capita figures

Total expenditure	$16,686,643
Total expenditure per capita, State	$5,813
Total expenditure per capita, U.S.	$6,427
Intergovernmental expenditure	$4,208,664
Direct expenditure	$12,477,979
Current operation	$8,756,128
Capital outlay	$1,088,586
Insurance benefits and repayments	$2,159,915
Assistance and subsidies	$201,483
Interest on debt	$271,867
Utility expenditure	$0
Liquor store expenditure	$0
Insurance trust expenditure	$2,159,915

Source: U.S. Census Bureau, 2011 Annual Survey of State Government Finances

State Government General Expenditures by Function, 2011

In thousands of dollars

Education	$5,966,159
Public welfare	$3,530,709
Hospitals	$1,227,935
Health	$322,888
Highways	$1,238,789
Police protection	$99,073
Correction	$341,552
Natural resources	$216,091
Parks and recreation	$34,783
Governmental administration	$456,464
Interest on general debt	$271,867
Other and unallocable	$820,418

Source: U.S. Census Bureau, 2011 Annual Survey of State Government Finances

State Government Finances, Cash and Debt, 2011

In thousands of dollars, except for per capita figures

Debt at end of fiscal year	
State, total	$6,893,030
State, per capita	$2,401
U.S., per capita	$3,635
Cash and security holdings	
State, total	$18,543,512
State, per capita	$6,460
U.S., per capita	$11,759

Source: U.S. Census Bureau, 2011 Annual Survey of State Government Finances

POLITICS

Composition of the Senate, 1995–2013

Congress (Year)	State/U.S	Dem	Rep	Total
104th (1995)	State delegates	0	2	2
	Total U.S.	48	52	100
105th (1997)	State delegates	0	2	2
	Total U.S.	45	55	100
106th (1999)	State delegates	0	2	2
	Total U.S.	45	55	100
107th (2001)	State delegates	0	2	2
	Total U.S.	50	50	100
108th (2003)	State delegates	0	2	2
	Total U.S.	48	51	100
109th (2005)	State delegates	0	2	2
	Total U.S.	44	55	100
110th (2007)	State delegates	0	2	2
	Total U.S.	49	49	100
111th (2009)	State delegates	0	2	2
	Total U.S.	57	41	100
112th (2011)	State delegates	0	2	2
	Total U.S.	51	47	100
113th (2013)	State delegates	0	2	2
	Total U.S.	54	45	100

Note: Figures are for the starts of first sessions; Totals include Democratic (Dem) and Republican (Rep) members as well as vacancies and seats held by independent party members
Source: U.S. Congress, Congressional Directory

Composition of the House of Representatives, 1995–2013

Congress (Year)	State/U.S	Dem	Rep	Total
104th (1995)	State delegates	0	4	4
	Total U.S.	204	230	435
105th (1997)	State delegates	4	0	4
	Total U.S.	207	226	435
106th (1999)	State delegates	1	3	4
	Total U.S.	211	223	435
107th (2001)	State delegates	1	3	4
	Total U.S.	212	221	435
108th (2003)	State delegates	1	3	4
	Total U.S.	205	229	435
109th (2005)	State delegates	1	3	4
	Total U.S.	202	231	435
110th (2007)	State delegates	2	2	4
	Total U.S.	233	198	435
111th (2009)	State delegates	1	3	4
	Total U.S.	256	178	435
112th (2011)	State delegates	0	4	4
	Total U.S.	193	242	435
113th (2013)	State delegates	0	4	4
	Total U.S.	201	234	435

Note: Figures are for the starts of first sessions; Totals include Democratic (Dem) and Republican (Rep) members as well as vacancies and seats held by independent party members
Source: U.S. Congress, Congressional Directory

Composition of State Legislature, 2004–2013

Year	Democrats	Republicans	Total
State Senate			
2004	10	30	40
2005	10	30	40
2006	10	30	40
2007	10	30	40
2008	10	30	40
2009	9	31	40
2010	9	31	40
2011	8	32	40
2012	8	32	40
2013	8	32	40
State House			
2004	45	80	125
2005	42	83	125
2006	42	83	125
2007	47	78	125
2008	47	78	125
2009	49	76	125
2010	49	76	125
2011	33	92	125
2012	33	92	125
2013	33	92	125

Note: Totals may include minor party members and vacancies
Source: The Council of State Governments, State Legislatures

Voter Participation in Presidential Elections, 1980–2012

Year	Voting-eligible State Population	State Voter Turnout Rate	U.S. Voter Turnout Rate
1980	1,704,420	57.5	54.2
1984	1,751,223	58.4	55.2
1988	1,774,451	56.0	52.8
1992	1,810,750	63.9	58.1
1996	1,856,507	57.3	51.7
2000	1,927,950	55.6	54.2
2004	1,928,764	61.6	60.1
2008	1,991,759	62.0	61.6
2012	2,034,892	57.0	58.2

Note: All figures are based on the voting-eligible population which excludes person ineligible to vote such as non-citizens, felons (depending on state law), and mentally-incapacitated persons. U.S. figures include the overseas eligible population (including military personnel).
Source: McDonald, Michael P., United States Election Project, Presidential Voter Turnout Rates, 1980–2012

Governors Since Statehood

Charles Robinson (R) 1861-1863
Thomas Carney (R) 1863-1865
Samuel J. Crawford (R) . . . . (r) 1865-1868
Nehemiah Green (R) 1868-1869
James M. Harvey (R) 1869-1873
Thomas A. Osborn (R) 1873-1877
George T. Anthony (R) 1877-1879
John P. St. John (R) 1879-1883
George W. Glick (D) 1883-1885
John A. Martin (R) 1885-1889
Lyman U. Humphrey (R) 1889-1893

Lorenzo D. Lewelling (O) 1893-1895
Edmund N. Morrill (R). 1895-1897
John W. Leedy (D) 1897-1899
William E. Stanley (R) 1899-1903
Willis J. Bailey (R). 1903-1905
Edward W. Hoch (R) 1905-1909
Walter R. Stubbs (R) 1909-1913
George H. Hodges (D) 1913-1915
Arthur Capper (R) 1915-1919
Henry J. Allen (R) 1919-1923
Jonathan M. Davis (D) 1923-1925
Benjamin S. Paulen (R) 1925-1929
Clyde M. Reed (R). 1929-1931
Harry H. Woodring (D) 1931-1933
Alfred M. Landon (R) 1933-1937
Walter A. Huxman (D). 1937-1939
Payne H. Ratner (R) 1939-1943
Andrew F. Schoeppel (R). 1943-1947
Frank Carlson (R) . . . . (r) 1947-1950
Frank L. Hagaman (R) 1950-1951
Edward F. Arn (R) 1951-1955
Fred L. Hall (R). . . . . (r) 1955-1957
John B. McCuish (R). 1957
George Docking (D). 1957-1961
John A. Anderson Jr. (R) 1961-1965
William H. Avery (R). 1965-1967
Robert B. Docking (D) 1967-1973
Robert F. Bennett (R) 1973-1979
John W. Carlin (D). 1979-1987
Mike Hayden (R) 1987-1991
Joan Finney (D) 1991-1995
Bill Graves (R). 1995-2003
Kathleen Sebelius (D) . . . . (r) 2003-2009
Mark Parkinson (R) 2009-2011
Sam Brownback (R). 2011-2015

Note: (D) Democrat; (R) Republican; (O) Other party; (r) resigned; (d) died in office; (i) removed from office

Kentucky

Location: Eastern central United States

Area and rank: 39,732 square miles (102,907 square kilometers); 40,411 square miles (104,664 square kilometers) including water; thirty-sixth largest state in area

Coastline: none

Population and rank: 4,380,415 (2012 estimate); twenty-sixth largest state in population

Capital city: Frankfort (25,527 people in 2010 census)

Largest city: Louisville (coterminous with Jefferson County since 2003) (741,096 people in 2010 census)

Entered Union and rank: June 1, 1792; fifteenth state

Present constitution adopted: 1891

Louisville, Kentucky's largest city, owes much of its historical growth to its position as a port on the Ohio River. (©The Pug Father/Flickr)

Counties: 120

State name: "Kentucky" is derived from an Iroquoian word, "Ken-tah-ten," which means "land of tomorrow"

State nickname: Bluegrass State

Motto: United we stand, divided we fall

State flag: Blue field with state seal, goldenrod sprigs below, and legend "Commonwealth of Kentucky" above

Highest point: Black Mountain—4,139 feet (1,262 meters)

Lowest point: Mississippi River—257 feet (78 meters)

Highest recorded temperature: 114 degrees Fahrenheit (46 degrees Celsius)—Greensburg, 1930

Lowest recorded temperature: −34 degrees Fahrenheit (−37 degrees Celsius)—Cynthiana, 1963

State song: "My Old Kentucky Home"

State tree: Tulip poplar

State flower: Goldenrod

State bird: Kentucky cardinal

National parks: Mammoth Cave

Kentucky History

Popularly known as the Bluegrass State, Kentucky was the first state west of the Appalachian Mountains populated by settlers from the original thirteen English colonies. From its earliest days it served as a gateway from east to west and as a border state between the North and South. For most of its history an agricultural and mining state, during the second half of the twentieth century Kentucky began a rapid transformation into a modern industrial economy.

Early History and Settlement. Evidence suggests that Native Americans first entered the area of modern Kentucky as long as fifteen thousand years ago and were primarily hunters and gatherers. Later, agriculture and trade were established, leading to a period around 450 B.C.E. known as the Adena culture, when burial mounds were constructed in the northern Kentucky area. Around 1000 C.E. two distinct Native American cultures developed in the area, the Missippippian in the west and the Fort Ancient in the east; the two groups had many similarities, including the cultivation of beans and corn from the south and the use of agricultural implements including the hoe. The first European explorers found the Cherokee, Delaware, Iroquois, and Shawnee Indian tribes in the territory, although the central portion was not permanently settled by any of these groups. Instead, it seems to have been used as a common hunting ground by all of them. It may also have been reserved for a battlefield for their disputes.

During the mid-eighteenth century, English settlers from the colonies on the East Coast, in particular from Virginia, began to push over the mountains into the area known as Kentucky. The word itself is derived from an Indian word which most likely means "land of tomorrow." Among these English explorers and settlers

President Abraham Lincoln is closely identified with Illinois, but he was born in what is now LaRue County, Kentucky, where this memorial marks his birthplace. (PhotoDisc)

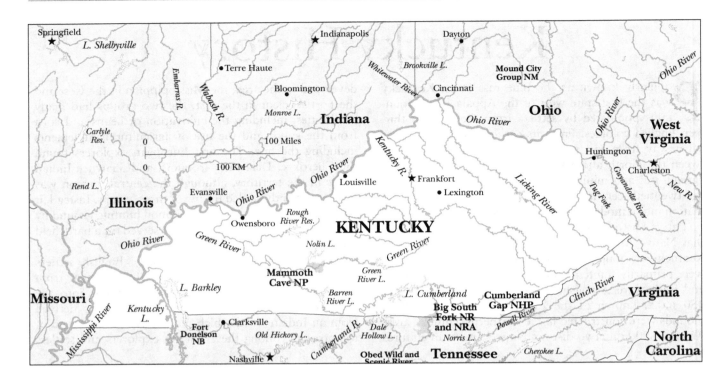

was Dr. Thomas Walker, who charted the Cumberland Gap, the entryway to Kentucky, and was the first European to build a permanent shelter in the area.

Another and more famous traveler was Daniel Boone, who explored the area first in 1767 and again in 1769. In his second journey, Boone reached as far as the central plateau of the state, soon known as "bluegrass country" from its distinctive vegetation. Boone's initial attempt at settlement in 1773 was a failure, but the following year James Harrod and colonists from Pennsylvania established Harrodstown. Boone returned the year after, and Fort Boonesborough was established in 1775. In 1776, the state of Virginia formally claimed the entire territory, giving it the name of the County of Kentucky.

Revolution and Statehood. Native Americans were bewildered and angered by the various treaties they had made with the settlers. The Native Americans felt that these treaties had robbed them of the use of the lands which had been common to all for generations; ownership, in the European sense of the word, was an alien concept to the American Indians. As a result, many tribes throughout the area beyond the mountains allied themselves with the British during the American Revolution, and their attacks on Kentucky threatened the entire American settlement. In response, pioneer George Rogers Clark launched an offensive against the British and Native American strongholds north of the Ohio River. In a campaign that pitted small forces against one another in extremely difficult terrain during the middle of winter, Clark won a crucial victory when he forced the besieged British to surrender the frontier

fort of Vincennes in 1779. However, Kentucky remained under threat from British and Native American attack until the Battle of Blue Licks in 1782, which has been called "the last battle of the Revolution."

Shortly after the Revolution ended in American independence, Kentuckians began agitating for their own independence, with the creation of a state separate from Virginia. During the 1780's, ten separate conventions were held, which gradually drafted the provisions that eventually established Kentucky as a state in its own right. On June 1, 1792, Kentucky was admitted to the Union as the fifteenth state, with Frankfort as its capital. It was the first state of the new United States established west of the Alleghenies.

During the years that followed, Kentucky encouraged one struggle, the War of 1812 against England, and sought to avoid a second, the American Civil War. Kentucky's most famous statesman of the years before the Civil War, Henry Clay, played a key role in both efforts. As a War Hawk congressman during the early nineteenth century, Clay advocated a conflict with Great Britain that he and others hoped could lead to the United States acquiring Canada. Later, as a U.S. Senator, Clay helped craft the Missouri Compromise of 1820 and the Compromise of 1850, which delayed, if they did not prevent, war between the states over slavery.

The Civil War and Early Modern Times. As a border state, Kentucky shared qualities of both the North and South. The majority of its residents were small farmers who owned few or no slaves, and they were inclined to neutrality in the Civil War. There were a number of slaveholders in the broad central portion of the state, and while their sympathies were with the South, they also sought to remain aloof from the struggle. The northern part of the state shared in the developing commerce of the Ohio Valley, and crops of tobacco and cotton were often shipped south down the Mississippi to New Orleans; thus all parts of the state feared that war would disrupt this commerce. Along the eastern, more mountainous portions of the state, where slaves were few, pro-Union sentiment was strongest. Perhaps the fact that most dramatically illustrated the state's precariously balanced position was the fact that both Abraham Lincoln, president of the Union, and Jefferson Davis, president of the Confederacy, were born in Kentucky within a year of one another.

As the controversy over slavery grew more intense and the nation drifted toward war, Kentucky hoped to find yet one more compromise to avert struggle. When the Civil War finally erupted in 1861, Kentucky declared its official neutrality and was promptly invaded by both the Confederacy and the Union, which seized strategic points in the state. Some seventy thousand Kentuckians served with the Union forces; approximately thirty thousand rallied to the Confederacy. After a powerful Confederate thrust north was turned back in the summer of 1862, Kentucky was kept firmly in Union hands for the duration of the war.

Following the Civil War, Kentucky continued to develop its agriculture, most notably the tobacco industry. In addition, the state expanded its reputation for outstanding horse breeding and racing; the first Kentucky Derby was held in Louisville in 1875. Whiskey, especially bourbon, had been produced in the state since the 1820's and became world famous for its quality. The expansion of the railroads into the eastern, more mountainous portions of the state opened new coal fields for exploitation, often through the destructive process of strip-mining, which left a barren wasteland behind. Life for coal miners and their families was hard and often dangerous.

The Great Depression, which began in 1929, coupled with years of drought and then flood, caused enormous damage to Kentucky's economy. By 1940 Kentucky ranked last in the nation for per-capita income. President Franklin Roosevelt's New Deal and then the economic energy unleashed by World War II brought a measure of recovery to the state, including even parts of the Appalachian Mountains. However, poverty remained an endemic problem, especially in Appalachia, even through President Lyndon Johnson's Great Society programs of the mid-1960's.

The Modern Era. After World War II, northern Kentucky in particular experienced an economic boom, with growth in manufacturing companies, which supplied industries in fields such as chemicals, automotives, office supplies, electric appliances, and wood products. In addition, the state took the lead in fields such as health care, with Humana, a Kentucky-formed company and one of the largest health care corporations in the United States, having established its headquarters in Louisville. State government actively sought to recruit industry, especially "light industry" which can fit into the Kentucky environment with minimal impact on natural resources. Such concerns are important, as horse breeding and tourism are major parts of Kentucky's overall economic picture and depend on precisely these natural resources for their continued viability.

Kentucky also took its place in the developing automobile industry in the Southeast. Under Democratic governor Martha Layne Collins, the state recruited a $3.5 billion investment by Japanese automaker Toyota in Kentucky, which, by the early 1990's, was employing more than twenty thousand workers. The success of Toyota in Kentucky was one of the reasons that other international automobile makers chose to locate in the area, most notably BMW in South Carolina in 1993 and Mercedes-Benz in Alabama in 1994. In addition to the automobile manufacturing plants themselves, the companies also attracted large numbers of suppliers for the parts needed in the production of the finished vehicle.

Tobacco Politics. In 2000, Kentucky, like other major tobacco-producing states, enacted a Tobacco Industry Shield Law. The law addressed the substantial liability that the tobacco industry regularly faces, costing many billions of dollars. If tobacco companies were required to post the bond that would otherwise be required against court judgments against such liability, they would be bankrupted. Kentucky, therefore, passed a Shield Law stating that the companies must put up only $25 million against their tobacco suit liability.

In 2003, tobacco also figured in the civic life of one of Kentucky's principal cities. Situated in a principal tobacco-growing state, citizens of the city of Lexington voted to ban smoking in most public buildings.

State Politics. During the 2000 general election, Kentucky residents watched as the most contested and expensive electoral race in Kentucky history took place. The race was between incumbent Republican Congress member Ernie Fletcher and former Democratic Congress member Scotty Baesler. Fletcher won over his Democratic opponent by 53-35 percent. A reform party candidate took 12 percent of the vote. In the presidential race, Kentucky gave its eight electoral votes to Texas governor George W. Bush.

In 2002 and 2003, Kentucky's political order was shaken by a scandal involving the state's popular governor, Paul E. Patton. He was said to have abused his office by giving business opportunities and other benefits to a lover. He admitted two violations and was given a five-thousand-dollar fine, as well as a public reprimand. He left office in 2003 and was succeeded by Fletcher.

Kentucky Derby, first held in 1875, is the oldest annual horse race in the United States. (Wikimedia Commons)

Kentucky's tilt to the political right continued in the 2004 general election. The referendum on gay marriage that was on the ballot was credited with drawing conservative voters to the polls. As in a number of other states, Kentucky voted to ban same-sex marriages. Senator Jim Bunning, a former baseball star, was reelected despite his sometimes erratic behavior in the final weeks of the campaign. Voters also elected a Republican to Congress in a seat vacated by a Democrat when Geoff Davis defeated Nick Clooney, father of Hollywood actor George Clooney. The state then had among its political representatives five Republicans and one Democrat. Nationally, President Bush added the state to his win column.

Demise of Great Racehorses. Kentucky, home of the famed Kentucky Derby, held annually in Louisville, the state's largest city, is known for its fondness for racehorses. The 125th running of the race took place in 1999. Kentuckians were therefore disappointed to learn in 2001 that Affirmed, the 1978 Triple Crown winner, had to be euthanized at the age of twenty-six in Lexington as a result of serious illness. The following year, Seattle Slew—at the time the only living Triple Crown winner—died in his sleep at the age of twenty-

eight. In 2006, thoroughbred racer Barbaro won the derby and was the heavy favorite for the Preakness Stakes soon after. However, the horse suffered a serious leg injury shortly after the beginning of that race which subsequently ended his racing career.

Church Versus State. In the first years of the 21st century, Kentucky drew national headlines because of the debate over displaying the Ten Commandments on public property. The division between popular support for an overt commitments to the fundamentals of the Judeo-Christian heritage and strict adherence to the principle of separation of church and state, supported by the American Civil Liberties Union (ACLU) found its way into the state and federal courts.

In 2005, in the case of *McCreary County v. ACLU of Kentucky*, the U.S. Supreme Court upheld a decision by a lower court that displaying the Ten Commandments in the Whitley City courthouse in Kentucky's McCreary County was unconstitutional. Later in 2005, the Sixth Circuit Court of Appeals, in the case of ACLU of *Kentucky v. Mercer County*, endorsed what was seen locally as a way through the problem. That court supported the idea that a display that included the Mayflower Compact, the Declaration of Independence, the Ten Commandments, the Magna Carta, "The Star-Spangled Banner," and the national motto could be erected in the courthouse. However, observers doubted whether that decision would set a precedent for other states or jurisdictions.

Economy. Expanding from its heritage in coal-mining and agriculture, Kentucky's economy has flourished in auto manufacturing and energy fuel production. The state ranked fourth in auto production. By 2010, 24 percent of electricity produced in the United States could be traced either to enriched uranium rods coming from the Paducah Gaseous Diffusion Plant (the only domestic site of low grade uranium enrichment), or to the more than 100,000 tons of coal produced from the state's two coal fields. The highest proportion of barge traffic on Kentucky waterways is coal that fuels many power plants located directly off the Ohio River.

Michael Witkoski
Updated by the Editor

Kentucky Time Line

1671	Thomas Batts and Robert Fallam of Virginia reach Ohio Valley.
1682	René-Robert Cavelier, sieur de La Salle, claims Kentucky as part of Louisiana Territory for France.
1750	Dr. Thomas Walker discovers Cumberland Gap.
1751	Christopher Gist explores area along Ohio River.
1763	France cedes Louisiana Territory to Britain.
1769	Daniel Boone and John Finley explore Kentucky.
1774	James Harrod founds Harrodstown, later Harrodsburg.
1775	Daniel Boone blazes Wilderness Road and founds Boonesborough.
Dec. 6, 1776	Kentucky County is created by Virginia.
1778	Settlers break American Indian siege of Boonesborough.
1778	George Rogers Clark organizes expedition against British in Ohio valley.
Aug. 19, 1782	Last battle of American Revolution fought at Blue Licks, near Mount Olivet.

Tipple of Mine at Black Mountain Corporation, September 1946, Harlan County, Kentucky. (National Archives and Records Administration)

June 1, 1792	Kentucky ratifies Constitution to become fifteenth state.
1794	General "Mad Anthony" Wayne defeats Native Americans at Fallen Timbers, ending their attacks on settlers in Kentucky.
1796	Wilderness Road opens to wagons.
1798	Legislature passes Kentucky Resolutions, opposing Alien and Sedition Acts.
1811	Henry Clay is elected to Congress.
1819	While drilling for salt, Martin Beatty finds petroleum in Cumberland River.
1830	Louisville and Portland Canal opens.
1849	Zachary Taylor, a Kentucky native, is elected twelfth president of United States.
1861	Kentucky declares itself neutral in Civil War, but is invaded by both Union and Confederate troops.
1862	Union forces win victory over Confederates at Perryville.
1865	University of Kentucky is founded at Lexington.
May 17, 1875	First Kentucky Derby is held at Churchill Downs near Louisville.
1891	New state constitution is adopted.
1926	Mammoth Cave National Park is established.
1937	Worst recorded flood of Ohio River occurs.
1937	United States builds gold depository at Fort Knox.
1944	Tennessee Valley Authority completes Kentucky Dam on Tennessee River.
1950	Atomic energy plant is built near Paducah.
1959	Cumberland Gap National Historical Park is dedicated.
1962	Federal government gives Kentucky control of certain nuclear energy materials, making it the first state granted this power.
1966	Kentucky passes a wide-ranging civil rights law, making it the first southern state to do so.
1966	Barkley Dam on Cumberland River is dedicated.
1982	Martha Layne Collins becomes first woman elected governor of Kentucky.
1985	Toyota automotive company announces construction of manufacturing plant near Georgetown, Kentucky.
1988	Voters approve state lottery.
2000	Kentucky passes a Tobacco Industry Shield Law setting a limit of $25 million for bonds that tobacco companies in the state must post against tobacco suit liability.
2001–2002	Famed racehorses Triple Crown winners Affirmed and Seattle Slew die.
2003	City of Lexington bans smoking in most public buildings.
2003	Governor Paul E. Patton leaves office in disgrace after being fined and receiving a public reprimand over charges of corruption.
Nov. 2, 2004	In general election, Nick Clooney is rejected in bid for congressional seat; Jim Bunning, one-time baseball great, is reelected to the U.S. Senate.
May 20, 2006	Thoroughbred Barbaro injures his leg, ending his racing career.
2010–2013	Kentucky's economy flourishes in auto manufacturing and energy fuel production, as opposed to its previous major industry, coal production.

Notes for Further Study

Published Sources. Two worthwhile books of introductory studies of Kentucky are M. Wharton's *Bluegrass Land and Life* (1992), which concentrates on the broad sweep of its historical development, economics, and popular culture, and Lowell H. Harrison and James C. Klotter's *A New History of Kentucky* (1997), a comprehensive survey of Kentucky from prehistoric to modern times, with a thorough review of developments in the twentieth century.

Klotter further contributes to this discussion with his edited volume titled *Our Kentucky: A Study of the Bluegrass State* (1992), in which a variety of authors and scholars examine the state's historical development and current status. *Running Mad for Kentucky: Frontier Travel Accounts* (2004), edited by Ellen Eslinger, offers one dozen firsthand accounts of travelers as they crossed the Appalachian Mountains in the eighteenth century. A geographical analysis of military tactics and civilian involvement during the Civil War can be found in Brian D. McKnight's *Contested Borderland: The Civil War in Appalachian Kentucky and Virginia (2006). Appalachians and Race: The Mountain South from Slavery to Segregation* (2001), edited by John C. Inscoe, examines the influences of African Americans on the region's economy, history, and culture.

The state's agriculture is discussed in Thomas D. Clark's *Agrarian Kentucky* (1977). *Kentucky Government and Politics* (1984), edited by Joel Goldstein, examines the state's political system. Economic difficulty in Kentucky's Appalachians is explored in *Poverty, Politics, and Health Care: An Appalachian Experience* (1975) by Richard A. Couto. Interesting Kentucky facts can be found in Ernie Couch and Jill Couch's *Kentucky Trivia* (1992). Readers will find nearly eight hundred pages of essays, statistics, photographs, and historical information about Kentucky's business and economy, the arts, sports, recreation, and family trends in *Clark's Kentucky Almanac and Book of Facts 2006*, edited by Sam Stephens (2006).

Web Resources. An excellent place to begin an Internet study of the state is the Commonwealth of Kentucky home page, the official Web site of the Kentucky state government (kentucky.gov/). This site is especially useful when supplemented with the home page of the Kentucky legislature (www.lrc.state.ky.us/home.htm) and the Kentucky State Government Links (www.govengine.com/stategov/kentucky.html), both of which are connected to a wealth of official information, statistics, and data. The Kentucky State History Center (history.ky.gov/) has a Web site worth visiting. Those interested in business conditions in the state should consult the Kentucky Chamber of Commerce (www.kychamber.com/). For contemporary events, the Lexington *Herald-Leader Online* (www.kentucky.com/heraldleader) has outstanding resources. As one of Kentucky's premiere newspapers, the *Herald-Leader* offers excellent insights into the state's economic, political, and cultural events.

The cultural and scenic sides of Kentucky can be found at a number of Web sites. The Kentucky Department of Tourism (www.kentuckytourism.com/) gives visitors a good overview of what the state has to offer. Kentucky has a wealth of folk art, especially in its Appalachian region, which can be studied through the Folk Art Center Web site (www.kyfolkart.org). For western Kentucky, and indeed the entire Ohio Valley, one of the most important natural wonders is Mammoth Cave, the Web site of which can be visited at Mammoth Cave Online (www.mammothcave.com).

Kentucky has no major league baseball team, but Louisville is famous for manufacturing baseball bats. This giant bat stands outside the Louisville Slugger Museum in Louisville. (©H. Michael Miley)

Counties

County	2012 Population	Pop. Rank	Land Area (sq. miles)	Area Rank
Adair	18,675	60	405.28	32
Allen	20,210	56	344.34	49
Anderson	21,728	52	201.83	101
Ballard	8,333	109	246.66	86
Barren	42,631	25	487.54	13
Bath	11,802	93	278.79	74
Bell	28,183	39	359.00	42
Boone	123,316	4	246.36	87
Bourbon	19,978	59	289.72	67
Boyd	49,164	19	159.86	115
Boyle	28,658	36	180.17	111
Bracken	8,494	106	205.61	98
Breathitt	13,635	82	492.41	12
Breckinridge	20,071	58	567.17	6
Bullitt	75,896	10	297.02	66
Butler	12,840	87	426.09	27
Caldwell	12,935	86	344.79	47
Calloway	37,655	27	385.02	36
Campbell	90,908	8	151.31	117
Carlisle	5,034	117	189.43	106
Carroll	10,900	96	128.57	118
Carter	27,348	40	409.50	31
Casey	16,082	71	444.23	20
Christian	75,427	11	717.50	2
Clark	35,787	30	252.46	83
Clay	21,556	53	469.25	15
Clinton	10,285	99	197.25	104
Crittenden	9,280	103	359.95	41
Cumberland	6,819	114	305.18	62
Daviess	97,847	7	458.35	18
Edmonson	12,071	91	302.88	63
Elliott	7,780	110	234.32	90

County	2012 Population	Pop. Rank	Land Area (sq. miles)	Area Rank
Estill	14,493	77	253.08	81
Fayette	305,489	2	283.65	71
Fleming	14,560	76	348.54	45
Floyd	38,949	26	393.34	34
Franklin	49,804	17	207.75	97
Fulton	6,525	115	205.50	99
Gallatin	8,479	107	101.23	119
Garrard	16,913	69	230.08	92
Grant	24,485	46	257.96	79
Graves	37,544	28	551.74	8
Grayson	25,964	43	496.70	11
Green	11,315	94	286.03	70
Greenup	36,707	29	344.40	48
Hancock	8,677	105	187.65	108
Hardin	107,025	6	623.28	4
Harlan	28,543	37	465.83	17
Harrison	18,624	61	306.36	60
Hart	18,366	62	412.09	30
Henderson	46,513	22	436.67	24
Henry	15,318	73	286.28	69
Hickman	4,754	118	242.27	88
Hopkins	46,718	21	542.00	9
Jackson	13,331	84	345.20	46
Jefferson	750,828	1	380.42	38
Jessamine	49,635	18	172.12	113
Johnson	23,383	51	261.95	77
Kenton	161,711	3	160.25	114
Knott	16,124	70	351.52	43
Knox	31,735	32	386.30	35
Larue	14,151	79	261.52	78
Laurel	59,462	16	433.95	25
Lawrence	15,848	72	415.60	29

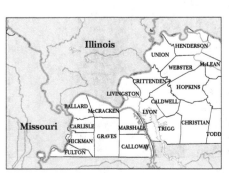

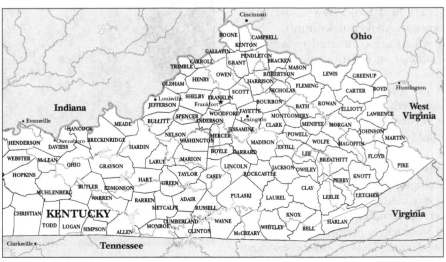

County	2012 Population	Pop. Rank	Land Area (sq. miles)	Area Rank
Lee	7,706	111	208.86	96
Leslie	11,170	95	400.84	33
Letcher	23,952	49	337.91	53
Lewis	13,835	80	482.84	14
Lincoln	24,461	47	334.09	54
Livingston	9,423	102	313.13	58
Logan	26,646	42	552.13	7
Lyon	8,351	108	213.84	95
Madison	84,786	9	437.29	23
Magoffin	13,041	85	308.44	59
Marion	20,090	57	343.01	50
Marshall	31,344	33	301.25	64
Martin	12,743	88	229.60	93
Mason	17,512	65	240.13	89
McCracken	65,549	12	248.74	85
McCreary	18,069	63	426.80	26
McLean	9,506	101	252.47	82
Meade	29,237	35	305.42	61
Menifee	6,220	116	203.58	100
Mercer	21,261	54	248.80	84
Metcalfe	9,969	100	289.65	68
Monroe	10,821	97	329.37	56
Montgomery	26,902	41	197.37	103
Morgan	13,668	81	381.13	37
Muhlenberg	31,181	34	467.08	16
Nelson	44,319	23	417.51	28
Nicholas	7,000	113	195.17	105
Ohio	24,075	48	587.27	5
Oldham	61,412	15	187.22	109
Owen	10,765	98	351.10	44
Owsley	4,722	119	197.41	102
Pendleton	14,604	75	277.16	75
Perry	28,241	38	339.67	52
Pike	64,178	13	786.83	1
Powell	12,483	90	178.98	112
Pulaski	63,593	14	658.41	3
Robertson	2,188	120	99.91	120
Rockcastle	17,006	68	316.54	57
Rowan	23,447	50	279.80	73
Russell	17,497	66	253.66	80
Scott	49,057	20	281.77	72
Shelby	43,614	24	379.64	39
Simpson	17,538	64	234.20	91
Spencer	17,416	67	186.68	110
Taylor	24,691	45	266.33	76
Todd	12,651	89	374.50	40
Trigg	14,447	78	441.43	21
Trimble	8,787	104	151.65	116
Union	14,850	74	342.85	51
Warren	117,110	5	541.60	10
Washington	11,833	92	297.27	65
Wayne	20,824	55	458.17	19
Webster	13,583	83	331.94	55
Whitley	35,499	31	437.83	22
Wolfe	7,164	112	222.17	94
Woodford	25,077	44	188.78	107

Source: U.S. Census Bureau, 2012 Population Estimates

Cities

With 10,000 or more residents

Legal Name	2010 Population	Pop. Rank	Land Area (sq. miles)	Area Rank
Ashland city	21,684	18	10.74	23
Bardstown city	11,700	33	10.49	24
Berea city	13,561	32	16.01	12
Bowling Green city	58,067	3	37.78	3
Burlington CDP	15,926	26	8.84	28
Covington city	40,640	5	13.20	18
Danville city	16,218	25	15.82	14
Elizabethtown city	28,531	11	25.36	5
Erlanger city	18,082	21	8.33	29
Florence city	29,951	8	10.31	25
Fort Campbell North CDP	13,685	31	5.04	36
Fort Knox CDP	10,124	39	20.62	7
Fort Thomas city	16,325	24	5.66	35
Frankfort city	25,527	14	14.32	17
Georgetown city	29,098	9	15.84	13
Glasgow city	14,028	30	15.45	15
Henderson city	28,757	10	15.30	16
Hopkinsville city	31,577	6	30.66	4
Independence city	24,757	16	17.44	11
Jeffersontown city	26,595	13	9.92	26
Lawrenceburg city	10,505	37	5.87	34

Legal Name	2010 Population	Pop. Rank	Land Area (sq. miles)	Area Rank
Lexington-Fayette urban county	295,803	2	283.65	2
Louisville/Jefferson County metro government	597,337	1	325.25	1
Lyndon city	11,002	36	3.60	39
Madisonville city	19,591	19	17.86	10
Mayfield city	10,024	40	6.89	33
Middlesborough city	10,334	38	7.54	32
Murray city	17,741	22	11.24	22
Newport city	15,273	27	2.72	40
Nicholasville city	28,015	12	13.01	19
Owensboro city	57,265	4	19.09	9
Paducah city	25,024	15	19.90	8
Radcliff city	21,688	17	12.39	20
Richmond city	31,364	7	22.81	6
St. Matthews city	17,472	23	4.31	38
Shelbyville city	14,045	29	8.06	30
Shepherdsville city	11,222	34	9.67	27
Shively city	15,264	28	4.57	37
Somerset city	11,196	35	11.32	21
Winchester city	18,368	20	7.84	31

Note: CDP–Census Designated Place
Source: U.S. Census Bureau, 2010 Census

Survey Says...

This section presents current rankings from dozens of public and private sources. It shows how this state ranks in a number of critical categories, including education, job growth, cost of living, teen drivers, energy efficiency, and business environment. Sources include *Forbes, Reuters, U.S. News and World Report, CNN Money, Gallup,* and *Huffington Post.*

- Kentucky ranked #33 in a government study measuring real gross domestic product (GDP)—the output of goods and services produced by labor and property located in the United States. The ranking is based on the percentage change compared with 2011 GDP.
  U.S. Department of Commerce, Bureau of Economic Analysis, June 2013; www.bea.gov

- Kentucky ranked #28 in a government study measuring real gross domestic product (GDP)—the output of goods and services produced by labor and property located in the United States. The ranking is based on the dollar value of its GDP.
  U.S. Department of Commerce, Bureau of Economic Analysis, June 2013; www.bea.gov

- Kentucky ranked #10 in the 17th edition of "Quality Counts; State of the States," Education Week's "report card" surveying key education indicators, policy efforts, and educational outcomes.
  Education Week, January 4, 2013 (online) and January 10, 2013 (print); www.edweek.org

- SERI (Science and Engineering Readiness Index) weighs the performance of the states' K-12 schools in preparing students in physics and calculus, the high school subjects considered most important for future scientists and engineers. Kentucky ranked #17.
  Newsletter of the Forum on Education of the American Physical Society, Summer 2011 issue; www.huffingtonpost.com, July 11, 2011; updated October 1, 2012

- Business website 24/7 Wall St. identified the states with the highest and lowest percentages of residents 25 or older with a college degree or higher. Of "America's Worst Educated States," Kentucky ranked #4 (#1 = worst).
  247wallst.com, posted October 15, 2012; consulted July 18, 2013

- MoneyRates.com ranked Kentucky #30 on its list of the best to worst states for making a living. Criteria: average income; inflation; employment prospects; and workers' Workplace Environment assessments according to the Gallup-Healthways Well-Being Index.
  www.money-rates.com, posted April 1, 2013

- *Forbes* analyzed business costs, labor supply, regulatory environment, current economic climate, growth prospects, and quality of life, to compile its "Best States for Business" rankings. Kentucky ranked #28.
  www.forbes.com. posted December 12, 2012

- In "The States People Are Fleeing in 2013," *Forbes* reported the results of United Van Lines's thirty-sixth annual survey of its "customer migration patterns." In percentage of outbound moves, Kentucky ranked #9 (1 = most).
  www.forbes.com, posted February 7, 2013

- The 2012 Gallup-Healthways Well-Being Index, surveyed American's opinions on economic confidence, workplace perceptions, community climate, personal choices, and health predictors to assess the "future livability" of each state. Kentucky ranked #48.
  "Utah Poised to Be the Best State to Live In," Gallup Wellbeing, www.gallup.com, August 7, 2012

- On CNBC's list of "America's Top States for Business 2013," Kentucky ranked #36. Criteria: measures of competitiveness developed with input from the National Association of Manufacturers, the Council on Competitiveness, and other business groups weighed with the states' own marketing criteria.
  www.cnbc.com, consulted July 19, 2013

- Kentucky ranked #12 on MoneyRates list of "Best-and Worst-States to Retire 2012." Criteria: life expectancy, crime rate, climate, economic conditions, taxes, job opportunities, and cost of living.
  www.money-rates.com, October 22, 2012

- Kentucky ranked #4 on the 2013 Bankrate "Best Places to Retire" list ranking the states and District of Columbia on various criteria relating to health, safety, and cost.
  www.bankrate.com, May 6, 2013

- Kentucky ranked #48 on the Social Science Research Council's "American Human Development Report: The Measure of America," assessing the 50 states plus the District of Columbia on health, education, and living-standard criteria.
  The Measure of America 2013-2014, posted June 19, 2013; www.measureofamerica.org

- Kentucky ranked #41 on the Foundation for Child Development's (FCD) Child Well-being Index (CWI). The FCD used the KIDS COUNT report and the National Survey of Children's Health, the only state-level source for several key indicators of child well-being.
  Foundation for Child Development, January 18, 2012; fcd-us.org

- Kentucky ranked #34 overall according to the 2013 KIDS COUNT Data Book, a project of the Annie E. Casey Foundation. Criteria: children's economic well-being, education, health, and family and community indicators.
  KIDS COUNT Data Center's Data Book, released June 20, 2013; http://datacenter.kidscount.org

- Kentucky ranked #32 in the children's economic well-being category by the 2013 KIDS COUNT Data Book, a project of the Annie E. Casey Foundation.
  KIDS COUNT Data Center's Data Book, released June 20, 2013; http://datacenter.kidscount.org

- Kentucky ranked #28 in the children's educational opportunities and attainments category by the 2013 KIDS COUNT Data Book, a project of the Annie E. Casey Foundation.
  KIDS COUNT Data Center's Data Book, released June 20, 2013; http://datacenter.kidscount.org

- Kentucky ranked #31 in the children's health category by the 2013 KIDS COUNT Data Book, a project of the Annie E. Casey Foundation.
  KIDS COUNT Data Center's Data Book, released June 20, 2013; http://datacenter.kidscount.org

- Kentucky ranked #38 in the family and community circumstances that factor into children's well-being category by the 2013 KIDS COUNT Data Book, a project of the Annie E. Casey Foundation.
  KIDS COUNT Data Center's Data Book, released June 20, 2013; http://datacenter.kidscount.org

- Kentucky ranked #49 in the 2012 Gallup-Healthways Well-Being Index. Criteria: emotional health; physical health; healthy behavior; work environment; basic access to food, shelter, health care; and a safe and satisfying place to live.
  2012 State of Well-Being, Gallup-Healthways Well-Being Index, released February 28, 2013; www.well-beingindex.com

- *U.S. News and World Report's* "Best States for Teen Drivers" rankings are based on driving and road safety laws, federal reports on driver's licenses, car accident fatality, and road-quality statistics. Kentucky ranked #28.
  U.S. News and World Report, March 18, 2010; www.usnews.com

- The Yahoo! Sports service Rivals.com ranks the states according to the strength of their high school football programs. Kentucky ranked #23.
  "Ranking the States: Where Is the Best Football Played?," November 18, 2011; highschool.rivals.com

- iVillage ranked the states by hospitable living conditions for women. Criteria: economic success, access to affordable childcare, health care, reproductive rights, female representation in government, and educational attainment. Kentucky ranked #46.
  iVillage, "50 Best to Worst States for Women," March 14, 2012; www.ivillage.com

- The League of American Bicyclists's "Bicycle Friendly States" ranked Kentucky #47. Criteria: legislation and enforcement, policies and programs, infrastructure and funding, education and advocacy, and evaluation and planning.
  "Washington Tops the Bicycle-Friendly State Ranking," May 1, 2013; bicycling.com

- The federal Corporation for National and Community Service ranked the states and the District of Columbia by volunteer rates. Kentucky ranked #39 for community service.
  "Volunteering and Civic Life in America 2012," www.volunteeringinamerica.gov, accessed July 24, 2013

- The Hospital Safety Score ranked states and the District of Columbia on their hospitals' performance scores. Kentucky ranked #23. Criteria: avoiding preventable harm and medical errors, as demonstrated by 26 hospital safety metrics.
  Spring 2013 Hospital Safety Score, May 8, 2013; www.hospitalsafetyscore.org

- GMAC Insurance ranked the states and the District of Columbia by the performance of their drivers on the GMAC Insurance National Drivers Test, comprised of DMV test questions. Kentucky ranked #23.
  "2011 GMAC Insurance National Drivers Test," www.gmacinsurance.com, accessed July 23, 2013

- Kentucky ranked #19 in a "State Integrity Investigation" analysis of laws and practices intended to deter corruption and promote accountability and openness in campaign finance, ethics laws, lobbying regulations and management of state pension funds.
  "What's Your State's Grade?," www.publicintegrity.org, accessed July 23, 2013

- Kentucky ranked #28 among the states and the District of Columbia in total rail miles, as tracked by the Association of American Railroads.
  "U.S. Freight Railroad Industry Snapshot: Railroads and States: Total Rail Miles by State: 2011"; www.aar.org, accessed July 23, 2013

- According to statistics compiled by the Beer Institute, Kentucky ranked #46 among the states and the District of Columbia in per capita beer consumption of persons 21 years or older.
  "Shipments of Malt Beverages and Per Capita Consumption by State 2012;" www.beerinstitute.org

- According to Concordia University's "Public Education Costs per Pupil by State Rankings," based on statistics gathered by the U.S. Census Bureau, which includes the District of Columbia, Kentucky ranked #38.
  Concordia University Online; education.cu-portland.edu, accessed July 24, 2013

- Kentucky ranked #22 among the states and the District of Columbia in population density based on U.S. Census Bureau data for resident population and total land area. "List of U.S. States by Population Density."
  www.wikipedia.org, accessed July 24, 2013

- In "America's Health Rankings, 2012 Edition," by the United Health Foundation, Kentucky ranked #44. Criteria included: rate of high school graduation; violent crime rate; incidence of infectious disease; childhood immunizations; prevalence of diabetes; per capita public-health funding; percentage of uninsured population; rate of children in poverty; and availability of primary-care physicians.
  United Health Foundation; www.americashealthrankings.org, accessed July 24, 2013

- The TechNet 2012 "State Broadband Index" ranked Kentucky #45 on the following criteria: broadband adoption; network quality; and economic structure. Improved broadband use is hoped to promote economic development, build strong communities, improve delivery of government services and upgrade educational systems.
  TechNet; www.technet.org, accessed July 24, 2013

- Kentucky was ranked #36 among the states and District of Columbia on the American Council for an Energy-Efficient Economy's "State Energy Efficiency Scorecard" for 2012.
  American Council for an Energy-Efficient Economy; aceee.org/sector/state-policy/scorecard, accessed July 24, 2013

Statistical Tables

DEMOGRAPHICS
Resident State and National Population, 1950-2012
Projected State and National Population, 2000-2030
Population by Age, 2012
Population by Race, 2012
Population by Hispanic Origin and Race, 2012

VITAL STATISTICS
Death Rates by Leading Causes, 2010
Death Rates by Selected Causes, 2010
Abortion Rates, 2009
Infant Mortality Rates, 1995-2009
Marriage and Divorce Rates, 2000-2011

ECONOMY
Nominal Gross Domestic Product by Industry, 2012
Real Gross Domestic Product, 2000-2012
Personal Income Per Capita, 1930-2012
Non-Farm Employment by Sector, 2012
Foreign Exports, 2000-2012
Energy Consumption, 2011

LAND AND WATER
Surface Area and Federally-Owned Land, 2007
Land Cover/Use of Non-Federal Rural Land, 2007
Farms and Crop Acreage, 2012

HEALTH AND MEDICAL CARE
Medical Professionals, 2012
Health Insurance Coverage, 2011
HIV, STD, and Tuberculosis Cases and Rates, 2011
Cigarette Smoking, 2011

HOUSING
Home Ownership Rates, 1995-2012
Home Sales, 2000-2010
Value of Owner-Occupied Homes, 2011

EDUCATION
School Enrollment, 2011
Educational Attainment, 2011
Public College Finances, FY 2012

TRANSPORTATION AND TRAVEL
Motor Vehicle Registrations and Drivers Licenses, 2011
Domestic Travel Expenditures, 2009
Retail Gasoline Prices, 2013
Public Road Length, 2011

CRIME AND LAW ENFORCEMENT
Full-Time Law Enforcement Officers, 2011
Prison Population, 2000-2012
Crime Rate, 2011

GOVERNMENT AND FINANCE
Local Governments by Type, 2012
State Government Revenue, 2011
State Government Expenditures, 2011
State Government General Expenditures by Function, 2011
State Government Finances, Cash and Debt, 2011

POLITICS
Composition of the Senate, 1995-2013
Composition of the House of Representatives, 1995-2013
Composition of State Legislature, 2004-2013
Voter Participation in Presidential Elections, 1980-2012
Governors Since Statehood

DEMOGRAPHICS

Resident State and National Population, 1950–2012

Year	State Population	U.S. Population	State Share
1950	2,945,000	151,326,000	1.95%
1960	3,038,000	179,323,000	1.69%
1970	3,220,711	203,302,031	1.58%
1980	3,660,777	226,545,805	1.62%
1990	3,685,296	248,709,873	1.48%
2000	4,042,193	281,424,600	1.44%
2010	4,339,367	308,745,538	1.41%
2012	4,380,415	313,914,040	1.40%

Note: 1950/1960 population figures are rounded to the nearest thousand.
Source: U.S. Census Bureau, Decennial Census 1950–2010; U.S. Census Bureau, 2012 Population Estimates

Projected State and National Population, 2000–2030

Year	State Population	U.S. Population	State Share
2000	4,041,769	281,421,906	1.44%
2005	4,163,360	295,507,134	1.41%
2010	4,265,117	308,935,581	1.38%
2015	4,351,188	322,365,787	1.35%
2020	4,424,431	335,804,546	1.32%
2025	4,489,662	349,439,199	1.28%
2030	4,554,998	363,584,435	1.25%
State population growth, 2000–2030			513,229
State percentage growth, 2000–2030			12.7%

Source: U.S. Census Bureau, Population Division, Interim State Population Projections, 2005

Population by Age, 2012

Age Group	State Population	Percent of Total Population	
		State	U.S.
Under 5 years	279,535	6.4%	6.4%
5 to 14 years	569,737	13.0%	13.1%
15 to 24 years	592,853	13.5%	14.0%
25 to 34 years	567,662	13.0%	13.5%
35 to 44 years	566,136	12.9%	12.9%
45 to 54 years	627,061	14.3%	14.1%
55 to 64 years	562,778	12.8%	12.3%
65 to 74 years	355,298	8.1%	7.6%
75 to 84 years	186,384	4.3%	4.2%
85 years and older	72,971	1.7%	1.9%
Under 18 years	1,018,238	23.2%	23.5%
65 years and older	614,653	14.0%	13.7%
Median age (years)	–	38.3	37.4

Source: U.S. Census Bureau, Annual Estimates of the Resident Population for Selected Age Groups by Sex for the United States, States, Counties, and Puerto Rico Commonwealth and Municipios: April 1, 2010 to July 1, 2012

Population by Race, 2012

Race	State Population	Percent of Total Population	
		State	U.S.
All residents	4,380,415	100.00%	100.00%
White	3,882,987	88.64%	77.89%
African American	354,119	8.08%	13.13%
Native American	12,429	0.28%	1.23%
Asian	55,336	1.26%	5.14%
Native Hawaiian	3,441	0.08%	0.23%
Two or more races	72,103	1.65%	2.39%

Source: U.S. Census Bureau, Population Division, Annual Estimates of the Resident Population by Sex, Race and Hispanic Origin for the United States, States, and Counties: April 1, 2010 to July 1, 2012

Population by Hispanic Origin and Race, 2012

Hispanic Origin/Race	State Population	Percent of Total Population	
		State	U.S.
All residents	4,380,415	100.00%	100.00%
All Hispanic residents	142,028	3.24%	16.89%
Hispanic			
White	121,985	2.78%	14.91%
African American	8,647	0.20%	0.79%
Native American	3,581	0.08%	0.49%
Asian	1,214	0.03%	0.17%
Native Hawaiian	1,101	0.03%	0.06%
Two or more races	5,500	0.13%	0.48%
Not Hispanic			
White	3,761,002	85.86%	62.98%
African American	345,472	7.89%	12.34%
Native American	8,848	0.20%	0.74%
Asian	54,122	1.24%	4.98%
Native Hawaiian	2,340	0.05%	0.17%
Two or more races	66,603	1.52%	1.91%

Source: U.S. Census Bureau, Population Division, Annual Estimates of the Resident Population by Sex, Race and Hispanic Origin for the United States, States, and Counties: April 1, 2010 to July 1, 2012

VITAL STATISTICS

Death Rates by Leading Causes, 2010

Cause	State	U.S.
Malignant neoplasms	225.4	186.2
Ischaemic heart diseases	133.7	122.9
Other forms of heart disease	73.1	53.4
Chronic lower respiratory diseases	63.9	44.7
Cerebrovascular diseases	47.1	41.9
Organic, incl. symptomatic, mental disorders	38.4	35.7
Other degenerative diseases of the nervous sys.	36.8	28.4
Other external causes of accidental injury	41.1	26.5
Diabetes mellitus	27.9	22.4
Hypertensive diseases	20.0	20.4
All causes	977.4	799.5

Note: Figures are age-adjusted death rates per 100,000 population
Source: CDC/NCHS, Underlying Cause of Death 1999–2010 on CDC WONDER Online Database

Death Rates by Selected Causes, 2010

Cause	State	U.S.
Assault	4.6	5.2
Diseases of the liver	15.4	13.9
Human immunodeficiency virus (HIV) disease	1.2	2.7
Influenza and pneumonia	22.6	16.2
Intentional self-harm	14.4	12.4
Malnutrition	1.4	0.9
Obesity and other hyperalimentation	2.5	1.8
Renal failure	22.8	14.4
Transport accidents	19.4	12.1
Viral hepatitis	2.1	2.4

Note: Figures are age-adjusted death rates per 100,000 population; A dash indicates that data was not available or was suppressed
Source: CDC/NCHS, Underlying Cause of Death 1999–2010 on CDC WONDER Online Database

Abortion Rates, 2009

Category	2009
By state of residence	
Total abortions	5,799
Abortion rate[1]	6.7%
Abortion ratio[2]	101
By state of occurrence	
Total abortions	4,120
Abortion rate[1]	4.8%
Abortion ratio[2]	72
Abortions obtained by out-of-state residents	11.0%
U.S. abortion rate[1]	15.1%
U.S. abortion ratio[2]	227

Note: (1) Number of abortions per 1,000 women aged 15–44 years; (2) Number of abortions per 1,000 live births; A dash indicates that data was not available
Source: CDC/NCHS, Morbidity and Mortality Weekly Report, November 23, 2012 (Abortion Surveillance, United States, 2009)

Infant Mortality Rates, 1995–2009

Category	1995	2000	2005	2009
All state residents	7.54	7.10	6.73	6.83
All U.S. residents	7.57	6.89	6.86	6.39
All state white residents	7.19	6.63	6.30	6.49
All U.S. white residents	6.30	5.71	5.73	5.33
All state black residents	11.08	11.31	11.19	10.76
All U.S. black residents	14.58	13.48	13.26	12.12

Note: Figures represent deaths per 1,000 live births of resident infants under one year old, exclusive of fetal deaths; A dash indicates that data was not available or was suppressed.
Source: Centers of Disease Control and Prevention, Division of Vital Statistics, Linked Birth/Infant Death Records on CDC Wonder Online

Marriage and Divorce Rates, 2000–2011

Year	Marriage Rate		Divorce Rate	
	State	U.S.	State	U.S.
2000	9.8	8.2	5.1	4.0
2002	9.0	8.0	5.2	3.9
2004	8.8	7.8	4.9	3.7
2006	8.4	7.5	5.0	3.7
2008	7.9	7.1	4.6	3.5
2010	7.4	6.8	4.5	3.6
2011	7.5	6.8	4.4	3.6

Note: Rates are based on provisional counts of marriages/divorces by state of occurrence and are per 1,000 total population residing in area
Source: CDC/NCHS, National Vital Statistics System

ECONOMY

Nominal Gross Domestic Product by Industry, 2012

In millions of current dollars

Industry	State GDP
Accommodation and food services	5,262
Administrative and waste management services	4,565
Agriculture, forestry, fishing, and hunting	2,090
Arts, entertainment, and recreation	883
Construction	6,081
Educational services	1,117
Finance and insurance	9,368
Health care and social assistance	14,713
Information	4,596
Management of companies and enterprises	2,491
Manufacturing	29,746
Mining	3,771
Other services, except government	3,977
Professional, scientific, and technical services	7,078
Real estate and rental and leasing	15,653
Retail trade	10,981
Transportation and warehousing	8,280
Utilities	3,561
Wholesale trade	10,978

Source: U.S. Department of Commerce, Bureau of Economic Analysis, Survey of Current Business

Real Gross Domestic Product, 2000–2012

In millions of chained 2005 dollars

Year	State GDP	U.S. GDP	State Share
2000	128,522	11,225,406	1.14%
2005	138,772	12,539,116	1.11%
2010	141,977	12,897,088	1.10%
2012	146,829	13,430,576	1.09%

Source: U.S. Department of Commerce, Bureau of Economic Analysis, Survey of Current Business

Personal Income Per Capita, 1930–2012

Year	State	U.S.
1930	$321	$618
1940	$317	$593
1950	$981	$1,503
1960	$1,617	$2,268
1970	$3,176	$4,084
1980	$8,113	$10,091
1990	$15,360	$19,354
2000	$24,785	$30,319
2010	$32,504	$39,791
2012	$35,041	$42,693

Source: U.S. Department of Commerce, Bureau of Economic Analysis, Regional Economic Accounts

Non-Farm Employment by Sector, 2012

In thousands

Sector	Employment
Construction	67.3
Education and health services	257.2
Financial activities	86.7
Government	337.1
Information	26.3
Leisure and hospitality	174.6
Mining and logging	20.7
Manufacturing	223.3
Other services	69.5
Professional and business services	191.2
Trade, transportation, and utilities	370.6
All sectors	1,824.4

Source: U.S. Bureau of Labor Statistics, State and Area Employment

Foreign Exports, 2000–2012

In millions of dollars

Year	State Exports	U.S. Exports	State Share
2000	9,612	712,054	1.35%
2002	10,680	649,940	1.64%
2004	13,055	768,554	1.70%
2006	17,254	973,994	1.77%
2008	19,120	1,222,545	1.56%
2010	19,346	1,208,080	1.60%
2012	22,125	1,478,268	1.50%

Note: U.S. figures exclude data from Puerto Rico, U.S. Virgin Islands, and unallocated exports
Source: U.S. Department of Commerce, International Trade Admin., Office of Trade and Industry Information, Manufacturing and Services

Energy Consumption, 2011

In trillions of BTUs, except as noted

Total energy consumption	
Total state energy consumption	1,911.4
Total U.S. energy consumption	97,387.3
State share of U.S. total	1.96%
Per capita consumption (in millions of BTUs)	
Total state per capita consumption	437.7
Total U.S. per capita consumption	312.6
End-use sectors	
Residential	381.8
Commercial	253.3
Industrial	804.3
Transportation	472.0
Sources of energy	
Petroleum	615.5
Natural gas	228.6
Coal	1,010.6
Renewable energy	82.7
Nuclear electric power	0.0

Source: U.S. Energy Information Administration, State Energy Data 2011: Consumption

LAND AND WATER

Surface Area and Federally-Owned Land, 2007

In thousands of acres

Category	State	U.S.	State Share
Total surface area	25,863.4	1,937,664.2	1.33%
Total land area	25,232.5	1,886,846.9	1.34%
Non-federal land	23,937.1	1,484,910.0	1.61%
Developed	2,093.1	111,251.2	1.88%
Rural	21,844.0	1,373,658.8	1.59%
Federal land	1,295.4	401,936.9	0.32%
Water area	630.9	50,817.3	1.24%

Source: U.S. Department of Agriculture, Natural Resources Conservation Service, 2007 National Resources Inventory

Land Cover/Use of Non-Federal Rural Land, 2007

In thousands of acres

Category	State	U.S.	State Share
Total rural land	21,844.0	1,373,658.8	1.59%
Cropland	5,173.0	357,023.5	1.45%
CRP[1] land	285.0	32,850.2	0.87%
Pastureland	5,242.1	118,615.7	4.42%
Rangeland	0.0	409,119.4	0.00%
Forest land	10,590.9	406,410.4	2.61%
Other rural land	553.0	49,639.6	1.11%

Note: (1) Conservation Reserve Program was created to assist private landowners in converting highly erodible cropland to vegetative cover.
Source: U.S. Department of Agriculture, Natural Resources Conservation Service, 2007 National Resources Inventory

Farms and Crop Acreage, 2012

Category	State	U.S.	State Share
Farms (in thousands)	85.5	2,170.0	3.94%
Acres (in millions)	14.0	914.0	1.53%
Acres per farm	163.7	421.2	–

Source: U.S. Department of Agriculture, National Agricultural Statistical Service, Quick Stats, 2012 Survey Data

HEALTH AND MEDICAL CARE

Medical Professionals, 2012

Profession	State Number	U.S. Number	State Share	State Rate[1]	U.S. Rate[1]
Physicians[2]	10,552	894,637	1.18%	241.6	287.1
Dentists	2,530	193,587	1.31%	57.9	62.1
Podiatrists	159	17,469	0.91%	3.6	5.6
Optometrists	557	45,638	1.22%	12.8	14.6
Chiropractors	865	77,494	1.12%	19.8	24.9

Note: (1) Rates are per 100,000 population; (2) Includes total, active Doctors of Osteopathic Medicine and Doctors of Medicine in 2011.
Source: U.S. Department of Health and Human Services, Bureau of Health Professions, Area Health Resource File, 2012-2013

Health Insurance Coverage, 2011

Category	State	U.S.
Total persons covered	3,689,000	260,214,000
Total persons not covered	621,000	48,613,000
Percent not covered	14.4%	15.7%
Children under age 18 covered	962,000	67,143,000
Children under age 18 not covered	47,000	6,965,000
Percent of children not covered	4.7%	9.4%

Source: U.S. Census Bureau, Current Population Survey, 2012 Annual Social and Economic Supplement

HIV, STD, and Tuberculosis Cases and Rates, 2011

Disease	State Cases	State Rate[1]	U.S. Rate[1]
Chlamydia	16,629	383.2	457.6
Gonorrhea	4,521	104.2	104.2
HIV diagnosis	342	9.4	15.8
HIV, stage 3 (AIDS)	173	4.8	10.3
Syphilis, early latent	109	2.5	4.3
Syphilis, primary/secondary	129	3.0	4.5
Tuberculosis	71	1.6	3.4

Note: (1) Rates are per 100,000 population
Source: Centers for Disease Control and Prevention

Cigarette Smoking, 2011

Category	State	U.S.
Adults who are current smokers	29.0%	21.2%
Adults who smoke everyday	23.6%	15.4%
Adults who smoke some days	5.4%	5.7%
Adults who are former smokers	24.3%	25.1%
Adults who never smoked	46.8%	52.9%

Source: Centers for Disease Control and Prevention, Behaviorial Risk Factor Surveillance System, Tobacco Use, 2011

HOUSING

Home Ownership Rates, 1995–2012

Area	1995	2000	2005	2010	2012
State	71.2%	73.4%	71.6%	70.3%	68.7%
U.S.	64.7%	67.4%	68.9%	66.9%	65.4%

Source: U.S. Census Bureau, Housing Vacancies and Homeownership, Annual Statistics

Home Sales, 2000–2010
In thousands of units

Year	State Sales	U.S. Sales	State Share
2000	66.0	5,174	1.28%
2002	73.5	5,632	1.31%
2004	89.3	6,778	1.32%
2006	96.9	6,478	1.50%
2008	75.3	4,913	1.53%
2010	70.3	4,908	1.43%

Note: Units include single-family homes, condos and co-ops
Source: National Association of Realtors, Real Estate Outlook, Market Trends & Insights

Value of Owner-Occupied Homes, 2011

Value	Total Units in State	Percent of Total, State	Percent of Total, U.S.
Less than $50,000	176,443	15.3%	8.8%
$50,000 to $99,000	282,927	24.6%	16.0%
$100,000 to $149,000	262,852	22.8%	16.5%
$150,000 to $199,000	174,442	15.1%	15.4%
$200,000 to $299,000	152,191	13.2%	18.2%
$300,000 to $499,000	71,365	6.2%	15.2%
$500,000 to $999,000	23,430	2.0%	7.9%
$1,000,000 or more	7,829	0.7%	2.0%
Median value	–	$120,600	$173,600

Source: U.S. Census Bureau, 2011 American Community Survey 1-Year Estimates

EDUCATION

School Enrollment, 2011

Educational Level	Students Enrolled in State	Percent of Total, State	Percent of Total, U.S.
All levels	1,127,708	100.0%	100.0%
Nursery school, preschool	62,994	5.6%	6.0%
Kindergarten	61,975	5.5%	5.1%
Elementary (grades 1–8)	456,465	40.5%	39.5%
Secondary (grades 9–12)	236,895	21.0%	20.7%
College or graduate school	309,379	27.4%	28.7%

Note: Figures cover the population 3 years and over enrolled in school
Source: U.S. Census Bureau, 2011 American Community Survey 1-Year Estimates

Educational Attainment, 2011

Highest Level of Education	State	U.S.
High school diploma	83.1%	85.9%
Bachelor's degree	21.1%	28.5%
Graduate/Professional degree	8.8%	10.6%

Note: Figures cover the population 25 years and over
Source: U.S. Census Bureau, 2011 American Community Survey 1-Year Estimates

Public College Finances, FY 2012

Category	State	U.S.
Full-time equivalent enrollment (FTE)[1]	159,305	11,548,974
Educational appropriations per FTE[2]	$6,959	$5,906
Net tuition revenue per FTE[3]	$5,927	$5,189
Total educational revenue per FTE[4]	$12,886	$11,043

(1) Full-time equivalent enrollment equates student credit hours to full time, academic year students, but excludes medical students; (2) Educational appropriations measure state and local support available for public higher education operating expenses including ARRA funds and excludes appropriations for independent institutions, financial aid for students attending independent institutions, research, hospitals, and medical education; (3) Net tuition revenue is calculated by taking the gross amount of tuition and fees, less state and institutional financial aid, tuition waivers or discounts, and medical student tuition and fees. Net tuition revenue used for capital debt service is included in the net tuition revenue figures; (4) Total educational revenue is the sum of educational appropriations and net tuition excluding net tuition revenue used for capital debt service.
Source: State Higher Education Executive Officers, State Higher Education Finance FY 2012

TRANSPORTATION AND TRAVEL

Motor Vehicle Registrations and Drivers Licenses, 2011

Vehicle Type	State	U.S.	State Share
Automobiles[1]	1,883,309	125,656,528	1.50%
Buses	10,639	666,064	1.60%
Trucks	1,770,584	118,455,587	1.49%
Motorcycles	98,495	8,437,502	1.17%
Drivers licenses	2,959,881	211,874,649	1.40%

Note: Motor vehicle registrations include private, commercial, and publicly-owned vehicles; (1) Includes taxicabs
Source: U.S. Department of Transportation, Federal Highway Administration

Domestic Travel Expenditures, 2009
In millions of dollars

Category	State	U.S.	State Share
Travel expenditures	$7,107	$610,200	1.16%

Note: Figures represent U.S. spending on domestic overnight trips and day trips of 50 miles or more, one way, away from home. Excludes spending by foreign visitors.
Source: U.S. Travel Association, Impact of Travel on State Economies, 2009

Retail Gasoline Prices, 2013

Gasoline Grade	State Average	U.S. Average
Regular	$3.57	$3.65
Mid	$3.69	$3.81
Premium	$3.81	$3.98
Diesel	$3.85	$3.88
Excise tax[1]	50.7 cents	49.4 cents

Note: Gasoline prices as of 7/26/2013; (1) Includes state and federal excise taxes and other state taxes as of July 1, 2013
Source: American Automobile Association, Daily Fuel Guage Report; American Petroleum Institute, State Motor Fuel Taxes, 2013

Public Road Length, 2011

Type	State Mileage	U.S. Mileage	State Share
Interstate highways	801	46,960	1.71%
Other highways	654	15,719	4.16%
Principal arterial	2,712	156,262	1.74%
Minor arterial	2,782	242,942	1.15%
Major collector	7,061	534,592	1.32%
Minor collector	9,489	266,357	3.56%
Local	55,721	2,814,925	1.98%
Urban	12,632	1,095,373	1.15%
Rural	66,588	2,982,383	2.23%
Total	79,220	4,077,756	1.94%

Note: Combined urban and rural road mileage equals the total of the other road types
Source: U.S. Department of Transportation, Federal Highway Administration, Public Road Length, 2011

CRIME AND LAW ENFORCEMENT

Full-Time Law Enforcement Officers, 2011

Gender	State Number	State Rate[1]	U.S. Rate[1]
Male officers	6,572	177.8	210.3
Female officers	473	12.8	28.1
Total officers	7,045	190.6	238.3

Note: (1) Rates are per 100,000 population
Source: Federal Bureau of Investigation, Uniform Crime Reports, Crime in the United States 2011

Prison Population, 2000–2012

Year	State Population	U.S. Population	State Share
2000	14,919	1,391,261	1.07%
2005	19,662	1,527,929	1.29%
2010	20,544	1,613,803	1.27%
2011	21,545	1,598,783	1.35%
2012	22,110	1,571,013	1.41%

Note: Figures include prisoners under the jurisdiction of state or federal correctional authorities.
Source: U.S. Department of Justice, Bureau of Justice Statistics, Prisoners in 2006, 2011, 2012 (Advance Counts)

Crime Rate, 2011
Incidents per 100,000 residents

Category	State	U.S.
Violent crimes	238.2	386.3
Murder	3.5	4.7
Forcible rape	33.5	26.8
Robbery	84.5	113.7
Aggravated assault	116.7	241.1
Property crimes	2,708.8	2,908.7
Burglary	745.0	702.2
Larceny/theft	1,811.1	1,976.9
Motor vehicle theft	152.7	229.6
All crimes	2,947.0	3,295.0

Source: Federal Bureau of Investigation, Uniform Crime Reports, Crime in the United States 2011

GOVERNMENT AND FINANCE

Local Governments by Type, 2012

Government Type	State	U.S.	State Share
All local governments	1,314	89,004	1.48%
County	118	3,031	3.89%
Municipality	418	19,522	2.14%
Town/Township	0	16,364	0.00%
Special District	604	37,203	1.62%
Ind. School District	174	12,884	1.35%

Source: U.S. Census Bureau, 2012 Census of Governments: Organization Component Preliminary Estimates

State Government Revenue, 2011
In thousands of dollars, except for per capita figures

Total revenue	$31,056,300
Total revenue per capita, State	$7,112
Total revenue per capita, U.S.	$7,271
General revenue	$23,572,816
Intergovernmental revenue	$9,025,194
Taxes	$10,203,241
General sales	$2,896,252
Selective sales	$1,998,095
License taxes	$472,828
Individual income taxes	$3,417,779
Corporate income taxes	$516,523
Other taxes	$901,764
Current charges	$3,087,125
Miscellaneous general revenue	$1,257,256
Utility revenue	$0
Liquor store revenue	$0
Insurance trust revenue[1]	$7,483,484

Note: (1) Within insurance trust revenue, net earnings of state retirement systems is a calculated statistic, and thus can be positive or negative. Net earnings is the sum of earnings on investments plus gains on investments minus losses on investments.
Source: U.S. Census Bureau, 2011 Annual Survey of State Government Finances

State Government Expenditures, 2011

In thousands of dollars, except for per capita figures

Total expenditure	$29,369,940
Total expenditure per capita, State	$6,726
Total expenditure per capita, U.S.	$6,427
Intergovernmental expenditure	$5,069,137
Direct expenditure	$24,300,803
Current operation	$16,042,722
Capital outlay	$2,041,224
Insurance benefits and repayments	$4,693,757
Assistance and subsidies	$831,120
Interest on debt	$691,980
Utility expenditure	$0
Liquor store expenditure	$0
Insurance trust expenditure	$4,693,757

Source: U.S. Census Bureau, 2011 Annual Survey of State Government Finances

State Government General Expenditures by Function, 2011

In thousands of dollars

Education	$9,415,111
Public welfare	$7,334,231
Hospitals	$1,135,081
Health	$770,728
Highways	$1,935,661
Police protection	$195,356
Correction	$518,890
Natural resources	$357,155
Parks and recreation	$110,142
Governmental administration	$879,616
Interest on general debt	$691,980
Other and unallocable	$1,332,232

Source: U.S. Census Bureau, 2011 Annual Survey of State Government Finances

State Government Finances, Cash and Debt, 2011

In thousands of dollars, except for per capita figures

Debt at end of fiscal year	
State, total	$14,522,026
State, per capita	$3,326
U.S., per capita	$3,635
Cash and security holdings	
State, total	$39,925,843
State, per capita	$9,143
U.S., per capita	$11,759

Source: U.S. Census Bureau, 2011 Annual Survey of State Government Finances

POLITICS

Composition of the Senate, 1995–2013

Congress (Year)	State/U.S	Dem	Rep	Total
104th (1995)	State delegates	1	1	2
	Total U.S.	48	52	100
105th (1997)	State delegates	1	1	2
	Total U.S.	45	55	100
106th (1999)	State delegates	0	2	2
	Total U.S.	45	55	100
107th (2001)	State delegates	0	2	2
	Total U.S.	50	50	100
108th (2003)	State delegates	0	2	2
	Total U.S.	48	51	100
109th (2005)	State delegates	0	2	2
	Total U.S.	44	55	100
110th (2007)	State delegates	0	2	2
	Total U.S.	49	49	100
111th (2009)	State delegates	0	2	2
	Total U.S.	57	41	100
112th (2011)	State delegates	0	2	2
	Total U.S.	51	47	100
113th (2013)	State delegates	0	2	2
	Total U.S.	54	45	100

Note: Figures are for the starts of first sessions; Totals include Democratic (Dem) and Republican (Rep) members as well as vacancies and seats held by independent party members
Source: U.S. Congress, Congressional Directory

Composition of the House of Representatives, 1995–2013

Congress (Year)	State/U.S	Dem	Rep	Total
104th (1995)	State delegates	2	4	6
	Total U.S.	204	230	435
105th (1997)	State delegates	1	5	6
	Total U.S.	207	226	435
106th (1999)	State delegates	1	5	6
	Total U.S.	211	223	435
107th (2001)	State delegates	1	5	6
	Total U.S.	212	221	435
108th (2003)	State delegates	1	5	6
	Total U.S.	205	229	435
109th (2005)	State delegates	1	5	6
	Total U.S.	202	231	435
110th (2007)	State delegates	2	4	6
	Total U.S.	233	198	435
111th (2009)	State delegates	2	4	6
	Total U.S.	256	178	435
112th (2011)	State delegates	2	4	6
	Total U.S.	193	242	435
113th (2013)	State delegates	1	5	6
	Total U.S.	201	234	435

Note: Figures are for the starts of first sessions; Totals include Democratic (Dem) and Republican (Rep) members as well as vacancies and seats held by independent party members
Source: U.S. Congress, Congressional Directory

Composition of State Legislature, 2004–2013

Year	Democrats	Republicans	Total
State Senate			
2004	16	22	38
2005	15	22	38
2006	15	22	38
2007	16	21	38
2008	15	22	38
2009	15	21	38
2010	17	20	38
2011	15	22	38
2012	15	22	38
2013	14	23	38
State House			
2004	63	36	100
2005	57	43	100
2006	57	43	100
2007	61	39	100
2008	64	36	100
2009	65	35	100
2010	65	35	100
2011	58	42	100
2012	59	40	100
2013	55	45	100

Note: Totals may include minor party members and vacancies
Source: The Council of State Governments, State Legislatures

Voter Participation in Presidential Elections, 1980–2012

Year	Voting-eligible State Population	State Voter Turnout Rate	U.S. Voter Turnout Rate
1980	2,562,572	50.5	54.2
1984	2,643,027	51.8	55.2
1988	2,680,364	49.3	52.8
1992	2,772,600	53.8	58.1
1996	2,880,808	48.2	51.7
2000	2,955,628	52.2	54.2
2004	3,057,741	58.7	60.1
2008	3,152,629	57.9	61.6
2012	3,248,303	55.3	58.2

Note: All figures are based on the voting-eligible population which excludes person ineligible to vote such as non-citizens, felons (depending on state law), and mentally-incapacitated persons. U.S. figures include the overseas eligible population (including military personnel).
Source: McDonald, Michael P., United States Election Project, Presidential Voter Turnout Rates, 1980–2012

Governors Since Statehood

Isaac Shelby (O) 1792-1796
James Garrard (O) 1796-1804
Christopher Greenup (O) 1804-1808
Charles Scott (O) 1808-1812
Isaac Shelby (O) 1812-1816
George Madison (O) . . . . (d) 1816
Gabriel Slaughter (O) 1816-1820
John Adair (O) 1820-1824
Joseph Desha (O) 1824-1828
Thomas Metcalfe (O) 1828-1832
John Breathitt (D) . . . . (d) 1832-1834

James T. Morehead (O) 1834-1836
James Clark (O) . . . . (d) 1836-1839
Charles A. Wickliffe (O) 1839-1840
Robert P. Letcher (O) 1840-1844
William Owsley (O) 1844-1848
John J. Crittenden (O) . . . . (r) 1848-1850
John L. Helm (O) 1850-1851
Lazarus W. Powell (D) 1851-1855
Charles S. Morehead (O) 1855-1859
Beriah Magoffin (D) . . . . (r) 1859-1862
James F. Robinson (O) 1862-1863
Thomas E. Bramlette (O) 1863-1867
John L. Helm (D) . . . . (d) 1867
John W. Stevenson (D) . . . . (r) 1867-1871
Preston H. Leslie (D) 1871-1875
James B. McCreary (D) 1875-1879
Luke P. Blackburn (D) 1879-1883
James Proctor Knott (D) 1883-1887
Simon B. Buckner (D) 1887-1891
John Young Brown (D) 1891-1895
William O. Bradley (R) . . . . (r) 1895-1899
William S. Taylor (R) . . . . (i) 1899-1900
William Goebel (D) . . . . (d) 1900
John C. W. Beckham (D) 1900-1907
Augustus E. Willson (R) 1907-1911
James B. McCreary (D) 1911-1915
Augustus O. Stanley (D) . . . . (r) 1915-1919
James D. Black (D) 1919
Edwin P. Morrow (R) 1919-1923
William J. Fields (D) 1923-1927
Flemon D. Sampson (R) 1927-1931
Ruby Laffoon (D) 1931-1935
Albert B. Chandler (D) . . . . (r) 1935-1939
Keen Johnson (D) 1939-1943
Simeon S. Willis (R) 1943-1947
Earle C. Clements (D) . . . . (r) 1947-1950
Lawrence W. Wetherby (D) 1950-1955
Albert B. Chandler (D) 1955-1959
Bert T. Combs (D) 1959-1963
Edward T. Breathitt (D) 1963-1967
Louis B. Nunn (R) 1967-1971
Wendell H. Ford (D) . . . . (r) 1971-1974
Julian M. Carroll (D) 1974-1980
John Y. Brown Jr. (D) 1980-1984
Martha Layne Collins (D) 1984-1987
Wallace G. Wilkinson (D) 1987-1991
Brereton C. Jones (D) 1991-1995
Paul E. Patton (D) 1995-2003
Ernie Fletcher (R) 2003-2007
Steve Beshear (D) . . . . 2007-2015 (term limits)

Note: (D) Democrat; (R) Republican; (O) Other party; (r) resigned; (d) died in office; (i) removed from office

Louisiana

Location: Gulf coast

Area and rank: 43,566 square miles (112,836 square kilometers); 51,843 square miles (134,273 square kilometers) including water; thirty-third largest state in area

Coastline: 397 miles (639 kilometers) on the Gulf of Mexico

Shoreline: 7,721 miles (12,426 kilometers)

Population and rank: 4,601,893 (2012 estimate); twenty-fifth largest state in population

Capital city: Baton Rouge (229,553 people in 2010 census)

Largest city: New Orleans (343,829 people in 2010 census, −29.1 percent since 2000 census, due to Hurricane Katrina in 2005)

State capitol building in Baton Rouge. (Wikimedia Commons)

Became territory: March 26, 1804

Entered Union and rank: April 30, 1812; eighteenth state

Present constitution adopted: 1974

Parishes (counties): 64

State name: Louisiana takes its name from France's King Louis XIV

State nickname: Pelican State; Sportsman's Paradise; Creole State; Sugar State

Motto: Union, justice, and confidence

State flag: Blue field with state seal design and the state motto on a banner below

Highest point: Driskill Mountain—535 feet (163 meters)

Lowest point: New Orleans— –8 feet (–2 meters)

Highest recorded temperature: 114 degrees Fahrenheit (46 degrees Celsius)—Plain Dealing, 1936

Lowest recorded temperature: –16 degrees Fahrenheit (–27 degrees Celsius)—Minden, 1899

State songs: "Give Me Louisiana"; "You Are My Sunshine" ("Belle Louisiane" is an unofficial French song)

State tree: Bald cypress

State flower: Magnolia

State bird: Pelican

Louisiana History

Much of Louisiana lies in the Mississippi Alluvial Plain, flat lands that stretch from each side of the Mississippi River. As the river moves south to the Gulf of Mexico, the elevation of the land becomes progressively lower, and most of it is damp and swampy. Far western and northwestern Louisiana is part of the West Gulf Coastal Plain. In the northern area of this region, the land is hilly, and it becomes prairie farther south. On the eastern side, near Mississippi, it lies in the East Gulf Coastal Plain, which is similar to the territory in the west. These three regions correspond roughly to the historical and cultural divisions of Louisiana. The swampy south central and southwestern areas have corresponded to French Roman Catholic Louisiana. The western region and the eastern region have been home to mostly Protestant, English-speaking people.

Early History. During prehistoric times, Louisiana was populated by people who lived in highly organized farming societies. These societies are often known as the Mound Builders, after the great ceremonial earth mounds they constructed. The Mound Builders may be divided into the people of the Hopewell culture, who flourished from about the first century until about 800 C.E., and the people of the Mississippian culture, who were present from about 800 C.E. until about 1500.

When the Europeans arrived, Louisiana was inhabited by Native Americans of three language groups. Those of the Caddoan language group lived in the northwestern area. Those who spoke Muskogean languages lived in east central Louisiana near the Mississippi River. Speakers of the Tunican languages generally lived near the coast of the Gulf of Mexico. Louisiana's Native American population

St. Philip Street at Royal Street, in the heart of the French Quarter, reflects the architecture of Louisiana's early history as a French colony. (Creative Commons)

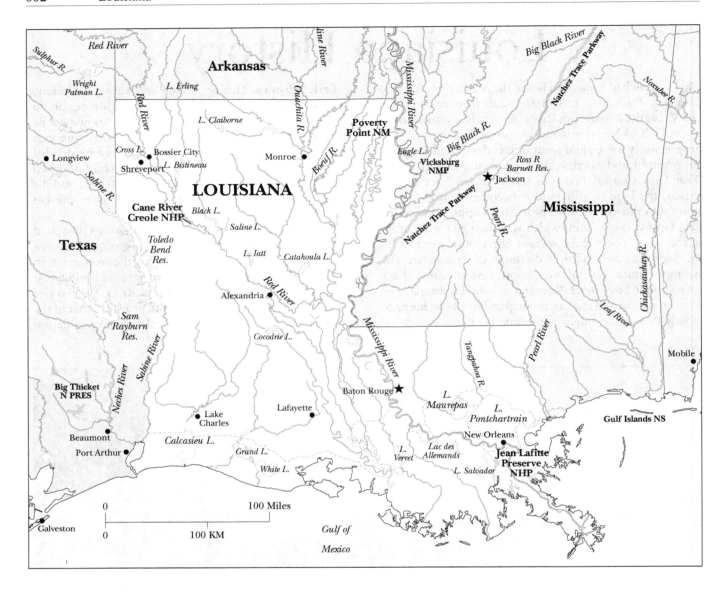

declined as a result of warfare, diseases introduced by the Europeans, and intermarriages with Americans of European and African descent. Some, such as the majority of the Choctaw nation, were forced westward into Indian territory in modern Oklahoma by the U.S. government during the 1830's. Contemporary Louisiana is home to communities of the Chitimacha, Houma, Tunica-Biloxi, Coushatta, and Choctaw.

Exploration and Settlement. The Spanish and the French were the first Europeans to explore the territory of the lower Mississippi River. In 1542, a Spanish expedition led by Hernando de Soto crossed through Louisiana. At the end of the seventeenth century, the French explorer René-Robert Cavelier, sieur de La Salle, journeyed down the Mississippi River to its mouth and claimed all of the land drained by the Mississippi in the name of France. La Salle named this huge expanse of territory Louisiana, in honor of King Louis XIV of France.

In 1718, the French explorer Jean-Baptiste Le Moyne de Bienville founded a settlement at a strategic location near the mouth of the Mississippi on the shores of the lake that the French had named Lake Pontchartrain. Bienville named his settlement Nouvelle-Orléans (New Orleans) in honor of the regent of France, the duke of Orleans. In 1722, New Orleans would become the capital of Louisiana.

The Acadians, or Cajuns, one of Louisiana's best-known population groups, arrived in the region between 1763 and 1788. These were French-speaking people from the former French colony of Acadia in Canada expelled by British troops in the French and Indian Wars (1754-1763). The Acadians settled in the swampy areas of southwestern Louisiana and on the Mississippi just north of New Orleans. Isolation enabled them to keep the French language. Although the use of French largely disappeared in other parts of Louisiana after World War

I, it would continue to be spoken in the Acadian region.

The British conquest of Canada also greatly reduced the strategic value of Louisiana for France. In order to entice the Spanish into entering the war against Britain, France transferred ownership of Louisiana to Spain in 1762. The following year, France and Spain lost the war. The Louisiana territories east of the Mississippi River became the property of Britain, and Spain was allowed to keep the lands west of the Mississippi, including New Orleans. Many of the French Louisianans had been born in America—Creoles—but they retained a devotion to France. The French Creoles revolted against Spanish rule, but Spanish troops quickly put down the rebellion. Spain, under the influence of French ruler Napoleon Bonaparte, returned the Louisiana territories to France in 1800. Bonaparte then sold the colony to the United States in 1803 in order to fund his own wars.

The American Period. The year after the United States purchased the huge Louisiana Territory, which extended the length of the Mississippi River, the United States split the region into the District of Louisiana and the District of Orleans. The District of Orleans became modern Louisiana. In 1810, American settlers in Spanish West Florida declared their independence from Spain and asked to join the United States. The American governor of Louisiana, William C. C. Claiborne, incorporated West Florida, as far as the Pearl River, into Orleans District. In 1812, the District of Orleans entered the United States as the state of Louisiana.

English-speaking settlers from other areas of the United States moved into Louisiana in large numbers. Most white Louisianans, both French-speaking and English-speaking, were small farmers. The most prosperous crops, though, were cotton and sugarcane. Both of these were plantation crops, which required intensive labor. As a result, slavery became a prominent part of the economic and social life of the state, especially in the southwestern bayou country, where the sugarcane

flourished. Slave markets also became important to the economy of New Orleans.

One of the unique racial characteristics of Louisiana was the existence of a large group of free people of mixed race, known as the *gens de couleur libres*, or free people of color. Free people of color were sometimes quite prosperous and even owned slaves. According to historian John Hope Franklin, 3,000 of the 10,689 free people of color in New Orleans were slave owners.

Civil War and Reconstruction. By the 1850's, the southern states, which were dependent on agriculture and slavery, were losing control of the U.S. Congress and presidency to the industrialized North. Many southerners believed that the southern way of life, including the institution of slavery, could only be preserved by seceding from the United States. In 1861, after the election of U.S. president Abraham Lincoln, southern states began declaring their independence. Louisiana withdrew from the union on April 12, 1861. One year later, though, the U.S. Navy captured New Orleans and soon afterward captured Baton Rouge.

Louisiana still had a large number of people of mixed race after the Civil War, and many of them were well educated. They made up the core of Louisiana's black political leadership during Reconstruction (1866-1877), when about one-third of the state's governmental leaders were black. In 1872, Louisiana's P. B. S. Pinchback became the first black governor in the United States.

After the withdrawal of Union troops, whites in the state reacted against Reconstruction violently. Taking control of the government, whites systematically excluded African Americans from many areas of public life. Legal segregation and the prevention of voting and political organization by African Americans continued until the 1960's, when Louisiana became a focal point of the Civil Rights movement.

Huey Long's Legacy. Louisiana continued to be a rural and agricultural state after the Civil War. During the

A barge that landed in the Lower 9th Ward of a New Orleans' neighborhood during Hurricane Katrina following the nearby Industrial Canal levee breach. (Creative Commons)

1920's, prices of agricultural goods, especially cotton, dropped. The charismatic politician Huey P. Long rose to power by championing the interests of workers and small farmers. One of Long's chief targets was Standard Oil Company, which had begun operating in Louisiana after the discovery of oil and gas deposits during the early twentieth century. Brilliant and ruthless, Long became governor in 1928. In 1930, he was elected U.S. senator, but he waited until 1932 to take his seat in the Senate, placing a hand-picked successor in the governor's position.

By the time Long was assassinated in 1935, he had almost total control over the Louisiana government. He helped to improve the lives of many Louisianans, but he also raised the level of corruption in state government. The Long political machine continued to operate under Huey's brother Earl Long through the 1950's, and the good and bad legacies of Huey Long would long remain with Louisiana politics.

Social and Economic Change. Although historically Louisiana has been a rural and agricultural state, the period after World War II saw substantial movement to cities. By 1990, 68 percent of Louisiana's people lived in urban areas. Sugarcane and rice farming continued to be economically important, but these agricultural activities became heavily mechanized and use only a small amount of human labor, mostly at planting and harvest times. Oil mining became increasingly important during the late twentieth century, and among the fifty states, Louisiana is second only to Texas in oil production.

Louisiana has one of the largest African American populations in the United States. About one out of every three Louisianans self-identified as African American in 1997. Despite the state's history of slavery and racial segregation, black Louisianans have made substantial progress toward political equality. During the 1990's, the state legislature was 16 percent black, and by 1992 two black Louisianans held elected office in the U.S. House of Representatives. One of these representatives, Cleo Fields, made it into the runoffs for governor in 1996. Despite these advances, incomes and living conditions of African Americans in Louisiana lagged far behind those of white residents. It also appeared that racism was still prevalent. David Duke, a former leader of the Ku Klux Klan, won a majority of white votes in the 1991 election for governor. Duke was defeated only because black voters turned out in record numbers.

Politics and Elections. Aspects of the 2000 election in Louisiana illustrated general tensions in the national electoral system. In early October, the U.S. Justice Department dispatched eight observers to St. Joseph, Louisiana, to ensure the fairness of the municipal primary election, in compliance with the Voting Rights Act of 1965. Their presence was necessary to ensure fair treatment of African American voters. In the general election, all seven incumbents to the U.S. House of Representatives were easily reelected. In presidential polling, Republican George W. Bush defeated Democrat Al Gore by 53–45 percent.

In 2002, with divided opposition, U.S. senator and Democratic incumbent Mary Landrieu retained her seat with less than 50 percent of the vote. In 2003, the first round of voting found Republican Piyush "Bobby" Jindal in the lead (33 percent) and Lieutenant Governor Kathleen Blanco trailing in second (18 percent). In the November runoff, however, Blanco, who ran as a pro-life Democrat, beat Jindal by 52 to 48 percent to become the state's first woman governor. In 2004, George W. Bush again won the state in presidential polling, this time with 57 percent of the vote. Republican David Vitter won the U.S. Senate seat vacated by retiring senator John Breaux, with 51 percent against a divided opposition.

Hurricane Katrina. On August 29, 2005, Hurricane Katrina made landfall in Louisiana, near the city of Buras-Triumph. The storm, a strong Category 3 hurricane that had just been downgraded from Category 4, had already made landfall in Florida, where it did considerable damage and killed fourteen people. It proceeded to do catastrophic damage to Louisiana and neighboring states Mississippi and Alabama, killing more than eighteen hundred people, including nearly sixteen hundred in Louisiana. Soon after the storm struck, its storm surge caused Lake Pontchartrain, on the northern edge of New Orleans, to rise and flood communities along its shores. Bridges were destroyed and some 900,000 people in the state were left without power.

The storm surge also caused breeches to the levees protecting the city of New Orleans. Since much of the city lay below the level of surrounding waters, the result was catastrophic flooding of about 80 percent of the city, as well as surrounding parishes. Although much of the city had been evacuated, thousands of residents who were unable, or in some cases unwilling, to leave were trapped inside their homes. About fifty-eight thousand National Guard members were deployed to keep order and rescue victims.

During the days that followed, thousands took refuge in the New Orleans Superdome, where terrible conditions added to the suffering. Looting and violence were commonplace in much of the city. Local, state, and federal government responses to the situation were inadequate. In the deluge of recriminations afterward, the Federal Emergency Management Agency (FEMA) was singled out for mismanagement. However, the City of New Orleans, its mayor, Ray Nagin, and Louisiana's state government led by Governor Blanco also shouldered much of the blame. Total damage was estimated at $150 billion.

FEMA spent hundreds of millions of dollars on relief, and by mid-2006 it was still housing 100,000 people in trailers. The Bush administration sought $105 billion for aid and reconstruction. The fallout from Katrina continued unabated, and by the one-year anniversary of the storm, tens of thousands of New Orleans residents had not returned and much of the city remained in ruin. Books and public conferences analyzed the catastrophe and spread copious amounts of blame and recrimination on all sides.

Deepwater Horizon. On April 20, 2010, the Deepwater Horizon oil rig exploded. Located about 41 miles off the coast of Louisiana, the resultant oil spill caused severe damage to the economy and natural environment of Louisiana, Mississippi, Alabama, and Florida. Louisiana was most directly and severely affected.

The disaster was the largest oil spill in history (excluding those caused intentionally during the Iraqi invasion of Kuwait in 1990–1991. The Deepwater Horizon accident is estimated to have released more than 4.9 million barrels of crude oil into Gulf of Mexico waters. British Petroleum at first denied this figure was an exaggeration, but during the surrounding controversy, confidential internal emails of the company revealed similar figures. As late as 2013, the discovery of tar mats and balls led to the closure of waters to commercial fishing.

The oil platform was a semi-submersible, mobile, floating rig designed to operate in water up to 10,000 feet in depth. The Korean-built rig was owned by Transocean, registered under the flag of the Marshall Islands, and was chartered to British Petroleum. At the time of the explosion, the rig was drilling a 35,000-foot-deep well under the seabed, some 5,100 feet below the surface of the sea. The accident came when high-pressure methane gas rose through the drilling pipes, igniting in the drilling rig. Most of the 126 crew members aboard survived, but the bodies of 11 workers were never located, despite extensive search by the Coast Guard.

Satellite imagery showed that the oil spill affected about 68,000 square miles of ocean, and oil washed ashore along some 125 miles of the Gulf States by June 2010, and by October, it had spread to Texas as well. By July 2011, the impacted shoreline was estimated to exceed 1000 miles. By early 2012, oil was still found on more than 200 miles of Louisiana shoreline, and in 2013, more than 2.7 million pounds of oiled material, including vegetation, sands, and absorbent barrier were removed from the Louisiana shoreline, and tar balls continued to wash ashore.

Carl L. Bankston III
Updated by the Editor

Scene of "Promiscuous Maskers on Canal Street" at New Orleans Mardi Gras in 1893, with the Henry Clay statue on Canal Street in the background. (Wikimedia Commons)

Louisiana Time Line

1500's	Mound Builder cultures flourish along the Mississippi River and in other areas of eastern North America.
1541-1542	Hernando de Soto discovers the Mississippi River.
Apr. 9, 1682	René-Robert Cavelier, sieur de La Salle, claims all territory drained by the Mississippi River for Louis XIV of France, for whom Louisiana is named.
1718	New Orleans is founded.
1722	France moves capital of the Louisiana colonies from Biloxi to New Orleans.
1763	Treaty of Paris transfers Louisiana to Spain.
1764	First Acadian families begin arriving in Louisiana.
Dec. 30, 1803	United States purchases the Louisiana Territory from France for fifteen million dollars.
Mar. 26, 1804	Louisiana is divided into the District of Orleans (modern Louisiana) and the District of Louisiana at 33 degrees latitude.
1810	American settlers in Spanish West Florida rebel against Spain; after a brief period of independence, West Florida becomes part of the District of Orleans.
Apr. 30, 1812	District of Orleans enters the United States as the state of Louisiana.
Jan. 8, 1815	U.S. general Andrew Jackson wins the Battle of New Orleans against the invading British.
1838	New Orleans holds its first Mardi Gras parade.
1849	State capital is moved from New Orleans to Baton Rouge.
Apr. 12, 1861	Louisiana votes to secede from the Union.
Apr. 25, 1862	U.S. Navy captures New Orleans.
1868	Louisiana ratifies a new state constitution, granting blacks social and civil rights, and is readmitted to the United States.
Nov. 1872	After the impeachment of Governor Henry C. Warmoth for corruption, Lieutenant Governor P. B. S. Pinchback becomes the first black governor in the United States.
1877	Reconstruction in Louisiana ends with the election of Democratic governor Francis T. Nicholls.
May 12, 1898	Louisiana adopts a new set of voting qualifications that take the vote away from almost all black Louisianans and many poor whites.
1901	First oil in Louisiana is discovered near the town of Jennings.
1915	New Orleans-style music becomes popularly known as "jazz."
1928	Huey P. Long is elected governor of Louisiana.
Sept. 8, 1935	Dr. Carl D. Weiss assassinates Long in Baton Rouge.
1947	Kerr-McGee Corporation drills the first deep-water, off-shore oil well off the Louisiana coast, with operations based in Morgan City.
1958	State legislature votes to close desegregated schools.
1963	In the midst of controversy over integration, Tulane University in New Orleans accepts first black students.
1975	Super Dome in New Orleans is completed.
1977	Ernest N. (Dutch) Morial is elected the first black mayor of New Orleans.
1979	David Treen becomes the first Republican governor of Louisiana since Reconstruction.
1983	Edwin W. Edwards becomes the first Louisiana governor to be elected to three terms.
1988	Louisiana has the country's highest high school dropout rate.
1991	Edwards wins a historic fourth term in a runoff against former Ku Klux Klansman David Duke.
Nov. 7, 2000	George W. Bush wins state's nine electoral votes; all seven congressional incumbents retain their seats.
Oct. 21, 2002	Four-term Louisiana governor Edwin Edwards begins serving ten-year sentence in federal prison for racketeering and conspiracy.
May 9, 2003	Russell Long, scion of the Long political dynasty and the only senator in U.S. history to be preceded in the Senate by both parents, dies at eighty-four.
Nov. 15, 2003	Kathleen Blanco wins runoff election to become the state's first woman governor.
Aug. 29, 2005	Hurricane Katrina makes landfall in Louisiana; storm surge causes breeches in New Orleans levees, subsequently flooding and ruining the city and killing hundreds.
Apr. 20, 2010	The Deepwater Horizon oil rig explodes 41 miles off the coast of Louisiana. The resultant oil spill causes severe damage to the economy and natural environment of Louisiana and several other states, however Louisiana is most directly and severely affected.

Notes for Further Study

Published Sources. Author Carl A. Brasseaux is one of the most prolific and respected authorities on Louisiana history, especially on the history of Acadian Louisiana. Brasseaux's *Acadian to Cajun: Transformation of a People, 1803–1877* (1992) is particularly recommended for its accurate, well-documented view of changing life in southwestern Louisiana. *Creoles of Color in the Bayou Country* (1996), also by Brasseaux, gives a fascinating account of Louisiana's free people of color. *The Historical Atlas of Louisiana* (1995) gives the places and facts of Louisiana history. For a short general overview of Louisiana history, readers should consult *A Guide to the History of Louisiana* (1982), edited by Light Townsend Cummins and Glen Jeansonne. *Creole: The History and Legacy of Louisiana's Free People of Color* (2000), edited by Sybil Kein, examines the ethnic roots of the Creoles and analyzes their contributions to the state's history.

Although an older title, one of the best books on Louisiana's complicated political history is T. Harry Williams's biography *Huey Long* (1969). Another book that details Long's career is Richard D. White, Jr.'s, *Kingfish: The Reign of Huey P. Long* (2006). For later political history, two books by Louisiana political commentator John Maginnis are highly recommended. *The Last Hayride* (1984) looks at the controversial political career of three-term governor Edwin W. Edwards. *In Cross to Bear* (1992), Maginnis looks at the 1991 Louisiana gubernatorial campaign, in which Edwards, who was accused of massive corruption and frequently indicted by federal authorities, ran against David Duke, former Grand Wizard of the Ku Klux Klan and alleged neo-Nazi. Wayne Parent explores modern state politics with *Inside the Carnival: Unmasking Louisiana Politics* (2004). Historian and New Orleans resident Douglas Brinkley examines a pre-eminent social and political event in Louisiana's history—Hurricane Katrina—in *The Great Deluge: Hurricane Katrina, New Orleans, and the Mississippi Gulf Coast* (2006).

New Orleans is the subject of many books and articles. *Classic New Orleans* (1993), with text by William R. Mitchell and photographs by James R. Lockhart, is a beautifully illustrated guide to the architecture and neighborhoods of the city. *Time and Place in New Orleans: Past Geographies in the Present Day* (2002) by Richard Campanella is an award-winning discussion of the way in which New Orleans's singular topography and geography influenced the city's growth and development. The second edition of the classic historical geography of New Orleans, Peirce F. Lewis's *New Orleans: The Making of an Urban Landscape*, was published in 2003.

Web Resources. A good starting place for obtaining information about Louisiana is the state of Louisiana Web site (louisiana.gov), which offers access to Louisiana state government sites. By clicking on Explore, the Internet user can find sites on the state's people, culture, history, demographics and census information, climate, and other topics. Those interested in the Civil War history of Louisiana should look at the Civil War in Louisiana site (www.civiliantraveler.com/TRANS/LA), which provides links to numerous short articles relating to the topic. American Civil War.com (www.americancivilwar.com/statepic/louisiana.html) also has a good map of critical battles fought within the state.

Louisiana.com (www.louisianatravel.com) offers updated news on entertainment and attractions in the state. Louisiana is known for its unique culture, especially for its music. Both LouisianaRadio.com (www.louisianaradio.com) and New Orleans Music (www.louisianamusicfactory.com/) are devoted entirely to local and regional music of Louisiana.

April 2010 Deepwater Horizon tragedy in the Gulf of Mexico. (U.S. Coast Guard)

Counties

Parish	2012 Population	Pop. Rank	Land Area (sq. miles)	Area Rank
Acadia	61,912	18	655.12	30
Allen	25,539	37	761.85	23
Ascension	112,286	13	289.98	58
Assumption	23,026	41	338.66	56
Avoyelles	41,632	28	832.43	18
Beauregard	36,281	31	1,157.34	7
Bienville	14,076	55	811.27	19
Bossier	122,197	12	840.06	17
Caddo	257,093	4	878.54	12
Calcasieu	194,493	7	1,063.66	9
Caldwell	10,004	60	529.42	46
Cameron	6,702	63	1,284.89	3
Catahoula	10,292	59	708.03	26
Claiborne	16,828	50	754.88	24
Concordia	20,365	48	696.92	27
De Soto	26,963	36	875.58	14

Parish	2012 Population	Pop. Rank	Land Area (sq. miles)	Area Rank
East Baton Rouge	444,526	1	455.37	48
East Carroll	7,526	62	420.70	50
East Feliciana	20,008	49	453.41	49
Evangeline	33,710	32	662.38	29
Franklin	20,561	47	624.59	35
Grant	22,068	44	643.03	33
Iberia	73,999	17	574.11	41
Iberville	33,228	33	618.63	37
Jackson	16,216	51	569.18	42
Jefferson	433,676	2	295.63	57
Jefferson Davis	31,432	34	651.33	31
LaSalle	14,927	54	624.68	34
Lafayette	227,055	6	268.72	60
Lafourche	97,029	15	1,068.21	8
Lincoln	46,953	24	471.74	47
Livingston	131,942	10	648.17	32

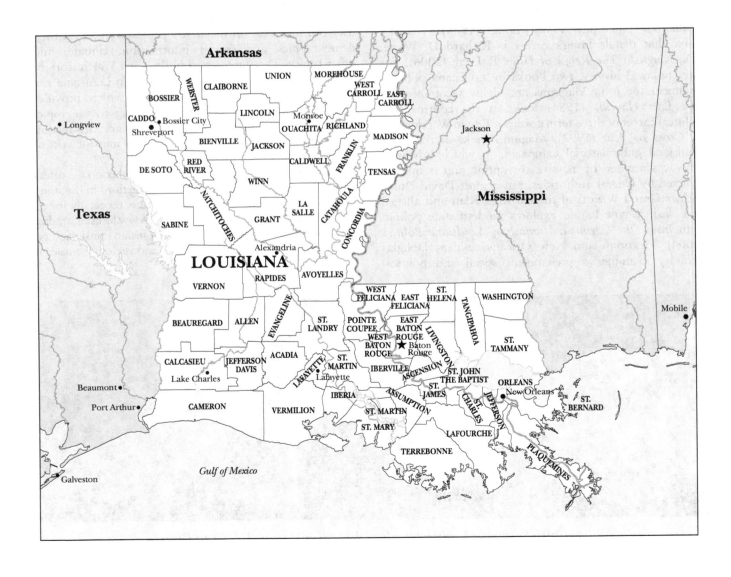

Parish	2012 Population	Pop. Rank	Land Area (sq. miles)	Area Rank
Madison	12,154	56	624.44	36
Morehouse	27,559	35	794.93	20
Natchitoches	39,436	30	1,252.25	4
Orleans	369,250	3	169.42	64
Ouachita	155,363	8	610.41	38
Plaquemines	23,921	40	779.91	22
Pointe Coupee	22,726	42	557.35	44
Rapides	132,373	9	1,317.96	2
Red River	8,983	61	389.09	53
Richland	20,921	46	559.04	43
Sabine	24,325	38	866.66	15
St. Bernard	41,635	27	377.52	54
St. Charles	52,681	23	279.08	59
St. Helena	11,071	58	408.40	51
St. James	21,722	45	241.54	61
St. John the Baptist	44,758	26	213.07	62
St. Landry	83,662	16	923.88	11
St. Martin	52,726	22	737.65	25
St. Mary	53,697	21	555.38	45
St. Tammany	239,453	5	845.55	16
Tangipahoa	123,441	11	791.27	21
Tensas	4,954	64	602.78	39
Terrebonne	111,893	14	1,231.81	5
Union	22,419	43	876.99	13
Vermilion	58,723	19	1,173.20	6
Vernon	53,869	20	1,327.91	1
Washington	46,670	25	669.52	28
Webster	40,940	29	593.03	40
West Baton Rouge	24,106	39	192.39	63
West Carroll	11,512	57	359.65	55
West Feliciana	15,405	52	403.21	52
Winn	15,000	53	950.09	10

Source: U.S. Census Bureau, 2012 Population Estimates

Cities

With 10,000 or more residents

Legal Name	2010 Population	Pop. Rank	Land Area (sq. miles)	Area Rank
Abbeville city	12,257	41	6.04	44
Alexandria city	47,723	10	28.41	9
Baker city	13,895	33	8.30	34
Bastrop city	11,365	49	8.90	33
Baton Rouge city	229,493	2	76.95	3
Bayou Blue CDP	12,352	40	23.26	13
Bayou Cane CDP	19,355	23	7.61	38
Belle Chasse CDP	12,679	38	24.91	10
Bogalusa city	12,232	42	9.50	31
Bossier City city	61,315	8	42.34	6
Central city	26,864	17	62.24	4
Chalmette CDP	16,751	27	7.15	40
Claiborne CDP	11,507	48	9.96	30
Crowley city	13,265	35	5.75	48
DeRidder city	10,578	52	9.14	32
Denham Springs city	10,215	56	7.29	39
Destrehan CDP	11,535	47	5.91	47

Legal Name	2010 Population	Pop. Rank	Land Area (sq. miles)	Area Rank
Estelle CDP	16,377	29	5.01	51
Eunice city	10,398	53	5.13	50
Gardere CDP	10,580	51	3.39	55
Gretna city	17,736	26	4.04	52
Hammond city	20,019	22	14.01	25
Harvey CDP	20,348	21	6.57	42
Houma city	33,727	11	14.42	24
Jefferson CDP	11,193	50	2.71	57
Jennings city	10,383	54	10.40	28
Kenner city	66,702	7	14.87	22
Lafayette city	120,623	5	49.23	5
Lake Charles city	71,993	6	42.06	7
Laplace CDP	29,872	14	21.19	18
Luling CDP	12,119	43	23.30	12
Mandeville city	11,560	45	6.71	41
Marrero CDP	33,141	12	7.94	35
Metairie CDP	138,481	4	23.22	14

Legal Name	2010 Population	Pop. Rank	Land Area (sq. miles)	Area Rank
Minden city	13,082	36	14.97	21
Monroe city	48,815	9	29.21	8
Morgan City city	12,404	39	5.98	46
Moss Bluff CDP	11,557	46	15.22	20
Natchitoches city	18,323	25	22.63	15
New Iberia city	30,617	13	11.14	27
New Orleans city	343,829	1	169.42	1
Opelousas city	16,634	28	7.91	37
Pineville city	14,555	32	12.63	26
Prairieville CDP	26,895	16	22.00	16
Raceland CDP	10,193	57	21.57	17
River Ridge CDP	13,494	34	2.80	56
Ruston city	21,859	19	20.85	19

Legal Name	2010 Population	Pop. Rank	Land Area (sq. miles)	Area Rank
Shenandoah CDP	18,399	24	6.21	43
Shreveport city	199,311	3	105.38	2
Slidell city	27,068	15	14.84	23
Sulphur city	20,410	20	9.99	29
Terrytown CDP	23,319	18	3.67	53
Thibodaux city	14,566	31	6.03	45
Timberlane CDP	10,243	55	1.50	58
Waggaman CDP	10,015	58	5.50	49
West Monroe city	13,065	37	7.94	35
Woodmere CDP	12,080	44	3.65	54
Zachary city	14,960	30	23.93	11

Note: CDP–Census Designated Place
Source: U.S. Census Bureau, 2010 Census

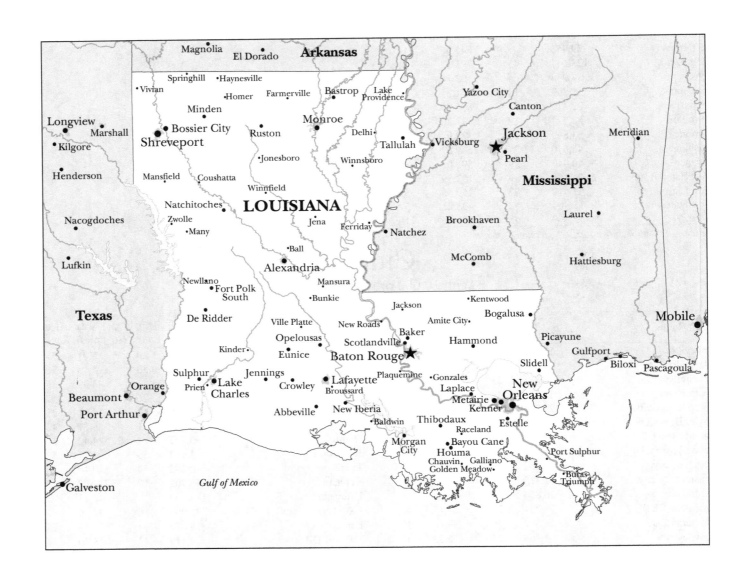

Survey Says...

This section presents current rankings from dozens of public and private sources. It shows how this state ranks in a number of critical categories, including education, job growth, cost of living, teen drivers, energy efficiency, and business environment. Sources include *Forbes, Reuters, U.S. News and World Report, CNN Money, Gallup,* and *Huffington Post.*

- CNN Money compiled a list of "Ten Most Entrepreneurial States" based on the Kauffman Index of Entrepreneurial Activity. Louisiana ranked #9 among the 50 states in 2012 for number of startups per 100,000 adult residents.
  CNN Money, June 20, 2013; money.cnn.com

- Louisiana ranked #30 in a government study measuring real gross domestic product (GDP)—the output of goods and services produced by labor and property located in the United States. The ranking is based on the percentage change compared with 2011 GDP.
  U.S. Department of Commerce, Bureau of Economic Analysis, June 2013; www.bea.gov

- Louisiana ranked #23 in a government study measuring real gross domestic product (GDP)—the output of goods and services produced by labor and property located in the United States. The ranking is based on the dollar value of its GDP.
  U.S. Department of Commerce, Bureau of Economic Analysis, June 2013; www.bea.gov

- Louisiana ranked #15 in the 17th edition of "Quality Counts; State of the States," Education Week's "report card" surveying key education indicators, policy efforts, and educational outcomes.
  Education Week, January 4, 2013 (online) and January 10, 2013 (print); www.edweek.org

- SERI (Science and Engineering Readiness Index) weighs the performance of the states' K-12 schools in preparing students in physics and calculus, the high school subjects considered most important for future scientists and engineers. Louisiana ranked #48.
  Newsletter of the Forum on Education of the American Physical Society, Summer 2011 issue; www.huffingtonpost.com, July 11, 2011; updated October 1, 2012

- Business website 24/7 Wall St. identified the states with the highest and lowest percentages of residents 25 or older with a college degree or higher. Of "America's Worst Educated States," Louisiana ranked #5 (#1 = worst).
  247wallst.com, posted October 15, 2012; consulted July 18, 2013

- MoneyRates.com ranked Louisiana #32 on its list of the best to worst states for making a living. Criteria: average income; inflation; employment prospects; and workers' Workplace Environment assessments according to the Gallup-Healthways Well-Being Index.
  www.money-rates.com, posted April 1, 2013

- *Forbes* analyzed business costs, labor supply, regulatory environment, current economic climate, growth prospects, and quality of life, to compile its "Best States for Business" rankings. Louisiana ranked #34.
  www.forbes.com. posted December 12, 2012

- The 2012 Gallup-Healthways Well-Being Index, surveyed American's opinions on economic confidence, workplace perceptions, community climate, personal choices, and health predictors to assess the "future livability" of each state. Louisiana ranked #43.
  "Utah Poised to Be the Best State to Live In," Gallup Wellbeing, www.gallup.com, August 7, 2012

- On CNBC's list of "America's Top States for Business 2013," Louisiana ranked #43. Criteria: measures of competitiveness developed with input from the National Association of Manufacturers, the Council on Competitiveness, and other business groups weighed with the states' own marketing criteria.
  www.cnbc.com, consulted July 19, 2013

- Louisiana ranked #5 on the "worst" end of the Christian Science Monitor's list of "States with the Best (and Worst) Job Growth," as indicated by year-over-year growth rates from May 2012 to May 2013.
  www.csmonitor.com, July 5, 2013

- Louisiana ranked #38 on MoneyRates list of "Best-and Worst-States to Retire 2012." Criteria: life expectancy, crime rate, climate, economic conditions, taxes, job opportunities, and cost of living.
  www.money-rates.com, October 22, 2012

- Louisiana ranked #2 on the 2013 Bankrate "Best Places to Retire" list ranking the states and District of Columbia on various criteria relating to health, safety, and cost.
  www.bankrate.com, May 6, 2013

- Louisiana ranked #46 on the Social Science Research Council's "American Human Development Report: The Measure of America," assessing the 50 states plus the District of Columbia on health, education, and living-standard criteria.
  The Measure of America 2013-2014, posted June 19, 2013; www.measureofamerica.org

- Louisiana ranked #48 on the Foundation for Child Development's (FCD) Child Well-being Index (CWI). The FCD used the KIDS COUNT report and the National Survey of Children's Health, the only state-level source for several key indicators of child well-being.
  Foundation for Child Development, January 18, 2012; fcd-us.org

- Louisiana ranked #46 overall according to the 2013 KIDS COUNT Data Book, a project of the Annie E. Casey Foundation. Criteria: children's economic well-being, education, health, and family and community indicators.
  KIDS COUNT Data Center's Data Book, released June 20, 2013; http://datacenter.kidscount.org

- Louisiana ranked #42 in the children's economic well-being category by the 2013 KIDS COUNT Data Book, a project of the Annie E. Casey Foundation.
  KIDS COUNT Data Center's Data Book, released June 20, 2013; http://datacenter.kidscount.org

- Louisiana ranked #45 in the children's educational opportunities and attainments category by the 2013 KIDS COUNT Data Book, a project of the Annie E. Casey Foundation.
  KIDS COUNT Data Center's Data Book, released June 20, 2013; http://datacenter.kidscount.org

- Louisiana ranked #41 in the children's health category by the 2013 KIDS COUNT Data Book, a project of the Annie E. Casey Foundation.
  KIDS COUNT Data Center's Data Book, released June 20, 2013; http://datacenter.kidscount.org

- Louisiana ranked #47 in the family and community circumstances that factor into children's well-being category by the 2013 KIDS COUNT Data Book, a project of the Annie E. Casey Foundation.
  KIDS COUNT Data Center's Data Book, released June 20, 2013; http://datacenter.kidscount.org

- Louisiana ranked #43 in the 2012 Gallup-Healthways Well-Being Index. Criteria: emotional health; physical health; healthy behavior; work environment; basic access to food, shelter, health care; and a safe and satisfying place to live.
  2012 State of Well-Being, Gallup-Healthways Well-Being Index, released February 28, 2013; www.well-beingindex.com

- *U.S. News and World Report's* "Best States for Teen Drivers" rankings are based on driving and road safety laws, federal reports on driver's licenses, car accident fatality, and road-quality statistics. Louisiana ranked #13.
  U.S. News and World Report, March 18, 2010; www.usnews.com

- The Yahoo! Sports service Rivals.com ranks the states according to the strength of their high school football programs. Louisiana ranked #4.
  "Ranking the States: Where Is the Best Football Played?," November 18, 2011; highschool.rivals.com

- iVillage ranked the states by hospitable living conditions for women. Criteria: economic success, access to affordable childcare, health care, reproductive rights, female representation in government, and educational attainment. Louisiana ranked #44.
  iVillage, "50 Best to Worst States for Women," March 14, 2012; www.ivillage.com

- The League of American Bicyclists's "Bicycle Friendly States" ranked Louisiana #29. Criteria: legislation and enforcement, policies and programs, infrastructure and funding, education and advocacy, and evaluation and planning.
  "Washington Tops the Bicycle-Friendly State Ranking," May 1, 2013; bicycling.com

- The federal Corporation for National and Community Service ranked the states and the District of Columbia by volunteer rates. Louisiana ranked #51 for community service.
  "Volunteering and Civic Life in America 2012," www.volunteeringinamerica.gov, accessed July 24, 2013

- The Hospital Safety Score ranked states and the District of Columbia on their hospitals' performance scores. Louisiana ranked #35. Criteria: avoiding preventable harm and medical errors, as demonstrated by 26 hospital safety metrics.
  Spring 2013 Hospital Safety Score, May 8, 2013; www.hospitalsafetyscore.org

- GMAC Insurance ranked the states and the District of Columbia by the performance of their drivers on the GMAC Insurance National Drivers Test, comprised of DMV test questions. Louisiana ranked #39.
  "2011 GMAC Insurance National Drivers Test," www.gmacinsurance.com, accessed July 23, 2013

- Louisiana ranked #15 in a "State Integrity Investigation" analysis of laws and practices intended to deter corruption and promote accountability and openness in campaign finance, ethics laws, lobbying regulations and management of state pension funds.
  "What's Your State's Grade?," www.publicintegrity.org, accessed July 23, 2013

- Louisiana ranked #23 among the states and the District of Columbia in total rail miles, as tracked by the Association of American Railroads.
  "U.S. Freight Railroad Industry Snapshot: Railroads and States: Total Rail Miles by State: 2011"; www.aar.org, accessed July 23, 2013

- According to statistics compiled by the Beer Institute, Louisiana ranked #11 among the states and the District of Columbia in per capita beer consumption of persons 21 years or older.
  "Shipments of Malt Beverages and Per Capita Consumption by State 2012;" www.beerinstitute.org

- According to Concordia University's "Public Education Costs per Pupil by State Rankings," based on statistics gathered by the U.S. Census Bureau, which includes the District of Columbia, Louisiana ranked #25.
  Concordia University Online; education.cu-portland.edu, accessed July 24, 2013

- Louisiana ranked #24 among the states and the District of Columbia in population density based on U.S. Census Bureau data for resident population and total land area. "List of U.S. States by Population Density."
  www.wikipedia.org, accessed July 24, 2013

- In "America's Health Rankings, 2012 Edition," by the United Health Foundation, Louisiana ranked #49. Criteria included: rate of high school graduation; violent crime rate; incidence of infectious disease; childhood immunizations; prevalence of diabetes; per capita public-health funding; percentage of uninsured population; rate of children in poverty; and availability of primary-care physicians.
  United Health Foundation; www.americashealthrankings.org, accessed July 24, 2013

- The TechNet 2012 "State Broadband Index" ranked Louisiana #47 on the following criteria: broadband adoption; network quality; and economic structure. Improved broadband use is hoped to promote economic development, build strong communities, improve delivery of government services and upgrade educational systems.
  TechNet; www.technet.org, accessed July 24, 2013

- Louisiana was ranked #43 among the states and District of Columbia on the American Council for an Energy-Efficient Economy's "State Energy Efficiency Scorecard" for 2012.
  American Council for an Energy-Efficient Economy; aceee.org/sector/state-policy/scorecard, accessed July 24, 2013

Statistical Tables

DEMOGRAPHICS
Resident State and National Population, 1950-2012
Projected State and National Population, 2000-2030
Population by Age, 2012
Population by Race, 2012
Population by Hispanic Origin and Race, 2012

VITAL STATISTICS
Death Rates by Leading Causes, 2010
Death Rates by Selected Causes, 2010
Abortion Rates, 2009
Infant Mortality Rates, 1995-2009
Marriage and Divorce Rates, 2000-2011

ECONOMY
Nominal Gross Domestic Product by Industry, 2012
Real Gross Domestic Product, 2000-2012
Personal Income Per Capita, 1930-2012
Non-Farm Employment by Sector, 2012
Foreign Exports, 2000-2012
Energy Consumption, 2011

LAND AND WATER
Surface Area and Federally-Owned Land, 2007
Land Cover/Use of Non-Federal Rural Land, 2007
Farms and Crop Acreage, 2012

HEALTH AND MEDICAL CARE
Medical Professionals, 2012
Health Insurance Coverage, 2011
HIV, STD, and Tuberculosis Cases and Rates, 2011
Cigarette Smoking, 2011

HOUSING
Home Ownership Rates, 1995-2012
Home Sales, 2000-2010
Value of Owner-Occupied Homes, 2011

EDUCATION
School Enrollment, 2011
Educational Attainment, 2011
Public College Finances, FY 2012

TRANSPORTATION AND TRAVEL
Motor Vehicle Registrations and Drivers Licenses, 2011
Domestic Travel Expenditures, 2009
Retail Gasoline Prices, 2013
Public Road Length, 2011

CRIME AND LAW ENFORCEMENT
Full-Time Law Enforcement Officers, 2011
Prison Population, 2000-2012
Crime Rate, 2011

GOVERNMENT AND FINANCE
Local Governments by Type, 2012
State Government Revenue, 2011
State Government Expenditures, 2011
State Government General Expenditures by Function, 2011
State Government Finances, Cash and Debt, 2011

POLITICS
Composition of the Senate, 1995-2013
Composition of the House of Representatives, 1995-2013
Composition of State Legislature, 2004-2013
Voter Participation in Presidential Elections, 1980-2012
Governors Since Statehood

DEMOGRAPHICS

Resident State and National Population, 1950–2012

Year	State Population	U.S. Population	State Share
1950	2,684,000	151,326,000	1.77%
1960	3,257,000	179,323,000	1.82%
1970	3,644,637	203,302,031	1.79%
1980	4,205,900	226,545,805	1.86%
1990	4,219,973	248,709,873	1.70%
2000	4,469,035	281,424,600	1.59%
2010	4,533,372	308,745,538	1.47%
2012	4,601,893	313,914,040	1.47%

Note: 1950/1960 population figures are rounded to the nearest thousand.
Source: U.S. Census Bureau, Decennial Census 1950–2010; U.S. Census Bureau, 2012 Population Estimates

Projected State and National Population, 2000–2030

Year	State Population	U.S. Population	State Share
2000	4,468,976	281,421,906	1.59%
2005	4,534,310	295,507,134	1.53%
2010	4,612,679	308,935,581	1.49%
2015	4,673,721	322,365,787	1.45%
2020	4,719,160	335,804,546	1.41%
2025	4,762,398	349,439,199	1.36%
2030	4,802,633	363,584,435	1.32%
State population growth, 2000–2030			333,657
State percentage growth, 2000–2030			7.5%

Source: U.S. Census Bureau, Population Division, Interim State Population Projections, 2005

Population by Age, 2012

Age Group	State Population	Percent of Total Population State	Percent of Total Population U.S.
Under 5 years	314,766	6.8%	6.4%
5 to 14 years	620,567	13.5%	13.1%
15 to 24 years	658,326	14.3%	14.0%
25 to 34 years	652,957	14.2%	13.5%
35 to 44 years	559,506	12.2%	12.9%
45 to 54 years	633,679	13.8%	14.1%
55 to 64 years	566,887	12.3%	12.3%
65 to 74 years	341,656	7.4%	7.6%
75 to 84 years	182,809	4.0%	4.2%
85 years and older	70,740	1.5%	1.9%
Under 18 years	1,117,803	24.3%	23.5%
65 years and older	595,205	12.9%	13.7%
Median age (years)	–	35.9	37.4

Source: U.S. Census Bureau, Annual Estimates of the Resident Population for Selected Age Groups by Sex for the United States, States, Counties, and Puerto Rico Commonwealth and Municipios: April 1, 2010 to July 1, 2012

Population by Race, 2012

Race	State Population	Percent of Total Population State	Percent of Total Population U.S.
All residents	4,601,893	100.00%	100.00%
White	2,930,137	63.67%	77.89%
African American	1,491,433	32.41%	13.13%
Native American	34,249	0.74%	1.23%
Asian	77,252	1.68%	5.14%
Native Hawaiian	2,781	0.06%	0.23%
Two or more races	66,041	1.44%	2.39%

Source: U.S. Census Bureau, Population Division, Annual Estimates of the Resident Population by Sex, Race and Hispanic Origin for the United States, States, and Counties: April 1, 2010 to July 1, 2012

Population by Hispanic Origin and Race, 2012

Hispanic Origin/Race	State Population	Percent of Total Population State	Percent of Total Population U.S.
All residents	4,601,893	100.00%	100.00%
All Hispanic residents	208,325	4.53%	16.89%
Hispanic			
White	174,566	3.79%	14.91%
African American	17,692	0.38%	0.79%
Native American	5,245	0.11%	0.49%
Asian	1,908	0.04%	0.17%
Native Hawaiian	1,077	0.02%	0.06%
Two or more races	7,837	0.17%	0.48%
Not Hispanic			
White	2,755,571	59.88%	62.98%
African American	1,473,741	32.02%	12.34%
Native American	29,004	0.63%	0.74%
Asian	75,344	1.64%	4.98%
Native Hawaiian	1,704	0.04%	0.17%
Two or more races	58,204	1.26%	1.91%

Source: U.S. Census Bureau, Population Division, Annual Estimates of the Resident Population by Sex, Race and Hispanic Origin for the United States, States, and Counties: April 1, 2010 to July 1, 2012

VITAL STATISTICS

Death Rates by Leading Causes, 2010

Cause	State	U.S.
Malignant neoplasms	213.7	186.2
Ischaemic heart diseases	134.5	122.9
Other forms of heart disease	82.9	53.4
Chronic lower respiratory diseases	46.3	44.7
Cerebrovascular diseases	47.9	41.9
Organic, incl. symptomatic, mental disorders	38.8	35.7
Other degenerative diseases of the nervous sys.	33.6	28.4
Other external causes of accidental injury	27.8	26.5
Diabetes mellitus	28.4	22.4
Hypertensive diseases	31.8	20.4
All causes	965.1	799.5

Note: Figures are age-adjusted death rates per 100,000 population
Source: CDC/NCHS, Underlying Cause of Death 1999–2010 on CDC WONDER Online Database

Death Rates by Selected Causes, 2010

Cause	State	U.S.
Assault	11.7	5.2
Diseases of the liver	15.3	13.9
Human immunodeficiency virus (HIV) disease	5.1	2.7
Influenza and pneumonia	21.5	16.2
Intentional self-harm	12.4	12.4
Malnutrition	1.7	0.9
Obesity and other hyperalimentation	2.2	1.8
Renal failure	27.1	14.4
Transport accidents	16.7	12.1
Viral hepatitis	2.4	2.4

Note: Figures are age-adjusted death rates per 100,000 population; A dash indicates that data was not available or was suppressed
Source: CDC/NCHS, Underlying Cause of Death 1999–2010 on CDC WONDER Online Database

Abortion Rates, 2009

Category	2009
By state of residence	
Total abortions	7,578
Abortion rate[1]	8.1%
Abortion ratio[2]	117
By state of occurrence	
Total abortions	8,167
Abortion rate[1]	8.8%
Abortion ratio[2]	126
Abortions obtained by out-of-state residents	2.1%
U.S. abortion rate[1]	15.1%
U.S. abortion ratio[2]	227

Note: (1) Number of abortions per 1,000 women aged 15–44 years; (2) Number of abortions per 1,000 live births; A dash indicates that data was not available
Source: CDC/NCHS, Morbidity and Mortality Weekly Report, November 23, 2012 (Abortion Surveillance, United States, 2009)

Infant Mortality Rates, 1995–2009

Category	1995	2000	2005	2009
All state residents	9.86	9.03	9.85	8.82
All U.S. residents	7.57	6.89	6.86	6.39
All state white residents	6.42	6.16	7.10	6.70
All U.S. white residents	6.30	5.71	5.73	5.33
All state black residents	14.90	13.05	14.08	12.20
All U.S. black residents	14.58	13.48	13.26	12.12

Note: Figures represent deaths per 1,000 live births of resident infants under one year old, exclusive of fetal deaths; A dash indicates that data was not available or was suppressed.
Source: Centers of Disease Control and Prevention, Division of Vital Statistics, Linked Birth/Infant Death Records on CDC Wonder Online

Marriage and Divorce Rates, 2000–2011

Year	Marriage Rate		Divorce Rate	
	State	U.S.	State	U.S.
2000	9.1	8.2	0.0	4.0
2002	8.1	8.0	3.3	3.9
2004	8.0	7.8	0.0	3.7
2006	0.0	7.5	0.0	3.7
2008	6.8	7.1	0.0	3.5
2010	6.9	6.8	0.0	3.6
2011	6.4	6.8	0.0	3.6

Note: Rates are based on provisional counts of marriages/divorces by state of occurrence and are per 1,000 total population residing in area
Source: CDC/NCHS, National Vital Statistics System

ECONOMY

Nominal Gross Domestic Product by Industry, 2012
In millions of current dollars

Industry	State GDP
Accommodation and food services	7,259
Administrative and waste management services	5,414
Agriculture, forestry, fishing, and hunting	2,059
Arts, entertainment, and recreation	2,330
Construction	11,332
Educational services	1,894
Finance and insurance	8,334
Health care and social assistance	14,897
Information	4,343
Management of companies and enterprises	2,406
Manufacturing	55,097
Mining	23,827
Other services, except government	5,315
Professional, scientific, and technical services	11,444
Real estate and rental and leasing	21,998
Retail trade	14,278
Transportation and warehousing	9,751
Utilities	4,967
Wholesale trade	10,594

Source: U.S. Department of Commerce, Bureau of Economic Analysis, Survey of Current Business

Real Gross Domestic Product, 2000–2012
In millions of chained 2005 dollars

Year	State GDP	U.S. GDP	State Share
2000	168,033	11,225,406	1.50%
2005	196,917	12,539,116	1.57%
2010	200,944	12,897,088	1.56%
2012	198,548	13,430,576	1.48%

Source: U.S. Department of Commerce, Bureau of Economic Analysis, Survey of Current Business

Personal Income Per Capita, 1930–2012

Year	State	U.S.
1930	$353	$618
1940	$362	$593
1950	$1,111	$1,503
1960	$1,683	$2,268
1970	$3,089	$4,084
1980	$8,767	$10,091
1990	$15,171	$19,354
2000	$23,554	$30,319
2010	$37,116	$39,791
2012	$39,413	$42,693

Source: U.S. Department of Commerce, Bureau of Economic Analysis, Regional Economic Accounts

Non-Farm Employment by Sector, 2012
In thousands

Sector	Employment
Construction	126.5
Education and health services	282.0
Financial activities	94.0
Government	350.1
Information	24.9
Leisure and hospitality	207.5
Mining and logging	54.6
Manufacturing	142.1
Other services	63.3
Professional and business services	202.5
Trade, transportation, and utilities	378.1
All sectors	1,925.6

Source: U.S. Bureau of Labor Statistics, State and Area Employment

Foreign Exports, 2000–2012
In millions of dollars

Year	State Exports	U.S. Exports	State Share
2000	16,814	712,054	2.36%
2002	17,583	649,940	2.71%
2004	19,920	768,554	2.59%
2006	23,476	973,994	2.41%
2008	41,908	1,222,545	3.43%
2010	41,370	1,208,080	3.42%
2012	62,892	1,478,268	4.25%

Note: U.S. figures exclude data from Puerto Rico, U.S. Virgin Islands, and unallocated exports
Source: U.S. Department of Commerce, International Trade Admin., Office of Trade and Industry Information, Manufacturing and Services

Energy Consumption, 2011

In trillions of BTUs, except as noted

Total energy consumption	
Total state energy consumption	4,055.3
Total U.S. energy consumption	97,387.3
State share of U.S. total	4.16%
Per capita consumption (in millions of BTUs)	
Total state per capita consumption	886.4
Total U.S. per capita consumption	312.6
End-use sectors	
Residential	371.5
Commercial	281.4
Industrial	2,679.7
Transportation	722.7
Sources of energy	
Petroleum	1,908.3
Natural gas	1,502.5
Coal	270.0
Renewable energy	127.1
Nuclear electric power	173.9

Source: U.S. Energy Information Administration, State Energy Data 2011: Consumption

LAND AND WATER

Surface Area and Federally-Owned Land, 2007

In thousands of acres

Category	State	U.S.	State Share
Total surface area	31,376.8	1,937,664.2	1.62%
Total land area	27,452.6	1,886,846.9	1.45%
Non-federal land	26,142.6	1,484,910.0	1.76%
Developed	1,862.8	111,251.2	1.67%
Rural	24,279.8	1,373,658.8	1.77%
Federal land	1,310.0	401,936.9	0.33%
Water area	3,924.2	50,817.3	7.72%

Source: U.S. Department of Agriculture, Natural Resources Conservation Service, 2007 National Resources Inventory

Land Cover/Use of Non-Federal Rural Land, 2007

In thousands of acres

Category	State	U.S.	State Share
Total rural land	24,279.8	1,373,658.8	1.77%
Cropland	5,107.3	357,023.5	1.43%
CRP[1] land	226.6	32,850.2	0.69%
Pastureland	2,458.1	118,615.7	2.07%
Rangeland	221.2	409,119.4	0.05%
Forest land	13,306.5	406,410.4	3.27%
Other rural land	2,960.1	49,639.6	5.96%

Note: (1) Conservation Reserve Program was created to assist private landowners in converting highly erodible cropland to vegetative cover.
Source: U.S. Department of Agriculture, Natural Resources Conservation Service, 2007 National Resources Inventory

Farms and Crop Acreage, 2012

Category	State	U.S.	State Share
Farms (in thousands)	29.0	2,170.0	1.34%
Acres (in millions)	8.0	914.0	0.87%
Acres per farm	274.1	421.2	–

Source: U.S. Department of Agriculture, National Agricultural Statistical Service, Quick Stats, 2012 Survey Data

HEALTH AND MEDICAL CARE

Medical Professionals, 2012

Profession	State Number	U.S. Number	State Share	State Rate[1]	U.S. Rate[1]
Physicians[2]	12,425	894,637	1.39%	271.6	287.1
Dentists	2,255	193,587	1.16%	49.3	62.1
Podiatrists	151	17,469	0.86%	3.3	5.6
Optometrists	411	45,638	0.90%	9.0	14.6
Chiropractors	614	77,494	0.79%	13.4	24.9

Note: (1) Rates are per 100,000 population; (2) Includes total, active Doctors of Osteopathic Medicine and Doctors of Medicine in 2011.
Source: U.S. Department of Health and Human Services, Bureau of Health Professions, Area Health Resource File, 2012-2013

Health Insurance Coverage, 2011

Category	State	U.S.
Total persons covered	3,568,000	260,214,000
Total persons not covered	938,000	48,613,000
Percent not covered	20.8%	15.7%
Children under age 18 covered	998,000	67,143,000
Children under age 18 not covered	131,000	6,965,000
Percent of children not covered	11.6%	9.4%

Source: U.S. Census Bureau, Current Population Survey, 2012 Annual Social and Economic Supplement

HIV, STD, and Tuberculosis Cases and Rates, 2011

Disease	State Cases	State Rate[1]	U.S. Rate[1]
Chlamydia	31,614	697.4	457.6
Gonorrhea	9,169	202.3	104.2
HIV diagnosis	1,376	36.6	15.8
HIV, stage 3 (AIDS)	842	22.4	10.3
Syphilis, early latent	488	10.8	4.3
Syphilis, primary/secondary	447	9.9	4.5
Tuberculosis	167	3.7	3.4

Note: (1) Rates are per 100,000 population
Source: Centers for Disease Control and Prevention

Cigarette Smoking, 2011

Category	State	U.S.
Adults who are current smokers	25.7%	21.2%
Adults who smoke everyday	19.3%	15.4%
Adults who smoke some days	6.4%	5.7%
Adults who are former smokers	22.0%	25.1%
Adults who never smoked	52.3%	52.9%

Source: Centers for Disease Control and Prevention, Behaviorial Risk Factor Surveillance System, Tobacco Use, 2011

HOUSING

Home Ownership Rates, 1995–2012

Area	1995	2000	2005	2010	2012
State	65.3%	68.1%	72.5%	70.4%	68.7%
U.S.	64.7%	67.4%	68.9%	66.9%	65.4%

Source: U.S. Census Bureau, Housing Vacancies and Homeownership, Annual Statistics

Home Sales, 2000–2010
In thousands of units

Year	State Sales	U.S. Sales	State Share
2000	66.8	5,174	1.29%
2002	71.7	5,632	1.27%
2004	79.6	6,778	1.17%
2006	92.3	6,478	1.42%
2008	59.1	4,913	1.20%
2010	51.6	4,908	1.05%

Note: Units include single-family homes, condos and co-ops
Source: National Association of Realtors, Real Estate Outlook, Market Trends & Insights

Value of Owner-Occupied Homes, 2011

Value	Total Units in State	Percent of Total, State	Percent of Total, U.S.
Less than $50,000	177,502	15.7%	8.8%
$50,000 to $99,000	224,450	19.9%	16.0%
$100,000 to $149,000	205,634	18.2%	16.5%
$150,000 to $199,000	213,048	18.8%	15.4%
$200,000 to $299,000	183,893	16.3%	18.2%
$300,000 to $499,000	91,548	8.1%	15.2%
$500,000 to $999,000	28,457	2.5%	7.9%
$1,000,000 or more	6,162	0.5%	2.0%
Median value	–	$139,400	$173,600

Source: U.S. Census Bureau, 2011 American Community Survey 1-Year Estimates

EDUCATION

School Enrollment, 2011

Educational Level	Students Enrolled in State	Percent of Total, State	Percent of Total, U.S.
All levels	1,213,228	100.0%	100.0%
Nursery school, preschool	84,369	7.0%	6.0%
Kindergarten	64,857	5.3%	5.1%
Elementary (grades 1–8)	508,755	41.9%	39.5%
Secondary (grades 9–12)	244,360	20.1%	20.7%
College or graduate school	310,887	25.6%	28.7%

Note: Figures cover the population 3 years and over enrolled in school
Source: U.S. Census Bureau, 2011 American Community Survey 1-Year Estimates

Educational Attainment, 2011

Highest Level of Education	State	U.S.
High school diploma	82.5%	85.9%
Bachelor's degree	21.1%	28.5%
Graduate/Professional degree	7.1%	10.6%

Note: Figures cover the population 25 years and over
Source: U.S. Census Bureau, 2011 American Community Survey 1-Year Estimates

Public College Finances, FY 2012

Category	State	U.S.
Full-time equivalent enrollment (FTE)[1]	181,589	11,548,974
Educational appropriations per FTE[2]	$5,551	$5,906
Net tuition revenue per FTE[3]	$3,587	$5,189
Total educational revenue per FTE[4]	$9,138	$11,043

(1) Full-time equivalent enrollment equates student credit hours to full time, academic year students, but excludes medical students; (2) Educational appropriations measure state and local support available for public higher education operating expenses including ARRA funds and excludes appropriations for independent institutions, financial aid for students attending independent institutions, research, hospitals, and medical education; (3) Net tuition revenue is calculated by taking the gross amount of tuition and fees, less state and institutional financial aid, tuition waivers or discounts, and medical student tuition and fees. Net tuition revenue used for capital debt service is included in the net tuition revenue figures; (4) Total educational revenue is the sum of educational appropriations and net tuition excluding net tuition revenue used for capital debt service.
Source: State Higher Education Executive Officers, State Higher Education Finance FY 2012

TRANSPORTATION AND TRAVEL

Motor Vehicle Registrations and Drivers Licenses, 2011

Vehicle Type	State	U.S.	State Share
Automobiles[1]	1,801,488	125,656,528	1.43%
Buses	13,427	666,064	2.02%
Trucks	2,169,221	118,455,587	1.83%
Motorcycles	68,460	8,437,502	0.81%
Drivers licenses	3,186,227	211,874,649	1.50%

Note: Motor vehicle registrations include private, commercial, and publicly-owned vehicles; (1) Includes taxicabs
Source: U.S. Department of Transportation, Federal Highway Administration

Domestic Travel Expenditures, 2009
In millions of dollars

Category	State	U.S.	State Share
Travel expenditures	$8,673	$610,200	1.42%

Note: Figures represent U.S. spending on domestic overnight trips and day trips of 50 miles or more, one way, away from home. Excludes spending by foreign visitors.
Source: U.S. Travel Association, Impact of Travel on State Economies, 2009

Retail Gasoline Prices, 2013

Gasoline Grade	State Average	U.S. Average
Regular	$3.50	$3.65
Mid	$3.68	$3.81
Premium	$3.85	$3.98
Diesel	$3.77	$3.88
Excise tax[1]	38.4 cents	49.4 cents

Note: Gasoline prices as of 7/26/2013; (1) Includes state and federal excise taxes and other state taxes as of July 1, 2013
Source: American Automobile Association, Daily Fuel Guage Report; American Petroleum Institute, State Motor Fuel Taxes, 2013

Public Road Length, 2011

Type	State Mileage	U.S. Mileage	State Share
Interstate highways	898	46,960	1.91%
Other highways	52	15,719	0.33%
Principal arterial	2,104	156,262	1.35%
Minor arterial	3,503	242,942	1.44%
Major collector	6,830	534,592	1.28%
Minor collector	3,153	266,357	1.18%
Local	45,096	2,814,925	1.60%
Urban	17,169	1,095,373	1.57%
Rural	44,466	2,982,383	1.49%
Total	61,635	4,077,756	1.51%

Note: Combined urban and rural road mileage equals the total of the other road types
Source: U.S. Department of Transportation, Federal Highway Administration, Public Road Length, 2011

CRIME AND LAW ENFORCEMENT

Full-Time Law Enforcement Officers, 2011

Gender	State Number	State Rate[1]	U.S. Rate[1]
Male officers	12,702	317.0	210.3
Female officers	2,870	71.6	28.1
Total officers	15,572	388.6	238.3

Note: (1) Rates are per 100,000 population
Source: Federal Bureau of Investigation, Uniform Crime Reports, Crime in the United States 2011

Prison Population, 2000–2012

Year	State Population	U.S. Population	State Share
2000	35,207	1,391,261	2.53%
2005	36,083	1,527,929	2.36%
2010	39,445	1,613,803	2.44%
2011	39,710	1,598,783	2.48%
2012	41,248	1,571,013	2.63%

Note: Figures include prisoners under the jurisdiction of state or federal correctional authorities.
Source: U.S. Department of Justice, Bureau of Justice Statistics, Prisoners in 2006, 2011, 2012 (Advance Counts)

Crime Rate, 2011
Incidents per 100,000 residents

Category	State	U.S.
Violent crimes	555.3	386.3
Murder	11.2	4.7
Forcible rape	27.7	26.8
Robbery	114.5	113.7
Aggravated assault	401.9	241.1
Property crimes	3,688.5	2,908.7
Burglary	1,012.5	702.2
Larceny/theft	2,476.6	1,976.9
Motor vehicle theft	199.4	229.6
All crimes	4,243.8	3,295.0

Source: Federal Bureau of Investigation, Uniform Crime Reports, Crime in the United States 2011

GOVERNMENT AND FINANCE

Local Governments by Type, 2012

Government Type	State	U.S.	State Share
All local governments	530	89,004	0.60%
County	60	3,031	1.98%
Municipality	304	19,522	1.56%
Town/Township	0	16,364	0.00%
Special District	97	37,203	0.26%
Ind. School District	69	12,884	0.54%

Source: U.S. Census Bureau, 2012 Census of Governments: Organization Component Preliminary Estimates

State Government Revenue, 2011
In thousands of dollars, except for per capita figures

Total revenue	$33,974,652
Total revenue per capita, State	$7,427
Total revenue per capita, U.S.	$7,271
General revenue	$26,939,024
Intergovernmental revenue	$12,532,918
Taxes	$8,865,421
General sales	$2,812,804
Selective sales	$2,318,406
License taxes	$351,398
Individual income taxes	$2,403,956
Corporate income taxes	$196,732
Other taxes	$782,125
Current charges	$3,299,702
Miscellaneous general revenue	$2,240,983
Utility revenue	$6,442
Liquor store revenue	$0
Insurance trust revenue[1]	$7,029,186

Note: (1) Within insurance trust revenue, net earnings of state retirement systems is a calculated statistic, and thus can be positive or negative. Net earnings is the sum of earnings on investments plus gains on investments minus losses on investments.
Source: U.S. Census Bureau, 2011 Annual Survey of State Government Finances

State Government Expenditures, 2011

In thousands of dollars, except for per capita figures

Total expenditure	$33,396,449
Total expenditure per capita, State	$7,300
Total expenditure per capita, U.S.	$6,427
Intergovernmental expenditure	$6,580,164
Direct expenditure	$26,816,285
Current operation	$18,352,257
Capital outlay	$2,631,116
Insurance benefits and repayments	$4,254,973
Assistance and subsidies	$535,045
Interest on debt	$1,042,894
Utility expenditure	$6,524
Liquor store expenditure	$0
Insurance trust expenditure	$4,254,973

Source: U.S. Census Bureau, 2011 Annual Survey of State Government Finances

State Government General Expenditures by Function, 2011

In thousands of dollars

Education	$8,904,101
Public welfare	$6,425,818
Hospitals	$2,205,036
Health	$597,955
Highways	$2,184,629
Police protection	$402,723
Correction	$757,363
Natural resources	$876,502
Parks and recreation	$343,450
Governmental administration	$981,958
Interest on general debt	$1,042,894
Other and unallocable	$4,412,523

Source: U.S. Census Bureau, 2011 Annual Survey of State Government Finances

State Government Finances, Cash and Debt, 2011

In thousands of dollars, except for per capita figures

Debt at end of fiscal year	
State, total	$18,447,200
State, per capita	$4,032
U.S., per capita	$3,635
Cash and security holdings	
State, total	$57,034,702
State, per capita	$12,467
U.S., per capita	$11,759

Source: U.S. Census Bureau, 2011 Annual Survey of State Government Finances

POLITICS

Composition of the Senate, 1995–2013

Congress (Year)	State/U.S	Dem	Rep	Total
104th (1995)	State delegates	2	0	2
	Total U.S.	48	52	100
105th (1997)	State delegates	2	0	2
	Total U.S.	45	55	100
106th (1999)	State delegates	2	0	2
	Total U.S.	45	55	100
107th (2001)	State delegates	2	0	2
	Total U.S.	50	50	100
108th (2003)	State delegates	2	0	2
	Total U.S.	48	51	100
109th (2005)	State delegates	1	1	2
	Total U.S.	44	55	100
110th (2007)	State delegates	1	1	2
	Total U.S.	49	49	100
111th (2009)	State delegates	1	1	2
	Total U.S.	57	41	100
112th (2011)	State delegates	1	1	2
	Total U.S.	51	47	100
113th (2013)	State delegates	1	1	2
	Total U.S.	54	45	100

Note: Figures are for the starts of first sessions; Totals include Democratic (Dem) and Republican (Rep) members as well as vacancies and seats held by independent party members
Source: U.S. Congress, Congressional Directory

Composition of the House of Representatives, 1995–2013

Congress (Year)	State/U.S	Dem	Rep	Total
104th (1995)	State delegates	4	3	7
	Total U.S.	204	230	435
105th (1997)	State delegates	2	5	7
	Total U.S.	207	226	435
106th (1999)	State delegates	2	5	7
	Total U.S.	211	223	435
107th (2001)	State delegates	2	5	7
	Total U.S.	212	221	435
108th (2003)	State delegates	3	4	7
	Total U.S.	205	229	435
109th (2005)	State delegates	2	5	7
	Total U.S.	202	231	435
110th (2007)	State delegates	2	5	7
	Total U.S.	233	198	435
111th (2009)	State delegates	1	6	7
	Total U.S.	256	178	435
112th (2011)	State delegates	1	6	7
	Total U.S.	193	242	435
113th (2013)	State delegates	1	5	6
	Total U.S.	201	234	435

Note: Figures are for the starts of first sessions; Totals include Democratic (Dem) and Republican (Rep) members as well as vacancies and seats held by independent party members
Source: U.S. Congress, Congressional Directory

Composition of State Legislature, 2004–2013

Year	Democrats	Republicans	Total
State Senate			
2004	24	15	39
2005	24	15	39
2006	24	15	39
2007	24	15	39
2008	25	14	39
2009	22	15	39
2010	24	15	39
2011	19	20	39
2012	15	24	39
2013	15	24	39
State House			
2004	68	37	105
2005	67	37	105
2006	67	37	105
2007	59	43	105
2008	60	43	105
2009	51	50	105
2010	52	50	105
2011	47	52	105
2012	45	58	105
2013	45	58	105

Note: Totals may include minor party members and vacancies
Source: The Council of State Governments, State Legislatures

Voter Participation in Presidential Elections, 1980–2012

Year	Voting-eligible State Population	State Voter Turnout Rate	U.S. Voter Turnout Rate
1980	2,868,792	54.0	54.2
1984	3,019,930	56.5	55.2
1988	2,941,023	55.4	52.8
1992	2,997,301	59.7	58.1
1996	3,087,693	57.8	51.7
2000	3,130,267	56.4	54.2
2004	3,182,762	61.1	60.1
2008	3,205,794	61.2	61.6
2012	3,302,514	60.4	58.2

Note: All figures are based on the voting-eligible population which excludes person ineligible to vote such as non-citizens, felons (depending on state law), and mentally-incapacitated persons. U.S. figures include the overseas eligible population (including military personnel).
Source: McDonald, Michael P., United States Election Project, Presidential Voter Turnout Rates, 1980–2012

Governors Since Statehood

William C. C. Claiborne 1812-1816
Jacques P. Villere 1816-1820
Thomas B. Robertson . . . . (r) 1820-1824
Henry S. Thibodaux 1824
Henry Johnson 1824-1828
Pierre A. C. B. Derbigny . . . . (d) 1828-1829
Armand Beauvais 1829-1830
Jacques Dupre 1830-1831
Andre B. Roman (O) 1831-1835
Edward D. White (O) 1835-1839
Andre B. Roman (O) 1839-1843

Alexandre Mouton (D) 1843-1846
Isaac Johnson (D) 1846-1850
Joseph M. Walker (D) 1850-1853
Paul O. Herbert (D) 1853
Robert C. Wickliffe (D) 1853-1860
Thomas O. Moore (D) 1860-1864
Henry W. Allen . . . . (i) 1864
George Michael D. Hahn . . . . (r) 1864-1865
J. Madison Wells (D) . . . . (i) 1865-1867
Benjamin F. Flanders (D) . . . . (i) 1867-1868
Joshua Baker (D) . . . . (i) 1868
Henry C. Warmoth (R) . . . . (r) 1868-1872
Pinckney B. S. Pinchback (R) 1872-1873
William P. Kellogg (R) 1873-1877
Francis R. T. Nicholls (D) 1877-1880
Louis A. Wiltz (D) . . . . (d) 1880-1881
Samuel D. McEnery (D) 1881-1888
Francis R. T. Nicholls (D) 1888-1892
Murphy J. Foster (D) 1892-1900
William W. Heard (D) 1900-1904
Newton C. Blanchard (D) 1904-1908
Jared Y. Sanders (D) 1908-1912
Luther E. Hall (D) 1912-1916
Ruffin G. Pleasant (D) 1916-1920
John M. Parker (D) 1920-1924
Henry L. Fuqua (D) . . . . (d) 1924-1926
Oramel H. Simpson (D) 1926-1928
Huey P. Long (D) . . . . (r) 1928-1932
Alvin O. King (D) 1932
Oscar K. Allen (D) . . . . (d) 1932-1936
James A. Noe (D) 1936
Richard W. Leche (D) . . . . (r) 1936-1939
Earl K. Long (D) 1939-1940
Sam Houston Jones (D) 1940-1944
James H. (Jimmie) Davis (D) 1944-1948
Earl K. Long (D) 1948-1952
Robert F. Kennon (D) 1952-1956
Earl K. Long (D) 1956-1960
James H. (Jimmie) Davis (D) 1960-1964
John J. McKeithen (D) 1964-1972
Edwin W. Edwards (D) 1972-1988
Charles E. Roemer III (D) 1988-1992
Edwin W. Edwards (D) 1992-1996
Murphy J. (Mike) Foster (R) 1996-2004
Kathleen Blanco (D) 2004-2008
Bobby Jindal (R) . . . . 2008-2016 (term limits)

Note: (D) Democrat; (R) Republican; (O) Other party; (r) resigned; (d) died in office; (i) removed from office

Maine

Location: New England

Area and rank: 30,865 square miles (79,939 square kilometers); 35,387 square miles (91,652 square kilometers) including water; thirty-ninth largest state in area

Coastline: 228 miles (367 kilometers) on the Atlantic Ocean

Shoreline: 3,478 miles (5,597 kilometers)

Population and rank: 1,329,192 (2012 estimate); forty-first largest state in population

Capital city: Augusta (19,136 people in 2010 census)

Largest city: Portland (66,194 people in 2010 census)

Entered Union and rank: March 15, 1820; twenty-third state

State capitol building in Augusta. (Maine Office of Tourism)

Present constitution adopted: 1820

Counties: 16

State name: "Maine" was first used to distinguish the region's mainland from its offshore islands; the name was also considered a compliment to English king Charles I's consort, Henrietta Maria, of France's Mayne province

State nickname: Pine Tree State

Motto: *Dirigo* (I lead)

State flag: Blue field with the state coat of arms

Highest point: Mount Katahdin—5,267 feet (1,605 meters)

Lowest point: Atlantic Ocean— sea level

Highest recorded temperature: 105 degrees Fahrenheit (41 degrees Celsius)— North Bridgton, 1911

Lowest recorded temperature: –48 degrees Fahrenheit (–44 degrees Celsius)—Van Buren, 1925

State song: "State of Maine Song"

State tree: White pine tree

State flower: White pine cone and tassel

State bird: Chickadee

State fish: Landlocked salmon

State animal: Moose

National parks: Acadia

Maine History

Maine, the largest of the six New England states, is filled with natural wonder and beauty. It has more than five thousand lakes and ponds, woodlands cover almost 90 percent of the state, and more than 3,400 miles of its Atlantic shoreline twist from New Hampshire to Canada. The harsh, brutal winters have always made living there difficult, and the state remains relatively sparsely populated.

As far as it is known, the first Native Americans to settle in the area were members of the Abenaki (people of the dawnland) tribe. They, and the tribes that followed them, were hunters and gatherers, living on fish, deer, moose, beavers, and bears. Like many Native Americans of New England, they lived in wigwams and were generally peaceful—until European settlers began to come.

Early Exploration and Settlement. Viking leader Leif Eriksson and other Norse sailors most likely explored part of Maine during their travels in 1000. John Cabot, sent by King Henry VII of England, claimed Maine as territory for England in 1497. In 1524, explorer Giovanni da Verrazano claimed Maine for France. In 1605, British captain George Weymouth landed in Maine, kidnapped five Abenaki men, and took them back to England. Upon meeting the American Indians and hearing stories of the land, King James I agreed to sponsor a settlement there, sending Sir Ferdinando Gorges and Sir John Popham to lead the exhibition. In 1607, the British explorers reached the coast where the Kennebec River meets the ocean. There they began the Popham colony, where they built the *Virginia*—the first English ship built in North America. Success was short-lived, however, as a typically bitter Maine winter, combined with attacks from the Abenakis, drove the entire colony back to England in 1608.

Soon, however, both English and French explorers returned and claimed different parts of the state for their kings. The English fought with the Native Americans often. Englishman John Winter founded one of Maine's first shipyards in 1637, and Maine was on its way to becoming a major shipbuilding center. The ships built in Maine supplied fish, fur, lumber, and masts to

With a population of fewer than twenty thousand people, Maine's capital city, Augusta, is only the ninth-largest city in the state. (PhotoDisc)

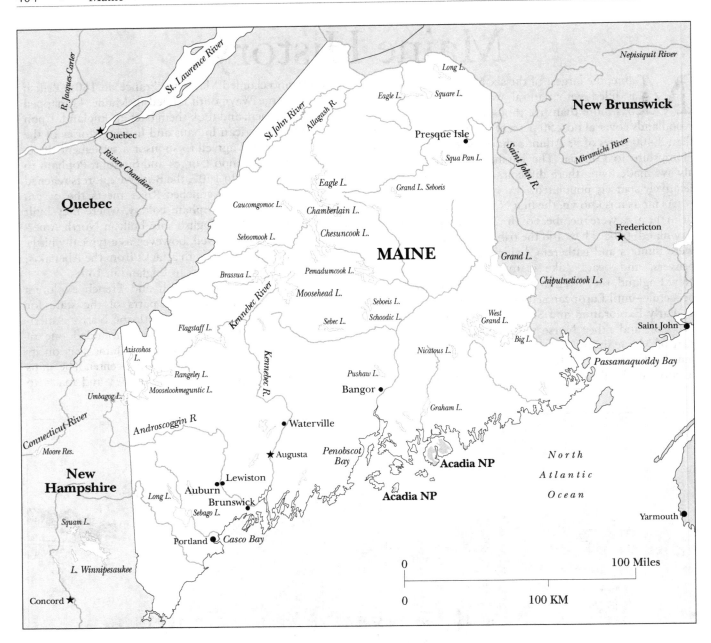

England's navy. The empty ships returning brought more settlers, and as settlers moved inland, farming gained importance. As in most of New England, native corn was Maine's primary crop. Primarily because of the harsh winters, Maine did not grow as quickly as the other New England colonies. The small population and weak government motivated the colonists there to merge with Massachusetts in 1658, and they remained part of it for nearly 150 years.

Two Wars. In 1754, tension over the colonies between France, which ruled Canada, and England broke into the French and Indian War. Thousands of Maine settlers fought against the French. The French and Indians were eventually defeated, and many of the warring tribes fled to Canada. The victory was costly, however, and it left Great Britain deeply in debt. When the war ended in 1763, Maine was doing well. The colony had twenty-five thousand settlers and nearly fifty towns. Each year, Maine shipped millions of pounds of fish and lumber to cities in Europe. Like the other colonies, Maine started resenting Britain's meddling. Britain, trying to relieve its war debt, continually raised the taxes of the colonists.

In 1774, a group of men from York, Maine, burned English tea to protest the high taxes in what would be called the York Tea Party. In 1775, the Revolutionary War began in Massachusetts. On June 12 of that year, the first sea battle of the war occurred off Maine, when colonists from Machias rowed out and attacked an English ship. Soon after that the English retaliated, and the city of Falmouth (later Portland) was bombarded and burned. By the time the Union won the war, about one thousand colonists from Maine had given their lives.

After the war, the Massachusetts government sold Maine land to new settlers for less than a dollar an acre. Maine's population increased significantly, and by 1785 Maine started lobbying for statehood. The new and growing country had other problems, however. In 1812, the United States again went to war with Great Britain. Britain, at that time at war with France, would attack and capture American ships and conscript Americans into service. Maine's growing dominance as a shipbuilder played a major role in the American success, and after the war, it pushed even harder for statehood.

Statehood. In 1820, in an effort to defuse the hotly contested issue of slavery in America, it was proposed that Missouri be admitted as a slave state if Maine were admitted as a free state, thus keeping a balance of eleven proslavery states and eleven antislavery states. Known as the Missouri Compromise, this agreement is credited with postponing civil war. Maine then separated from

Massachusetts and became the twenty-third state, and the last New England state accepted into the Union. Portland served as the state capital until 1832, when the more centrally located Augusta became the capital. By then, potatoes were replacing corn as the most profitable crop, and lumbering became the state's largest industry. The city of Bath became the leading shipbuilding city in the country.

Maine was admitted to the Union as a free state, as it had a history of supporting people of African descent: When Bowdoin College opened in Brunswick in 1802, it was the first U.S. college to admit black students. John Russwurm, the college's first black graduate, co-founded *Freedom's Journal*, the country's first black-run newspaper, in 1827.

Antislavery Maine governor Hannibal Hamlin became President Abraham Lincoln's vice president in 1861. The Civil War erupted that year, and many Mainers heeded the call to arms. In the election of 1864, Lincoln was in political trouble, and he quietly allowed moderate southern Democrat Andrew Johnson to replace Hamlin as his vice president to ensure his reelection. By the time

Although Maine ranks only thirty-ninth in area among the states, it has nearly 3,500 miles of shoreline and is famous for its numerous lighthouses. (Wikimedia Commons)

the Civil War ended in 1865, about 7,500 Maine soldiers had been killed fighting.

Industrial Revolution. During the 1850's, the Industrial Revolution began to influence American cities, and Maine came to operate textile and leather factories. Like the rest of New England, Maine was successful at building factories, and thousands of French Canadians crossed the border to find jobs. Many Irish escaped the horrible potato famine that began during the 1840's and came to Maine. In 1894, the Arrostock Railroad was completed, and trains began to move the wealth of Maine potatoes to the markets of other American cities. During this time Maine became one of the country's great potato-growing areas.

Economic Decline. During the twentieth century, tourists discovered Maine: its mystique, unspoiled beauty, and lack of crowded cities. The upsurge in tourists helped Maine's economy, as the state's other industries began to falter. The development of iron steamships damaged Maine's wooden-ship building industry, and the traditional activities of lumbering, fishing, and farming did not provide enough jobs for everyone.

There was a small break in economic decline when World War I began in 1914. Many Mainers did not wait for the United States to enter the war and joined Canada's armed forces to fight the Germans. The United States entered the war in 1917, and 35,000 Mainers joined the U.S. forces. Maine's shipbuilding industry sprang back to life, and farmers and fisherman saw a significant increase in price for their harvests. After the war ended, however, times were difficult in Maine. When the country entered World War II in 1941, Maine again sprang back to life. During the 1950's and 1960's, Air Force bases were built, which employed many locals, but unemployment remained higher in Maine than in the rest of the nation.

Modern Era. In 1954, Edmund Muskie became the first modern Democrat elected governor in the traditionally Republican state. In 1957, he was the first Maine Democrat elected to the Senate. The popular senator went on to run unsuccessfully for the vice presidency in 1968 and the presidential nomination of the Democratic Party in 1972.

In 1972, Maine's Native Americans filed a lawsuit against the United States, claiming their lands had been wrongly seized and showing a 1794 treaty as proof. In 1980, the federal government paid the tribes $81.5 million for their land. It was the largest such settlement ever awarded to Native Americans.

During the 1980's, the state's economy became strong again, particularly in the largest city, Portland, although industry declined to the point that service industries represented 70 percent of the state's economy. Maine lobster is often referred to the best in the country, and the state produces 22 million pounds of it each year. Maine also produces 98 percent of the nation's blueberries.

The state is relatively underpopulated, with only about one million residents. In the northern part of the state, there are few developed cities. During the 1990's, less than 1 percent of the population was Native American, and most Mainers are descendants of emigrants from Great Britain, France, and Canada.

State Politics. Although often considered a Republican state, Maine does not always stay true to that category when it comes to presidential politics. An old saying that "so Maine goes, so goes the nation" could not apply in the instances of Democratic Party victories in 2000. In that year, all of Maine's four electoral votes went to Democratic Party candidate Vice President Al Gore, by a margin of 49 percent to 44 percent. Republican U.S. senator Olympia Snowe was reelected, as were the state's two Democrats in the House of Representatives. The Maine state senate went to the Republican Party.

With a population of fewer than twenty thousand people, Maine's capital city, Augusta, is only the ninth-largest city in the state. A number of important initiatives were on the ballot in 2000. Voters narrowly rejected a gay rights initiative that barred discrimination on the basis of sexual orientation by 51 percent to 49 percent. By the same margin, they also turned down an assisted suicide measure that would have allowed doctors to help certain patients to die at their own hands. For the third time in three years, Maine voters also were not interested in allowing a video-based lottery, with 61 percent dissenting. Finally, voters rejected curbs in cutting the state's timber by the lopsided margin of 71 percent to 29 percent.

In 2004, Maine voters repeated their year 2000 performance in presidential politics, voting the state's electoral votes to Democrat senator John Kerry from neighboring Massachusetts by a 53–45 percent margin. An initiative decided upon at the ballot box was a proposal to ban hunting bears with bait, traps, or dogs. Voters rejected the measure, which pitted animal rights activists against hunters, by a 54–46 percent margin. Voters also rejected a measure modeled after California's Proposition 13 that would have limited real estate taxes to 1 percent of assessed value.

Although Maine has been seen as in the mainstream of liberal political positions characteristic of the Northeast and New England, the election of Tea Party candidate Paul LePage as governor in 2010 has challenged that perception. LePage, the first Maine governor of French-Canadian ancestry, has a personal background of childhood poverty and a hard struggle to success as a businessman. LePage had served as Mayor of Waterville from 2003 to 2011. In the 2010 primary election, he took the Republican nomination with 38 percent of the vote against six other candidates. An outspoken critic of the Obama administration and the federal government in his victory speech LePage announced that he would shrink

Lobster boats in Bass Harbor, Mount Desert Island. (Wikimedia Commons)

government, lower taxes, decrease business regulation, and put the people ahead of politics.

Legal Disputes Settled. In 2001, the long border dispute between Maine and New Hampshire—sometimes called a "border war"—was finally settled by a decision of the U.S. Supreme Court. The border issue, which stretched back to 1827, revolved around whether the Portsmouth Navy Yard was in Maine or in New Hampshire. If it were in the latter, citizens of New Hampshire, which did not have a state income tax, would be able to stop paying Maine's state income tax. In an 8-0 decision, the Court ruled that New Hampshire could not change the border that had been agreed with Maine in 1977.

When asked at the polls on two occasions, Maine voters said that mentally ill people who are under guardianship should not be allowed to vote. In 2001, however, a federal judge overturned their decision, ruling that barring the mentally ill from voting violates the equal protection clause of the Fourteenth Amendment to the U.S. Constitution.

During his administration, he continued to be criticized on a number of counts, including nepotism, insulting the labor movement, outspoken criticism of the Internal Revenue Service and other federal agencies,

disrespect for the president, and for vetoing many bills passed by the Democratic-controlled state legislature. Supporters, however, praised him for being outspoken and frank about his beliefs. LePage vetoed 82 bills during the first session of the 126th legislature. Five of the vetoes were overridden, including the 2013–2014 state budget; on its passage he stated that he might not run for re-election, because he believed the state could not recover from the effect of the budget.

Same-sex marriage. Maine retained its liberal image, however, with a number of measures. Among them was the fact that same-sex marriage became legal in the state on December 29, 2012. The bill for legalization was approved by voters in the November 2012 elections. Maine joined Maryland and Washington as the first U.S. states to legalize same-sex marriage by popular vote. An earlier bill allowing same-sex marriages had been signed into law in May 2009, but was rejected by a popular referendum in November 2009. When the law had been signed, it represented the first time a state had legalized same-sex marriage by approval of the state legislature and governor signature.

Kevin M. Mitchell
Updated by the Editor

Maine Time Line

1400	Abenaki tribe inhabits Maine area.
1497	John Cabot claims Maine for England.
1524	Explorer Giovanni da Verrazano claims Maine for France.
1605	Captain George Weymouth kidnaps five Native Americans and takes them to England.
1607	Gorge Popham establishes a settlement near Kennebec River; the first English ship, the *Virginia*, is built.
1620's	Smallpox wipes out many Abenaki.
1628	Plymouth Pilgrims establish several fur-trading posts in Maine territory.
1634	First sawmill in Maine begins operation.
1637	First shipyard in Maine opens.
1640's	French establish missions and begin converting Indians.
1649	Government grants all Christians the right to form churches.
1652	Maine becomes a part of the Massachusetts Bay Colony.
1690's	French and Indians from Canada pillage Maine until only four English settlements remain inhabited.
1774	Patriots burn English tea to protest high taxes in York Tea Party.
May 12, 1775	Maine patriots capture English ship in first naval battle of the American Revolution.
1778	Continental Congress divides Massachusetts into three districts, including one province called Maine.
1785	Maine's first newspaper, the *Falmouth Gazette*, is published.
1791	First lighthouse on the Atlantic Coast begins operation in Portland.
1801	First free public library opens in Castine.
1802	Bowdoin College opens in Brunswick.
1819	Maine state representatives vote to separate from Massachusetts and adopt a state constitution.
Mar. 15, 1820	Maine gains statehood under terms of Missouri Compromise, becoming the twenty-third state of the Union.
1832	State capital is moved to Augusta.
1834	Maine's Antislavery Society is formed in Augusta.
1850's	Most remaining Native Americans live on reservations.
1851	Anti-drinking legislation passes making Maine the first dry state.
1855	State militia fires on civilians as they descend upon Portland's City Hall, looking for liquor; one man is killed.
1861	Maine Republican Hannibal Hamlin is elected vice president of the United States.
1894	Arrostock Railroad is completed; trains move potatoes to the markets of other American cities.
1912	Leon Bean founds clothing mail-order business L. L. Bean in Freeport.
1950	Margaret Chase Smith becomes the first woman elected to both houses of the U.S. Congress.
1957	Governor Edmund S. Muskie is first Maine Democrat elected to the U.S. Senate.
1979	Maine's three Indian reservations have a total population of 1,247.
1981	Tourism continues to lead all industries; more than $500 million is spent by out-of-state visitors in Maine.
1999	Children's Rights Council names Maine the best state in which to raise children.
Nov. 7, 2000	Maine voters give the state's four electoral votes to Al Gore and reelect Republican Olympia Snowe to the U.S. Senate.
May 29, 2001	Long-standing border dispute with New Hampshire is settled in Maine's favor by the U.S. Supreme Court.
Nov. 4, 2003	Voters reject a proposal by two Indian tribes, the Passamaquoddy Tribe and the Penobscot Nation, to build a $650 million casino resort.
Nov. 2, 2004	Maine voters choose Senator John Kerry for president, reject an initiative limiting the means by which bears are hunted, and also reject an initiative that would have limited real estate taxes to 1 percent of assessed value.
Dec. 29, 2012	Same sex marriage becomes legal in Maine.

Notes for Further Study

Published Sources. For younger readers, information about Maine's history, culture, and social and political development can be found in Margaret Coull Phillips's *Maine* (2004), Terry Allan Hicks's *Maine* (2006), and *Maine History! Surprising Secrets About Our State's Founding Mothers, Fathers and Kids!* (1996) by Carole Marsh. *Maine: A Narrative History* (1990) by Neil Rolde offers a more in-depth view of the state. *Maine: Heads of Families at the First Census of the U.S. Taken in 1790* (1987), edited by Robert Danbury, offers insight to Maine's early settlers and the first families of the state. Gail Underwood Parker gives readers a lively narrative of Maine history from the first colony in the early

seventeenth century to the modern era in *It Happened in Maine* (2004).

The French and Indian War (1997) by Christopher Collier and James Lincoln Collier covers the many battles that took place on Maine's soil, as well as the hundred years between initial colonization and the American Revolution. *The Maine Reader: The Down East Experience, 1614 to the Present* (1997), edited by Charles Shain and Samuella Shain, offers a sweeping history of the state through literature. Covering everything from ferry boats to the islands, in addition to coastal architecture, is *The Coast of Maine Book: A Complete Guide* (1999) by Rick Ackermann and Kathryn Buxton. *The Lobster Coast:*

Founded in Freeport, Maine, in 1912, L.L. Bean is one of the largest mail-order clothing businesses in the United States. (Maine Office of Tourism)

Rebels, Rusticators, and the Struggle for a Forgotten Frontier (2004) by Colin Woodard describes the political developments and environmental issues of the state by focusing on the coast's fishing and lobstering communities.

For those readers interested in all aspects of Maine's politics and politicians, author Christian P. Potholm covers these topics thoroughly with three books: *An Insider's Guide to Maine Politics* (1998), *This Splendid Game: Maine Campaigns and Elections, 1940-2002* (2003), and *Maine: The Dynamics of Political Change* (2006). Editor Richard Barringer, in *Changing Maine 1960-2010* (2004), brings together presentations from speakers in a 2003-2004 public lecture series presented by the Muskie School of Public Service University of Southern Maine. The lectures examine Maine's changing economic, political, and social landscape over several decades.

The Maine Handbook (1998) by Kathy Brandes provides information on all of Maine's natural beauty destinations, as does *Maine: An Explorer's Guide* (13th ed., 2006) by Christina Tree and Nancy English. *Maine Trivia* (1998), compiled by John N. Cole, is an entertaining, insightful, small volume of the facts, figures, and firsts of the Pine Tree State.

Web Resources. There are many Maine sites on the Internet, and those listed here often give valuable links to others. A good starting point is the Center for Maine History (www.mainehistory.org/). The center comprises the Maine Historical Society Research Library, the Maine History Gallery, and the historic Wadsworth-Longfellow House. The official state of Maine home page (www.state.me.us/) is a collection of information and other Web sites on such topics as history, finance, and politics. Visit Maine (www.visitmaine.com/home.php) is the state's official tourism site.

The U.S. Census Bureau provides its so-called QuickFacts for each of the fifty states; those for Maine can be found at quickfacts.census.gov/qfd/states/23000.html. Information on Margaret Chase Smith and the organization that she inspired can be found at Margaret Chase Smith Library (www.mcslibrary.org/). The state's largest newspaper, the *Portland Press Herald* (pressherald.mainetoday.com/home.html), offers updated news on state happenings. The Portland Harbor Museum (www.portlandharbormuseum.org/) is a fascinating maritime museum with information on the city's port and working lighthouse.

The view from the top of the northwestern slopes of Saddleback Mountain in Franklin County, Maine. (Wikimedia Commons)

Counties

County	2012 Population	Pop. Rank	Land Area (sq. miles)	Area Rank
Androscoggin	107,609	5	467.93	13
Aroostook	70,868	6	6,671.33	1
Cumberland	283,921	1	835.24	11
Franklin	30,630	15	1,696.61	7
Hancock	54,558	8	1,586.89	8
Kennebec	121,853	4	867.52	10
Knox	39,668	10	365.13	15
Lincoln	34,180	13	455.82	14
Oxford	57,481	7	2,076.84	6
Penobscot	153,746	3	3,397.36	4

County	2012 Population	Pop. Rank	Land Area (sq. miles)	Area Rank
Piscataquis	17,290	16	3,960.86	2
Sagadahoc	35,191	12	253.69	16
Somerset	51,910	9	3,924.40	3
Waldo	38,820	11	729.92	12
Washington	32,462	14	2,562.66	5
York	199,005	2	990.71	9

Source: *U.S. Census Bureau, 2012 Population Estimates*

Cities
With 10,000 or more residents

Legal Name	2010 Population	Pop. Rank	Land Area (sq. miles)	Area Rank
Auburn city	23,055	5	59.33	1
Augusta city	19,136	9	55.13	2
Bangor city	33,039	3	34.26	11
Biddeford city	21,277	6	30.09	13
Brunswick town	20,278	8	46.73	7
Brunswick CDP	15,175	16	14.51	18
Falmouth town	11,185	18	29.38	14
Gorham town	16,381	14	50.62	4
Kennebunk town	10,798	19	35.05	10
Lewiston city	36,592	2	34.15	12
Orono town	10,362	20	18.19	16

Legal Name	2010 Population	Pop. Rank	Land Area (sq. miles)	Area Rank
Portland city	66,194	1	21.31	15
Saco city	18,482	11	38.46	9
Sanford town	20,798	7	47.78	5
Scarborough town	18,919	10	47.61	6
South Portland city	25,002	4	11.99	20
Waterville city	15,722	15	13.58	19
Westbrook city	17,494	12	17.12	17
Windham town	17,001	13	46.56	8
York town	12,529	17	54.67	3

Note: CDP–Census Designated Place
Source: U.S. Census Bureau, 2010 Census

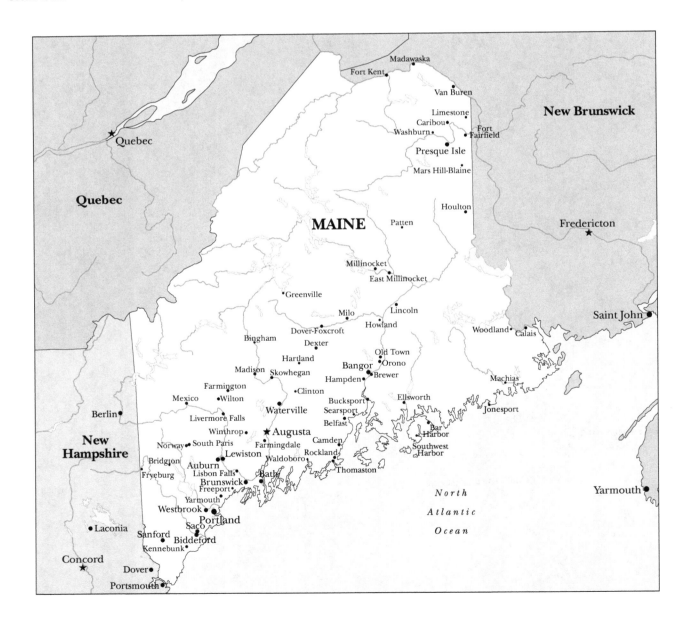

Survey Says...

This section presents current rankings from dozens of public and private sources. It shows how this state ranks in a number of critical categories, including education, job growth, cost of living, teen drivers, energy efficiency, and business environment. Sources include *Forbes, Reuters, U.S. News and World Report, CNN Money, Gallup,* and *Huffington Post.*

- Maine ranked #44 in a government study measuring real gross domestic product (GDP)—the output of goods and services produced by labor and property located in the United States. The ranking is based on the percentage change compared with 2011 GDP.

  U.S. Department of Commerce, Bureau of Economic Analysis, June 2013; www.bea.gov

- Maine ranked #44 in a government study measuring real gross domestic product (GDP)—the output of goods and services produced by labor and property located in the United States. The ranking is based on the dollar value of its GDP.

  U.S. Department of Commerce, Bureau of Economic Analysis, June 2013; www.bea.gov

- Maine ranked #33 in the 17th edition of "Quality Counts; State of the States," Education Week's "report card" surveying key education indicators, policy efforts, and educational outcomes.

  Education Week, January 4, 2013 (online) and January 10, 2013 (print); www.edweek.org

- SERI (Science and Engineering Readiness Index) weighs the performance of the states' K-12 schools in preparing students in physics and calculus, the high school subjects considered most important for future scientists and engineers. Maine ranked #10.

  Newsletter of the Forum on Education of the American Physical Society, Summer 2011 issue; www.huffingtonpost.com, July 11, 2011; updated October 1, 2012

- MoneyRates.com ranked Maine #40 on its list of the best to worst states for making a living. Criteria: average income; inflation; employment prospects; and workers' Workplace Environment assessments according to the Gallup-Healthways Well-Being Index.

  www.money-rates.com, posted April 1, 2013

- *Forbes* analyzed business costs, labor supply, regulatory environment, current economic climate, growth prospects, and quality of life, to compile its "Best States for Business" rankings. Maine ranked #50.

  www.forbes.com. posted December 12, 2012

- In "The States People Are Fleeing in 2013," *Forbes* reported the results of United Van Lines's thirty-sixth annual survey of its "customer migration patterns." In percentage of outbound moves, Maine ranked #8 (1 = most).

  www.forbes.com, posted February 7, 2013

- The 2012 Gallup-Healthways Well-Being Index, surveyed American's opinions on economic confidence, workplace perceptions, community climate, personal choices, and health predictors to assess the "future livability" of each state. Maine ranked #40.

  "Utah Poised to Be the Best State to Live In," Gallup Wellbeing, www.gallup.com, August 7, 2012

- On CNBC's list of "America's Top States for Business 2013," Maine ranked #38. Criteria: measures of competitiveness developed with input from the National Association of Manufacturers, the Council on Competitiveness, and other business groups weighed with the states' own marketing criteria.

  www.cnbc.com, consulted July 19, 2013

- Maine ranked #43 on MoneyRates list of "Best-and Worst-States to Retire 2012." Criteria: life expectancy, crime rate, climate, economic conditions, taxes, job opportunities, and cost of living.

  www.money-rates.com, October 22, 2012

- Maine ranked #46 on the 2013 Bankrate "Best Places to Retire" list ranking the states and District of Columbia on various criteria relating to health, safety, and cost.

  www.bankrate.com, May 6, 2013

- Maine ranked #25 on the Social Science Research Council's "American Human Development Report: The Measure of America," assessing the 50 states plus the District of Columbia on health, education, and living-standard criteria.

  The Measure of America 2013-2014, posted June 19, 2013; www.measureofamerica.org

- Maine ranked #17 on the Foundation for Child Development's (FCD) Child Well-being Index (CWI). The FCD used the KIDS COUNT report and the National Survey of Children's Health, the only state-level source for several key indicators of child well-being.

  Foundation for Child Development, January 18, 2012; fcd-us.org

- Maine ranked #13 overall according to the 2013 KIDS COUNT Data Book, a project of the Annie E. Casey Foundation. Criteria: children's economic well-being, education, health, and family and community indicators.

  KIDS COUNT Data Center's Data Book, released June 20, 2013; http://datacenter.kidscount.org

- Maine ranked #20 in the children's economic well-being category by the 2013 KIDS COUNT Data Book, a project of the Annie E. Casey Foundation.

  KIDS COUNT Data Center's Data Book, released June 20, 2013; http://datacenter.kidscount.org

- Maine ranked #20 in the children's educational opportunities and attainments category by the 2013 KIDS COUNT Data Book, a project of the Annie E. Casey Foundation.

  KIDS COUNT Data Center's Data Book, released June 20, 2013; http://datacenter.kidscount.org

- Maine ranked #1 in the children's health category by the 2013 KIDS COUNT Data Book, a project of the Annie E. Casey Foundation.

  KIDS COUNT Data Center's Data Book, released June 20, 2013; http://datacenter.kidscount.org

- Maine ranked #6 in the family and community circumstances that factor into children's well-being category by the 2013 KIDS COUNT Data Book, a project of the Annie E. Casey Foundation.
  KIDS COUNT Data Center's Data Book, released June 20, 2013; http://datacenter.kidscount.org

- Maine ranked #21 in the 2012 Gallup-Healthways Well-Being Index. Criteria: emotional health; physical health; healthy behavior; work environment; basic access to food, shelter, health care; and a safe and satisfying place to live.
  2012 State of Well-Being, Gallup-Healthways Well-Being Index, released February 28, 2013; www.well-beingindex.com

- *U.S. News and World Report's* "Best States for Teen Drivers" rankings are based on driving and road safety laws, federal reports on driver's licenses, car accident fatality, and road-quality statistics. Maine ranked #30.
  U.S. News and World Report, March 18, 2010; www.usnews.com

- The Yahoo! Sports service Rivals.com ranks the states according to the strength of their high school football programs. Maine ranked #42.
  "Ranking the States: Where Is the Best Football Played?," November 18, 2011; highschool.rivals.com

- iVillage ranked the states by hospitable living conditions for women. Criteria: economic success, access to affordable childcare, health care, reproductive rights, female representation in government, and educational attainment. Maine ranked #13.
  iVillage, "50 Best to Worst States for Women," March 14, 2012; www.ivillage.com

- The League of American Bicyclists's "Bicycle Friendly States" ranked Maine #13. Criteria: legislation and enforcement, policies and programs, infrastructure and funding, education and advocacy, and evaluation and planning.
  "Washington Tops the Bicycle-Friendly State Ranking," May 1, 2013; bicycling.com

- The federal Corporation for National and Community Service ranked the states and the District of Columbia by volunteer rates. Maine ranked #12 for community service.
  "Volunteering and Civic Life in America 2012," www.volunteeringinamerica.gov, accessed July 24, 2013

- The Hospital Safety Score ranked states and the District of Columbia on their hospitals' performance scores. Maine ranked #1. Criteria: avoiding preventable harm and medical errors, as demonstrated by 26 hospital safety metrics.
  Spring 2013 Hospital Safety Score, May 8, 2013; www.hospitalsafetyscore.org

- GMAC Insurance ranked the states and the District of Columbia by the performance of their drivers on the GMAC Insurance National Drivers Test, comprised of DMV test questions. Maine ranked #16.
  "2011 GMAC Insurance National Drivers Test," www.gmacinsurance.com, accessed July 23, 2013

- Maine ranked #46 in a "State Integrity Investigation" analysis of laws and practices intended to deter corruption and promote accountability and openness in campaign finance, ethics laws, lobbying regulations and management of state pension funds.
  "What's Your State's Grade?," www.publicintegrity.org, accessed July 23, 2013

- Maine ranked #40 among the states and the District of Columbia in total rail miles, as tracked by the Association of American Railroads.
  "U.S. Freight Railroad Industry Snapshot: Railroads and States: Total Rail Miles by State: 2011"; www.aar.org, accessed July 23, 2013

- According to statistics compiled by the Beer Institute, Maine ranked #10 among the states and the District of Columbia in per capita beer consumption of persons 21 years or older.
  "Shipments of Malt Beverages and Per Capita Consumption by State 2012;" www.beerinstitute.org

- According to Concordia University's "Public Education Costs per Pupil by State Rankings," based on statistics gathered by the U.S. Census Bureau, which includes the District of Columbia, Maine ranked #14.
  Concordia University Online; education.cu-portland.edu, accessed July 24, 2013

- Maine ranked #38 among the states and the District of Columbia in population density based on U.S. Census Bureau data for resident population and total land area. "List of U.S. States by Population Density."
  www.wikipedia.org, accessed July 24, 2013

- In "America's Health Rankings, 2012 Edition," by the United Health Foundation, Maine ranked #9. Criteria included: rate of high school graduation; violent crime rate; incidence of infectious disease; childhood immunizations; prevalence of diabetes; per capita public-health funding; percentage of uninsured population; rate of children in poverty; and availability of primary-care physicians.
  United Health Foundation; www.americashealthrankings.org, accessed July 24, 2013

- The TechNet 2012 "State Broadband Index" ranked Maine #40 on the following criteria: broadband adoption; network quality; and economic structure. Improved broadband use is hoped to promote economic development, build strong communities, improve delivery of government services and upgrade educational systems.
  TechNet; www.technet.org, accessed July 24, 2013

- Maine was ranked #25 among the states and District of Columbia on the American Council for an Energy-Efficient Economy's "State Energy Efficiency Scorecard" for 2012.
  American Council for an Energy-Efficient Economy; aceee.org/sector/state-policy/scorecard, accessed July 24, 2013

Statistical Tables

DEMOGRAPHICS
Resident State and National Population, 1950-2012
Projected State and National Population, 2000-2030
Population by Age, 2012
Population by Race, 2012
Population by Hispanic Origin and Race, 2012

VITAL STATISTICS
Death Rates by Leading Causes, 2010
Death Rates by Selected Causes, 2010
Abortion Rates, 2009
Infant Mortality Rates, 1995-2009
Marriage and Divorce Rates, 2000-2011

ECONOMY
Nominal Gross Domestic Product by Industry, 2012
Real Gross Domestic Product, 2000-2012
Personal Income Per Capita, 1930-2012
Non-Farm Employment by Sector, 2012
Foreign Exports, 2000-2012
Energy Consumption, 2011

LAND AND WATER
Surface Area and Federally-Owned Land, 2007
Land Cover/Use of Non-Federal Rural Land, 2007
Farms and Crop Acreage, 2012

HEALTH AND MEDICAL CARE
Medical Professionals, 2012
Health Insurance Coverage, 2011
HIV, STD, and Tuberculosis Cases and Rates, 2011
Cigarette Smoking, 2011

HOUSING
Home Ownership Rates, 1995-2012
Home Sales, 2000-2010
Value of Owner-Occupied Homes, 2011

EDUCATION
School Enrollment, 2011
Educational Attainment, 2011
Public College Finances, FY 2012

TRANSPORTATION AND TRAVEL
Motor Vehicle Registrations and Drivers Licenses, 2011
Domestic Travel Expenditures, 2009
Retail Gasoline Prices, 2013
Public Road Length, 2011

CRIME AND LAW ENFORCEMENT
Full-Time Law Enforcement Officers, 2011
Prison Population, 2000-2012
Crime Rate, 2011

GOVERNMENT AND FINANCE
Local Governments by Type, 2012
State Government Revenue, 2011
State Government Expenditures, 2011
State Government General Expenditures by Function, 2011
State Government Finances, Cash and Debt, 2011

POLITICS
Composition of the Senate, 1995-2013
Composition of the House of Representatives, 1995-2013
Composition of State Legislature, 2004-2013
Voter Participation in Presidential Elections, 1980-2012
Governors Since Statehood

DEMOGRAPHICS

Resident State and National Population, 1950–2012

Year	State Population	U.S. Population	State Share
1950	914,000	151,326,000	0.60%
1960	969,000	179,323,000	0.54%
1970	993,722	203,302,031	0.49%
1980	1,124,660	226,545,805	0.50%
1990	1,227,928	248,709,873	0.49%
2000	1,274,779	281,424,600	0.45%
2010	1,328,361	308,745,538	0.43%
2012	1,329,192	313,914,040	0.42%

Note: 1950/1960 population figures are rounded to the nearest thousand.
Source: U.S. Census Bureau, Decennial Census 1950–2010; U.S. Census Bureau, 2012 Population Estimates

Projected State and National Population, 2000–2030

Year	State Population	U.S. Population	State Share
2000	1,274,923	281,421,906	0.45%
2005	1,318,557	295,507,134	0.45%
2010	1,357,134	308,935,581	0.44%
2015	1,388,878	322,365,787	0.43%
2020	1,408,665	335,804,546	0.42%
2025	1,414,402	349,439,199	0.40%
2030	1,411,097	363,584,435	0.39%
State population growth, 2000–2030			136,174
State percentage growth, 2000–2030			10.7%

Source: U.S. Census Bureau, Population Division, Interim State Population Projections, 2005

Population by Age, 2012

Age Group	State Population	Percent of Total Population	
		State	U.S.
Under 5 years	66,904	5.0%	6.4%
5 to 14 years	150,113	11.3%	13.1%
15 to 24 years	164,594	12.4%	14.0%
25 to 34 years	148,099	11.1%	13.5%
35 to 44 years	161,566	12.2%	12.9%
45 to 54 years	210,092	15.8%	14.1%
55 to 64 years	201,448	15.2%	12.3%
65 to 74 years	125,691	9.5%	7.6%
75 to 84 years	70,212	5.3%	4.2%
85 years and older	30,473	2.3%	1.9%
Under 18 years	265,918	20.0%	23.5%
65 years and older	226,376	17.0%	13.7%
Median age (years)	–	43.5	37.4

Source: U.S. Census Bureau, Annual Estimates of the Resident Population for Selected Age Groups by Sex for the United States, States, Counties, and Puerto Rico Commonwealth and Municipios: April 1, 2010 to July 1, 2012

Population by Race, 2012

Race	State Population	Percent of Total Population	
		State	U.S.
All residents	1,329,192	100.00%	100.00%
White	1,266,849	95.31%	77.89%
African American	17,603	1.32%	13.13%
Native American	8,859	0.67%	1.23%
Asian	14,810	1.11%	5.14%
Native Hawaiian	513	0.04%	0.23%
Two or more races	20,558	1.55%	2.39%

Source: U.S. Census Bureau, Population Division, Annual Estimates of the Resident Population by Sex, Race and Hispanic Origin for the United States, States, and Counties: April 1, 2010 to July 1, 2012

Population by Hispanic Origin and Race, 2012

Hispanic Origin/Race	State Population	Percent of Total Population	
		State	U.S.
All residents	1,329,192	100.00%	100.00%
All Hispanic residents	18,599	1.40%	16.89%
Hispanic			
White	15,484	1.16%	14.91%
African American	1,032	0.08%	0.79%
Native American	515	0.04%	0.49%
Asian	287	0.02%	0.17%
Native Hawaiian	76	0.01%	0.06%
Two or more races	1,205	0.09%	0.48%
Not Hispanic			
White	1,251,365	94.14%	62.98%
African American	16,571	1.25%	12.34%
Native American	8,344	0.63%	0.74%
Asian	14,523	1.09%	4.98%
Native Hawaiian	437	0.03%	0.17%
Two or more races	19,353	1.46%	1.91%

Source: U.S. Census Bureau, Population Division, Annual Estimates of the Resident Population by Sex, Race and Hispanic Origin for the United States, States, and Counties: April 1, 2010 to July 1, 2012

VITAL STATISTICS

Death Rates by Leading Causes, 2010

Cause	State	U.S.
Malignant neoplasms	202.5	186.2
Ischaemic heart diseases	99.0	122.9
Other forms of heart disease	53.8	53.4
Chronic lower respiratory diseases	50.0	44.7
Cerebrovascular diseases	37.2	41.9
Organic, incl. symptomatic, mental disorders	44.1	35.7
Other degenerative diseases of the nervous sys.	31.9	28.4
Other external causes of accidental injury	23.9	26.5
Diabetes mellitus	23.5	22.4
Hypertensive diseases	9.1	20.4
All causes	800.9	799.5

Note: Figures are age-adjusted death rates per 100,000 population
Source: CDC/NCHS, Underlying Cause of Death 1999–2010 on CDC WONDER Online Database

Death Rates by Selected Causes, 2010

Cause	State	U.S.
Assault	2.0	5.2
Diseases of the liver	14.1	13.9
Human immunodeficiency virus (HIV) disease	–	2.7
Influenza and pneumonia	14.4	16.2
Intentional self-harm	13.4	12.4
Malnutrition	–	0.9
Obesity and other hyperalimentation	1.9	1.8
Renal failure	14.2	14.4
Transport accidents	13.2	12.1
Viral hepatitis	2.3	2.4

Note: Figures are age-adjusted death rates per 100,000 population; A dash indicates that data was not available or was suppressed
Source: CDC/NCHS, Underlying Cause of Death 1999–2010 on CDC WONDER Online Database

Abortion Rates, 2009

Category	2009
By state of residence	
Total abortions	2,355
Abortion rate[1]	9.6%
Abortion ratio[2]	175
By state of occurrence	
Total abortions	2,413
Abortion rate[1]	9.8%
Abortion ratio[2]	179
Abortions obtained by out-of-state residents	2.3%
U.S. abortion rate[1]	15.1%
U.S. abortion ratio[2]	227

Note: (1) Number of abortions per 1,000 women aged 15–44 years; (2) Number of abortions per 1,000 live births; A dash indicates that data was not available
Source: CDC/NCHS, Morbidity and Mortality Weekly Report, November 23, 2012 (Abortion Surveillance, United States, 2009)

Infant Mortality Rates, 1995–2009

Category	1995	2000	2005	2009
All state residents	6.40	4.85	6.87	5.72
All U.S. residents	7.57	6.89	6.86	6.39
All state white residents	6.12	4.93	6.81	5.82
All U.S. white residents	6.30	5.71	5.73	5.33
All state black residents	–	–	–	–
All U.S. black residents	14.58	13.48	13.26	12.12

Note: Figures represent deaths per 1,000 live births of resident infants under one year old, exclusive of fetal deaths; A dash indicates that data was not available or was suppressed.
Source: Centers of Disease Control and Prevention, Division of Vital Statistics, Linked Birth/Infant Death Records on CDC Wonder Online

Marriage and Divorce Rates, 2000–2011

Year	Marriage Rate State	Marriage Rate U.S.	Divorce Rate State	Divorce Rate U.S.
2000	8.8	8.2	5.0	4.0
2002	8.4	8.0	4.6	3.9
2004	8.6	7.8	4.3	3.7
2006	7.8	7.5	4.2	3.7
2008	7.4	7.1	4.2	3.5
2010	7.1	6.8	4.2	3.6
2011	7.2	6.8	4.2	3.6

Note: Rates are based on provisional counts of marriages/divorces by state of occurrence and are per 1,000 total population residing in area
Source: CDC/NCHS, National Vital Statistics System

ECONOMY

Nominal Gross Domestic Product by Industry, 2012
In millions of current dollars

Industry	State GDP
Accommodation and food services	2,005
Administrative and waste management services	1,482
Agriculture, forestry, fishing, and hunting	808
Arts, entertainment, and recreation	514
Construction	2,070
Educational services	745
Finance and insurance	4,070
Health care and social assistance	6,176
Information	1,011
Management of companies and enterprises	780
Manufacturing	5,497
Mining	7
Other services, except government	1,275
Professional, scientific, and technical services	2,893
Real estate and rental and leasing	7,367
Retail trade	4,545
Transportation and warehousing	1,251
Utilities	1,052
Wholesale trade	2,699

Source: U.S. Department of Commerce, Bureau of Economic Analysis, Survey of Current Business

Real Gross Domestic Product, 2000–2012
In millions of chained 2005 dollars

Year	State GDP	U.S. GDP	State Share
2000	41,715	11,225,406	0.37%
2005	45,520	12,539,116	0.36%
2010	45,564	12,897,088	0.35%
2012	45,986	13,430,576	0.34%

Source: U.S. Department of Commerce, Bureau of Economic Analysis, Survey of Current Business

Personal Income Per Capita, 1930–2012

Year	State	U.S.
1930	$570	$618
1940	$525	$593
1950	$1,187	$1,503
1960	$1,901	$2,268
1970	$3,413	$4,084
1980	$8,333	$10,091
1990	$17,211	$19,354
2000	$26,699	$30,319
2010	$36,629	$39,791
2012	$39,481	$42,693

Source: U.S. Department of Commerce, Bureau of Economic Analysis, Regional Economic Accounts

Non-Farm Employment by Sector, 2012
In thousands

Sector	Employment
Construction	25.6
Education and health services	121.2
Financial activities	31.4
Government	101.3
Information	7.9
Leisure and hospitality	61.7
Mining and logging	2.5
Manufacturing	50.8
Other services	19.9
Professional and business services	58.0
Trade, transportation, and utilities	117.4
All sectors	597.6

Source: U.S. Bureau of Labor Statistics, State and Area Employment

Foreign Exports, 2000–2012
In millions of dollars

Year	State Exports	U.S. Exports	State Share
2000	1,778	712,054	0.25%
2002	1,980	649,940	0.30%
2004	2,431	768,554	0.32%
2006	2,641	973,994	0.27%
2008	3,016	1,222,545	0.25%
2010	3,162	1,208,080	0.26%
2012	3,047	1,478,268	0.21%

Note: U.S. figures exclude data from Puerto Rico, U.S. Virgin Islands, and unallocated exports
Source: U.S. Department of Commerce, International Trade Admin., Office of Trade and Industry Information, Manufacturing and Services

Energy Consumption, 2011

In trillions of BTUs, except as noted

Total energy consumption	
Total state energy consumption	412.5
Total U.S. energy consumption	97,387.3
State share of U.S. total	0.42%
Per capita consumption (in millions of BTUs)	
Total state per capita consumption	310.5
Total U.S. per capita consumption	312.6
End-use sectors	
Residential	86.2
Commercial	63.7
Industrial	139.6
Transportation	123.0
Sources of energy	
Petroleum	190.5
Natural gas	74.0
Coal	1.5
Renewable energy	160.4
Nuclear electric power	0.0

Source: U.S. Energy Information Administration, State Energy Data 2011: Consumption

LAND AND WATER

Surface Area and Federally-Owned Land, 2007

In thousands of acres

Category	State	U.S.	State Share
Total surface area	20,966.2	1,937,664.2	1.08%
Total land area	19,709.6	1,886,846.9	1.04%
Non-federal land	19,502.4	1,484,910.0	1.31%
Developed	851.1	111,251.2	0.77%
Rural	18,651.3	1,373,658.8	1.36%
Federal land	207.2	401,936.9	0.05%
Water area	1,256.6	50,817.3	2.47%

Source: U.S. Department of Agriculture, Natural Resources Conservation Service, 2007 National Resources Inventory

Land Cover/Use of Non-Federal Rural Land, 2007

In thousands of acres

Category	State	U.S.	State Share
Total rural land	18,651.3	1,373,658.8	1.36%
Cropland	372.8	357,023.5	0.10%
CRP[1] land	29.7	32,850.2	0.09%
Pastureland	141.6	118,615.7	0.12%
Rangeland	0.0	409,119.4	0.00%
Forest land	17,632.1	406,410.4	4.34%
Other rural land	475.1	49,639.6	0.96%

Note: (1) Conservation Reserve Program was created to assist private landowners in converting highly erodible cropland to vegetative cover.
Source: U.S. Department of Agriculture, Natural Resources Conservation Service, 2007 National Resources Inventory

Farms and Crop Acreage, 2012

Category	State	U.S.	State Share
Farms (in thousands)	8.1	2,170.0	0.37%
Acres (in millions)	1.4	914.0	0.15%
Acres per farm	166.7	421.2	–

Source: U.S. Department of Agriculture, National Agricultural Statistical Service, Quick Stats, 2012 Survey Data

HEALTH AND MEDICAL CARE

Medical Professionals, 2012

Profession	State Number	U.S. Number	State Share	State Rate[1]	U.S. Rate[1]
Physicians[2]	4,300	894,637	0.48%	323.7	287.1
Dentists	733	193,587	0.38%	55.2	62.1
Podiatrists	78	17,469	0.45%	5.9	5.6
Optometrists	216	45,638	0.47%	16.3	14.6
Chiropractors	331	77,494	0.43%	24.9	24.9

Note: (1) Rates are per 100,000 population; (2) Includes total, active Doctors of Osteopathic Medicine and Doctors of Medicine in 2011.
Source: U.S. Department of Health and Human Services, Bureau of Health Professions, Area Health Resource File, 2012-2013

Health Insurance Coverage, 2011

Category	State	U.S.
Total persons covered	1,196,000	260,214,000
Total persons not covered	134,000	48,613,000
Percent not covered	10.1%	15.7%
Children under age 18 covered	252,000	67,143,000
Children under age 18 not covered	17,000	6,965,000
Percent of children not covered	6.3%	9.4%

Source: U.S. Census Bureau, Current Population Survey, 2012 Annual Social and Economic Supplement

HIV, STD, and Tuberculosis Cases and Rates, 2011

Disease	State Cases	State Rate[1]	U.S. Rate[1]
Chlamydia	3,094	232.9	457.6
Gonorrhea	272	20.5	104.2
HIV diagnosis	59	5.2	15.8
HIV, stage 3 (AIDS)	22	1.9	10.3
Syphilis, early latent	8	0.6	4.3
Syphilis, primary/secondary	12	0.9	4.5
Tuberculosis	9	0.7	3.4

Note: (1) Rates are per 100,000 population
Source: Centers for Disease Control and Prevention

Cigarette Smoking, 2011

Category	State	U.S.
Adults who are current smokers	22.8%	21.2%
Adults who smoke everyday	17.6%	15.4%
Adults who smoke some days	5.2%	5.7%
Adults who are former smokers	31.6%	25.1%
Adults who never smoked	45.6%	52.9%

Source: Centers for Disease Control and Prevention, Behaviorial Risk Factor Surveillance System, Tobacco Use, 2011

HOUSING

Home Ownership Rates, 1995–2012

Area	1995	2000	2005	2010	2012
State	76.7%	76.5%	73.9%	73.8%	74.1%
U.S.	64.7%	67.4%	68.9%	66.9%	65.4%

Source: U.S. Census Bureau, Housing Vacancies and Homeownership, Annual Statistics

Home Sales, 2000–2010

In thousands of units

Year	State Sales	U.S. Sales	State Share
2000	27.6	5,174	0.53%
2002	28.8	5,632	0.51%
2004	33.6	6,778	0.50%
2006	30.7	6,478	0.47%
2008	20.6	4,913	0.42%
2010	22.8	4,908	0.46%

Note: Units include single-family homes, condos and co-ops
Source: National Association of Realtors, Real Estate Outlook, Market Trends & Insights

Value of Owner-Occupied Homes, 2011

Value	Total Units in State	Percent of Total, State	Percent of Total, U.S.
Less than $50,000	32,701	8.3%	8.8%
$50,000 to $99,000	53,517	13.7%	16.0%
$100,000 to $149,000	68,586	17.5%	16.5%
$150,000 to $199,000	79,594	20.3%	15.4%
$200,000 to $299,000	86,169	22.0%	18.2%
$300,000 to $499,000	50,532	12.9%	15.2%
$500,000 to $999,000	16,131	4.1%	7.9%
$1,000,000 or more	4,467	1.1%	2.0%
Median value	–	$171,600	$173,600

Source: U.S. Census Bureau, 2011 American Community Survey 1-Year Estimates

EDUCATION

School Enrollment, 2011

Educational Level	Students Enrolled in State	Percent of Total, State	Percent of Total, U.S.
All levels	304,531	100.0%	100.0%
Nursery school, preschool	15,365	5.0%	6.0%
Kindergarten	15,201	5.0%	5.1%
Elementary (grades 1–8)	124,147	40.8%	39.5%
Secondary (grades 9–12)	66,335	21.8%	20.7%
College or graduate school	83,483	27.4%	28.7%

Note: Figures cover the population 3 years and over enrolled in school
Source: U.S. Census Bureau, 2011 American Community Survey 1-Year Estimates

Educational Attainment, 2011

Highest Level of Education	State	U.S.
High school diploma	90.9%	85.9%
Bachelor's degree	28.4%	28.5%
Graduate/Professional degree	10.5%	10.6%

Note: Figures cover the population 25 years and over
Source: U.S. Census Bureau, 2011 American Community Survey 1-Year Estimates

Public College Finances, FY 2012

Category	State	U.S.
Full-time equivalent enrollment (FTE)[1]	37,897	11,548,974
Educational appropriations per FTE[2]	$6,071	$5,906
Net tuition revenue per FTE[3]	$8,027	$5,189
Total educational revenue per FTE[4]	$14,097	$11,043

(1) Full-time equivalent enrollment equates student credit hours to full time, academic year students, but excludes medical students; (2) Educational appropriations measure state and local support available for public higher education operating expenses including ARRA funds and excludes appropriations for independent institutions, financial aid for students attending independent institutions, research, hospitals, and medical education; (3) Net tuition revenue is calculated by taking the gross amount of tuition and fees, less state and institutional financial aid, tuition waivers or discounts, and medical student tuition and fees. Net tuition revenue used for capital debt service is included in the net tuition revenue figures; (4) Total educational revenue is the sum of educational appropriations and net tuition excluding net tuition revenue used for capital debt service.
Source: State Higher Education Executive Officers, State Higher Education Finance FY 2012

TRANSPORTATION AND TRAVEL

Motor Vehicle Registrations and Drivers Licenses, 2011

Vehicle Type	State	U.S.	State Share
Automobiles[1]	530,057	125,656,528	0.42%
Buses	4,631	666,064	0.70%
Trucks	586,265	118,455,587	0.49%
Motorcycles	50,327	8,437,502	0.60%
Drivers licenses	1,014,826	211,874,649	0.48%

Note: Motor vehicle registrations include private, commercial, and publicly-owned vehicles; (1) Includes taxicabs
Source: U.S. Department of Transportation, Federal Highway Administration

Domestic Travel Expenditures, 2009

In millions of dollars

Category	State	U.S.	State Share
Travel expenditures	$2,490	$610,200	0.41%

Note: Figures represent U.S. spending on domestic overnight trips and day trips of 50 miles or more, one way, away from home. Excludes spending by foreign visitors.
Source: U.S. Travel Association, Impact of Travel on State Economies, 2009

Retail Gasoline Prices, 2013

Gasoline Grade	State Average	U.S. Average
Regular	$3.79	$3.65
Mid	$3.91	$3.81
Premium	$4.03	$3.98
Diesel	$3.97	$3.88
Excise tax[1]	49.9 cents	49.4 cents

Note: Gasoline prices as of 7/26/2013; (1) Includes state and federal excise taxes and other state taxes as of July 1, 2013
Source: American Automobile Association, Daily Fuel Guage Report; American Petroleum Institute, State Motor Fuel Taxes, 2013

Public Road Length, 2011

Type	State Mileage	U.S. Mileage	State Share
Interstate highways	368	46,960	0.78%
Other highways	19	15,719	0.12%
Principal arterial	931	156,262	0.60%
Minor arterial	1,250	242,942	0.51%
Major collector	3,750	534,592	0.70%
Minor collector	2,180	266,357	0.82%
Local	14,377	2,814,925	0.51%
Urban	3,007	1,095,373	0.27%
Rural	19,867	2,982,383	0.67%
Total	22,874	4,077,756	0.56%

Note: Combined urban and rural road mileage equals the total of the other road types
Source: U.S. Department of Transportation, Federal Highway Administration, Public Road Length, 2011

CRIME AND LAW ENFORCEMENT

Full-Time Law Enforcement Officers, 2011

Gender	State Number	State Rate[1]	U.S. Rate[1]
Male officers	2,121	159.8	210.3
Female officers	136	10.2	28.1
Total officers	2,257	170.0	238.3

Note: (1) Rates are per 100,000 population
Source: Federal Bureau of Investigation, Uniform Crime Reports, Crime in the United States 2011

Prison Population, 2000–2012

Year	State Population	U.S. Population	State Share
2000	1,679	1,391,261	0.12%
2005	2,023	1,527,929	0.13%
2010	2,154	1,613,803	0.13%
2011	2,145	1,598,783	0.13%
2012	2,108	1,571,013	0.13%

Note: Figures include prisoners under the jurisdiction of state or federal correctional authorities.
Source: U.S. Department of Justice, Bureau of Justice Statistics, Prisoners in 2006, 2011, 2012 (Advance Counts)

Crime Rate, 2011

Incidents per 100,000 residents

Category	State	U.S.
Violent crimes	123.2	386.3
Murder	2.0	4.7
Forcible rape	29.6	26.8
Robbery	27.8	113.7
Aggravated assault	63.8	241.1
Property crimes	2,545.5	2,908.7
Burglary	591.3	702.2
Larceny/theft	1,873.0	1,976.9
Motor vehicle theft	81.2	229.6
All crimes	2,668.7	3,295.0

Source: Federal Bureau of Investigation, Uniform Crime Reports, Crime in the United States 2011

GOVERNMENT AND FINANCE

Local Governments by Type, 2012

Government Type	State	U.S.	State Share
All local governments	841	89,004	0.94%
County	16	3,031	0.53%
Municipality	22	19,522	0.11%
Town/Township	466	16,364	2.85%
Special District	238	37,203	0.64%
Ind. School District	99	12,884	0.77%

Source: U.S. Census Bureau, 2012 Census of Governments: Organization Component Preliminary Estimates

State Government Revenue, 2011

In thousands of dollars, except for per capita figures

Total revenue	$10,611,116
Total revenue per capita, State	$7,987
Total revenue per capita, U.S.	$7,271
General revenue	$8,249,133
Intergovernmental revenue	$3,241,435
Taxes	$3,675,810
General sales	$1,010,241
Selective sales	$672,404
License taxes	$248,730
Individual income taxes	$1,420,982
Corporate income taxes	$208,997
Other taxes	$114,456
Current charges	$791,648
Miscellaneous general revenue	$540,240
Utility revenue	$0
Liquor store revenue	$33
Insurance trust revenue[1]	$2,361,950

Note: (1) Within insurance trust revenue, net earnings of state retirement systems is a calculated statistic, and thus can be positive or negative. Net earnings is the sum of earnings on investments plus gains on investments minus losses on investments.
Source: U.S. Census Bureau, 2011 Annual Survey of State Government Finances

State Government Expenditures, 2011
In thousands of dollars, except for per capita figures

Total expenditure	$9,099,085
Total expenditure per capita, State	$6,849
Total expenditure per capita, U.S.	$6,427
Intergovernmental expenditure	$1,301,692
Direct expenditure	$7,797,393
Current operation	$5,730,549
Capital outlay	$492,329
Insurance benefits and repayments	$1,089,136
Assistance and subsidies	$236,004
Interest on debt	$249,375
Utility expenditure	$4,801
Liquor store expenditure	$0
Insurance trust expenditure	$1,089,136

Source: U.S. Census Bureau, 2011 Annual Survey of State Government Finances

State Government General Expenditures by Function, 2011
In thousands of dollars

Education	$2,121,288
Public welfare	$2,905,192
Hospitals	$54,358
Health	$445,881
Highways	$647,106
Police protection	$71,468
Correction	$142,410
Natural resources	$168,925
Parks and recreation	$25,230
Governmental administration	$286,203
Interest on general debt	$249,375
Other and unallocable	$887,712

Source: U.S. Census Bureau, 2011 Annual Survey of State Government Finances

State Government Finances, Cash and Debt, 2011
In thousands of dollars, except for per capita figures

Debt at end of fiscal year	
State, total	$5,904,221
State, per capita	$4,444
U.S., per capita	$3,635
Cash and security holdings	
State, total	$17,780,804
State, per capita	$13,384
U.S., per capita	$11,759

Source: U.S. Census Bureau, 2011 Annual Survey of State Government Finances

POLITICS

Composition of the Senate, 1995–2013

Congress (Year)	State/U.S	Dem	Rep	Total
104th (1995)	State delegates	0	2	2
	Total U.S.	48	52	100
105th (1997)	State delegates	0	2	2
	Total U.S.	45	55	100
106th (1999)	State delegates	0	2	2
	Total U.S.	45	55	100
107th (2001)	State delegates	0	2	2
	Total U.S.	50	50	100
108th (2003)	State delegates	0	2	2
	Total U.S.	48	51	100
109th (2005)	State delegates	0	2	2
	Total U.S.	44	55	100
110th (2007)	State delegates	0	2	2
	Total U.S.	49	49	100
111th (2009)	State delegates	0	2	2
	Total U.S.	57	41	100
112th (2011)	State delegates	0	2	2
	Total U.S.	51	47	100
113th (2013)	State delegates	0	2	2
	Total U.S.	54	45	100

Note: Figures are for the starts of first sessions; Totals include Democratic (Dem) and Republican (Rep) members as well as vacancies and seats held by independent party members
Source: U.S. Congress, Congressional Directory

Composition of the House of Representatives, 1995–2013

Congress (Year)	State/U.S	Dem	Rep	Total
104th (1995)	State delegates	1	1	2
	Total U.S.	204	230	435
105th (1997)	State delegates	2	0	2
	Total U.S.	207	226	435
106th (1999)	State delegates	2	0	2
	Total U.S.	211	223	435
107th (2001)	State delegates	2	0	2
	Total U.S.	212	221	435
108th (2003)	State delegates	2	0	2
	Total U.S.	205	229	435
109th (2005)	State delegates	2	0	2
	Total U.S.	202	231	435
110th (2007)	State delegates	2	0	2
	Total U.S.	233	198	435
111th (2009)	State delegates	2	0	2
	Total U.S.	256	178	435
112th (2011)	State delegates	2	0	2
	Total U.S.	193	242	435
113th (2013)	State delegates	2	0	2
	Total U.S.	201	234	435

Note: Figures are for the starts of first sessions; Totals include Democratic (Dem) and Republican (Rep) members as well as vacancies and seats held by independent party members
Source: U.S. Congress, Congressional Directory

Composition of State Legislature, 2004–2013

Year	Democrats	Republicans	Total
State Senate			
2004	18	17	35
2005	19	16	35
2006	19	16	35
2007	18	17	35
2008	18	17	35
2009	20	15	35
2010	20	15	35
2011	14	20	35
2012	14	20	35
2013	19	15	35
State House			
2004	80	67	151
2005	76	73	151
2006	76	73	151
2007	89	60	151
2008	90	59	151
2009	95	55	151
2010	96	54	151
2011	72	78	151
2012	72	77	151
2013	58	89	151

Note: Totals may include minor party members and vacancies
Source: The Council of State Governments, State Legislatures

Voter Participation in Presidential Elections, 1980–2012

Year	Voting-eligible State Population	State Voter Turnout Rate	U.S. Voter Turnout Rate
1980	799,746	65.4	54.2
1984	840,251	65.8	55.2
1988	888,612	62.5	52.8
1992	915,082	74.3	58.1
1996	929,970	65.2	51.7
2000	969,292	67.2	54.2
2004	1,003,792	73.8	60.1
2008	1,036,242	70.6	61.6
2012	1,047,901	68.1	58.2

*Note: All figures are based on the voting-eligible population which
excludes person ineligible to vote such as non-citizens, felons (depending
on state law), and mentally-incapacitated persons. U.S. figures include
the overseas eligible population (including military personnel).*
*Source: McDonald, Michael P., United States Election Project,
Presidential Voter Turnout Rates, 1980–2012*

Governors Since Statehood

William King (O)	(r) 1820-1821
William D. Williamson (O)	(r) 1821
Benjamin Ames (O)	1821-1822
Albion K. Parris (O)	1822-1827
Enoch Lincoln (O)	(d) 1827-1829
Nathan Cutler (O)	1829-1830
Joshua Hall (O)	1830
Jonathan G. Hunton (O)	1830-1831
Samuel E. Smith (O)	1831-1834
Robert P. Dunlap (D)	1834-1838
Edward Kent (O)	1838-1839
John Fairfield (D)	1839-1841
Edward Kent (O)	1841-1842
John Fairfield (D)	(r) 1842-1843
Edward Kavanagh (D)	1843-1844
Hugh J. Anderson (D)	1844-1847
John W. Dana (D)	1847-1850
John Hubbard (D)	1850-1853
William G. Crosby (O)	1853-1855
Anson P. Morrill (R)	1855-1856
Samuel Wells (D)	1856-1857
Hannibal Hamlin (R)	1857
Joseph H. Williams (R)	1857-1858
Lot M. Morrill (R)	1858-1861
Israel Washburn Jr. (R)	1861-1863
Abner Coburn (R)	1863-1864
Samuel Cony (R)	1864-1867
Joshua L. Chamberlain (R)	1867-1871
Sidney Perham (R)	1871-1874
Nelson Dingley Jr. (R)	1874-1876
Sheldon Connor (R)	1876-1879
Alonzo Garcelon (D)	1879-1880
Daniel F. Davis (R)	1880-1881
Harris M. Plaisted (O)	1881-1883
Frederick Robie (R)	1883-1887
Joseph R. Bodwell (R)	(d) 1887
Sebastian S. Marble (R)	1887-1889
Edwin C. Burleigh (R)	1889-1893
Henry B. Cleaves (R)	1893-1897
Llewellyn Powers (R)	1897-1901
John F. Hill (R)	1901-1905
William T. Cobb (R)	1905-1909
Bert M. Fernald (R)	1909-1911
Frederick W. Plaisted (D)	1911-1913
William T. Haines (R)	1913-1915
Oakley C. Curtis (D)	1915-1917
Carl E. Milliken (R)	1917-1921
Frederic H. Parkhurst (R)	(d) 1921
Percival P. Baxter (R)	1921-1925
Ralph O. Brewster (R)	1925-1929
William T. Gardiner (R)	1929-1933
Louis J. Brann (R)	1933-1937
Lewis O. Barrows (D)	1937-1941
Sumner Sewall (R)	1941-1945
Horace A. Hildreth (R)	1945-1949
Frederick G. Payne (R)	(r) 1949-1952
Burton M. Cross (R)	1952-1955
Edmund S. Muskie (D)	(r) 1955-1959
Robert N. Haskell (R)	1959
Clinton A. Clauson (D)	(d) 1959
John H. Reed (R)	1959-1967
Kenneth M. Curtis (D)	1967-1975
James B. Longley (O)	1975-1979
Joseph E. Brennan (D)	1979-1987
John R. McKernan Jr. (R)	1987-1995
Angus S. King Jr. (O)	1995-2003
John Baldacci (D)	2003-2011
Paul LePage (R)	2011-2015

*Note: (D) Democrat; (R) Republican; (O) Other party; (r) resigned;
(d) died in office; (i) removed from office*

Maryland

Location: Atlantic coast

Area and rank: 9,775 square miles (25,316 square kilometers); 12,407 square miles (32,134 square kilometers) including water; forty-second largest state in area

Coastline: 31 miles (50 kilometers) on the Atlantic Ocean

Shoreline: 3,190 miles (5,134 kilometers)

Population and rank: 5,884,563 (2012 estimate); nineteenth largest state in population

Capital city: Annapolis (38,394 people in 2010 census)

Largest city: Baltimore (620,961 people in 2010 census)

Entered Union and rank: April 28, 1788; seventh state

Present constitution adopted: 1867

Counties: 23, as well as 1 independent city

State name: Maryland was named to honor of Henrietta Maria, the queen of Charles I of England

State nicknames: Free State; Old Line State

State capitol building in Annapolis. (©Rudy Riet/Flickr)

Motto: *Fatti maschii, parole femine* (Manly deeds, womanly words; or, Strong deeds, gentle words)

State flag: Two quarters bear the arms of the Calvert family in gold and black; two quarters show the arms of the Crossland family in red and white

Highest point: Backbone Mountain—3,360 feet (1,024 meters)

Lowest point: Atlantic Ocean—sea level

Highest recorded temperature: 109 degrees Fahrenheit (43 degrees Celsius)—Cumberland and Frederick, 1936

Lowest recorded temperature: –40 degrees Fahrenheit (–40 degrees Celsius)—Oakland, 1912

State song: "Maryland! My Maryland!"

State tree: White oak

State flower: Black-eyed susan

State bird: Baltimore oriole

State fish: Rockfish

Maryland History

In many ways, Maryland is a microcosm of much of the United States, combining elements from the north, south, east, and west. Physically located in the middle of the English colonies, it was the center state of the new nation and thus the logical site for a capital, which is located in the District of Columbia. After the Revolution, Maryland led efforts to develop the nation westward; it remained in the Union during the Civil War but sent soldiers to both the North and the South during that conflict. After World War II, the state managed to preserve its historic traditions and environmental legacy while advancing into the future.

Early History and Settlement. It is uncertain when Native Americans first entered the area now known as Maryland, but tribes of the Iroquoian and Algonquian peoples were certainly present several hundred years prior to European arrival. The major Iroquoian tribe was the Susquehannock, sometimes known as Conestoga, who came south from the Pennsylvania area. The Algonquians included the Choptank, Portobago, and Wicomico, names which still survive on the map of Maryland. The major Algonquian tribes were the Piscataway on the western shore (the mainland) of the Chesapeake Bay, and the Nanticoke on the eastern shore (the peninsula between the Chesapeake Bay and the Atlantic coast). Both Iroquoian and Algonquian Indians lived and farmed in permanent settlements.

The Algonquian tribes welcomed the English settlers, but the Susquehannock proved hostile, although their attacks were aimed as much against Native American allies of the English as against the English themselves. In any event, the colonists successfully defended themselves and in 1652 concluded a peace with the Susquehannock, which included the American Indians' departure from

Antietam, the site of the single bloodiest battle fought during the Civil War. (Wikimedia Commons)

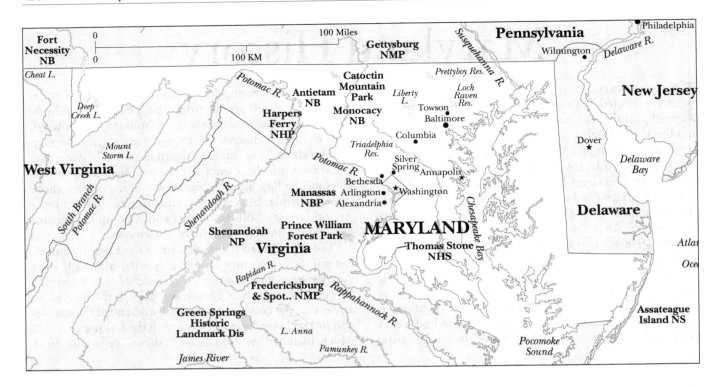

Maryland. Between the 1690's and the mid-eighteenth century, first the Piscataway and then the other Native Americans also moved away from the area.

The Spanish were the first Europeans to explore the area, but the English were the first permanent settlers. English colonists from Virginia under Councilman William Claiborne established a trading post on Kent Island in Chesapeake Bay in 1631. The following year, King Charles I granted Baron Baltimore land north of the Potomac River, which included Maryland. It was on this land that Baltimore established a colony in 1634. Led by Leonard Calvert, half brother of Cecil, the colonists included many Roman Catholics, among them two priests. At this time Roman Catholics were forbidden by British law from voting or holding office. In part, Maryland was founded with the tacit understanding that it would be a refuge for English Catholics. In fact, the name of the colony, while officially honoring Queen Henrietta Maria of England, was often interpreted as referring to the Virgin Mary. In 1649, the colony adopted an "Act Concerning Religion," the first act of religious toleration in the colonies. Soon afterward, a group of Puritans arrived from Virginia.

In the meantime, Maryland settlers under Leonard Calvert disputed Virginia's claims to Kent Island. In 1654, Virginian Claiborne led the Puritans in a revolt that exiled Calvert, an action recognized by the English Commonwealth that had overthrown and executed Charles I. However, in 1658 Calvert and proprietary government were restored to Maryland. In 1692, Maryland became a royal colony, and the Church of England was declared the established, or official, church. In 1718, Roman Catholics were denied the right to vote.

By far the most important influence on Maryland's history has been the Chesapeake Bay, the largest inlet on the East Coast. The bay is nearly two hundred miles long from north to south and as wide as twenty-five miles and is important for commercial fishing, oystering, and crabbing. At the head of the bay is Baltimore, one of the major American ports since its founding in 1729 and Maryland's largest city.

Revolution and Growth. Marylanders joined with other colonists in their distaste for the high taxes imposed by Britain, and in 1774 a group of patriots boarded the *Peggy Stewart* in Annapolis Harbor and destroyed more than two thousand pounds of its cargo of tea. During the American Revolution, when the British threatened the capital of Philadelphia, the Continental Congress moved to Baltimore, then to Annapolis. Maryland troops were among the best in the Continental Army, and their straight ranks and orderly battle lines earned Maryland the nickname "The Old Line State" from General George Washington. After ratifying the Constitution of the newly independent United States, Maryland officially entered the Union in 1788.

In 1791, Maryland and Virginia ceded land to the United States to create the District of Columbia as the site of the new national capital. Construction of the White House began in 1793 and of the Capitol in 1794. In 1800, Congress moved to the new capital city from Philadelphia. During the War of 1812, British forces seized Washington and burned the White House but were unable to force their way past Fort McHenry to capture Baltimore. It was while watching this bombardment from Baltimore harbor that Francis Scott Key composed the poem "The Star Spangled Banner," which later became the national anthem of the United States.

In its key central position, Maryland took a leading role in the growth of the new nation, especially in its westward advancement. The Cumberland Road, also known as the National Pike, was a prime avenue for settlers heading into the interior of the continent; by 1818 it reached the Ohio River. Maryland was also active in the construction of canals, essential for transport of cargo during that period. Two vital waterways, the Chesapeake and Delaware and the Chesapeake and Ohio, connected the bay to those two rivers. The state also took the forefront in exploiting the new technology of the steam railroad, with the Baltimore and Ohio (B&O) starting operations in 1830 as the first American railroad to carry both passengers and freight.

A number of battles were fought in Maryland during the Civil War, the largest being that of Antietam, fought in 1862. Antietam was the single bloodiest day of battle of the war, with more than twenty-three thousand casualties. It was a narrow Union victory, but enough for President Abraham Lincoln to feel justified in announcing the Emancipation Proclamation, which freed the slaves in the Confederacy and transformed the nature of the war to a crusade for liberty. During the summer of 1863, Confederate general Robert E. Lee's Army of Northern Virginia passed through the state on its way to the Battle of Gettysburg. In 1864, Confederate forces under General Jubal Early threatened Washington but were driven back at the last moment by federal reinforcements.

Post-Civil War Progress. Agriculture had been dominant in Maryland prior to the Civil War, with the major crop of tobacco being shipped through the port of Baltimore. However, after the war the state's economy shifted toward manufacturing. Baltimore remained a key shipbuilding and weaponry production center; in the twentieth century the city would make rockets and missiles for the U.S. military. Both shipbuilding and

Few states have cities as dominant as Baltimore, whose population is more than seven times greater than that of Maryland's next-largest city, Columbia. (PhotoDisc)

weapons manufacture were spurred by government purchases during the two world wars.

Education in the state received an infusion of resources during the second half of the nineteenth century, especially with donations from philanthropists such as Johns Hopkins, who provided the financial backing to create the prestigious university that bears his name. Later, during the 1960's, federal funds were allocated for the National Institutes of Health at Bethesda and the Goddard Space Flight Center.

Toward the Future. As the twentieth century advanced, Maryland's agriculture remained important, with the chief crops being tobacco, corn, hay, and soybeans. Manufacturing continued to expand, primarily in shipbuilding, transportation equipment, and modern technology such as electronics. Fishing in the renewed Chesapeake Bay provided much of the seafood sold nationally. However, it was commerce which led Maryland's revitalization, especially in its largest city.

Throughout most of Maryland's history, trade and commerce focused on Baltimore, which underwent a striking revival starting during the 1950's. Under Kurt Schmoke, the first African American elected mayor of the city, Baltimore completed an ambitious reconstruction of its inner harbor, with its centerpiece being the USS *Constellation*, the first warship commissioned by the U.S. Navy, in 1797. In 1992, the Baltimore Orioles opened their new stadium, Camden Yards, widely hailed as one of the best designed and most attractive of modern baseball parks.

Perhaps Maryland's most visible success is its reclaiming of Chesapeake Bay and its adoption of a policy of smart growth to combat urban sprawl. After decades of environmental neglect, including drainage of agriculture chemicals, unregulated dumping of waste, and overfishing, the bay was seriously endangered. Governor Marvin Mandel established a Chesapeake Bay Interagency Planning Committee, and a widespread Save the Bay organization was created—two parts of a comprehensive effort that linked grassroots activists, government, and the private sector in addressing the problem. Spurred by the growing success of this effort, an association of environmental and citizen groups known as the Thousand Friends of Maryland began to campaign for strategic planning and "smart growth" to control urban sprawl, save Maryland's traditional farmlands, and preserve its small towns and their unique character. Supported by Governor Parris Glendening, who made smart growth an issue in his reelection campaign, the Maryland smart growth program became a national trendsetter for the twenty-first century.

Politics and Politicians. In the 2000 election, Maryland, which leans to the Democratic Party, gave its electoral votes to Vice President Al Gore. Senator Paul Sarbanes, a popular Democrat, had little trouble being reelected, garnering 63 percent of the vote to his opponent's 37 percent. In a contested Maryland race, Republican representative Constance Morella defeated a former lobbyist who had been involved in questionable loan practices with a member of Congress.

A controversial issue in November, 2001, concerned legislation barring discriminatory treatment toward homosexuals in public accommodations, housing, and employment. The measure passed the Maryland legislature

Cadets lining up at the U.S. Naval Academy, which opened at Maryland's state capital, Annapolis, in 1845. (Middleton Evans/ Courtesy Maryland Office of Tourism)

and became law. Opponents announced they could not force a referendum on the issue because they were unable to collect sufficient signatures. Passage of the measure had been a top priority of Governor Glendening.

On May 9, 2002, taking part in national soul-searching over the death penalty, Governor Glendening ordered a moratorium on the death penalty. The moratorium was to remain in force at least until a study could be completed on whether racial bias was involved in its application. In the 2002 midterm elections, Maryland's congressional delegation changed dramatically, as two Republicans seats were lost to Democrats, including the seat of eight-term member Constance Morella. At the same time, a new governor was elected, when Robert Ehrlich, Jr., defeated Kathleen Kennedy Townsend, ending thirty-six years of Democrat domination of the statehouse. In 2004, Maryland gave its ten electoral votes to Democratic challenger John Kerry by 56-43 percent. At the same time, it reelected Senator Barbara Mikulski. The $7 million spent on the Senate race set a record in the state.

Martin Joseph O'Malley was elected governor of Maryland in 2006, defeating incumbent Governor Robert Ehrlich. O'Malley won again in 2010, again running against Ehrlich. Prior to being elected as governor, O'Malley had served as mayor of Baltimore from 1999 to 2007. A committed Democrat, he chaired the Democratic Governors Association from 2011 to 2013.

Sniper Killings. Between October 2 and October 24, 2002, two persons, later identified as forty-one-year-old John Allen Muhammad and seventeen-year-old John Lee Malvo, perpetrated a series of fatal shootings in Washington, D.C., and its suburbs, including Maryland and Virginia. Residents were terrorized for weeks as the random attacks continued. Some motivation for the crimes, it was later said, was the men's plot to extort $10 million from the U.S. government. When the spree ended with the capture of the two, ten persons had been killed and three others critically wounded. Some fifteen hundred federal agents and thousands of state and local law enforcement personnel had hunted the snipers. More than seventy thousand calls from the public were received on a hotline by October 21. Most of the incidents occurred in Maryland, where six died and one was injured. The two snipers were apprehended at a Maryland highway rest stop.

Hurricane Isabel. In mid-September, 2003, the state was hit by Hurricane Isabel, which had been downgraded to a tropical storm when it arrived. The storm mainly affected coastal cities, where there was serious flooding. In Baltimore, the state's largest city, water was waist deep; in Annapolis, the state capital, water reached a depth of more than 7.5 feet in the city's streets.

Marijuana. On May 2, 2013 Governor O'Malley signed a law that made medical marijuana legal in Maryland. The law, HB 1101, took effect October 1st. Maryland thus became the nineteenth state to legalize medical marijuana. However, the law is not likely to go into full effect before 2016. The law allows academic medical centers to participate in a "trial program," which would be the only source for patients to get medical marijuana; however some prominent medical centers stated that they would not participate.

Economy. In 2012, the Maryland economy, already in trouble, was further hit by sequestration, which resulted in unpaid furloughs of federal employees. Due to the fact that a large proportion of Maryland residents work for the federal government, either in the District of Columbia or in federal offices located in Maryland, the state was particularly vulnerable to the layoffs. By July 2013, the unemployment rate in the state topped seven percent.

Michael Witkoski
Updated by the Editor

Maryland Time Line

1608	English Captain John Smith charts Chesapeake Bay region.
1631	Councilman William Claiborne establishes trading post on Kent Island as outpost of Virginia.
June 20, 1632	English King Charles I grants Lord Baltimore the province of Maryland.
1634	Governor Leonard Calvert and settlers found St. Mary's City.
1635	St. Mary's City settlers fight Claiborne's colonists.
Apr. 21, 1649	Maryland enacts "Act Concerning Religion," the first act of religious toleration in the colonies.
1652	Peace treaty is made with Susquehannock Indians.
1654	English Commonwealth ends Maryland's proprietary government.
1658	Proprietary government is restored by English Parliament.
1692	Maryland becomes a royal colony; Church of England made state church.
1694	Capital is moved to Annapolis.

1718	Roman Catholics lose the right to vote.
Oct. 19, 1774	Patriots burn cargo of tea aboard *Peggy Stewart* in Annapolis Harbor.
1776	Maryland Provincial Convention votes for independence; adopts state constitution.
1776	Continental Congress, fearing capture by British, flees Philadelphia to Baltimore.
Jan. 14, 1784	Continental Congress meets at Annapolis to sign Treaty of Paris.
Apr. 28, 1788	Maryland ratifies U.S. Constitution, becoming seventh state.
1791	Maryland cedes land to District of Columbia.
1796	Baltimore City is incorporated.
1809	First Roman Catholic parochial school in Union opens in Baltimore.
1812	University of Maryland is founded at Baltimore.
1814	British are defeated in attack on Fort McHenry outside Baltimore; Francis Scott Key writes "The Star-Spangled Banner."
1818	Cumberland Road (National Pike) reaches Ohio River.
1824–1829	Chesapeake and Delaware Canal is constructed.
1827	Baltimore and Ohio Railroad is chartered.
1828–1850	Chesapeake and Ohio Canal is constructed.
1830	Locomotive *Tom Thumb* races on Baltimore and Ohio Railroad line, the first U.S. railroad to carry both passengers and freight.
May 24, 1844	First telegraph line in United States links Baltimore with Washington, D.C.
1845	U.S. Naval Academy opens at Annapolis.
1849	Edgar Allan Poe dies in Baltimore.
Apr. 19, 1861	Baltimore mob attacks Union troops passing through state; sixteen are killed.
Sept. 16–17, 1862	Union wins a bloody victory over Confederate army at Antietam.
1864	State adopts new constitution abolishing slavery.
1867	State adopts revised constitution.
1876	Johns Hopkins University opens in Baltimore.
1904	Great Baltimore Fire destroys downtown.
1920	Governor Albert Ritchie refuses to enforce national prohibition law.
1942	President Franklin D. Roosevelt establishes Shangri-La (now Camp David) as presidential retreat in Catoctin Mountains of Maryland.
1950	Friendship International Airport opens.
July 1954	Chesapeake Bay Bridge is completed near Annapolis.
Sept. 1954	Baltimore desegregates public schools.
1957	Baltimore Harbor Tunnel opens.
1970	Perren Mitchell is elected to Congress, the first African American to represent Maryland.
1972	Maryland adopts state lottery.
1973	Parallel bridge of Chesapeake Bay Bridge is completed.
1980	Baltimore opens Harborplace, centerpiece of the renewed city.
1983	Chesapeake Bay Agreement to improve water quality and living resources of the bay is enacted.
1987	Updated and revised Chesapeake Bay Agreement to restore and protect the bay is enacted.
1987	Kurt Schmoke becomes first African American mayor of Baltimore.
1992	Baltimore Orioles open Camden Yards baseball stadium.
1992	Maryland is first state to require public high school students to perform community service to graduate.
1994	Maryland adopts Smart Growth initiative to control urban sprawl.
Nov. 22, 2001	Legislation barring various forms of discrimination against gays and lesbians becomes law when opponents concede they are unable to obtain the voter signatures required to force a referendum.
May 9, 2002	Governor Parris Glendening orders moratorium on use of the death penalty.
Oct. 2–24, 2002	Ten people are shot dead and three wounded by two men in a series of sniper incidents in the Washington, D.C., area. Most incidents take place in Maryland, where six die.
Nov. 5, 2002	Robert Ehrlich, Jr., becomes Maryland's governor.
Sept. 18–19, 2003	Maryland is hit by Tropical Storm Isabel.
2013	Medical marijuana becomes legal in Maryland.
July 2013	Unemployment in Maryland tops seven percent.

Notes for Further Study

Published Sources. Maryland's history may best be studied in Robert J. Brugger's *Maryland: A Middle Temperament, 1684-1980* (1989), a traditional but solid history that examines the state's unique character and contributions from colonial times to the modern era. For young adults interested in the state's history and culture, *Maryland* (2006) by Michael Burgan, Roberta Wiener and James R. Arnold's *Maryland* (2004), and Liz Sonneborn's *Colony of Maryland* (2005) are good choices. *Maryland Lost and Found: People and Places from Chesapeake to Appalachia* (1986) by Eugene Meyer is a genial approach to the cultures, communities, and diversity found between Maryland's coast and mountains. Two excellent guides to the state are *Maryland: A New Guide to the Old Line State* (2d ed., 1999) by Earl Arnett with Robert J. Brugger and Edward C. Papenfuse and *The Chesapeake Bay Book: A Complete Guide* (4th ed., 2005) by Alison Blake and Tracy Sahler. Robert B. Harmon's *Government and Politics in Maryland* (1990) offers some excellent information and insights into Maryland's economic, cultural, and historical trends, as does Theodore Sheckles's *Maryland Politics and Political Communication, 1950-2005* (2006). Readers interested in learning about the way in which the Civil Rights movement played out in Maryland will appreciate *Civil War on Race Street: The Civil Rights Movement in Cambridge, Maryland* (2003) by Peter B. Levy. It offers a detailed examination of a local protest by African Americans that had national ramifications. *African-American Leaders of Maryland: A Portrait Gallery* (2004) by Suzanne Ellery Chapelle and Glenn O. Phillips focuses both on Civil Rights leaders and on prominent African Americans from earlier decades and centuries.

Web Resources. A good starting point for information on the state is the Maryland government page (www.maryland.gov/), which has links to various state agencies and departments and their wealth of resources. The state's office of tourism (http://visitmaryland.org) has an informative site for visitors. Of particular interest is the Maryland State Archives site (www.mdarchives.state.md.us), which has much material on Maryland's history and development from its settlement. A good supplement to these two sites is that of the Maryland Historical Society (www.mdhs.org). Two generalized sites are Maryland Manual Online (http://msa.maryland.gov/msa/mdmanual/html/mmtoc.html) and Maryland Online (www.maryland.com), both of which contain information about contemporary Maryland. More specialized are the sites devoted to Maryland's Eastern Shore (www.easternshore.com/) and to Maryland's women (http://msa.maryland.gov/msa/stagser/s1259/153/html/0044/womenhist/womentoc.html).

A Maryland horse farm. (Middleton Evans/Courtesy Maryland Office of Tourism)

Counties

County	2012 Population	Pop. Rank	Land Area (sq. miles)	Area Rank
Allegany	74,012	15	424.16	12
Anne Arundel	550,488	4	414.90	13
Baltimore	817,455	3	598.30	3
Calvert	89,628	14	213.15	23
Caroline	32,718	19	319.42	19
Carroll	167,217	8	447.59	10
Cecil	101,696	12	346.27	17
Charles	150,592	9	457.75	9
Dorchester	32,551	20	540.77	4
Frederick	239,582	7	660.22	1
Garrett	29,854	21	647.10	2
Harford	248,622	6	437.09	11
Howard	299,430	5	250.74	22

County	2012 Population	Pop. Rank	Land Area (sq. miles)	Area Rank
Kent	20,191	23	277.03	20
Montgomery	1,004,709	1	491.25	5
Prince George's	881,138	2	482.69	6
Queen Anne's	48,595	17	371.91	15
Somerset	26,253	22	319.72	18
St. Mary's	108,987	11	357.18	16
Talbot	38,098	18	268.54	21
Washington	149,180	10	457.78	8
Wicomico	100,647	13	374.44	14
Worcester	51,578	16	468.28	7

Source: U.S. Census Bureau, 2012 Population Estimates

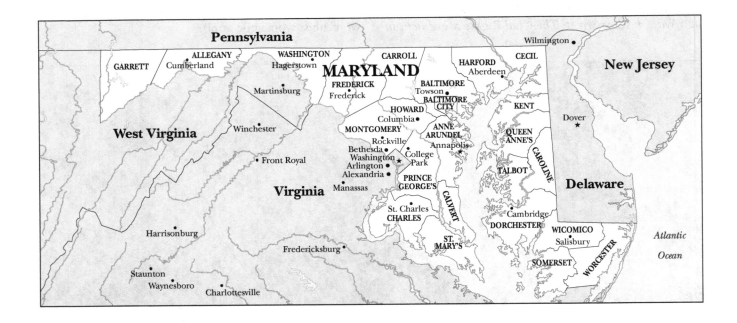

Cities
With 10,000 or more residents

Legal Name	2010 Population	Pop. Rank	Land Area (sq. miles)	Area Rank
Aberdeen city	14,959	90	6.80	71
Accokeek CDP	10,573	118	27.43	6
Adelphi CDP	15,086	89	2.74	113
Annapolis city	38,394	24	7.18	61
Annapolis Neck CDP	10,950	113	6.95	67
Arbutus CDP	20,483	62	6.52	77
Arnold CDP	23,106	57	10.82	36
Aspen Hill CDP	48,759	15	9.62	47
Ballenger Creek CDP	18,274	68	10.82	36
Baltimore city	620,961	1	80.94	1
Bel Air town	10,120	122	2.93	111
Bel Air North CDP	30,568	36	16.06	18
Bel Air South CDP	47,709	17	15.67	20
Beltsville CDP	16,772	76	7.16	62
Bensville CDP	11,923	106	16.89	15
Bethesda CDP	60,858	11	13.29	29
Bowie city	54,727	14	18.43	10
Brooklyn Park CDP	14,373	92	4.20	97
California CDP	11,857	107	12.78	31
Calverton CDP	17,724	69	4.60	92
Cambridge city	12,326	102	10.34	40
Camp Springs CDP	19,096	65	7.69	60
Carney CDP	29,941	40	6.97	65
Catonsville CDP	41,567	21	13.96	24
Chesapeake Ranch Estates CDP	10,519	119	4.32	93
Chillum CDP	33,513	30	3.41	106
Clarksburg CDP	13,766	93	8.21	55

Legal Name	2010 Population	Pop. Rank	Land Area (sq. miles)	Area Rank
Clinton CDP	35,970	28	25.00	8
Cloverly CDP	15,126	88	10.05	46
Cockeysville CDP	20,776	61	11.39	35
Colesville CDP	14,647	91	5.03	89
College Park city	30,413	38	5.64	80
Columbia CDP	99,615	2	31.93	4
Crofton CDP	27,348	43	6.61	76
Cumberland city	20,859	60	10.08	45
Damascus CDP	15,257	86	11.56	34
Dundalk CDP	63,597	9	13.07	30
East Riverdale CDP	15,509	84	1.62	120
Easton town	15,945	81	10.56	39
Edgewood CDP	25,562	47	17.78	11
Eldersburg CDP	30,531	37	39.69	2
Elkridge CDP	15,593	83	8.39	53
Elkton town	15,443	85	8.35	54
Ellicott City CDP	65,834	7	29.96	5
Essex CDP	39,262	23	9.26	50
Fairland CDP	23,681	55	4.92	90
Ferndale CDP	16,746	77	3.98	100
Forestville CDP	12,353	101	3.92	101
Fort Washington CDP	23,717	54	13.79	25
Frederick city	65,239	8	21.99	9
Gaithersburg city	59,933	12	10.20	44
Germantown CDP	86,395	3	17.00	14
Glassmanor CDP	17,295	73	2.35	118
Glen Burnie CDP	67,639	6	17.32	13
Glenmont CDP	13,529	94	2.80	112

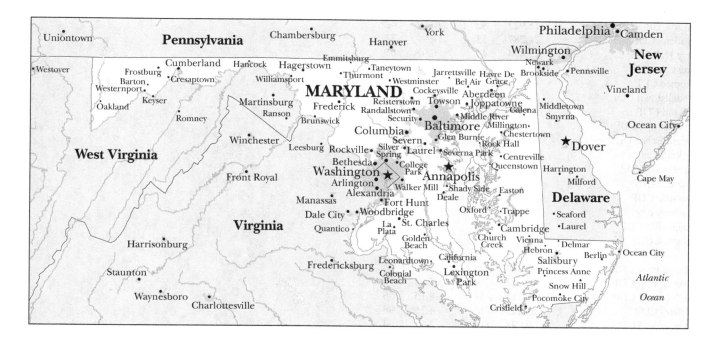

Legal Name	2010 Population	Pop. Rank	Land Area (sq. miles)	Area Rank
Glenn Dale CDP	13,466	95	7.12	63
Greenbelt city	23,068	59	6.28	79
Hagerstown city	39,662	22	11.79	33
Halfway CDP	10,701	116	4.66	91
Havre de Grace city	12,952	96	5.50	83
Hillcrest Heights CDP	16,469	79	2.49	117
Hyattsville city	17,557	71	2.67	114
Ilchester CDP	23,476	56	10.75	38
Joppatowne CDP	12,616	99	6.73	72
Kemp Mill CDP	12,564	100	2.54	116
Kettering CDP	12,790	97	5.50	83
Lake Shore CDP	19,477	63	13.45	27
Landover CDP	23,078	58	4.07	98
Langley Park CDP	18,755	66	0.99	122
Lanham CDP	10,157	121	3.53	105
Largo CDP	10,709	115	3.06	108
Laurel city	25,115	50	4.30	94
Lexington Park CDP	11,626	109	5.62	81
Linthicum CDP	10,324	120	5.46	85
Lochearn CDP	25,333	48	5.59	82
Maryland City CDP	16,093	80	7.74	59
Mays Chapel CDP	11,420	110	3.71	103
Middle River CDP	25,191	49	7.78	58
Milford Mill CDP	29,042	41	6.94	68
Mitchellville CDP	10,967	112	5.05	88
Montgomery Village CDP	32,032	32	4.00	99
New Carrollton city	12,135	105	1.53	121
North Bethesda CDP	43,828	20	8.85	52
North Potomac CDP	24,410	51	6.52	77
Ocean Pines CDP	11,710	108	6.66	73
Odenton CDP	37,132	27	14.78	22
Olney CDP	33,844	29	16.19	17
Overlea CDP	12,275	103	3.00	110
Owings Mills CDP	30,622	35	9.54	48
Oxon Hill CDP	17,722	70	6.62	75
Parkville CDP	30,734	34	4.29	95
Parole CDP	15,922	82	10.27	42
Pasadena CDP	24,287	53	14.94	21
Perry Hall CDP	28,474	42	6.97	65
Pikesville CDP	30,764	33	12.35	32
Potomac CDP	44,965	18	25.11	7
Randallstown CDP	32,430	31	10.22	43
Redland CDP	17,242	75	7.06	64
Reisterstown CDP	25,968	45	5.16	87
Riviera Beach CDP	12,677	98	2.63	115
Rockville city	61,209	10	13.51	26
Rosaryville CDP	10,697	117	9.18	51
Rosedale CDP	19,257	64	6.90	69
Rossville CDP	15,147	87	5.37	86
Salisbury city	30,343	39	13.40	28
Scaggsville CDP	24,333	52	10.29	41
Seabrook CDP	17,287	74	3.02	109
Severn CDP	44,231	19	17.71	12
Severna Park CDP	37,634	26	16.49	16
Silver Spring CDP	71,452	4	7.92	57
South Laurel CDP	26,112	44	8.15	56
Suitland CDP	25,825	46	4.25	96
Summerfield CDP	10,898	114	3.63	104

Legal Name	2010 Population	Pop. Rank	Land Area (sq. miles)	Area Rank
Takoma Park city	16,715	78	2.08	119
Towson CDP	55,197	13	14.15	23
Travilah CDP	12,159	104	15.83	19
Waldorf CDP	67,752	5	36.22	3
Walker Mill CDP	11,302	111	3.16	107
Westminster city	18,590	67	6.63	74
Wheaton CDP	48,284	16	6.90	69
White Oak CDP	17,403	72	3.78	102
Woodlawn CDP	37,879	25	9.54	48

Note: CDP–Census Designated Place
Source: U.S. Census Bureau, 2010 Census

Survey Says...

This section presents current rankings from dozens of public and private sources. It shows how this state ranks in a number of critical categories, including education, job growth, cost of living, teen drivers, energy efficiency, and business environment. Sources include *Forbes, Reuters, U.S. News and World Report, CNN Money, Gallup,* and *Huffington Post.*

- Maryland ranked #15 in a government study measuring real gross domestic product (GDP)—the output of goods and services produced by labor and property located in the United States. The ranking is based on the percentage change compared with 2011 GDP.
  U.S. Department of Commerce, Bureau of Economic Analysis, June 2013; www.bea.gov

- Maryland ranked #15 in a government study measuring real gross domestic product (GDP)—the output of goods and services produced by labor and property located in the United States. The ranking is based on the dollar value of its GDP.
  U.S. Department of Commerce, Bureau of Economic Analysis, June 2013; www.bea.gov

- Maryland ranked #1 in the 17th edition of "Quality Counts; State of the States," Education Week's "report card" surveying key education indicators, policy efforts, and educational outcomes.
  Education Week, January 4, 2013 (online) and January 10, 2013 (print); www.edweek.org

- SERI (Science and Engineering Readiness Index) weighs the performance of the states' K-12 schools in preparing students in physics and calculus, the high school subjects considered most important for future scientists and engineers. Maryland ranked #7.
  Newsletter of the Forum on Education of the American Physical Society, Summer 2011 issue; www.huffingtonpost.com, July 11, 2011; updated October 1, 2012

- Business website 24/7 Wall St. identified the states with the highest and lowest percentages of residents 25 or older with a college degree or higher. Of "America's Best Educated States," Maryland ranked #2 (#1 = best).
  247wallst.com, posted October 15, 2012; consulted July 18, 2013

- MoneyRates.com ranked Maryland #26 on its list of the best to worst states for making a living. Criteria: average income; inflation; employment prospects; and workers' Workplace Environment assessments according to the Gallup-Healthways Well-Being Index.
  www.money-rates.com, posted April 1, 2013

- *Forbes* analyzed business costs, labor supply, regulatory environment, current economic climate, growth prospects, and quality of life, to compile its "Best States for Business" rankings. Maryland ranked #16.
  www.forbes.com. posted December 12, 2012

- The 2012 Gallup-Healthways Well-Being Index, surveyed American's opinions on economic confidence, workplace perceptions, community climate, personal choices, and health predictors to assess the "future livability" of each state. Maryland ranked #10.
  "Utah Poised to Be the Best State to Live In," Gallup Wellbeing, www.gallup.com, August 7, 2012

- On CNBC's list of "America's Top States for Business 2013," Maryland ranked #40. Criteria: measures of competitiveness developed with input from the National Association of Manufacturers, the Council on Competitiveness, and other business groups weighed with the states' own marketing criteria.
  www.cnbc.com, consulted July 19, 2013

- Maryland ranked #42 on MoneyRates list of "Best-and Worst-States to Retire 2012." Criteria: life expectancy, crime rate, climate, economic conditions, taxes, job opportunities, and cost of living.
  www.money-rates.com, October 22, 2012

- Maryland ranked #44 on the 2013 Bankrate "Best Places to Retire" list ranking the states and District of Columbia on various criteria relating to health, safety, and cost.
  www.bankrate.com, May 6, 2013

- Reuters ranked Maryland #5 on its list of the "Ten Most Expensive States in America." Rankings are based on the U.S. Commerce Department's prototype cost-of-living index comparing price levels across the states for a standardized mix of goods and services.
  www.huffingtonpost.com, posted June 12, 2013

- Maryland ranked #5 on the Social Science Research Council's "American Human Development Report: The Measure of America," assessing the 50 states plus the District of Columbia on health, education, and living-standard criteria.
  The Measure of America 2013-2014, posted June 19, 2013; www.measureofamerica.org

- Maryland ranked #9 on the Foundation for Child Development's (FCD) Child Well-being Index (CWI). The FCD used the KIDS COUNT report and the National Survey of Children's Health, the only state-level source for several key indicators of child well-being.
  Foundation for Child Development, January 18, 2012; fcd-us.org

- Maryland ranked #10 overall according to the 2013 KIDS COUNT Data Book, a project of the Annie E. Casey Foundation. Criteria: children's economic well-being, education, health, and family and community indicators.
  KIDS COUNT Data Center's Data Book, released June 20, 2013; http://datacenter.kidscount.org

- Maryland ranked #14 in the children's economic well-being category by the 2013 KIDS COUNT Data Book, a project of the Annie E. Casey Foundation.
  KIDS COUNT Data Center's Data Book, released June 20, 2013; http://datacenter.kidscount.org

- Maryland ranked #5 in the children's educational opportunities and attainments category by the 2013 KIDS COUNT Data Book, a project of the Annie E. Casey Foundation.
  KIDS COUNT Data Center's Data Book, released June 20, 2013; http://datacenter.kidscount.org

- Maryland ranked #8 in the children's health category by the 2013 KIDS COUNT Data Book, a project of the Annie E. Casey Foundation.
  KIDS COUNT Data Center's Data Book, released June 20, 2013; http://datacenter.kidscount.org

- Maryland ranked #20 in the family and community circumstances that factor into children's well-being category by the 2013 KIDS COUNT Data Book, a project of the Annie E. Casey Foundation.
  KIDS COUNT Data Center's Data Book, released June 20, 2013; http://datacenter.kidscount.org

- Maryland ranked #11 in the 2012 Gallup-Healthways Well-Being Index. Criteria: emotional health; physical health; healthy behavior; work environment; basic access to food, shelter, health care; and a safe and satisfying place to live.
  2012 State of Well-Being, Gallup-Healthways Well-Being Index, released February 28, 2013; www.well-beingindex.com

- *U.S. News and World Report's* "Best States for Teen Drivers" rankings are based on driving and road safety laws, federal reports on driver's licenses, car accident fatality, and road-quality statistics. Maryland ranked #4.
  U.S. News and World Report, March 18, 2010; www.usnews.com

- The Yahoo! Sports service Rivals.com ranks the states according to the strength of their high school football programs. Maryland ranked #17.
  "Ranking the States: Where Is the Best Football Played?," November 18, 2011; highschool.rivals.com

- iVillage ranked the states by hospitable living conditions for women. Criteria: economic success, access to affordable childcare, health care, reproductive rights, female representation in government, and educational attainment. Maryland ranked #3.
  iVillage, "50 Best to Worst States for Women," March 14, 2012; www.ivillage.com

- The League of American Bicyclists's "Bicycle Friendly States" ranked Maryland #11. Criteria: legislation and enforcement, policies and programs, infrastructure and funding, education and advocacy, and evaluation and planning.
  "Washington Tops the Bicycle-Friendly State Ranking," May 1, 2013; bicycling.com

- The federal Corporation for National and Community Service ranked the states and the District of Columbia by volunteer rates. Maryland ranked #23 for community service.
  "Volunteering and Civic Life in America 2012," www.volunteeringinamerica.gov, accessed July 24, 2013

- GMAC Insurance ranked the states and the District of Columbia by the performance of their drivers on the GMAC Insurance National Drivers Test, comprised of DMV test questions. Maryland ranked #49.
  "2011 GMAC Insurance National Drivers Test," www.gmacinsurance.com, accessed July 23, 2013

- Maryland ranked #40 in a "State Integrity Investigation" analysis of laws and practices intended to deter corruption and promote accountability and openness in campaign finance, ethics laws, lobbying regulations and management of state pension funds.
  "What's Your State's Grade?," www.publicintegrity.org, accessed July 23, 2013

- Maryland ranked #43 among the states and the District of Columbia in total rail miles, as tracked by the Association of American Railroads.
  "U.S. Freight Railroad Industry Snapshot: Railroads and States: Total Rail Miles by State: 2011"; www.aar.org, accessed July 23, 2013

- According to statistics compiled by the Beer Institute, Maryland ranked #47 among the states and the District of Columbia in per capita beer consumption of persons 21 years or older.
  "Shipments of Malt Beverages and Per Capita Consumption by State 2012;" www.beerinstitute.org

- According to Concordia University's "Public Education Costs per Pupil by State Rankings," based on statistics gathered by the U.S. Census Bureau, which includes the District of Columbia, Maryland ranked #9.
  Concordia University Online; education.cu-portland.edu, accessed July 24, 2013

- Maryland ranked #5 among the states and the District of Columbia in population density based on U.S. Census Bureau data for resident population and total land area. "List of U.S. States by Population Density."
  www.wikipedia.org, accessed July 24, 2013

- In "America's Health Rankings, 2012 Edition," by the United Health Foundation, Maryland ranked #19. Criteria included: rate of high school graduation; violent crime rate; incidence of infectious disease; childhood immunizations; prevalence of diabetes; per capita public-health funding; percentage of uninsured population; rate of children in poverty; and availability of primary-care physicians.
  United Health Foundation; www.americashealthrankings.org, accessed July 24, 2013

- The TechNet 2012 "State Broadband Index" ranked Maryland #4 on the following criteria: broadband adoption; network quality; and economic structure. Improved broadband use is hoped to promote economic development, build strong communities, improve delivery of government services and upgrade educational systems.
  TechNet; www.technet.org, accessed July 24, 2013

- Maryland was ranked #9 among the states and District of Columbia on the American Council for an Energy-Efficient Economy's "State Energy Efficiency Scorecard" for 2012.
  American Council for an Energy-Efficient Economy; aceee.org/sector/state-policy/scorecard, accessed July 24, 2013

Statistical Tables

DEMOGRAPHICS

Resident State and National Population, 1950–2012

Year	State Population	U.S. Population	State Share
1950	2,343,000	151,326,000	1.55%
1960	3,101,000	179,323,000	1.73%
1970	3,923,897	203,302,031	1.93%
1980	4,216,975	226,545,805	1.86%
1990	4,781,468	248,709,873	1.92%
2000	5,296,647	281,424,600	1.88%
2010	5,773,552	308,745,538	1.87%
2012	5,884,563	313,914,040	1.87%

Note: 1950/1960 population figures are rounded to the nearest thousand.
Source: U.S. Census Bureau, Decennial Census 1950–2010; U.S. Census Bureau, 2012 Population Estimates

Projected State and National Population, 2000–2030

Year	State Population	U.S. Population	State Share
2000	5,296,486	281,421,906	1.88%
2005	5,600,563	295,507,134	1.90%
2010	5,904,970	308,935,581	1.91%
2015	6,208,392	322,365,787	1.93%
2020	6,497,626	335,804,546	1.93%
2025	6,762,732	349,439,199	1.94%
2030	7,022,251	363,584,435	1.93%
State population growth, 2000–2030			1,725,765
State percentage growth, 2000–2030			32.6%

Source: U.S. Census Bureau, Population Division, Interim State Population Projections, 2005

Population by Age, 2012

Age Group	State Population	Percent of Total Population	
		State	U.S.
Under 5 years	365,224	6.2%	6.4%
5 to 14 years	746,144	12.7%	13.1%
15 to 24 years	800,172	13.6%	14.0%
25 to 34 years	802,102	13.6%	13.5%
35 to 44 years	775,155	13.2%	12.9%
45 to 54 years	896,020	15.2%	14.1%
55 to 64 years	736,727	12.5%	12.3%
65 to 74 years	431,361	7.3%	7.6%
75 to 84 years	225,850	3.8%	4.2%
85 years and older	105,808	1.8%	1.9%
Under 18 years	1,343,800	22.8%	23.5%
65 years and older	763,019	13.0%	13.7%
Median age (years)	–	38.1	37.4

Source: U.S. Census Bureau, Annual Estimates of the Resident Population for Selected Age Groups by Sex for the United States, States, Counties, and Puerto Rico Commonwealth and Municipios: April 1, 2010 to July 1, 2012

Population by Race, 2012

Race	State Population	Percent of Total Population	
		State	U.S.
All residents	5,884,563	100.00%	100.00%
White	3,579,276	60.82%	77.89%
African American	1,766,990	30.03%	13.13%
Native American	32,275	0.55%	1.23%
Asian	352,347	5.99%	5.14%
Native Hawaiian	5,674	0.10%	0.23%
Two or more races	148,001	2.52%	2.39%

Source: U.S. Census Bureau, Population Division, Annual Estimates of the Resident Population by Sex, Race and Hispanic Origin for the United States, States, and Counties: April 1, 2010 to July 1, 2012

Population by Hispanic Origin and Race, 2012

Hispanic Origin/Race	State Population	Percent of Total Population	
		State	U.S.
All residents	5,884,563	100.00%	100.00%
All Hispanic residents	512,010	8.70%	16.89%
Hispanic			
White	408,988	6.95%	14.91%
African American	54,673	0.93%	0.79%
Native American	18,027	0.31%	0.49%
Asian	5,784	0.10%	0.17%
Native Hawaiian	2,884	0.05%	0.06%
Two or more races	21,654	0.37%	0.48%
Not Hispanic			
White	3,170,288	53.87%	62.98%
African American	1,712,317	29.10%	12.34%
Native American	14,248	0.24%	0.74%
Asian	346,563	5.89%	4.98%
Native Hawaiian	2,790	0.05%	0.17%
Two or more races	126,347	2.15%	1.91%

Source: U.S. Census Bureau, Population Division, Annual Estimates of the Resident Population by Sex, Race and Hispanic Origin for the United States, States, and Counties: April 1, 2010 to July 1, 2012

VITAL STATISTICS

Death Rates by Leading Causes, 2010

Cause	State	U.S.
Malignant neoplasms	184.0	186.2
Ischaemic heart diseases	130.9	122.9
Other forms of heart disease	43.5	53.4
Chronic lower respiratory diseases	37.2	44.7
Cerebrovascular diseases	41.4	41.9
Organic, incl. symptomatic, mental disorders	47.2	35.7
Other degenerative diseases of the nervous sys.	19.1	28.4
Other external causes of accidental injury	15.2	26.5
Diabetes mellitus	21.4	22.4
Hypertensive diseases	24.0	20.4
All causes	778.6	799.5

Note: Figures are age-adjusted death rates per 100,000 population
Source: CDC/NCHS, Underlying Cause of Death 1999–2010 on CDC WONDER Online Database

Death Rates by Selected Causes, 2010

Cause	State	U.S.
Assault	7.4	5.2
Diseases of the liver	11.1	13.9
Human immunodeficiency virus (HIV) disease	5.3	2.7
Influenza and pneumonia	16.8	16.2
Intentional self-harm	8.6	12.4
Malnutrition	0.5	0.9
Obesity and other hyperalimentation	1.6	1.8
Renal failure	12.6	14.4
Transport accidents	9.6	12.1
Viral hepatitis	2.0	2.4

Note: Figures are age-adjusted death rates per 100,000 population; A dash indicates that data was not available or was suppressed
Source: CDC/NCHS, Underlying Cause of Death 1999–2010 on CDC WONDER Online Database

Abortion Rates, 2009

Category	2009
By state of residence	
Total abortions	–
Abortion rate[1]	–%
Abortion ratio[2]	–
By state of occurrence	
Total abortions	–
Abortion rate[1]	–%
Abortion ratio[2]	–
Abortions obtained by out-of-state residents	–%
U.S. abortion rate[1]	15.1%
U.S. abortion ratio[2]	227

Note: (1) Number of abortions per 1,000 women aged 15–44 years; (2) Number of abortions per 1,000 live births; A dash indicates that data was not available
Source: CDC/NCHS, Morbidity and Mortality Weekly Report, November 23, 2012 (Abortion Surveillance, United States, 2009)

Infant Mortality Rates, 1995–2009

Category	1995	2000	2005	2009
All state residents	8.87	7.51	7.30	7.22
All U.S. residents	7.57	6.89	6.86	6.39
All state white residents	5.81	4.74	5.04	4.19
All U.S. white residents	6.30	5.71	5.73	5.33
All state black residents	15.44	12.97	11.54	12.97
All U.S. black residents	14.58	13.48	13.26	12.12

Note: Figures represent deaths per 1,000 live births of resident infants under one year old, exclusive of fetal deaths; A dash indicates that data was not available or was suppressed.
Source: Centers of Disease Control and Prevention, Division of Vital Statistics, Linked Birth/Infant Death Records on CDC Wonder Online

Marriage and Divorce Rates, 2000–2011

Year	Marriage Rate		Divorce Rate	
	State	U.S.	State	U.S.
2000	7.5	8.2	3.3	4.0
2002	7.1	8.0	3.4	3.9
2004	6.9	7.8	3.2	3.7
2006	6.6	7.5	3.0	3.7
2008	5.9	7.1	2.8	3.5
2010	5.7	6.8	2.8	3.6
2011	5.8	6.8	2.9	3.6

Note: Rates are based on provisional counts of marriages/divorces by state of occurrence and are per 1,000 total population residing in area
Source: CDC/NCHS, National Vital Statistics System

ECONOMY

Nominal Gross Domestic Product by Industry, 2012

In millions of current dollars

Industry	State GDP
Accommodation and food services	9,018
Administrative and waste management services	9,699
Agriculture, forestry, fishing, and hunting	900
Arts, entertainment, and recreation	2,607
Construction	14,356
Educational services	4,771
Finance and insurance	18,419
Health care and social assistance	24,700
Information	11,990
Management of companies and enterprises	3,487
Manufacturing	18,657
Mining	188
Other services, except government	8,261
Professional, scientific, and technical services	35,411
Real estate and rental and leasing	50,827
Retail trade	17,643
Transportation and warehousing	6,557
Utilities	7,598
Wholesale trade	14,014

Source: U.S. Department of Commerce, Bureau of Economic Analysis, Survey of Current Business

Real Gross Domestic Product, 2000–2012

In millions of chained 2005 dollars

Year	State GDP	U.S. GDP	State Share
2000	209,712	11,225,406	1.87%
2005	247,241	12,539,116	1.97%
2010	264,321	12,897,088	2.05%
2012	274,930	13,430,576	2.05%

Source: U.S. Department of Commerce, Bureau of Economic Analysis, Survey of Current Business

Personal Income Per Capita, 1930–2012

Year	State	U.S.
1930	$713	$618
1940	$711	$593
1950	$1,636	$1,503
1960	$2,349	$2,268
1970	$4,558	$4,084
1980	$11,164	$10,091
1990	$22,681	$19,354
2000	$34,678	$30,319
2010	$48,621	$39,791
2012	$51,971	$42,693

Source: U.S. Department of Commerce, Bureau of Economic Analysis, Regional Economic Accounts

Non-Farm Employment by Sector, 2012

In thousands

Sector	Employment
Construction	145.2
Education and health services	415.2
Financial activities	143.0
Government	505.2
Information	39.9
Leisure and hospitality	244.5
Mining and logging (data combined with construction)	0.0
Manufacturing	108.6
Other services	112.2
Professional and business services	410.2
Trade, transportation, and utilities	450.6
All sectors	2,574.5

Source: U.S. Bureau of Labor Statistics, State and Area Employment

Foreign Exports, 2000–2012

In millions of dollars

Year	State Exports	U.S. Exports	State Share
2000	4,592	712,054	0.65%
2002	4,476	649,940	0.69%
2004	5,756	768,554	0.75%
2006	7,600	973,994	0.78%
2008	11,383	1,222,545	0.93%
2010	10,167	1,208,080	0.84%
2012	11,741	1,478,268	0.79%

Note: U.S. figures exclude data from Puerto Rico, U.S. Virgin Islands, and unallocated exports
Source: U.S. Department of Commerce, International Trade Admin., Office of Trade and Industry Information, Manufacturing and Services

Energy Consumption, 2011

In trillions of BTUs, except as noted

Total energy consumption	
Total state energy consumption	1,426.4
Total U.S. energy consumption	97,387.3
State share of U.S. total	1.46%
Per capita consumption (in millions of BTUs)	
Total state per capita consumption	244.3
Total U.S. per capita consumption	312.6
End-use sectors	
Residential	417.9
Commercial	428.0
Industrial	146.1
Transportation	434.3
Sources of energy	
Petroleum	478.5
Natural gas	199.1
Coal	241.2
Renewable energy	76.7
Nuclear electric power	150.7

Source: U.S. Energy Information Administration, State Energy Data 2011: Consumption

LAND AND WATER

Surface Area and Federally-Owned Land, 2007

In thousands of acres

Category	State	U.S.	State Share
Total surface area	7,869.9	1,937,664.2	0.41%
Total land area	6,208.3	1,886,846.9	0.33%
Non-federal land	6,039.4	1,484,910.0	0.41%
Developed	1,496.7	111,251.2	1.35%
Rural	4,542.7	1,373,658.8	0.33%
Federal land	168.9	401,936.9	0.04%
Water area	1,661.6	50,817.3	3.27%

Source: U.S. Department of Agriculture, Natural Resources Conservation Service, 2007 National Resources Inventory

Land Cover/Use of Non-Federal Rural Land, 2007

In thousands of acres

Category	State	U.S.	State Share
Total rural land	4,542.7	1,373,658.8	0.33%
Cropland	1,413.0	357,023.5	0.40%
CRP[1] land	10.7	32,850.2	0.03%
Pastureland	463.4	118,615.7	0.39%
Rangeland	0.0	409,119.4	0.00%
Forest land	2,317.4	406,410.4	0.57%
Other rural land	338.2	49,639.6	0.68%

Note: (1) Conservation Reserve Program was created to assist private landowners in converting highly erodible cropland to vegetative cover.
Source: U.S. Department of Agriculture, Natural Resources Conservation Service, 2007 National Resources Inventory

Farms and Crop Acreage, 2012

Category	State	U.S.	State Share
Farms (in thousands)	12.8	2,170.0	0.59%
Acres (in millions)	2.1	914.0	0.22%
Acres per farm	160.2	421.2	–

Source: U.S. Department of Agriculture, National Agricultural Statistical Service, Quick Stats, 2012 Survey Data

HEALTH AND MEDICAL CARE

Medical Professionals, 2012

Profession	State Number	U.S. Number	State Share	State Rate[1]	U.S. Rate[1]
Physicians[2]	23,288	894,637	2.60%	398.8	287.1
Dentists	4,092	193,587	2.11%	70.1	62.1
Podiatrists	382	17,469	2.19%	6.5	5.6
Optometrists	747	45,638	1.64%	12.8	14.6
Chiropractors	723	77,494	0.93%	12.4	24.9

Note: (1) Rates are per 100,000 population; (2) Includes total, active Doctors of Osteopathic Medicine and Doctors of Medicine in 2011.
Source: U.S. Department of Health and Human Services, Bureau of Health Professions, Area Health Resource File, 2012-2013

Health Insurance Coverage, 2011

Category	State	U.S.
Total persons covered	5,009,000	260,214,000
Total persons not covered	803,000	48,613,000
Percent not covered	13.8%	15.7%
Children under age 18 covered	1,229,000	67,143,000
Children under age 18 not covered	136,000	6,965,000
Percent of children not covered	10.0%	9.4%

Source: U.S. Census Bureau, Current Population Survey, 2012 Annual Social and Economic Supplement

HIV, STD, and Tuberculosis Cases and Rates, 2011

Disease	State Cases	State Rate[1]	U.S. Rate[1]
Chlamydia	27,212	471.3	457.6
Gonorrhea	6,458	111.9	104.2
HIV diagnosis	1,771	36.4	15.8
HIV, stage 3 (AIDS)	1,169	24.0	10.3
Syphilis, early latent	332	5.8	4.3
Syphilis, primary/secondary	452	7.8	4.5
Tuberculosis	233	4.0	3.4

Note: (1) Rates are per 100,000 population
Source: Centers for Disease Control and Prevention

Cigarette Smoking, 2011

Category	State	U.S.
Adults who are current smokers	19.1%	21.2%
Adults who smoke everyday	13.7%	15.4%
Adults who smoke some days	5.4%	5.7%
Adults who are former smokers	22.6%	25.1%
Adults who never smoked	58.3%	52.9%

Source: Centers for Disease Control and Prevention, Behaviorial Risk Factor Surveillance System, Tobacco Use, 2011

HOUSING

Home Ownership Rates, 1995–2012

Area	1995	2000	2005	2010	2012
State	65.8%	69.9%	71.2%	68.9%	68.5%
U.S.	64.7%	67.4%	68.9%	66.9%	65.4%

Source: U.S. Census Bureau, Housing Vacancies and Homeownership,
Annual Statistics

Home Sales, 2000–2010
In thousands of units

Year	State Sales	U.S. Sales	State Share
2000	100.5	5,174	1.94%
2002	117.6	5,632	2.09%
2004	140.6	6,778	2.07%
2006	113.2	6,478	1.75%
2008	63.8	4,913	1.30%
2010	74.5	4,908	1.52%

Note: Units include single-family homes, condos and co-ops
Source: National Association of Realtors, Real Estate Outlook, Market
Trends & Insights

Value of Owner-Occupied Homes, 2011

Value	Total Units in State	Percent of Total, State	Percent of Total, U.S.
Less than $50,000	42,003	2.9%	8.8%
$50,000 to $99,000	57,403	4.0%	16.0%
$100,000 to $149,000	104,180	7.2%	16.5%
$150,000 to $199,000	175,443	12.2%	15.4%
$200,000 to $299,000	389,609	27.1%	18.2%
$300,000 to $499,000	420,659	29.3%	15.2%
$500,000 to $999,000	211,492	14.7%	7.9%
$1,000,000 or more	36,658	2.6%	2.0%
Median value	–	$287,100	$173,600

Source: U.S. Census Bureau, 2011 American Community Survey 1-Year
Estimates

EDUCATION

School Enrollment, 2011

Educational Level	Students Enrolled in State	Percent of Total, State	Percent of Total, U.S.
All levels	1,577,839	100.0%	100.0%
Nursery school, preschool	97,216	6.2%	6.0%
Kindergarten	74,892	4.7%	5.1%
Elementary (grades 1–8)	582,658	36.9%	39.5%
Secondary (grades 9–12)	316,806	20.1%	20.7%
College or graduate school	506,267	32.1%	28.7%

Note: Figures cover the population 3 years and over enrolled in school
Source: U.S. Census Bureau, 2011 American Community Survey 1-Year
Estimates

Educational Attainment, 2011

Highest Level of Education	State	U.S.
High school diploma	88.9%	85.9%
Bachelor's degree	36.9%	28.5%
Graduate/Professional degree	16.5%	10.6%

Note: Figures cover the population 25 years and over
Source: U.S. Census Bureau, 2011 American Community Survey 1-Year
Estimates

Public College Finances, FY 2012

Category	State	U.S.
Full-time equivalent enrollment (FTE)[1]	242,955	11,548,974
Educational appropriations per FTE[2]	$6,668	$5,906
Net tuition revenue per FTE[3]	$7,256	$5,189
Total educational revenue per FTE[4]	$13,924	$11,043

(1) Full-time equivalent enrollment equates student credit hours to full
time, academic year students, but excludes medical students;
(2) Educational appropriations measure state and local support available
for public higher education operating expenses including ARRA funds
and excludes appropriations for independent institutions, financial aid
for students attending independent institutions, research, hospitals, and
medical education; (3) Net tuition revenue is calculated by taking the
gross amount of tuition and fees, less state and institutional financial aid,
tuition waivers or discounts, and medical student tuition and fees. Net
tuition revenue used for capital debt service is included in the net tuition
revenue figures; (4) Total educational revenue is the sum of educational
appropriations and net tuition excluding net tuition revenue used for
capital debt service.
Source: State Higher Education Executive Officers, State Higher
Education Finance FY 2012

TRANSPORTATION AND TRAVEL

Motor Vehicle Registrations and Drivers Licenses, 2011

Vehicle Type	State	U.S.	State Share
Automobiles[1]	2,088,130	125,656,528	1.66%
Buses	14,558	666,064	2.19%
Trucks	1,682,819	118,455,587	1.42%
Motorcycles	120,122	8,437,502	1.42%
Drivers licenses	3,856,604	211,874,649	1.82%

Note: Motor vehicle registrations include private, commercial, and
publicly-owned vehicles; (1) Includes taxicabs
Source: U.S. Department of Transportation, Federal Highway
Administration

Domestic Travel Expenditures, 2009
In millions of dollars

Category	State	U.S.	State Share
Travel expenditures	$11,675	$610,200	1.91%

Note: Figures represent U.S. spending on domestic overnight trips and
day trips of 50 miles or more, one way, away from home. Excludes
spending by foreign visitors.
Source: U.S. Travel Association, Impact of Travel on State Economies,
2009

Retail Gasoline Prices, 2013

Gasoline Grade	State Average	U.S. Average
Regular	$3.69	$3.65
Mid	$3.88	$3.81
Premium	$4.07	$3.98
Diesel	$3.86	$3.88
Excise tax[1]	45.4 cents	49.4 cents

Note: Gasoline prices as of 7/26/2013; (1) Includes state and federal excise taxes and other state taxes as of July 1, 2013
Source: American Automobile Association, Daily Fuel Guage Report; American Petroleum Institute, State Motor Fuel Taxes, 2013

Public Road Length, 2011

Type	State Mileage	U.S. Mileage	State Share
Interstate highways	481	46,960	1.02%
Other highways	306	15,719	1.95%
Principal arterial	1,531	156,262	0.98%
Minor arterial	2,274	242,942	0.94%
Major collector	3,308	534,592	0.62%
Minor collector	1,770	266,357	0.66%
Local	22,649	2,814,925	0.80%
Urban	17,998	1,095,373	1.64%
Rural	14,323	2,982,383	0.48%
Total	32,321	4,077,756	0.79%

Note: Combined urban and rural road mileage equals the total of the other road types
Source: U.S. Department of Transportation, Federal Highway Administration, Public Road Length, 2011

CRIME AND LAW ENFORCEMENT

Full-Time Law Enforcement Officers, 2011

Gender	State Number	State Rate[1]	U.S. Rate[1]
Male officers	13,402	237.0	210.3
Female officers	2,050	36.3	28.1
Total officers	15,452	273.2	238.3

Note: (1) Rates are per 100,000 population
Source: Federal Bureau of Investigation, Uniform Crime Reports, Crime in the United States 2011

Prison Population, 2000–2012

Year	State Population	U.S. Population	State Share
2000	23,538	1,391,261	1.69%
2005	22,737	1,527,929	1.49%
2010	22,645	1,613,803	1.40%
2011	22,558	1,598,783	1.41%
2012	21,522	1,571,013	1.37%

Note: Figures include prisoners under the jurisdiction of state or federal correctional authorities.
Source: U.S. Department of Justice, Bureau of Justice Statistics, Prisoners in 2006, 2011, 2012 (Advance Counts)

Crime Rate, 2011

Incidents per 100,000 residents

Category	State	U.S.
Violent crimes	494.1	386.3
Murder	6.8	4.7
Forcible rape	20.5	26.8
Robbery	177.5	113.7
Aggravated assault	289.3	241.1
Property crimes	2,860.2	2,908.7
Burglary	614.0	702.2
Larceny/theft	1,970.5	1,976.9
Motor vehicle theft	275.7	229.6
All crimes	3,354.3	3,295.0

Source: Federal Bureau of Investigation, Uniform Crime Reports, Crime in the United States 2011

GOVERNMENT AND FINANCE

Local Governments by Type, 2012

Government Type	State	U.S.	State Share
All local governments	347	89,004	0.39%
County	23	3,031	0.76%
Municipality	157	19,522	0.80%
Town/Township	0	16,364	0.00%
Special District	167	37,203	0.45%
Ind. School District	0	12,884	0.00%

Source: U.S. Census Bureau, 2012 Census of Governments: Organization Component Preliminary Estimates

State Government Revenue, 2011

In thousands of dollars, except for per capita figures

Total revenue	$41,716,504
Total revenue per capita, State	$7,144
Total revenue per capita, U.S.	$7,271
General revenue	$32,998,746
Intergovernmental revenue	$11,335,533
Taxes	$16,002,529
General sales	$3,896,700
Selective sales	$2,757,314
License taxes	$739,482
Individual income taxes	$6,644,962
Corporate income taxes	$775,845
Other taxes	$1,188,226
Current charges	$3,248,535
Miscellaneous general revenue	$2,412,149
Utility revenue	$152,836
Liquor store revenue	$0
Insurance trust revenue[1]	$8,564,922

Note: (1) Within insurance trust revenue, net earnings of state retirement systems is a calculated statistic, and thus can be positive or negative. Net earnings is the sum of earnings on investments plus gains on investments minus losses on investments.
Source: U.S. Census Bureau, 2011 Annual Survey of State Government Finances

State Government Expenditures, 2011

In thousands of dollars, except for per capita figures

Total expenditure	$37,672,576
Total expenditure per capita, State	$6,451
Total expenditure per capita, U.S.	$6,427
Intergovernmental expenditure	$8,124,451
Direct expenditure	$29,548,125
Current operation	$19,699,511
Capital outlay	$2,605,932
Insurance benefits and repayments	$4,474,946
Assistance and subsidies	$1,702,594
Interest on debt	$1,065,142
Utility expenditure	$891,776
Liquor store expenditure	$0
Insurance trust expenditure	$4,474,946

Source: U.S. Census Bureau, 2011 Annual Survey of State Government Finances

State Government General Expenditures by Function, 2011

In thousands of dollars

Education	$11,212,610
Public welfare	$9,274,305
Hospitals	$495,596
Health	$1,848,976
Highways	$2,195,643
Police protection	$521,332
Correction	$1,383,744
Natural resources	$467,720
Parks and recreation	$128,763
Governmental administration	$1,308,637
Interest on general debt	$1,065,142
Other and unallocable	$2,403,386

Source: U.S. Census Bureau, 2011 Annual Survey of State Government Finances

State Government Finances, Cash and Debt, 2011

In thousands of dollars, except for per capita figures

Debt at end of fiscal year	
State, total	$25,250,138
State, per capita	$4,324
U.S., per capita	$3,635
Cash and security holdings	
State, total	$58,515,287
State, per capita	$10,020
U.S., per capita	$11,759

Source: U.S. Census Bureau, 2011 Annual Survey of State Government Finances

Composition of the Senate, 1995–2013

Congress (Year)	State/U.S	Dem	Rep	Total
104th (1995)	State delegates	2	0	2
	Total U.S.	48	52	100
105th (1997)	State delegates	2	0	2
	Total U.S.	45	55	100
106th (1999)	State delegates	2	0	2
	Total U.S.	45	55	100
107th (2001)	State delegates	2	0	2
	Total U.S.	50	50	100
108th (2003)	State delegates	2	0	2
	Total U.S.	48	51	100
109th (2005)	State delegates	2	0	2
	Total U.S.	44	55	100
110th (2007)	State delegates	2	0	2
	Total U.S.	49	49	100
111th (2009)	State delegates	2	0	2
	Total U.S.	57	41	100
112th (2011)	State delegates	2	0	2
	Total U.S.	51	47	100
113th (2013)	State delegates	2	0	2
	Total U.S.	54	45	100

Note: Figures are for the starts of first sessions; Totals include Democratic (Dem) and Republican (Rep) members as well as vacancies and seats held by independent party members
Source: U.S. Congress, Congressional Directory

Composition of the House of Representatives, 1995–2013

Congress (Year)	State/U.S	Dem	Rep	Total
104th (1995)	State delegates	4	4	8
	Total U.S.	204	230	435
105th (1997)	State delegates	4	4	8
	Total U.S.	207	226	435
106th (1999)	State delegates	4	4	8
	Total U.S.	211	223	435
107th (2001)	State delegates	4	4	8
	Total U.S.	212	221	435
108th (2003)	State delegates	6	2	8
	Total U.S.	205	229	435
109th (2005)	State delegates	6	2	8
	Total U.S.	202	231	435
110th (2007)	State delegates	6	2	8
	Total U.S.	233	198	435
111th (2009)	State delegates	7	1	8
	Total U.S.	256	178	435
112th (2011)	State delegates	6	2	8
	Total U.S.	193	242	435
113th (2013)	State delegates	7	1	8
	Total U.S.	201	234	435

Note: Figures are for the starts of first sessions; Totals include Democratic (Dem) and Republican (Rep) members as well as vacancies and seats held by independent party members
Source: U.S. Congress, Congressional Directory

Composition of State Legislature, 2004–2013

Year	Democrats	Republicans	Total
State Senate			
2004	33	14	47
2005	33	14	47
2006	33	14	47
2007	33	14	47
2008	33	14	47
2009	33	14	47
2010	33	14	47
2011	35	12	47
2012	35	12	47
2013	35	12	47
State House			
2004	98	43	141
2005	98	43	141
2006	98	43	141
2007	104	37	141
2008	104	37	141
2009	104	36	141
2010	104	36	141
2011	98	43	141
2012	98	43	141
2013	98	43	141

Note: Totals may include minor party members and vacancies
Source: The Council of State Governments, State Legislatures

Voter Participation in Presidential Elections, 1980–2012

Year	Voting-eligible State Population	State Voter Turnout Rate	U.S. Voter Turnout Rate
1980	2,964,704	52.0	54.2
1984	3,113,967	53.8	55.2
1988	3,325,582	51.6	52.8
1992	3,440,015	57.7	58.1
1996	3,530,148	50.4	51.7
2000	3,649,631	55.5	54.2
2004	3,797,264	62.9	60.1
2008	3,925,117	67.0	61.6
2012	4,091,886	66.2	58.2

Note: All figures are based on the voting-eligible population which excludes person ineligible to vote such as non-citizens, felons (depending on state law), and mentally-incapacitated persons. U.S. figures include the overseas eligible population (including military personnel).
Source: McDonald, Michael P., United States Election Project, Presidential Voter Turnout Rates, 1980–2012

Governors Since Statehood

Thomas Johnson	1777-1779
Thomas Sim Lee	1779-1782
William Paca	1782-1785
William Smallwood	1785-1788
John Eager Howard (O)	1788-1791
George Plater (O)	(d) 1791-1792
James Brice (O)	1792
Thomas Sim Lee (O)	1792-1794
John Hoskins Stone (O)	1794-1797
John Henry (O)	1797-1798
Benjamin Ogle (O)	1798-1801
John Francis Mercer (O)	1801-1803
Robert Bowie (O)	1803-1806
Robert Wright (O)	(r) 1806-1809
James Butcher (O)	1809
Edward Lloyd (O)	1809-1811
Robert Bowie (O)	1811-1812
Levin Winder (O)	1812-1816
Charles Carnan Ridgley (O)	1816-1819
Charles Goldsborough (O)	1819
Samuel Sprigg (O)	1819-1822
Samuel Stevens Jr. (O)	1822-1826
Joseph Kent (O)	1826-1829
Daniel Martin (O)	1829-1830
Thomas King Carroll (O)	1830-1831
Daniel Martin (O)	(d) 1831
George Howard (O)	1831-1833
James Thomas (O)	1833-1836
Thomas Ward Veazey (O)	1836-1839
William Grason (D)	1839-1842
Francis Thomas (D)	1842-1845
Thomas George Pratt (O)	1845-1848
Philip Francis Thomas (D)	1848-1851
Enoch Louis Lowe (D)	1851-1854
Thomas Watkins Ligon (D)	1854-1858
Thomas Holliday Hicks (O)	1858-1862
Augustus W. Bradford (O)	1862-1866
Thomas Swann (O)	1866-1869
Oden Bowie (D)	1869-1872
William Pinkney Whyte (D)	(r) 1872-1874
James Black Groome (D)	1874-1876
John Lee Carroll (D)	1876-1880
William Thomas Hamilton (D)	1880-1884
Robert Milligan McLane (D)	(r) 1884-1885
Henry Lloyd (D)	1885-1888
Elihu Emory Jackson (D)	1888-1892
Frank Brown (D)	1892-1896
Lloyd Lowndes (R)	1896-1900
John W. Smith (D)	1900-1904
Edwin Warfield (D)	1904-1908
Austin L. Crothers (D)	1908-1912
Phillips L. Goldsborough (R)	1912-1916
Emerson C. Harrington (D)	1916-1920
Albert C. Ritchie (D)	1920-1935
Harry W. Nice (R)	1935-1939
Herbert R. O'Conor (D)	1939-1947
William P. Lane Jr. (D)	1947-1951
Theodore R. McKeldin (R)	1951-1959
J. Millard Tawes (D)	1959-1967
Spiro T. Agnew (R)	(r) 1967-1969
Marvin Mandel (D)	(i) 1969-1977
Blair Lee III (D)	1977-1979
Harry R. Hughes (D)	1979-1987
William Donald Schaefer (D)	1987-1991
Parris N. Glendening (D)	1995-2003
Robert L. Ehrlich (R)	2003-2007
Martin O'Malley (D)	2007-2015 (term limits)

Note: (D) Democrat; (R) Republican; (O) Other party; (r) resigned; (d) died in office; (i) removed from office

Massachusetts

Location: New England

Area and rank: 7,838 square miles (20,300 square kilometers); 10,555 square miles (27,337 square kilometers) including water; forty-fifth largest state in area

Coastline: 192 miles (309 kilometers) on the Atlantic Ocean

Shoreline: 1,519 miles (2,445 kilometers)

Population and rank: 6,646,144 (2012); fourteenth largest state in population

Capital and largest city: Boston (617,594 people in 2010 census)

Entered Union and rank: February 6, 1788; sixth state

Present constitution adopted: 1780 (oldest U.S. state constitution in effect today)

Counties: 14

Known as the Massachusetts State House, the state capitol buiding in Boston houses both the legislature and the offices of the governor. (Wikimedia Commons)

State name: "Massachusetts" is named after a Native American society of the same name

State nicknames: Bay State; Old Colony State

Motto: *Ense petit placidam sub libertate quietem* (By the sword we seek peace, but peace only under liberty)

State flag: White field with state coat of arms in blue and yellow

Highest point: Mount Greylock—3,487 feet (1,063 meters)

Lowest point: Atlantic Ocean—sea level

Highest recorded temperature: 107 degrees Fahrenheit (42 degrees Celsius)—New Bedford and Chester, 1975

Lowest recorded temperature: −34 degrees Fahrenheit (−37 degrees Celsius)—Birch Hill Dam, 1957

State songs: "All Hail to Massachusetts"; "Massachusetts" (official folk song); "The Road to Boston" (official ceremonial march)

State tree: American elm

State flower: Trailing arbutus (Mayflower)

State bird: Chickadee

Massachusetts History

Massachusetts was one of the original thirteen colonies, and its capital, Boston, is considered the cradle of the American Revolution. The state was home to some of the greatest American leaders. Its reputation for excellent education is due to its many great universities and colleges, including the world-famous Harvard University and Massachusetts Institute of Technology (MIT). Geographically, the state forms a narrow rectangle. Relatively small, it is forty-fifth in area among the states, yet thirteenth in state population.

Native American History. The Algonquians were a large family of tribes, related by language and customs, who lived throughout the northeastern United States. Several of these tribes made their homes in the fertile farming and hunting grounds of the area. The Nauset lived on Cape Cod, while the Wampanoag, the Massachusetts (for whom the state is named), and the Patuxet fished and hunted along the coast. Women played a central role in Algonquian society. They owned the tribe's land, which they cleared and farmed communally. When a young man married, he left home to become a member of his bride's family.

Early Exploration and the Pilgrims. In 1602, English navigator Bartholomew Gosnold visited Massachusetts Bay and named it Cape Cod. Two years later explorer Samuel de Champlain explored the coast, followed by Captain John Smith in 1614.

In September of 1620, an English merchant ship called the *Mayflower* set sail from the port of Southhampton with 102 passengers bound for the Americas. Of these passengers, 41 were Separatists, members of a renegade congregation that had broken away from the Church of England. These people considered themselves religious pilgrims. Before the pilgrims and the others left England, the group leaders wrote and signed a document that became the foundation of American democracy, the Mayflower Compact. It decreed a representative government.

Despite legend, the ship did not land at Plymouth Rock, but rather at the tip of Cape Cod, the site of modern Provincetown. After a little exploring, Plymouth proved a

The landing of English pilgrims at Plymouth Rock in 1620 is traditionally considered the beginning of British North America. (Library of Congress)

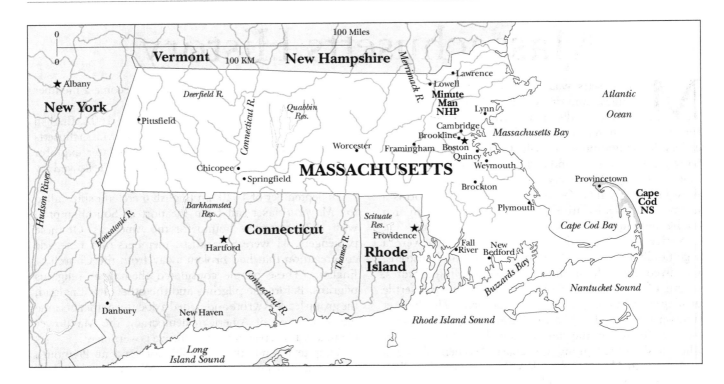

better place to found a village. After the harsh winter of 1621, however, half the settlers were dead. Spring came, and the pilgrims met a Patuxet Indian named Squanto. Years earlier he had been captured by slave traders and sold in Spain. After escaping to England and becoming fluent in English, he made his way back to his homeland, only to find his tribe wiped out by disease. Squanto taught the pilgrims how to farm and served as an interpreter, making treaties with other tribes. After the first harvest in October, 1621, for three days the pilgrims hosted about ninety Native Americans in a feast. It became the first Thanksgiving, a tradition that would long be celebrated in the United States.

The colony began to prosper, and every year brought more colonists seeking religious freedom. In 1630, John Winthrop, with a charter for "The Governor and Company of the Massachusetts Bay in New England," landed at Salem with more than one thousand colonists. Winthrop and his followers did not want to separate from the church, but they believed it needed to be purified from within and thus were called Puritans. The Puritans felt the law must be strictly obeyed if the community were to be strong. A set of wooden stocks stood in the center of many towns, and wrongdoers were put there for crimes as small as swearing.

The Witch Trials. Ironically, while Winthrop and his followers left England to seek religious freedom, they had little tolerance of others' religious philosophies. During the 1660's, Puritan authorities hanged several Quakers as heretics. By 1692 this intolerance, mixed with superstition, turned into one of the New World's most shameful chapters, the Salem witch trials. Tituba, a West Indian slave woman, told locals tales of African magic. When some of the girls began to have fainting spells, they accused Tituba of casting spells over them. When Salem reverend Samuel Parris demanded to know who else had been practicing the evil arts, the girls started falsely accusing neighbors of witchery, and soon everyone was accusing everyone else. Nineteen men and women were burned as witches, and nearly 150 more were awaiting trail when authorities in Boston stopped the proceedings. Although the Puritans initiated an atmosphere of intolerance and fear in their society, they must also be remembered for their dedication to hard work and their respect for education; they founded Harvard, the first institution of higher learning in North America.

The American Revolution. By the mid-eighteenth century, Massachusetts was the center of shipbuilding and commerce in the British colonies. The people there were successful, well educated, and accustomed to managing their own affairs. The French and Indian War was won by the British, but at a great cost. To raise more money, Great Britain heavily taxed the colonies. The colonists were particularly upset about this because they were being taxed with no representation in Parliament: "No taxation without representation!" was the frequent cry of colonial protesters. The merchants of Boston led a boycott of British goods, and Britain responded by stationing troops in the city. One night in March of 1770, mounting tension exploded in a skirmish that became known as the Boston Massacre. Five were killed, the first being a young black man named Crispus Attucks.

On December 16, 1773, a group of Boston men crept aboard three British ships and dumped the tea cargoes in the harbor to protest the high taxes, in what became known as the Boston Tea Party. In April of 1775, the British, intent on quelling the patriots by force, planned to send armed men to Lexington, Concord, and then Boston. Paul Revere, among others, was able to warn the Minutemen, Massachusetts fighters. While the British were able to take Lexington and then Concord in small battles, the patriots were able to defend Boston for a while. Eventually, however, the city succumbed to British force. The Revolutionary War had begun.

The next year, General George Washington took Boston back, chasing the British out of Massachusetts forever. The Treaty of Paris of 1783 granted independence to the colonies. No other colony had contributed more men or money to the war for independence than Massachusetts. In 1788, Massachusetts formally joined the newly independent United States as the sixth state.

War and Immigration. The United States went to war with Britain again in 1812 for interfering with American trade, pirating U.S. ships, and forcing Americans to fight the British war with France. Boston, the largest American city of the time, suffered greatly. Boston developed industries to maintain the economy.

During the 1840's, the potato famine in Ireland sent more than one million Irish men and women to the United States, and hundreds of thousands settled in Massachusetts. They found work in the factories of Boston, Lawrence, Lowell, and Worcester. Many residents saw the flood of Irish Catholics as a threat to their Anglo-Protestant society. Discrimination against the Irish was prevalent, and it was not uncommon to see a Help Wanted sign include a No Irish Need Apply slogan. However, any labor was needed eventually as the state became a leader in the American Industrial Revolution. New mills producing textile, paper, boots, and shoes sprang up all over the state.

The Late Nineteenth Century. The Civil War began in 1861, and Massachusetts was the first state to respond, with a regiment of fifteen hundred soldiers. Throughout the war, the state supplied guns, uniforms, and boots to the Union army. When the war was over, the Irish, many of whom served in the war, began climbing the social ladder. They founded businesses, saved money, and bought their own homes. Still, they were discriminated against, and they looked to politics as a way to fight back. In 1880, Hugh O'Brien became Boston's first Irish mayor. In 1892, Patrick Joseph "P. J." Kennedy, son of an East Boston barrel maker, was elected to the state

Now a picturesque resort region, Cape Cod is the actual site of the first pilgrim landing in 1620. (PhotoDisc)

senate. Yet discrimination against the Irish, as well as all immigrants, continued.

During the 1880's and 1890's, fresh waves of immigrants poured in. In 1896, U.S. Senator Henry Cabot Lodge, a descendant of Boston's most elite families, sponsored a bill to restrict immigration. He claimed scientific evidence to prove that southern and eastern Europeans were racially inferior and prone to crime. It was vetoed by the U.S. president but signed into law in 1924.

Economic Hard Times. By 1900 Massachusetts was an industrial state, yet the large mills in the state would not always run smoothly. In 1912, more than twenty-two thousand textile workers staged a strike in Lawrence. There would be other labor problems, and men and women began to organize into unions to fight for better working conditions and higher wages.

After World War I, Massachusetts slipped into recession. When the country fell into the Depression of the 1930's, Massachusetts was hit hard. By 1931 only 44 percent of the state's workers were employed full-time. When World War II began in 1941, Massachusetts factories and shipyards rebounded. The state achieved almost full employment, and thousands of African Americans migrated from southern states to work in the war plants. After the war, the factories fell on hard times yet again. However, another industry, education, led by MIT and Harvard, proved to entice many great minds— and federal grants—to the state. Boston, meanwhile, emerged as a center for banking, insurance, and medicine.

The Kennedy Dynasty. Joseph Kennedy, the son of P. J. Kennedy, graduated from Harvard in 1912 and entered the world of banking. At twenty-five, he became the youngest bank president in the nation. He rose in stature and was eventually named ambassador to England. His political career was ruined, however, when he supported appeasement with German leader Adolf Hitler. Three of his nine children would fulfill his ambitions by going into politics.

In 1961, his son and Massachusetts senator John F. Kennedy became the first Irish Catholic president of the United States. He would not be allowed to finish out his term, however, and the nation grieved when the young president was assassinated in Dallas in 1963. His brother, Robert, was also killed when running for president, in 1968. Joseph Kennedy's youngest son, Edward "Ted" Kennedy, served in the U.S. Senate for many years, serving as the patriarch of the ill-fated family. Several of the next generation of Kennedys served in politics as well.

Great politicians and diversity continued to be strengths of the state. Michael S. Dukakis was the first Greek American to be elected governor, in 1972. He later won the Democratic nomination for U.S. president in 1988 but lost to George H. W. Bush.

Liberal Politics. Geographically small Massachusetts remained a major intellectual force in the nation, especially the area around Boston, where Harvard University, the Massachusetts Institute of Technology (MIT), and many other colleges and universities are located. Moreover, the state's representation in Congress, especially that of Senator Ted Kennedy, was a potent liberal influence in politics. The state's liberalism was manifest in May, 2004, as Massachusetts became the first state in the Union to issue official same-sex marriage licenses.

Massachusetts voters chose Vice President Al Gore for the state's twelve electoral votes in the 2000 presidential election. As expected, Senator Kennedy was reelected by a landslide margin, winning 73 percent of the vote. The state's voters declined to return a single Republican to Washington, as ten Democrats were reelected to the House of Representatives. Five of them ran unopposed. Similar electoral sentiment was apparent in 2002 and 2004, when Massachusetts's "favorite son," Democrat senator John Kerry, took the state's electoral votes for president by a lopsided 62-37 percent margin.

The liberal tradition suffered a hit in 2001, however, when Maxwell Kennedy, son of slain Senator Robert F. Kennedy, declined to run for public office. In another episode, which took place on May 4, 2006, Representative Patrick J. Kennedy, son of Ted and Joan Kennedy, crashed his car into a barricade on Capitol Hill at 2:45 a.m., after spending time in two bars. He later pleaded guilty to driving under the influence of prescription medicine.

The "Big Dig." The Central Artery/Tunnel Project, nicknamed the Big Dig, was designed to transform a limited-access highway running through the heart of Boston into a 3.5-mile tunnel. The project also included construction of a second tunnel and a bridge over the Charles River from Boston to Cambridge. Conceived during the 1970's, the project got underway officially in 1982, when planning began. Congress appropriated major funding in 1987, overriding President Ronald Reagan's veto. Work began in 1991, and by the end of 2004, it was 95 percent complete. Projected to cost $5.8 billion, its actual cost became more than $15 billion, the most expensive highway project in the nation's history.

The epic project spawned epic problems and scandals. Major obstacles delayed construction. Provision of substandard cement and evidence of doctored records led to arrests for those deemed responsible. In 2004, an official report found some four hundred leaks in the tunnels were found, but other sources said there were thousands. The city of Cambridge objected to the proposed bridge's design and sued. In 2006, the state demanded return of more than $100 million from companies accused of incompetence or worse.

On July 10, 2006, sections of the ceiling of a connector tunnel fell on a car, killing a passenger. The site of the collapse was treated as a crime scene and the possibility of criminal charges was suggested. The resignation of the state agency in charge of the project was demanded by the governor and others. A complete investigation into the safety of the entire project was also demanded.

"Curse of the Bambino" Broken. In 2004, the Boston Red Sox finally broke what had been called the "curse of the Bambino" and won baseball's World Series for the first time since 1918. For years it had been said that the team's fateful trade of George Herman "Babe" Ruth to the New York Yankees, where he blossomed into one of the greatest players in the game, had placed a curse on the team. Now, the team and its loyal followers in Boston and throughout the country, known as the Red Sox Nation, were free at last.

Superstorm Sandy. The hurricane, downgraded to a "superstorm" when it came ashore in October 2012, brought power outages to some 200,000 customers in Massachusetts at the height of the storm. The storm also disrupted travel, shut down schools, and sank a 50-foot barge. Winds knocked down trees and power lines into the roadways, while rainwater flooded Route 28, halting all traffic. However, there was far less damage to homes and waterfront properties than experienced in New York and New Jersey.

Boston Marathon Bombing. During the Boston Marathon on April 15, 2013, two bombs, found to have been constructed in pressure cookers, exploded at 2:49 pm. The bombs killed three people and injured 264 others near the Marathon finish line on Boylston Street. The FBI ran the investigation, and after examining thousands of still and video images, publicized photographs and surveillance video of two suspects on April 18. Later on the 18th, the FBI identified the suspects as the brothers Dzhokhar and Tamerlan Tsarnaev, young immigrants from the Caucasus region of Russia.

Shortly after the publication of the pictures of the two suspects, they allegedly killed a college police officer from the Massachusetts Institute of Technology, then hijacked an SUV and had an extended gunfight with local police in Watertown. As Dzhokhar drove off in the SUV, the vehicle ran over Tamerlan and killed him. A massive manhunt and unprecedented shutdown of the region followed; most public transportation, schools, and businesses were closed. At about 7 pm on April 19, the younger Tsarnaev brother was found hiding in a covered boat in a Watertown backyard and arrested. On July 10, 2012, he pled not guilty to all charges and awaited trial.

Kevin M. Mitchell
Updated by the Editor

Harbor of Massachusetts's capital and largest city, Boston. (PhotoDisc)

Massachusetts Time Line

1620	*Mayflower* lands and begins settlement at Plymouth.
1621	Patuxet Indian named Squanto befriends the pilgrims and teaches them farming.
Oct., 1621	First Thanksgiving takes place.
1634	Boston Commons is established, making it the first city park in the nation.
1636	Harvard, America's first institution of higher learning, is founded.
1692	Salem witch trials begin, resulting in nineteen people being burned as witches.
Mar. 5, 1770	Five are killed, the first being Crispus Attucks, in Boston Massacre.

Witchcraft trials at Salem Village, 1692. (Wikimedia Commons)

Dec. 16, 1773	Patriots sneak aboard a British cargo ship and dump tea into the harbor to protest high taxes during the Boston Tea Party.
1775	First battle of the Revolutionary war occurs at Lexington; Paul Revere makes "midnight ride" to warn patriots.
1780	State constitution is adopted.
1783	Treaty of Paris is signed, ending the Revolutionary War and granting the thirteen colonies independence.
1783	Massachusetts abolishes slavery.
1786	Pelham farmer Daniel Shay leads an armed uprising protesting high taxes from Boston in Shay's Rebellion.
Feb. 6, 1788	Massachusetts, led by Samuel Adams and John Hancock, ratifies Constitution, becoming the sixth state.
1797	John Adams of Massachusetts becomes second president of the United States.
1815	Newburyport businessman Francis Cabot Lowell, inspired by England and Scotland's textile mills, opens the state's first mill at Waltham.
1825	John Quincy Adams, son of the second president, becomes the fifth president of the United States.
1829	Journalist William Lloyd Garrison begins publishing his antislavery newspaper, the *Liberator*, in Boston.
1832	Perkins Institute, the first school for the blind in the Union, is founded.
1881	Boston Symphony is founded.
1897	First Boston Marathon is held.
1908	P. J. Kennedy is elected to the state senate.
1912	More than twenty-two thousand textile workers stage a massive strike in Lawrence.
1919	Republican governor Calvin Coolidge sends in state police to restore order in the Boston Police strike.
1924	Newly installed U.S. president Coolidge signs into law Massachusetts senator Henry Cabot Lodge's bill limiting immigration.
1937	Joseph Kennedy named ambassador to England, becomes the first Irish American to represent the country.
1946	John F. Kennedy is elected to House of Representatives.
1956	Foster Furcolo becomes first Italian American governor of Massachusetts.
1966	Republican Edward Brooke is first black man elected U.S. senator in nearly a century.
1974	Federal judge orders Boston to start busing students in order to integrate its public schools, sparking years of turmoil.
July 1999	John F. Kennedy, Jr., son of the slain president, is killed in a plane crash near Martha's Vineyard.
Sept. 11, 2001	Two jetliners from Boston's Logan Airport bound for California are hijacked by terrorists and crashed into the World Trade Center in Manhattan.
May 2004	Massachusetts becomes first state to issue same-sex marriage licenses.
Oct. 27, 2004	Boston Red Sox win baseball's World Series for the first time since 1918.
Dec. 2004	Officials announce that 95 percent of Boston's Big Dig Project is complete.

Jul. 10, 2006	Sections of a tunnel ceiling in the Big Dig fall on automobiles, killing one person.
October 2012	Superstorm Sandy brings power outages to about 200,000 residents. The storm also greatly disrupts state infrastructure.
April 15, 2013	During the Boston Marathon, two bombs constructed in pressure cookers, exploded at 2:49 pm, killing three people and injuring 264 others near the Marathon finish line on Boylston Street.

Notes for Further Study

Published Sources. Those interested in learning about Massachusetts history will find a wealth of materials on all aspects of the state's early years. For short, informational histories, readers should consult *Massachusetts* (1998) by Sylvia McNair and *Massachusetts: From Sea to Shining Sea* (1994) by Dennis B. Fradin. *Massachusetts Bay Company and Its Predecessors* (1974) by Frances Rose-Troup offers an in-depth overview of the earliest European settlers and their trials and tribulations. *Massachusetts: A Concise History* (rev. and exp. ed., 2000) by Richard D. Brown and Jack Tager also provides a good overview of the state's history. Marcia Sewall's *The Pilgrims of Plymouth* (1996) chronicles in text and illustrations the day-to-day life of the early pilgrims of the Plymouth Colony. *Pilgrims and Puritans: 1620-1676* (1994) by Christopher Collier and James Lincoln Collier recounts the religious, political, and social history of the Massachusetts Bay Colony and its influence on modern life. Using as its basis the discovery of artifacts along what was once the colonists' line of defense at the northwest boundary of Massachusetts, Michael Coe's *The Line of Forts: Historical Archaeology on the Colonial Frontier of Massachusetts* (2006) weaves a narrative of eighteenth century American life. Although focused specifically on the Boston area, Jacqueline Barbara Carr's *After the Siege: A Social History of Boston, 1775–1800* (2005) allows the reader to discern the general aftereffects of the American Revolution and how state leaders attempted to bring the economy and daily life back to normalcy.

The Salem Witch Trials (1991) by Earle Rice covers the social, legal, and political realities surrounding the trials, as does *Salem Witch Trials: A Primary Source History of the Witchcraft Trials in Salem, Massachusetts* (2003) by Jenny Macbain. For a personal view of the American Revolution and such key events as the Tea Party and the Boston Massacre, a Boston shoemaker's account is available in *The Shoemaker and the Tea Party: Memory and the American Revolution* (1999), edited by Alfred F. Young. *Civil War Boston: Home Front and Battlefield* (1999) by Thomas H. O'Connor examines the dramatic ways that the Civil War affected Bostonians on the home front and discusses how residents contributed to the Union cause, focusing on businessmen, Irish Catholic immigrants, African Americans, and women. *The Boston Irish: A Political History* (1996), also by Thomas H. O'Connor, discusses how Irish political dominance in Boston grew out of generations of bitter and unyielding conflict between Yankees and Irish Catholic immigrants. Massachusetts political insider Richard A. Hogarty brings forth a discussion of the state's political arena, including the workings of the executive, legislative, and judicial branches, as well as the administrative bureaucracy, in *Massachusetts Politics and Public Policy: Studies in Power and Leadership* (2002). In *Extraordinary Tenure: Massachusetts and the Making of the Nation: From John Adams to Tip O'Neill* (2004) by Neil J. Savage, the lives and times of presidents, governors, senators, congress members, diplomats, and cabinet members who came out of Massachusetts to serve the interests of the nation are explored. There are a great deal of books available on the Kennedys, including *The Sins of the Father: Joseph P. Kennedy and the Dynasty He Founded* (1996) by Ronald Kessler.

Web Resources. There are many Massachusetts Internet sites, and those listed here often give valuable links to others. The state's official home page (www.mass.gov/) is a good launching point, providing comprehensive information about the state's government agencies, as well as information targeted to residents and visitors. A thorough overview of historical Massachusetts, as well as a Boston African American database, can be found at the Massachusetts Historical Society (www.masshist.org/).

Massachusetts' early history can be accessed at Mayflower and Early Families (www.mayflowerfamilies.com/) and the Wampanoag site (www.tolatsga.org/wampa.html). For information regarding the Salem witchcraft hysteria, visit Salem's city guide (www.salemweb.com/guide/witches.shtml), Destination Salem (www.salem.org/17th_Century.asp), and the University of Virginia's page about this period (etext.virginia.edu/salem/witchcraft/). The Kennedy Presidential Library and Museum, located in Boston, has a site (www.jfklibrary.org/) that is useful not only for learning more about the Kennedy political dynasty but also for keeping up with statewide travel information.

Counties

County	2012 Population	Pop. Rank	Land Area (sq. miles)	Area Rank
Barnstable	215,423	9	393.72	11
Berkshire	130,016	11	926.82	2
Bristol	551,082	6	553.10	7
Dukes	17,041	13	103.25	12
Essex	755,618	3	492.56	9
Franklin	71,540	12	699.32	4
Hampden	465,923	8	617.14	6
Hampshire	159,795	10	527.26	8
Middlesex	1,537,215	1	817.82	3
Nantucket	10,298	14	44.97	14
Norfolk	681,845	5	396.11	10
Plymouth	499,759	7	659.08	5
Suffolk	744,426	4	58.15	13
Worcester	806,163	2	1,510.77	1

Source: U.S. Census Bureau, 2012 Population Estimates

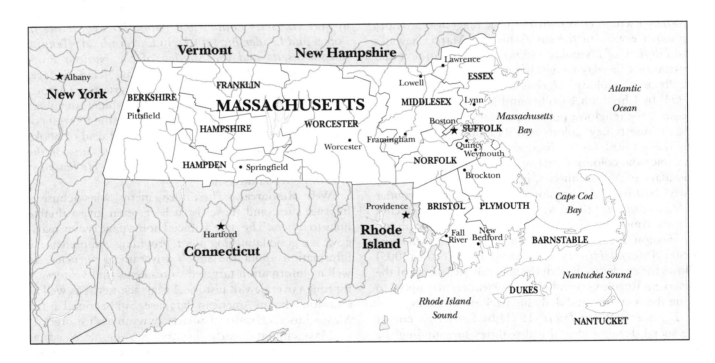

Cities

With 10,000 or more residents

Legal Name	2010 Population	Pop. Rank	Land Area (sq. miles)	Area Rank	Legal Name	2010 Population	Pop. Rank	Land Area (sq. miles)	Area Rank
Abington town	15,985	122	9.65	152	Amherst town	37,819	41	27.60	40
Acton town	21,924	87	19.87	89	Amherst Center CDP	19,065	97	4.94	173
Acushnet town	10,303	178	18.43	96	Andover town	33,201	47	30.85	31
Agawam Town city	28,438	61	23.31	58	Arlington town	42,844	30	5.15	171
Amesbury Town city	16,283	119	12.26	137	Ashland town	16,593	117	12.33	134

Legal Name	2010 Population	Pop. Rank	Land Area (sq. miles)	Area Rank
Athol town	11,584	163	32.29	27
Attleboro city	43,593	29	26.81	43
Auburn town	16,188	120	15.48	115
Barnstable Town city	45,193	27	59.80	4
Bedford town	13,320	150	13.66	124
Belchertown town	14,649	133	52.64	5
Bellingham town	16,332	118	18.35	98
Belmont town	24,729	76	4.65	175
Beverly city	39,502	38	15.09	116
Billerica town	40,243	36	25.57	50
Boston city	617,594	1	48.28	7
Bourne town	19,754	96	40.64	16
Braintree Town city	35,744	42	13.75	123
Bridgewater town	26,563	70	27.32	41
Brockton city	93,810	7	21.33	72
Brookline town	58,732	18	6.75	163
Burlington town	24,498	78	11.73	138
Cambridge city	105,162	5	6.39	164
Canton town	21,561	89	18.80	92
Carver town	11,509	164	37.40	18
Charlton town	12,981	154	42.18	15
Chelmsford town	33,802	46	22.37	64
Chelsea city	35,177	44	2.21	183
Chicopee city	55,298	22	22.83	60
Clinton town	13,606	146	5.65	169
Concord town	17,668	105	24.52	52
Danvers town	26,493	71	13.28	127
Dartmouth town	34,032	45	60.92	3
Dedham town	24,729	76	10.25	146
Dennis town	14,207	137	20.51	82
Dracut town	29,457	54	20.63	80
Dudley town	11,390	167	20.82	77

Legal Name	2010 Population	Pop. Rank	Land Area (sq. miles)	Area Rank
Duxbury town	15,059	129	23.74	55
East Bridgewater town	13,794	141	17.21	103
East Longmeadow town	15,720	126	13.01	129
Easthampton Town city	16,053	121	13.33	126
Easton town	23,112	83	28.75	36
Everett city	41,667	31	3.43	179
Fairhaven town	15,873	123	12.33	134
Fall River city	88,857	10	33.13	23
Falmouth town	31,531	52	44.07	12
Fitchburg city	40,318	35	27.83	38
Foxborough town	16,865	114	19.85	90
Framingham town	68,318	14	25.04	51
Franklin Town city	31,635	51	26.63	44
Gardner city	20,228	94	22.08	68
Gloucester city	28,789	57	26.20	49
Grafton town	17,765	104	22.81	61
Greenfield Town city	17,456	111	21.43	71
Groton town	10,646	175	32.76	26
Hanover town	13,879	140	15.61	114
Hanson town	10,209	181	15.05	117
Harwich town	12,243	157	20.88	75
Haverhill city	60,879	15	32.97	24
Hingham town	22,157	85	22.21	66
Holbrook town	10,791	174	7.25	159
Holden town	17,346	113	35.08	21
Holliston town	13,547	147	18.64	94
Holyoke city	39,880	37	21.28	73
Hopkinton town	14,925	130	26.26	48
Hudson town	19,063	98	11.52	140
Hudson CDP	14,907	131	5.74	167
Hull town	10,293	180	2.80	182
Ipswich town	13,175	152	32.11	28

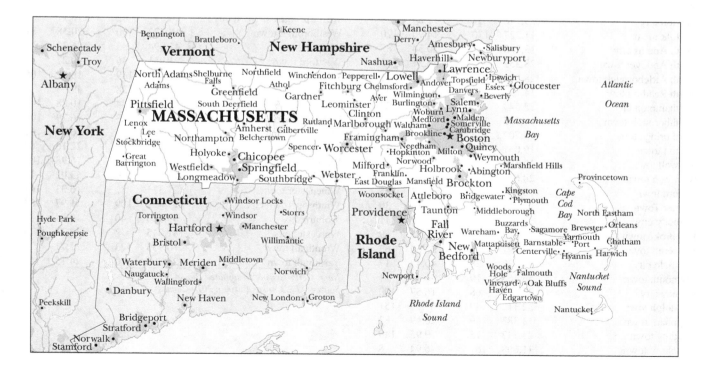

Legal Name	2010 Population	Pop. Rank	Land Area (sq. miles)	Area Rank
Kingston town	12,629	156	18.66	93
Lakeville town	10,602	176	29.56	34
Lawrence city	76,377	12	6.93	162
Leicester town	10,970	172	23.25	59
Leominster city	40,759	34	28.81	35
Lexington town	31,394	53	16.43	110
Longmeadow town	15,784	125	9.12	153
Lowell city	106,519	4	13.58	125
Ludlow town	21,103	92	27.20	42
Lunenburg town	10,086	184	26.48	46
Lynn city	90,329	9	10.74	143
Lynnfield town	11,596	162	9.88	150
Malden city	59,450	17	5.04	172
Mansfield town	23,184	81	20.09	87
Marblehead town	19,808	95	4.39	176
Marlborough city	38,499	39	20.87	76
Marshfield town	25,132	72	28.62	37
Mashpee town	14,006	139	23.39	57
Maynard town	10,106	183	5.21	170
Medfield town	12,024	159	14.40	122
Medford city	56,173	20	8.10	156
Medway town	12,752	155	11.54	139
Melrose city	26,983	67	4.68	174
Methuen Town city	47,255	26	22.25	65
Middleborough town	23,116	82	69.07	2
Milford town	27,999	64	14.75	121
Milford CDP	25,055	73	10.16	147
Millbury town	13,261	151	15.71	113
Milton town	27,003	66	13.01	129
Nantucket town	10,172	182	44.97	11
Natick town	33,006	48	14.95	119
Needham town	28,886	56	12.29	136
New Bedford city	95,072	6	20.00	88
Newburyport city	17,416	112	8.35	154
Newton city	85,146	11	17.84	99
Norfolk town	11,227	170	14.90	120
North Adams city	13,708	145	20.34	85
North Andover town	28,352	63	26.31	47
North Attleborough town	28,712	58	18.87	91
North Reading town	14,892	132	13.14	128
Northampton city	28,549	60	34.24	22
Northborough town	14,155	138	18.48	95
Northbridge town	15,707	127	17.26	102
Norton town	19,031	99	27.81	39
Norwell town	10,506	177	20.93	74
Norwood town	28,602	59	10.37	144
Oxford town	13,709	144	26.53	45
Palmer Town city	12,140	158	31.58	30
Peabody city	51,251	25	16.21	111
Pembroke town	17,837	103	21.78	69
Pepperell town	11,497	165	22.60	63
Pittsfield city	44,737	28	40.47	17
Plymouth town	56,468	19	96.46	1
Quincy city	92,271	8	16.57	109
Randolph town	32,112	49	9.83	151
Raynham town	13,383	149	20.49	83
Reading town	24,747	75	9.95	149
Rehoboth town	11,608	161	46.94	8

Legal Name	2010 Population	Pop. Rank	Land Area (sq. miles)	Area Rank
Revere city	51,755	24	5.69	168
Rockland town	17,489	110	10.32	145
Salem city	41,340	32	8.28	155
Sandwich town	20,675	93	42.74	14
Saugus town	26,628	69	10.79	142
Scituate town	18,133	102	17.63	101
Seekonk town	13,722	143	18.37	97
Sharon town	17,612	107	23.44	56
Shrewsbury town	35,608	43	20.73	78
Somerset town	18,165	101	7.90	157
Somerville city	75,754	13	4.12	177
South Hadley town	17,514	108	17.71	100
South Yarmouth CDP	11,092	171	6.96	160
Southbridge Town city	16,719	116	20.28	86
Spencer town	11,688	160	32.83	25
Springfield city	153,060	3	31.87	29
Stoneham town	21,437	90	6.02	166
Stoughton town	26,962	68	16.09	112
Sudbury town	17,659	106	24.27	53
Swampscott town	13,787	142	3.02	180
Swansea town	15,865	124	22.69	62
Taunton city	55,874	21	46.70	9
Tewksbury town	28,961	55	20.70	79
Tyngsborough town	11,292	168	16.77	107
Uxbridge town	13,457	148	29.59	33
Wakefield town	24,932	74	7.36	158
Walpole town	24,070	79	20.44	84
Waltham city	60,632	16	12.73	131
Wareham town	21,822	88	35.86	20
Watertown Town city	31,915	50	3.99	178
Wayland town	12,994	153	15.05	117
Webster town	16,767	115	12.37	133
Webster CDP	11,412	166	3.00	181
Wellesley town	27,982	65	10.02	148
West Springfield Town city	28,391	62	16.71	108
Westborough town	18,272	100	20.58	81
Westfield city	41,094	33	46.32	10
Westford town	21,951	86	30.27	32
Weston town	11,261	169	16.82	105
Westport town	15,532	128	49.84	6
Westwood town	14,618	134	10.88	141
Weymouth Town city	53,743	23	16.79	106
Whitman town	14,489	135	6.94	161
Wilbraham town	14,219	136	22.16	67
Wilmington town	22,325	84	16.98	104
Winchendon town	10,300	179	43.02	13
Winchester town	21,374	91	6.03	165
Winthrop Town city	17,497	109	1.97	184
Woburn city	38,120	40	12.64	132
Worcester city	181,045	2	37.37	19
Wrentham town	10,955	173	21.71	70
Yarmouth town	23,793	80	24.15	54

Note: CDP–Census Designated Place
Source: U.S. Census Bureau, 2010 Census

Survey Says…

This section presents current rankings from dozens of public and private sources. It shows how this state ranks in a number of critical categories, including education, job growth, cost of living, teen drivers, energy efficiency, and business environment. Sources include *Forbes, Reuters, U.S. News and World Report, CNN Money, Gallup,* and *Huffington Post.*

- Massachusetts ranked #19 in a government study measuring real gross domestic product (GDP)—the output of goods and services produced by labor and property located in the United States. The ranking is based on the percentage change compared with 2011 GDP.
  U.S. Department of Commerce, Bureau of Economic Analysis, June 2013; www.bea.gov

- Massachusetts ranked #12 in a government study measuring real gross domestic product (GDP)—the output of goods and services produced by labor and property located in the United States. The ranking is based on the dollar value of its GDP.
  U.S. Department of Commerce, Bureau of Economic Analysis, June 2013; www.bea.gov

- Massachusetts ranked #2 in the 17th edition of "Quality Counts; State of the States," Education Week's "report card" surveying key education indicators, policy efforts, and educational outcomes.
  Education Week, January 4, 2013 (online) and January 10, 2013 (print); www.edweek.org

- SERI (Science and Engineering Readiness Index) weighs the performance of the states' K-12 schools in preparing students in physics and calculus, the high school subjects considered most important for future scientists and engineers. Massachusetts ranked #1.
  Newsletter of the Forum on Education of the American Physical Society, Summer 2011 issue; www.huffingtonpost.com, July 11, 2011; updated October 1, 2012

- Business website 24/7 Wall St. identified the states with the highest and lowest percentages of residents 25 or older with a college degree or higher. Of "America's Best Educated States," Massachusetts ranked #1 (#1 = best).
  247wallst.com, posted October 15, 2012; consulted July 18, 2013

- MoneyRates.com ranked Massachusetts #13 on its list of the best to worst states for making a living. Criteria: average income; inflation; employment prospects; and workers' Workplace Environment assessments according to the Gallup-Healthways Well-Being Index.
  www.money-rates.com, posted April 1, 2013

- *Forbes* analyzed business costs, labor supply, regulatory environment, current economic climate, growth prospects, and quality of life, to compile its "Best States for Business" rankings. Massachusetts ranked #17.
  www.forbes.com. posted December 12, 2012

- The 2012 Gallup-Healthways Well-Being Index, surveyed American's opinions on economic confidence, workplace perceptions, community climate, personal choices, and health predictors to assess the "future livability" of each state. Massachusetts ranked #11.
  "Utah Poised to Be the Best State to Live In," Gallup Wellbeing, www.gallup.com, August 7, 2012

- On CNBC's list of "America's Top States for Business 2013," Massachusetts ranked #16. Criteria: measures of competitiveness developed with input from the National Association of Manufacturers, the Council on Competitiveness, and other business groups weighed with the states' own marketing criteria.
  www.cnbc.com, consulted July 19, 2013

- Massachusetts ranked #46 on MoneyRates list of "Best-and Worst-States to Retire 2012." Criteria: life expectancy, crime rate, climate, economic conditions, taxes, job opportunities, and cost of living.
  www.money-rates.com, October 22, 2012

- Massachusetts ranked #36 on the 2013 Bankrate "Best Places to Retire" list ranking the states and District of Columbia on various criteria relating to health, safety, and cost.
  www.bankrate.com, May 6, 2013

- Reuters ranked Massachusetts #8 on its list of the "Ten Most Expensive States in America." Rankings are based on the U.S. Commerce Department's prototype cost-of-living index comparing price levels across the states for a standardized mix of goods and services.
  www.huffingtonpost.com, posted June 12, 2013

- Massachusetts ranked #2 on the Social Science Research Council's "American Human Development Report: The Measure of America," assessing the 50 states plus the District of Columbia on health, education, and living-standard criteria.
  The Measure of America 2013-2014, posted June 19, 2013; www.measureofamerica.org

- Massachusetts ranked #2 on the Foundation for Child Development's (FCD) Child Well-being Index (CWI). The FCD used the KIDS COUNT report and the National Survey of Children's Health, the only state-level source for several key indicators of child well-being.
  Foundation for Child Development, January 18, 2012; fcd-us.org

- Massachusetts ranked #3 overall according to the 2013 KIDS COUNT Data Book, a project of the Annie E. Casey Foundation. Criteria: children's economic well-being, education, health, and family and community indicators.
  KIDS COUNT Data Center's Data Book, released June 20, 2013; http://datacenter.kidscount.org

- Massachusetts ranked #13 in the children's economic well-being category by the 2013 KIDS COUNT Data Book, a project of the Annie E. Casey Foundation.
  KIDS COUNT Data Center's Data Book, released June 20, 2013; http://datacenter.kidscount.org

- Massachusetts ranked #1 in the children's educational opportunities and attainments category by the 2013 KIDS COUNT Data Book, a project of the Annie E. Casey Foundation.
  KIDS COUNT Data Center's Data Book, released June 20, 2013; http://datacenter.kidscount.org

- Massachusetts ranked #11 in the children's health category by the 2013 KIDS COUNT Data Book, a project of the Annie E. Casey Foundation.
  KIDS COUNT Data Center's Data Book, released June 20, 2013; http://datacenter.kidscount.org

- Massachusetts ranked #7 in the family and community circumstances that factor into children's well-being category by the 2013 KIDS COUNT Data Book, a project of the Annie E. Casey Foundation.
  KIDS COUNT Data Center's Data Book, released June 20, 2013; http://datacenter.kidscount.org

- Massachusetts ranked #10 in the 2012 Gallup-Healthways Well-Being Index. Criteria: emotional health; physical health; healthy behavior; work environment; basic access to food, shelter, health care; and a safe and satisfying place to live.
  2012 State of Well-Being, Gallup-Healthways Well-Being Index, released February 28, 2013; www.well-beingindex.com

- *U.S. News and World Report's* "Best States for Teen Drivers" rankings are based on driving and road safety laws, federal reports on driver's licenses, car accident fatality, and road-quality statistics. Massachusetts ranked #24.
  U.S. News and World Report, March 18, 2010; www.usnews.com

- The Yahoo! Sports service Rivals.com ranks the states according to the strength of their high school football programs. Massachusetts ranked #32.
  "Ranking the States: Where Is the Best Football Played?," November 18, 2011; highschool.rivals.com

- iVillage ranked the states by hospitable living conditions for women. Criteria: economic success, access to affordable childcare, health care, reproductive rights, female representation in government, and educational attainment. Massachusetts ranked #4.
  iVillage, "50 Best to Worst States for Women," March 14, 2012; www.ivillage.com

- The League of American Bicyclists's "Bicycle Friendly States" ranked Massachusetts #6. Criteria: legislation and enforcement, policies and programs, infrastructure and funding, education and advocacy, and evaluation and planning.
  "Washington Tops the Bicycle-Friendly State Ranking," May 1, 2013; bicycling.com

- The federal Corporation for National and Community Service ranked the states and the District of Columbia by volunteer rates. Massachusetts ranked #36 for community service.
  "Volunteering and Civic Life in America 2012," www.volunteeringinamerica.gov, accessed July 24, 2013

- The Hospital Safety Score ranked states and the District of Columbia on their hospitals' performance scores. Massachusetts ranked #2. Criteria: avoiding preventable harm and medical errors, as demonstrated by 26 hospital safety metrics.
  Spring 2013 Hospital Safety Score, May 8, 2013; www.hospitalsafetyscore.org

- GMAC Insurance ranked the states and the District of Columbia by the performance of their drivers on the GMAC Insurance National Drivers Test, comprised of DMV test questions. Massachusetts ranked #47.
  "2011 GMAC Insurance National Drivers Test," www.gmacinsurance.com, accessed July 23, 2013

- Massachusetts ranked #12 in a "State Integrity Investigation" analysis of laws and practices intended to deter corruption and promote accountability and openness in campaign finance, ethics laws, lobbying regulations and management of state pension funds.
  "What's Your State's Grade?," www.publicintegrity.org, accessed July 23, 2013

- Massachusetts ranked #42 among the states and the District of Columbia in total rail miles, as tracked by the Association of American Railroads.
  "U.S. Freight Railroad Industry Snapshot: Railroads and States: Total Rail Miles by State: 2011"; www.aar.org, accessed July 23, 2013

- According to statistics compiled by the Beer Institute, Massachusetts ranked #40 among the states and the District of Columbia in per capita beer consumption of persons 21 years or older.
  "Shipments of Malt Beverages and Per Capita Consumption by State 2012;" www.beerinstitute.org

- According to Concordia University's "Public Education Costs per Pupil by State Rankings," based on statistics gathered by the U.S. Census Bureau, which includes the District of Columbia, Massachusetts ranked #8.
  Concordia University Online; education.cu-portland.edu, accessed July 24, 2013

- Massachusetts ranked #3 among the states and the District of Columbia in population density based on U.S. Census Bureau data for resident population and total land area. "List of U.S. States by Population Density."
  www.wikipedia.org, accessed July 24, 2013

- In "America's Health Rankings, 2012 Edition," by the United Health Foundation, Massachusetts ranked #4. Criteria included: rate of high school graduation; violent crime rate; incidence of infectious disease; childhood immunizations; prevalence of diabetes; per capita public-health funding; percentage of uninsured population; rate of children in poverty; and availability of primary-care physicians.
  United Health Foundation; www.americashealthrankings.org, accessed July 24, 2013

- The TechNet 2012 "State Broadband Index" ranked Massachusetts #2 on the following criteria: broadband adoption; network quality; and economic structure. Improved broadband use is hoped to promote economic development, build strong communities, improve delivery of government services and upgrade educational systems.
  TechNet; www.technet.org, accessed July 24, 2013

- Massachusetts was ranked #1 among the states and District of Columbia on the American Council for an Energy-Efficient Economy's "State Energy Efficiency Scorecard" for 2012.
  American Council for an Energy-Efficient Economy; aceee.org/sector/state-policy/scorecard, accessed July 24, 2013

Statistical Tables

DEMOGRAPHICS
Resident State and National Population, 1950-2012
Projected State and National Population, 2000-2030
Population by Age, 2012
Population by Race, 2012
Population by Hispanic Origin and Race, 2012

VITAL STATISTICS
Death Rates by Leading Causes, 2010
Death Rates by Selected Causes, 2010
Abortion Rates, 2009
Infant Mortality Rates, 1995-2009
Marriage and Divorce Rates, 2000-2011

ECONOMY
Nominal Gross Domestic Product by Industry, 2012
Real Gross Domestic Product, 2000-2012
Personal Income Per Capita, 1930-2012
Non-Farm Employment by Sector, 2012
Foreign Exports, 2000-2012
Energy Consumption, 2011

LAND AND WATER
Surface Area and Federally-Owned Land, 2007
Land Cover/Use of Non-Federal Rural Land, 2007
Farms and Crop Acreage, 2012

HEALTH AND MEDICAL CARE
Medical Professionals, 2012
Health Insurance Coverage, 2011
HIV, STD, and Tuberculosis Cases and Rates, 2011
Cigarette Smoking, 2011

HOUSING
Home Ownership Rates, 1995-2012
Home Sales, 2000-2010
Value of Owner-Occupied Homes, 2011

EDUCATION
School Enrollment, 2011
Educational Attainment, 2011
Public College Finances, FY 2012

TRANSPORTATION AND TRAVEL
Motor Vehicle Registrations and Drivers Licenses, 2011
Domestic Travel Expenditures, 2009
Retail Gasoline Prices, 2013
Public Road Length, 2011

CRIME AND LAW ENFORCEMENT
Full-Time Law Enforcement Officers, 2011
Prison Population, 2000-2012
Crime Rate, 2011

GOVERNMENT AND FINANCE
Local Governments by Type, 2012
State Government Revenue, 2011
State Government Expenditures, 2011
State Government General Expenditures by Function, 2011
State Government Finances, Cash and Debt, 2011

POLITICS
Composition of the Senate, 1995-2013
Composition of the House of Representatives, 1995-2013
Composition of State Legislature, 2004-2013
Voter Participation in Presidential Elections, 1980-2012
Governors Since Statehood

DEMOGRAPHICS

Resident State and National Population, 1950–2012

Year	State Population	U.S. Population	State Share
1950	4,691,000	151,326,000	3.10%
1960	5,149,000	179,323,000	2.87%
1970	5,689,170	203,302,031	2.80%
1980	5,737,037	226,545,805	2.53%
1990	6,016,425	248,709,873	2.42%
2000	6,349,364	281,424,600	2.26%
2010	6,547,629	308,745,538	2.12%
2012	6,646,144	313,914,040	2.12%

Note: 1950/1960 population figures are rounded to the nearest thousand.
Source: U.S. Census Bureau, Decennial Census 1950–2010; U.S. Census Bureau, 2012 Population Estimates

Projected State and National Population, 2000–2030

Year	State Population	U.S. Population	State Share
2000	6,349,097	281,421,906	2.26%
2005	6,518,868	295,507,134	2.21%
2010	6,649,441	308,935,581	2.15%
2015	6,758,580	322,365,787	2.10%
2020	6,855,546	335,804,546	2.04%
2025	6,938,636	349,439,199	1.99%
2030	7,012,009	363,584,435	1.93%
State population growth, 2000–2030			662,912
State percentage growth, 2000–2030			10.4%

Source: U.S. Census Bureau, Population Division, Interim State Population Projections, 2005

Population by Age, 2012

Age Group	State Population	Percent of Total Population	
		State	U.S.
Under 5 years	365,557	5.5%	6.4%
5 to 14 years	782,468	11.8%	13.1%
15 to 24 years	938,951	14.1%	14.0%
25 to 34 years	891,511	13.4%	13.5%
35 to 44 years	854,097	12.9%	12.9%
45 to 54 years	1,005,035	15.1%	14.1%
55 to 64 years	850,031	12.8%	12.3%
65 to 74 years	508,386	7.6%	7.6%
75 to 84 years	296,995	4.5%	4.2%
85 years and older	153,113	2.3%	1.9%
Under 18 years	1,401,415	21.1%	23.5%
65 years and older	958,494	14.4%	13.7%
Median age (years)	–	39.3	37.4

Source: U.S. Census Bureau, Annual Estimates of the Resident Population for Selected Age Groups by Sex for the United States, States, Counties, and Puerto Rico Commonwealth and Municipios: April 1, 2010 to July 1, 2012

Population by Race, 2012

Race	State Population	Percent of Total Population	
		State	U.S.
All residents	6,646,144	100.00%	100.00%
White	5,560,222	83.66%	77.89%
African American	525,799	7.91%	13.13%
Native American	31,172	0.47%	1.23%
Asian	387,770	5.83%	5.14%
Native Hawaiian	6,304	0.09%	0.23%
Two or more races	134,877	2.03%	2.39%

Source: U.S. Census Bureau, Population Division, Annual Estimates of the Resident Population by Sex, Race and Hispanic Origin for the United States, States, and Counties: April 1, 2010 to July 1, 2012

Population by Hispanic Origin and Race, 2012

Hispanic Origin/Race	State Population	Percent of Total Population	
		State	U.S.
All residents	6,646,144	100.00%	100.00%
All Hispanic residents	674,073	10.14%	16.89%
Hispanic			
White	522,299	7.86%	14.91%
African American	92,927	1.40%	0.79%
Native American	19,275	0.29%	0.49%
Asian	5,719	0.09%	0.17%
Native Hawaiian	3,698	0.06%	0.06%
Two or more races	30,155	0.45%	0.48%
Not Hispanic			
White	5,037,923	75.80%	62.98%
African American	432,872	6.51%	12.34%
Native American	11,897	0.18%	0.74%
Asian	382,051	5.75%	4.98%
Native Hawaiian	2,606	0.04%	0.17%
Two or more races	104,722	1.58%	1.91%

Source: U.S. Census Bureau, Population Division, Annual Estimates of the Resident Population by Sex, Race and Hispanic Origin for the United States, States, and Counties: April 1, 2010 to July 1, 2012

VITAL STATISTICS

Death Rates by Leading Causes, 2010

Cause	State	U.S.
Malignant neoplasms	184.1	186.2
Ischaemic heart diseases	99.0	122.9
Other forms of heart disease	52.7	53.4
Chronic lower respiratory diseases	32.8	44.7
Cerebrovascular diseases	33.6	41.9
Organic, incl. symptomatic, mental disorders	48.2	35.7
Other degenerative diseases of the nervous sys.	24.4	28.4
Other external causes of accidental injury	23.0	26.5
Diabetes mellitus	14.3	22.4
Hypertensive diseases	12.1	20.4
All causes	722.1	799.5

Note: Figures are age-adjusted death rates per 100,000 population
Source: CDC/NCHS, Underlying Cause of Death 1999–2010 on CDC WONDER Online Database

Death Rates by Selected Causes, 2010

Cause	State	U.S.
Assault	3.1	5.2
Diseases of the liver	12.4	13.9
Human immunodeficiency virus (HIV) disease	1.8	2.7
Influenza and pneumonia	17.1	16.2
Intentional self-harm	8.9	12.4
Malnutrition	0.5	0.9
Obesity and other hyperalimentation	1.1	1.8
Renal failure	17.2	14.4
Transport accidents	6.1	12.1
Viral hepatitis	2.0	2.4

Note: Figures are age-adjusted death rates per 100,000 population; A dash indicates that data was not available or was suppressed
Source: CDC/NCHS, Underlying Cause of Death 1999–2010 on CDC WONDER Online Database

Abortion Rates, 2009

Category	2009
By state of residence	
Total abortions	23,252
Abortion rate[1]	17.1%
Abortion ratio[2]	310
By state of occurrence	
Total abortions	22,945
Abortion rate[1]	16.9%
Abortion ratio[2]	306
Abortions obtained by out-of-state residents	3.4%
U.S. abortion rate[1]	15.1%
U.S. abortion ratio[2]	227

Note: (1) Number of abortions per 1,000 women aged 15–44 years; (2) Number of abortions per 1,000 live births; A dash indicates that data was not available
Source: CDC/NCHS, Morbidity and Mortality Weekly Report, November 23, 2012 (Abortion Surveillance, United States, 2009)

Infant Mortality Rates, 1995–2009

Category	1995	2000	2005	2009
All state residents	5.18	4.61	5.13	5.09
All U.S. residents	7.57	6.89	6.86	6.39
All state white residents	4.63	3.98	4.68	4.64
All U.S. white residents	6.30	5.71	5.73	5.33
All state black residents	10.03	10.14	8.30	8.35
All U.S. black residents	14.58	13.48	13.26	12.12

Note: Figures represent deaths per 1,000 live births of resident infants under one year old, exclusive of fetal deaths; A dash indicates that data was not available or was suppressed.
Source: Centers of Disease Control and Prevention, Division of Vital Statistics, Linked Birth/Infant Death Records on CDC Wonder Online

Marriage and Divorce Rates, 2000–2011

Year	Marriage Rate		Divorce Rate	
	State	U.S.	State	U.S.
2000	5.8	8.2	2.5	4.0
2002	5.9	8.0	2.5	3.9
2004	6.5	7.8	2.2	3.7
2006	5.9	7.5	2.3	3.7
2008	5.7	7.1	2.0	3.5
2010	5.6	6.8	2.5	3.6
2011	5.5	6.8	2.7	3.6

Note: Rates are based on provisional counts of marriages/divorces by state of occurrence and are per 1,000 total population residing in area
Source: CDC/NCHS, National Vital Statistics System

ECONOMY

Nominal Gross Domestic Product by Industry, 2012
In millions of current dollars

Industry	State GDP
Accommodation and food services	12,351
Administrative and waste management services	11,142
Agriculture, forestry, fishing, and hunting	749
Arts, entertainment, and recreation	3,968
Construction	12,334
Educational services	11,828
Finance and insurance	37,017
Health care and social assistance	39,736
Information	19,785
Management of companies and enterprises	9,408
Manufacturing	41,629
Mining	131
Other services, except government	8,628
Professional, scientific, and technical services	49,441
Real estate and rental and leasing	56,951
Retail trade	18,273
Transportation and warehousing	6,830
Utilities	5,286
Wholesale trade	20,231

Source: U.S. Department of Commerce, Bureau of Economic Analysis, Survey of Current Business

Real Gross Domestic Product, 2000–2012
In millions of chained 2005 dollars

Year	State GDP	U.S. GDP	State Share
2000	301,565	11,225,406	2.69%
2005	323,314	12,539,116	2.58%
2010	340,159	12,897,088	2.64%
2012	353,717	13,430,576	2.63%

Source: U.S. Department of Commerce, Bureau of Economic Analysis, Survey of Current Business

Personal Income Per Capita, 1930–2012

Year	State	U.S.
1930	$836	$618
1940	$780	$593
1950	$1,651	$1,503
1960	$2,496	$2,268
1970	$4,472	$4,084
1980	$10,570	$10,091
1990	$22,797	$19,354
2000	$38,222	$30,319
2010	$51,143	$39,791
2012	$54,687	$42,693

Source: U.S. Department of Commerce, Bureau of Economic Analysis, Regional Economic Accounts

Non-Farm Employment by Sector, 2012
In thousands

Sector	Employment
Construction	114.6
Education and health services	688.1
Financial activities	206.2
Government	437.3
Information	86.8
Leisure and hospitality	324.3
Mining and logging	1.0
Manufacturing	251.8
Other services	121.9
Professional and business services	491.0
Trade, transportation, and utilities	550.7
All sectors	3,273.6

Source: U.S. Bureau of Labor Statistics, State and Area Employment

Foreign Exports, 2000–2012
In millions of dollars

Year	State Exports	U.S. Exports	State Share
2000	20,514	712,054	2.88%
2002	16,705	649,940	2.57%
2004	21,899	768,554	2.85%
2006	24,056	973,994	2.47%
2008	28,369	1,222,545	2.32%
2010	26,304	1,208,080	2.18%
2012	25,612	1,478,268	1.73%

Note: U.S. figures exclude data from Puerto Rico, U.S. Virgin Islands, and unallocated exports
Source: U.S. Department of Commerce, International Trade Admin., Office of Trade and Industry Information, Manufacturing and Services

Energy Consumption, 2011

In trillions of BTUs, except as noted

Total energy consumption	
Total state energy consumption	1,395.1
Total U.S. energy consumption	97,387.3
State share of U.S. total	1.43%
Per capita consumption (in millions of BTUs)	
Total state per capita consumption	211.2
Total U.S. per capita consumption	312.6
End-use sectors	
Residential	424.4
Commercial	277.8
Industrial	234.8
Transportation	458.0
Sources of energy	
Petroleum	570.0
Natural gas	461.2
Coal	43.0
Renewable energy	70.5
Nuclear electric power	53.2

Source: U.S. Energy Information Administration, State Energy Data 2011: Consumption

LAND AND WATER

Surface Area and Federally-Owned Land, 2007

In thousands of acres

Category	State	U.S.	State Share
Total surface area	5,339.0	1,937,664.2	0.28%
Total land area	4,972.4	1,886,846.9	0.26%
Non-federal land	4,875.3	1,484,910.0	0.33%
Developed	1,716.4	111,251.2	1.54%
Rural	3,158.9	1,373,658.8	0.23%
Federal land	97.1	401,936.9	0.02%
Water area	366.6	50,817.3	0.72%

Source: U.S. Department of Agriculture, Natural Resources Conservation Service, 2007 National Resources Inventory

Land Cover/Use of Non-Federal Rural Land, 2007

In thousands of acres

Category	State	U.S.	State Share
Total rural land	3,158.9	1,373,658.8	0.23%
Cropland	237.7	357,023.5	0.07%
CRP[1] land	0.0	32,850.2	0.00%
Pastureland	135.4	118,615.7	0.11%
Rangeland	0.0	409,119.4	0.00%
Forest land	2,589.0	406,410.4	0.64%
Other rural land	196.8	49,639.6	0.40%

Note: (1) Conservation Reserve Program was created to assist private landowners in converting highly erodible cropland to vegetative cover.
Source: U.S. Department of Agriculture, Natural Resources Conservation Service, 2007 National Resources Inventory

Farms and Crop Acreage, 2012

Category	State	U.S.	State Share
Farms (in thousands)	7.7	2,170.0	0.35%
Acres (in millions)	0.5	914.0	0.06%
Acres per farm	67.5	421.2	–

Source: U.S. Department of Agriculture, National Agricultural Statistical Service, Quick Stats, 2012 Survey Data

HEALTH AND MEDICAL CARE

Medical Professionals, 2012

Profession	State Number	U.S. Number	State Share	State Rate[1]	U.S. Rate[1]
Physicians[2]	32,580	894,637	3.64%	493.1	287.1
Dentists	5,931	193,587	3.06%	89.8	62.1
Podiatrists	412	17,469	2.36%	6.2	5.6
Optometrists	1,156	45,638	2.53%	17.5	14.6
Chiropractors	1,489	77,494	1.92%	22.5	24.9

Note: (1) Rates are per 100,000 population; (2) Includes total, active Doctors of Osteopathic Medicine and Doctors of Medicine in 2011.
Source: U.S. Department of Health and Human Services, Bureau of Health Professions, Area Health Resource File, 2012-2013

Health Insurance Coverage, 2011

Category	State	U.S.
Total persons covered	6,304,000	260,214,000
Total persons not covered	219,000	48,613,000
Percent not covered	3.4%	15.7%
Children under age 18 covered	1,387,000	67,143,000
Children under age 18 not covered	36,000	6,965,000
Percent of children not covered	2.5%	9.4%

Source: U.S. Census Bureau, Current Population Survey, 2012 Annual Social and Economic Supplement

HIV, STD, and Tuberculosis Cases and Rates, 2011

Disease	State Cases	State Rate[1]	U.S. Rate[1]
Chlamydia	22,764	347.7	457.6
Gonorrhea	2,353	35.9	104.2
HIV diagnosis	1,262	22.5	15.8
HIV, stage 3 (AIDS)	666	11.9	10.3
Syphilis, early latent	233	3.6	4.3
Syphilis, primary/secondary	266	4.1	4.5
Tuberculosis	196	3.0	3.4

Note: (1) Rates are per 100,000 population
Source: Centers for Disease Control and Prevention

Cigarette Smoking, 2011

Category	State	U.S.
Adults who are current smokers	18.2%	21.2%
Adults who smoke everyday	13.3%	15.4%
Adults who smoke some days	4.9%	5.7%
Adults who are former smokers	28.3%	25.1%
Adults who never smoked	53.5%	52.9%

Source: Centers for Disease Control and Prevention, Behaviorial Risk Factor Surveillance System, Tobacco Use, 2011

HOUSING

Home Ownership Rates, 1995–2012

Area	1995	2000	2005	2010	2012
State	60.2%	59.9%	63.4%	65.3%	65.8%
U.S.	64.7%	67.4%	68.9%	66.9%	65.4%

Source: U.S. Census Bureau, Housing Vacancies and Homeownership, Annual Statistics

Home Sales, 2000–2010
In thousands of units

Year	State Sales	U.S. Sales	State Share
2000	112.3	5,174	2.17%
2002	115.9	5,632	2.06%
2004	141.7	6,778	2.09%
2006	128.1	6,478	1.98%
2008	103.8	4,913	2.11%
2010	105.3	4,908	2.15%

Note: Units include single-family homes, condos and co-ops
Source: National Association of Realtors, Real Estate Outlook, Market Trends & Insights

Value of Owner-Occupied Homes, 2011

Value	Total Units in State	Percent of Total, State	Percent of Total, U.S.
Less than $50,000	30,088	1.9%	8.8%
$50,000 to $99,000	28,017	1.8%	16.0%
$100,000 to $149,000	70,346	4.5%	16.5%
$150,000 to $199,000	151,080	9.6%	15.4%
$200,000 to $299,000	408,182	25.9%	18.2%
$300,000 to $499,000	578,071	36.7%	15.2%
$500,000 to $999,000	253,835	16.1%	7.9%
$1,000,000 or more	53,660	3.4%	2.0%
Median value	–	$326,300	$173,600

Source: U.S. Census Bureau, 2011 American Community Survey 1-Year Estimates

EDUCATION

School Enrollment, 2011

Educational Level	Students Enrolled in State	Percent of Total, State	Percent of Total, U.S.
All levels	1,764,471	100.0%	100.0%
Nursery school, preschool	115,161	6.5%	6.0%
Kindergarten	81,223	4.6%	5.1%
Elementary (grades 1–8)	629,133	35.7%	39.5%
Secondary (grades 9–12)	346,200	19.6%	20.7%
College or graduate school	592,754	33.6%	28.7%

Note: Figures cover the population 3 years and over enrolled in school
Source: U.S. Census Bureau, 2011 American Community Survey 1-Year Estimates

Educational Attainment, 2011

Highest Level of Education	State	U.S.
High school diploma	89.2%	85.9%
Bachelor's degree	39.1%	28.5%
Graduate/Professional degree	16.8%	10.6%

Note: Figures cover the population 25 years and over
Source: U.S. Census Bureau, 2011 American Community Survey 1-Year Estimates

Public College Finances, FY 2012

Category	State	U.S.
Full-time equivalent enrollment (FTE)[1]	170,221	11,548,974
Educational appropriations per FTE[2]	$5,259	$5,906
Net tuition revenue per FTE[3]	$5,526	$5,189
Total educational revenue per FTE[4]	$10,786	$11,043

(1) Full-time equivalent enrollment equates student credit hours to full time, academic year students, but excludes medical students; (2) Educational appropriations measure state and local support available for public higher education operating expenses including ARRA funds and excludes appropriations for independent institutions, financial aid for students attending independent institutions, research, hospitals, and medical education; (3) Net tuition revenue is calculated by taking the gross amount of tuition and fees, less state and institutional financial aid, tuition waivers or discounts, and medical student tuition and fees. Net tuition revenue used for capital debt service is included in the net tuition revenue figures; (4) Total educational revenue is the sum of educational appropriations and net tuition excluding net tuition revenue used for capital debt service.
Source: State Higher Education Executive Officers, State Higher Education Finance FY 2012

TRANSPORTATION AND TRAVEL

Motor Vehicle Registrations and Drivers Licenses, 2011

Vehicle Type	State	U.S.	State Share
Automobiles[1]	3,180,009	125,656,528	2.53%
Buses	11,590	666,064	1.74%
Trucks	2,344,721	118,455,587	1.98%
Motorcycles	159,007	8,437,502	1.88%
Drivers licenses	4,683,323	211,874,649	2.21%

Note: Motor vehicle registrations include private, commercial, and publicly-owned vehicles; (1) Includes taxicabs
Source: U.S. Department of Transportation, Federal Highway Administration

Domestic Travel Expenditures, 2009
In millions of dollars

Category	State	U.S.	State Share
Travel expenditures	$12,419	$610,200	2.04%

Note: Figures represent U.S. spending on domestic overnight trips and day trips of 50 miles or more, one way, away from home. Excludes spending by foreign visitors.
Source: U.S. Travel Association, Impact of Travel on State Economies, 2009

Retail Gasoline Prices, 2013

Gasoline Grade	State Average	U.S. Average
Regular	$3.75	$3.65
Mid	$3.90	$3.81
Premium	$4.02	$3.98
Diesel	$3.94	$3.88
Excise tax[1]	41.9 cents	49.4 cents

Note: Gasoline prices as of 7/26/2013; (1) Includes state and federal excise taxes and other state taxes as of July 1, 2013
Source: American Automobile Association, Daily Fuel Guage Report; American Petroleum Institute, State Motor Fuel Taxes, 2013

Public Road Length, 2011

Type	State Mileage	U.S. Mileage	State Share
Interstate highways	573	46,960	1.22%
Other highways	345	15,719	2.19%
Principal arterial	1,992	156,262	1.27%
Minor arterial	4,137	242,942	1.70%
Major collector	4,062	534,592	0.76%
Minor collector	775	266,357	0.29%
Local	24,417	2,814,925	0.87%
Urban	28,315	1,095,373	2.58%
Rural	7,988	2,982,383	0.27%
Total	36,303	4,077,756	0.89%

Note: Combined urban and rural road mileage equals the total of the other road types
Source: U.S. Department of Transportation, Federal Highway Administration, Public Road Length, 2011

CRIME AND LAW ENFORCEMENT

Full-Time Law Enforcement Officers, 2011

Gender	State Number	State Rate[1]	U.S. Rate[1]
Male officers	14,962	230.6	210.3
Female officers	1,363	21.0	28.1
Total officers	16,325	251.6	238.3

Note: (1) Rates are per 100,000 population
Source: Federal Bureau of Investigation, Uniform Crime Reports, Crime in the United States 2011

Prison Population, 2000–2012

Year	State Population	U.S. Population	State Share
2000	10,722	1,391,261	0.77%
2005	10,701	1,527,929	0.70%
2010	11,313	1,613,803	0.70%
2011	11,623	1,598,783	0.73%
2012	11,308	1,571,013	0.72%

Note: Figures include prisoners under the jurisdiction of state or federal correctional authorities.
Source: U.S. Department of Justice, Bureau of Justice Statistics, Prisoners in 2006, 2011, 2012 (Advance Counts)

Crime Rate, 2011

Incidents per 100,000 residents

Category	State	U.S.
Violent crimes	428.4	386.3
Murder	2.8	4.7
Forcible rape	24.7	26.8
Robbery	102.7	113.7
Aggravated assault	298.1	241.1
Property crimes	2,258.7	2,908.7
Burglary	554.6	702.2
Larceny/theft	1,540.3	1,976.9
Motor vehicle theft	163.7	229.6
All crimes	2,687.1	3,295.0

Source: Federal Bureau of Investigation, Uniform Crime Reports, Crime in the United States 2011

GOVERNMENT AND FINANCE

Local Governments by Type, 2012

Government Type	State	U.S.	State Share
All local governments	852	89,004	0.96%
County	5	3,031	0.16%
Municipality	53	19,522	0.27%
Town/Township	298	16,364	1.82%
Special District	412	37,203	1.11%
Ind. School District	84	12,884	0.65%

Source: U.S. Census Bureau, 2012 Census of Governments: Organization Component Preliminary Estimates

State Government Revenue, 2011

In thousands of dollars, except for per capita figures

Total revenue	$56,636,798
Total revenue per capita, State	$8,572
Total revenue per capita, U.S.	$7,271
General revenue	$44,897,892
Intergovernmental revenue	$14,136,989
Taxes	$22,089,530
General sales	$4,920,521
Selective sales	$2,188,175
License taxes	$854,458
Individual income taxes	$11,597,152
Corporate income taxes	$1,931,571
Other taxes	$597,653
Current charges	$4,576,524
Miscellaneous general revenue	$4,094,849
Utility revenue	$208,690
Liquor store revenue	$0
Insurance trust revenue[1]	$11,530,216

Note: (1) Within insurance trust revenue, net earnings of state retirement systems is a calculated statistic, and thus can be positive or negative. Net earnings is the sum of earnings on investments plus gains on investments minus losses on investments.
Source: U.S. Census Bureau, 2011 Annual Survey of State Government Finances

State Government Expenditures, 2011

In thousands of dollars, except for per capita figures

Total expenditure	$52,550,586
Total expenditure per capita, State	$7,954
Total expenditure per capita, U.S.	$6,427
Intergovernmental expenditure	$8,826,190
Direct expenditure	$43,724,396
Current operation	$27,811,681
Capital outlay	$2,758,230
Insurance benefits and repayments	$9,141,544
Assistance and subsidies	$795,029
Interest on debt	$3,217,912
Utility expenditure	$228,034
Liquor store expenditure	$0
Insurance trust expenditure	$9,141,544

Source: U.S. Census Bureau, 2011 Annual Survey of State Government Finances

State Government General Expenditures by Function, 2011

In thousands of dollars

Education	$12,334,213
Public welfare	$14,715,542
Hospitals	$515,094
Health	$1,112,022
Highways	$1,907,814
Police protection	$759,139
Correction	$1,050,827
Natural resources	$349,346
Parks and recreation	$237,973
Governmental administration	$1,648,292
Interest on general debt	$3,131,246
Other and unallocable	$5,419,500

Source: U.S. Census Bureau, 2011 Annual Survey of State Government Finances

State Government Finances, Cash and Debt, 2011

In thousands of dollars, except for per capita figures

Debt at end of fiscal year	
State, total	$74,315,823
State, per capita	$11,248
U.S., per capita	$3,635
Cash and security holdings	
State, total	$94,697,510
State, per capita	$14,333
U.S., per capita	$11,759

Source: U.S. Census Bureau, 2011 Annual Survey of State Government Finances

POLITICS

Composition of the Senate, 1995–2013

Congress (Year)	State/U.S	Dem	Rep	Total
104th (1995)	State delegates	2	0	2
	Total U.S.	48	52	100
105th (1997)	State delegates	2	0	2
	Total U.S.	45	55	100
106th (1999)	State delegates	2	0	2
	Total U.S.	45	55	100
107th (2001)	State delegates	2	0	2
	Total U.S.	50	50	100
108th (2003)	State delegates	2	0	2
	Total U.S.	48	51	100
109th (2005)	State delegates	2	0	2
	Total U.S.	44	55	100
110th (2007)	State delegates	2	0	2
	Total U.S.	49	49	100
111th (2009)	State delegates	2	0	2
	Total U.S.	57	41	100
112th (2011)	State delegates	1	1	2
	Total U.S.	51	47	100
113th (2013)	State delegates	2	0	2
	Total U.S.	54	45	100

Note: Figures are for the starts of first sessions; Totals include Democratic (Dem) and Republican (Rep) members as well as vacancies and seats held by independent party members
Source: U.S. Congress, Congressional Directory

Composition of the House of Representatives, 1995–2013

Congress (Year)	State/U.S	Dem	Rep	Total
104th (1995)	State delegates	8	2	10
	Total U.S.	204	230	435
105th (1997)	State delegates	10	0	10
	Total U.S.	207	226	435
106th (1999)	State delegates	10	0	10
	Total U.S.	211	223	435
107th (2001)	State delegates	10	0	10
	Total U.S.	212	221	435
108th (2003)	State delegates	10	0	10
	Total U.S.	205	229	435
109th (2005)	State delegates	10	0	10
	Total U.S.	202	231	435
110th (2007)	State delegates	10	0	10
	Total U.S.	233	198	435
111th (2009)	State delegates	10	0	10
	Total U.S.	256	178	435
112th (2011)	State delegates	10	0	10
	Total U.S.	193	242	435
113th (2013)	State delegates	9	0	9
	Total U.S.	201	234	435

Note: Figures are for the starts of first sessions; Totals include Democratic (Dem) and Republican (Rep) members as well as vacancies and seats held by independent party members
Source: U.S. Congress, Congressional Directory

Composition of State Legislature, 2004–2013

Year	Democrats	Republicans	Total
State Senate			
2004	34	6	40
2005	34	6	40
2006	34	6	40
2007	35	5	40
2008	35	5	40
2009	35	5	40
2010	35	5	40
2011	36	4	40
2012	36	4	40
2013	36	4	40
State House			
2004	136	23	160
2005	136	21	160
2006	138	21	160
2007	141	19	160
2008	140	19	160
2009	142	16	160
2010	143	16	160
2011	128	31	160
2012	125	33	160
2013	129	29	160

Note: Totals may include minor party members and vacancies
Source: The Council of State Governments, State Legislatures

Voter Participation in Presidential Elections, 1980–2012

Year	Voting-eligible State Population	State Voter Turnout Rate	U.S. Voter Turnout Rate
1980	4,110,721	61.4	54.2
1984	4,273,437	59.9	55.2
1988	4,385,728	60.0	52.8
1992	4,346,897	63.8	58.1
1996	4,385,268	58.4	51.7
2000	4,517,052	59.9	54.2
2004	4,533,859	64.2	60.1
2008	4,612,550	66.8	61.6
2012	4,781,421	66.3	58.2

Note: All figures are based on the voting-eligible population which excludes person ineligible to vote such as non-citizens, felons (depending on state law), and mentally-incapacitated persons. U.S. figures include the overseas eligible population (including military personnel).
Source: McDonald, Michael P., United States Election Project, Presidential Voter Turnout Rates, 1980–2012

Governors Since Statehood

John Hancock	(r) 1780-1785
Thomas Cushing	1785
James Bowdoin	1785-1787
John Hancock	(d) 1787-1793
Samuel Adams (O)	1793-1797
Increase Sumner (O)	(d) 1797-1799
Moses Gill (O)	(d) 1799-1800
Thomas Dawes (O)	1800
Caleb Strong (O)	1800-1807
James Sullivan (O)	(d) 1807-1808
Levi Lincoln (O)	1808-1809
Christopher Gore (O)	1809-1810
Elbridge Gerry (O)	1810-1812
Caleb Strong (O)	1812-1816
John Brooks (O)	1816-1823
William Eustis (O)	(d) 1823-1825
Marcus Morton (O)	1825
Levi Lincoln Jr. (O)	1825-1834
John Davis (O)	(r) 1834-1835
Samuel T. Armstrong (O)	1835-1836
Edward Everett (O)	1836-1840
Marcus Morton (D)	1840-1841
John Davis (O)	1841-1843
Marcus Morton (D)	1843-1844
George N. Briggs (O)	1844-1851
George S. Boutwell (D)	1851-1853
John H. Clifford (O)	1853-1854
Emory Washburn (O)	1854-1855
Henry J. Gardner (O)	1855-1858
Nathaniel P. Banks (R)	1858-1861
John A. Andrew (R)	1861-1866
Alexander H. Bullock (R)	1866-1869
William Claflin (R)	1869-1872
William B. Washburn (R)	(r) 1872-1874
William Talbot (R)	1874-1875
William Gaston (D)	1875-1876
Alexander H. Rice (R)	1876-1879
Thomas Talbot (R)	1879-1880
John D. Long (R)	1880-1883
Benjamin F. Butler (D)	1883-1884
George D. Robinson (R)	1884-1887
Oliver Ames (R)	1887-1890
John Q. A. Brackett (R)	1890-1891
William E. Russell (D)	1891-1894
Frederic T. Greenhalge (R)	(d) 1894-1896
Roger Wolcott (R)	1896-1900
Winthrop Murray Crane (R)	1900-1903
John L. Bates (R)	1903-1905
William L. Douglas (D)	1905-1906
Curtis Guild Jr. (R)	1906-1909
Eben S. Draper (R)	1909-1911
Eugene N. Foss (D)	1911-1914
David T. Walsh (D)	1914-1916
Samuel W. McCall (R)	1916-1919
Calvin Coolidge (R)	1919-1921
Channing H. Cox (R)	1921-1925
Alvan T. Fuller (R)	1925-1929
Frank G. Allen (R)	1929-1931
Joseph B. Ely (D)	1931-1935
James M. Curley (D)	1935-1937
Charles F. Hurley (D)	1937-1939
Leverett Saltonstall (R)	1939-1945
Maurice J. Tobin (D)	1945-1947
Robert F. Bradford (R)	1947-1949
Paul A. Dever (D)	1949-1953
Christian A. Herter (R)	1953-1957
Foster Furcolo (D)	1957-1961
John A. Volpe (R)	1961-1963
Endicott Peabody (D)	1963-1965
John A. Volpe (R)	(r) 1965-1969
Francis W. Sargent (R)	1969-1975
Michael S. Dukakis (D)	1975-1979
Edward J. King (D)	1979-1983
Michael S. Dukakis (D)	1983-1991
William Weld (R)	(r) 1991-1997
Argeo Paul Cellucci (R)	(a) 1997-2001
Jane Swift (R)	(a) 2001-2003
W. Mitt Romney (R)	2003-2007
Deval Patrick (D)	2007-2015 (retiring)

Note: (D) Democrat; (R) Republican; (O) Other party; (r) resigned; (d) died in office; (i) removed from office

Michigan

Location: Upper Midwest

Area and rank: 58,110 square miles (150,504 square kilometers); 96,810 square miles (250,738 square kilometers) including water; twenty-first largest state in area

Coastline: none

Population and rank: 9,883,360 (2012 estimate); ninth largest state in population

Capital city: Lansing (114,297 people in 2010 census)

Largest city: Detroit (713,777 people in 2010 census)

State capitol building in Lansing. (Travel Michigan)

Became territory: January 11, 1805

Entered Union and rank: January 26, 1837; twenty-sixth state

Present constitution adopted: April 1, 1963 (effective January 1, 1964)

Counties: 83

State name: "Michigan" comes from the Indian word "Michigana," meaning "great or large lake"

State nickname: Wolverine State

Motto: *Si quaeris peninsulam amoenam circumspice* (If you seek a pleasant peninsula, look around you)

State flag: Blue field with state coat of arms

Highest point: Mount Arvon—1,979 feet (603 meters)

Lowest point: Lake Erie—571 feet (174 meters)

Highest recorded temperature: 112 degrees Fahrenheit (44 degrees Celsius)—Mio, 1936

Lowest recorded temperature: –51 degrees Fahrenheit (–46 degrees Celsius)—Vanderbilt, 1934

State song: "Michigan, My Michigan"

State tree: White pine

State flower: Apple blossom

State bird: Robin

State fish: Trout; brook trout

National parks: Isle Royale

Michigan History

Michigan's abundant natural resources and access to major waterways, including four of the five Great Lakes, have made it an important area of human activity for more than ten thousand years. The unique geographic situation of Michigan, with the state divided into two separate land masses, has had a profound influence on its history. The southern land mass, known as the Lower Peninsula, developed into a heavily populated area of agriculture, forestry, and industry. The northern land mass, known as the Upper Peninsula, remained sparsely populated but provided important mineral resources.

Early History. The first inhabitants of the region hunted and fished about eleven thousand years ago. They also made tools from copper found in the Upper Peninsula. This is the earliest known use of metal in the New World. About three thousand years ago, agriculture began to develop in the southwestern part of the Lower Peninsula.

By the time Europeans arrived in North America, Michigan was primarily inhabited by Native Americans belonging to the Algonquian language group. These peoples included the Ottawa, the Ojibwa, the Miami, and the Potawatomi, mostly living in the northern regions. In the south lived the Huron, a Native American tribe belonging to the Iroquois language group. During the middle of the seventeenth century, conflict with other Iroquois peoples to the east drove the Huron and the Ottawa westward. At about the same time, the development of the French fur trade led many Native Americans in northern Michigan to move south.

Exploration and Settlement. The first European known to have visited the area was Étienne Brulé, who reached the Upper Peninsula from Canada in 1622. Another French explorer, Jean Nicolet, traveled through the narrow strait that separates the two peninsulas in 1634 during a journey from Canada to Wisconsin. The

Ford Motor Company's Model T factory at Highland Park, Michigan, where assembly-line production began in 1913. (Library of Congress)

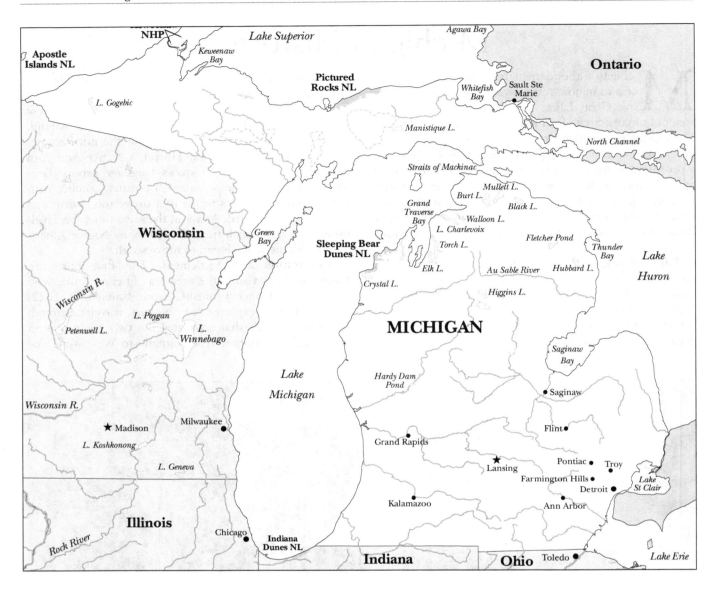

earliest permanent European settlements, located in the Upper Peninsula, were founded by the French missionary Jacques Marquette at Sault Sainte Marie in 1668 and St. Ignace in 1671.

During the late seventeenth and early eighteenth centuries, several French missionary, fur trading, and military posts were established on both peninsulas. In 1701, Detroit was founded by Antoine Laumet de La Mothe, sieur de Cadillac. It soon became the most important French settlement in the Great Lakes region.

During the French and Indian War, a struggle between France and England for control of North America, Detroit was surrendered to the British in 1760. After the war, control of the region went to Great Britain. Fearful that the British would bring many more settlers to the area, many Native Americans united under the Ottawa leader Pontiac. After capturing several British forts in the area, Pontiac's forces laid siege to Detroit for nearly six

months in 1763. Pontiac was forced to abandon the siege in October, and the British remained in control.

Steps to Statehood. Although the end of the American Revolution officially brought the area under American control, the British did not leave Detroit and other military posts until 1796. Michigan was part of the Northwest Territory from 1787 to 1800, when it became part of the newly created Indiana Territory. The Michigan Territory was created in 1805. In the same year, a fire destroyed several buildings in Detroit.

After being rebuilt, Detroit was an important military objective in the War of 1812, a conflict between the United States and England. Detroit was captured by the British in August of 1812 but recaptured in September of 1813. Control of the Great Lakes region was restored to the United States the same month, when American naval forces commanded by Oliver Hazard Perry defeated the British in the Battle of Lake Erie.

Michigan began growing quickly after the war. Settlement was encouraged by the beginning of steamship transportation on Lake Erie from Buffalo to Detroit. The completion of the Erie Canal in 1825, linking the Hudson River to Lake Erie, also led to rapid population growth. From 1820 to 1840, the number of settlers, mostly from eastern states, increased from less than 9,000 to more than 200,000. During this time, many Native Americans gave up their lands or were forced to leave. However, some remained on reservations that still exist.

Michigan reached the population of sixty thousand required for statehood as early as 1833. Before statehood could be approved by Congress, however, a border dispute arose between Michigan and Ohio. Ohio claimed lands in the southeastern part of the Michigan Territory. In the Toledo War of 1835, Michigan militia prevented Ohio officials from occupying the area. Michigan eventually gave up the disputed region in return for a large increase in the size of its lands in the Upper Peninsula. It became the twenty-sixth state in 1837.

Economic Development. Despite an economic depression during the late 1830's, Michigan experienced rapid growth in the two decades after statehood. Many of the new residents were immigrants from Germany, Ireland, and the Netherlands. The vast majority of settlers were drawn to Michigan by the rich, productive soil found in the southern part of the Lower Peninsula. During the 1850's, about 85 percent of the population was involved in agriculture.

The pine forests of the northern part of the Lower Peninsula and the mineral resources of the Upper Peninsula were also important parts of the state's economy. Iron, copper, and salt deposits began to be mined during the 1840's. Immigrants from Finland and Cornwall, a region of southwestern England, were involved in the development of the mining industry. An important stimulus to economic growth in the Upper Peninsula was the completion in 1855 of a series of locks at Sault Sainte Marie which allowed ships to travel from Lake Huron to Lake Superior. The growing importance of the northern regions of the state was a factor in the decision to move the capital from Detroit to Lansing in 1847.

Republicans and the Civil War. The Democratic Party dominated Michigan politics from before statehood until the national crisis over slavery during the 1850's. In 1854, antislavery members of the Democratic Party joined with members of the Whig Party and the Free-Soil Party to form the Republican Party in Jackson. The new party would dominate Michigan politics for the next eight decades.

During the Civil War about ninety thousand residents of Michigan fought for the Union, and around fourteen thousand were killed. Among the forces representing Michigan was a regiment of African Americans drawn from several states.

The Rise of Industry. The late nineteenth century saw the beginnings of modern manufacturing in Michigan. Grand Rapids became a center of furniture making. Kalamazoo dominated the paper industry. The Dow Chemical Company and the Upjohn Company made the chemical and pharmaceutical industries an important part of the state's economy. Perhaps the most distinctive industry to arise in Michigan at this time was the manufacture of breakfast cereal. This industry, which grew out of health resorts in the state that developed these products as part of a vegetarian diet, is centered in the city of Battle Creek.

By far the most important industry in Michigan during the twentieth century was automobile manufacturing. The industry began in 1901, when Ransom Eli Olds began marketing the Oldsmobile, the first successful American automobile. Inspired by this success, other automobile manufacturing companies soon appeared in the state. Henry Ford organized the Ford Motor Company in 1903 and began manufacturing the highly successful Model T in 1908. The same year, William C. Durant created the General Motors Corporation. Walter P. Chrysler founded the Chrysler Corporation in 1925. These and many other companies made the cities of Detroit, Flint, Pontiac, and Lansing dominant in the automobile industry.

The Twentieth Century. During the late nineteenth and early twentieth centuries, large numbers of immigrants from Ireland, Italy, Poland, and other European nations entered the state. At about the same time, African Americans from southern states began to arrive in large numbers. From 1900 to the late twentieth century, the number of African Americans in the state rose from less than sixteen thousand to well over one million. In the last few decades of the century, immigrants also arrived from Latin America, Asia, and the Middle East.

The Great Depression of the 1930's devastated the automobile industry. By 1932 half the industrial workers in Michigan were unemployed. This crisis ended the dominance of the Republican Party in the state. It also made organized labor an important force in Michigan. The entire automobile industry was unionized by the United Automobile Workers by 1941.

World War II revitalized industry in the state as automobile manufacturers turned to making military vehicles. Prosperity continued from the end of the war until the nationwide recession of the 1980's, which brought much higher unemployment to Michigan than to most other states. During the late 1980's and 1990's, the state made efforts to lessen its economic dependence on the automobile industry, particularly by developing technological industries and tourism.

Economic Setbacks. As the twenty-first century neared, Michigan endured economic reverses in a mainstay of its economy, the automobile industry. In 2000, General Motors closed its production of Oldsmobiles, the oldest automobile make in the nation, with the loss of fifteen

General Motors' headquarters at Renaissance Center in Michigan's largest city, Detroit. (Wikimedia Commons)

thousand jobs. The following year, DaimlerChrysler, a German-owned successor to the Chrysler Corporation, announced the closing of a Michigan plant and the layoff of twenty thousand workers in the process. In 2002, the Ford Motor Company announced the closing of five of its forty-four plants in North America.

Michigan was among the states losing jobs. Altogether, Ford laid off 10 percent of its workforce. The company also announced that it was discontinuing several of its models, including well-known cars such as the Ford Escort and the Lincoln Continental. At the same time, General Motors said it would lay off thousands more workers. Given such economic conditions, there was little surprise that, according to the 2000 census, Michigan's population did not keep up national trends of population increase. As a result, the state lost one member of Congress.

Electoral Trends. In the 2000 presidential election, Michigan cast its eighteen electoral votes for Vice President Al Gore over Texas governor George W. Bush by a 51-47 percent margin. Democrats also took five seats

in the Michigan state senate that were previously held by Republicans. Moreover, in the race for U.S. senator, Democrat Deborah Ann Stabenow unseated her Republican opponent, Senator Spencer Abraham, by 50 to 49 percent in a closely watched race. A Republican, however, took Stabenow's seat in the House.

In 2002, voters reelected Democrat Carl Levin to the U.S. Senate, but Republicans returned two new members to Congress. In the race for the statehouse, Democrat Jennifer Granholm, Michigan's attorney general, beat the state's Republican lieutenant governor to become the state's first female elected governor. In 2004, Michigan again chose a Democrat to receive its electoral votes, as Senator John Kerry carried the state by a 51-48 percent margin. All fourteen incumbents were reelected, and a Republican victory in the fifteenth race retained a Republican seat when its holder retired.

Affirmative Action. Two University of Michigan lawsuits in 2003 (*Grutter v. Bollinger* and *Gratz v. Bollinger*) were important both for the state and for the nation. In

December, 2000, a federal judge upheld a challenge to the University of Michigan's use of race in its admissions policies, which awarded undergraduate applicants points (20 points in a total of 150) for racial criteria. This policy differed from a previous policy of racial quotas that had been outlawed by the U.S. Supreme Court. When the case was appealed in 2003, the U.S.

Supreme Court denied the validity of awarding such points since the policy did not use race in a "narrowly tailored" way. However, in a separate case decided the same day involving University of Michigan law school admissions, the Court, while continuing to ban admission quotas, upheld the use of race as a "plus" for applicants as individuals because the law school had a compelling state interest in attaining a diverse student body. The Court did ban any "mechanical" application of race that fails to consider each applicant as an individual.

Economy. Michigan was particularly hard hit by the economic downturn that followed the economic crisis of 2008. Michigan led the nation in unemployment for the next four years, but finally dropped out of the top 10 when state unemployment slid to 9.3 percent in December 2011. Some 67,000 jobs were created in Michigan in 2011. Unemployment peaked at 14.1 percent in the fall of 2009. However, economists noted that the main reason the unemployment rate dropped was because the labor force itself was shrinking from retirement, emigration, and jobless workers simply giving up looking for work. The year 2011 was the first year since 2004 that all three major U.S. auto manufacturers showed a profit, two years after the 2009 bailout by the federal government.

Politics. Democrat Jennifer Granholm, a Democrat, was elected governor in 2002 and re-elected in 2006. She was prohibited by the state's constitution from seeking a third term. In 2010, a large pool of candidates led to two Democrats and five Republicans in the primaries. Since it was anticipated that a Republican would win, the Republican primary race was highly competitive.

Analysts suspected that a large portion of Democrats crossed party lines to vote for Rick Snyder, who actively sought bipartisan and independent support. Snyder was a businessman and venture capitalist. In Michigan, voters may vote in either primary regardless of their registration. Snyder gained almost a 10-point lead over Pete Hoekstra. In the general election, Snyder took over 58 percent of the vote against his Democratic opponent, Virg Bernero.

Rose Secrest
Updated by the Editor

Known as the Big House, the University of Michigan stadium is the world's largest facility built for American football. It regularly sells out to crowds of 100,000 people. (©Andrew Horne/Wikimedia Commons)

Michigan Time Line

1622	French explorer Étienne Brulé reaches the Upper Peninsula.
1634	Jean Nicolet journeys between the Upper and Lower Peninsulas.
1668	Father Jacques Marquette founds Sault Sainte Marie.
1671	Marquette founds St. Ignace.
July 24, 1701	Antoine Laumet de La Mothe, sieur de Cadillac, founds Detroit.
Nov. 29, 1760	Detroit surrenders to the British during the French and Indian War.
1763	Native American forces under Pontiac unsuccessfully lay siege to Detroit; end of the war brings the area under British control.
1783	End of the American Revolution brings the area under American control.
1787	Michigan becomes part of the Northwest Territory;
July 11, 1796	British leave Detroit.
1800	Michigan becomes part of the Indiana Territory.
Jan. 11, 1805	Michigan Territory is created with Detroit as the capital.
1805	Fire devastates Detroit.
1806	First post office in the state is established in Detroit.
Aug. 16, 1812	Detroit surrenders to the British during the War of 1812.
1813	Detroit is recaptured by the United States; Michigan returns to American control after the defeat of the British in the Battle of Lake Erie.
1818	Steamship travel begins between Buffalo and Detroit.
1820	Number of settlers reaches nearly nine thousand.
1825	Opening of the Erie Canal allows water transportation from New York City to Detroit.
1833	Population reaches sixty thousand.
1835	Toledo War, a border dispute between Michigan and Ohio, breaks out.
1836	First railroad is completed, linking Toledo and Arian.
Jan. 26, 1837	Michigan is admitted to the Union as the twenty-sixth state.
1837	University of Michigan is founded at Ann Arbor.
1840	Population reaches more than 200,000.
May 18, 1846	Michigan is first state to abolish the death penalty.
1847	Capital is moved to Lansing.
1854	Republican Party is founded at a convention in Jackson.
1855	Locks are completed at Sault Sainte Marie, linking Lake Huron and Lake Superior.
1901	Ransom Eli Olds begins selling the Oldsmobile.
1903	Henry Ford founds the Ford Motor Company.
1908	Ford begins manufacturing the Model T; William C. Durant founds the General Motors Corporation.
1914	Auto industry is responsible for 37 percent of state's manufacturing.
1920	For the first time, a majority of Michigan residents live in cities.
1925	Walter P. Chrysler founds the Chrysler Corporation.
1926	Commercial air travel from Detroit begins.
1932	Half of the state's industrial workers are unemployed due to the Great Depression.
1941	United Automobile Workers unionize the entire automobile industry.
June 20–21, 1943	Race riot breaks out in Detroit, leaving thirty-four dead.
1957	Mackinac Bridge connects the Upper and Lower Peninsulas.
1963	New state constitution is the first in the nation to create a Department of Civil Rights.
July 21–23, 1967	Race riot occurs in Detroit, leaving forty-three dead.
1973	Coleman Young is elected the first African American mayor of Detroit.
Aug. 9, 1974	Michigan resident Gerald R. Ford becomes president of United States.
1982	Due to a nationwide recession, unemployment reaches 17.3 percent.
1988	Less than one-quarter of all wage earners work in factories, a decline of 30 percent in ten years.
1998	Population reaches 9.8 million.
1998	Chrysler Corporation merges with German automaker Daimler-Benz to form DaimlerChrysler.
2000	General Motors announces discontinuation of the Oldsmobile, the oldest automobile make in the U.S.

2002	Ford Motor Company announces major job reductions and discontinues manufacture of several major car models.
Nov. 5, 2002	Michigan attorney general Jennifer Granholm is elected the state's first woman governor.
June 23, 2003	In deciding two cases, the U.S. Supreme Court accepts the University of Michigan's use of race as one of many factors in determining admissions but bans any "mechanical" application of race.
2006	Jennifer Granholm is re-elected as governor.
2011	Still ravaged by the recession, Michigan's unemployment slips back to 9.3 percent.

Notes for Further Study

Published Sources. For students new to the subject, several books intended for a general audience provide a basic introduction to the state. *Michigan* (1998) by Martin Hintz is a good place to start, with a clear, simple account of the state's geography, plant and animal life, history, economy, culture, and people. Similar information about Michigan and its neighboring states is found in *Eastern Great Lakes: Indiana, Michigan, Ohio* (1995) by Thomas G. Aylesworth; *Michigan History* (2003) by Marcia Schonberg; and *Michigan, the Great Lakes State: An Illustrated History* (2005) by George S. May and Joellen Vinyard. General information, with an emphasis on tourist attractions, is also found in Tina Lassen's *Michigan Handbook* (1999) and in *Michigan* (2006) by David Lee Poremba, which offers readers good information about the people who have called the state home over the centuries, the state's industries and politics, and its cultural and political development.

An enjoyable way to learn about the state is *Michigan Trivia* (1995) by Ernie and Jill Couch. The importance of industry in the state is the subject of Burton W. Folsom's *Empire Builders: How Michigan Entrepreneurs Helped Make America Great* (1998). *Wheels for the World: Henry Ford, His Company, and a Century of Progress* (2003) by Douglas Brinkley provides a good survey of the life and work of Ford and the way in which the automobile industry transformed Detroit. Howard P. Seagal, in *Recasting the Machine Age: Henry Ford's Village Industries* (2005), details Ford's efforts to decentralize his automobile production from Detroit and into communities surrounding that city.

Of the many volumes concerning the state's past, *A Historical Album of Michigan* (1996) by Charles Wills is a good introduction. *Traveling Through Time: A Guide to Michigan's Historical Markers* (rev. ed., 2005), edited by Laura Rose Ashlee, introduces readers to nearly fifteen hundred historical sites in the state and provides information about each one's significance. A more scholarly account is found in *Michigan: A History of the Wolverine State* (1995) by Willis F. Dunbar and George S. May. The early history of the state's major city is the topic of Annick Hivert-Carthew's *Cadillac and the Dawn of Detroit* (1995). The important role of race relations in the city is the subject of Thomas J. Sugrue's *The Origins of the Urban Crisis: Race and Inequality in Postwar Detroit* (1996); the same subject is discussed in *Someone Else's House: America's Unfinished Struggle for Integration* (1998) by Tamar Jacoby, which compares the situation in Detroit to those in New York City and Atlanta.

In *William G. Milliken: Michigan's Passionate Moderate* (2006), Dave Dempsey argues that Milliken, a three-term governor, set in place a number of characteristics of modern-day politics in Michigan; the book gives readers good insight into state politics. *French Canadians of Michigan: Their Contribution to the Development of the Saginaw Valley and the Keweenaw Peninsula, 1840–1914* (2003) by Jean Lamarre (translated by Howard Keillor and Hermione Jack) details the French Canadians' substantial impact on the state's development.

Web Resources. An enormous variety of Internet resources exists with information about Michigan. A good place to begin exploring the many Web sites available is the state's official site (www.michigan.gov/), which covers government, travel and recreation, education and children's services, and business and economic growth, among other topics. The importance of farming to the state is studied at Michigan Department of Agriculture (www.michigan.gov/mda). Statistical information is available in great detail from the U.S. Census Bureau State and County QuickFacts (quickfacts.census.gov/qfd/states/26000.html). Of the many sites devoted to the state's history, one of the best is Michigan Historical Center (www.michigan.gov/michiganhistory), which provides information on state archives and museums, as well as biographies of famous residents. Access Genealogy has a good Web page that describes Michigan tribes and allows users to research Native American ancestry (www.accessgenealogy.com/native/michigan/). The Saginaw-Chippewa tribe has its own Web page (www.sagchip.org/), as does the Sault tribe of the Chippewa (www.saulttribe.com/).

Counties

County	2012 Population	Pop. Rank	Land Area (sq. miles)	Area Rank
Alcona	10,635	75	674.59	30
Alger	9,541	76	915.07	12
Allegan	112,039	18	825.23	18
Alpena	29,234	49	571.86	39
Antrim	23,406	61	475.70	76
Arenac	15,477	68	363.19	81
Baraga	8,683	78	898.26	14
Barry	58,990	33	553.09	58
Bay	106,935	20	442.30	79
Benzie	17,465	65	319.70	83

County	2012 Population	Pop. Rank	Land Area (sq. miles)	Area Rank
Berrien	156,067	15	567.75	42
Branch	43,868	38	506.37	69
Calhoun	135,099	17	706.23	26
Cass	52,242	35	490.06	74
Charlevoix	26,023	53	416.34	80
Cheboygan	25,835	54	715.26	25
Chippewa	38,917	42	1,558.42	2
Clare	30,753	48	564.32	50
Clinton	76,001	25	566.41	44
Crawford	14,009	70	556.28	55

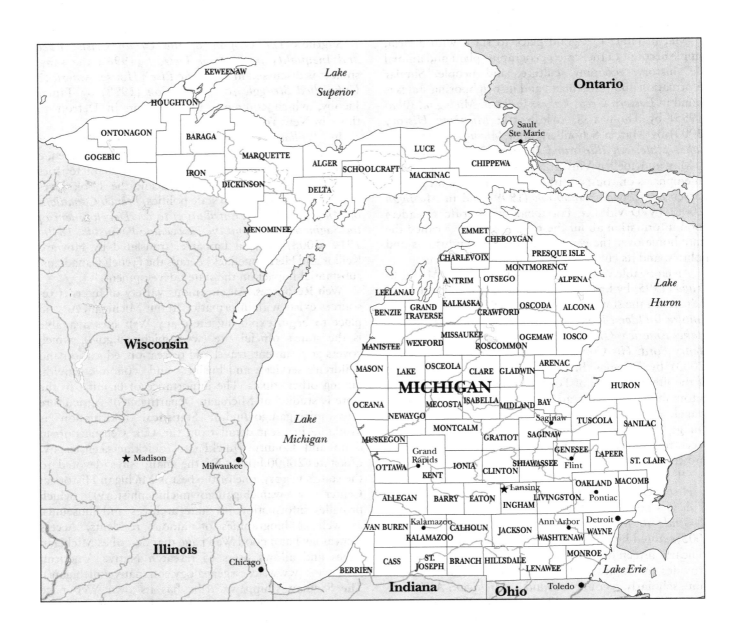

County	2012 Population	Pop. Rank	Land Area (sq. miles)	Area Rank
Delta	36,884	43	1,171.10	5
Dickinson	26,220	52	761.40	22
Eaton	108,008	19	575.17	37
Emmet	32,915	45	467.49	77
Genesee	418,408	5	636.98	33
Gladwin	25,484	55	501.78	70
Gogebic	16,084	67	1,101.85	7
Grand Traverse	89,112	22	464.33	78
Gratiot	42,063	41	568.46	41
Hillsdale	46,229	37	598.13	36
Houghton	36,520	44	1,009.10	10
Huron	32,463	47	835.71	17
Ingham	281,723	7	556.12	56
Ionia	63,941	30	571.30	40
Iosco	25,357	56	549.10	60
Iron	11,587	72	1,166.15	6
Isabella	70,617	27	572.68	38
Jackson	160,309	14	701.67	29
Kalamazoo	254,580	9	561.66	53
Kalkaska	17,099	66	559.86	54
Kent	614,462	4	846.95	16
Keweenaw	2,215	83	540.11	63
Lake	11,498	73	567.37	43
Lapeer	88,173	23	643.01	32
Leelanau	21,607	63	347.17	82
Lenawee	98,987	21	749.55	23
Livingston	182,838	11	565.25	47
Luce	6,522	81	899.08	13
Mackinac	11,137	74	1,021.57	9
Macomb	847,383	3	479.22	75
Manistee	24,672	57	542.15	62
Marquette	67,906	29	1,808.40	1
Mason	28,680	50	495.07	73
Mecosta	43,318	39	555.07	57
Menominee	23,815	60	1,044.08	8
Midland	83,822	24	516.25	66
Missaukee	15,031	69	564.73	49
Monroe	151,048	16	549.39	59
Montcalm	63,097	31	705.40	28
Montmorency	9,476	77	546.66	61
Muskegon	170,182	12	499.25	72
Newaygo	47,959	36	813.20	19
Oakland	1,220,657	2	867.66	15
Oceana	26,310	51	512.07	68
Ogemaw	21,437	64	563.49	51
Ontonagon	6,413	82	1,311.22	3
Osceola	23,276	62	566.39	45
Oscoda	8,592	79	565.73	46
Otsego	24,020	59	514.97	67
Ottawa	269,099	8	563.47	52
Presque Isle	13,129	71	658.72	31
Roscommon	24,106	58	519.64	65
Saginaw	198,353	10	800.11	21
Sanilac	42,268	40	962.57	11
Schoolcraft	8,343	80	1,171.36	4
Shiawassee	69,232	28	530.67	64
St. Clair	160,644	13	721.17	24
St. Joseph	60,796	32	500.59	71

County	2012 Population	Pop. Rank	Land Area (sq. miles)	Area Rank
Tuscola	54,662	34	803.13	20
Van Buren	75,454	26	607.47	35
Washtenaw	350,946	6	705.97	27
Wayne	1,792,365	1	612.08	34
Wexford	32,608	46	565.00	48

Source: U.S. Census Bureau, 2012 Population Estimates

Cities

With 10,000 or more residents

Legal Name	2010 Population	Pop. Rank	Land Area (sq. miles)	Area Rank	Legal Name	2010 Population	Pop. Rank	Land Area (sq. miles)	Area Rank
Ada township	13,142	162	36.04	20	Bath charter township	11,598	180	31.83	72
Adrian city	21,133	99	7.95	158	Battle Creek city	52,347	31	42.61	5
Allen Park city	28,210	71	7.00	164	Bay City city	34,932	52	10.17	145
Allendale charter township	20,708	101	31.13	76	Bedford township	31,085	60	39.19	8
Allendale CDP	17,579	118	22.73	111	Beecher CDP	10,232	204	5.88	173
Alpena city	10,483	197	8.54	152	Benton charter township	14,749	138	32.37	68
Alpine township	13,336	159	35.90	22	Benton Harbor city	10,038	207	4.43	187
Ann Arbor city	113,934	6	27.83	91	Berkley city	14,970	136	2.61	205
Antwerp township	12,182	170	34.69	39	Beverly Hills village	10,267	203	4.00	193
Auburn Hills city	21,412	95	16.60	121	Big Rapids city	10,601	195	4.36	189
Bangor charter township	14,641	143	14.10	133	Birmingham city	20,103	105	4.79	185

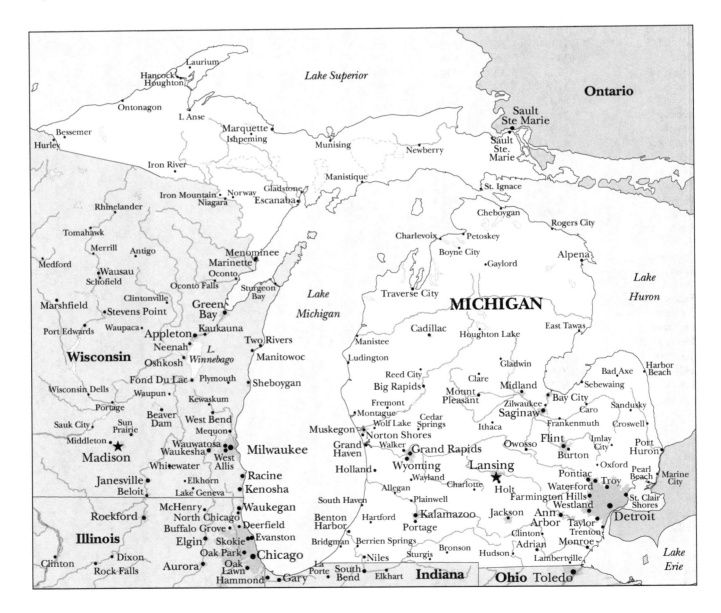

Legal Name	2010 Population	Pop. Rank	Land Area (sq. miles)	Area Rank
Blackman charter township	24,051	83	31.71	73
Bloomfield charter township	41,070	43	24.63	102
Brandon charter township	15,175	134	35.11	34
Bridgeport charter township	10,514	196	34.43	40
Brighton township	17,791	116	32.96	64
Brownstown charter township	30,627	62	22.19	112
Burton city	29,999	66	23.36	107
Byron township	20,317	104	36.10	18
Cadillac city	10,355	202	7.16	162
Caledonia township	12,332	169	34.91	38
Cannon township	13,336	159	35.26	32
Canton charter township	90,173	12	36.11	17
Cascade charter township	17,134	120	33.88	49
Chesterfield township	43,381	40	27.58	92
Clawson city	11,825	174	2.20	207
Clinton charter township	96,796	11	28.10	90
Coldwater city	10,945	187	8.03	157
Commerce charter township	40,186	45	27.45	93
Comstock charter township	14,854	137	33.31	58
Comstock Park CDP	10,088	206	3.88	194
Cooper charter township	10,111	205	36.33	13
Cutlerville CDP	14,370	149	5.87	174
Davison township	19,575	109	33.32	57
DeWitt charter township	14,321	150	31.03	77
Dearborn city	98,153	9	24.22	104
Dearborn Heights city	57,774	27	11.74	138
Delhi charter township	25,877	77	28.61	88
Delta charter township	32,408	58	32.46	67
Detroit city	713,777	1	138.75	1
East Bay township	10,663	192	39.93	7
East Grand Rapids city	10,694	191	2.93	201
East Lansing city	48,579	34	13.59	134
East Lansing city	46,610	38	10.04	146
Eastpointe city	32,442	57	5.14	183
Emmett charter township	11,770	176	32.00	71
Escanaba city	12,616	167	12.88	135
Farmington city	10,372	200	2.66	204
Farmington Hills city	79,740	15	33.28	59
Fenton charter township	15,552	130	23.80	105
Fenton city	11,756	177	6.68	166
Ferndale city	19,900	107	3.88	194
Flint city	102,434	8	33.42	55
Flint charter township	31,929	59	23.28	108
Flushing charter township	10,640	194	31.37	75
Forest Hills CDP	25,867	78	49.27	2
Fort Gratiot charter township	11,108	185	15.96	125
Fraser city	14,480	148	4.14	191
Frenchtown township	20,428	103	41.82	6
Fruitport charter township	13,598	157	29.98	83
Gaines charter township	25,146	80	35.70	25
Garden City city	27,692	72	5.87	174
Garfield charter township	16,256	126	26.59	97
Genesee charter township	21,581	93	29.06	86
Genoa township	19,821	108	34.05	47

Legal Name	2010 Population	Pop. Rank	Land Area (sq. miles)	Area Rank
Georgetown charter township	46,985	37	33.17	61
Grand Blanc charter township	37,508	49	32.70	66
Grand Haven charter township	15,178	133	28.68	87
Grand Haven city	10,412	199	5.77	178
Grand Rapids city	188,040	2	44.40	4
Grand Rapids charter township	16,661	122	15.34	129
Grandville city	15,378	131	7.27	161
Green Oak township	17,476	119	34.30	44
Grosse Ile township	10,371	201	9.20	148
Grosse Pointe Park city	11,555	181	2.17	208
Grosse Pointe Woods city	16,135	127	3.25	198
Hamburg township	21,165	98	32.24	69
Hamtramck city	22,423	90	2.09	209
Harper Woods city	14,236	152	2.61	205
Harrison charter township	24,587	82	14.46	131
Hartland township	14,663	142	35.86	24
Haslett CDP	19,220	111	15.37	128
Hazel Park city	16,422	124	2.82	202
Highland charter township	19,202	112	34.11	46
Highland Park city	11,776	175	2.97	200
Holland charter township	35,636	50	27.03	95
Holland city	33,051	56	16.59	122
Holland city	26,035	74	8.39	153
Holly township	11,362	183	34.38	41
Holt CDP	23,973	86	15.67	127
Huron charter township	15,879	128	35.35	31
Independence charter township	34,681	53	34.99	37
Inkster city	25,369	79	6.25	170
Ionia city	11,394	182	5.35	179
Jackson city	33,534	55	10.86	143
Jenison CDP	16,538	123	5.85	176
Kalamazoo city	74,262	17	24.68	100
Kalamazoo charter township	21,918	91	11.68	139
Kentwood city	48,707	33	20.90	113
Lansing city	114,297	5	36.05	19
Lansing city	109,563	7	33.17	61
Lenox township	10,470	198	38.71	9
Leoni township	13,807	156	48.54	3
Lincoln charter township	14,691	140	17.91	117
Lincoln Park city	38,144	48	5.89	172
Livonia city	96,942	10	35.70	25
Lyon charter township	14,545	146	30.95	78
Macomb township	79,580	16	36.23	15
Madison Heights city	29,694	67	7.09	163
Marquette city	21,355	97	11.39	141
Melvindale city	10,715	190	2.72	203
Meridian charter township	39,688	46	30.49	81
Midland city	41,863	41	33.69	52
Midland city	41,706	42	33.25	60
Milford charter township	15,736	129	32.99	63
Monitor charter township	10,735	189	36.78	11
Monroe charter township	14,568	144	16.90	119
Monroe city	20,733	100	9.17	149

Legal Name	2010 Population	Pop. Rank	Land Area (sq. miles)	Area Rank
Mount Clemens city	16,314	125	4.07	192
Mount Morris township	21,501	94	31.51	74
Mount Pleasant city	26,016	75	7.74	159
Mundy township	15,082	135	36.03	21
Muskegon charter township	17,840	114	22.94	110
Muskegon city	38,401	47	14.21	132
Muskegon Heights city	10,856	188	3.19	199
New Baltimore city	12,084	171	4.61	186
Niles township	14,164	153	37.32	10
Niles city	11,600	178	5.79	177
Niles city	11,599	179	5.14	183
Northview CDP	14,541	147	10.34	144
Northville township	28,497	70	16.19	124
Norton Shores city	23,994	84	23.24	109
Novi city	55,224	29	30.26	82
Oak Park city	29,319	68	5.16	182
Oakland charter township	16,779	121	36.30	14
Oceola township	11,936	173	36.12	16
Okemos CDP	21,369	96	16.76	120
Orion charter township	35,394	51	33.33	56
Oshtemo charter township	21,705	92	35.87	23
Owosso city	15,194	132	5.23	181
Oxford charter township	20,526	102	33.78	50
Park township	17,802	115	19.20	116
Pittsfield charter township	34,663	54	27.26	94
Plainfield charter township	30,952	61	35.04	35
Plymouth charter township	27,524	73	15.93	126
Pontiac city	59,515	26	19.97	115
Port Huron charter township	10,654	193	12.84	136
Port Huron city	30,184	63	8.08	155
Portage city	46,292	39	32.22	70
Redford charter township	48,362	35	11.24	142
Riverview city	12,486	168	4.40	188
Rochester city	12,711	166	3.82	196
Rochester Hills city	70,995	22	32.82	65
Romulus city	23,989	85	35.61	27
Roseville city	47,299	36	9.83	147
Royal Oak city	57,236	28	11.78	137
Saginaw charter township	40,840	44	24.50	103
Saginaw city	51,508	32	17.34	118
St. Joseph charter township	10,028	208	6.65	167
Sault Ste. Marie city	14,144	154	14.77	130
Scio township	20,081	106	33.73	51
Shelby charter township	73,804	18	34.26	45
South Lyon city	11,327	184	3.73	197
Southfield city	71,739	20	26.27	98
Southfield township	14,547	145	8.05	156
Southgate city	30,047	64	6.85	165
Spring Lake township	14,300	151	16.48	123
Springfield charter township	13,940	155	35.43	29
St. Clair Shores city	59,715	25	11.62	140
Sterling Heights city	129,699	4	36.50	12
Sturgis city	10,994	186	6.49	168
Summit township	22,508	89	29.09	85
Superior charter township	13,058	163	35.21	33
Taylor city	63,131	24	23.60	106
Texas charter township	14,697	139	34.38	41
Thomas township	11,985	172	30.61	80

Legal Name	2010 Population	Pop. Rank	Land Area (sq. miles)	Area Rank
Traverse City city	14,674	141	8.33	154
Trenton city	18,853	113	7.28	160
Troy city	80,980	14	33.47	54
Tyrone township	10,020	209	35.40	30
Union charter township	12,927	164	28.16	89
Van Buren charter township	28,821	69	33.97	48
Vienna charter township	13,255	161	35.01	36
Walker city	23,537	88	24.94	99
Warren city	134,056	3	34.38	41
Washington township	25,139	81	35.48	28
Waterford charter township	71,707	21	30.66	79
Waverly CDP	23,925	87	9.07	151
Wayne city	17,593	117	6.02	171
West Bloomfield charter township	64,690	23	27.01	96
Westland city	84,094	13	20.42	114
White Lake charter township	30,019	65	33.52	53
Wixom city	13,498	158	9.15	150
Woodhaven city	12,875	165	6.39	169
Wyandotte city	25,883	76	5.27	180
Wyoming city	72,125	19	24.64	101
Ypsilanti charter township	53,362	30	29.93	84
Ypsilanti city	19,435	110	4.33	190

Note: CDP–Census Designated Place
Source: U.S. Census Bureau, 2010 Census

Survey Says...

This section presents current rankings from dozens of public and private sources. It shows how this state ranks in a number of critical categories, including education, job growth, cost of living, teen drivers, energy efficiency, and business environment. Sources include *Forbes, Reuters, U.S. News and World Report, CNN Money, Gallup,* and *Huffington Post.*

- Michigan ranked #18 in a government study measuring real gross domestic product (GDP)—the output of goods and services produced by labor and property located in the United States. The ranking is based on the percentage change compared with 2011 GDP.
  U.S. Department of Commerce, Bureau of Economic Analysis, June 2013; www.bea.gov

- Michigan ranked #13 in a government study measuring real gross domestic product (GDP)—the output of goods and services produced by labor and property located in the United States. The ranking is based on the dollar value of its GDP.
  U.S. Department of Commerce, Bureau of Economic Analysis, June 2013; www.bea.gov

- Michigan ranked #24 in the 17th edition of "Quality Counts; State of the States," Education Week's "report card" surveying key education indicators, policy efforts, and educational outcomes.
  Education Week, January 4, 2013 (online) and January 10, 2013 (print); www.edweek.org

- SERI (Science and Engineering Readiness Index) weighs the performance of the states' K-12 schools in preparing students in physics and calculus, the high school subjects considered most important for future scientists and engineers. Michigan ranked #26.
  Newsletter of the Forum on Education of the American Physical Society, Summer 2011 issue; www.huffingtonpost.com, July 11, 2011; updated October 1, 2012

- MoneyRates.com ranked Michigan #16 on its list of the best to worst states for making a living. Criteria: average income; inflation; employment prospects; and workers' Workplace Environment assessments according to the Gallup-Healthways Well-Being Index.
  www.money-rates.com, posted April 1, 2013

- *Forbes* analyzed business costs, labor supply, regulatory environment, current economic climate, growth prospects, and quality of life, to compile its "Best States for Business" rankings. Michigan ranked #47.
  www.forbes.com. posted December 12, 2012

- In "The States People Are Fleeing in 2013," *Forbes* reported the results of United Van Lines's thirty-sixth annual survey of its "customer migration patterns." In percentage of outbound moves, Michigan ranked #6 (1 = most).
  www.forbes.com, posted February 7, 2013

- The 2012 Gallup-Healthways Well-Being Index, surveyed American's opinions on economic confidence, workplace perceptions, community climate, personal choices, and health predictors to assess the "future livability" of each state. Michigan ranked #35.
  "Utah Poised to Be the Best State to Live In," Gallup Wellbeing, www.gallup.com, August 7, 2012

- On CNBC's list of "America's Top States for Business 2013," Michigan ranked #29. Criteria: measures of competitiveness developed with input from the National Association of Manufacturers, the Council on Competitiveness, and other business groups weighed with the states' own marketing criteria.
  www.cnbc.com, consulted July 19, 2013

- Michigan ranked #51 on MoneyRates list of "Best-and Worst-States to Retire 2012." Criteria: life expectancy, crime rate, climate, economic conditions, taxes, job opportunities, and cost of living.
  www.money-rates.com, October 22, 2012

- Michigan ranked #36 on the 2013 Bankrate "Best Places to Retire" list ranking the states and District of Columbia on various criteria relating to health, safety, and cost.
  www.bankrate.com, May 6, 2013

- Michigan ranked #32 on the Social Science Research Council's "American Human Development Report: The Measure of America," assessing the 50 states plus the District of Columbia on health, education, and living-standard criteria.
  The Measure of America 2013-2014, posted June 19, 2013; www.measureofamerica.org

- Michigan ranked #23 on the Foundation for Child Development's (FCD) Child Well-being Index (CWI). The FCD used the KIDS COUNT report and the National Survey of Children's Health, the only state-level source for several key indicators of child well-being.
  Foundation for Child Development, January 18, 2012; fcd-us.org

- Michigan ranked #31 overall according to the 2013 KIDS COUNT Data Book, a project of the Annie E. Casey Foundation. Criteria: children's economic well-being, education, health, and family and community indicators.
  KIDS COUNT Data Center's Data Book, released June 20, 2013; http://datacenter.kidscount.org

- Michigan ranked #36 in the children's economic well-being category by the 2013 KIDS COUNT Data Book, a project of the Annie E. Casey Foundation.
  KIDS COUNT Data Center's Data Book, released June 20, 2013; http://datacenter.kidscount.org

- Michigan ranked #32 in the children's educational opportunities and attainments category by the 2013 KIDS COUNT Data Book, a project of the Annie E. Casey Foundation.
  KIDS COUNT Data Center's Data Book, released June 20, 2013; http://datacenter.kidscount.org

- Michigan ranked #23 in the children's health category by the 2013 KIDS COUNT Data Book, a project of the Annie E. Casey Foundation.
  KIDS COUNT Data Center's Data Book, released June 20, 2013; http://datacenter.kidscount.org

- Michigan ranked #27 in the family and community circumstances that factor into children's well-being category by the 2013 KIDS COUNT Data Book, a project of the Annie E. Casey Foundation.
  KIDS COUNT Data Center's Data Book, released June 20, 2013; http://datacenter.kidscount.org

- Michigan ranked #36 in the 2012 Gallup-Healthways Well-Being Index. Criteria: emotional health; physical health; healthy behavior; work environment; basic access to food, shelter, health care; and a safe and satisfying place to live.
  2012 State of Well-Being, Gallup-Healthways Well-Being Index, released February 28, 2013; www.well-beingindex.com

- *U.S. News and World Report's* "Best States for Teen Drivers" rankings are based on driving and road safety laws, federal reports on driver's licenses, car accident fatality, and road-quality statistics. Michigan ranked #35.
  U.S. News and World Report, March 18, 2010; www.usnews.com

- The Yahoo! Sports service Rivals.com ranks the states according to the strength of their high school football programs. Michigan ranked #20.
  "Ranking the States: Where Is the Best Football Played?," November 18, 2011; highschool.rivals.com

- iVillage ranked the states by hospitable living conditions for women. Criteria: economic success, access to affordable childcare, health care, reproductive rights, female representation in government, and educational attainment. Michigan ranked #21.
  iVillage, "50 Best to Worst States for Women," March 14, 2012; www.ivillage.com

- The League of American Bicyclists's "Bicycle Friendly States" ranked Michigan #12. Criteria: legislation and enforcement, policies and programs, infrastructure and funding, education and advocacy, and evaluation and planning.
  "Washington Tops the Bicycle-Friendly State Ranking," May 1, 2013; bicycling.com

- The federal Corporation for National and Community Service ranked the states and the District of Columbia by volunteer rates. Michigan ranked #32 for community service.
  "Volunteering and Civic Life in America 2012," www.volunteeringinamerica.gov, accessed July 24, 2013

- The Hospital Safety Score ranked states and the District of Columbia on their hospitals' performance scores. Michigan ranked #7. Criteria: avoiding preventable harm and medical errors, as demonstrated by 26 hospital safety metrics.
  Spring 2013 Hospital Safety Score, May 8, 2013; www.hospitalsafetyscore.org

- GMAC Insurance ranked the states and the District of Columbia by the performance of their drivers on the GMAC Insurance National Drivers Test, comprised of DMV test questions. Michigan ranked #20.
  "2011 GMAC Insurance National Drivers Test," www.gmacinsurance.com, accessed July 23, 2013

- Michigan ranked #44 in a "State Integrity Investigation" analysis of laws and practices intended to deter corruption and promote accountability and openness in campaign finance, ethics laws, lobbying regulations and management of state pension funds.
  "What's Your State's Grade?," www.publicintegrity.org, accessed July 23, 2013

- Michigan ranked #12 among the states and the District of Columbia in total rail miles, as tracked by the Association of American Railroads.
  "U.S. Freight Railroad Industry Snapshot: Railroads and States: Total Rail Miles by State: 2011"; www.aar.org, accessed July 23, 2013

- According to statistics compiled by the Beer Institute, Michigan ranked #36 among the states and the District of Columbia in per capita beer consumption of persons 21 years or older.
  "Shipments of Malt Beverages and Per Capita Consumption by State 2012;" www.beerinstitute.org

- According to Concordia University's "Public Education Costs per Pupil by State Rankings," based on statistics gathered by the U.S. Census Bureau, which includes the District of Columbia, Michigan ranked #23.
  Concordia University Online; education.cu-portland.edu, accessed July 24, 2013

- Michigan ranked #17 among the states and the District of Columbia in population density based on U.S. Census Bureau data for resident population and total land area. "List of U.S. States by Population Density."
  www.wikipedia.org, accessed July 24, 2013

- In "America's Health Rankings, 2012 Edition," by the United Health Foundation, Michigan ranked #37. Criteria included: rate of high school graduation; violent crime rate; incidence of infectious disease; childhood immunizations; prevalence of diabetes; per capita public-health funding; percentage of uninsured population; rate of children in poverty; and availability of primary-care physicians.
  United Health Foundation; www.americashealthrankings.org, accessed July 24, 2013

- The TechNet 2012 "State Broadband Index" ranked Michigan #31 on the following criteria: broadband adoption; network quality; and economic structure. Improved broadband use is hoped to promote economic development, build strong communities, improve delivery of government services and upgrade educational systems.
  TechNet; www.technet.org, accessed July 24, 2013

- Michigan was ranked #12 among the states and District of Columbia on the American Council for an Energy-Efficient Economy's "State Energy Efficiency Scorecard" for 2012.
  American Council for an Energy-Efficient Economy; aceee.org/sector/state-policy/scorecard, accessed July 24, 2013

Statistical Tables

DEMOGRAPHICS
- Resident State and National Population, 1950-2012
- Projected State and National Population, 2000-2030
- Population by Age, 2012
- Population by Race, 2012
- Population by Hispanic Origin and Race, 2012

VITAL STATISTICS
- Death Rates by Leading Causes, 2010
- Death Rates by Selected Causes, 2010
- Abortion Rates, 2009
- Infant Mortality Rates, 1995-2009
- Marriage and Divorce Rates, 2000-2011

ECONOMY
- Nominal Gross Domestic Product by Industry, 2012
- Real Gross Domestic Product, 2000-2012
- Personal Income Per Capita, 1930-2012
- Non-Farm Employment by Sector, 2012
- Foreign Exports, 2000-2012
- Energy Consumption, 2011

LAND AND WATER
- Surface Area and Federally-Owned Land, 2007
- Land Cover/Use of Non-Federal Rural Land, 2007
- Farms and Crop Acreage, 2012

HEALTH AND MEDICAL CARE
- Medical Professionals, 2012
- Health Insurance Coverage, 2011
- HIV, STD, and Tuberculosis Cases and Rates, 2011
- Cigarette Smoking, 2011

HOUSING
- Home Ownership Rates, 1995-2012
- Home Sales, 2000-2010
- Value of Owner-Occupied Homes, 2011

EDUCATION
- School Enrollment, 2011
- Educational Attainment, 2011
- Public College Finances, FY 2012

TRANSPORTATION AND TRAVEL
- Motor Vehicle Registrations and Drivers Licenses, 2011
- Domestic Travel Expenditures, 2009
- Retail Gasoline Prices, 2013
- Public Road Length, 2011

CRIME AND LAW ENFORCEMENT
- Full-Time Law Enforcement Officers, 2011
- Prison Population, 2000-2012
- Crime Rate, 2011

GOVERNMENT AND FINANCE
- Local Governments by Type, 2012
- State Government Revenue, 2011
- State Government Expenditures, 2011
- State Government General Expenditures by Function, 2011
- State Government Finances, Cash and Debt, 2011

POLITICS
- Composition of the Senate, 1995-2013
- Composition of the House of Representatives, 1995-2013
- Composition of State Legislature, 2004-2013
- Voter Participation in Presidential Elections, 1980-2012
- Governors Since Statehood

DEMOGRAPHICS

Resident State and National Population, 1950–2012

Year	State Population	U.S. Population	State Share
1950	6,372,000	151,326,000	4.21%
1960	7,823,000	179,323,000	4.36%
1970	8,881,826	203,302,031	4.37%
1980	9,262,078	226,545,805	4.09%
1990	9,295,297	248,709,873	3.74%
2000	9,938,823	281,424,600	3.53%
2010	9,883,640	308,745,538	3.20%
2012	9,883,360	313,914,040	3.15%

Note: 1950/1960 population figures are rounded to the nearest thousand.
Source: U.S. Census Bureau, Decennial Census 1950–2010; U.S. Census Bureau, 2012 Population Estimates

Projected State and National Population, 2000–2030

Year	State Population	U.S. Population	State Share
2000	9,938,444	281,421,906	3.53%
2005	10,207,421	295,507,134	3.45%
2010	10,428,683	308,935,581	3.38%
2015	10,599,122	322,365,787	3.29%
2020	10,695,993	335,804,546	3.19%
2025	10,713,730	349,439,199	3.07%
2030	10,694,172	363,584,435	2.94%
State population growth, 2000–2030			755,728
State percentage growth, 2000–2030			7.6%

Source: U.S. Census Bureau, Population Division, Interim State Population Projections, 2005

Population by Age, 2012

Age Group	State Population	Percent of Total Population	
		State	U.S.
Under 5 years	575,714	5.8%	6.4%
5 to 14 years	1,278,829	12.9%	13.1%
15 to 24 years	1,411,002	14.3%	14.0%
25 to 34 years	1,178,030	11.9%	13.5%
35 to 44 years	1,221,551	12.4%	12.9%
45 to 54 years	1,453,683	14.7%	14.1%
55 to 64 years	1,321,837	13.4%	12.3%
65 to 74 years	795,854	8.1%	7.6%
75 to 84 years	442,946	4.5%	4.2%
85 years and older	203,914	2.1%	1.9%
Under 18 years	2,266,870	22.9%	23.5%
65 years and older	1,442,714	14.6%	13.7%
Median age (years)	–	39.4	37.4

Source: U.S. Census Bureau, Annual Estimates of the Resident Population for Selected Age Groups by Sex for the United States, States, Counties, and Puerto Rico Commonwealth and Municipios: April 1, 2010 to July 1, 2012

Population by Race, 2012

Race	State Population	Percent of Total Population	
		State	U.S.
All residents	9,883,360	100.00%	100.00%
White	7,920,263	80.14%	77.89%
African American	1,415,107	14.32%	13.13%
Native American	69,751	0.71%	1.23%
Asian	259,806	2.63%	5.14%
Native Hawaiian	3,720	0.04%	0.23%
Two or more races	214,713	2.17%	2.39%

Source: U.S. Census Bureau, Population Division, Annual Estimates of the Resident Population by Sex, Race and Hispanic Origin for the United States, States, and Counties: April 1, 2010 to July 1, 2012

Population by Hispanic Origin and Race, 2012

Hispanic Origin/Race	State Population	Percent of Total Population	
		State	U.S.
All residents	9,883,360	100.00%	100.00%
All Hispanic residents	456,330	4.62%	16.89%
Hispanic			
White	386,335	3.91%	14.91%
African American	29,075	0.29%	0.79%
Native American	14,168	0.14%	0.49%
Asian	3,556	0.04%	0.17%
Native Hawaiian	1,350	0.01%	0.06%
Two or more races	21,846	0.22%	0.48%
Not Hispanic			
White	7,533,928	76.23%	62.98%
African American	1,386,032	14.02%	12.34%
Native American	55,583	0.56%	0.74%
Asian	256,250	2.59%	4.98%
Native Hawaiian	2,370	0.02%	0.17%
Two or more races	192,867	1.95%	1.91%

Source: U.S. Census Bureau, Population Division, Annual Estimates of the Resident Population by Sex, Race and Hispanic Origin for the United States, States, and Counties: April 1, 2010 to July 1, 2012

VITAL STATISTICS

Death Rates by Leading Causes, 2010

Cause	State	U.S.
Malignant neoplasms	197.0	186.2
Ischaemic heart diseases	146.8	122.9
Other forms of heart disease	53.0	53.4
Chronic lower respiratory diseases	48.2	44.7
Cerebrovascular diseases	42.3	41.9
Organic, incl. symptomatic, mental disorders	33.4	35.7
Other degenerative diseases of the nervous sys.	26.8	28.4
Other external causes of accidental injury	25.7	26.5
Diabetes mellitus	25.7	22.4
Hypertensive diseases	23.4	20.4
All causes	840.5	799.5

Note: Figures are age-adjusted death rates per 100,000 population
Source: CDC/NCHS, Underlying Cause of Death 1999–2010 on CDC WONDER Online Database

Death Rates by Selected Causes, 2010

Cause	State	U.S.
Assault	6.2	5.2
Diseases of the liver	14.2	13.9
Human immunodeficiency virus (HIV) disease	1.5	2.7
Influenza and pneumonia	14.5	16.2
Intentional self-harm	12.7	12.4
Malnutrition	1.3	0.9
Obesity and other hyperalimentation	1.9	1.8
Renal failure	13.6	14.4
Transport accidents	11.2	12.1
Viral hepatitis	2.1	2.4

Note: Figures are age-adjusted death rates per 100,000 population; A dash indicates that data was not available or was suppressed
Source: CDC/NCHS, Underlying Cause of Death 1999–2010 on CDC WONDER Online Database

Abortion Rates, 2009

Category	2009
By state of residence	
Total abortions	22,175
Abortion rate[1]	11.3%
Abortion ratio[2]	189
By state of occurrence	
Total abortions	22,357
Abortion rate[1]	11.4%
Abortion ratio[2]	191
Abortions obtained by out-of-state residents	2.4%
U.S. abortion rate[1]	15.1%
U.S. abortion ratio[2]	227

Note: (1) Number of abortions per 1,000 women aged 15–44 years; (2) Number of abortions per 1,000 live births; A dash indicates that data was not available
Source: CDC/NCHS, Morbidity and Mortality Weekly Report, November 23, 2012 (Abortion Surveillance, United States, 2009)

Infant Mortality Rates, 1995–2009

Category	1995	2000	2005	2009
All state residents	8.25	8.19	7.89	7.60
All U.S. residents	7.57	6.89	6.86	6.39
All state white residents	6.40	6.29	6.12	5.80
All U.S. white residents	6.30	5.71	5.73	5.33
All state black residents	16.51	16.86	16.39	14.79
All U.S. black residents	14.58	13.48	13.26	12.12

Note: Figures represent deaths per 1,000 live births of resident infants under one year old, exclusive of fetal deaths; A dash indicates that data was not available or was suppressed.
Source: Centers of Disease Control and Prevention, Division of Vital Statistics, Linked Birth/Infant Death Records on CDC Wonder Online

Marriage and Divorce Rates, 2000–2011

Year	Marriage Rate		Divorce Rate	
	State	U.S.	State	U.S.
2000	6.7	8.2	3.9	4.0
2002	6.5	8.0	3.8	3.9
2004	6.2	7.8	3.5	3.7
2006	5.9	7.5	3.5	3.7
2008	5.6	7.1	3.4	3.5
2010	5.5	6.8	3.5	3.6
2011	5.7	6.8	3.4	3.6

Note: Rates are based on provisional counts of marriages/divorces by state of occurrence and are per 1,000 total population residing in area
Source: CDC/NCHS, National Vital Statistics System

ECONOMY

Nominal Gross Domestic Product by Industry, 2012
In millions of current dollars

Industry	State GDP
Accommodation and food services	11,578
Administrative and waste management services	14,342
Agriculture, forestry, fishing, and hunting	4,110
Arts, entertainment, and recreation	3,056
Construction	11,300
Educational services	3,343
Finance and insurance	25,823
Health care and social assistance	35,799
Information	10,218
Management of companies and enterprises	8,033
Manufacturing	66,230
Mining	1,155
Other services, except government	10,630
Professional, scientific, and technical services	31,359
Real estate and rental and leasing	44,918
Retail trade	27,272
Transportation and warehousing	10,610
Utilities	9,967
Wholesale trade	24,966

Source: U.S. Department of Commerce, Bureau of Economic Analysis, Survey of Current Business

Real Gross Domestic Product, 2000–2012
In millions of chained 2005 dollars

Year	State GDP	U.S. GDP	State Share
2000	372,148	11,225,406	3.32%
2005	375,753	12,539,116	3.00%
2010	329,812	12,897,088	2.56%
2012	348,867	13,430,576	2.60%

Source: U.S. Department of Commerce, Bureau of Economic Analysis, Survey of Current Business

Personal Income Per Capita, 1930–2012

Year	State	U.S.
1930	$656	$618
1940	$680	$593
1950	$1,717	$1,503
1960	$2,437	$2,268
1970	$4,198	$4,084
1980	$10,291	$10,091
1990	$18,719	$19,354
2000	$29,400	$30,319
2010	$34,326	$39,791
2012	$37,497	$42,693

Source: U.S. Department of Commerce, Bureau of Economic Analysis, Regional Economic Accounts

Non-Farm Employment by Sector, 2012
In thousands

Sector	Employment
Construction	127.3
Education and health services	632.1
Financial activities	196.2
Government	610.3
Information	53.1
Leisure and hospitality	387.1
Mining and logging	7.8
Manufacturing	536.9
Other services	168.3
Professional and business services	576.6
Trade, transportation, and utilities	728.5
All sectors	4,024.2

Source: U.S. Bureau of Labor Statistics, State and Area Employment

Foreign Exports, 2000–2012
In millions of dollars

Year	State Exports	U.S. Exports	State Share
2000	33,845	712,054	4.75%
2002	33,969	649,940	5.23%
2004	35,949	768,554	4.68%
2006	40,499	973,994	4.16%
2008	45,135	1,222,545	3.69%
2010	44,851	1,208,080	3.71%
2012	56,993	1,478,268	3.86%

Note: U.S. figures exclude data from Puerto Rico, U.S. Virgin Islands, and unallocated exports
Source: U.S. Department of Commerce, International Trade Admin., Office of Trade and Industry Information, Manufacturing and Services

Energy Consumption, 2011
In trillions of BTUs, except as noted

Total energy consumption	
Total state energy consumption	2,802.7
Total U.S. energy consumption	97,387.3
State share of U.S. total	2.88%
Per capita consumption (in millions of BTUs)	
Total state per capita consumption	283.8
Total U.S. per capita consumption	312.6
End-use sectors	
Residential	762.4
Commercial	610.5
Industrial	708.1
Transportation	721.8
Sources of energy	
Petroleum	797.2
Natural gas	787.3
Coal	691.1
Renewable energy	159.5
Nuclear electric power	344.2

Source: U.S. Energy Information Administration, State Energy Data 2011: Consumption

LAND AND WATER

Surface Area and Federally-Owned Land, 2007
In thousands of acres

Category	State	U.S.	State Share
Total surface area	37,349.2	1,937,664.2	1.93%
Total land area	36,228.4	1,886,846.9	1.92%
Non-federal land	32,954.8	1,484,910.0	2.22%
Developed	4,227.6	111,251.2	3.80%
Rural	28,727.2	1,373,658.8	2.09%
Federal land	3,273.6	401,936.9	0.81%
Water area	1,120.8	50,817.3	2.21%

Source: U.S. Department of Agriculture, Natural Resources Conservation Service, 2007 National Resources Inventory

Land Cover/Use of Non-Federal Rural Land, 2007
In thousands of acres

Category	State	U.S.	State Share
Total rural land	28,727.2	1,373,658.8	2.09%
Cropland	7,844.1	357,023.5	2.20%
CRP[1] land	192.0	32,850.2	0.58%
Pastureland	2,213.9	118,615.7	1.87%
Rangeland	0.0	409,119.4	0.00%
Forest land	16,568.3	406,410.4	4.08%
Other rural land	1,908.9	49,639.6	3.85%

Note: (1) Conservation Reserve Program was created to assist private landowners in converting highly erodible cropland to vegetative cover.
Source: U.S. Department of Agriculture, Natural Resources Conservation Service, 2007 National Resources Inventory

Farms and Crop Acreage, 2012

Category	State	U.S.	State Share
Farms (in thousands)	54.7	2,170.0	2.52%
Acres (in millions)	9.9	914.0	1.08%
Acres per farm	181.0	421.2	–

Source: U.S. Department of Agriculture, National Agricultural Statistical Service, Quick Stats, 2012 Survey Data

HEALTH AND MEDICAL CARE

Medical Professionals, 2012

Profession	State Number	U.S. Number	State Share	State Rate[1]	U.S. Rate[1]
Physicians[2]	30,847	894,637	3.45%	312.3	287.1
Dentists	6,494	193,587	3.35%	65.8	62.1
Podiatrists	718	17,469	4.11%	7.3	5.6
Optometrists	1,433	45,638	3.14%	14.5	14.6
Chiropractors	2,484	77,494	3.21%	25.1	24.9

Note: (1) Rates are per 100,000 population; (2) Includes total, active Doctors of Osteopathic Medicine and Doctors of Medicine in 2011.
Source: U.S. Department of Health and Human Services, Bureau of Health Professions, Area Health Resource File, 2012-2013

Health Insurance Coverage, 2011

Category	State	U.S.
Total persons covered	8,493,000	260,214,000
Total persons not covered	1,210,000	48,613,000
Percent not covered	12.5%	15.7%
Children under age 18 covered	2,164,000	67,143,000
Children under age 18 not covered	123,000	6,965,000
Percent of children not covered	5.4%	9.4%

Source: U.S. Census Bureau, Current Population Survey, 2012 Annual Social and Economic Supplement

HIV, STD, and Tuberculosis Cases and Rates, 2011

Disease	State Cases	State Rate[1]	U.S. Rate[1]
Chlamydia	49,568	501.5	457.6
Gonorrhea	12,901	130.5	104.2
HIV diagnosis	793	9.6	15.8
HIV, stage 3 (AIDS)	506	6.1	10.3
Syphilis, early latent	132	1.3	4.3
Syphilis, primary/secondary	286	2.9	4.5
Tuberculosis	170	1.7	3.4

Note: (1) Rates are per 100,000 population
Source: Centers for Disease Control and Prevention

Cigarette Smoking, 2011

Category	State	U.S.
Adults who are current smokers	23.3%	21.2%
Adults who smoke everyday	17.3%	15.4%
Adults who smoke some days	6.0%	5.7%
Adults who are former smokers	25.7%	25.1%
Adults who never smoked	51.0%	52.9%

Source: Centers for Disease Control and Prevention, Behaviorial Risk Factor Surveillance System, Tobacco Use, 2011

HOUSING

Home Ownership Rates, 1995–2012

Area	1995	2000	2005	2010	2012
State	72.2%	77.2%	76.4%	74.5%	74.8%
U.S.	64.7%	67.4%	68.9%	66.9%	65.4%

Source: U.S. Census Bureau, Housing Vacancies and Homeownership, Annual Statistics

Home Sales, 2000–2010
In thousands of units

Year	State Sales	U.S. Sales	State Share
2000	185.0	5,174	3.58%
2002	203.5	5,632	3.61%
2004	213.4	6,778	3.15%
2006	182.4	6,478	2.82%
2008	155.6	4,913	3.17%
2010	150.8	4,908	3.07%

Note: Units include single-family homes, condos and co-ops
Source: National Association of Realtors, Real Estate Outlook, Market Trends & Insights

Value of Owner-Occupied Homes, 2011

Value	Total Units in State	Percent of Total, State	Percent of Total, U.S.
Less than $50,000	409,930	15.1%	8.8%
$50,000 to $99,000	707,551	26.1%	16.0%
$100,000 to $149,000	555,568	20.5%	16.5%
$150,000 to $199,000	444,042	16.4%	15.4%
$200,000 to $299,000	355,727	13.1%	18.2%
$300,000 to $499,000	163,110	6.0%	15.2%
$500,000 to $999,000	53,442	2.0%	7.9%
$1,000,000 or more	16,910	0.6%	2.0%
Median value	–	$118,100	$173,600

Source: U.S. Census Bureau, 2011 American Community Survey 1-Year Estimates

EDUCATION

School Enrollment, 2011

Educational Level	Students Enrolled in State	Percent of Total, State	Percent of Total, U.S.
All levels	2,695,641	100.0%	100.0%
Nursery school, preschool	145,290	5.4%	6.0%
Kindergarten	129,698	4.8%	5.1%
Elementary (grades 1–8)	1,030,070	38.2%	39.5%
Secondary (grades 9–12)	566,119	21.0%	20.7%
College or graduate school	824,464	30.6%	28.7%

Note: Figures cover the population 3 years and over enrolled in school
Source: U.S. Census Bureau, 2011 American Community Survey 1-Year Estimates

Educational Attainment, 2011

Highest Level of Education	State	U.S.
High school diploma	88.8%	85.9%
Bachelor's degree	25.6%	28.5%
Graduate/Professional degree	9.9%	10.6%

Note: Figures cover the population 25 years and over
Source: U.S. Census Bureau, 2011 American Community Survey 1-Year Estimates

Public College Finances, FY 2012

Category	State	U.S.
Full-time equivalent enrollment (FTE)[1]	423,198	11,548,974
Educational appropriations per FTE[2]	$4,185	$5,906
Net tuition revenue per FTE[3]	$8,963	$5,189
Total educational revenue per FTE[4]	$13,148	$11,043

(1) Full-time equivalent enrollment equates student credit hours to full time, academic year students, but excludes medical students; (2) Educational appropriations measure state and local support available for public higher education operating expenses including ARRA funds and excludes appropriations for independent institutions, financial aid for students attending independent institutions, research, hospitals, and medical education; (3) Net tuition revenue is calculated by taking the gross amount of tuition and fees, less state and institutional financial aid, tuition waivers or discounts, and medical student tuition and fees. Net tuition revenue used for capital debt service is included in the net tuition revenue figures; (4) Total educational revenue is the sum of educational appropriations and net tuition excluding net tuition revenue used for capital debt service.
Source: State Higher Education Executive Officers, State Higher Education Finance FY 2012

TRANSPORTATION AND TRAVEL

Motor Vehicle Registrations and Drivers Licenses, 2011

Vehicle Type	State	U.S.	State Share
Automobiles[1]	4,742,808	125,656,528	3.77%
Buses	20,209	666,064	3.03%
Trucks	4,111,481	118,455,587	3.47%
Motorcycles	308,349	8,437,502	3.65%
Drivers licenses	7,059,509	211,874,649	3.33%

Note: Motor vehicle registrations include private, commercial, and publicly-owned vehicles; (1) Includes taxicabs
Source: U.S. Department of Transportation, Federal Highway Administration

Domestic Travel Expenditures, 2009
In millions of dollars

Category	State	U.S.	State Share
Travel expenditures	$14,148	$610,200	2.32%

Note: Figures represent U.S. spending on domestic overnight trips and day trips of 50 miles or more, one way, away from home. Excludes spending by foreign visitors.
Source: U.S. Travel Association, Impact of Travel on State Economies, 2009

Retail Gasoline Prices, 2013

Gasoline Grade	State Average	U.S. Average
Regular	$3.70	$3.65
Mid	$3.83	$3.81
Premium	$3.97	$3.98
Diesel	$3.93	$3.88
Excise tax[1]	57.9 cents	49.4 cents

Note: Gasoline prices as of 7/26/2013; (1) Includes state and federal excise taxes and other state taxes as of July 1, 2013
Source: American Automobile Association, Daily Fuel Guage Report; American Petroleum Institute, State Motor Fuel Taxes, 2013

Public Road Length, 2011

Type	State Mileage	U.S. Mileage	State Share
Interstate highways	1,244	46,960	2.65%
Other highways	705	15,719	4.49%
Principal arterial	4,500	156,262	2.88%
Minor arterial	9,801	242,942	4.03%
Major collector	20,190	534,592	3.78%
Minor collector	4,294	266,357	1.61%
Local	81,352	2,814,925	2.89%
Urban	35,490	1,095,373	3.24%
Rural	86,596	2,982,383	2.90%
Total	122,086	4,077,756	2.99%

Note: Combined urban and rural road mileage equals the total of the other road types
Source: U.S. Department of Transportation, Federal Highway Administration, Public Road Length, 2011

CRIME AND LAW ENFORCEMENT

Full-Time Law Enforcement Officers, 2011

Gender	State Number	State Rate[1]	U.S. Rate[1]
Male officers	15,366	156.0	210.3
Female officers	2,322	23.6	28.1
Total officers	17,688	179.6	238.3

Note: (1) Rates are per 100,000 population
Source: Federal Bureau of Investigation, Uniform Crime Reports, Crime in the United States 2011

Prison Population, 2000–2012

Year	State Population	U.S. Population	State Share
2000	47,718	1,391,261	3.43%
2005	49,546	1,527,929	3.24%
2010	44,165	1,613,803	2.74%
2011	42,940	1,598,783	2.69%
2012	43,636	1,571,013	2.78%

Note: Figures include prisoners under the jurisdiction of state or federal correctional authorities.
Source: U.S. Department of Justice, Bureau of Justice Statistics, Prisoners in 2006, 2011, 2012 (Advance Counts)

Crime Rate, 2011
Incidents per 100,000 residents

Category	State	U.S.
Violent crimes	445.3	386.3
Murder	6.2	4.7
Forcible rape	44.0	26.8
Robbery	105.2	113.7
Aggravated assault	289.9	241.1
Property crimes	2,612.1	2,908.7
Burglary	724.9	702.2
Larceny/theft	1,629.0	1,976.9
Motor vehicle theft	258.2	229.6
All crimes	3,057.4	3,295.0

Source: Federal Bureau of Investigation, Uniform Crime Reports, Crime in the United States 2011

GOVERNMENT AND FINANCE

Local Governments by Type, 2012

Government Type	State	U.S.	State Share
All local governments	2,877	89,004	3.23%
County	83	3,031	2.74%
Municipality	533	19,522	2.73%
Town/Township	1,240	16,364	7.58%
Special District	445	37,203	1.20%
Ind. School District	576	12,884	4.47%

Source: U.S. Census Bureau, 2012 Census of Governments: Organization Component Preliminary Estimates

State Government Revenue, 2011
In thousands of dollars, except for per capita figures

Total revenue	$64,440,454
Total revenue per capita, State	$6,524
Total revenue per capita, U.S.	$7,271
General revenue	$54,727,497
Intergovernmental revenue	$19,914,367
Taxes	$23,540,253
General sales	$9,477,156
Selective sales	$3,442,475
License taxes	$1,403,872
Individual income taxes	$6,391,544
Corporate income taxes	$719,890
Other taxes	$2,105,316
Current charges	$7,395,302
Miscellaneous general revenue	$3,877,575
Utility revenue	$0
Liquor store revenue	$812,140
Insurance trust revenue[1]	$8,900,817

Note: (1) Within insurance trust revenue, net earnings of state retirement systems is a calculated statistic, and thus can be positive or negative. Net earnings is the sum of earnings on investments plus gains on investments minus losses on investments.
Source: U.S. Census Bureau, 2011 Annual Survey of State Government Finances

State Government Expenditures, 2011

In thousands of dollars, except for per capita figures

Total expenditure	$63,108,508
Total expenditure per capita, State	$6,390
Total expenditure per capita, U.S.	$6,427
Intergovernmental expenditure	$19,878,322
Direct expenditure	$43,230,186
Current operation	$28,235,945
Capital outlay	$2,246,088
Insurance benefits and repayments	$10,245,923
Assistance and subsidies	$1,364,321
Interest on debt	$1,137,909
Utility expenditure	$0
Liquor store expenditure	$660,861
Insurance trust expenditure	$10,245,923

Source: U.S. Census Bureau, 2011 Annual Survey of State Government Finances

State Government General Expenditures by Function, 2011

In thousands of dollars

Education	$23,146,215
Public welfare	$14,926,663
Hospitals	$2,522,008
Health	$1,156,070
Highways	$2,464,441
Police protection	$299,994
Correction	$1,663,416
Natural resources	$282,791
Parks and recreation	$86,884
Governmental administration	$823,221
Interest on general debt	$1,137,909
Other and unallocable	$3,692,112

Source: U.S. Census Bureau, 2011 Annual Survey of State Government Finances

State Government Finances, Cash and Debt, 2011

In thousands of dollars, except for per capita figures

Debt at end of fiscal year	
State, total	$30,975,273
State, per capita	$3,136
U.S., per capita	$3,635
Cash and security holdings	
State, total	$72,279,169
State, per capita	$7,318
U.S., per capita	$11,759

Source: U.S. Census Bureau, 2011 Annual Survey of State Government Finances

POLITICS

Composition of the Senate, 1995–2013

Congress (Year)	State/U.S	Dem	Rep	Total
104th (1995)	State delegates	1	1	2
	Total U.S.	48	52	100
105th (1997)	State delegates	1	1	2
	Total U.S.	45	55	100
106th (1999)	State delegates	1	1	2
	Total U.S.	45	55	100
107th (2001)	State delegates	2	0	2
	Total U.S.	50	50	100
108th (2003)	State delegates	2	0	2
	Total U.S.	48	51	100
109th (2005)	State delegates	2	0	2
	Total U.S.	44	55	100
110th (2007)	State delegates	2	0	2
	Total U.S.	49	49	100
111th (2009)	State delegates	2	0	2
	Total U.S.	57	41	100
112th (2011)	State delegates	2	0	2
	Total U.S.	51	47	100
113th (2013)	State delegates	2	0	2
	Total U.S.	54	45	100

Note: Figures are for the starts of first sessions; Totals include Democratic (Dem) and Republican (Rep) members as well as vacancies and seats held by independent party members
Source: U.S. Congress, Congressional Directory

Composition of the House of Representatives, 1995–2013

Congress (Year)	State/U.S	Dem	Rep	Total
104th (1995)	State delegates	9	7	16
	Total U.S.	204	230	435
105th (1997)	State delegates	10	6	16
	Total U.S.	207	226	435
106th (1999)	State delegates	10	6	16
	Total U.S.	211	223	435
107th (2001)	State delegates	9	7	16
	Total U.S.	212	221	435
108th (2003)	State delegates	6	9	15
	Total U.S.	205	229	435
109th (2005)	State delegates	6	9	15
	Total U.S.	202	231	435
110th (2007)	State delegates	6	9	15
	Total U.S.	233	198	435
111th (2009)	State delegates	8	7	15
	Total U.S.	256	178	435
112th (2011)	State delegates	7	8	15
	Total U.S.	193	242	435
113th (2013)	State delegates	5	9	14
	Total U.S.	201	234	435

Note: Figures are for the starts of first sessions; Totals include Democratic (Dem) and Republican (Rep) members as well as vacancies and seats held by independent party members
Source: U.S. Congress, Congressional Directory

Composition of State Legislature, 2004–2013

Year	Democrats	Republicans	Total
State Senate			
2004	16	22	38
2005	16	22	38
2006	16	22	38
2007	17	21	38
2008	17	21	38
2009	16	21	38
2010	16	22	38
2011	12	26	38
2012	12	26	38
2013	11	26	38
State House			
2004	63	47	110
2005	52	58	110
2006	50	58	110
2007	58	52	110
2008	58	52	110
2009	67	43	110
2010	66	43	110
2011	47	63	110
2012	46	62	110
2013	51	59	110

Note: Totals may include minor party members and vacancies
Source: The Council of State Governments, State Legislatures

Voter Participation in Presidential Elections, 1980–2012

Year	Voting-eligible State Population	State Voter Turnout Rate	U.S. Voter Turnout Rate
1980	6,374,955	61.3	54.2
1984	6,407,156	59.3	55.2
1988	6,608,812	55.5	52.8
1992	6,786,593	63.0	58.1
1996	6,954,059	55.3	51.7
2000	7,070,702	59.9	54.2
2004	7,263,024	66.6	60.1
2008	7,229,512	69.2	61.6
2012	7,317,247	64.7	58.2

Note: All figures are based on the voting-eligible population which excludes person ineligible to vote such as non-citizens, felons (depending on state law), and mentally-incapacitated persons. U.S. figures include the overseas eligible population (including military personnel).
Source: McDonald, Michael P., United States Election Project, Presidential Voter Turnout Rates, 1980–2012

Governors Since Statehood

Stevens T. Mason (D)	1835-1840
William Woodbridge (O)	(r) 1840-1841
James Wright Gordon (O)	1841-1842
John S. Barry (D)	1842-1846
Alpheus Felch (D)	(r) 1846-1847
William L. Greely (D)	1847-1848
Epaphroditus Ransom (D)	1848-1850
John S. Barry (D)	1850-1852
Robert McClelland (D)	(r) 1852-1853
Andrew Parsons (D)	1853-1855
Kinsley S. Bingham (R)	1855-1859

Moses Wisner (R)	1859-1861
Austin Blair (R)	1861-1865
Henry H. Crapo (R)	1865-1869
Henry P. Baldwin (R)	1869-1873
John J. Bagley (R)	1873-1877
Charles M. Crosswell (R)	1877-1881
David H. Jerome (R)	1881-1883
Josiah W. Begole (O)	1883-1885
Russell A. Alger (R)	1885-1887
Cyrus G. Luce (R)	1887-1891
Edwin B. Winans (D)	1891-1893
John T. Rich (R)	1893-1897
Hazen S. Pingree (R)	1897-1901
Aaron T. Bliss (R)	1901-1905
Fred M. Warner (R)	1905-1911
Chase M. Osborn (R)	1911-1913
Woodbridge N. Ferris (D)	1913-1917
Albert E. Sleeper (R)	1917-1921
Alexander J. Groesbeck (R)	1921-1927
Fred W. Green (R)	1927-1931
Wilbur M. Brucker (R)	1931-1933
William A. Comstock (D)	1933-1935
Frank D. Fitzgerald (R)	1935-1937
Frank Murphy (D)	1937-1939
Frank D. Fitzgerald (R)	(d) 1939
Luren D. Dickinson (R)	1939-1941
Murray D. Van Wagoner (D)	1941-1943
Harry F. Kelly (R)	1943-1947
Kim Sigler (R)	1947-1949
Gerhard Mennon Williams (D)	1949-1961
John B. Swainson (D)	1961-1963
George W. Romney (R)	(r) 1963-1969
William G. Milliken (R)	1969-1983
James J. Blanchard (D)	1983-1991
John Engler (R)	1991-2003
Jennifer Granholm (D)	2003-2011
Rick Snyder (R)	2011-2015

Note: (D) Democrat; (R) Republican; (O) Other party; (r) resigned; (d) died in office; (i) removed from office

Minnesota

Location: Upper Midwest

Area and rank: 79,617 square miles (206,207 square kilometers); 86,943 square miles (225,182 square kilometers) including water; fourteenth largest state in area

Coastline: none

Population and rank: 5,379,139 (2012 estimate); twenty-first largest state in population

Capital city: St. Paul (285,068 people in 2010 census)

Largest city: Minneapolis (382,578 people in 2010 census)

Became territory: March 3, 1849

State capitol building at St. Paul. (©James Blank/Weststock)

Entered Union and rank: May 11, 1858; thirty-second state

Present constitution adopted: 1858

Counties: 87

State name: "Minnesota" is derived from a Dakota Indian word that means "sky-tinted water"

State nickname: North Star State; Gopher State; Land of 10,000 Lakes

Motto: *L'Etoile du nord* (The North Star)

State flag: Blue field with detail from state seal, name "Minnesota," and nineteen stars

Highest point: Eagle Mountain—2,301 feet (701 meters)

Lowest point: Lake Superior—602 feet (183 meters)

Highest recorded temperature: 114 degrees Fahrenheit (46 degrees Celsius)—Moorhead, 1936

Lowest recorded temperature: −59 degrees Fahrenheit (−51 degrees Celsius)—Pokegama Dam, 1903

State song: "Hail! Minnesota"

State tree: Red (or Norway) pine

State flower: Pink-and-white lady's slipper

State bird: Common loon (also known as great northern diver)

State fish: Walleye

National parks: Voyageurs

Minnesota History

Reaching farther north than any other state except Alaska, Minnesota was settled more slowly than other states in the center of the United States, which were more accessible to heavily populated eastern states. Despite its isolation, the fertile soils of the south and west, the pine forests of the northeast, and the hardwood forests between these regions eventually attracted settlers. The state's access to Lake Superior, numerous rivers, and countless lakes also brought economic growth to the area. Much of Minnesota remains rural, in sharp contrast to the Twin Cities of Minneapolis and St. Paul near the eastern edge of the state.

Early History. The earliest people to inhabit the area, known as the Paleo-Indian culture, hunted bison and other large animals more than ten thousand years ago. About seven thousand years ago, the people of the Eastern Archaic culture hunted small and large animals and made tools from copper. The Woodland culture, starting about three thousand years ago, introduced the use of pottery and burial mounds. Starting about one thousand years ago, the Mississippian culture built large, permanent villages located in fertile river valleys and raised corn, beans, and squash.

Both the Woodland culture and Mississippian culture lifestyles lasted until Europeans arrived about three hundred years ago. Until the middle of the nineteenth century, Minnesota was primarily inhabited by the Ojibwa in the north and east and the Dakota in the south and west. Conflicts between these peoples led to the Ojibwa forcing the Dakota to move farther southwest during the middle of the eighteenth century.

Exploration and Settlement. The first European explorers to reach the area were the French fur traders

Located near the confluence of Minnehaha Creek and the Mississippi River, Minnehaha Falls is a popular tourist attraction because of its association with Henry Wadsworth Longfellow's 1855 poem The Song of Hiawatha. *During the winter months, the falls often freeze solid.* (National Park Service)

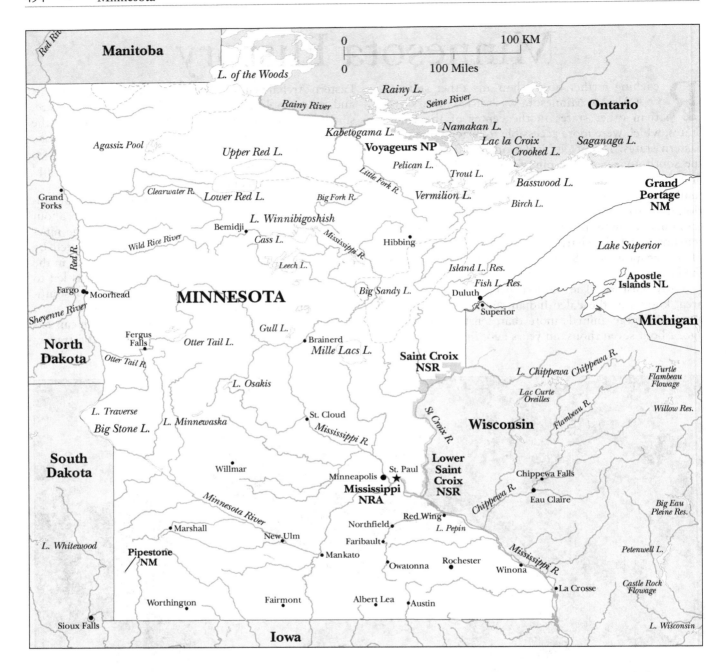

Pierre Esprit Radisson and Médard Chouart des Gro-seilliers, who traveled from Canada through Wisconsin and into eastern Minnesota in 1658. In September of 1679, Daniel Greysolon, sieur du Lhut, met with Native Americans near Mille Lacs Lake near the center of the region. As a result of this meeting, peaceful relations were established among the French, the Ojibwa, and the Dakota. Du Lhut also claimed the area for King Louis XIV of France.

In January of 1680, the French missionary Louis Hennepin began a journey north along the Mississippi River into eastern Minnesota. In April, Hennepin was captured by the Dakota. During his captivity, Hennepin

named a waterfall on the Mississippi River the Falls of St. Anthony, near the future site of the Twin Cities. Hennepin was rescued by Du Lhut in July.

In 1682, the French explorer René-Robert Cavelier, sieur de La Salle, claimed the entire valley of the Missis-sippi River for France. He named this vast area, includ-ing western Minnesota, Louisiana. Meanwhile, French fur traders had established the first permanent European settlement in the region in the far north, at Grand Portage. Grand Portage soon became the center of the prosperous fur trade. Among the many noted French explorers who established settlements in the area were Nicolas Perrot, who founded Fort Antoine in 1686, and Pierre Gaultier de

Varennes, sieur de La Vérendrye, who founded Fort Saint Charles in 1731.

The British and Americans. The wealth generated by the fur trade was part of the struggle for control of North America between France and England that led to the French and Indian War (1754–1763). The British took control of Minnesota east of the Mississippi River after the war. Western Minnesota, with the rest of Louisiana, had been ceded to Spain in 1762 but was returned to France in 1800.

Spain did little to settle the area, but England quickly established the North West Company at Grand Portage to take advantage of the lucrative fur trade. At the end of the American Revolution (1775–1783), eastern Minnesota officially became part of the United States. The North West Company did not leave Grand Portage until 1803, when it moved to Canada. It was replaced by the American Fur Company, established in 1808.

Eastern Minnesota became part of the newly created Northwest Territory in 1787. It became part of several different territories as the vast Northwest Territory was reorganized during the early nineteenth century. Between 1800 and 1858, it was part of Indiana Territory, Illinois Territory, Michigan Territory, Wisconsin Territory, and Minnesota Territory.

Meanwhile, the United States purchased Louisiana, including western Minnesota, from France in 1803. From 1834 to 1849, western Minnesota was part of Michigan Territory, Wisconsin Territory, the Iowa Territory, again Wisconsin Territory, and Minnesota Territory.

Becoming a State. During this time, Minnesota remained a sparsely populated area isolated from the rest of the United States. In 1805, a military expedition led by Zebulon Pike failed to locate the source of the Mississippi but did manage to secure lands along a river from the Dakota Indians. In 1818, a treaty with England added a large area of land to northern Minnesota. In 1819, Fort Saint Anthony was established as the first permanent American settlement in the area. The site was renamed Fort Snelling in 1825 and went on to become the most important settlement in the area until the middle of the century.

The fur trade began to decline in 1837, with the first in a series of treaties with the Dakota and Ojibwa Indians that ceded large amounts of land to the United States. This encouraged settlers to enter the region and

Mass execution of participants in the Minnesota Dakota Sioux uprising of 1862. (Library of Congress)

eventually made the lumber industry and agriculture more important than the fur trade.

The Minnesota Territory had about four thousand settlers in 1849, mostly near Fort Snelling. Most of these early settlers were from New England, although many had entered Minnesota from Canada. Within one year, the population jumped to more than six thousand. As the lumber industry grew more important, the population grew even more quickly. By 1857 the number of Minnesota residents, mostly from eastern states, reached more than 150,000. The majority of new residents settled in the southeast part of the territory, near Fort Snelling. In the same area, St. Paul was founded in 1838 and became the territory capital in 1849. The nearby city of Minneapolis was founded in 1855. Minnesota became the thirty-second state, with much of its western lands removed and added to the Nebraska Territory, in 1858.

Wars and Industry. Minnesota was the first state to send volunteers to fight for the Union during the Civil War. More than twenty thousand residents of the state served in the war. Meanwhile, Minnesota faced its own violent conflict. In 1862, a rebellion by the Dakotas, confined to reservations within the state, eventually led to more than five hundred deaths within a few weeks. The defeated Dakotas were forced into reservations in western territories. The Ojibwas remained on reservations created for them in the north of the state.

After the Civil War, growth continued at a rapid pace. Germans, Swedes, and Norwegians arrived in large numbers. Other important sources of new immigrants were Finland, Poland, Bohemia, Ireland, France, Canada, the Netherlands, Belgium, Iceland, Denmark, Wales, and Switzerland. During the 1880's, the period of the state's fastest growth, most settlers were homesteaders in western Minnesota or worked in the lumber industry. Flour milling was also a major industry in the Twin Cities, both of which tripled in population during this decade. Mining of iron ore began in 1884 and soon became a major source of income.

The Twentieth Century. Immigration during the early twentieth century was mostly to the Twin Cities and included Finns, Italians, Slovakians, Croatians, Serbs, Greeks, Jews, Ukrainians, Russians, and Hispanics. African Americans from southern states moved to the Twin Cities also. In later years, Asians also immigrated.

Throughout the twentieth century Minnesota tended to be politically independent. It traditionally supported a wide variety of small political parties that influenced the policies of the major parties. The modern Democratic Party in Minnesota incorporates many of the ideas of the Farmer-Labor Party, while the modern Republican Party in the state is influenced by independents.

Loss of natural resources led to changes in the state's economy during the twentieth century. Much of the most valuable lumber was cut by 1920, forcing the industry to turn to other trees. At about the same time, flour milling was moved from Minneapolis to Buffalo. The best iron ore was depleted by the late 1950's. New techniques for using lower-grade iron ore led to a revitalization of the industry during the 1960's, but low-cost imports led to another decline during the 1980's. Despite a decline in agriculture after World War II, agriculture was still the state's largest industry.

The early 1980's brought a drop in crop prices, bringing hardship to farmers throughout the state. However, the nationwide recession of the late 1980's had only a minimal effect on Minnesota. During the 1990's, the state's economy turned to industries such as printing, health care, scientific instruments, chemicals, and recreational equipment.

Governor Ventura. From January, 1999, until January, 2003, Minnesota's governor was a colorful and sometimes controversial figure, Jesse Ventura. The name was his stage name as a professional wrestler and actor. Ventura was elected as a third-party reformer and gained office when the vote was split three ways. Describing himself as "fiscally conservative and socially liberal," Ventura achieved remarkable levels of public approval, which at one point soared to nearly 75 percent, despite his holding of sometimes-divisive views. As governor, he supported property tax reform, gay rights, medical marijuana, and abortion rights and was outspoken in his preference for atheism. He was also an outspoken advocate of a light rail system for the state. He vetoed many pieces of legislation, but his vetoes were frequently overridden and he was given derisive treatment by the media. In 2002, he refused to run for reelection, complaining about the focus of the press on politicians' private lives.

Hmong Citizenship. In 2000, an issue from Minnesota's past finally reached a climax. The issue involved the citizenship status of the many of the Hmong, a people mainly from Laos in Southeast Asia. Some 160,000 Hmong immigrated after the Vietnam War to the United States, and among them, about 60,000 settled in Minnesota. Tens of thousands had assisted the U.S. Army fighting and wished their sacrifices to be recompensed with lower barriers to citizenship. They wished to become citizens but found the language requirement daunting. They were vigorously supported in this regard by Democratic senator Paul Wellstone. On May 26, 2000, President Bill Clinton signed into law a measure exempting up to 45,000 Hmong immigrants from the English requirement for citizenship.

2002 Elections. Just before the 2002 general election, a tragic accident aggrieved many Minnesotans. Senator Wellstone, who had held office since 1991, was killed with his wife and daughter in a small plane crash. Wellstone, a former political science professor, was campaigning for reelection. The televised memorial service for him was turned into a political rally by his supporters. Others in attendance, such as Governor Ventura, who were not always allied with Wellstone's politics, decried being part of an impromptu rally, since they believed the event had a different purpose.

In the 2002 general election, the death of Senator Wellstone left the Democratic Party without a candidate. Implored to fill the position, former senator and vice president Walter Mondale agreed to assume the vacancy. He was not successful at the election, however. St. Paul mayor Norm Coleman, a Republican, in one of the closest observed and contested races in the country, defeated him by 50 to 47 percent. At the same election, Republican Tim Pawlenty, a Minnesota House of Representatives leader, was elected governor in a three-way race. Two years later, Democrat John Kerry defeated George W. Bush 51 to 48 percent to win the state's ten electoral votes.

Politics. Michele Bachmann was elected to Congress in 2006 and was re-elected three times. She decided not run for re-election in 2013. Bachman was a candidate for the Republican nomination in the 2012 U.S. presidential election. She won the Ames Iowa Straw Poll in August 2011 but dropped out of contention in January 2012 after she came in sixth in the Iowa state-wide caucuses. She was the first Republican woman to represent the state in Congress, was a supporter of the Tea Party movement, and a founder of the Tea Party Caucus in the House of Representatives. In Minnesota, she has been strongly opposed by environmental groups.

Timothy Pawlenty served as the 39th governor of Minnesota (2003–2011). He previously served in the Minnesota House of Representatives (1993–2003), where he was majority leader for two terms. In 2011 he was one of several candidates seeking the Republican presidential nomination; he was also named as a potential vice presidential nominee. Pawlenty won a three-party election for governor in 2002, and in 2006 he was re-elected by a less than one percent margin. In 2007–2008, he chaired the National Governors Association. In September 2012 he left Mitt Romney's presidential campaign to become a Washington lobbyist for financial institutions.

Rose Secrest
Updated by the Editor

Minnesota's largest city, Minneapolis, is separated from the capital city, St. Paul, by the Mississippi River. The side-by-side cities are popularly known as the Twin Cities. (PhotoDisc)

Minnesota Time Line

1658	Pierre Esprit Radisson and Médard Chouart des Groseilliers are the first Europeans to explore the region.
1679	Daniel Greysolon, sieur Du Lhut, meets with Native Americans and claims the area for France.
1680	Father Louis Hennepin explores the area, is captured by the Dakota, and is rescued by Du Lhut.
1682	René-Robert Cavelier, sieur de La Salle, claims the entire valley of the Mississippi River for France, naming it Louisiana.
1686	Nicolas Perrot founds Fort Antoine.
1731	Pierre Gaultier de Varennes, sieur de La Vérendrye, founds Fort Saint Charles.
1762	Louisiana is ceded to Spain.
1763	End of the French and Indian War brings eastern Minnesota under British control.
1783	End of the American Revolution brings eastern Minnesota under American control.
1787	Eastern Minnesota becomes part of the Northwest Territory.
1800	Louisiana is returned to France; Eastern Minnesota becomes part of Indiana Territory.
1803	United States purchases Louisiana Territory from France.
1805	Explorer Zebulon Pike leads a military expedition to the region.
1808	American Fur Company is established.
1809	Eastern Minnesota becomes part of Illinois Territory.
1818	Eastern Minnesota becomes part of Michigan Territory.
1818	Part of Canada is ceded to the United States by England and is incorporated into Minnesota.

Civil War Veterans gather for Fourth of July in Ortonville, Minnesota in 1880. (U.S. National Archives and Records Administration)

1884 photograph showing construction of the original timber dam at Winnibigoshish Lake, Minnesota. (Library of Congress)

1819	Fort Saint Anthony (later Fort Snelling) is established.
1834	Western Minnesota becomes part of Michigan Territory
1836	Minnesota becomes part of Wisconsin Territory.
1837	Treaties with Native Americans open new lands for settlers.
1838	St. Paul is founded.
1838	Western Minnesota becomes part of Iowa Territory.
1846	Western Minnesota is returned to Wisconsin Territory.
Mar. 3, 1849	Minnesota Territory is created, with St. Paul as the capital.
1849	Population is about four thousand.
1850	Population is more than six thousand.
1851	University of Minnesota is established.
1855	Minneapolis is founded.
1857	Population reaches 150,000.
May 11, 1858	Minnesota is admitted to the Union as the thirty-second state.
1862	Rebellion by the Dakota Indians leads to five hundred deaths.
1862	First railroad, linking the Twin Cities, is built.
1867	Railroads link the Twin Cities to Chicago.
1880's	Minnesota experiences its period of fastest growth.
1880	Minneapolis surpasses St. Paul in population.
1884	Mining of iron ore begins.
1890's	Immigration shifts from rural areas to the Twin Cities.
1920's	Flour milling and lumber industries decline in importance.
1950's	High-grade iron ore is depleted.
1959	Great Lakes are opened to oceangoing vessels.
1960's	Methods are developed to use low-grade iron ore.
1970's	Asian immigrants begin to arrive in Minnesota.
1980's	Crop prices decline, leading to economic hardship.
1980's	Low-cost foreign iron ore leads to a decline in the iron business.
1990	Population reaches nearly 4.4 million; more than half live in the Minneapolis-St. Paul metro area.
1998	Population reaches 4.7 million.
1998	In a campaign that draws national attention, former professional wrestler Jesse Ventura is elected governor, the first Reform Party member to win a statewide office.

May 26, 2000	President Bill Clinton signs bill exempting up to 45,000 Hmong immigrants from the English language requirement for citizenship.
Oct. 25, 2002	Senator Paul Wellstone is killed in an airplane crash while campaigning.
Nov. 5, 2002	St. Paul mayor Norm Coleman defeats Walter Mondale for the U.S. Senate; Tim Pawlenty is elected governor with 44 percent of the vote.
Jan. 6, 2003	Controversial Governor Jesse Ventura, who reached the highest level of public approval of any governor in U.S. history, leaves office.
2004	Light-rail Hiawatha Line advocated by Governor Ventura in 1999 is completed; public use exceeds all estimates.
2013	Congresswoman Michele Bachmann decides not run for a fourth term.

Notes for Further Study

Published Sources. Of the many books that offer general information about the state, one of the most enjoyable for beginning students may be *Minnesota Trivia* (1990) by Laurel Winter. Minnesota's scenic beauty has led to the publications of many books about the land and the living things that reside there. Two of the best are *Minnesota's Natural Heritage: An Ecological Perspective* (1995), edited by John R. Tester and Mary Keinstead, and *Natural Wonders of Minnesota: Parks, Preserves, and Wild Places* (1997) by Martin Hintz. An interesting look at new ways of influencing political decisions, using the issue of school choice in Minnesota as an example, can be found in *Transforming Public Policy: Dynamics of Policy Entrepreneurship and Innovation* (1996) by Nancy C. Roberts and Paula J. King. Jennifer A. Delton, in *Making Minnesota Liberal: Civil Rights and the Transformation of the Democratic Party* (2002), delves into the roots of Minnesota political culture to answer why a largely white state became a springboard for civil rights and social justice movements.

For students of the state's history, an excellent starting place is *A Historical Album of Minnesota* (1993) by Jeffrey D. Carlson or *A Popular History of Minnesota* (2005) by Norman K. Risjord. A more scholarly account is found in *Minnesota: A History* (1998) by William E. Lass. An interesting account of Native Americans in the state is offered in Samuel W. Pond's *The Dakota or Sioux in Minnesota as They Were in 1834* (1986). A colorful account of the early days of fur trading can be found in *The Grand Portage Story* (1992) by Carolyn Gilman. Kurt D. Bergemann's *Battalion: Minnesota Cavalry in the Civil War and Dakota War* (2004) details how a modestly trained group of volunteers from Minnesota lived to serve longer and see more action than any other Minnesota unit engaged in the Civil War; it later played a pivotal role during the uprising of the Dakota Indians. The Minnesota Historical Society has published a number of excellent books in its People of Minnesota Series, which explore the ethnic roots of the state, including *African Americans in Minnesota* (2002) by David Vassar, *Jews in Minnesota* (2002) by Hyman Berman and Linda Mack Schloff, and *Chinese in Minnesota* (2004) by Sherri Gebert Fuller. The modern history of the state is discussed in detail in *Minnesota in a Century of Change: The State and Its People Since 1900* (1989), edited by Cliford E. Clark.

Web Resources. A wide variety of Web sites dealing with all aspects of Minnesota can be found on the Internet. Many of these are associated with the state government, which maintains a large number of informative sites. Minnesota.gov (mn.gov/portal/) serves as a general portal to a wide range of information about the state, including government, business, health and safety, and travel and leisure. Explore Minnesota (www.exploreminnesota.com/) is a good place to begin the search for tourist-related information. At the Minnesota Department of Natural Resources site (www.dnr.state.mn.us/index.html), users can study native plants, see photos of state wildlife, and learn about the region's climate, among many other features. On the University of Minnesota's Geological Survey page (www.mngs.umn.edu/) users can view topographical maps or regional rocks. Statistical information from the U.S. Census Bureau can be found at Minnesota QuickFacts (quickfacts.census.gov/qfd/states/27000.html).

Detailed information on economic activity in the state is available at Minnesota's Department of Employment and Economic Development (www.deed.state.mn.us/index.htm). An unusual Web site, dealing with public policy issues such as crime and the environment, can be found at Minnesota Planning (www.mnplan.state.mn.us). Of the many Web sites devoted to the state's past, a good starting place is Minnesota Historical Society (www.mnhs.org/index.htm), which offers information about the state's historical museums, archives, and libraries. Minnesota Genealogy (www.rootsweb.com/~mngenweb/) allows users to search for ancestor information by county. Information about the state's political process can be found at Minnesota's State Legislature (www.leg.state.mn.us/).

Counties

County	2012 Population	Pop. Rank	Land Area (sq. miles)	Area Rank
Aitkin	15,927	53	1,821.66	9
Anoka	336,414	4	423.01	81
Becker	33,000	32	1,315.20	15
Beltrami	45,375	21	2,504.94	4
Benton	38,865	25	408.30	83
Big Stone	5,164	83	499.02	67
Blue Earth	65,091	13	747.84	34
Brown	25,425	41	611.09	51
Carlton	35,348	30	861.38	27
Carver	93,707	11	354.33	86

County	2012 Population	Pop. Rank	Land Area (sq. miles)	Area Rank
Cass	28,357	37	2,021.54	6
Chippewa	12,135	62	581.12	54
Chisago	53,452	18	414.86	82
Clay	60,155	16	1,045.37	19
Clearwater	8,703	74	998.94	21
Cook	5,185	82	1,452.28	12
Cottonwood	11,597	63	638.61	47
Crow Wing	62,882	15	999.09	20
Dakota	405,088	3	562.17	58
Dodge	20,231	49	439.28	74

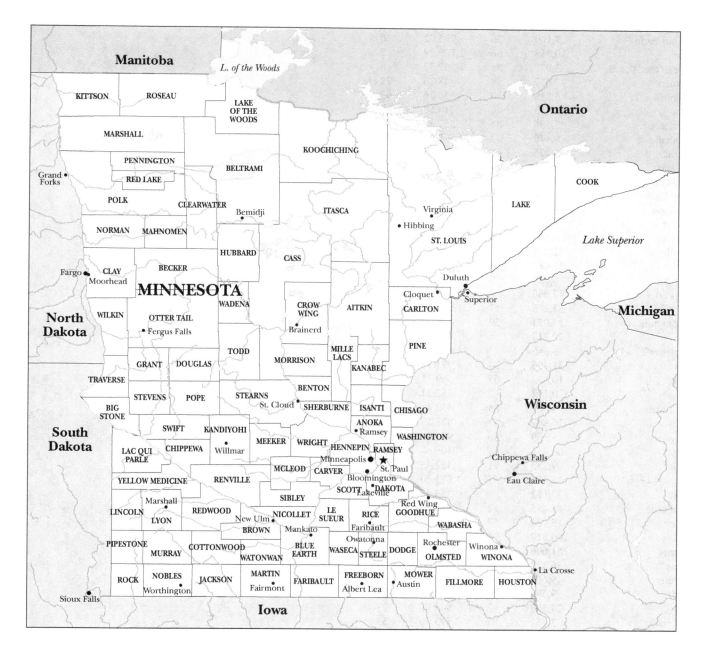

County	2012 Population	Pop. Rank	Land Area (sq. miles)	Area Rank
Douglas	36,415	27	637.30	48
Faribault	14,263	58	712.48	38
Fillmore	20,834	46	861.30	28
Freeborn	31,054	35	707.09	41
Goodhue	46,336	20	756.84	32
Grant	5,944	79	548.16	62
Hennepin	1,184,576	1	553.59	60
Houston	18,837	51	552.06	61
Hubbard	20,347	48	925.67	24
Isanti	38,248	26	435.79	75
Itasca	45,221	22	2,667.72	3
Jackson	10,281	67	702.98	43
Kanabec	16,005	52	521.59	66
Kandiyohi	42,379	23	796.78	29
Kittson	4,493	84	1,098.80	18
Koochiching	13,208	61	3,104.07	2
Lac qui Parle	7,109	76	765.02	30
Lake	10,818	66	2,109.29	5
Lake of the Woods	3,973	86	1,297.87	16
Le Sueur	27,677	38	448.76	72
Lincoln	5,818	80	536.76	63
Lyon	25,543	40	714.56	37
Mahnomen	5,536	81	557.88	59
Marshall	9,449	72	1,775.07	10
Martin	20,475	47	712.35	39
McLeod	36,053	29	491.47	69
Meeker	23,061	43	608.18	52
Mille Lacs	25,740	39	572.31	56
Morrison	33,052	31	1,125.06	17
Mower	39,372	24	711.33	40
Murray	8,577	75	704.70	42
Nicollet	32,929	33	448.49	73
Nobles	21,487	44	715.11	36
Norman	6,634	77	872.79	26
Olmsted	147,066	8	653.35	46
Otter Tail	57,288	17	1,972.07	7
Pennington	14,074	59	616.57	50
Pine	29,218	36	1,411.29	13
Pipestone	9,345	73	465.05	71
Polk	31,416	34	1,971.13	8
Pope	10,892	65	669.71	44
Ramsey	520,152	2	152.21	87
Red Lake	4,087	85	432.41	78
Redwood	15,847	54	878.57	25
Renville	15,369	56	982.91	22
Rice	64,854	14	495.68	68
Rock	9,553	71	482.45	70
Roseau	15,476	55	1,671.60	11
Scott	135,152	9	356.48	85
Sherburne	89,455	12	432.92	77
Sibley	15,123	57	588.78	53
St. Louis	200,319	6	6,247.40	1
Stearns	151,606	7	1,343.13	14
Steele	36,322	28	429.65	79
Stevens	9,663	69	563.60	57
Swift	9,594	70	742.08	35
Todd	24,509	42	944.98	23
Traverse	3,451	87	573.90	55

County	2012 Population	Pop. Rank	Land Area (sq. miles)	Area Rank
Wabasha	21,476	45	522.98	65
Wadena	13,767	60	536.27	64
Waseca	19,237	50	423.36	80
Washington	244,088	5	384.28	84
Watonwan	11,187	64	434.95	76
Wilkin	6,585	78	750.96	33
Winona	51,629	19	626.21	49
Wright	127,336	10	661.46	45
Yellow Medicine	10,158	68	759.10	31

Source: U.S. Census Bureau, 2012 Population Estimates

Cities

With 10,000 or more residents

Legal Name	2010 Population	Pop. Rank	Land Area (sq. miles)	Area Rank	Legal Name	2010 Population	Pop. Rank	Land Area (sq. miles)	Area Rank
Albert Lea city	18,016	63	12.59	57	Brooklyn Center city	30,104	31	7.96	76
Alexandria city	11,070	93	15.96	45	Brooklyn Park city	75,781	6	26.07	34
Andover city	30,598	30	33.88	16	Buffalo city	15,453	70	7.17	79
Anoka city	17,142	65	6.70	85	Burnsville city	60,306	14	24.91	35
Apple Valley city	49,084	19	16.86	44	Champlin city	23,089	43	8.17	74
Austin city	24,718	38	11.79	59	Chanhassen city	22,952	45	20.19	38
Bemidji city	13,431	79	12.92	56	Chaska city	23,770	40	16.97	43
Big Lake city	10,060	99	6.91	83	Cloquet city	12,124	88	35.20	11
Blaine city	57,186	15	33.66	17	Columbia Heights city	19,496	59	3.41	97
Bloomington city	82,893	5	34.68	13	Coon Rapids city	61,476	12	22.61	36
Brainerd city	13,590	76	11.90	58	Cottage Grove city	34,589	27	33.62	18

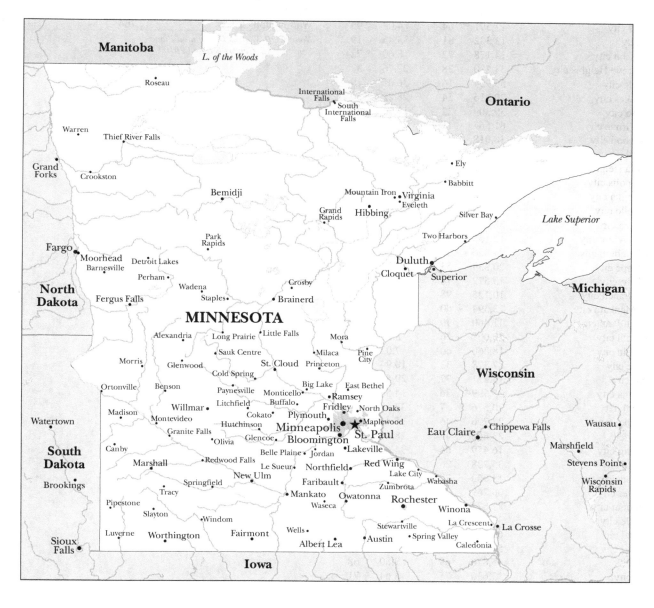

Legal Name	2010 Population	Pop. Rank	Land Area (sq. miles)	Area Rank
Crystal city	22,151	48	5.78	89
Duluth city	86,265	4	67.79	2
Eagan city	64,206	9	31.12	26
East Bethel city	11,626	89	44.80	6
Eden Prairie city	60,797	13	32.45	24
Edina city	47,941	20	15.45	47
Elk River city	22,974	44	42.29	7
Fairmont city	10,666	97	15.04	50
Faribault city	23,352	42	15.32	49
Farmington city	21,086	51	14.69	51
Fergus Falls city	13,138	82	14.11	54
Forest Lake city	18,375	61	30.56	27
Fridley city	27,208	34	10.17	64
Golden Valley city	20,371	52	10.19	63
Grand Rapids city	10,869	95	22.56	37
Ham Lake city	15,296	71	34.39	15
Hastings city	22,172	47	10.00	66
Hibbing city	16,361	68	181.83	1
Hopkins city	17,591	64	4.08	95
Hugo city	13,332	81	33.45	19
Hutchinson city	14,178	72	8.60	72
Inver Grove Heights city	33,880	28	27.76	32
Lakeville city	55,954	16	36.05	9
Lino Lakes city	20,216	54	28.22	30
Mankato city	39,309	22	17.91	41
Maple Grove city	61,567	11	32.63	23
Maplewood city	38,018	24	16.98	42
Marshall city	13,680	74	10.07	65
Mendota Heights city	11,071	92	9.15	69
Minneapolis city	382,578	1	53.97	4
Minnetonka city	49,734	18	26.93	33
Monticello city	12,759	85	8.94	70
Moorhead city	38,065	23	19.80	39
Mounds View city	12,155	87	4.03	96
New Brighton city	21,456	50	6.46	86
New Hope city	20,339	53	5.04	92
New Ulm city	13,522	78	9.92	67
North Branch city	10,125	98	35.60	10
North Mankato city	13,394	80	5.86	88
North St. Paul city	11,460	90	2.85	98
Northfield city	20,007	56	8.56	73
Northfield city	18,860	60	7.02	80
Oakdale city	27,378	33	10.94	60
Otsego city	13,571	77	29.56	28
Owatonna city	25,599	36	14.53	52
Plymouth city	70,576	7	32.68	22
Prior Lake city	22,796	46	15.44	48
Ramsey city	23,668	41	28.81	29
Red Wing city	16,459	66	34.60	14
Richfield city	35,228	26	6.87	84
Robbinsdale city	13,953	73	2.79	99
Rochester city	106,769	3	54.59	3
Rosemount city	21,874	49	33.22	20
Roseville city	33,660	29	13.00	55
St. Cloud city	65,842	8	40.04	8
St. Cloud city	52,661	17	31.86	25
Sartell city	15,876	69	9.80	68
Sartell city	13,630	75	8.64	71

Legal Name	2010 Population	Pop. Rank	Land Area (sq. miles)	Area Rank
Sauk Rapids city	12,773	83	6.10	87
Savage city	26,911	35	15.63	46
Shakopee city	37,076	25	28.01	31
Shoreview city	25,043	37	10.77	61
South St. Paul city	20,160	55	5.65	90
St. Louis Park city	45,250	21	10.64	62
St. Michael city	16,399	67	32.73	21
St. Paul city	285,068	2	51.98	5
St. Peter city	11,196	91	5.59	91
Stillwater city	18,225	62	6.96	82
Vadnais Heights city	12,302	86	6.98	81
Waconia city	10,697	96	4.34	94
West St. Paul city	19,540	58	4.91	93
White Bear township	10,949	94	7.30	78
White Bear Lake city	23,797	39	8.02	75
Willmar city	19,610	57	14.15	53
Winona city	27,592	32	18.84	40
Woodbury city	61,961	10	34.73	12
Worthington city	12,764	84	7.34	77

Note: CDP–Census Designated Place
Source: U.S. Census Bureau, 2010 Census

Survey Says...

This section presents current rankings from dozens of public and private sources. It shows how this state ranks in a number of critical categories, including education, job growth, cost of living, teen drivers, energy efficiency, and business environment. Sources include *Forbes, Reuters, U.S. News and World Report, CNN Money, Gallup,* and *Huffington Post.*

- Minnesota ranked #5 in a government study measuring real gross domestic product (GDP)—the output of goods and services produced by labor and property located in the United States. The ranking is based on the percentage change compared with 2011 GDP.
  U.S. Department of Commerce, Bureau of Economic Analysis, June 2013; www.bea.gov

- Minnesota ranked #17 in a government study measuring real gross domestic product (GDP)—the output of goods and services produced by labor and property located in the United States. The ranking is based on the dollar value of its GDP.
  U.S. Department of Commerce, Bureau of Economic Analysis, June 2013; www.bea.gov

- Minnesota ranked #39 in the 17th edition of "Quality Counts; State of the States," Education Week's "report card" surveying key education indicators, policy efforts, and educational outcomes.
  Education Week, January 4, 2013 (online) and January 10, 2013 (print); www.edweek.org

- SERI (Science and Engineering Readiness Index) weighs the performance of the states' K-12 schools in preparing students in physics and calculus, the high school subjects considered most important for future scientists and engineers. Minnesota ranked #2.
  Newsletter of the Forum on Education of the American Physical Society, Summer 2011 issue; www.huffingtonpost.com, July 11, 2011; updated October 1, 2012

- Business website 24/7 Wall St. identified the states with the highest and lowest percentages of residents 25 or older with a college degree or higher. Of "America's Best Educated States," Minnesota ranked #10 (#1 = best).
  247wallst.com, posted October 15, 2012; consulted July 18, 2013

- MoneyRates.com ranked Minnesota #6 on its list of the best to worst states for making a living. Criteria: average income; inflation; employment prospects; and workers' Workplace Environment assessments according to the Gallup-Healthways Well-Being Index.
  www.money-rates.com, posted April 1, 2013

- *Forbes* analyzed business costs, labor supply, regulatory environment, current economic climate, growth prospects, and quality of life, to compile its "Best States for Business" rankings. Minnesota ranked #20.
  www.forbes.com. posted December 12, 2012

- The 2012 Gallup-Healthways Well-Being Index, surveyed American's opinions on economic confidence, workplace perceptions, community climate, personal choices, and health predictors to assess the "future livability" of each state. Minnesota ranked #2.
  "Utah Poised to Be the Best State to Live In," Gallup Wellbeing, www.gallup.com, August 7, 2012

- On CNBC's list of "America's Top States for Business 2013," Minnesota ranked #15. Criteria: measures of competitiveness developed with input from the National Association of Manufacturers, the Council on Competitiveness, and other business groups weighed with the states' own marketing criteria.
  www.cnbc.com, consulted July 19, 2013

- Minnesota ranked #19 on MoneyRates list of "Best-and Worst-States to Retire 2012." Criteria: life expectancy, crime rate, climate, economic conditions, taxes, job opportunities, and cost of living.
  www.money-rates.com, October 22, 2012

- Minnesota ranked #43 on the 2013 Bankrate "Best Places to Retire" list ranking the states and District of Columbia on various criteria relating to health, safety, and cost.
  www.bankrate.com, May 6, 2013

- Minnesota ranked #7 on the Social Science Research Council's "American Human Development Report: The Measure of America," assessing the 50 states plus the District of Columbia on health, education, and living-standard criteria.
  The Measure of America 2013-2014, posted June 19, 2013; www.measureofamerica.org

- Minnesota ranked #6 on the Foundation for Child Development's (FCD) Child Well-being Index (CWI). The FCD used the KIDS COUNT report and the National Survey of Children's Health, the only state-level source for several key indicators of child well-being.
  Foundation for Child Development, January 18, 2012; fcd-us.org

- Minnesota ranked #4 overall according to the 2013 KIDS COUNT Data Book, a project of the Annie E. Casey Foundation. Criteria: children's economic well-being, education, health, and family and community indicators.
  KIDS COUNT Data Center's Data Book, released June 20, 2013; http://datacenter.kidscount.org

- Minnesota ranked #6 in the children's economic well-being category by the 2013 KIDS COUNT Data Book, a project of the Annie E. Casey Foundation.
  KIDS COUNT Data Center's Data Book, released June 20, 2013; http://datacenter.kidscount.org

- Minnesota ranked #7 in the children's educational opportunities and attainments category by the 2013 KIDS COUNT Data Book, a project of the Annie E. Casey Foundation.
  KIDS COUNT Data Center's Data Book, released June 20, 2013; http://datacenter.kidscount.org

- Minnesota ranked #15 in the children's health category by the 2013 KIDS COUNT Data Book, a project of the Annie E. Casey Foundation.
  KIDS COUNT Data Center's Data Book, released June 20, 2013; http://datacenter.kidscount.org

- Minnesota ranked #5 in the family and community circumstances that factor into children's well-being category by the 2013 KIDS COUNT Data Book, a project of the Annie E. Casey Foundation.
  KIDS COUNT Data Center's Data Book, released June 20, 2013; http://datacenter.kidscount.org

- Minnesota ranked #3 in the 2012 Gallup-Healthways Well-Being Index. Criteria: emotional health; physical health; healthy behavior; work environment; basic access to food, shelter, health care; and a safe and satisfying place to live.
  2012 State of Well-Being, Gallup-Healthways Well-Being Index, released February 28, 2013; www.well-beingindex.com

- *U.S. News and World Report's* "Best States for Teen Drivers" rankings are based on driving and road safety laws, federal reports on driver's licenses, car accident fatality, and road-quality statistics. Minnesota ranked #8.
  U.S. News and World Report, March 18, 2010; www.usnews.com

- The Yahoo! Sports service Rivals.com ranks the states according to the strength of their high school football programs. Minnesota ranked #25.
  "Ranking the States: Where Is the Best Football Played?," November 18, 2011; highschool.rivals.com

- iVillage ranked the states by hospitable living conditions for women. Criteria: economic success, access to affordable childcare, health care, reproductive rights, female representation in government, and educational attainment. Minnesota ranked #8.
  iVillage, "50 Best to Worst States for Women," March 14, 2012; www.ivillage.com

- The League of American Bicyclists's "Bicycle Friendly States" ranked Minnesota #4. Criteria: legislation and enforcement, policies and programs, infrastructure and funding, education and advocacy, and evaluation and planning.
  "Washington Tops the Bicycle-Friendly State Ranking," May 1, 2013; bicycling.com

- The federal Corporation for National and Community Service ranked the states and the District of Columbia by volunteer rates. Minnesota ranked #4 for community service.
  "Volunteering and Civic Life in America 2012," www.volunteeringinamerica.gov, accessed July 24, 2013

- The Hospital Safety Score ranked states and the District of Columbia on their hospitals' performance scores. Minnesota ranked #3. Criteria: avoiding preventable harm and medical errors, as demonstrated by 26 hospital safety metrics.
  Spring 2013 Hospital Safety Score, May 8, 2013; www.hospitalsafetyscore.org

- GMAC Insurance ranked the states and the District of Columbia by the performance of their drivers on the GMAC Insurance National Drivers Test, comprised of DMV test questions. Minnesota ranked #4.
  "2011 GMAC Insurance National Drivers Test," www.gmacinsurance.com, accessed July 23, 2013

- Minnesota ranked #25 in a "State Integrity Investigation" analysis of laws and practices intended to deter corruption and promote accountability and openness in campaign finance, ethics laws, lobbying regulations and management of state pension funds.
  "What's Your State's Grade?," www.publicintegrity.org, accessed July 23, 2013

- Minnesota ranked #8 among the states and the District of Columbia in total rail miles, as tracked by the Association of American Railroads.
  "U.S. Freight Railroad Industry Snapshot: Railroads and States: Total Rail Miles by State: 2011"; www.aar.org, accessed July 23, 2013

- According to statistics compiled by the Beer Institute, Minnesota ranked #29 among the states and the District of Columbia in per capita beer consumption of persons 21 years or older.
  "Shipments of Malt Beverages and Per Capita Consumption by State 2012;" www.beerinstitute.org

- According to Concordia University's "Public Education Costs per Pupil by State Rankings," based on statistics gathered by the U.S. Census Bureau, which includes the District of Columbia, Minnesota ranked #22.
  Concordia University Online; education.cu-portland.edu, accessed July 24, 2013

- Minnesota ranked #31 among the states and the District of Columbia in population density based on U.S. Census Bureau data for resident population and total land area. "List of U.S. States by Population Density."
  www.wikipedia.org, accessed July 24, 2013

- In "America's Health Rankings, 2012 Edition," by the United Health Foundation, Minnesota ranked #5. Criteria included: rate of high school graduation; violent crime rate; incidence of infectious disease; childhood immunizations; prevalence of diabetes; per capita public-health funding; percentage of uninsured population; rate of children in poverty; and availability of primary-care physicians.
  United Health Foundation; www.americashealthrankings.org, accessed July 24, 2013

- The TechNet 2012 "State Broadband Index" ranked Minnesota #19 on the following criteria: broadband adoption; network quality; and economic structure. Improved broadband use is hoped to promote economic development, build strong communities, improve delivery of government services and upgrade educational systems.
  TechNet; www.technet.org, accessed July 24, 2013

- Minnesota was ranked #9 among the states and District of Columbia on the American Council for an Energy-Efficient Economy's "State Energy Efficiency Scorecard" for 2012.
  American Council for an Energy-Efficient Economy; aceee.org/sector/state-policy/scorecard, accessed July 24, 2013

Statistical Tables

DEMOGRAPHICS
Resident State and National Population, 1950-2012
Projected State and National Population, 2000-2030
Population by Age, 2012
Population by Race, 2012
Population by Hispanic Origin and Race, 2012

VITAL STATISTICS
Death Rates by Leading Causes, 2010
Death Rates by Selected Causes, 2010
Abortion Rates, 2009
Infant Mortality Rates, 1995-2009
Marriage and Divorce Rates, 2000-2011

ECONOMY
Nominal Gross Domestic Product by Industry, 2012
Real Gross Domestic Product, 2000-2012
Personal Income Per Capita, 1930-2012
Non-Farm Employment by Sector, 2012
Foreign Exports, 2000-2012
Energy Consumption, 2011

LAND AND WATER
Surface Area and Federally-Owned Land, 2007
Land Cover/Use of Non-Federal Rural Land, 2007
Farms and Crop Acreage, 2012

HEALTH AND MEDICAL CARE
Medical Professionals, 2012
Health Insurance Coverage, 2011
HIV, STD, and Tuberculosis Cases and Rates, 2011
Cigarette Smoking, 2011

HOUSING
Home Ownership Rates, 1995-2012
Home Sales, 2000-2010
Value of Owner-Occupied Homes, 2011

EDUCATION
School Enrollment, 2011
Educational Attainment, 2011
Public College Finances, FY 2012

TRANSPORTATION AND TRAVEL
Motor Vehicle Registrations and Drivers Licenses, 2011
Domestic Travel Expenditures, 2009
Retail Gasoline Prices, 2013
Public Road Length, 2011

CRIME AND LAW ENFORCEMENT
Full-Time Law Enforcement Officers, 2011
Prison Population, 2000-2012
Crime Rate, 2011

GOVERNMENT AND FINANCE
Local Governments by Type, 2012
State Government Revenue, 2011
State Government Expenditures, 2011
State Government General Expenditures by Function, 2011
State Government Finances, Cash and Debt, 2011

POLITICS
Composition of the Senate, 1995-2013
Composition of the House of Representatives, 1995-2013
Composition of State Legislature, 2004-2013
Voter Participation in Presidential Elections, 1980-2012
Governors Since Statehood

DEMOGRAPHICS

Resident State and National Population, 1950–2012

Year	State Population	U.S. Population	State Share
1950	2,982,000	151,326,000	1.97%
1960	3,414,000	179,323,000	1.90%
1970	3,806,103	203,302,031	1.87%
1980	4,075,970	226,545,805	1.80%
1990	4,375,099	248,709,873	1.76%
2000	4,919,631	281,424,600	1.75%
2010	5,303,925	308,745,538	1.72%
2012	5,379,139	313,914,040	1.71%

Note: 1950/1960 population figures are rounded to the nearest thousand.
Source: U.S. Census Bureau, Decennial Census 1950–2010; U.S. Census Bureau, 2012 Population Estimates

Projected State and National Population, 2000–2030

Year	State Population	U.S. Population	State Share
2000	4,919,479	281,421,906	1.75%
2005	5,174,743	295,507,134	1.75%
2010	5,420,636	308,935,581	1.75%
2015	5,668,211	322,365,787	1.76%
2020	5,900,769	335,804,546	1.76%
2025	6,108,787	349,439,199	1.75%
2030	6,306,130	363,584,435	1.73%
State population growth, 2000–2030			1,386,651
State percentage growth, 2000–2030			28.2%

Source: U.S. Census Bureau, Population Division, Interim State Population Projections, 2005

Population by Age, 2012

Age Group	State Population	Percent of Total Population State	Percent of Total Population U.S.
Under 5 years	348,338	6.5%	6.4%
5 to 14 years	713,620	13.3%	13.1%
15 to 24 years	720,566	13.4%	14.0%
25 to 34 years	737,095	13.7%	13.5%
35 to 44 years	667,219	12.4%	12.9%
45 to 54 years	787,115	14.6%	14.1%
55 to 64 years	675,419	12.6%	12.3%
65 to 74 years	391,725	7.3%	7.6%
75 to 84 years	225,423	4.2%	4.2%
85 years and older	112,619	2.1%	1.9%
Under 18 years	1,276,148	23.7%	23.5%
65 years and older	729,767	13.6%	13.7%
Median age (years)	–	37.6	37.4

Source: U.S. Census Bureau, Annual Estimates of the Resident Population for Selected Age Groups by Sex for the United States, States, Counties, and Puerto Rico Commonwealth and Municipios: April 1, 2010 to July 1, 2012

Population by Race, 2012

Race	State Population	Percent of Total Population State	Percent of Total Population U.S.
All residents	5,379,139	100.00%	100.00%
White	4,654,134	86.52%	77.89%
African American	297,962	5.54%	13.13%
Native American	68,961	1.28%	1.23%
Asian	235,120	4.37%	5.14%
Native Hawaiian	3,206	0.06%	0.23%
Two or more races	119,756	2.23%	2.39%

Source: U.S. Census Bureau, Population Division, Annual Estimates of the Resident Population by Sex, Race and Hispanic Origin for the United States, States, and Counties: April 1, 2010 to July 1, 2012

Population by Hispanic Origin and Race, 2012

Hispanic Origin/Race	State Population	Percent of Total Population State	Percent of Total Population U.S.
All residents	5,379,139	100.00%	100.00%
All Hispanic residents	264,359	4.91%	16.89%
Hispanic			
White	224,263	4.17%	14.91%
African American	10,648	0.20%	0.79%
Native American	12,315	0.23%	0.49%
Asian	2,887	0.05%	0.17%
Native Hawaiian	1,066	0.02%	0.06%
Two or more races	13,180	0.25%	0.48%
Not Hispanic			
White	4,429,871	82.35%	62.98%
African American	287,314	5.34%	12.34%
Native American	56,646	1.05%	0.74%
Asian	232,233	4.32%	4.98%
Native Hawaiian	2,140	0.04%	0.17%
Two or more races	106,576	1.98%	1.91%

Source: U.S. Census Bureau, Population Division, Annual Estimates of the Resident Population by Sex, Race and Hispanic Origin for the United States, States, and Counties: April 1, 2010 to July 1, 2012

VITAL STATISTICS

Death Rates by Leading Causes, 2010

Cause	State	U.S.
Malignant neoplasms	179.3	186.2
Ischaemic heart diseases	73.1	122.9
Other forms of heart disease	46.7	53.4
Chronic lower respiratory diseases	37.0	44.7
Cerebrovascular diseases	38.7	41.9
Organic, incl. symptomatic, mental disorders	47.8	35.7
Other degenerative diseases of the nervous sys.	28.0	28.4
Other external causes of accidental injury	27.4	26.5
Diabetes mellitus	19.0	22.4
Hypertensive diseases	11.1	20.4
All causes	708.1	799.5

Note: Figures are age-adjusted death rates per 100,000 population
Source: CDC/NCHS, Underlying Cause of Death 1999–2010 on CDC WONDER Online Database

Death Rates by Selected Causes, 2010

Cause	State	U.S.
Assault	2.1	5.2
Diseases of the liver	11.0	13.9
Human immunodeficiency virus (HIV) disease	0.9	2.7
Influenza and pneumonia	10.5	16.2
Intentional self-harm	11.4	12.4
Malnutrition	0.4	0.9
Obesity and other hyperalimentation	1.4	1.8
Renal failure	13.5	14.4
Transport accidents	10.3	12.1
Viral hepatitis	1.1	2.4

Note: Figures are age-adjusted death rates per 100,000 population; A dash indicates that data was not available or was suppressed
Source: CDC/NCHS, Underlying Cause of Death 1999–2010 on CDC WONDER Online Database

Abortion Rates, 2009

Category	2009
By state of residence	
Total abortions	11,908
Abortion rate[1]	11.4%
Abortion ratio[2]	169
By state of occurrence	
Total abortions	12,388
Abortion rate[1]	11.8%
Abortion ratio[2]	175
Abortions obtained by out-of-state residents	8.0%
U.S. abortion rate[1]	15.1%
U.S. abortion ratio[2]	227

Note: (1) Number of abortions per 1,000 women aged 15–44 years; (2) Number of abortions per 1,000 live births; A dash indicates that data was not available
Source: CDC/NCHS, Morbidity and Mortality Weekly Report, November 23, 2012 (Abortion Surveillance, United States, 2009)

Infant Mortality Rates, 1995–2009

Category	1995	2000	2005	2009
All state residents	6.78	5.62	5.09	4.59
All U.S. residents	7.57	6.89	6.86	6.39
All state white residents	6.12	4.89	4.53	4.06
All U.S. white residents	6.30	5.71	5.73	5.33
All state black residents	15.83	13.93	9.57	8.46
All U.S. black residents	14.58	13.48	13.26	12.12

Note: Figures represent deaths per 1,000 live births of resident infants under one year old, exclusive of fetal deaths; A dash indicates that data was not available or was suppressed.
Source: Centers of Disease Control and Prevention, Division of Vital Statistics, Linked Birth/Infant Death Records on CDC Wonder Online

Marriage and Divorce Rates, 2000–2011

Year	Marriage Rate		Divorce Rate	
	State	U.S.	State	U.S.
2000	6.8	8.2	3.2	4.0
2002	6.5	8.0	3.1	3.9
2004	6.0	7.8	2.8	3.7
2006	6.0	7.5	0.0	3.7
2008	5.4	7.1	0.0	3.5
2010	5.3	6.8	0.0	3.6
2011	5.6	6.8	0.0	3.6

Note: Rates are based on provisional counts of marriages/divorces by state of occurrence and are per 1,000 total population residing in area
Source: CDC/NCHS, National Vital Statistics System

ECONOMY

Nominal Gross Domestic Product by Industry, 2012
In millions of current dollars

Industry	State GDP
Accommodation and food services	6,855
Administrative and waste management services	6,911
Agriculture, forestry, fishing, and hunting	7,449
Arts, entertainment, and recreation	2,985
Construction	10,582
Educational services	2,940
Finance and insurance	28,799
Health care and social assistance	25,963
Information	10,101
Management of companies and enterprises	11,253
Manufacturing	40,441
Mining	831
Other services, except government	6,564
Professional, scientific, and technical services	18,456
Real estate and rental and leasing	36,504
Retail trade	16,342
Transportation and warehousing	8,220
Utilities	5,040
Wholesale trade	19,878

Source: U.S. Department of Commerce, Bureau of Economic Analysis, Survey of Current Business

Real Gross Domestic Product, 2000–2012
In millions of chained 2005 dollars

Year	State GDP	U.S. GDP	State Share
2000	211,529	11,225,406	1.88%
2005	237,813	12,539,116	1.90%
2010	240,418	12,897,088	1.86%
2012	252,971	13,430,576	1.88%

Source: U.S. Department of Commerce, Bureau of Economic Analysis, Survey of Current Business

Personal Income Per Capita, 1930–2012

Year	State	U.S.
1930	$545	$618
1940	$519	$593
1950	$1,427	$1,503
1960	$2,143	$2,268
1970	$4,050	$4,084
1980	$10,229	$10,091
1990	$19,710	$19,354
2000	$32,599	$30,319
2010	$42,528	$39,791
2012	$46,227	$42,693

Source: U.S. Department of Commerce, Bureau of Economic Analysis, Regional Economic Accounts

Non-Farm Employment by Sector, 2012
In thousands

Sector	Employment
Construction	94.8
Education and health services	478.1
Financial activities	177.1
Government	411.8
Information	53.7
Leisure and hospitality	244.3
Mining and logging	7.0
Manufacturing	305.4
Other services	116.1
Professional and business services	336.3
Trade, transportation, and utilities	503.3
All sectors	2,727.6

Source: U.S. Bureau of Labor Statistics, State and Area Employment

Foreign Exports, 2000–2012
In millions of dollars

Year	State Exports	U.S. Exports	State Share
2000	10,302	712,054	1.45%
2002	10,398	649,940	1.60%
2004	12,697	768,554	1.65%
2006	16,349	973,994	1.68%
2008	19,186	1,222,545	1.57%
2010	18,903	1,208,080	1.56%
2012	20,826	1,478,268	1.41%

Note: U.S. figures exclude data from Puerto Rico, U.S. Virgin Islands, and unallocated exports
Source: U.S. Department of Commerce, International Trade Admin., Office of Trade and Industry Information, Manufacturing and Services

Energy Consumption, 2011

In trillions of BTUs, except as noted

Total energy consumption	
Total state energy consumption	1,866.6
Total U.S. energy consumption	97,387.3
State share of U.S. total	1.92%
Per capita consumption (in millions of BTUs)	
Total state per capita consumption	349.1
Total U.S. per capita consumption	312.6
End-use sectors	
Residential	397.6
Commercial	341.7
Industrial	655.0
Transportation	472.4
Sources of energy	
Petroleum	605.8
Natural gas	425.0
Coal	315.6
Renewable energy	228.1
Nuclear electric power	125.1

Source: U.S. Energy Information Administration, State Energy Data 2011: Consumption

LAND AND WATER

Surface Area and Federally-Owned Land, 2007

In thousands of acres

Category	State	U.S.	State Share
Total surface area	54,009.9	1,937,664.2	2.79%
Total land area	50,865.0	1,886,846.9	2.70%
Non-federal land	47,528.9	1,484,910.0	3.20%
Developed	2,395.2	111,251.2	2.15%
Rural	45,133.7	1,373,658.8	3.29%
Federal land	3,336.1	401,936.9	0.83%
Water area	3,144.9	50,817.3	6.19%

Source: U.S. Department of Agriculture, Natural Resources Conservation Service, 2007 National Resources Inventory

Land Cover/Use of Non-Federal Rural Land, 2007

In thousands of acres

Category	State	U.S.	State Share
Total rural land	45,133.7	1,373,658.8	3.29%
Cropland	20,693.9	357,023.5	5.80%
CRP[1] land	1,453.8	32,850.2	4.43%
Pastureland	3,759.8	118,615.7	3.17%
Rangeland	0.0	409,119.4	0.00%
Forest land	16,541.2	406,410.4	4.07%
Other rural land	2,685.0	49,639.6	5.41%

Note: (1) Conservation Reserve Program was created to assist private landowners in converting highly erodible cropland to vegetative cover.
Source: U.S. Department of Agriculture, Natural Resources Conservation Service, 2007 National Resources Inventory

Farms and Crop Acreage, 2012

Category	State	U.S.	State Share
Farms (in thousands)	79.4	2,170.0	3.66%
Acres (in millions)	26.8	914.0	2.93%
Acres per farm	337.5	421.2	–

Source: U.S. Department of Agriculture, National Agricultural Statistical Service, Quick Stats, 2012 Survey Data

HEALTH AND MEDICAL CARE

Medical Professionals, 2012

Profession	State Number	U.S. Number	State Share	State Rate[1]	U.S. Rate[1]
Physicians[2]	16,474	894,637	1.84%	308.1	287.1
Dentists	3,444	193,587	1.78%	64.4	62.1
Podiatrists	184	17,469	1.05%	3.4	5.6
Optometrists	838	45,638	1.84%	15.7	14.6
Chiropractors	2,543	77,494	3.28%	47.6	24.9

Note: (1) Rates are per 100,000 population; (2) Includes total, active Doctors of Osteopathic Medicine and Doctors of Medicine in 2011.
Source: U.S. Department of Health and Human Services, Bureau of Health Professions, Area Health Resource File, 2012-2013

Health Insurance Coverage, 2011

Category	State	U.S.
Total persons covered	4,798,000	260,214,000
Total persons not covered	487,000	48,613,000
Percent not covered	9.2%	15.7%
Children under age 18 covered	1,193,000	67,143,000
Children under age 18 not covered	82,000	6,965,000
Percent of children not covered	6.4%	9.4%

Source: U.S. Census Bureau, Current Population Survey, 2012 Annual Social and Economic Supplement

HIV, STD, and Tuberculosis Cases and Rates, 2011

Disease	State Cases	State Rate[1]	U.S. Rate[1]
Chlamydia	16,902	318.7	457.6
Gonorrhea	2,284	43.1	104.2
HIV diagnosis	318	7.2	15.8
HIV, stage 3 (AIDS)	215	4.9	10.3
Syphilis, early latent	121	2.3	4.3
Syphilis, primary/secondary	139	2.6	4.5
Tuberculosis	137	2.6	3.4

Note: (1) Rates are per 100,000 population
Source: Centers for Disease Control and Prevention

Cigarette Smoking, 2011

Category	State	U.S.
Adults who are current smokers	19.1%	21.2%
Adults who smoke everyday	13.2%	15.4%
Adults who smoke some days	5.9%	5.7%
Adults who are former smokers	26.2%	25.1%
Adults who never smoked	54.7%	52.9%

Source: Centers for Disease Control and Prevention, Behaviorial Risk Factor Surveillance System, Tobacco Use, 2011

HOUSING

Home Ownership Rates, 1995–2012

Area	1995	2000	2005	2010	2012
State	73.3%	76.1%	76.5%	72.6%	72.0%
U.S.	64.7%	67.4%	68.9%	66.9%	65.4%

Source: U.S. Census Bureau, Housing Vacancies and Homeownership, Annual Statistics

Home Sales, 2000–2010
In thousands of units

Year	State Sales	U.S. Sales	State Share
2000	96.3	5,174	1.86%
2002	122.6	5,632	2.18%
2004	137.4	6,778	2.03%
2006	115.4	6,478	1.78%
2008	96.2	4,913	1.96%
2010	89.7	4,908	1.83%

Note: Units include single-family homes, condos and co-ops
Source: National Association of Realtors, Real Estate Outlook, Market Trends & Insights

Value of Owner-Occupied Homes, 2011

Value	Total Units in State	Percent of Total, State	Percent of Total, U.S.
Less than $50,000	93,527	6.1%	8.8%
$50,000 to $99,000	165,280	10.8%	16.0%
$100,000 to $149,000	260,784	17.1%	16.5%
$150,000 to $199,000	336,656	22.1%	15.4%
$200,000 to $299,000	373,386	24.5%	18.2%
$300,000 to $499,000	214,508	14.1%	15.2%
$500,000 to $999,000	67,978	4.5%	7.9%
$1,000,000 or more	13,330	0.9%	2.0%
Median value	–	$183,500	$173,600

Source: U.S. Census Bureau, 2011 American Community Survey 1-Year Estimates

EDUCATION

School Enrollment, 2011

Educational Level	Students Enrolled in State	Percent of Total, State	Percent of Total, U.S.
All levels	1,423,499	100.0%	100.0%
Nursery school, preschool	93,785	6.6%	6.0%
Kindergarten	72,448	5.1%	5.1%
Elementary (grades 1–8)	562,788	39.5%	39.5%
Secondary (grades 9–12)	295,125	20.7%	20.7%
College or graduate school	399,353	28.1%	28.7%

Note: Figures cover the population 3 years and over enrolled in school
Source: U.S. Census Bureau, 2011 American Community Survey 1-Year Estimates

Educational Attainment, 2011

Highest Level of Education	State	U.S.
High school diploma	92.0%	85.9%
Bachelor's degree	32.4%	28.5%
Graduate/Professional degree	10.5%	10.6%

Note: Figures cover the population 25 years and over
Source: U.S. Census Bureau, 2011 American Community Survey 1-Year Estimates

Public College Finances, FY 2012

Category	State	U.S.
Full-time equivalent enrollment (FTE)[1]	214,055	11,548,974
Educational appropriations per FTE[2]	$4,607	$5,906
Net tuition revenue per FTE[3]	$7,589	$5,189
Total educational revenue per FTE[4]	$12,196	$11,043

(1) Full-time equivalent enrollment equates student credit hours to full time, academic year students, but excludes medical students; (2) Educational appropriations measure state and local support available for public higher education operating expenses including ARRA funds and excludes appropriations for independent institutions, financial aid for students attending independent institutions, research, hospitals, and medical education; (3) Net tuition revenue is calculated by taking the gross amount of tuition and fees, less state and institutional financial aid, tuition waivers or discounts, and medical student tuition and fees. Net tuition revenue used for capital debt service is included in the net tuition revenue figures; (4) Total educational revenue is the sum of educational appropriations and net tuition excluding net tuition revenue used for capital debt service.
Source: State Higher Education Executive Officers, State Higher Education Finance FY 2012

TRANSPORTATION AND TRAVEL

Motor Vehicle Registrations and Drivers Licenses, 2011

Vehicle Type	State	U.S.	State Share
Automobiles[1]	2,248,879	125,656,528	1.79%
Buses	17,519	666,064	2.63%
Trucks	2,402,947	118,455,587	2.03%
Motorcycles	240,289	8,437,502	2.85%
Drivers licenses	3,306,139	211,874,649	1.56%

Note: Motor vehicle registrations include private, commercial, and publicly-owned vehicles; (1) Includes taxicabs
Source: U.S. Department of Transportation, Federal Highway Administration

Domestic Travel Expenditures, 2009
In millions of dollars

Category	State	U.S.	State Share
Travel expenditures	$9,887	$610,200	1.62%

Note: Figures represent U.S. spending on domestic overnight trips and day trips of 50 miles or more, one way, away from home. Excludes spending by foreign visitors.
Source: U.S. Travel Association, Impact of Travel on State Economies, 2009

Retail Gasoline Prices, 2013

Gasoline Grade	State Average	U.S. Average
Regular	$3.62	$3.65
Mid	$3.70	$3.81
Premium	$3.94	$3.98
Diesel	$3.86	$3.88
Excise tax[1]	47.0 cents	49.4 cents

Note: Gasoline prices as of 7/26/2013; (1) Includes state and federal excise taxes and other state taxes as of July 1, 2013
Source: American Automobile Association, Daily Fuel Guage Report; American Petroleum Institute, State Motor Fuel Taxes, 2013

Public Road Length, 2011

Type	State Mileage	U.S. Mileage	State Share
Interstate highways	914	46,960	1.95%
Other highways	166	15,719	1.06%
Principal arterial	4,256	156,262	2.72%
Minor arterial	9,178	242,942	3.78%
Major collector	18,422	534,592	3.45%
Minor collector	12,031	266,357	4.52%
Local	93,735	2,814,925	3.33%
Urban	20,817	1,095,373	1.90%
Rural	117,885	2,982,383	3.95%
Total	138,702	4,077,756	3.40%

Note: Combined urban and rural road mileage equals the total of the other road types
Source: U.S. Department of Transportation, Federal Highway Administration, Public Road Length, 2011

CRIME AND LAW ENFORCEMENT

Full-Time Law Enforcement Officers, 2011

Gender	State Number	State Rate[1]	U.S. Rate[1]
Male officers	7,749	147.2	210.3
Female officers	1,040	19.8	28.1
Total officers	8,789	167.0	238.3

Note: (1) Rates are per 100,000 population
Source: Federal Bureau of Investigation, Uniform Crime Reports, Crime in the United States 2011

Prison Population, 2000–2012

Year	State Population	U.S. Population	State Share
2000	6,238	1,391,261	0.45%
2005	9,281	1,527,929	0.61%
2010	9,796	1,613,803	0.61%
2011	9,800	1,598,783	0.61%
2012	9,938	1,571,013	0.63%

Note: Figures include prisoners under the jurisdiction of state or federal correctional authorities.
Source: U.S. Department of Justice, Bureau of Justice Statistics, Prisoners in 2006, 2011, 2012 (Advance Counts)

Crime Rate, 2011
Incidents per 100,000 residents

Category	State	U.S.
Violent crimes	221.2	386.3
Murder	1.4	4.7
Forcible rape	31.1	26.8
Robbery	63.4	113.7
Aggravated assault	125.4	241.1
Property crimes	2,549.4	2,908.7
Burglary	481.3	702.2
Larceny/theft	1,915.1	1,976.9
Motor vehicle theft	153.1	229.6
All crimes	2,770.6	3,295.0

Source: Federal Bureau of Investigation, Uniform Crime Reports, Crime in the United States 2011

GOVERNMENT AND FINANCE

Local Governments by Type, 2012

Government Type	State	U.S.	State Share
All local governments	3,633	89,004	4.08%
County	87	3,031	2.87%
Municipality	854	19,522	4.37%
Town/Township	1,785	16,364	10.91%
Special District	569	37,203	1.53%
Ind. School District	338	12,884	2.62%

Source: U.S. Census Bureau, 2012 Census of Governments: Organization Component Preliminary Estimates

State Government Revenue, 2011
In thousands of dollars, except for per capita figures

Total revenue	**$45,684,189**
Total revenue per capita, State	$8,543
Total revenue per capita, U.S.	$7,271
General revenue	$33,451,689
Intergovernmental revenue	$9,819,493
Taxes	$18,952,919
General sales	$4,657,395
Selective sales	$3,578,288
License taxes	$1,113,909
Individual income taxes	$7,482,396
Corporate income taxes	$1,003,657
Other taxes	$1,117,274
Current charges	$2,782,199
Miscellaneous general revenue	$1,897,078
Utility revenue	$0
Liquor store revenue	$0
Insurance trust revenue[1]	$12,232,500

Note: (1) Within insurance trust revenue, net earnings of state retirement systems is a calculated statistic, and thus can be positive or negative. Net earnings is the sum of earnings on investments plus gains on investments minus losses on investments.
Source: U.S. Census Bureau, 2011 Annual Survey of State Government Finances

State Government Expenditures, 2011

In thousands of dollars, except for per capita figures

Total expenditure	$38,488,350
Total expenditure per capita, State	$7,198
Total expenditure per capita, U.S.	$6,427
Intergovernmental expenditure	$11,102,449
Direct expenditure	$27,385,901
Current operation	$18,649,448
Capital outlay	$1,617,046
Insurance benefits and repayments	$5,701,467
Assistance and subsidies	$825,431
Interest on debt	$592,509
Utility expenditure	$116,378
Liquor store expenditure	$0
Insurance trust expenditure	$5,701,467

Source: U.S. Census Bureau, 2011 Annual Survey of State Government Finances

State Government General Expenditures by Function, 2011

In thousands of dollars

Education	$12,406,335
Public welfare	$10,872,302
Hospitals	$288,254
Health	$633,406
Highways	$2,565,152
Police protection	$396,442
Correction	$508,237
Natural resources	$690,585
Parks and recreation	$280,770
Governmental administration	$905,382
Interest on general debt	$592,509
Other and unallocable	$2,531,131

Source: U.S. Census Bureau, 2011 Annual Survey of State Government Finances

State Government Finances, Cash and Debt, 2011

In thousands of dollars, except for per capita figures

Debt at end of fiscal year	
State, total	$12,896,921
State, per capita	$2,412
U.S., per capita	$3,635
Cash and security holdings	
State, total	$60,605,879
State, per capita	$11,334
U.S., per capita	$11,759

Source: U.S. Census Bureau, 2011 Annual Survey of State Government Finances

POLITICS

Composition of the Senate, 1995–2013

Congress (Year)	State/U.S	Dem	Rep	Total
104th (1995)	State delegates	1	1	2
	Total U.S.	48	52	100
105th (1997)	State delegates	0	2	2
	Total U.S.	45	55	100
106th (1999)	State delegates	1	1	2
	Total U.S.	45	55	100
107th (2001)	State delegates	2	0	2
	Total U.S.	50	50	100
108th (2003)	State delegates	1	1	2
	Total U.S.	48	51	100
109th (2005)	State delegates	1	1	2
	Total U.S.	44	55	100
110th (2007)	State delegates	1	1	2
	Total U.S.	49	49	100
111th (2009)	State delegates	2	0	2
	Total U.S.	57	41	100
112th (2011)	State delegates	2	0	2
	Total U.S.	51	47	100
113th (2013)	State delegates	2	0	2
	Total U.S.	54	45	100

Note: Figures are for the starts of first sessions; Totals include Democratic (Dem) and Republican (Rep) members as well as vacancies and seats held by independent party members
Source: U.S. Congress, Congressional Directory

Composition of the House of Representatives, 1995–2013

Congress (Year)	State/U.S	Dem	Rep	Total
104th (1995)	State delegates	6	2	8
	Total U.S.	204	230	435
105th (1997)	State delegates	6	2	8
	Total U.S.	207	226	435
106th (1999)	State delegates	6	2	8
	Total U.S.	211	223	435
107th (2001)	State delegates	5	3	8
	Total U.S.	212	221	435
108th (2003)	State delegates	4	4	8
	Total U.S.	205	229	435
109th (2005)	State delegates	4	4	8
	Total U.S.	202	231	435
110th (2007)	State delegates	5	3	8
	Total U.S.	233	198	435
111th (2009)	State delegates	5	3	8
	Total U.S.	256	178	435
112th (2011)	State delegates	4	4	8
	Total U.S.	193	242	435
113th (2013)	State delegates	5	3	8
	Total U.S.	201	234	435

Note: Figures are for the starts of first sessions; Totals include Democratic (Dem) and Republican (Rep) members as well as vacancies and seats held by independent party members
Source: U.S. Congress, Congressional Directory

Composition of State Legislature, 2004–2013

Year	Democrats	Republicans	Total
State Senate			
2004	35	31	67
2005	35	31	67
2006	35	31	67
2007	44	23	67
2008	45	22	67
2009	46	21	67
2010	46	21	67
2011	30	37	67
2012	30	37	67
2013	39	28	67
State House			
2004	53	81	134
2005	66	68	134
2006	66	68	134
2007	85	49	134
2008	85	48	134
2009	87	47	134
2010	87	47	134
2011	62	72	134
2012	62	72	134
2013	73	61	134

Note: Totals may include minor party members and vacancies
Source: The Council of State Governments, State Legislatures

Voter Participation in Presidential Elections, 1980–2012

Year	Voting-eligible State Population	State Voter Turnout Rate	U.S. Voter Turnout Rate
1980	2,882,406	71.2	54.2
1984	2,982,015	69.9	55.2
1988	3,087,194	67.9	52.8
1992	3,187,255	73.7	58.1
1996	3,319,509	66.1	51.7
2000	3,506,432	69.5	54.2
2004	3,609,185	78.4	60.1
2008	3,740,142	77.8	61.6
2012	3,876,752	75.7	58.2

Note: All figures are based on the voting-eligible population which excludes person ineligible to vote such as non-citizens, felons (depending on state law), and mentally-incapacitated persons. U.S. figures include the overseas eligible population (including military personnel).
Source: McDonald, Michael P., United States Election Project, Presidential Voter Turnout Rates, 1980–2012

Governors Since Statehood

Henry H. Sibley (D)	1858-1860
Alexander Ramsey (R)	(r) 1860-1863
Henry A. Swift (R)	1863-1864
Stephen Miller (R)	1864-1868
William R. Marshall (R)	1868-1870
Horace Austin (R)	1870-1874
Cushman K. Davis (R)	1874-1876
John S. Pillsbury (R)	1876-1882
Lucius F. Hubbard (R)	1882-1887
Andrew R. McGill (R)	1887-1889
William R. Merriam (R)	1889-1893
Knute Nelson (R)	(r) 1893-1895
David M. Clough (R)	1895-1899
John Lind (D)	1899-1901
Samuel R. Van Sant (R)	1901-1905
John A. Johnson (D)	(d) 1905-1909
Adolph O. Eberhart (R)	1909-1915
Winfield S. Hammond (D)	(d) 1915
Joseph A. A. Burnquist (R)	1915-1921
Jacob A. O. Preus (R)	1921-1925
Theodore Christianson (R)	1925-1931
Floyd B. Olson (O)	(d) 1931-1936
Hjalmar Petersen (O)	1936-1937
Elmer A. Benson (O)	1937-1939
Harold E. Stassen (R)	(r) 1939-1943
Edward J. Thye (R)	1943-1947
Luther W. Youngdahl (R)	(r) 1947-1951
Clyde Elmer Anderson (R)	1951-1955
Orville L. Freeman (O)	1955-1961
Elmer L. Anderson (R)	1961-1963
Karl F. Rolvaag (O)	1963-1967
Harold P. LeVander (R)	1967-1971
Wendell R. Anderson (O)	(r) 1971-1976
Rudy Perpich (O)	1976-1979
Albert H. Quie (R)	1979-1983
Rudolph Perpich (O)	1983-1991
Arne Carlson (R)	1991-1999
Jesse Ventura (O)	1999-2003
Tim Pawlenty (R)	2003-2011
Mark Dayton (D)	2011-2015

Note: (D) Democrat; (R) Republican; (O) Other party; (r) resigned; (d) died in office; (i) removed from office

Mississippi

Location: Gulf coast

Area and rank: 46,914 square miles (121,506 square kilometers); 48,434 square miles (125,444 square kilometers) including water; thirty-first largest state in area

Coastline: 44 miles (71 kilometers) on the Gulf of Mexico

Shoreline: 359 miles (578 kilometers)

Population and rank: 2,984,926 (2012 estimate); thirty-first largest state in population

Capital and largest city: Jackson (173,514 people in 2010 census)

Became territory: April 7, 1798

Entered Union and rank: December 10, 1817; twentieth state

Present constitution adopted: 1890
Counties: 82

State name: Mississippi takes its name from an Indian expression for "father of waters"

State nickname: Magnolia State

Motto: *Virtute et armis* (By valor and arms)

State capitol building in Jackson. (Mississippi Division of Tourism Development)

State flag: Modified Confederate flag in upper left corner, over red, white, and blue stripes

Highest point: Woodall Mountain—806 feet (246 meters)

Lowest point: Gulf of Mexico—sea level

Highest recorded temperature: 115 degrees Fahrenheit (46 degrees Celsius)—Holly Springs, 1930

Lowest recorded temperature: –19 degrees Fahrenheit (–28 degrees Celsius)—Corinth, 1966

State song: "Go, Mississippi"

State tree: Magnolia

State flower: Magnolia

State bird: Mockingbird

State fish: Largemouth or black bass

Mississippi History

Mississippi's climate has greatly influenced its history. Located in the Deep South of the United States, just above the Gulf of Mexico, Mississippi has long, humid summers and generally short, mild winters. Consequently the growing season throughout the state is more than two hundred days long. In the far South, the growing season can be as long as 280 days. This long growing period, combined with abundant rain, has made agriculture a prominent economic activity. Outside the hilly region in the north, the soils are finely textured, composed of clays, sands, and other components.

In the nineteenth century, when cotton became a major export crop for the United States, climate and soil tended to make the state heavily dependent on production of cotton. The prominence of cotton, a plantation crop requiring heavy investment of labor, contributed to the development of slavery as a major feature of life before the Civil War. Slavery gave Mississippi a large African American population, and the legacy of slavery produced racial inequality and troubled race relations. Continuing reliance on agriculture also tended to make Mississippi one of the least industrialized and poorest states in the United States throughout the twentieth century.

Early History. During prehistoric times, the area of Mississippi was populated by people who lived in highly organized farming societies. These societies are known as the Mound Builders, after the great ceremonial earth mounds they constructed. The Mound Builders may be divided into the people of the Hopewell culture, who flourished from about the first century until about 800 C.E., and the people of the Mississippian culture, who lived from about 800 C.E. until about 1500. When the earliest French settlers arrived in what is now the southwestern part of Mississippi, the Natchez Indians were still building mounds, which were used for burials and as sites for public buildings.

By the time of European settlement in this area of North America, there were three major Native American nations in the Mississippi region, as well as a host of small Native American groups. The nation of the Choctaw was the largest of the three. The Choctaw controlled most of central and southern Mississippi. In southwestern Mississippi, the Natchez nation was dominant. In the northern part of what is now the state of Mississippi, the Chickasaw were the largest and most powerful group.

The Choctaw were an agricultural people who lived in thatched-roof cabins made of mud and bark. The Chickasaw were closely related to the Choctaw, and both groups

Modern Mississippi riverboat recalls the great age of nintheenth century steamboating on the Mississippi River. (PhotoDisc)

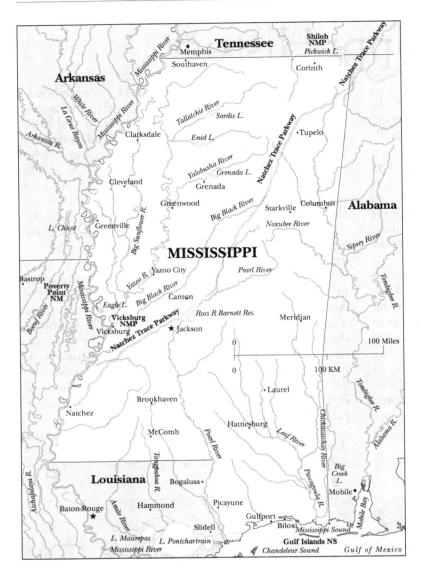

modern state of Mississippi. At the end of the seventeenth century, the French explorer René-Robert Cavelier, sieur de La Salle, journeyed down the Mississippi River to its mouth and claimed all of the land drained by the Mississippi in the name of France. La Salle named this huge expanse of territory Louisiana, in honor of King Louis XIV of France.

After the French and Indian War between France and Great Britain, from 1754 to 1763, France ceded all of the French land east of the Mississippi River to Great Britain. Although the British attempted to reserve the land of northern Mississippi for Native Americans and forbade white settlement in that region, white Ameri-cans were drawn to the region for its rich soil. In 1783, the Spanish, who had acquired the Louisiana territories from France, took southern Mississippi from the British. In 1798, Spain recognized the northern part of modern Mississippi as territory of the new United States. That same year, the U.S. Congress organized this region as the Mississippi Territory.

American colonists in West Florida, the areas of modern Louisiana and southern Mississippi still under Spanish rule, revolted against Spain in 1810. West Florida became independent briefly, then it was annexed to the United States. In 1817, Mississippi was admitted to the United States as the twentieth state.

Cotton and the Civil War. In 1800, there were only 7,600 settlers in Mississippi. By 1820 this number had grown to 75,448. Ten years later, the U.S. Census put the state's population at 136,621. The 1860 census showed a population of 791,305. Much of this rapid growth was due to the immigration of farmers who were looking for land to grow cotton. Cotton was Mississippi's most important crop, and, by the eve of the Civil War, Mississippi produced more cotton than any other state. Although only a small minority of the whites in the state were large plantation owners, owners of the big plantations held most of the economic and political power. Reliance on slave labor meant that the state had a huge slave population, with slaves of African descent outnumbering whites. Because there were so many people held in bondage, Mississippi's slave laws were among the harshest in the South.

About eighty thousand Mississippians fought for the Confederacy, and almost one-third of them died in the Civil War. Many counties in Mississippi also saw internal civil wars, as small farmers who opposed secession organized themselves to fight against the Confederacy. Fighting ravaged the state, and the forces of U.S. general

spoke languages of the Muskogean family, but they were traditional enemies before European settlement. The Natchez were the largest and most unified group in the area. However, war broke out between the Natchez and French settlers during the early eighteenth century. The French joined with the Choctaw to destroy the Natchez in 1729. Some Natchez were sold into slavery, and others were absorbed into other tribes. The Choctaw and Chickasaw continued to live in the Mississippi region, adopting many of the ways of European society. By 1842 though, the U.S. government, under pressure from land-hungry white settlers, forced most of the Native Americans of the Southeast to relocate to Indian Territory in Oklahoma.

Exploration and Settlement. The Spanish and the French were the first Europeans to explore the territory of the lower Mississippi River. From 1539 to 1543, the Spaniard Hernando de Soto led an expedition that is believed to have crossed the northern part of the

William T. Sherman were especially destructive in their efforts to defeat the rebellious southerners.

The Legacy of War and Slavery. Mississippi's history of slavery and civil war led to continuing problems of racial inequality. During Reconstruction, the period following the Civil War when northern troops occupied the defeated lands of the Confederacy, the state's freed slaves entered political life, although few had sufficient education or experience to hold more than minor offices.

By 1875, though, the whites of Mississippi began to retake power. They instituted segregation and, by the early twentieth century, excluded African Americans from public life by laws and terrorism. In some of the counties of the Mississippi Delta, the region where the Mississippi and Yazoo Rivers join together, 80 to 90 percent of the people were African American. Most of them worked as sharecroppers, farmers working the land for a share of the crop, on land owned by whites.

As a consequence of this legacy of slavery, Mississippi became a central battleground of the Civil Rights movement. In 1964, black and white college students working with civil rights organizations traveled to the state for Freedom Summer, to provide educational opportunities to local African Americans and to encourage minority voter registration. After the passage of the Civil Rights Act of 1964 and the Voting Rights Act of 1965, segregation became illegal in the United States, and black Mississippians began to enter public life. By the 1990's, the Mississippi legislature had the highest percentage of African Americans of any state legislature in the nation. Nevertheless, racial prejudice and poverty in Mississippi's black population continued to be problems.

Economy and Population After the War. Mississippi continued to have an economy based on agriculture well into the twentieth century. However, declining prices for cotton and other agricultural goods contributed to making it the poorest state in the nation by many measures. In 1936, Governor Hugh L. White began an effort to bring industry into the state with his Balance Agriculture with Industry (BAWI) program. World War II helped industrialization, especially in the shipbuilding industry along the Gulf Coast.

Modern machine harvesting cotton, the product on which Mississippi's agricultural economy was built during the nineteenth century. (Mississippi Division of Tourism Development)

The period following World War II saw rapid industrialization. By 1990 less than 3 percent of Mississippi's labor force were employed in agriculture, while almost 23 percent were employed in factories. The state's largest areas of employment during the late twentieth century were lumber and wood products, furniture, food products, and the manufacture of clothing.

With the disappearance of agricultural jobs, many black Mississippians left the state. The state's African American population declined from 60 percent of all Mississippians in 1900 to 36 percent in 1990. Most small towns and villages grew smaller or even disappeared after World War II. Most of the state's population growth in this period took place in the urban areas of Jackson, Biloxi-Gulfport, and Pascagoula-Moss Point. By 1990 nearly half of all the people in the state lived in cities.

History and Tradition. Despite economic and social progress in the state, issues from the past arose from time to time as a new decade began. When students at the University of Mississippi waved Confederate flags at football games in 2000, the university banned them. Students took the university to court for the right to wave the flags, but a state appeals court sided with the university. The Confederate flag issue resurfaced the following year in a referendum, and two-thirds of the state's voters chose to approve retaining the symbol of the Old South as the official flag of the state. At that, the National Association for the Advancement of Colored People (NAACP) announced a boycott of the state.

In 2001, another public issue tugged at the public's sense of traditionalism. Governor Ronnie Musgrove signed a law requiring schools to show the motto In God We Trust in classrooms, auditoriums, and cafeterias. In response, the American Civil Liberties Union (ACLU) threatened to sue. Backers of the law countered that the display of the motto was justified by its being a national motto of the United States, found on U.S. currency.

In April of the same year, Mississippi reached a $500 million settlement to end a twenty-six-year-old class action suit to desegregate the state's public colleges and universities. Plaintiffs said that the state's three historically black colleges were chronically underfunded. Nearly all of the settlement funds went to those colleges.

Early in December, 2002, Mississippi senator Trent Lott, majority leader in the Senate, raised a national furor for remarks he made at an event for South Carolina senator Strom Thurmond. Lott said that the nation "wouldn't have had all these problems over the years" if it had elected Thurmond in 1948, when the South Carolina senator ran for president on a segregationist platform. The torrent of criticism that followed caused Lott to make profuse public apologies, calling Mississippi segregation "wrong and wicked." Nevertheless, just before Christmas he resigned as Senate majority leader.

Another echo of the state's racist past was heard when, in 2003, a seventy-two-year-old man, Ernest Avants, was convicted in federal court of aiding and abetting the murder of a black sharecropper, sixty-seven-year-old Ben Chester White, in 1966. Avants had been tried and found innocent in 1967, but the case was reopened in 1999 when it was found that the murder had taken place on federal land. Avants was sentenced to life in prison and died there in June, 2004.

Hurricane Katrina. The state's coast suffered catastrophic damage when Hurricane Katrina made landfall on August 29, 2005. The Category 3 storm, with sustained winds of 120 miles per hour, was responsible for the deaths of 238 people; 67 remained missing. The hurricane's damage in Mississippi, which occurred throughout the state, amounted to billions of dollars. Officials determined that 90 percent of the buildings and other structures within one-half mile of the coast were destroyed.

Politics. Mississippi remains a somewhat enigmatic state when outside analysts attempt to explain the voting patterns of the state. With African Americans constituting 37 percent of the electorate, and with the state being among those highest in receiving federal money, the interests of the population would appear to favor voting for liberal candidates committed to federal expenditure. However, a wide variety of opinion polls rank Mississippi as the single most conservative state, and the most religious state in the nation.

Voters were torn in the 2012 election, because Mitt Romney, as a Mormon, was unpalatable to born-again Christians who viewed the Church of Latter-day Saints as a cult. On the other hand, while Barack Obama attracted the African American vote, his political positions ran strictly against the conservatism of the majority of Mississippians. In the 2012 election, Romney and his running mate, Paul Ryan, won Mississippi with 55.3 percent of the popular vote to Obama's and Biden's 43.8 percent. Even so, Mississippi was one of only six states in which Obama gained in proportion over his 2008 vote. Analysts attributed the slight increase to the fact that black voters turned out in higher numbers in 2012.

Deepwater Horizon. Although Mississippi has a relative short coastline on the Gulf of Mexico, only 44 miles, the shortest of those states impacted by the 2010 Deepwater Horizon explosion, the state has been active in supporting citizens' claims for damage. Senator Roger Wicker from Mississippi (appointed in 2007 to fill out the term of Trent Lott, and re-elected in 2008 and 2012), served on the Senate Committee on Commerce, Science and Transportation, which included a focus on ocean pollution issues. Wicker took an active part in ensuring that Mississippi citizens received reimbursement for damages resulting from the oil spill.

Carl L. Bankston III
Updated by the Editor

Mississippi Time Line

1500's	Mound Builder cultures flourish along the Mississippi River and in other areas of eastern North America
1540	Spanish explorer Hernando de Soto's expedition enters the northern part of modern Mississippi.
1682	René-Robert Cavalier, sieur de La Salle, travels down the Mississippi to its mouth and claims all lands along the river in the name of France.
1699	French found Biloxi, the first permanent European settlement in Mississippi.
1729	French and the Choctaw together destroy the Natchez nation.
1763	Great Britain takes control of the Mississippi region after the French and Indian Wars.
Apr. 7, 1798	Spain recognizes northern Mississippi as part of the United States; U.S. Congress organizes the Mississippi Territory.
1816	Chickasaw sign a treaty ceding their lands to the United States.
Dec. 10, 1817	Mississippi is admitted to the United States as the twentieth state.
1822	Capital of Mississippi is moved from Columbia to Jackson.
1830	Choctaw sign a treaty ceding their lands in Mississippi to the United States.
1844	University of Mississippi is chartered by the state legislature.
Jan. 9, 1861	Mississippi is the second state to secede from the Union, joining the Confederacy.
Apr. 12, 1861	Civil War begins when Confederate forces attack Fort Sumter, South Carolina.
Feb. 22, 1862	Former U.S. senator Jefferson Davis of Mississippi is made Confederate president.
July 4, 1863	Vicksburg, Mississippi, falls to Union forces.
Feb. 23, 1870	Mississippi is readmitted to the Union.
1875	Democratic Party takes control of the Mississippi legislature from the Republicans, essentially ending Reconstruction in Mississippi.
1890	Mississippi legislature adopts a constitution that formally establishes racial segregation in the state and effectively takes the vote away from most black citizens.
1908	Mississippi state legislature prohibits the sale and consumption of alcohol.
1926	Public schools are forbidden to teach evolution.
Apr. 21, 1927	Mississippi River floods and devastates many areas of Mississippi.
1936	Governor Hugh L. White begins attempting to industrialize Mississippi with the Balance Agriculture with Industry (BAWI) program.
Apr. 5, 1955	Governor White signs a bill providing fines and a jail sentence for white students who attend schools with African Americans.
Sept. 28, 1962	U.S. Court of Appeals orders Mississippi governor Ross R. Barnett to stop interfering with desegregation at the University of Mississippi.
Oct. 1, 1962	James Meredith is admitted to the University of Mississippi after riots that result in two deaths.
June 12, 1963	Medgar N. Evers, a Mississippi official of the National Association for the Advancement of Colored People, is shot to death.
June 1964	Three young civil rights workers are murdered in Mississippi.
1969	Charles Evers, brother of Medgar Evers, becomes mayor of Fayette, making him the first black mayor in Mississippi.
1973	U.S. Supreme Court rules unconstitutional a Mississippi law enabling the state to purchase textbooks and distribute them free to segregated private schools.
1978	Mississippi elects its first Republican senator since Reconstruction.
1983	Unemployment is at a record high of 13.8 percent.
1988	Three southern governors, including Mississippi's, agree to improve conditions in the extremely impoverished Mississippi Delta.
1991	Kirk Fordice is elected the first Republican governor in Mississippi since Reconstruction.
June 30, 1992	U.S. Supreme Court rules that Mississippi has still not sufficiently erased segregation from its state university system.
2000	University of Mississippi wins law suit allowing it to ban the waving of Confederate flags at football games.
2001	Mississippians vote in referendum to retain the Confederate flag as the state's official flag.

Jan. 2001	Byron De La Beckwith, convicted in 1994 of murdering civil rights activist Medgar Evers in 1963, dies in prison at the age of eighty.
Dec. 20, 2002	Mississippi senator Trent Lott resigns as majority leader of the U.S. Senate after furor erupts at his comments about the segregationist policies advocated in 1948 by Senator Strom Thurmond of South Carolina.
Feb. 2, 2003	Ernest Avants is convicted in Jackson of the 1966 murder of black sharecropper Ben Chester White and is later sentenced to life in prison.
Aug. 29, 2005	Hurricane Katrina savages Mississippi's Gulf Coast, with 238 dead, 67 missing, and billions of dollars in damage.
2012	Though having less than 50 miles of coastline, Mississippi is damaged by the Deepwater Horizon catastrophe in which an offshore oil rig exploded, resulting in an oil spill of 4.9 million barrels.

Notes for Further Study

Published Sources. One of the most readable introductions to Mississippi history and the legacy of this history is Anthony Walton's *Mississippi: An American Journey* (1997). Walton, from a Mississippi family, weaves the story of his own family together with the history of the state and gives a moving and sympathetic account of Mississippi's past and present. *Mississippi: A Documentary History* (2003) by Bradley G. Bond also offers a scholarly survey of the state's history. Those interested in Mississippi's pre-European past would do well to consult *Archeology of Mississippi* (1992) by Calvin S. Brown. *Mississippi Women: Their Histories, Their Lives* (2003), edited by Martha H. Swain, Elizabeth Anne Payne, and Marjorie Julian Spruill, brings together seventeen biographies of historically important women.

Readers interested in the Civil War period will want to look at *A Mississippi Rebel in the Army of Northern Virginia: The Civil War Memoirs of Private David Holt* (1995), written by war veteran David Holt and edited by Thomas D. Cockrell and Michael B. Ballard. Holt's memoirs begin well before the Civil War, so they provide an excellent view of middle-class life in Mississippi in the antebellum years. *Jefferson Davis: The Man and His Hour* (1991) by William C. Davis is a good biography of the Mississippian who led the Confederacy. *Jefferson Davis: The Essential Writings* (2003), edited by William J. Cooper, brings together Davis's letters and speeches.

The literature on the civil rights era in Mississippi is vast. Eric R. Burner's *And Gently He Shall Lead Them: Robert Parris Moses and Civil Rights in Mississippi* (1994) tells the story of the organization of civil rights activists in Mississippi by relating the story of one of the central organizers. *Have No Fear: The Charles Evers Story* (1996) is the autobiography of Charles Evers, a prominent black Mississippi civil rights activist and brother of Medgar Evers, who was murdered by a white supremacist in 1963. *I've Got the Light of Freedom: The Organizing Tradition and the Mississippi Freedom Struggle* (1995) by Charles M. Payne uses archives and interviews with participants in the Civil Rights movement to present a social history of the struggle. J. Todd Moye, in his use of extensive oral history interviews and archival research, provides a window into how struggles over civil rights and democracy in Mississippi played out against national developments in the Civil Rights movement with *Let the People Decide: Black Freedom and White Resistance Movements in Sunflower County, Mississippi* (2004). Paul Hendrickson's award-winning book *Sons of Mississippi: A Story of Race and Its Legacy* (2003) uses a racist event that occurred in 1962 to expose the wider issues surrounding race in the state.

Web Resources. One of the best online sources for general information about Mississippi is the home page of the state (www.state.ms.us). This offers connections to all of the Mississippi state government Web sites, sites for federal government officials and agencies in Mississippi, educational institution home pages, and a variety of other sites. For students of state government, the Mississippi Legislature site (www.ls.state.ms.us/) provides links to elected officials, the legislative calendar, and a good graphic showing how a bill becomes a law in Mississippi. For outdoor enthusiasts, the Mississippi Wildlife, Fisheries, and Parks site (www.mdwfp.com/) has information on a range of recreational activities and natural attractions. Those interested in detailed information about Mississippi history should go to the site of the Mississippi Department of Archives and History (www.mdah.state.ms.us), which gives material on historical landmarks in the state, as well as genealogical records and primary historical sources. The Visit Mississippi site (www.visitmississippi.org/) has an extensive and well-designed collection of historical information, including links to the state's experiences with the Civil War and the Civil Rights movement, as well as narratives on the Native American and African American heritage within the region.

Counties

County	2012 Population	Pop. Rank	Land Area (sq. miles)	Area Rank
Adams	32,122	26	462.41	57
Alcorn	37,164	20	400.04	82
Amite	12,957	62	730.10	12
Attala	19,157	50	734.98	11
Benton	8,730	76	406.62	78
Bolivar	33,904	25	876.57	2
Calhoun	14,843	60	586.57	36
Carroll	10,423	70	628.24	30
Chickasaw	17,416	54	501.78	48
Choctaw	8,346	77	418.18	69

County	2012 Population	Pop. Rank	Land Area (sq. miles)	Area Rank
Claiborne	9,349	74	487.41	51
Clarke	16,556	55	691.55	22
Clay	20,427	47	410.08	74
Coahoma	25,709	38	552.44	43
Copiah	28,955	30	777.24	6
Covington	19,607	48	413.79	72
DeSoto	166,234	3	476.15	53
Forrest	76,894	9	466.31	56
Franklin	7,918	78	563.78	42
George	22,930	42	478.71	52

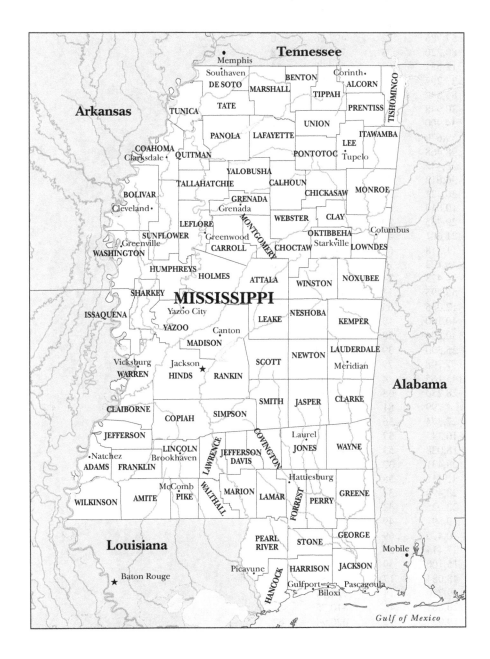

County	2012 Population	Pop. Rank	Land Area (sq. miles)	Area Rank
Greene	14,311	61	712.76	16
Grenada	21,682	44	422.11	66
Hancock	45,255	18	473.75	54
Harrison	194,029	2	573.99	40
Hinds	248,643	1	869.74	3
Holmes	18,796	52	756.70	10
Humphreys	9,189	75	418.49	68
Issaquena	1,386	82	413.05	73
Itawamba	23,340	40	532.79	45
Jackson	140,298	5	722.75	14
Jasper	16,523	56	676.24	25
Jefferson	7,638	80	519.93	46
Jefferson Davis	12,032	66	408.44	76
Jones	68,641	10	694.80	21
Kemper	10,335	71	766.18	8
Lafayette	49,495	15	631.71	29
Lamar	57,786	12	497.06	50
Lauderdale	80,220	8	703.63	18
Lawrence	12,551	63	430.67	64
Leake	23,297	41	583.00	38
Lee	85,042	7	449.95	61
Leflore	30,948	27	592.54	33
Lincoln	34,900	23	586.11	37
Lowndes	59,670	11	505.51	47
Madison	98,468	6	714.51	15
Marion	26,442	37	542.38	44
Marshall	36,612	21	706.19	17
Monroe	36,421	22	765.09	9
Montgomery	10,614	68	406.98	77
Neshoba	29,785	29	570.14	41
Newton	21,601	45	578.10	39
Noxubee	11,218	67	695.14	20
Oktibbeha	48,192	16	458.20	58
Panola	34,473	24	685.14	23
Pearl River	55,295	13	810.86	4
Perry	12,086	65	647.25	26
Pike	40,100	19	409.01	75
Pontotoc	30,594	28	497.69	49
Prentiss	25,390	39	414.98	71
Quitman	7,798	79	405.01	79
Rankin	145,165	4	775.48	7
Scott	28,250	33	609.18	31
Sharkey	4,799	81	431.72	63
Simpson	27,374	36	589.16	34
Smith	16,345	57	636.25	28
Stone	18,028	53	445.48	62
Sunflower	28,431	32	697.75	19
Tallahatchie	15,111	58	645.29	27
Tate	28,490	31	404.76	80
Tippah	22,025	43	457.81	59
Tishomingo	19,591	49	424.25	65
Tunica	10,475	69	454.67	60
Union	27,414	35	415.60	70
Walthall	15,100	59	403.94	81
Warren	48,084	17	588.50	35
Washington	49,750	14	724.74	13
Wayne	20,661	46	810.75	5
Webster	10,039	72	420.94	67

County	2012 Population	Pop. Rank	Land Area (sq. miles)	Area Rank
Wilkinson	9,432	73	678.11	24
Winston	19,029	51	607.24	32
Yalobusha	12,401	64	467.13	55
Yazoo	28,195	34	922.95	1

Source: U.S. Census Bureau, 2012 Population Estimates

Cities
With 10,000 or more residents

Legal Name	2010 Population	Pop. Rank	Land Area (sq. miles)	Area Rank
Biloxi city	44,054	5	38.22	8
Brandon city	21,705	19	25.91	15
Brookhaven city	12,513	34	21.64	22
Byram city	11,489	36	18.36	26
Canton city	13,189	31	21.24	23
Clarksdale city	17,962	23	13.89	32
Cleveland city	12,334	35	7.30	41
Clinton city	25,216	11	41.82	6
Columbus city	23,640	17	22.06	21

Legal Name	2010 Population	Pop. Rank	Land Area (sq. miles)	Area Rank
Corinth city	14,573	28	30.16	12
Gautier city	18,572	21	30.23	11
Greenville city	34,400	8	26.89	14
Greenwood city	15,205	26	12.34	35
Grenada city	13,092	32	30.01	13
Gulfport city	67,793	2	55.59	2
Hattiesburg city	45,989	4	53.39	4
Hernando city	14,090	29	25.73	16
Horn Lake city	26,066	10	16.02	29

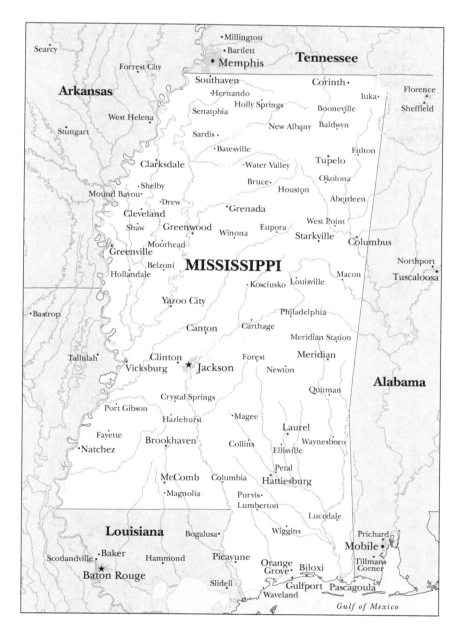

Legal Name	2010 Population	Pop. Rank	Land Area (sq. miles)	Area Rank
Indianola city	10,683	40	8.57	40
Jackson city	173,514	1	111.05	1
Laurel city	18,540	22	16.24	28
Long Beach city	14,792	27	10.00	38
Madison city	24,149	13	25.22	18
McComb city	12,790	33	11.57	36
Meridian city	41,148	6	53.74	3
Moss Point city	13,704	30	24.16	19
Natchez city	15,792	25	13.20	33
Ocean Springs city	17,442	24	11.52	37
Olive Branch city	33,484	9	36.70	9
Oxford city	18,916	20	15.83	30
Pascagoula city	22,392	18	15.38	31
Pearl city	25,092	12	23.60	20
Petal city	10,454	41	16.87	27
Picayune city	10,878	39	12.96	34
Ridgeland city	24,047	14	19.61	25
Southaven city	48,982	3	41.25	7
Starkville city	23,888	15	25.51	17
Tupelo city	34,546	7	51.14	5
Vicksburg city	23,856	16	32.98	10
West Point city	11,307	38	20.88	24
Yazoo City city	11,403	37	9.84	39

Note: CDP–Census Designated Place
Source: U.S. Census Bureau, 2010 Census

Survey Says...

This section presents current rankings from dozens of public and private sources. It shows how this state ranks in a number of critical categories, including education, job growth, cost of living, teen drivers, energy efficiency, and business environment. Sources include *Forbes, Reuters, U.S. News and World Report, CNN Money, Gallup,* and *Huffington Post.*

- CNN Money compiled a list of "Ten Most Entrepreneurial States" based on the Kauffman Index of Entrepreneurial Activity. Mississippi ranked #5 among the 50 states in 2012 for number of startups per 100,000 adult residents.
  CNN Money, June 20, 2013; money.cnn.com

- Mississippi ranked #17 in a government study measuring real gross domestic product (GDP)—the output of goods and services produced by labor and property located in the United States. The ranking is based on the percentage change compared with 2011 GDP.
  U.S. Department of Commerce, Bureau of Economic Analysis, June 2013; www.bea.gov

- Mississippi ranked #36 in a government study measuring real gross domestic product (GDP)—the output of goods and services produced by labor and property located in the United States. The ranking is based on the dollar value of its GDP.
  U.S. Department of Commerce, Bureau of Economic Analysis, June 2013; www.bea.gov

- Mississippi ranked #48 in the 17th edition of "Quality Counts; State of the States," Education Week's "report card" surveying key education indicators, policy efforts, and educational outcomes.
  Education Week, January 4, 2013 (online) and January 10, 2013 (print); www.edweek.org

- SERI (Science and Engineering Readiness Index) weighs the performance of the states' K-12 schools in preparing students in physics and calculus, the high school subjects considered most important for future scientists and engineers. Mississippi ranked #50.
  Newsletter of the Forum on Education of the American Physical Society, Summer 2011 issue; www.huffingtonpost.com, July 11, 2011; updated October 1, 2012

- Business website 24/7 Wall St. identified the states with the highest and lowest percentages of residents 25 or older with a college degree or higher. Of "America's Worst Educated States," Mississippi ranked #2 (#1 = worst).
  247wallst.com, posted October 15, 2012; consulted July 18, 2013

- MoneyRates.com ranked Mississippi #49 on its list of the best to worst states for making a living. Criteria: average income; inflation; employment prospects; and workers' Workplace Environment assessments according to the Gallup-Healthways Well-Being Index.
  www.money-rates.com, posted April 1, 2013

- *Forbes* analyzed business costs, labor supply, regulatory environment, current economic climate, growth prospects, and quality of life, to compile its "Best States for Business" rankings. Mississippi ranked #46.
  www.forbes.com. posted December 12, 2012

- The 2012 Gallup-Healthways Well-Being Index, surveyed American's opinions on economic confidence, workplace perceptions, community climate, personal choices, and health predictors to assess the "future livability" of each state. Mississippi ranked #49.
  "Utah Poised to Be the Best State to Live In," Gallup Wellbeing, www.gallup.com, August 7, 2012

- On CNBC's list of "America's Top States for Business 2013," Mississippi ranked #41. Criteria: measures of competitiveness developed with input from the National Association of Manufacturers, the Council on Competitiveness, and other business groups weighed with the states' own marketing criteria.
  www.cnbc.com, consulted July 19, 2013

- Mississippi ranked #5 on the "worst" end of the Christian Science Monitor's list of "States with the Best (and Worst) Job Growth," as indicated by year-over-year growth rates from May 2012 to May 2013.
  www.csmonitor.com, July 5, 2013

- Mississippi ranked #33 on MoneyRates list of "Best-and Worst-States to Retire 2012." Criteria: life expectancy, crime rate, climate, economic conditions, taxes, job opportunities, and cost of living.
  www.money-rates.com, October 22, 2012

- Mississippi ranked #5 on the 2013 Bankrate "Best Places to Retire" list ranking the states and District of Columbia on various criteria relating to health, safety, and cost.
  www.bankrate.com, May 6, 2013

- Mississippi ranked #51 on the Social Science Research Council's "American Human Development Report: The Measure of America," assessing the 50 states plus the District of Columbia on health, education, and living-standard criteria.
  The Measure of America 2013-2014, posted June 19, 2013; www.measureofamerica.org

- Mississippi ranked #49 on the Foundation for Child Development's (FCD) Child Well-being Index (CWI). The FCD used the KIDS COUNT report and the National Survey of Children's Health, the only state-level source for several key indicators of child well-being.
  Foundation for Child Development, January 18, 2012; fcd-us.org

- Mississippi ranked #49 overall according to the 2013 KIDS COUNT Data Book, a project of the Annie E. Casey Foundation. Criteria: children's economic well-being, education, health, and family and community indicators.
  KIDS COUNT Data Center's Data Book, released June 20, 2013; http://datacenter.kidscount.org

- Mississippi ranked #50 in the children's economic well-being category by the 2013 KIDS COUNT Data Book, a project of the Annie E. Casey Foundation.
  KIDS COUNT Data Center's Data Book, released June 20, 2013; http://datacenter.kidscount.org

- Mississippi ranked #48 in the children's educational opportunities and attainments category by the 2013 KIDS COUNT Data Book, a project of the Annie E. Casey Foundation.
  KIDS COUNT Data Center's Data Book, released June 20, 2013; http://datacenter.kidscount.org

- Mississippi ranked #48 in the children's health category by the 2013 KIDS COUNT Data Book, a project of the Annie E. Casey Foundation.
  KIDS COUNT Data Center's Data Book, released June 20, 2013; http://datacenter.kidscount.org

- Mississippi ranked #50 in the family and community circumstances that factor into children's well-being category by the 2013 KIDS COUNT Data Book, a project of the Annie E. Casey Foundation.
  KIDS COUNT Data Center's Data Book, released June 20, 2013; http://datacenter.kidscount.org

- Mississippi ranked #48 in the 2012 Gallup-Healthways Well-Being Index. Criteria: emotional health; physical health; healthy behavior; work environment; basic access to food, shelter, health care; and a safe and satisfying place to live.
  2012 State of Well-Being, Gallup-Healthways Well-Being Index, released February 28, 2013; www.well-beingindex.com

- *U.S. News and World Report's* "Best States for Teen Drivers" rankings are based on driving and road safety laws, federal reports on driver's licenses, car accident fatality, and road-quality statistics. Mississippi ranked #40.
  U.S. News and World Report, March 18, 2010; www.usnews.com

- The Yahoo! Sports service Rivals.com ranks the states according to the strength of their high school football programs. Mississippi ranked #13.
  "Ranking the States: Where Is the Best Football Played?," November 18, 2011; highschool.rivals.com

- iVillage ranked the states by hospitable living conditions for women. Criteria: economic success, access to affordable childcare, health care, reproductive rights, female representation in government, and educational attainment. Mississippi ranked #50.
  iVillage, "50 Best to Worst States for Women," March 14, 2012; www.ivillage.com

- The League of American Bicyclists's "Bicycle Friendly States" ranked Mississippi #36. Criteria: legislation and enforcement, policies and programs, infrastructure and funding, education and advocacy, and evaluation and planning.
  "Washington Tops the Bicycle-Friendly State Ranking," May 1, 2013; bicycling.com

- The federal Corporation for National and Community Service ranked the states and the District of Columbia by volunteer rates. Mississippi ranked #35 for community service.
  "Volunteering and Civic Life in America 2012," www.volunteeringinamerica.gov, accessed July 24, 2013

- The Hospital Safety Score ranked states and the District of Columbia on their hospitals' performance scores. Mississippi ranked #30. Criteria: avoiding preventable harm and medical errors, as demonstrated by 26 hospital safety metrics.
  Spring 2013 Hospital Safety Score, May 8, 2013; www.hospitalsafetyscore.org

- GMAC Insurance ranked the states and the District of Columbia by the performance of their drivers on the GMAC Insurance National Drivers Test, comprised of DMV test questions. Mississippi ranked #46.
  "2011 GMAC Insurance National Drivers Test," www.gmacinsurance.com, accessed July 23, 2013

- Mississippi ranked #6 in a "State Integrity Investigation" analysis of laws and practices intended to deter corruption and promote accountability and openness in campaign finance, ethics laws, lobbying regulations and management of state pension funds.
  "What's Your State's Grade?," www.publicintegrity.org, accessed July 23, 2013

- Mississippi ranked #29 among the states and the District of Columbia in total rail miles, as tracked by the Association of American Railroads.
  "U.S. Freight Railroad Industry Snapshot: Railroads and States: Total Rail Miles by State: 2011"; www.aar.org, accessed July 23, 2013

- According to statistics compiled by the Beer Institute, Mississippi ranked #12 among the states and the District of Columbia in per capita beer consumption of persons 21 years or older.
  "Shipments of Malt Beverages and Per Capita Consumption by State 2012;" www.beerinstitute.org

- According to Concordia University's "Public Education Costs per Pupil by State Rankings," based on statistics gathered by the U.S. Census Bureau, which includes the District of Columbia, Mississippi ranked #46.
  Concordia University Online; education.cu-portland.edu, accessed July 24, 2013

- Mississippi ranked #32 among the states and the District of Columbia in population density based on U.S. Census Bureau data for resident population and total land area. "List of U.S. States by Population Density."
  www.wikipedia.org, accessed July 24, 2013

- In "America's Health Rankings, 2012 Edition," by the United Health Foundation, Mississippi ranked #50. Criteria included: rate of high school graduation; violent crime rate; incidence of infectious disease; childhood immunizations; prevalence of diabetes; per capita public-health funding; percentage of uninsured population; rate of children in poverty; and availability of primary-care physicians.
  United Health Foundation; www.americashealthrankings.org, accessed July 24, 2013

- The TechNet 2012 "State Broadband Index" ranked Mississippi #42 on the following criteria: broadband adoption; network quality; and economic structure. Improved broadband use is hoped to promote economic development, build strong communities, improve delivery of government services and upgrade educational systems.
  TechNet; www.technet.org, accessed July 24, 2013

- Mississippi was ranked #51 among the states and District of Columbia on the American Council for an Energy-Efficient Economy's "State Energy Efficiency Scorecard" for 2012.
  American Council for an Energy-Efficient Economy; aceee.org/sector/state-policy/scorecard, accessed July 24, 2013

Statistical Tables

DEMOGRAPHICS

Resident State and National Population, 1950–2012

Year	State Population	U.S. Population	State Share
1950	2,179,000	151,326,000	1.44%
1960	2,178,000	179,323,000	1.21%
1970	2,216,994	203,302,031	1.09%
1980	2,520,638	226,545,805	1.11%
1990	2,573,216	248,709,873	1.03%
2000	2,844,754	281,424,600	1.01%
2010	2,967,297	308,745,538	0.96%
2012	2,984,926	313,914,040	0.95%

Note: 1950/1960 population figures are rounded to the nearest thousand.
Source: U.S. Census Bureau, Decennial Census 1950–2010; U.S. Census Bureau, 2012 Population Estimates

Projected State and National Population, 2000–2030

Year	State Population	U.S. Population	State Share
2000	2,844,658	281,421,906	1.01%
2005	2,915,696	295,507,134	0.99%
2010	2,971,412	308,935,581	0.96%
2015	3,014,409	322,365,787	0.94%
2020	3,044,812	335,804,546	0.91%
2025	3,069,420	349,439,199	0.88%
2030	3,092,410	363,584,435	0.85%
State population growth, 2000–2030			247,752
State percentage growth, 2000–2030			8.7%

Source: U.S. Census Bureau, Population Division, Interim State Population Projections, 2005

Population by Age, 2012

Age Group	State Population	Percent of Total Population	
		State	U.S.
Under 5 years	203,828	6.8%	6.4%
5 to 14 years	417,376	14.0%	13.1%
15 to 24 years	435,250	14.6%	14.0%
25 to 34 years	388,609	13.0%	13.5%
35 to 44 years	369,947	12.4%	12.9%
45 to 54 years	402,569	13.5%	14.1%
55 to 64 years	363,272	12.2%	12.3%
65 to 74 years	232,211	7.8%	7.6%
75 to 84 years	124,635	4.2%	4.2%
85 years and older	47,229	1.6%	1.9%
Under 18 years	745,333	25.0%	23.5%
65 years and older	404,075	13.5%	13.7%
Median age (years)	–	36.3	37.4

Source: U.S. Census Bureau, Annual Estimates of the Resident Population for Selected Age Groups by Sex for the United States, States, Counties, and Puerto Rico Commonwealth and Municipios: April 1, 2010 to July 1, 2012

Population by Race, 2012

Race	State Population	Percent of Total Population	
		State	U.S.
All residents	2,984,926	100.00%	100.00%
White	1,788,664	59.92%	77.89%
African American	1,116,367	37.40%	13.13%
Native American	17,501	0.59%	1.23%
Asian	28,255	0.95%	5.14%
Native Hawaiian	1,715	0.06%	0.23%
Two or more races	32,424	1.09%	2.39%

Source: U.S. Census Bureau, Population Division, Annual Estimates of the Resident Population by Sex, Race and Hispanic Origin for the United States, States, and Counties: April 1, 2010 to July 1, 2012

Population by Hispanic Origin and Race, 2012

Hispanic Origin/Race	State Population	Percent of Total Population	
		State	U.S.
All residents	2,984,926	100.00%	100.00%
All Hispanic residents	85,260	2.86%	16.89%
Hispanic			
White	68,619	2.30%	14.91%
African American	8,885	0.30%	0.79%
Native American	3,099	0.10%	0.49%
Asian	662	0.02%	0.17%
Native Hawaiian	753	0.03%	0.06%
Two or more races	3,242	0.11%	0.48%
Not Hispanic			
White	1,720,045	57.62%	62.98%
African American	1,107,482	37.10%	12.34%
Native American	14,402	0.48%	0.74%
Asian	27,593	0.92%	4.98%
Native Hawaiian	962	0.03%	0.17%
Two or more races	29,182	0.98%	1.91%

Source: U.S. Census Bureau, Population Division, Annual Estimates of the Resident Population by Sex, Race and Hispanic Origin for the United States, States, and Counties: April 1, 2010 to July 1, 2012

VITAL STATISTICS

Death Rates by Leading Causes, 2010

Cause	State	U.S.
Malignant neoplasms	218.1	186.2
Ischaemic heart diseases	131.5	122.9
Other forms of heart disease	108.2	53.4
Chronic lower respiratory diseases	58.6	44.7
Cerebrovascular diseases	54.6	41.9
Organic, incl. symptomatic, mental disorders	31.0	35.7
Other degenerative diseases of the nervous sys.	35.0	28.4
Other external causes of accidental injury	33.1	26.5
Diabetes mellitus	32.5	22.4
Hypertensive diseases	42.9	20.4
All causes	1,028.3	799.5

Note: Figures are age-adjusted death rates per 100,000 population
Source: CDC/NCHS, Underlying Cause of Death 1999–2010 on CDC WONDER Online Database

Death Rates by Selected Causes, 2010

Cause	State	U.S.
Assault	9.6	5.2
Diseases of the liver	15.2	13.9
Human immunodeficiency virus (HIV) disease	4.1	2.7
Influenza and pneumonia	20.7	16.2
Intentional self-harm	13.4	12.4
Malnutrition	1.5	0.9
Obesity and other hyperalimentation	3.0	1.8
Renal failure	24.6	14.4
Transport accidents	24.5	12.1
Viral hepatitis	1.8	2.4

Note: Figures are age-adjusted death rates per 100,000 population; A dash indicates that data was not available or was suppressed
Source: CDC/NCHS, Underlying Cause of Death 1999–2010 on CDC WONDER Online Database

Abortion Rates, 2009

Category	2009
By state of residence	
Total abortions	6,193
Abortion rate[1]	10.2%
Abortion ratio[2]	144
By state of occurrence	
Total abortions	2,438
Abortion rate[1]	4.0%
Abortion ratio[2]	57
Abortions obtained by out-of-state residents	2.6%
U.S. abortion rate[1]	15.1%
U.S. abortion ratio[2]	227

Note: (1) Number of abortions per 1,000 women aged 15–44 years; (2) Number of abortions per 1,000 live births; A dash indicates that data was not available
Source: CDC/NCHS, Morbidity and Mortality Weekly Report, November 23, 2012 (Abortion Surveillance, United States, 2009)

Infant Mortality Rates, 1995–2009

Category	1995	2000	2005	2009
All state residents	10.38	10.64	11.46	10.09
All U.S. residents	7.57	6.89	6.86	6.39
All state white residents	6.86	6.97	6.94	7.28
All U.S. white residents	6.30	5.71	5.73	5.33
All state black residents	14.39	15.08	17.04	13.50
All U.S. black residents	14.58	13.48	13.26	12.12

Note: Figures represent deaths per 1,000 live births of resident infants under one year old, exclusive of fetal deaths; A dash indicates that data was not available or was suppressed.
Source: Centers of Disease Control and Prevention, Division of Vital Statistics, Linked Birth/Infant Death Records on CDC Wonder Online

Marriage and Divorce Rates, 2000–2011

Year	Marriage Rate		Divorce Rate	
	State	U.S.	State	U.S.
2000	6.9	8.2	5.0	4.0
2002	6.4	8.0	4.9	3.9
2004	6.1	7.8	4.5	3.7
2006	5.7	7.5	4.8	3.7
2008	5.1	7.1	4.3	3.5
2010	4.9	6.8	4.3	3.6
2011	4.9	6.8	4.0	3.6

Note: Rates are based on provisional counts of marriages/divorces by state of occurrence and are per 1,000 total population residing in area
Source: CDC/NCHS, National Vital Statistics System

ECONOMY

Nominal Gross Domestic Product by Industry, 2012
In millions of current dollars

Industry	State GDP
Accommodation and food services	4,066
Administrative and waste management services	2,407
Agriculture, forestry, fishing, and hunting	2,313
Arts, entertainment, and recreation	676
Construction	5,291
Educational services	809
Finance and insurance	4,939
Health care and social assistance	7,612
Information	2,129
Management of companies and enterprises	1,166
Manufacturing	15,254
Mining	1,374
Other services, except government	2,649
Professional, scientific, and technical services	3,488
Real estate and rental and leasing	9,479
Retail trade	8,144
Transportation and warehousing	3,555
Utilities	3,200
Wholesale trade	4,551

Source: U.S. Department of Commerce, Bureau of Economic Analysis, Survey of Current Business

Real Gross Domestic Product, 2000–2012
In millions of chained 2005 dollars

Year	State GDP	U.S. GDP	State Share
2000	76,050	11,225,406	0.68%
2005	81,360	12,539,116	0.65%
2010	85,363	12,897,088	0.66%
2012	86,396	13,430,576	0.64%

Source: U.S. Department of Commerce, Bureau of Economic Analysis, Survey of Current Business

Personal Income Per Capita, 1930–2012

Year	State	U.S.
1930	$197	$618
1940	$210	$593
1950	$764	$1,503
1960	$1,227	$2,268
1970	$2,628	$4,084
1980	$7,005	$10,091
1990	$13,117	$19,354
2000	$21,555	$30,319
2010	$30,841	$39,791
2012	$33,073	$42,693

Source: U.S. Department of Commerce, Bureau of Economic Analysis, Regional Economic Accounts

Non-Farm Employment by Sector, 2012
In thousands

Sector	Employment
Construction	48.3
Education and health services	133.3
Financial activities	44.2
Government	246.2
Information	12.5
Leisure and hospitality	121.9
Mining and logging	9.2
Manufacturing	137.0
Other services	37.9
Professional and business services	96.9
Trade, transportation, and utilities	215.9
All sectors	1,103.4

Source: U.S. Bureau of Labor Statistics, State and Area Employment

Foreign Exports, 2000–2012
In millions of dollars

Year	State Exports	U.S. Exports	State Share
2000	2,725	712,054	0.38%
2002	3,064	649,940	0.47%
2004	3,178	768,554	0.41%
2006	4,484	973,994	0.46%
2008	7,323	1,222,545	0.60%
2010	8,223	1,208,080	0.68%
2012	11,786	1,478,268	0.80%

Note: U.S. figures exclude data from Puerto Rico, U.S. Virgin Islands, and unallocated exports
Source: U.S. Department of Commerce, International Trade Admin., Office of Trade and Industry Information, Manufacturing and Services

Energy Consumption, 2011

In trillions of BTUs, except as noted

Total energy consumption	
Total state energy consumption	1,163.4
Total U.S. energy consumption	97,387.3
State share of U.S. total	1.19%
Per capita consumption (in millions of BTUs)	
Total state per capita consumption	390.7
Total U.S. per capita consumption	312.6
End-use sectors	
Residential	228.6
Commercial	164.2
Industrial	410.8
Transportation	359.9
Sources of energy	
Petroleum	409.0
Natural gas	439.0
Coal	107.5
Renewable energy	69.6
Nuclear electric power	108.2

Source: U.S. Energy Information Administration, State Energy Data 2011: Consumption

LAND AND WATER

Surface Area and Federally-Owned Land, 2007

In thousands of acres

Category	State	U.S.	State Share
Total surface area	30,527.3	1,937,664.2	1.58%
Total land area	29,637.4	1,886,846.9	1.57%
Non-federal land	27,842.6	1,484,910.0	1.88%
Developed	1,811.9	111,251.2	1.63%
Rural	26,030.7	1,373,658.8	1.89%
Federal land	1,794.8	401,936.9	0.45%
Water area	889.9	50,817.3	1.75%

Source: U.S. Department of Agriculture, Natural Resources Conservation Service, 2007 National Resources Inventory

Land Cover/Use of Non-Federal Rural Land, 2007

In thousands of acres

Category	State	U.S.	State Share
Total rural land	26,030.7	1,373,658.8	1.89%
Cropland	4,703.9	357,023.5	1.32%
CRP[1] land	780.0	32,850.2	2.37%
Pastureland	3,249.3	118,615.7	2.74%
Rangeland	0.0	409,119.4	0.00%
Forest land	16,826.8	406,410.4	4.14%
Other rural land	470.7	49,639.6	0.95%

Note: (1) Conservation Reserve Program was created to assist private landowners in converting highly erodible cropland to vegetative cover.
Source: U.S. Department of Agriculture, Natural Resources Conservation Service, 2007 National Resources Inventory

Farms and Crop Acreage, 2012

Category	State	U.S.	State Share
Farms (in thousands)	42.3	2,170.0	1.95%
Acres (in millions)	11.2	914.0	1.22%
Acres per farm	263.6	421.2	–

Source: U.S. Department of Agriculture, National Agricultural Statistical Service, Quick Stats, 2012 Survey Data

HEALTH AND MEDICAL CARE

Medical Professionals, 2012

Profession	State Number	U.S. Number	State Share	State Rate[1]	U.S. Rate[1]
Physicians[2]	5,541	894,637	0.62%	186.1	287.1
Dentists	1,247	193,587	0.64%	41.9	62.1
Podiatrists	62	17,469	0.35%	2.1	5.6
Optometrists	306	45,638	0.67%	10.3	14.6
Chiropractors	268	77,494	0.35%	9.0	24.9

Note: (1) Rates are per 100,000 population; (2) Includes total, active Doctors of Osteopathic Medicine and Doctors of Medicine in 2011.
Source: U.S. Department of Health and Human Services, Bureau of Health Professions, Area Health Resource File, 2012-2013

Health Insurance Coverage, 2011

Category	State	U.S.
Total persons covered	2,458,000	260,214,000
Total persons not covered	476,000	48,613,000
Percent not covered	16.2%	15.7%
Children under age 18 covered	696,000	67,143,000
Children under age 18 not covered	69,000	6,965,000
Percent of children not covered	9.0%	9.4%

Source: U.S. Census Bureau, Current Population Survey, 2012 Annual Social and Economic Supplement

HIV, STD, and Tuberculosis Cases and Rates, 2011

Disease	State Cases	State Rate[1]	U.S. Rate[1]
Chlamydia	21,216	715.0	457.6
Gonorrhea	5,814	195.9	104.2
HIV diagnosis	617	25.3	15.8
HIV, stage 3 (AIDS)	399	16.4	10.3
Syphilis, early latent	313	10.5	4.3
Syphilis, primary/secondary	191	6.4	4.5
Tuberculosis	91	3.1	3.4

Note: (1) Rates are per 100,000 population
Source: Centers for Disease Control and Prevention

Cigarette Smoking, 2011

Category	State	U.S.
Adults who are current smokers	26.0%	21.2%
Adults who smoke everyday	18.8%	15.4%
Adults who smoke some days	7.1%	5.7%
Adults who are former smokers	21.3%	25.1%
Adults who never smoked	52.8%	52.9%

Source: Centers for Disease Control and Prevention, Behaviorial Risk Factor Surveillance System, Tobacco Use, 2011

HOUSING

Home Ownership Rates, 1995–2012

Area	1995	2000	2005	2010	2012
State	71.1%	75.2%	78.8%	74.8%	74.2%
U.S.	64.7%	67.4%	68.9%	66.9%	65.4%

Source: U.S. Census Bureau, Housing Vacancies and Homeownership, Annual Statistics

Home Sales, 2000–2010
In thousands of units

Year	State Sales	U.S. Sales	State Share
2000	38.7	5,174	0.75%
2002	48.0	5,632	0.85%
2004	58.1	6,778	0.86%
2006	63.8	6,478	0.98%
2008	50.4	4,913	1.03%
2010	42.1	4,908	0.86%

Note: Units include single-family homes, condos and co-ops
Source: National Association of Realtors, Real Estate Outlook, Market Trends & Insights

Value of Owner-Occupied Homes, 2011

Value	Total Units in State	Percent of Total, State	Percent of Total, U.S.
Less than $50,000	162,076	21.5%	8.8%
$50,000 to $99,000	215,691	28.6%	16.0%
$100,000 to $149,000	137,578	18.2%	16.5%
$150,000 to $199,000	105,128	13.9%	15.4%
$200,000 to $299,000	85,859	11.4%	18.2%
$300,000 to $499,000	33,903	4.5%	15.2%
$500,000 to $999,000	10,884	1.4%	7.9%
$1,000,000 or more	3,544	0.5%	2.0%
Median value	–	$99,900	$173,600

Source: U.S. Census Bureau, 2011 American Community Survey 1-Year Estimates

EDUCATION

School Enrollment, 2011

Educational Level	Students Enrolled in State	Percent of Total, State	Percent of Total, U.S.
All levels	830,815	100.0%	100.0%
Nursery school, preschool	55,300	6.7%	6.0%
Kindergarten	44,214	5.3%	5.1%
Elementary (grades 1–8)	338,221	40.7%	39.5%
Secondary (grades 9–12)	174,839	21.0%	20.7%
College or graduate school	218,241	26.3%	28.7%

Note: Figures cover the population 3 years and over enrolled in school
Source: U.S. Census Bureau, 2011 American Community Survey 1-Year Estimates

Educational Attainment, 2011

Highest Level of Education	State	U.S.
High school diploma	81.1%	85.9%
Bachelor's degree	19.8%	28.5%
Graduate/Professional degree	7.3%	10.6%

Note: Figures cover the population 25 years and over
Source: U.S. Census Bureau, 2011 American Community Survey 1-Year Estimates

Public College Finances, FY 2012

Category	State	U.S.
Full-time equivalent enrollment (FTE)[1]	142,031	11,548,974
Educational appropriations per FTE[2]	$6,033	$5,906
Net tuition revenue per FTE[3]	$5,430	$5,189
Total educational revenue per FTE[4]	$11,464	$11,043

(1) Full-time equivalent enrollment equates student credit hours to full time, academic year students, but excludes medical students;
(2) Educational appropriations measure state and local support available for public higher education operating expenses including ARRA funds and excludes appropriations for independent institutions, financial aid for students attending independent institutions, research, hospitals, and medical education; (3) Net tuition revenue is calculated by taking the gross amount of tuition and fees, less state and institutional financial aid, tuition waivers or discounts, and medical student tuition and fees. Net tuition revenue used for capital debt service is included in the net tuition revenue figures; (4) Total educational revenue is the sum of educational appropriations and net tuition excluding net tuition revenue used for capital debt service.
Source: State Higher Education Executive Officers, State Higher Education Finance FY 2012

TRANSPORTATION AND TRAVEL

Motor Vehicle Registrations and Drivers Licenses, 2011

Vehicle Type	State	U.S.	State Share
Automobiles[1]	1,050,978	125,656,528	0.84%
Buses	9,012	666,064	1.35%
Trucks	948,456	118,455,587	0.80%
Motorcycles	28,078	8,437,502	0.33%
Drivers licenses	1,926,603	211,874,649	0.91%

Note: Motor vehicle registrations include private, commercial, and publicly-owned vehicles; (1) Includes taxicabs
Source: U.S. Department of Transportation, Federal Highway Administration

Domestic Travel Expenditures, 2009
In millions of dollars

Category	State	U.S.	State Share
Travel expenditures	$5,842	$610,200	0.96%

Note: Figures represent U.S. spending on domestic overnight trips and day trips of 50 miles or more, one way, away from home. Excludes spending by foreign visitors.
Source: U.S. Travel Association, Impact of Travel on State Economies, 2009

Retail Gasoline Prices, 2013

Gasoline Grade	State Average	U.S. Average
Regular	$3.41	$3.65
Mid	$3.58	$3.81
Premium	$3.76	$3.98
Diesel	$3.74	$3.88
Excise tax[1]	37.2 cents	49.4 cents

Note: Gasoline prices as of 7/26/2013; (1) Includes state and federal excise taxes and other state taxes as of July 1, 2013
Source: American Automobile Association, Daily Fuel Guage Report; American Petroleum Institute, State Motor Fuel Taxes, 2013

Public Road Length, 2011

Type	State Mileage	U.S. Mileage	State Share
Interstate highways	703	46,960	1.50%
Other highways	71	15,719	0.45%
Principal arterial	2,920	156,262	1.87%
Minor arterial	4,626	242,942	1.90%
Major collector	13,260	534,592	2.48%
Minor collector	2,299	266,357	0.86%
Local	51,241	2,814,925	1.82%
Urban	11,011	1,095,373	1.01%
Rural	64,107	2,982,383	2.15%
Total	75,119	4,077,756	1.84%

Note: Combined urban and rural road mileage equals the total of the other road types
Source: U.S. Department of Transportation, Federal Highway Administration, Public Road Length, 2011

CRIME AND LAW ENFORCEMENT

Full-Time Law Enforcement Officers, 2011

Gender	State Number	State Rate[1]	U.S. Rate[1]
Male officers	3,669	182.1	210.3
Female officers	367	18.2	28.1
Total officers	4,036	200.3	238.3

Note: (1) Rates are per 100,000 population
Source: Federal Bureau of Investigation, Uniform Crime Reports, Crime in the United States 2011

Prison Population, 2000–2012

Year	State Population	U.S. Population	State Share
2000	20,241	1,391,261	1.45%
2005	20,515	1,527,929	1.34%
2010	21,067	1,613,803	1.31%
2011	21,386	1,598,783	1.34%
2012	22,319	1,571,013	1.42%

Note: Figures include prisoners under the jurisdiction of state or federal correctional authorities.
Source: U.S. Department of Justice, Bureau of Justice Statistics, Prisoners in 2006, 2011, 2012 (Advance Counts)

Crime Rate, 2011

Incidents per 100,000 residents

Category	State	U.S.
Violent crimes	269.8	386.3
Murder	8.0	4.7
Forcible rape	29.0	26.8
Robbery	83.7	113.7
Aggravated assault	149.1	241.1
Property crimes	3,025.5	2,908.7
Burglary	1,037.7	702.2
Larceny/theft	1,822.5	1,976.9
Motor vehicle theft	165.4	229.6
All crimes	3,295.3	3,295.0

Source: Federal Bureau of Investigation, Uniform Crime Reports, Crime in the United States 2011

GOVERNMENT AND FINANCE

Local Governments by Type, 2012

Government Type	State	U.S.	State Share
All local governments	991	89,004	1.11%
County	82	3,031	2.71%
Municipality	297	19,522	1.52%
Town/Township	0	16,364	0.00%
Special District	448	37,203	1.20%
Ind. School District	164	12,884	1.27%

Source: U.S. Census Bureau, 2012 Census of Governments: Organization Component Preliminary Estimates

State Government Revenue, 2011

In thousands of dollars, except for per capita figures

Total revenue	**$23,606,197**
Total revenue per capita, State	$7,928
Total revenue per capita, U.S.	$7,271
General revenue	$17,807,309
Intergovernmental revenue	$8,726,548
Taxes	$6,714,180
General sales	$2,932,859
Selective sales	$1,386,826
License taxes	$455,473
Individual income taxes	$1,447,751
Corporate income taxes	$353,057
Other taxes	$138,214
Current charges	$1,764,127
Miscellaneous general revenue	$602,454
Utility revenue	$0
Liquor store revenue	$263,321
Insurance trust revenue[1]	$5,535,567

Note: (1) Within insurance trust revenue, net earnings of state retirement systems is a calculated statistic, and thus can be positive or negative. Net earnings is the sum of earnings on investments plus gains on investments minus losses on investments.
Source: U.S. Census Bureau, 2011 Annual Survey of State Government Finances

State Government Expenditures, 2011

In thousands of dollars, except for per capita figures

Total expenditure	$20,157,417
Total expenditure per capita, State	$6,770
Total expenditure per capita, U.S.	$6,427
Intergovernmental expenditure	$5,253,307
Direct expenditure	$14,904,110
Current operation	$10,740,372
Capital outlay	$1,255,919
Insurance benefits and repayments	$2,397,687
Assistance and subsidies	$242,417
Interest on debt	$267,715
Utility expenditure	$0
Liquor store expenditure	$213,348
Insurance trust expenditure	$2,397,687

Source: U.S. Census Bureau, 2011 Annual Survey of State Government Finances

State Government General Expenditures by Function, 2011

In thousands of dollars

Education	$5,518,603
Public welfare	$5,436,907
Hospitals	$1,073,347
Health	$434,010
Highways	$1,377,654
Police protection	$103,889
Correction	$354,626
Natural resources	$307,107
Parks and recreation	$82,824
Governmental administration	$395,498
Interest on general debt	$267,715
Other and unallocable	$2,194,202

Source: U.S. Census Bureau, 2011 Annual Survey of State Government Finances

State Government Finances, Cash and Debt, 2011

In thousands of dollars, except for per capita figures

Debt at end of fiscal year	
State, total	$6,768,371
State, per capita	$2,273
U.S., per capita	$3,635
Cash and security holdings	
State, total	$31,204,875
State, per capita	$10,480
U.S., per capita	$11,759

Source: U.S. Census Bureau, 2011 Annual Survey of State Government Finances

POLITICS

Composition of the Senate, 1995–2013

Congress (Year)	State/U.S	Dem	Rep	Total
104th (1995)	State delegates	0	2	2
	Total U.S.	48	52	100
105th (1997)	State delegates	0	2	2
	Total U.S.	45	55	100
106th (1999)	State delegates	0	2	2
	Total U.S.	45	55	100
107th (2001)	State delegates	0	2	2
	Total U.S.	50	50	100
108th (2003)	State delegates	0	2	2
	Total U.S.	48	51	100
109th (2005)	State delegates	0	2	2
	Total U.S.	44	55	100
110th (2007)	State delegates	0	2	2
	Total U.S.	49	49	100
111th (2009)	State delegates	0	2	2
	Total U.S.	57	41	100
112th (2011)	State delegates	0	2	2
	Total U.S.	51	47	100
113th (2013)	State delegates	0	2	2
	Total U.S.	54	45	100

Note: Figures are for the starts of first sessions; Totals include Democratic (Dem) and Republican (Rep) members as well as vacancies and seats held by independent party members
Source: U.S. Congress, Congressional Directory

Composition of the House of Representatives, 1995–2013

Congress (Year)	State/U.S	Dem	Rep	Total
104th (1995)	State delegates	4	1	5
	Total U.S.	204	230	435
105th (1997)	State delegates	2	3	5
	Total U.S.	207	226	435
106th (1999)	State delegates	3	2	5
	Total U.S.	211	223	435
107th (2001)	State delegates	3	2	5
	Total U.S.	212	221	435
108th (2003)	State delegates	2	2	2
	Total U.S.	205	229	435
109th (2005)	State delegates	2	2	4
	Total U.S.	202	231	435
110th (2007)	State delegates	2	2	4
	Total U.S.	233	198	435
111th (2009)	State delegates	3	1	4
	Total U.S.	256	178	435
112th (2011)	State delegates	1	3	4
	Total U.S.	193	242	435
113th (2013)	State delegates	1	3	4
	Total U.S.	201	234	435

Note: Figures are for the starts of first sessions; Totals include Democratic (Dem) and Republican (Rep) members as well as vacancies and seats held by independent party members
Source: U.S. Congress, Congressional Directory

Composition of State Legislature, 2004–2013

Year	Democrats	Republicans	Total
State Senate			
2004	30	22	52
2005	28	24	52
2006	28	24	52
2007	25	27	52
2008	27	25	52
2009	27	25	52
2010	27	25	52
2011	25	27	52
2012	21	31	52
2013	20	31	52
State House			
2004	80	42	122
2005	75	47	122
2006	74	47	122
2007	74	47	122
2008	75	47	122
2009	74	48	122
2010	74	48	122
2011	69	53	122
2012	58	64	122
2013	56	65	122

Note: Totals may include minor party members and vacancies
Source: The Council of State Governments, State Legislatures

Voter Participation in Presidential Elections, 1980–2012

Year	Voting-eligible State Population	State Voter Turnout Rate	U.S. Voter Turnout Rate
1980	1,704,163	52.4	54.2
1984	1,766,654	53.3	55.2
1988	1,792,847	52.0	52.8
1992	1,854,797	52.9	58.1
1996	1,949,309	45.9	51.7
2000	2,024,650	49.1	54.2
2004	2,068,766	55.7	60.1
2008	2,113,347	61.0	61.6
2012	2,152,832	59.7	58.2

Note: All figures are based on the voting-eligible population which excludes person ineligible to vote such as non-citizens, felons (depending on state law), and mentally-incapacitated persons. U.S. figures include the overseas eligible population (including military personnel).
Source: McDonald, Michael P., United States Election Project, Presidential Voter Turnout Rates, 1980–2012

Governors Since Statehood

David Holmes (O)	1817-1820
George Poindexter (O)	1820-1822
Walter Leake (O)	(d) 1822-1825
Gerard C. Brandon (O)	1825-1826
David Holmes (O)	(r) 1826
Gerard C. Brandon (O)	1826-1832
Abram M. Scott (O)	(d) 1832-1833
Charles Lynch (O)	1833
Hiram G. Runnells (O)	1833-1835
John A. Quitman (O)	1835-1836
Charles Lynch (O)	1836-1838
Alexander G. McNutt (D)	1838-1842
Tilghman M. Tucker (D)	1842-1844
Albert G. Brown (D)	1844-1848
Joseph M. Matthews (D)	1848-1850
John A. Quitman (D)	(r) 1850-1851
John I. Guion (D)	1851
James Whitfield (D)	1851-1852
Henry S. Foote (D)	(r) 1852-1854
John J. Pettus (D)	1854
John J. McRae (D)	1854-1857
William McWillie (D)	1857-1859
John J. Pettus (D)	1859-1863
Charles Clark (D)	(i) 1863-1865
William L. Sharkey (D)	(i) 1865
Benjamin G. Humphreys (D)	(i) 1865-1868
Adelbert Ames (R)	1868-1870
James L. Alcorn (R)	(r) 1870-1871
Ridgely C. Powers (R)	1871-1874
Adelbert Ames (R)	(r) 1874-1876
John M. Stone (D)	1876-1882
Robert Lowry Jr. (D)	1882-1890
John M. Stone (D)	1890-1896
Anselm J. McLaurin (D)	1896-1900
Andrew H. Longbird (D)	1900-1904
James K. Vardman (D)	1904-1908
Edmund F. Noel (D)	1908-1912
Earl L. Brewer (D)	1912-1916
Theodore G. Bilbo (D)	1916-1920
Lee M. Russell (D)	1920-1924
Henry L. Whitfield (D)	(d) 1924-1927
Dennis Murphree (D)	1927-1928
Theodore G. Bilbo (D)	1928-1932
Martin S. Conner (D)	1932-1936
Hugh L. White (D)	1936-1940
Paul B. Johnson (D)	(d) 1940-1943
Dennis Murphree (D)	1943-1944
Thomas L. Bailey (D)	(d) 1944-1946
Fielding L. Wright (D)	1946-1952
Hugh L. White (D)	1952-1956
James F. Coleman (D)	1956-1960
Ross R. Barnett (D)	1960-1964
Paul B. Johnson Jr. (D)	1964-1968
John Bell Williams (D)	1968-1972
William L. Waller (D)	1972-1976
Cliff Finch (D)	1976-1980
William Winter (D)	1980-1984
Bill Allain (D)	1984-1988
Ray Mabus (D)	1988-1992
Kirk Fordice (R)	1992-2000
Ronnie Musgrove (D)	2000-2004
Haley Barbour (R)	2004-2012
Phil Bryant (R)	2012-2016

Note: (D) Democrat; (R) Republican; (O) Other party; (r) resigned; (d) died in office; (i) removed from office

Missouri

Location: Midwest

Area and rank: 68,898 square miles (178,446 square kilometers); 69,709 square miles (180,546 square kilometers) including water; eighteenth largest state in area

Coastline: none

Population and rank: 6,021,988 (2012 estimate); eighteenth largest state in population

Capital city: Jefferson City (43,079 people in 2010 census)

Largest city: Kansas City (459,787 people in 2010 census)

Became territory: June 4, 1812

Entered Union and rank: August 10, 1821; twenty-fourth state

Present constitution adopted: 1945

Counties: 114, as well as 1 independent city

State name: Missouri takes its name from the Missouri Indians, whose name means "town of the large canoes"

State nickname: Show-Me State

Motto: *Salus populi suprema lex esto* (The welfare of the people shall be the supreme law)

State capitol building in Jefferson City. (Missouri Division of Tourism)

State flag: Red, white, and blue stripes with state coat of arms surrounded by twenty-four stars

Highest point: Taum Sauk Mountain—1,772 feet (540 meters)

Lowest point: St. Francis River—230 feet (70 meters)

Highest recorded temperature: 118 degrees Fahrenheit (48 degrees Celsius)— Warsaw and Union, 1954

Lowest recorded temperature: –40 degrees Fahrenheit (–40 degrees Celsius)—Warsaw, 1905

State song: "Missouri Waltz"

State tree: Flowering dogwood

State flower: Hawthorn

State bird: Bluebird

State fish: Paddlefish; channel catfish

State animal: Mule

Missouri History

Missouri lies almost in the center of the forty-eight contiguous states. It is the southernmost midwestern state. Its eastern boundary is the Mississippi River, its western boundary the Missouri River. It is bordered by eight states: west of Missouri are Nebraska, Kansas, and Oklahoma. To its east are Illinois and Kentucky. Iowa borders it on the north, and Arkansas and Tennessee are on the south. Missouri is about 300 miles from east to west and about 280 miles from north to south.

The earliest settlers in the area probably lived there more than twelve thousand years ago. By the seventeenth century, the Missouri and Osage Indian tribes were there. The first Europeans in the region were Jacques Marquette, a French missionary, and Louis Jolliet, a fur trader, known to be there in 1673. In 1683, René-Robert Cavelier, sieur de La Salle, claimed a vast expanse of land, including present-day Missouri, for France, calling it Louisiana after King Louis XIV.

Early Settlements. The first permanent French settlement in Missouri was Sainte Genevieve, on the Mississippi River south of present-day St. Louis, established in 1735. In 1764, Pierre Laclède and René Auguste Chouteau founded St. Louis, also on the Mississippi River.

In 1762, Spain claimed France's Louisiana territory and futilely attempted to coerce Spaniards to move there. When the United States became independent in 1776, Spain invited Americans east of the Mississippi to move into Missouri. Substantial numbers of farmers and miners accepted. By 1799 groups of settlers inhabited the area.

In 1800, France reclaimed the Louisiana territory, which, through the Louisiana Purchase, it sold to the United States for fifteen million dollars in 1803. The Missouri Territory, which included Kansas, had a population of about twenty thousand by 1812. Most settled on land that had been the property of Native Americans, who sought to reclaim it. Various treaties were signed between the indigenous people and the new arrivals, but by 1825, almost no American Indians remained in Missouri.

The Missouri Compromise. Black slaves came to Missouri as early as 1720, owned by French miners searching for gold and other minerals. These slaves were

Modern depiction of a wagon train leaving Missouri to follow the Oregon Trail to the west. (Library of Congress)

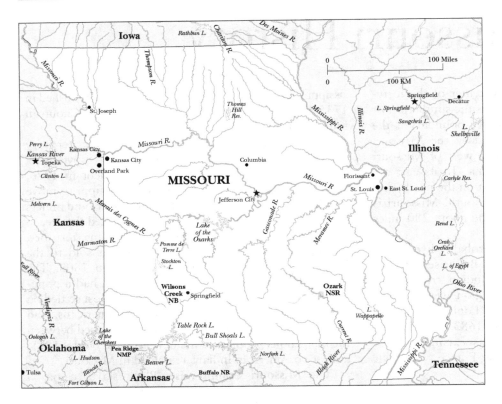

The potato famine in Ireland during the mid-1840's resulted in an influx of Irish into Missouri, where they worked on railroad construction or as day laborers. Missouri was growing so fast that extra hands were welcome. By the late 1840's, a wave of Germans seeking a better life came to the area around St. Louis.

Slavery. Slavery was a contentious matter in Missouri. By 1860, nearly 115,000 slaves were held in servitude in Missouri, many of them working on farms in the western part of the state. Some 3,600 free African Americans also lived in the state prior to the Civil War, most of them settling around St. Louis.

Dred Scott and his wife, Harriet, were slaves in Missouri. In 1846, the Scotts sued for their freedom, claiming that they were humans, not chattel. Their case reached the U.S. Supreme Court in 1857. The Court ultimately ruled that the Scotts were property owned by the master who had bought them. As such, they had no rights as citizens. This decision enraged northern abolitionists and was one of the crucial factors that led to the Civil War, which started in 1861.

Missouri and the Confederacy. In 1861, the southern slave states formed the Confederacy, a separate nation with its own government. As a border state, Missouri, despite pressure from many of its slave owners, voted to remain in the Union, although nearly thirty-five thousand Missourians joined the Confederate armed forces.

Months before the war ended, Missouri freed all of its slaves, many of whom remained in the state. At the end of the twentieth century, Missouri had an African American population of nearly 11 percent. During the Civil War, more than a thousand battles were fought in Missouri, which sent more than 150,000 of its men to fight. About 115,000 of these fought in the Union forces.

Urban Growth. Missouri's strategic location and access to waterways and major trails resulted in the establishment of towns and cities along trade routes and encouraged urban development. The two cities that emerged as preeminent were St. Louis in the east and Kansas City on the western border with Kansas. Both cities became railroad centers, and Kansas City was known for its stockyards, first established in 1870, which still contribute substantially to its economy.

involved in building Missouri's first cities. Soon southern farmers and plantation owners relocated in Missouri, bringing their slaves with them.

Missouri applied to join the United States in 1818, coming in as a slave state. This would have made for one extra slave state in the country, and the federal government could not sanction an imbalance between slave and free states. The solution was the Missouri Compromise of 1821, which assured that the number of slave states and free states would remain equal. Maine was to be admitted as a free state, thereby permitting Missouri statehood as a slave state. In 1821, Missouri became the twenty-fourth state.

Early Economy. Missouri's land became fertile when advancing glaciers deposited rich topsoil upon it thousands of years ago. The state also has excellent river transportation in the east and the west. Steamboats carried their cargos to points along the rivers that eventually became thriving ports. Trails running west from Missouri led into the Rocky Mountains, where independent fur traders lived.

Soon there were permanent settlements and thriving towns along the river banks and trade routes. In 1822, the Santa Fe Trail was opened between Independence, in western Missouri, and Santa Fe, New Mexico, then a possession of Mexico. The beginning of the two thousand-mile-long Oregon Trail was in Independence. When the Gold Rush to California began in 1848, thousands of prospectors passed through Missouri.

St. Louis became a major manufacturing center. In 1904, the city held a World's Fair that attracted people from around the world. In the same year, St. Louis also became the first U.S. city chosen as the site of the Olympic Games.

By 1990, 75 percent of Missouri's residents lived in urban areas. Chief among these, besides Kansas City and St. Louis, were Springfield, Joplin, St. Joseph, and Columbia, the site of the University of Missouri's main campus, established in 1841.

Other Factors in the Economy. Agriculture is a major contributor to Missouri's economy. Soybeans are the state's most lucrative crop, but Missouri farms produce sorghum, wheat, and hay as well. Cattle, hogs, and turkeys are also raised.

Its agricultural production notwithstanding, manufacturing became the largest and most important factor in Missouri's economy. Among the major industries located in the state are General Motors and Ford, whose plants produce automobiles and trucks, McDonnell-Douglas, which makes commercial and private airplanes,

and the Hallmark Card Company.

Tourism and commerce are also major factors in the economy. Tourists bring more than five billion dollars per year into the state, coming there to sightsee, gamble in the riverboat casinos, and attend the many shows in Branson, where nearly thirty well-known singers own theaters.

Missouri's Attractions. Besides the riverboat casinos and Branson's theaters, tourists are drawn to the state to view such attractions as the Gateway Arch in St. Louis, designed by Eero Saarinen and opened in 1965, which commemorates St. Louis as the jumping-off point for many pioneers heading into the western frontier.

Tourists also flock into New Madrid, a town on the Mississippi River that in 1811 and 1812 was rocked by three of the worst earthquakes ever recorded in North America. The New Madrid Museum provides detailed information about these earthquakes, which were so destructive they were felt as far away as Washington, D.C., and changed the course of the Mississippi River.

The Ozark Mountains and Lake of the Ozarks in southern Missouri offer excellent recreational facili-

The Great Pike of the 1904 St. Louis World's Fair. Scenes from the fair were re-created in the 1944 film Meet Me in St. Louis. (Library of Congress)

St. Louis's skyline is dramatically framed by the Gateway Arch, which opened in 1965. The arch was built to symbolize the city's history as the gateway through which the American West was developed. (Wikimedia Commons)

ties. This area attracts both tourists and retirees in large numbers. Tourists also flock into Florida and Hannibal in the north to visit the birthplace of Mark Twain and the town in which he grew up and used as the setting for some of his most popular stories.

Electoral Politics and Controversies. As the year 2000 arrived, Missouri politics were bifurcated, leaning right of center and to left of center. In presidential politics, the state leaned slightly to the right, as Republican candidate George W. Bush took Missouri's eleven electoral votes by 51-47 percent over Vice President Al Gore. On the other hand, the Democrats won a seat in the U.S. Senate previously held by Republican John Ashcroft, who lost the race to a deceased candidate, the late governor, Mel Carnahan. Voters chose Carnahan despite his death on October 16 in a plane crash amid the campaign; Senator Ashcroft lost the vote by two percentage points. The interim governor, Roger B. Wilson, appointed Carnahan's widow Jean in her late husband's place. A critical factor in the election was the stance of each candidate regarding gun control. Ashcroft made an issue of Carnahan's opposition to a proposed law that would allow carrying concealed weapons.

A controversial measure on the ballot that went down to defeat by a wide margin was a proposal to tax large businesses in order to help candidates who voluntarily agree to limit their acceptance of special interest contributions. Two-thirds of the voters opposed it. The election was marred by the inability to vote by some voters in largely African American St. Louis precincts. Crowds were so large as the polls' closing time approached that it was clear that some would be unable to vote. The Democratic Party proposed that the polls be allowed to remain open until 10:00 p.m. The Republican Party opposed this, and in the end the polls closed forty-five minutes later than their usual time. It was later determined that votes of those unable to cast their ballots would not have changed the electoral outcome.

After the election, a suit was filed and four members of the St. Louis Election Board were ousted by the governor. He explained that he was replacing them because of charges of irregularities that excluded hundreds of black voters from voting, mainly on account of crowding. In the governor's race, the outcome was decided by a hair, as the Democratic candidate Bob Holden edged out Republican Jim Talent by fewer than 22,000 votes among more than 2.3 million votes cast. Third-party candidates played a possibly decisive role in collecting more than 60,000 votes. Two years later, when Talent ran for U.S. Senate, however, he won the very close race. Running against Jean Carnahan for a full Senate term, Talent won by fewer than 23,000 out of some 1.87 million votes cast.

By 2004, however, Missouri voters made a clear choice, though by no means of landslide proportions. This time, George W. Bush won the state by 53-46 percent over challenger John Kerry. In the governor's race, Republican Matt Blunt defeated his opponent by nearly 84,000 votes; and in the race for U.S. Senate, Republican Kit Bond won by 13 percent, which translated into more than 360,000 votes. In races for House seats, all incumbents were reelected. No incumbent received less than 59 percent of the vote; most had more than 60 percent and up to 75 percent, a huge margin.

A newly elected member of the House was Democrat Russ Carnahan, son of the late governor and Jean Carnahan. He ran for the seat vacated by long-time congressional leader and presidential candidate Richard Gephardt, who opted for retirement. One key factor in the shift to the right of public opinion was the impact of the terrorist attacks in September, 2001. While this effect was felt everywhere in the nation, it was especially felt in Missouri because the Gateway Arch in St. Louis was closed as a possible terrorist target.

Environment. A major statewide environmental concern in Missouri in the first decade of the 21st century was confined-animal feeding operations (CAFOs), such as chicken, turkey, and pig facilities that produce excessive amounts of animal waste. State environmental organizations have focused on the CAFO issue, as well as river pollution and the larger issue of human-caused global warming. All of these issues severely divided local interests and elected political officials.

Casinos. Another divisive issue has been the opening of eleven casinos in the state, including several on either stationary or movable riverboats. Authorized in 1992, the casinos have provided a source of state revenue; the state imposes a loss-limit of $500 every two hours on gamblers. Several riverboat casinos are stationary, never leaving the dock, at St. Charles, St. Louis, Caruthersville, La Grange, and the Isle of Capri at Boonville.

Politics. In 2004, Republican Matt Blunt won the governorship in a tight race against former state auditor Claire McGaskill; Republicans also gained a majority in the state General Assembly, the first time in 80 years that Republicans held both the governorship and a majority in the Assembly. In 2008, Blunt chose not to run for re-election. He claimed he had achieved all that he set out to do; however, polls showed he had a low approval rating that suggested he would have a difficult chance at re-election. In that election, Democrat Jay Nixon, who had served as the state attorney general since 1993, defeated Republican Congressman Kenny Hulshof for the governorship with 58 percent of the votes. Nixon ran again in 2012, defeating the Republican candidate, businessman Dave Spence.

R. Baird Shuman
Updated by the Editor

Kansas City, Missouri's largest city. (PhotoDisc)

Missouri Time Line

1673   Jacques Marquette, a missionary, and Louis Jolliet, a fur trader, sail the Mississippi, exploring Missouri and Tennessee.

1682   René-Robert Cavelier, sieur de La Salle, claims the Mississippi River Valley for France, naming it Louisiana.

1720   Philip Renault, searching for silver, brings black slaves to Missouri.

1724   Fort Orleans is built to protect French settlers from Spanish.

1750   Founding of Sainte Genevieve, the first permanent French settlement.

1763   Treaty of Paris cedes all of Canada and land west of the Mississippi River to Britain.

1764   René Auguste Chouteau and Pierre Laclède found St. Louis.

President Harry S. Truman riding in a convertible down main street in Bolivar, Missouri on July 4, 1948. (Wikimedia Commons)

1799	Spanish encourage Americans to settle in Missouri.
1800	Spain returns western Louisiana territory to France.
1803	France sells area to the United States in Louisiana Purchase.
1804	Meriwether Lewis and William Clark leave St. Louis on their cross-country exploration.
1811	First of three earthquakes rocks New Madrid area.
June 4, 1812	Missouri becomes a territory.
1815	Indians in Missouri sign peace treaty with the United States.
1818	Missouri applies for statehood as a slave state.
1819	Steamship *Independence* sails the Missouri River, proving its navigability.
1820	Henry Clay brings the Missouri Compromise before Congress, which approves it.
Aug. 10, 1821	Missouri admitted to Union as twenty-fourth state.
1834	*St. Louis Herald*, first daily paper in the state, published in St. Louis.
1836	Missouri gains six northern counties from American Indians in Platte Purchase.
1839	University of Missouri chartered.
1841	University of Missouri opens in Columbia.
1847	St. Louis linked to eastern United States by telegraph.
1849	Major fire devastates much of the center of St. Louis.
1853	State opens first public high school in St. Louis.
1857	U.S. Supreme Court renders Dred Scott decision, denying him freedom.
1859	First railroad across Missouri links St. Joseph and Hannibal.
Apr. 3, 1860	First Pony Express service begins in St. Joseph.
Mar. 6, 1861	Missouri votes against seceding from Union.
1865	Civil War ends; new Missouri constitution bans slavery.
1866	Lincoln Institute is founded for recently freed slaves.
1867	First women admitted to University of Missouri.
1869	First bridge across Missouri River opens at Kansas City.
1875	New constitution restores voting rights to Confederate sympathizers.
1880	First newspaper in Missouri for African Americans, the *Advocate*, is established.
1904	St. Louis hosts Olympic Games and World's Fair.
1908	University of Missouri launches first journalism school in the United States.
1921	Missouri's first radio station, WEW, begins broadcasting at St. Louis University.
1931	Bagnell Dam on Osage River opens and forms Lake of the Ozarks.
1945	Harry S. Truman of Independence becomes the thirty-third president of the United States.
1945	Missouri's present constitution is adopted.
1952	Drought ravishes Missouri.
1955	Tornados kill 115 people in Missouri and Kansas.
1957	Harry S Truman Library opens in Independence.
1959	Tornadoes kill 22 and injure 5,350 in St. Louis.
1965	Gateway Arch opens in St. Louis.
1973	Floods devastate Missouri, causing $100 million in damage.
1982	Dioxin contamination closes Times Beach, threatens fifty other localities.
1986	State, suffering economic recession, institutes lottery.
1988	Court orders desegregation of Kansas City public schools.
1990	Governor signs educational bill allowing parental choice in public schools their children will attend.
1991	Kansas City elects its first black mayor, Emanuel Cleaver.
1993	St. Louis elects its first black mayor, Freeman Bosley, Jr.
1993	Floods cause five billion dollars damage in eastern Missouri.
Oct. 16, 2000	Governor Mel Carnahan, a candidate for U.S. Senate, is killed in airplane crash.
Nov. 7, 2000	Governor Carnahan is elected posthumously to the U.S. Senate; the state's interim governor appoints his widow to the seat.
Sept. 11, 2001	Gateway Arch in St. Louis is temporarily closed as a suspected terrorist target.
Jan., 2005	Richard Gephardt, longtime congressional member and House Democratic leader, retires from Congress after failing in bid for presidential nomination.
May 22, 2011	An EF5 tornado strikes the city of Joplin, killing 158 people. It is the costliest tornado in U.S. history, causing well over $2 billion in damage.

Notes for Further Study

Published Sources. P. C. Nagel's *Missouri: A History* (1988) is useful and readable. It should be read in conjunction with M. D. Rafferty's *Missouri: A Geography* (1982), which gives graphic descriptions of the state's topography. Michael J. O'Brien delves into Missouri's distant past in *Paradigms of the Past: The Story of Missouri Archeology* (1996). W. E. Foley views the development of Missouri from a wilderness to a state in *The Genesis of Missouri: From Wilderness to Statehood* (1989), while Walter D. Kamphoefner considers the nineteenth century German immigration into the state in *The Westphalians: From Germany to Missouri* (1987). More specialized is John E. Farley's *Earthquake Fears, Predictions, and Preparations in Mid-America* (1998), which offers a detailed account of the New Madrid earthquakes and explains the underlying geological structure that makes Missouri earthquake prone. Also somewhat specialized but of exceeding importance is Paul Finkelman's *Dred Scott v. Sandford: A Brief History with Documents* (1997). It offers a explanation of the case that helped to start the Civil War.

David Thelen's *Paths of Resistance: Tradition and Dignity in Industrializing Missouri* (1996) offers information about the industrialization of the state and the obstacles that the shift from agriculture to industry involved. *Dino, Godzilla, and the Pigs: My Life on Our Missouri Hog Farm* (1993) by Mary Elizabeth Fricke is a beguiling memoir that chronicles the author's growing up on a Missouri farm. It is interesting when read along with R. Douglas Hurt's *Agriculture and Slavery in Missouri's Little Dixie* (1992), focusing on the matter of what slavery meant to Missouri's agricultural economy. Joan Gilbert in *The Trail of Tears Across Missouri* (1996) deals with the dispossession of the Cherokee Indians from North Carolina and Tennessee, who were forced to go west to Missouri and Oklahoma. *American Confluence: The Missouri Frontier from Borderland to Border State* (2006) by Stephen Aron provides a window to frontier and pioneer life in the Missouri River region. *The Other Missouri History: Populists, Prostitutes, and Regular Folk* (2004), edited by Thomas M. Spencer, is a fascinating narrative of the state's social history. *Women in Missouri History: In Search of Power and Influence* (2004), edited by LeeAnn Whites, Mary C. Neth, and Gary R. Kremer, offers a collection of lively essays profiling several important women from the period of colonial settlement through the mid-twentieth century.

The Off the Beaten Path series typically delivers a solid blend of photographs and interesting text designed to guide travelers through the state; the series' *Missouri* (7th ed., 2004) by Patti DeLano is a worthwhile read. Among the best accounts of the state aimed at juvenile readers are Patricia K. Kummer's *Missouri* (rev. ed., 2002), Dennis B. and Judith Bloom Fradin's *Missouri* (1994), Rita C. LaDoux's *Missouri* (rev. ed., 2001), and William R. Sanford's *America the Beautiful: Missouri* (1990).

Web Resources. The state of Missouri Web site (www.mo.gov) offers comprehensive information about Missouri and its economy and leads users to other pertinent Web sites. The state's tourist bureau provides a site (www.visitmo.com/) offering voluminous information about tourism in Missouri and will direct viewers to lodgings, restaurants, and tourist attractions, including the twenty-two caves in the state open to tourists. People interested in Branson and its offerings should consult some of its fourteen Web sites, among them Branson.com (www.branson.com) and BransonInfo.com (www.bransoninfo.com). Lake of the Ozarks Web sites include Lake of the Ozarks (www.funlake.com/) and Lake of the Ozarks State Park (www.mostateparks.com/lakeozark .htm).

The Missouri Historical Society (www.mohistory.org/) should be the first stop for a wide range of information regarding the state's past. The Guide to the State of Missouri (www.theus50.com/missouri/) offers a detailed historical time line. Access Genealogy maintains pages that detail states' Indian tribes; those of Missouri can be found at www.accessgenealogy.com/missouri/. Web sites that detail cultural attractions include the St. Louis Art Museum (www.slam.org) and the Kansas City Museum (kansascitymuseum.org). The Harry S. Truman site (www.nps.gov/hstr) provides information about Truman, his home, and the Truman Library. Information about higher education in the state is best obtained from the Missouri Department of Higher Education site (www.dhe.mo.gov/). The state's Department of Natural Resources (www.dnr.mo.gov/index.html) provides visitors with information about state parks, conservation, and environmental issues.

Counties

County	2012 Population	Pop. Rank	Land Area (sq. miles)	Area Rank	County	2012 Population	Pop. Rank	Land Area (sq. miles)	Area Rank
Adair	25,581	42	567.32	61	Cape Girardeau	76,950	14	578.53	59
Andrew	17,417	63	432.70	100	Carroll	9,086	93	694.62	29
Atchison	5,517	107	547.30	67	Carter	6,262	105	507.36	78
Audrain	25,621	41	692.23	30	Cass	100,376	10	696.84	27
Barry	35,546	31	778.25	15	Cedar	13,799	74	474.48	89
Barton	12,337	81	591.92	58	Chariton	7,649	99	751.18	21
Bates	16,709	65	836.69	6	Christian	79,824	13	562.64	64
Benton	18,962	56	704.06	25	Clark	6,969	101	504.69	80
Bollinger	12,382	80	617.91	50	Clay	227,577	5	397.30	111
Boone	168,535	7	685.41	31	Clinton	20,508	53	418.96	106
Buchanan	89,706	12	408.03	109	Cole	76,363	15	393.75	112
Butler	43,053	25	694.67	28	Cooper	17,520	62	564.77	62
Caldwell	9,145	92	426.39	102	Crawford	24,832	45	742.52	23
Callaway	44,305	23	834.57	7	Dade	7,568	100	490.01	87
Camden	43,845	24	655.92	40	Dallas	16,799	64	540.77	70

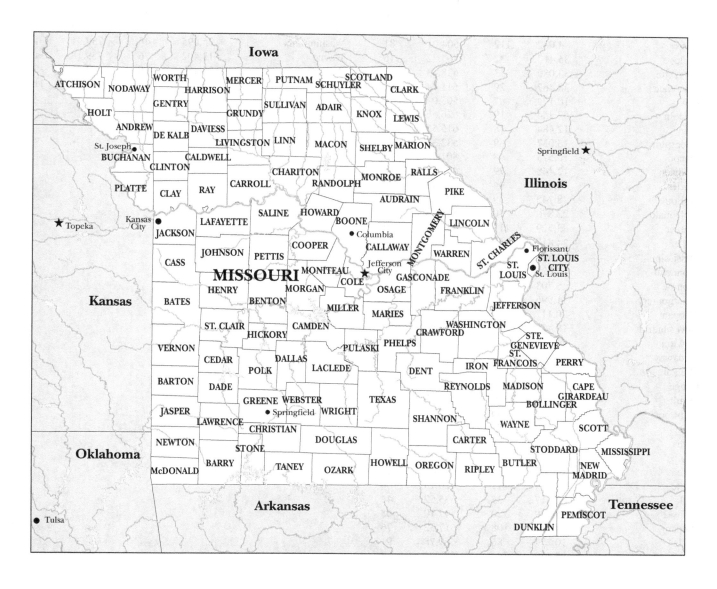

County	2012 Population	Pop. Rank	Land Area (sq. miles)	Area Rank
Daviess	8,239	98	563.24	63
DeKalb	12,940	77	421.36	103
Dent	15,647	66	752.79	20
Douglas	13,585	75	813.63	11
Dunklin	31,826	35	541.07	69
Franklin	101,412	9	922.68	4
Gasconade	14,972	70	517.80	75
Gentry	6,777	102	491.42	86
Greene	280,626	4	675.30	34
Grundy	10,338	85	435.28	99
Harrison	8,728	95	722.50	24
Henry	22,153	51	696.95	26
Hickory	9,391	91	399.09	110
Holt	4,655	110	462.69	94
Howard	10,169	88	463.85	93
Howell	40,629	27	927.25	3
Iron	10,374	84	550.26	66
Jackson	677,377	2	604.46	53
Jasper	115,258	8	638.49	43
Jefferson	220,209	6	656.63	39
Johnson	54,397	18	829.28	8
Knox	4,082	112	504.01	81
Laclede	35,417	32	764.72	16
Lafayette	33,080	33	628.43	47
Lawrence	38,467	29	611.74	52
Lewis	10,174	87	505.04	79
Lincoln	53,354	19	626.56	48
Linn	12,484	78	615.56	51
Livingston	15,037	69	532.33	73
Macon	15,573	68	801.23	13
Madison	12,448	79	494.39	84
Maries	9,014	94	526.98	74
Marion	28,745	39	436.92	97
McDonald	22,876	50	539.48	71
Mercer	3,729	113	453.84	95
Miller	24,817	46	592.59	56
Mississippi	14,322	71	411.58	108
Moniteau	15,625	67	415.03	107
Monroe	8,703	96	647.65	42
Montgomery	11,996	82	536.25	72
Morgan	20,117	54	597.63	55
New Madrid	18,488	59	674.84	35
Newton	59,069	17	624.76	49
Nodaway	23,419	47	876.96	5
Oregon	10,997	83	789.80	14
Osage	13,858	73	604.35	54
Ozark	9,601	89	744.97	22
Pemiscot	18,111	60	492.54	85
Perry	19,018	55	474.35	90
Pettis	42,319	26	682.22	32
Phelps	44,987	22	671.78	36
Pike	18,565	58	670.44	37
Platte	92,054	11	420.19	104
Polk	31,017	37	635.52	44
Pulaski	53,259	20	547.10	68
Putnam	4,931	108	517.32	76
Ralls	10,277	86	469.78	91
Randolph	25,330	43	482.68	88

County	2012 Population	Pop. Rank	Land Area (sq. miles)	Area Rank
Ray	23,064	49	568.81	60
Reynolds	6,667	103	808.48	12
Ripley	14,036	72	629.54	46
Saline	23,339	48	755.50	19
Schuyler	4,370	111	307.30	113
Scotland	4,877	109	436.67	98
Scott	39,139	28	419.99	105
Shannon	8,318	97	1,003.82	2
Shelby	6,234	106	500.86	82
St. Charles	368,666	3	560.44	65
St. Clair	9,474	90	669.98	38
St. Francois	65,917	16	451.89	96
St. Louis	1,000,438	1	507.80	77
Ste. Genevieve	17,740	61	499.15	83
Stoddard	29,795	38	823.22	10
Stone	31,568	36	464.03	92
Sullivan	6,546	104	647.98	41
Taney	52,956	21	632.44	45
Texas	25,810	40	1,177.27	1
Vernon	20,748	52	826.40	9
Warren	32,753	34	428.60	101
Washington	25,095	44	759.91	17
Wayne	13,402	76	759.18	18
Webster	36,351	30	592.56	57
Worth	2,079	114	266.61	114
Wright	18,629	57	681.77	33

Source: U.S. Census Bureau, 2012 Population Estimates

Cities

With 10,000 or more residents

Legal Name	2010 Population	Pop. Rank	Land Area (sq. miles)	Area Rank
Affton CDP	20,307	35	4.60	78
Arnold city	20,808	34	11.58	45
Ballwin city	30,404	20	8.99	58
Bellefontaine Neighbors city	10,860	78	4.32	81
Belton city	23,116	30	14.25	33
Blue Springs city	52,575	10	22.27	18
Bolivar city	10,325	82	8.28	62
Branson city	10,520	81	20.63	20
Bridgeton city	11,550	72	14.60	31
Cape Girardeau city	37,941	16	28.43	15
Carthage city	14,378	59	11.65	44
Chesterfield city	47,484	14	31.77	12
Clayton city	15,939	53	2.48	85
Columbia city	108,500	5	63.08	7
Concord CDP	16,421	49	5.48	75

Legal Name	2010 Population	Pop. Rank	Land Area (sq. miles)	Area Rank
Crestwood city	11,912	69	3.60	83
Creve Coeur city	17,833	44	10.27	50
Dardenne Prairie city	11,494	74	4.92	77
Eureka city	10,189	84	10.35	49
Excelsior Springs city	11,084	75	10.42	48
Farmington city	16,240	51	9.35	54
Ferguson city	21,203	33	6.19	69
Festus city	11,602	71	5.71	74
Florissant city	52,158	12	12.56	38
Fort Leonard Wood CDP	15,061	54	96.18	2
Fulton city	12,790	66	12.26	39
Gladstone city	25,410	28	8.05	63
Grain Valley city	12,854	65	6.06	70
Grandview city	24,475	29	14.73	29
Hannibal city	17,916	43	15.73	26

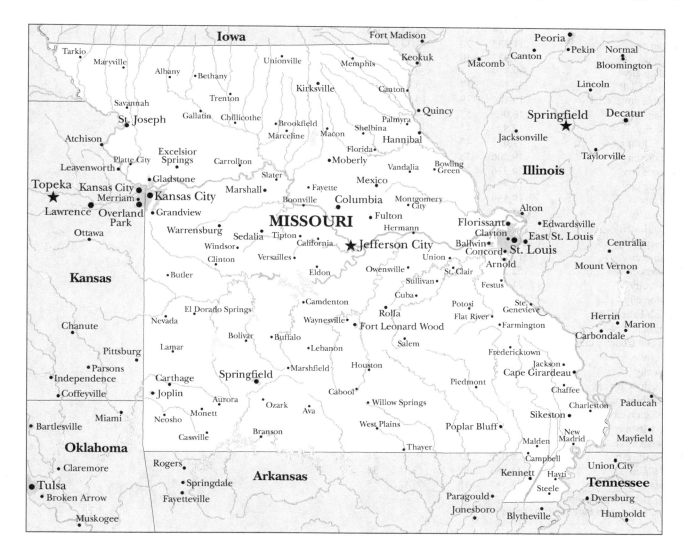

Legal Name	2010 Population	Pop. Rank	Land Area (sq. miles)	Area Rank
Harrisonville city	10,019	85	9.88	53
Hazelwood city	25,703	27	16.02	24
Independence city	116,830	4	77.57	4
Jackson city	13,758	62	10.94	47
Jefferson City city	43,079	15	35.95	10
Jennings city	14,712	56	3.70	82
Joplin city	50,150	13	35.56	11
Kansas City city	459,787	1	314.95	1
Kennett city	10,932	77	6.96	68
Kirksville city	17,505	46	14.39	32
Kirkwood city	27,540	25	9.16	56
Lake St. Louis city	14,545	57	7.91	64
Lebanon city	14,474	58	14.63	30
Lee's Summit city	91,364	6	63.35	6
Lemay CDP	16,645	48	4.37	79
Liberty city	29,149	22	29.03	14
Manchester city	18,094	42	5.08	76
Marshall city	13,065	63	10.22	51
Maryland Heights city	27,472	26	21.83	19
Maryville city	11,972	68	5.77	73
Mehlville CDP	28,380	24	7.46	65
Mexico city	11,543	73	12.00	41
Moberly city	13,974	61	12.22	40
Neosho city	11,835	70	15.73	26
Nixa city	19,022	40	8.48	61
O'Fallon city	79,329	7	29.19	13
Oakville CDP	36,143	17	15.93	25
Old Jamestown CDP	19,184	39	14.94	28
Overland city	16,062	52	4.36	80
Ozark city	17,820	45	11.10	46
Poplar Bluff city	17,023	47	12.90	37
Raymore city	19,206	38	17.58	22
Raytown city	29,526	21	9.93	52
Republic city	14,751	55	13.30	35
Rolla city	19,559	37	11.83	42
St. Ann city	13,020	64	3.18	84
St. Charles city	65,794	9	23.65	16
St. Joseph city	76,780	8	43.99	9
St. Louis city	319,294	2	61.91	8
St. Peters city	52,575	10	22.37	17
Sedalia city	21,387	32	13.29	36
Sikeston city	16,318	50	17.32	23
Spanish Lake CDP	19,650	36	7.42	66
Springfield city	159,498	3	81.72	3
Town and Country city	10,815	79	11.68	43
Troy city	10,540	80	7.30	67
Union city	10,204	83	9.16	56
University City city	35,371	19	5.90	71
Warrensburg city	18,838	41	8.85	59
Washington city	13,982	60	9.34	55
Webb City city	10,996	76	8.63	60
Webster Groves city	22,995	31	5.90	71
Wentzville city	29,070	23	19.96	21
West Plains city	11,986	67	13.31	34
Wildwood city	35,517	18	66.42	5

Note: CDP–Census Designated Place
Source: U.S. Census Bureau, 2010 Census

Survey Says...

This section presents current rankings from dozens of public and private sources. It shows how this state ranks in a number of critical categories, including education, job growth, cost of living, teen drivers, energy efficiency, and business environment. Sources include *Forbes, Reuters, U.S. News and World Report, CNN Money, Gallup,* and *Huffington Post.*

- Missouri ranked #25 in a government study measuring real gross domestic product (GDP)—the output of goods and services produced by labor and property located in the United States. The ranking is based on the percentage change compared with 2011 GDP.

  U.S. Department of Commerce, Bureau of Economic Analysis, June 2013; www.bea.gov

- Missouri ranked #22 in a government study measuring real gross domestic product (GDP)—the output of goods and services produced by labor and property located in the United States. The ranking is based on the dollar value of its GDP.

  U.S. Department of Commerce, Bureau of Economic Analysis, June 2013; www.bea.gov

- Missouri ranked #41 in the 17th edition of "Quality Counts; State of the States," Education Week's "report card" surveying key education indicators, policy efforts, and educational outcomes.

  Education Week, January 4, 2013 (online) and January 10, 2013 (print); www.edweek.org

- SERI (Science and Engineering Readiness Index) weighs the performance of the states' K-12 schools in preparing students in physics and calculus, the high school subjects considered most important for future scientists and engineers. Missouri ranked #33.

  Newsletter of the Forum on Education of the American Physical Society, Summer 2011 issue; www.huffingtonpost.com, July 11, 2011; updated October 1, 2012

- MoneyRates.com ranked Missouri #14 on its list of the best to worst states for making a living. Criteria: average income; inflation; employment prospects; and workers' Workplace Environment assessments according to the Gallup-Healthways Well-Being Index.

  www.money-rates.com, posted April 1, 2013

- *Forbes* analyzed business costs, labor supply, regulatory environment, current economic climate, growth prospects, and quality of life, to compile its "Best States for Business" rankings. Missouri ranked #29.

  www.forbes.com, posted December 12, 2012

- The 2012 Gallup-Healthways Well-Being Index, surveyed American's opinions on economic confidence, workplace perceptions, community climate, personal choices, and health predictors to assess the "future livability" of each state. Missouri ranked #37.

  "Utah Poised to Be the Best State to Live In," Gallup Wellbeing, www.gallup.com, August 7, 2012

- On CNBC's list of "America's Top States for Business 2013," Missouri ranked #26. Criteria: measures of competitiveness developed with input from the National Association of Manufacturers, the Council on Competitiveness, and other business groups weighed with the states' own marketing criteria.

  www.cnbc.com, consulted July 19, 2013

- Missouri ranked #33 on MoneyRates list of "Best-and Worst-States to Retire 2012." Criteria: life expectancy, crime rate, climate, economic conditions, taxes, job opportunities, and cost of living.

  www.money-rates.com, October 22, 2012

- Missouri ranked #11 on the 2013 Bankrate "Best Places to Retire" list ranking the states and District of Columbia on various criteria relating to health, safety, and cost.

  www.bankrate.com, May 6, 2013

- Missouri ranked #37 on the Social Science Research Council's "American Human Development Report: The Measure of America," assessing the 50 states plus the District of Columbia on health, education, and living-standard criteria.

  The Measure of America 2013-2014, posted June 19, 2013; www.measureofamerica.org

- Missouri ranked #29 on the Foundation for Child Development's (FCD) Child Well-being Index (CWI). The FCD used the KIDS COUNT report and the National Survey of Children's Health, the only state-level source for several key indicators of child well-being.

  Foundation for Child Development, January 18, 2012; fcd-us.org

- Missouri ranked #27 overall according to the 2013 KIDS COUNT Data Book, a project of the Annie E. Casey Foundation. Criteria: children's economic well-being, education, health, and family and community indicators.

  KIDS COUNT Data Center's Data Book, released June 20, 2013; http://datacenter.kidscount.org

- Missouri ranked #22 in the children's economic well-being category by the 2013 KIDS COUNT Data Book, a project of the Annie E. Casey Foundation.

  KIDS COUNT Data Center's Data Book, released June 20, 2013; http://datacenter.kidscount.org

- Missouri ranked #21 in the children's educational opportunities and attainments category by the 2013 KIDS COUNT Data Book, a project of the Annie E. Casey Foundation.

  KIDS COUNT Data Center's Data Book, released June 20, 2013; http://datacenter.kidscount.org

- Missouri ranked #32 in the children's health category by the 2013 KIDS COUNT Data Book, a project of the Annie E. Casey Foundation.

  KIDS COUNT Data Center's Data Book, released June 20, 2013; http://datacenter.kidscount.org

- Missouri ranked #26 in the family and community circumstances that factor into children's well-being category by the 2013 KIDS COUNT Data Book, a project of the Annie E. Casey Foundation.

  KIDS COUNT Data Center's Data Book, released June 20, 2013; http://datacenter.kidscount.org

- Missouri ranked #38 in the 2012 Gallup-Healthways Well-Being Index. Criteria: emotional health; physical health; healthy behavior; work environment; basic access to food, shelter, health care; and a safe and satisfying place to live.
  2012 State of Well-Being, Gallup-Healthways Well-Being Index, released February 28, 2013; www.well-beingindex.com

- *U.S. News and World Report's* "Best States for Teen Drivers" rankings are based on driving and road safety laws, federal reports on driver's licenses, car accident fatality, and road-quality statistics. Missouri ranked #36.
  U.S. News and World Report, March 18, 2010; www.usnews.com

- The Yahoo! Sports service Rivals.com ranks the states according to the strength of their high school football programs. Missouri ranked #27.
  "Ranking the States: Where Is the Best Football Played?," November 18, 2011; highschool.rivals.com

- iVillage ranked the states by hospitable living conditions for women. Criteria: economic success, access to affordable childcare, health care, reproductive rights, female representation in government, and educational attainment. Missouri ranked #36.
  iVillage, "50 Best to Worst States for Women," March 14, 2012; www.ivillage.com

- The League of American Bicyclists's "Bicycle Friendly States" ranked Missouri #30. Criteria: legislation and enforcement, policies and programs, infrastructure and funding, education and advocacy, and evaluation and planning.
  "Washington Tops the Bicycle-Friendly State Ranking," May 1, 2013; bicycling.com

- The federal Corporation for National and Community Service ranked the states and the District of Columbia by volunteer rates. Missouri ranked #15 for community service.
  "Volunteering and Civic Life in America 2012," www.volunteeringinamerica.gov, accessed July 24, 2013

- The Hospital Safety Score ranked states and the District of Columbia on their hospitals' performance scores. Missouri ranked #28. Criteria: avoiding preventable harm and medical errors, as demonstrated by 26 hospital safety metrics.
  Spring 2013 Hospital Safety Score, May 8, 2013; www.hospitalsafetyscore.org

- GMAC Insurance ranked the states and the District of Columbia by the performance of their drivers on the GMAC Insurance National Drivers Test, comprised of DMV test questions. Missouri ranked #8.
  "2011 GMAC Insurance National Drivers Test," www.gmacinsurance.com, accessed July 23, 2013

- Missouri ranked #16 in a "State Integrity Investigation" analysis of laws and practices intended to deter corruption and promote accountability and openness in campaign finance, ethics laws, lobbying regulations and management of state pension funds.
  "What's Your State's Grade?," www.publicintegrity.org, accessed July 23, 2013

- Missouri ranked #10 among the states and the District of Columbia in total rail miles, as tracked by the Association of American Railroads.
  "U.S. Freight Railroad Industry Snapshot: Railroads and States: Total Rail Miles by State: 2011"; www.aar.org, accessed July 23, 2013

- According to statistics compiled by the Beer Institute, Missouri ranked #18 among the states and the District of Columbia in per capita beer consumption of persons 21 years or older.
  "Shipments of Malt Beverages and Per Capita Consumption by State 2012;" www.beerinstitute.org

- According to Concordia University's "Public Education Costs per Pupil by State Rankings," based on statistics gathered by the U.S. Census Bureau, which includes the District of Columbia, Missouri ranked #29.
  Concordia University Online; education.cu-portland.edu, accessed July 24, 2013

- Missouri ranked #28 among the states and the District of Columbia in population density based on U.S. Census Bureau data for resident population and total land area. "List of U.S. States by Population Density."
  www.wikipedia.org, accessed July 24, 2013

- In "America's Health Rankings, 2012 Edition," by the United Health Foundation, Missouri ranked #42. Criteria included: rate of high school graduation; violent crime rate; incidence of infectious disease; childhood immunizations; prevalence of diabetes; per capita public-health funding; percentage of uninsured population; rate of children in poverty; and availability of primary-care physicians.
  United Health Foundation; www.americashealthrankings.org, accessed July 24, 2013

- The TechNet 2012 "State Broadband Index" ranked Missouri #32 on the following criteria: broadband adoption; network quality; and economic structure. Improved broadband use is hoped to promote economic development, build strong communities, improve delivery of government services and upgrade educational systems.
  TechNet; www.technet.org, accessed July 24, 2013

- Missouri was ranked #43 among the states and District of Columbia on the American Council for an Energy-Efficient Economy's "State Energy Efficiency Scorecard" for 2012.
  American Council for an Energy-Efficient Economy; aceee.org/sector/state-policy/scorecard, accessed July 24, 2013

Statistical Tables

DEMOGRAPHICS
Resident State and National Population, 1950-2012
Projected State and National Population, 2000-2030
Population by Age, 2012
Population by Race, 2012
Population by Hispanic Origin and Race, 2012

VITAL STATISTICS
Death Rates by Leading Causes, 2010
Death Rates by Selected Causes, 2010
Abortion Rates, 2009
Infant Mortality Rates, 1995-2009
Marriage and Divorce Rates, 2000-2011

ECONOMY
Nominal Gross Domestic Product by Industry, 2012
Real Gross Domestic Product, 2000-2012
Personal Income Per Capita, 1930-2012
Non-Farm Employment by Sector, 2012
Foreign Exports, 2000-2012
Energy Consumption, 2011

LAND AND WATER
Surface Area and Federally-Owned Land, 2007
Land Cover/Use of Non-Federal Rural Land, 2007
Farms and Crop Acreage, 2012

HEALTH AND MEDICAL CARE
Medical Professionals, 2012
Health Insurance Coverage, 2011
HIV, STD, and Tuberculosis Cases and Rates, 2011
Cigarette Smoking, 2011

HOUSING
Home Ownership Rates, 1995-2012
Home Sales, 2000-2010
Value of Owner-Occupied Homes, 2011

EDUCATION
School Enrollment, 2011
Educational Attainment, 2011
Public College Finances, FY 2012

TRANSPORTATION AND TRAVEL
Motor Vehicle Registrations and Drivers Licenses, 2011
Domestic Travel Expenditures, 2009
Retail Gasoline Prices, 2013
Public Road Length, 2011

CRIME AND LAW ENFORCEMENT
Full-Time Law Enforcement Officers, 2011
Prison Population, 2000-2012
Crime Rate, 2011

GOVERNMENT AND FINANCE
Local Governments by Type, 2012
State Government Revenue, 2011
State Government Expenditures, 2011
State Government General Expenditures by Function, 2011
State Government Finances, Cash and Debt, 2011

POLITICS
Composition of the Senate, 1995-2013
Composition of the House of Representatives, 1995-2013
Composition of State Legislature, 2004-2013
Voter Participation in Presidential Elections, 1980-2012
Governors Since Statehood

DEMOGRAPHICS

Resident State and National Population, 1950–2012

Year	State Population	U.S. Population	State Share
1950	3,955,000	151,326,000	2.61%
1960	4,320,000	179,323,000	2.41%
1970	4,677,623	203,302,031	2.30%
1980	4,916,686	226,545,805	2.17%
1990	5,117,073	248,709,873	2.06%
2000	5,596,564	281,424,600	1.99%
2010	5,988,927	308,745,538	1.94%
2012	6,021,988	313,914,040	1.92%

Note: 1950/1960 population figures are rounded to the nearest thousand.
Source: U.S. Census Bureau, Decennial Census 1950–2010; U.S. Census Bureau, 2012 Population Estimates

Projected State and National Population, 2000–2030

Year	State Population	U.S. Population	State Share
2000	5,595,211	281,421,906	1.99%
2005	5,765,166	295,507,134	1.95%
2010	5,922,078	308,935,581	1.92%
2015	6,069,556	322,365,787	1.88%
2020	6,199,882	335,804,546	1.85%
2025	6,315,366	349,439,199	1.81%
2030	6,430,173	363,584,435	1.77%
State population growth, 2000–2030			834,962
State percentage growth, 2000–2030			14.9%

Source: U.S. Census Bureau, Population Division, Interim State Population Projections, 2005

Population by Age, 2012

Age Group	State Population	Percent of Total Population	
		State	U.S.
Under 5 years	379,246	6.3%	6.4%
5 to 14 years	785,738	13.0%	13.1%
15 to 24 years	832,017	13.8%	14.0%
25 to 34 years	791,739	13.1%	13.5%
35 to 44 years	730,782	12.1%	12.9%
45 to 54 years	856,529	14.2%	14.1%
55 to 64 years	762,756	12.7%	12.3%
65 to 74 years	487,289	8.1%	7.6%
75 to 84 years	275,607	4.6%	4.2%
85 years and older	120,285	2.0%	1.9%
Under 18 years	1,403,475	23.3%	23.5%
65 years and older	883,181	14.7%	13.7%
Median age (years)	–	38.1	37.4

Source: U.S. Census Bureau, Annual Estimates of the Resident Population for Selected Age Groups by Sex for the United States, States, Counties, and Puerto Rico Commonwealth and Municipios: April 1, 2010 to July 1, 2012

Population by Race, 2012

Race	State Population	Percent of Total Population	
		State	U.S.
All residents	6,021,988	100.00%	100.00%
White	5,049,604	83.85%	77.89%
African American	706,079	11.73%	13.13%
Native American	31,631	0.53%	1.23%
Asian	107,092	1.78%	5.14%
Native Hawaiian	7,821	0.13%	0.23%
Two or more races	119,761	1.99%	2.39%

Source: U.S. Census Bureau, Population Division, Annual Estimates of the Resident Population by Sex, Race and Hispanic Origin for the United States, States, and Counties: April 1, 2010 to July 1, 2012

Population by Hispanic Origin and Race, 2012

Hispanic Origin/Race	State Population	Percent of Total Population	
		State	U.S.
All residents	6,021,988	100.00%	100.00%
All Hispanic residents	225,314	3.74%	16.89%
Hispanic			
White	193,119	3.21%	14.91%
African American	11,420	0.19%	0.79%
Native American	6,823	0.11%	0.49%
Asian	2,000	0.03%	0.17%
Native Hawaiian	1,414	0.02%	0.06%
Two or more races	10,538	0.17%	0.48%
Not Hispanic			
White	4,856,485	80.65%	62.98%
African American	694,659	11.54%	12.34%
Native American	24,808	0.41%	0.74%
Asian	105,092	1.75%	4.98%
Native Hawaiian	6,407	0.11%	0.17%
Two or more races	109,223	1.81%	1.91%

Source: U.S. Census Bureau, Population Division, Annual Estimates of the Resident Population by Sex, Race and Hispanic Origin for the United States, States, and Counties: April 1, 2010 to July 1, 2012

VITAL STATISTICS

Death Rates by Leading Causes, 2010

Cause	State	U.S.
Malignant neoplasms	199.9	186.2
Ischaemic heart diseases	145.9	122.9
Other forms of heart disease	57.5	53.4
Chronic lower respiratory diseases	55.8	44.7
Cerebrovascular diseases	47.1	41.9
Organic, incl. symptomatic, mental disorders	37.4	35.7
Other degenerative diseases of the nervous sys.	31.9	28.4
Other external causes of accidental injury	33.5	26.5
Diabetes mellitus	22.6	22.4
Hypertensive diseases	15.4	20.4
All causes	875.8	799.5

Note: Figures are age-adjusted death rates per 100,000 population
Source: CDC/NCHS, Underlying Cause of Death 1999–2010 on CDC WONDER Online Database

Death Rates by Selected Causes, 2010

Cause	State	U.S.
Assault	7.3	5.2
Diseases of the liver	12.2	13.9
Human immunodeficiency virus (HIV) disease	1.8	2.7
Influenza and pneumonia	18.7	16.2
Intentional self-harm	14.3	12.4
Malnutrition	0.9	0.9
Obesity and other hyperalimentation	1.9	1.8
Renal failure	18.3	14.4
Transport accidents	15.0	12.1
Viral hepatitis	2.5	2.4

Note: Figures are age-adjusted death rates per 100,000 population; A dash indicates that data was not available or was suppressed
Source: CDC/NCHS, Underlying Cause of Death 1999–2010 on CDC WONDER Online Database

Abortion Rates, 2009

Category	2009
By state of residence	
Total abortions	13,534
Abortion rate[1]	11.4%
Abortion ratio[2]	172
By state of occurrence	
Total abortions	6,881
Abortion rate[1]	5.8%
Abortion ratio[2]	87
Abortions obtained by out-of-state residents	8.1%
U.S. abortion rate[1]	15.1%
U.S. abortion ratio[2]	227

Note: (1) Number of abortions per 1,000 women aged 15–44 years; (2) Number of abortions per 1,000 live births; A dash indicates that data was not available
Source: CDC/NCHS, Morbidity and Mortality Weekly Report, November 23, 2012 (Abortion Surveillance, United States, 2009)

Infant Mortality Rates, 1995–2009

Category	1995	2000	2005	2009
All state residents	7.37	7.19	7.52	7.07
All U.S. residents	7.57	6.89	6.86	6.39
All state white residents	6.31	6.09	6.53	6.03
All U.S. white residents	6.30	5.71	5.73	5.33
All state black residents	13.16	13.94	13.61	13.02
All U.S. black residents	14.58	13.48	13.26	12.12

Note: Figures represent deaths per 1,000 live births of resident infants under one year old, exclusive of fetal deaths; A dash indicates that data was not available or was suppressed.
Source: Centers of Disease Control and Prevention, Division of Vital Statistics, Linked Birth/Infant Death Records on CDC Wonder Online

Marriage and Divorce Rates, 2000–2011

Year	Marriage Rate		Divorce Rate	
	State	U.S.	State	U.S.
2000	7.8	8.2	4.5	4.0
2002	7.3	8.0	4.0	3.9
2004	7.1	7.8	3.8	3.7
2006	6.9	7.5	3.8	3.7
2008	6.8	7.1	3.7	3.5
2010	6.5	6.8	3.9	3.6
2011	6.6	6.8	3.9	3.6

Note: Rates are based on provisional counts of marriages/divorces by state of occurrence and are per 1,000 total population residing in area
Source: CDC/NCHS, National Vital Statistics System

ECONOMY

Nominal Gross Domestic Product by Industry, 2012
In millions of current dollars

Industry	State GDP
Accommodation and food services	7,593
Administrative and waste management services	8,046
Agriculture, forestry, fishing, and hunting	3,299
Arts, entertainment, and recreation	3,559
Construction	9,238
Educational services	3,112
Finance and insurance	17,079
Health care and social assistance	23,257
Information	13,584
Management of companies and enterprises	7,740
Manufacturing	32,275
Mining	315
Other services, except government	6,853
Professional, scientific, and technical services	16,715
Real estate and rental and leasing	26,737
Retail trade	16,872
Transportation and warehousing	9,232
Utilities	5,204
Wholesale trade	15,891

Source: U.S. Department of Commerce, Bureau of Economic Analysis, Survey of Current Business

Real Gross Domestic Product, 2000–2012
In millions of chained 2005 dollars

Year	State GDP	U.S. GDP	State Share
2000	204,918	11,225,406	1.83%
2005	216,336	12,539,116	1.73%
2010	216,681	12,897,088	1.68%
2012	221,702	13,430,576	1.65%

Source: U.S. Department of Commerce, Bureau of Economic Analysis, Survey of Current Business

Personal Income Per Capita, 1930–2012

Year	State	U.S.
1930	$558	$618
1940	$516	$593
1950	$1,421	$1,503
1960	$2,190	$2,268
1970	$3,855	$4,084
1980	$9,306	$10,091
1990	$17,582	$19,354
2000	$27,885	$30,319
2010	$36,406	$39,791
2012	$39,049	$42,693

Source: U.S. Department of Commerce, Bureau of Economic Analysis, Regional Economic Accounts

Non-Farm Employment by Sector, 2012
In thousands

Sector	Employment
Construction	104.0
Education and health services	412.5
Financial activities	164.1
Government	437.4
Information	58.2
Leisure and hospitality	275.1
Mining and logging	4.1
Manufacturing	248.3
Other services	114.0
Professional and business services	337.9
Trade, transportation, and utilities	513.8
All sectors	2,669.4

Source: U.S. Bureau of Labor Statistics, State and Area Employment

Foreign Exports, 2000–2012
In millions of dollars

Year	State Exports	U.S. Exports	State Share
2000	6,497	712,054	0.91%
2002	6,786	649,940	1.04%
2004	9,021	768,554	1.17%
2006	12,781	973,994	1.31%
2008	12,852	1,222,545	1.05%
2010	12,924	1,208,080	1.07%
2012	13,927	1,478,268	0.94%

Note: U.S. figures exclude data from Puerto Rico, U.S. Virgin Islands, and unallocated exports
Source: U.S. Department of Commerce, International Trade Admin., Office of Trade and Industry Information, Manufacturing and Services

Energy Consumption, 2011

In trillions of BTUs, except as noted

Total energy consumption	
Total state energy consumption	1,878.1
Total U.S. energy consumption	97,387.3
State share of U.S. total	1.93%
Per capita consumption (in millions of BTUs)	
Total state per capita consumption	312.5
Total U.S. per capita consumption	312.6
End-use sectors	
Residential	536.9
Commercial	413.6
Industrial	360.2
Transportation	567.4
Sources of energy	
Petroleum	642.0
Natural gas	274.9
Coal	825.6
Renewable energy	88.7
Nuclear electric power	98.1

Source: U.S. Energy Information Administration, State Energy Data 2011: Consumption

LAND AND WATER

Surface Area and Federally-Owned Land, 2007

In thousands of acres

Category	State	U.S.	State Share
Total surface area	44,613.9	1,937,664.2	2.30%
Total land area	43,747.6	1,886,846.9	2.32%
Non-federal land	41,828.2	1,484,910.0	2.82%
Developed	2,931.5	111,251.2	2.64%
Rural	38,896.7	1,373,658.8	2.83%
Federal land	1,919.4	401,936.9	0.48%
Water area	866.3	50,817.3	1.70%

Source: U.S. Department of Agriculture, Natural Resources Conservation Service, 2007 National Resources Inventory

Land Cover/Use of Non-Federal Rural Land, 2007

In thousands of acres

Category	State	U.S.	State Share
Total rural land	38,896.7	1,373,658.8	2.83%
Cropland	13,285.7	357,023.5	3.72%
CRP[1] land	1,463.3	32,850.2	4.45%
Pastureland	10,950.4	118,615.7	9.23%
Rangeland	83.1	409,119.4	0.02%
Forest land	12,430.1	406,410.4	3.06%
Other rural land	684.1	49,639.6	1.38%

Note: (1) Conservation Reserve Program was created to assist private landowners in converting highly erodible cropland to vegetative cover.
Source: U.S. Department of Agriculture, Natural Resources Conservation Service, 2007 National Resources Inventory

Farms and Crop Acreage, 2012

Category	State	U.S.	State Share
Farms (in thousands)	106.0	2,170.0	4.88%
Acres (in millions)	29.0	914.0	3.17%
Acres per farm	273.6	421.2	–

Source: U.S. Department of Agriculture, National Agricultural Statistical Service, Quick Stats, 2012 Survey Data

HEALTH AND MEDICAL CARE

Medical Professionals, 2012

Profession	State Number	U.S. Number	State Share	State Rate[1]	U.S. Rate[1]
Physicians[2]	17,069	894,637	1.91%	284.1	287.1
Dentists	3,034	193,587	1.57%	50.5	62.1
Podiatrists	268	17,469	1.53%	4.5	5.6
Optometrists	969	45,638	2.12%	16.1	14.6
Chiropractors	1,831	77,494	2.36%	30.5	24.9

Note: (1) Rates are per 100,000 population; (2) Includes total, active Doctors of Osteopathic Medicine and Doctors of Medicine in 2011.
Source: U.S. Department of Health and Human Services, Bureau of Health Professions, Area Health Resource File, 2012-2013

Health Insurance Coverage, 2011

Category	State	U.S.
Total persons covered	5,020,000	260,214,000
Total persons not covered	878,000	48,613,000
Percent not covered	14.9%	15.7%
Children under age 18 covered	1,249,000	67,143,000
Children under age 18 not covered	162,000	6,965,000
Percent of children not covered	11.5%	9.4%

Source: U.S. Census Bureau, Current Population Survey, 2012 Annual Social and Economic Supplement

HIV, STD, and Tuberculosis Cases and Rates, 2011

Disease	State Cases	State Rate[1]	U.S. Rate[1]
Chlamydia	27,887	465.6	457.6
Gonorrhea	7,802	130.3	104.2
HIV diagnosis	562	11.2	15.8
HIV, stage 3 (AIDS)	361	7.2	10.3
Syphilis, early latent	124	2.1	4.3
Syphilis, primary/secondary	136	2.3	4.5
Tuberculosis	96	1.6	3.4

Note: (1) Rates are per 100,000 population
Source: Centers for Disease Control and Prevention

Cigarette Smoking, 2011

Category	State	U.S.
Adults who are current smokers	25.0%	21.2%
Adults who smoke everyday	19.4%	15.4%
Adults who smoke some days	5.6%	5.7%
Adults who are former smokers	25.0%	25.1%
Adults who never smoked	50.0%	52.9%

Source: Centers for Disease Control and Prevention, Behaviorial Risk Factor Surveillance System, Tobacco Use, 2011

HOUSING

Home Ownership Rates, 1995–2012

Area	1995	2000	2005	2010	2012
State	69.4%	74.2%	72.3%	71.2%	70.8%
U.S.	64.7%	67.4%	68.9%	66.9%	65.4%

Source: U.S. Census Bureau, Housing Vacancies and Homeownership, Annual Statistics

Home Sales, 2000–2010
In thousands of units

Year	State Sales	U.S. Sales	State Share
2000	110.2	5,174	2.13%
2002	115.2	5,632	2.05%
2004	141.8	6,778	2.09%
2006	135.3	6,478	2.09%
2008	108.7	4,913	2.21%
2010	94.6	4,908	1.93%

Note: Units include single-family homes, condos and co-ops
Source: National Association of Realtors, Real Estate Outlook, Market Trends & Insights

Value of Owner-Occupied Homes, 2011

Value	Total Units in State	Percent of Total, State	Percent of Total, U.S.
Less than $50,000	182,035	11.4%	8.8%
$50,000 to $99,000	342,114	21.5%	16.0%
$100,000 to $149,000	358,607	22.5%	16.5%
$150,000 to $199,000	285,475	17.9%	15.4%
$200,000 to $299,000	245,415	15.4%	18.2%
$300,000 to $499,000	126,123	7.9%	15.2%
$500,000 to $999,000	43,297	2.7%	7.9%
$1,000,000 or more	9,965	0.6%	2.0%
Median value	–	$136,900	$173,600

Source: U.S. Census Bureau, 2011 American Community Survey 1-Year Estimates

EDUCATION

School Enrollment, 2011

Educational Level	Students Enrolled in State	Percent of Total, State	Percent of Total, U.S.
All levels	1,569,557	100.0%	100.0%
Nursery school, preschool	105,239	6.7%	6.0%
Kindergarten	81,135	5.2%	5.1%
Elementary (grades 1–8)	614,703	39.2%	39.5%
Secondary (grades 9–12)	323,644	20.6%	20.7%
College or graduate school	444,836	28.3%	28.7%

Note: Figures cover the population 3 years and over enrolled in school
Source: U.S. Census Bureau, 2011 American Community Survey 1-Year Estimates

Educational Attainment, 2011

Highest Level of Education	State	U.S.
High school diploma	87.6%	85.9%
Bachelor's degree	26.1%	28.5%
Graduate/Professional degree	9.7%	10.6%

Note: Figures cover the population 25 years and over
Source: U.S. Census Bureau, 2011 American Community Survey 1-Year Estimates

Public College Finances, FY 2012

Category	State	U.S.
Full-time equivalent enrollment (FTE)[1]	196,360	11,548,974
Educational appropriations per FTE[2]	$4,984	$5,906
Net tuition revenue per FTE[3]	$4,885	$5,189
Total educational revenue per FTE[4]	$9,870	$11,043

(1) Full-time equivalent enrollment equates student credit hours to full time, academic year students, but excludes medical students; (2) Educational appropriations measure state and local support available for public higher education operating expenses including ARRA funds and excludes appropriations for independent institutions, financial aid for students attending independent institutions, research, hospitals, and medical education; (3) Net tuition revenue is calculated by taking the gross amount of tuition and fees, less state and institutional financial aid, tuition waivers or discounts, and medical student tuition and fees. Net tuition revenue used for capital debt service is included in the net tuition revenue figures; (4) Total educational revenue is the sum of educational appropriations and net tuition excluding net tuition revenue used for capital debt service.
Source: State Higher Education Executive Officers, State Higher Education Finance FY 2012

TRANSPORTATION AND TRAVEL

Motor Vehicle Registrations and Drivers Licenses, 2011

Vehicle Type	State	U.S.	State Share
Automobiles[1]	2,440,765	125,656,528	1.94%
Buses	16,087	666,064	2.42%
Trucks	2,572,195	118,455,587	2.17%
Motorcycles	140,947	8,437,502	1.67%
Drivers licenses	4,277,037	211,874,649	2.02%

Note: Motor vehicle registrations include private, commercial, and publicly-owned vehicles; (1) Includes taxicabs
Source: U.S. Department of Transportation, Federal Highway Administration

Domestic Travel Expenditures, 2009
In millions of dollars

Category	State	U.S.	State Share
Travel expenditures	$11,351	$610,200	1.86%

Note: Figures represent U.S. spending on domestic overnight trips and day trips of 50 miles or more, one way, away from home. Excludes spending by foreign visitors.
Source: U.S. Travel Association, Impact of Travel on State Economies, 2009

Retail Gasoline Prices, 2013

Gasoline Grade	State Average	U.S. Average
Regular	$3.52	$3.65
Mid	$3.66	$3.81
Premium	$3.84	$3.98
Diesel	$3.70	$3.88
Excise tax[1]	35.7 cents	49.4 cents

Note: Gasoline prices as of 7/26/2013; (1) Includes state and federal excise taxes and other state taxes as of July 1, 2013
Source: American Automobile Association, Daily Fuel Guage Report; American Petroleum Institute, State Motor Fuel Taxes, 2013

Public Road Length, 2011

Type	State Mileage	U.S. Mileage	State Share
Interstate highways	1,207	46,960	2.57%
Other highways	1,432	15,719	9.11%
Principal arterial	3,242	156,262	2.07%
Minor arterial	5,984	242,942	2.46%
Major collector	18,812	534,592	3.52%
Minor collector	6,496	266,357	2.44%
Local	94,495	2,814,925	3.36%
Urban	23,839	1,095,373	2.18%
Rural	107,827	2,982,383	3.62%
Total	131,667	4,077,756	3.23%

Note: Combined urban and rural road mileage equals the total of the other road types
Source: U.S. Department of Transportation, Federal Highway Administration, Public Road Length, 2011

CRIME AND LAW ENFORCEMENT

Full-Time Law Enforcement Officers, 2011

Gender	State Number	State Rate[1]	U.S. Rate[1]
Male officers	13,062	221.0	210.3
Female officers	1,424	24.1	28.1
Total officers	14,486	245.1	238.3

Note: (1) Rates are per 100,000 population
Source: Federal Bureau of Investigation, Uniform Crime Reports, Crime in the United States 2011

Prison Population, 2000–2012

Year	State Population	U.S. Population	State Share
2000	27,543	1,391,261	1.98%
2005	30,823	1,527,929	2.02%
2010	30,623	1,613,803	1.90%
2011	30,833	1,598,783	1.93%
2012	31,247	1,571,013	1.99%

Note: Figures include prisoners under the jurisdiction of state or federal correctional authorities.
Source: U.S. Department of Justice, Bureau of Justice Statistics, Prisoners in 2006, 2011, 2012 (Advance Counts)

Crime Rate, 2011

Incidents per 100,000 residents

Category	State	U.S.
Violent crimes	447.4	386.3
Murder	6.1	4.7
Forcible rape	24.3	26.8
Robbery	104.3	113.7
Aggravated assault	312.7	241.1
Property crimes	3,308.8	2,908.7
Burglary	745.7	702.2
Larceny/theft	2,308.3	1,976.9
Motor vehicle theft	254.8	229.6
All crimes	3,756.2	3,295.0

Source: Federal Bureau of Investigation, Uniform Crime Reports, Crime in the United States 2011

GOVERNMENT AND FINANCE

Local Governments by Type, 2012

Government Type	State	U.S.	State Share
All local governments	3,752	89,004	4.22%
County	114	3,031	3.76%
Municipality	955	19,522	4.89%
Town/Township	312	16,364	1.91%
Special District	1,837	37,203	4.94%
Ind. School District	534	12,884	4.14%

Source: U.S. Census Bureau, 2012 Census of Governments: Organization Component Preliminary Estimates

State Government Revenue, 2011

In thousands of dollars, except for per capita figures

Total revenue	$38,606,945
Total revenue per capita, State	$6,425
Total revenue per capita, U.S.	$7,271
General revenue	$27,082,904
Intergovernmental revenue	$12,015,114
Taxes	$10,109,918
General sales	$2,972,654
Selective sales	$1,654,538
License taxes	$573,309
Individual income taxes	$4,534,346
Corporate income taxes	$323,593
Other taxes	$51,478
Current charges	$2,778,187
Miscellaneous general revenue	$2,179,685
Utility revenue	$0
Liquor store revenue	$0
Insurance trust revenue[1]	$11,524,041

Note: (1) Within insurance trust revenue, net earnings of state retirement systems is a calculated statistic, and thus can be positive or negative. Net earnings is the sum of earnings on investments plus gains on investments minus losses on investments.
Source: U.S. Census Bureau, 2011 Annual Survey of State Government Finances

State Government Expenditures, 2011

In thousands of dollars, except for per capita figures

Total expenditure	$30,646,880
Total expenditure per capita, State	$5,100
Total expenditure per capita, U.S.	$6,427
Intergovernmental expenditure	$5,948,493
Direct expenditure	$24,698,387
Current operation	$16,709,191
Capital outlay	$1,767,540
Insurance benefits and repayments	$4,874,147
Assistance and subsidies	$525,418
Interest on debt	$822,091
Utility expenditure	$0
Liquor store expenditure	$0
Insurance trust expenditure	$4,874,147

Source: U.S. Census Bureau, 2011 Annual Survey of State Government Finances

State Government General Expenditures by Function, 2011

In thousands of dollars

Education	$8,854,989
Public welfare	$7,586,724
Hospitals	$1,492,957
Health	$1,402,255
Highways	$2,032,506
Police protection	$218,447
Correction	$720,834
Natural resources	$307,101
Parks and recreation	$37,915
Governmental administration	$532,697
Interest on general debt	$822,091
Other and unallocable	$1,764,217

Source: U.S. Census Bureau, 2011 Annual Survey of State Government Finances

State Government Finances, Cash and Debt, 2011

In thousands of dollars, except for per capita figures

Debt at end of fiscal year	
State, total	$20,682,303
State, per capita	$3,442
U.S., per capita	$3,635
Cash and security holdings	
State, total	$70,741,709
State, per capita	$11,773
U.S., per capita	$11,759

Source: U.S. Census Bureau, 2011 Annual Survey of State Government Finances

POLITICS

Composition of the Senate, 1995–2013

Congress (Year)	State/U.S	Dem	Rep	Total
104th (1995)	State delegates	0	2	2
	Total U.S.	48	52	100
105th (1997)	State delegates	1	1	2
	Total U.S.	45	55	100
106th (1999)	State delegates	0	2	2
	Total U.S.	45	55	100
107th (2001)	State delegates	0	2	2
	Total U.S.	50	50	100
108th (2003)	State delegates	0	2	2
	Total U.S.	48	51	100
109th (2005)	State delegates	0	2	2
	Total U.S.	44	55	100
110th (2007)	State delegates	1	1	2
	Total U.S.	49	49	100
111th (2009)	State delegates	1	1	2
	Total U.S.	57	41	100
112th (2011)	State delegates	1	1	2
	Total U.S.	51	47	100
113th (2013)	State delegates	1	1	2
	Total U.S.	54	45	100

Note: Figures are for the starts of first sessions; Totals include Democratic (Dem) and Republican (Rep) members as well as vacancies and seats held by independent party members
Source: U.S. Congress, Congressional Directory

Composition of the House of Representatives, 1995–2013

Congress (Year)	State/U.S	Dem	Rep	Total
104th (1995)	State delegates	6	3	9
	Total U.S.	204	230	435
105th (1997)	State delegates	5	4	9
	Total U.S.	207	226	435
106th (1999)	State delegates	5	4	9
	Total U.S.	211	223	435
107th (2001)	State delegates	4	5	9
	Total U.S.	212	221	435
108th (2003)	State delegates	4	5	9
	Total U.S.	205	229	435
109th (2005)	State delegates	4	5	9
	Total U.S.	202	231	435
110th (2007)	State delegates	4	5	9
	Total U.S.	233	198	435
111th (2009)	State delegates	4	5	9
	Total U.S.	256	178	435
112th (2011)	State delegates	3	6	9
	Total U.S.	193	242	435
113th (2013)	State delegates	2	6	8
	Total U.S.	201	234	435

Note: Figures are for the starts of first sessions; Totals include Democratic (Dem) and Republican (Rep) members as well as vacancies and seats held by independent party members
Source: U.S. Congress, Congressional Directory

Composition of State Legislature, 2004–2013

Year	Democrats	Republicans	Total
State Senate			
2004	14	20	34
2005	10	22	34
2006	11	22	34
2007	13	21	34
2008	14	20	34
2009	11	23	34
2010	11	23	34
2011	7	26	34
2012	8	26	34
2013	10	24	34
State House			
2004	73	90	163
2005	66	97	163
2006	64	96	163
2007	71	92	163
2008	71	92	163
2009	74	89	163
2010	74	88	163
2011	57	106	163
2012	56	106	163
2013	52	109	163

Note: Totals may include minor party members and vacancies
Source: The Council of State Governments, State Legislatures

Voter Participation in Presidential Elections, 1980–2012

Year	Voting-eligible State Population	State Voter Turnout Rate	U.S. Voter Turnout Rate
1980	3,529,489	59.5	54.2
1984	3,617,948	58.7	55.2
1988	3,696,905	56.6	52.8
1992	3,792,675	63.1	58.1
1996	3,919,885	55.1	51.7
2000	4,052,255	58.2	54.2
2004	4,180,960	65.3	60.1
2008	4,327,572	67.6	61.6
2012	4,410,813	62.5	58.2

Note: All figures are based on the voting-eligible population which excludes person ineligible to vote such as non-citizens, felons (depending on state law), and mentally-incapacitated persons. U.S. figures include the overseas eligible population (including military personnel).
Source: McDonald, Michael P., United States Election Project, Presidential Voter Turnout Rates, 1980–2012

Governors Since Statehood

Alexander McNair (O) 1820-1824
Frederick Bates (O) . . . . (d) 1824-1825
Abraham J. Williams (O) 1825-1826
John Miller (O) 1826-1832
Daniel Dunkin (D) . . . . (r) 1832-1836
Lillburn W. Boggs (D) 1836-1840
Thomas Reynolds (D) . . . . (d) 1840-1844
Meredith M. Marmaduke (D) 1844
John C. Edwards (D) 1844-1848
Austin A. King (D) 1848-1853
Sterling Price (D) 1853-1857

Truston Polk (D) 1857
Hancock L. Jackson (D) 1857
Robert M. Stewart (D) 1857-1861
Claiborne F. Jackson (D) . . . . (i) 1861
Hamilton R. Gamble (O) . . . . (d) 1861-1864
Willard P. Hall (O) 1864-1865
Thomas C. Fletcher (R) 1865-1869
Joseph W. McClurg (R) 1869-1871
Benjamin Gratz Brown (R) 1871-1873
Silas Woodson (D) 1873-1875
Charles H. Hardin (D) 1875-1877
John S. Phelps (D) 1877-1881
Thomas T. Crittenden (D) 1881-1885
John S. Marmaduke (D) . . . . (d) 1885-1887
Albert P. Morehouse (D) 1887-1889
David R. Francis (D) 1889-1893
William J. Stone (D) 1893-1897
Lon V. Stephens (D) 1897-1901
Alexander M. Dockery (D) 1901-1905
Joseph W. Polk (D) 1905-1909
Herbert S. Hadley (R) 1909-1913
Elliott W. Major (D) 1913-1917
Frederick D. Gardner (D) 1917-1921
Arthur M. Hyde (R) 1921-1925
Samuel A. Baker (R) 1925-1929
Henry S. Caulfield (R) 1929-1933
Guy B. Park (D) 1933-1937
Lloyd C. Stark (D) 1937-1941
Forrest C. Donnell (R) 1941-1945
Phillip M. Donnelly (D) 1945-1949
Forest Smith (D) 1949-1953
Phillip M. Donnelly (D) 1953-1957
James T. Blair Jr. (D) 1957-1961
John M. Dalton (D) 1961-1965
Warren E. Hearnes (D) 1965-1973
Christopher S. Bond (R) 1973-1977
Joseph P. Teasdale (D) 1977-1981
Christopher S. Bond (R) 1981-1985
John D. Ashcroft (R) 1985-1993
Mel Carnahan (D) . . . . (d) 1993-2000
Roger B. Wilson (D) 2000-2001
Robert Lee Holden Jr. (D) 2001-2005
Matthew Roy Blunt (R) 2005-2009
Jay Nixon (D) . . . . 2009-2017 (term limits)

Note: (D) Democrat; (R) Republican; (O) Other party; (r) resigned; (d) died in office; (i) removed from office

Montana

Location: Northwestern United States

Area and rank: 145,556 square miles (376,991 square kilometers); 147,046 square miles (380,849 square kilometers) including water; fourth largest state in area

Coastline: none

Population and rank: 1,005,141 (2012 estimate); forty-fourth largest state in population

Capital city: Helena (28,190 people in 2010 census)

Largest city: Billings (104,170 people in 2010 census)

State capitol building in Helena, Montana. (Travel Montana/Donnie Sexton)

Became territory:
May 26, 1864

Entered Union and rank:
November 8, 1889;
forty-first state

**Present constitution
adopted:** 1972

Counties: 56, as well
as a small part of
Yellowstone National
Park

State name: "Montana" is
a Latinized form for a
Spanish word meaning
"mountainous."

State nickname: Treasure State

Motto: *Oro y plata* (Gold and silver)

State flag: Dark blue field with the state seal emblem and
name "Montana" above

Highest point: Granite Peak—12,799 feet (244 meters)

Lowest point: Kootenai
River—1,800 feet (549 meters)

Highest recorded temperature: 117
degrees Fahrenheit (47 degrees
Celsius)—Medicine Lake, 1937

Lowest recorded temperature: –70
degrees Fahrenheit (–57 degrees
Celsius)—Rogers Pass, 1954

State songs: "Montana"; "Montana
Melody"

State tree: Ponderosa pine

State flower: Bitterroot

State bird: Western meadowlark

National parks: Glacier, Yellowstone

Montana History

One of the six Rocky Mountain states, Montana lies directly south of the Canadian provinces of Saskatchewan and Alberta. To its east are North and South Dakota. Wyoming lies south of it, and Idaho borders it to the south and west. It is 570 miles from east to west. From Canada in the north to Wyoming in the south is 315 miles. With an area exceeding 147,000 square miles, it ranks fourth in size among the fifty states.

With a population density of 5.5 people per square mile, Montana ranks forty-fourth among the states in population. Montana lost population between 1980 and 1990 but experienced a slight population upsurge during the 1990's.

The Rocky Mountains dominate the western two-fifths of the state. The eastern three-fifths consist mostly of rolling hills and plains. The climate is dry and, in winter, extremely cold. Summers are hot. The rich soil of the plains, the hot summers, and the long summer days in this latitude are ideal for agriculture.

Early History. When French Canadian explorers first visited the area, it had already been inhabited by humans for more than nine thousand years. Evidence exists of cultures that date to 8000 B.C.E. Among the native tribes in the area were the Arapaho, Assiniboine, Blackfoot, Cheyenne, Crow, Kalispel, Kutenai, and Salish Indians.

In prehistoric times, dinosaurs roamed Montana. A nest of duck-billed dinosaur fossils was discovered there in 1978. In 1988, the most complete skeleton of a tyrannosaur ever unearthed was discovered. The earliest human inhabitants hunted bison and other indigenous animals with spears.

Early Exploration. The earliest known explorers to reach Montana were François and Louis Joseph de La Vérendrye, French Canadian brothers who arrived in

Decision Point, at the confluence of the Marias and Missouri Rivers—a key site in Meriwether Lewis and William Clark's exploration of the Louisiana Territory during the nineteenth century. (Travel Montana / Victor Bjornberg)

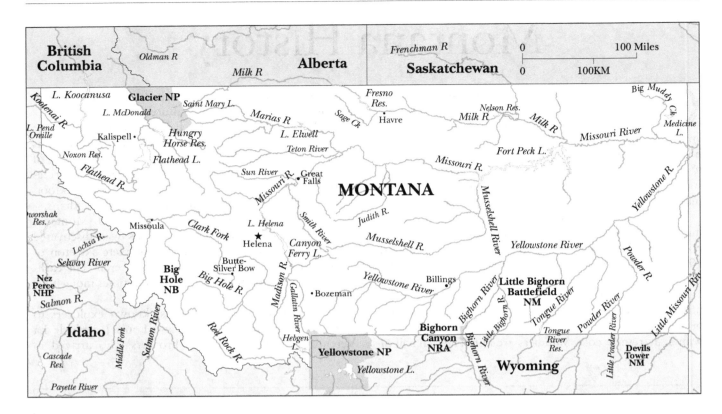

1743. Montana became part of the United States in 1803 through the Louisiana Purchase.

Explorers Meriwether Lewis and William Clark, guided by a young American Indian woman, Sacagawea, crossed the territory in 1805 en route to America's northwest coast. They returned in 1806 on their trip east. A Spanish trader, Manuel Lisa, established the Missouri Fur Company and went on a trading expedition up the Yellowstone River. In 1807, he established Montana's first trading post, Fort Manuel.

The following year Canadian David Thompson established a trading post on the Kootenai River and, in 1809, founded Salish House near Thompson Falls. By 1829, both the Hudson Bay Company and the American Fur Company traded in this area.

Montana's rivers and low mountain passes encouraged transportation. The second longest river in the United States, the 2,315-mile-long Missouri, begins in Montana. Other rivers—including the Madison, the Gallatin, and the Yellowstone—criss-cross the state.

By 1850 fur traders had overhunted and exploited Montana to the extent that most of the fur-bearing animals had been killed. Whole herds of bison, fox, and deer were wiped out by voracious traders.

The Discovery of Gold. When gold was discovered in California in 1848, thousands of easterners rushed across the country seeking instant wealth. Meanwhile, residents of Montana searched for gold in their area. In 1862, John White discovered small gold deposits at Grasshopper Creek. By 1863 more than five hundred miners had come there.

Soon a gold strike was made nearby. A settlement, Virginia City, which by 1865 had ten thousand inhabitants, sprang into being. Gold was discovered at Last Chance Gulch, where its discovery spawned another city, Helena. Meanwhile, rich veins of copper and silver were found around Butte in the Rocky Mountains.

Lawlessness soon became a considerable problem. Gangsters robbed stagecoaches of the gold and silver they transported. During 1863 one gang killed more than one hundred people. In the following year, vigilantes captured and hanged more than twenty such criminals, thereby reducing crime substantially.

Miners flocked into the area as well as merchants, who arrived with their families to open stores and to establish an infrastructure. Cattle ranchers came to eastern Montana. In 1863, schools were opened in Bannack and Nevada City.

The Road to Statehood. Congress created the Montana Territory in 1864. In 1875, Helena became its capital. American Indian uprisings raged. In 1876, the Sioux and Cheyenne Indians killed Lieutenant Colonel George Custer in the Battle of the Little Bighorn, but in 1877, Chief Joseph of the Nez Perce tribe surrendered, ending the American Indian wars that plagued the territory. By 1880, Montana's Native American population was deployed to seven American Indian reservations within the territory.

In 1880, the Utah and Northern Railroad laid tracks across Montana, enabling Montanans to ship produce and cattle to eastern markets. Montana's first bid for statehood in 1866 was premature because the state had a very small population, little access to eastern markets, and continuing problems with American Indian wars. Because the expansion of the railroad into the state resulted in the population quadrupling within a decade, a constitutional convention was called in 1884, and statehood was again requested but refused for political reasons.

In 1889, President Grover Cleveland signed an enabling bill guaranteeing that if North Dakota, South Dakota, Washington, and Montana submitted acceptable constitutions, statehood would be granted. Montana held a constitutional convention in July of that year, offered a constitution to its electorate, and was granted statehood in November, 1889, becoming the forty-first state. In 1894, Montana voters chose Helena as the capital.

Copper Mining in Montana. Although early prospectors found gold and silver around Butte, it was copper that brought the greatest wealth to Montana. Marcus Daly, seeking silver in the area, discovered one of the richest copper deposits in the world and in 1881 opened his copper mine in Anaconda. William Clark soon opened a copper operation nearby in Butte.

The copper found here was so abundant that Butte Hill was nicknamed "the Richest Hill on Earth." The copper industry attracted immigrants, mostly from Great Britain, to work in the mines. Daly established the Anaconda Copper Company, and in 1926 Clark's Butte holdings were sold to that corporation.

Montana Politics and Education. The two powerful copper barons who emerged from the Butte-Anaconda area, Marcus Daly and William Clark, were business and political rivals. They engaged in a heated campaign to have their own towns declared capital of the state, with Clark prevailing. Each owned the newspaper in his respective town. Clark was elected to the U.S. Senate in 1891 but resigned when a scandal, perpetrated by reports accusing him of bribery in Daly's newspaper, the *Anaconda Standard*, cast doubt upon Clark's integrity.

Little Bighorn, the battlefield on which the Sioux and their allies annihilated the U.S. cavalry troops commanded by George Armstrong Custer, has been consecrated as a national monument. (PhotoDisc)

He was, nevertheless, elected to the Senate when he ran again in 1900.

Montana was the first state to elect a woman to Congress. Jeanette Rankin was elected in 1917 and served for two years. She served again from 1941 to 1943. Rankin was the only member of Congress to vote against the U.S. entry into World War I in 1917 and into World War II in 1941.

Montana's first constitution, ratified in 1889, was replaced when a constitutional convention called in 1972 produced a new constitution, narrowly ratified by the electorate and put into effect in 1973. This constitution combined more than one hundred state agencies into fifteen departments, whose heads report to the governor. In 1974, the constitution was amended to change the annual sixty-day legislative session to a ninety-day session to meet in odd-numbered years.

Montana prides itself on valuing education. Its 1990 literacy rate of 92 percent is 5 percent above the national average. Seventy-five percent of Montanans are high school graduates, whereas the national average is 67 percent.

Industrial Expansion. Natural gas was discovered in Glendive, near Montana's eastern border, in 1913. This was an important discovery because where there is natural gas, there is usually oil. It was not until 1950, however, that vast oil deposits were discovered on the Montana-North Dakota border. Oil revenues spurred the state's faltering economy. The strip mining of bituminous coal in the eastern part of the state also helped to advance Montana's economy, changing the nature of the plains considerably. Nevertheless, the Montana plains are among the most prolific producers of wheat in the United States.

In 1955, the Anaconda Aluminum Company began operation in Columbia Falls in northwestern Montana. In 1983, however, the once-powerful Anaconda Copper Company, having mined out the area around Butte, suspended operations.

Located on Montana's border with Canada, Glacier National Park was established by the U.S. Congress in 1910. (PhotoDisc)

Natural Disasters. Between 1917 and 1920, Montana suffered greatly from droughts that caused many farmers and cattle ranchers in eastern Montana to fail. In 1929, another drought began that again devastated eastern Montana and lasted for several years, during which the economic contractions of the Great Depression also affected that state's economy. During 1935 Helena was struck by more than one hundred earthquakes. Although no lives were lost, property damage was severe.

With federal aid, Montana strove to avert the devastation earlier droughts had inflicted upon the state. Although Flathead Lake, which covers two hundred square miles, is the largest freshwater lake west of the Mississippi River, it proved insufficient to provide irrigation during droughts. In 1934, Montana began a dam-building project that, in 1940, culminated in the creation of the four-hundred-square-mile Lake Peck and several other artificial lakes that provide irrigation and hydroelectric power for Montana's farms and cattle ranches.

Elections. During the year 2000 elections, Montana voters chose Republican candidate George W. Bush for its three electoral votes by a wide margin, 58 percent to 34 percent. Republican victories set the tone for other races, as a Republican retained the state's at-large member of Congress, Senator Conrad Burns retained his seat in the U.S. Senate, and Lieutenant Governor Judy Martz, also a Republican, took the governor's mansion by 51 percent to 48 percent vote. Voters also decided to repeal the state's inheritance taxes.

In the 2004 presidential race, Montana again chose Republican candidate George W. Bush. In the race for governor, however, Brian Schweitzer, a Democrat, beat Republican Bob Brown, Montana's secretary of state, by a 50–46 percent margin. A principal campaign issue was whether Montanans should be able to import inexpensive prescription drugs from Canada, a position that Schweitzer strongly backed.

Cultural and Environmental Issues. The state's reputation for conservatism suffered a setback the following year, however, when voters in the state's capital, Helena, decided to ban indoor smoking in public places within

Women taking place of men on Great Northern Railway at Great Falls. Montana, in 1918, during World War I. (Wikimedia Commons)

the city, including bars and restaurants. Other issues that captured public attention during the early years of the new millennium was a 2002 proposal to drill for oil at Sacred Valley, a site of rock drawings thought to be among the most significant in the area. The proposal was not approved.

Another issue was the environmental impact of the use of snowmobiles in Yellowstone National Park, a part of which lies in Montana and which is frequently visited by Montanans. In this case, the U.S. House of Representatives rejected a proposal for a complete snowmobile ban in the park. In 2004, a further environmental issue came to the fore as oil and gas exploration companies planned drilling in the state's Rocky Mountain Front, the largest concentration of wilderness in the nation except for Alaska. Most Montanans opposed the exploration plans, and in October of that year, the federal Bureau of Land Management suspended its plan for drilling.

Wildfires. In common with a number of other Western states, Montana endured tremendous damage from wildfires that burned out of control in the summer of 2000 and in succeeding years. In 2000, at least thirty-three major wildfires burned across the West, affecting 380,000 acres—a Level 5 condition, the worst on the standard scale. Some 22,600 firefighters fought the blazes. In 2003, two firefighters were killed near Missoula, and the fires consumed great portions of Glacier National Park. In July, 2006, five major fires burned in the southern and eastern parts of the state, engulfing about 294 square miles.

Politics. Montana's political environment evolved in the first decade of the 21st century, with issues resembling some of the other Western and mountain region states. Montana is characterized by low density of population and reliance on extractive industries such as mining and lumbering; the state has distinct regional economies, and scenic beauty and outdoor recreation give further inputs to the political climate.

The high population growth rates in some counties, with influx of new residents from California and other states, all contribute to the evolution of a new type of voter in the high-growth counties of the western and central parts of the state. These new voters tended to be conservative on fiscal issues and progressive on environmental issues.

Furthermore, the three regions of Montana vary in political alignment. The western region is dominated by residents who tend not be involved in either the agricultural and traditional mining and lumbering economy of the state. They tend not to be as concerned with employment opportunities that might be impacted by stricter environmental policies.

In the eastern region, which is more dependent on agriculture and extractive industries, voters tend to be far less eager to sacrifice jobs in the interest of environmental protection. Issues such as water quality, forest fire protection, land use, and zoning have been particularly contentious in Montana through the early years of the 21st century.

As a result of the mix of political viewpoints, Democrats tended to do well on the statewide level, but the state voted a more conservative position in the national elections. In 2008, Democrat Brian Schweitzer was elected governor. In 2012, Democrat Steve Bullick took the governorship, with 49 percent of the popular vote. In both elections, the state voted for the Republican candidates for president, John McCain and Mitt Romney.

R. Baird Shuman
Updated by the Editor

Montana Time Line

c. 8000 B.C.E.	People first settle Montana.
1743 C.E.	French Canadians Francois and Louis de La Vérendrye explore the area.
1803	United States gains most of Montana through the Louisiana Purchase.
1805	Explorers Meriwether Lewis and William Clark are guided through Montana by American Indian Sacagawea.
1807	Spanish trader Manuel Lisa establishes Montana's first fur-trading post.
1846	Fort Benton is built.
1862	John White discovers gold at Grasshopper Creek.
1863	Virginia City is established near Grasshopper Creek gold strike.
May 26, 1864	Montana Territory is created.
1875	Helena becomes capital of the territory.
June 25, 1876	Battle of the Little Bighorn takes place between Sioux and U.S. Army; Lieutenant Colonel George Custer is killed.
Oct. 5, 1877	Chief Joseph of the Nez Perce surrenders, ending the American Indian wars.
1880	Most of Montana's Native Americans are placed on reservations.
Nov. 8, 1889	Montana becomes the forty-first state.
1893	Four public institutions of higher learning open in Montana.
1910	Congress establishes Glacier National Park.
1917	Jeannette Rankin becomes the first female member of Congress.
1917–1918	More than forty thousand Montanans serve in World War I.
1917–1920	Severe droughts devastate Montana farms and ranches.
1934	Work begins on Fort Peck Dam.

1935	Helena is hit by more than one hundred earthquakes.
1940	Jeannette Rankin is elected to a second term in Congress.
1941–1945	Some fifty-seven thousand Montanans serve in World War II.
1950	Large oil strike is made in eastern Montana.
1955	Anaconda Aluminum Company begins operation.
1959	Huge earthquake creates Quake Lake on Madison River.
1973	New state constitution is instituted.
1983	Anaconda Copper Company closes its Butte mining operations.
1984	Forest fires ravage state.
1996	Native Americans sue state over voting precinct districting.
1997	Montana farmers seek right to kill buffalo outside Yellowstone Park to control brucellosis.
1998	Montana farmers block border point to protest low Canadian produce prices.
1999	Montana replaces "reasonable and prudent" speed limit with one of 75 miles per hour on most highways.
2000	Wildfires devastate thousands of acres of Montana along with similar devastation across the West.
2004	Secretary of Agriculture Ann Venem announces repeal of the "roadlessrule" under which roads could not be built in any of the nearly sixty million acres of federal lands.
Oct. 1, 2004	Federal Bureau of Land Management suspends plans for oil drilling along Montana's Rocky Mountain Front.
Nov. 2, 2004	Democrat Brian Schweitzer defeats Republican Bob Brown for governorship.
July 2006	Five wildfires engulf some 294 square miles of the southern and eastern parts of the state, mostly east of Billings.
2008	Democrat Brian Schweitzer is elected governor.
2012	Schweitzer is re-elected governor.

Notes for Further Study

Published Sources. The most comprehensive study of Montana is *Montana: A History of Two Centuries* (Rev. ed., 2003) by Michael P. Malone, Richard B. Roeder, and William L. Lang. This richly illustrated book presents the history of the state, considering its cultural, educational, and economic development. *Montana Legacy: Essays on History, People, and Place* (2002), edited by Harry W. Fritz, Mary Murphy, and Robert R. Swartout, Jr., brings together sixteen essays that detail the people, cultures, places, and events that shaped present-day Montana. Donald Spritzer's *Roadside History of Montana* (1999) is divided into chapters corresponding to the state's six geographical areas and follows highway routes as a device to reveal the state's history. Readers interested in statistical and demographic data might enjoy perusing *Montana: 2000, Summary Social, Economic, and Housing Characteristics* (2003), published by the U.S. Census Bureau.

Janice Cohn in *The Christmas Menorahs: How a Town Fought Hate* (1995) explains how citizens of Billings, Montana, defended a Jewish family that fell victim to hate crimes. R. E. Mather in *Vigilante Victims: Montana's Hanging Spree* (1991) discusses the vigilantes who broke the Montana crime wave of the 1860's. Laura Ross focuses on America's dealings with Montana's Native Americans in *Inventing the Savage: The Social Construction of Native American Criminality* (1998). In *The Mechanics of Optimism: Mining Companies, Technology, and the Hot Spring Gold Rush* (2004), Jeffrey J. Safford examines the boom-bust cycles of mining in nineteenth century Montana by focusing on the failed Hot Springs District, a gold-mining camp.

Richard Allan Fox, Jr., discusses the Battle of the Little Bighorn and George Custer's defeat in *Archeology, History, and Custer's Last Battle: The Little Big Horn Reexamined* (1993), updating *Archeological Insights into the Custer Battle: The Assessment of the 1984 Field Season* (1987) by Douglas D. Scott and Richard A. Fox, Jr. Duane A. Smith's *Rocky Mountain West: Colorado, Wyoming, and Montana* (1991) emphasizes the western part of the state, in which most of its mining occurs.

General audiences will enjoy *Hidden Montana* (5th ed., 2005); John Gottberg provides detailed maps, Internet information for each listing, suggested itineraries, and walking and driving tours, among other features. Younger readers will find Ann Heinrichs's *Montana* (2005) clear, well written, and detailed. Rita Ladoux's *Montana* (Rev. and exp. ed., 2002) is written for a teenage audience.

Holter Dam on the Missouri River in Lewis & Clark County, was built by the United Missouri River Power Company in 1918. As of 2010, it had a 50 megawatt generating capacity. (National Park Service/Kristi Hager)

Web Resources. The best Internet source for information about the government of Montana is its home page (www.mt.gov). For tourist information, consult the Web sites of the tourist service (www.visitmt. com), Glacier National Park (www.glacierparkinc. com/), and Yellowstone National Park (www.nps.gov/ yell). Information about hunting and fishing can be found at the state's Fish, Wildlife, and Parks Web site (fwp.mt.gov/default.html) or the Montana Bowhunters site (www.mtba.org). *Montana Outdoors* (http://fwp. mt.gov/mtoutdoors) provides a number of online articles from its back issues. Links directing users to a range of business and commerce sites can be found at Montana Business Assistance Connection (www.mbac. biz/). For information about legal matters, the Montana Bar Association's Web site (www.montanabar.org) is useful. The Montana Education Association maintains a Web site (www.mea-mft.org/).

For those interested in the state's historical and cultural past, several sites offer valuable information. Montana History (http://www.visitmt.com/Experiences/) and Montana History.net (www.montanahistory.net/) are all good starting points. Indian Nations of Montana (indiannations.visitmt.com/) is an attractive site that details the history and culture of tribes such as the Blackfeet and Crow, as well as locales that are important to these communities. For young Web users, Montana Is for Kids (montanakids.com/) is an entertaining site that discusses plants and animals, cultural history, and regional attractions.

Counties

County	2012 Population	Pop. Rank	Land Area (sq. miles)	Area Rank
Beaverhead	9,346	23	5,541.62	1
Big Horn	13,061	14	4,995.46	5
Blaine	6,683	30	4,227.55	9
Broadwater	5,756	34	1,192.54	51
Carbon	10,127	21	2,048.79	33
Carter	1,177	51	3,340.75	15
Cascade	81,723	5	2,698.16	21
Chouteau	5,904	33	3,972.49	10
Custer	11,888	15	3,783.36	11
Daniels	1,786	47	1,426.10	48
Dawson	9,249	24	2,371.86	28
Deer Lodge	9,227	25	736.53	55
Fallon	3,024	42	1,620.77	45
Fergus	11,435	16	4,339.80	8
Flathead	91,633	4	5,087.66	3
Gallatin	92,614	3	2,602.69	24
Garfield	1,261	50	4,675.36	7
Glacier	13,711	13	2,995.94	17
Golden Valley	839	54	1,175.34	52
Granite	3,109	41	1,727.41	40
Hill	16,366	11	2,898.95	18
Jefferson	11,401	18	1,656.26	42
Judith Basin	2,024	45	1,869.82	35
Lake	28,986	9	1,490.15	46
Lewis and Clark	64,876	6	3,458.83	14
Liberty	2,392	43	1,430.05	47
Lincoln	19,491	10	3,612.92	12
Madison	7,733	27	3,587.48	13
McCone	1,701	49	2,643.17	22

County	2012 Population	Pop. Rank	Land Area (sq. miles)	Area Rank
Meagher	1,924	46	2,391.91	26
Mineral	4,167	37	1,219.44	50
Missoula	110,977	2	2,593.42	25
Musselshell	4,665	36	1,868.16	36
Park	15,567	12	2,803.06	19
Petroleum	511	56	1,654.87	43
Phillips	4,128	38	5,140.03	2
Pondera	6,165	31	1,622.86	44
Powder River	1,763	48	3,297.30	16
Powell	7,096	29	2,326.39	30
Prairie	1,157	52	1,736.74	39
Ravalli	40,617	7	2,390.82	27
Richland	10,810	20	2,084.14	32
Roosevelt	10,927	19	2,354.79	29
Rosebud	9,396	22	5,010.40	4
Sanders	11,408	17	2,760.52	20
Sheridan	3,580	40	1,677.08	41
Silver Bow	34,403	8	718.48	56
Stillwater	9,195	26	1,795.35	38
Sweet Grass	3,605	39	1,855.20	37
Teton	6,053	32	2,272.37	31
Toole	5,220	35	1,915.65	34
Treasure	736	55	977.40	53
Valley	7,505	28	4,925.82	6
Wheatland	2,104	44	1,423.19	49
Wibaux	1,057	53	889.26	54
Yellowstone	151,882	1	2,633.29	23

Source: U.S. Census Bureau, 2012 Population Estimates

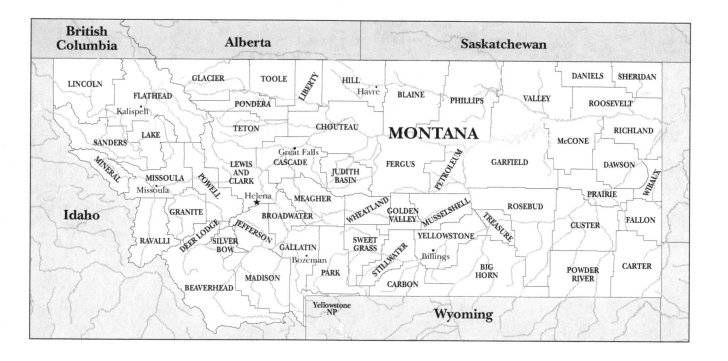

Cities

With 5,000 or more residents

Legal Name	2010 Population	Pop. Rank	Land Area (sq. miles)	Area Rank
Anaconda-Deer Lodge County	9,298	9	736.53	1
Belgrade city	7,389	14	3.25	19
Billings city	104,170	1	43.41	3
Bozeman city	37,280	4	19.12	7
Butte-Silver Bow (balance)	33,525	5	716.25	2
Evergreen CDP	7,616	13	8.61	12
Great Falls city	58,505	3	21.79	6
Havre city	9,310	8	3.28	18
Helena city	28,190	6	16.35	8
Helena Valley Southeast CDP	8,227	11	14.31	9
Helena Valley West Central CDP	7,883	12	26.50	5

Legal Name	2010 Population	Pop. Rank	Land Area (sq. miles)	Area Rank
Kalispell city	19,927	7	11.64	11
Laurel city	6,718	17	2.14	21
Lewistown city	5,901	19	5.32	16
Livingston city	7,044	15	6.02	14
Lockwood CDP	6,797	16	12.90	10
Miles City city	8,410	10	3.34	17
Missoula city	66,788	2	27.51	4
Orchard Homes CDP	5,197	20	6.00	15
Sidney city	5,191	21	2.66	20
Whitefish city	6,357	18	6.43	13

Note: CDP–Census Designated Place
Source: U.S. Census Bureau, 2010 Census

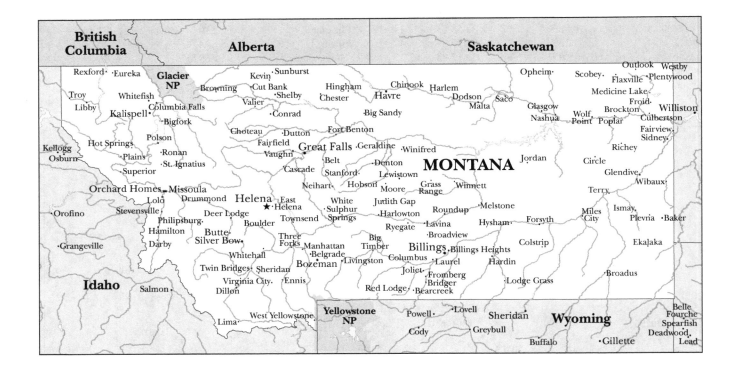

Survey Says...

This section presents current rankings from dozens of public and private sources. It shows how this state ranks in a number of critical categories, including education, job growth, cost of living, teen drivers, energy efficiency, and business environment. Sources include *Forbes, Reuters, U.S. News and World Report, CNN Money, Gallup,* and *Huffington Post.*

- CNN Money compiled a list of "Ten Most Entrepreneurial States" based on the Kauffman Index of Entrepreneurial Activity. Montana ranked #1 among the 50 states in 2012 for number of startups per 100,000 adult residents.
  CNN Money, June 20, 2013; money.cnn.com

- Montana ranked #21 in a government study measuring real gross domestic product (GDP)—the output of goods and services produced by labor and property located in the United States. The ranking is based on the percentage change compared with 2011 GDP.
  U.S. Department of Commerce, Bureau of Economic Analysis, June 2013; www.bea.gov

- Montana ranked #49 in a government study measuring real gross domestic product (GDP)—the output of goods and services produced by labor and property located in the United States. The ranking is based on the dollar value of its GDP.
  U.S. Department of Commerce, Bureau of Economic Analysis, June 2013; www.bea.gov

- Montana ranked #44 in the 17th edition of "Quality Counts; State of the States," Education Week's "report card" surveying key education indicators, policy efforts, and educational outcomes.
  Education Week, January 4, 2013 (online) and January 10, 2013 (print); www.edweek.org

- SERI (Science and Engineering Readiness Index) weighs the performance of the states' K-12 schools in preparing students in physics and calculus, the high school subjects considered most important for future scientists and engineers. Montana ranked #29.
  Newsletter of the Forum on Education of the American Physical Society, Summer 2011 issue; www.huffingtonpost.com, July 11, 2011; updated October 1, 2012

- MoneyRates.com ranked Montana #34 on its list of the best to worst states for making a living. Criteria: average income; inflation; employment prospects; and workers' Workplace Environment assessments according to the Gallup-Healthways Well-Being Index.
  www.money-rates.com, posted April 1, 2013

- *Forbes* analyzed business costs, labor supply, regulatory environment, current economic climate, growth prospects, and quality of life, to compile its "Best States for Business" rankings. Montana ranked #26.
  www.forbes.com. posted December 12, 2012

- The 2012 Gallup-Healthways Well-Being Index, surveyed American's opinions on economic confidence, workplace perceptions, community climate, personal choices, and health predictors to assess the "future livability" of each state. Montana ranked #24.
  "Utah Poised to Be the Best State to Live In," Gallup Wellbeing, www.gallup.com, August 7, 2012

- On CNBC's list of "America's Top States for Business 2013," Montana ranked #19. Criteria: measures of competitiveness developed with input from the National Association of Manufacturers, the Council on Competitiveness, and other business groups weighed with the states' own marketing criteria.
  www.cnbc.com, consulted July 19, 2013

- Montana ranked #16 on MoneyRates list of "Best-and Worst-States to Retire 2012." Criteria: life expectancy, crime rate, climate, economic conditions, taxes, job opportunities, and cost of living.
  www.money-rates.com, October 22, 2012

- Montana ranked #16 on the 2013 Bankrate "Best Places to Retire" list ranking the states and District of Columbia on various criteria relating to health, safety, and cost.
  www.bankrate.com, May 6, 2013

- Montana ranked #40 on the Social Science Research Council's "American Human Development Report: The Measure of America," assessing the 50 states plus the District of Columbia on health, education, and living-standard criteria.
  The Measure of America 2013-2014, posted June 19, 2013; www.measureofamerica.org

- Montana ranked #33 on the Foundation for Child Development's (FCD) Child Well-being Index (CWI). The FCD used the KIDS COUNT report and the National Survey of Children's Health, the only state-level source for several key indicators of child well-being.
  Foundation for Child Development, January 18, 2012; fcd-us.org

- Montana ranked #28 overall according to the 2013 KIDS COUNT Data Book, a project of the Annie E. Casey Foundation. Criteria: children's economic well-being, education, health, and family and community indicators.
  KIDS COUNT Data Center's Data Book, released June 20, 2013; http://datacenter.kidscount.org

- Montana ranked #15 in the children's economic well-being category by the 2013 KIDS COUNT Data Book, a project of the Annie E. Casey Foundation.
  KIDS COUNT Data Center's Data Book, released June 20, 2013; http://datacenter.kidscount.org

- Montana ranked #13 in the children's educational opportunities and attainments category by the 2013 KIDS COUNT Data Book, a project of the Annie E. Casey Foundation.
  KIDS COUNT Data Center's Data Book, released June 20, 2013; http://datacenter.kidscount.org

- Montana ranked #50 in the children's health category by the 2013 KIDS COUNT Data Book, a project of the Annie E. Casey Foundation.
  KIDS COUNT Data Center's Data Book, released June 20, 2013; http://datacenter.kidscount.org

- Montana ranked #14 in the family and community circumstances that factor into children's well-being category by the 2013 KIDS COUNT Data Book, a project of the Annie E. Casey Foundation.
  KIDS COUNT Data Center's Data Book, released June 20, 2013; http://datacenter.kidscount.org

- Montana ranked #6 in the 2012 Gallup-Healthways Well-Being Index. Criteria: emotional health; physical health; healthy behavior; work environment; basic access to food, shelter, health care; and a safe and satisfying place to live.
  2012 State of Well-Being, Gallup-Healthways Well-Being Index, released February 28, 2013; www.well-beingindex.com

- *U.S. News and World Report's* "Best States for Teen Drivers" rankings are based on driving and road safety laws, federal reports on driver's licenses, car accident fatality, and road-quality statistics. Montana ranked #43.
  U.S. News and World Report, March 18, 2010; www.usnews.com

- The Yahoo! Sports service Rivals.com ranks the states according to the strength of their high school football programs. Montana ranked #44.
  "Ranking the States: Where Is the Best Football Played?," November 18, 2011; highschool.rivals.com

- iVillage ranked the states by hospitable living conditions for women. Criteria: economic success, access to affordable childcare, health care, reproductive rights, female representation in government, and educational attainment. Montana ranked #26.
  iVillage, "50 Best to Worst States for Women," March 14, 2012; www.ivillage.com

- The League of American Bicyclists's "Bicycle Friendly States" ranked Montana #39. Criteria: legislation and enforcement, policies and programs, infrastructure and funding, education and advocacy, and evaluation and planning.
  "Washington Tops the Bicycle-Friendly State Ranking," May 1, 2013; bicycling.com

- The federal Corporation for National and Community Service ranked the states and the District of Columbia by volunteer rates. Montana ranked #18 for community service.
  "Volunteering and Civic Life in America 2012," www.volunteeringinamerica.gov, accessed July 24, 2013

- The Hospital Safety Score ranked states and the District of Columbia on their hospitals' performance scores. Montana ranked #9. Criteria: avoiding preventable harm and medical errors, as demonstrated by 26 hospital safety metrics.
  Spring 2013 Hospital Safety Score, May 8, 2013; www.hospitalsafetyscore.org

- GMAC Insurance ranked the states and the District of Columbia by the performance of their drivers on the GMAC Insurance National Drivers Test, comprised of DMV test questions. Montana ranked #13.
  "2011 GMAC Insurance National Drivers Test," www.gmacinsurance.com, accessed July 23, 2013

- Montana ranked #31 in a "State Integrity Investigation" analysis of laws and practices intended to deter corruption and promote accountability and openness in campaign finance, ethics laws, lobbying regulations and management of state pension funds.
  "What's Your State's Grade?," www.publicintegrity.org, accessed July 23, 2013

- Montana ranked #21 among the states and the District of Columbia in total rail miles, as tracked by the Association of American Railroads.
  "U.S. Freight Railroad Industry Snapshot: Railroads and States: Total Rail Miles by State: 2011"; www.aar.org, accessed July 23, 2013

- According to statistics compiled by the Beer Institute, Montana ranked #3 among the states and the District of Columbia in per capita beer consumption of persons 21 years or older.
  "Shipments of Malt Beverages and Per Capita Consumption by State 2012;" www.beerinstitute.org

- According to Concordia University's "Public Education Costs per Pupil by State Rankings," based on statistics gathered by the U.S. Census Bureau, which includes the District of Columbia, Montana ranked #26.
  Concordia University Online; education.cu-portland.edu, accessed July 24, 2013

- Montana ranked #48 among the states and the District of Columbia in population density based on U.S. Census Bureau data for resident population and total land area. "List of U.S. States by Population Density."
  www.wikipedia.org, accessed July 24, 2013

- In "America's Health Rankings, 2012 Edition," by the United Health Foundation, Montana ranked #29. Criteria included: rate of high school graduation; violent crime rate; incidence of infectious disease; childhood immunizations; prevalence of diabetes; per capita public-health funding; percentage of uninsured population; rate of children in poverty; and availability of primary-care physicians.
  United Health Foundation; www.americashealthrankings.org, accessed July 24, 2013

- The TechNet 2012 "State Broadband Index" ranked Montana #43 on the following criteria: broadband adoption; network quality; and economic structure. Improved broadband use is hoped to promote economic development, build strong communities, improve delivery of government services and upgrade educational systems.
  TechNet; www.technet.org, accessed July 24, 2013

- Montana was ranked #25 among the states and District of Columbia on the American Council for an Energy-Efficient Economy's "State Energy Efficiency Scorecard" for 2012.
  American Council for an Energy-Efficient Economy; aceee.org/sector/state-policy/scorecard, accessed July 24, 2013

Statistical Tables

DEMOGRAPHICS
Resident State and National Population, 1950-2012
Projected State and National Population, 2000-2030
Population by Age, 2012
Population by Race, 2012
Population by Hispanic Origin and Race, 2012

VITAL STATISTICS
Death Rates by Leading Causes, 2010
Death Rates by Selected Causes, 2010
Abortion Rates, 2009
Infant Mortality Rates, 1995-2009
Marriage and Divorce Rates, 2000-2011

ECONOMY
Nominal Gross Domestic Product by Industry, 2012
Real Gross Domestic Product, 2000-2012
Personal Income Per Capita, 1930-2012
Non-Farm Employment by Sector, 2012
Foreign Exports, 2000-2012
Energy Consumption, 2011

LAND AND WATER
Surface Area and Federally-Owned Land, 2007
Land Cover/Use of Non-Federal Rural Land, 2007
Farms and Crop Acreage, 2012

HEALTH AND MEDICAL CARE
Medical Professionals, 2012
Health Insurance Coverage, 2011
HIV, STD, and Tuberculosis Cases and Rates, 2011
Cigarette Smoking, 2011

HOUSING
Home Ownership Rates, 1995-2012
Home Sales, 2000-2010
Value of Owner-Occupied Homes, 2011

EDUCATION
School Enrollment, 2011
Educational Attainment, 2011
Public College Finances, FY 2012

TRANSPORTATION AND TRAVEL
Motor Vehicle Registrations and Drivers Licenses, 2011
Domestic Travel Expenditures, 2009
Retail Gasoline Prices, 2013
Public Road Length, 2011

CRIME AND LAW ENFORCEMENT
Full-Time Law Enforcement Officers, 2011
Prison Population, 2000-2012
Crime Rate, 2011

GOVERNMENT AND FINANCE
Local Governments by Type, 2012
State Government Revenue, 2011
State Government Expenditures, 2011
State Government General Expenditures by Function, 2011
State Government Finances, Cash and Debt, 2011

POLITICS
Composition of the Senate, 1995-2013
Composition of the House of Representatives, 1995-2013
Composition of State Legislature, 2004-2013
Voter Participation in Presidential Elections, 1980-2012
Governors Since Statehood

DEMOGRAPHICS

Resident State and National Population, 1950–2012

Year	State Population	U.S. Population	State Share
1950	591,000	151,326,000	0.39%
1960	675,000	179,323,000	0.38%
1970	694,409	203,302,031	0.34%
1980	786,690	226,545,805	0.35%
1990	799,065	248,709,873	0.32%
2000	902,200	281,424,600	0.32%
2010	989,415	308,745,538	0.32%
2012	1,005,141	313,914,040	0.32%

Note: 1950/1960 population figures are rounded to the nearest thousand.
Source: U.S. Census Bureau, Decennial Census 1950–2010; U.S. Census Bureau, 2012 Population Estimates

Projected State and National Population, 2000–2030

Year	State Population	U.S. Population	State Share
2000	902,195	281,421,906	0.32%
2005	933,005	295,507,134	0.32%
2010	968,598	308,935,581	0.31%
2015	999,489	322,365,787	0.31%
2020	1,022,735	335,804,546	0.30%
2025	1,037,387	349,439,199	0.30%
2030	1,044,898	363,584,435	0.29%
State population growth, 2000–2030			142,703
State percentage growth, 2000–2030			15.8%

Source: U.S. Census Bureau, Population Division, Interim State Population Projections, 2005

Population by Age, 2012

Age Group	State Population	Percent of Total Population	
		State	U.S.
Under 5 years	60,964	6.1%	6.4%
5 to 14 years	123,272	12.3%	13.1%
15 to 24 years	136,258	13.6%	14.0%
25 to 34 years	126,267	12.6%	13.5%
35 to 44 years	112,927	11.2%	12.9%
45 to 54 years	140,331	14.0%	14.1%
55 to 64 years	146,833	14.6%	12.3%
65 to 74 years	89,742	8.9%	7.6%
75 to 84 years	47,466	4.7%	4.2%
85 years and older	21,081	2.1%	1.9%
Under 18 years	221,980	22.1%	23.5%
65 years and older	158,289	15.7%	13.7%
Median age (years)	–	40.1	37.4

Source: U.S. Census Bureau, Annual Estimates of the Resident Population for Selected Age Groups by Sex for the United States, States, Counties, and Puerto Rico Commonwealth and Municipios: April 1, 2010 to July 1, 2012

Population by Race, 2012

Race	State Population	Percent of Total Population	
		State	U.S.
All residents	1,005,141	100.00%	100.00%
White	901,340	89.67%	77.89%
African American	5,679	0.56%	13.13%
Native American	65,164	6.48%	1.23%
Asian	7,315	0.73%	5.14%
Native Hawaiian	774	0.08%	0.23%
Two or more races	24,869	2.47%	2.39%

Source: U.S. Census Bureau, Population Division, Annual Estimates of the Resident Population by Sex, Race and Hispanic Origin for the United States, States, and Counties: April 1, 2010 to July 1, 2012

Population by Hispanic Origin and Race, 2012

Hispanic Origin/Race	State Population	Percent of Total Population	
		State	U.S.
All residents	1,005,141	100.00%	100.00%
All Hispanic residents	31,552	3.14%	16.89%
Hispanic			
White	24,517	2.44%	14.91%
African American	481	0.05%	0.79%
Native American	3,777	0.38%	0.49%
Asian	247	0.02%	0.17%
Native Hawaiian	127	0.01%	0.06%
Two or more races	2,403	0.24%	0.48%
Not Hispanic			
White	876,823	87.23%	62.98%
African American	5,198	0.52%	12.34%
Native American	61,387	6.11%	0.74%
Asian	7,068	0.70%	4.98%
Native Hawaiian	647	0.06%	0.17%
Two or more races	22,466	2.24%	1.91%

Source: U.S. Census Bureau, Population Division, Annual Estimates of the Resident Population by Sex, Race and Hispanic Origin for the United States, States, and Counties: April 1, 2010 to July 1, 2012

VITAL STATISTICS

Death Rates by Leading Causes, 2010

Cause	State	U.S.
Malignant neoplasms	172.7	186.2
Ischaemic heart diseases	93.5	122.9
Other forms of heart disease	59.5	53.4
Chronic lower respiratory diseases	53.9	44.7
Cerebrovascular diseases	44.5	41.9
Organic, incl. symptomatic, mental disorders	45.6	35.7
Other degenerative diseases of the nervous sys.	28.4	28.4
Other external causes of accidental injury	32.1	26.5
Diabetes mellitus	20.4	22.4
Hypertensive diseases	13.8	20.4
All causes	803.7	799.5

Note: Figures are age-adjusted death rates per 100,000 population
Source: CDC/NCHS, Underlying Cause of Death 1999–2010 on CDC WONDER Online Database

Death Rates by Selected Causes, 2010

Cause	State	U.S.
Assault	2.8	5.2
Diseases of the liver	15.3	13.9
Human immunodeficiency virus (HIV) disease	–	2.7
Influenza and pneumonia	15.0	16.2
Intentional self-harm	22.2	12.4
Malnutrition	0.0	0.9
Obesity and other hyperalimentation	2.8	1.8
Renal failure	10.8	14.4
Transport accidents	20.9	12.1
Viral hepatitis	2.3	2.4

Note: Figures are age-adjusted death rates per 100,000 population; A dash indicates that data was not available or was suppressed
Source: CDC/NCHS, Underlying Cause of Death 1999–2010 on CDC WONDER Online Database

Abortion Rates, 2009

Category	2009
By state of residence	
Total abortions	1,977
Abortion rate[1]	10.8%
Abortion ratio[2]	161
By state of occurrence	
Total abortions	2,223
Abortion rate[1]	12.2%
Abortion ratio[2]	181
Abortions obtained by out-of-state residents	12.4%
U.S. abortion rate[1]	15.1%
U.S. abortion ratio[2]	227

Note: (1) Number of abortions per 1,000 women aged 15–44 years; (2) Number of abortions per 1,000 live births; A dash indicates that data was not available
Source: CDC/NCHS, Morbidity and Mortality Weekly Report, November 23, 2012 (Abortion Surveillance, United States, 2009)

Infant Mortality Rates, 1995–2009

Category	1995	2000	2005	2009
All state residents	7.09	6.02	7.25	6.20
All U.S. residents	7.57	6.89	6.86	6.39
All state white residents	7.20	5.39	6.96	5.52
All U.S. white residents	6.30	5.71	5.73	5.33
All state black residents	–	–	–	–
All U.S. black residents	14.58	13.48	13.26	12.12

Note: Figures represent deaths per 1,000 live births of resident infants under one year old, exclusive of fetal deaths; A dash indicates that data was not available or was suppressed.
Source: Centers of Disease Control and Prevention, Division of Vital Statistics, Linked Birth/Infant Death Records on CDC Wonder Online

Marriage and Divorce Rates, 2000–2011

Year	Marriage Rate		Divorce Rate	
	State	U.S.	State	U.S.
2000	7.3	8.2	4.2	4.0
2002	7.1	8.0	4.0	3.9
2004	7.5	7.8	3.8	3.7
2006	7.4	7.5	4.4	3.7
2008	7.6	7.1	4.1	3.5
2010	7.4	6.8	3.9	3.6
2011	7.8	6.8	4.0	3.6

Note: Rates are based on provisional counts of marriages/divorces by state of occurrence and are per 1,000 total population residing in area
Source: CDC/NCHS, National Vital Statistics System

ECONOMY

Nominal Gross Domestic Product by Industry, 2012
In millions of current dollars

Industry	State GDP
Accommodation and food services	1,490
Administrative and waste management services	928
Agriculture, forestry, fishing, and hunting	1,387
Arts, entertainment, and recreation	468
Construction	2,033
Educational services	182
Finance and insurance	2,088
Health care and social assistance	3,736
Information	927
Management of companies and enterprises	200
Manufacturing	2,860
Mining	1,949
Other services, except government	1,075
Professional, scientific, and technical services	2,100
Real estate and rental and leasing	4,805
Retail trade	2,698
Transportation and warehousing	1,929
Utilities	1,125
Wholesale trade	2,100

Source: U.S. Department of Commerce, Bureau of Economic Analysis, Survey of Current Business

Real Gross Domestic Product, 2000–2012
In millions of chained 2005 dollars

Year	State GDP	U.S. GDP	State Share
2000	25,816	11,225,406	0.23%
2005	30,054	12,539,116	0.24%
2010	31,918	12,897,088	0.25%
2012	33,374	13,430,576	0.25%

Source: U.S. Department of Commerce, Bureau of Economic Analysis, Survey of Current Business

Personal Income Per Capita, 1930–2012

Year	State	U.S.
1930	$497	$618
1940	$562	$593
1950	$1,654	$1,503
1960	$2,066	$2,268
1970	$3,624	$4,084
1980	$9,038	$10,091
1990	$15,346	$19,354
2000	$23,457	$30,319
2010	$34,405	$39,791
2012	$37,370	$42,693

Source: U.S. Department of Commerce, Bureau of Economic Analysis, Regional Economic Accounts

Non-Farm Employment by Sector, 2012
In thousands

Sector	Employment
Construction	22.9
Education and health services	67.5
Financial activities	21.4
Government	89.9
Information	6.9
Leisure and hospitality	58.3
Mining and logging	9.3
Manufacturing	17.5
Other services	17.4
Professional and business services	41.1
Trade, transportation, and utilities	88.3
All sectors	440.5

Source: U.S. Bureau of Labor Statistics, State and Area Employment

Foreign Exports, 2000–2012
In millions of dollars

Year	State Exports	U.S. Exports	State Share
2000	540	712,054	0.08%
2002	386	649,940	0.06%
2004	566	768,554	0.07%
2006	900	973,994	0.09%
2008	1,394	1,222,545	0.11%
2010	1,393	1,208,080	0.12%
2012	1,576	1,478,268	0.11%

Note: U.S. figures exclude data from Puerto Rico, U.S. Virgin Islands, and unallocated exports
Source: U.S. Department of Commerce, International Trade Admin., Office of Trade and Industry Information, Manufacturing and Services

Energy Consumption, 2011

In trillions of BTUs, except as noted

Total energy consumption	
Total state energy consumption	397.5
Total U.S. energy consumption	97,387.3
State share of U.S. total	0.41%
Per capita consumption (in millions of BTUs)	
Total state per capita consumption	398.4
Total U.S. per capita consumption	312.6
End-use sectors	
Residential	86.9
Commercial	78.3
Industrial	113.4
Transportation	119.0
Sources of energy	
Petroleum	171.9
Natural gas	79.5
Coal	165.7
Renewable energy	143.6
Nuclear electric power	0.0

Source: U.S. Energy Information Administration, State Energy Data 2011: Consumption

LAND AND WATER

Surface Area and Federally-Owned Land, 2007

In thousands of acres

Category	State	U.S.	State Share
Total surface area	94,110.0	1,937,664.2	4.86%
Total land area	93,070.6	1,886,846.9	4.93%
Non-federal land	65,978.6	1,484,910.0	4.44%
Developed	1,047.0	111,251.2	0.94%
Rural	64,931.6	1,373,658.8	4.73%
Federal land	27,092.0	401,936.9	6.74%
Water area	1,039.4	50,817.3	2.05%

Source: U.S. Department of Agriculture, Natural Resources Conservation Service, 2007 National Resources Inventory

Land Cover/Use of Non-Federal Rural Land, 2007

In thousands of acres

Category	State	U.S.	State Share
Total rural land	64,931.6	1,373,658.8	4.73%
Cropland	13,930.5	357,023.5	3.90%
CRP[1] land	3,315.7	32,850.2	10.09%
Pastureland	3,960.1	118,615.7	3.34%
Rangeland	36,953.4	409,119.4	9.03%
Forest land	5,488.1	406,410.4	1.35%
Other rural land	1,283.8	49,639.6	2.59%

Note: (1) Conservation Reserve Program was created to assist private landowners in converting highly erodible cropland to vegetative cover.
Source: U.S. Department of Agriculture, Natural Resources Conservation Service, 2007 National Resources Inventory

Farms and Crop Acreage, 2012

Category	State	U.S.	State Share
Farms (in thousands)	28.6	2,170.0	1.32%
Acres (in millions)	58.8	914.0	6.43%
Acres per farm	2,055.9	421.2	–

Source: U.S. Department of Agriculture, National Agricultural Statistical Service, Quick Stats, 2012 Survey Data

HEALTH AND MEDICAL CARE

Medical Professionals, 2012

Profession	State Number	U.S. Number	State Share	State Rate[1]	U.S. Rate[1]
Physicians[2]	2,200	894,637	0.25%	220.5	287.1
Dentists	655	193,587	0.34%	65.7	62.1
Podiatrists	42	17,469	0.24%	4.2	5.6
Optometrists	184	45,638	0.40%	18.4	14.6
Chiropractors	354	77,494	0.46%	35.5	24.9

Note: (1) Rates are per 100,000 population; (2) Includes total, active Doctors of Osteopathic Medicine and Doctors of Medicine in 2011.
Source: U.S. Department of Health and Human Services, Bureau of Health Professions, Area Health Resource File, 2012-2013

Health Insurance Coverage, 2011

Category	State	U.S.
Total persons covered	806,000	260,214,000
Total persons not covered	180,000	48,613,000
Percent not covered	18.3%	15.7%
Children under age 18 covered	192,000	67,143,000
Children under age 18 not covered	27,000	6,965,000
Percent of children not covered	12.3%	9.4%

Source: U.S. Census Bureau, Current Population Survey, 2012 Annual Social and Economic Supplement

HIV, STD, and Tuberculosis Cases and Rates, 2011

Disease	State Cases	State Rate[1]	U.S. Rate[1]
Chlamydia	3,406	344.2	457.6
Gonorrhea	85	8.6	104.2
HIV diagnosis	22	2.6	15.8
HIV, stage 3 (AIDS)	12	1.4	10.3
Syphilis, early latent	1	0.1	4.3
Syphilis, primary/secondary	7	0.7	4.5
Tuberculosis	8	0.8	3.4

Note: (1) Rates are per 100,000 population
Source: Centers for Disease Control and Prevention

Cigarette Smoking, 2011

Category	State	U.S.
Adults who are current smokers	22.1%	21.2%
Adults who smoke everyday	16.4%	15.4%
Adults who smoke some days	5.7%	5.7%
Adults who are former smokers	26.9%	25.1%
Adults who never smoked	51.0%	52.9%

Source: Centers for Disease Control and Prevention, Behaviorial Risk Factor Surveillance System, Tobacco Use, 2011

HOUSING

Home Ownership Rates, 1995–2012

Area	1995	2000	2005	2010	2012
State	68.7%	70.2%	70.4%	68.1%	67.8%
U.S.	64.7%	67.4%	68.9%	66.9%	65.4%

Source: U.S. Census Bureau, Housing Vacancies and Homeownership, Annual Statistics

Home Sales, 2000–2010
In thousands of units

Year	State Sales	U.S. Sales	State Share
2000	17.4	5,174	0.34%
2002	22.6	5,632	0.40%
2004	24.2	6,778	0.36%
2006	26.8	6,478	0.41%
2008	19.9	4,913	0.41%
2010	20.4	4,908	0.42%

Note: Units include single-family homes, condos and co-ops
Source: National Association of Realtors, Real Estate Outlook, Market Trends & Insights

Value of Owner-Occupied Homes, 2011

Value	Total Units in State	Percent of Total, State	Percent of Total, U.S.
Less than $50,000	27,857	10.1%	8.8%
$50,000 to $99,000	33,062	12.0%	16.0%
$100,000 to $149,000	40,811	14.9%	16.5%
$150,000 to $199,000	49,032	17.9%	15.4%
$200,000 to $299,000	66,328	24.2%	18.2%
$300,000 to $499,000	36,424	13.3%	15.2%
$500,000 to $999,000	14,932	5.4%	7.9%
$1,000,000 or more	6,124	2.2%	2.0%
Median value	–	$184,100	$173,600

Source: U.S. Census Bureau, 2011 American Community Survey 1-Year Estimates

EDUCATION

School Enrollment, 2011

Educational Level	Students Enrolled in State	Percent of Total, State	Percent of Total, U.S.
All levels	242,981	100.0%	100.0%
Nursery school, preschool	17,521	7.2%	6.0%
Kindergarten	13,763	5.7%	5.1%
Elementary (grades 1–8)	94,501	38.9%	39.5%
Secondary (grades 9–12)	50,108	20.6%	20.7%
College or graduate school	67,088	27.6%	28.7%

Note: Figures cover the population 3 years and over enrolled in school
Source: U.S. Census Bureau, 2011 American Community Survey 1-Year Estimates

Educational Attainment, 2011

Highest Level of Education	State	U.S.
High school diploma	92.3%	85.9%
Bachelor's degree	28.2%	28.5%
Graduate/Professional degree	8.6%	10.6%

Note: Figures cover the population 25 years and over
Source: U.S. Census Bureau, 2011 American Community Survey 1-Year Estimates

Public College Finances, FY 2012

Category	State	U.S.
Full-time equivalent enrollment (FTE)[1]	40,847	11,548,974
Educational appropriations per FTE[2]	$4,007	$5,906
Net tuition revenue per FTE[3]	$4,834	$5,189
Total educational revenue per FTE[4]	$8,841	$11,043

(1) Full-time equivalent enrollment equates student credit hours to full time, academic year students, but excludes medical students; (2) Educational appropriations measure state and local support available for public higher education operating expenses including ARRA funds and excludes appropriations for independent institutions, financial aid for students attending independent institutions, research, hospitals, and medical education; (3) Net tuition revenue is calculated by taking the gross amount of tuition and fees, less state and institutional financial aid, tuition waivers or discounts, and medical student tuition and fees. Net tuition revenue used for capital debt service is included in the net tuition revenue figures; (4) Total educational revenue is the sum of educational appropriations and net tuition excluding net tuition revenue used for capital debt service.
Source: State Higher Education Executive Officers, State Higher Education Finance FY 2012

TRANSPORTATION AND TRAVEL

Motor Vehicle Registrations and Drivers Licenses, 2011

Vehicle Type	State	U.S.	State Share
Automobiles[1]	435,575	125,656,528	0.35%
Buses	4,789	666,064	0.72%
Trucks	731,783	118,455,587	0.62%
Motorcycles	47,011	8,437,502	0.56%
Drivers licenses	752,483	211,874,649	0.36%

Note: Motor vehicle registrations include private, commercial, and publicly-owned vehicles; (1) Includes taxicabs
Source: U.S. Department of Transportation, Federal Highway Administration

Domestic Travel Expenditures, 2009
In millions of dollars

Category	State	U.S.	State Share
Travel expenditures	$2,757	$610,200	0.45%

Note: Figures represent U.S. spending on domestic overnight trips and day trips of 50 miles or more, one way, away from home. Excludes spending by foreign visitors.
Source: U.S. Travel Association, Impact of Travel on State Economies, 2009

Retail Gasoline Prices, 2013

Gasoline Grade	State Average	U.S. Average
Regular	$3.70	$3.65
Mid	$3.78	$3.81
Premium	$3.91	$3.98
Diesel	$3.91	$3.88
Excise tax[1]	46.2 cents	49.4 cents

Note: Gasoline prices as of 7/26/2013; (1) Includes state and federal excise taxes and other state taxes as of July 1, 2013
Source: American Automobile Association, Daily Fuel Guage Report; American Petroleum Institute, State Motor Fuel Taxes, 2013

Public Road Length, 2011

Type	State Mileage	U.S. Mileage	State Share
Interstate highways	1,192	46,960	2.54%
Other highways	0	15,719	0.00%
Principal arterial	2,814	156,262	1.80%
Minor arterial	3,224	242,942	1.33%
Major collector	7,377	534,592	1.38%
Minor collector	8,817	266,357	3.31%
Local	51,456	2,814,925	1.83%
Urban	3,182	1,095,373	0.29%
Rural	71,698	2,982,383	2.40%
Total	74,880	4,077,756	1.84%

Note: Combined urban and rural road mileage equals the total of the other road types
Source: U.S. Department of Transportation, Federal Highway Administration, Public Road Length, 2011

CRIME AND LAW ENFORCEMENT

Full-Time Law Enforcement Officers, 2011

Gender	State Number	State Rate[1]	U.S. Rate[1]
Male officers	1,793	180.0	210.3
Female officers	114	11.4	28.1
Total officers	1,907	191.4	238.3

Note: (1) Rates are per 100,000 population
Source: Federal Bureau of Investigation, Uniform Crime Reports, Crime in the United States 2011

Prison Population, 2000–2012

Year	State Population	U.S. Population	State Share
2000	3,105	1,391,261	0.22%
2005	3,532	1,527,929	0.23%
2010	3,716	1,613,803	0.23%
2011	3,678	1,598,783	0.23%
2012	3,609	1,571,013	0.23%

Note: Figures include prisoners under the jurisdiction of state or federal correctional authorities.
Source: U.S. Department of Justice, Bureau of Justice Statistics, Prisoners in 2006, 2011, 2012 (Advance Counts)

Crime Rate, 2011
Incidents per 100,000 residents

Category	State	U.S.
Violent crimes	267.5	386.3
Murder	2.8	4.7
Forcible rape	35.8	26.8
Robbery	16.9	113.7
Aggravated assault	212.0	241.1
Property crimes	2,319.7	2,908.7
Burglary	339.6	702.2
Larceny/theft	1,834.0	1,976.9
Motor vehicle theft	146.1	229.6
All crimes	2,587.2	3,295.0

Source: Federal Bureau of Investigation, Uniform Crime Reports, Crime in the United States 2011

GOVERNMENT AND FINANCE

Local Governments by Type, 2012

Government Type	State	U.S.	State Share
All local governments	1,240	89,004	1.39%
County	54	3,031	1.78%
Municipality	129	19,522	0.66%
Town/Township	0	16,364	0.00%
Special District	736	37,203	1.98%
Ind. School District	321	12,884	2.49%

Source: U.S. Census Bureau, 2012 Census of Governments: Organization Component Preliminary Estimates

State Government Revenue, 2011
In thousands of dollars, except for per capita figures

Total revenue	$7,950,510
Total revenue per capita, State	$7,969
Total revenue per capita, U.S.	$7,271
General revenue	$5,768,585
Intergovernmental revenue	$2,414,552
Taxes	$2,303,516
General sales	$0
Selective sales	$533,372
License taxes	$307,838
Individual income taxes	$812,629
Corporate income taxes	$123,985
Other taxes	$525,692
Current charges	$605,674
Miscellaneous general revenue	$444,843
Utility revenue	$0
Liquor store revenue	$73,456
Insurance trust revenue[1]	$2,108,469

Note: (1) Within insurance trust revenue, net earnings of state retirement systems is a calculated statistic, and thus can be positive or negative. Net earnings is the sum of earnings on investments plus gains on investments minus losses on investments.
Source: U.S. Census Bureau, 2011 Annual Survey of State Government Finances

State Government Expenditures, 2011
In thousands of dollars, except for per capita figures

Total expenditure	$7,105,366
Total expenditure per capita, State	$7,122
Total expenditure per capita, U.S.	$6,427
Intergovernmental expenditure	$1,352,917
Direct expenditure	$5,752,449
Current operation	$3,811,860
Capital outlay	$730,434
Insurance benefits and repayments	$946,281
Assistance and subsidies	$108,377
Interest on debt	$155,497
Utility expenditure	$13,609
Liquor store expenditure	$63,464
Insurance trust expenditure	$946,281

Source: U.S. Census Bureau, 2011 Annual Survey of State Government Finances

State Government General Expenditures by Function, 2011
In thousands of dollars

Education	$1,840,578
Public welfare	$1,390,134
Hospitals	$47,762
Health	$170,135
Highways	$709,293
Police protection	$48,159
Correction	$188,537
Natural resources	$259,715
Parks and recreation	$31,274
Governmental administration	$420,478
Interest on general debt	$155,497
Other and unallocable	$820,450

Source: U.S. Census Bureau, 2011 Annual Survey of State Government Finances

State Government Finances, Cash and Debt, 2011
In thousands of dollars, except for per capita figures

Debt at end of fiscal year	
State, total	$4,266,731
State, per capita	$4,277
U.S., per capita	$3,635
Cash and security holdings	
State, total	$16,596,265
State, per capita	$16,635
U.S., per capita	$11,759

Source: U.S. Census Bureau, 2011 Annual Survey of State Government Finances

POLITICS

Composition of the Senate, 1995–2013

Congress (Year)	State/U.S	Dem	Rep	Total
104th (1995)	State delegates	1	1	2
	Total U.S.	48	52	100
105th (1997)	State delegates	1	1	2
	Total U.S.	45	55	100
106th (1999)	State delegates	1	1	2
	Total U.S.	45	55	100
107th (2001)	State delegates	1	1	2
	Total U.S.	50	50	100
108th (2003)	State delegates	1	1	2
	Total U.S.	48	51	100
109th (2005)	State delegates	1	1	2
	Total U.S.	44	55	100
110th (2007)	State delegates	2	0	2
	Total U.S.	49	49	100
111th (2009)	State delegates	2	0	2
	Total U.S.	57	41	100
112th (2011)	State delegates	2	0	2
	Total U.S.	51	47	100
113th (2013)	State delegates	2	0	2
	Total U.S.	54	45	100

Note: Figures are for the starts of first sessions; Totals include Democratic (Dem) and Republican (Rep) members as well as vacancies and seats held by independent party members
Source: U.S. Congress, Congressional Directory

Composition of the House of Representatives, 1995–2013

Congress (Year)	State/U.S	Dem	Rep	Total
104th (1995)	State delegates	1	0	1
	Total U.S.	204	230	435
105th (1997)	State delegates	0	1	1
	Total U.S.	207	226	435
106th (1999)	State delegates	0	1	1
	Total U.S.	211	223	435
107th (2001)	State delegates	0	1	1
	Total U.S.	212	221	435
108th (2003)	State delegates	0	1	1
	Total U.S.	205	229	435
109th (2005)	State delegates	0	1	1
	Total U.S.	202	231	435
110th (2007)	State delegates	0	1	1
	Total U.S.	233	198	435
111th (2009)	State delegates	0	1	1
	Total U.S.	256	178	435
112th (2011)	State delegates	0	1	1
	Total U.S.	193	242	435
113th (2013)	State delegates	1	0	1
	Total U.S.	201	234	435

Note: Figures are for the starts of first sessions; Totals include Democratic (Dem) and Republican (Rep) members as well as vacancies and seats held by independent party members
Source: U.S. Congress, Congressional Directory

Composition of State Legislature, 2004–2013

Year	Democrats	Republicans	Total
State Senate			
2004	21	29	50
2005	27	23	50
2006	27	23	50
2007	26	24	50
2008	26	24	50
2009	23	27	50
2010	23	27	50
2011	22	28	50
2012	22	28	50
2013	21	29	50
State House			
2004	47	53	100
2005	50	50	100
2006	50	50	100
2007	49	50	100
2008	49	50	100
2009	50	50	100
2010	50	50	100
2011	32	68	100
2012	32	68	100
2013	39	61	100

Note: Totals may include minor party members and vacancies
Source: The Council of State Governments, State Legislatures

Voter Participation in Presidential Elections, 1980–2012

Year	Voting-eligible State Population	State Voter Turnout Rate	U.S. Voter Turnout Rate
1980	554,636	65.6	54.2
1984	578,925	66.4	55.2
1988	568,014	64.4	52.8
1992	593,345	69.2	58.1
1996	645,052	63.1	51.7
2000	667,525	61.6	54.2
2004	699,114	64.4	60.1
2008	741,853	66.3	61.6
2012	773,147	62.6	58.2

Note: All figures are based on the voting-eligible population which excludes person ineligible to vote such as non-citizens, felons (depending on state law), and mentally-incapacitated persons. U.S. figures include the overseas eligible population (including military personnel).
Source: McDonald, Michael P., United States Election Project, Presidential Voter Turnout Rates, 1980–2012

Governors Since Statehood

Joseph K. Toole (D) 1889-1893
John E. Rickards (R) 1893-1897
Robert B. Smith (O) 1897-1901
Joseph K. Toole (D) . . . . (r) 1901-1908
Edwin L. Norris (D) 1908-1913
Samuel V. Stewart (D) 1913-1921
Joseph M. Dixon (R) 1921-1925
John E. Erickson (D) . . . . (r) 1925-1933
Frank H. Cooney (D) . . . . (d) 1933-1935
William Elmer Hoyt (D). 1935-1937
Roy E. Ayers (D) 1937-1941

Samuel C. Ford (R) 1941-1949
John W. Bonner (D) 1949-1953
John Hugo Aronson (R) 1953-1961
Donald G. Nutter (R) . . . . (d) 1961-1962
Tim M. Babcock (R) 1962-1969
Forrest H. Anderson (D). 1969-1973
Thomas L. Judge (D) 1973-1981
Ted Schwinden (D) 1981-1989
Stan Stephens (R). 1989-1993
Marc Racicot (R) 1993-2001
Judy Martz (R) 2001-2005
Brian Schweitzer (D) 2005-2013
Steve Bullock (D). 2013-2017

Note: (D) Democrat; (R) Republican; (O) Other party; (r) resigned; (d) died in office; (i) removed from office